HANDBOOK
of
HEALTH CARE
HUMAN
RESOURCES
MANAGEMENT

HANDBOOK of HEALTH CARE HUMAN RESOURCES MANAGEMENT

Second Edition

Edited by
Norman Metzger
Edmond A. Guggenheim Professor
Department of Health Care Management
Mount Sinai School of Medicine
New York, New York

AN ASPEN PUBLICATION®
Aspen Publishers, Inc.
Rockville, Maryland
1990

Library of Congress Cataloging-in-Publication Data

Handbook of health care human resources management/edited by
Norman Metzger. --2nd. ed.
p. cm.
"An Aspen publication."
Includes bibliographical references.
ISBN: 0-8342-0094-5
1. Health facilities--Personnel management--Handbooks, manuals, etc.
2. Hospitals--Personnel management--Handbooks, manuals, etc.
I. Metzger, Norman, 1924
[DNLM: 1. Health Manpower--organization & administration.
2. Personnel Management. W 88 H236]
RA971.35.H36   1989   362.1′1′0683--dc20
DGPO/DLC
for Library of Congress
89-17693
CIP

Editorial Services: Ruth Bloom

Library of Congress Catalog Card Number: 89-17693
ISBN: 0-8342-0094-5

Printed in the United States of America

1 2 3 4 5

To Bart

Whom I learn from in each
conversation, exchange,
written word, and deed

When a business manager who is fully committed to this ethic is asked, "What are you in business for?" the answer may be: "I am in the business of growing people—people who are stronger, healthier, more autonomous, more self-reliant, more competent. Incidentally, we also make and sell for a profit things that people want to buy so we can pay for all this. We play that game hard and well and we are successful by the usual standards, but that is really incidental. . . ."

Robert K. Greenleaf, *Servant Leadership: A Journey into the Nature of Legitimate Power and Greatness.*
(New York: Paulist Press, 1977), 156.

Table of Contents

Preface

In one of my earliest books, *Personnel Administration in the Health Services Industry*, I discussed the need to "arrange" the institutional MOs—i.e., methods of operation in general from doctors to porters—so that the deliverers of patient care can achieve *their* goals by directing their efforts toward *institutional* objectives. Achieving personal goals and institutional objectives are not mutually exclusive. A well-staffed and well-led human resources department can add immeasurably to the fabric of the institution as it pertains to the delivery of quality patient care. I went on to remark that the assemblage of people—professionals and paraprofessionals, skilled and nonskilled—in an efficient group, fully cognizant of institutional goals and committed to their fulfillment, is not happenstance.

In the past two decades, human resources administration has developed into a key responsibility in the complex world of hospital administration. Labor expenditures accounted for 54 percent of total hospital budgets in 1986.[1] The managing and inspiring of this largest of components of our delivery system is at the heart of human resources administration.

During the remaining years of this century, the challenges and responsibilities of human resources departments will not only increase but will also radically change. The need to develop trust, which is a particularly difficult task, will be critical. The establishment of enduring trusting relationships depends on the creation of an overall climate of justice and fairness, which will be one of the responsibilities of the human resources manager. Such individuals will need to direct their maximum efforts to the essential core of human relations—building trust, building a structure of participatory management, and creating flexible and ingenious reward systems.

This *Handbook* is the second edition of the 1981 comprehensive compilation of articles in the field of human resources management, benefits administration, and labor relations. The first edition became a "must read" book for all those who found it imperative to keep up with the most recent developments in the field.

Once again I was assisted by several distinguished experts in the field. These illustrious scholars and practitioners nominated contributors and recommended subject matter for coverage. Bill Abelow and Tom Helfrich, respectively president and counsel and senior vice-president and counsel of the League of Voluntary Hospitals and Homes of New York, were as always extremely helpful. Sam Levey, professor and director of the Graduate Program in Health and Hospital Administration at the College of Medicine, University of Iowa, once again tapped his national network of scholars for contributions to this edition. Tony Gajda, principal at William M. Mercer-Meidinger-Hansen, brought together several of his associates to write key articles in the benefits area. James B. Williams, vice-president and worldwide director of industry consulting of the Hay Management Group, solicited his partners to participate. Charles Joiner, senior associate dean of the School of Community and Allied Health, University of Alabama, a prolific writer in his own right, solicited several authors in addition to contributing on his own.

My publisher, Aspen, opened up its voluminous storeroom of books that they have published in the field for my review and permitted me to reprint outstanding articles.

In order to bring together the large number of contributors, the task of assembling, organizing, and following through once again fell to my talented associate, Irene Wehr. I no longer have to ask her how she does it—she does it magnificently.

Of all the books that I have written or edited—this is my fifteenth—I am most proud of this effort. I strongly recommend this collection to teachers and scholars in the field of health care human resources administration and to the practitioners who are *doing* what we are writing about. This *Handbook* once again presents in a simple and logical form a storehouse of up-to-date ideas and usable wisdom. It highlights the enormity of the task of those who are in the field attempting to grapple with a changing work force and a changing society.

It is an extremely timely compendium; given the new financial realities of health care delivery, there is an obvious need to develop well-motivated and productive work forces. To the human resources manager fall the responsibilities to play a key part in such programs and to assume the critical role of leader as well as catalyst for change—for *change* is the order of the day!

Let me conclude by referring to a wonderful book by Robert Levering, *A Great Place To Work*, in which he talks about moving toward a new workplace ethic. He suggests that our society is in many ways at an economic crossroads. He also quotes a "little noticed volume," *Servant Leadership* by Robert Greenleaf:

> When a business manager who is fully committed to this ethic is asked, "What are you in business for?" the answer may be: "I am in the business of growing people—people who are stronger, healthier, more autonomous,

more self-reliant, more competent. Incidentally, we also make and sell for profit things that people want to buy so we can pay for all this. We play that game here and well and we are successful by the usual standards, but that is really incidental. . . .[2]

Levering then concludes that if, indeed, our society is at an economic crossroads, we should, instead of falling back on old reflexes because of this crisis, use this opportunity to engage in a major rethinking, not just about where we are going but how we expect to get there. He believes that being the best means "not just producing the best quality," but also that "We could become known as the place where people at all levels are treated decently because work is seen as an end in and of itself. The workplace in this vision, becomes a place for people, not for people who feel like robots."[3] To achieve a work place that would appear in the next *A Great Place To Work*, we need some radical reshaping of the work place and the work ethic.

Norman Metzger

NOTES

1. American Hospital Association, *Hospital Statistics* (Chicago: American Hospital Association, 1987).

2. Robert Levering, *A Great Place To Work* (New York: Random House, Inc., 1988), 269, quoting Robert K. Greenleaf, *Servant Leadership: A Journey into the Nature of Legitimate Power and Greatness* (New York: Paulist Press, 1977).

3. Ibid., 259.

Contributors

Steven G. Allen, PhD
Professor of Economics and Business
North Carolina State University
Raleigh, North Carolina

Laura Avakian, MA
Vice President, Human Resources
Beth Israel Hospital
Boston, Massachusetts

Lawrence C. Bassett, CMC
President
The Bassett Consulting Group, Inc.
Thornwood, New York

L. Robert Batterman, Esquire
Partner
Proskauer Rose Goetz & Mendelsohn
New York, New York

Richard E. Berger, BA
William M. Mercer Meidinger Hansen, Inc.
New York, New York

Patricia Berger-Friedman, MA
Associate and Consultant
William M. Mercer Meidinger Hansen, Incorporated
New York, New York

Michael I. Bernstein, Esquire
Benetar Isaacs Bernstein & Schair
New York, New York

David A. Bjork, PhD
Director—HMO Consulting
The Hay Group
Minneapolis, Minnesota

John D. Blair, PhD
College of Business Administration
Texas Tech University
Lubbock, Texas

Phyllis C. Borzi, Esquire
Counsel for Pensions and Employee Benefits
Sub-Committee on Labor Management Relations
Committee on Education and Labor
Washington, D.C.

Mark E. Brossman, JD
Chadbourne & Parke
New York, New York

Jerad D. Browdy, JD
President
Jerad D. Browdy Associates
Evanston, Illinois

Mary S. Case, BA
Principal
William M. Mercer Meidinger Hansen, Incorporated
New York, New York

Marco L. Colosi, BS, MA, DPA
Vice President, Human Resources and Labor Relations
Bronx-Lebanon Hospital Center
Bronx, New York

Michael R. Cooper, PhD
World-Wide Managing Director—Hay Research for
   Management
The Hay Group
Philadelphia, Pennsylvania

Brian G. Costello, SPHR
Vice President
Garofolo, Curtiss & Company
Philadelphia, Pennsylvania

Donald Crow, BBA
Vice-President, Operations
Methodist Health Care Network
Houston, Texas

Janet R. Douglas, MPH, OTR
William M. Mercer Meidinger Hansen, Incorporated
Deerfield, Illinois

E.J. Dowling, MBA
Vice President, Human Resources
Yale-New Haven Hospital
New Haven, Connecticut

Catherine A. Duran, MBA, MS
College of Business Administration
Texas Tech University
Lubbock, Texas

Norbert F. Elbert, DBA
Professor of Management
Bellarmine College
Louisville, Kentucky

Gregory T. Finnegan, MBA
Director, Management Systems
Robert Wood Johnson University Hospital
New Brunswick, New Jersey

Thomas P. Flannery, Jr., PhD
Regional Director-Health Care Consulting
The Hay Group
St. Louis, Missouri

Myron D. Fottler, PhD
Professor
Department of Health Services Administration
School of Health Related Professions
University of Alabama at Birmingham
Birmingham, Alabama

Anthony J. Gajda, PhD
Principal
William M. Mercer Meidinger Hansen, Incorporated
New York, New York

James J. Gallagher, PhD
Partner
King Chapman Broussard & Gallagher, Inc.
New York, New York

Robin Gourlay
Professor of Health Care Management
The International Management Centre from Buckingham
   England
Director, Mercia Publications, Ltd.
Keele, Staffordshire, England

Fred W. Graumann, JD
Senior Vice President, Human Resources
Robert Wood Johnson University Hospital
New Brunswick, New Jersey

E.J. Holland, Jr., Esquire
Managing Partner
Spencer Fane Britt & Browne
Kansas City, Missouri

James R. Hudek, LLB
Managing Partner
Head, Employee Benefits Group
Spencer Fane Britt & Browne
Kansas City, Missouri

Sanford M. Jacoby, PhD
Associate Professor
Anderson Graduate School of Management
University of California-Los Angeles
Los Angeles, California

Richard E. Johnson, BA
William M. Mercer Meidinger Hansen, Incorporated
Chicago, Illinois

Charles L. Joiner, PhD
Professor and Associate Dean
University of Alabama
Birmingham, Alabama

Arnold D. Kaluzny, MHA, PhD
Professor
Department of Health Policy and Administration
School of Public Health
University of North Carolina at Chapel Hill
Chapel Hill, North Carolina

Howard L. Kane, FSA
Vice President & Chief Actuary
Noble Lowndes
New York, New York

Elliott A. Kellman, MPA
Senior Vice President, Human Resources
Baystate Health Systems
Springfield, Massachusetts

David Lance, BS
President
American Horizon Consulting
Shawn, Massachusetts

Jack M. Marco, BA
President
The Marco Consulting Group
Chicago, Illinois

Kenneth A. Mason, JD
Associate
Spencer Fane Britt & Browne
Kansas City, Missouri

Martin H. Meisel, BA
President
Martin H. Meisel Associates, Inc.
New York, New York

V. Brandon Melton, MA
Corporate Vice President, Human Resources
Catholic Health Corporation
Omaha, Nebraska

Bart Metzger, MA
Director of Human Resources
Georgetown University Medical Center
Washington, D.C.

Norman Metzger
Professor
Mount Sinai School of Medicine and The Mount Sinai
    Medical Center
New York, New York

Arnold Milstein, MD, MPH
Medical Audit Services
William M. Mercer Meidinger Hansen, Incorporated
San Francisco, California

Daniel H. Mundt, JD
Proprietor
Mundt and Associates
Duluth, Minnesota

Gail E. Nethercut, PhD
Director, National Medical Audit's Workers' Compensation
    Medical Cost Containment
William M. Mercer Meidinger Hansen, Incorporated
San Francisco, California

Mark F. Peterson, PhD
Area of Management
College of Business Administration
Texas Tech University
Lubbock, Texas

Jeffrey P. Petertil, MBA
William M. Mercer Meidinger Hansen, Incorporated
Chicago, Illinois

Robert L. Phillips, PhD
Area of Management
College of Business Administration
Texas Tech University
Lubbock, Texas

Bettina B. Plevan, PhD
Partner, Proskauer Rose Goetz & Mendelsohn
New York, New York

Kevin Renner, MBA
Associate
The Hay Group
Walnut Creek, California

Rhonda Rhodes, JD
Senior Counsel
Office of Legal & Regulatory Affairs
American Hospital Association
Chicago, Illinois

Susan S. Robfogel, Esquire
Nixon, Hargrave, Devans & Doyle
Rochester, New York

James A. Rodeghero, PhD
Director—Physician's Compensation Consulting
The Hay Group
Los Angeles, California

Kent E. Romanoff, MA
Consultant
The Hay Group
San Francisco/Walnut Creek, California

William A. Rothman, MS, HA
Formerly with Gaylord Hospital
Wallingford, Connecticut

Grant T. Savage, PhD
Area of Management
College of Business Administration
Texas Tech University
Lubbock, Texas

Amarjit S. Sethi, PhD
Associate Professor
Master in Health Administration Program
Faculty of Administration
University of Ottawa
Ottawa, Canada

Howard L. Smith, PhD
Anderson School of Management
University of New Mexico
Albuquerque, New Mexico

Edward J. Speedling, PhD
Director of Organizational Development
Associate Professor of Community Medicine
The Mount Sinai Medical Center
New York, New York

Paula L. Stamps, PhD
Professor, Health Policy and Management Program
Division of Public Health
School of Health Sciences
University of Massachusetts
Amherst, Massachusetts

Julius M. Steiner, JD
Myerson & Kuhn
Philadelphia, Pennsylvania

James H. Stephens, JD
Chairman
National Labor Relations Board
Washington, D.C.

Alexander Sussman, FSA
President and Consulting Actuary
Noble Lowndes
Garden City, New York

Eugene D. Ulterino, LLB
Partner and Chairman, Labor and Employment
Nixon, Hargrave, Devans & Doyle
Rochester, New York

Susan Warner, JD
Director, Human Resources and Administrative Services
United Way
Philadelphia, Pennsylvania

Thomas J. Welling, CLU, CH, FC
Welling Associates, Inc.
Bronxville, New York

Carlton J. Whitehead, PhD
Area of Management
College of Business Administration
Texas Tech University
Lubbock, Texas

James B. Williams, MBA
Director, Worldwide Healthcare Consulting
The Hay Group
San Francisco/Walnut Creek, California

Sharon Winn, MS
President
Winn & Associates, Inc.
and
Clinical Associate Professor
Department of Health Services
School of Public Health and Community Medicine
University of Washington
Seattle, Washington

John A. Witt
National Advisor
Witt Associates, Inc.
Oak Brook, Illinois

Paul Yager, MS, ILR
Director, Retired
Eastern Region
Federal Mediation and Conciliation Service
Metuchen, New Jersey

Part I

Human Resources Management

The change agent of the organization—the Human Resource Department—has been going through some changes of its own lately. Departmental reorganization, shifts and accountability and increasing specialization among department personnel are helping to make human resources a strategically oriented department that's impacting the bottom line.*

It has become quite clear that human resources management is strategic management. In recognition of this clear and primary responsibility three articles on human resources strategic planning have been included in this part. V. Brandon Melton gives us his view, Myron D. Fottler adds his to our deliberations, and E.J. Dowling and Elliott Kellman present a case study in human resources strategic planning.

Whereas the first edition of this handbook began with an article entitled "There's More To It Than People Shuffling," which, indeed, seemed to be defensive at the least, the coverage of human resources management in this edition begins with an explicit message from John A. Witt, "Values and Integrity in Health Care." He asks us to consider the following: "Do you sense some of the feelings of frustration of your employees, managers, and executives as they feel abandoned in the 'caring' portion of their professional responsibilities?" The more advanced human resources departments in health care are addressing this "caring" ingredient.

It matters not what some may think are sound human relations approaches. More important for our consideration is the review of what *works*, of what produces the following for the institution and its employees:

- attainment of the organization's goals
- efficiency, productivity, and, of course, quality
- fulfilling and meaningful work
- rewards recognized as being based on contribution

In this part the contributors attempt to respond to Witt's question. Their concerns run the gamut, including quality control circles, compensation systems and trends, guest relations, work satisfaction, executive search, documentation, negotiation skills, gainsharing, and outplacement.

I am proud to include an excellent research paper by Paula L. Stamps, "The Stamps-Piedmonte Index of Work Satisfaction: Linking Job Satisfaction to Job Redesign," and I am quite excited about the reaction to David Lance's provocative article, "The Revolution in Human Resources: Money, Motivation, Mythology." Pride is not sufficient to describe my feeling about my son, Bart Metzger, who is director of human resources at the Georgetown University Medical Center in Washington, D.C., and his article entitled "Human Resources Administration: An Alternative Model." In that article he states

The face of health care human resources administration is being reconfigured as we go about our daily ministrations.

---

*Linda Stockman Bines, "Dissecting the Human Resources Department," *Human Resource Executive;* 2, No. 7 (July-August 1988): 20.

1

We practice today at a critical juncture of the discipline, but unless we lift our heads from the fray, we are liable to miss it. Buffeted by forces extrinsic to our environment, the human resources function is in the process of being relegated to the margins of the health care organization. To arrest this process of marginalization, we must see more clearly the contours of our new face and look more closely at the forces that are driving that change. Only by doing so will we be able to play a role in recasting our discipline.

It is toward achievement of this end—to see more clearly the contours of our face and to look more closely at the forces that are driving that change—that this part is directed.

John A. Witt

Values and Integrity in Health Care

1

Winds of change are blowing across American health care organizations. Generations of trust are being blown away like so many dry leaves in these fall winds. Miracles of modern health care and medicine built by you and your preceptors once earned you the respect of the public, your employees, and your patients. Today there is a building fear and frustration among many health care professionals, distrust and disdain from many government officials, and an opportunistic press waiting to make either your success or your failure its next opportunity to second-guess you.

My observations have been made as I travel to large and small organizations in all sections of the country. What I have seen and heard in the board room, the doctor's lounge, the executive suite, or the employee cafeteria has caused me to raise a few questions for your consideration today. In team-building seminars we discuss service strategy, human development, and the differences between success and fulfillment. We never talk about how to really listen to what your people are *feeling*. It is my view that too many CEOs are spending too much time on positioning the organization with strategies and competitive advantages while overlooking some of their key leadership responsibilities.

I have jotted down here a few lines of inquiry that I want to walk through with you, because I am convinced that we need to re-examine some basic matters.

Note: From a presentation at the 1987 Shareholders' Meeting, Voluntary Hospitals of America, Inc., October 29, 1987. Reprinted with permission of John A. Witt, National Advisor, Witt Associates, Inc., Oak Brook, Illinois.

Do you sense some of the feelings of frustration of your employees, managers, and executives as they feel abandoned in the "caring" portion of their professional responsibilities?

Hospital employees are not dumb. Emphasizing budgets and clerical work more than caring confuses people. Most people selected health occupations not because of the potential for high salaries, but because they have a sense of caring and social justice. They made trade-offs and sacrifices for their values saying, in effect, "I will give needed care, my patients will get better, and I will receive appreciation."

Are you aware of how health care professionals are feeling about changing values in the work place?

Unless we allow our employees and managers to talk about, discuss, and process their feelings, we will not deliver the caring quality service our ads are promoting. Employees are being asked to increase their productivity while sometimes sending patients home earlier than they may feel is right. Are employees encouraged to discuss these changing values, or are those who raise these questions branded as disloyal? The ethical concerns of many professionals are raising strong feelings, and if those feelings are not processed, their attitudes will be affected. Excellent leaders will recognize the problem and promote ethical responsibility in discussing the issue.

Do we publicly profess to want the highest quality service, but privately congratulate the cost-cutters who produce bigger bottom lines?

As this entire field structures and restructures, bundles and unbundles its services, how many of your new business plans reward quality service? I have been asked as a consultant in compensation matters to structure many risk-reward systems that focus on quantified results. Very seldom am I asked by executives or their boards to help them reward quality. Where are the rewards for defining quality by department, for delivering quality, or for teaching quality?

Do we integratively deal with human weaknesses, or do we circumvent the "problem" people by cutting their responsibilities and bringing in new people?

In the last several years, I have been struck by the lack of integrity that is shown when the board has decided to release its CEO. Severance agreements are essential, and what about the spectacle of everyone lying through his teeth as to why the person is being terminated?

That is not to exonerate the CEOs in this field who have obviously learned those lessons well—the same scenario occurs when vice-presidents are moved aside or moved out. Long-service people who were loyal, dedicated and produced to the best of their ability are unceremoniously dumped.

As the organization's needs change, some people will plateau out. This is not fatal; it is natural that some people's jobs outgrow them. But what can be distressing is how people at all levels are dealing with this. People unaware they have deficiencies never get the support to learn, grow, and change. Rather, their organizations avoid communication and make the person a negative role model of how people are to be treated. In other situations titles are given less to reflect what a person or group does than what will look good or sound nice.

All these small elements, taken together, will shape the attitudes of people in a service organization. You can develop attitudes that are positive, caring, and concerned or attitudes that are negative, uncaring, unconcerned, and unfeeling. And the attitudes create the level of care that will be delivered.

Are the contracts, joint ventures, and agreements we make with our physicians in the public's best interest, or are we helping to ensure the monopoly privilege that protects the physicians' economic interests and our own?

If we believe that competition will be the prevailing climate for the next 10 years in health care, the voluntary-model health care organization has one large problem. That problem: All the organization's programs and strategies are based on alliances with independent physicians, and every move that is made has one underlying theme called, "Make the doctors happy; *at all costs*, make the private-practice doctors happy."

If your attempts to preserve private practice result in lower costs, better distribution of physicians throughout the population, and better quality service, all these new ventures could earn some health care executive the Nobel Peace Prize. I would like to see it happen—but I am not holding my breath.

Do we say people are our most important resources, but only spend annual performance appraisal time (if that) on coaching and developing tomorrow's leaders?

As I view many of the people in the top spots in health care, I recall their preceptors, who gave them golden opportunities to learn and grow. Hours of coaching and endless time to question those mentors helped to develop strong vision and clear thinking. I see too few CEOs today spending that kind of time with our next generation of leaders.

A CEO of a system I met with some months ago had a budget of several hundred million dollars and numerous projects going internally and externally, but he had no designated successor. The person in the number-two position was universally distrusted, he said. That CEO is making time for a lot of things, but developing people is not a priority, apparently. What CEO's duty or responsibility is of greater importance than developing tomorrow's leaders and managers?

Do we cloak our mission statements in the humanitarian language of social service agencies, but write Machiavellian business and action plans that seek to crush our professional peers like grapes?

As a speaker at several board retreats in the last few months, I have watched boards and their key executives discuss their mission statements. Much of the mission statement is loaded with the language of their former nonprofit hospitals, honoring apple pie, motherhood, and the flag—but do not bother to try to square that up with their business plans.

If people are to work together effectively in an organization, I am convinced they must have a set of shared beliefs. The challenge is to make our philosophies and corporate purposes integrative, so that service professionals at all levels can truly buy into our missions.

Values that take their nutrition from the mission statement are what employees are hungering for. They want a sense of purpose that will serve themselves and their employer.

Do we expect our boards, bankers, and suppliers to treat us as businesses, but never publish or widely distribute our financial results?

The fundamental measures used in most businesses to indicate their financial results are gross sales, net profit, return on investment, or return on equity. My experience is that outside observers will want to make comparisons in judging an organization's success or viability. If you make the comparisons and publish the financial data early and often, you will avoid giving the public the impression you are trying to put something over on someone.

If you fail to do this, it will not be a matter of *whether* there will be a financial analyst looking at your organization, but *when*. Long after government and the press forget Jim and Tammy Bakker, they and the general public will remember the Bakkers were spawned by their not-for-profit status and got as far as they did because of it.

Are you ready to be interviewed by the investigative reporter who wants this story: Who profits in the nonprofit industries and why?

Do we ask our people to be honest and open, even providing programs on how to display feelings and caring, but never share our own feelings in an integrative way with our key people?

I cannot help but notice the number of people in this industry who bury their feelings. Last year, for example, I interviewed executives in three organizations who had been brutalized verbally by their CEOs. I asked all of these vice-presidents how they felt, and both the men and women used these phrases: "It doesn't bother me," "I'm thick-skinned," "He thinks he will get to me, but I won't give him the satisfaction of letting him know.''

Each of those individuals is a sure bet for future physical and emotional problems. That pseudo-macho mentality is a guarantee to everyone in psychiatric counseling that future business will be very good.

Life skills and job skills blend very nicely. Psychologists and company trainers are learning the value of people with high self-esteem who can say:

- ''Thank you.''
- ''You hurt my feelings when . . .''
- ''Are you displeased with something I've done or said?''

The pseudo-macho types may conclude this is sissy talk. Those in the business of building caring attitudes in organizations that are in the business of caring will see a direct relationship between building better people and building better organizations.

What are your values? How far are you willing to go for them? What beliefs are you willing to stand up for? How integrative are you in your dealings?

Standing up for principles in the future will be critical. This country's problems will cause us soon to see how people and the meaning of work have been reduced to purely economic mechanisms. Our people are becoming consuming mechanisms who must somehow obtain enough to buy goods and services not just for survival but to compensate for the pain of being alive. What a grim reality we face, if we do not change it.

Standing up for integrative practices and values may sound like an ethical discussion for philosophy professors. However, I am reminded how essentially practical it is to stand up for principles by some thoughts that were born in the ghastly crucible of Germany during World War II. The author was Pastor Martin Niemoeller, a German Lutheran minister.

> In Germany they came first for the Communists, and I did not speak up because I was not a Communist.
>
> Then they came for the Jews, and I did not speak up because I was not a Jew.
>
> Then they came for the trade unionists, and I did not speak up because I was not a trade unionist.
>
> Then they came for the Catholics, and I did not speak up because I was a Protestant.
>
> Then they came for me but, by that time, no one was left to speak up.

Bart Metzger

Human Resources Administration: An Alternative Model

2

INTRODUCTION

Occupational disciplines almost invariably evolve in small and often imperceptible increments. Quantum leaps of progression are rare, and critical junctures are usually transparent to the practitioner, becoming manifest only in retrospective analysis. As practitioners, we are too often mired in the day-to-day exigencies of the administrative process to take stock of the structural changes that frame and inform our organizational existence. Even as our objective functions change, we continue to think about ourselves without reference to those changes. As a result, our capacity to apprehend the change process is diminished.

The face of health care human resources administration is being reconfigured as we go about our daily ministrations. We practice today at a critical juncture of the discipline, but unless we lift our heads from the fray, we are liable to miss it. Buffeted by forces extrinsic to our environment, the human resources function is in the process of being relegated to the margins of the health care organization. To arrest this process of marginalization, we must see more clearly the contours of our new face and look more closely at the forces that are driving that change. Only by doing so will we be able to play a role in recasting our discipline.

The changes in the structure of health care delivery in our society have transformed the fabric of our organizational existence, and with it the cultural norms within which we function. Personnel practices are the most important variables in the determination of organizational culture. In the composite, they reflect the very basis of the employment relationship; outwardly, they reflect the internal essence of an organization.

We refer here to personnel practices in the widest possible sense, including not only the rules, regulations, policies, and procedures but also the daily interactions with the work force, forms of management intervention, and quality of work supervision. Indeed, the defining features of organizational culture are visible in the way an organization *conceives of* its employees; the manner in which employees are treated and required to function will flow directly from the manner in which they are conceived.

Prospective payment is altering the way hospitals and health care institutions conceive of their employees. The role of the human resources function in that changing conception has thus far been passive and, at best, ancillary in nature. As a direct result, the industry's response to the new set of imperatives has been determined largely in the absence of a personnel perspective. Those sectors within health care administration that have formulated the industry's response have followed a model that views the work force as human capital that needs to be disciplined into higher levels of productivity or replaced by those who will be more compliant. In short, this is a model of organizational dynamics that has failed to break with the old practices, methods, and techniques. Arguably suited to the old environment, this model will prove a prescription for failure in confronting the new age in health care delivery.

Indeed, the strategies that the industry has thus far developed in response to the inexorable pressures of efficiency have involved little more than a tightening of the screws, *more* rather than *different kinds* of management. Human resources administrators have increasingly been assigned the role of captain of the managerial army of screw tighteners, and the results thus far have been predictably dismal. In fact, there is evidence of little, if any, productivity increases, and the organizational costs have been quite high. Layoffs, hiring freezes, reductions in benefits, increased turnover, higher levels of disciplinary action, more rigorous and inflexible enforcement of work rules, and lower levels of tolerance of employee dissent and involvement have been the results thus far of the industry's response to the prospective payment system (PPS).

An unprecedented number of hospitals has closed over the last five years, and many more will follow over the next five years. Layoffs and operating deficits are rapidly becoming the norm, but even in the face of structural crisis, health care institutions have by and large been unwilling to question the efficacy of their response model. Clearly, some hospitals and health care facilities ought to close, but the industry's shrinkage should be planned and orderly and should proceed from rational and tenable social criteria. Instead, the pattern of shrinkage has been haphazard at best and has followed the fault lines of managerial arrogance and incompetence. The result is not only an industry flailing helplessly in the face of crisis but also shrinkage of the health care delivery system in ways that impact detrimentally on the medical needs of our society.

The inner logic of PPS forces the health care industry to render its "product" more efficiently with fewer resources. In this sense, the industry can avail itself of two response models to meet the new imperatives. Because each of these models is the negation of the other, however, it is as though a person were standing on two different legs, only one of which could make him walk.

The "right" leg is what I will call the Theory X leg. In this conception, only increased work discipline forcibly imposed on a recalcitrant work force will result in the higher levels of productivity that the industry now requires. The managers and supervisors who inhabit this world carry screwdrivers in their pockets and blank warning notices under their arms. They regard themselves as their organizations' enforcers, and their importance is confirmed to them by their higher salaries and their policing powers. They construe the new challenges that confront them as purely *technical* issues that can be met with purely technical responses. Here, employees are implacable adversaries who, if left to their own devices, will systematically sabotage organizational goals and objectives.

The "left" leg is what I will refer to as the Theory Y leg. In this response model, a recognition flourishes that higher levels of productivity in a resource-scarce environment are possible only when the work force is empowered, motivated, and consulted. In this conception, managers are facilitators who view the knowledge, abilities, and learning capacities of employees as the instrumentalities through which organizational growth is achieved and who view their fundamental tasks to be training and motivating the work force. In short, these are managers whose *raison d'etre* is to free employee potentialities through encouraging employee involvement and participation in the decision-making processes of their work environment.

Once again, we return to the idea that these response models are based on different and opposing *conceptions* of health care workers, in terms of both their ability to make self-directed contributions to desired organizational outcomes and their placement within the organizational hierarchy. The process through which the industry will formulate its response to prospective payment will in the final analysis proceed from the basic assumptions regarding the work force held by those who dominate that process—that is, from the ways in which they conceive the work force. Their choice between these alternative conceptions, if we can speak of it in this way, will determine the future of health care human resources because each alternative will configure the human resources function in a vastly different way. I will explore the nature of these choices and trace the configuration that is likely to follow from each. In addition, I will look at possible strategies to facilitate involvement by human resources administrators in the process that will determine the ultimate complexion of the industry's adaptation to the prospective payment system.

THE INDUSTRY'S MANAGEMENT MODEL

A plethora of "experts" has emerged over the last five years to herald the "pursuit of excellence" through enlightened management. In their wake, seminar upon seminar followed in a feverish attempt to spread the ostensibly new gospel. Despite the fact that virtually all the organizational models cited in the "excellence" literature are based on private sector, for-profit institutions, health care administrators have appeared to take up the gauntlet. The almost obsessive emphasis on excellence within the industry has coincided quite nicely with the advent of prospective payment; indeed, tens of thousands of health care employees have by now been nearly bludgeoned half to death with the new mantra. So insistent and pervasive have the exhortations been that they have eroded any meaning that a reasoned discussion of organizational excellence might have. In short, the concept of excellence has been reduced to a set of ritual incantations.

We ought not be surprised that the new emphasis has not been accompanied by any of the managerial and organizational support mechanisms that would make its attainment possible. With some exceptions, the managers of the health care industry have been unwilling to subject their own assumptions and practice patterns to the same level of scrutiny they have applied to the books and seminars of Peters and Waterman and their colleagues. In this sense, the industry has adopted the theme songs and argot of the new management ideology but has clearly rejected its programmatic substance. To understand why this would be, we need to take stock of the traditional management model that has and continues to dominate health care administration.

The roots of modern management theory and practice in this country lie in the scientific management system of work organization and managerial ideology created by Frederick Winslow Taylor in the early years of the twentieth century.

Taylor's seminal premise was that the needs of efficiency and profit require the *dissociation of the labor process.* Quite simply, this involved the separation of each constituent element of a formerly unified craft into discrete components, each of which was, of course, simpler than the whole.[1] Taylor understood that the labor required to perform each alienated element of the work process could be purchased more cheaply than the labor of the craftsman, whose worth derived from his mastery over the entire labor process.[2]

Prior to scientific management, managers had involved themselves in a general process of setting work tasks but had fully yielded to the craftsman or artisan in matters related to the actual performance of the work. Taylor posited that yielding to the worker in this way made the inner workings of the production process effectively inaccessible to the manager and, therefore, put them beyond his *control.* Taylor's management methodology was consequently designed to transfer control over the work process from the worker to the manager, and thereby to the organization. Simply stated, scientific management can be seen (and *was* seen by Taylor) as the means through which managers would seize control over "the actual mode of performance of every labor activity, from the simplest to the most complicated."[3] In doing so, it defined the essence of modern management as *control*—control, that is, over each aspect of the work process.

If there is genius to Taylor's formulations, it resides in his insights into what I will call the mechanics of control. Scientific management proceeded from Taylor's belief that control over work requires control over "the decisions that are made in the course of work."[4] But an insidious contradiction lurks at the heart of Taylor's system: in order to realize the quantum increases in labor productivity that are the hallmark of scientific management, the once-unified labor process must be atomized into its lowest common denominators; it must be *deskilled.* The process of doing so, however, creates a new class of unskilled workers whose relationship to the work process and work product is newly marginalized and whose investment in the work is therefore marginal. In his preeminent emphasis on the efficiency windfall, Taylor failed to see the human and psychological dynamics associated with the logic of the process. Scientific management could win the body of the work force, but not its heart and mind.

By dissociating the work process into its constituent elements, Taylor effectively separated conception from execution. The newly deskilled workers, relegated to the rote performance of routinized tasks over which they had little control, were now placed under the strict jurisdiction of a small army of thinkers, planners, measurers, and evaluators. Not noted for his subtlety, Taylor stated frankly that the goals of scientific management "will not have been realized until almost all of the machines in the shop are run by men who are of small calibre and attainments, and who are therefore cheaper than those required under the old system."[5]

So thoroughly did Taylor remove from the shop floor the conceptual features of the work process that he created a vast spectrum of job functions bereft of any meaningful content beyond their sheer execution. The "scientific" managers arrogated unto themselves the preconception of the work process prior to its execution, the definition of each aspect of the work, the determination of the exact manner in which it is to be performed and the time to be alloted to it, and the checking, measurement, and evaluation of each stage of the process. It is a short step indeed to the point at which each worker "operates like a hand, watched, corrected, and controlled by a distant brain."[6] As a necessary byproduct of the separation of conception from execution, not only is the hand separated from the brain, but also the conceivers and executors who grow up around those functions become divided and adversarial. Even more importantly, the work itself becomes something *less than human.*

Perhaps the most insidious consequences of the organization of work in accordance with the principles of scientific management relate to the behavioral and psychological aspects of the deskilling of human labor. As their work is systematically robbed of meaning and self-control, growing numbers of workers treat their jobs as though they were meaningless. In Hoxie's words

> It is evident . . . that the native efficiency of the working class must suffer from the neglect of apprenticeship, if no other means of industrial education is forthcoming. Scientific managers, themselves, have complained bitterly of the poor and lawless material from which they recruit their workers, compared with the efficient and self-respecting craftsman who applied for employment twenty years ago.[7]

The modern equivalent of this phenomenon is found in the often-heard complaints regarding the demise of the so-called work ethic. While I will be returning to this issue later, suffice it to note at this point that if there has in fact been an erosion of the work ethos, it is inextricably bound to the deskilling of work itself. Absent any sense of ownership in the work process, workers often become indifferent, recalcitrant, and unproductive. The defining irony of scientific management is that its virtual obsession with productivity and efficiency culminates in its negation, the alienation of the disenfranchised worker.

In this peculiar sense, the disciplines of industrial psychology and personnel administration were called into being by the human consequences of scientific management. Their essential subject was the alienation of the work force, and their essential mission was the facilitation of workers' adaptation to their deskilled job function and their organizational powerlessness. By definition, this undertaking concerned itself not with the intrinsic nature of the deskilled work process but rather with the reaction of workers to the routinization of their work. Braverman has referred to this process as the habituation of workers to their work.[8] In too many ways, modern-day industrial psychology has progressed little beyond the original conception, which viewed the fundamental problem not in terms of the degradation of work but rather in terms of the need to produce a more acclimated work force.

This returns us to our home territory, health care management. Too many of us fail to see ourselves as functioning within the traditions of scientific management. We have been falsely lulled into a kind of organizational complacency in distinguishing our environment from the manufacturing sector. Although historically immune from the private sector exigencies of profit and efficiency, the health care industry has nonetheless been characterized by a management methodology and a management mindset that fall decidedly within the mainstream of American management norms. Our industry has become as fully stratified, hierarchical, and organizationally fragmented as any other, and in some ways more so.

This is not meant to imply that health care management practices have assumed all the features of scientific management. To be sure, the absence of a profit motive and the industry's relative immunity from market forces have softened and diluted the virulent aspects of the system of work organization and the forms of management that obtain in much of the private sector. These differences, however, are ones of degree rather than kind. The health care industry has organized work in such a way as to encourage a proliferation of low-skilled job functions (euphemistically termed "disciplines"), with minimal authority and less power, and has adopted a management model that is based on a rigid, unyielding separation of conception from execution, of order giving from order taking. In this fundamental sense, health care management must be placed within the tradition of scientific management. The institutionalization of PPS will almost certainly erase even those few features that have distinguished the industry's management from that of its private sector counterparts.

We need to return to the issue of the division between order giving and order taking.[9] This division both mimics and reflects the separation of conception from execution, although there are indeed order givers who are themselves locked out of the planning and conception process (such as line supervisors and entry-level managers). Even a cursory review of the evolution of the industry's management practices and culture reveals a relentless and largely successful effort to remove responsibility from health care workers. We ought not to be surprised, then, if segments of our work force, particularly at the lower ends of the occupational hierarchy, have acted irresponsibly. In general, we have treated the division of labor between conceiving and executing as a virtual truism, a given, a natural basis of work organization. The nature of industrial relations within the industry has proceeded logically from this division. If we are to meet the challenges that confront us, we must begin with the proposition that the conception/execution dichotomy, far from being natural, is a structural impediment. In Peter Drucker's words

> It does not follow from the separation of planning and doing in the analysis of work that the planner and the doer should be two different people. It does not follow that the industrial world should be divided into two classes of people; the few who decide what is to be done, design the job, set the pace, rhythm and motions and order others about; and the many who do what and as they are being told.[10]

Before moving on to alternative approaches to the management function, let us recapitulate the essential features of the traditional management model as handed down to us by scientific management.

- The overarching needs of efficiency require the separation of the conception of the work process from its execution. The functions of planning, measuring, and evaluating the work process must therefore be removed from the worker.
- The fundamental mission of management is to maintain and exercise control over each aspect of the work process. The reduction of work to its lowest skill components is an essential precondition of management control and the single most important factor serving the interests of efficiency.
- If left "unmanaged," workers will naturally malinger, aimlessly socialize, and otherwise sabotage the process of efficient production. Accordingly, the interests of efficiency dictate extremely close levels of supervision, the removal of all but nominal decision-making power from the work unit, the stringent application of disciplinary policies, and the absolute and unquestioned tyranny of the order givers over the order takers.
- The institutional role of disciplining and otherwise pacifying the work force in the interests of efficiency resides in the personnel function.
- Work autonomy is inimical to the interests of the order givers. It must therefore be kept to an absolute minimum, and mechanisms must be developed to discipline its emergence.

AN ALTERNATIVE MODEL

Because the traditional management model has so completely dominated American management practices since at least the turn of the century, it is tempting to view both its assumptions and its methodology as natural, fixed, and immutable. In fact, alternative models do exist and, in more instances than are generally known, have been implemented and have been effective. My first task, therefore, is to debunk the notion that it cannot be otherwise, that the humanization of the work place is a fantasy that exists in the minds of theorists but is alien to and unworkable in the real world of bottom lines and business competition.

Alternative models of management must be based on alternative conceptions of people and of workers if they are to constitute true alternatives. They need to be based on concepts of motivation rather than merely on discipline, on freeing creative energies and potentialities rather than on suppressing them, on developing organizational conventions and norms that facilitate employee investment rather than on fostering alienation, on empowerment rather than subjugation. Most importantly, they need to be based on the notion that the most basic function of management is to motivate workers through their inclusion in the planning, design, and organization of their work.

One of the few corporate leaders in this society who has understood and been willing to struggle against the bankruptcy of the traditional model is Rene McPherson, formerly the chief executive officer of Dana and now Dean of the Stanford University Business School. McPherson has in a sense reformulated the issue of employee motivation and in the process has redefined its essential nature: "We don't motivate people. They are motivated by their upbringing, education, and other things. What we are doing is taking the handcuffs off by giving workers responsibility and a voice in how their jobs are done."[11] For McPherson, one of the ways to accomplish this objective is to create a breed of managers who do not reduce their essential function merely to telling people what to do and how to do it and who are not threatened by asking workers what they think.[12]

Any attempt to flesh out an alternative and opposing model of management will cross the path of the works of Douglas McGregor. Athough the body of his work is a subject unto itself, let us look briefly at his Theory X/Theory Y with a view toward integrating it into our subject matter.

McGregor posited two generic forms of management, arbitrarily assigning to them the categories Theory X and Theory Y. Most of us have been exposed on numerous occasions to this theoretical dichotomy in college and graduate school and in management literature. As is the case with many seminal works and ideas, McGregor's X/Y theory has been significantly watered down through the years and wrenched from its original context. The dominant interpretation has treated the opposing theories as though they connote management *styles* rather than fundamentally different conceptions of human motivation and of people themselves. What is at issue here is not the *affects* of managers as they go about their job of managing but rather the assumptions that frame and animate their actions.

The Theory X construct closely conforms to those assumptions, characteristics, and practices we have defined as dominating the traditional management model. It construes workers as having an inherent dislike of work and an unlimited capacity to devise ways to avoid it; as preferring direction and the avoidance of responsibility to autonomy and self-directed accomplishment; as needing large measures of control, coercion, and externally imposed discipline; and as having little or no interest in contributing to the attainment of organizational goals and objectives, unless forced to do so.

Moving from the theoretical to the practical realm, Theory X management is characterized by a high ratio of managers to employees in order to maximize managerial control; an almost obsessive concern with quantification, measurement, and evaluation mechanisms; highly stratified and hierarchical organizational structures; and a low threshold for employee

dissent or, for that matter, innovation outside the limits of the basic job function.

The Theory Y model proceeds from a vastly different and opposing set of assumptions regarding work, workers, and human nature itself. The managers who inhabit this model believe that workers have a natural desire to work hard and that under "normal" conditions, the average employee will not attempt to avoid work; that self-motivation is an inherent quality in most people and that the desire and willingness to contribute to organizational goals does not have to be coerced out of most employees; that the average person both accepts and seeks responsibility; that creative and innovative capacities and inclinations are widely rather than narrowly distributed throughout the general population; and that the intellectual and technical potentialities of most people are woefully underutilized under the existing system of work organization.[13]

Levitan and Johnson have cited survey results in support of the general assumptions that animate and inform the Theory Y model.

> Even recent survey results confirm a continuing attachment to work—a Roper Organization survey found that one in five people place more emphasis on their personal satisfaction than on working hard and doing a good job, and 85 percent of those interviewed . . . believe that success in life is dependent on their working hard. If we are really about to abandon work, somebody had better tell the workers.[14]

The management practices that characterize the Theory Y model are directed toward forms of work organization in which the nucleus is the worker and the work unit, toward practices that are designed to liberate rather than confine and circumscribe the potentialities that are seen to be inherent in the work force. Theory Y managers conceive of workers not simply as "a variable factor in the efficiency of an organization"[15] but rather as the determining factor, and they seek to organize work and design organizational policies around that conception. In this environment, quality assurance and quality control are transformed into mechanisms through which workers advise the organization on ways to improve organizational efficiency rather than being just another form of managerial surveillance.

Theory Y management involves less management and therefore fewer managers. The surveillance metaphor is particularly instructive here. When the *sine qua non* of management is defined as control over each aspect of the work process, work must be organized in ways that facilitate and maximize managerial control. Rather than being natural, this control must be enforced on a daily basis. The management structure that arises to fulfill this enforcement function must by definition be both extensive and intensive if it is to accomplish its defining mission. These managers are, in the final analysis, gendarmes, constituting a kind of industrial police force. That is to say, a surveillance function has become their defining activity. The alternative and opposing model, which as we have seen is based on a conception of people as largely being self-directed *under the appropriate conditions*, calls into being managers who view creating those conditions as their primary function. In this latter case, the requirements of managerial intervention are consequently of a far lesser magnitude insofar as managers are cast in the role of facilitators and coordinators rather than that of an occupation army. This is precisely why organizations built on Theory Y foundations invariably have lower ratios of managers to employees than do those built in the tradition of scientific management.

THE EFFECTS OF PROSPECTIVE PAYMENT

The specific ways in which health care administration has conformed to the Theory X model have in general been poorly understood. As managers, we have considered the health care industry *sui generis*, unique and incomparable, creating the illusion that we somehow function in an industrial vacuum. As we have previously noted, it is unquestionably true that the industry is characterized by certain unique features that distinguish it from the corporate norms of the private, for-profit sector. Indeed, the very fact that our "product" is health care is a distinguishing attribute *per se*. Moreover, at least until recently, the forms in which our costs were reimbursed reflected the peculiar and distinguishing nature of our business. We have also noted, however, that as managers, we have been functioning very much within the framework of the traditional organizational model, the uniqueness of our industry notwithstanding.

Although we are hard pressed to compare health care workers to Taylor's pig-iron workers, or to production workers in general, we have managed them as though the differences were cosmetic in nature. The typical health care institution is literally riddled with several hundred job classifications and "disciplines," the overwhelming proportion of which require minimal skill levels; it is managed by a large cadre of supervisory and managerial overseers who not only see themselves as enforcers but also are punished and rewarded on the basis of their enforcement skills; and it is organized in an extremely hierarchical structure that inhibits and otherwise suppresses employee involvement in patient care management. Administrative overhead in the industry increased by 20 percent between 1980 and 1985, thus constituting the fastest-growing component of health care expenditures.[16]

Although the health care industry has to a large extent been immunized from the pressures of profit and efficiency under the systems of cost reimbursement that preceded PPS, it is simply fallacious to argue that our forms of management and our conception of workers have been outside the framework of the traditional model. The most we can say is that the *intensity* of management has been of a lesser magnitude in the absence of market forces. It is somewhat remarkable that even in the absence of the kind of profit motives that drive the private sector, we have engendered forms of work organization based on a rigid division between order givers and order takers and have been largely impervious to even the mildest and most benign forms of employee involvement and participation.

The prospective payment system has gone a long way in eradicating most of the features that have distinguished health care management from its private sector counterparts. With the gradual infusion of market forces into the delivery of health care, the industry has become more than ever a "business" reducing medical care for the sick and dying to the status of the commodity. In the process, human suffering itself has in a sense been similarly transformed into a marketable product.[17] As with any business that must compete in the (more or less) open market, health care institutions have been compelled by the logic of PPS to take any and all measures that make financial survival more likely. Quite simply, the result is an industry in transformation. The evidence of this transformation has taken a variety of forms. Its indexes have included the following:

- An unprecedented number of hospitals has closed since the advent of PPS. Many more waver on the precipice of fiscal insolvency. Forty-nine hospitals closed in 1985, seventy-one in 1986, and seventy-nine in 1987.[18] We can expect the next several years to witness even higher levels of closure.

- The aggregate number of health care workers has been significantly reduced. Downsizing has become the new mantra, and with it an entirely new cadre of consultants has emerged to ostensibly guide us through the contraction. The logic of prospective payment is in this regard ineluctable. Fewer and fewer health care institutions that fail to diminish their work force will be able to survive. It will be interesting to see whether the ranks of health care managers will be reduced commensurately. The logic of the Theory X methodology, as we have noted elsewhere, would suggest that they will not be.

- Entirely new functions have been called into being with the mission of marketing the health care "product." With the burgeoning of these marketing functions, the traditional public relations function has been transformed into an adjunct of the marketing process. Indeed, a growing share of scarce health care resources has been siphoned into these undertakings, and we can expect this trend to accelerate. With the new status accorded to marketing, the idiom of health care administration is itself changing. The words on the lips of health care administrators are now likely to be "consumer profiles," "focus groups," and "product line management." What were once patients in need of health care services are now consumers and clients. This new language reflects the larger forces acting on the industry and its transformation from provider to vendor.

- Only five years into prospective payment, the system has already gone a long way in reconfiguring the face of the health care industry. Lengths of stay and hospital admissions are down to unprecedented levels; hospital occupancy has fallen almost 13 percent on a national level since 1983 (from 72.6 percent to 60 percent). Over and above hospital closures, the reduction of beds is spreading across the industry like fire (22,000 beds closed in 1984 alone), and the Health Care Financing Administration, the agency responsible for the administration of the prospective payment system, projects that PPS will ultimately close one of every six hospital beds.[19] As a result of the system's reimbursement biases, new services such as ambulatory surgery have emerged, and outpatient services in general have proliferated. Meanwhile, the aggressive search for new sources of patients to counteract decreasing utilization and admissions has resulted in the spread of health maintenance organizations (HMOs) and preferred provider organizations (PPOs). Indeed, the number of physicians employed by HMOs increased 40 percent from 1980 to 1983 (from 50,000 to 70,000).[20]

The industry's response to these new conditions has been extremely discouraging, but perhaps not surprising. This response has consisted largely of an intensification of the status quo; we have simply reached down deeper into the traditional arsenal of rules, regulations, policies, and procedures in the interest of fostering higher levels of work discipline and productivity—*but that dog won't hunt*. Prospective payment has increased the level of organizational stress within the industry to what must surely be its highest point in the modern era. Based on the current response model, we ought to expect a growing rather than a diminishing level of stress. Confronted with this pressure, health care workers are exhibiting a declining tolerance for the industry's adversarial forms of supervision and management, they are showing a growing interest in union organization as a means to protect themselves against the onslaught, and more and more they are demanding a role in the changing health care delivery process beyond the mere execution of their job functions. In short, they are exhibiting a diminished capacity and a disinclination to tolerate their institutional marginalization. As we have noted, the industry's response has been to demand further marginalization of its work force in the mistaken belief that disciplined and overmanaged employees are productive employees. Given the management model from which the industry operates, it perhaps could not be otherwise.

Insofar as we are wedded to the Theory X model of management, the arsenal with which our industry has confronted the imperatives of prospective payment is fixed and limited. Ask the Theory X chief executive officer what measures he or she has implemented and plans to implement to deal with the new exigencies of prospective payment, and I assure you that you will hear a litany of belt tightening, downsizing, heightened disciplinary standards, and more vigilant union-avoidance strategies. The notion that the enfranchisement and empowerment of health care workers might make sense under the new circumstances, not for liberal reasons but for *business* reasons,

will in all probability be dismissed as either naive or irrelevant, or both.

As human resources administrators, we will simply have to be more effective in insinuating ourselves and our perspective into the front lines of the industry's response to PPS. If not, we cannot reasonably expect that the Theory Y approach will prevail—or even be considered. We need to get into the board rooms and planning offices to make it clear that the path of training, motivating, and empowering the health care work force is the path of organizational survival. Not only does the fate of our individual institutions hinge on the manner in which we manage the PPS juggernaut, but the nature and complexion of health care human resources administration do as well.

Let us now proceed to a closer look at the nature of this causation: the ways in which our mission as human resources administrators will be conditioned and determined by the industry's response to the new imperatives.

HUMAN RESOURCES ADMINISTRATION UNDER PPS

As a general proposition and with some notable exceptions, human resources administration has not figured prominently in the determination of organizational outcomes in the health care industry. Too many of us have passively accepted our subordination in the organizational power matrix and have allowed or been helpless to prevent our relegation to the margins of management. At best, we have functioned as a type of maintenance crew for the human machinery, a function that has itself symbolized our subordination.

As a result, the norms and texture of health care organizational culture have largely been determined without our input or involvement. To the extent that personnel policies have a determining effect on organizational value formation, we have in a sense been closed out of our own jurisdiction. It is critical to understand that our marginalization follows logically and directly from the marginalization of the work force. At the risk of simplifying the matter, the premium an organization places on its human resources function is an expression of the premium it places on its employees. To the precise extent that an organization understands its work force is its single most critical element, it empowers its human resources function.

In this sense, the nature of human resources administration is determined by the manner in which an organization perceives its employees. When employees are viewed as organizational instrumentalities, as mere factors of production, human resources administration will be assigned the role of maintenance crew, and its organizational perspective will reflect that function. When, on the other hand, employees are understood to be the lifeblood of the organization, and to be freely willing to contribute to and enrich the organization if only allowed to do so, the human resources function will be assigned the role of facilitating that contribution through employee involvement, empowerment, and due process.

It should be clear that these alternative scenarios correspond to the alternative management models that we examined above. We can speak of a series of defining activities that characterize human resources administration in Theory X and Theory Y organizations.

Theory X human resources administration

- construes its primary function as that of "prosecuting attorney" for management in the application of personnel policies, with a pre-eminent emphasis on disciplinary policies
- is assigned the role of institutional enforcer of the pre-rogatives of management over/against the work force
- accordingly views the human resources function as an adjunct of management/administration and relegates its employee advocacy and employee-management liaison functions to an ancillary status
- places virtually exclusive emphasis on the maintenance functions of human resources administration—forms processing, records and benefits administration, labor relations, and contract administration—while under-developing or neglecting the developmental functions of training, staff and career development, employee assistance, and employee advocacy
- consumes most of its energies in its bureaucratic func-tions, the primacy of which it jealously guards like the family fortune

Theory Y human resources administration

- defines its primary functions as training, career develop-ment, and employee advocacy and develops organiza-tional structures within the department to reflect that mission
- provides institutional leadership in the development of employee recognition, reward, and involvement mechanisms
- designs and develops personnel policies that reflect employee-oriented values and encourages work auton-omy and employee-directed forms of work organization
- develops and administers wage and salary policies that are performance-driven and impartially applied
- facilitates job definition in ways that make workers more rather than less responsible, for process as well as for outcomes
- involves employees at all levels of the organizational hierarchy in determining performance standards, evalua-tion mechanisms, and personnel policies
- views due process safeguards as a virtual organizational religion and consistently disciplines their violation

Which form of human resources administration a particular institution encourages is less an expression of the proclivities of the individual human resources administrator than it is an expression of the set of assumptions and beliefs inherent in the institution's management model. It is precisely these assump-tions and beliefs that form the foundations of organizational values.

The most compelling challenge facing health care human resources administrators over the next several years is to identify to the industry's leadership the inextricable link between humanized work and working conditions on the one hand and the levels of productivity that survival requires on the other. We need to insist that compassionate and efficiently rendered patient care *is not possible* without a humanized and democratically organized work environment. We need to link organizational health and survival with the empowerment of health care workers. If health care administrators cannot be expected to speak and understand the language of social justice within the work place, then we need to speak to them in the idiom of institutional survival.

CONCLUSION

The initial signs are not encouraging. Five years into pro-spective payment, the heirs of scientific management—plan-ners, efficiency experts, and work simplifiers—dominate the health care industry and, therefore, dominate the industry's response to prospective payment. There are indeed excep-tions, but they remain a distinctly minority phenomenon.

Exclusion from the essential features of patient care man-agement and the absence of work autonomy are the two most consistently cited sources of dissatisfaction for health care workers. We need to begin to see these factors as an instru-mental part of the destructive process through which we make adversaries of our employees. Despite its historically low levels of productivity, the industry has failed to move beyond a classification structure based on fractionalized job functions that serve to routinize and deskill job functions rather than expand them.

There are still opportunities, however, to advance the alter-native model. Indeed, the failures of the present strategy may eventually make the alternatives more attractive to health care administrators, even if only out of desperation. We have already seen that in several instances the requirements of the burgeoning marketing function have caused some health care institutions to probe the issue of job satisfaction. That this concern has emerged from a patient relations perspective rather than out of a concern for the working lives of health care workers need not deter us.

The present course is a prescription for industrial conflict and will almost certainly result in higher levels of successful union organizing, even as the proportion of unionized employ-ees in other sectors of our economy continues to decline. More importantly, it is a prescription for failure.

Once again, we return to the image of a person standing on two different legs, only one of which can make him walk. If we throw the wrong leg out, we will be vanquished by the logic of prospective payment.

NOTES

1. H. Braverman, *Labor and Monopoly Capital: The Degradation of Work in the Twentieth Century* (New York and London: Monthly Review Press, 1974), 81.

2. Ibid.

3. Ibid., 90.

4. Ibid., 107.

5. F.W. Taylor, *Shop Management* (New York: Harper & Row, 1911), 105.

6. Braverman, *Labor and Monopoly Capital*, 125.

7. R.F. Hoxie, *Scientific Management and Labor* (New York: Kelley, 1915), 134.

8. Braverman, *Labor and Monopoly Capital*, 139.

9. J. Simmons and W. Mares, *Working Together: Employee Participation in Action* (New York: New York University Press, 1986), 16.

10. P. Drucker, *The Practice of Management* (New York: Harper & Row, 1954), 284.

11. Simmons and Mares, *Working Together*, 161.

12. Ibid., 213.

13. D. McGregor, *The Human Side of Enterprise* (New York: McGraw-Hill Book Co., 1960), 138–40.

14. S.A. Levitan and C.M. Johnson, *Second Thoughts on Work* (Kalamazoo, Mich.: W.E. Upjohn Institute for Employment Research, 1982), 9.

15. Ibid., 153.

16. J. Fineglass, "Living with Bottomline Health Care," *Zeta Magazine* (October 1988): 96.

17. R. Kotelchuck, "In the Grip of P.P.S.," *Health PAC Bulletin* 15, no. 2 (November 1986), 12.

18. "Small Inner-City Hospitals Face Threat of Financial Failure," *New York Times*, 2 August 1988.

19. R. Kotelchuck, "In the Grip of P.P.S.," *Health PAC Bulletin* 15, no. 1 (September 1986), 7.

20. J. Fineglass, "Living with Bottomline Health Care," 96.

V. Brandon Melton

Human Resources Strategic Planning: The Human Resources Professional As Architect

3

In a recent survey of over 800 human resources executives in the health care industry, human resources strategic planning was identified as the most critical issue they will face in the coming years. It is no wonder. The health care industry is in its most revolutionary period since the first U.S. hospital was founded in another revolutionary time—1776.

Prior to the mid-1980s the health care industry experienced a 25-year period of growth and prosperity. Hospitals became larger, and many changed their names to medical centers and then to health centers, but their basic structure did not undergo significant change. Most hospitals remained stand-alone business entities with one primary mission—to provide acute inpatient care. In addition, the post–World War II "baby boomers" provided a seemingly endless supply of well-educated individuals interested in nursing, medicine, and other health-related professions. Today, all of this has changed.

Diversification, outsizing, joint ventures, mergers, acquisitions, buy outs, closures, executive management turnover, and downsizing are subjects that consume the agendas of hospital governing board meetings. Health care futurist Russell Coile coined a new health care acronym, "O.W.A.," to describe the extent and complexity of the diversification our industry has experienced. O.W.A. stands for "Other Weird Arrangements." Although the acute care inpatient setting continues to serve as the anchor for most hospital corporations, the diversity and number of alternative delivery settings and services are growing rapidly.

Ambulatory care, outpatient surgery, home health care, satellite clinics, urgi/emergicenters, women's health care, hospices, and wellness centers are all important components of many of today's successful health care systems. If the human resources function is to be truly relevant to the success of our organizations, we human resources professionals must play an important role in helping to ensure the success of these new ventures. We must become as critical to their success as are the lawyers who negotiate the contracts, the accountants who manage the finances of these enterprises, and the architects who design the facilities.

While lawyers, accountants, and architects work for months or even years planning a new venture, human resources professionals often are called in at the last moment, with little consideration given to what level of competence is needed to staff the new enterprise or where the staff will come from. One of the more unfortunate effects of this late entry on the part of human resources is that it provides little time to retrain or cross train current hospital staff to assume new roles. As a result, valuable employees are laid off from the acute care hospital, while newly hired employees assume positions in the new alternative delivery settings. The human suffering, not to mention the financial costs, from simultaneously downsizing current staff and recruiting others is considerable. A human resources strategic plan enables an organization to utilize current staff to assume new roles and responsibilities. As a result, the organization can plan well in advance to use more humane methods of downsizing, such as voluntary reductions of hours or pay, transfers, promotions, and early retirement.

THE PLAN

Norman Metzger, one of the leading human resources executives in the United States, stresses that the key to the success of any human resources function is relevancy. Another leading human resources executive, Kerma Jones, has said that "human resources professionals will be in alignment with their organizations when they lay awake nights worrying about the same things their CEOs lay awake nights worrying about." In order to be truly relevant and fully aligned, human resources executives must develop human resources strategic plans that mirror their organization's overall strategic plans. We must help each organization's most important and expensive resource—its people—move in the same direction its governing board and senior management staff are moving. If the hospital is contemplating a new venture, we must determine the skills and competencies required to manage and staff it successfully. If it is contemplating a merger, we must determine ways to integrate the staffs of the merging organizations. Whatever the direction the governing board and senior executive staff are taking the organization in, we must look for ways to help them get there. In "A Guide to Strategic Human Resource Planning for the Health Care Industry," Thomas Wilson (1986) defined human resources planning as "the process for determining an organization's human resources requirements, and the plans for how these resources can best be acquired, developed, managed, and deployed." This how-to manual further describes human resources planning as having the following four key phases.

1. *Situation analysis.* Situation analysis is the systemic identification of the human resources challenges facing the organization. This is accomplished through a comprehensive analysis of the external environment and the organization's current strategic goals and objectives. In assessing the organization's external environment, a number of factors need to be examined, including anticipated changes in the legislative and regulatory arena, economic forces, technological advances, changes in the demographic makeup of the marketplace, and shifts in consumer attitudes and values. A second key issue to be examined in this phase of the human resources planning process is the organization's current strengths and weaknesses, as well as its strategic plans for the future. Which lines of business or services are expected to grow in the coming years, and which are expected to be less important to the organization's overall success in the future? A thorough assessment of the external environment, coupled with an examination of the organization's strategic goals and objectives, will complete the situation analysis.

2. *Demand analysis.* Once the current and future situations have been analyzed, the examination of demand is the next major phase in the human resources planning process. This step involves an analysis of the current and future requirements for staffing to fulfill the organization's business strategy. As part of the demand analysis, the human resources planner examines whether staffing should be increased or decreased in each of the organization's existing staff positions. Are changes needed in the existing skill mix? Will new positions need to be expanded to meet new demands dictated by either the organization's external environment or its strategic goals and objectives? In addition to the examination of staffing requirements, the demand analysis phase may also call for adjustments to the organization's structure, its management philosophy, or its corporate culture.

3. *Supply analysis.* This phase of the human resources planning process calls for a projection of the number and skill mix of professional and support staff available to fully meet the demand. This analysis should include a thorough assessment of the current staff available as well as an examination of external labor markets. Supply analysis should in fact begin with a thorough assessment of the existing job incumbents' capabilities and potentials. The assessment of existing staff has significant implications for a number of critical human resources functions, such as staff education and training, succession planning, performance management, and reductions in force or resizing. An examination of external labor markets includes a thorough assessment of the supply and skill mix of individuals available to enter the health care work force. This analysis should encompass individuals involved in midcareer changes as well as those entering the labor force for the first time.

4. *The human resources plan.* The human resources plan is in large part an identification of the gaps, overlaps, and issues raised when comparing the human resources demand with the projected supply. The gaps identified in this phase indicate those areas where the organization is at risk of failing to achieve its strategic goals and objectives. Once the human resources gaps have been identified, the organization can develop action plans for filling them. The human resources plan should also address those areas for which there is likely to be excess capacity or staffing. Essential to the development of a human resources plan is the possibility of shifting personnel from areas of excess capacity to those in which workers are anticipated to be in short supply. When it is determined that workers will be in short supply in particular areas, specific action plans can be developed to help close these gaps. In some cases, closing these gaps may be possible by retraining and cross training current staff. If this strategy is not sufficient to provide an adequate supply, recruitment and development of staff from outside the organization will be necessary. The human resources plan should contain action plans for the development of specific objectives, action steps, timetables, responsibilities, and resources needed to provide ade-

quate staff to meet the organization's future human resources requirements. To be both effective and relevant, the organization's human resources plan should be re-evaluated on at least an annual basis. In the rapidly changing and complex health care environment, it is essential that the human resources plan remain a dynamic document, sensitive to the many internal and external forces that affect the organization.

SUCCESS FACTORS

The successful development and implementation of a human resources plan in a health care organization is dependent on a number of key factors.

- The human resources planning process must be integrated with the organization's overall strategic and corporate planning systems.
- The specific action plans, goals, and objectives outlined in the human resources plan need to become part of each manager's performance planning and evaluation system.
- The responsibility for human resources planning should rest with line managers, with the human resources professional playing the role of expert consultant and facilitator.
- Human resources planning must be supported by the organization's senior executive management staff.
- Because the human resources planning process is a systematic, ongoing function, the plan should be re-evaluated on an annual basis, and adjustments should be made as needed.

Competition, diversification, and a dwindling labor force will characterize the health care industry through the end of this century. To remain competitive and to be flexible enough to respond to a rapidly changing environment, health care organizations will have to identify and adjust to the changing supply and demand for human resources talent, as well as to the dramatic changes that are occurring in our industry. Because human capital is our most vital asset, we must develop human resources strategic plans to ensure the sustained success of our organizations today and in the future.

BIBLIOGRAPHY

Dowling, Edward J., and Kellman, Elliott A. "The Strategic Management of Human Resources." Paper presented at the Region I Educational Conference, American Society for Hospital Personnel Administration, Newport, R.I., September 1985.

Eisenberg, B. "Strategic Human Resource Plans Help Providers Survive Changing Conditions." *Modern Healthcare* 16, No. 39 (March 28, 1986): 154.

"Human Resource Planning: Trends and Issues." *Management Memo,* The Hay Group, Inc., no. 340, Philadelphia, PA.

Leshner, M., and Coleman, S. "Human Resource Planning That Works: A Case Study." *Personnel Journal* (April 1985): 57.

Mills, P.Q. "Planning with People in Mind." *Harvard Business Review* 63, No. 4 (July-August 1985): 97.

National Association for Health Service Personnel Officers and Hay Management Consultants. "Human Resource Planning in Healthcare—A Guide for Managers and Human Resource Professionals." National Association of Health Service Personnel Officers (London) and Hay Management Consultants, 1988.

Wilson, Thomas B. "A Guide to Strategic Human Resource Planning for the Health Care Industry." Chicago: American Society for Healthcare Human Resources Administration of the American Hospital Association, 1986, 21.

Myron D. Fottler

Strategic Human Resources Management

4

INTRODUCTION

The external environment in which health care organizations must exist has become increasingly complex and turbulent. Changing financing mechanisms, the emergence of new competitors in various markets, declining inpatient hospital occupancy rates, changes in physician health care organization relations, the growth of multi-institutional systems, capital shortages, and changes in work force demographics are some of the major environmental factors affecting health care. In response to these changes, health care organizations are closing facilities, undertaking corporate reorganization, canceling major construction projects, instituting staffing freezes and/or reductions in their work force, providing services with fewer resources, changing their organizational structures, and developing leaner management structures with fewer levels and wider spans of control.

Developing appropriate strategic responses to the challenging external environment received an enormous amount of attention from both academicians and health care executives during the 1980s. As a result, strategic planning is now well accepted in health care organizations. The major competitive strategies currently being pursued include

- becoming a low-cost provider of traditional health services
- providing the highest-quality patient services through extra high technical quality or customer service
- specializing in a few clinical areas
- diversifying into related health care businesses

- diversifying into nonrelated health care fields that utilize existing capabilities[1]

One of the problems with strategic planning in health care organizations is a *failure of implementation*.[2] Such a failure may be due to two factors. First, all the individuals and groups who have to execute a given strategy may not have had input into the strategy. The result is an ill-conceived strategy. Second, the strategy may draw on input from all the appropriate individuals and groups and may be well conceived. However, the execution of the strategy may be deficient because implementation issues may not have been considered when the strategy was conceived.

For example, the use of human resources management as a key factor in the successful implementation of a strategy has not received much attention. Yet McManis has noted that "While many hospitals have elegant and elaborate strategic plans, they often do not have supporting human resource strategies to ensure that the overall corporate plan can be implemented. But strategies don't fail, people do."[3] Peters and Waterman also have pointed out that all the excellent organizations they surveyed made effective use of their human resources as a strategic activity.[4]

The perspective that business strategies might be linked to human resources practices has just begun to emerge in the health care industry. Eisenberg identifies this linkage as essential to organizational survival.[5] Cerne sees it as a method of avoiding shortages of key personnel, which could impede attainment of the strategic objectives.[6] Health care organizations tend to develop a linkage between strategy and human resources when new strategies significantly impact the way work is done, staffing problems inhibit productivity or growth, changes in the organization's structure impact job requirements, and/or significant turnover is occurring (or about to occur) in key positions.

This chapter will (1) define the concept of strategic human resources management; (2) provide a rationale for how it could enhance organizational outcomes in health care organizations; (3) define the steps involved in strategically managing human resources; (4) provide some examples of how human resources can be managed strategically; and (5) identify factors that can enhance the success of this approach.

DEFINITION AND RATIONALE

Definition

For purposes of this chapter, strategic human resources management is defined as follows:

> Strategic human resources management is the planning and implementation of systems of human resources planning, career planning, recruitment, selection, training, performance appraisal, compensation, and labor relations that insure qualified personnel are available to staff the portfolio of business units and reinforce the business strategy of the organization.[7]

The strategic management of human resources involves attention to the effect of external environmental and internal components on human resources practices.[8] As a result of the critical role of health professionals in delivering services in this labor-intensive industry, a major concern of health care executives should be the development of personnel policies and practices that are closely related to, influenced by, and supportive of the strategic thrust of the organization.

Figure 4-1 provides a graphic illustration of the strategic human resources management (SHRM) process. The corporate and business unit strategy is formulated after an assessment of internal strengths and weaknesses, environmental opportunities and threats, and the organizational mission. Once the strategy has been formulated, it has to be implemented through a wide range of management processes, including marketing, finance, information systems, and human resources. Only the latter is shown in Figure 4-1 because human resources are the focus of the present chapter.

Strategy implementation through SHRM begins with an assessment of the organization's human resources requirements in terms of numbers, characteristics, and human resources systems. These human resources requirements are then compared to existing human resources numbers, characteristics, and systems to determine the existence and nature of any gaps. These gaps, in turn, drive the human resources strategy, which should be implemented through modified human resources systems and practices geared to reinforce the business strategy. This mutual reinforcement should result in improved individual and organizational outcomes, such as efficiency, effectiveness, and competitive advantage.

Rationale

Why should a health care organization adopt the process of SHRM described above? First, the benefits of such a linkage have been demonstrated in other industries. During the 1981–82 recession, employers who had linked human resources planning to strategy were able to minimize employee layoffs through hiring freezes, attrition, and other types of advanced actions.[9] Almost three-quarters of these corporations in a variety of industries were also certain that SHRM improved their profitability. Other research has found a strong positive correlation between the exporting success of 300 manufacturing corporations and their use of SHRM.[10]

As noted earlier, health care organizations tend to engage in some form of SHRM when new strategies require new skills, staffing problems inhibit productivity or growth, significant turnover is occurring in key positions, or changes in the organization's structure impact job requirements. One example of the latter is a for-profit, national chain of mental health and substance abuse hospitals. This chain is attempting to restructure internally by moving from a functional structure to a product-line structure. The purposes are to increase staff productivity and to become more responsive to patient needs. Such a shift in organizational structure also requires a change in the job requirements for many positions, such as nurse, psychologist, and medical social worker. The corporation is now in the process of using SHRM to identify the new tasks, task combinations, required skills and abilities, and the necessary consequent training of existing personnel and/or recruitment of new personnel from outside the corporation.

Another example is a rapidly growing health maintenance organization in the Southeast. This organization discovered that a lack of qualified middle management personnel was leading to significant problems in enrollee and physician service as well as to a slowing rate of increase in enrollment. Moreover, potential turnover in key positions would have put the whole organization at risk. The SHRM process resulted in a plan for staffing various middle management positions over a three-year period through both external recruitment and the development of various management training programs for present management personnel. At the time of this writing, some new positions have been defined in terms of functions and responsibilities (i.e., job descriptions), and internal and external recruitment is underway.

More generally, the result of SHRM is an enhanced ability to attract and retain qualified personnel who are motivated to perform the right functions at the right time and place. The improved matching of human resources to the organization's human resources needs should result in improved profitability, lower turnover, higher service quality, lower unit costs, and more rapid acceptance and implementation of the corporate and business unit strategy.

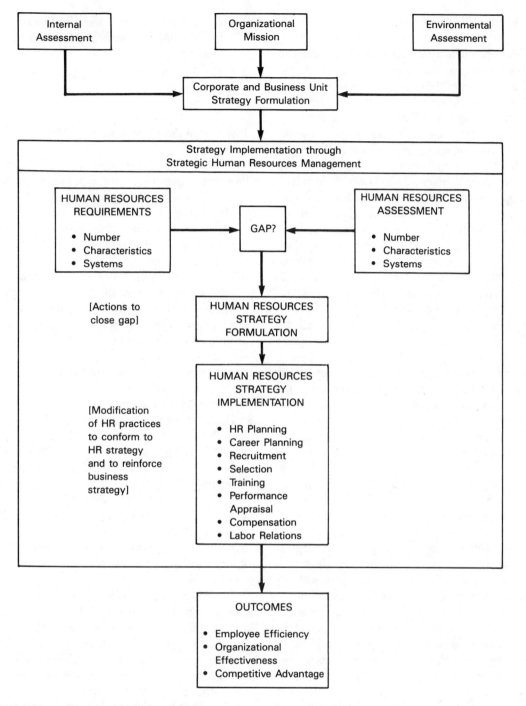

Figure 4-1 The Strategic Human Resources Management Process

IMPLEMENTATION STEPS

The steps involved in implementing the process of SHRM are implicit in Figure 4-1: (1) formulate the corporate and business unit strategy after assessing the external environment, internal corporate strengths and weaknesses, and the organizational mission; (2) determine the human resources requirements in terms of the numbers, characteristics, and systems required to implement the strategy; (3) assess the current status of human resources in terms of numbers, characteristics, and systems; (4) compare the human resources requirements to the current human resources situation to determine what gap (if any) exists; (5) formulate a strategy for closing the gap identified in (4) above; (6) implement the human resources strategy through appropriate changes in human resources practices; and (7) measure the impact of these modified practices on various outcomes, such as efficiency, effectiveness, and competitive position.

Formulating the Strategy

Space limitations preclude a detailed discussion of strategy formulation. The first step in the process involves an external environmental assessment of the organization's *opportunities* and *threats*. Possible environmental factors to consider are demographics, technological changes, economic changes, regulatory/reimbursement changes, consumer attitudes and values, and increased competition in particular markets. For any particular health care organization, some of the factors will be more important than others. To be in a position to take advantage of opportunities that are anticipated to occur, as well as to minimize potential threats from changed conditions or from competitor initiatives, health care managers must have detailed knowledge of the current and future operating environments. An external environmental assessment allows the organization to consider the market attractiveness of various service areas based on competitive pressures, entry barriers, profitability, and expected volume.

Assessment of internal strengths and weaknesses allows management to develop plans based on an accurate assessment of the organization's ability to perform in the various specific services in which it might compete. Examples of factors that might be considered are the organization's market share for various segments, quality of service, price competitiveness, community reputation, and managerial strengths.

The mission of the organization must also be considered in making final decisions because it may encourage or constrain particular choices. Certain strategies may not be consistent with the general goals and operating philosophy of the mission statement.

Based on the organization's assessment of both the market attractiveness of various market segments and the organization's internal competitive strengths, the corporate strategy is formulated. Those services that are attractive from both perspectives are slated for increased growth and investment. A moderate degree of attractiveness on both dimensions might lead the organization to maintain its market share and increase investment only in response to increased patient demand. A low degree of attractiveness on both dimensions would imply that the organization might "harvest" or "divest" that service. A "harvest" strategy would produce short-term cash flow from a service by decreasing operating costs (i.e., staff and maintenance), while maintaining prices. Eventually, the service will be terminated or sold. The "divest" strategy means the organization will abandon the market immediately.

The organization must then decide how it will compete in those markets for the services that will be increased or maintained. It must determine what general approach it will use to achieve competitive advantage within each market segment. These basic strategies have been found to lead to sustained competitive advantage.

- *Overall cost leadership:* Become the low-cost producer for a given service.

- *Differentiation:* Offer a service that is unique on important dimensions, such as technical quality or patient amenities.
- *Focus:* Target a narrow scope of competition within the community.[11]

Identifying the Human Resources Gap

The human resources gap is determined by comparing the human resources requirements for implementing the strategy or strategies selected at the corporate and business unit levels to the current human resources situation. Both the human resources requirements and the current human resources situation are assessed in terms of numbers, characteristics, and systems (see Figure 4-1).

The requirements are determined by identifying the human resources implications of the corporate strategy. For example, a strategy of growth through investment in certain attractive service areas will imply or emphasize recruitment, selection, and training of employees capable of providing the particular service. Alternatively, if the corporate strategy is to harvest or divest particular services, then the human resources emphasis will be on cost containment through staff freezes, reduction, and redeployment to other service areas.

Human resources implications are determined by forecasting which functional areas (e.g., nursing), divisions (e.g., ABC Health Center), job levels (e.g., professionals), and job families (e.g., physicians) are most important to the implementation of the strategic plan. For each of these impacted employee categories, the specific implications are determined. These might include increasing or decreasing staff in existing positions, changing the skill mix or job requirements of existing jobs, adding new positions, or enhancing productivity through training, job restructuring, quality circles, or other methods.[12]

Forecasting the expected demand for each occupational category that will be impacted by the strategy can be accomplished through a variety of methods. These include management estimates, staffing tables, regression analysis, delphi techniques, and computer simulations.[13] Discussion of these techniques of human resources demand forecasting is beyond the scope of this chapter. However, all of these approaches attempt to relate the human resources requirements to the volume and types of services an organization expects to provide in the future.

Assessing the internal supply of human resources can be done using a variety of methods. The specific method or methods used should fit the needs and requirements of the organization. Labor force analysis involves preparing an inventory of the numbers, backgrounds, career preferences, capabilities (strengths and weaknesses), and potential to meet future demands for all employees in the impacted units. Markov analysis examines the internal movement of employees (i.e., where they come from and where they go) in terms of the various levels, functions, and units. Expected employee turnover by position is also factored into the analysis. Labor market analysis looks at the primary external labor markets and those trends that impact on the organization's human resources function. Finally, a computer simulation can be used to forecast labor supply using various assumptions and mathematical models.

Determining the human resources gap involves the comparing of projected human resources demand to supply for the areas expected to be impacted by the strategy. Managers should attempt to summarize the primary human resources issues facing the organization. Examples might be projected human resources needs, shortages of skills and capabilities, excess capability, and critical training and development issues. Common human resources problems in health care organizations today include an excess number of employees delivering inpatient services, a shortage of qualified personnel in emerging areas, too many management levels, and training programs that are irrelevant to the new staffing requirements.

Formulating and Implementing a Human Resources Strategy

Once the nature of the human resources gap is identified, the organization needs to formulate and implement a human resources strategy to close that gap. The strategies formulated obviously depend on the nature of the gap. Examples of possible strategies include job restructuring, employee layoffs, hiring freezes, career ladders, external recruitment for new positions, more sophisticated selection criteria, revamped training programs, revised performance appraisal criteria, and incentive compensation.

The implementation of the human resources strategies should not be left to chance. Each strategy should have clear objectives and well-organized action steps. Examples of action steps might be to broaden the search and recruitment of registered nurses to institute periodic employee morale surveys to increase retention of nurses and to study the present nurse compensation system to eliminate perceived or real inequities.

Implementation also requires a clear statement of who is responsible for what action, when, and with what type of assistance or support. Examples of the latter include internal staff, external consultants, and external recruiters.

Finally, effective mechanisms for feedback and strategy adjustment need to be built in so that progress is monitored at periodic intervals. Several types of human resources measures can be monitored periodically to determine the success of the process.

- voluntary and involuntary turnover
- unfilled job vacancies
- employee attitude surveys

- physician and patient attitude surveys
- financial outcomes
- growth of service volume
- employee deficiencies identified in performance appraisals
- proportion of new positions filled internally

As noted in Figure 4-1, a successful SHRM process should result in higher levels of employee efficiency and employee effectiveness, as well as an advantage vis-à-vis competitors. Whenever the degree of success experienced by the organization, the results need to be fed back as part of the organization's internal assessment for the next round in the process. The SHRM process should be a continual cycle of strategic change, compatible human resources changes, monitoring of results, feedback, and adjustment of both corporate and human resources strategies.

SUCCESS FACTORS

Merely following the steps outlined in the previous section will not guarantee successful implementation of SHRM. Two additional factors are required to achieve such success: the *competence* of the chief human resources executive and the *process* by which SHRM is implemented.

First, human resources managers must understand the health care business generally, as well as the financial, strategic, and technological capabilities of their own organization. They need to understand (1) financial statements and issues associated with the cost of capital, revenue sources, and cost determinants; (2) the competitor and customer pressures, the nature of the organization's services, and the strategic direction of the organization; and (3) the technology of their organization in terms of what it means for physicians and patients.

Obviously, human resources managers must be competent in understanding the role that the human resources function can play in helping the organization reach its strategic objectives. In addition to their expertise in narrowly defined human resources matters, they should also be knowledgeable about the organization's structure, communication networks, control processes, change processes, and political processes. The latter is particularly important because the SHRM process requires strong support from senior management. As a result, human resources managers must understand and respond to the needs of the senior line managers.

The senior human resources manager should pursue an active, helping, and consultative role with top management. This means providing the types of services and support that enable management to do its job more effectively and efficiently. He or she also needs to educate, involve, and commit the line managers so that they consider human resources when making significant decisions. Rather than trying to excel in each functional area, the human resources manager should identify and focus on those human resources practices that are most critical to strategic success. This should enhance the perception and reality of human resources as a strategic business partner.

SHRM should be viewed as a multipurpose process. It should be proactive in terms of addressing issues before they become major problems. It should also develop effective action plans to enhance management communication and teamwork. It should be aimed at developing the line managers' skills and abilities by making them more sensitive to human resources issues in their daily decision making. As in the case of any significant activity, the goals of the human resources plan need to be tied into the performance measures on which the line managers' rewards are based.

CONCLUSION

A health care organization's growth, prosperity, and survival are dependent on its gaining and retaining competitive advantage. Although there are many paths toward that end, one that is frequently not recognized is capitalizing on superior human resources management. While more health care organizations recognize the growing importance of their human resources, few are conceptualizing them in strategic terms. As a result, most forgo the opportunity to sieze competitive advantage through human resources practice initiatives. This neglect of strategic human resources considerations is particularly surprising in a labor-intensive service industry currently undergoing severe shortages in certain occupations that require the right people in the right jobs at the right time. No business strategy can be successful if the latter conditions do not exist.

The SHRM concepts presented here challenge health care executives to manage human resources strategically as an integral part of strategic management. More high-quality output from the human resources function is needed if competitive advantage is to be achieved. In the future, the human resources department should be seen as more than just an operational or staff function. Rather, it should be seen as a facilitator of strategic change. Executives should consciously formulate human resources strategies that are linked to the broader strategic posture of the organization and that facilitate the management of its strategy. This process should stretch management thinking about human resources and impact on decisions affecting people. It should also be ongoing so that it is modified over time as executives learn the process and as issues facing the organization change.

NOTES

1. T.B. Wilson, *A Guide to Strategic Human Resources Planning for the Health Industry* (Chicago: American Society for Health Care Human Resources Administration of the American Hospital Association, 1986), 13.

2. R. Zalloro, B. Joseph, and N. Furey, "Do Hospitals Practice Strategic Planning? An Empirical Study," *Health Care Strategic Management* 2, no. 2 (1984): 16–20.

3. G.L. McManis, "Managing Competitively: The Human Factor," *Healthcare Executive* 2, no. 6 (1987): 20–21.

4. T.J. Peters and R.H. Waterman, *In Search of Excellence* (New York: Warner Books, 1982).

5. Eisenberg, "Strategic Human Resource Plans Help Providers Survive Changing Conditions," *Modern Healthcare* 16, no. 6 (1986): 154–156.

6. F. Cerne, "Human Resources: Plan Today for Tomorrow's Workforce Needs," *Hospitals* 62, no. 20 (1988): 95.

7. Wilson, *A Guide*, 22–23.

8. M.D. Fottler, S.R. Hernandez, and C.L. Joiner, eds. *Strategic Management of Human Resources in Health Services Organizations* (New York: John Wiley & Sons, Inc., 1988), 6–18.

9. D.Q. Mills, "Planning with People in Mind," *Harvard Business Review* 63, no. 4 (1985): 97–105.

10. L.R. Gomez-Mejia, "The Role of Human Resources Strategy in Export Performance: A Longitudinal Study," *Strategic Management Journal* 9, no. 4 (1988): 493–505.

11. M.E. Porter, *Competitive Advantage: Creating and Sustaining Superior Performance* (New York: Free Press, 1985): 1–43.

12. Wilson, *A Guide*, 55.

13. Wilson, *A Guide*, 60.

Edward J. Dowling
Elliott A. Kellman

5

A Case Study in Human Resources Strategic Planning

INTRODUCTION

Human resources strategic planning is a relatively new concept, not only in the field of human resources management but also in the health care field.

The U.S. health care system has entered an era of radical transformation. Hospital executives face enormous challenges as they plan effective responses to a new health care environment, which is both intensely competitive and highly regulated. In response to the emerging trends and issues that are shaping health care, new priorities have been established by the entire health care constituency. Pressures from board members, government agencies, community groups, and medical staff require a new level of managerial responsiveness, effectiveness, and fundamental leadership. Successful health care executives must develop organizational plans that anticipate emerging business and environmental demands in order to keep their organizations economically sound while maintaining high-quality patient care.

> *KEY ISSUE*: Human resources professionals should take the lead in developing a strategic plan that complements and meets the overall goals and objectives of the health care organization.

Figure 5-1 illustrates responses to the unique health care environment.

The health care field is labor intensive, and it is clear from current studies that effective management of human resources is a component of highly successful organizations. In these organizations there is an ingrained belief that the work force is the source of quality, productivity, and profit. In order to survive the regulatory and competitive pressures, medical facilities must pay greater attention to the management of human resources as an organizational asset for which the boundaries of organizational performance and productivity must continue to be expanded.

The initiation of a human resources strategic planning process will require health care managers to analyze and assess factors that are critical to the survival, growth, profitability, and quality of their organizations. This process will provide top management with an essential "piece of the puzzle" necessary to successfully compete under the dynamic market conditions that are emerging.

WHAT IS HUMAN RESOURCES STRATEGIC PLANNING?

Human resources strategic planning can be defined as a process of analyzing, setting objectives, and then measuring the progress of a series of interactive human resources management decisions. In any organization, large or small, dozens of key human resources decisions are made daily. These decisions range from who receives a promotion to what salary level is appropriate to attract qualified staff nurses.

1. Commits to excellence in service to patients
2. Views human resources as an asset
3. Establishes fair and equitable policies and practices
4. Supports initiative and creativity
5. Focuses on productivity

Figure 5-1 Responses to the Health Care Environment

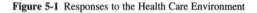

It is important to note, however, that these decisions can all fit into a broader organizational plan and, thus, create a synergy that gives an institution clearer priorities and leads to greater accomplishments. In the absence of a defined human resources strategy, many actions can be seen as ineffective or, even worse, contradictory. Effective human resources strategic planning stimulates thinking and services as a framework within which to further shape, refine, and provide an organizational sensitivity to the human resources dimension of business planning.

Human resources strategic planning requires a fundamental change from periodic reaction to key events or circumstances that affect human resources decisions. A successful human resources strategy, however, provides for continuous evaluation and assessment of those crucial external and internal environmental factors that are essential to the long-term success of the organization. For example, the external factors might include the aforementioned trends and pressures facing the health care industry, while the internal forces might be the existing organizational concerns, attitudes, and values, as well as the personal priorities of senior management. The ability to manage staff and make human resources decisions in a timely manner directly relates to the importance and commitment the organization places in that ability. Defining and understanding these internal and external forces will allow an organization to exploit opportunities and reduce threats posed by the external environment, while capitalizing on its strengths and minimizing its weaknesses in the internal milieu.

The consistent application of these planning processes leads to the establishment of organizational values, which permeate the entire management process and determine effective human resources management responses. By articulating and defining a strategic approach to its human resources, the organization is encouraged to think about its decisions in a conscious way. It then begins to shape and positively influence the way things are done.

WHAT ARE THE UNIQUE CHARACTERISTICS OF STRATEGIC PLANNING IN HEALTH CARE?

After an extended period that saw the health care industry move from the Hill-Burton financial incentives for facility construction to the program expansion encouraged by Medicare, we have progressed to the point where the widespread conclusion is that the delivery of health care services in this country has grown too expensive and must be curtailed and controlled. This realization has brought about a dramatic change in how health care organizations view their future. As a result of these forces, the health care field has shifted its focus from societal issues and priorities to economic issues and priorities.

In essence, the health care environment is currently being shaped by three dominant forces. First is the increased competition, as providers emerge from all sides to compete for different (or more lucrative) shares of the health care services market. These competitors include physicians who see an opportunity to extend and protect their patient services through urgi-centers, drop-in clinics, etc., as well as through organizations such as HMOs, which are playing an accelerating role in dictating where patients will go for care in this price-sensitive area. This increased competition, which ranges from sophisticated transplant services to the dramatic growth of home health care organizations, has left the traditional health care facility with a shrinking census. Many hospitals are left with a population of indigent patients who are unable to pay, creating further financial pressures and raising important moral issues.

The second emerging force is the increasing pressure exerted by both federal and state regulatory agencies. With the introduction of the Diagnostic Related Group (DRG) method of respective reimbursement, an entirely new financing mechanism now determines how institutions view census, length of stay data, and the utilization of various medical services. In addition to this federal effort to limit its payment under the Medicare and Medicaid programs, state regulatory commissions, such as those in Connecticut, Massachusetts, and Maryland, and voluntary prospective rating programs, such as that in Rhode Island, continue to exert considerable influence over health care organizations' financial survival and profitability. Despite the increase in the number of health care organizations that have initiated corporate reorganization and/or downsizing in an effort to avoid regulatory control, the pressure from both state and federal regulatory agencies will continue because the health care industry has a tremendous impact on both national and local resources. Further, health care provides a service in the public interest and, therefore, is a business section in which government agencies feel impelled to remain actively and directly involved.

The third emerging force is the changing expectations of consumers—both the ones who receive the health care services and the ones who pay through insurers for available services. As these consumers/patients grow more discerning, they will start to exercise more control over the treatment and delivery modes of care. For example, the vast growth of outpatient facilities and health promotion activities signals the potential long-term impact individuals can make on the health care marketplace. Similarly, the ability of employers and insurers to radically affect a hospital's census level through a Preferred Provider Organization (PPO) arrangement is emerging as a new dimension in health care management considerations. Through these PPOs, a contract is established with a specific institution to provide medical services for an employee population.

These three unique characteristics found in the health care industry require an increased emphasis on human resources strategic planning.

IS HUMAN RESOURCES STRATEGIC PLANNING ESSENTIAL TO TOP MANAGEMENT?

Yes. Health care executives are facing enormous challenges as they plan an effective response to this new environment. As mentioned, pressures from board members, government agencies, and community groups, labor unrest, and medical staff frustration all demand a new level of managerial effectiveness and fundamental leadership.

As the health care executive surveys a future characterized by strong regulatory control and expanding competition for a static population base, the development of a cohesive, well-thought-out multiyear strategy becomes more and more essential to organizational results. In the labor-intensive health care industry, it is clear that the human resources component requires greater attention in the form of data development, performance analysis, goal formulation, audit, and follow-up. As management views the growing challenges and complexities of organizing, planning, and directing a health care enterprise, the human resource dimension becomes more critical; it becomes an essential ingredient for organizational success.

These pressures dictate a new outlook and a fresh set of priorities for managerial and executive leadership. Senior executives must progress toward an organizational philosophy that sees the emerging health care environment as dictating the organization's business which, in turn, must be supported by proactive, integrated human resources, financial, and marketing strategies. Clearly, the human resources strategy must become part of the organization's overall business device, not something "extra" that managers are asked to do.

HUMAN RESOURCES STRATEGY AND ORGANIZATIONAL VALUES

More and more organizational studies indicate that the long-term success of an organization is not guaranteed by specific products, marketing campaigns, or financial studies. Rather, employers are acknowledging that how employees *feel* about their jobs, their supervisors, the organization's mission, their working environment, and the leadership that they receive is equal to or more important than elaborate planning documents

or lengthy management analysis reports. Consequently, corporate values, being the sum of employee feelings and work standards, significantly affect employee productivity, teamwork, cooperation, creativity, attendance, turnover, commitment, and, ultimately, overall organizational performance. This conscious consideration and definition of human resources values and principles can and do change behavior that impacts on the quality, service, and performance standards of an organization.

GOALS OF THE HUMAN RESOURCES STRATEGIC PLAN

An effective human resources strategic plan is one that *supports the overall strategic plan of the organization.* This overall business plan may be one of growth or consolidation, one introducing new services or improving current programs, one of specialization or diversification. In any event, the human resources strategy and management responses must complement and enhance the possibility of a successful outcome.

Second, the strategic plan *must define the organization's benefits and values.* Employees at all levels must be permitted to understand the culture and contribute to the common beliefs and expectations that employees have for each other and for how their jobs should be performed, from simple phone courtesy to the detailed training of surgical teams.

Finally, *the plan must encourage the development of specific and measurable objectives* to determine success and to allow individuals to see results and participate in shaping and influencing these outcomes. The leadership and work force values that emanate from the thoughtful consideration of these factors must reflect the organization's values of quality and service: how it relates to the patient; how it views itself as an organization; and how it will carry out its commitment to cost containment, service, and efficiency. The successful integration of these values in an organization requires the commitment of senior management. Management practices and attitudes need to ensure that the medical facility's labor force is seen not merely as a necessary expense, but rather as a crucial asset requiring wise investment and sound management in order to realize significant return.

THE ROLE OF THE HUMAN RESOURCES DIRECTOR

Before embarking on the development of a human resources strategic plan, the human resources director needs to assess the readiness of the organization to develop an effective plan. Questions that should be asked include the following:

• What are the key organizational concerns or goals expressed by senior management?

- Which of these critical concerns or goals depend on human resources for success?
- How does your organization view its work force: As an asset? As an expense?
- How would you judge your own performance and the human resources department's level of performance?
- Are you part of the senior planning group? If not, why not?
- Have you thought hard about the long-term implications of a changing health care environment for the human resources aspects of your organization?
- Are you prepared to raise and persist in the discussion of difficult and complex human resources issues for which there appear to be no easy or convenient solutions?

Thus, the human resources director can only model the organization's commitment to a concept that treats human resources as a valuable organizational asset to be managed for an investment return, like any other asset. By adopting this philosophy, the human resources director will be required to oversee four important responsibilities essential to a human resources strategic plan.

1. *Install information systems to establish an employee data base*. The human resources director must ensure that the information systems and data are available to enable the organization to understand how human resources can and should be measured. These data range from a comprehensive organizational employee attitude survey to turnover statistics, benefit utilization, and work force demographics. In short, the organization must be able to measure and understand the tremendous investment that it has in a labor-intensive organization such as a hospital or medical group.
2. *Train and educate management and staff concerning human resources management issues*. The human resources leadership must play a central role in training and developing employees and managers with regard to their approach to human resources management. This will require consultation and support from other departments because the human resources function will be in a unique position to articulate the organizational values and principles regarding the human resources department.
3. *Participate in the development and redesign of human resources policies, procedures, and practices*. The human resources director will be required to oversee and/or participate in the development or modification of organizational policies, procedures, and practices regarding human resources. These operational revisions may include the discussion and consideration of staffing patterns and compensation policies, as well as manpower or training programs.
4. *Prioritize human resources responsibilities*. The human resources director must assess and prioritize the tasks of

the human resources department and his or her own functional responsibilities. A department that is awash in paperwork compliance and consumed by urgent operational issues will not be effective in a strategic environment, which requires a director to give greater emphasis to broader organizational issues and the planning necessary to achieve the desired results.

ENCOURAGING ORGANIZATIONAL ACCEPTANCE OF THE HUMAN RESOURCES STRATEGIC PLAN

Although there is no simple blueprint for assuring that a human resources strategic plan will be embraced by the organization, four steps are essential for a successful introduction.

1. The senior management of the organization must be involved sufficiently to develop "ownership" in the human resources strategic plan. They must have argued about, challenged, designed, and accepted a strategy of human resources principles that they feel are critical to the long-term success of the medical facility.
2. The human resources strategy must have a clarity and directness about it so that employees, at all levels, understand it. While a human resources strategy will, of necessity, touch on numerous facets of the organization, the strategy must have a cohesiveness that provides a reference point for key human resources decisions and programs.
3. There must be an explicit commitment to preserve the adopted human resources principles during the communications and implementation phases. Recognizing the limitations and resistance that will exist in any organization, particularly one as diverse and complex as a health care delivery organization, it is important that management visibly demonstrate "ownership" of the human resources strategy. The recognition that the establishment of these key human resource principles is a multi-year effort will temper unrealistic expectations and minimize frustration.
4. The human resources function must have the credibility, influence, and expertise to allow the human resources strategy to be communicated effectively and instituted throughout the organization. Not only must the communication process allow information to flow regularly to employees, but also it must allow information from employees to reach the decision and policy makers of the organization. This results not only in the reinforcement of and adherence to key human resources principles but also in the sharing of human resources values, standards, and key organizational principles.

Figure 5-2 illustrates the strategic role of the human resources department at Yale–New Haven Hospital. The vice president of human resources coordinated the hospital's

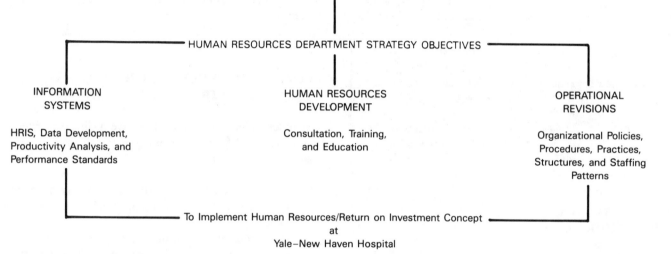

THE STRATEGIC ROLE OF HUMAN RESOURCES
MANAGEMENT AT YALE–NEW HAVEN HOSPITAL

CORPORATE LEADERSHIP

Corporate Mission of Excellence
Clarification of Values

MANGEMENT OF YALE–NEW HAVEN
HOSPITAL'S HUMAN RESOURCES

Adoption of Human Resources/Return on Investment Concept

HUMAN RESOURCES DEPARTMENT STRATEGY OBJECTIVES

INFORMATION SYSTEMS	HUMAN RESOURCES DEVELOPMENT	OPERATIONAL REVISIONS
HRIS, Data Development, Productivity Analysis, and Performance Standards	Consultation, Training, and Education	Organizational Policies, Procedures, Practices, Structures, and Staffing Patterns

To Implement Human Resources/Return on Investment Concept
at
Yale–New Haven Hospital

Figure 5-2 The Strategic Role of Human Resources Management at Yale–New Haven Hospital

human resources management and professional staff in developing and implementing this successful strategic plan.

THE HUMAN RESOURCES STRATEGIC PLANNING PROCESS

The key to effective human resources planning is the analysis of factors representing change that potentially affects the survival, growth, profitability, efficiency, and quality of the health care institution.

Key Point: Developing a human resources strategic plan is a process. The discussions and interaction required in this planning stage are more important than the creation of a planning document.

The human resources strategic planning process includes

- *Evaluation*: Evaluating your environment is the first step in the planning process. Two factors should be reviewed in depth during the evaluation phase.

1. External environment: trends and pressures facing the health care industry
2. Internal forces: concerns, attitudes, values, personnel management priorities of senior management, and major changes planned

- *Design*: After evaluating your environment and obtaining the involvement and commitment of senior management, you are ready to design your plan. When designing your plan, identify different strategic options that can be evaluated for inclusion in the final planning document.

- *Implementation*: You are now ready to implement your strategic plan. Refer to the section on "Encouraging Organizational Acceptance of the Human Resources Strategic Plan."

- *Audit*: Last in the process is auditing your plan to determine if it has achieved the established goals. Your audit should assess the planning outcomes and link them to both the human resources strategic plan and the organization's business plan.

Exhibit 5-1 is an example of the human resources strategic plan that was designed and implemented at Yale–New Haven Hospital.

Exhibit 5-1 Yale–New Haven Hospital Human Resources Strategic Plan

STRATEGIC STATEMENT:	Instilling a commitment of excellence in service to patients, thereby maximizing the return on our investment in human resources to support and achieve overall organizational goals.
STRATEGY 1:	Instill in the entire work force commitment to excellence in service to patients.
STRATEGY 2:	Instill the self-worth and value of each employee to the organization by expanding his/her skills, knowledge, and competencies.
STRATEGY 3:	Recognizing the diversity of Yale–New Haven Hospital's work force, maintain fair and equitable personnel policies and practices throughout all levels of the organization.
STRATEGY 4:	Support initiative, creativity, and the exploration of new ideas on the part of all employees.
STRATEGY 5:	Establish productivity indicators for programs and services, incorporating performance criteria and productivity targets.
NOTE:	There are delineated objectives within each strategy with measurable outcomes and targeted completion dates.

RESULTS OF HUMAN RESOURCES STRATEGIC PLANNING

The impact that a successful human resources strategy has on the organization can be observed in several ways. A critical change occurs in how the human resources function is viewed within the organization. If the importance of human resources is understood, then effective human resources management becomes part of every manager's job. Similarly, the human resources staff must now fulfill the role of internal consultant to assist other managers in shaping a positive work environment. The expectation will exist that personnel policies and practices "fit" within the overall human resources strategy of the organization.

The organizational outcomes now become linked to the return on the investment, which is made in the human resources component. Sustained high performance, increased employee initiatives, greater understanding and commitment to organizational goals, and a higher degree of collaboration and cooperation between various work groups are all part of the investment return. Needless to say, in this climate there are greater expectations regarding the performance level and the capability of the human resources function necessary to support and enhance these initiatives.

Of primary importance are the strategic results that are made possible as the human resources strategy becomes accepted and becomes part of the management process. For example, the human resources staff has an explicit sense of direction, as opposed to merely fulfilling a bureaucratic record keeping responsibility or reacting to the regular daily crisis. Human resources management becomes an implicit part of every manager's job and is no longer something that only a staff department is supposed to be concerned about. There is also improved coordination of diverse human resources programs: compensation planning fits with staffing goals; training programs anticipate organizational needs; and communication levels allow the organization to respond smoothly and effectively to emerging marketplace considerations.

Finally, there is a greater probability that the overall business strategy will succeed.

Key Point: Successful human resources initiatives will link strategic, operational, and financial planning into a cohesive plan.

ELEMENTS OF SUCCESSFUL HUMAN RESOURCES STRATEGIC PLANNING

In order for human resources initiatives to link the strategic, operational, and financial planning of the organization, four conditions are essential.

1. Human resource values, principles, and personnel policies must be endorsed and supported by senior management.
2. The accountability for implementing critical personnel practices must become an integral part of line management's responsibilities.
3. The human resources staff will need to develop and maintain a highly credible image and expertise.
4. The effect of human resources strategies on the organization must be audited and evaluated on an ongoing basis.

Finally, if the human resources strategic planning process is successfully integrated into the organization, the following results will be achieved:

- excellence and quality of patient care services
- improved productivity
- greater collaboration between management and the medical staff
- establishment of a strong position in core business markets

The human resources strategic planning process is more important than the human resources strategic plan itself. Human resources professionals can take the leadership role in assisting the organization in reaching its overall goals and objectives by initiating, designing, and implementing a human resources strategic plan. In today's competitive health care environment, success will be determined by how effectively an organization is able to utilize its human resources talent to accomplish its critical goals.

David Lance

The Revolution in Human Resources: Money, Motivation, Mythology

6

You couldn't tell by most enthusiastic articles or presentations at professional conferences, but there is an ill-defined uneasiness with the status of the personnel or human resources department. The scent of change hangs, as if it were some elusive musk, hinting at portents on the horizon.

Oblivion. Is that where the human resources department, as we know it, is headed? Is it a matter of anachronistic overhead routed through the path of least resistance? Is the very purpose of such a department unclear and built on a consortium of ideas based on hollow and shifting ground?

Most CEOs, regardless of the industry sector, who fancy themselves as alert and aware are already rethinking the purpose for, and payoff from, such departments. Too often this has resulted in simplistically capping or, even worse, downsizing the personnel staff while the plate for the remainder continues to grow in an erratic spiraling fashion. And that's a shame since most personnel management practitioners have noble intentions, but increasingly find themselves lacking enough horsepower to see them through.

While the natural, erratic process of evolution plods on, the survival needs, if not the leaders of our people-filled organizations, cry out for revolution in our profession. Yours and mine. They seek new thinking, supportive leadership, and consultative action. They sense that the state of the art, today, is in deep trouble because today is not yesterday, and tomorrow finds us sadly unprepared to meet its challenges. They see us as collectively confused about who we are, what we believe, whom we serve, and how we serve.

Earlier in this decade it became fashionable for personnel departments to call themselves human resources departments. Most reports indicate that as many as half of our collaborative functions are so named. But what's in a name if, fundamentally, you continue to do as personnel departments have done for many years?

The concept of a personnel department is a relatively recent one in the long history of American business. Its history is a rich and intriguing one, but it is comparatively brief and embryonic, with less claim as an integral professional component of business than accounting, marketing, or production. To be sure, a formal human resources management department remains a nonexistent component in most small businesses.

The personnel executive was *born*, with a whimper, as a matter of convenience shortly after the turn of the century. For perhaps a decade, coincident with World War I, this executive took the first infantile steps in the realm of employment, records, and recruitment only to be *extinguished and eradicated by a line management revolution*, during a dark age beginning about 1920. Line managers had concluded that personnel management was the very essence of management, i.e., something *they did* as a part of *their job*. They felt it unnecessary to tolerate a central control—and abolished it. Thus, line managers, not personnel executives, led what I refer to as *the first revolution in human resources*.[1]

Years later, the personnel executive was *resurrected and reincarnated* as a union fighter. Years later still, this union fighter *evolved* at a staggering pace, to become first a researcher, then a 'do gooder,' later a policeman.

Finally, and most sadly, this personnel executive evolved to become a bureaucrat, captured in a tent of too much breadth, with too little support, and too many colors. One might conclude that this current status is a natural result of a role that was perfunctory to begin with, dashing to each fad and fetish in search of justification for its existence.[2]

But, mark me well. Following the dark age in our history, there was indeed a *golden age* of the personnel profession. It took place from about 1945 to 1975. For three solid decades, the personnel department took root, blossomed, and bore fruit. Has it yet to bear consistent fruit of great quality or abundance?[3]

Thinkers, such as myself, often on the outside looking in at human resources management functions, systems, and departments, have wondered at signals we have noted regarding *a potential second revolution in human resources.*

For the past decade, I believe that human resources management executives, and their departments, have been in the "eye of the storm." It has been a period during which human resources has been accorded a limbolike existence, with labor unions in a coma, new developments relegated to management by best seller (merely providing a helter-skelter regurgitation of past truths), and a general de-escalation of newly produced employer/employee law.

One would imagine that during this eye of the storm, the human resources profession would have sorted out the valuable lessons of its golden age and reached agreement on the answers to some questions that are critical to every profession. Who are we? What do we call ourselves? What does it mean to be one of us? How does one become one of us? What do we believe? Who is the client we serve? How do we serve? What do we expect, in the way of a fee, for such service? How long does it take to become one of us? How do we police our own profession?

Professional memberships, rudimentary certification programs based on empirical recall, overpowering data bases, and journals were manifest during this past decade. But have we answered, *really answered*, fundamental questions with one voice. I think not.

Perhaps human resources management is far more art than science. And perhaps it is less a profession than an engagement for several types of specialists by several types of chief executives.

Most reporters agree that less than 50 percent of all human resource departments report to the CEO. I presume that the CEO of an organization should be the client of the human resources executive (chief personnel or labor relations officer). It is on behalf of the CEO that classical attributes of a staff function, such as advice, service, and control, are granted. It is my premise that *it is the CEO* who is accountable to employees, managers, and consumers.

Fuzzy thinking to the contrary, human resources executives merely advise, recommend, analyze, and otherwise serve to the advantage or disadvantage of the CEO who employs them. If there is a vice-president for human resources, the president of human resources is the CEO.

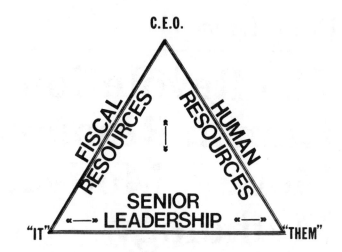

Figure 6-1 The "Triangle of Effective Organization" Model compares interdependence of the two principal *staff* resources (fiscal, the "it") versus (human, the "them") as component considerations for senior leadership (*line*); the CEO relies on all of these, balancing actions by people, for people, as the leader of leaders. *Source:* Reprinted from *RENAISSANCE—The Ultimate Leadership Development*, copyright 1986, 1988 by The American Healthcare Consulting Corporation, Sharon, Massachusetts.

That president carries the burden of organization, both the "it" and the "them" of organization. The chief financial officer represents the realm of "it" as fiscal resources, and the chief personnel officer represents the realm of "them" as human resources.

> Both the "it" and the "them" of organization must be in balance if a CEO expects to carry on business effectively in the longer run. Barring that, a board can only expect indecision and procrastination, rather than leadership, from its appointed CEO. Any CEO without the "it" and the "them" of organization clearly in a balance of resourcefulness, who attempts to lead, may be worse for the business than no leader at all.[4]
>
> This, then, looms as an indictment of many CEOs, not merely those in the health care industry where people are apparently our greatest expense. People, of course, are our only expense. Beyond compensation and employee benefits, people are our only spenders. Thus, all forms of productivity are in the province of people. They are not merely assets; they are the essence of the organization.[5]

To be sure, fiscal resources are the circulatory system of the organization and, thus, vital to its livelihood. That there is an imbalance manifested in the actions of many CEOs who favor fiscal resources with their time, attention, and effort is clearly a matter of record. You need only review the index of articles in any magazine that CEOs read routinely. By sheer number alone, fiscal resources is the focus of nearly unilateral attention. How many CEOs have you met that would long tolerate a CEO they felt was below par? Human resources, on the other hand, too often is felt to be for the birds!

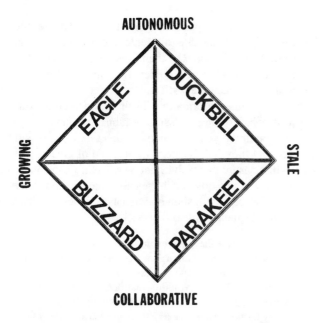

AUTONOMOUS

EAGLE   DUCKBILL

GROWING   STALE

BUZZARD   PARAKEET

COLLABORATIVE

Figure 6-2 The "Birds of a Feather" Model compares individual status (*growing* versus *stale*) to style inclination (*autonomous* versus *collaborative*) resulting in four distinct types: eagle, duckbill, buzzard, parakeet. *Source:* Reprinted from *RENAISSANCE—The Ultimate Leadership Development*, copyright 1986, 1988 by The American Healthcare Consulting Corporation, Sharon, Massachusetts.

There are at least four kinds of birds, which many CEOs feel may now be leading our human resources management functions (see Figure 6-2). They are

1. *Eagles.* A rare, powerful bird nearing extinction. Once prolific. Tends to invent and tailor make whatever he/she puts his/her name to. An autonomous bird, with a nest that is often far removed from others and guarded fiercely. Typically viewed as a one-bird show. Believes he/she has the answers, if only there were the opportunity to apply them. Where answers don't exist, relentlessly hunts them down. Often proves to be right through sheer determination alone. Has a tendency to bite off more than can be chewed. As a result, swallows a lot or chokes.

2. *Parakeets.* A most prolific bird, enthusiastic with its own kind. Preens its own feathers and grooms constantly. Often seen at personnel conferences, warbling the tunes and buzzwords of the day. Composed of plastic to greater or lesser degrees. This is a bird gifted in mimicry. He/She passionately believes everything that should passionately be believed, as dictated by his/her professional peer group. Sustains shock if beliefs are challenged. Incapable of independent thinking. Hive mentality. Rarely reads, but if he/she does read, rarely applies. Hires others to apply effort, and critiques them based on political acceptability of the action. Delegates (projects) accountability and responsibility, but holds tight to authority. Accepts praise well when others are successful, becomes a piranha when they're not. Regur-

gitates whatever it is fed, thus saps the strength of the organization with banter more than substance.

3. *Buzzards.* A bird that fancies itself a survivor. Keen eyesight (not necessarily insight) causes it to find sustenance where others might not notice. Constantly on the move, a seeker in flight. Steal an idea from this one, part of a system from that one, half the technique of another one. . . . Be mindful of plagiarism and copyrights, but mix together and voilà! A dish to fit a king, tailor made at no cost to the boss. If indigestion doesn't kill the organization with these Frankenstein-like creations, it will muddle through. The buzzard has learned the song of open-ended questions and general inquisitiveness, but sings only to its own kind. Most prolific in the cost-contained environment, it finds sustenance in whatever it is fed—be it fresh or carrion. If it seems OK, if other buzzards are picking at it, and if it sticks to the ribs without much cost or effort, it may be good enough for the organization.

4. *Duckbills.* No one is sure whether this is a bird! Has a defined territory after years of holding ground. Exactly what is done there and by whom is unknown. We do know many lay blame there, often righteous blame. A bird without song, silent, withdrawn, rarely seen, independent. Accepts whatever it is given, but does not feed. Stores it away for a rainy day. Unhappy with today's environment. Dreams of leaving, but holds on to little, desperately. Rarely fights for much, unless discovered, cornered, and seriously threatened. Resists flying because of clipped wings. Avoids the company of high-flying birds, assuming they are predators.[6]

You might ask me, "Exactly how does this analogy fit in?" Permit me to focus.

> Our client, the CEO, too often permits the existence of one of these birds in a role that is vital to the business and people of his or her organization. It may be the CEO is entertained by, or sorry for, or fears, or identifies with, the bird. It may be he or she helped to create the bird, or perhaps inherited and tolerates its company. In either alternative, to do so is self-destructive behavior. It can make an enormous difference to the success of our CEO if he or she can acquire what he or she feels is *the right* chief personnel or labor relations officer.[7]

Of paramount importance is the principle that the client CEO determines what is "right." It is the CEO's burden. It goes with the territory. One can indifferently permit the status quo, or one can change. One can play the cards as dealt or cut them first. It is the CEO's job and cannot be avoided with indifference, if it is to be deemed as a job well done.

To permit the status quo signals that the CEO is assured, as a client must be assured, that the advice and service of the personnel professional will provide all he or she needs to help deliver organizational success (see Figure 6-1). To change signals that the CEO will take the responsibility himself or get someone new to do it.

And herein lies the pivotal point of a second revolution in human resources. Will it be the CEO or the human resource executive who rises as the fifth bird, "phoenixlike," from the ashes of the previous four. It will take a phoenix to re-enter the storm.

We are at the beginning of what futurist John Naisbett has called "The Information Age" and are experiencing the need for "Reinvention of the Corporation." Information or knowledge, however, is not power in and of itself. It will take power to reinvent the corporation. It will take action to distinguish information, formulate vision, and empower people or groups of people, if CEOs are to succeed in the business of metamorphosing our organizations of people.

For such reasons, and with no intention to slight Naisbett's writings, I prefer to refer to the times before us as "The Leadership Age."[8]

It will be a time of enormous change for the CEOs of our organizations. Perhaps the unprecedented turnover of hospital CEOs in the past two years signals that the storm has already been re-entered. One thing is clear. The challenges of the Leadership Age are pointed squarely at the CEO. It is his or her storm.

If the CEO is to survive, matters of image and political feasibility will become paramount, as they relate to all constituencies of people. It will become abundantly apparent that in his or her office lies the locus of the business and the locus of the employer. If it hasn't dawned on the CEO yet that he or she most obviously carries this double-barreled burden, it will soon.

Would we predict that the human resources department will be prepared, in the eyes of its client CEO, to rise to the challenge of assuring his or her success among people as the leader of people? No, we would not. We think few will.

Unless the human resources executive is prepared to embark on professional rethinking and strategic reformation, the human resources management department will be rendered to the status of an anachronism, or a vestigial organ of the organization.

Many will not be prepared to rethink and reform. They will resist the call for reformation, spellbound as part of the "Medusa" herself. They will cower, waiting for the CEO to enter their arena and slay the human resources management department. They will be counting on past indifference. But when the CEO's survival is threatened, barring adaptation to the new environment, the "leopard" will change his or her spots. After all, there is an excess of "tigers" always available to replace a CEO.

Some will rise above birdlike stereotypes, only to find that changing their role in support of the CEO's image is impossible within the organization to which they have contributed their effort. These will take flight from the past and scatter to other endeavors.

Only a few will rise from the ashes, phoenix-like, sprung from the head of the slain Medusa. Perhaps these few will have slain the Medusa themselves, prior to the metamorphosis.

It is a sobering supposition that most human resources executives will not be able to re-enter the storm and initiate a renaissance brought about by their personal rethinking of what we learned during the past golden age. Most will find themselves unable to accurately sift and then direct such knowledge toward the coming reformation. Their failure to do so will not be catastrophic to the profession of human resources.

To the contrary, *fewer* human resources executives will be needed—but they will be alert, aware, and of greater gauge. They will measure themselves not by what they can control or direct, but rather by how much they do influence the success of others. Their realm will shun maintenance of their service and favor improvement of others' services.

> These few are the quiet revolutionaries of today, initiating the inevitable metamorphosis of their profession, and discontent with the slow process of its erratic evolution. They know that an evolution that does not adapt one's purpose, method, and contribution to the environment in a timely fashion results in extinction, and that a thinker who does not challenge thinking atrophies.[9]

During the decade of the nineties, these few human resources executives will "come out of the closet" as a new phoenix. They will appear to be much less like directors of personnel and more like political campaign "handlers." They will be consultative *to* the CEO and *for* the CEO's senior leadership group (previously known as top management). They will be the in-house experts in the art of unleashing and improving the potential of human resources. They will be in demand by any business that seeks its competitive edge by the people, for the people. They will have realized that "everyone in management thought they knew how to manage people, but few in management know how to lead people."[10] *These leaders will be the new phoenix.*

"But what of the others of us?" you may ask. They may view the following with alarm, for the memo below conjures up a scenario in which the CEO portrays himself as an agent of change and a practitioner of leadership. Whether right or wrong, on any or all counts, the CEO below has initiated a second revolution in human resources by attacking matters central to money, motivation, and the mythology of human resources management departments.

Place yourself in the role of a line operational vice-president as you read Exhibit 6-1.

It might be tremendously difficult to maintain a role of *line* vice-president, if you are not one, while reviewing the preceding exhibit memo. Interestingly, my own unofficial polling suggests that most line officers and chief financial officers typically are intrigued by the exhibit, while many human resources executives typically grow cold somewhere after the first four paragraphs.

Taken as one, the actions of I.M. Tiger, newly appointed CEO of St. Generic, would probably doom the organization by too much change—too quickly. However, you will certainly find substance in a variety of the actions he suggests. Not all, but some of his behavior is predictable.

Exhibit 6-1 "Memorandum." Disclaimer applied, as an imaginative work of intentional fiction, except where footnoted.

ST. GENERIC GENERAL HOSPITAL
Everywhere, U.S.A.

CONFIDENTIAL MEMORANDUM:

To: Senior Leadership Group (Top Management)
From: I.M. Tiger, Your New CEO
Subject: Human Resources Management Department;
     Some Revolutionary Changes

We have less than 45 days before I arrive in the office of the President on a full-time basis. This memo will convey the high points of our verbal discussions, your commitments, and our resolutions over two days last week.

As you are all aware, Fred Leopard, Ph.D., F.A.C.H.E., was "gunned down" by the board several months ago. It was a clean shot, right between the eyes; he went brain dead and humbly evaporated. He is a richer man for the experience. Charlie Bird, A.E.P., your V.P. for Human Resources, followed Fred at my suggestion. It was clear he missed him and his ways. Together they make an interesting team. We wish them good luck!

It is very important for you to portray yourselves as enthusiastic and positive about all changes at St. Generic, and the future course of events. I require your enthusiastic commitment to anything we do together, if you are to remain a Vice-President for me. If my way is not your way, you should tell me before we go any farther. I'll help you find a more harmonious employment situation elsewhere. You won't be on my team (let alone a leader of my team) if you don't fully and positively manifest support for its plans and actions.

There is a critical element of theatric ability necessary to the role you will be privileged to perform. People of our organization will look to you and interpret your every act. Do not be false.

Consider yourself to be a winner among winners. Be proud of who you are and who you are among. Express your opinions freely before we resolve; afterwards your opinions must be synonymous with *our* opinions. Together we dare great things, and I will lead you to be a leader of successful people. Love it and live it. Don't pretend, or I'll extinguish your career.

Charlie Bird did leave me some notes and suggestions regarding Human Resources Management:

1. *The Human Resources Department is understaffed and under-budgeted.* (by Charlie)

We resolved: Our intention is to close the Human Resources Department, and utilize its space for a revenue-producing function. What the Human Resources Department has done, that needs to be done, can be done better elsewhere by others in the organization. Of course, the closing of the Human Resources Department will be planned to phase in over several months, with contingency planning for a shorter period.

Staff will be advised by me, shortly after my starting date, that they may refer themselves to you for the first available position for which they qualify, and which is acceptable to them. Otherwise, they will be laid off, not subject to recall.

2. *Department heads (middle managers) are complaining about lack of recognition for their special burden of responsibilities.* (by Charlie)

We resolved: Our intention is to eliminate as many department head positions as possible, as well as all "assistants to." This will be accomplished in three waves over 18–24 months, or by attrition, whichever is sooner. We will utilize these positions to hire more knowledge workers in each discipline. We will experiment heavily with self-governance leadership systems, particularly among knowledge workers, in place of management. We will do everything possible to bring all working people close to senior leadership, without bureaucratic barriers. It is their contribution that defines who we are, and we owe them no less.

Management at St. Generic has failed miserably in the realm of *leadership*. It has been so successful at *managing* that the organization has become mediocre. No one who is interested in doing more than passing time is going to be interested in identifying themselves with mediocrity for long. It is time to stop taking care to tend the "store." Instead, we need to help our people evolve the "store" to be more than we ever believed it could be.

Our intention is to recognize that the genie is out of the bottle; it can no longer be ignored or contained. In the leadership age, we must "inspirate, instigate, and irrigate toward growing rather than satiating or obviating people."[11] Failing this, we will remain unattractive to all, save the most desperate or lethargic of people.

"As we all know, most of the last decade has reflected a spiraling rate of middle management elimination, worldwide. Business of all kinds has sought the elusive competitive edge, in harnessing the potential of people. You don't do that through counting activity, or controlling people. You do it through empowering people to do well in a worthy cause. It's called leadership, and it's not pulling people, or pushing people, or donkey/carrot/stick-type motivation. It is initiating and supporting behavior that grows winners in an organization orchestrated by winners."[12] We'll never succeed at this without trimming out levels of management. You can't do it without eradicating the middle management obstacle, and moving from bureaucracy to leadership.

3. *Someone has been trying to sell us a management training program. The managers could sure use one. It's been a long time.* (by Charlie)

We resolved: We do not wish to train *managers* to make the wrong moves better. Further, altogether too much time has been spent on counseling them to contain or control people and the behavior of people.

Management is a bankrupted concept. It can only thrive where competition is nonexistent and collaboration or monopoly is a way of life. This is no longer the hallmark of the health care industry, or any industry for that matter.

Quality, as a result of personal effort, is the gauge by which consumers judge products or services. Therefore, how consumers feel about quality from our personal effort will determine if staying in business is worthwhile. In this regard, the stakes could not be higher.

We will begin with ourselves, CEO and Vice-Presidents, to engage in a *learning* program, regarding leadership. A credible Human Resources Consultant, David Lance, has written that "Leadership is about winning. Leadership is taking a person on a quest to win, for something he thinks is worth winning, with people and resources that assure him that winning is possible. Those who are led do not have a job. They have a quest for a cause to dare their actions among great people, for rewards they deem suitable. Winning reinforces winning, even in the happenstance of losing."[13]

Your quest, as senior leadership people, is to help me lead. You will do this by clarifying, then strategizing, and then marketing the quest, the rewards, the winning image of me, and everything and everyone associated with me. Together, we will be an organization by people, for people.

Lance writes on: "For the sake of the people inside and outside of the organization, the CEO must be perceived as a winner and, in fact, often win. The test of his success will be in the realm of charisma, and he may read it in the faces and feelings of those who are led in this very personal

Exhibit 6-1 continued

experience. Charisma, after all, is accorded (or not) to him by people, as their perception and reception of the CEO's intentions. It is their interpretation of his actions and inactions. It's as nearly inseparable from corporate culture as the organization is from the CEO. In the conscious and subconscious of the employee, these are all one thing."[14]

We agree that we cannot be *trained* to lead an organization. We can, however, *learn* to lead an organization. Learning implies that while reading, hearing, or witnessing something, we know we will have to apply it. The test of learning is the action of applying it. And we are resolved to do so.

Lance writes on: "Among the major misnomers of management is the allusion that they somehow motivate people. The key to motivation is on the inside of the door to each of us. All people are motivated. Their motivation is easy to identify. It is striving behavior, the priceless gift of human effort. Each decides how much motivation, if any, to lend toward a given task based on a personal assessment of its perceived risk vs. return, for the doing or not doing of it. Those in command positions of organizations, who wish to lead, must pay special and constant attention to this principle. They can inspirate, instigate, or irrigate amidst people at work; they can orchestrate, but they do not motivate. The people themselves do that, by choice and for their own purposes."[15]

We are motivated to try to make our organization the preferred choice of people, by and for people. We must do that by learning leadership and applying it.

4. *Turnover is up, and we have had a tough time filling vacancies for what we are paying. Line management has become too choosy amidst a diminished supply of applicants. A perfect example is the Executive Secretary position.* (by Charlie)

We resolved: Our intention is to cease wasting our time, confusing and losing our people, and being generally unattractive as an employer. There is a fundamental failure in basic personnel management technique that has been there since it was copied from the military by smokestack industries in the 1940s and 1950s. The failure is that many major methods of personnel management never have been made to work very well in any industry. Faulty thinking amidst false beliefs, when repetitively copied, do not withstand the test of time when times change.

We will not be successful in the leadership age unless we adapt our organization to succeed in the times before it. We need to rethink, resolve, and act, as one.

Turning to the writings of Lance again, "There is a growing labor shortage in this country, not just related to registered nurses, engineers, and computer experts. This time it's an across-the-board shortage that will increase its pain for all business organizations until it peaks sometime in the late 1990s. Think of it this way. We can identify the number of preteens today for jobs in the future, compared to retirement, deaths, and the probable creation of new jobs. There just aren't going to be enough people readily available tomorrow to conduct business as we've known it. We've begun a bidder's war because of a baby bust."[16]

"You can count on people becoming impatient for money, choosier about organizations to commit to, with overt preference for the smaller, downsized, personalized, decentralized organization. Such an organization must have a cause to share that is attractive and will share it in a less structured, less controlled, very personal, but more competitive way. It will accomplish this by admitting, in one voice, that people do not work for 'us'; they work for themselves."[17]

"Since all human motivation is based on needs a person feels are unmet, leaders of organizations will come to realize a fundamental tenet of organizational behavior. *Unless you grow people, you had better really be prepared to buy people, and keep buying.*"[18]

We choose to grow people, and we will compensate them well. We need turnover of the wrong people. We will cull them from the back door of our organization, away from the in-house of our organization. We need to

identify, attract, and foster the right people in-house, and personally see to the front door of our organization. There are several major changes in store.

First, recruitment and selection will be decentralized. Applications, new hires, transfers, and promotions will be recorded in the Payroll Department. Prior to the recording, however, it will be you, the line Vice-Presidents, who will assess those who would wish to contribute and, in turn, authorize or reject their recording.

We will stop insulting those people who compliment us, with their interests in becoming one of us, by eliminating the past system of "hurdles." Leaping the hurdles of receptionist, Personnel Department, department head, supervisor, and God knows who else is an untenable way to encourage people to join our cause. It denies that the right people are always in short supply, especially in the coming decade. It is too impersonal to be satisfactory to the "persona" our organization wishes to project.

We will see to it that we learn new methods of selection that will require more of your time and the time of your administrative assistant. Together, each line Vice-President's office will be the Human Resources office, in the best meaning of the term. The Payroll office will be the receptacle of paper, data, and simple compliance reporting. That Payroll has been redundant with Personnel in the past will not prevent us from eliminating that redundancy in the future.

It is paramount that you know, authorize, and support those whom you lead. You are accountable for whom they are, why they are here, and how they feel about doing things as a member of us. Your objective, as a leader, is to select them personally and carefully; then apply them to their best contribution; then grow them to greater, more versatile contributions. We will positively hang together on this accountability and share as a team, or you will hang separately.

The second major change involves the in-house employment leadership pattern. You will note that the Nurse Recruiter position has been eliminated, and that in Nursing we now have two new line Vice-Presidents. Each line Vice-President has a personal administrative assistant, upon whom each will rely as an extension and representation of himself.

No Vice-President will have charge to directly lead more than 150 people. It will be as if each of you were an entrepreneur amidst other entrepreneurs, on whom you must rely. You will get to know your people personally, and they will see and speak with you routinely. Where they are is where it's happening—not in your office.

In your office is your principal representative. No longer just a receptionist and typist and file clerk, your *administrative assistant will be called a Liaison Officer*. She (or he, as the case may be) will not only be your Executive Secretary; she or he will be charged with being you, when you are not in your office.

All Liaison Officers will be paid the same, $50,000.00 per annum. Annually, the replacement value of this critical role will be redetermined based upon "market competitive positioning."[19]

Judge now whether you can bet your career on your current Executive Secretary growing, with your coaching, into the Liaison Officer role.

Closer to where it is happening in the organization is a critical part of the substitute for Departmental Directors. Our objective, for example, is that over a period of time, there will be no Director of Pharmacy or Director of Telecommunications. There will be a Pharmacy Unit Leader and a Telecommunications Unit Leader, and in like kind a leader for every unit of organization.

The focus of these leaders will be today and in the short run. They will mostly be doing the work as a worker, but they will also serve a double-barreled role. They will represent the workers' interest to you and represent your interests to the workers. In doing so, by definition, they will represent me for all of our collective interests.

To do so, they will accomplish becoming an important resource for quality assurance as a communicator and doer. They will be charged with

Exhibit 6-1 continued

appraising work, not people. They will coach people, as if they were the lubricant to successful operations by people, removing or reducing obstacles to personal peak performance within discretionary limits of leadership authority. You will define those limits and delegate that authority. Accordingly, the people themselves will self-govern on our behalf and appraise themselves on our behalf, by simplified peer review.

All Unit Leaders will be paid the same, $10,000.00 per annum more than the highest paid worker in the Unit Peer group. They will serve in the capacity for up to one year, with potential annual reappointment by you. Failing reappointment, their salary will be reduced to their prior annual salary or the "target" rate of their peer group, whichever is greater.

Judge now whether you can bet your career on the current *informal* leader in each work unit of your given charge. Can you grow them, with your coaching, into the Unit Leader role? If not, what will you do to remove or reduce the obstacle that the informal leader may present to your new Unit Leader?

5. *Promotional bidding is down. Anniversary merit pay budgets are too low. Perhaps you should consider an overhaul of the compensation system.* (by Charlie)

We resolved: Each line Vice-President will post available roles (positions), and *any* employee can see *any* Vice-President for *any* purpose, through appointment granted on a priority basis. Our unwritten rule, regarding promotions, is that when an employee has *close* to the required qualifications, skills, and background for a given role, the employee will be awarded that role.

We'll do everything moral and reasonable to help an employee gain full qualifications before we go to the outside market. What counts most in your consideration is the contribution the employee has given to the organization, and the investment the organization has made, and may make in the employee.

If you might be able to increase the return on investment through a promotion, do so. Assemble your facts and analyze your feelings. Consider taking the risk to improve the return. Be predisposed to accept the gamble, but gamble legally and well.

As a leader of people, each of us is responsible for the "attracting, retaining, and entertaining of people" in the interest of our business, which is carried on by people. People of our organization, as do all people, place high symbolic value in money as it relates to pay. We therefore need to learn about money and to use it for its maximum effect on pay. Our objective, in this regard, is "to pay fewer, better people more."[20]

Lance has written that "There have always been two sides to the coin of pay: for the employee, time and effort represent a perishable commodity; for the employer, an idea or action that is untapped represents a potential market that may be tapped by other employers. In the truly successful organization of the Leadership Age, both sides will land heads up."[21]

"In such successful organizations, leaders will proclaim that employees are *not* paid to incite them toward working harder or smarter, or to do more with less. Rather, employees are paid because leaders are predisposed to believe that they will work their hardest, they are smart, and they want to contribute greatly. The never-ending ambition of a leadership-oriented CEO is to succeed in helping employees win on behalf of his organization."[22]

"To do that, we must rethink and reform pay. If all motivation is striving toward unmet needs, those who accept base salary should be satiated about money each time they cash their paycheck. The paycheck would have to be large enough to symbolically meet a security status as the employee personally defines it. For the employee, it is a matter of personal decision making: risk (how much effort is devoted) versus return (how valuable the result of effort is)."[23]

"Beyond that, a human being judges if risk versus return is *roughly* in balance, to conclude whether the pay is deemed fair, and whether satiation of his need has been accomplished. If the paychecks are predictable, and

the employee's assessment of personal risk versus return is constant, one might conclude that base pay, alone, should satisfy the employee, about money. And it would be that way were it not for the fact that human beings and their environments are more complex than laboratory animals. Human beings make complex value judgments about right and wrong, particularly when it comes to money."[24]

"Money is a motivator until it is perceived as right. Money is a demotivator if it is perceived as wrong. When organizations try to inspire motivation with money, they will eventually hit a satiation point, where more money buys increasingly less motivation. What's worse is the more complex and pseudosophisticated they become about pay, the less trusting employees become in the upper leadership of the organization. That leads to poor commitment to an organization, not just poor motivation about the work."[25]

"What can a CEO do about people and pay? Two things."[26]

"First, simplify when adjusting pay upward by role (position) to a *specific* market competitive point of pay (the Target) twice per year, if warranted by the market. Do this by disregarding performance appraisal. Continuing base pay, and the market adjusting of it, represents full pay for performance of a role in a satisfactory or better (honorable) fashion. When an employee can do that consistently, he has peaked on the learning curve. It doesn't take an employee 10 years (worth 10 steps) to peak on the learning curve for a given role. It never did."[27]

"If you can afford it, move all your postprobationary employees to maximum of their published scale; then stop publishing scales and eliminate max from the organization's vocabulary. The salary objective of every employee is to reach Target pay for their role. They do that in a short time, commensurate with the learning curve for their role. Once an employee reaches Target, market forces dictate the degree of movement upward, returning to a predefined competitive position. That position is specific, as no more and no less than what the organization wishes to pay for a given role, honorably performed, at a given time."[28]

"Second, compete by offering Behavioral Lease Agreements. Simply stated they might be expressed as follows:

> If you agree to join us, in any role, we expect you to do everything legal and moral to help us remain and grow as a winning team of people. In such a role, we will start your pay high, move it quickly to what we pay others in such a role, and stay aware of that role's market. We will try to provide for adequate and reasonable employee benefits for the security of yourself and your immediate family. We wish through this agreement to lease, not police, your effort and behavior. We will try to help you grow, and you must try to help us grow to be justifiably proud of yourself and those you are among. We are not just in business to make money; we are in it for people (consumers). In that sense, you will also be in our business, if you join us. This lease can terminate at the will of either of the parties by notice to the other. It may be reviewed by either, from time to time, for honorable compliance.[29]

I have not incorporated Lance's writings on the subject of incentives, "ownership systems," perks, and executive incentives because we haven't discussed and resolved these considerations yet. However, we have agreed to retain an outside consultant to help *us* create a "Target" pay system, survey the market biannually, and recommend to *us*, as well as help *us* define and communicate, a "Behavioral Lease Process."

6. *Employees have told me that the number one problem at St. Generic is communications. We have had very few formal grievances. The suggestion box is empty. Perhaps we should improve cafeteria benefit plans.* (by Charlie)

We resolved: The number one problem at St. Generic is *not* communications. It is definition. We need to define who we are, how we do business, why a person should become one of us . . . and the list goes on. We need to stop communicating that which has not been defined. Polite idle conversa-

Exhibit 6-1 continued

tion and supposition have resulted in confusion about the intentions of leadership, and the intentions of those who are led. Actions by both have signaled rewards for "coffee table" communications by the grapevine, "baronial" cliquish behavior, and an overabundance of one-way communications that breed guarded suspicion. We favor plain speaking, with matters of substance, once we *define* our organization.

There is folly in the formal grievance procedure because it is based on a predisposition of adversarial relationships. Tear it up. Open your door to *any* employee with *any* concern or idea. Visit them where they are, soliciting their concerns or ideas. Tell *any* employee you think he's doing well, or not so well. Forget about chain of command and protocol. Take the responsibility for the soothing of feathers with other leaders on yourself. Remember that if an employee with a concern or idea is not dealt with in a friendly, verbal, comfortable fashion, to the satisfaction of the employee, my door will be manifestly open to them, and you, as an encouraging last resort.

In time, we shall review the writings of Lance regarding morale and opinion surveys. We will explore "conducting routine, brief, ongoing opinion polls of our employee population and adopt them as a way of organizational life."[30]

We concluded that all employee benefit plans need a review and overhaul with an eye toward simplicity. If an employee cannot understand a benefit (such as the pension plan), there is no benefit worth paying for. If we are going to cost shift, by deductibles to employees, we are going to provide less of a benefit to those we wish to benefit. If we provide new "living" benefits that healthy employees may access as an alternative, experience will rise and so will the cost. The result will be less total benefits to those we wish to benefit. We do not want to compete on employee benefits, as we do regarding pay. Our organization will probably never wish to afford that.

Lance has written that "Organizations are being duped into hazing up the line between pay and benefits because of a misunderstanding of total compensation, complicated by tax considerations. Pay is for spending power external to the organization, a support to self-determination. Incentives, perks, and ownership concepts are also part of pay, but benefits should not be."[31]

"Benefits assume an economy of scale by limiting choice, in order to spread personal security risk as in health, life, disability, and, perhaps, pension. An employee should be able to look toward the employer to relieve his mind of basic fear of personal misfortune or tragedy."[32]

"Getting fancy, beyond the basics, usually tempts an employee to take risks with the basics. Thus, an employee population becomes vulnerable, when the original intention was to minimize the group's vulnerability. To play it safe on benefits is to spend dollars *equivalently* to competing organizations for the basics of security. Extra dollars should be spent on competing with pay, in its many forms."[33]

"Paternalism has its role only in benefits. Trying to take out paternalism in favor of free choice may be tempting, but you'll risk overspending someone's limited dollars to do so."[34]

"Do not be deceived. Insurance companies are in business to make money. They are professional gamblers. Believing that you can buy more benefits, to be used by more people, for less money, is like believing there are "skunk apes" from Atlantis in those flying saucers from Loch Ness. Instead, buy the best benefits you can afford, for use by fewer people. Realize that too much food purchased in the "cafeteria" of insurance companies may be pleasing to the eye but will lie uncomfortably on the stomach of your organization and its people. The only exception to this rule may be Section 125 salary reduction agreements (but that's a story unto itself)."[35]

We resolved that we will secure the services of an independent insurance broker to help us reduce the out-of-control cafeteria aspect of our benefit plans. We will self-insure or trigger-insure what we should and competitively bid the remainder. We will need his help to explain this to employees in a planned, organized way. We will also need his help regarding the transfer of all benefit compliance responsibility to accounting. There, knowledge of the IRS requirements and accounts payable considerations has always been, and should be.

To prevent foolish vested interests, and the potential conflict of interest, we will pay the broker a direct consulting fee, in lieu of insurance company kickbacks (commissions).

7. *You will want to initiate a search for my replacement. As there is no one better qualified to appreciate what department heads, personnel staff, and employees want, I'd be glad to help locate the right candidate.* (by Charlie)

We resolved: The important thing is what senior leadership wants. At this time, it would not choose to replace Charlie.

I resolved: To do two things we did not discuss at our meeting.

First: Quite a while ago, I retained Ms. Ida Phoenix as a strategist and advisor. She has been a key contributor to many of the thoughts and considerations that I have brought before you, and that together we have resolved. She describes herself as a reformer in human resources, who was formerly a cross between an eagle and a buzzard, whatever that means.

I am pleased to announce that Ms. Phoenix will be joining us on a retainer basis for half the annual hours, and about the same total compensation accorded to Charlie's position. However, *she is not going to do what Charlie did.* She will not be a bureaucrat, a legislator, a tender of data, or a police officer; nor will she have contact with employees. Instead, she will be consultative to me, and all line Vice-Presidents, as a tactician, "spin doctor," "consigliori," or campaign manager. She will be an inspiration, a sounding board, and a ghost writer who will help *us* portray *our* organization as one dedicated to winning for people, by people.

Ms. Phoenix and I agree that every day is a campaign for the hearts, minds, and hands of those *we* lead. Use Ms. Phoenix's talents liberally, but note that she is not a leader in our organization. She is "staff" to the "line."

Second: Of equal importance is the subject of fiscal resources. Our CEO, Genghis, has accepted a role and status somewhat similar to Ms. Phoenix.

At our next scheduled meeting of senior leadership, we will first review this letter, but then focus on fiscal resources. Genghis will be in attendance, as well as Ms. Phoenix. We have also invited Attila, our Controller, to discuss his new role and title.

I realize that the road before us will be a hard and treacherous one. The times before us are filled with change. Leadership at St. Generic will not be comfortable or secure. The "line" will be repositioned in revolutionary ways, and we will all be learning to lead. Staff will be repositioned to *support* the actions of the line.

"Anyone who says he has leadership 'figured out' is a simpleton, a charlatan, or a fool."[36] I am none of those things. What I am is your new President. I need your help, as the leader of leaders, to win for all the people of St. Generic.

This documentation of our resolutions has not been brief. Take this as an indication that I do not appreciate trading salient facts for brevity. If I am to lead you well, I want to read and hear what you think, and how you think, and why you think the way you do. I want to feel where you feel we are, as you feel it. Never assume that I know what is in your head and your heart. Check. Learn to read, write, speak, and listen well. Then I will be increasingly confident that you can lead others, *on my behalf,* as well as one must to remain with me.

"Statistics from many sources indicate that well over 50 percent of all hospital CEO positions became vacant in the past two years. Outside of hospitals, a number of surveys have suggested that the greatest fear of CEOs is 'takeover,' and their most reluctant action is in firing people. Regardless of industry, the odds are that you are destined for a new CEO, if your current one isn't amenable to thinking and doing something about leadership in place of management."[37]

"Perhaps arbitragers (takeover artists) and turnaround consultants have unwittingly given us a clue to the future direction of CEO leadership in organizations. I classify their method as the five Ts."[38]

1. "Take 'em over."
2. "Trim 'em down."
3. "Tune 'em up."
4. "Turn 'em on (around)."
5. "Teach 'em to win."

You will note an assortment of statements addressing all five aspects of this method in reviewing Exhibit 6-1.

The role for human resources executives in modern, competitive organizations, despite lip service to the contrary, is becoming more perfunctory as we enter the Leadership Age. Founded on a kitbag of services and systems that supported or defined the management process, human resources executives may find management itself to be an outdated concept.

"Work, and the world of work, have been revolutionized by people. The modern employee no longer identifies with a 'fair day's work for a fair day's pay.' Now work is much more a psychological contract, with adequate contributions by both parties for membership. Truly, work had been a place and time; now it is much more a state of mind. And for each individual there are choices, more prolific than at any time in human history."[39]

"Human resources executives are being swept into a time when new application of old ways will prove disastrous. Those ways are founded on the presumption that people are disposable, or replaceable, or classifiable. Those ways are themselves classifiable as a batch processing mentality about people and the needs of people."[40]

"As people, and organizations of people, adapt to the challenges of the Leadership Age, such presumptions and ways will become passé. With them will go those human resources executives who cannot bring themselves to tailor roles to fit people, but instead exhaustively analyze jobs with simplicity of tasks and minimum requirements."[41]

Ask yourself about fascination with straightjacketed job definition; mute allegiance to formal education and certification/registration requirements; "hurdles" in the selection process; dedication to differential review of past task performance, rather than futuristic goal setting; poor portions of "merit" pay, rather than achievement incentives; a focus on employment at will, rather than "ownership systems" or gainsharing; and strategic planning for job requirements, rather than the inciting of personal growth ambitions. Do such behaviors do much to convince a person to commit a major portion of his or her energy and effort to your organization?[42]

Perhaps they do not. Perhaps it shows. Perhaps it is being noticed. Perhaps we are re-entering the storm.

For those few human resources executives who recognize a ring of truth in the bell I have sounded, there will be new ways coming in the Leadership Age (though not all at once, to the contrary of Exhibit 6-1). To you, I recommend the following initiative:

- *Rethink and reform* outdated beliefs and rituals regarding motivation to work, commitment to organization, compensation, employment, and employee relations.
- *Stop* controlling, limiting, and batch processing behavior. *Start* facilitating, and *foster* leading behavior.
- *Do more* than decentralizing the human resources department. *Downsize* it, *relegating* routine, ongoing aspects of it, with discretionary prerogatives, back to the upper line. Those charged with first-line leadership should seek their counsel, not yours.
- *Redefine* your organization as one of people, by people, for people. *Communicate* that well, and *initiate* the learning of it. Make the payroll department the receptacle of data regarding employees.
- *Focus* on the client CEO's image. Do everything possible to cause him or her to appear to be, and be in fact, a winner, in business for people, by people. Offer your time and effort to *his* or *her* line senior leadership people.

Most important to the above five elements of prescription is that you *investigate and sift* carefully through the past history of the personnel profession and management milestones. (See Exhibit 6-2 at the conclusion of this chapter.) As the personnel department evolved in answer to the needs of management, you as a phoenix will need to *instigate* a revolution in answer to the new needs of leadership.

It has been said that "Those who ignore history are condemned to repeat it." It has also been said that "The trails of history are littered with inevitabilities that never came to be." *Balance* these critically, and practice the art of *timing*.

Formulate your own vision of the future, and *act* on it. The future, after all, is yours. You hold within yourself, as do all people, the motivation to win. Choose to win at reducing the human resources department's maintenance and control functions. Become more strategic and consultative for the sake of your CEO, yourself, your profession, the people of your organization, and those served by them.

Take your best shot at the Leadership Age. And, for everyone's sake, do so soon, before someone else does it for you!

Winston Churchill said, "The price of greatness is responsibility." I say, "There is no profession more accountable for the revolution of growing a winning organization, made up of winning people, than human resources. *If you don't, someone else should—and will.*"

Exhibit 6-2 "Roots and Tubers, The Incomplete TAHCC Version of History: A Sketch of Personnel (H.R.M.)." Datelined are some significant events and some significant publications representing the evolution of the personnel profession and management milestones.

Pre-1900

- Some separate departments of Finance, Accounting, Production, Marketing. No Personnel Department. First federal law in 1868 re 8-hour workday.

1902

- First Personnel Department called "Labor Department" by John Patterson, owner and president of NCR, Dayton, Ohio. Responsibilities included:
  Employment
  Grievances
  Wage administration
  Improved working conditions
  Record keeping
  Training (including "worker improvement")

World War I: 1914–1918

- Shortage of civilian labor.
- Army officer selection/training needs result in intelligence tests called Army Alpha and Army Beta (illiterates)–foundation of personnel testing and appraisal systems.
- 1916–*The Principles of Scientific Management* published one year after death of Frederick Winslow Taylor.

Prohibition: 1920–1933

- First textbook on personnel management, *Personnel Administration* by Ordway Tead and Henry C. Metcalf (1920), defines personnel job as "the direction and coordination of the human relations of any organization with a view to getting the maximum necessary production with a minimum of effort and friction, with proper regard for the genuine well-being of the workers."
- Personnel departments *become extinct* (1920–1923). **Line management revolutions** against employment managers usurping authority in hiring. Several consulting firms formed, accent on benefits/medical/workers' compensation (majority of states now have what federal government had in 1908).
- American Management Association (P.K.A. National Personnel Association—P.K.A. National Association of Employment Managers) formed. *Precipitating reason:* Personnel not an isolated function, line has authority to deal directly with workers (1923). 1926—first method of point job evaluation published in *Wage Scales and Job Evaluation* by Merril R. Lott. Inspiration to AMA and NMTA.
- "Yellow dog" contracts proliferate, attempt to kill off labor movement.
- Norris-LaGuardia Act of 1932 (prohibits "yellow dog" contracts).

Crash/Depression to World War II: 1929–1939

- Tiny informal research departments slowly begin to form in big companies re: attitudes, job analysis, productivity.
- October 1929—Wall Street Crash.
- 1935—Wagner Act (government's purpose to actively encourage growth of trade unions and restrain management interference). NLRB formed.
- 1935—Social Security Act/Unemployment compensation.
- 1938—Fair Labor Standards (wage/hour) Act.

World War II: 1939–1945

- War Manpower Commission gives advice and birth to concepts of Manpower Planning, Job Instruction Training (J.I.T.), training the trainer, and O.J.T.

- War Labor Board administers direct authority over private employers. Controls give birth to wage and salary administration and labor relations functions.
- 1941—report of Hawthorne Studies in *Readers' Digest*.
- 1943—Maslow's *Theory of Human Motivation* is published.
- 1944—report of the first Institute on Hospital Personnel Management. Bulletin #224.

Post-War to 1960s

- 1947—Taft-Hartley Act. (Unions had grown another 50 percent and grew 25 percent more over the seven years following Taft-Hartley.) Management got some rights.
- 1948—ASPA formed as a comprehensive professional organization with under 100 members.
- Human relations training abounds (happy means productive).
- 1950—Edward Hay publishes a five-page article, "Techniques of Securing Agreement in Job Evaluation Committees" (6 to 10 members; "pooled judgment" by averaging or discussion.)
- 1954—Peter Drucker publishes *The Practice of Management*, asking "Is personnel management bankrupt?" Coins the concept of M.B.O.
- 1954—First textbook on *Hospital Personnel Administration* published by Norman D. Bailey, then administrator of Grant Hospital in Chicago.
- 1955—AFL–CIO merger.
- 1957—Douglas McGregor publishes "An Uneasy Look at Performance Appraisal." Publishes "The Human Side of Enterprise" (theory X/Y) (1960) and refines M.B.O.; gives birth to organizational development (O.D.).
- 1957—*Parkinson's Law and Other Studies in Administration* published by C. Northcote Parkinson.
- 1958—L.M.R.D.A. of Landrum-Griffin Act.
- 1959—Warren Bennis publishes *Leadership Theory and Administrative Behavior: The Problem of Authority*.

1960s to Late 1970s

- 1963—Equal Pay Act.
- 1964—Civil Rights Act.
- Blake & Mouton publish *The Managerial Grid* (1964).
- Chris Argyris publishes his concepts of *T-Groups for Organizational Effectiveness* (1964) and *Integrating the Individual and the Organization*.
- First paid CEO of ASPA, Len Brice (1964).
- *Creative Management* published by Shigeru Kobayashi, managing director of The Sony Corp. (1966).
- *Management and Machiavelli, an Inquiry into the Politics of Corporate Life* published by Antony Jay (1967).
- 1967–1968—Frederick Herzberg publishes his theories of motivation.
- 1969—ASHPA formed. *The Peter Principle* published by Dr. L. Peter.
- 1969—Age Discrimination Act (BFOQ).
- Executive Order of 1970 (affirmative action).
- OSHA begins in 1970.
- *Up the Organization (How To Stop the Corporation from Stifling People and Strangling Profits)* by Robert Townsend. Suggests "Fire the whole Personnel Dept." (1970) (seven-month best seller).
- 1971—*Griggs v. Duke Power Co.* (test result, not employer's intent—substantially reduces use of employment tests).

Exhibit 6-2 continued

- 1971—Pay freezes.
- 1973—HMO Act.
- 1974—Health care amendments to NLRA.
- 1974—Watergate.
- 1974—Saul Gellerman publishes "In Praise of Those Who Leave."
- 1974—ERISA.
- *Power! How to Get it, How to Use it* published by Michael Korda (1975).
- World Federation of Personnel Management Association chartered in 1976.

- Full-time Washington office for ASPA opens in 1977.
- *Managing in Turbulent Times* published by Peter Drucker (1980).

Since Then

- *Some Law Evolving* (Labor, EEO, R.E.A., COBRA, Immigration, "Employment at Will").
- *Some Awareness Evolving by Rediscovery* (competition/quality/teamwork/customer relations/coaching and best sellers. Personnel now called Human Resources in about 50 percent of cases). Effort, with mixed review, at accreditation.

Have the 1980s been the eye of the storm?

Source: Reprinted from *RENAISSANCE—The Ultimate Leadership Development,* copyright 1986, 1988 by The American Healthcare Consulting Corporation, Sharon, Massachusetts.

NOTES

1. David Lance, "The Revolution in Human Resources: Money, Motivation, Mythology." Oral presentation and distribution of papers at the 24th annual meeting of the Human Resource Institute of the Hospital Association of New York State.

2. Ibid.

3. Ibid.

4. "RENAISSANCE—The Ultimate Leadership Development" (Sharon, Mass.: American Healthcare Consulting Corporation, 1988).

5. Ibid.

6. Ibid.

7. Ibid.

8. Ibid.

9. Lance, "The Revolution."

10. "RENAISSANCE."

11. "QUEST—The Supportive Process" (Sharon, Mass.: American Healthcare Consulting Corporation, 1988).

12. Ibid.

13. "RENAISSANCE."

14. "The PROBE Analytic Series" (Sharon, Mass.: American Healthcare Consulting Corporation, 1989).

15. "RENAISSANCE."

16. Lance, "The Revolution."

17. Ibid.

18. "PRICER/SHADOW—Strategy and Tactics" (Sharon, Mass.: American Healthcare Consulting Corporation, 1988).

19. Ibid.

20. "RENAISSANCE."

21. Ibid.

22. Ibid.

23. Ibid.

24. Ibid.

25. Ibid.

26. Ibid.

27. Ibid.

28. "PRICER/SHADOW."

29. "RENAISSANCE."

30. "The PROBE."

31. "PRICER/SHADOW."

32. Ibid.

33. Ibid.

34. Ibid.

35. Ibid.

36. "RENAISSANCE."

37. Ibid.

38. Ibid.

39. "QUEST."

40. "RENAISSANCE."

41. Ibid.

42. Ibid.

Laura Avakian

Human Resources Leadership—A Perspective from the Trenches

7

Because the profession is plagued with an image of mushy-headed, bureaucratic reactiveness, ''human resources leadership'' might be considered an oxymoron by many outside and even within the field. In 1978 Addison Bennett wrote, ''The needs and conditions do exist to set the stage for making personnel people in hospitals 'The new corporate heros.'''[1] Yet after more than a decade of acknowledgment that human resources expertise belongs in the board room, the profession must ask itself why it still does not have the clout it seeks and needs if it is to be effective. But it must answer quickly. There is no time for brooding introspection. The future of the health care industry in many ways rests with how its individual organizations are managing their human resources . . . now.

WHY HUMAN RESOURCES LEADERSHIP IS NECESSARY

Hospitals have always been complex organizations. They often have multiple missions—patient care, physician education, medical research, community service. They are extraordinarily labor-intensive and tough to administer because they defy many time-honored priniciples of good management.

To be effective, they have needed to combine the latest technological advances with highly personalized customer service in cost-effective ways. While some other industries, such as the telephone company, may have similar demands, none has greater consequences from its successes or failures than a hospital with its impact on human life and well-being.

These descriptors of intensity and complexity and consequence have always applied to health care operations. Yet the

decade of the eighties brought new tumult to this already churning industry. A number of external factors—nearly all of them reflective of problems with the availability, capability, and/or cost of human resources—put severe pressure on hospitals' ability to deliver services.

Not the least among these factors is the shortage of skilled health care workers. The American Hospital Association reported a 13.6-percent vacancy rate for registered nurse positions in the United States in 1986 (more than double the 1985 rate),[2] and a decline of baccalaureate nursing school graduates of 13 percent between 1986 and 1996 is projected by the National League of Nursing.[3] Also in short supply are radiographers, medical technologists, and respiratory and physical therapists. And in many areas of the country, there is a dearth of clerical and service workers as well.

Not infrequently, the results of these shortages have been either closed beds or weary, frustrated care givers who are demanding the near-impossible of their employment office staffs. Another consequence has been the rapid escalation of pay rates for some of these occupations, in radical contrast to others, creating dissension among employees and throwing havoc into job evaluation and pay systems.

The already stressful hospital environment is rendered more so by the presence of AIDS victims and a whole subset of related human resources issues, such as confidentiality of records and employee safety and education. Further, with the growth of outpatient services, acuity levels of inpatients have worsened, and yet expectations by patients and family members of high-quality care keep rising.

Another external force affecting all industries' human resources management is increasing government involvement

45

in virtually every aspect of work life. From minimum wage laws to retirement plan regulations, from labor law to parental leave to employment-at-will, legislative and regulatory bodies have ensured a need for knowledgeable human resources staffs and lifetimes of work for attorneys.

All these external forces document the need for strong human resources expertise but do not necessarily demonstrate a demand for leadership. That pressure, rather, is now generated from within organizations. *In Search of Excellence* and other commentaries on corporate successes reflect the importance of a strong, internally directed organizational culture. Some management consultants said it this way: ''As the economy shifts from an industrial base to a service and informational base, business increasingly depends on competent, well-managed human resources. In this new economic environment, human skills and ability determine what organizations can accomplish.''[4] And another authority noted

> A highly qualified, innovative human resources function is more important to companies today than ever before. Why? Because of such factors as the need to step up productivity in the face of foreign competition, the need to comply with an increasing number of regulations and laws, and the increasing need to compete with other companies for highly skilled employees.[5]

WHY HUMAN RESOURCES LEADERSHIP IS SCARCE

Some similar perceptions about human resources professionals' shortcomings are held by practitioners, as well as by observers of the field. A common theme resounds in comments like these sprinkled throughout the literature on human resources management.

- ''It is crucial that human resources professionals realize that company survival and cost control are also their problems.''[6]
- ''The personnel professional is going to have to get more into the language and syntax of business people to be understood and also to understand issues such as cost effectiveness and value added.''[7]
- ''Management had a sense that the personnel department was doing valuable work, but management failed to understand what HR was doing or why it was relevant to competitive strategy, cost controls, and business results.''[8]
- ''Top management often sees the HR staff as incompetent and lacking in the skills needed to deal with such crucial company concerns as productivity, government regulations, and human resources planning.''[9]

In short, the discrepancy between an organization's business needs and the human resources department's ability to understand them—much less to meet them—is made more glaring by the competitive, pressured environment of contemporary industries.

Where not so long ago it was manufacturing companies that bore the brunt of these pressures, generated largely by foreign competition, these same kinds of demands have now hit service industries, and health care is certainly among them. And while the acknowledgment is pervasive that human resources professionals need to form a bond with line management in developing business strategies, it simply has not happened in the human resources sector, or at least with the speed necessary.

Why not? Human resources professionals have spent a long time becoming specialists, specialists who have woven such a web of mystery around their craft that line managers have yielded much of their personnel direction to human resources and yet are suspicious of it. Some of the unfortunate results are that affirmative action is seen as a human resources function, that employee grievances are the property of human resources, and that job evaluation is a system to be tricked if employees are to be paid right. Human resources specialists toss acronyms about as if they were stirring alphabet soup—EEOC, ERISA, NLRB, FLSA—shaking their heads at managers' ignorance and noncompliance. But who can blame human resources? After all, someone has, in fact, needed to worry about these regulations and the appropriate responses to them.

Regardless of where ''fault'' lies, the alienation of human resources and the distrust of line managers exist, and these facts are making it tough for human resources to do its job right—or even to do the right job.

Another major hurdle is posed by human resources professionals' standard approach to problem resolution. The traditional response is (a) do a survey, (b) develop a program, and (c) do (or at least promise to do) program evaluation. That evaluation has often consisted of recording the number of employees who participate and making some subjective judgments about program quality as it has related to such areas as recruitment or employee morale.

To help their organizations solve today's problems, human resources staffs need to be as expert at planning strategies as they have been at planning programs. And they need a knowledge base that includes techniques of cost control, productivity improvement, and organizationwide human resources planning. In short, they must stop being reactors and become leaders committed to solving the business needs of their organizations.

HOW TO DEVELOP HUMAN RESOURCES INTO A LEADERSHIP FUNCTION

For many reasons, these roles of leadership and business partnership are not so easily achieved. Among them is the fact that the human resources function must continue to provide expert specialists in salary and benefits administration, in employment, in labor relations, and in employee health and safety. Additionally, more government involvement and regulation can be expected, not less. And the negative stereotyping of human relations departments' competence and helpfulness will not change overnight.

With so many hats to wear and hurdles to leap, how can the human resources leader emerge? First, senior human resources people must assess the mission and priorities of their department. These should mirror the mission and priorities of the larger organization. As one management consultant admonishes the human resources executive, "One must develop a 'mindset' that reflects and assesses the enterprise and where it is heading—rather than one that mechanically thinks, says, that the company should have a dental plan because other companies have it."[10] A highly regarded human resources executive has advised

> Go back to the mission statement of the HR function—helping management achieve the maximum utilization of the employer resources and, at the same time, being the employee advocate. The real key is having that mission statement viewed as a management position, not simply as an HR posture.[11]

Further, human resources professionals must have, or develop, solid leadership skills. Albert A. Vicere, an educator and management consultant, has cited the need for four critical competencies.

1. a detailed understanding of the strategic management process
2. an in-depth knowledge of the organization's business and its competitive environment
3. a thorough working knowledge of the organization itself from both a line and a staff perspective
4. a firm grasp on the role of the human resources professional as a catalyst in the implementation of strategic change through carefully developed human resources selection, appraisal, reward, and development systems[12]

These competencies may be developed in a variety of ways. Vicere advocates methods that include using a self-assessment tool to become aware of the skills required by strategic management and taking time to learn the business. He also urges spending time on site with line managers to really understand their functions, problems, and roles in the organization's strategic efforts.[13]

A human resources executive, addressing a conference of the Human Resource Planning Society, advised his audience, "Do your homework."[14] It is the facts and figures of one's business that form the bases for evaluation and strategic planning.

In describing how dollar-oriented data serve to attract management's attention, a consultant with Hay points out that human resources executives too often describe abstract concepts, such as employee development, to their colleagues, or they list the pure costs of a program. They should, rather,

demonstrate the impact of these concepts or costs on the company's business or income.[15]

Further, there is a variety of tools and techniques at hand, including the following, that could be used with great impact.

- *Employee Attitude/Climate Assessment Surveys:* Periodic employee opinion surveys provide rich data for program evaluation. They also help management determine when and how to implement changes and can test for employees' understanding of goals and support for the leadership.
- *Communications Programs:* Human resources should evaluate the effectiveness of all written employee communications and propose means of ensuring that there is upward communication in the organization as well as a variety of vehicles for dialogue across departments.
- *Succession Planning:* A vital part of planning an organization's future is to consider its leaders-to-be and how they are being developed. Helping the CEO and other administrators plan for transitions is an important human resources role.
- *Focus Groups:* These provide a way of testing opinion and the impact of changes before they are implemented. Like formal opinion surveys, focus groups provide excellent data for planning and evaluation.
- *Skills Inventories:* A tool to assist in management planning, inventories of employee skills help with the development of training programs and succession planning.

The human resources staff has expertise in administering these processes. Beyond their use as evaluation methods, the data that result should become fodder for organizational planning. Strategies for involving employees in fulfilling the hospital's mission, for conducting cost-benefit analyses of employer-related expenses, and for anticipating future manpower needs and ways of meeting them can all be derived by using these tools. In initiating such study, the human resources staff is not viewed as superimposing time-consuming programs on line management. Rather, they are leading a process aimed at achieving organizational goals.

DEVELOPING HUMAN RESOURCES STAFF

It is not sufficient that the vice-president for human resources direct his or her own thinking and activity toward a strategic planning process. The mindset and commitment must filter throughout the human resources staff. However, there is a risk of romanticizing all this "fun" activity of influencing the leadership of the organization at the expense of good, basic personnel administration. Compensation, benefits, employment, contract and regulation compliance, and other ongoing programs must be well managed.

In helping human resources staff maintain their expertise in their specialized functions, yet still assume this new kind of leadership role, these strategies for their development are recommended.

- *Provide opportunities for external education and professional affiliation.* Many educational programs, both in specific areas of human resources and in business administration, are available at reasonable cost at universities, at junior colleges, and through professional seminars. Also, membership in professional societies, such as the American Society for Healthcare Human Resources Administration (ASHHRA) or the American Society for Personnel Administration (ASPA), or their local or state chapters, is not expensive and provides stimulating exchange among colleagues. A portion of the human resources budget devoted to the professional development of staff is money well spent.

- *Send human resources staff out into the hospital to do their work.* If they do all their work in their offices, expecting employees always to come to them when they need assistance, their function will never be perceived as proactive. "Road shows" are one effective way to expose human resources staff to the environment they need to know and understand. For example, an employee relations specialist might ask to speak at various departmental meetings on such subjects as the disciplinary policy or the grievance procedure. Or people from the employment or compensation areas might do an educational "road show" on promotions and transfers. By having human resources staff appear in other departments, such as the laundry or a nursing conference room, respect for those functions is conveyed. This also allows the human resources staff to get more in-depth knowledge of their customers' issues.

- *Create interdisciplinary work teams.* When projects are undertaken, involve staff from a variety of human resources areas as well as from other departments. For example, if an exit interview program is being developed, line managers should participate with human resources people in devising the questionnaire and deciding how the data will be used. The process assures support for the program but, more importantly, results in a product that reflects issues important to the whole organization. Other opportunities for expanding staff members' knowledge of the organization can be created in the form of ongoing committees on such topics as employee health and safety and employee recognition programs. Also, internal experts could be invited to attend human resources staff functions. A physician speaking on the research going on in the organization, a development officer talking about the hospital's reliance on fund raising, a facilities engineer describing how buildings are planned and maintained—all serve to open human resources staff's eyes to the broader scope and purposes of the organization.

- When possible, *expose human resources staff to top management and members of the board of trustees.* Hearing those who are ultimately accountable for the effectiveness of the organization reinforces the importance of its mission and the value of all employees in supporting it. If such opportunities do not exist, the human resources staff could initiate activities and events to create a dialogue throughout the hospital.

- *Teaching and mentoring are important functions* in assuring that human resources staff rise to the level of competence needed to lead the organization. They can learn the principles and mechanisms of strategic planning, and they can follow the excellent example set by top-flight human resources executives, both within their institution and in others.

CONCLUSION

The cry for human resources leadership from within health care organizations is a loud one. The challenge of delivering quality patient care with increasingly scarce resources is enormous, and many of the answers lie in effective planning and people management.

While this is not the first opportunity human resources professionals have had to use their expertise to influence the work environment, the issues calling for their leadership have never been more graphic, nor the consequences of inaction so potentially devastating.

Human resources must become a partner with line management and must be able to define and evaluate its contribution to the business of the hospital. The profession can no longer excuse itself by claiming that others in the organization do not understand the importance of human resources. Even though they do so with some skepticism and distrust, line managers are opening the board room door to human resources professionals and inviting them to contribute their expertise in placement, utilization, and development and recognition of employees, knowing that success in these areas is needed if the hospital is to gain a competitive edge.

The future of human resources and the future of health care are more vitally linked than ever. This time let's walk through that door.

NOTES

1. Addison Bennett, "There's More to It Than People Shuffling," *Hospitals* 52, no. 23 (1 Dec. 1978).

2. American Hospital Association, "The Nursing Shortage: Facts and Figures and Feeling," in *Research Report* (AHA, 1987).

3. Nursing Data Review, 1985-1986, New York's National League of Nursing, 1986.

4. Lloyd Baird and Ilan Meshoulam, "A Second Chance for Human Resources To Make the Grade," *Personnel* (April 1986): 47.

5. Edward F. McDonough III, "How Much Power Does Human Resources Have, and What Can It Do To Win More?" *Personnel* (January 1986): 18.

6. "Regaining the Competitive Edge," *Personnel Administrator* (July 1986): 36.

7. Ibid.

8. Baird and Meshoulam, "A Second Chance," 46.

9. McDonough, "How Much Power," p. 23.

10. George G. Gordon, "Getting in Step," *Personnel Administrator* (April 1987): 134.

11. "Regaining the Competitive Edge," 40.

12. Albert A. Vicere, "Break the Mold: Strategies for Leadership," *Personnel Journal* (May 1987): 69.

13. Ibid., 70–71.

14. Gordon, "Getting in Step," 48.

15. Ibid., 46.

Paula L. Stamps

The Stamps-Piedmonte Index of Work Satisfaction: Linking Job Satisfaction and Job Redesign

8

INTRODUCTION AND BACKGROUND

There are over five million people employed in health-related occupations nationally, and in some states the health industry has more employees than any other sector of the economy. The largest single group within the health industry is nurses, who compose one-half of the total work force.[1] In view of numbers alone, one would expect a vigorous and flourishing profession. Instead, members are leaving nursing at fairly high rates, high turnover rates exist for those who are choosing to stay in the field as they move around from job to job, and extremely low levels of occupational satisfaction are consistently reported.

The published literature is full of studies documenting low levels of occupational satisfaction on the part of nursing staff. Some of the studies have very large samples, including one in Florida that involved 3,700 nurses.[2] Hospital nurses have been involved in many of the studies, including the largest single survey of nurses ever done, which involved 17,000 responses; 78 percent of staff nurses reported that they were "barely" satisfied.[3] Long-term and chronic care nursing has also been the setting for several studies, with major issues of dissatisfaction involving lower pay and fewer benefits than in acute care settings; fewer opportunities for autonomy; unrealistic staffing patterns, and a generally perceived low level of understanding of the work of the professional nurse in long-term care.[4]

Some of these studies are smaller and on more specific issues, such as pay, self-esteem, lack of autonomy in relation to the larger issue of oppression of women, and the continuing problem of the most appropriate clinical role for nurses. Other studies focus on employee withdrawal behaviors, including turnover, absenteeism, and burnout that leads nurses to leave the profession entirely. Most of these studies have included demographic, education, and staffing variables.

This literature leaves the reader with several strong impressions. One is the strength of what Corwin many years ago termed the "calling" part of the nurse's role,[5] which seems to keep nurses in nursing, even in the face of obvious and sometimes overwhelming occupational dissatisfaction. Another very strong impression is the lack of standardization that characterizes all of these studies. Even though they are all looking at the same large issue—occupational satisfaction of nurses—there is no agreement on how to measure this, or on which are dependent or independent variables, or even on the definition of satisfaction. It is impossible to summarize the findings, and it is also impossible to generalize the findings of those many specific studies. The one clear sense that arises from this literature is a need to be able to document and describe the nature of job satisfaction for nurses in such a way as to be able to generalize about issues. This has caused a research team, led by the author, to become involved in a ten-year research project, the major objective of which has been to develop a statistically valid and reliable measurement tool that can be used to describe occupational satisfaction of nurses and that can also be utilized as a management tool to modify the work environments of nurses. After more than 10 years, the scale has been validated and has now been prepared for general use.[6] The purpose of this chapter is to briefly describe the development of this tool and then to focus on the use of it, particularly in hospital settings.

THE STAMPS—PIEDMONTE INDEX OF WORK SATISFACTION

After reviewing the literature and talking to staff nurses, administrative nurses, and occupational sociologists, we attempted the first scale definition in 1972. Since that time, many revisions have occurred, although the most recent ones involve scoring and other scale mechanics rather than significant content analysis.

The theoretical structure of the scale is based on the need fulfillment theory and the social reference group or equity theory.[7] Additionally, two other assumptions have guided the development of this scale. First is the notion that work satisfaction is made up of more than one simple variable. One who attempts to measure this complex, multifaceted concept must first carefully separate it into its components. Second, is the acceptance of the general idea that personal satisfaction is partly a result of balancing expectations and rewards, so that a measurement instrument must include items related to the components that people value in their occupations, as well as their perceptions of the degree to which their current work fulfills those ideal expectations. This means that both the components of work satisfaction and the current level of satisfaction with each component must be included in a measurement instrument.

The components we have used to define satisfaction so that it will be specific to the health field are the following:

- *Pay:* dollar remuneration and fringe benefits received for work done
- *Autonomy:* amount of job-related independence, initiative, and freedom either permitted or required in daily work activities
- *Task requirements:* tasks that must be done as a regular part of the job
- *Organizational policies:* management policies and procedures put forward by the hospital and nursing administrators
- *Interaction:* opportunities and requirements for both formal and informal social contact during working hours; divided into two subcomponents: nurse-nurse interaction and nurse-physician interaction
- *Job prestige/status:* overall importance or significance felt about the job at the personal level and to the organization

Description of the Measurement Instrument

These components then become the first section of the questionnaire that measures the relative importance or ideal expectations of the elements of job satisfaction. This section essentially consists of a statement of ideal expectations. It compares the six components of satisfaction in a forced choice among all possible combinations of pairs. That is, the respondents are asked to choose the member of each of 15 pairs (e.g., autonomy or pay, task requirements or autonomy) that is more important to them as a contributor to their own level of satisfaction. The relative importance of each component is weighted by modification of the paired comparisons test described by Edwards.[8] In this procedure, the frequency with which the component is chosen more important is determined, and this number is converted into a proportion; the porportion is then converted into a Z-statistic and, through two more transformations, into a rank on a scale from zero to one, zero being the value arbitrarily assigned to the least important component. These rankings then serve as the weighting to determine both a weighted score for each component and the total score. This section of the questionnaire is known as Part A or Paired Comparisons.

The second section of the measurement instrument (Part B) is a Likert-type attitude scale that measures current levels of satisfaction for each of the six components. The items are arranged randomly throughout the questionnaire so that the respondent does not become aware of the specific component being examined. The response mode is on a seven-point scale with a neutral midpoint. Half of the items within each component are phrased positively and half negatively. In the process of scoring, the negative scores are reversed so that a higher component score denotes a higher level of satisfaction with that component. Each of the six components is treated as a separate dimension of current level of satisfaction. Each component, therefore, yields a separate score; a total score also may be derived from the entire scale. The rankings of the level of satisfaction with the components (based on the attitude scores for each component) may then be compared with the rankings of the importance of the components (derived from the scale values of the paired comparisons).

One additional step is then taken in developing an overall index: to produce one score that reflects both importance and actual satisfaction, the average component score is multiplied by its appropriate weighting coefficient, thereby producing weighted component scores. These six scores are summed to produce a single figure, the Index of Work Satisfaction (IWS). This weighted scoring procedure produces a total index that emphasizes the relative importance of the components so that more heavily weighted components have a greater influence on the total score.

The early phases of the research necessary for the development of this instrument have been reported in the literature.[9] Throughout this process, statistical estimates of reliability were obtained through the use of Cronbach's Alpha coefficient and Kendall's Tau. Statistical estimates of validity were obtained through the use of factor analytic techniques. The scale has performed well throughout the various analyses and revisions, with each revision strengthening the scale.

The final validation study phase consisted of surveying the people who had used the scale and performing a comparative analysis of their data which involved comparing not only results but also the statistical analysis for estimates of reliability and validity. The questionnaire was then modified one last time as a result of these analyses and was administered in two additional community hospital settings. The instrument was revised based on the results of the analysis of these two last studies and, because of the strong statistical analysis, is now considered to be a valid and reliable tool to be used for measuring the level of satisfaction of nurses.[10]

Exhibit 8-1 gives the attitude scale in its final validated form. The construction of the scale is such that seven items are used to measure Professional Status (2, 9, 15, 27, 34, 38, 41), six items are used to measure Task Requirements (4, 11, 22, 24, 29, 36), six items are used to measure Pay (1, 8, 14, 21, 32, 44), seven items are used to measure Organizational Policies (5, 12, 18, 25, 33, 40, 42), and eight items are used to measure Autonomy (7, 13, 17, 20, 26, 30, 31, 43). The final component, Interaction, is divided into two subcomponents: the first, Physician-Nurse Interaction, is measured by items 6, 19, 35, 37, and 39; the second, Nurse-Nurse Interaction, is measured by items 3, 10, 16, 23, and 28.

Table 8-1 shows the numerical data from one of the last two administrations. This table presents the actual scores of Part A (the Component Weighting Coefficient developed from the Paired Comparisons), the actual mean scores for each of the components (from Part B, the Attitude Scale), and the mean score for each component. For each of these, the range of scores is also given. Table 8-1 also shows the adjusted scores (the scores from Part B weighted by the level of importance), as well as the total IWS (Index of Work Satisfaction) score. The range for each of these is also given.

Data Analysis and Interpretation

Several levels of analysis are possible, including both quantitative and qualitative data. These have been described completely elsewhere,[11] but some important issues will be summarized here.

Exhibit 8-1 The Stamps-Piedmonte Index of Work Satisfaction: Part B (Attitude Scale)

1. My present salary is satisfactory.
2. Most people do not sufficiently appreciate the importance of nursing care to hospital patients.
3. The nursing personnel on my service do not hesitate to pitch in and help one another out when things get in a rush.
4. There is too much clerical and "paperwork" required of nursing personnel in this hospital.
5. The nursing staff has sufficient control over scheduling their own work shifts in my hospital.
6. Physicians in general cooperate with nursing staff on my unit.
7. I feel that I am supervised more closely than is necessary.
8. Excluding myself, it is my impression that a lot of nursing personnel at this hospital are dissatisfied with their pay.
9. Nursing is a long way from being recognized as a profession.
10. New employees are not quickly made to "feel at home" on my unit.
11. I think I could do better job if I did not have so much to do all the time.
12. There is a great gap between the administration of this hospital and the daily problems of the nursing service.
13. I feel I have sufficient input into the program of care for each of my patients.
14. Considering what is expected of nursing service personnel at this hospital, the pay we get is reasonable.
15. There is no doubt whatever in my mind that what I do on my job is really important.
16. There is a good deal of teamwork and cooperation between various levels of nursing personnel on my service.
17. I have too much responsibility and not enough authority.
18. There are not enough opportunities for advancement of nursing personnel at this hospital.
19. There is a lot of teamwork between nurses and doctors on my own unit.
20. On my service, my supervisors make all the decisions. I have little direct control over my own work.
21. The present rate of increase in pay for nursing service personnel at this hospital is not satisfactory.
22. I am satisfied with the types of activities that I do on my job.
23. The nursing personnel on my service are not as friendly and outgoing as I would like.

24. I have plenty of time and opportunity to discuss patient care problems with other nursing service personnel.
25. There is ample opportunity for nursing staff to participate in the administrative decision-making process.
26. A great deal of independence is permitted, if not required, of me.
27. What I do on my job does not add up to anything really significant.
28. There is a lot of "rank consciousness" on my unit. Nursing personnel seldom mingle with others of lower ranks.
29. I have sufficient time for direct patient care.
30. I am sometimes frustrated because all of my activities seem programmed for me.
31. I am sometimes required to do things on my job that are against my better professional nursing judgment.
32. From what I hear from and about nursing service personnel at other hospitals, we at this hospital are being fairly paid.
33. Administrative decisions at this hospital interfere too much with patient care.
34. It makes me proud to talk to other people about what I do on my job.
35. I wish the physicians here would show more respect for the skill and knowledge of the nursing staff.
36. I could deliver much better care if I had more time with each patient.
37. Physicians at this hospital generally understand and appreciate what the nursing staff does.
38. If I had the decision to make all over again, I would still go into nursing.
39. The physicians at this hospital look down too much on the nursing staff.
40. I have all the voice in planning policies and procedures for this hospital and my unit that I want.
41. My particular job really doesn't require much skill or "know how."
42. The nursing administrators generally consult with the staff on daily problems and procedures.
43. I have the freedom in my work to make important decisions as I see fit, and can count on my supervisors to back me up.
44. An upgrading of pay schedules for nursing personnel is needed at this hospital.

Response made is on a 1–7 scale, from Strongly Disagree to Strongly Agree.

Source: Reprinted from *Nurses and Work Satisfaction: An Index for Measurement* by Paula L. Stamps and Eugene B. Piedmonte, with permission of Health Administration Press, a division of the Foundation of the American College of Healthcare Executives, © 1986.

Table 8-1 gave the complete scores, along with the ranges for all the quantitative scores that result from an administration of the Stamps-Piedmonte Index of Work Satisfaction. Table 8-2 shows a comparison of two community hospitals. The ranges for each of the numbers, although not shown on this table, are the same as for Table 8-1.

As can be seen, the rankings and the values for Part A are very similar for these two hospitals. This reinforces the conclusion that for nurses in community hospital settings, it is not necessary to administer the first part of the questionnaire every time. The rankings and the values are constant enough that the component weighting coefficient may be used from the weights that have been recently reported. Table 8-1 also showed the rankings of components on current level of satisfaction (Part B), including the component score, the mean component score, and the adjusted component score, which is the mean component score weighted by the component weighting coefficient.[12]

Interpretation of these data is best done on a relative basis because satisfaction is itself a relative phenomenon. The scale is best interpreted by quartiles, and for each of the numeric scores given in Table 8-1, quartiles have been calculated.

Using this approach, it is easy to take any score falling below the 50th percentile as being an indicator of dissatisfaction. Using this criterion, all scores reported in Table 8-1 are low. In fact, the only two components with scores above the 50th percentile are Interaction and Professional Status. Hospital 2 is relatively more dissatisfied than Hospital 1, with three components (Organizational Policies, Task Requirements, and Pay) just at or slightly below the first quartile. This means that the scores on these three components fall under or at 25 percent of the total possible score.

As expected, the final summary figure—the Index of Work Satisfaction—is also quite low for both hospitals. The values for the IWS range from 0.5 to 39.7, with the quartiles being 10.5–20.0–29.7–39.7. The values of 12.5 and 12.0 for these two hospitals place this just above the first quartile but not at all close to the 50th-percentile criterion.

These numeric scores are probably most useful in comparing results of two or more hospitals and are meant to be used in the development of norms that may be used to compare many hospitals. However, the primary purpose of this scale must be remembered: it is to be used to develop a program within an institution that improves the morale of the nursing staff. In

Table 8-1 Numerical Values for the Scale, Ranges, and Quartiles

Component	Component Weighting Coefficient (from Part A)	Component Scale Scores (from Part B), Range, and Quartiles	Component Mean Score (from Part B)	Adjusted Scores
Autonomy	3.61	35.2 Range: 8–56 20–32–44–56	4.4	15.8
Pay	3.5	16.2 Range: 6–42 15–24–33–42	2.7	9.4
Professional Status	3.3	37.8 Range: 7–49 17–28–38–49	5.4	17.8
Interaction	3.0	46.0 Range: 10–70 25–40–55–70	4.6	13.8
a. Nurse-Nurse	3.4	26.5 Range: 5–35 13–20–27–35	5.3	18.0
b. Physician-Nurse	2.8	19.8 Range: 5–35 13–20–27–35	3.9	10.9
Task Requirements	2.8	16.8 Range: 6–42 15–24–33–42	2.8	7.8
Organizational Policies	2.4	19.6 Range: 7–49 17–28–38–49	2.8	6.7

Range: 0.9 to 5.3	IWS: 12	Range: 1–7	Range: 0.9–37.1
Quartiles: 2.0–3.1–4.2–5.3	Range: 0.5 to 39.7	Quartiles: 2.5–4.0–5.5–7.0	Quartiles: 9.9–19.0–28.1–37.1
	Percentiles: 10.3–20.0–29.7–39.7		

Table 8-2 Summary of Numerical Values for Index of Work Satisfaction in Two Community Hospitals

Rankings of Components: Part A		
Components	Component Weighting Coefficient	
	Hospital 1	Hospital 2
Autonomy	3.56	3.61
Pay	3.36	3.46
Professional Status	3.27	3.26
Interaction	2.93	3.00
Task Requirements	2.91	2.82
Organizational Policies	2.55	2.43

Rankings of Components: Part B			
Components	Component Score	Mean Component Score	Adjusted Component Score
Hospital 1:			
Professional Status	38.36	5.4	17.28
Autonomy	37.84	4.7	16.92
Interaction	48.66	4.8	13.92
Pay	21.09	3.5	11.55
Task Requirements	17.88	3.0	8.7
Organizational Policies	18.34	2.6	6.5
IWS			12.5
Hospital 2:			
Professional Status	38.36	5.4	17.69
Autonony	35.23	4.4	16.09
Interaction	46.00	4.6	13.98
Pay	16.25	2.7	9.45
Task Requirements	16.87	2.8	8.1
Organizational Policies	18.2	2.8	6.9
IWS			12.0

Sources: "An Analysis of the Stamps-Piedmonte Index of Work Satisfaction as a Tool for Measuring Job Satisfaction of Nursing Personnel" by Mary Kit, unpublished thesis, University of Massachusetts, 1985; and "The Relationship of Absenteeism and Occupational Satisfaction" by P. Di Tomasso, unpublished thesis, University of Massachusetts, 1987.

order to accomplish this, it is important not only to examine these numeric scores but also to analyze the frequency distribution of responses to the individual items, as shown in Table 8-3. The combination of the numeric results and the pattern of responses to the individual items should be used to direct organizational efforts at resolving some of the problems perceived by the nursing staff.

It is an ironic quirk of our highly technological society that we have a sense of dissatisfaction with our limited ability to do more with these numbers. It is very important to remember that until now, we could not say (with authority) anything specific about why nurses seemed so dissatisfied. With a few more administrations of this scale, we will be able to report to a hospital or nursing director the fact that, for example, 75 percent of the nurses in a similar hospital are more satisfied than the nurses in theirs. As a first step in achieving comparative

analyses, relating the scores to quartiles is the most appropriate mechanism.

It is also important to remember what is gained by standardization. For the immediate future, until we know the range of numerical scores, investigators and administrators who use this scale should try to use it as it has been designed, without major modifications. This is clearly a loss of flexibility for some specific studies, but it is important to try to gain an understanding of the normative values. In the long run, the nursing profession will be better off with a solid understanding of the normative values. As more research is conducted, revisions to this instrument will make it a stronger and more sensitive measurement.

USING THE STAMPS–PIEDMONTE INDEX OF WORK SATISFACTION

This research project started out as an effort to develop a valid measurement instrument. It is, of course, necessary to be able to trust a particular measurement instrument, and because of this, we have spent a lot of time developing the necessary statistical basis for this attitude scale. This has been the first objective.

The second objective has been to make the measurement instrument simple enough to be used by busy hospital and nurse administrators who may not have any specific training in either survey research or data analysis. This has also now been accomplished with the publication of a book that gives all necessary information for scoring and for completing a study of nurses. As has been noted here, continued work on this area will improve our measurement ability.

Now, we are obligated to answer the "So what do we do now?" question: the third objective of our research concerns the ability of an organization to use this now-validated IWS as a part of a management information system. When used in this way, the IWS provides valuable insights into nurses' occupational satisfaction in such a way as to facilitate structural changes where they work. No other attitude scale has been developed to accomplish all three of these objectives.

This section will concentrate on defining a management information system and identifying the ways in which personnel and satisfaction measures can be included. This is a technical aspect of our work. The second concern of this section is largely philosophical—and more controversial. It relates to our willingness and our ability to change organizations as a result of what we learn from the information contained in our managment information systems. Before we can address these two topics, a brief discussion of planning and motivation is in order.

Planning and Motivation

It is very important to prepare adequately for the administration of this scale. It should not be given simply to "do

Table 8-3 Item Analysis of Responses in Two Community Hospitals

	Agree		No Opinion		Disagree	
	Hosp. 1	Hosp. 2	Hosp. 1	Hosp. 2	Hosp. 1	Hosp. 2
Pay						
1. My present salary is satisfactory.	57.7	38.6	1.2	1.2	41.1	60.2
2. Excluding myself, it is my impression that a lot of nursing personnel at this hospital are dissatisfied with their pay.	62.5	81.4	10.1	4.5	27.4	14.1
3. Considering what is expected of nursing service personnel at this hospital, the pay we get is reasonable.	36.9	19.7	2.4	2.9	60.7	77.4
4. The present rate of increase in pay for nursing service personnel at this hospital is satisfactory.	62.3	79.8	4.2	3.7	33.5	16.5
5. From what I hear from and about nursing service personnel at other hospitals, we at this hospital are being fairly paid.	67.3	48.2	13.1	9.5	19.6	42.3
6. An upgrading of pay schedules for nursing personnel is needed at this hospital.	82.6	89.4	6.6	4.5	10.8	6.1
Autonomy						
1. I feel that I am supervised more closely than is necessary.	11.4	19.2	1.8	7.0	86.8	73.8
2. I feel I have sufficient input into the program of care for each of my patients.	75.5	72.0	6.0	6.7	18.6	21.3
3. I have too much responsibility and not enough authority.	44.7	46.3	9.5	9.8	45.8	43.9
4. On my service, my supervisors make all the decisions. I have little direct control over my own work.	22.1	26.7	3.0	3.7	74.9	69.6
5. A great deal of independence is permitted, if not required, of me.	75.2	56.7	4.2	6.9	20.6	36.4
6. I am sometimes frustrated because all of my activities seem programmed for me.	45.2	52.2	11.4	9.4	43.4	38.4
7. I am sometimes required to do things on my job that are against my better professional nursing judgment.	49.4	47.1	6.0	5.0	44.6	47.9
8. I have the freedom in my work to make important decisions as I see fit, and can count on my supervisors to back me up.	53.6	38.8	4.9	6.2	41.5	55.0
Task Requirements						
1. There is too much clerical and "paperwork" required of nursing personnel in this hospital.	91	87.8	1.2	2.9	7.8	9.3
2. I think I could do a better job if I did not have so much to do all the time.	70.7	72.3	4.2	6.2	25.1	21.5
3. I am satisfied with the types of activities that I do on my job.	75.5	71.1	1.2	2.9	23.4	26.0
4. I have plenty of time and opportunity to discuss patient care problems with other nursing service personnel.	32.3	34.5	3.6	3.7	64.1	61.8
5. I have sufficient time for direct patient care.	70.3	76.8	9.7	8.3	20.0	14.9
6. I could deliver much better care if I had more time with each patient.	87.4	89.1	3.0	5.0	9.6	5.9
Job Status/Prestige						
1. Most people do not sufficiently appreciate the importance of nursing care to hospital patients.	90.5	89.1	2.4	1.6	7.1	9.3
2. Nursing is a long way from being recognized as a profession.	55.3	63.3	1.8	2.5	42.9	34.2
3. There is no doubt whatever in my mind that what I do on my job is really important.	95.8	92.2	1.2	1.6	3.0	6.2

Table 8-3 continued

	Agree		No Opinion		Disagree	
	Hosp. 1	Hosp. 2	Hosp. 1	Hosp. 2	Hosp. 1	Hosp. 2
4. What I do on my job does not add up to anything really significant.	7.2	8.3	1.2	2.0	91.6	89.7
5. It makes me proud to talk to other people about what I do on my job.	68.9	71.2	4.3	7.0	26.8	21.8
6. If I had the decision to make all over again, I would still go into nursing.	54.6	59.1	9.0	10.8	36.4	30.1
7. My particular job really doesn't require much skill or "know how."	4.8	5.3	0.6	0.8	94.6	93.9

Interaction

	Agree		No Opinion		Disagree	
1. The nursing personnel on my service do not hesitate to pitch in and help one another out when things get in a rush.	84.3	88.1	3.0	0.8	12.7	11.1
2. Physicians in general cooperate with the nursing staff on my unit.	23.4	34.3	9.5	5.7	67.1	60.0
3. New employees are not quickly made to "feel at home" on my unit.	33.7	42.5	4.3	2.5	62.0	55.0
4. There is a good deal of teamwork and cooperation between various levels of nursing personnel on my service.	82	75.3	1.2	4.5	16.8	20.2
5. There is a lot of teamwork between nurses and doctors on my own unit.	67.6	56.1	8.4	7.4	24.0	36.5
6. The nursing personnel on my service are not as friendly and outgoing as I would like.	23.4	23.7	2.3	2.5	74.3	73.8
7. There is a lot of "rank consciousness" on my unit. Nursing personnel seldom mingle with others of lower ranks.	13.2	15.1	3.0	3.7	83.8	81.2
8. I wish the physicians here would show more respect for the skill and knowledge of the nursing staff.	76.6	77.2	3.6	5.7	19.8	17.1
9. Physicians at this hospital generally understand and appreciate what the nursing staff does.	61.7	57.3	3.6	4.5	34.7	38.2
10. The physicians at this hospital look down too much on the nursing staff.	38.1	52.8	8.9	8.7	53.0	38.5

Organizational Policies

	Agree		No Opinion		Disagree	
1. The nursing staff has sufficient control over scheduling their own work shifts.	65.5	80.0	8.9	4.1	25.6	15.9
2. There is a great gap between the administration of this hospital and the daily problems of the nursing service.	87.5	91.7	2.4	0.8	10.1	7.5
3. There are not enough opportunities for advancement of nursing personnel at this hospital.	76.8	75.4	5.4	7.4	17.9	17.2
4. There is ample opportunity for nursing staff to participate in the administrative decision-making processes.	9.6	10.6	4.2	3.3	86.2	86.1
5. Administrative decisions at this hospital interfere too much with patient care.	60.7	66.9	12.5	7.9	26.8	25.2
6. I have all the voice in planning policies and procedures for this hospital and my unit that I want.	23.8	30.0	4.8	4.2	71.4	65.8
7. The nursing administrators generally consult with the staff on daily problems and procedures.	19.2	16.8	6.6	3.7	74.2	79.5

Sources: "An Analysis of the Stamps-Piedmonte Index of Work Satisfaction as a Tool for Measuring Job Satisfaction of Nursing Personnel" by Mary Kit, unpublished thesis, University of Massachusetts, 1985; and "The Relationship of Absenteeism and Occupational Satisfaction" by P. Di Tomasso, unpublished thesis, University of Massachusetts, 1987.

something about nurses.'' All levels of the organization should be involved in the preparatory steps. Lines of communication should be opened between the administration and nursing staff, especially with respect to later implementation strategies. An atmosphere of trust is very important in the questionnaire's administration. This depends on the nurse respondents' believing that the administration really wants to make necessary changes to help them.

Of paramount importance in this preparation process is the honest estimation of motivation for using this instrument. This is important for two reasons: to reduce the potential for manipulation and to increase participation of all the staff. Both of these will be specifically discussed later.

This measurement tool is only a technique; it cannot substitute for effective management. This technique does allow a sharing of perceptions from two important viewpoints: that of the nursing staff and that of the administrators. And it can be used to assist both groups in understanding their particular needs and constraints. This measurement tool will be most productive in those organizations that have as their primary motivation the desire to increase communication between nurses and the administration but lack the technical ability to do so.

The most important aspect of ensuring successful administration of this scale is an appropriate planning phase. The first step requires a clear delineation of motivation of all levels within the organization. To ensure maximum success and to make sure that motivation has been carefully thought about, all levels of personnnel within the administrative hierarchy should be involved. For example, if nurses in a hospital are to be surveyed, not only should hospital administrators be involved, but also nurse administrators, staff nurses, and nurse leadership in the union (if any) should be included. Ideally, the use of this scale should arise from a concern to translate often ubiquitous staff dissatisfaction into discrete areas that are amenable to correction. The more that all levels are involved in the planning phase, the more successful the venture will be. Additionally, other areas of concern may be included.

A specific part of the planning phase is an explicit discussion of the objectives the organization wants to achieve by measuring level of nurse satisfaction. These objectives should be written down and discussed by all members of the nursing hierarchy. Additionally, each level should develop its own objectives and compare them. For example, the nursing staff may have objectives separate from the nursing administrators. Communication can be improved only when these objectives are shared and the scope of responsibility identified.

It is difficult to separate implementation issues from planning issues. The single most important thought about implementation is this: *the IWS is designed to be translated into some type of organizational action based on the understanding gained from the questionnnaire.* Work satisfaction is a relative phenomenon and may be very specific to the work situation. Although the first part of this chapter provided a mechanism for comparison with other groups, the main reason for implementation is to create change *within* a specific organization.

The ability to build direct management strategies on this scale is partly related to three more technical issues: adequate response rate, grouped data and, interpretation of the data. The most important of these is an adequate response rate.

It is absolutely imperative to try to maximize the reponse rate. A larger and more representative sample will obviously allow for more valid statistical analysis and, therefore, make it possible to interpret subtle differences more accurately. A more practical concern is related to the issues discussed previously, however. Since the information is to be used to make decisions, it is imperative that everybody be represented.

There are several effective methods for distributing the questionnaire: with paychecks to individuals or in groups; in person; or by mail to homes. Retrieving the completed questionnaires is more complex and is related to another issue of critical importance. The use of this data collection instrument triggers an increase in information flow and communication throughout the organization. Respondents must be assured that their responses will remain absolutely confidential. If this assurance cannot be made credibly, the respondents may either fail to answer the questionnaire or give only those answers that they feel are acceptable. Either will bias the data.

The seriousness with which the respondents answer the questionnaire is influenced by their estimation of the management's respect for their candid opinions. Therefore, it is important that no one who has direct supervisory or administrative authority over the group being surveyed actually handle the questionnaires or be involved in the data analysis. Those surveyed can mail their questionnaires back in an envelope that is provided. A data collection box that is locked and placed in a nonthreatening location is an alternative strategy. The best strategy is to have the questionnaires personally picked up by someone outside the hospital administration.

An additional method for assuring a high response rate is to deal sensitively with the issue of confidentiality. It should be emphasized that no respondent will be identifiable. Most managers will want some demographic or organizational characteristics included, such as units, floors, work assignments, or shift assignments. As long as individual nurses cannot be recognized, these may add important information. However, any necessary compromise must be in the direction of increasing confidentiality rather than increasing data. All possible cross-tabulations of research and demographic variables should be arrayed in ''dummy tables'' with no fewer than seven persons in the most narrowly defined category (for example, full-time medical/surgical RNs on the fifth floor). In addition, no person who has supervisory authority should handle the raw questionnaires. It is also neither wise nor necessary to have identifying personal characteristics on the questionnaire.

A final caution is this: the Stamps-Piedmonte Index of Work Satisfaction gives management information about various areas of dissatisfaction. This information may enable management to manipulate the working environment solely to its own benefit. This could be done by discovering the relative importance and level of satisfaction of components of work and then by linking incentives to some of these while ignoring others. For example, if pay is a source of dissatisfaction, but it is not valued highly, it may be easier to change scheduled work shifts than to deal with possible inequities in salary. It is this potential for manipulation that makes the honest estimation of motivation for using this scale so important. This manipulative use should be avoided because in the long run it does not contribute to anything but further alienation of providers and administrators. When the scale is properly used, it can open channels of communication between various levels of health professionals and managers. It can also make possible specific changes in the organization by balancing administrative constraints with expectations and satisfactions of the health care providers.

Communication and Information

Communication and information are critical to any organization. Management is impossible without communication, which is at its simplest the process of exchanging information between all organization members and the decision centers. Information is potential knowledge; it must be shared if it is to provide a motivation for action. The collection of information for its own sake does not accomplish any purpose. Both researchers and managers spend far too much time gathering and processing information and far too little time on the more critical role of sharing that information—which is the process of communication.

Even the most casual reading of the literature on nursing satisfaction reveals the prominent role played by dissatisfaction with communication. Firsthand observation and personal discussion with nurses quickly confirm this impression. And, of course, communication is related to power. The struggle for organizational power and professional power magnifies the problem of poor communication.

Every organization faces the problem of maintaining adequate communication; it is, of course, far worse in the hierarchical organizations in which many nurses work. Most organizations tend to deal with this by developing some sort of management information system, although they may not always use this term.

The need for information and its storage, retrieval, and use in decision making is not new. What is new, however, is the information explosion that has forced both the amount and the variety of information to grow at an exponential rate. Most administrators now feel they must "manage information" lest they be buried by an avalanche of data, much of it superfluous and redundant. This usually leads to an increasingly technical view of information and an increasingly formal management information system. This has caused much anxiety among those who feel they do not understand or cannot participate in a technological, empirical managment information system.

This recent trend is unfortunate because it clouds the real issue. Information is intended to facilitate effective decision making. In order to accomplish this, it is necessary to disseminate information to appropriate members of the organization. Because we want such information to be of high quality and useful, we have focused first on the technical nature of collecting and processing it. However, of even greater importance is its dissemination, basically a philosophical problem which is dealt with in the last section of this chapter.

Management information systems are increasingly common in the health field. It is ironic that in such a labor-intensive field, personnel supervision is often omitted from an organized management information system. Financial systems of the organization obviously require data collection in a systematic and organized fashion; these data are most commonly part of a management information system. Increasingly, interest is also developing in the clinical area, as more experiments in standardizing medical records require methods of collecting, extracting, and communicating information.

The need for organized and systematic information is no less great in personnel supervision. Data are collected in this area; however, the collection is usually sporadic and almost never includes direct measures of occupational satisfaction. The two most common measures are estimates of turnover, exit interviews completed at job termination, or some sort of performance evaluation of continuing employees. It is possible to meet the technical requirements of a management information system even if just using turnover rates, exit interviews, or even performance evaluations. More importantly, however, the development of the IWS now also allows the systematic collection of direct information about the level of satisfaction. All three of these sources of information should be used within the context of a management information system.

Generic solutions to nurse dissatisfaction do not exist. Individual approaches must be used, and in order to do that, the work environment itself must be considered as part of the problem. This requires a certain philosophical approach to job satisfaction that includes the ideas inherent in job redesign. This is the philosophical level of management.

From Work Satisfaction to Job Redesign

It is not the purpose of this chapter to go into great detail on job redesign: other chapters in this volume do that. However, as we have discussed our scale with nurses, administrators, and other health care professionals, we have become increasingly aware of the "so what" phenomenon. What *use* is to be made of this new ability to measure work satisfaction? Reflecting on the answer to this question had led us into the field of work alienation, which is a concept new to the health field.

The term *worker alienation* is a strong one. Its use sometimes cuts off discussion of improving work satisfaction, a much easier concept with which to deal. However, the framework for work alienation is more comprehensive than the framework for work satisfaction because it incorporates organizational concerns, not just individual ones. In the European literature this is often called "industrial democracy." In Japan it is a system of informational discussions and consultations with management, with management retaining the power to make final decisions, but with these decisions being based on common interests among the individual workers and management. In the United States it is "quality of work life." The objective of "quality of work life" is to improve individual work satisfaction as a basis for building more effective management, so that management spends less time on day-to-day problem solving and more time on long-range policy formulation and planning.

Traditional approaches to understanding occupational dissatisfaction have not been effective, mainly because of the common focus on the worker as an individual employee. Through experience, most employees express a dislike for the organizational structure itself, but most people have also learned that this structure is considered to be an unchangeable variable. Therefore, it is far more likely that we express dissatisfaction with supervisory style, peer relations, pay, or other components we have identified as being related to job satisfaction.

Moving from work satisfaction measures to job redesign is both complex and simple. It is complex in that it involves a whole set of assumptions about work, alienation, and organizations. At the same time it is simple because it provides a way out of the frustration of measuring work satisfaction without being able to decrease turnover or have any impact on satisfaction itself. There is no shortage of work satisfaction studies, but the great majority do not go beyond the measurement of individual employee attitudes, so it is difficult to show any impact on satisfaction, productivity, turnover, or other variables.

This is resolved by going beyond individual measures of satisfaction to a consideration of the role an organization plays or, better yet, to an explicit enrichment strategy. For example, the initiation of a program to reduce turnover in a hospital should not begin with the individual nurses, but with factors related to the organization. In fact, both the initial recruiting interview and the orientation strategy should be viewed as serious organization efforts to retain nursing staff. One objective of the personnel supervision system itself should be the retention of this critical labor force. Although evidence of such problems as nurse turnover is revealed in individual behavior, solutions for this problem require looking first at the organization and its management. Based on exit interviews, information from the Stamps-Piedmonte IWS, and anecdotal evidence, a list of problems, grievances, or annoyances can be drawn up. For each one on the list, the administrator should ascertain whether he/she has direct control. If such administrative control is lacking, the manager most likely to influence the situation should be identified. The cost and benefit of each possible change then should be noted, with as much discussion with relevant nurses as possible. Results of this process, along with suggested administrative and/or organizational changes, can then be shared with the entire staff.

Obviously, this goes far beyond the traditional solution: to "put a nurse on a committee." It ultimately involves sharing decision-making power. However, it also involves sharing constraints that are equally real. Not all situations can be influenced even by the top administrator of an organization. Other changes that can be influenced by the administrator may have too high a price when all the needs of the organization are considered. Staff nurses all too often are concerned with only their own issues and problems while top hospital administrators often have little sensitivity to nurses' concerns. An organization that has an open and honest information exchange allows both of these groups to better understand the perspective of the other.

Any progressive organization is in a constant state of change, and new programs frequently mean individuals must adapt, often resulting in feelings of alienation, frustration, and dissatisfaction. In the health field, this usually involves the changing roles of nurses and auxiliary health personnel. It is important for a manager or administrator to be aware of and sensitive to these feelings. The development of this work satisfaction instrument allows for the practical assessment of this attitude before and after the implementation of a new program or rearrangement of responsibilities.

The philosophical notion behind this work satisfaction instrument is to compare actual work satisfaction with an "ideal" work situation. This information, built into the management information system, should allow administrators to make necessary changes to improve work satisfaction and, in turn, nursing effectiveness. The mechanism for this is a management information system in which input from the employees can be systemically collected, evaluated, and acted on.

It is important to note that a survey of work satisfaction cannot be viewed as a one-time only study; rather, the study itself should act to start the whole communication process. Addtionally, use of this tool does not in and of itself open communication. This requires the adequate follow-up of specific efforts at job redesign.

The decade that has gone into the development of the Stamps-Piedmonte Index of Work Satisfaction was necessary in order to develop a statistically valid and reliable measurement instrument that is practical to use. Although continuing research in this area will be helpful in order to make the instrument stronger and more sensitive, it is very important to now begin to deal specifically with the possibilities for using the results of a survey to change the working environment of nurses. Only by concentrating on these job redesign strategies can we begin to create health care organizations that enable health professionals to function more productively and in a manner that enhances personal and professional development.

NOTES

1. P.R. Torrens and C.E. Lewis, "Health Care Personnel," in S.J. Williams and P.R. Torrens, eds., *Introduction to Health Services*, 2d ed. (New York: John Wiley & Sons, Inc., 1982): 96.

2. G.C. Hallas, "Why Nurses Are Giving It Up," *RN* 43 (July 1980): 17–21.

3. M.A. Godfrey, "Job Satisfaction or Should That Be Dissatisfaction: How Nurses Feel About Nursing," Parts I–III, *Nursing 78* 8, no. 4: 89–104; 8, no. 5: 105–20; 8, no. 6: 81–95.

4. L.H. Aiken, "Nursing Priorities for the 1980's: Hospitals and Nursing Homes," *American Journal of Nursing* 81 (February 1981): 324–30. L.H. Aiken and R.J. Blendon, "The National Nurse Shortage," *National Journal* (May 1981): 948–53. L.H. Aiken, R.J. Blendon, and D.E. Rogers, "The Shortage of Hospital Nurses: A New Perspective," *American Journal of Nursing* 81, no. 9 (1981): 1612–18.

5. R. Corwin, "The Professional Employee: A Study of Conflict in Nursing Roles," in J. Skipper and R. Leonard, eds., *Social Interaction and Patient Care* (Philadelphia: J.B. Lippincott Co., 1965), 341–56.

6. P.L. Stamps and E.B. Piedmonte, *Nurses and Work Satisfaction: An Index for Measurement* (Ann Arbor, Mich.: Health Administration Press, 1986).

7. J.S. Adams, "Toward an Understanding of Inequity," in E.E. Lawler, *Motivation in Work Organizations* (Los Angeles: Brooks/Cole, 1973). A. Korman, *Industrial and Organizational Psychology* (Englewood Cliffs, N.J.: Prentice-Hall, Inc., 1971). L. Porter, E. Lawler, and J.P. Hackman, *Behavior in Organizations* (New York: McGraw-Hill Book Co., 1975).

8. A.L. Edwards, *Techniques of Attitude Scale Construction* (New York: Appleton-Century-Crofts, 1957): 19–51.

9. P.L. Stamps et al., "Measurement of Work Satisfaction among Health Professionals," *Medical Care* 16 (April 1978): 337–52. D.B. Slavitt et al., "Nurses' Satisfaction with Their Work Situation." *Nursing Research* 27 (March/April 1978): 114–20. P.L. Stamps, "Satisfaction of Direct Care Providers," in *Evaluation of Outpatient Facilities*, vol. 3 of *Ambulatory Care Systems* (Lexington, Mass.: D.C. Heath, 1978), 75–106. D.B. Slavitt, "Measuring Nurses' Job Satisfaction." *Hospital and Health Services Administration* 24, no. 3 (Summer 1979): 62–77. P.L. Stamps and B. Shopnik, "Emergency Medical Technicians' Perception of Acceptance by Nurses and Physicians," *Journal of Ambulatory Care Management* 4 (November 1981): 69–86.

10. Stamps and Piedmonte, *Nurses and Work Satisfaction*.

11. Ibid., pp. 55–64.

12. Ibid., p. 57.

Edward J. Speedling

Motivation

9

INTRODUCTION

People make choices in all spheres of their lives, including work. Motivational theorists attempt to understand the social and psychological dimensions of people's choices, those who employ strategies of motivation use this knowledge to influence choices made in the work place. In the course of this century we have witnessed a tremendous shift in theories and practices of motivation, which reflects a continuing evolution in our understanding of human behavior and in the meaning of work in people's lives.

In his recent book, *Productive Workplaces,*[1] Weisbord charts the history of ideas and strategies employed over the past century to influence the way in which people approach and carry out their work roles. The beginning and end of the twentieth century are like opposing points on a spectrum. The revolution in management thinking sparked by the ideas of Frederick Taylor introduced unprecedented rational order and control to work places that were all too often managed in an arbitrary and haphazard fashion. The time and motion studies of expert management engineers provided workers with precise guidelines that they were expected to follow faithfully. By design, worker choice was minimized, and control, while based on objective rather than subjective criteria, remained external to the worker.

We can, of course, find vestiges of this thinking alive and well today. But over the course of this century, such people as Lewin, Maslow, Herzberg, and McGregor have demonstrated that "we are likely to modify our own behavior when we participate in problem analysis and solution and likely to carry

out decisions we have helped make."[2] Today, we are thinking of how to expand the arena for participation of workers in designing incentives, systems, and rewards in the work place. In some organizations, workers have become stakeholders, supervisors are coaches, and people are part of high-performing teams. To improve efficiency and productivity, we are expanding the choices available to workers and relying more and more on self-control rather than external control.

It is important to note that while pragmatic considerations, such as competitiveness and productivity, are very much behind the new thinking about motivation, so are societal values. Optimizing choice is very consistent with democratic ideals. A society that places high value on achievement is fertile ground for sharing the benefits of mutual risk and participation. And is it surprising that in our culture, which has been so hospitable to the development of humanistic psychology and psychotherapy, people are demanding that they be treated with dignity and given a chance to grow—intellectually and emotionally—on the job?

In this chapter we will examine motivation in health care settings. What principles can guide us toward human resources policies that are effective in achieving the stated purposes of our institutions and that at the same time are consistent with our historic values?

THE ALTRUISTIC OPTION

Many theories of motivation are based on principles of self-interest. It is presumed that workers will choose to behave in accordance with corporate goals and objectives when they perceive a connection between their efforts and the desired outcomes, such as financial reward, recognition, self-expression, etc. We can see this principle being applied in health care today. Faced with unprecedented competitive pressures, hospitals are appealing to their staffs to improve the quality of patient care services, reduce costs, and increase efficiency for the sake of what is called "the competitive edge" for their institutions. Some hospitals are installing various kinds of gainsharing plans, which motivate employees by offering financial incentives for productivity gains.

Rather than arguing the merits of competition and utilitarianism, I would like to offer alternative approaches to bring out the best efforts of the people who staff our health care facilities. These are not based on self-interest; rather, they derive from people's desire for connectedness with others and with institutions that gives purpose and meaning to our lives.

Titmus tells us that humans have a social and biological need to help.[3] Indeed, around the world and through the ages, societies have symbolized this deep feeling of connectedness, this need for social order, through ritualized gift giving. And while contemporary society seems to have deritualized helping behavior, the instinct to give of oneself to strangers without expectation of reward is evident in the behavior of millions of people today. It is estimated, for example, that in 1988 some 20 million people volunteered five or more hours a week to various causes and that 80 million people volunteered a total of 14.9 billion hours. It is further estimated that 75 percent of all families in America each give almost $1000 a year to charity.[4] Sharing what we have to give—be it time, money, or services—is habitual rather than unusual. If the norm in our private lives is to be altruistic, why need it be otherwise in our public lives?

The fact is, of course, that people who work in health care transcend the boundaries of their job descriptions to respond to patients' personal human needs all the time. These acts are done quietly and are often unrecognized except by those involved in the caring encounter. Sometimes exemplary individuals are recognized formally through an institution's award program. However, ordinary people—most of us—are simply not encouraged enough to bring this "no strings attached" dimension to our efforts.

Yet we know that people are attracted to work in the health care field out of a desire to be of service to their fellow men and women. This is true for professionals and nonprofessionals. Wessen found in a study that for hospital employees in low-status positions, "such intangible advantages as security and the satisfaction of 'helping people' mean more to them than the increased salaries they could earn on the outside."[5]

We have learned through studies that altruism is irrepressible, that it breaks through even the most insidious attempts to suppress it. We also know that altruistic behavior can be encouraged through social policy. Titmus' classic study of blood donation in different societies demonstrated this. He concluded

> The way in which society organizes and structures its social institutions . . . can encourage or discourage the Altruistic in man; such systems can foster integration or alienation; they can allow the "theme of gift—of generosity toward strangers—to spread among and between social groups and generations."[6]

Even in the Oliners' study, *The Altruistic Personality,*[7] which argues that the roots of altruistic behavior are laid down in the family during the formative years, most subjects performed helping acts after *being asked* to do so. It is important to note that once asked, these subjects who risked their lives to help Jews escape Nazi persecution responded almost immediately.

I suggest there are several barriers standing in the way of motivating our staff members through appeals to their most generous instincts. One is a fear that management will lose control unless behavior is closely regulated. Because altruistic behavior springs from a generous impulse, is often a spontaneous response to an unpredicted human need, and occurs outside of the view of all but those immediately involved, it is not subject to our normal systems for regulating behavior in institutions. But as Greenly and Schoenherr found in a study of the organizational determinants of humaneness of service in health and human service organizations, more, not less, autonomy given to staff members leads to clients' experiencing greater humaneness with the service.[8] While it is true that people who lack judgment, are poorly informed, or do not communicate well can make matters worse despite the best of intentions, people can be educated to use discretion, seek advice, and interact with sensitivity in the course of bringing compassion and generosity to their work roles. The failure on the part of management to let go and to place trust in employees is counterproductive and, as Greenly and Schoenherr argue, "may be a key factor in explaining why highly structured or bureaucratic human service organizations are often observed to give unsatisfactory service and why their staffs are seen as inflexible, unresponsive and uninterested."[9]

The value placed on individual autonomy and utilitarianism is so high in our country that sometimes it is hard to imagine that people act for the common good. A bias toward viewing the world in individualistic terms hinders our ability to nurture an altruistic response among our staff members. But utilitarianism cannot be the sole language we speak when attributing motivation to human actions. And just as it would be incorrect to suggest that self-interest has no legitimate place in our health care institutions, we impoverish ourselves by excluding from our institutional vocabularies terms like *commitment, service, selflessness, charity,* and *love of fellow man.*

It is apparent that our patients expect us to act toward them with higher motives than self-interest or utilitarianism. Cousins expresses it this way.

> I became convinced that nothing a hospital could provide in the way of technological marvels was as helpful as an atmosphere of compassion. . . . But for most people the

facts of hospital life involve discontinuity, fractioned care, and inadequate protection against surprise. . . . The central question to be asked of hospitals . . . is whether they inspire the patient with confidence that he or she is in the right place; whether they enable him to have trust in those who seek to heal him; in short, whether he has the expectation that good things will happen.[10]

For patients in an acute care hospital, the feeling of being cared about is the most powerful influence on their experience.[11] The vulnerability that is inherent in patienthood can only be relieved by a sensitive human presence.

By encouraging our staff members to respond freely to the human need they encounter in the course of their daily rounds—be it medical, nursing, or housekeeping—we can bring patients what they tell us over and over they want: compassionate, personal attention to their psychosocial as well as biological needs. Our appeal must be to the altruistic inclinations within our staffs. While we can and should establish standards of behavior for all health care workers to govern their relations with patients, we run a serious risk if we attempt to regulate, control, or mandate compassion. If, for example, we made caring and compassionate behavior part of a formal performance appraisal system, or even if we used patient feedback on these matters as a basis for systematic reward and punishment, we would thereby create a situation in which marketplace rules replace altruistic expressions of fellowship. Patients would become objects of gain or deficit and subject to manipulation. The situation would militate against the partnership so vital to the ends of health care. Staff would lose, too, because they would be denied the freedom to give freely and fulfill deep human longings for commitment and interpersonal connectedness.

MOTIVATING THROUGH TEAM MEMBERSHIP

A century of collective wisdom about people and work comes down to this: men and women prefer involvement—not alienation; a chance to make a contribution through active participation—not complacency; collegiality and mutual respect among coworkers and superiors—not confrontation or hierarchy for its own sake; partnership and integration—not mindless battles over status or turf.

The complexity that has accompanied rapid technological advances in health care has resulted in much specialization of functions and differentiation of roles in our institutions. Effective health care requires that we integrate the many different contributions people have to make into a coherent whole. Successfully motivating each and every individual requires that everyone be aware and be recognized for the contribution that he or she makes to the central task before us: patient well-being.

It would help us create a sense of team spirit if we rid ourselves of the archaic thinking represented by terms such as

ancillary and *hotel services*. Although these terms are meant to be descriptive and not evaluative, they have connotations that may be pejorative. Ancillary means subsidiary, of secondary importance. We have seen enough evidence to know that the therapeutic mission of a hospital cannot be fully realized unless curative technique is combined with positive, caring, and sensitive interpersonal relationships. If we create an impression that what large numbers of our staff members do is unconnected to what the hospital is in business for, the effect on morale and performance will be obvious.

The fact is that when we foster teamwork, patient care is enhanced. In a study entitled "An Evaluation of Outcome from Intensive Care in Major Medical Centers,"[12] a search was undertaken to explain differential mortality rates in 13 sophisticated intensive care settings, all of which had similar technical capabilities. The findings are impressive. After searching for associations between mortality and variables related to organization, staffing, commitment to teaching, research, and education, the only significant differences between high- and low-mortality units related to interaction and communication between physicians and nurses. The authors clearly state that "involvement and interaction of critical care personnel can directly influence outcome from critical care."[13] Good communication characterized units with relatively low mortality rates. In one such unit, "excellent communications between physicians and nursing staff was ongoing to insure that all patients' care needs were met. In a high mortality unit, in contrast, frequent disagreement . . . occurred, and there was an atmosphere of distrust."[14]

What we are talking about transcends lip service about being a part of "one big family." Think of the sheer volume of interactions between patients and personnel other than doctors and nurses. Think of the amount of coordination it takes to implement a treatment plan. Think of how rarely we credit support personnel for their contribution to creating a climate that enhances patient well-being. Think of the feeling of self-worth such sincere recognition would bring to support staffers. Instead of employing motivational strategies as means to some end, we need to bring into sharp focus the real value of what our people do all day in our institutions. Instead of importing language from the hotel and hospitality industries, we should be expanding the language of patient care to include each and every member of the health care field.

Team membership promotes feelings of common purpose with the institution because it translates the lofty mission statement into language, and action, that people can understand. Moreover, the daily reinforcement that occurs through face-to-face interaction with teammates who value what they do personalizes and allows us to identify with institutional goals that might otherwise seem arcane. The bonds of affection that grow for team members add a balance to the impersonality that is a real aspect of work today. Warm interpersonal relations among people who value each other's contributions to the common good allow people to be more expressive, more creative, and more satisfied with their work.

TOWARD A HEALTH CARE COMMUNITY

Although we have, in our society, tended to place individualism high on our priority list of values, Americans have a long tradition of involvement in activities that build and maintain community. For many people, participation in institutions that serve the general welfare fulfills a sense of responsibility felt to be part of good citizenship. It allows them to transcend the narrow confines of self-interest and provides a sense of moral purpose to their daily activities.[15]

For some organizations, the mission statement may be seen as an attempt to take the moral high ground by placing corporate goals in a larger social context. A mission statement can be a vehicle for expressing the social purpose of the enterprise and for articulating valued principles on how business is conducted. It is as much a message to those who work in the organization as it is to clients and the public at large. It is one way to create a corporate identity that employees can respect, relate to, and use to give their efforts a meaning that goes beyond the paycheck.

At a time when health care organizations are facing competitive pressures and adopting more businesslike postures than we have seen previously, we must not lose sight of our traditional humanitarian values and community-oriented purposes. We must, as McNernery tells us, "take full advantage of the many efficiencies of good business practices without sacrificing or diminishing the sense of social mission and the dedication to social purpose that have been the distinctive characteristics of health enterprise in the past."[16]

The mission statements of our health care institutions are valid and compelling rallying cries, which can coalesce our diverse work force. What we stand for is universal; what we offer our employees is participation in other-directed activities that provide dignity and significance across the spectrum of work in our institutions.

Those who work in health care are in a unique position. They can satisfy their needs for security and status; they can experience the personal satisfaction that comes from achievement; and they can, if they so desire, aspire to rise to the top of their professional and occupational fields. But they can also identify themselves with a cause and experience a sense of belonging in a community in which committed participation confers dignity.

NOTES

1. M.R. Weisbord, *Productive Workplaces: Organizing and Managing for Dignity, Meaning and Community* (San Francisco: Jossey-Bass Inc., Pubs. 1988).

2. Ibid., 89.

3. R.M. Titmus, *The Gift Relationship: From Human Blood to Social Policy* (New York: Pantheon Books, 1971).

4. B. O'Connell, "Already 1,000 Points of Light," *The New York Times* (January 25, 1989): A23.

5. A.F. Wessen, "Hospital Ideology and Communication between Ward Personnel," in E.G. Jaco, ed., *Patients, Physicians and Illness: A Sourcebook in Behavioral Science and Health,* 2d ed. (New York: Free Press, 1972), 341.

6. Titmus, *The Gift Relationship,* p. 235.

7. S.P. Oliner and P.M. Oliner, *The Altruistic Personality* (New York: Free Press, 1988).

8. J.R. Greenly and R.A. Schoenherr, "Organization Effects on Client Satisfaction with Humaneness of Service," *Journal of Health and Social Behavior* 22 (March 1981): 2–17.

9. Ibid., 15.

10. N. Cousins, *Anatomy of an Illness As Perceived by the Patient: Reflections on Healing and Regeneration* (New York: Bantam Books, 1979), 154.

11. E. Speedling and D. Rose, "Building an Effective Doctor-Patient Relationship: From Patient Satisfaction to Patient Participation," *Social Science and Medicine* 21 (1985): 116.

12. W.A. Znaus, E.A. Draper, D.P. Wagner, and J.E. Zimmerman, "An Evaluation of Outcome from Intensive Care in Major Medical Centers," *Annals of Internal Medicine* 104 (1986): 410–18.

13. Ibid., 416.

14. Ibid., 415–16.

15. R.H. Bellah et al., *Habits of the Heart: Individualism and Commitment in American Life* (Berkeley: University of California Press, 1985).

16. J. McNernery, "The Evolution in Health Services Management," in *Handbook of Health, Health Care, and the Health Professions* (New York: The Free Press, 1983), p. 530.

James B. Williams
Kevin Renner

Human Resources' Role in Managing Staff Costs and Productivity in Health Care Organizations

10

BACKGROUND

The intense pressures on cost control in the health care industry are well documented. Not so well documented is the surge in U.S. hospital overhead costs in the past decade. In the last four years alone, hospital overhead (defined as total non-revenue-producing expense) has risen from 37 percent to more than 40 percent of operating costs—representing an increase of over 12 percent per year.[1]

How and why has this happened? How can hospital and health system managers reverse this trend? What specifically can human resources managers do? Before addressing directly those questions, a brief discussion of overhead will add perspective to the problem.

Contrary to popular belief, staff overhead (incurred by such functions as human resources staffs, legal services, accounting departments, etc.) is not necessarily the corporate quicksand in which all of American enterprise is sinking. Historically, staff size grew as organizations evolved into the bureaucratic form to take advantage of expertise, specialization, and economies of scale.

Unfortunately, few managers look analytically at overhead staff functions as *an investment*. Yet overhead is exactly that—an investment, which should be managed as such. And like any other investment, its returns should be examined and measured regularly. Perhaps this scarce analysis of overhead investments has contributed to overhead's growth in health care institutions. Also contributing to overhead growth are the

changes in the health industry; health care today is a much more complicated business, operating in a more complicated environment and, therefore, more costly to manage.

As part of our major, ongoing data base of organization effectiveness, Hay Management Consultants has been examining staff costs and productivity in more than 35 health care systems nationwide. Our detailed study is supplemented by data from over 100 other systems, as well as from similar studies of regional hospitals. This study focuses on numerous aspects of organizational effectiveness: strategy, organization structure, staff roles/accountabilities, staff costs, and productivity, as well as management culture, processes, and characteristics.

By examining the top-performing health care organizations from our study, we have identified numerous management practices associated with successful for-profit and not-for-profit health management companies. Among the findings that stand out is that staff costs and allocation do matter: successful companies *manage* their staff costs. Moreover, the high-performing systems spend less on staff (and get higher staff productivity) than their lower-performing peers. The key, of course, is finding the fine balance between too much and too little staff overhead.

Managing staff costs involves three fundamental steps: assessment, decision making, and implementation, each of which is discussed below. Implicit in the discussion is the fact that human resources managers play a central role in each of these three important steps. Whether they assume the leading role or a supportive function, human resources managers should be key players in the diagnosis, decision making, and implementation of staff cost analyses or reallocations.

ASSESSMENT

The thoughtful investor regularly compares a portfolio's performance against others' and also examines the portfolio internally for nonperforming investments. The same should hold true when managing staff.

Managing staff levels begins with making practical analyses and comparisons, such as assessing job tasks and work flows, conducting external comparisons, and more. Important analytical steps are discussed below.

Analyzing Internal Costs and Trends

Health care organizations can benefit greatly from a regular audit of staff levels and costs, as well as of how costs are shifting and how they compare from one function to another. For example, consider the following questions:

- For each function, how do our costs and staffing levels today compare with those of three years ago?
- What is our relative return on investment for each function?

Measuring Staff Output and Value

The above step clearly demands measurement tools and procedures that tell management what it is getting from its staff. There are three complementary methods of measuring staff output and value.

1. quantitative, tangible measurements of output—e.g., units of service, such as benefits claims processed, accounts receivable days
2. qualitative descriptions of service, such as programs and activities
3. management's perceptions of the efficiency, effectiveness, and value of the various staff functions (This can be done through a written survey to assure confidentiality and validity. See Figure 10-1.)

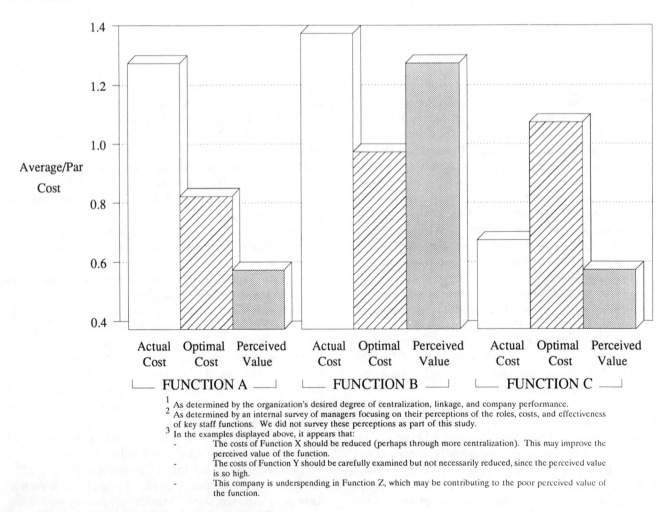

[1] As determined by the organization's desired degree of centralization, linkage, and company performance.
[2] As determined by an internal survey of managers focusing on their perceptions of the roles, costs, and effectiveness of key staff functions. We did not survey these perceptions as part of this study.
[3] In the examples displayed above, it appears that:
-     The costs of Function X should be reduced (perhaps through more centralization). This may improve the perceived value of the function.
-     The costs of Function Y should be carefully examined but not necessarily reduced, since the perceived value is so high.
-     This company is underspending in Function Z, which may be contributing to the poor perceived value of the function.

Figure 10-1 Assess Perceived Value vs. Optimal and Actual Costs

Conducting External Comparisons

Is a $10-million finance and accounting staff too big or too small? It all depends on the standard of comparison. A 160-pound athlete is too big to ride as a jockey and too small to play professional football. Trying to diagnose overhead costs at *all* organizational levels (corporate, regional, and hospital) without some relevant references would similarly offer little information of value. (See Figures 10-2 and 10-3.)

Such comparisons in the past have been difficult, if not impossible. Our research and the resulting data base have enabled these comparisons to be made. Among the most compelling findings of that data base are the following:

- As might be expected, work force size accounts for most of the variance in staff costs. Another important component is compensation level: higher-performing health care companies actually pay individual staff members *higher* than average salaries and run with leaner staffs. Pay and performance are clearly linked in these environments. We also found that higher levels of outside purchased services are associated with lower *overall* staff costs (of which purchased services are a component). (See Figure 10-4.)

- Highly centralized health care systems benefiting from economies of scale have the lowest levels of aggregate staff costs, but decentralized systems were not far behind. It was those companies "stuck in the middle" that reported the lowest levels of staff productivity.

- Health care systems pursuing a horizontal strategy invest less in staff costs than do vertically integrated health care companies. On average, vertically integrated systems invest 50 percent more in staff costs than do systems that pursue a horizontal strategy. This is primarily because of the difficulty and cost of developing linkages among different types of business units.

Successful health care systems allocate as much as one-third more to their human resources, planning/marketing, and public relations functions than do their lower-performing counterparts, adjusted for size differences among the health care systems.

Assessing Job Tasks and Work Flow

It is important to examine the nature of staff work and work flow. A helpful approach to doing this is to carefully analyze

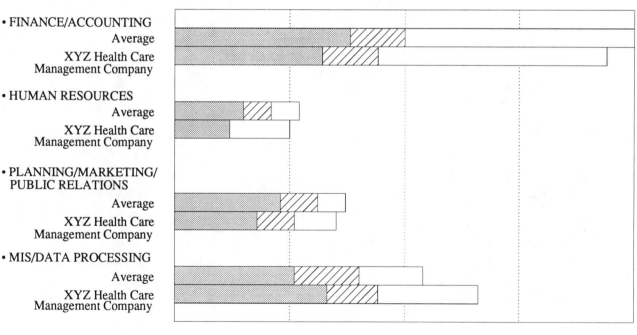

AVERAGE FUNCTIONAL STAFF COSTS*
(As percentage of adjusted organization size)

▨ Corporate ▨ Regional ☐ Unit

XYZ's staff functions are smaller than average, adjusted for organization size. They also are less centralized, with the exception of a large, centralized MIS department. These findings suggest that XYZ should initially focus on 1) the cost effectiveness of its MIS function and 2) possibly increasing the centralization of costs in the Finance/Accounting function to obtain better economies of scale.

Figure 10-2 Amount and Allocation of Staff Costs

the efficiency of the flow of work (e.g., Are too many people involved?), as well as to prioritize each job's tasks as

- critical
- important, but not critical
- desirable

The key here is the process of setting and communicating priorities—and having operating unit and department managers active in the process.

Identifying System and Service Needs

Too often, staff changes are made without identifying line managers' true staff support needs. More importantly, it is vital to reassess how well systems and processes fit with the new organization. Frequently, a staff that has been reduced is still asked to (1) provide the same level of service and (2) maintain systems and processes that were established for (and by) a larger number of people. Thus, take a fresh look at your systems and processes to ensure they fit with the ''new'' organization's structure and culture.

Considering Labor Market Dynamics

Given critical skill shortages in the health care industry, it is crucial to know where important labor shortages are now and to project where they will be. Thoughtful human resources planning will help assure logical continuity and development of staff, while helping to reduce the costs of turnover.

DECISION MAKING

Following the assessment stage, health executives face critical and difficult decisions. The necessary internal and external comparisons suggest issues and approaches, but assessment does not lay out definitive answers. Because no two situations are alike, each decision and each implementation plan require their own considerations. As a starting point, however, health care organizations must ask how staff functions will fit with the organization's strategy and organizing concept (e.g., centralization vs. decentralization, autonomy vs. linkage).

Our ongoing research is addressing whether staff allocation is moving closer to the patient (i.e., away from corporate

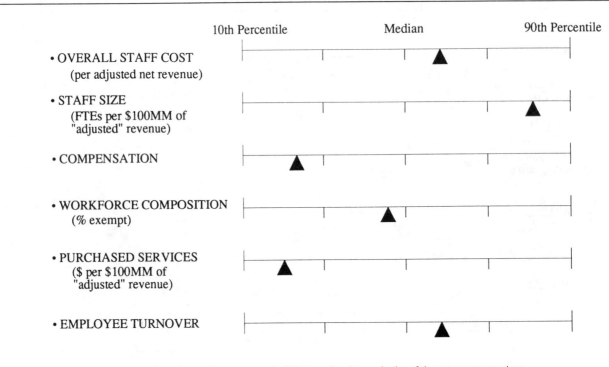

XYZ's overall Finance/Accounting costs are at the 75th percentile. An examination of the cost components above reveals that staffing levels are high while compensation and purchased services are relatively low. The data also suggest that:

- staffing levels should be carefully examined (and probably reduced);
- automated processes or improved workflow/management controls needs to be developed;
- compensation competitiveness must be improved, to match the leaner yet better-paying structures of top-performing medical centers.

 = XYZ Medical Center

Figure 10-3 Components of Staff Costs

levels and toward hospitals and business units), given the pressures on health care organizations to be more responsive. Also our research is examining whether "response-oriented" staff functions, such as marketing, will become more decentralized, under the hypothesis that improved responsiveness outweighs the lost economies of scale from centralization. Similarly, we may find that for those functions in which local responsiveness is less crucial, such as finance, the lost responsiveness from centralizing is less important than the gain in economies of scale.

For now, research indicates that more local autonomy is required in more turbulent markets and environments. Not only is the health care industry as a whole facing the most turbulent environment in its history, but also many regional markets face excruciating unpredictability and instability. In those areas especially, appropriate autonomy and responsiveness will become essential.

Other fundamental questions require decision makers' attention.

- How will key programs, functions, or services be affected? What changes will take place in the level and range of services provided?
- What changes must be proposed to continue meeting business objectives and the company mission?
- What are the financial and nonfinancial impacts?
- What are the implementation considerations?

IMPLEMENTATION

Following assessments and decisions, several issues must be effectively confronted if staff is to be restructured or resized.

- A *humane, efficient redeployment of human resources* is imperative. Health care administrators must address transition, placement, and, if staff is reduced, severance assistance. The restructured work force may need supervisory training.
- *Effective communication of change* is also essential. The first element of that communication is usually symbolic: management must commit itself significantly and visibly to the change process. Channels must be selected for answering employees' questions and addressing their apprehensions. An appointed communications coordinator may prove to be helpful.
- Given the nature of the change, managers may have to move quickly to *"pick up the pieces" and rebuild* the

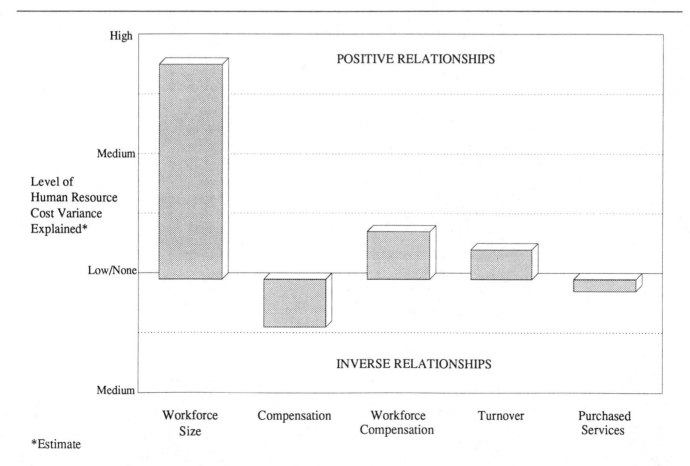

*Estimate

Figure 10-4 Staff Cost Variance Explained by Key Components. *Source*: "Health Care Organizational Effectiveness and Human Resource Productivity Base," Hay Management Consultants, 1989.

team. While they should acknowledge feelings that will inevitably arise, they must balance the organization's past practices with emerging business needs.

- Managers should expect the *long-term benefits to be clouded by significant short-term disruption*. Yet the cost of not acting can be considerable. For one large hospital that was forced to institute a plan to reduce costs, first-year savings amounted to $5.4 million. Seen differently, the cost of not acting was $104,000 a week.

In summary, reallocating or reducing staff costs requires hard decisions that must be made at the top. How this unpleasant task is done will largely determine the "new" organization's success. The most effective health care organizations are proactive in this area: They measure, compare, and rationalize their staff costs *before* a crisis. They involve key people and build commitment at each level. They communicate openly. They create a sense of urgency regarding change and tailor organization design and costs to their own competitive strategy.

If effectively managed, such restructuring can create a shared feeling of momentum, a more focused and cost-effective organization, and the knowledge that future evolution is inevitable.

NOTE

1. *Health Care Investment Analysts*. Baltimore, MD.: Health Care Investment Analysts, 1989.

Sanford M. Jacoby

Employee Attitude Surveys in American Industry: An Historical Perspective

11

Union leaders and their supporters have long been suspicious of behavioral scientists. As researchers, behavioral scientists have been criticized for their unitary premises and consequent disregard of unions. As practitioners, they have been characterized as "servants of power" and "cow sociologists" because they purportedly help employers to suppress unions and control their employees. In the past, however, little evidence was offered to sustain this latter claim. Most critics of the human relations movement directed their fire at the writings of such prominent researchers as Elton Mayo but rarely considered how these writings were translated into industrial practice (Landsberger 1958).

Recently, however, a growing body of research has verified the important role played by applied behavioral science in the post-1960 growth of industry's nonunion sector. According to this research, the nonunion sector was at one time primarily reactive, borrowing personnel innovations (e.g., fringe benefits and seniority rules) from the more dynamic unionized sector of the economy. But over the last 25 years, nonunion firms have become proactive, leading the way in the application of behavioral science "technology" to the work place (Foulkes 1980; Verma 1983; Verma and Kochan 1985). Unfortunately, the reasons for this transformation are not clear. One explanation, proposed by Kochan and Capelli (1984, 146), is that a set of "psychology-based, individual-oriented

personnel policies" became available after 1960 and that non-union firms were the first to adopt these policies and to demonstrate their labor relations potential. In fact, however, much of this behavioral science technology—including personnel counseling, participative management, and group dynamics—was available before the 1960s.

One technique with a particularly long history in both the union and the nonunion sectors is employee attitude testing: the use of surveys and other methods to assess employee attitudes toward management and its policies. Attitude testing began in the 1920s and remains popular to this day, after suffering something of a decline in the late 1950s and experiencing a renaissance in the late 1960s. As will be discussed later, these shifts in the technique's popularity can be analyzed using an economic model of technological diffusion in which an innovation's diffusion rate is a function of its cost and of its perceived profitability, which in this case hinges on the gains to be reaped from achieving or maintaining a nonunion status. This chapter focuses chiefly on industry's use of attitude testing prior to the 1960s, a period that researchers have not adequately examined.

While relatively easy to carry out, employee attitude testing is based on a complex mix of scientific methods and concepts: attitude constructs, scaling theory, interview methodology, and statistical methods, such as sampling and factor analysis. Indeed, one could argue that attitude research constitutes the intellectual core of the behavioral sciences. Thus, the history of employee attitude testing provides a paradigm of how behavioral science has been applied by management as a problem-solving tool.

Note: This is an expanded version of an article which appeared in *Industrial Relations*, Vol. 27, No. 1, Winter 1988. © 1988 Regents of the University of California, Berkeley. Reprinted with permission.

DEVELOPMENT OF ATTITUDE SURVEYS

Thomas and Znaniecki's *The Polish Peasant in Europe and America* (1918) was the first modern social science study to apply the term *attitude* to a purely mental state, as opposed to its original meaning of bodily position or posture, the sense in which it was used by nineteenth-century biologists and physiologists seeking a scientific explanation for human behavior (Fleming 1967). *The Polish Peasant* was followed by numerous studies during the 1920s and 1930s that applied the term to both individual and group behavior. Although precise definitions varied (Allport 1935), attitudes were generally viewed as orientations toward action. More than just feelings, they had cognitive and normative content, and they could be measured (Converse 1985).

There was some disagreement, however, over how best to assess attitudes. One group, made up of sociologists (e.g., the "Chicago School"; see Madge 1962) and anthropologists (e.g., Radcliffe-Brown 1922), thought of attitudes as deep-seated or unconscious beliefs that had to be ferreted out by unstructured interviews, case studies, and field work. Another group, consisting largely of psychologists, was more inclined to accept self-stated opinions as valid measures of attitudes and relied on quantitative questionnaire data to document those opinions (Converse 1987; Kiesler, Collins, and Miller 1969). Hence, the development of attitude scaling methods by Thurstone (1928), Likert (1932), and others constituted a major breakthrough for this latter approach. But members of both groups recognized the value of a syncretic methodology. Sociologists acknowledged the importance of validating interviews with quantitative data (Bogardus 1924; Bulmer 1981), while psychometricians such as Thurstone (1935) developed techniques—notably factor analysis—for sifting through questionnaire responses to uncover latent attitude clusters.

The first significant commercial application of attitude surveys occurred in the area of market research. In the 1920s, manufacturers and advertising agencies conducted surveys of consumer attitudes toward particular products and advertising media (Haring 1936; Lockley 1950). By the early 1930s, several organizations—A.C. Nielsen, Market Research Corporation of America, and Psychological Corporation, a consortium of academic psychologists—offered market research services to industry. Most market research during this period was rather unsophisticated, consisting chiefly of informal interviews and "objective" (e.g., multiple-choice) questionnaires (Converse 1987; White 1931). A notable exception was the work of Paul F. Lazarsfeld (1934, 1935, 1937), which emphasized careful item construction, causal analysis of consumer motives, and the use of qualitative methods to probe for underlying attitudes.

It was but a short methodological step from surveying consumer attitudes to surveying voters on political and social issues. Gallup, Crossley, and Roper, now well known as public opinion pollsters, began their careers in market research, establishing their reputations in the political arena when they correctly predicted Roosevelt's landslide in the 1936 presidential election (Converse 1987; Jensen 1980). After this, polling became a standard feature of the American political landscape, and research began to explore such topics as opinion formation and mass communication (Lazarsfeld 1940; Murphy and Likert 1938).

THE EARLY YEARS: EMPLOYEE SURVEYS THROUGH 1941

Another area closely tied to market research was employee attitude testing. Here the pioneering practitioner was J. David Houser of Houser Associates. After training as an educational psychologist, Houser began his career in the early 1920s conducting consumer attitude studies for large public utilities (Houser 1924). Among the marketing studies then being done, his work was notable for going beyond mere description and was praised for its careful causal analysis and its reliance on sampling theory (Houser 1924, 1932, 1938a; Strong 1938; Wheeler 1935).

Houser's studies of employee attitudes were similarly sophisticated. Others had published journalistic accounts of worker attitudes (Williams 1920), but Houser was the first to take a quantitative approach and to demonstrate its utility to employers. Prior to World War I, most American managers were more concerned with their employees' actions and behavior than with their attitudes and inner states (Bendix 1956). But wartime strikes and labor shortages forced companies to adopt more systematic and scientific forms of personnel administration. According to economist Sumner Slichter (1929, 401) this new emphasis reflected "a growing realization by managers of the close relationship between industrial morale and efficiency." It also created an environment favorable to studying employee attitudes for knowledge as well as for profit.

While a Wertheim Fellow at Harvard University in 1924–25, Houser interviewed a number of top executives and discovered that few of them had accurate information on their employees' morale and attitudes toward management. This ignorance was unfortunate, said Houser (1927, 164), because low morale caused employees to "express resentment through sabotage, 'soldiering' in their work, wage demands, and strikes." To gauge employee morale, Houser had interviewers ask employees a set of standardized questions about various factors in the work environment. Responses were then coded on a scale from 1 to 5, ranging from enthusiasm through indifference to hostility. In this way, Houser was able to compute an overall "morale score": a single number that, when averaged over all employees in a unit, allowed for comparisons across departments or firms.

The publication of Houser's book *What the Employer Thinks* in 1927 was followed by a steadily growing number of academic studies that analyzed employee morale and job satisfaction. Some studies, concerned with such broad social issues as occupational maladjustment, sampled employees from throughout a given community (Cole 1940; Hoppock 1935;

Lazarsfeld 1931; Watson 1940). But most focused on the employees of single organizations and were conducted under employer auspices. They were marked by what was to become a characteristic feature of academic research on employee attitudes: the blending of theoretical concerns with practical suggestions for managers.

The industrial and social psychologists who conducted much of this early research relied heavily on standardized questionnaires and morale scales.[1] But they were more inclined to supplement these sources with interviews than were psychologists conducting research on other kinds of attitudes. There were several reasons for this proclivity. First, industrial psychology had its roots in vocational guidance, a field with a tradition of educational counseling (Bingham and Moore 1931; Edgerton 1926). Second, surveying employees in the work place posed special difficulties. Workers were often suspicious of attitude surveys, fearing that they might suffer unpleasant consequences if their replies were too negative. Interviews added a personal touch that eased these anxieties and allowed for "free and frank expression, with no fears of reprisals and no doubts that personal confidences will be absolutely respected" (Kornhauser and Sharp 1932, 395). The final factor was the considerable influence of the Hawthorne studies, which began at Western Electric in 1927.

Between 1928 and 1931, the Hawthorne researchers conducted over 21,000 interviews with employees. Originally intended to provide material for supervisory training programs, these interviews soon became an end in themselves because of their cathartic effect on employees. Workers enjoyed this form of "participating jointly with the company in its endeavor to improve supervision and working conditions"; they got "a lift" from "expressing freely their feelings and emotions" (Roethlisberger and Dickson 1939, 227; see also Putnam 1930). The interview technique used at Hawthorne was nondirective: the employee was allowed to choose the topics and speak without any substantive interference from the interviewer. Like the projective techniques developed in later years (Campbell 1950), nondirective interviewing was somewhat manipulative in that it penetrated a person's conscious barriers and brought out latent or unconscious "sentiments." As Roethlisberger and Dickson acknowledged (1939, 272), their interview method owed much to the depth orientation of the sociological and anthropological strand in attitude research, as well as to the free association techniques widely used by psychiatrists (Jelliffe 1918; Lasswell 1930).[2]

By the end of the 1930s, the issues that would inform employee attitude research for the next 20 years or so had become clear. Among them were human relations concerns, such as the importance of supervision and the relative unimportance of pecuniary factors as determinants of employee morale (Houser 1938b; Kornhauser and Sharp 1932; Likert and Willits 1940; Roethlisberger and Dickson 1939); the consequences of high morale, particularly individual productivity (Hersey 1932; Kornhauser 1933); and the development of conceptually refined and psychometrically sensible measures of morale (Chant 1932; Kolstad 1938).

Despite this growing body of research, employee attitude surveys were not widely used by industry prior to World War II. A handful of progressive firms adopted the technique during the late 1930s when private consultants, such as Houser Associates, Stech Associates, and Opinion Research Corporation, began to promote attitude testing as a tool for avoiding unionization or for mitigating the impact of recently organized unions. Sounding a common theme, Houser (1938b, 1) warned that "the gates are open wide to a flood of unionization" because of management's "dangerous and costly misconceptions and oversimplifications concerning the motives of men in their work." More specifically, he and others believed that managers overestimated the importance of pay and promotion in determining morale and underestimated the importance of such nonpecuniary factors as participation in management decisions, fair supervision, and interesting work (Bergen 1942; Employee Relations Bureau 1939; Mayo 1933; Moore 1941). With attitude surveys, said Houser (1938b, 20), business could get "a true picture of workers' motives and desires," thereby avoiding "the dangers inherent in complete unionization." These arguments were bound to appeal to employers because they suggested, first, that union demands for wage increases did not reflect employees' true desires and, second, that less expensive and more effective ways of deterring unions could be found.

Of course, managers had other reasons for conducting attitude surveys. Imitating Western Electric, firms such as Westinghouse, one of Houser's clients, used survey results in their foreman training classes (Burke 1939). In addition, many managers now took it as an article of faith that productivity could be raised by improving employee morale. Nevertheless, their dominant motive was the desire for a solution to the complex labor relations problem that confronted them.

In unionized firms, attitude surveys allowed managers to bypass the union as a source of information on worker attitudes and, thus, stay one step ahead in the competition for employee loyalty (*Personnel Journal* 1938). Moreover, they gave management a negotiating advantage during collective bargaining because the company could safely reject any union demand that employees did not support or did not care about deeply (Bergen 1942). Finally, they could function as a subtle form of communication. For instance, in a questionnaire booklet distributed in 1938 and again in 1940, Armstrong Cork (which was partially unionized) reminded employees of the company's largesse by asking them detailed questions about its various welfare programs (Evans 1941).

Attitude surveys were also a useful device for firms seeking to avoid unionization (Bergen 1939; Brown 1941; Hersey 1937; Smith 1942). By identifying issues, departments, or employee groups that were potential "fuel for the fire of revolt" (Moore 1941, 363), the surveys enabled management to improve its policies and programs. They allowed large firms with many unorganized facilities to monitor the success of local managers in maintaining employee loyalty to, and satisfaction with, the company. The largest prewar survey program was run by Sears, Roebuck and Company, which hired Houser

Associates to conduct attitude surveys at its predominantly nonunion stores and warehouses. Between 1939 and 1942, Houser surveyed over 37,000 Sears employees by means of a questionnaire that asked for opinions on specific work place practices. The questionnaire also contained a 10-item scale that measured the employee's overall attitude toward the company, producing an employee's "morale score." After a local unit had been surveyed, the findings were discussed with the unit's manager, who was then expected to devise a written plan for remedying the problems uncovered (Hull 1939; Hull and Kolstad 1942; Jones 1961).

WARTIME DEVELOPMENTS

Although the outbreak of World War II brought a temporary halt to the Sears survey program, elsewhere—notably in aircraft manufacturing, shipbuilding, and other defense industries—experimentation with attitude surveys increased. With labor scarce and with wages frozen by the War Labor Board, firms in these rapidly growing industries had to be especially attentive to worker complaints; attitude surveys aided in this endeavor (*Factory Management* 1942, 1943). These firms also hired employee counselors to help defense workers with housing, child care, and many other problems they faced. As at Western Electric, which started a model counseling program in 1936 (Dickson and Roethlisberger 1966; Wilensky and Wilensky 1951), wartime counselors were expected to raise morale by listening sympathetically to complaints, thus giving workers an opportunity to "let off steam"; these complaints were then summarized (with care taken to preserve anonymity) and reported to management (Baker 1944; Cantor 1945; Fuller 1944; Tead 1943).

Corporate survey activity was overshadowed by that of the federal government, which commissioned numerous polls and surveys during the war. Gallup and Roper worked for the government, as did a large number of behavioral and social scientists, including over a fifth of the nation's psychologists (Viteles 1945).[3] With their help the War Department's Morale Services Division conducted over 250 surveys of soldier attitudes, and these led to studies of topics that had obvious relevance for industry, such as the relationship between combat performance and troop morale (Elinson 1949; Katz 1951; Stouffer and DeVinney 1949).

Because of the importance attached to winning the war on the home front, government researchers directed much of their attention to the civilian population. To assess civilian morale, the Office of War Information (OWI) employed public opinion pollsters such as Gallup, as well as a more academic group of social psychologists headed by Rensis Likert, who was then based in the Department of Agriculture (Harding 1944; Likert 1947; Marquis 1944; Skott 1943).[4] The OWI was especially interested in the morale of the nation's defense workers and its relationship to productivity and absenteeism, issues that Likert's group studied by surveying workers in shipyards and other defense plants (Katz and Hyman 1947a, 1947b).

THE POSTWAR BOOM, 1945–1955

Employee attitude surveys jumped in popularity toward the end of the war and spread throughout industry during the following decade. Each year after 1944 saw a steady increase in the number of firms using surveys, and by 1954, when the growth curve began to flatten out, about two in five large firms had conducted at least one survey (Table 11-1). The most common users were large firms and firms that had previous experience either with consumer surveys or with psychological selection testing—hence, the prevalence of surveying in nonmanufacturing industries, such as retailing and public utilities.[5]

What accounts for this surge in popularity? First, because of their contributions to the war effort, the behavioral and social sciences enjoyed great prestige outside the university. Employers were more eager than ever before to hire technical personnel specialists to design training, selection, and compensation programs, as well as to conduct attitude surveys. One psychologist said that employers had become "psychologically minded" (Canter 1948), ready to embrace the notion that "the whole question of efficiency and productivity boils down to one thing: understanding the MOTIVATIONS of your employees and taking steps to SATISFY them" (Research Institute of America 1949). By 1948, 30 percent of large corporations had a psychologist on staff, while others employed sociologists, psychiatrists, and anthropologists (Baritz 1960; Bennett 1948; Gordon 1952; Tiffin 1958). A

Table 11-1 Industrial Use of Attitude Surveys, 1947–1982 (percentage of firms that had conducted at least one survey)

	1947	1954	1963	1981	1982
All Firms	7	N/A	N/A	N/A	45
Type of Firm					
Manufacturing	6	—	21	45	—
Nonmanufacturing	11	—	—	—	47
Employees Surveyed					
Hourly	—	15	17	44	—
Nonexempt Salaried	—	21	18	45	—
Number of Employees in Firm					
500–1,000	—	—	21	—	33
1,000–4,999	11	15	21	—	42
5,000 and over	19	38	38	—	67

Note: The 1954 data on size refer to hourly employees, 92 percent of whom were employed in manufacturing. All of the 1963 data are for manufacturing employees.

Sources: 1947: "Personnel Activities in American Business," National Industrial Conference Board (NICB), Studies in Personnel Policy (SPP), no. 86 (1947), p. 32; 1954: "Personnel Practices in Factory and Office," fifth ed., NICB, SPP no. 145 (1954), pp. 55, 109; 1963: "Personnel Practices in Factory and Office-Manufacturing," NICB, SPP no. 194 (1964), pp. 55–56; 1981: Harriet Gorlin, "Personnel Practices III: Employee Services, Work Rules," Conference Board Information Bulletin no. 95 (1981), pp. 24–25; 1982: New York Stock Exchange, Office of Economic Research, *People and Productivity: A Challenge to Corporate America* (1982), pp. 25, 44–47.

related development was the rapid growth of corporate personnel departments during and after the war. To justify their larger budgets, these departments needed some quantitative measure that would prove their effectiveness, and surveys of employee morale levels provided one such indicator (BNA 1954; Stock and Lubin 1946).

Second, labor relations concerns fueled the interest in attitude surveys, just as in the late 1930s. But now, more confident than before, management was ready to launch a well-financed offensive against organized labor. Although unions had grown in size and stature during the war, a wave of strikes in 1945 and 1946 damaged their public image. Perceiving "a window of opportunity," employers set about the task of reclaiming their authority in national affairs. On the legislative front they pushed for passage of the Taft-Hartley Act, at the same time embarking on a campaign to convince the public of the virtues inherent in the free enterprise system, an effort that continued even after the act was passed (Harris 1982; Whyte 1952). To guide this campaign, companies relied heavily on surveys of public opinion, just as the government had relied on polls to shape its wartime propaganda. Opinion Research Corporation (ORC), for example, conducted polls for industry on such topics as "Collectivist Ideology in America" and "Collectivist Ideology and Economic Ignorance" (Viteles 1953).

The work place itself was the vital center and chief target of this public relations campaign. Both unionized and nonunion firms bombarded their employees with films, magazines, pamphlets, and personal letters, all designed to convince them that management was a generous, friendly, and trustworthy guardian of their interests. Attitude surveys played a crucial role in this effort because they provided the data necessary to plan "downward" communications and to gauge employee reactions to them. Consultants such as ORC and Psychological Corporation did a brisk business, conducting attitude surveys to evaluate communications programs at such companies as Alcoa, Pittsburgh Plate Glass, and General Electric, which had a communications program designed by Lemuel Boulware, a former GE marketing vice-president (Boulware 1948; *Business Week* 1953a). Often the survey itself became an instrument of propaganda, as when workers received glossy postsurvey brochures announcing that "97 percent of employees think this is an above-average plant" (*Factory Management* 1948, 90; Hurst 1948). Moreover, because surveys gave employees "an outlet for their dissatisfactions," they were widely acknowledged to be a direct and relatively inexpensive way for companies not only to measure but also to raise employee morale. For this reason, four out of five companies surveyed all the employees in a given unit, rather than selecting a representative sample (Campbell 1948; McMurry 1946, 215; Raube 1951).

Attitude surveys also had more specific labor relations functions, just as before the war. Those firms that had managed to remain nonunion were well aware that, as one manager put it, "Unions would have far less control and influence in this country if industry had been listening, and once having devel-oped the art of listening, reacted as it should have to what it heard" (BNA 1951, 12). One prominent nonunion company, Thompson Products (later TRW), fended off several organizing drives during the 1940s by combining a pugnacious communications program with periodic employee opinion polls that were used to debunk claims made by union organizers (*Factory Management* 1946; *Iron Age* 1944).

At Sears, which renewed its survey program in 1946, attitude testing became the critical element in a "firefighting" strategy whereby units thought to be especially vulnerable to union organizing efforts—because of poor local management, employee complaints, or location in a heavily unionized community—were targeted for surveys. Those in charge of the program claimed it could accurately forecast union activity in a particular department or division. According to Burleigh B. Gardner (1985), an anthropologist who served as a consultant to Sears, "You could see it coming clear as day [and could] predict trouble in six months unless you acted." In these surveys, employees at the store completed a questionnaire designed by Gardner and David G. Moore; then, employees were selected for nondirective interviewing.[6] Managers of units with an average "morale score" below 35 (the questionnaire scale ran to 100) were advised to "start looking where your trouble is and start figuring out how to do something about it" (Gardner 1985).[7]

Although some managers argued that attitude surveys were unnecessary at heavily unionized firms (BNA 1954), this was a minority point of view. In the postwar period, the managers of heavily unionized firms made determined efforts to contain union inroads on their prerogatives, while at the same time aggressively competing for the rank and file's trust and loyalty. According to several contemporary studies of what was called the "dual loyalty" issue, even in situations in which union solidarity was high, workers could have very positive attitudes toward management, though a conflict of values existed (Gottlieb and Kerr 1950; Katz 1949a; Rose 1952; Stagner et al. 1954). Among other things, this suggested that the proper managerial response to a popular union was not fatalistic quiescence but rather the kind of sophisticated aggressiveness displayed by such firms as General Motors, General Electric, Ford, and Monsanto, each of which made attitude surveys part of its labor relations strategy. Surveys provided a legal means to undercut the union's role as the workers' exclusive representative, thus making it possible for managers to "give" before the union "demanded and won," and to "separate a demand by a union business agent from a request by the majority of workers" (Irwin 1945, 42; see also *Business Week*, 1953b; *Fortune* 1943). Three prominent psychologists summarized the logic behind this approach: "In the competition between employers and unions . . . whichever side achieves a more accurate and deeper understanding of the motivations involved to that extent improves its ability to accomplish its own purposes" (French, Kornhauser, and Marrow 1946, 10).

Exceptionally effective in this regard was General Motors (GM), the first of the Big Three automobile manufacturers to develop a coherent labor relations strategy. GM's approach was Janus-like: the unions were faced with a tough adversary in bargaining and contract administration, while the employees saw a more human visage as the company sought to establish direct and personal ties with them. To carry out the latter objective, GM established an Employee Relations Department in 1945. Its director, Harry B. Coen, was an ardent opponent of the United Auto Workers who once said, "I do not believe in making the union contact the only one between our employees and ourselves . . . I am hopeful that . . . we as a staff can deal with it in such a manner that the union aspect will be only one little segment, or whatever segment it cares to be" (quoted in Bendix 1956, 329). Coen picked L.N. Laseau, formerly with GM's customer research staff, to head the department's employee research section, and over the next two years Laseau developed an attitude survey program for GM.[8]

In 1947, the company announced a giant contest in which employees were to write essays on "My Job and Why I Like It." Such prominent persons as Peter Drucker and George W. Taylor were hired to judge the essays, and more than $150,000 in prizes—including 40 new cars and 65 refrigerators—was set aside. The contest had two objectives. The first was to raise morale directly by encouraging employees to reflect on the company's positive attributes and by creating the impression that GM was a fun place to work. To promote the contest, Laseau distributed banners, flyers, and pamphlets to all GM plants, some of which also sponsored parades and parties with hired orchestras. The second objective was to ascertain employees' attitudes toward the company, information that would be useful in dealing with the union and in modifying company policies so as to improve morale. Laseau's staff prepared special manuals to code the content of the essays and was thus able to identify 58 major themes. Divisions were given the results and asked to prepare action plans to correct problems. GM also asked university researchers to analyze the contest data. This request spurred a variety of projects, including the compilation of an industrial workers' word list to be used as a guide in corporate communications, as well as several studies by Lazarsfeld, who used the data to test his method of latent structure analysis, a variant of factor analysis. In addition, GM hired ORC to find out what employees thought of the contest. Although the contest itself was never repeated, ORC in subsequent years conducted periodic attitude surveys at GM plants around the country (*Business Week* 1949; Evans and Laseau 1950).

The United Automobile Workers (UAW), which represented most of GM's workers, was quick to condemn both the contest and some of the company's other surveys. Its president, Walter Reuther, called the contest "an attempt to conduct a one-sided opinion poll" (*Mill & Factory* 1948), and most local union newspapers also criticized it. In some plants, contest posters were torn down, and handbills were distributed saying that the contest was part of an effort to destroy the union. The most publicized union attack on GM's survey

program occurred in 1955, after ORC conducted structured interviews with workers at the company's Flint plant. During these interviews workers were asked several questions on the topic of the guaranteed annual wage (GAW). Since the union was planning to demand a GAW in its upcoming bargaining sessions with GM, Reuther claimed that these questions were biased or "designed to elicit answers that could be damaging to the union." Reuther added that he was not opposed to attitude surveys per se, so long as they were "properly and honestly applied" (*Business Week* 1955, 31). Indeed, in at least one instance the UAW cooperated with the management of a small Illinois auto parts firm in conducting a survey (*Business Week* 1956; Mason 1949).

Such cooperative endeavors were, however, the exception rather than the rule. While 85 percent of a group of union leaders favored the joint survey approach (Raube 1951), management usually rejected it. In fact, nearly half of all the companies studied by the National Industrial Conference Board did not even inform the union beforehand about their plans to conduct a survey, and 60 percent did not share survey findings with union officers (McMurry 1946; Raube 1951). One manager said he did not involve the union in his company's survey program because he feared that the union would "attempt to control the views of the membership and thus defeat the true purpose of such a survey" (BNA 1951, 4). Some university-based consultants (e.g., Michigan's Institute for Social Research) refused to conduct a survey that did not have union approval. But most consultants did not share this inhibition (Kornhauser 1961).[9]

Hence, it is not surprising that union leaders were suspicious both of attitude surveys and of the people conducting them: industrial and social psychologists and professional pollsters (Habbe 1961; Kornhauser 1947; Raube 1951). Although this suspicion did not always erupt into outspoken opposition, there was, nevertheless, the underlying fear that, as one union spokesman said, attitude surveys would undermine the most fundamental aspects of unionism by "stealing the prestige for the solution of problems [from the grievance and bargaining mechanisms] and arrogating it completely to a management-controlled device" (Barkin 1952, 82). The unions themselves made little use of the survey technique to study their own members: neither the AFL nor the CIO knew of any such studies conducted prior to 1950, and only a handful were done during the 1950s (Davis and St. Germain 1951; Kirchner and Uphoff 1955; Rosen and Rosen 1955). The reasons for this lack are not clear, but it is likely that union leaders thought of the attitude survey as a tainted, rather than a neutral, device and viewed survey consultants in a similarly unfavorable way (Barkin 1961; Katz 1949).[10]

PRACTICAL AND PROFESSIONAL PROBLEMS

Despite its popularity, surveying was fraught with problems attributable to the inexperience of corporate surveyors and the expedient nature of their surveys, which were often little more than a "potpourri of items thrown together by harried personnel workers" (Taylor 1959, 981). Attitude surveys purported to be measuring something called "employee morale" or "job satisfaction." Yet this key concept was neither carefully defined nor operationalized, and as a result, the term took on a plethora of meanings (Guion 1958; McNemar 1946). To the extent a central tendency could be observed, however, the *assumption* seems to have been that morale was a unidimensional continuum reflecting an employee's attitude toward the company and his or her identification with its management (Brayfield and Crockett 1955; Gordon 1955; Kornhauser 1944).

Another problem was that those conducting the surveys were naive about what Viteles (1953) referred to as the "bias of the auspices": the fact that employees were less likely to speak truthfully to their employer or to someone representing him than to a more impartial and less threatening person (Dunnette and Heneman 1956). While many employers took steps to encourage a sense of anonymity—including locked "ballot boxes" and the omission of coding numbers on questionnaires—such efforts were not always enough to overcome suspicion and bias. (Benge 1946; McMurry 1946). To cite one egregious example, at Westinghouse in the late 1930s, some employees signed their questionnaires even though they were told not to. But far from eliciting skepticism about response validity, the manager in charge boasted that this behavior proved that the employees "felt sure that the questionnaire would not be misused" (Burke 1939, 27).

The questionnaires themselves were often poorly constructed, used leading questions and emotionally toned words, and encouraged a rigid patterning of responses. Few were designed to systematically measure relationships between variables or to assess causal relationships. Although some of the more sophisticated surveys collected demographic and other factual data, most failed to take account of the age, occupation, and other salient characteristics of the surveyed employee groups (Katz 1950; Viteles 1953). Moreover, because the questionnaires were customized instruments containing firm-specific rather than standardized questions, survey results were rarely comparable across firms. The lack of external norms meant that companies had no idea of how their employees stacked up against those in similar firms.

One consequence of these problems was that employee attitude surveys contributed little to scientific research. Given the absence of careful controls and systematic research designs, it is not surprising that behavioral scientists tended to ignore the literally tons of data collected by corporate survey programs. To serious researchers, the typical survey represented little more than a mere "counting procedure" (Katz 1950, 212).

To the extent that these problems led to trivial or biased results, they reinforced management's doubts about the practical value of the surveys. Almost a fifth of all firms questioned by the National Industrial Conference Board admitted that they learned little or nothing about their employees from attitude surveys (Raube 1951), while another study found a significant minority who faulted attitude surveys because of poor design and because employees systematically lied on them (BNA 1954). Of course, employers had other reasons for their dissatisfaction. Some feared that surveys might give the union ammunition with which to attack the company, while others felt that they would awaken "sleeping dogs" by suggesting complaints and misgivings to employees (McMurry 1946). As a result, companies were often wary of reporting survey results to their workers, and survey follow-ups were poorly done.[11] For all of these reasons, then, attitude surveys were less widespread than other psychological techniques such as selection tests[12] and were usually one-shot affairs rather than part of a continuing program, as at Sears or Monsanto.

A MILITARY–INDUSTRIAL COMPLEX

At the same time that attitude testing was catching on in the corporate world, research on employee attitudes was burgeoning among behavioral and social scientists in the universities. Three times as many studies relating job factors to employee attitudes were published between 1950 and 1954 as had appeared between 1940 and 1944 (Herzberg et al. 1957). The military—through such agencies as the Office of Naval Research—heavily supported research in this area, including the Ohio State University leadership studies and the employee morale studies done at the University of Michigan.[13] Private companies also funded many of these studies by hiring university researchers to survey their employees and by contributing funds for the development of new survey instruments. These ties among government, universities, and corporate personnel departments were not unprecedented; similar research nexuses had developed during and immediately after World War I (Noble 1977). What was new was the large volume of subsidized research and the extent to which behavioral scientists became dependent upon it.

The relationship between industry and academia was symbiotic: both sides profited from it. For behavioral scientists interested in employee attitudes, industry provided research issues, research sites, and support for scientists and for the new industrial relations institutes established after the war. To take advantage of these opportunities, academics had to learn a whole new etiquette for establishing cooperative research relationships with business clients (Likert and Lippitt 1953). For industry, linking up with the universities had two advantages. First, it conferred legitimacy on attitude testing and other personnel techniques, casting them in a neutral, scientific light and allaying the suspicions of workers and union leaders. Thus, when Pitney-Bowes hired researchers from Dartmouth's Tuck School to conduct an attitude survey, the employees were given a brochure describing the Tuck staff and containing photographs of the school, of sealed questionnaire cartons being loaded into a car headed for Dartmouth, and of the Tuck researchers tabulating the survey data (Raube 1951). The second and more important benefit of the academic connection was technical assistance in solving the various problems that beset employee surveys. The contribution made by academia can best be understood by examining the activities of several key university groups involved in employee attitude research.

The Industrial Relations Center (IRC) at the University of Chicago was headed by Robert K. Burns and supported by a number of local companies, including Sears, Roebuck. In the late 1940s, Sears became dissatisfied with its existing survey instrument because, like other questionnaires then in use, it was difficult to administer, lacked psychometric rigor, and provided no basis for external comparisons. Sears turned to the IRC for help, and in 1950, a group of Chicago faculty members including Burns, L.L. Thurstone, and David G. Moore, a former Sears manager, joined forces under the aegis of the IRC to develop an employee attitude questionnaire that Sears as well as other companies could use. By applying item analysis, factor analysis, and other statistical techniques, the Chicago group developed a sophisticated, self-administering instrument known as the Employee Inventory (EI). Science Research Associates (SRA), a testing company founded by Burns, published the EI and sold it, along with scoring and analysis services, to firms wishing to survey their employees (Baehr 1953; Burns 1952; Moore 1985). Easy to use and bearing good academic credentials, the Inventory soon became industry's most popular employee attitude questionnaire (BNA 1954). Because so many firms purchased the EI, SRA was able to develop national norms for the Inventory, thus allowing firms such as Sears to compare their EI scores to those of other users (Burns 1954; Minaker 1953; Moore and Burns 1956). A similarly sophisticated questionnaire, the Triple Audit, was developed in 1948 at the University of Minnesota's Industrial Relations Center, but it was more frequently used for research purposes and had less commercial success than the Chicago instrument (England, Korman, and Stein 1961; Hamel and Reif 1952; Yoder, Heneman, and Cheit 1951).

Also more research oriented than the Chicago IRC was the Institute for Social Research (ISR) at the University of Michigan, which conducted a series of landmark studies examining the relationships among morale, supervision, and performance. Using questionnaires and structured interviews, the Michigan researchers studied workers at a number of major companies, including Caterpillar Tractor, Studebaker, Detroit Edison, Prudential Life Insurance, and the Chesapeake and Ohio Railroad. Not only did the ISR group contribute significantly to an understanding of the determinants of employee morale, but also it blazed a methodological trail by demonstrating that employee attitude surveys could be designed both to yield valuable generalizations for the behavioral sciences and to produce useful results for the companies sponsoring the research (Kahn 1956; Likert 1953; Likert and Katz 1948).

While conducting surveys for Detroit Edison in the late 1940s, the ISR group also developed the technique known as *survey feedback*, an interesting blend of theory and practice (Mann 1957; Mann and Likert 1952; Schwab 1953). On the surface, feedback appeared to be no more than a modest device for improving survey follow-ups and for ensuring the widespread dissemination of survey findings, both weak spots in survey practice. But, in actuality, it turned the survey into a powerful tool for *changing*, as well as monitoring, employee attitudes. At Detroit Edison, for instance, survey findings were presented to employees through an interlocking chain of group meetings that took place over a two-year period following the survey. First, the company's top executives discussed the findings and planned remedial actions, and then they held similar meetings with their subordinates. The process was repeated down the managerial ranks to the first-line supervisors and their work groups. According to the ISR researchers, this consultative approach had a number of positive effects on employees: it deepened their interest in the survey, helped them identify more closely with it, and made them readier to accept and support corrective measures introduced as a result of its findings. (One might add that these group meetings had great symbolic value, allowing management to demonstrate its concern for the employees and their opinions.) This procedure was consistent with the human relations tenets of Kurt Lewin and his students, who emphasized the change processes associated with employee participation and small groups (Coch and French 1948; Lewin 1948).

The ISR studies were also among the first to employ factor analysis as a method for more precisely defining employee morale. Rather than being a single factor, morale was found to comprise four dimensions: intrinsic job satisfaction, satisfaction with the company, satisfaction with supervision, and financial and job status satisfaction (Katz et al. 1951; Katz and Kahn 1952). Other university researchers also experimented with factor analytic definitions of employee morale. Some, such as the Chicago group working on the Employee Inventory, received support from private sources (Baehr 1954), while others were funded by the Air Force, which became interested in factor analysis after the war (Gordon 1955; Smith and Westen 1951). Even though this research helped to refine the definition of morale statistically, it left plenty of room for disagreement over how to apply and interpret factor analyses of employee surveys (Katzell 1958; Wherry 1954). Moreover, critics contended that researchers and managers still used "high employee morale" as a euphemism to describe workers who were "happy, contented, but typically docile" (Wilensky 1957, 39).

While the "fit" between industry and academia was generally good, each partner had its own agenda and did not always provide what the other side wanted. Employers were dismayed by researchers who insisted that the union be involved in any survey, and researchers had to deal with clients who were indifferent to, and ignorant of, a survey's contributions to the theoretical literature. Thus, even though numerous studies failed to confirm any direct causal link between morale and performance, 86 percent of managers polled in 1957 asserted that such a relationship existed (BNA 1957).[14]

SURVEYING SINCE THE MID–1950s: AN OVERVIEW

After more than a decade of rapid growth, the number of new users of attitude surveys began to taper off after the mid-1950s, as indicated in Table 11-1: Between 1954 and 1963, the proportion of firms conducting surveys of their hourly or salaried employees changed very little; while surveying became more common among medium-sized firms over this period, the proportion of large firms using the techniques remained constant. These trends failed to register in academia: the number of research studies dealing with employee attitudes did not decline noticeably, but fewer articles on surveying appeared in management-oriented magazines and journals.[15]

These trends may be illusory, the result of faulty data. But a more plausible explanation for the appearance of stasis is that by the late 1950s and early 1960s, management was feeling more secure of its standing with the public, the unions, and its employees than at any time during the previous three decades. In the realm of public relations, business had regained much of the prestige eroded by the Great Depression. In politics, it bested the unions in the battle over Taft-Hartley and won a smaller, though still significant victory with the passage of the Landrum-Griffin Act in 1959. Confident of their ability to control industrial relations problems, managers of unionized firms adopted a "mature" view by finally accepting unions as a permanent feature of the environment and by concentrating their energies on stabilizing labor-management relations. In the unorganized sector, unions posed less of a threat because they had lost their organizing momentum: after the mid-1950s, they represented a declining proportion of the labor force. Thus, employers throughout industry felt less pressure to experiment with such esoteric techniques as attitude surveys.

This is not to say that companies with existing survey programs disbanded them. They did not. In fact, in the late 1950s a number of firms began to include managerial and professional employees in their programs (Dunham and Smith 1979; Habbe 1961; Laitin 1961). In addition, the introduction of high-speed computers led to a variety of innovations in survey technology. Using machine-readable survey forms, Sears was able to survey all 200,000 of its employees in 1959, while AT&T in 1960 conducted factor analyses of thousands of employee questionnaires (Clarke and Grant 1961; Smith 1985). But those companies that had never previously utilized attitude surveys were now less willing to adopt them than in the immediate postwar years.

The situation changed again starting in the late 1960s and early 1970s: the proportion of manufacturing firms conducting employee attitude surveys rose from 21 percent in 1963 to 45 percent in 1981 (see Table 11-1), with most of these programs being adopted after 1972 (New York Stock Exchange 1982; see also BNA 1964, 1975). One driving force behind this change was industry's growing reliance on behavioral science tools to solve work place problems (Rush 1969). These tools included the innovations in work organization associated with the "quality of work life (QWL)" rubric, as well as a variety of organization development (OD) techniques, such as participative problem solving, task forces, team building, and employee involvement programs. While the precise mix of techniques has varied from company to company, once a firm uses some of them, it is more likely to adopt others, including attitude surveys. Thus, according to one study that distinguished between companies that were heavy and light users of OD techniques, the OD group was more than twice as likely as the non-OD group to have survey programs and made more extensive use of participatory mechanisms, such as survey feedback, in conducting these programs (Rush 1973; see also Nadler 1977).

But the proliferation of attitude surveys and other practices based on behavioral science stemmed from deeper and more significant developments in the labor relations arena. Not only did union organization among private firms decline steadily during the 1960s and 1970s, but at the same time there emerged a dynamic nonunion sector comprising both unorganized firms, such as those in high tech industry, and new, nonunion divisions within older, unionized companies (Verma and Kochan 1985). These firms employed large numbers of white-collar technical and professional workers, a highly educated group with special needs. Managing these employees required personnel policies that promoted communication and group decision making—precisely the outcomes that could be achieved through the use of attitude surveys and survey feedback, as well as other personnel techniques grounded in behavioral science. Today, managers of some nonunion firms remain wary of surveying because they regard it as too group oriented (like unionism), but this is a minority view. Modern managers tend to be more educated and even more "psychologically minded" than their predecessors. Hence, they are less reluctant to interact with behavioral scientists. They also understand that attitude surveys can function as a "voice" substitute for unionism, keeping an organization responsive to employee problems which, if ignored, could provide an opening wedge for unionization (Sherman 1969). As the vice-president of one large nonunion company said, "Management is convinced the survey is an effective tool of remaining nonunion. It allows us to keep our finger on the pulse, and we don't have to justify the budget request for the survey" (Foulkes 1980, 263).

These developments were not limited to the nonunion sector. During the past 15 years, as the union-nonunion wage gap has widened and as unions have declined in popularity, the managers of unionized firms have adopted a more aggressive posture and have shifted their priorities from maintaining stability in union-management relations to confronting weak unions and, where possible, undermining or even eliminating them. Today's managers are less likely to accept the inevitability of unions and are less skeptical of behavioral science techniques than were their predecessors of the 1940s and 1950s (Kochan and Capelli 1984). Management's greater reliance on attitude surveys in unionized firms has weakened the union's position as the employees' representative. In 1964,

96 percent of the managers in unionized firms reported that they depended on union representatives to supply them with information on employee concerns; by 1975, this figure had fallen to 56 percent (BNA 1964, 1975).

CONCLUSION

One important conclusion to be drawn from the history of employee attitude testing is that industry's reliance on behavioral science is neither a recent (i.e., post-1960) phenomenon nor one that has developed in a linear fashion, gradually becoming more prevalent over time. Rather, the diffusion of behavioral science throughout industry has followed a rational pattern not unlike that of capital-embodied innovations, in which the rate at which an innovation spreads throughout industry is positively related to its perceived profitability and inversely related to the size of the initial investment required to implement the technology (Mansfield 1961).

In the case of employee attitude testing, which can be used to repel or to weaken unions, managerial perceptions of profitability have been influenced by shifts in the expense of dislodging or deterring unions relative to the benefits of operating without them, including lower relative wage and strike costs. Thus, managers in organized firms have perceived the technique to be most profitable during periods when unions were regarded as vincible (the late 1930s), costly (the immediate postwar years), or both (the recent period that started sometime in the early 1970s). During the 1950s and 1960s— the heyday of mature collective bargaining—managers in unionized firms were able to absorb or pass along the costs of unionization; they also realized that their bargaining partners could not easily be dislodged and reluctantly accepted them as part of the status quo. In the nonunion sector, managers have perceived attitude testing to be most profitable when the threat of organization was high (during the 1930s and 1940s when the labor movement was expanding) or when the cost of unionization was high (during the recent period when the union-nonunion wage differential began to widen, a factor that also affects the union sector).

In contrast to these shifts in perceived profitability, the cost of implementing attitude testing has been steadily falling since its introduction in the 1920s, leading, in turn, to a steady rise in use of the technique. This has occurred in several ways. First, the growth of the behavioral sciences in academia and their receipt of support from government and military sources have created a social infrastructure that serves to reduce the private cost of implementing applied behavioral science programs. Second, out-of-pocket implementation costs have fallen over time because of improvements in the technology, such as machine-readable questionnaires, and because of scale economies associated with the growing use of other behavioral science techniques. (For example, companies with a staff of behavioral scientists overseeing an OD program need not hire additional staff to launch an attitude survey.) Finally, the

rising education level of managers, including their exposure to behavioral science concepts in business schools, has made it easier for behavioral scientists to interact with them and to "sell" them on the virtues of such techniques as attitude testing. Educated managers are also more predisposed to perceive those techniques as profitable. The net result of these cyclical (union cost) and secular (implementation cost) factors is the diffusion pattern shown in Table 11-1 and discussed here: increasing incidence over time, but with alternating periods of rapid diffusion and relative stasis.

The model's plausibility is buttressed when we look at the situation in such countries as Canada and Great Britain. These two nations have industrial relations systems similar to that of the United States, but their employers are more likely to see unions as inevitable and their union-nonunion wage gaps are narrower (Abbott and Stengos 1986). Although precise evidence is lacking, the United States also probably has a more extensive social infrastructure linking academia, government, and business, a nexus that reduces the private cost of behavioral science programs. As a result, attitude testing and other behavioral science techniques are far less prevalent in those countries than in the United States (Thomson and Warner 1981; Xishan et al. 1983).

In appraising employee attitude testing, one must ask whether it is simply a neutral technology or, rather, a form of communication that is inherently less democratic than other available channels, such as those provided by union representation and similar participatory mechanisms. In an illuminating essay on the history of attitude research, Donald Fleming (1967, 358) argues that the development of the modern concept of attitude over the last 70 to 80 years coincides—not by accident—with the incorporation of the masses into public affairs: "Their preferences, their response to public issues, became of crucial importance, if only to . . . manipulate them from above." Although Fleming does not say so, this period saw the rise not only of mass political democracy but also of industrial democracy, as a work force increasingly insistent of its rights forced organizations to become more sensitive to the thoughts and desires of their employees. Attitude testing represents one response of industrial elites to this development. Although the technique benefits employees by bringing their problems to the attention of management, it tends to do so in a fashion that encourages employee passivity and enhances top-down, expert-led solutions. The history of attitude testing demonstrates that applied behavioral science is a double-edged sword, one that management uses to solve employee problems but also wields as a weapon in the struggle for control of the work place.

NOTES

1. See, for example, the research done by Uhrbrock (1934) for Procter and Gamble, a firm that also pioneered in the use of psychological selection tests.

2. The Hawthorne experiments—though more extensive than anything done previously—were not the first industrial application of these techniques. Earlier, White (1924) had used "free interviewing" to assess employee atti-

tudes, while R.H. Macy & Co. in the mid-1920s hired psychiatrists and social workers to run an interviewing and counseling program for its employees (Anderson 1929).

3. Of course, many of these social scientists worked in areas other than attitude research, such as the armed forces' personnel selection and classification program.

4. For a fascinating analysis of a wartime *methodenstreit* between these two groups, see Converse (1984). After the war, Likert's group became the core of the new Institute for Social Research at the University of Michigan.

5. In 1947, nonmanufacturing firms were twice as likely as manufacturing firms to use attitude surveys (11 percent vs. 6 percent) and selection tests (32 percent vs. 15 percent). Within the manufacturing sector, attitude surveys were most prevalent in the aircraft, instruments, oil, glass, and paint industries, all of which (with the exception of paint) were also heavy users of selection tests (Raube 1947).

6. After the war, a growing number of companies besides Sears, including clients of ORC and of Michigan's Institute for Social Research, supplemented their written questionnaires with nondirective, "depth," or "open-ended" interviewing (*Business Week* 1953a; Likert and Katz 1948). A few companies also experimented with projective interviewing techniques, such as incomplete sentences (Friesen 1952; Kornhauser 1949). Proponents argued that this kind of interviewing helped to reveal the deep feelings and meaning behind an employee's questionnaire responses; critics charged that it was expensive and unreliable (Carey et al. 1951; Katz 1950; Weddell and Smith 1951). Similar debate occurred in other branches of survey research and continues to this day (Seltiz et al. 1959; Webb et al. 1966).

7. Recent research done by Sears bears out these claims: a correlation of .57 was found between a unit's scores on certain survey items and subsequent unionization attempts (Hamner and Smith 1978). The survey's ability to predict union activity is not surprising, given that Sears identified high-morale employees as those who made "positive and willing adjustments to the demands of the organization" and had "ideological sentiments" akin to management's (Moore and Gardner 1946).

8. In 1946 Ford followed GM's lead—as usual—by replacing its notorious Service Department with a new Industrial Relations Department, which immediately established a "human engineering program" and inaugurated a survey of the company's employees. In later years, Elmo Roper conducted regular employee opinion polls for Ford (Baird 1952; *Business Week* 1948; *Factory Management* 1947).

9. In the early 1950s, two-thirds of all surveys were conducted by outside consultants; this figure held steady through the early 1960s and has only recently begun to decline (Gorlin 1981; NICB 1964; Raube 1951).

10. A number of postwar studies found that union leaders were no better able than managers to predict employee responses to attitude surveys: both groups overemphasized pecuniary factors as determinants of employee morale. Researchers said that this resulted from a lack of "empathy" between leaders and workers and that it demonstrated the need for more attitude surveys and human relations training on both sides (Arthur 1950; Herzberg et al. 1957; Raube 1951).

11. Of the companies conducting attitude surveys, only a fifth shared all findings with their employees, usually in the form of a special report or booklet; 42 percent did not report any of this information to their nonsupervisory employees (Day 1949; Raube 1951).

12. See note 5.

13. On their own, the armed forces also conducted attitude surveys of their enlisted and civilian employees, as had been done during World War II (Elinson 1949; England 1952; Holdredge 1949).

14. Overzealous consultants were partly to blame for some of these misunderstandings. For example, in its advertisements for the Employee Inventory, SRA made the unsubstantiated claim that "high morale almost invariably means: high productivity, low absenteeism and turnover, confidence in management, [and] a harmonious and creative atmosphere" (Taylor 1959, 930).

15. Publishing trends were ascertained by counting citations in the *Business Periodicals Index* and the *Psychological Abstracts Index*.

REFERENCES

Abbott, Michael G., and Thonasis Stengos. 1986. Alternative estimates of union-nonunion and public-private wage differentials in Ontario, 1981. Working Paper 1987–4. Kingston, Ontario: Industrial Relations Centre, Queens University.

Allport, Gordon W. 1935. "Attitudes." In *A handbook of social psychology*, ed. Carl Murchison. Worcester, Mass.: Clark University Press.

Anderson, V.V. 1929. *Psychiatry in industry*. New York: Harper & Bros.

Arthur, Guy B., Jr. 1950. Employee opinion surveys that help management. *Personnel Journal* 29 (December): 261–65.

Baehr, Melanie E. 1953. A simplified procedure for the measurement of employee attitudes. *Journal of Applied Psychology* 37 (June): 163–67.

———. 1954. A factorial study of the SRA Employee Inventory. *Personnel Psychology* 7 (Autumn): 319–36.

Baird, D.G. 1952. What Ford gets from its employee opinion surveys. *Mill & Factory* 50 (January): 141–43.

Baker, Helen. 1944. *Employee counseling: A survey of a new development in personnel relations*. Princeton, N.J.: Industrial Relations Section, Princeton University.

Baritz, Loren. 1960. *The servants of power: A history of the use of social science in American industry*. Middletown, Conn.: Wesleyan University Press.

Barkin, Solomon. 1952. "Discussion." Conn.: In *Proceedings of the fourth annual meeting of the Industrial Relations Research Association, Boston, December 1948*. Champaign, Ill.: IRRA.

———. 1961. Psychology as seen by a trade unionist. *Personnel Psychology* 14 (Autumn): 259–70.

Bendix, Reinhard. 1956. *Work and authority in industry*. New York: John Wiley & Sons, Inc.

Benge, Eugene J. 1946. Morale survey improves management-employee relations. *Paper Industry and Paper World* 28 (November): 1141–43.

Bennett, George K. 1948. A new era in business and industrial psychology. *Personnel Psychology* 1 (Winter): 473–77.

Bergen, Harold B. 1939. Finding out what employees are thinking. *Management Record* 1 (April): 53–58.

———. 1942. Measuring attitudes and morale in wartime. *Management Record* 4 (April): 101–104.

Bingham, Walter V., and Bruce V. Moore. 1931. *How to interview*. New York: Macmillan Publishing Co., Inc.

BNA (Bureau of National Affairs). 1951. Is management listening? Personnel Policies Forum, no. 3. Washington, D.C.: BNA.

———. 1954. Evaluating a P–IR program. Personnel Policies Forum, no. 23. Washington, D.C.: BNA.

———. 1957. Employee job satisfaction. Personnel Policies Forum, no. 43. Washington, D.C.: BNA.

———. 1964. Upward communications. Personnel Policies Forum, no. 76. Washington, D.C.: BNA.

———. 1975. Employee communications. Personnel Policies Forum, no. 110. Washington, D.C.: BNA.

Bogardus, Emory S. 1924. Personal experiences and social research. *Journal of Applied Sociology* 8 (May): 294–303.

Boulware, L.R. 1948. How G.E. is trying to sell employees on giving full skill, care, and effort at work. *Printers' Ink* 225 (10 December): 76–77.

Brayfield, Arthur H., and Walter H. Crockett. 1955. Employee attitudes and employee performance. *Psychological Bulletin* 52 (September): 396–424.

Brown, Gerald. 1941. Job attitudes: Store employees. *Personnel Journal* 20 (September): 98–104.

Bulmer, Martin. 1981. Quantification and Chicago social science in the 1920s: A neglected tradition. *Journal of the History of the Behavioral Sciences* 17 (July): 312–31.

Burke, J.T. 1939. Sensing employee attitudes. In *Addresses on industrial relations: 1939*. Ann Arbor: Bureau of Industrial Relations, University of Michigan.

Burns, Robert K. 1952. Employee morale: Its meaning and measurement. In *Proceedings of the fourth annual meeting of the Industrial Relations Research Association, Boston, December 1951*. Champaign, Ill.: IRRA.

———. 1954. Attitude surveys and the diagnosis of organization needs. Personnel Series, no. 157. New York: American Management Association.

Business Week. 1948. Human engineering program pays off for Ford. (30 October): 88–95.

———. 1949. How do you feel? GM asks its workers. (31 December): 48–50.

———. 1953a. Inside a worker's head. (31 January): 81–82.

———. 1953b. Asking for labor criticism. (7 November): 167.

———. 1955. The worker's poll that kicked up a fuss. (19 February): 30–31.

———. 1956. Joining in attitude survey proves a move toward peace. (14 April): 57–60.

Campbell, Donald T. 1950. The indirect assessment of social attitudes. *Psychological Bulletin* 47: 15–38.

Campbell, James W. 1948. An attitude survey in a typical manufacturing firm. *Personnel Psychology* 1 (Spring): 31–39.

Canter, Ralph R., Jr. 1948. Psychologists in industry. *Personnel Psychology* 1 (Summer): 145–61.

Cantor, Nathaniel. 1945. *Employee counseling: A new viewpoint in industrial psychology*. New York: McGraw-Hill Book Co.

Carey, James F., Jr., et al. 1951. Reliability of ratings of employee satisfaction based on written interview methods. *Journal of Applied Psychology* 35 (August): 252–55.

Chant, S.N.F. 1932. Measuring the factors that make a job interesting. *Personnel Journal* 11 (June): 1–4.

Child, Irvin L. 1941. Morale: A bibliographical review. *Psychological Bulletin* 38 (June): 393–420.

Clarke, Ann V., and Donald L. Grant. 1961. Application of a factorial method in selecting questions from employee attitude surveys. *Personnel Psychology* 14 (Summer): 131–39.

Coch, L., and J.R.P. French. 1948. Overcoming resistance to change. *Human Relations* 1 (August): 512–32.

Cole, Remsen J. 1940. A survey of employee attitudes. *Public Opinion Quarterly* 4 (September): 487–506.

Converse, Jean M. 1984. Strong arguments and weak evidence: The open/closed questioning controversy of the 1940s. *Public Opinion Quarterly* 48 (Spring): 267–82.

———. 1985. Attitude measurement in psychology and sociology: The early years. In *Surveying subjective phenomena*, ed. Charles F. Turner and Elizabeth Martin. Vol. 1. New York: Russell Sage Press.

———. 1987. *Survey research in the United States: Roots and emergence, 1890–1960*. Berkeley: University of California Press.

Davis, Keith, and Edward E. St. Germain. 1951. An opinion survey of a regional union group. *Journal of Applied Psychology* 35 (December): 392–400.

Day, O.H. 1949. What do utility employees think of the company? *Public Utilities Fortnightly* 43 (26 May): 683–89.

Dickson, William J., and F.J. Roethlisberger. 1966. *Counseling in an organization: A sequel to the Hawthorne researches*. Boston: Harvard Graduate School of Business Administration.

Dunham, Randall B., and Frank J. Smith. 1979. *Organizational surveys: An internal assessment of organizational health*. Glenview, Ill.: Scott, Foresman & Co.

Dunnette, Marvin, and H.G. Heneman, Jr. 1956. Influence of scale administrator on employee attitude responses. *Journal of Applied Psychology* 40 (February): 73–78.

Edgerton, A.H. 1926. *Vocational guidance and counselling*. New York: Macmillan Publishing Co., Inc.

Elinson, Jack. 1949. Attitude research in the Army. *Journal of Applied Psychology* 33 (February): 1–5.

Employee Relations Bureau, National Retail Dry Goods Association. 1939. Your employee wants you to know him. *Personnel Journal* 17 (April): 357–63.

England, Arthur O. 1952. How we survey attitudes periodically. *Personnel Journal* 31 (November): 202–208.

England, George, Abraham K. Korman, and Carroll I. Stein. 1961. Overcoming contradictions in attitude surveys. *Personnel Administration* 24 (May): 36–40.

Evans, Chester E., and La Verne N. Laseau. 1950. *My job contest*. Washington, D.C.: Personnel Psychology.

Evans, J.J., Jr. 1941. Interchanging ideas between management and employees. Personnel Services, no. 46, 8–19. New York: American Management Association.

Factory Management and Maintenance. 1942. Invited workers to "let down their hair"—and they did. 100 (November): 110–11.

———. 1943. Poll of employees reveals confidence in management. 101 (October): 252–56.

———. 1946. Two way information flow pays off. 104 (May): 108–12.

———. 1947. Employee opinion survey aids Ford in policy making. 105 (June): 132–33.

———. 1948. How to find out what your workers think of you. 106 (August): 81–91.

Fleming, Donald. 1967. Attitude: The history of a concept. *Perspectives in American History* 1: 287–365.

Fortune. 1943. Polling the employees. 27 (February): 72–80.

Foulkes, Fred K. 1980. *Personnel policies in large nonunion companies*. Englewood Cliffs, N.J.: Prentice-Hall, Inc.

French, J.R.P., Jr., A. Kornhauser, and A. Marrow, eds. 1946. Conflict and cooperation in industry. *Journal of Social Issues* 2 (February): 1–56.

Friesen, Edward P. 1952. The incomplete sentence technique as a measure of employee attitudes. *Personnel Psychology* 5 (Winter): 329–45.

Fuller, S.E. 1944. Goodyear Aircraft employee counseling. *Personnel Journal* 23 (October): 145–53; 23 (November): 176–84.

Gardner, Burleigh B. 1985. Interview with author, 23 March.

Gordon, Gerald. 1952. Industrial psychiatry: Five year plant experience. *Industrial Medicine and Surgery* 21 (December): 585–88.

Gordon, Oakley J. 1955. A factor analysis of human needs and industrial morale. *Personnel Psychology* 8 (Spring): 1–18.

Gorlin, Harriet. 1981. Personnel practices III: Employee services, work rules. Conference Board Information Bulletin No. 95.

Gottlieb, Bertram, and Willard A. Kerr. 1950. An experiment in industrial harmony. *Personnel Psychology* 3 (Winter): 445–53.

Guion, Robert M. 1958. The problem of terminology. *Personnel Psychology* 11 (Spring): 59–64.

Habbe, Stephen. 1961. Following up attitude survey findings. Studies in Personnel Policy, no. 181. New York: National Industrial Conference Board.

Hamel, La Verne, and Hans G. Reif. 1952. Should attitude questionnaires be signed? *Personnel Psychology* 5 (Spring): 35–40.

Hamner, W. Clay, and Frank J. Smith. 1978. Work attitudes as predictors of unionization activity. *Journal of Applied Psychology* 63 (August): 415–21.

Harding, J. 1944. The measurement of civilian morale. In *Gauging public opinion*, ed. Hadley Cantril. Princeton, N.J.: Princeton University Press.

Haring, Albert. 1936. The evolution of marketing research technique. *National Marketing Review* 1 (Winter): 268–72.

Harris, Howell John. 1982. *The right to manage: Industrial relations policies of American business in the 1940s*. Madison: University of Wisconsin Press.

Hersey, Rexford B. 1932. *Workers' emotions in shop and home*. Philadelphia: University of Pennsylvania Press.

———. 1937. Employees rate plant policies. *Personnel Journal* 16 (September): 71–80.

Herzberg, Frederick, et al. 1957. *Job attitudes: Review of research and opinion*. Pittsburgh: Psychological Service of Pittsburgh.

Holdredge, Fred E., Jr. 1949. Implementing an employee opinion survey. *Journal of Applied Psychology* 33 (October): 428–35.

Hoppock, Robert. 1935. *Job satisfaction*. New York: Harper & Bros.

Houser, J. David. 1924. Letter to F.W. Taussig, 6 September. Wertheim Fellowship Papers. Harvard University Archives.

———. 1927. *What the employer thinks: Executives' attitudes toward employees*. Cambridge: Harvard University Press.

———. 1932. Measuring consumer attitudes. *Bulletin of the Taylor Society* 17 (April): 50–52.

———. 1938a. Measurement of the vital products of business. *Journal of Marketing* 2 (January): 181–89.

———. 1938b. *What people want from business*. New York: McGraw-Hill Book Co.

Hull, Richard L. 1939. Measuring employee attitudes: A proving ground for personnel policy and practices. *Management Record* 1 (November): 165–72.

Hull, Richard L., and Arthur Kolstad. 1942. Morale on the job. In *Civilian morale*, ed. Goodwin Watson. Boston: Houghton Mifflin.

Hurst, Peter F. 1948. This small plant made a morale survey. *Factory Management and Maintenance* 106 (May): 78–79.

Iron Age. 1944. Thompson employee survey points toward better labor relations. 154 (9 November): 108.

Irwin, James W. 1945. Sampling workers' opinions. *Dun's Review* 53 (November): 32–42.

Jelliffe, S.E. 1918. *The technique of psychoanalysis*. New York: Mental and Nervous Disease Publishing Co.

Jensen, Richard. 1980. Democracy by the numbers. *Public Opinion* 3 (March): 53–59.

Jones, Virginia. 1961. History of the employee morale survey program. Chicago: Sears, Roebuck National Personnel Department.

Kahn, Robert L. 1956. The prediction of productivity. *Journal of Social Issues* 12: 41–49.

Katz, Daniel. 1949a. Employee groups: What motivates them and how they perform. *Advanced Management* 14 (September): 119–24.

———. 1949b. The attitude survey approach. In *Psychology of Labor-Management Relations*, ed. A.W. Kornhauser. Champaign, Ill.: IRRA.

———. 1950. Good and bad practices in attitude surveys in industrial relations. In *Second annual proceedings of the Industrial Relations Research Association, New York, 1949*. Champaign, Ill.: IRRA.

———. 1951. Studies in social psychology in World War II. *Psychological Bulletin* 48 (November): 512–19.

Katz, Daniel, et al. 1951. *Productivity, supervision, and morale among railroad workers*. Ann Arbor: Institute for Social Research, University of Michigan.

Katz, Daniel, and Herbert Hyman. 1947a. Industrial morale and public opinion methods. *International Journal of Opinion and Attitude Research* 1 (September): 13–30.

———. 1947b. Morale in war industry. In *Readings in social psychology*, ed. Theodore Newcomb and Eugene L. Hartley. New York: Henry Holt.

Katz, Daniel, and Robert L. Kahn. 1952. *Some recent findings in human relations research*. Ann Arbor: University of Michigan, Survey Research Center.

Katzell, Raymond. 1958. Measurement of morale. *Personnel Psychology* 11 (Spring): 71–78.

Kiesler, C.A., B.E. Collins, and N. Miller. 1969. *Attitude change: A critical analysis of theoretical approaches*. New York: John Wiley & Sons, Inc.

Kirchner, Wayne K., and Walter Uphoff. 1955. The effect of grouping scale items in union-attitude measurement. *Journal of Applied Psychology* 39 (June): 182–83.

Kochan, Thomas A., and Peter Capelli. 1984. The transformation of the industrial relations and personnel function. In *Internal Labor Markets*, ed. Paul Osterman. Cambridge: MIT Press.

Kolstad, Arthur. 1938. Employee attitudes in a department store. *Journal of Applied Psychology* 22 (October): 470–79.

Kornhauser, Arthur W. 1933. The technique of measuring employee attitudes. *Personnel* 9 (May): 99–107.

———. 1944. Psychological studies of employee attitudes. *Journal of Consulting Psychology* 8 (May): 127–43.

———. 1947. Are public opinion polls fair to organized labor? *Public Opinion Quarterly* 10 (Winter): 484–500.

———. 1949. The contribution of psychology to industrial relations research. In *First proceedings of the Industrial Relations Research Association, Cleveland, 1948*. Champaign, Ill.: IRRA.

———. 1961. Observations on the psychological study of labor-management relations. *Personnel Psychology* 14 (Autumn): 241–49.

Kornhauser, Arthur W., and Agnes A. Sharp. 1932. Employee attitudes: Suggestions from a study in a factory. *Personnel Journal* 10 (April): 393–404.

Laitin, Yale J. 1961. How to make employee attitude surveys pay off. *Personnel* 38 (July): 23–33.

Landsberger, Henry A. 1958. *Hawthorne revisited*. Ithaca, N.Y.: Cornell University Press.

Lasswell, Harold D. 1930. *Psychopathology and politics*. New York: Viking Press.

Lazarsfeld, Paul F., ed. 1931. *Jugend und Beruf: Kritik und Material*. Jena: G. Fischer.

Lazarsfeld, Paul F. 1934. The psychological aspect of market research. *Harvard Business Review* 13 (October): 54–71.

———. 1935. The art of asking why in marketing research. *National Marketing Review* 1 (Summer): 26–38.

———. 1937. The use of detailed interviews in market research. *Journal of Marketing* 2 (July): 3–8.

———. 1940. *Radio and the printed page*. New York: Duell, Sloan, and Pearce.

Lewin, Kurt. 1948. *Resolving social conflicts*. New York: Harper.

Likert, Rensis A. 1932. A technique for the measurement of attitudes. *Archives of Psychology* 22: 1–55.

———. 1947. The effects of strategic bombing on German morale. Morale Division, U.S. Strategic Bombing Survey. Washington, D.C.: U.S. Government Printing Office.

———. 1953. Motivation: The core of management. Personnel series, no. 155, 3–21. New York: American Management Association.

Likert, Rensis A., and Daniel Katz. 1948. Supervisory practices and organization structures as they affect employee productivity and morale. Personnel Series, no. 120, 14–24. New York: American Management Association.

Likert, Rensis A., and Ronald Lippitt. 1953. The utilization of social science. In *Research methods in the behavioral sciences*, ed. Leon Festinger and Daniel Katz. New York: Dryden Press.

Likert, Rensis A., and Joseph M. Willits. 1940. *Morale and agency management*. 4 vols. Hartford: Life Insurance Sales Research Bureau.

Lockley, Lawrence C. 1950. Notes on the history of marketing research. *Journal of Marketing* 14 (April): 733–36.

McMurry, Robert N. 1946. Management's reaction to employee opinion polls. *Journal of Applied Psychology* 30 (April): 212–19.

McNemar, Quinn. 1946. Opinion-attitude methodology. *Psychological Bulletin* 43 (July): 289–374.

Madge, John. 1962. *The origins of scientific sociology*. New York: Free Press.

Mann, Floyd C. 1957. Studying and creating change: A means to understanding social organization. In *Research in industrial human relations*, ed. C.M. Arensberg. New York: Harper.

Mann, Floyd C., and Rensis Likert. 1952. The need for research on the communication of research results. *Human Organization* 11 (Winter): 15–19.

Mansfield, Edwin. 1961. Technical change and the rate of imitation. *Econometrics* 29 (October): 741–66.

Marquis, Donald G. 1944. Social psychologists in national war agencies. *Psychological Bulletin* 41 (February): 115–26.

Mason, Ralph L. 1949. Experiences with employee opinion surveys. *Advanced Management* 14 (September): 98–100.

Mayo, Elton. 1933. *The human problems of an industrial civilization*. New York: Macmillan Publishing Co., Inc.

Mill & Factory. 1948. Employees tell why they like their jobs. 42 (February): 102–104.

Minaker, F.C. 1953. How employee opinion poll aids company communications. *American Business* 23 (October): 26–30.

Moore, David G. 1985. Letter to author, 25 April.

Moore, David G., and Robert K. Burns. 1956. How good is good morale? *Factory Management and Maintenance* 114 (February): 130–36.

Moore, David G., and Burleigh B. Gardner. 1946. Factors related to morale. Reprint. Jones, Virginia. 1961. History of the employee morale survey program. Chicago: Sears, Roebuck National Personnel Department.

Moore, Herbert. 1941. Employee attitude surveys. *Personnel Journal* 19 (April): 360–63.

Murphy, Gardner, and Rensis Likert. 1938. *Public opinion and the individual*. New York: Harper & Bros.

Nadler, David A. 1977. *Feedback and organization development: Using data-based methods*. Reading, Mass.: Addison-Wesley Publishing Co., Inc.

NICB (National Industrial Conference Board). 1964. Personnel practices in factory and office—Manufacturing. Studies in Personnel Policy, no. 194. New York: NICB.

New York Stock Exchange, Office of Economic Research. 1982. *People and productivity: A challenge to corporate America*. New York: NYSE.

Noble, David F. 1977. *America by design: Science, technology, and the rise of corporate capitalism*. New York: Alfred A. Knopf., Inc.

Personnel Journal. 1938. A review of how to learn worker attitudes. 16 (January): 258–64.

Putnam, M.L. 1930. Improving employee relations: A plan which uses data obtained from employees. *Personnel Journal* 8 (February): 314–25.

Radcliffe-Brown, A.R. 1922. *The Andaman Islanders*. Cambridge: Cambridge University Press.

Raube, S. Avery. 1947. Personnel activities in American business. Studies in Personnel Policy, no. 86. New York: National Industrial Conference Board.

———. 1951. Experience with employee attitude surveys. Studies in Personnel Policy, no. 115. New York: National Conference Board.

Research Institute of America. 1949. *Employee motivation*. New York: RIA.

Roethlisberger, F.J., and William J. Dickson. 1939. *Management and the worker*. Cambridge: Harvard University Press.

Rose, A.M. 1952. *Union solidarity*. Minneapolis: University of Minnesota Press.

Rosen, R.A. Hudson, and Hjalmar Rosen. 1955. A suggested modification in job satisfaction surveys. *Personnel Psychology* 8 (Autumn): 303–14.

Rush, Harold M.F. 1969. *Behavioral science: Concepts and applications*. New York: The Conference Board.

———. 1973. *Organization development: A reconnaissance*. New York: The Conference Board.

Schwab, Robert E. 1953. Motivation and human relations principles. Personnel Series, no. 155, 30–39. New York: American Management Association.

Seltiz, Claire, et al. 1959. *Research methods in social relations*. New York: Holt.

Sherman, V. Clayton. 1969. Unionism and the nonunion company. *Personnel Journal* 48 (June): 413–22.

Skott, Hans. 1943. Attitude research in the Department of Agriculture. *Public Opinion Quarterly* 7 (Summer): 280–92.

Slichter, Sumner H. 1929. The current labor policies of American industries. *Quarterly Journal of Economics* 43 (May): 393–435.

Smith, Frank J. 1985. Interview with author, 20 March.

Smith, McGregor. 1942. Mending our weakest links. *Advanced Management* 7 (April): 77–83.

Smith, R.G., and R.J. Westen. 1951. *Studies of morale methodology and criteria*. Research Bulletin 51–29. San Antonio: U.S. Air Force Air Training Command, Human Resources Research Center.

Stagner, Ross, et al. 1954. Dual allegiance to union and management: A symposium. *Personnel Psychology* 7 (Spring): 41–80.

Stock, J. Stevens, and Harriet Lubin. 1946. Indices of personnel management. *Personnel* 23 (July): 6–16.

Stouffer, Samuel A., and Leland C. DeVinney. 1949. *The American soldier*. 2 vols. Princeton, N.J.: Princeton University Press.

Strong, Edward K., Jr. 1938. *Psychological aspects of business*. New York: McGraw-Hill Book Co.

Taylor, Edwin K. 1959. SRA Employee Inventory. In *The fifth mental measurement yearbook*, ed. Oscar K. Buros. Highland Park, N.J.: Gryphon Press.

Tead, Ordway. 1943. Employee counseling: A new personnel assignment—Its status and its standards. *Advanced Management* 8 (July): 97–103.

Thomas, William I., and Florian Znaniecki. 1918. *The Polish peasant in Europe and America*. 2 vols. Chicago: University of Chicago Press.

Thomson, Andrew, and Malcolm Warner. 1981. *The behavioral sciences and industrial relations*. Aldershot, United Kingdom: Gower.

Thurstone, L.L. 1928. Attitudes can be measured. *American Journal of Sociology* 33 (January): 529–54.

———. 1935. *Vectors of mind: Multiple factor analysis for the isolation of primary traits*. Chicago: University of Chicago Press.

Tiffin, Joseph. 1958. How psychologists serve industry. *Personnel Journal* 36 (March): 372–76.

Uhrbrock, Richard S. 1934. Attitudes of 4430 employees. *Journal of Social Psychology* 5 (August): 365–77.

Verma, Anil. 1983. Union and nonunion industrial relations systems at the plant level. Ph.D. diss. MIT.

Verma, Anil, and Thomas A. Kochan. 1985. The growth and nature of the nonunion sector within a firm. In *Challenges and choices facing American labor*, ed. Thomas A. Kochan. Cambridge: MIT Press.

Viteles, Morris S. 1945. Wartime applications of psychology: Their value to industry. Personnel Series, no. 93, 3–12. New York: American Management Association.

———. 1953. *Motivation and morale in industry*. New York: W.W. Norton & Co., Inc.

Watson, Goodwin. 1940. Work satisfaction. In *Industrial conflict: A psychological interpretation*, ed. George W. Hartmann and Theodore Newcomb. New York: Cordon.

Webb, Eugene, et al. 1966. *Unobtrusive measures: Nonreactive research in the social sciences*. Chicago: Rand-McNally.

Weddell, Carl, and Karl U. Smith. 1951. Consistency of interview methods in appraisal of attitudes. *Journal of Applied Psychology* 35 (December): 392–400.

Wheeler, Ferdinand C. 1935. New methods and results in market research. *American Marketing Journal* 2 (April): 35–39.

Wherry, Robert J. 1954. An orthogonal rerotation of the Baehr and Ash studies of the SRA Employee Inventory. *Personnel Psychology* 7 (Autumn): 365–80.

White, Leonard D. 1924. Methods used in a study of morale in the municipal employment of Chicago. *Journal of Personnel Research* 4 (June): 215–21.

White, Percival. 1931. *Marketing research technique*. New York: Harper & Bros.

Whyte, William H., Jr. 1952. *Is anybody listening?* New York: Simon & Schuster.

Wilensky, Harold L. 1957. Human relations in the workplace: An appraisal of some recent research. In *Research in industrial human relations*, ed. C.M. Arensberg. New York: Harper.

Wilensky, Jeanne L., and Harold L. Wilensky. 1951. Personnel counseling: The Hawthorne Case. *American Journal of Sociology* 57 (November): 265–80.

Xishan, Yang, et al. 1983. Behavioral science applications in Vancouver based firms. *Relations Industrielles* 38: 120–39.

Yoder, Dale, Herbert G. Heneman, Jr., and Earl F. Cheit. 1951. *Triple audit of industrial relations*. Bulletin 11. Minneapolis: University of Minnesota Industrial Relations Center.

Norman Metzger

Achieving Excellence: A Challenge To Change One's Management Style

12

You, as a supervisor, must accept the fact that by improved managerial practices and attention to the proper utilization of people and technology, you can increase the satisfaction and productivity of the people who work for you. This is made clear by much of the theory and research on organizational motivation, satisfaction, and productivity. Such research indicates that people bring to the work area different mental and physical abilities. Supervisors must deal with varying personalities and varying levels of experience.

Need fulfillment and frustration produce constructive behavior and defensive behavior, respectively. How often have you noted tensions in employees who seem to be dissatisfied with their work? Such dissatisfaction produces behavior designed to relieve that tension. Employees whose needs are not met become defensive; they employ defense mechanisms, such as withdrawal, aggression, substitution, or compensation. You must have seen employees who do very little talking; they seem withdrawn, and you have great difficulty in communicating with them. Other dissatisfied employees channel their frustration into constructive behavior by looking outside the work area for fulfillment; they join clubs, teams, or unions. Defensive behavior may work against the goals of the department and the institution. Dissatisfaction on the job exacts a high cost. It produces friction on the job, low productivity, high absenteeism, excessive turnover, and, of course, strikes. Many employees seek more satisfaction from their work than is available to them under present managerial structures. There is little question that employee motivation results in increased productivity and higher efficiency. Such motivation can be enhanced by a supervisory style that encompasses the knowledge and appreciation of employee motives.

A relationship between a supervisor and workers that includes mutual understanding and agreement on goals and rewards is an ideally effective one. Supervisors are responsible for getting results from their work team. Therefore, they must demand such results; however, demanding results does not necessarily guarantee results. Supervisors must be willing to move from authority-obedience styles of supervision to involvement-participation-commitment styles. More and more evidence has been produced to indicate that the old authority-obedience approach is not result oriented. Yet the involvement-participation-commitment style of supervision is difficult and complex. The new approach involves reaching consensus on what the real problem to be solved is in any given case; listening for reservations and doubts, rather than for signs of compliance; encouraging people to express their diverse views; and dealing with conflicts in an open and candid way.[1]

Research and experience clearly indicate that a supervisor is indeed able to meet the needs of employees and thereby make them more productive. Although there is no one sure way to make employees more efficient, there is a central theme that weaves through the mass of research and literature on this subject. This central theme, which found its way through the works of Herzberg, McGregor, and Mayo and which was emblazoned in the singular study *Work in America*, points an accusing finger at the typical organization. Employees who start a new job bring with them a caring attitude and a high level of motivation. The subsequent lack of productivity and efficiency is usually caused by the organization, which by its inherent noncaring style destroys an employee's natural desire to care about work and to do it well.

It falls then to the supervisor to restructure the work situation for the employee. This restructuring includes an objective review of work content with an eye toward enriching, redesigning, and broadening responsibilities. This is necessary because worker motivation derives from the task itself. In addition to the challenge of improving the job, attention must be directed toward improving the environment. Recognition is necessary at every level of the organization. Communication is just as important to the porter as it is to the surgeon. Everyone wants to be in on things. Employees want to know what the supervisor is thinking and what management is thinking and planning. They want to feel that management knows that they are there—that they are not invisible. Alienation and frustration will develop if employees feel nobody is listening or paying attention to their needs. The wise supervisor who directs his or her attention toward maximizing opportunities for effective work teams will keep these conclusions in mind and not be confused by long-ingrained beliefs and myths that are counterproductive to getting the job done.

Successful managers display leadership traits such as the following:

- They are willing to take risks. Those who play it safe—and there are legions of such managers in health care—may survive in the organization. But who will know that they are there?
- They are decision makers. This means they understand the need to make decisions even if they are unpopular. Decisiveness is a trait found in most successful leaders. Decisiveness and persistence are the hallmarks of those who move ahead in management. Passing the buck may well permit you to survive. But who will follow you?
- They have a deep concern for the human aspects of management. Such managers believe that caring counts. It has been proved time and time again that employees will follow you to the ends of the earth if they feel that you care about them as human beings. Caring does pay off.
- They are always sensitive to protect the dignity of others. Shorris said, "A manager who knows that his subordinates are his equals becomes the equal of his superiors."[2] The manager who moves ahead, who is effective, who has the most productive work team is the one who is constantly sensitive to the need for protecting the dignity of subordinates and, indeed, gets in return the protection of his or her own dignity. Support your people and they will support you; respect your people and they will respect you.
- These managers have a "high touch" style of management. They are not reluctant to share credit and give rewards. There is an old Oriental adage that says, "If you wish your merit to be known, acknowledge that of other people." They are the ones Blanchard and Johnson are referring to when they suggest "Catch someone doing something right."[3]

- They are willing to accept mistakes. To err is human; to admit that you make mistakes at times seems superhuman. People appreciate honesty. The "blame-throwers" of the world develop alienated workers.
- They view development of subordinates as a priority responsibility. Effective supervision is based on the belief that people are by nature neither passive nor resistant to organizational needs. It is the manager's responsibility to enable the employees to fulfill their own needs and goals, as well as the organization's needs and goals. The successful manager treats employees as resources that, if cultivated, will yield economic returns to the institution.

> What we all once thought of as "authority" is undergoing significant changes in our society. We are moving away from authority based strictly on power and status to authority based on knowledge and ability. Authority is granted by constituents to their leaders only so long as these leaders satisfy the needs and standards of the governed. This startling change applies equally to managerial authority.[4]

NEW EMPLOYEES: NEW CHALLENGES FOR MANAGERS

It is time to take inventory. We are not dealing with the same employees with whom we have dealt in the past, though some of them have been around for a while. Perceptions and needs have changed within the American work force. Let us look at the new breed of employee.

A survey was conducted recently to answer this critical question: "Do employees feel that they make a difference where they work?"[5] The major survey finding is that a manager or supervisor who has a relaxed style and who invites employee participation in decision making is more likely to have employees with a high level of organizational self-esteem than a more "traditional" manager is. The managers whose employees have higher self-esteem show an interest in each employee's contribution, status, and well-being; show an interest in each employee's personal situation; and offer employees variety, a degree of autonomy, significant work experience, and a chance to use valued skills. A most important finding is that the extent to which an employee is permitted participation in departmental decision making is related to the employee's level of organizational self-esteem. Both experiencing meaningfulness of work and experiencing responsibility for work outcome show significant correlation with organizational self-esteem. Employees who could trust both their supervisor and the management of their organization in general had higher levels of self-esteem than did those employees who found themselves working with supervisors and/or management that they could not trust. Faith in the employee's capacity to direct him- or herself was related; so was a show of satisfaction in the employee.

Research conducted on the effective management of people indicates the following trends:

- Each employee group is less optimistic about its chances for advancement.
- Feelings of security, though still high, are beginning to deteriorate.
- Employees still like their jobs, and most still find their employers credible, but there is evidence of a growing malaise, a gradual but persistent loss of optimism.[6]

Further findings indicate work values, notably loyalty and commitment, are in decline because employees no longer feel that their employers are loyal and committed to them. The net effect is diminished commitment at all levels of the organization and even in some firms that are performing well.

THE NEW WORK FORCE

Many observers believe that there is a growing mismatch between the characteristics and aspirations of the work force and the ability of the work place, as it is now constituted, to satisfy these new expectations. Kanter states that

> Promotion opportunities (one of the major sources of increase in pay, challenge and influence in a large corporation) were thought to be declining. Increased competition from a large number of aspirants, an aging workforce postponing retirement, and a slower growth economy prevented the organizational pyramid from expanding to accommodate all those seeking the ''better'' jobs.[7]

The new work force is comprised of employees who expect a greater voice in decisions at work and who want opportunities beyond those contained in their present jobs. They are more educated and, therefore, less fulfilled. More educated employees invariably come with elevated hopes of more attractive jobs, higher earnings, and greater opportunities for career advancement. This may well set the stage for worker disillusionment and discontent because in many instances, unfortunately, opportunities lag behind such expectations. Levitan and Johnson tell us that

> Job satisfaction surveys have identified the combination of longer schooling and low pay as one of the most potent formulas for dissatisfaction in the workplace, reflecting the belief that education credentials implicitly promise or guarantee future success. In sending them to school for longer stints, we prepare a veritable ''powderkeg'' of expectations among new entrants to the labor force, who by virtue of youth and inexperience are most likely to suffer from the inadequacies of the labor market.[8]

The legitimacy of traditional systems is eroding, and foremost among the challenges to the traditional bureaucracy are the changing pay-for-performance systems, which reflect the new work ethic. Our employees expect greater meaning from their work and, indeed, want to feel that they make a difference. This feeling comes from a desire to innovate.[9] Innovation cannot take place in an organization that stifles employees' ability to contribute. This ability to contribute requires an atmosphere where risk taking is not only permissible but also encouraged. Peterfruend believes that hardly an organization exists today in which climate, culture, or management systems support and motivate risk taking below the executive level. He states, ''The amount of risk individuals dare to take is adversely conditioned in most organizations by the belief (strongly entrenched as a result of past experience) that the rewards for successful risk-taking are *far* outweighed by the penalties for failure.'' An organization that is innovative provides the wherewithal for its employees, at all levels, to take risks. Such risks are taken if employees believe that the rewards for success are in proper balance with the penalties for failure.[10] Inherent then in such an organization is the ability to share in the successes of the organization. Equally as important is the diminishing of fear—the fear of both ostracism and failure. There is a pervasive fear of criticism that employees evidence in traditional organizations. This stifles suggestions, contributions, and commitment. An employee must feel that there is freedom to make mistakes—to make ''silly'' suggestions—and, finally, to participate in problem solving and decision making as a *partner*, and not as a *junior* partner.

It is time to turn our backs on the myth that only top management is omniscient—that the only ideas worthwhile to the organization can come from those presently in power. Ideas worth considering and implementing *can* come from people at all levels in the organization—professional, nonprofessional, high up in the hierarchy, low down in the hierarchy. Therefore, it is your responsibility to encourage employees to be innovative and to contribute. Through such innovation and contribution we can maximize employee commitment and thereby ensure the excellence of the organization.

Brown and Weiner point out that today's young workers are immersed in a legacy of the late 1960s.[11] Five overriding factors have emerged since that period:

1. the introduction of two-wage-earner households
2. a broadened social awareness and search for ''meaning''
3. the explosive growth of the service economy
4. the economic, demographic, and technological challenge to middle management positions
5. the reality of being forced to live in a time of rapid change and future uncertainty

WORKER ALIENATION

One of the results of these changing times is worker alienation. It is easy to recognize the symptoms of such alienation: low productivity, high absenteeism, lateness, and confrontational relationships. The key to understanding such alienation is the realization that an alienated worker believes that his or her behavior cannot determine the outcome of what he or she seeks.[12] Dickinson, referring to a Harris survey,[13] shows the index of alienation of workers rising perceptibly in the 1970s. Of the individuals surveyed, 64 percent answered affirmatively to this statement: "Most people with power try to take advantage of people like yourself." Also, 59 percent agreed with this statement: "What you think does not count very much anymore."[14] An alienated worker does not believe that his or her work can give that worker fulfillment and meaning. Ruch and Goodman tell us that fulfillment and meaningful work experiences are characterized by four components:

1. *Knowledge*: Employees want to know what's going on in the company and why certain actions are taken.
2. *Care*: Employees want to know that management cares about what they are doing, and they themselves want to care about what they are doing.
3. *Respect*: Such respect derives from one's humanity. Indeed, it is the respect for people's humanness that makes people feel fulfilled at the job.
4. *Responsibility*: People want to have a feeling that they are responsible for *something*; they want to be accountable.[15]

These four factors, K.C.R.R., are at the heart of combating alienation; they are the ingredients of fulfilling and meaningful work.

To deal with worker alienation, you must communicate more openly and more frequently. The new breed of employee has an enormous appetite for information. We can no longer be gatekeepers of such information; rather, we must be expediters. We must let them know what is going on; let them know how they will be affected by changes in the organization; let them share in our plans; and, indeed, let them share in the planning. People want to feel "in" on things. It is essential that you facilitate that process.

Being knowledgeable also means being equipped to face changing requirements. The new employee wants to grow, to improve skills, and to take on additional responsibilities. That again is your challenge. No matter how many times you have heard the expression "Caring counts," it is not a cliché but a truism. The art of management is being reshaped. Old myths must be discarded. The key element of leadership is a genuine interest in people. Good people relations produce good patient care. If employees believe that we truly value their ideas, that we will consider their suggestions objectively, and that they can be free to voice their concerns to us, then, and only then, will we have employees who are committed to the goals of the organization. Caring means that you have a primary concern for the human aspect of management, that you have as much respect for human capital as for economic capital, and that you have a belief in basic values: dignity, human fallibility, and human needs. Bettelheim made this profound observation: "If we hope to live not just from moment-to-moment but in true

consciousness of our existence, then our greatest need and most difficult achievement is to find meaning in our lives."[16]

It is your responsibility to make such meaning appear from the redesign of workers' responsibilities. Workers respond best and, indeed, more creatively not when they are tightly controlled by management, placed in narrowly defined jobs, and treated like an unwelcome necessity, but rather when they are given broader responsibilities, encouraged to contribute, and helped to take satisfaction in their work.[17]

TRADITIONAL VERSUS CONTEMPORARY VALUES

As a supervisor and manager, you will be exposed to a variety of employee values. Employees, in general, can be categorized as those with traditional values and those with contemporary values. Those with traditional values are usually best supervised by managers who express a high locus of control, high self-esteem, low tolerance for ambiguity, low social judgment, and low risk taking.[18] Such managers believe that advancement depends on achievement and that they have a great deal of control over subordinates' behavior. They also place high priority on employee feedback; work best in structured, unambiguous situations; tend not to let personal feelings interfere with work; and are stable and cautious. On the other hand, many of your employees are those with contemporary values and are best supervised by supervisors with a high tolerance for ambiguity (i.e., the ability to function well in unstructured, ambiguous situations), high social judgment (i.e., sensitivity and good interpersonal relationships), and high risk taking (i.e., the valuing of change and excitement above the status quo).

Knowing whether your employees' values are contemporary or traditional is very important. Knowing your own value system is equally as important, whether such values are traditional or contemporary. More and more evidence indicates that the personal qualities most admired in the work place are responsibility and honesty. This has not changed very much, although the composition of the work force has. Just a generation ago the typical worker was a man working full time to provide complete support for his wife and children. Now more than two out of five mothers of children aged six or younger work for pay. More and more members of the work force have college degrees, and we can expect these educational trends to continue. Such increases in the educational level of workers will have a serious impact on the work force and on the work place. The challenge will be to utilize such education because surveys continue to show that over one-half of all college graduates feel underutilized in their jobs, compared to only one-third of non–college graduates. The members of this more educated work force are looking for better jobs. They expect more equal treatment, and they expect to be listened to, regardless of their job categories. They are less likely to accept differences in privilege and status.[19]

As the work force changes, representing growth in the number of women employed and the number of workers who will be in the "prime age" years, we must reassess some of the old approaches to employee policies and supervisory techniques. Because the number of workers with children is increasing in the work force, flexible work schedules should be considered. Innovative work schedules, including flexible hours, part-time employment, and job sharing are likely to involve more than half of the American work force by the beginning of the 1990s. At the beginning of this decade, a report by Work in America Institute concluded that changes in society and the composition of the work force, particularly the sharp increase in the number of working mothers, are providing an "irresistible force propelling employees in the direction of further experimentation with new work schedules." It states that the new work schedules "go beyond the employees' freedom to balance competing demands of work, family, and personal life. There are rewards for employees in increased productivity; for unions in fewer layoffs of members; and for the general public in less traffic congestion, energy consumption and air pollution." That study found that the single most important obstacle to flexible scheduling is "the autocratic tradition of supervision," developed by custom and practice under the theory that rigid work schedules are essential to efficiency.[20]

THE WORK ETHIC: DEAD OR ALIVE

There is a great fear that Americans have or will abandon work, that people are less committed to the work ethic. People do work for different reasons, but most truly want to work. Labor force data suggest that increased proportions of Americans are working more, not less, and opting for leisure only when that step is consistent with the continuing identification of established work rules.[21]

We are inundated with statistics on falling productivity levels, which are challenged by other statistics that indicate the contrary. Siegel has a clearer vision of the "true facts."

> Whatever the "true facts" about the nation's productivity performance since the mid-1960s, and whatever the merit of anecdotal and other evidence and surmises regarding the flabbiness of "the work ethic" it is more important to stress the improvability of both. It is also necessary to repeat that management, public as well as private, has ample scope and unavoidable responsibilities for upgrading both. Management has to recognize and respond strongly to the challenge and interest of maintaining customary living standards and maintaining competitiveness of American products in domestic and foreign markets.[22]

That, indeed, is the challenge. We can spend our idle hours bemoaning the loss of the work ethic. However, continuing improvement is possible. Job commitment is necessary for such improvement; job commitment flows from understanding the needs of the new breed of employee. It requires restructuring our present organizations, changing hierarchical relationships, and moving from organizations that may be anchored in authority-obedience management styles and propelled by paper rather than by people to organizations that are based on involvement, participation, and commitment. Self-reliant, trusting, and decisive managers are able to develop self-reliant and efficient subordinates, even if the work ethic has changed.

Many new employees do express a cynical view of work. Yankelovich had documented that an overwhelming 84 percent of all Americans feel a certain resentment and belief that those who work harder and live by the rules end up on the short end of the stick.[23] Yes, our employees are less content and less likely to be trustful of management's intentions. But the response has to be a broadening concern with aspects of people's lives, a broadening attempt to include employees in the deliberations on how to provide the services of the institution and how to satisfy their own needs. Indifference and frustration result from employees' being excluded from the planning function and being overlooked in the communication network. You can change the organizational climate to a more positive direction if

- your employees feel that they can solve problems and that you will help them to do so
- you help your employees develop a sense of independence and trust your employees' judgments
- you encourage your employees to take increased responsibility

You do this by helping your employees see that their rewards and recognition outweigh threats and criticism and that there is a promotion system that will enable them to move onward and upward and, most importantly, by ensuring that rewards are related to excellence of performance.

HOW TO DEAL WITH THE NEW BREED OF EMPLOYEES

- We are moving away from authority based strictly on power and status to authority based on knowledge and ability.
- A manager or supervisor who has a relaxed style and who invites employee participation in decision making is more likely to have employees with a high level of organizational self-esteem.
- The new work force is made up of employees who expect a greater voice in decisions at work and who want opportunities beyond those contained in their present jobs. It is up to you to meet those needs.
- Our employees expect greater meaning from their work and want to feel that they make a difference; this feeling comes from a desire to innovate. Innovation cannot take

place in an organization that stifles an employee's ability to contribute.

- The work place is full of employees with good ideas. Ideas worth considering and implementing *can* come from people at all levels of the organization.

- Many of our employees are alienated; to deal with worker alienation, you must communicate more openly and more frequently.

- The new employees respond best and most creatively when you give them broader responsibilities, encourage them to contribute, and help them to take satisfaction in their work.

- If you believe that the work ethic has deteriorated, it is important that you understand that it can be improved.

- Even if the work ethic has changed, self-reliant, trusting, and decisive managers are able to develop self-reliant and efficient subordinates.

- Involve your employees in goal setting, and assist them in recognizing that the goals of the organization and their own goals are not mutually exclusive.

- To meet their changing needs, help employees develop a sense of independence, and encourage them to take increased responsibilities.

THE NEW MANAGEMENT CREDO: THE ROAD TO EXCELLENCE

Caring about people is the backbone of organizational strength and success. The new management credo includes the broadening concern with aspects of people's lives, both individually and collectively, which, unfortunately, received little attention in the past. The thousands of health care employees who have been little, but invisible people are demanding attention. They want their contributions appreciated, and they want an end to the alienated feeling that results when they have no stake in the outcome. The modern supervisor and manager must lead the drive to make positive changes in the organizational climate. He or she looks for common ground, is not easily angered, feels positive about him- or herself, encourages boat rockers, and is a truth teller.

In many of our organizations there is a strong immediate pressure on the individual to conform. The typical health care hierarchical structure has as its role model a doctor, a financial expert, or a strategic planner, all of whom are often so preoccupied with their own expertise that all other concerns—e.g., interpersonal relationships—are at best secondary. We often find a troubling adversarial relationship between groups in an institution; goal definition and agreement receive little or no attention. Too often decision making is protected by the chosen few, and control is unshared. Hayes, in discussing the utility of industrial democracy, states

> This movement towards greater participation of employees in the decisions that affect their everyday work lives—

not the politically-oriented power thrust of some movements toward "industrial democracy"—seems to reflect the desire of free men to have greater control over their own lives. To the extent that this occurs, and to the extent that free men commit themselves to the goals of the organization because of their participation in its decisions, we are likely to have organizations of spirited, vivacious people who are working together to accomplish their common goals—not bossed, not "hired" but free committed men.[24]

Such outcomes require a new management style within a new management organization. Kanter tells us

> In short, while workplace reform has the potential to fulfill many of the expectations of the new workforce, it also points to more fundamental problems in the design of organizations. The ideal-typical twentieth century bureaucracy could be showing cracks and strains, tension and contradictions which point to the need for a new concept of the corporation.[25]

These cracks and strains call out for organizational restructuring. What is necessary is to change the culture of the organization. Many researchers and observers believe that we must transform individuals—who selfishly have been assigned limited tasks and have worked with neither the drive for interdependence nor the awareness of how jobs interrelate within the entire organization—into groups of employees who perforce have a broader understanding of commitment to the total enterprise.[26] It is clear that the new employees expect greater meaning in their work, a feeling of making a difference. A fear of insignificance is pervasive in our large institutions. Kanter warns us

> This new workplace involves opportunities for greater employee initiative, for entrepreneurial effort, and for greater participation in problem-solving. However, this new workplace cannot exist easily in the conventional command-and-control hierarchy of status and authority relations that have been the dominant organizational form in the twentieth century.[27]

There is a need to reshape organizations that are built around an environment with policies that control and implement freedom for all but a few. Drucker states

> Far too few of today's managers realize that management is defined by responsibility and not by power. Far too few fight the debilitating disease of bureaucracy: the belief that big budgets and a huge staff are accomplishments rather than incompetence.[28]

The successful supervisor and manager is so defined not because of the power that he or she harnesses but rather because of the accomplishments of the work force that he or she manages. It is time to empower others. The work arena has too long defined success by a selfish accumulation of power.

Sharing power does not mean abdicating responsibility. On the contrary, the most responsible act a manager can take is to broaden the base of decision making and problem solving. If we encourage democratic collaboration, it is likely that our employees who are involved in that process will help us sharpen and refine ideas. If we listen to what others have to say and offer, we may change our own positions. Contrary to a common myth, tasks performed cooperatively rather than competitively are accomplished more efficiently, and the participants have a higher degree of motivation and morale. When an employee believes it is his or her idea or suggestion that we are implementing, he or she is more likely to make it work. It, therefore, should be clear that the hallmark of the restructured organization is a pervasive willingness to share power.

It is equally clear that the successful health care organization of the future will be less bureaucratic with fewer managerial levels. Less is better when it comes to the hierarchical structure. In building such a thin managerial structure, attention must be paid to encouraging subordinates to feel free to tell the truth, free to make suggestions, and free to participate in problem solving and decision making. Research studies continue to indicate a strong desire on the part of employees to be involved in their jobs. The new management credo insists on the sharing of managerial prerogatives with line supervisors and workers on a systematic institutional basis. There is a need to revamp the workplace.

THE NEW MANAGEMENT CREDO: CHALLENGE TO HEALTH CARE SUPERVISORS

The singular challenge is presented to you to create some of the basic conditions of human community that are absent from many of our health care institutions—that is, to provide work experiences that make people feel that "they make a difference." This requires an inordinate amount of trust and confidence in your own ability and judgment and a willingness to change. Let us embark on a new management style directed toward achieving excellence. To do that, we must understand the following:

- Your effectiveness is built on your own strength, on the strengths of your superiors and colleagues, and, not the least, on the strengths of your subordinates.
- There is a self-fulfilling prophecy in management: if you expect superior performance, you are more likely to get it.
- An effective supervisor must understand and appreciate employee motivations and needs.
- The behavioral scientists indicate a clear road to employee commitment: the lesson of the Hawthorne studies is the big difference that the little difference of paying attention to employees makes to them.
- Need fulfillment and frustration produce constructive behavior and defensive behavior, respectively; concen-

trate on identifying the needs of your employees and the methods to fulfill them.
- The critical relationship between you and the people who work for you includes mutual understanding and agreement on goals and rewards.
- It is up to you to restructure the work situation; such restructuring must include enriching, redesigning, and broadening of the responsibilities of each job.
- The successful supervisor is a people-centered supervisor; good people relations produce good patient care.
- *Possibility* is the watchword for excellent supervision; grasping possibilities should be a constant goal of managers.
- Good leadership includes the willingness to be a risk taker.
- You must build an atmosphere in which your people are willing to take risks; they need to know that you will tolerate mistakes and that they can grow with their experiences.
- A manager who knows that subordinates are his or her equals becomes the equal of his or her superiors.
- Successful managers have a "high touch" style of management; they share credit and give rewards.
- Immediate positive recognition is a necessary stimulus for continued efficiency. Once-a-year performance evaluation is not the answer; ongoing communication of appreciation or redirection is much more important.
- Work performance is improved appreciably when the employee knows that it is possible to influence the expected results.
- Strive for self-commitment among your employees; self-motivation and self-discipline are the strongest forces for a plan to obtain excellence.
- To be successful, an organization requires managers who can recognize the *need* for change, *initiate* change, and *adapt* to change. You do this through communication.
- The key to the process of effecting change is establishing a plan aimed toward ameliorating the effect of the change on the person involved.
- Active listening—sitting up and listening—plays an important role in supervisor-employee relationships; you *must* want to listen.
- Most employees are desperately seeking answers to four basic questions: "Where am I going?" "How am I going to get there?" "Who will I be when I arrive?" "Can I feel good about myself in the process?"
- Self-discipline develops when employees trust their supervisor and management, feel that their job is important and appreciated, and feel that they belong.
- Authority is granted by constituents to their leaders only so long as these leaders satisfy the needs and standards of the governed.
- The new work force is comprised of employees who expect a greater voice in decisions at work and want

opportunities beyond those contained in their present jobs.

- Our employees expect greater meaning from their work; they want to be able to innovate; they want to be able to contribute.

- You must develop an atmosphere of trust that permits employees to participate in problem solving and decision making as partners and not as junior partners.

- An alienated worker does not believe that his or her work can give that worker fulfillment and meaning.

- Fulfilling and meaningful work comes from a relationship characterized by trust, appreciation, and caring.

- Workers respond best and most creatively not when they are tightly controlled by management but rather when they are given broader responsibilities and helped to take satisfaction in their work.

- You must be sensitive to contemporary work values. The new employee expects more equal treatment; expects to be listened to, regardless of his or her job category; and is less likely to accept differences in privilege and status.

- Whatever the status of the work ethic, it is within your grasp to improve it.

- When employees are permitted to be *collaborators* rather than tools of management, they will be less alienated.

- You must devise plans to help workers develop the ability to *manage themselves*.

- The sharing of managerial prerogatives with your workers will bring us the excellence we so desperately need in the health care industry.

- It is time to empower employees by having them participate in the organization's decision making and goal setting.

CONCLUSION

What we have been discussing is a plan for excellence: the new management credo for an organization that has at its core a creative orientation. This organization encourages diversity of vision and permits people to take risks, participate, collaborate, and share in the rewards. Such an organization has an open system rather than a rigid, hierarchical, and bureaucratic one. In such organizations you, the manager and supervisor, assume the roles of coach, mentor, and visionary. You go down a new path. It is time to shed the inane propensity to move along the comfortable road of redundancy and obscurity.

NOTES

1. Robert R. Blake and Jane Srygley Mouton, *The Grid for Supervisory Effectiveness* (Austin, Tex: Scientific Methods, 1975), 3.

2. Earl Shorris, *The Oppressed Middle* (Garden City, N.Y.: Anchor Press/Doubleday, 1981), 373.

3. Kenneth Blanchard and Spencer Johnson, *The One-Minute Manager* (New York: Berkeley Books, 1983), 39.

4. Thomas L. Quick, *Understanding People at Work* (New York: Executive Enterprises Publications, 1976), vii.

5. "The Management-Employee Climate and Its Impact upon the Employee's Organizational Self-Esteem," in *The 1986 ASPA/CCH Survey*, conducted by John L. Pierce (Duluth, Minn.: Center for Organizational Management Research, School of Business and Economics, University of Minnesota), June 13, 1986: 1, 4.

6. *Achieving Competitive Advantage through the Effective Management of People, 1986–87* (Philadelphia: Hay Group, 1986), 1–14. (Research provided by Strategic Management Associates of the Hay Group and by Yankelovich, Clancy and Shulman, wholly owned subsidiaries of Saachi and Saachi, PLC.

7. Rosabeth Moss Kanter, "The New Workforce Meets the Changing Workplace," *Human Resources Management* 25 (Winter 1986): 517–18.

8. Sar A. Levitan and Clifford M. Johnson, "The Survival of Work," in *A Critical Analysis*, Work Ethic Series (New York: Industrial Relations Research Association, 1983), 21.

9. Kanter, "The New Workforce," 526.

10. Stanley Peterfruend, "Making Change: Risk-Taking" (Occasional paper prepared for New York Telephone, November 1986), 8.

11. Arnold Brown and Edith Weiner, *Supermanaging* (New York: New American Library, 1984), chap. 9.

12. Robert S. Ruch and Ronald Goodman, *Image at the Top: Crisis and Renaissance of Corporate Leadership* (New York: Free Press, 1983), chap. 4.

13. The Harris Survey, *ABC News*, 11 December 1980.

14. Ibid.

15. Robert S. Ruch and Ronald Goodman, *Image at the Top*, 51–64.

16. Bruno Bettelheim, *On the Uses of Enchantment* (New York: Random House, Inc., 1976), 48.

17. Richard E. Walton, "From Control to Commitment in the Workplace," *Harvard Business Review* 2 (March-April 1985): 77.

18. This section was developed from Mark G. Mindell and William I. Gordon, "Employee Values in a Changing Society," in *AMA Management Briefing* (New York: AMACOM, Div. American Management Association, 1981): 57, 59, 60.

19. Rosabeth Moss Kanter, "Forces for Work Improvement in the Public Sector," *QWL Review* 1, no. 1 (1981): 3–4.

20. *New Work Schedules for a Changing Society* (Scarsdale, N.Y.: Work in America Institute, 1981): 4, 5.

21. Levitan and Johnson, "The Survival of Work," 24.

22. Irving H. Siegel, "Work Ethic and Productivity," in *A Critical Analysis*, Work Ethic Series (New York: Industrial Relations Research Association, 1983), 39.

23. Daniel Yankelovich (Address to the National Conference on Human Resources, Dallas, Texas, 25 October 1978).

24. James L. Hayes, *Memos for Management Leadership* (New York: AMACOM, Division of American Management Association, 1983), 14.

25. Rosabeth Moss Kanter, "The New Workforce Meets the Changing Workplace: Strains, Dilemmas and Contradictions in Attempts To Implement Participative and Entrepreneurial Management," *Human Resources Management* 25, no. 4 (Winter 1986): 516.

26. R.J. Bullock and E. Lawler, "Gainsharing: A Few Questions and Fewer Answers," *Human Resources Management* 23 (Spring 1984): 123.

27. Rosabeth Moss Kanter, "The New Workforce," 534–35.

28. Peter F. Drucker, "A New Discipline," *Success* (January-February 1981): 18.

Arnold D. Kaluzny
Sharon Winn

13

Transforming Middle Management: Challenges and Opportunities

In the last few years health care organizations have undergone a revolution in structure and operations. Nowhere is this more apparent than in the role and function of middle management. Yet who constitutes this group? What is their character and function? And what special challenges do they face now when health care organizations are expected to manage more effectively and efficiently with fewer resources? This chapter explores the issues faced by middle management and the approaches for transforming middle management to better meet the challenges of the future.

WHO IS MIDDLE MANAGEMENT?

Middle management is an eclectic group of individuals, including department heads, clinical managers, unit supervisors, charge nurses, and numerous other people who have some managerial responsibility within their organization. While eclectic, these middle managers are constantly challenged to lead their respective units in the delivery of evermore compassionate, complex, and accessible care. It is likely, however, that this will be done by an increasingly smaller group of middle managers. Peter Drucker[1] suggests that there may be fewer middle managers in the future simply because organizations will be composed largely of specialists who

direct and discipline their own performance through feedback from colleagues, customers, and headquarters. Moreover, these remaining middle managers themselves will be technical experts and what Lorsch and Mathais[2] term "producing managers"—i.e., individuals who are both formally responsible for managing activities and actively engaged in providing client services.

FUNCTIONS OF MIDDLE MANAGEMENT

Are there specific skills or functions required of this group? While the general management literature and studies in health services have tended to focus on the role of top management, vis à vis the total organization, it is possible to speculate on some of the functions that need to be performed at this middle management level. Since middle management—by definition—operates within a larger organizational context defined by larger policies developed at the upper levels of management, the role of middle management is to use that structure and/or interpolate structure to implement existing policies and reach existing organizational goals, as described by Katz and Kahn:

> The critical task of the intermediate levels of management is to piece out the organizational structure or guide subordinates to do so, in ways which optimize organizational functioning. On the cognitive side this involves some degree of internal system perspective, specifically technical know-how about tasks of the relevant subsystems and knowledge of their relationship with immediately adjacent subsystems. In terms of affective orientation, the

Note: Sections of this chapter are based on material originally presented at the 24th Annual Forum on Hospital and Health Affairs, Duke University, May 1988, and published in *Hospital & Health Services Administration*, Vol. 34, No. 1, © 1989.

basic requirement is the ability to integrate primary and secondary relationships. This type of orientation has been associated with human relations skills.[3]

How well individuals perform these functions depends on the particular view of the organization and how this view affects their role within the organization. Given the siege mentality facing the industry and the prevailing strategies of downsizing, hiring freezes, and aggressive marketing, a central theme in all of these approaches appears to be the idea of *control*. From this perspective, a great deal of attention is given to job definitions, assigned accountability, measurable standards, and status differentials. As described by Walton,[4] "at the heart of this traditional mode is the wish to establish order, exercise control and achieve efficiency in the application of the work force." Moreover, as resources become increasingly scarce, efforts to enhance control increase.

While this approach has always had difficulty, given the unique characteristics of the health services system—e.g., level of professionalization of personnel, ambiguity, and uncertainty of the task—its limitations are becoming increasingly apparent as a result of a number of developments within the health care field. For example, health care organizations are characterized by an ever-increasing technology, which contributes to increasing costs. The development of new organizational roles to ensure delivery of this technology presents difficult organizational problems not only because of the emergent nature of the technologies and structures, but also because of the fact that the processes and interrelationships are quite incompatible with many of the stringent requirements, either implict of explicit, in the control perspective. Similarly, health service organizations are undergoing such unprecedented changes in sociodemographics, the level of competition, and the regulatory environment that it is quite difficult to provide the necessary specificity in job definitions and accountability. The application of the control perspective requires a certain level of stability that simply does not reflect the realities of the health care field.

Finally, attention must be given to changes in the work force itself, which further stresses the utility of the control perspective. There is increasing evidence that workers are less willing to simply follow orders on the basis of positional authority as reflected in job definitions and *a priori* assigned standards. An equally important finding is that employees would like to have significantly more influence on a range of issues, including how they do their work, the scheduling of work, pay raises, promotions, hiring, and the making of organizational policy.[5]

An alternative approach—which is gaining a great deal of visibility within industrial organizations[6] and is far more compatible with the character of health services and the particular environment within which they function—is that of involvement and commitment. Here attention is given to individual initiatives, interdisciplinary skills, information sharing, and thoughtful participation within the decision-making process of the organization. Under this approach, information and decision making do not simply flow from the top with the expecta-

tion of only trivial modifications. Instead, the model places a great deal of emphasis on individual initiative to constantly upgrade the system, and specific attention is given to continually improving the ongoing operation of the organization. Since a variety of skills and perspectives are necessary to adequately perform these tasks, interdisciplinary teams become the basic accountability units within the organization, rather than individuals. Information is shared widely with full assurance that candid and thoughtful participation will not result in loss of jobs and/or stature within the organization.

CHALLENGES AND OPPORTUNITIES

The use of the involvement and commitment approach at the middle management level faces a number of challenges:

- prevailing values that emphasize cost and cost containment—often at the expense of quality
- an emphasis on formal structure—without understanding the true and informal character of many health service organizations
- an emphasis on strategic planning—without adequate consideration for the implementation of the plan within the larger organization
- a managerial style that is based on the underlying assumptions of control, rather than on involvement and commitment

Below we consider each of these issues and suggest approaches and skills that will help transform middle management into more effective members of the managerial team.

Shared Values

Current Challenges

Health care professionals at all levels share a commitment to quality care. Quality of care as a shared value has historically linked middle managers to each other, to their departments, to their supervisors, and to patients. Each provider delivered quality services, and the organization was reimbursed for the cost of these services.

The implementation of prospective reimbursement with ever-increasing cost containment efforts has changed the role of the middle manager from an easy collegial relationship to one of competition for scarce resources with upper management, and with other middle managers. Many middle managers feel alienated by what appears to be the disappearance of quality as a shared and basic value of the organization. Organizational needs are often perceived to be in conflict with stated values, such as quality and compassionate care delivered with dignity.

Far too often individual middle managers have not been given a chance to be involved in and committed to cost control and "value added" services, and, thus, they do not see these as challenges; instead, they view these efforts as threats to their basic commitment to quality. Middle managers and their subordinates require organizational involvement and commitment to something of substance—and there is no better candidate than the idea of quality: it is essential that they see quality as enhanced, not diminished, by the new emphasis on costs.

Approaches

Some organizations have been able to infuse their departments and work units with a clear understanding of and commitment to how their group supports the quality mission of the organization. The focus on quality as the overarching goal of the organization and its restatement within various departments and roles provide a critical base for building a common departmental/organizational vision. This approach fulfills several functions: it unites and inspires members, thus justifying extra effort; it establishes criteria on which to base decisions; it makes clear the direction toward which the unit should be striving; and it defines the future.[7]

Middle managers need the opportunity to reaffirm, review, and reinforce their shared commitment to quality. Consider the following approaches.

Reaffirmation. In contrast to many industrial organizations,[8] persons who work in health service organizations share a sense of individual worth and justice—values that are basic to assuring quality. Emphasizing the compatibility, rather than apologizing for the structural anomalies of health care organizations, will provide a unique opportunity for middle managers to reaffirm their commitment to quality.

Moreover, quality appeals to the social as well as the economic values of health care personnel. Failing to recognize or underestimating the importance of these social motives will limit the ability of leaders to retain competent middle managers. The desire to protect and advocate for their patients is an equal, if not stronger motivational force than purely economic rewards. The challenge is to structure the process to channel this energy in a constructive direction, given financial, logistical, and cultural constraints.[9]

Consider this approach: in recruiting personnel, one health care organization asks its applicants to review its shared values and mission and to identify *their* individual/personal strengths and weaknesses in view of the written mission statement.

Review. Written state-of-the-organization and department reviews in which actual style, strategy, and structure are compared to stated values and goals provide another opportunity to confront shared values. While a review of actual behavior against stated values can be threatening, permanent attitudinal change can occur when individuals confront discrepancies in their own value system.[10]

A review of stated values against performance may also lead to some level of dissatisfaction with the existing state because there is often a discrepancy between values and performance.[11] This strategy provides an opportunity for informed

change on the part of organizational decision makers. The ground rules—established in advance—must allow these decision makers to change either stated values or performance to assure greater alignment.

As an illustration, a Seattle, Washington, hospital conducted a serious review of shared values. Starting at the executive level, participants identified how they wanted their behavior to align with their shared values. In the safety of a process and environment structured by an outside facilitator, the executive group agreed on norms for executive behavior that better expressed their stated values. For example, executives decided to solve problems, no matter how controversial they might be, in face-to-face encounters with the individuals concerned. This behavior reinforced a value of the dignity of the individual. Three years later, conflicts are still being resolved without gossip.

Reinforcement. The structure and process of the organization itself need to reinforce shared values. For example, the dignity and worth of the patient is a value that hospital patient relations programs may reinforce by providing training to all personnel. But training is not enough. The decisions and the decision-making process of the governing body and executives are more telling than a training program. In one medical center the orientation for new employees includes time to work with another manager outside of the intact work group. The resulting relationships reinforce informal access to role models of effective involvement and commitment that cut across departmental boundaries. Similarly, the structure of a quality assurance program that includes both nurses and physicians reinforces the dignity and worth of the nursing service and institutionalizes the organization's commitment to quality as a multidimensional concept.

Perhaps most telling is how the governing board and management handle downsizing and layoffs of personnel. Some organizations do this better than others. For example, in one health care organization employees were laid off, but the physician partnership and the governing body did not share in this cutback. As the management of the organization, they chose to exempt themselves from personal commitment to and involvement in being part of the solution. In contrast, some health care and non–health care organizations facing similar choices have developed more equitable solutions so that few or none of the employees were terminated.

While these approaches may be useful in a variety of health care organizations, past experience indicates that it is important to avoid the following:

- telling middle managers that the governing body or top executives have reaffirmed shared values, rather than asking managers to participate in a way that allows for two-way dialogue

- assuming that a written announcement or plan without discussion or follow-up commits middle managers to your shared values

- assuming middle managers can internalize shared values without time to meet and prepare, the opportunity to participate, and encouragement by supervisors
- avoiding the legitimate and difficult discussion needed, starting at the top, when actual institutional behavior doesn't support its stated values
- suppressing or avoiding the conflict needed for a meaningful discussion about trade-offs between individual and organizational values
- assuming that all individuals' values can and will be met within your organization
- assuming your employees have the same values as you
- underestimating the power of service and contribution rather than economics as a value for health care professionals
- analyzing personal and organizational values on an abstract level without assessing whether stated values are consistent with behavior.

Skills

The development of a sense of shared values required skills in conflict resolution. A set of shared values will not be achieved without a certain amount of conflict. Bright, dedicated people interacting on substantive issues are likely to disagree on fundamental points, particularly given the level of uncertainty facing health service organizations. Thus, persons responsible for clarifying shared values require special skills in negotiation and conflict management. These skills must be first role modeled within upper management, at which point leadership defines, discusses, and decides on shared values. The issue is not how to avoid the problem but how to structure the group and interpersonal processes to assure that middle managers receive clear and consistent messages about the fundamental values of the organization.

Structure

Current Challenges

Health care organizations are assuming the terminology, if not the very character, of industrial-type organizations. Administrators are now presidents, assistant administrators are vice-presidents, patients are customers, and services are product lines. These changes mask the fundamental character of health service organizations as informal coalitions of professionals providing services to patients. Significant actors within the coalition are not only employees of the organizations but also autonomous professionals who form coalitions for the acquisition and distribution of resources. This rather amorphous and dynamic process is in contrast to the more formal structure of health care that involves a series of very specific roles, activities, and incentives.

Given the difference between formal and informal structures within health services organizations, it is not surprising that 6 out of 10 middle managers report that the most important unsolved problem in their organizations involves intergroup rivalries.[12] The formal structure competes with the informal. The tension created by these two structures places great demands on the ability of middle management to deal with the situation. For example, 30 percent of medical staff in three hospitals did not know the purpose of, participants in, and results expected from the groups in which they had participated.[13]

Approaches

To deal with these problems, middle management needs to consider a number of approaches that have proved effective in industrial organization settings and have considerable application to the problems facing health services.

Temporary Working Groups. Many activities involving midlevel managers are nonroutine, and, thus, coordination cannot be programmed. Therefore, temporary work groups come together to solve the problem and then disband. Patient care conferences are one example of such a temporary work group.

A temporary work group requires

- a person to whom the group is accountable and a defined purpose (Who authorizes the charge and resources for the team?)
- a chairperson (Who leads discussions?)
- agendas (What will be discussed?)
- summaries (What was discussed?)
- skills at group process (Was interchange effective?)
- homework (Did the group get the information it needed in a timely and effective format?)

Effective, Naturally Occurring Work Groups. Middle managers most often participate in defining and resolving problems on a routine basis. The middle manager who chairs or staffs one of these groups needs all of the tools described above for the temporary work group, plus

- the authorization of time and funds needed to support the ongoing effective functioning of the group (Meeting social needs may be more important for intact work groups than for temporary work groups, for example.)
- the ability to acknowledge and resolve differences of opinion among highly trained, credentialed experts
- the ability to summarize these discussions in a concrete manner
- the ability to lead the group in setting and implementing ground rules

One farsighted health care organization provides each middle manager with two to four hours per month of confidential coaching from an expert in group development. The manager chooses whether to use this expert to brainstorm, observe, or facilitate. This monthly support replaces travel and seminar time and gives the manager on-the-job training to solve real-world problems.

Skills

In the structure of the future, the middle manager will

- Build an involved and committed team. Given the clear mandate for quality throughout the patient care process, the inclusion of a range of disciplines relative to that process requires a high level of interdependency, as described by Bradford and Cohen:

    > The problems of bringing together all the necessary information and producing all the coordination are growing each year at increasing speed. . . . The solution is not to work harder and run faster, but instead to build a team that shares in the responsibility of managing. . . .[14]

- Lead and participate in more effective meetings. A team is composed of individuals; these individuals must have certain skills if the group is to function effectively. Since the involvement/commitment approach requires that individuals have both technical and behavioral skills, the role of middle management is to develop these skills among subordinates as needed to improve team decision making. Special attention must be given to the development of interpersonal skills because these skills receive the least amount of attention in formal technical training programs and are the least developed but most critical to consensual decision making.

Strategy

Current Pressures

The strategic-planning process is often viewed as a panacea for many of the problems facing health service organizations. Unfortunately, these expectations far exceed reality. Two specific problems can be identified. First, the process itself presents an elegant exercise that underestimates the level of uncertainty facing the organization. As described by McKelvey and Aldrich:

> What may be radically wrong with many clients' strategic processes is that they are too organized. By the time they have defined what they mean by mission, goal, strategy, objective, plan, business unit and the like, they may have so narrowly defined the boundaries as to proscribe experimentation.[15]

A second limitation is that the strategic-planning process itself often represents a pro forma exercise that involves top management and a series of outside experts and that fails to adequately include middle management people who are ultimately responsible for implementing the strategic-planning product. This is not to say that middle managers should or desire to control strategy; instead, they need to be involved in the definition of issues and participate in the dialogue necessary for effective implementation. Lack of involvement is one of the major shortcomings of most strategic-planning efforts.

Approaches

Empowering middle managers requires that they have substantive input at various points of the planning process. The annual review of the strategic plan and the setting of institutional goals require a top-down and bottom-up interaction that can be carefully constructed and managed to assure that managers and departments "own" and are committed to appropriate priorities. Persons who participate in setting individual and group goals and objectives will be more productive than persons who set only individual objectives.[16] Moreover, management at all levels must define and recognize new constituent groups and ways to implement change; yet in hospitals under labor contract and associations negotiating with organized labor, failure to recognize and involve organized labor in the design and development of the program limits the implementation at its onset.

A variety of planning processes can be systematically applied. These processes tend to focus on defining the mission, identifying the target results wanted in critical areas, identifying what has to be done to achieve success in each area, and then setting priorities. Critical to the success of the entire effort, however, is the following: involving all the key players in planning, achieving consensus, and assuring follow-through. All members of the team must be involved from the onset. As described by some proponents, "If even one member of the team cannot attend—wait. [The process] requires a buy in from everyone not only to identify what is needed but also to commit to the process."[17]

Skills

The implementation of strategic plans requires that middle managers develop a basic and realistic understanding of the implementation process. Implementation involves a series of stages beginning with recognizing the problem and then identifying a solution vis-à-vis that problem, implementing the solution, and finally institutionalizing the change within the organization.[18] Because organizations and units within these organizations will be at different stages in the process, an accurate identification of stage is critical. Failure to accurately determine the stage of the organization/unit will greatly limit the ability to facilitate the effective implementation of the plan. For example, efforts to build involved and committed teams or "continual improvement programs" as part of the strategic effort are likely to encounter resistance if the problems that the solutions address are not recognized. Equally critical is the recognition that different units and components of the organization may be at different stages, and where discrepancies exist, management must be capable of recognizing these differences and acting accordingly.

For effective implementation to occur, managers need to develop some level of dissatisfaction with the existing state. Several approaches are possible. First, managers might provide opportunities to compare the organization with similar organizations and the departments with similar departments. Comparative data have historically been used to highlight performance gaps, thereby initiating a search for viable solutions. While this approach may be worthy of further exploration, one major limitation is the fact that it tends to foster denial and defensive behavior on the part of critical actors within the organization, thus reinforcing the control model. An alternative approach is for the organization—and, within organizations, the departments and work units—to self-compare over time. Research reveals that when results fall short of what individuals desire, motiviation for change increases,[19] thus facilitating the implementation process. This strategy is far less threatening and provides an opportunity for a great deal of learning on the part of organizational decision makers.

Managerial Style

Current Challenges

"Control of costs" easily slips into the implied strategy of "controlling people." Thousands of hours and dollars have been spent on job definition, assigned accountability, measurable standards, and status differentials. These efforts translate into a set of norms that describe how many middle managers feel they *should* act.

- The good manager knows at all times what is going on in the department.
- The good manager should have more technical expertise than any subordinate.
- The good manager should be able to solve quickly any problems that come up (or at least solve the problem before the subordinate).
- The good manager should be the primary (if not the only) person responsible for how the department is functioning.[20]

These norms implicitly or explicitly guide managerial decision making throughout health care organizations. Given the complexity and uncertainty facing most middle managers, these are unrealistic, if not inappropriate, guides to behavior. Meeting the challenges of the 1990s requires a major shift in styles to support changes occurring in values, structure, and strategy. In order for middle-level managers to redefine their style, executives must also redefine the way they relate to middle management. A new way of thinking about superior-subordinate and professional-nonprofessional relationships must pervade each health care organization. The shift is from control to involvement and commitment.

Approaches

Short of changing leaders, can a style of control be changed to a style of involvement and commitment? The grounding for what works starts at the individual level. If individuals are effective, groups will be effective. If groups are effective, the organization will provide effective and efficient health services. Therefore, revitalizing decision making for middle managers rests, finally, on the willingness of individuals—starting with the governing body—to develop their own attitudes and styles so they rest firmly on a paradigm of involvement and commitment, rather than control. Middle managers will be revitalized to work in an environment that acknowledges that reality. Activities used successfully for this leadership development process include the following:

- Involve teams of board members, executives, and managers through the same development process so that they share the same new vocabulary and expectations.
- Commit two to five years to the process. (The first year is start-up at the executive management level; the second year is start-up for middle managers; the remaining period is for institutionalizing this process. Each participant will spend about 16 to 20 days in the change process before it is institutionalized.[21])
- Commit major resources to the process. (A minimum budget is often $100,000 a year for consulting services alone, with additional discretionary funds required.)
- Apply a comprehensive change strategy in which the governing body provides role models for executives, and executives train midlevel managers. Change occurs on the job, not in seminars without follow-up.

Skills

Developing skills that facilitate involvement/commitment requires role modeling and day-to-day communication, not brokering of outside seminars. A range of options is available, including continuing education programs and career counseling. However, in reality, the development of technical and behavioral skills is probably best served by an in-house developmental process.[22] Under this approach, tasks are assigned to broaden subordinates' knowledge and skills with appropriate coaching and feedback by middle managers. Middle managers themselves will require mentoring and support over time as they engage in these activities. For example, in the implementation of the Hospital Corporation of America continuing improvement program, each manager has a designated mentor to provide counseling and support. This approach provides an opportunity to constructively convert behavioral problems into learning opportunities and can be quite motivating to both midlevel managers and their subordinates. Obviously, not all individuals have the appropriate levels of interest, motivation, and ability; yet the role of management is to assure that all individuals have the opportunity to realize their full potential.

CONCLUSIONS

The approaches and skills associated with sharing values, recognizing the structure of the organization, carrying out realistic strategic planning, and developing the styles required by middle managers have far-reaching implications for the ability of health service organizations to manage effectively, given high expectations and reduced resources. This transformation, however, will not be easy. It is particularly difficult because both middle management and top management confront an organization that suffers from a combination of genetic and iatrogenic disorders that inhibit any involvement of middle management with the decision-making process of the organization. Genetically, these organizations have high levels of inertia because of their structural characteristics and because of the characteristics of certain key actors. Structurally, health care organizations in general, and hospitals in particular, are "loosely coupled." Their organizational units are not coordinated in any systematic manner; while they may share a common mission, there are few integrating mechanisms to sustain coordinated activities over time. With uncoordinated units it is difficult to initiate and sustain change; each unit has the option to sabotage, veto, or simply ignore the process. Health service organizations are composed of individuals who by background and technical training have commitments and orientations independent of their organizations. In contrast to many industrial organizations in which the main line of advancement is into general management positions, health professionals have limited interest and/or expectations of becoming managers. In fact, many have considerable contempt for the entire management process.

An iatrogenic disorder (one inadvertently caused by the health care process) that cannot be ignored is the level of cynicism among health care personnel. For the last 10 years, health care organizations have been in constant transition, and there is a pervasive attitude among personnel that "We have seen it all!" Hospital personnel have been subjected to MBO, DRGs, performance evaluation systems, and quality-of-work-life programs—all with high expectations for solving major organizational problems. Because each program has fallen far short of expectations, any new attempts to transform health care organizations along the lines we have suggested will have to overcome employee skepticism.

Despite these obstacles, middle and top management must confront the realities of the organization and the role of middle management within that organization. Confrontation will facilitate the transformation and, in so doing, empower middle management to more effectively deal with the challenges and opportunities faced by health care organizations.

NOTES

1. P. Drucker, "The Coming of the New Organization," *Harvard Business Review* 66, no. 1 (January-February 1988): 45–53.10.

2. J.W. Lorsch and P. Mathais, "When Professionals Have To Manage," *Harvard Business Review* 65, no. 4 (July-August 1987): 78–83.

3. D. Katz and R.L. Kahn, *The Social Psychology of Organizations*, 2d ed. (New York: John Wiley & Sons, Inc., 1978), 547–48.

4. R.E. Walton, "From Control to Commitment in the Work Place," *Harvard Business Review* 63, no. 2 (March-April 1985): 78.

5. E.E. Lawler, P.A. Renwick, and R.J. Bullock, "Employee Influence on Decisions: An Analysis," *Journal of Occupational Behavior* 2 (1981): 115–23.

6. R.E. Walton, *Innovating To Compete* (San Francisco: Jossey-Bass Inc., Pubs., 1987).

7. D.L. Bradford and A.R. Cohen, *Managing for Excellence* (New York: John Wiley & Sons, Inc., 1984).

8. Walton, *Innovating*.

9. G. Shea, "The View from the Union" (Paper prepared for the Twenty-fourth Annual Forum on Hospital and Health Affairs, Duke University, Durham, North Carolina, May 1988).

10. M. Rockeach, *The Nature of Human Values* (New York: Free Press, 1973).

11. E.E. Lawler III. "Transformation from Control to Involvement," in *Corporate Transformation*, ed. R.H. Kilmann and T.J. Covin (San Francisco: Jossey-Bass, Inc., Pubs., 1988).

12. Chris Argyris, *Reasoning, Learning and Action: Individual and Organizational* (San Francisco: Jossey-Bass Inc., Pubs., 1982).

13. Sandra Gill (Speech for Selected Topics in Management, Estes Park Institute, Seattle, 1983).

14. Bradford and Cohen, *Managing*, 169.

15. B. McKelvey and H. Aldrich, "Applied Population Science," *Administrative Science Quarterly* 28 (March 1983): 101–28.

16. Charles Gowen, "Managing Work Group Performance by Individual Goals and Group Goals for an Interdependent Group Task," *Journal of Organizational Behavior Management* 7, no. 3/4 (Fall-Winter 1985–86): 5–27.

17. M. Hardacker and B.K. Ward, "Getting Things Done," *Harvard Business Review* 64, no. 6 (November-December 1986): 112–15, 118, 120.

18. M.A. Scheirer, *Program Implementation: The Organizational Context* (Beverly Hills, Calif.: Sage Publications, 1981).

19. Lawler, "Transformation," 115–123.

20. Bradford and Cohen, *Managing*.

21. Jerry I. Porras and P.O. Berg, "The Impact of Organizational Development," *Academic of Management Review* 3 (April 1978): 249–66.

22. Bradford and Cohen, *Managing*.

Michael R. Cooper
James B. Williams

Managing Cultural Change To Achieve Competitive Advantage

14

HEALTH CARE'S TURBULENCE: THE IMPETUS FOR CULTURE

Health care organizations are experiencing an unprecedented pace of change. Reimbursement practices, labor shortages, high vacancy rates, and the growing clout of purchasers are but a few of the major changes intensifying the industry's turbulence. This external turbulence, coupled with changing values and a decreasing supply of health care employees, demands well-managed cultural changes internal to the organization. In fact, turbulence in the U.S. (and worldwide) health care industry has *accelerated*, causing an unprecedented level of competition—in many cases for the sheer *survival* of the organization. Thus, in today's health care environment, *creating a culture for competitive advantage* is more than important—it is essential.

Organizational change and transformation require attention by health care executives and human resources professionals in three areas: mission, strategy, and culture. This process is illustrated in Figure 14-1.

The *mission* of the organization is the most fundamental of the three. It anticipates the environment, reflects the values of the organization, and sets the stage for strategy.

Strategy focuses on allocating the organization's resources to provide it with a sustainable competitive advantage in accomplishing its mission.

Note: Portions of this chapter have been reprinted with permission from *Handbook of Business Strategy*, Copyright 1988 by Warren, Gorham & Lamont, Inc., 210 South Street, Boston, MA 02111. All rights reserved.

Once the mission has been redefined and the strategy formulated, the supporting structures, processes, and management of the organization—its *culture*—must be brought into alignment with the mission and the structure. This often demands significant realignment to achieve effective implementation of the new mission and strategy. (See Figure 14-2.)

What Is Culture?

Culture is a body of *learned practices* that employees of an organization share and that they transmit to new employees. Simply stated, culture is "the way things get done in the organization."

Culture within health care organizations is often changed in an unplanned, haphazard way. As their markets and goals change, too many organizations find their organizational culture hampers their new strategic objectives. For example, within a multifacility health care system, responding quickly to new programs and services at the local level may be the new dictum, but successfully carrying out this strategy is exceedingly difficult where the time-honored practice is to get every decision approved at the regional and corporate offices. Clearly, a supportive cultural change is needed here, and it cannot be accomplished by a companywide memo or mandate.

With the unprecedented changes in the health care market, more and more health care organizations find their culture is inconsistent with new strategies required to be competitive. Many health care organizations that have operated in relatively stable environments find themselves forced to make dramatic changes to survive. These providers often have large numbers

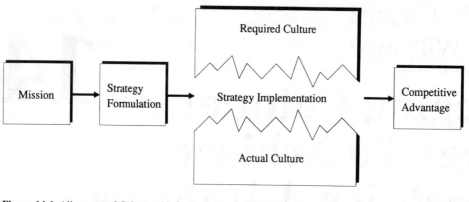

Figure 14-1 Alignment of Culture with Strategic Needs To Achieve Competitive Advantage

of people who work best in stable environments and have management processes that were built to reinforce stability. Certainly, such organizations must make new and significant changes. And many of these changes will be counter to the type of organization preferred by their current management and nonmanagement employees. This fundamental conflict between organizational need and employee values/expectations makes the culture change process in health care organizations all the more difficult. Managing culture within a health care organization takes on a unique complexity, given the nature and number of constituents (managers, employees, physicians, community, governing board, government) that impact on a hospital.

Managers are trained to manage and be responsible for the organization's resources and performance (including quality). Yet their job is exceptionally difficult for, among others, these key reasons: (1) they don't have true control over the physicians, who in most cases are the true ''gatekeepers'' of patients; (2) the governing board and the community are typ-

ically quite active and concerned about the hospital—often having significant impact on the internal day-to-day operations of the organization; and (3) historically many were trained in the art and science of hospital administration—and are not oriented to (or, as noted in 1 and 2 above, do not have the resources/control for) managing a market-driven, highly competitive business.

Health care professionals typically identify more with the profession than with the organization. This, however, is changing as (1) the shakeout of ''winners'' and ''losers'' continues in health care, and (2) the labor shortage of health care professionals and technical employees has given them greater freedom to choose their employer—and has caused hospitals to focus equally on nonmonetary factors to attract and retain employees in these areas.

Health care executives have long embraced the notion of strategic planning. They have always recognized strategy formulation as one of their foremost accountabilities. Often, however, the well-thought-out strategic plan on paper turns

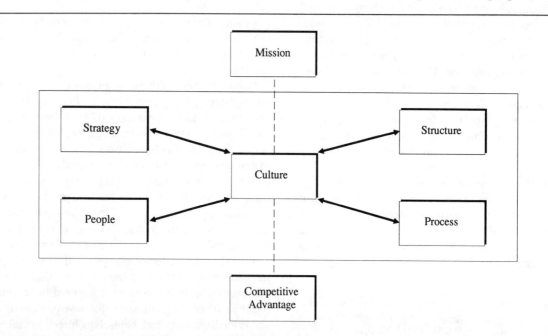

Figure 14-2 Alignment of Mission with Organizational Culture To Achieve Competitive Advantage

into a paper tiger. Why? Because like all planning, it is only as good as its implementation. Elaborate strategic plans cannot be implemented, much less sustained, without the appropriate organizational culture to support them.

Managing the culture for competitive advantage is the key to successful implementation of strategy, and executive management must take the lead. The role of the chief executive officer and the executive management team can no longer be limited to formulating strategy. They must ask probing questions about the culture of their organization and whether it is suitable in light of strategic business objectives. What is the culture? Does it complement the strategy? How can it be managed to gain competitive advantage?

Determining the optimal culture and ensuring that this optimal culture is developed and maintained are the responsibility of the health care organization's senior executives and human resources staff. This is a responsibility every bit as important as setting strategy itself.

MEASURING ORGANIZATIONAL CHANGE

Every health care organization has its own culture—one that can be measured, compared with the cultures of similar organizations, and managed to complement mission and strategy. The two principal approaches for measuring culture are the anecdotal approach and the quantitative approach.

The Anecdotal Approach

Anyone who has worked in a health care or other organization develops a sense of the culture. Talk to people in that organization, and the stories will begin to provide a picture of the culture. This is what is meant by the anecdotal approach. Although these stories and company myths provide a picture of the culture, they are not measurable, and their "fit" with a particular strategy can be difficult for the health care executive or human resources manager to evaluate.

The Quantitative Approach

The quantitative approach to culture measurement relies on objective data about the organization and its culture. These data are gathered through face-to-face interviews; observation; analysis of organizational levels, staff size, and reporting ratios; and systematic collection of culture perceptions through questionnaires. Information is collected about *management practices*—what managers do and how they do it. With this approach, culture can be measured in a way that enables comparison to other organizations and provides a basis for making changes in the organization's culture and monitoring their effects.

Out of Hay's extensive experience in measuring culture over the past many years, a framework has been developed to organize and condense information about culture in a meaningful and useful way. The core dimensions that are examined in each culture assessment are

- *Clarity of direction:* the extent to which the organization relies on formal and complete planning systems and has established clear courses of action (Have plans and goals been well formulated? Have the strategy and the plans and goals been communicated to appropriate management down the line?)

- *Decision making/organization:* the degree to which decisions are systematically formulated, implemented, and reviewed (Are information systems providing the information needed for decision making? How centralized is the decision-making process? Are the organizational structure and staffing levels appropriate in light of the strategy?)

- *Organization integration:* the degree of coordination, cooperation, and communication among units in the organization

- *Management style:* the pattern of encouragement and support for initiative taking and openness (How much freedom to act do managers have? Are managers encouraged to take risks, or does top management send out a "play it safe" message? How are conflicts aired and resolved?)

- *Performance orientation:* the extent of emphasis placed on individual accountability for clearly defined end results (Are the managers held accountable for achieving these results?)

- *Organizational vitality:* the dynamic nature of an organization as reflected by its responsiveness to change in its business environment, the development of pace-setting programs, and the creation of venturesome goals (Is this a fast-paced, market-responsive organization, or is it conservative and slow paced?)

- *Management compensation:* the extent to which the compensation system is seen as internally equitable, externally competitive, and tied to performance (Is the compensation program consistent with the business strategy and designed to elicit appropriate behavior?)

- *Management development:* the degree to which the organization provides opportunities for advancement and developmental experiences to prepare people for higher-level jobs

- *Identity:* the organization as a place to work and the image projected to employees and outside constituencies

- *Quality of care:* the perceived extent to which the organization delivers high-quality health care, encourages employees to focus on providing quality care, and provides them with the necessary resources, direction, and support to accomplish this goal; also, the degree to which employees judge their work to be of high quality

DATA BASES—MAKING NORMATIVE AND VALID COMPARISONS

The Hay Group maintains two extensive data bases (within and outside of the health care industry) for use in culture assessment. One data base consists of the perceptions of managers about the culture of their organization. Data are collected by means of written questionnaires in which managers are asked to describe the various components of their organization's culture. The data base includes the views of more than 200,000 managers in hundreds of organizations. A second data base consists of extensive comparative data concerning the design and staffing of organizations. A given organization can be compared to competitor/peer organizations on such variables as number of management levels, span of control, size of staff, and function versus matrix design.

These data bases, coupled with other Hay data bases on work force values, performance improvement programs, management competencies, etc., provide powerful tools to make meaningful, normative comparisons against comparable health care organizations. Making normative comparisons, particularly in the unique health care industry, is critical to assure the validity of a culture assessment. More bluntly, a culture or attitude survey that does not rely on external (and, eventually, internal historical) norms within the health care industry will probably lead to an improper assessment—and, therefore, an inappropriate priority for action.

CULTURE MEASUREMENT

The framework of cultural dimensions outlined previously forms the core for measuring an organization's culture. Where the purpose of the culture measurement is to determine the culture's suitability for the business strategy, a comprehensive picture of the strategy and culture is needed.

The measurement process generally includes the following elements:

- understanding the overall mission and strategy, the mission and strategy of each individual business unit, and the corresponding objectives for major departments and functions
- exploring the values shared by management in terms of what the values "are" versus what they "should be"
- examining the key management systems and the degree to which they support the mission and strategy
- assessing the current organizational culture and identifying the structure, process, and people components needed to support the strategy

A typical framework for determining the required culture is shown in Figure 14-3. Down the left-hand side of the matrix is listed a series of *critical success factors* that represent the unique ways that a particular organization competes or plans to compete in its marketplace. Across the top is listed a series of

key organizational and managerial attributes. These include the core cultural dimensions described previously, as well as additional attributes that are associated with successful implementation of the strategy.

Determining the culture requires trade-offs. Some of the ways to "manage" shown in Figure 14-3 will need to be emphasized, and some will need to be de-emphasized. For example, what is the required culture for an HMO that has identified superior member service as the key to its success in the marketplace? How formal should the planning process be? How much freedom to act must managers have?

IS THERE A UNIVERSAL CULTURE FOR COMPETITIVE ADVANTAGE?

Toward a Culture for Success: A Typology of Strategy

One of the great contributions made by strategists in the 1970s was getting managers to think about their operations as part of an industry. An industry has definable markets, economics, and competitors that make similar products. Within most industries there are several fundamental competitive options. Each option has certain characteristics in its organization/culture mix that distinguish it from others, and there is a culture for success that fits each of these configurations of strategy and structure. Several typologies of strategy and structure have been developed by organization theorists and strategy researchers. One such typology includes the four generic configurations discussed below.

The Cost-Driven Organization

Strategically, these organizations are production-driven and compete with low costs. Cost advantage is often achieved through size, scale, or centralization. The structure of the production-driven firm is usually functional. Many of the management practices are "hardwired" by plant design and process constraints, as are many cultural factors.

The Technology-Driven Organization

The technology-driven organization's strategy is to achieve differentiation—and, hence, premium prices—for its products and services by relying on a stream of new and innovative offerings that always keep it one step ahead of the competition. Technology-driven organizations often experience cultural schizophrenia as they mature because the culture for success changes as a product moves through its life cycle. Thus, these organizations may need to manage for low cost in an older business that has become commoditylike, while still needing to encourage risk taking and innovation in a younger business.

The Sales-Driven Organization

While this option has some elements in common with the first two (e.g., sales volume leads to scale advantages), the focus is on sales volume—getting the order, covering the market, and dis-

ORGANIZATIONAL/MANAGERIAL ATTRIBUTES
- Ways to Manage -

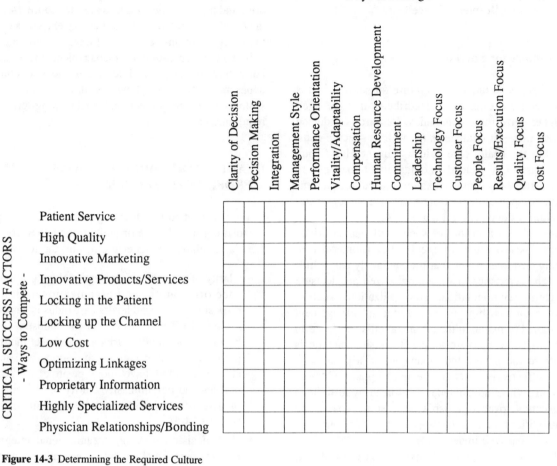

Figure 14-3 Determining the Required Culture

tributing the product and/or providing the service. Senior managers in sales-driven organizations usually have significant line experience and well-established sales records. Sales-driven organizations sell harder and cut prices when competitors move to take market share away.

The Market-Driven Organization

The market-driven organization seeks to identify customer needs that it uniquely can fulfill. As businesses move through their life cycle, the key factors for market-driven success change. The role of distributors, for example, may be insignificant at first when the customer has a high need for education and is willing to pay high prices for the advantages of a new product. As the product matures and becomes commoditylike, distributors can play a very significant role in the marketing mix. Customers start to base their purchases on availability and price, rather than on product attributes.

Within this framework health care organizations are now differentiating themselves with several different types of strategy, including

- *Vertical integration:* in a defined local or regional geographic market, developing and linking a continuum of health care services (e.g., acute, long-term, psychiatric, ambulatory) and, often, financing. A key tenet of this strategy is to attract and retain patients within the system. These organizations tend to be more costly, complex, and difficult to manage. They often need to operate in a centralized manner in order to "manage" vertical integration and obtain economies of scale.

- *Horizontal integration:* in a defined regional, national, or international marketplace, delivering a single type of service. A key focus of this strategy is on achieving significant economies of scale. A key challenge in these organizations is balancing the need to centralize/consolidate certain staff functions and resources (to obtain economies of scale) against the need to delegate decision making to allow local administrators autonomy to respond. Typically, the more turbulence that is occurring in the local marketplace, the more decentralization that is required.

- *Medical Specialty:* in a defined local or regional market, serving as a specialist in one or more service areas—often through creating "centers of excellence."

Is There a Culture for Success?

Although there is no universal "culture for success," it is possible to identify certain cultural attributes that are often found in higher-performing companies. Research conducted across a broad range of companies (as well as specific comparisons within the health care industry) in the Hay Group Culture Database, has yielded findings about the keys to success. It is particularly useful to examine the culture patterns of successful companies at opposite ends of a strategy-category continuum, as depicted in Figure 14-4.

Figure 14-5 shows a profile of successful market-driven organizations. These organizations seek to be customer-driven by identifying customer needs that they uniquely can fulfill. The culture characteristics that are emphasized are decision making, performance orientation, and organizational vitality. In these organizations, high focus is found in management systems designed to maintain the organization's shorter-term paybacks in dynamic marketplaces: (1) decision making is pushed close to the patient with managers in a position to quickly and effectively react to the marketplace; (2) pace setting for competitive advantage is reinforced by fostering a sense of urgency to accomplish venturesome goals; and (3) accountabilities for end results are clearly spelled out, well communicated, and well understood.

Successful cost-driven organizations evidence a very different set of common culture characteristics. For example, in successful utilities, where the core business demands reliability and consistency of service, high focus is found in management systems designed to maintain the organization's memory banks (human resources development, organizational integration, and planning systems), as seen in Figure 14-6. Assuring the know-how for reliable and consistent service delivery in these organizations requires (1) development and continuity of the next generation of management and employees for know-how transfer, (2) integration and cooperation across departments for know-how coordination, and (3) planning systems that can project and ensure long-term know-how requirements.

HEALTH CARE ORGANIZATIONS: CULTURE PROFILES OF SUCCESS

With respect to the differing health care strategies, high-performing health care organizations generally emphasize (and have relatively higher profiles in) the following:

- Clarity of direction, organizational integration, performance orientation, and organizational vitality—with respect to the overall health care industry (as displayed in Figures 14-7 and 14-8). As the industry continues to become more market-driven, we expect that the higher-performing health care organizations will increasingly emphasize (and have more positive) decision-making profiles and de-emphasize clarity of direction, as in the profile of successful market-driven organizations (Figure 14-5).
- High decision making, organizational integration, and management development in vertically integrated organizations. This is due to the necessary complexity of their management structure and the unique cultures and types of people that must be developed.

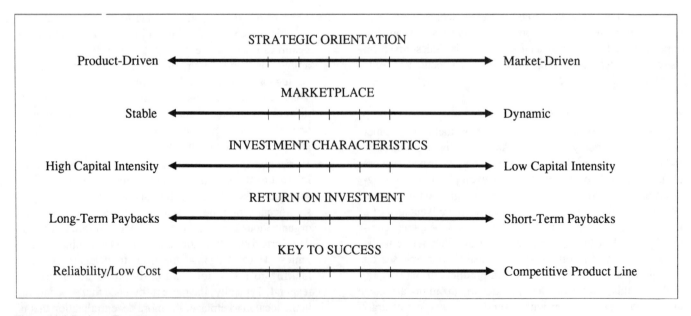

Figure 14-4 Business Contrasts

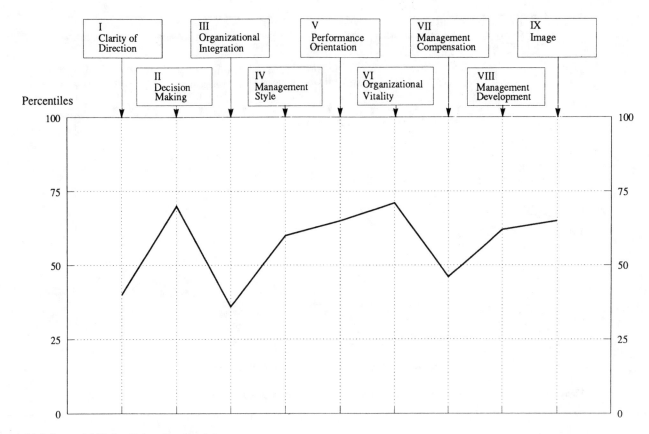

Figure 14-5 Successful Market-Driven Organizations

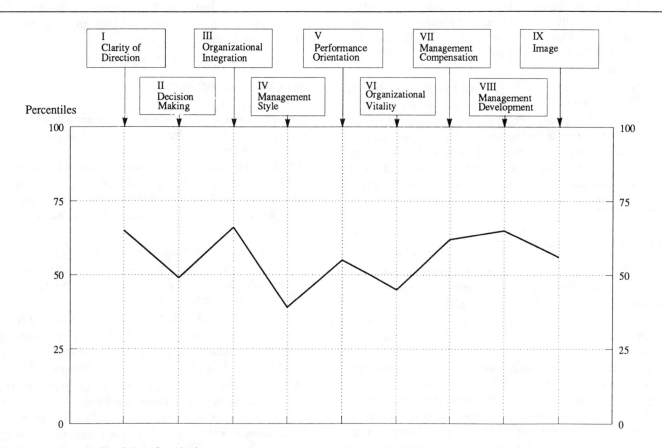

Figure 14-6 Successful Cost-Driven Organizations

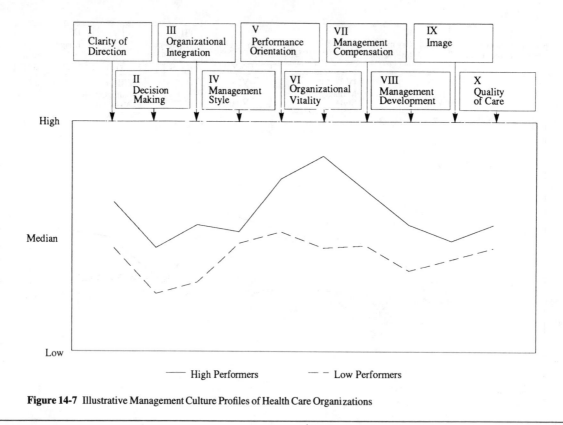

Figure 14-7 Illustrative Management Culture Profiles of Health Care Organizations

- High organizational vitality and performance orientation and low clarity of direction in horizontal health care companies. This is particularly true of those high-performing horizontal companies that operate in very turbulent markets.

- High quality of care, image, and management style in those organizations that are focused on medical specialties. The quality of care and image factors are critical for service differentiation and market penetration. Positive management style is a requirement in these organizations in which attracting, retaining, and motivating top-level specialists and maintaining a very strong physician orientation are imperative.

Linking Culture with Strategy

As illustrated in the previous section, there is no culture that fits all organizations. If a market-oriented strategy is implemented in an organization that traditionally has emphasized a maintenance and control decision-making process, then the strategy and the culture do not fit: they pull in opposite directions.

In an industry as competitive and turbulent as health care, culture must support strategy. When culture and strategy work together, the chances for high performance increase dramatically. Every health care organization's success depends on finding and building the best culture to support its mission and strategy. The critical challenge for health care organizations in

the 1990s will be effective strategy implementation: determining the optimal culture needed and then ensuring that this culture is developed and sustained.

CAN CULTURE BE MANAGED?

Indeed, organizational culture *can* be managed. Managing culture requires, first, a clear comprehension of the organization's mission and strategy, as well as existing management systems and practices. Human resources leaders can facilitate the management of culture by taking executives through the following analytical steps, beginning with an examination of current and required cultures. Fundamental questions include

- *Where are we?* This entails an assessment of the organization's culture, structure, and staffing. Executive management needs to compare these management systems to strategic/peer organizations.

- *Where do we want to be?* Certainly, it is important for an organization to know where it currently is—but knowing where it should be is essential. Gaps between where it is and where it should be are areas that demand attention.

- *What are the gaps?* Relative to strategic/peer organizations, executive management must agree on top priority strengths to be sustained and on selective competitive weaknesses to be changed. This requires understanding, commitment to change, and high focus.

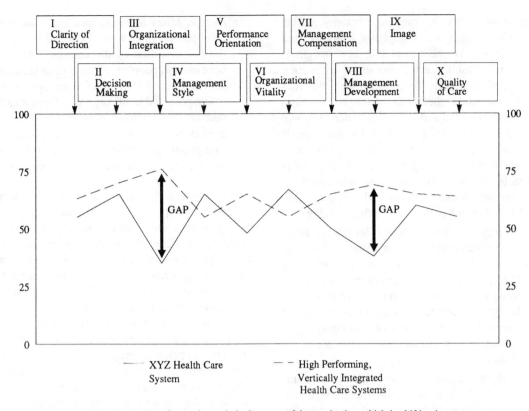

Figure 14-8 Illustrative Management Culture Profile

In this example, XYZ Health Care Systen is a relatively successful organization which is shifting its strategy to a more exclusive focus on vertical integration within its statewide market. In assessing its culture relative to other high-performing, vertically integrated systems, it is clear the XYZ's prioritized, specific actions to change culture should focus on enhancing organizational integration (interunit understanding of objectives, cooperation, etc.) and management development (formal training, promotion from within, succession planning, etc.). These actions will clearly help XYZ effectively compete, given its vertical strategy, particularly over the longer term.

- *How can the gaps be closed?* What elements of the management systems need change: Strategy? Structure? Process? People?

- *How rapidly can identified gaps be closed?* What is the organization's tolerance for change?

- *Where and how do we begin to act?* Management must emphasize practices consistent with strategy objectives, and executive management commitment to change must be both visible and sustained.

- *Are we progressing?* Progress must be measured against internal trends and peer organizations to find out where and why success is occurring. Winning and losing business units within the organization should be compared.

The process of aligning strategy and culture encompasses the following basic steps, starting preferably with step 1, but in practice with any of steps 1, 2, 3, or 4.

Step 1: Clarify mission/strategy
Step 2: Analyze critical success factors
Step 3: Describe the required culture: key organizational/ managerial attributes

Step 4: Assess the current culture
Step 5: Identify gaps with the required culture
Step 6: Adjust the levers
Step 7: Monitor the alignment

In step 6 the organization takes the appropriate actions to better align the strategy and the culture. Levers available to facilitate change are strategy, structure, process, and people. The sequence of level implementation typically depends on the degree of change required and accepted by executive management.

- *Strategy.* It may be necessary to rethink and revise the strategy itself. To be successful, the strategy must be in accord with external and internal realities. No matter how well the organization is geared up to implement strategy, it is not likely to succeed if the strategy is based on incorrect or incomplete assumptions about the external business environment. It is often necessary to retest the underlying assumptions about the competitive environment and the company's strengths and weaknesses in order to separate any myths from reality. A variety of studies can be used to test the company's strategy: market analyses, industry analyses, competitor analyses, and company analyses. To the extent that new insight is gleaned from these studies, a different strategic direction might be needed. Similarly, the culture diagnostic process will have identified whether the strategy is in alignment with internal realities of the organization. In some cases it is advisable to modify the business direction, if possible, rather than the culture. This is so when it becomes clear that pursuing a given strategic direction is not executable, given cultural obstacles, and that these cannot be overcome sufficiently or quickly enough to stay in tune with the pace of change in a defined market.

- *Structure.* Changes in organizational design can bring about changes in decision making, information flow, and management style. Functions or units may be centralized or decentralized to create new linkages to better implement the strategy. Changes in reporting levels can contribute to changing the nature of decision making. Levels may be eliminated to provide for more managerial latitude, or they may be added to increase control and introduce redundancy.

- *Process.* Management processes can be changed to reinforce the strategy. The mission and the strategic plan may not have been articulated or disseminated throughout the organization in a way that affects people who must be involved in the implementation of strategy. Or managers may not understand the real meaning and personal implications of the new values and required behaviors. There is always a gap between newly articulated values and the translation of these into required day-to-day behaviors. For example, what do terms like *customer focus*, *risk taking*, and *individual accountability* mean to the veteran manager who has never been encouraged to live up to—or been rewarded for living up to—these values?

Changes can be made in the recruiting process to attract people with a different skills base or management style. Management compensation programs can be redesigned, changing the amount, mix, and/or leverage of incentive compensation to better align it with the strategy. Performance planning can be enhanced by changing goal-setting and performance appraisal techniques and criteria. Systems and processes in specific functional areas can be targeted for improvement to bring about changes in cost control, market intelligence, and management information systems.

- *People.* Many issues surface about the current management/professional work force and its suitability for the (future) direction of the company. Does the company have enough people with the type of skills that are needed for the future? Does it have enough people with leadership potential to fill key slots? Does it have enough risk takers? Does it have enough marketeers? Assessment centers, training programs, career planning, and succession planning programs are some of the actions that can be taken to address these types of concerns.

In addition to initiating change through strategy, structure, process, and/or people levers, a fundamental ingredient in all cultural change involves executive and senior leadership in modeling the kinds of behaviors that are needed to shape the new required culture. Words in mission and strategy documents and corporate values statements, when not supported by the actions of leadership, can have a negative effect in that employee cynicism will develop out of these contradictions.

It cannot be overstated that the health care organization's CEO and executive management team must be actively involved in reshaping organizational culture. When the issue is implementing a culture that is consistent with the strategy, nothing less than top management involvement will do. This accountability is as important as formulating the business strategy itself.

CONCLUSION

> When she was a little girl in the nineteenth century, the future Queen Wilhelmina of the Netherlands paid a visit to Emperor Wilhelm II of Germany. "See," said the Kaiser to the Dutch Princess, "my guards are 7 feet tall and yours are only shoulder high to them." "Quite true, your majesty," replied Wilhelmina. "Your guards are 7 feet tall. But when we open our dikes, the water is 10 feet deep."*

The need for health care managers to identify and use organization strengths in new and different ways for competitive advantage, as well as to identify and correct organization weaknesses, has never been greater. The changes occurring in the industry today are so monumental that providers everywhere are overhauling their missions and strategies in an effort to survive, and health organizations' prospects for success are dramatically enhanced when culture is managed for compatibility with mission and strategy.

---

*Source: Unknown.

Norbert F. Elbert
Howard L. Smith

Hospital Staff Development

15

A fundamental shift in orientation needs to occur. While corporate America has taken off its green eye shades and shed its "training as cost" perspective, and now sees training and staff development as an investment—an investment in its employees—hospitals and health care organizations still view staff development as an expendable activity. When employees are viewed as important assets, then staff development remains even during organizational downswings. Unfortunately, hospitals are often more guilty of viewing "training as cost" than corporate America ever was.

LUXURY OR NECESSITY?

Each day hospitals and health care organizations confront a wide variety of critical issues, such as third-party reimbursement, quality of care, cost control, productivity, and competition. In most instances, solutions and strategies that address these issues are formed around the skills of many people. Physicians, nurses, administrators, ancillary staff, and other hospital staff members ultimately determine the success of these responses. They are the individuals who are primarily responsible for the daily provision of services. It is on people and their productivity—whether related to ideas or skills—that hospital performance is based.

Yet what level of performance is achieved when staff members lack necessary training or education, are not properly oriented to a hospital's standard operating procedures, or have

become dated in the knowledge that contributes to their expertise? Eventually, education and skill deficiencies in hospital and health care personnel become evident in suboptimal performance. Therefore, hospital managers, such as department heads and supervisors, must be especially alert to staff training and development needs if optimal performance is to be reached.

Staff development and training programs and inservice education programs have generally been treated as luxuries and not necessities in hospital budgets. The main exception is continuing medical education for physicians and nurses. In this instance, inservice education is often maintained to meet state and federal regulations. In contrast, when funds are adequate, participation in staff development by other clinical and nonclinical personnel may be considered a reward for good performance. However, in lean years when resources lessen, staff development and inservice education of this nature are items usually at or near the top of the nonessential list. Significant budget cuts in the staff development effort can result. Training and development have been sacrificed in some instances to make room for what is often perceived to be a more cost-effective allocation of resources.

When hospital staff development is viewed as an expendable activity, the cost and quality of health services delivery can be jeopardized. Such a philosophy may produce indifferently trained personnel. For example, consider the trend among hospitals to diversify into home health care. A home health agency that only occasionally orients its home health aides to the need for courteous and dignified treatment of clients during visitations minimizes its control over the consistency of services provided. Some of the aides may be highly

Note: Adapted from *The Health Care Supervisor's Guide to Staff Development* by H.L. Smith and N.F. Elbert, Aspen Publishers, Inc., © 1986.

conscious of the need to be courteous, polite, and patient because of their participation in an orientation or training program. Other aides who have not received the training may believe that their attitude toward the client is less important than the services they provide. The lack of consistent training among all staff members, therefore, leaves the quality of service to chance. There has been no attempt to standardize, and there is a lack of uniformity in services provided.

Until it is recognized that staff development is just as crucial to the performance of hospitals and other health care organizations as other resource expenditures, staff development will continue to be viewed as convenient, but not essential. Such an attitude is unfortunate. Ultimately, not having an inservice education, training, orientation, or staff development program that encourages and nurtures employee development may be very costly to the efficient and effective performance of any hospital or health care facility.

Many professionals and support personnel are questioning whether staff development is a necessity for hospitals. Such an attitude is counterproductive because staff development has so much that it can potentially add to the performance of any hospital, nursing home, health maintenance organization, or department within a health institution. The answer to the problem of misperception is to link staff development with better performance by employees, their clinical and nonclinical departments, and their hospitals. In other words, the credibility of staff development programs can be established only when it can be proved that the resources invested have raised the efficiency or effectiveness of hospital care.

Until prospective payment and its cost-containment pressures arrived, there was little incentive to link resource expenditures with tangible end results. The phasing out of cost-pass-through reimbursement creates a context in which staff development can be perceived as a major contributor to hospital performance.

WHAT IS STAFF DEVELOPMENT?

Since there is an extensive array of staff development programs throughout the hospital and health field, it is first appropriate to define the components of staff development. These components could include one or more of the following:

- inservice education
- continuing education
- orientation training
- training
- management development

Other variations can be suggested, but this list is representative of what many hospital professionals envision as staff development.

Inservice Education

Inservice education is the most traditional type of staff development. Basically, it involves a program within a health institution devoted to teaching staff members about various facts and topics.[1] A good example is inservice education for nursing services.[2] Since medical diagnosis and treatment protocols vary according to developments in medical research, it is often necessary for hospitals to update nurses on new techniques, methods, or findings.[3] This sort of learning can take place on site without a massive expenditure of time or travel money because the teaching objectives are limited and well defined. Programmatically the teaching sessions are usually combined under one authority—the director of inservice education.

Whether nurses, physicians, physical therapists, or other members of the health services team, hospital personnel must remain current on changes in knowledge in a given profession.[4] For example, hospital department heads must be capable of translating the impact of prospective payment on their departments' budgets. Inservice education helps accomplish this goal. It also may help new professionals more easily transfer their academic preparation to the job site. Few experienced hospital personnel are able to function effectively without some initial inservice preparation, even if it only means limited orientation training. In sum, inservice education has a diverse set of teaching goals, but it is generally limited to on-site incremental training without the intent of granting course credits, degrees, or diplomas.

Continuing Education

Continuing education is another component of staff development. It may be a separate program, or it may be combined with other education programs (e.g., inservice education) within hospitals. The goal of continuing education is to help staff members remain current in their knowledge base and to expand on that base when feasible.[5] Continuing medical education in a hospital-based multispecialty group practice offers a good example of this concept. The program might be responsible for fulfilling physician and nurse education needs to maintain professional license standards. In addition, the continuing education director or department head might integrate courses designed to improve managerial skills in team leaders. In this manner the knowledge base is not only retained but expanded as well.

Continuing education is distinguished from inservice education by its orientation and goals. Continuing education is usually designed to fulfill externally imposed standards. External learning resources (e.g., university courses) may be relied on to a large degree. Inservice education by comparison is more internally oriented and seeks to achieve organizational goals. Clearly, there is room for overlap.[6]

Orientation Training

A more fundamental education program is aimed at orienting new hospital employees.[7] There are few jobs for which some form of orientation is not needed. This is especially true for most hospitals and health care organizations in which jobs must be completed faithfully according to predefined procedures. If the standardized procedures are not followed, there is risk of serious complications.

The orientation phase is the first contact between a staff member and the hospital. It may establish predispositions that are indelible. Hence, every effort should be made to ensure that the impressions and attitudes that evolve are compatible with hospital goals and intentions.

Most hospitals and related health care institutions discover that employee orientation is needed more extensively at some levels than at others. For example, orientation training of nursing aides in hospitals is often very comprehensive (unless a supply of experienced personnel is available). This investment in orientation training may not really represent a problem solved (i.e., a self-created supply of knowledgeable nursing aides). Health facilities such as nursing homes have discovered that they serve as a training ground for nursing aides who then parlay their knowledge and experience into higher wages at hospitals. Hospitals, however, are not immune to these marketplace forces of supply, demand, and price (i.e., wages or salaries). As a result, the specific investment of resources in staff development varies according to each hospital and its context.

Training

Training may constitute another component of hospital staff development. According to Goldstein, training is the "systematic acquisition of skills, rules, concepts, or attitudes that results in improved performance in another environment."[8] Unlike initial orientation efforts that usually introduce staff members to the organization's culture and methods of operation, training is more skill oriented (although it also may constitute attitude formation). Training is more methodical than continuing education because a structured program is usually repeated with predominately in-house resources, although sometimes supplemented with external resources). Training is more synonymous with inservice education, and the differences between the two may blur to the point of nondistinction. Inservice, though, is usually centered on health professionals. Training refers to the process by which employees are taught the necessary skills to maintain an acceptable performance level.

Management Development

Development assumes that these necessary skills are present. It focuses on the growth and improvement of employees as integral parts of the hospital and as people. Management development may include education oriented toward supervisors, department heads, staff personnel, and executive-level positions in the hospital or health institution. Management development is education designed to improve the administrative and managerial skills of the management team.[9] It is the most recent topic to be included in staff development

because of the growing importance of management in hospital and health organization performance. Bures has studied the growth of management development in the health care sector. In his analysis of 472 hospitals nationwide, he discovered that management development has generally centered on the following topics:

- leadership
- motivation
- problem solving
- industrial/labor relations
- delegation/authority/responsibility[10]

Although this finding may reflect only the programs available to hospitals and not specific needs, the list conveys the thrust of management development.

Management development may be broader in actual application in hospitals than implied by the aforementioned study. This is because management development is increasingly being extended to all hospital staff members. Normally, management development was reserved for the administrative staff. Clinical managers—department heads, for example—were usually not included in this group because of the basic line functions they performed. Consequently, directors of nursing service were viewed as clinicians first and managers second. The exceptions were the ancillary department heads who were responsible for support services used by clinical departments. This approach permitted nurses and physicians to concentrate on their clinical skills and other line department heads to concentrate on supervisory activities (as opposed to broader management responsibilities).

The evolution of the hospital management team has rapidly outgrown these former distinctions. As a result, there has been a blurring of the differentiation between clinician and manager. The implication for staff development is a sharing of a common concern by team members for more extensive exposure to improved management skills training. Not only must the director of purchasing and materials management be capable of performing all management functions but the director of nursing must have this capability as well. Lack of ability by one team member may jeopardize the performance of personnel, supervisors, or departments.

Management development itself has also acquired a broader scope than that implied in the Bures study. For many health care organizations and hospitals, management development is viewed as a multiple-goal process.

- improvement in the conceptual knowledge base of the managing process
- development of specific skills that implement that knowledge (e.g., planning, organizing, controlling, motivating, leading)
- application of skills to the relevant hospital job assignment
- nurturance and expansion of skills and knowledge over time

- integration of the manager's perspective to attain a holistic organizational perspective (i.e., organization culture)
- development of a positive attitude toward managing and a commitment to the hospital (i.e., organization)
- renewed focus on coaching staff members toward improved job performance (i.e., higher productivity and quality of output)
- understanding and attainment of a performance orientation—improvement in end results for the department and the hospital

When seen in this light, it should be apparent that management development is more than training in specific management skills. Yet it would be unwise to separate the training and development functions. Employees must not only be trained in the specific skill areas related to their responsibilities, but also have a knowledge base broad enough to allow them to learn the new skills needed to respond to rapid changes and resulting demands.

Defining Staff Development

Considering the diversity of the preceding definitions, it is clear that staff development has many different definitions and implications for people. We will refer to staff development in the broad sense of the word, which encompasses all of these individual components. Even though terminology is important, it is also crucial to remember that results count in the final analysis. Thus, we will look beyond terms and program definition to the end results of staff development performance. Here is where attention should be focused.

By dwelling on improved performance as the guiding rationale behind hospital staff development, it is possible to take such a program toward the higher level of endeavor that it deserves. Not conveying the broader performance ramifications of staff development to the chief operating officer or other key decision makers ensures that the program will never command the respect or resource allocations it deserves.

Staff development should be viewed as one of the most vital expenditures of hospital resources because it provides a basis from which better personnel productivity and job accomplishment begin. The only certain way in which this realization will ever be attained is for staff development directors to document program goals attained. Most trainers and inservice directors do not go that extra step in the documentation phase. They are very adept at documenting the process and immediate end results of a training session. Yet they seldom determine transfer, retention, and outcomes from staff development. They need a bottom-line orientation.

These ideas are substantially magnified under prospective payment. To the extent that a staff development director can document the efficiency of invested program resources, there is greater opportunity for continued or higher levels of funding. But remember that hospitals are looking for ways to trim costs as a result of prospective payment. Until staff development programs can substantiate tangible results, there is every reason to believe that they will experience continued funding problems. With prospective payment, there is no substitute for substantiated performance.

THE ROLE OF PERFORMANCE

Having defined staff development, it is appropriate to explain what is meant by a performance-oriented approach to staff development. Performance represents the tangible end results of individual, departmental, and organizational efforts. Performance is the measurable outcome(s) from the expenditure of resources.

LEVEL OF EFFORT OR ACTIVITY:	ILLUSTRATION OF PERFORMANCE:
Individual	Meals prepared in one hour by a dietary aide
Department	Number of purchase orders processed in one month by the purchasing department
Organizational	Number of patient days served

As these illustrations suggest, performance may be broadly defined as the level of return on resources invested and expended over a given period of time.

Clearly, performance is an ambiguous, somewhat global concept that has different meanings depending on perspective. This elusiveness in accurately defining performance has caused many managers and supervisors to forgo attempting to reach a meaningful operating definition for their subordinates, departments, or organization. The rationale is that performance means different things to different people—so why bother? It is precisely this attitude that creates an environment in which subordinates, departments, or organizations are not results oriented. No one is truly interested in raising the standard of performance—that is, increasing the return on resources expended for a given period of time.

We are going to provide some assistance in coming to grips with operationally defining performance and in explaining how performance should be related to staff development. For the moment, a meaningful framework that supervisors can use in defining performance includes

- the level of analysis
- the presence of multiple criteria
- the focus of performance
- the time frame
- the method of measuring performance

This framework offers a beginning for creating a performance-oriented approach to staff development.

The level of analysis reflects the unit that is measured. It usually involves individual, departmental (or work unit), or organizationwide performance criteria (i.e., multiple criteria). Determining who or what is performing (i.e., the performance focus) is the central issue. Organizational criteria, for example, might include the multiple criteria of profitability and effective care. Organizational performance might then be ascertained as good or bad to the degree that measures such as return on investment, medical audit results, and utilization findings improve relative to past performance and/or performance by similar organizations.

Performance criteria, of course, exist only within a specified time frame that can conveniently be broken down into short, intermediate, or long-term measures. Finally, performance measures need to be rigidly defined so that progress is recognized and consistently tracked. While quantitative measures (e.g., frequency of absenteeism) are preferred, qualitative measures (e.g., attitude surveys) may be just as valid.

PROBLEMS WITH HOSPITAL STAFF DEVELOPMENT

The current reputation of staff development programs in hospital and health care organizations is less than admirable. While nursing and continuing medical education have continued to maintain a high standard and reputation (professional licensure may be working effectively in this regard), in contrast, other forms of hospital staff development have suffered greatly. This may be an artifact of underdeveloped or unsupported (in terms of resources) human resources management and personnel administration.

Some programs have continually trained staff in concepts or skills that were not needed. Other programs have centered on skills that were covered in academic programs. Still other programs have attempted to make do with a limited amount of resources. Many programs have not evaluated the outcomes from training. Others have tried, but they have used suspect methodology. Finally, continuing education programs by professional associations are often viewed suspiciously because they fail to concentrate on organization-specific needs.

Moore and Dutton indicate that the poor reception of most programs arises from several factors.

- the periodic and infrequent nature of the programs
- their crisis intervention
- the lack of coordination with other functions within the organization.[11]

Bures's analysis of 472 hospitals suggests that the problem is mainly one of the programs' not being relevant.[12]

The impression that emerges from examining the preceding research and discussions with many health professionals is that staff development is needed—but current programs are not offering the program design or forethought that distinguishes a good effort from a bad one. More systematic analysis and thought could feasibly resolve these limitations and make staff development programs something to be desired, rather than avoided, in hospitals.

A SUPERFLUOUS EXTRA?

Staff development programs in the hospital field should be able to demonstrate sufficient positive results to justify continued resource allocations. Most large health care facilities, such as hospitals and health maintenance organizations, have recognized the contribution that properly training personnel at all levels can make toward improving the "quality" of care. However, less attention has been directed to efficiency and productivity. Prospective payment helps reverse these trends. More nutritious meals served at correct temperatures with an appealing setting by dietary workers in a hospital can be as important as continuing education delivered to nursing staff members on proper intravenous injections. This awareness of the need for efficiency-oriented performance is being expanded as health providers attack cost-containment issues.

Inservice education can prove effective in creating practical programs aimed at managing hospital costs. The attitude and procedures for controlling costs in housekeeping—inventory control and prevention of waste of cleaning materials—are just as important as attempts at energy conservation for the entire hospital. New licensing and certification standards for hospital personnel will further stimulate the growth of staff development. Meanwhile, community health education and facility outreach can extend other forms of training to health consumers. When seen in this light, it is apparent that staff development programs possess a broader base than typically thought by most hospital and health care professionals.

Ironically, a countervailing factor against the growth of staff development programs in hospitals and other health-related organizations is the necessity for cost containment—the need to hold down all costs.[13] Meaningful staff development requires resources, but with the growing restriction on health care reimbursement, there will be less of a budgetary pie to divide.

However, the drive to hold down health costs may also ultimately fuel an increased demand for staff development programs in hospitals. Cost-containment training programs could help focus personnel attention on providing high-quality care and reduced (or at least stable) operating costs. Staff development programs have valuable potential for helping achieve quality of care with low costs by instilling an operational awareness about cost control. That potential, however, is dependent first on the commitment of the hospital's management to staff development and second on its sincere effort to mount a program in which performance receives primary consideration.

Another trend that suggests hospital staff development is not a superfluous extra is employee mobility. Positional vacancies—due to employee turnover—occur in all organizations. However, the failure to adequately plan for or actively address the replacement of critical personnel has long remained a problem for many hospitals and health care facilities. Hospitals traditionally have encountered problems in obtaining and retaining registered nurses. Although this problem has recently been alleviated for some urban hospitals, there is always an issue of staffing with the best personnel. Nursing homes, for example, have consistently experienced difficulty in acquiring quality licensed practical nurses. The growth and success of nursing registries or personnel pools serve as an obvious comment on human resources management issues within health care institutions.

GENERATING INTEREST IN STAFF DEVELOPMENT

A primary dilemma confronting the health care field is determining how to provide adequate services with the resources available. Prospective payment exacerbates the search for a fundamental solution. This problem will more than likely increase in magnitude in the future. Health workers represent one of the largest cost centers in hospital budgets. Therefore, health care supervisors must be concerned with establishing conditions under which staff members can become more productive while maintaining high-quality services and controlling costs.

Sophisticated patient care equipment and access to the latest information (via computerized literature searches or through professional meetings) exemplify a few of the technologies that improve a hospital or nursing home's effectiveness in developing a more productive, efficient, and effective staff. Equally important, each employee must be oriented and trained to complete a job correctly.

For example, a radiology technician may be presented with the most recent imaging equipment available. If that technician does not receive correct instruction in its use, or if consistent errors in its use are allowed to recur, then the technician's productivity, efficiency, and effectiveness have deteriorated. Staff development presents a valuable alternative for preventing these problems before they occur. It also offers a means for maintaining staff knowledge after training has occurred.

Hospital training and staff development must support other management interventions, and they must be implemented as a continuous function. It will take courage, perseverance, and dedication to sustain staff development programs in the face of increasing economic and inflationary pressures. Many health care professionals may wonder whether it is worthwhile to support staff development. The answer may come from another question: is there really an alternative?

THE "TRAINING PILL"

A frequently occurring sequence of training needs determination and fulfillment might follow this scenario:

A hospital administrator has noticed the high cost of providing orientation to new medical assistants and concludes that a turnover problem exists. She mentions this to the director of human resources, along with making a recommendation that a training program may be in order to reduce employee turnover in the hospital. The director, in turn, believes that a training session on interpersonal relations for departmental supervisors would improve the situation because the supervisors are the first line in the management defense and, thus, closest to the problem. A notice is sent to the supervisors requesting that they attend a training program on human relations skills at the local university. At the conclusion of the program, the director passes out a questionnaire, asking for impressions of the program.

The preceding scenario can best be described as the diagnosis and prescription of the "training pill." Whenever an organizational problem appears (e.g., ancillary worker turnover), an initial reactionary response by hospital administrators is to consider staff development as a quick cure. The inservice education or training director is usually assigned responsibility for dealing with the problem.

Time and money are invested to rectify the situation. But what has been accomplished? Other than satisfying the request for training (thus demonstrating compliance with top authority), few positive outcomes have resulted. In essence, symptoms have been treated with a questionable prescription, rather than undertaking corrective surgery. It is unlikely that turnover will improve. It is not even certain that the hospital supervisors will appreciate the opportunity to attend the program without incurring any expenses because it may be scheduled at such times as to be more of a hindrance than a reward.

Utilizing emergency on-the-job training instead of planned staff development can be very costly in terms of increased operating mistakes, higher personnel administration costs, and eventually declining use of the training program. The time selected to attend the training session may conflict with personal or departmental plans. Instead of nurturing positive attitudes toward staff development, good intentions may have created deep resentment toward the program. It should be obvious that the "training pill" approach, as common as it might be, is not an effective method for solving a hospital or health care organization's personnel problems.

DETERMINING TRAINING NEEDS

Too often hospital administrators and supervisors fail to probe deeply enough into training and inservice education requests to identify the real staff development needs. For example, the business office staff in a hospital may receive a series of training sessions in how to coordinate work more effectively with medical records to improve the processing of Medicare paperwork. The real problem may actually have been spatial location. The decision to conduct a training program is often made after first noticing a symptom (e.g., mistakes in DRG classification), rather than diagnosing the deeper malady.

Frequently, a top administrative officer contacts the director of staff development, explains the nature of a problem, and requests immediate assistance. This crisis management approach is not unusual and conveys the impression that the administrator is a valuable authority for solving any problem. While many hospital administrators learn from their own errors and the misfortunes of not having planned a staff development program, the trial-and-error approach is inefficient. Furthermore, some hospital supervisors never learn from their mistakes, and these poor management techniques tend to become permanent work habits.

Hospital managers must also remember that inappropriate staff development raises the possibility of demotivating supervisors.[14] For example, department heads in a hospital may have viewed a training program (designed to resolve employee dissatisfaction) as an attempt to transfer top management responsibility for a serious turnover problem to them. Other department heads might have misread the number of problems. A quick-reaction approach is oftentimes only a facade that is deliberately (and as often unintentionally) designed to validate managerial aspiration and competence. Nevertheless, the training director is inevitably forced to respond in a quick and decisive manner to the urgent problem. In these cases, the responsibility for diagnosing the problem and ascertaining what solution should be developed is transferred to the director of staff development.

It is usually the personnel director, director of human resources, or director of staff development who is responsible for determining the training needs of a hospital. Even so, this individual may find himself or herself in the uncomfortable position of not knowing when to suggest that alternative administrative interventions be utilized to solve the particular problem of interest. For example, the head of obstetrics in a hospital may request a program in time management for staff nurses after deciding that nurses are wasting too much time in administrative record keeping. The problem may not be the nurses' utilization of their time, but rather the department head's continual development and implementation of new forms and reports.

Similarly, when a quick diagnosis and recommendation are made by a chief executive officer, the better part of valor recommends acquiescence. However, if the original diagnosis results in a poor decision, it is not unusual for the director of staff development to take responsibility. The primary responsibility for determining training needs rests with the director, not with the chief executive officer of the hospital.

A director of inservice education or health care supervisor may discover that an external consultant is helpful in determining training needs. This decision to acquire outside assistance in the diagnosis of education/training/development issues may indicate gaps in a staff development program. Such assistance may also highlight the inadequacy of an employee evaluation system. Performance that is good may have been mistakenly measured as bad. For these reasons, the director of inservice education in any health care organization must strive to maintain open communications between the training department and those that it serves.

In other instances, the inservice department does not possess sufficient resources in a skill to effectively present a program.[15] This may contribute to hesitancy in comprehensively ascertaining training needs. For this and the preceding problems, it is recommended that external training components be integrated as part of an inservice or staff development program. The key to selecting a successful external education source is finding a source that has the ability to address the specific training issue at hand. This usually requires some searching, but the time expended in the process can be repaid by a better match between training needs and resources. If budgetary constraints are too severe, a last resource may be the selection of a prepackaged training program from a reliable source.

PREPACKAGED PROGRAMS

Hospitals inadvertently incorporate training on a continuing basis for many reasons.

- It may help solve a problem.
- It indicates a specific response—action—by a hospital manager to a potential problem (whether training-related or not).
- It delays further decisions and actions until the training is complete.
- It builds confidence in staff and management that the hospital is responsive to individual needs.
- It suggests that the hospital training program is actually doing something.
- It engenders an attitude that all is progressing smoothly within the hospital.

The question is whether the "training pill" really produces results.

An even more unsatisfactory choice (when there is no overall planned program design) by many hospitals is the selection of a prepackaged training program. Prospective payment may encourage staff development directors and supervisors to look seriously at prepackaged programs because of budget restrictions and the new demands accompanying the reimbursement change. Training program budget restrictions emanating from prospective payment cost control force staff development and inservice directors to capitalize on cost-effective options. Prepackaged programs are especially beneficial in this regard: they offer substantial content for a reasonable price. However, as we will see, there are significant trade-offs.

Prepackaged programs are also attractive because they offer timely content. With the pervasive impact of prospective payment throughout the entire hospital, supervisors must fulfill a tremendous knowledge vacuum. Staff need to know how to perform and manage in view of prospective payment. Since few internal training hospital training programs have the ability to meet all of these needs, it is likely that prepackaged programs will be adopted. Such a decision should not be made without careful consideration.

Many hospitals utilize prepackaged programs presented by universities, professional organizations, and consultants. Hospitals and health care institutions that are small, lack adequate internal staff resources, or operate within a frugal budget may depend on external training programs to develop and train workers. In some cases, money expended on external training programs is well spent, and the benefits far outweigh the costs. More often than not, however, the training program will be viewed as a virtual waste of time and money. This results from the failure to match inservice content with skill deficiencies.[16] Such a predicament need not occur.

The trouble with prepackaged programs is that they are often marketed with catchy titles that entice the unwary participant. For example, topics that everyone in the industry is talking about (e.g., prospective payment, DRGs, corporate culture, MBO, and stress management) and topics that appear to have a high entertainment rating (e.g., listening skills) are frequently the programs that are popular and sell well.

Attendance at exotic training locations (e.g., Atlantic City and Las Vegas) is especially tantalizing to a hospital administrator who has a surplus of funds with which to work. Rather than end the fiscal year with unused funds, health services administrators and programs may fall prey to a ritual of expending funds to maintain the next budget cycle's allocation. When the end of the fiscal year draws near, it is not unusual to hear of expenditures for strange objects, equipment, and trips related to staff development. In contrast to esoteric outlays, the justification for funding staff development programs often appears rational and needed, even if they do take place in Honolulu, Hawaii.

While the situations described above do happen, most hospital administrators and directors of staff development have to be and are quite cost conscious. With the introduction of prospective payment they may have very little choice to be otherwise. This concern for costs can become obsessive. As paradoxical as it may seem, the institution seeking a staff training program is usually more concerned about the cost of the program than its relevance to staff development needs. Every attempt should be made to locate a learning resource such as a workshop seminar in the community and contract for it at a fair price. However, costs and quality must be judiciously balanced.

It is also important to remember that research into the continued education of allied health personnel indicates that staff generally do not want to participate in education programs that are located far from the health facility.[17] This finding has specific meaning for improving hospital personnel development. It suggests that staff are interested in content first and style or atmosphere second.

Hospital managers are susceptible to being easily satisfied with low-cost training packages. Through contact with either professional consultants or universities, a packaged program is negotiated in which the contract fee is too good to overlook.

An opportunity to hear a seminar at half price may be too tempting for a director of staff development to pass up. After all, a program devoted to stress management, for example, is certain to be helpful to someone in the hospital.

Besides cost, other reasons expressed for using a professional trainer are

- He/she is funny.
- He/she is physically attractive.
- He/she has great presence (even though the material is less than useful).
- He/she gives attendees something to think about.

In essence, many training and education programs are entertaining. The consultant trainer usually has developed a smooth, thoroughly professional show that provides the audience with a cursory exposure to topics, while simultaneously maintaining some general relevance to their concerns. Throw in a binder full of handouts, a few jokes, an entertaining film, and a cocktail hour, and the training program evaluations will indicate a positive reaction to the consultant and further enhance her or his reputation. The positive evaluations will also make the administrator or staff development director responsible for arranging the training program look good.

After attending a few such training programs that entertain more than inform, health care personnel may begin to expect a good time. The opportunity to attend can, therefore, become a reward (rather than the satisfaction of a need), and not being invited can be seen as a punishment. Staff development under such circumstances is not development at all, but rather a retreat of sorts in disguise. It is this type of program that has given staff development the reputation of being a nonessential luxury the health care field cannot afford.

Another consideration in selecting prepackaged training programs is the site of the presentation. Most inservice directors do not have to worry about arranging facilities within which to conduct the training. Their organizations possess seminar rooms. Smaller health care organizations, such as nursing homes, clinics, or rural health centers, must either improvise or designate a suitable room (e.g., the cafeteria) as a part-time learning center. In these cases, it is not likely that a director has been hired specifically to supervise the staff development program, but, nevertheless, a successful program still can be pursued.

Greater flexibility must be built into smaller-scale programs, increasing the use of external training methods both on and off the premises. Funding for travel to the training site will also be more limited in these instances, thereby preventing the holiday syndrome. However, hospital administrators can also consider the increased motivation that might be attained through attendance at a regional or national professional conference. In the final analysis, the important principle to remember is judicious control over the use of prepackaged training programs.

TRAINING IS NOT A PANACEA

The use of the "training pill" and prepackaged programs suggests that staff development, training, or inservice education is often viewed as a panacea. Hospital executives, staff members, and inservice directors must come to recognize that staff development alone will not resolve all the problems confronting hospitals in a prospective payment environment. Training may establish conditions under which a hospital begins to formulate a comprehensive plan of action and to implement such a plan. But inservice education cannot itself change the external reimbursement constraints.

Two critical aspects of staff development should be kept in mind by hospital supervisors who contemplate expanded inservice education to resolve their organizations' woes: (1) staff development cannot substitute for purposeful employee selection, and (2) staff development is most relevant when training needs are objectively determined, rather than intuitively estimated. These ideas clearly underscore the realization that staff development is not a panacea—it is a means for helping hospitals manage problems (such as prospective payment) in a more efficient and effective manner.

Substituting Training for Selection

Staff development is not a remedy for poor selection of personnel when filling job vacancies. Extensive staff development will do little good when the individuals have neither the motivation and aptitude nor the personality attributes for developing into more effective performers. When expectations are too great, personnel may become frustrated and lapse into destructive or defensive behavioral mechanisms (e.g., aggression, regression, and the like).

The failure of staff development directors to understand that staff development should not be substituted for improper employee selection can put incredible stress on the individual as he or she is confronted with impossible demands, not to mention the dysfunctions it causes for the hospital.

Using Intuition Alone

The use of casual approaches for diagnosing staff development needs in hospitals and health care organizations is inadequate, considering the generally high degree of professionalism and education among health workers. Effective inservice education should be based on precise and continuous research into ascertaining possible training needs. Such analysis should consist of more than a subjective perception of the problem confronting a nursing unit, technical department, or other structural unit within a hospital. Merely applying an intuitive approach is an open invitation to misread a health care organization's pulse. What health care supervisors, educators, trainers, and directors of inservice education often identify as the problem is not truly the problem at all, but rather one portion of a larger problem or merely a symptom—not the cause. Until that problem is well defined, proposing a training solution is tantamount to solving a dilemma with insufficient knowledge or resources.[18]

Yet how many bad decisions, wasted efforts, and unneeded expenses are needed before hospital administrators and inservice directors gain adequate experience in accurately diagnosing training needs? Most trainers concede that it took years and countless mistakes to refine their perspective on training needs.

Is intuition in conflict with a systematic approach? Not at all. The two complement each other quite well. Intuition that is based on years of experience, observation, and judgment can make a systematic approach to staff development more viable and valid. However, unless a hospital manager or inservice director has dependable intuition, the diagnosis of training needs can be imprecise. A more systematic approach is both desirable and essential.[19]

STAFF DEVELOPMENT IS A LIFETIME COMMITMENT

Staff training and development in the health care field will rise to greater prominence as inservice education and training programs are more systematically developed. Hospital supervisors should understand that training programs can have positive effects on the productivity, efficiency, and effectiveness of health care services. Furthermore, training should not be viewed as a superfluous extra, but rather as an integral part of an ongoing management program designed to improve the provision of health services. In the final analysis, staff development is lifetime education and demands hospital lifetime commitment.

The judicious hospital has always recognized the importance of training, inservice education, and staff development. Under the current prospective payment environment, this wisdom and the resource investment it has generated should pay high dividends. Staff development under this management approach is a continuing investment in personnel, the hospital, and its patients. It is not a cure-all, quick fix, or tangential aspect of human resources management. Hospitals that have maintained this latter approach are usually disappointed by the program results and consequently tend to offer support on a sporadic basis in incremental levels. This approach will probably continue in the future in spite of prospective payment. The cycle will not be broken until hospitals can point to specific improvements in employee and organizational performance from staff development expenditures.

Staff development is a necessity, whether hospitals like to admit it or not. Because the prognosis for hospitals and medical care is an increasingly constrained reimbursement environment, it is essential that staff development programs contribute substantially to the management of these constraints. By demonstrating tangible end results in terms of improved performance, staff development will acquire greater recognition as a necessity, rather than a nicety.

NOTES

1. M.B. Straus et al., "The Impact of Continuing Education on the Nursing Profession: Historical Perspectives and Future Implications," *Journal of Continuing Education in Nursing* 13 (1982): 6–12.

2. R.C. Swanburg, *Inservice Education* (New York: G.P. Putnam's Sons, 1968). F.S. Curtis et al., *Continuing Education in Nursing* (Boulder, Colo.: Western Interstate Commission for Higher Education [WICHE], 1969).

3. E.C. Lambertson, "Inservice Education for Emergency Nursing Service," *Nursing Clinics of North America* 2 (1967): 237–343.

4. N.D. Medearis and E.S. Popiel, "Guidelines for Organizing Inservice Education," in *Staff Development* (Wakefield, Mass.: Contemporary Publishing, 1975).

5. M.M. Cantor, "Education for Quality Care," in *Staff Development* (Wakefield, Mass.: Contemporary Publishing, 1975).

6. D.J. Del Bueno, "Continuing Education: Spinach and Other Good Things," *Journal of Nursing Administration* 7 (1977): 32–34. B.R. Rudnick and I.M. Bolte, "The Case for On-Going Inservice Education," in *Staff Development* (Wakefield, Mass.: Contemporary Publishing, 1975).

7. W. McGehee and P.W. Thayer, *Training in Business and Industry* (New York: John Wiley & Sons, Inc., 1961).

8. I.L. Goldstein, *Training: Program Development and Evaluation* (Monterey, Calif.: Brooks/Cole, 1974), 3.

9. C.C. Snow and J.T. Grant, "Answers to Questions about Management Development Programs," *Hospital and Health Services Administration* 25 (1980): 36–53.

10. A.L. Bures, "Management Development in the Health Care Sector: An Empirical Study," *Hospital and Health Services Administration* 28 (1983): 8–23.

11. M.L. Moore and P. Dutton, "Training Needs Analysis Review and Critique," *Academy of Management Review* 3, no. 3 (1978): 533.

12. Bures, "Management Development," 8–23.

13. K.P. Larson, "Taking Action To Contain Health Care Costs," *Personnel Journal* 59, no. 8 (1980): 640–44.

14. D.L. Kirkpatrick, *Supervisor Training and Development* (Reading, Mass.: Addison-Wesley Publishing Co., Inc., 1971).

15. M.M. Broadwell, *The Supervisor As Instructor* (Reading, Mass.: Addison-Wesley Publishing Co., Inc., 1968). J. Dittrich, G. Lang, and J. White, "Nurses' Management Problems and Their Training Implications," *Personnel Journal* 58, no. 5 (May 1979): 317.

16. K. Rechnagel, "Why Management Training Fails and How To Make It Succeed," *Personnel Journal* 53, no. 8 (August 1984): 595–597.

17. D.C. Broski and S.C. Upp, "What Allied Health Professionals Want from Continuing Education Programs," *Journal of Allied Health* 14 (1979): 24–28.

18. D.F. Michalak and E.G. Yager, *Making the Training Process Work* (New York: Harper & Row, 1979). B.M. Bass and J.A. Vaughan, *Training in Industry: The Management of Learning* (Monterey, Calif.: Brooks/Cole, 1966).

19. H.L. Smith and N.F. Elbert, "An Integrated Approach to Performance Evaluation in the Health Care Field," *Health Care Management Review* 5 (1980): 59–67. R. Blomberg, E. Levy, and A. Anderson, "Assessing the Value of Employee Training," *Health Care Management Review* 13, no. 1 (1988): 63–70.

Fred W. Graumann
Gregory T. Finnegan

16

Productivity: The Dilemma of the Non-Revenue-Producing Department

THE PRODUCTIVITY IMPERATIVE

The hospitals in this country are a major component of a mature industry in a declining market. Patient days increased unabated through 1982. But since then, with the advent of the DRG prospective payment system, patient days have been declining steadily. And they are projected to continue to decline steadily (American Hospital Association 1987).

The last 25 years are worthy of note because during these years hospitals experienced what marketing calls a *product life cycle*. A product life cycle is the time covering the initiation of a product into a market, its expansion, and finally the end of expansion and competitiveness within the market, which is now well defined and no longer growing. During these years development and growth hit limits, and there began to be consolidations, closings, and purchases of hospitals. Finally, the industry as a whole began to cope with the limitations of all available resources (Boston Consulting Group 1972).

Beginning in the 1960s and into the early 1970s, the access to health care was broadened substantially and culminated with the advent of Medicare and Medicaid. More people were able to get more quality medical care with ease than ever before. With a major focus on access, length of stay increased. The cost-reimbursement system indirectly encouraged more. Increasing the range and utilization of services for each patient was financially rewarding to hospitals. Increasing the number of beds increased patients days, market share, and revenue. Large cost increases would be met with even larger revenue gains (Jennings 1988).

In the seventies, the cost containment effort emerged as a way for hospitals to monitor and curtail some costs. Health care costs rose to $458 billion which was 11 percent of the country's gross national product ($458 billion) (Freeland and Schendler 1987). Success at this cost control effort would show that federal regulatory intervention was unnecessary. Hospitals set up cost containment committees and directed department heads to look for ways to cut or limit costs. There are varied opinions as to the level of success of the effort; while costs were reduced, there were still many attempts at individual growth through expansion of beds and services. Capital costs tended to continue to increase.

As we know, DRGs have drastically changed what is rewarding. Access-to-care questions remain, but more and bigger is no longer necessarily "better"; efficiency is better. The financial rewards go to those capable of reducing length of stay, eliminating "unnecessary" services, reducing patient utilization of inpatient services, increasing outpatient activity, and maximizing current bed capacity, resources, and throughput. From 1970 to 1980, hospital occupancy decreased 2.6 percent, from 78 percent to 75.4 percent. From 1980 to 1986, it decreased 11.2 percent, from 75.4 percent to 64.2 percent. By 1988, some estimates placed unused beds at nearly 50 percent. DRGs in an all-payer environment have spurred competition for patients, as well as for the resources to provide care for them (Jennings 1988).

In the next 10 years, Medicare will continue to drive down reimbursement both to hospitals and physicians. Legislators in Washington, D.C., apparently do not see people getting hurt by reimbursement reductions to hospitals, and a limit to the expansion of this segment of the economy is a priority concern (Cavarrochi 1988). Rather, they see decreased profits to hospitals. They will continue their attempts to reduce beds.

The Joint Commission on Accreditation of Healthcare Organizations has identified quality assurance as the key to hospital evaluation in the decade from 1990 to 2000 (Jennings 1988). Hospitals that survive the changes of the DRG prospective payment system will be directed to focus their attention on the quality of the service provided. Quality assurance has already been a major concern and thrust of the DRG system. The challenge is not to look at quality assurance as revisiting the DRG effort; rather, it will be an emphasis on yet another look—a quality assurance look that takes into account the maturity of the whole market. Such a view focuses on the residual issues of providing optimal care with decreasing financial and human resources, redesigning how service is delivered and measured, and emphasizing customer satisfaction as an important ingredient to demonstrating successful health care delivery.

Issues to Consider in Productivity Programs

The shift in focus across the last three decades from access to cost control and, now, to quality, in the face of price control, has fostered the re-emergence of a focus on productivity.

When Robert Wood Johnson University Hospital began its exploration of productivity issues, we managers knew one thing. We wanted to make sure that there was linkage between the performance of individuals and the performance of groups. Our belief was that top-down-driven efforts at productivity can yield only what individuals and the group (formal as well as informal) have agreed to give. Our experience is that peer group pressure or peer group norms yield an additional level of result. We felt that if groups were properly prepared for good work performance, individuals in the group who might otherwise be prone to poor or marginal performance would be affected by the group norm. Because individuals tend to desire to meet the expectation of the group, they would, therefore, improve their work habits, behavior, and work results.

With these "truths" in hand, we began reviewing productivity-monitoring programs that were available on the market. We found the following:

- They typically reported on indicators that were removed from direct performance. There was a strong reliance on classic productivity indicators, such as cost per admission, cost per full-time equivalent (FTE), or cost per square foot. These measures are often attempted for non-revenue-producing departments. Unfortunately, their language has no discernible bearing on performance. To report to Security that its cost per square foot went up or down does not inherently suggest anything about the department's performance or ability to fulfill its mission—or how to fix what is allegedly "wrong" with that department. That is to say that a vacancy, while driving down the cost per square foot, does not suggest improved or even good performance by the department or the manager. The ability of the Personnel Department to keep its cost per hospital FTE stable has little bearing on the service it provides to its constituency. There is no suggestion of improved service, performance, or productivity in the activity of FTEs and the supposed relevance to the Personnel Department's functions.

- Package programs frequently use language that is not understood or is difficult to translate and suggest indicators that are even more difficult to track. Relative value units (RVUs) make a lot of sense theoretically. But like the cost per hospital FTE, it is an indicator not tied to observable performance. As an indicator it does not provide guidance as to where something might be wrong. There can be as much time spent in interpreting the result of the analysis as is spent to obtain the analysis. People do not think in terms of relative value units. We think that people might be able to make judgments on RVUs in smaller applications—e.g., daily chart work done by medical records coders—but it is difficult to manage as a major feedback mechanism for department operations.

- These packages do not address investigation and action for improvement. It is not apparent what to do when some of these indicators suggest a problem. If the threshold for Admitting is cost per admission, it is not terribly apparent what to do when the cost goes up ten cents per admission, or maybe even one dollar per admission. It is good information to have, but we find that there is little tie-in of such broad-based indicators to performance at work group and individual levels. When an indicator suggests a problem, the department head is oftentimes forced to analyze what few records are available or to try to make some intuitive judgment as to why the variance occurred. Frequently, the first defense involves standard reasons: the census was up, the invoices from the previous month hit the books a month late, etc. There should be a better tie-in between the focus of major indicators and the work done by individuals and groups.

- The package is generally installed without any employee input. It is difficult enough to get support for a productivity-monitoring program; implementing a program without some kind of employee involvement in determining measures, standards, and reporting mechanism would most likely greatly diminish the effectiveness of the program.

- These programs are very expensive. The price for one department multiplied by only several possible departments quickly gets to six figures. Programs involving on-site consultants typically generate six- or seven-figure costs and involve a very few departments—and then only revenue-producing departments.

Based on our view of what was available to us, we decided to take a closer look at how we could accomplish what we did not see available in the market in a form or at a cost that we liked. Because we decided to consider performance as our focus, our goal became to set up a performance-monitoring program. This distinction is more than cosmetic. Employees are as used to having performance measured as they are "frightened" by productivity monitoring. We came to consider productivity a subset to performance. We would define where we were going, why we were heading that way, and how we were going to get there.

CREATING A SUCCESSFUL PERFORMANCE-MONITORING PROGRAM

We began with the goal of linking individual and group performance. We knew also that we wanted to create specific incentives for proven worthy performance. To accomplish this, we developed the following guidelines as our strategy map.

Feedback must be tied to performance. We wanted it to be more apparent to staff which action is necessary when the feedback suggests poor or deteriorating performance. Therefore, feedback to various levels, groups, and individuals is stated in performance language. For example, feedback that "95 percent of personnel action forms for pay raises were done within two working days" suggests a performance that the employee can relate to. While there may be further detail that can be reported with the 95 percent in this example, the employee can interpret the feedback and focus independently on behavior that can improve this performance.

Language must be understood. We wanted to avoid any language that needs further interpretation. The language used is the language of the employee.

Employees need to be involved in the whole process. There are some principles about performance monitoring that are not up for a vote: there will be monitoring, there will be measures and standards, and there will be improvements, as appropriate. Everything else is up for discussion. In fact, the discussion in itself is valuable. It is a way for employees to "get their heads"—individually and collectively—into the performance improvement effort. Further, it acknowledges that the employee is the expert at that job and knows where performance improvement can take place.

Again, there are certain principles that must be met to ensure overall effectiveness and fairness. Many problem areas raised would be improved by employee suggestions. Examples where discussion and consensus or compromise could help prepare people include setting up simplified systems or procedures for collecting data, recording data, preparing the feedback mechanism, displaying the data, and analyzing data to help determine standards. In fact, as the U.S. economy has become more service oriented, most business executives believe that improvement of American productivity will be nearly impossible without the workers' support (Franke, Harrick, and Klein 1982). The investment in employees will increase productivity and overall patient care (Alpert 1986).

We were determined to build *a management tool to be interactively used rather than a record-keeping document.*

Wherever possible, we wanted to include a troubleshooting guide for people. The measures that are tracked should not have to wait for monthly reporting before there is a "read on the situation," which determines that a problem exists and that appropriate action is necessary. Problems that are recurring suggest the appropriateness of troubleshooting guides that allow individuals and groups to respond to deficiencies and act appropriately in a timely fashion to make improvements when they are spotted. In fact, part of the reporting to supervisors and department heads should include the frequency and type of these problems.

Typically, most people see pieces of a group's operation; few see the whole. Work groups may concentrate on accomplishing the standards of their performance measure and never realize that their good performance is adversely affecting the performance of another work group. It can be more likely that individuals in small work groups work effectively within those limited settings, but more significant inefficiencies occur between/among large work groups and departments. It is critical that a work group monitor its interfaces.

Supervisors should look at what happens between work groups. They are in a position to influence people to alter or improve what they do when their performance adversely affects others. The same is true for department heads who can influence supervisors or work groups when they see that problems are being created for other departments. The reporting of information from employees to supervisors and from supervisors to department heads is an essential part of the process of monitoring individual, group, and department performance. In the final analysis, it is quite probable that most problems are the result of managerial decisions that affect job definition, controls, and work flow (Sayles 1973). However, performance feedback and simple goal setting will improve performance (Still 1986).

If there is one more principle that guided us, it was the belief that *behavior that is rewarded will be repeated.* The work of Herzberg, Maslow, and others has suggested for years that people are motivated by select characteristics depending on what they have and do not have, what they need and what they want. People—at work or in their private lives—desire recognition that what they do is appreciated and valued. Relationships in general thrive when such recognition is tangible.

At work, recognition has to be ongoing. There has to be an environment that people find personally supportive. People do not have to "be themselves," but they do need to feel that they belong, that they can be at ease, and that they are supported. At intervals—both regular and irregular—there should be commendation that recognizes the achievement and effort individuals and groups make toward some commonly held or stated goal. The recognition can be verbal and should be varied from formal to informal. In fact, employees often trust informal feedback more than the formal because of the spontaneity of the informal (Veninga 1975). Not only should recognition for a job well done be expressed to the person who performed well; it should be shared with others as individuals and told to the group as well. When other members of the group are engaged in a similar activity, they should be encouraged to talk to the good performer to discuss their ideas or opinions. This activity is good for new, inexperienced, or less confident members of a group. While the neophyte learns from someone who is a positive model, the good performer, in turn, is getting individual and group recognition. All manner of recognition, verbal and nonverbal, should be provided regularly and irregularly.

Incentives represent a more innovative approach to recognizing worthy performance. More attempts need to be made to create incentives. Popular incentives include sick time buy-back and gainsharing programs. If a sick time buy-back program succeeds, it reduces the dollars expended to cover for call-ins, while maintaining quality of service over the days that would have been affected by increased sick time use. Another approach is attendance incentives whereby incentives are given for *not* having unscheduled absences. In this example, the incentive paid for optimal attendance over a set time period reduces overtime dollars (King 1988). Performance problems need to be analyzed for their impact to the bottom line. Recurring problems, such as the sick time problem, can be corrected over time if there is an incentive to do so. These incentives should be group incentives to ensure that individuals within the group will help each other, maximize their performance, and work as a team to create the desired performance level for the department.

PUTTING PERFORMANCE MONITORING TOGETHER

There are four building blocks to achieving a successful program that is geared toward performance improvement, and these must be considered in any implementation strategy.

1. selecting performance indicators
2. setting up a monitoring and feedback system
3. implementing the performance system—a context for optimizing performance
4. creating performance incentives

Selecting Performance Indicators

The objective of this program is to maximize the ability of employees and supervisors to the "read" what is happening over the day and the week and, when appropriate, to act independently to correct deficiencies.

In our model, there are three levels of performance indicators: (1) a single productivity indicator that identifies total cost over a single output parameter, (2) three to five major indicators that feed directly either to cost or to service output, and (3) several supporting indicators which are tracked daily or weekly by employees that feed directly to the major indicators.

The purpose of the productivity indicator is simply to measure the overall expense of the operation against some major volume of output. This is the broadest view of "how we are doing." Productivity indicators are easier to see in revenue-producing departments—cost per test, cost per patient day, cost per procedure. This single indicator is insufficient by itself to be helpful to non-revenue-producing departments, such as accounting, personnel, security, admitting, and medical records. Being responsive to requisitions, admitting patients, and completing charts are performances that can suffer while the productivity indicator could be improving. An increase in volume or an increase in staff vacations can show an improvement when the service actually becomes slower or worse in some other way. Non-revenue-producing departments have to look at more discrete indicators to properly gauge their effectiveness.

The manager needs to review three to five major indicators of performance that tell how well the work group is accomplishing its goal(s). Two indicators may be financial, while three may be process indicators. Admitting should track the percentage of credit reviews it receives from the credit department before admission. It should be 100 percent, but if it is less, then some number of patients are being admitted without a deposit or credit approval.

At the same time, Medical Records should report the number of completed charts, regardless of the reasons for charts being incomplete. The overall effectiveness of the department is measured by the percentages of complete and incomplete charts.

The manager may review all available indicators used at all levels, but these three to five major indicators are those that the manager reports regularly to his administrator. These indicators create conversations on work group performance between the administrator and the manager and between the manager and the supervisor. These indicators are reported anywhere from daily to weekly. They are the objective statements of current day-to-day operations. They also remove the misunderstandings and vague comments between levels and indicate how good or how bad things are. While the preference would always be that data for analysis are a byproduct of regular work procedures, sometimes it may be necessary to build a tracking system apart from work routine.

Supporting performance indicators are worker-level indicators that are tracked by employees and reported to supervisors. The issue is not one of close supervision; in fact, many of these indicators will be on subjects in part beyond the employees' control. For example, Medical Records may have as one major indicator "number of completed charts versus number initiated into the system." Supporting indicators may include the number of attempts to get the physician to complete the chart, the aging of incomplete charts by 10-day increments, and the number of days each chart is completed after discharge by each physician. The number of days that a chart is incomplete can be the cue for an employee or supervisor to call a physician's office.

In summary, the focus of any indicator should be on performance. Good indicators will direct people toward departmental effectiveness, excellence in service from the client's perspective, and a tendency toward improvement. If Admitting tracks the number of missing records for patients on the day of their same-day surgery, they will be in a better position to reduce the number of missing records. At first this is difficult for Admitting personnel to support because they do not control the performance of doctors, clinical departments, or patients necessary to get the needed records to Admitting the day prior to surgery. It would seem that the number of preadmission testing registrations processed would be a fairer indicator to judge the effectiveness of an admitting coordinator.

But the problems created by missing records remain untouched. Omitting such a performance indicator fails to represent what is good for the hospital and the department, as well as for patients and physicians. Missing records delay patients' going to the O.R., result in inadequate clinical and demographic information, back up patient transfers and admissions throughout the day, and increase the waiting and aggravation factor for patients and physicians. The effectiveness of the department warrants monitoring the indicator of missing records.

Likewise in Training, an obvious performance indicator is the number of student hours generated by the department and by individual. Monitoring such an indicator—student hours—creates a priority. The number of student hours will increase. However, the drive toward increased student hours may be counterproductive. If training is offered in response to a performance problem, the measure of effectiveness is not in the number of hours or of students taught; it is also not in the quality of instruction. It is not even in the cost per student hour. The effectiveness of the training is determined by the extent to which the problem has been affected. Something should have improved: accuracy, quality, volume, cost, frequency, or rate. The focus of performance indicators for Training is on the improved performance of those trained.

In Personnel, the effectiveness of the department is tied directly to the service it provides. It is a pyrrhic victory to say that the internal processing of pay changes was done within a standard time if 20 percent of the employees did not receive the pay increase when they expected it. Including Payroll in the goal—and then influencing Payroll employees to meet it—will create a hospitalwide success and customer satisfaction and recognition of Personnel's achievement.

In the examples given above, the performance indicators do not shrink from control outside of one's purview. The fact that the admitting coordinator does not control physician behavior and the fact that the trainer does not control on-the-job supervision are disregarded in pursuit of a larger result—namely, that performance indicators that tie individuals to group effectiveness will create avenues to improve communication with other work groups that will improve the organizational area most in need of improvement—the interface between departments.

Setting Up a Monitoring and Feedback System

Monitoring is a tracking system. It tracks where we have been and, just like a road map, tracks where we are headed. Having plotted our course, or objectives, we monitor our path, and our progress, to give ourselves sufficient feedback to ensure that we are headed as planned. Detours of any kind, small or great, can be tolerated or explained when we know that they are occurring and when we take action as necessary to get us back on our path.

The monitoring system is the vehicle for determining who reports what to whom and in what form. This question is answered after the indicators are determined and people know what they are tracking. The display, or printed format, is best expressed as a graph showing activity over time—daily, weekly, etc. The reporting "up" may be informal and scratched on slips of paper, but the reporting "down" should be more formal. Tables or graphs that show performance over time are preferred.

Often, the monitoring system redefines what supervisors do. Typically, supervisors begin collecting information from subordinates that they never collected before, except in a crisis or for occasional management reports. They now collect this information on a regular basis from employees who have the expectation that they will collect or prepare simple data and pass it on to the supervisor. Employees feed data to supervisors who collate and pass it on to department managers. Oftentimes in these two transfers, there is a simple discussion of how things are going.

The act of monitoring is done relative to the way things ought to be. If a personnel clerk is expected to process 85 percent of change of status forms in a day and reports only 60 percent to the supervisor, (s)he will probably exchange information to address the performance gap. Special priority work could be the explanation, or a problem in getting the work done may be identified. While a weekly or monthly summary will record the level of performance in that day, the daily exchange of information can generate follow-up activity by the supervisor to resolve any difficulties in future performance immediately. When the admitting coordinator reports that 95 percent of the next day PAT patients are registered, but only 50 percent have all of the necessary paperwork in, the supervisor can take immediate action to address the problem. Likewise, when the supervisor reports summaries of indicators to the manager, problem areas can be addressed for follow-up activity.

But monitoring performance is not enough. The aim is to improve performance. Improvements need not wait until reports are written and passed up and down two or more levels. Each indicator should be reviewed to determine under which circumstances someone, employee or supervisor, will take some corrective action. The goal is to empower individuals to initiate improvement in areas where necessary corrective action is predictable.

On a regular basis, performance indicators are then fed back to the people who provide the performance. Daily, weekly, and/or monthly summaries of performance are displayed for all to see. An indicated above, this should be on paper and, when possible, should be displayed as a graph. In any event, the display should show actual performance relative to some standard. The standard can be a target based on past performance or based on what other work groups in other hospitals are able to accomplish. Feedback that is quantitative and made relative to a goal, or standard, provides information that many employees desire—namely, "let me know how I'm doing."

In summary, once performance indicators are selected, the next step is to create the information loop to the people providing the service. This means setting up a monitoring system that defines who will report the performance indicators to whom and what they will do with the information. Then the information is displayed in some way and fed back to the performers. Finally, where possible, the information represents standards or triggers that will suggest when appropriate action is needed. This entire process of identifying indicators, tracking them, feeding them back to people who generate them, and making improvement where possible is one that collectively creates a drive toward improvement. Often, the activity of monitoring performance will create improvement (Luthans, Maciag, and Rosenkrantz 1983). In many cases, however, the data will suggest a problem where the solution is not readily discernible. In such cases, some analysis of performance is required to identify the cause of the performance problem. A system of analyzing performance causes that will complete the drive toward improvements now becomes critical.

Implementing the Performance System—A Context for Optimizing Performance

Creating some of the indicators in the last section may seem foreign to Human Resources. Under the DRG system, though, we have to re-evaluate the way we measure ourselves. Some indicators sound like management engineering. Historically, that may be true. We would say that while the management engineers have contributed to the performance improvement effort, they have been least likely to be able to help create improvements in human performance. On the other hand, *work load analysis provides definite benefit*. It helps to match labor resources to workload needs. The management engineering approach will aim to level workload and reduce discretionary work through incorporation of productivity goals (Greidanus 1988).

The skills of the manager need to be expanded to go beyond problem situations and involve the entire work situation, or performance system. We find that there are some specific situations under which people will perform well at work. The settings in which people perform well are well documented and have long been known. The role of supervision is to create the environment in which the desired performance can take place. If any of the elements is missing or lacking, performance problems will occur. The manager needs to focus on the broader performance system; he or she needs to look systematically at performance. The elements of a performance model include good feedback, procedures supporting performance, balanced consequences to performance, an environment supporting performance, and adequate knowledge and skill to do the job well.

Feedback needs to be clear, given in a timely manner, and given regularly. The biggest single cause of performance problems is the lack, or inadequacy, of feedback. Too often feedback is not clear; language is used that does not make sense or is too vague to direct workers toward improved performance. Feedback such as "You weren't courteous to that woman" is too vague, as well as too judgmental, to allow a person to focus on how to handle the same situation better at a future time.

When feedback is given, it can be a real determinant of the success of improving the performance. The general principle is to give feedback as close to a performance as possible. Someone answering the phone by saying "Hello" without identifying the department or giving his or her name should be given feedback immediately afterward as to how everyone is asked to answer the phone (e.g., "Good Morning, Accounting Department," etc.). This is an occasion when immediate feedback makes sense because the likelihood of that person's answering the phone soon is great. They will have the opportunity to quickly use what they heard and improve their performance. At the same time, feedback prior to a performance can be enormously helpful in improving performance. In this case, an inability to perform a specific task well that occurs infrequently can be better addressed prior to its next occurrence.

Feedback also needs to be given regularly. When feedback is irregular, it stands the chance of being negative. When feedback is irregular, people draw a conclusion that supports mediocre to poor performance: "I guess everything is OK; nobody says anything."

The conclusion is erroneous, of course, but understandable. Without regular feedback, people have no gauge to go by except when things are very wrong. Then the manager puts on the heat. There is a flurry of activity, and the problem—or rather the symptom of a real problem—appears to go away. People settle down and eventually return to the way they usually do things. In this type of setting, the stage is set for the fulfillment of a very unhappy prophecy.

Setting up simple feedback systems can improve performance measurably. When analyzing performance problems, feedback should be the first element looked at. Again, managers assume that people know how well they are doing when they do not. Feedback can take time. It can involve time to collect data for feedback to people, time to give the feedback in a constructive way, and time to deal with any discomfort associated with the feedback. A frequent lament by people at work, including managers, is "I don't know where I stand." Setting up simple feedback systems can improve performance measurably.

In most cases when a poor performance can be traced to the way things get done—procedures—it is not necessarily true that the procedure is wrong, or faulty, or ill conceived. Oftentimes the procedure can work, except it will not work in the present construct of time, resources, and other procedures. Employees generically have to accomplish many tasks requiring varied times, set procedures, carry out simple and complex communications, and work under various levels of stress to accomplish major objectives in a given shift. Some procedures will simply not get done well, or as well as planned. The reason has less to do with people and more to do with the procedure's chance for success, given the context of accomplishing several competing objectives.

Procedures that are constructed without appropriate allowance for their context are probably doomed to failure, or at least inadequate compliance. What will work in a vacuum will create predictable performance problems in the real world. These problems will be blamed on people. People will suffer, as will the operation. Consideration for procedures includes concern not only for how things are done but also for when they are done, by whom, how often, and to what end. Some procedures will be more successful at other times, if done by someone else, or if done less frequently; they may even be eliminated entirely if there is insufficient reason to continue. Tom Peters (1985) points out that simplifying routines, eliminating steps, and organizing better not only will improve quality but also will lower cost.

One way to ensure that worthy performance is achieved and repeated when desired is to make sure that a positive consequence is derived from doing that which is desired. Creating positive consequences for all the tasks done throughout a day is impossible, unrealistic, and even unnecessary. It is, however, a managerial error not to consider where positive consequences do and do not occur.

A corollary to this principle is to make sure that a positive consequence does not support a competing, or undesirable, performance. A very real reason why some things do not get done on time, well, or at all is that something of a lower priority has a positive consequence for an employee. This positive consequence can be personal time, an easier workload, friendlier people to deal with, supervisory accolades, etc.

A more common corollary to the general principle of positive reinforcement is that poor performance should be met with negative consequences. If people cannot change the consequences from the negative, they will find ways to avoid these negative consequences. Their attempts to minimize their pain can result in tasks not done or done late. If the negative feedback from a supervisor has to do with time to complete a task, the employee may find the most expedient way to complete that portion of the task that will suggest completion, thereby achieving the desired end of avoiding negative feedback.

Balancing consequences means looking for ways to positively reinforce good performance, to eliminate—or reduce—any negatives that impede good performance, and to remove any positive reinforcements that focus people in the wrong direction.

Resources are needed to adequately accomplish most tasks. In general, people, time, and supplies are needed. More specifically, people need supplies, space, time, other people, information, and equipment in order to get their jobs done. An insufficient quantity of any of these can impede the quality or quantity of their work. When resources are available only at insufficient levels, it is appropriate to ask questions about how things get done: to what extent can we do things differently and accomplish the same end? This question can direct work groups to better handle accomplishments when resources are in short supply.

People need to know how to do things. When they don't know how to do something, they should receive skill training. Training is the easiest solution to poor performance problems when lack of knowledge is the cause of the problem. This is especially true of supervisors who too frequently receive little supervisory training. To some extent their role and work get redefined in a performance monitoring system. When they see that getting the job done is the context for the monitoring, they will be better able to see the value in the system for themselves and their supervisory accomplishments (Key 1987).

However, an essential aspect of job knowledge is knowing what is expected in accomplishing the objectives of a department. Creating clear expectations of what contributes to operational success is critical. People need to operate from a mission they can articulate. The fulfillment of work is tied to accomplishments, or attempts toward achieving a mission. In this context, tasks getting done efficiently and effectively succeed beyond themselves. Success involving a change of status form lies not just in the fact that it was processed within one day of receipt; rather, the success involves meeting an urgent need by the laboratory to fill a position for the following week.

Another critical issue overlooked around the factors of knowledge is the ability of people to discriminate regarding cues that indicate either when to perform some task or which task is needed for a certain set of conditions. A cue is some signal that says, "Now is when you do X." A nurse may be qualified beyond question to treat decubiti—bed sores. However, if she or he is unable to discern the onset of decubiti, she or he is unable to provide a larger good—namely, preventing the spread of bed sores that causes serious problems later. The inability of people to identify when to take action, or which action to take from their collection of skills, will create performance problems.

Finally, people may know how to do something, but they are unable to perform as desired. They lack the skill or capacity to accomplish a task the way it should be done, or at the rate it should be done. If the issue involves something done occasionally, practice time can improve mastery of the task. If the task occurs only occasionally, a performance guide may be the best way to improve performance. Performance guides are drawings or decision tables or flow charts that show someone how to make the right judgments or do the right things in the appropriate sequence to perform well.

Creating Performance Incentives

Positive reinforcement of any behavior will result in the repetition of that behavior. It is difficult to predict the outcome of punitive feedback. The child who is paddled for running into the street after a ball without looking both ways will not necessarily look both ways the next time. In fact, it is very likely that the next time the child runs into the street, he or she will not look both ways. Instead, the child will look back to see if a parent is watching. Similarly, the manager who never gives feedback unless something is wrong allows people to mistakenly assume that things are going well, or that their performance is as it should be. If feedback is neither positive nor negative, but is somewhere between nonexistent to insufficient, people's performance will deteriorate over time. They will assume that all is well and learn to respond to brush fires identified by management, rather than actively making improvements when they are needed. It is very important, then, to keep the reinforcement desirable, while at the same time monitoring its effectiveness (Healy 1987).

Positive recognition is a primary management tool for motivating employees. The manager can predict that good performance can be improved and maintained as a result of it. Public and private compliments, simple performance achievement celebrations, coaching, professional development talks, and merit reviews are ways the manager has to reinforce worthy and desired performance. An innovative method for extending this recognition and, in fact, creating the basis for driving a group toward performance excellence is to use incentives.

We associate incentive programs primarily with for-profit manufacturing environments. While obvious differences exist in manufacturing and health care products, look at the goals of James Lincoln (1951), owner of Lincoln Electric, the world leader in arc welding: "The primary goal of any industry to be successful continuously must be to make a better and better product to be sold to more and more people at a lower and lower price. Every design can be bettered. Every method can be improved. Every skill can be increased" (1951). Lincoln's faith in people and their recognition created many successes, including a turnover rate that is one-sixth the industry average, no strikes, no unions, excellent productivity, and employee year-end bonuses that average 97.6 percent of payroll for everyone. Since 1934, Lincoln Electric has achieved the goal stated by Lincoln by encouraging pride in employees' work and by giving a year-end bonus proportional to the work group's contribution to the year's success (Shore 1986).

The principles certainly transfer to any other industry, and the goal as Lincoln states it is transferable as well. The difference may be that the reimbursement structures in health care are driving the price down. Lincoln's view of getting more service to more people is replaced in health care with a similar suggestion regarding competition where number of beds, length of stay, and admissions are being driven down, resulting in increased competition for fewer patients.

Pat Groner, executive director of Baptist Hospital in Pensacola, Florida, outlines hospitalwide attempts at creating departmental incentives beginning in the 1950s (Groner, Appleyard, and Hicks 1977). So, though incentives are not new to health care, very limited use has been made of them. However, today group incentives are becoming increasingly visible around the country. Incentives help to focus a work group on work group effectiveness rather than on personal reward. When properly focused, individuals will have a stronger identity with the overall accomplishments of the group. There are several steps in setting up an incentive program.

- Set group versus individual goals.
- Set targets for eligibility.
- Determine the incentive.
- If dollars are used, determine the source of the dollars.
- Determine the payment mechanism.

Group incentives create the increases in performance and productivity anticipated in such a program. When the group is rewarded, the behavior and accomplishments of everyone become the concern of everyone. With group incentives, people fill in for fellow group members who are sick, tardy, taking personal days, and on vacation. When the workload fluctuates, the group works together to complete tasks for the whole group.

Conversely, this penchant toward teamwork is not supported with individual incentives. If individual initiative is rewarded, that initiative will be evident. But, very likely, it will be at the expense of the group and the group's effectiveness. If the quantity of service is the indicator for an incentive, people may use their initiative and ingenuity to get the easier job or the job that takes the least amount of time. More difficult or time-consuming jobs will be left for others. This will warrant a system of fairly parceling out the hard or time-consuming jobs to everyone. Not only might this create bad feelings as individuals charge unfairness in the allocation system, but also the emphasis on the hard jobs might be out of proportion to the value they have for the group or department. In Medical Records, the difficult cases are the ones that frequently represent the most charges. In Personnel, the difficult recommendations for wage changes will be those where the duties have not changed, but the market conditions have. In Escort, the patients on upper floors may have to wait longer because of the allocation system.

Individual incentives can improperly focus employees on their own interests, rather than on accomplishing the mission of the work group. Therefore, the group incentive is highly desirable as a means to focus a group on the effectiveness of the group.

The next step is to set targets for eligibility. For example, the Admitting PAT personnel would have a performance indicator such as 90 percent of PAT patients for the following day are preregistered. Ninety-percent compliance becomes a minimal standard for saying that we are doing well. Ninety-five percent becomes the threshold for eligibility for an incentive. No matter what the incentive is, no one in PAT will be eligible unless the group—not individuals—achieves 95 percent preregistration of PAT patients for the next day.

The incentive itself needs to be something that is perceived as valuable by individuals and the group. Options include money, prizes, vacations, and free time. The best way to determine what a work group's members value is to ask them. Perhaps the best incentive is money. Money overcomes the differences in taste and preferences of individuals. Rather than having individuals determine their liking for particular prizes as a condition of their effort, money provides a common ground that tells people to get what they prefer with the monetary incentive they earn. However, some use non-monetary incentives after determining what employees like (Young 1984).

A monetary incentive is also easily divided among individuals and work groups. A common method of distribution is according to a percentage of salary. The available dollars that will be given to employees are divided by the total salary dollars for the eligible employees. This results in a percentage that is then multiplied by each eligible employee's salary for the time period to determine the personal incentive. Another method would be to determine a set dollar amount to reward each employee, regardless of her or his salary level. Some health care organizations report very large payouts. One, in Southfield, Michigan, paid out $4.3 million in its first year by sharing gains 50–50 with employees (Droste 1987).

The dollars awarded should come from the reduced expenses realized by teamwork. These dollars can come from reduced overtime expense, reduced purchased labor expense, reduced costs for materials, and other cost reduction efforts.

The payment mechanism is best handled with a separate check from Payroll. Payment can be by pay period, monthly, or annually. The advantage of a by-pay-period system lies in the principle of immediate gratification and reinforcement. Money received after one or two weeks provides an immediate payoff. On the other hand, the advantage of annual payments is that the dollars can be held in a bank and earn interest during the year. The annual payment can then be timed to coincide with the Christmas holiday, for example.

EXAMPLES OF OUTCOMES

Whether or not a department generates revenue, it must still interact with many other departments. Although typically not recognized, each department is the client of every other department. The ability to satisfy one's client—even another department—is one general measure of success. Likewise, one's own effectiveness is dependent on the client departments as well. It is a rare exception where a department in a hospital can act independently with no regard for the interface with other departments—that is, without negative repercussions to one or more departments. The continual resource drain felt by the industry since the cost containment effort of the 1970s has forced most departments to think of themselves and what they need. Departments as a result maximize their efficiencies, often at the expense of overall organizational effectiveness.

A hospital's credit department has the responsibility to verify insurance carriers and coverage for patients coming in for elective surgery. Oftentimes this is a high-volume task that quickly becomes a mess when calls to carriers are unanswered or calls have to be returned. After just a few days, the credit department not only has the regular calls to make for cases the next day, but also must now make up an equal number of calls that were unanswered during the last few days. One way to handle this dilemma is to let patients come in and then have them wait while the call is made. Of course, this creates a wait for patients and an annoyance about credit at the worst possible time—just before surgery. Patient evaluations will show displeasure with the wait, and typically patients will identify Admitting as the problem.

At the same time, Admitting will not receive all the paperwork necessary for all the admissions. Among the missing items will be EKGs, history and physicals, orders, consents, and X-ray reports. These omissions will cause delays in surgical procedures for same-day-stay patients and morning surgical admits. Again, patients will express frustration or anger over the wait, and once again Admitting will be identified as the offender.

This scenario, repeated throughout the hospital industry, suggests two major performance indicators for Admitting: one is the number of credit logs completed the afternoon before admission; the other is the precentage of admissions having completed paperwork at the time of admission. At first it would appear that the credit log indicator is appropriate for Credit, not Admitting. And the tracking of missing paperwork might be a better indicator of the performance of other people. Interestingly, though, these indicators suggest a major component of the effectiveness of the admitting process. If patient flow suffers, so does patient satisfaction. If there is a void in clinical information, physicians and residents may be called to rush to floors to see patients to prevent cases from being delayed.

The effectiveness of the Admitting Department is closely tied to that of the hospital in these performances. Admitting is in the best position to track and directly influence part of the outcome. Tracking these indicators will suggest supervisory activity to reduce the number of missing papers, and strategies to increase compliance by physicians in submitting all paperwork will probably increase. The indicators will direct corrective activity that will benefit the hospital, Admitting, Surgery, same-day-stay patients, etc. As the number of missing credit logs, orders, etc., decreases, fewer patients will be delayed, and the flow of patients will be improved. Admitting will have improved its effectiveness.

This performance indicator requires that employees and supervisors initiate action for correction. In fact, the supervisor's role may be altered to allow for the activity. While a certain percentage of the problem is under the control of others, the supervisor and department head will show activity that attempts to negotiate, persuade, or cajole them into compliance. Typically, the very act of giving feedback regularly to people will improve their performance. The overall result will be that Admitting has greatly reduced the problem and provided benefits to many people, many departments, and the hospital.

A further example in Personnel could be the tracking of the number of payroll changes that come into the department the requested number of days prior to the expected payroll change. Frequently, employees are angry with Personnel and question the service the entire department provides when they open their check and do not find their increase. Monthly feedback to department heads on the percentage of payroll changes received by the deadlines will help increase the compliance on their part. Similarly, the percentage of status changes completed by Personnel within three days of arrival could be shared if there is value in showing the efficiency of the department and highlighting the number of "late" submissions.

Another Personnel or Risk Management concern relates to workers' compensation claims or to claims by employees for use of hospital services elsewhere. A major expenditure of hospital dollars in these areas suggests the need for active performance monitoring. The quick response is to say that these are outside the control of Personnel or Risk Management. At first they are. Yet a major concern when it comes to workers' compensation is to both review cases after they have been started and show a proactive approach toward prevention. There are issues of education for managers that can help in this process. There are attempts to curb or control workers' compensation expenditures that need to be visible.

Likewise, issues arise when employees use other hospitals. While many benefit packages offer a discount on deductibles for employees using the hospital that employs them, some employees will use another hospital because of some other preference. Where mileage from home is substantial, it will be very difficult to entice employees to use their own hospital. On the other hand, it may be possible to influence certain units—e.g., labor and delivery—to provide some added service to employees who use the facility. Something as simple as employee programs to review benefits may help the situation. At issue is whether Personnel or Risk Management monitors indicators and then takes an interest in bringing those indicators in line with the desire of the hospital.

Additionally, Personnel can act as a consultant to department managers to help them get employee input into the design of jobs, encourage employee feedback on standards and accomplishment, identify equitable rewards, and secure and train a competent work force (Burton 1981).

CONCLUSION

Performance indicators that focus on effectiveness are the primary concern of revenue-generating and non-revenue-generating departments. The issue of efficiency, doing more with less, when work volumes do not vary drastically is a misfocus. The workload does not vary in some non-revenue-producing departments the way it does in revenue-producing departments—e.g., Personnel, Safety and Security, and Accounting. Other non-revenue-producing departments, such as Medical Records, Admitting, and Patient Accounts, will see workloads with greater variability. Still, all of these departments share a mission of providing support to the clinical purpose of a hospital—namely, to provide trained personnel capable of controlling the flow of patients and related information through a health care system. The outcome is the restoration of health or improved conditions in a smooth and efficient manner from booking to billing. Many of these departments are involved in key transfer points for information or people. The effectiveness of these departments is tied not only to the performance of their own employees but also to a great degree to their ability to influence the compliance of others. A concentration on performance will improve the effectiveness of the service in a more efficient way. Incentives will sharpen the focus on optimal performance. Productivity gains will be realized, and the work place will support the desired human performance.

REFERENCES

Alpert, M.S. 1986. Employee motivation: Training, idea generation, incentive approaches. *Journal of the American Medical Records Association* 57, no. 5 (May): 14–17.

American Hospital Association. 1987. *Hospital statistics, 1951–1987*. American Hospital Association.

Boston Consulting Group. 1972. *Perspective on experience*. Boston: Boston Consulting Group.

Browdy, J.D. 1985. Tips for tailoring an incentive compensation plan to your employees' needs. *Trustee* 38, no. 7 (July): 29–32.

Bruggen, P., and S. Bourne. 1982. The distinction awards system in England and Wales 1980. *British Medical Journal* 284 (May 22): 1577–80.

Burton, E.K. 1981. Productivity: A plan for personnel. *Personnel Administrator* 26, no. 9 (September): 85–92.

Carkhuff, R. 1983. *Sources of human productivity*. Amherst, Mass.: Human Resource Development Press.

Cavarrochi, Nicholas. 1988. Speech on government regulations presented at seminar on Managing Health Care into the 1990s. (New Brunswick, N.J., Robert Wood University Hospital, May 10).

Connellan, T. 1978. *How to improve human performance: Behaviorism in business and industry*. New York: Harper & Row.

Daniels, A., and T. Rosen. 1984. *Performance management: Improving quality and productivity through positive reinforcement*. Tucker, Ga: Performance Management Publications, Inc. 1983.

Desnoyer, J.M., N.J. Barr, and M.K. O'Brien. 1987. Standards of performance: A model for development in health care. *Journal of Healthcare Education and Training* 2, no. 1 (Spring): 1–3.

Droste, T. 1987. Gainsharing: The newest way to up productivity. *Hospitals* 61, no. 11 (June 5): 71.

Fenger, L. 1988. Keep current with fore-incentive plans: A bibliography (1980–present). *Journal of American Medical Records Association* 59, no. 4 (April): 53.

Fodor, J., III, and A. Salvekar. 1987. Productivity monitoring of the non-technical staff. *Radiology Management* 9, no. 1 (Winter): 32–34.

Franke, A.G., E.J. Harrick, and A.J. Klein. 1982. The role of personnel in improving productivity. *Personnel Administrator* 27, no. 3 (March): 83–88.

Freeland, M.S., and C.E. Schendler. 1987. Health spending in the 1980's: Integration of clinical practice patterns with management. *Health Care Finance Review* 8, no. 4 (Summer): 1–68.

Gilbert, T. 1978. *Human competence, engineering worthy performance.* New York: McGraw-Hill Book Co.

Grayson, M.A. 1985a. Auditing innovation. *Multis* 2, no. 5 (October 1): M18.

———. 1985b. Call out the stars. *Multis* 2, no. 5 (October 1): M26.

Greidanus, J. 1988. The cost of human resources: Controlling the size and productivity of the work force. *Public Utilities Fortnightly* 121, no. 7 (March 31): 17–20.

Groner, P., J. Appleyard, and H.J. Hicks. 1977. *Cost containment through employee incentives programs.* Rockville, Md.: Aspen Publishers, Inc., 144.

Harless, J. 1975. *An ounce of analysis (is worth a pound of objectives).* Newnan, Ga.: Harless Performance Guild, Inc.

Harrison, J. 1978. *Improving performance and productivity.* Reading, Mass.: Addison-Wesley Publishing Co., Inc.

Healy, C.D. 1987. Positive reinforcement: A management alternative. *Radiology Management* 9, no. 1 (Winter): 35–36.

Jennings, Marian C. 1988. Speech on Planning and Marketing presented at seminar on Managing Health Care into the 1990s. (New Brunswick, N.J., Robert Wood Johnson University Hospital, January 21).

Key, P. 1987. Time to change culture. *Health Service Journal* 97 (October 22): 1235.

King, J.H. 1988. Creative pay scales can give providers a competitive edge. *Provider* 14, no. 5 (May): 29.

Lincoln, J.F. 1951. Incentive management. Cleveland: Lincoln Electric Company.

Luthans, F., W.S. Maciag, and S.A. Rosenkrantz. 1983. O.B. mod.: Meeting the productivity challenge with human resources management. *Personnel* 60, no. 2 (March-April): 28–36.

MacDonald, R.A. 1983. Productivity improvement through human resource systems. *Business Quarterly* 48, no. 3 (Fall): 32–33.

Peters, T. 1987. In search of excellence: A road map for CEOs. *Hospitals* 61, no. 9 (May 5): 91–92.

Powills, S. 1987. Rewards spur employee use of WI provider. *Hospitals* 61, no. 18 (September 20): 60–61.

Sayles, L.R. 1973. Managing human resources for higher productivity. *Conference Board Record* 10, no. 7 (July): 57–58.

Shore, H. 1986. Mr. Lincoln and his system. *Business Quarterly* 51, no. 2 (Summer): 10–12.

Spencer, Lyle M., Jr. 1986. *Calculating human resource costs and benefits.* New York: John Wiley & Sons, Inc.

Stull, M.K. 1986. Staff nurse performance, effects of goal-setting and performance feedback. *Journal of Nursing Administration* 16, nos. 7 and 8 (July-August): 26–30.

Veninga, R. 1975. Interpersonal feedback: A cost-benefit analysis. *Journal of Nursing Administration* (February): 40–43.

Ventrone, J.M., M. Zanotti, and M. Morava-Heidtman. 1988. Dressing for success: Measuring productivity can ensure continuing success. *Healthcare Financial Management* 42, no. 8 (August): 31–40.

Young, B. 1984. A patient and employee advocacy program—How to get productivity and harmony. *Hospital Topics* 62, no. 2 (March-April): 22–23.

Robert L. Phillips
Catherine A. Duran
John D. Blair
Mark F. Peterson
Grant T. Savage
Carlton J. Whitehead

17

Quality Circles in Health Care Organizations: Pitfalls and Promises

The health care literature is assimilating an increasing number of examples of possible applications of Japanese management techniques in general and of quality circles (QCs) in particular. The twin imperative of cost containment (fee limitations and increased competition), coupled with the decreasing availability of nurses, has impelled several health care organizations to adopt, experiment with, or at least consider organizational changes that promise increased employee motivation and retention, as well as improved efficiency and effectiveness. To be sure, such promises are becoming increasingly vociferous, especially when made by authors and speakers who make their living (wholly or in part) by selling QC-related facilitative services.

The purpose of this chapter is to review the history and evolution of the QC concept, to discern the theoretical basis for the expected application outcomes, and to address several critical questions concerning QCs, especially with respect to their application in health care organizations. The specific questions we address are as follows:

- What has been the history of performance of QCs in Japanese and American industry, and especially in health care organizations?
- What are the key factors that might determine success or failure?
- What are the fundamental problems with the implementation of QCs in health care organizations?
- What might be done to increase the chances for success of a health care QC program?

- How important is it for an organization to implement an organizationwide participative management program in order for QCs to survive?
- What are the alternatives to QCs?

HISTORY AND EVOLUTION OF QUALITY CIRCLES

Quality circles represent a blending of ideas from two different schools of management thought from the United States with the Japanese labor tradition and culture existing in the decade of the sixties. Specifically, many of the precepts of statistical quality control stemming from the scientific management school, primarily as a result of the work of Deming, were merged with participative management concepts from the human relations school (findings, for example, from the Hawthorne studies and the American Soldier studies, research on reference group theory, and the work of the Institute for Social Research at the University of Michigan) and placed in the Japanese organizational culture. Several Japanese organizations, including the Japan Union of Scientists and Engineers (JUSE) and the Japan Management Association, had prominent roles in contributing to the modification of U.S. ideas to the Japanese situation. The Japan Group Dynamics Association affiliated with Kyushu University acted as a clearinghouse for such information, particularly about U.S. human relations practices, and provided documentation and assessments of

QC-related program effects.[1] In other words, Japanese organizations were applying the results of research and theory developed in the United States to their established work organizations as part of their general absorption with American technology and culture following World War II. The Japanese system already contained the traditions of recruiting newly graduated employees and providing them with organization-specific skills, the seniority system for pay (wage tied to the person and not to the job description), and lifetime employment.

Further, QCs had as much to do with the participative management prescriptions from the human relations school as with the classical statistical control techniques advocated by Deming. It was the idea of the Japanese to combine the two notions of quality control (some believe more out of respect to Deming than from the purpose of the circle) and participative management. The first QC began in 1962 with a foreman circle that acted as a template for subsequent circles.[2] Quality circles are now firmly established in Japanese industry with over 80,000 registered with the Japanese Association of Science and Technology.[3] The first U.S. company to employ the QC concept on a large-scale basis was Lockheed Missile and Space Company, which began its program in 1974.[4] As would be expected, the QC concept in the United States was modified and now generally consists of a group of 6 to 12 employees that meet on a regular basis in order to address problems affecting the group's work area. Usually, QC members are trained in problem-solving and quality control techniques. Most meetings are held on "company time," either during regular working hours or on an overtime basis. A facilitator normally helps design the program, train the participants, and oversee the operation of the process. Usually, companies tailor the QC concept to their respective structure and culture. It is estimated that over 90 percent of the Fortune 500 companies have tried QC programs at some time.[5] However, it is quite interesting to note that a Japan External Trade Organization study found that only 8 percent of the 238 Japanese-owned U.S. subsidiaries had a QC program as of 1981.[6]

Since William Ouchi's book *Theory Z* is the prototype for many U.S. managers' understanding of Japanese management, it is a good starting point for theoretically understanding the Japanese context for QCs. Ouchi notes the Japanese management policies of lifetime employment, investment in organization-specific skills, the balancing of explicit and implicit criteria in decision making, participative decision making, and the development of a holistic view of people. These practices are suggested to lead to trust, greater job satisfaction, and higher productivity.[7] In other words, these practices help establish an "Industrial Clan" in which workers' needs are met more by the organization and members of a work group than by the general society, not unlike a deployed military organization during wartime, and in which the employees become highly committed to organizational goals. In a critique of *Theory Z*, Sullivan suggested that Ouchi's formulation was open to attack on theoretical grounds;[8] also, certain empirical evidence suggests that decision making in Japanese firms

functions as a "top-down *consultative* process under the facade of a bottom-up *concensus* process."[9]

However, if we examine the history and reasoning at the time of implementation of QCs in Japan, the expected outcomes of implementing QCs are found to be based on the original democratic/participative management theory from the United States. The issue of the superiority of U.S.-style democracy was practically and emotionally significant in the years following U.S. occupation. As indicated earlier, the findings from small group research as well as, we suspect, the results of early U.S. applications of initial participative interventions substantially influenced the Japanese experiments.[10] Further, in Japanese corporations, the norm is for workers to share in increased profits, a condition that is relatively rare in U.S. industry and rarer still in health care organizations. Thus, it is expected that by involving employees in decisions affecting their work, an organization will realize specific suggestions for product improvement, higher employee morale and productivity, greater employee retention, and increased commitment to the organization. Of course, the above outcomes are predicated on the assumption of management and organization reciprocation in the form of recognition, promotion, and perhaps the sharing of any increased profits resulting from improved productivity. Thus, if we are to stick with the theory that forms the impetus for the QC movement, a key question is the degree to which any given QC program is truly participative—i.e., involves employees in influencing decision making. We will return to this consideration after examining the impact of QC programs on a number of corporations—manufacturing as well as health care organizations.

A HISTORY OF QC PROGRAM PERFORMANCE

Since QCs emerged in Japan (in the 1960s) and in the United States (in the 1970s), there has been a plethora of reports on their successes and failures. Moreover, QCs have been implemented in a wide range of countries besides Japan and the United States, including Taiwan, Mexico, Brazil, Thailand, Malaysia, the Netherlands, Belgium, Denmark, and the U.K.[11] However, the history of performance is not consistent.

Ingle notes two successful QC programs in the United States: one at Mercury Marine (an outboard motor manufacturer) that had been going on for four years and one at Brunswick Corporation (a sports equipment manufacturer).[12] A successful QC program was also seen at White Sands Missile Range, where in 1983 there were several circles with 300 participating employees, contributing an estimated cost savings of $33,000.[13] Another success story is in a military maintenance organization in which five departments implemented QCs; the participants indicated in surveys that improvements were seen in such areas as job performance and job satisfaction. However, even in this "success story," two of the original participating departments dropped out of the QC program during the period of study. An example of a failed QC program is provided by Pati, Salitore, and Brady in looking at Lake Financial Corporation (a banking institution).[14] In the early 1980s, Lake Financial started and then tried to revitalize their dying program; the participants called the program "a nuisance, a joke, very non-productive, boring, dull, and intimidating."[15]

Griffin conducted a three-year longitudinal study of a QC program in two manufacturing plants of an electronics company. He concluded that although attitudes, behaviors, and effectiveness improved initially, there was a drop to previous levels after about 24 months, and that the financial impact of the QCs had diminished.[16] On a more positive note, Cornell reports that several service organizations have had success with QCs. For example, through the use of QCs, the Jacksonville, Florida, branch of the Federal Reserve Board in Atlanta reduced employee turnover, Hawaiian Airlines reduced fuel costs, and a Sheraton hotel reduced the incidence of guest complaints.[17] Federal and state governmental agencies have also implemented QC programs. In 1987 there were 125 QCs operating in the Missouri state government with estimated cost savings in several departments. In the Florida Department of Transportation, "Quality Improvement Teams" were started in 1984. In 1988, these teams were still functioning, but warnings were given that "refresher courses" and "midcourse corrections" were necessary to avoid failure.[18]

Because of the publicity surrounding QC programs in industry and some service organizations, health care institutions began looking at this technique. Miller and Miller believe that the "industrial quality model" can naturally be applied to health care because, after all, there is a great emphasis on the need for quality in health care, as well as the need for cost awareness.[19] Many health care institutions have implemented QCs. For example, organizations such as Veterans Medical Center in Albany, New York,[20] St. Joseph's Hospital in Fort Wayne, Indiana,[21] Lakeshore Mental Health Institute of Knoxville, Tennessee,[22] and Barnes Hospital in St. Louis, Missouri[23] have reported such positive results as increased employee morale and motivation and cost improvements due to QCs. Most of these QCs were in staff support functions, such as nursing, housekeeping, dietetics, etc. One QC program specific to nursing was implemented at Central Middlesex Hospital in 1985 and, as a result, one of the circles reduced the incidence of pressure sores.[24] Foothills Provincial General Hospital in Calgary, Canada, implemented a QC program in the early 1980s that was successful in terms of human resources development (education and training), quality of care, productivity, and efficiency, although the results were not quantified.[25] Henry Ford Hospital in Detroit, Michigan, had an extensive QC program that was said to be successful.[26]

In addition to the reports of successful QC programs in hospitals, there are also documentations of failures. One study of a military medical facility showed that a QC program involving 165 people reaped "little detectable improvement" in job performance and job satisfaction and concluded that if a QC program is done badly, it may actually do more harm than good.[27] Mt. Sinai Hospital in Miami, Florida, had a QC program that included such diverse areas as word processing, housekeeping, recovery room, pharmacy, and respiratory from which actual cost savings were observed and documented.[28] However, the Mt. Sinai QC program had been disbanded for over two years. Another hospital in the southern region in the United States had a QC program that in 1984 was justified by its "people building" aspects;[29] however, this program has also been discontinued. Moreover, one comprehensive study of a large quality of worklife (QWL) program with elements similar to QCs in a hospital in the eastern U.S. concluded that over a three-and-a-half-year period (1974–1978), there were some intangible improvements in employee morale and communications, but that the results did not justify the financial and human resource costs.[30]

Considering the above examples, it is not clear whether QCs are effective. One problem in evaluating the performance of QCs, either in industry or in health care organizations, is that measuring QC effectiveness is extremely difficult or ambiguous. Barwick and Alexander reviewed 33 studies that dealt with QCs in a variety of organizations (industrial, service, health care, etc.) in an attempt to classify these by effectiveness outcomes. Overall, they found that about 49 percent showed positive results, while 51 percent showed mixed, nonsignificant, or negative results. Of the three hospitals that were included in their review, one showed positive results, and two showed mixed or nonsignificant results.[31] Greenbaum, Kaplan, and Metlay point out that, in most cases, there is no formal system of evaluation for QC programs. They believe that evaluation is imperative for the survival and improvement of QC programs.[32]

Another issue raised by the above examples is the length of time that QC programs are viable. Often, even the "success stories" do not seem to continue. Lawler and Mohrman present a life-cycle model of QCs. They explicate six phases in the life of a QC, each of which has its own key activities and potential threats for the QC programs: (1) start-up, (2) initial problem solving, (3) approval of initial suggestions, (4) implementation, (5) expansion of problem solving, and (6) decline. The reason for the somewhat pessimistic forecast by Lawler and Mohrman is that their analysis suggests that a QC program is basically an unstable organizational structure. However, they do offer some suggestions concerning methods to make a QC program viable, which we discuss in a later section.[33]

Considering the many examples of successful and failed QCs (with the additional problem of how success or failure is measured), it is evident that sometimes QCs work and sometimes they do not. As discussed above, several studies showed that QCs improve quality, reduce costs, and improve morale and communications; yet there were also several studies that demonstrated that QC programs failed to live up to their expectations. Obviously, whether QC programs are successful depends on the differing situations in which they are attempted and the various ways they are implemented.

A CONTINGENCY APPROACH

The performance of QC programs in the United States is a mixed bag. We believe there are at least two reasons for such results. First, many of the reports of success may be coming from QC programs in the early stages of development; that is, they result from what Lawler and Mohrman call the "honeymoon period" where there is pressure by top management on middle management to accept initial suggestions.[34] Recall that Griffin, using a longitudinal and experimental design to track QCs over a three-year period, found impressive initial results with a decline after 12 to 36 months.[35] Second, it appears to us that what is being called a quality circle varies greatly across organizations. Some descriptions of QC implementations might be considered, at least from the information given, simply problem-solving groups and others not much more than discussion groups. Based on the evolution and the theoretical considerations, we suggest that in order to fit the implied definition prevalent in the literature, a QC must involve genuine participation in decisions concerning the methods of work of the circle members. Thus, group discussion or suggestion programs keyed only to the production of recommendations may not carry the potentially threatening baggage of a more extensive program involving the sharing of authority and might have a better chance of earning a favorable report, at least on the part of management.

Clearly, the success or failure of QCs seems to be contingent on a number of considerations. Many general factors must be considered in trying to assess the likelihood of successful institutionalization of QCs. These factors are of two kinds: (1) those that deal with the program itself, and (2) those that deal with contingencies outside the program. These latter factors provide the context in which the program operates. What are these contingencies? In Figure 17-1, we identify and illustrate several classes of variables that will affect the quality of QCs to survive.

The sections that follow have two different purposes. First, we describe in general terms the kinds of contingency variables of concern at each level in the model (individual, work setting, organizational, environmental). Second, we illustrate each class of variables by discussing selected factors that affect the survival of QCs. We do not identify all relevant contingency variables at each level of analysis, and we do not discuss all the negative or positive factors within the set of variables identified at that level. Our objective here is to illustrate selectively the utility of the contingency model in directing attention to the kinds of variables outside of the program itself that have an effect on the ability of QCs to survive.

Individual Factors

Of consequence for industrial QC programs are individuals' education, age, and gender; their attitudes toward the organization, the work group, and their jobs; and their needs for autonomy and challenge. In a hospital setting, individual factors are more complicated because of the various professional groups involved in the delivery of quality. Thus, those formulating a QC program will have to consider the various professional groups when designing specific tasks to be addressed.

Dealing with these characteristics and needs from the perspective of the QC technique involves a reconceptualization of the locus of expertise in an organization. Taylorism started from the perspective that it was the manager's job to tell the workers what to do, and the workers' role was to do exactly that.[36] Planning and doing were separate functions.

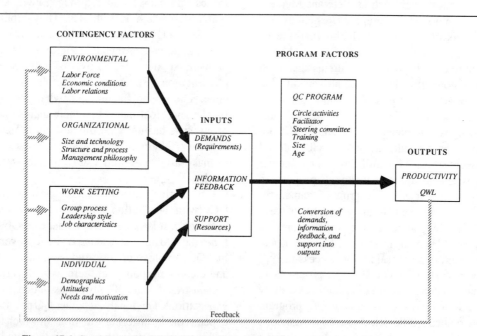

Figure 17-1 Contingency Model of a Quality Circle Program

The assumption underlying the quality circle approach is that those who do the work have a great deal of expertise. Workers have the ability to identify and solve problems that create impediments to quality and productivity, provided they are given both the opportunity and the appropriate training in problem solving. Tapping into this underutilized skill, insight, and expertise benefits the organization. The quality circle technique can also generate substantial motivation. Because QC participation is voluntary—at least that is what is strongly recommended in a later section—participants are self-selected. The training in problem-solving techniques and the experiences of identifying and analyzing problems and of developing, communicating, and defending solutions provide a mechanism for personal development. Members can take pride in developing successful solutions and enjoy the recognition they receive from management and other members of the organization, especially when their solutions are publicized. The desire for autonomy is at least partially satisfied.

The philosophy of QCs is generally consistent with the need theories of motivation, including the literature on job enrichment.[37] Quality circles enrich the job through supplementary activities, rather than by changing the nature of the job itself, and job supplements may be easier to implement than job redesign.

In addition, from the perspective of the expectancy theory, QCs provide the conditions for increasing the effort-to-performance and the performance-to-outcome expectancies, as well as outcome valences. According to the theory, the higher the expectancies and outcome valences, the higher the level of motivation.[38]

As presently constituted, most American QC programs rely primarily on intrinsic rewards derived from participation and secondarily on extrinsic reinforcement from various means of recognition. This lack of monetary (or other gainsharing) reinforcement could have a major effect on QC members' motivation and desire to participate after the initial euphoria from increased participation has decreased. For example, in a recent review of several hundred employee motivation studies, Locke found that the use of monetary rewards was the most powerful source of motivation for productivity improvement and, when combined with other motivational approaches, significantly enhanced the results obtained.[39] Of course, because health care organizations have a community purpose, one would suppose that the expectation of monetary reward for ideas to improve the quality of health care would be less than the expectation in an industrial setting.

Work Setting Factors

The second set of contingency variables includes group process variables, as well as the characteristics of the jobs themselves in a particular work setting. The characteristics of QCs are consistent with those of effective small groups.[40] They also emphasize congruence between group and organizational goals.

However, the operating level poses a number of potential problems for QCs. First, the level of participation can be a problem. The voluntary participation of only a small proportion of the members in a work unit, or of the work units themselves, tends to result in pressure on those participating and makes implementation of changes difficult. In Japan, volunteerism and nearly total participation are quite consistent. In the United States, they are not. In addition, major problems might reside in those work units that are not participating.

Further, professional employees, especially in a health care setting, already have considerable autonomy and some input into decision making. Hence, the feasibility of QCs in systems with highly skilled or high technology personnel performing relatively autonomous tasks is questionable.[41]

Finally, fundamental problems outside of the scope of the QCs may be of much greater significance than the ones addressed by the QCs. That is why QCs by themselves cannot be expected to create effective and efficient organizations.

Organizational Factors

The third set of contingencies comes from the organization itself. These include the organization's size, its dominant technology, its structure (centralized or decentralized), and its processes (decision-making procedures and communication flows), as well as its general management philosophy (including the level of management support for QCs specifically and for employee involvement generally).

The QC process can be an important vehicle for development and change in the organization. Training in problem identification and problem-solving processes are valuable to both workers and managers alike. In addition, QC experiences may increase the members' appreciation for the complexities of solving problems in the work place and also increase their awareness of the overall complexities of management and organization processes. Likewise, managers may develop a deeper appreciation for workers and their problems and capacities.

The organization's processes for coping with and solving problems are enhanced. Calling attention to problems is legitimized, as is requesting information necessary for identifying and solving problems. Quality circles communicate their results to management which, in turn, gives feedback to the circles.

Dealing openly with problems and having more open communication can lead to a supportive, as opposed to a defensive, organizational climate. A supportive organizational climate can enhance both the performance and the development of organization members, as well as reduce conflict between workers and management. The overall performance and innovative capacity of the organization should be improved.[42]

The QC process provides an apparently safe and legitimate approach for a major organizational intervention because it focuses on quality and productivity improvement. Management can justify and accept this approach more readily than one that emphasizes quality of work life with the hope that there will be a productivity payoff. In addition, management maintains control over the key decisions and at least maintains the illusion of being in control of the QC process. The QC members have the incentive of gaining enhanced roles in the organization. At a minimum, the process provides the opportunity to cope with some of the irritants in the work environment. In addition, it has the advantage of being a bottom-up approach. However, there can also be problems because the QC structure often bypasses middle managers, threatening their autonomy and control.

The QC approach also provides a structure for sustaining the change. By providing a structured process for problem solving and decision making with a continuing facilitating and coordinating mechanism, the QC approach has a distinct advantage over other approaches that are short term and have a specified beginning and end.

Environmental Factors

The fourth set of contingency variables results from the fact that the organization in which a quality circle must survive must itself exist in an uncertain environment determined by the characteristics of the labor force (skills, availability, and expectation), economic conditions (plant closings and foreign competition), and the state of labor relations (unionized or not, relatively cooperative or characterized by conflict). The current concern in the United States with improving organizational effectiveness, especially in terms of quality and productivity, creates a generally favorable climate for QCs. They provide a limited structural intervention that is compatible with both people- and technology-oriented interventions. However, some characteristics of the American environment limit the ability of people to implement and sustain quality circles.

American, as opposed to Japanese, organizations have traditionally used labor force adjustments to cope with economic cycles.[43] Both seasonal and cyclical economic cycles that result in major fluctuations in the labor force pose major problems for QCs. Quality circles are not likely to work well under conditions of instability or uncertainty about the member's future in the organization. Instability creates problems in training costs and discontinuity in circle membership, among other things.

In addition, the resistance of union leadership to QCs could severely limit participation. Although lack of union support is not inevitable, failure to inform and involve the union could make efforts to start and sustain a program unsuccessful.[44]

Quality circles are emerging in the United States during a period of economic stress. The intrinsic satisfaction of participation coupled with the economic reality of workers' saving their jobs by increasing quality and productivity might be sufficient to sustain QCs in American organizations in the short run. However, their long-run viability might depend on

sharing the monetary benefits of productivity improvements.[45] Even the Japanese rely on an annual bonus system for their employees.[46]

Overview of the Contingency Model

Now that we have discussed and illustrated in some detail contingency variables at the individual, work setting, organizational, and environmental levels, let us return to a more general consideration of the model and its implications for understanding the survivability of QCs. The contingency variables affect the demands of requirements being placed on the program. They will also affect, to some degree, the provision of support or resources for the program—including employee willingness to participate. Finally, from the program context will come informational feedback about how the program is being received. Demands, support, and information feedback provide the critical inputs into the QC program as a subsystem of the host organization.

All the contingency factors then affect the nature of the inputs into the program and have possible consequences for the outputs of the QC effort, such as changes in productivity and the quality of products or services or in the quality of work life, as reflected in absenteeism and turnover. All these potential outputs are purported consequences of QC programs. The outputs, of course, have feedback effects on the contingency factors and, in turn, affect the nature of the new organizational inputs to the QC system and its long-term survival.

This feedback process is more complicated than the old adage that "nothing succeeds like success." In fact, a major problem for QC programs is that successful ones can breed the conditions for their own failure. For example, top management may go on to other projects once they feel that this "successful" program no longer needs their attention, or the program may be expanded too quickly or into inappropriate areas because the pilot program was a success. Of course, all this is not to deny that successful programs will generate increased interest, broader management support, and other resources. They will, however, also generate raised expectations and other new demands.

THE CRITICAL PROGRAM IMPLEMENTATION CONSIDERATION

Up to this point, we have attempted to present specific considerations concerning the advisability of attempting a QC program, based upon the Blair and Whitehead contingency notions and recent reviews and research.[47] The question arises now as to how best to go about establishing a QC program. The literature is replete with a variety of prescriptions and specific "rules." But the critical question is how far an organization must go toward a participative management program in order to implement a successful QC program. Unfortunately, whether an organization must adopt a companywide participative management program in order for a QC program to survive is somewhat ambiguous. Certainly, some organizational theorists are very convincing in advancing the argument that it is, indeed, necessary for the larger organization to convert to a participative management structure in order for a QC program to work.[48] Others simply suggest that QC programs work best when part of a larger organizational development effort.[49] Finally, there are several accounts of successful QC programs in which the authors do not address the larger issue of a companywide organizational development, Theory Z, or participative management programs. Thus, one might conclude that the jury is still out on the issue. However, if we return to an earlier conclusion concerning the definition of a QC, we note a requirement for some sort of group control over some aspect of the problem-solving process. Further, we speculate that the greater the degree of participative latitude, the more the organization requires a wider, supportive, participative decision-making philosophy. There might be cases of "limited QCs" or a quality circle analogue, such as those extracted from the Lawler and Mohrman recommendations (discussed in a later section), where the delegation of decision-making authority is not necessary.[50] In such cases, the QCs would not constitute a participative program. In essence, then, we are simply suggesting that the greater the coincidence between the QC program structure in terms of participative processes and the structure of the larger organization, the greater the chances for survival of the QC intervention.

However, launching an organizationwide participative program is not an easy proposition. First, one must consider that participative decision making has important consequences for managers. While certain decisions may be delegated to specific work groups, the responsibility for the decision—i.e., the consequences—ultimately resides with a manager.[51] The resulting tension may create a reluctance on the part of management to accept participative principles. A second consideration is that usually top management decides to implement a QC program. However, it is the first-line and middle management that must share power. There is a danger that if top management is not careful, it might elicit apparent compliance with the QC principles, yet be faced with unstated resentment and opposition.

More fundamental to the entire question of adopting a Theory Z–type organization process is what Shortell suggests are four different features of the nature of work organization in health care institutions.

1. the differences between the needs of the organization and the needs of the professionals working in the organization
2. the differing cultures due to the differences in the education and training of the several professional groups
3. the nature of the work process
4. the purpose of a hospital in that it has a social as well as technical mission

These four fundamental considerations suggest that implementing a Japanese-developed program designed for manufacturing organizations may need significant modification or at least considerable thought prior to implementation. Shortell also lists some opportunities as a result of the above features that might aid in participative decision-making development.[52] Nevertheless, by any account, the adaptation of an organization's culture from a traditional hospital management structure to a Japanese management structure would be a major, and probably lengthy, undertaking.

If we return to one of the basic issues—the sharing of power—it is interesting to note that Kelley and Brown surveyed 15 hospitals that have not used the QC approach. Of the 15, 10 replied that they were not considering the QC concept. The primary reason given was that it would require a delegation of power. Kelley and Brown also surveyed a group of registered nurses and nurse recruiters holding midlevel management positions who were prospective participants in a QC program. The results indicated that in the respective organizations of the survey group, the delegation of power was a major stumbling block in any decision to adopt a QC strategy.[53]

SPECIFIC RECOMMENDATIONS ON THE ESTABLISHMENT OF A QC PROGRAM

Mohrman and Ledford conducted an extensive assessment of nine sites of a large divisionalized company. They found six critical design features of QCs: (1) having measurable goals, (2) providing training for many or all participants, (3) making resource specialists available to QC groups, (4) maintaining thorough records of activities, (5) establishing links to higher management groups, and (6) conducting weekly or biweekly meetings.[54]

Further specific recommendations are based not only on the evaluative articles but also on the cluster of articles in the literature that seem to unreservedly advocate QC programs. If we examine the broadly diverse prescriptions and cautions, we find several recommendations in common.

1. *Management must be supportive.* This is rather a broad statement with a variety of meanings and suggestions. Of course, if management is not supportive, no program will work. However, the basic consideration has to do with whether the organization has in place a larger participative management program. But there are other important considerations.

A very important aspect of management support is the expectations of general management. To help shape expectations, as well as to determine whether a QC program is advisable, a careful diagnosis of the organization should be undertaken. Such a diagnosis ensures that a QC program is appropriate and determines exactly what would be expected from such a program. A random grab of what some might consider to be the latest fad in order to apply a quick fix to some "people problems" does not seem to hold a great deal of promise. Is a QC program an appropriate solution for the problem at hand? If so, the diagnosis should yield clear, specific objectives. Management should not introduce QCs into organizations under extreme stress; further, QCs do not appear to be a substitute for good labor-management relations.[55] Quality circles seem to work best when implemented in a stable firm.[56] If one or more unions are involved, it is just as important to have the union management on board with the program prior to its launch.

A diagnosis should also include an estimate of cost and employee time requirements in order to minimize unpleasant surprises. Management should start a QC program slowly, allow for adjustments, and then expand from a base of success. Management should expect some QCs fail and not realize their objectives. Management should also recognize the length of time it may take to effect certain improvements. Further, a QC program should not be overpromised with respect to the degree of improvement. Finally, management should expect that some of the initially successful QCs will subsequently fail.[57]

Management support also means a willingness to accept at least some proposals and implement them. In a diagnosis of a large-scale quality-of-work-life program in a large hospital, Hanlon and Gladstein concluded

> The Parkside case suggests that the critical factor is not whether employees working in problem-solving groups are able to diagnose organizational shortcomings and offer solutions—the answer in this case is strongly affirmative. The critical factor is whether or not management is willing to provide the support necessary to implement proposals for change.[58]

2. *Training is necessary*. Training represents the second most discussed imperative in the implementation of QCs. Training can be construed broadly—as preparing the organization to receive the QC program intervention—or narrowly—as providing instruction to individual members on problem-solving techniques. In the broader sense, the preparation of the organization to receive a QC program in at least some organizations borders on a "religious conversion." There need to be pronouncements as to the good expected and assurances of the support of the organization as a whole, as well as support in specific departments. A pilot program should be considered.[59] Quality circle leaders need to be trained in methods of facilitation as well as in problem-solving techniques.[60] Individual members need to have the benefits of the QC program explained and to receive training in problem solving. The training of group members should emphasize that QC meetings are not complaint sessions.[61] If supervisors are used as QC leaders, the organization should provide additional training to complement the QC-related training as part of a larger training program on good supervision.[62]

3. *The program needs to be voluntary*. The voluntary participation principle has strong support.[63] Herkimer listed five reasons for QC program failure from "The National Productivity Report."[64] One of the five was "restricting voluntary features by goading people into joining or enforcing joining by edict." Incidentally, the other four reasons were inadequate

management support, emphasis of a "people using" rather than a "people-building" theme, inadequate training, and an emphasis on individual rather than on team effort.[65]

4. *The program needs to be conducted within certain limits*. Again, a large number of articles recommend that meetings connected with a QC program occur on "company time," either during normal working hours or on an overtime basis. Further, although QCs should be able to choose their own problems, they should be restricted to working on those problems affecting their immediate work area.[66] Also, do not use a "canned" program without attempting to adapt the program to the specific organization. An excellent reference on establishing a QC program has been published by the American Management Association. It contains a large number of specific suggestions on the content of training programs, the conduct of a diagnosis, the program design, and evaluation techniques.[67]

5. *Establish some sort of evaluation technique*. Our review of the literature shows many missed opportunities to cite specific cost-benefit estimations of large-scale QC programs. If the support of management, as well as the willing support of participants, is important, then we suggest that evaluations go beyond short-term, attitudinal data.

ALTERNATIVE CONSIDERATIONS

Aside from the several articles reviewed above that advocate specific policies or procedures with respect to the implementation of QC programs, we were struck by the very different approach taken by Lawler and Mohrman. As discussed in an earlier section, they pointed out that QCs are basically unstable organizational structures that are likely to "self-destruct"; however, they suggested three "sensible ways" in which organizations could employ a QC program.

1. Use QCs as basically a group suggestion program in which ideas are collected from the individuals closest to the work. Management could establish QCs, rotate memberships, and stop the program if and when it made sense to do so.
   (a) Potential benefits: good ideas that result in improvements (higher quality, increased savings); improved upward communications; greater emphasis on quality and productivity; plus no requirement for management to shift to a more participative style
   (b) Potential dangers: lack of cooperation by employees who may feel manipulated and perhaps disappointed if their ideas go unheeded
2. Use QCs on special projects to deal with temporary or critical organizational issues. When the critical issue is resolved, disband the program.
   (a) Potential benefits: greater acceptance of change and greater commitment

(b) Potential dangers: employees may believe the organization is taking advantage of them—the company benefits, but they don't

3. Use QCs as a transitional device to effect an entire cultural change.[68]

Incidentally, Griffin agreed with Lawler and Mohrman's formulation.[69]

Whereas suggestions 1 and 2 above are designed to limit the impact of a QC program in the organization, using the program as an interim device increases the impact of the intervention. An organization could establish a QC program, examine its advantages and disadvantages, and then make adjustments as it moves the program toward a larger participative culture—e.g., semiautonomous work groups.

CONCLUSION

Although there is an extensive literature on the subject of QC programs in the United States and in health care organizations, there is no clear consensus that QC programs are indeed an organizational palliative. Further, there are some well-documented cases in which QCs have caused more problems than they have solved. Yet, in certain quarters, enthusiasm runs very high. We would be more favorably disposed to QC programs if so much of the enthusiastic literature did not come from the consulting segment whose livelihood, at least in part, comes from the demand for such programs. Nevertheless, with the foregoing as a caveat, we are not ready to conclude that a health care organization ought not to try such a program. There are too many reported cases of success for us to ignore the promise of a QC program intervention. However, we do suggest that health care executives carefully consider the various contingency factors affecting such programs, and we do recommend a careful reading of the several prescriptions offered by the various researchers that we cited in the section entitled "Specific Recommendations on the Establishment of a QC Program."

NOTES

1. Jyuji Misumi, "Japanese Management and Behavioral Science: Japanese Management Evolves," typescript.

2. Naoki Ikegami and Seth B. Goldsmith, "Quality Circles: The Myth and Reality of Hospital Management," *Health Care Management Review* 10, no. 3 (1985): 45–53. Misumi, "Japanese Management."

3. Ikegami and Goldsmith, "Quality Circles," 46.

4. John D. Blair, Stanley L. Cohen, and Jerome V. Hurwitz, "Quality Circles: Practical Considerations for Public Managers," *Public Productivity Review* 6, nos. 1–2 (March-June 1982): 10.

5. Edward E. Lawler III and Susan A. Mohrman, "Quality Circles After the Fad," *Harvard Business Review* 63, no. 1 (January-February 1985): 66.

6. R.E. Cole and D.S. Tachike, "Forging Institutional Links: Making Quality Circles Work in the U.S.," *National Productivity Review* 3, no. 4 (Autumn 1984): 417–29.

7. William Ouchi, *Theory Z: How American Business Can Meet the Japanese Challenge* (Reading, Mass.: Addison-Wesley Publishing Co., Inc., 1981).

8. Jeremiah J. Sullivan, "A Critique of Theory Z," *Academy of Management Review* 8, no. 1 (1983): 132–42.

9. N. Hatvany and V. Pucik, "Japanese Management Practices and Productivity," *Organizational Dynamics* 9, no. 4 (1981): 5–21.

10. Misumi, "Japanese Management." L. Coch and J.R.P. French, Jr., "Overcoming Resistance to Change," *Human Relations* 1 (1948): 512–32.

11. Sud Ingle, "How To Avoid Quality Circle Failure in Your Company," *Training and Development Journal* 36, no. 6 (June 1982): 59.

12. Ingle, "How To Avoid Quality Circle Failure."

13. Arthur A. Whatley and Wilma Hoffman, "Quality Circles Earn Union Respect," *Personnel Journal* 66, no. 12 (December 1987): 93.

14. Gopal C. Pati, Robert Salitore, and Sandra Brady, "What Went Wrong with Quality Circles?" *Personnel Journal* 66, no. 12 (December 1987): 83–87.

15. Ibid., 84.

16. Ricky W. Griffin, "Consequences of Quality Circles in an Industrial Setting: A Longitudinal Assessment," *Academy of Management Journal* 31, no. 2 (1988): 338–58.

17. Leonard Cornell, "Quality Circles in the Service Industries," *Quality Progress* 17, no. 7 (July 1984): 22–24.

18. Robert B. Denhardt, James Pyle, and Allen C. Bluedorn, "Implementing Quality Circles," *Public Administration Review* 7, no. 7 (July-August 1987): 304–309. James S. Bowman and Jane I. Steele, "Quality Teams in a State Agency," *Public Productivity Review* 47, no. 4 (Summer 1988): 11–31.

19. Laird Miller and Joanne Miller, "What Can Industry Teach Medicine about Quality?" *Medical Interface* (January 1989): 11.

20. Cornell, "Quality Circles in the Service Industries."

21. Leonard Cornell, "Quality Circles: A New Cure for Hospital Dysfunctions?" *Hospital and Health Services Administration* 29, no. 5 (September-October 1984): 88–93. Martha M. McKinney, "The Newest Miracle Drug: Quality Circles in Hospitals," *Hospital and Health Services Administration* 29, no. 5 (September-October 1984): 74–87.

22. Cornell, "Quality Circles: A New Cure?"

23. Marlene K. Strader, "Adapting Theory Z to Nursing Management," *Nursing Management* 18, no. 4 (April 1987): 61–64.

24. Susan Osborne, "A Quality Circle Investigation," *Nursing Times* 83, no. 7 (February 1987): 73–76.

25. Cheryl M. McColl, "Managers and Staff—Improve Quality of Working Life," *Dimensions in Health Services* 64, no. 1 (February 1987): 37–39.

26. McKinney, "The Newest Miracle Drug."

27. Robert P. Steel, Anthony J. Mento, Benjamin L. Dilla, and Russell F. Lloyd, "Factors Influencing the Success and Failure of Two Quality Circle Programs," *Journal of Management* 11, no. 1 (1985): 115.

28. McKinney, "The Newest Miracle Drug." Cornell, "Quality Circles: A New Cure?"

29. McKinney, "The Newest Miracle Drug," 85.

30. Martin D. Hanlon and Deborah L. Gladstein, "Improving the Quality of Work Life in Hospitals," *Hospital and Health Services Administration* 29, no. 5 (September-October 1984): 94–107.

31. Murray R. Barrick and Ralph A. Alexander, "A Review of Quality Circle Efficacy and the Existence of Positive-Findings Bias," *Personnel Psychology* 40, no. 3 (1987): 579–91.

32. Howard H. Greenbaum, Ira T. Kaplan, and William Metlay, "Evaluation of Problem-Solving Groups: The Case of Quality Circle Programs," *Group and Organization Studies* 13, no. 2 (June 1988): 133–47.

33. Lawler and Mohrman, "Quality Circles After the Fad."

34. Edward E. Lawler III and Susan A. Mohrman, "Quality Circles: After the Honeymoon," *Organizational Dynamics* 15, no. 4 (Spring 1987): 42–54.

35. Griffin, "Consequences of Quality Circles."

36. Henry Mintzberg, *The Structuring of Organizations* (Englewood Cliffs, N.J.: Prentice-Hall, Inc., 1979). J. Richard Hackman and Greg R. Oldham,

Work Redesign (Reading, Mass.: Addison-Wesley Publishing Co., Inc., 1980).

37. Abraham Maslow, *Motivation and Personality* (New York: Harper & Bros., 1954). Frederick I. Herzberg, "One More Time: How Do You Motivate Employees?" *Harvard Business Review* (January-February 1968): 53–62. Hackman and Oldham, *Work Redesign.*

38. Victor H. Vroom, *Work and Motivation* (New York: John Wiley & Sons, Inc., 1964). David Nadler and Edward E. Lawler III, "Motivation: A Diagnostic Approach," in J.R. Hackman, E.E. Lawler III, and L.W. Porter, eds., *Perspectives on Behavior in Organizations*, 2d ed. (New York: McGraw-Hill Book Co., 1983): 67–78.

39. Edward Locke, "Employee Motivation: A Discussion," *Journal of Contemporary Business* 11, no. 2 (1982): 71–81.

40. Alvin F. Zander, *Groups at Work* (San Francisco: Jossey-Bass Inc., Pubs., 1977). Linda Jewell and H. Joseph Reitz, *Group Effectiveness in Organizations* (Glenview, Ill.: Scott, Foresman, & Co., 1981).

41. Robert W. Elwood, "Quality Circles and the Knowledge Worker," in *Transactions of the Fourth Annual Conference of the International Association of Quality Circles* (1982): 421–28.

42. Mariann Jelinek, *Institutionalizing Innovation: A Study of Organizational Learning Systems* (New York: Praeger, 1979); Robert Zager and Michael Rosow, *The Innovative Organization* (Elmsford, N.Y.: Pergamon, 1982).

43. Robert E. Cole, *Work Mobility and Participation: A Comparative Study of American and Japanese Industry* (Los Angeles: University of California Press, 1979).

44. Frank M. Gryna, Jr., *Quality Circles: A Team Approach to Problem Solving* (New York: AMACOM, 1981): 35–36. Robert E. Cole, "Will Quality Circles Work in the U.S.?" *Quality Progress* 13, no. 7 (July 1980): 30. Saeed Samiee, "How Auto Workers Look at Productivity Measures: Lessons from Overseas," *Business Horizons* 25, no. 3 (May-June 1982): 91.

45. Locke, "Employee Motivation." Barry A. Macy, "The Bolivar Quality of Work Life Project: Success or Failure?" in Robert Zager and Michael P. Rosow, eds., *The Innovative Organization: Productivity Programs in Action* (New York: Pergamon, 1982), 184–221. Y.K. Shetty, "Key Elements of Productivity Improvement Programs," *Business Horizons* 25, no. 2 (March-April 1982): 15–22. Samiee, "How Auto Workers Look at Productivity Measures."

46. Cole, "Work Mobility and Participation." Jon P. Alston, "Awarding Bonuses the Japanese Way," *Business Horizons* 25, no. 5 (September-October 1982): 46–50.

47. John D. Blair and Carlton J. Whitehead, "Can Quality Circles Survive in the United States?" *Business Horizons* (September-October 1984): 17–23.

48. Misumi, "Japanese Management." A. Aaron Kelley and Mary Brady Brown, "Quality Circles in the Hospital Setting: Their Current Status and

Potential for the Future," *Health Care Management Review* 12, no. 1 (Winter 1987): 55–59. Ingle, "How To Avoid Quality Circle Failure."

49. McKinney, "The Newest Miracle Drug." Howard L. Smith and R. Clay Burchell, "Japanese Management: Implications for Healthcare Administration," *Hospital and Health Services Administration* 29, no. 2 (March-April 1984): 72–83.

50. Lawler and Mohrman, "Quality Circles After the Fad."

51. Stephen M. Shortell, "Theory Z: Implications and Relevance for Health Care Management," *Health Care Management Review* (Fall 1982): 7–21.

52. Ibid.

53. Kelley and Brown, "Quality Circles," 57.

54. S.A. Mohrman and G.E. Ledford, "The Design of Effective Employee Participation Groups: Implications for Human Resources Management," *Human Resource Management* 24, no. 4 (Winter 1985).

55. John D. Blair and Kenneth D. Ramsing, "Quality Circles and Production/Operations Management," *Journal of Operations Management* 4, no. 1 (November 1983): 8.

56. Kelley and Brown, "Quality Circles."

57. Blair and Ramsing, "Quality Circles." Lawler and Mohrman, "Quality Circles After the Fad." Griffin, "Consequences of Quality Circles."

58. Hanlon and Gladstein, "Improving the Quality of Work Life," 106.

59. Ingle, "How To Avoid Quality Circle Failure."

60. Allen G. Herkimer, Jr., "Quality Circles—New Wave or Fad?" *Healthcare Financial Management* 38, no. 7 (July 1984): 34. Julie A. Wine and John E. Baird, Jr., "Improving Nursing Management and Practice Through Quality Circles," *Journal of Nursing Administration* 13, no. 5 (May 1983): 5–10.

61. Pati, Salitore, and Brady, "What Went Wrong with Quality Circles?", 86.

62. Ibid., 86.

63. Blair and Ramsing, "Quality Circles." Herkimer, "Quality Circles—New Wave or Fad?" McKinney, "The Newest Miracle Drug." Pati, Salitore, and Brady, "What Went Wrong with Quality Circles?" Steel, Mento, Dilla, and Lloyd, "Factors Influencing the Success and Failure." George Munchus III, "Employer-Employee Based Quality Circles in Japan: Human Resource Policy Implications for American Firms," *Academy of Management Review* 8, no. 2 (1983): 255–61. McColl, "Managers and Staff—Improve Quality of Working Life."

64. Herkimer, "Quality Circles—New Wave or Fad?"

65. Ibid., 38.

66. McKinney, "The Newest Miracle Drug," 79.

67. Gryna, "Quality Circles."

68. Lawler and Mohrman, "Quality Circles After the Fad," 69–71.

69. Griffin, "Consequences of Quality Circles."

Kent E. Romanoff
James B. Williams

18

Gainsharing: A Powerful and Proven Method for Improving Hospital Productivity and Quality

In health care today, with so many hospitals watching their profit margins dwindle or disappear entirely, a dollar saved is worth more than a dollar earned; it may be worth dozens. This is why hospitals across the nation are exploring every conceivable way to save money, including headcount reductions, reorganizations, technological redeployment, capital restructuring—the list goes on and on. Such an environment of severe cost containment takes a toll on everyone involved, from managers, employees, and boards of directors to investors, shareholders, and even patients.

The flurry of cost-cutting activity set in motion with the advent of diagnostic related groups (DRGs) has been with us now for more than five years, and managers are weary. Yet they continue to face one simple reality: cut costs or go broke.

Employees have it as bad as or worse than their managers. So many hospitals have experienced dramatic staff reductions that the ones laid off may be the lucky ones. Those remaining not only toil under the specter of further cutbacks but also are being asked to accomplish more with less—less staff, less supplies, less money.

The industry is in a Darwinian crisis. Hospitals are closing at an alarming rate, and the National Committee for Quality Health Care predicts that 40 percent of the nation's hospitals may close by 2000.[1] Several chapters in this edition discuss the myriad approaches and interventions intended to stem this attrition. Here we will discuss one in particular—*gainsharing*.

To some, gainsharing is a retread, "old wine in a new bottle." To most, however, it is one of the last win-win propositions left in human resources management. In this chapter we will describe gainsharing and its history, discuss how it is implemented in a hospital setting, and dispel some of the myths that have developed around it.

WHAT IS GAINSHARING?

Gainsharing is an organizational program designed to improve productivity, enhance quality, and reduce cost. The benefits that accrue from these improvements are then shared in cash with the employees who produced them.

Gainsharing is a group incentive program with the emphasis on teamwork. Furthermore, gainsharing is intended to capture the numerous small savings that collectively add up to substantial savings. And what's more, gainsharing creates an environment for sustained, continual improvements.

The concept of gainsharing is simple. First, the hospital calculates its historic rates of productivity (and, where measurable, quality). Then, new targets are set. If performance reaches the new targets, the hospital and its employees share the monetary gains. Because it involves money that the hospital otherwise would not have saved or earned, the program is self-funding. In this sense, it is a win-win program for both the hospital and its employees.

Although gainsharing has only recently come to the attention of many hospital managers, the concept is not new. Prototype Scanlon plans appeared in the late 1930s and Rucker plans in the early 1940s. In fact, six major forms of gainsharing are currently in use in the United States: Scanlon plans, Rucker plans, Improshare plans, productivity and waste bonus programs, combined work-group/plantwide plans, and standard hour plans. Each type has its own philosophy, approach, structure, measurement system, and provisions for employee involvement. The six major types are thoroughly discussed and documented in the literature so we will not rehash them here (see Suggested Reading list). In practice, most programs are highly eclectic, borrowing features freely from the various

147

types and adding a measure of creativity to fit the specific organization.

HOW IS GAINSHARING IMPLEMENTED IN A HOSPITAL SETTING?

The optimal way to implement gainsharing depends entirely on the needs and conditions of the hospital. Therefore, be wary of canned approaches. Gainsharing touches so many hospital employees that a flawed design and/or implementation could deal a blow to the organization from which it may not soon recover.

There is, however, a proven process for successfully designing a gainsharing plan. That process involves the following eight steps:

1. buy-in
2. assessment
3. design
4. review/acceptance
5. preparation/training of supervisors
6. program introduction
7. monitoring
8. revision

We will explore each of these steps in detail on the following pages, but first a few observations are in order.

One Size Does Not Fit All

Unfortunately, many human resources programs in health care suffer from the "me too" syndrome. That is, what has proven to work well in one organization is copied by another. Frequently, this understandable desire to not "reinvent the wheel" backfires because of

- a program design that doesn't fit with the needs and circumstances of the institution
- weak implemention and buy-in

Thus, our first key message is this: *one size does not fit all*. In fact, gainsharing programs usually fail when a proper assessment does not precede a well-tailored design and an effective implementation.

Don't Overdesign

For some reason, gainsharing programs seem more susceptible to overdesign than do other types of programs. We at Hay are frequently called in to "induce labor" on plans that have been gestating in design committees for years. Why does it take so long? Probably because the idea of giving employees

cash for doing their jobs better creates a strong desire to avoid giveaways. This keeps designers searching for every possible contingency. The result can be debilitating. The message is clear: *don't overdesign*. In gainsharing, as in most change-oriented employee involvement programs, an "80–20" rule applies: If you spend 80 percent of your time and money designing the program and 20 percent implementing it, you will almost surely fail. However, if you spend 20 percent of your time designing and 80 percent implementing, you stand a much better chance for success. Thus, it is imperative to keep the program simple, but not simplistic.

There are two ways to keep the gainsharing design process going smoothly. First, it is important to create an awareness of the cost of *not* implementing gainsharing. Consider the following. If a hospital has a controllable expense budget of $150 million dollars, a 2-percent savings (a conservative estimate of what's achievable) equals $3 million dollars. Even after paying 50 percent of this savings to employees, it is costing the hospital $30,000 every week it waits to implement a gainsharing program. Second, developing a systematic approach to the design process assures hospital management that all contingencies have been covered and that nothing has been overlooked.

Let's consider such an approach, one step at a time.

Step 1. Buy-In

Gainsharing benefits from extensive administrative and physician buy-in from the start. Administrators want assurances that the program is not a giveaway. Physicians want assurances that employees will not sacrifice quality care. In the early stages these assurances can usually be accomplished with a few meetings to clarify objectives and approaches. Later on there will need to be further meetings and discussions on specific design elements.

Achieving this early buy-in provides the requisite senior management team that is committed to the program. Other influential constituencies, like the board of directors and corporate staff, also need to be exposed to the idea of gainsharing early on to secure their support.

Step 2. Assessment

An effective predesign assessment is critical to a successful gainsharing program. Not every hospital is ready for gainsharing, and not all gainsharing programs are alike. Gainsharing in a hospital that is not ready can be counterproductive. Remember, once the program is implemented, employees will have high expectations of receiving a payout. If the system breaks down and they receive none, they will probably be very frustrated and disappointed.

To avoid this potential setback, all hospitals should assess their overall gainsharing readiness. Hay management consultants have developed a four-part diagnostic process that provides a comprehensive assessment of a hospital's gainsharing readiness. The four elements of the diagnostic are

1. management interviews
2. gainsharing readiness audit
3. employee focus groups
4. systems review

The result of the overall assessment process is rarely a "go–no go" decision. Rather, it produces a plan for strengthening any weak spots before proceeding. The elements of the various assessment approaches are described below. As you read them, remember that each provides a different perspective on overall readiness.

Management Interviews

Management interviews serve the dual purpose of testing management readiness and gaining acceptance. These interviews center around perceived hindrances and obstructions that could impede a successful gainsharing implementation. They provide a firsthand impression of the "personality" and values of the hospital, as expressed through its management. These interviews provide an ideal setting to test and corroborate initial design hypotheses for further discussion in employee focus groups. Management interviews are usually held one on one, and the discussions are confidential. The results from all the interviews are normally condensed into a brief report to management that includes feedback on all aspects of the overall assessment process.

Gainsharing Readiness Audit

Hay management consultants have created a standardized questionnaire of over 100 items designed to assess employee attitudes and management culture in 11 critical areas. This survey provides a powerful analytical tool for assessing a hospital's gainsharing readiness and prescribing the best design and implementation strategy to meet each hospital's unique needs. Tailored to each hospital's specific situation, it is administered either to all employees or to a statistically meaningful sample. The specific factors are defined in Table 18-1.

While all factors in the gainsharing readiness audit provide important and useful insights, Supervisory Capability and Trust tend to correlate most closely with ultimate program success. We discuss this correlation more fully later in the sections on design and implementation.

Hay's gainsharing readiness audit is different from other employee attitude surveys in one important respect: it is supported by a data base of the collected responses from each hospital. This data base is used to help hospitals determine the relative favorability of their responses. From this we can produce a profile of hospitals that have successfully implemented gainsharing and compare it to any individual hospital. We can also use the data base to help assess the readiness of individual departments, as Figure 18-1 illustrates.

Employee Focus Groups

Employee focus groups permit the testing of hypotheses about employee reactions to special design considerations. By engaging 10–15 employees in discussions on the critical issues that have arisen in the other phases of the assessment process, one can sample both the employee reaction and the depth of emotions generated by these issues. This enables the design team to gauge how various approaches are likely to be received by the employees once the program is implemented. The composition of focus groups is critical to their value and success. As a general rule we don't mix managers and their subordinates or levels within the organization because this tends to obstruct candor. In addition, it is desirable to have both homogeneous and heterogeneous groups by function. A typical hospital's functional groupings for employee focus groups might look like this.

- nursing supervisors
- clinical (non-nursing) supervisors
- administrative supervisors
- mixed supervisors
- nursing staff
- clinical (non-nursing) staff
- administrative staff
- mixed staff

Decisions on focus group composition and participation are very important and must be carefully planned so as not to skew the results, create false expectations on the part of the participants, or insult important individuals/groups not chosen to participate. During focus groups, every effort is made to assure confidentiality. Participation in an employee focus group is voluntary, and individuals should not be asked to identify themselves. Notes are usually taken, but direct quotes should be avoided. Such sessions are best conducted by neutral third parties, but representatives of the hospital often sit in on one or several meetings to help interpret comments. Like the findings for the management interviews, focus group results are provided to management, the Design Task Force, and focus group participants, but care must be taken not to breach confidences or identify individuals.

Systems Review

A complete review of the hospital's relevant operational and management systems early on in the design process is important and necessary. It helps ascertain whether the hospital has the systems and measurement capability necessary to support gainsharing. When certain capabilities are lacking, the early warning allows the program to be postponed until correction or additions can be made. The types of systems reviewed are

- *Productivity measurement systems.* Here one checks for the presence of historical baselines; the accuracy, reliability, and timeliness of the information; the ability to flex

Table 18-1 Factors Considered in the Gainsharing Readiness Audit

Factor	Definition
1. Organizational Vitality	The overall place and sense of urgency exhibited by the organization as indicated by the venturesomeness of goals, the timeliness of decision making, the responsiveness to change, the degree of innovation, and the orientation toward risk taking
2. Clarity of Direction	The extent to which goals provide a useful context for daily action/decision making and are thoughtfully planned, well defined, clearly communicated, and well understood
3. Performance Orientation	The extent to which individuals are encouraged to stretch toward demanding goals, are held personally accountable for results, and understand what's expected of them
4. Measurement Credibility	The extent to which current measurement systems (i.e., budgets, revenue reports, performance appraisals, productivity reports) are perceived as being accurate, timely, complete, fairly compiled, and a true reflection of actual accomplishments
5. Teamwork	The degree to which employees work well together and need to work well together; the overall extent to which organizational integration, inter- and intradepartmental cooperation, lateral communication, and open discussion are used constructively to resolve conflict
6. Supervisory Capability	How well supervisors are perceived as knowing their job, holding people accountable for performance, treating employees fairly, providing timely and appropriate feedback, responding to problems, encouraging suggestions for improvements, recognizing and appreciating good work, and rewarding superior performance
7. Trust	The overall level of trust that employees have in the organization and their management with regard to reliability of information, level of commitment to employees, and willingness to provide directions
8. Productivity	The extent to which individuals feel that their job equipment and systems are designed to achieve the desired results, that they personally contribute to the results in their area, and that they are working at peak efficiency and productivity
9. Quality of Care	The extent to which the organization delivers high-quality health care, encourages employees to focus on providing high-quality care, and provides employees with the necessary resources, direction, and support to accomplish this goal; the degree to which employees judge their work to be of high quality
10. Job Satisfaction	The extent to which individuals find their jobs challenging and interesting, feel their jobs make good use of their skills and abilities, and are provided with sufficient information, authority, and discretion to do their jobs effectively
11. Rewards	Employees' overall satisfaction with current compensation and benefits policies and practices, their level of understanding of programs, and the extent to which nonmonetary rewards are provided and valued

for census, acuity, and severity; the usefulness of the measures; the amount, extent, and nature of employee impact on what is being measured; and the way reports are formatted and used by management.

- *Financial measurement systems.* Here, again, one looks at the accuracy, reliability, and timeliness of the information; its sensitivity to patient and staffing variations; the ability to extract controllable costs; and the presence of historical baselines linked to a coherent budgeting process.

- *Quality measurement systems.* In order to assure that productivity gains are not made at the expense of quality, it is essential for the hospital to develop a means for tracking and measuring the quality of its care. Here one is concerned with the types of measures used and how they are used on short- and long-term bases to monitor and control quality.

- *Performance management systems.* Since gainsharing is a group rather than an individual incentive program, it is

important to understand the hospital's philosophies, programs, and practices with respect to rewarding individual performance in order to reinforce them, not undermine or contradict them. In addition, one must fully understand the nature of the other systems in use to motivate individuals in order to make sure that gainsharing does not force individuals to make choices between their own interest and the interest of the group.

- *Compensation systems.* Gainsharing programs are greatly affected by employee perceptions of the other compensation approaches in the hospital. In hospitals where the pay is perceived as high, gainsharing may be viewed with indifference by employees who are content with their pay. In hospitals where the pay is perceived as low, gainsharing can be viewed either positively as a way to supplement income or negatively as a way to get people to work harder without guaranteeing them any more money. In order to manage employee expectations about gainsharing, it is important to understand the equity and competitiveness of the overall pay program.

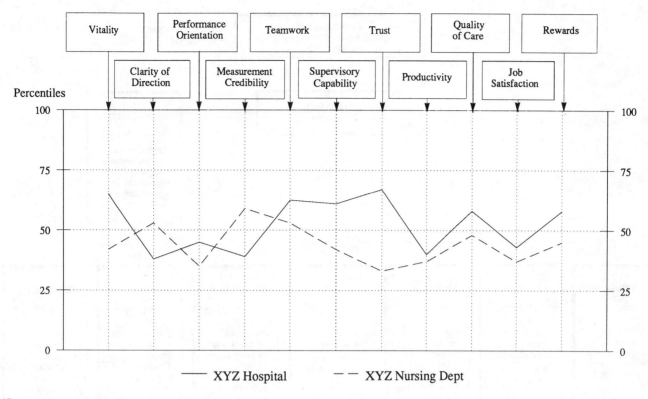

*Represents normative data base of over 200 U.S. hospitals

This illustration highlights an interesting and important relationship between employee perceptions of trust and the credibility of productivity/quality/performance measurement systems. Below are types of implications that emerge.

- Given XYZ Hospital's reservoir of trust and relative lack of measurement credibility, the hospital does not need to overspecify measures and targets, and it is well positioned to make midcourse adjustments.

- However, the dangerously low "trust" levels in the nursing department probably call for a separate nursing program that clearly specifies measures, targets, and payout opportunities and that is intensively communicated to assure that the program is understood and accepted.

Figure 18-1 Gainsharing Readiness Audit—Illustrative Departmental Comparison

---

- *Other employee involvement systems.* Many hospitals have a variety of employee involvement programs, some of which could conflict with gainsharing. Examples of such programs include employee suggestion box programs, perfect quality programs, patient complaint programs, and productivity enhancement schemes. In general, such programs are a plus and contribute to an overall environment that is favorable toward gainsharing. On the other hand, employees will want to know how all the various programs fit together. The Gainsharing Design Team must be aware of the various issues that could arise in order to deal constructively with any conflicts that occur.

Step 3. Design

Before delving into the specific considerations of the actual gainsharing design, it may be helpful to describe the makeup of a typical design team. This team usually takes the form of a

large task force out of which several smaller sub-task forces are created. Figure 18-2 shows the organization and responsibilities of a typical task force.

The Gainsharing Task Force usually involves from 5 to 15 individuals, the majority of whom are at the department head level and above (with some employee participation recommended). Members should represent both line and staff functions from all participating units or facilities. Furthermore, at least one physician representative should serve on this task force to convey physician concerns and represent their interests. Such a broad-based, multidisciplinary design task force helps secure additional buy-in and incorporates specific knowledge and expertise about the hospital's systems and processes. Members of the task force should be recognized leaders in the organization. It is particularly important to involve those key managers who are skeptical of or concerned about the program in order to secure their early support.

A key role in the task force is that of the task force chairperson. Far from being a figurehead, this person is essential to ultimate program success. The chairperson serves as the or-

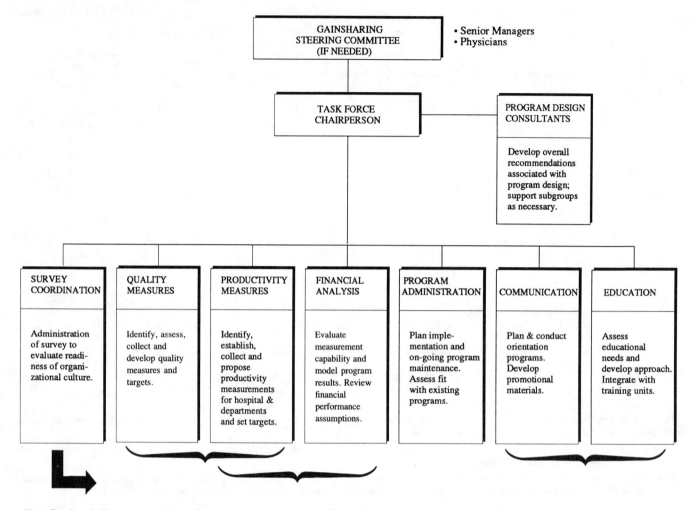

Note: Brackets indicate groups that are frequently combined. Arrow indicates that members of this group typically serve on other groups when tasks are completed.

Figure 18-2 Gainsharing Task Force

ganization's principal gainsharing proponent and fulfills these important roles.

- consensus builder
- information conduit
- coordinator
- custodian of the organization's mission and values
- link to the steering committee

The chairperson not only needs to be committed to the program's success, but also should be action oriented and well regarded throughout the organization. Without this individual, gainsharing may never materialize.

The Gainsharing Design Task Force usually reports to a steering committee and/or the organization's senior management group. In smaller organizations, the steering committee is replaced by the CEO. The senior management/steering committee role is to review and approve the final design.

Members of the steering committee are usually senior managers and physicians who are typically not eligible to participate directly in the plan. As such, they are best positioned to assess the plan objectively.

In Figure 18-2 the brackets indicate subgroups that are frequently combined. The arrow under Survey Coordination indicates that members of this subgroup typically serve on other subgroups when the gainsharing readiness audit is complete. During the design process the emphases are on the Quality, Productivity, and Financial Analysis subgroups. Thus, there is a temptation to postpone forming the other subgroups (i.e., Program Administration, Communication, and Education) until later when they are needed. This is a mistake. If members of these subgroups are to be ready when called on, they must understand the issues underpinning the design decisions.

The roles and accountabilities of the principal design sub–task forces are described below.

Quality Sub–Task Force

As mentioned earlier, a hospital gainsharing program must not overlook the quality of care. Preserving or enhancing the quality of care must be the overriding concern of the development process. It is the specific job of the Quality Sub–Task Force to assure that this is accomplished. This is done typically using the following steps:

- Inventory the existing quality measurement systems.
- Assess the quality and effectiveness of existing quality measures in terms of
  1. coverage (patients, MDs, clerical departments, staff departments)
  2. accuracy
  3. reliability
  4. availability of historical data
  5. timeliness
  6. understandability/clarity
  7. methods of communication
- Document significant quality measures that are lacking.
- Recommend one or two appropriate quality measures for each department.
  1. one clinical (if possible)
  2. one perceptive (if possible)
- Consider potential department clusters to share a single measure.
- Recommend three to five appropriate total-hospital-quality measures.
- Propose preliminary threshold quality levels for all measures.

Members of the Quality Sub–Task Force usually work closely both with members of the hospital Quality Assurance Department and with other department heads, especially when recommending departmental quality measures and standards.

Financial Analysis and Productivity Measure Sub–Task Forces

These groups are considered together because their activities are so closely related. The purposes of these groups are to

- establish hospital and departmental productivity measures and targets
- evaluate the hospital's measurement capability and model program results based on financial performance assumptions

Activities undertaken by these groups usually involve some combination of the following steps:

- Inventory existing productivity measurement, budgeting, and/or cost accounting systems.
- Assess the effectiveness of existing productivity measurement systems in terms of
  1. accuracy
  2. flexibility needed to accommodate shifts in volume
  3. reliability
  4. relevance to the gainsharing program
  5. availability of historical data
  6. difficulty in achieving targets
  7. level of employee impact/control on measures
  8. difficulty in measuring/tracking
  9. level of use/understanding at the department head/ supervisory level
- Document significant measures that are lacking.
- Recommend one or two appropriate measures for each department or cluster of departments.
- Recommend total hospital measures (if applicable).
- Propose preliminary threshold productivity levels for all measures.
- Model payout scenarios under various performance criteria.

As with the Quality Sub–Task Force, members of the Productivity Sub–Task Force work frequently and closely with others, including financial analysts, management engineers, and department heads.

Now that we have discussed the makeup of the Gainsharing Design Team, let's look at the following specific design elements:

- elgibility
- measures
- payouts
- hospital/employee share

Eligibility

Options as to which employees should participate in the gainsharing program are many and varied. Most hospitals choose to involve all employees, but other options include

- All employees who have passed normal probation
- All full-time employees
- All regular employees
- All nonmanagement employees
- All nonexempt employees
- Selected departments or facilities (pilot programs)

The ultimate decision is usually based on the program's purpose and the employees' eligibility in other similar programs. Because part-time employees make up such a large part of most hospitals' staffs and because their productivity is so important to overall hospital success, they are typically eligible to participate in the gainsharing program.

Measures

We discussed how measures are determined above. Let us now look at examples of the types of measures that are used. (See Table 18-2.)

Be careful not to use too many measures. Doing so will make it difficult for employees to focus on what's important. We recommend that no more than three qualifiers be used for each department and that all departments have at least one of each type (quality and productivity).

Once the actual measures are selected, how are they used? Table 18-3 presents the two major options available for a gainsharing plan that includes both quality and productivity measures. Typically, Option 1 is selected for hospitalwide programs because determining payouts at the total hospital level minimizes departmental rivalry, cost shifting, and sub-optimizing at the department level. Under this option, each department must achieve set productivity and quality standards in order for employees in that department to be eligible to receive a payout. The size of the payout is determined by overall hospital performance. Quality standards are also frequently set at the total hospital level, but many hospitals feel this is unnecessary if quality is adequately monitored at the departmental level.

It is worthwhile noting that in very sophisticated gainsharing programs, one or more of the qualifiers are replaced by modifiers that vary the payout based on a comparison of the level of performance with the standards, rather than simply turning the payout on or off.

If a hospital chooses to focus its gainsharing plan on quality, it can determine the payout on that basis instead. This is problematic, however, because of the difficulties associated

Table 18-2 Gainsharing Measures

	Hospitalwide	Departmental
Productivity/ Cost Measures	Targeted Costs − Actual Costs = Savings Net Adjusted Revenues − Actual Costs = Operating Surplus Targeted Cost per Patient − Actual Cost per Patient × Patient Day = Savings Reimbursement for DRG Inlier Activities − Actual Costs = Savings $\frac{Output}{Input}$ = $\frac{Aggregate\ Units\ of\ Service}{Cost}$ = Overall Productivity Index $\frac{Output}{Input}$ = $\frac{Aggregate\ Units\ of\ Service}{Human\ Resources\ Cost}$ = Human Resources Productivity Index	Cost per Unit of Service Cost per Test Cost per Discharge Cost per Square Foot Cost per FTE Cost per Admission Cost per Visit Cost per RVU Net Bad Debt Receivable Days
Quality Measures	Joint Commission Accreditation Board of Directors' Approval Physician Satisfaction Index Overall Patient Satisfaction Index	Patient Satisfaction Index Performance of Safety Checks Completing Treatment Plans Postoperative Complications (Therapies) Tests Ordered But Not Done Call Backs or Re-do's Breakage and Waste Documentation Completeness and Timeliness

Table 18-3 Use of Gainsharing Measures

OPTION 1

		Hospitalwide	Departmental
Productivity		Determiner	Qualifier
Quality		Qualifier	Qualifier

OPTION 2

		Hospitalwide	Departmental
Productivity		Qualifier	Qualifier
Quality		Determiner	Determiner

Determiner: determines the *size* of the actual payout
Qualifier: establishes who will be eligible to receive a payout

with valuing the savings that result from quality improvements.

Payouts

Like eligibility, there are numerous options for both the frequency and the method for allocating the gainsharing payout. For motivational reasons, payouts should be made as frequently as possible, provided that doing so doesn't place unreasonable burdens on the payroll system. We recommend payouts at least quarterly. Some hospitals pay bimonthly or even monthly. Pay annually or semiannually only if you must. If possible, make the payout in a separate check to highlight its special nature. Some hospitals choose to send checks only once a year, but to provide more frequent reports that indicate how each individual is faring. In our view there is no substitute for cash in hand to motivate and stimulate involvement. Furthermore, if you are going to calculate individual earning reports, most of the work is already done, and you might as well cut the check.

Most hospitals debate whether payouts should be equal in size for all eligible (qualifying) employees or whether they should vary depending on salary. (Equal share payouts are usually based on hours worked in order to allow for part-time employees.) The basic formula for each type of calculation appears below.

Equal Shares:

$$\frac{\text{Total employee share (\$)}}{\text{Total hours worked}} = \text{Share per Hour}$$

$$\begin{array}{c}\text{Individual} \\ \text{hours worked} \\ \text{in period}\end{array} \times \begin{array}{c}\text{Share} \\ \text{per hour}\end{array} = \begin{array}{c}\text{Individual} \\ \text{Employee} \\ \text{Share}\end{array}$$

Unequal Shares:

$$\frac{\text{Total employee share (\$)}}{\text{Total payroll for period}} = \text{Payout Percentage}$$

$$\begin{array}{c}\text{Individual} \\ \text{earnings for} \\ \text{period}\end{array} \times \begin{array}{c}\text{Payout} \\ \text{percentage}\end{array} = \begin{array}{c}\text{Individual} \\ \text{Employee} \\ \text{Share}\end{array}$$

The choice is made based on whom you consider gainsharing to be intended to motivate. If you believe that gainsharing is intended to reward lower-level employees, equal shares would be appropriate. If, on the other hand, you feel that the ultimate success of gainsharing rests with the commitment of supervisors, managers, and other professionals to make it work, you may consider it unfair for all employees to receive the same dollar share.

In our view, this is not such a difficult choice. Since the amount of money required to motivate a higher-level employee, such as a pharmacist, is different from the amount required to motivate a lower-level employee, such as a pot washer, offering equal shares will overcompensate the lower-level employee and not motivate the higher-level employee. This is a particularly undesirable outcome when you consider that successful gainsharing programs depend on the support and participation of department heads and supervisors and often put the most pressure on these individuals.

Hospital/Employee Share

There is range of options for dividing gainsharing savings between the hospital and the employees. Most hospitals opt for a 50-50 split because of its apparent fairness. The split does not have to be equal, however. Some hospitals have even decided to institute a three-way split with the final third going to charity. The decision is based on the hospital's philosophy and the type of message it wishes to pass to its employees.

The actual split, however, is less important than whether or not the hospital chooses to hold some of the employees' payout in reserve as insurance against overpayment. Overpayment can occur when payouts are made more frequently than once a year. The risk when increasing payout frequency is that superior performance early in the year could result in large payouts, but a later reversal could find the employees owing the hospital money. To avoid this, we recommend that 10 or 20 percent of the employee share be held in reserve against down periods and paid out at the end of the year if a positive balance remains.

This concludes the discussion of the major decisions that are made during the design phase of the program. There are, of course, numerous smaller considerations that go beyond the scope of this chapter. Examples include overtime treatment, capital expenditures, and major unplanned investments.

Step 4. Review/Acceptance

The preliminary design, once completed, usually is returned to the Steering Committee for review and approval. The Steering Committee will probably be most concerned about the accuracy and flexibility of the measures and the mechanisms that control for extenuating circumstances (e.g., to avoid payouts when the hospital is performing poorly). The design is usually finalized jointly in these meetings between the Steering Committee and the Design Task Force.

Step 5. Preparation/Training of Supervisors

Supervisory resistance to gainsharing occurs in varying degrees in almost all hospitals. Supervisors must be taught the skills and behaviors they will need in order to flourish in the new environment gainsharing represents. Examples of these skills and behaviors include

- openness to change
- willingness to admit errors
- confidence in the abilities of others
- willingness to allow the free flow of information

These valuable qualities do not suddenly appear when you decide to implement a gainsharing program. On the contrary, introducing a gainsharing program often produces the opposite result—supervisory intransigence. Supervisors who feel that they have been made vulnerable through exposure to subordinates' challenges and that they appear weaker to higher management may respond with passive nonsupport, or even subtle or overt sabotage of the gainsharing program.

To counter this tendency, the Education Sub–Task Force must be prepared to address the specific improvement that was identified during the gainsharing readiness audit and the employee focus groups. Approaches that can be used include

- training supervisors in participatory management
- encouraging supervisors with the correct skills to assume leadership roles in training others

- employing outside facilitators to conduct interactive sessions to enhance supervisory skills

Step 6. Program Introduction

The importance of this phase to the ultimate success of the gainsharing program can scarcely be overemphasized. As with any employee involvement program, getting it off to a good start is critical. The Communication Sub–Task Force is accountable for managing this effort. Its job is to create early momentum. By making use of the task force approach described earlier, the Communication Sub–Task Force members will have a reserve of trained, knowledgeable, involved people who can help get the message out.

Early on, employees will desire a great deal of information about the new program. Don't get caught unprepared. Make a plan that identifies all the audiences and what information they need. A sample draft of a communication plan appears in Table 18-4.

Communications should do more than merely describe the mechanics of the program; they should also include ideas and suggestions about how gains are made. Furthermore, visible top-management commitment is most important at this time. In the critical early days employees will be looking for tangible signs that gainsharing is not a passing fancy or a management whim, but a program to which all levels of management are committed.

The best communication approach is a multimedia one involving special events with posters, slide shows, video

Table 18-4 Communication Plan

Audiences	Objectives	Messages	Media	Success Factors	Timing	Responsibilities
• All employees	• Find out what's in it for me • Determine how it works	• Improves quality • Supports mission • Enhances justice and fairness	• Memos • Newsletters			
• Management/ supervisors	• Determine how it works • Overcome resistance	• Sustains business success • Rewards success	• Training materials • Glossary • Charts/graphs			
• Physicians	• Improve quality of care	• Improves quality of care	• Newsletters • Meetings			
• Special committees	• Show progress & results		• Memos • Newsletters			
• Corporate parent	• Communicate results		• Memos • Newsletters • Meetings			
• Task force members	• Provide updates and show progress		• Memos • Newsletters			

tapes, buttons, whatever is customary for your organization. Extensive use should be made of posters and charts that clearly display progress on a frequent basis. Ideally, every department will have two charts (one for productivity and one for quality) posted in a visible public area, and a similar chart should be displayed in the cafeteria showing the total hospital measure(s). Don't skimp here. Do a sharp, professional job, and the returns will cover the investment many times over.

Step 7. Monitoring

Once the gainsharing program is designed, announced, and in effect, performance and results must be monitored. This is the job of the Program Administration Sub–Task Force. Mechanisms for this monitoring should be in place prior to implementing the program. This monitoring should occur both at the total hospital level (if payments will be based on total hospital performance) and at the department level.

Step 8. Revision

The perfect gainsharing program has yet to be created on the first try. Even the best design needs to be tuned after it is implemented. We have found it useful to reconvene the entire Design Task Force monthly at the outset to discuss any necessary revisions. In all likelihood there will be questions about the measures that require judgment and forgiveness. It is preferable to offer forgiveness on a temporary basis, rather than making midyear changes to measures or the standards. The Design Task Force may need to secure guidance from the Steering Committee regarding which revisions they are free to make and which will need the Steering Committee's review and approval. In our experience, it takes an entire plan cycle (usually one year) to iron out most of the bugs.

WHY DO GAINSHARING PLANS FAIL?

Although the majority of thoughtfully designed and conscientiously implemented hospital gainsharing plans succeed, some do occasionally fail. The reasons for this failure include

- lack of top management commitment
- recalcitrance from first-line supervisors
- excessive complexity
- lack of employee trust in management
- unattainable goals
- poor communications
- inappropriate culture and management style
- inadequate management training
- lack of employee involvement in program design and implementation

With so many pitfalls, why do any hospitals attempt such a plan? Because gainsharing mines the hospital's last untapped resources: the enthusiasm, creativity, and commitment of its employees.

WHAT IS THE RESULT?

For the health care gainsharing programs in place, first-year productivity increases are averaging around 12 percent.* Subsequent years' increases are less, but still significant. The first-year gainsharing results reported by one 375-bed, not-for-profit community hospital are telling.

- Overall productivity increased 9 percent, yielding cost savings of almost $2 million.
- Cost per adjusted admission was reduced 6 percent from the previous year's level.
- Supply and expense costs per admission were reduced 3 percent.
- Quality of care improved, according to surveys, physician surveys, and clinical data.
- Employee commitment and motivation improved significantly.
- Employees' gainsharing awards averaged 5 percent of their annual salaries.

As you can see from these statistics, gainsharing results can be dramatic. Perhaps the most striking result is the size of the payout (5 percent). In an economy with relatively low inflation, it is possible for gainsharing rewards to meet or exceed an employee's normal raise. This is particularly important in light of the pressures on hospitals to recruit and retain scarce talent in an environment of severe cost sensitivity.

CONCLUSION

Many health care managers are somewhat uncomfortable with incentive and bonus programs that traditionally work well in other industries. But merely sticking to the basic knitting of quality care is not enough to survive in these turbulent times. Managers must attend to the financial viability of their institution and work to involve their employees in the effort. Only the collective energy, creativity, and commitment of all employees will assure success.

Gainsharing can and does help. It is a proven technique for helping employees feel like and behave like shareholders in the organization. Gainsharing's track record both inside and outside of health care is impressive. There is considerable risk, however, to both managers and employees, given Gainsharing's visibility and impact. If well designed and implemented,

---

*Source of data is recently completed gainsharing program designed by and implemented in conjunction with the authors.

gainsharing will contribute to improved hospital performance. If poorly designed and implemented, it could damage the morale of the organization.

Remember our two basic themes to improve your organization's chances of producing a successful program.

1. *One size does not fit all*. Tailor the program to fit your hospital's needs and circumstances.
2. *Don't overdesign*. Keep the program as simple (not simplistic) and understandable as possible.

If you do these things, you will have a program that induces managers to run their departments as if they were their own businesses. If they don't, their employees will remind them that they should.

NOTE

1. "The Year in Review," *Hospitals*, December 20, 1988.

SUGGESTED READINGS

Doyle, Robert J. Gainsharing and Productivity. New York: American Management Association, 1983.

Fein, Mitchell. *Improshare: An Alternative to Traditional Managing*. New Jersey, Mitchell Fein, Inc., 1981.

Frost, Carl F. *The Scanlon Plan for Organization Development*. East Lansing, Mich.: Michigan State University Press, 1979.

Productivity Sharing Programs: Can They Contribute to Productivity Improvement? Staff Report. Washington, D.C.: U.S. General Accounting Office, 1981.

David A. Bjork

Incentive Compensation in For-Profit and Not-For-Profit Organizations: A Comparison

19

INTRODUCTION

It is almost a truism that not-for-profit organizations have less flexibility than for-profit organizations in motivating their executives through incentive compensation programs. Managers and governing board members of not-for-profit organizations can point with envy to the ease with which for-profit organizations can encourage and reward outstanding performance with bonuses or incentive awards based on profit, or with stock options or stock grants that allow executives to share in any rewards provided to shareholders. The root of this matter can be found in differences in mission (and legal structure), as well as in organizational values and regulatory climate. Although both for-profit and not-for-profit organizations are designed to provide health care and comparable services to the same public, for-profit organizations do so to generate a return to their shareholders, whereas the not-for-profits do so to be in position to underwrite charitable care.

The investor-owned organization seems to have a clearer objective, a better yardstick for measuring performance, and a ready-made pool for funding rewards in profit or return on shareholder equity. The for-profit organization has a clearer rationale for motivating executives, as well as for rewarding them, in the profit motive, generating shareholder value and profit sharing. The not-for-profit organization, by contrast, has to worry about the concept of inurement and take great pains to avoid anything that could be construed as profit sharing.

Note: Reprinted from *Managing and Motivating Health Care Executive Performance* with permission of Pluribus Press, © 1989.

In terms of long-term incentives, the for-profits have a clearer rationale for motivating and rewarding executive performance in the "ownership theory," which argues that managers will do a better job of creating shareholder wealth if they are allowed to reap the same rewards as shareholders. This theory is absolutely contrary to the notion of a not-for-profit organization and would, in fact, result in inurement. Whereas investor-owned organizations work to generate profits, not-for-profits concentrate on generating surplus. The for-profits, in a general sense, belong to shareholders, but surplus is meant to fund charitable care and replacement or renovation of facilities. Theoretically, if some profit is good, more profit is better for the investor-owned organization. For the not-for-profit organization, on the other hand, too large an operating surplus can be an embarrassment—or even a potential tax liability, on the theory that it should have been used to fund more charitable care, to maintain facilities, or to improve the quality of care.

The underlying rationale for executive incentive programs in the for-profit sector is to provide a means of sharing a portion of the profits so that executives will be encouraged to generate more. The traditional values of the not-for-profit sector are far removed from the profit motive: providing high-quality patient care, underwriting charitable care, being of service to the community, and breaking even or covering costs. Behind the stated differences in using incentive compensation programs to motivate and reward executives are fundamental differences in mission or purpose, in culture and values, and often in the type of person who chooses to work in one sector over the other.

The not-for-profit sector traditionally has shied away from using incentive compensation, viewing it as inappropriate.

Aside from the difficulty of defining performance objectives and measuring performance, not-for-profits have viewed incentives as unseemly in the context of a charitable mission, looking on them as only enriching executives, rather than motivating and rewarding their performance. Perhaps because of their tight linkage with profits in the for-profit sector, executive incentives have been viewed by the not-for-profit sector almost as a kind of profit taking. "Why should our administrators get paid extra just for doing what they are given salaries for?"

If one looks beyond the overcharged terminology, however, it becomes evident that the differences between the for-profit and the not-for-profit sectors in health care are not all that great—and certainly not great enough to warrant significantly different approaches to motivating and managing executive behavior. The for-profits and not-for-profits are engaged in the same business and operate the same kinds of institutions. They compete in the same economic environment for the same patients and operate within the same system of health care financing. Both use the same type of operational objectives—for example, maintaining high enough occupancy rates to cover patient costs, with enough left over to finance expansion or improvement of facilities and acquistion or replacement of equipment.

As the environment becomes more competitive, and as the concept of "cost-plus reimbursement" by third-party payers fades into the past, not-for-profits are coming to realize just how closely their objectives resemble those of for-profit health care providers. They must capture enough market share to survive, find ways of increasing productivity as reimbursement rates decline, generate enough surplus to maintain their attractiveness to patients, and, where possible, find ways to increase efficiency and staying power through growth. For these reasons the not-for-profit sector today has less reason than in the past to avoid using incentive compensation. Two perspectives are important.

1. Incentive compensation is just as important as a pay system and a management tool, and is a process that ought to produce greater benefits to the organization than to the recipient. Incentives are a tool for focusing executive attention on important organizational objectives, for reinforcing strategy by aligning executives' interests with those of the organization, and for motivating executives to make the kinds of improvements in organizational performance that alone can ensure long-term success and survival.
2. Incentive pay is not extra pay, but rather a different form of pay. If the right rate of pay for a senior executive is, say, $90,000, the executive could be paid $90,000 in straight salary or $80,000 in base salary with an opportunity to earn $90,000 on average through an incentive pay program that would actually pay more than $90,000 for unusually good performance but less than that for a less outstanding performance. If not-for-profit organizations intend to pay their executives competitively, they must provide a total compensation package that is competitive with what other organizations pay, even if it is made up of salary plus bonus or incentive pay. They can do so either by paying a high base salary and guaranteeing a highly competitive rate of pay, regardless of performance, or by paying a moderate base salary plus offering an incentive pay opportunity that rewards executives according to their actual achievement.

The health care field has many challenges facing it in the years ahead. It must find ways of becoming more cost effective and must refocus its values on productivity and efficiency without losing sight of quality of care and its responsibility for providing charitable care. Whether incentive pay is appropriate in health care is no longer questionable. The real question now is whether an organization can meet coming challenges without using incentive pay to capture executives' attention, underscore the urgency of making fundamental changes, and provide strong motivation for making such changes.

INCENTIVES USED BY FOR–PROFIT ORGANIZATIONS

Incentive compensation plans in the for-profit health care sector can be placed broadly in two groups—those that reserve a portion of profits for executives, or reward them for generating profit, and those that, in effect, reserve shares of common stock for executives, or reward them in proportion to gains experienced by shareholders. The first type of plan focuses on near- or medium-term financial results, rewarding executives directly for producing "good results," whereas the second type focuses on treating executives as shareholders in order to draw their attention to generating wealth for shareholders. The first group of plans typically emphasizes cash rewards, whereas the second group typically is based on stock or stock surrogates. Although both groups could be divided into several subgroups or types of plans, the clearer differences among stock-related vehicles allow them to be classified as (1) profit pools, (2) stock appreciation vehicles, (3) performance plans, and (4) stock retention vehicles.

Profit Pools

The simplest and perhaps most common kind of short-term incentive is a profit pool that reserves a portion of profit for the executives who generated it. The pool can be defined as a flat percentage of either operating profit or net income or as a percentage of incremental profit above a threshold that provides a reasonable return to shareholders. This type of plan may be more highly structured so that it rewards executives for reaching certain goals, but the goals are typically profit objectives, even though other goals may also be involved. Whether or not the profit pool is explicitly defined and funded, short-term incentive plans in the for-profit sector typically are tied directly to profits generated.

The same concept is sometimes exended to what is, in effect, a profit pool accumulated over a two- to five-year period. Longer-term plans are less likely to define the rewards so clearly in terms of a profit pool; yet behind a framework of multiple objectives can generally be found a structure that is little more than a fund accumulated in proportion to cumulative profits. Profit may, of course, be defined in terms of return on equity, earnings per share, or growth in earnings per share, but the effect is the same. Rewards may be distributed from this pool in any number of ways: in direct proportion to salary, in proportion to individual contribution or performance, or in some other way. The distribution formula may obscure the underlying profit pool and make it appear that the rewards are directly related to individual performance; in truth, however, these rewards are seldom paid unless profit is large enough to fund them.

Stock Appreciation Vehicles

The underlying assumption of most stock-related incentive plans is that the ultimate goal of any investor-owned organization is to create shareholder wealth, whether in the form of appreciation in share value or in the form of a dividend stream. Although it may seem self-evident that the way to create shareholder wealth is to create profit, the matter is more complex than that; share value depends on many factors in addition to last year's or this year's profits or next year's anticipated profits. Because profit is defined by accounting principles, it does not adequately reflect changing dollar values. Investors are interested in the total return on their investment, a combination of appreciation in share value and dividend income. Even steadily increasing profits do not necessarily generate a positive total real return to shareholders, inasmuch as share value can fall as dividend income grows. Share value, most theorists argue, is largely dependent on investors' expectations of the company's future income stream, which is linked to competitive strength, growth through investment, and other factors that can even hold down earnings in current years to generate greater income in future years. For that reason, for-profit companies like to tie incentives and rewards for top executives to share value, rather than current profits, to align executives' interests with those of shareholders and focus their attention on long-term growth in the company's value.

Stock Options

The most common way to motivate and reward senior executives through stock value is with grants of *stock options*. Stock options are not only the most common type of long-term incentive vehicles, but also they are the only type in many for-profit health care management companies. They are almost always the first type used by a for-profit company. Stock options are of two principal types: "incentive stock options," which qualify for special treatment under IRS regulation, and "nonqualified stock options," which do not. The two types

have different tax and accounting treatments for both the company and the executive. Because the tax and accounting treatments are constantly changing, however, it is not possible to describe these aspects here.

A stock option gives the recipient the right to purchase a specified number of shares of common stock at some time in the future at a specified price, which is usually the market price ("fair market value") on the day the option is granted. The underlying assumption is that managers given stock options will strive to increase the value of the company because they will benefit from increased share value. Once vesting requirements are met and before the option expires, the option holder can generally exercise his or her right to buy the shares at his or her own convenience. Any vesting requirements are set by the company at the time the option is granted, as is the life of the option.

With the grant of a stock option, the company says to the executive, "We want you to work to increase the value of the company, and we are willing to reward you for doing that. We think it's only right that you should share in the value you create for our shareholders. Therefore, we will give you the right to purchase some shares of our stock at any time in the next 10 years, once you complete another year of service with the company. You will have to purchase the shares yourself, but the price will be set at today's market price. If the company prospers through your efforts, the shares will rise in value, and you will be able to capture that gain by buying the stock. We don't know how much the shares will be worth later on, of course, but that's partly up to you. The more they are worth, the better off our shareholders will be and the happier we'll be. There are a few laws and regulations, and we'll be glad to explain those to you."

The stock option is intended to focus executives' attention on the long-term objective of increasing the value of the company, rather than on the short-term objective of increasing this year's profits. It is intended to align executives' interests with those of the company's shareholders. Because the option allows executives to gain from any increase in share value, it is often considered just as effective as share ownership in getting executives to think like shareholders. On the other hand, should the underlying shares decline in value, the option carries no risk of loss.

The greatest strength of the stock option is its simplicity. It requires no goal setting, no internal measurement of management performance, and no complex administrative rules. It requires no debates over what the best measures of performance are, over what level of performance is good enough, and, after the fact, whether the goals were too easy or impossible to achieve or whether some unforeseen, external factors made it easy or difficult to earn the award. It provides a very direct reward for a very specific achievement, in direct proportion to the achievement.

The principal weakness of the stock option is that many factors other than management performance affect share value. Macroeconomic factors, such as the rate of inflation, interest rates, industry-specific structural changes, or demographic changes, can effect major changes in stock market values regardless of how well individual companies are performing. Although the most successful companies, or those with the brightest prospects, may lose less value than the others, even the best management is unlikely to be able to overcome a strong downward market trend. Likewise, when market values for a whole industry rise, share values of badly performing companies benefit, thereby delivering rewards from previously granted stock options even to ineffective management teams. One can legitimately argue, however, that macroeconomic factors and industrywide structural changes affect share values more in the short run than in the long run, and that in the long run, well-managed and successful companies will see their stock significantly outperform both industry and general market averages.

Stock Appreciation Rights

Another vehicle that works like a stock option is a stock appreciation right. A stock appreciation right, which is often coupled with stock options, provides an alternative means of delivering the reward due executives from appreciation in share value. In common use in the health care field, it finds most use among large and established companies, for the reason that it can result in significant charges against earnings.

A stock appreciation right gives the recipient the right to receive any appreciation in share value for a specified number of shares, above a specified price, which is usually the market price on the day the stock appreciation right is granted. The principal difference between a stock appreciation right and a stock option is that the executive need not buy stock in order to capture the gain. The executive simply exercises his or her right to be paid the full amount of the gain by the company either in stock or cash or in a combination of the two. The terms of a stock appreciation right are generally similar to those of a stock option, except that the executive can exercise the right only during a short "window period" following the publication of quarterly or annual reports.

A stock appreciation right generally is used in one of two ways. Typically, it is designed as an alternative form of settling stock options, so that the recipient can exercise either the option or the stock appreciation right, but not both. Sometimes, however, a stock appreciation right is used to facilitate the exercise of stock options by providing the executive with a cash award sufficient to cover the tax due on exercise of the option. In this case, the recipient typically can exercise the stock appreciation right only if he exercises an option to purchase an equivalent number of shares.

The assumptions underlying a stock appreciation right are more or less the same as those underlying a stock option, and the two are used in about the same way. However, because a stock appreciation right does not require that the executive purchase stock, it is often viewed as being less effective than the stock option in aligning the executive's interest with those of shareholders. Except when it requires the concurrent exercise of stock options, the stock appreciation right can be seen simply as an easy way for executives to capture any increase in share value without any of the risk of share ownership. It does, however, provide a number of real advantages to the recipient, who avoids cash-flow difficulties and entanglement in regulations governing stock trading by corporate insiders.

Performance Plans

Performance plans originated as substitutes for the stock option during the 1970s, when the stock market was sluggish and was not delivering significant appreciation in share value even to companies which considered themselves well managed. More recently, they have come to be seen as a better vehicle than stock options for motivating and rewarding executives because the link between performance and pay seems to be much more direct. In essence, long-term performance plans are "stretched-out" annual incentive plans, with goals defined over a three-, four-, or five-year performance cycle. Executives are rewarded to the degree that they achieve those long-term goals. Significant effort has gone into determining which types of goals are most likely to be beneficial to shareholders—which, in other words, "create shareholder value" or raise share price.

Theoretically, performance plans should work much like stock options, except that they exclude marketwide or industrywide changes in share value. In other words, they should reward executives solely for managerial performance—for achieving the company's strategic objectives, for achieving goals established by the board. Whereas performance plans do reward executives for achieving these goals even if there is no subsequent increase in share value, they do not reward executives who fail to achieve long-term objectives, even if share price does increase.

The most common type of performance plan actually is tied to changes in share value in that it either defines a unit of value in terms of a share of common stock or couples the performance grant with a grant of stock options. Recent experience with performance plans has shown that macroeconomic factors and industrywide changes can have as great an effect on a company's ability to achieve its long-term objectives as on the market's evaluation of its stock. For that reason, performance plans are often paired with stock appreciation vehicles in the hope that one or the other may work well, if not both.

Performance plans require a well-established and reasonably sophisticated long-term planning process that allows the company to define with reasonable precision what its performance objectives are over a three-, four-, or five-year period, as well as a range of possible outcomes above and below the target for which different levels of reward should be paid. For this reason, performance plans are rarely found in new or fast-growing companies, which usually rely on stock options. Although they have become quite common in large industrial firms, performance plans are not yet used much in the health care industry, except by some of the larger, more mature firms, or by those that do not have publicly traded stock. For-profit companies that do not have publicly traded stock, such as subsidiaries of larger companies or joint ventures, often turn to performance plans because they are arguably the best alternative to stock options for motivating and rewarding superior executive performance.

Of the two common types of performance plans, one (performance share plan) is tied to share value and the other (performance unit plan) is not. A performance share plan defines the unit of value as a share of common stock, so that at the end of the performance period, executives are given an award equivalent to the then-current value of the number of shares they have earned over the period. If they reach the maximum performance level defined at the beginning of the period, they earn the total number of shares granted at the beginning of the period. If performance fell short of the definition, they receive only some of the shares they were contingently granted at the beginning of the period. Thus, the ultimate value of the award is tied to achievement of long-term objectives and to changes in the price of the company's common stock.

A performance unit plan, by contrast, defines value in terms of a specific dollar amount that does not change over the performance period. If the company achieves its long-term objectives over a performance period, the executive will be given a reward for "on-plan" performance. If the company exceeds its goals, the reward will be proportionately higher; if goals are not achieved, any award paid will be less.

With the contingent grant of performance units or shares, the company says to the executive, "We want you to work to see that the company achieves its strategic objectives, and we are willing to reward you for doing that. We believe that by achieving our goals, we create value for our shareholders, and we think it's only right that you should share in what you create. Therefore, we will give you the opportunity to earn an award (dollars in a performance unit plan or shares in a performance share plan) over the next three years. In our planning process, we established a set of long-term objectives that you agreed were obtainable over the next three years. If we reach those objectives, we will reward you. If we do better than we plan, the reward will be bigger, and if we do less well than we plan, it will be smaller." In the case of a performance share plan, the discussion will continue, "Because we are giving you the opportunity to earn shares of common stock, the value of the reward will depend partly on how well our stock does. If the share price rises, the ultimate value of the reward will be greater than the same number of shares would be today. Of course, if our stock falls in price, the opposite will be true. In either event, you are treated just like our shareholders. If you make money for them, you'll earn more for yourself."

The greatest strength of a performance plan is its ability to link pay directly to performance, to reinforce strategy by focusing executive attention on the company's strategic objectives, and to tailor a long-term incentive precisely to the company's circumstances, plans, and objectives. It allows the company to enter into what amounts to a "performance contract" with its executives that precisely defines performance expectations and award opportunities. Such a plan permits executives to play a major role in shaping the plans and objectives to which their rewards will be tied, and requires them to reach agreement with the company's directors on what kind of performance is expected. Also, it gives directors an effective tool for assessing the longer-term performance of the executive team.

The greatest weakness of a performance plan is that because it is built on the company's internally developed plans and objectives, its effectiveness depends on the appropriateness of the objectives specified. The planning process must be strong because the stakes riding on that process are high. If objectives are set too high or too low, a performance plan can deliver inappropriately large or small rewards. Performance plans work best in a stable environment, and changes in the environment can make it easier or harder than expected to achieve the company's long-term goals. Purely external factors, in other words, can provide a windfall or deprive executives of a reward for good performance in the context of the new circumstances. Another weakness of a performance plan is that its effectiveness in motivating executives is strictly limited to the duration of the performance cycle; it provides no longer-term incentive. Yet another weakness is its inflexibility as to timing—performance is measured precisely at the end of the performance period. Unlike stock options and stock appreciation rights, performance plans do not allow executives to choose the time for measuring and rewarding performance. On the other hand, a series of overlapping performance plans can minimize some of these problems as can after-the-fact review of the appropriateness of corporate objectives and modification of rewards in the light of end-of-the-period circumstances.

Stock Retention Vehicles

Stock retention vehicles, by their very design, place greater emphasis on retaining executives than on motivating performance. Insofar as they are stock based, however, they can provide significant incentive value over the long term. A grant of stock, contingent only on continued service to the company over a period of years, can be a powerful tool for motivating and rewarding executive performance, inasmuch as the reward increases or decreases in value in direct porportion to share price and dividends paid. Just as stock options and stock appreciation rights motivate executives to act in ways that will increase share value, so also do grants of stock earned through continued service. More important, because the executive actually owns the stock, the grant should motivate him or her to try to avoid any drop in share value. Grants of stock earned through service also can foster a longer-term orientation, because the ultimate value of the award does not depend on the executive's selecting the most advantageous moment to exercise the option or the appreciation right, but rather on long-term appreciation and value.

Restricted stock, the most common stock retention vehicle involves an outright grant of stock. The stock is earned by the recipient over a specified restriction period during which the recipient cannot sell the stock or use it otherwise as collateral. In a *restricted stock option*, another variation, the recipient typically is allowed to purchase shares of common stock at a deep discount, with restrictions on resale of the stock until a specified period of service is completed. Neither type of stock retention vehicle is all that common in the health care industry, or in general industry either for that matter; however, both are being used increasingly as an alternative to other types of long-term incentives in connection with mergers and acquisitions, when retention of key individuals is particularly important. Both vehicles also are coming to be viewed as reasonable alternatives to performance plans, inasmuch as they do not depend for their efficacy on the company's ability to plan, forecast, and set goals.

A grant of restricted stock gives the recipient full title to a specified number of shares of stock even during the restriction period, typically with both voting and dividend rights, but prevents sale or other use of the stock during the restriction period. Once the recipient has completed the required term of service (typically one to five years) all restrictions lapse. If the executive does not complete the required term of service, he or she forfeits ownership of the stock. The underlying assumptions are threefold: First, the executive will remain to help the company prosper; second, he or she will strive to increase the value of the company's stock; and third, if the company does not perform well, the executive may not remain an employee long enough to earn free title to the stock.

In granting restricted stock or a restricted stock option, the company says to the executive, "We want you to work to increase the value of the company, and we are willing to reward you for doing that. Because we want you to be a shareholder, so that your interests are the same as those of our other shareholders, we will give you some shares; however, you cannot sell or use them in any other way until you have completed five years of service. At the end of this period, you will own the shares free and clear. If the company prospers through your efforts, the shares will rise in value, but they might fall in value, too. The more they are worth, the better off our shareholders will be and the happier we will be. Even during the restriction period, you will receive dividends and have the right to vote, just like any other shareholder."

Stock retention vehicles are intended primarily to retain key executives, but also to align their interests with those of shareholders and focus their attention on increasing share value over the long term. Because stock vehicles benefit executives regardless of company performance, they are sometimes seen as a "giveaway." They do, however, work much like stock appreciation vehicles in offering an opportunity for long-term gain. They also offer a greater certainty of reward and a greater predictability of reward value, much like a performance plan.

The greatest strength of restricted stock is its simplicity. Like the stock option, it requires no goal setting, no internal measurement of management performance, and no complex administrative rules. Better yet, it avoids the unpredictability of gain, a major drawback of the stock option or stock appreciation right. The principal weakness of restricted stock is that the reward is not tied to performance but relies heavily on the premise that executives who do not perform well will not complete the required period of service. However, in recent years, some companies have overcome this weakness by allowing restrictions to lapse earlier when performance is good.

LONG-TERM INCENTIVES IN NOT-FOR-PROFIT ORGANIZATIONS

The questions confronting the not-for-profit organization as it wrestles with motivating and managing executive performance with incentive compensation are

- Should the not-for-profit organization use incentive compensation?
- Should it use long-term incentives in addition to short-term incentives?
- Without stock, what kind of long-term incentives can it use?
- What principles should guide design of a long-term incentive plan?

The first question has been answered by describing incentive compensation not as "extra pay" but as variable pay, which rewards executives in proportion to their success in achieving the organization's goals. Variable pay may not be appropriate for every organization, but it can be appropriate for any organization that has clearly defined and quantifiable goals and is willing to measure and reward executives relative to achievement of those goals. Given the difficult challenges confronting health care oranizations, the issue may well be whether a not-for-profit organization can achieve its goals in an increasingly competitive environment without using incentive compensation as a tool for motivating and managing performance. The remaining three questions are discussed in the sections that follow.

Should Long-Term Incentives Be Used?

Not-for-profit organizations only recently have begun using incentive compensation. Many have not yet taken the first step of adopting short-term incentives, and even those that have done so have often found that short-term incentives don't work quite as well as they would like. Then why should they even consider using long-term incentives? The answer is that long-term incentives are probably more appropriate than short-term incentives for the not-for-profit health care field. The true measure of organizational success is long-term viability as an independent organization, remaining a survivor by maintaining competitive strength and financial stability. The best measure of executive performance is whether the executive can make the organization stronger over the long run. Short-term goals may be stepping stones toward achieving long-term success and useful yardsticks in measuring short-term executive performance, but that is *all* they are. The real strategic challenges are longer term—increasing or at least maintaining market share, increasing or at least maintaining operating margins, increasing productivity, gaining greater control over the organization's destiny through vertical integration, and improving utililization of assets. Any one of these objectives required long-term effort that outweighs the importance of achieving short-term goals. If organizations could identify and quantify their longer-term objectives as easily as short-term goals, and if they were able and willing to measure executive performance over a three-, four-, or five-year period, long-term incentives would often make more sense than short-term incentives.

The strategic challenges confronting most health care organizations require transforming the organization, not making incremental changes. Major initiatives and sustained effort over a period of years are required to make changes in the nature of the organization, in the way it does business, and in its approach to the marketplace. Also required are a vision of the organization's future and a commitment to that future, innovation, risk taking, and entrepreneurship—typically with some sacrifice of short-term stability and short-term success as measured by occupancy rates and operating margins. Gaining the commitment of executives and focusing their attention on the overriding importance of achieving the organization's long-term goals are no easy matter, and long-term incentives can be an effective tool for doing just that. Health care organizations can no longer afford to define executive accountabilities in terms of administration, stewardship, or caretaking; in most cases, maintaining the strength and stability of the organization merely by continuing to manage it in traditional fashion is virtually impossible. Short-term incentives often focus on incremental improvement, of doing the same thing better. Long-term incentives can focus on accomplishing major changes in the business or on doing the right thing, rather than just doing things right.

Which Long-Term Incentives Can Be Used?

Not-for-profit organizations cannot use the simplest, most common types of incentives used by for-profit organizations, which are based on shares of ownership in the organization. Even if not-for-profits did have stock, or defined a kind of surrogate stock or stock substitute sometimes used by for-profits when stock is not publicly traded (such as "book value shares"), they would still have to avoid using such stock substitutes in executive incentive plans because they represent inurement—in the form of an ownership right to "profits" produced by the not-for-profit organization.

Theoretically, not-for-profits could use stock surrogates designed to reward executives for increasing the value of the organization (like a stock option or a stock appreciation right) or designed to retain the executive (like restricted stock), just so long as the surrogate was stripped of any right to an income stream in perpetuity (in the form of dividends) and any voting right representing ownership in the organization. As long as the reward is for increasing the value of the organization to the community it serves or increasing its ability to provide charitable care, the stock surrogate can avoid inurement. At this point, however, the surrogate would be a cash reward tied to achievement of objectives—more of a performance plan than a real stock surrogate. The risks might then outweigh the benefit. The mere resemblance of stock, or comparison with stock, should raise a red flag to anyone concerned about avoiding inurement. Why encourage anyone to raise the question?

The one type of vehicle ideally suited to the not-for-profit environment is the performance plan. It allows the organization to reward executives for achieving any properly defined objectives, be they related to the financial strength of the organization (its ability to continue funding charitable care), its competitive strength, its productivity, or its quality of care. Any of the kinds of measures appropriate for short-term incentive plans could be appropriate for long-term plans as well. Also appropriate would be longer-term strategic achievements—such as producing 10 percent of revenues from non-hospital businesses, achieving significant vertical integration by controlling payers or physicians representing 15 percent of inpatient revenues, developing a new product or service line that makes use of an empty wing or facility, disposing of unproductive facilities, or consummating a merger that boosts productivity. To avoid any semblance of inurement, financial goals can be defined in terms of strategic imperatives rather than profitability—in terms of productive use of assets (generating enough operating surplus to renew and replace all depreciable assets, to support charitable care, and to fund any investment necessary to ensure survival), financial stability (improving the organization's ability to provide charitable care and to continue serving the community), or the role of the organization as a low-cost provider (therefore ensuring a reasonable operating surplus).

A performance plan gives a not-for-profit organization almost unlimited flexibility in designing a long-term incentive to suit its unique characteristics, fit its organizational culture and management style, and reinforce its strategy. Such a plan may be defined to last any length of time, include any number of participants, focus on almost any kind of quantifiable goal, and provide any reasonable amount of reward. Control of the plan is left in the hands of the board, and organizational objectives and performance expectations can be clearly communicated.

Designing and implementing an effective performance plan in a not-for-profit setting are no easy matter, of course. Considerable effort is required, particularly in establishing clear-cut long-range goals and an operating strategy that makes those goals achievable. Some negotiation is required between management and the board over what level of performance is realistic and attainable. Both management and the board must be willing to make a strong commitment to achieving those objectives, and the board must be willing to administer the plan.

What Design Principles Should Be Used for Long-Term Incentive Plans?

The most important design principle of any incentive plan in a not-for-profit organization is that the plan should support the charitable mission of the organization. Coincident with that is the principle that the plan must take precautions to avoid inurement. Among the necessary precautions are

- placing administration of the plan in the hands of a disinterested party (typically the board)
- defining eligibility and participation one year at a time (to avoid implication of any right to participate)
- measuring performance at least partly in terms other than "profit" or other related financial measures
- ensuring that total compensation is not unreasonable (not above the normal range of compensation for comparable positions in comparable organizations)
- avoiding any funding formula (which could imply reserving a share of profits for executives)
- avoiding defining rewards as directly proportional to "profits" or operating surplus

Any other design principles are more or less the same as they would be in the for-profit sector. They are not absolute principles, in the way that the first two are; rather, they are concepts that, if followed, can make the plan more effective than it might be otherwise.

Eligibility

Eligibility should be limited to senior executive positions that have significant impact on the overall success of the organization. Participation in a long-term incentive plan is usually more restricted than in a short-term incentive plan because fewer positions play a significant role in determining the longer-term success of an organization. Positions that should be considered for eligibility are those that particpate in—or have a major role in—strategic planning (as opposed to operational planning), are responsible for making strategic decisions and major capital investment decisions, and are important in determining the shape and effectiveness of the organization. A long-term incentive plan generally should not include positions focused primarily on managing day-to-day operations. A typical organization might have 4 to 8 participants in a long-term plan, and even a very large organization rarely has more than 15 or 20 participants. The right number depends on the size of the organization, its structure, its

management style, and the design of senior executive positions.

Incentive Opportunity

Incentive opportunity under a long-term plan should be enough to counterbalance the short-term incentive plan and enough to motivate exceptional effort among participants. Organizations adopting long-term incentive plans for the first time often make the mistake of providing so little incentive opportunity that the long-term plan fails to capture the attention of participants or suffers in comparison with annual bonus or incentive opportunity. A primary reason for adopting a long-term incentive plan is to focus executive attention on the importance of achieving long-term strategic results, even at the cost of not achieving near-term operational goals. The risk of providing too little incentive opportunity is that the shorter-term operational objectives can appear to be more meaningful (at least in terms of monetary reward to participants) than the overriding strategic goals of the organization.

Performance Measures

The purpose of a long-term incentive plan is to reinforce organizational strategy by focusing executive attention on the most important long-term strategic goals of the organization. Performance measures chosen for this purpose should represent the most important goals over the cycle of the long-term incentive plan. Insofar as possible, they should be coincident with or complementary to the performance measures of a short-term incentive plan, so that the two incentive plans are not pulling executives in opposite directions. In the for-profit sector, there is a strong tendency to select one of the two overriding financial measures of success, such as return on equity and growth in earnings. In the not-for-profit sector, selecting just one or two financial measures such as these might carry considerable risk because of the obvious implications of inurement. Just as important, such financial measures may not adequately represent an organization's strategic objectives. Among nonfinancial measures that may also be important are market share, productivity improvement, and achievement of major operational components of a strategic plan that require organizational transformation to become more vertically integrated. Because long-term incentive plans generally are defined as group incentives, a single set of measures generally applies to all participants. However, more and more diversified, multibusiness organizations are basing long-term incentive rewards on measures tailored to the various business units. Because this approach obviously complicates the plan, a single set of measures may be preferable.

Focus on Organizational Success

Short-term incentive plans often place considerable weight on the success of individual business units, functions, or positions. By contrast, long-term incentives generally focus on overall organizational success. If a position does not contribute enough to overall organizational success to earn rewards on that basis, it probably does not belong in a long-term incentive plan. One attractive byproduct of a long-term incentive plan is that it can help build strong team identification, encourage teamwork, and overcome any tendency toward competitiveness among organizational units. A long-term incentive plan should encourage optimal utilization of resources so that the organization as a whole succeeds, even at the cost of individual units.

Duration

Long-term incentive plans typically measure performance over three- to five-year periods that are coincident with the organization's planning cycle. In times of rapid change, five-year plans can seem remote or—worse—fail to anticipate significant environmental changes and the shifts in strategic direction that may be required to accommodate them. For that reason, many organizations experienced in long-term planning and long-term incentive plans are shortening the long-term incentive plan to two, three, or four years.

The test of the effectiveness of either a long-term or a short-term incentive plan is whether it helps the organization achieve its objectives by motivating behavior, shaping decisions, and building commitment to the organization's vision of its future. If a long-term incentive can do that, the results are likely to be improved enough to justify the expense and administrative effort required. If it cannot do this, the plan is not effective, even if it does pay rewards and thereby satisfies participants.

Thomas P. Flannery, Jr.

20

Managing Base Compensation for Key Executives

For purposes of discussion *base compensation* is defined as the cash salary paid—at least once each month—for expected levels of performance. Base compensation, often stated in annual dollar terms, is usually the largest portion of the compensation package for the health care executive.

HOW MUCH SHOULD WE PAY?

Establishing a salary for executives often becomes a difficult and frustrating experience for the board of directors and for the chief executive officer (CEO). Opinion often clouds the issue because so few facts are available on which to base an informed decision. Although trustees and executives have a natural tendency to maintain pay at a reasonable level, they approach the experience with a different perspective. Many board members evaluate the executive salary package in light of their own incomes. If these incomes are low, the organization may not be able to recruit and retain competent personnel. The executive understands the risk inherent in a senior appointed position and so desires a reward commensurate with that perceived risk. Despite the different perspectives, however, both the executive and the board members are concerned that the organization develop and maintain the highest level of service and quality of care.

Only by understanding the pay-setting process itself can we begin to comprehend executive pay. This requires a review of

Note: Reprinted from *Managing and Motivating Health Care Executive Performance* with permission of Pluribus Press, © 1989.

the steps involved in determining pay and an appreciation of the many variables that influence the decision-making process.

It should be kept in mind at the outset that each organization has an existing pay practice, whether good or bad, defined or undefined. The question to ask is: Does the current pay program achieve the organization's overall objectives? Several indicators of the quality of the existing pay program serve to answer this question. These are

- *Turnover.* Is the organization losing executives to other organizations? Is the reason compensation, or do they stay in the job for extended periods?
- *Vacancies.* When the organization has vacancies, do pay scales make it difficult to get candidates to apply for jobs or to accept job offers? How long do positions remain vacant?
- *Market Data.* In reviewing published salary survey data, do your salaries appear out of line?
- *Complaints.* Do executives constantly complain about pay levels?

Because these are rough indicators, a health care organization must exercise care in interpreting them. Just because an executive remains for 20 years in the same organization does not necessarily suggest that pay levels are too high. If no one leaves the organization, it may be a pay issue. It may also be some other factor. For example, if one individual stays for 20 years, it may be an issue of family, life style, or location. On the other hand, if senior executives are being recruited away with offers of more pay, it is a good indication that the organization's pay program may be noncompetitive.

A health care organization should conduct a formal review of its executive compensation program whenever uncertainty about the program exists. Also, this review should be conducted whenever a major event occurs, such as the retirement of the CEO or a shift in the organization's business strategy. The review should be updated periodically to ensure that the organization maintains its desired compensation position. Two such reviews are available. The first, an in-depth evaluation of the compensation program's adequacy, is usually conducted every four to five years. The second is an annual update designed to help the organization maintain its desired compensation position relative to the market.

ESTABLISHING AN EXECUTIVE COMPENSATION PROGRAM

The first step in designing or conducting an in-depth evaluation of the organization's compensation program is to acquire a conceptual understanding of the organization's current pay position relative to the executive job market. This is easily accomplished by a simple model. This model is shown in Figure 20-1. The horizontal axis represents job challenge, which can be defined several ways, including organizational size, job size, annual revenue, or number of full-time equivalents (FTEs). The vertical axis represents annual salary dollars. This model shows the CEO's current annual salary, around which is a "safety zone." The safety zone defines the threshold level at which it becomes unlikely that the incumbent will leave the organization, either for more pay or for a different challenge. The size of the safety zone is a personal decision, over which the organization or its board of directors has little control. In normal circumstances, it is unlikely that an executive will leave for less pay or for a bigger job at the same level of pay. It *is* likely, however, that an executive will leave for a job of the same size or for a bigger job at a higher pay level. Some say that an executive will not typically change jobs for less than a 10- to 15-percent increase in salary.

Breaking the chart into four quadrants allows one to determine an organization's level of vulnerability to losing the executive. The greatest threat comes from any outside organization with a vacancy that offers compensation higher than the executive now receives. This is represented in quadrants I and II. The individual who leaves for a larger job at the same pay level is probably attracted by the job challenge, advancement opportunities, location, or some other reason unrelated to pay. Pay may be a useful defensive tool here, but only if an organization can match the factors inducing the executive to move. It is unlikely that an organization will lose an executive to a lower-paying job strictly for pay reasons.

An organization is most vulnerable to employers in quadrant I who offer more challenging jobs and higher pay. Quadrant II (more pay, smaller job challenge) is the next level of vulnerability, followed by organizations in quadrant III (less

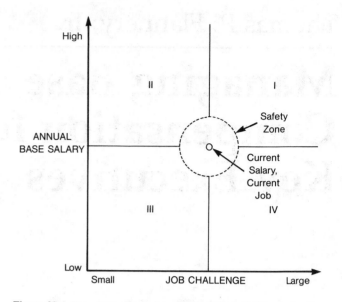

Figure 20-1 Determining Your Organization's Vulnerability to Losing an Executive Because of Pay or Job Challenge Opportunities

pay, smaller job challenge) and quadrant IV (less pay, bigger job challenge).

In reviewing the vulnerability of the organization, the board must understand that it cannot eliminate the risk of losing an executive over pay issues. There will always exist an organization that will offer higher remuneration. The challenge the board faces involves setting executive compensation at a level that allows the organization to attract, motivate, and retain competent executives. Meeting that challenge means developing a decision-making process that explores the salary market for health care executives.

PROGRAM DESIGN CRITERIA

The second step in evaluating the executive compensation program is to determine design criteria. Affordability and desire to pay represent two key criteria. Affordability to pay, which represents the dollars the organization can invest in an executive compensation program, is primarily an economic issue. Affordability to pay is sometimes offset by desire to pay: An organization may desire to pay at certain salary levels but be quite unable to afford the cost. The affordability and desire issues frequently arise when the organization begins to recruit. A candidate who requires a high salary may find that the health care organization needs his or her talents, but may believe it can find an equivalent candidate for fewer dollars. At another organization, the same candidate may find that the health care organization desires to pay the price but is unable to afford the cost. The health care organization should begin resolving the issues of affordability and desire to pay at the outset. Failing to do so will only postpone the questions and complicate the decision-making process.

Internal equity is an additional important factor. "Internal equity" is defined as the perceived relative fairness of each person's pay. A pay plan that is perceived as unfair can demoralize members of the management team. Often, the unfairness is unintentional. For example, one health care system brought in a less-experienced hospital administrator at the same rate of pay as one of the system's veteran administrators. The veteran learned of the new administrator's pay. He felt that his contribution and loyalty were not considered sufficiently valuable because the new person's pay was almost the same as his. Rather than stay with the system, the administrator left. It would have been simpler if the system had made an adjustment to the veteran's pay package and communicated its positive feelings about the executive's loyalty and performance.

When finalizing the pay package for a new executive, consideration should be given to how the package relates to the pay of current members of the team.

In some instances, an executive will hire a subordinate and compensate the individual at the same rate of pay as a veteran but assume that the veteran will not learn the new person's pay. Although many tactics can be used to keep pay issues confidential, it is risky to assume that pay will be kept secret. If pay levels are ever made fully or partially public, a well-designed, carefully considered pay program will prevent the embarrassment that capriciously set salaries are sure to cause.

JOB EVALUATION TO ACHIEVE INTERNAL EQUITY

Job evaluation is the process of "measuring" the content of jobs through use of a disciplined approach, in which compensation factors are defined and used to generate a ranking of jobs. Achieving internal equity through job evaluation is most useful in very large organizations where it is virtually impossible to use market data, where job titles in the market are misleading, or where a more refined approach to ranking jobs for pay-setting purposes is required.

As an example, a multihospital system may have five hospitals with about the same number of beds, employees, and revenue. Although on the surface the hospitals may appear to be the same, one is in a highly competitive market and another is the only hospital in its market. The hospital in the competitive market may require talents beyond those required of an administrator who operates the only hospital in a market. A formal job evaluation process can help the hospital sort through the differences to determine if, in fact, the differences are sufficiently important to justify different pay opportunities.

A note of caution when using job evaluation techniques: Pay structures must be internally equitable and result in pay ranges that can compete effectively in the executive salary market. Internal equity must be tempered with external competitiveness; that is, the organization should assess the functional skills required for a given job and reflect the market salary rates for those skills in the pay hierarchy.

In some cases, internal equity and external competitiveness clearly conflict. Perhaps the best example involves the case of an organization with a medical director who reports to the CEO. A structure that is strictly equitable internally will result in the CEO's being paid more than the medical director. Medical directors often are paid relative to a physician market, which is often higher than the hospital administrative market. The choices in this situation are to:

- Compensate so there is internal equity between the positions, in which case the options will be as follows:
  —Compensate the medical director at market, resulting in the CEO being compensated above the CEO market
  —Compensate the CEO at market, resulting in the medical director being compensated below the medical director market
  —Compensate both positions above the market for each position
  —Compensate both positions below the market for each position
- Ignore internal equity and compensate each position relative to the market for each position.

The only internal equity option that will eliminate short-term compensation problems is to compensate both positions above the respective markets. Choosing to ignore internal equity and compensating each position relative to the respective market is the option of choice for many health care organizations.

STATING THE PAY PROGRAM'S OBJECTIVES

Criteria used to establish the compensation program should be formalized and articulated so they can be easily communicated to top executives and clearly understood by them. Health care organizations that take a positive approach to compensation develop a statement of compensation philosophy. An example of one organization's compensation philosophy is

> The total salary and benefits provided by the hospital are for the purpose of attracting, motivating, and retaining competent health care executives to provide the services at a level established by the board of directors. Specific salary and benefit levels will be determined on the basis of internal equity, external competitiveness, and fiscal ability. The target rate is the total cash compensation median of the executive health care market for hospitals between 300 and 600 beds.

An additional point: Whatever the executive compensation philosophy and program established, they should be simple enough to be administered by the compensation committee of the board for the CEO, and by the CEO for the other executives. After establishing the design criteria and articulating a compensation philosophy, the process of actual program design can begin.

THE MARKET

The salary market is not monolithic. It consists of many different jobs in different types of health care and nonhealth care organizations and involves functional skills. Figure 20-2 represents the executive salary market. Within this market are health care and nonhealth care organizations, and within each group are subgroups that can be further subdivided. Shown is a simple subdivision for hospitals: pediatric and adult acute care. Adult acute care is divided into religious and community. Across the bottom are functional skills that cut across organizational types. For example, it is possible to find physicians as CEOs of for-profit and not-for-profit hospitals; as medical directors in hospitals, HMOs, public health agencies, and insurance companies; and as direct care providers.

To evaluate an executive compensation program one must assess the market segment or segments in which the organization plans to compete for talent. This can be assessed by asking: From where do we want to recruit and—if we were to lose an executive—to what part of the market would that incumbent go? At this point philosophy enters the picture. It is possible to narrow the definition of the market from which the organization plans to recruit. For example, a religious health care system may choose to recruit only from other religious organizations, whereas a second religious health care system may be willing to recruit from all health care market segments.

A sound evaluation of the executive compensation program assesses job markets in several ways, including definition of primary and secondary markets. Some jobs, such as chief of nursing services, are found primarily in health care organiza-

tions, suggesting that the primary market for these executives is health care organizations. Other jobs, such as head of data processing, are not industry specific; thus, it is appropriate to define the market for these jobs as the data processing market and to include segments outside the health care industry.

Caution must be exercised in comparing the data processing needs in health care to those in a large manufacturing environment. Data processing skills demanded in health care are often very different from those in general industry. For example, a large manufacturer may have multiple data processing sites across the United States, whereas a hospital's data processing system may be a single inhouse main frame, or it may subscribe to a time-sharing service. These factors will affect the type of talent and level of pay required.

An example of how for-profit and not-for-profit religious and secular health care organizations might define market comparators is shown in the matrix in Table 20-1. It should be remembered that no single right answer exists and that it is advisable to consider a primary and a secondary market.

When defining the market, organizations usually want to further narrow the basis of comparison. This is often performed on the basis of standard criteria. The criterion most frequently used in health care and other industries is size, often defined by revenues. Other criteria include assets, number of beds, type of services provided, and location. Thus, as its comparators for the CEO's salary, a not-for-profit secular organization located in the Midwest may use other Midwest not-for-profit secular teaching hospitals with comparable annual revenues. A market comparator matrix sensitive to an organization's needs should be developed for each of its executives. An example is shown in Table 20-2.

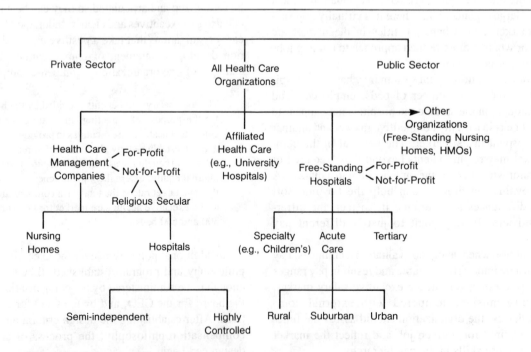

Figure 20-2 Taxonomy of Health Care Organizations

Table 20-1 Example of Market Competitors for Executive Matrix

	Recruitment Source for Executive Talent by Sector					
	For-Profit		Secular Not-for-Profit		Religious Not-for-Profit	
Position	Primary	Secondary	Primary	Secondary	Primary	Secondary
CEO	All Health Care	All Industry	Hospitals	General Health Care	Religious Hospitals	Secular Health Care
CFO	All Health Care Finance	Industry Finance	Hospitals	Industry Health Care	Religious Health Care Hospitals	Industry Finance
Head of Nursing	Health Care Management Companies Nursing Executive	Hospitals Nursing Executive	Hospitals Nursing Executive	All Health Care Nursing Executive	Religious Health Care Nursing Executives	All Health Care Nursing Executive

Table 20-2 Market Comparator Matrix

Position	Primary Market	Secondary Market
Chief Executive Officer	Health care system, 4+ hospitals, 750–1000 beds	Large urban hospital, 750–1000 beds
Chief Financial Officer	Health care system, $250–300 million in revenue	Financial positions with data processing responsibilities
VP Human Resources	Hospital, no union, 750+ bed	Professional service organization, 2500+ employees

SALARY SURVEYS

Salary surveys, the primary source of market data for compensation-setting purposes, are available by subscription. Subscriptions usually cost several thousand dollars, but a good survey outweighs its price. A bad survey eventually will cost more when the poor quality of its data is discovered. In evaluating a survey, several questions should be asked.

1. Does the survey cover similar types of organizations? For a free-standing hospital, a survey of health care management companies (HCMCs)* or industrial organizations will be of limited utility. HCMCs are typically much larger and more complex organizations than some free-standing hospitals, and industrial organizations do not represent the labor market for health care executives.
2. Does the survey have enough comparators with the organizational characteristics that are considered impor-

tant? A survey dominated by rural participants will not provide a fair representation of an urban hospital market.
3. Can the survey data be subdivided so that the user organization can compare its pay levels with a select or representative group of comparators? A good survey should allow such subdivision so that the user is able to assess pay trends in the broad market as well as in more specific markets.
4. Does the survey have a wide range of jobs similar to those in your organization? Although no survey will include every job in the user's organization, a sufficient number should be present.
5. Does the survey cover all the relevant compensation elements? A quality compensation survey will contain such data as base salary, total cash opportunity (long- and short-term incentives), and total cash received.

Additionally, salary surveys of acceptable quality address compensation trends and salary administration issues. The best surveys also include data on executive benefits and perquisites and, recognizing the evolving interest in performance compensation, contain data on executive pay relative to organizational performance.

For reasons that will be indicated later in this chapter, two other criteria should be considered when selecting a survey: First, the survey should have well-described jobs; and second, the survey should contain demographic information to compare the relative size of survey jobs with jobs in the user organization.

TYPES OF SALARY SURVEYS

A *fee survey* is one that is purchased. Often, the survey can be obtained only if an organization submits its own data. Fee surveys are generally of excellent quality because the sponsors, typically consulting organizations, have a vested interest

---

*Health care management companies are multihospital/facility systems having vertical and/or horizontal integration.

in ensuring high quality. They will frequently meet the criteria defined in the previous section.

In a *club survey*, a group of organizations sponsor the survey and contract with a consulting organization to conduct it. Because they reflect the sponsors' definition of their market, these surveys are often the best available source of data. If an organization is invited to participate, it may have the opportunity to help shape the survey, get valuable data about its executive pay market, and simplify its market comparisons, all for a cost that is shared among the sponsoring organizations.

Occasionally one sponsor will fund an entire survey. In return for an organization's participation, the sponsor will provide it with a free copy. Because the cost of conducting a valid and reliable survey is so high, however, the survey may be conducted only once, creating a data vacuum for future years. But often the value of the survey is recognized, and the participants share the cost of continuing the survey in future years.

QUALITY OF DATA

The value of a survey depends, of course, on its quality. As mentioned earlier, the two elements that should be evaluated when selecting a survey are well-described jobs and demographic data with which to compare the jobs. These two issues may appear to be "technical," but they go to the heart of the user's ability to correctly use market data in establishing its pay program. Title comparison surveys attempt to demonstrate pay relationship without considering these essential components, but they are generally ineffective in doing so. For example, simply comparing an organization's chief financial officer with a survey job entitled "chief financial officer" can produce misleading results, because all jobs named chief financial officer are not alike. Many jobs entitled chief financial officer actually are controller positions reporting to the head of corporate finance. The corporate-level chief financial officer may be responsible for tax reimbursement, risk management, budgetary control, and equity financing, and may function as corporation treasurer. The hospital-based finance position may be subordinate to this corporate position and

have only limited local authority over accounting, facility budget, and inventory control.

Table 20-3 compares the average compensation for six financial positions. Note the difference in base salaries for each. When the survey questionnaires were completed, many of the jobs were reported as having the title of chief financial officer. However, the jobs were matched to survey descriptions not only of the chief financial officer but also of corporate controller, hospital chief financial officer, hospital controller, and regional controller. Again, titles are very misleading.

The table shows that the chief of finance in a system is paid two-and-one-half times what a head of finance in a subsidiary hospital is paid. The chief financial officer of a free-standing hospital with more than 500 beds is paid almost twice as much as the head of finance in a subsidiary hospital. If a survey user selects the wrong comparison group, the organization can end up with an inappropriate pay level. The user must know the titles in a survey, must know which organizations are included in the survey, and must make sure that comparisons are valid.

Demographics can be used to enhance the quality of the data available to the user. By selecting the appropriate market comparison, survey users can be more certain that they are using the survey data to the fullest extent possible.

A MORE ACCURATE APPROACH: THE JOB CONTENT SURVEY

The survey approach having the greatest accuracy is a *job content controlled survey*. With this survey, the content of all jobs is assessed, using defined criteria as a base. The Hay *Guide Chart-Profile Method of Job Evaluation* is perhaps the method most widely used. With this approach, each job in the survey is evaluated according to the fixed criteria of know-how, problem solving, and accountability. A value is generated for each job in the survey, making it possible to specifically compare the job content of a specific organization's executive jobs with that of jobs in organizations included in the survey. This approach has an added benefit in that it allows an organization to establish a pay hierarchy that is internally equitable. Balanced with market competitiveness, it is an excellent method to construct a sound compensation program.

Table 20-3 Average Base Salary, Selected Financial Positions, 1988–1989 Data (in thousands of dollars)

Position	Chief Financial Officer	Corporate Treasurer	Corporate Controller	Regional Controller	Head of Financial Hospital Subsidiary	Chief Financial Officer, Free-Standing Hospital	
						<500 Beds	>500 Beds
1988–1989 Base Salary Average	$126.7	$86.7	$74.9	$69.2	$50.5	$77.1	$91.8

Source: 1988 Hay Management Consultants Survey of Health Care Management Companies.

The organization must consider the total compensation program and the context of the position. Following are some of the factors which should be considered:

- mix between cash compensation (base and incentive) and noncash compensation (benefits and perquisites)
- degree to which the board can accept turnover
- ability to recruit internally and externally for the position
- prestige of the organization
- talent required to respond to a competitive market
- challenge of the job at the hospital in question:
  1. trustee support
  2. physician support
  3. age of facilities
  4. resources available

WHERE IN THE MARKET SHOULD WE PAY?

Determining where in the market any one job or a number of executive positions should be paid involves using high-quality market data and developing an understanding of an organization's needs to make informed decisions. Despite what many believe, there is no single right answer. Consider, for example, the following recent cases:

- A 350-bed hospital in a metropolitan area with more than 30 competing hospitals is one of the highest payers for a CEO within its market. The reason: Several years ago, major issues of poor quality placed the hospital on the front pages of the local newspaper. The trustees looked for a CEO with the ability to turn the organization around. The trustees paid top dollar for a top performer and realized superior results. Today the hospital's beds are filled, and physician and employee morale are high.

- A rural hospital in the Rocky Mountain region pays in the first quartile. Its executive turnover is low. The location is highly desirable. It is an acute care facility that offers a limited number of specialties. There is no competition because it is the only hospital in a community of 50,000, and the nearest town with a hospital is more than 50 miles away. The trustees do not feel pressured to pay higher because when the last two executive positions needed to be filled, they received an abundance of qualified applicants.

- A religious system pays all of its administrators above-average salaries, even in rural areas where this level of pay is unnecessary. However, the system moves its administrators every five years and does not want its pay program to be a barrier.

- A large research and teaching hospital pays above-average salaries for its executives, but because it is affiliated with a public university, it cannot provide incentive compensation. The total cash compensation position is low relative to many hospitals.

- A religious system, unable to afford paying above the first quartile, provides rapid internal advancement opportunities and extensive training programs. As a result, it has been able to increase its retention of CEOs from 18 months to 3 years.

The health care organization is challenged to identify those variables that are important and to incorporate them into the base pay program. Every several years, the organization should assess whether the pay program continues to meet organizational needs and be willing to adapt if circumstances dictate. It should be prepared to address the critical issues of the affordability of a market position as well as its desire to pay at a given level. In the final analysis, a well-designed base compensation program is an investment and not a cost. It will enable the organization to retain and motivate executives to high levels of performance.

Lawrence C. Bassett

21

Job Evaluation Systems: Increasing Return on Payroll Dollars

The changes that have taken place in the health care industry have focused attention on the need to increase employee productivity. One objective is to get optimum return on each payroll dollar by lowering the cost of each "unit" of work by employees in all categories, including management. Developing a strategy to achieve this goal is prudent and practical. However, many hospital managements are spending much time, effort, and money to streamline operations, only to lose their gains because of archaic or malfunctioning compensation administration.

In a passionate effort to reduce costs, many a management actually has increased costs by paying employees at low levels that turn them off on the organization or at levels too high for the value of the work performed.

* * * *

Paying employees less than the work they perform is worth is false value at best. And the hidden cost of paying employees more than necessary is a double whammy. It is wasteful on a common-sense level, but it is even more harmful because of its impact on employees who see other employees whose jobs have less responsibility than theirs being paid above what they perceive as fair.

If productivity increases are to achieve their desired effect, they must be accompanied by a sound system of compensation that assures that each payroll dollar brings the best possible return in terms of employee good will, sense of satisfaction, and sense of fairness.

* * * *

There is a time- and experience-tested tool that addresses these issues fully, effectively, and inexpensively. It is the process of job evaluation.

THE OBJECTIVES OF A SOUND COMPENSATION PROGRAM

If an organization is to remain competitive and able to attract and keep a staff of competent and motivated employees, it must achieve two objectives.

External Equity

Maintaining external equity means that the organization's levels of pay compare favorably and competitively with the salaries offered by comparable organizations within the competitive labor market for similar jobs. Essentially, external equity is achieved by making certain that highly visible generic positions are being paid at levels that salary surveys and other data indicate are going rates in the marketplace from which employees are recruited. Maintaining external equity appears relatively simple. For example, when salaries for such a barometer position as Registered Nurse are advertised and publicized at a given level, an organization can respond accordingly. Similarly, salaries of an X-ray or laboratory technologist can be ascertained and adjustments in salary made.

Many organizations maintain external equity and believe that this is sufficient to satisfy employees. They also may be living under the delusion that this is all that is necessary to have a sound corporate compensation program. This is a costly self-deception.

* * * *

Obviously, it is necessary to be competitive in order to attract new employees, but there is an element of compensation even more important to employees, particularly in relation to improving the retention of key employees. In fact, if an organization has a choice between these two elements, the maintaining of external equity would come in second. We are referring to *internal equity*.

Internal Equity

A cornerstone of good employee relations is the paying of salaries that each employee believes reflect his or her level of responsibility and value compared with those of other employees. When employees believe that management is not recognizing their contributions or service to the hospital, external equity drops in importance. More significant is the fact that even if there is sound external equity, an employee who believes his or her salary is not ''fair'' will find fault with the organization's overall pay structure and most likely will conclude that external equity, or competitiveness, also is poor.

* * * *

When internal equity is not present, employees become soured on management, and the cost of maintaining external equity largely is wasted because employees may not believe that it exists. An employee's sense of the organization's entire pay policy is tainted by perceptions of how that individual is treated.

* * * *

SOLUTION—JOB EVALUATION

It is reasonable to assume that every successful major organization maintains external equity. Without the salaries to attract workers, these organizations couldn't survive. It is just as reasonable to assume that every organization that considers itself to be successful and a leader in its field has developed and maintained a strong internal equity as well. What these organizations have in place is some form *job evaluation*.

By definition, job evaluation is a method of determining the relative worth of every position in the organization to all others. It is a compensation tool that recognizes the inherent responsibility and functions of each job and determines how they compare with the responsibilities and duties of other jobs. Proper placement is the key step in constructing salary scales that reflect the relative worth of jobs to the organization in a pattern that is seen as fair by employees.

A job evaluation should be seen as an investment and not as a cost. Its value in ensuring sound employee relations is far greater than any start-up cost, and from a more pragmatic view, the economies realized as payroll dollars are used more effectively provide an excellent return on investment. On a straight bottom-line calculation, the cost of a job evaluation program should be paid back in less than three to three-and-a-half years.

THE HEART OF ALL JOB EVALUATION SYSTEMS: THE JOB DESCRIPTION

Job descriptions are often maligned, but when it comes to job evaluation, they are the indispensable core on which all pay scales should be built. The job description is no more than a photograph of what the person does, and though it has many valuable uses (in orienting and training new employees, serving as a focus for performance appraisal, clarifying duties between manager and employee, etc.), it is the only assurance management has that payroll dollars are being spent for responsibilities and not for job titles or false assumptions.

Though job descriptions should have a consistent style and format, it is more important that they be accurate, no matter how they are written. And because employees know their jobs better than anyone, including their supervisors, the involvement of employees in the preparation of job descriptions should be mandatory. In this way, there is the highest assurance that the job description is accurate, while the employees' participation tends to build in greater acceptance of the end results.

While sound job descriptions are frequently best developed with outside assistance, they also can be developed by the human resources department. In smaller organizations with few employee relations specialists, recruiting a number of job description writers from throughout the staff is a practical alternative. Every organization has people who enjoy writing and who are good at it. They can be taught how to write job descriptions, thus providing the organization with a permanent in-house capability.

JOB EVALUATION METHODOLOGY

A number of basic techniques can be employed, the most suitable being determined by the characteristics of the organization, including its size, the number of jobs (not people), the level of sophistication of the jobs involved, the time available for the study, the past experience of those responsible for the effort, and other organizational traditions.

1. Qualitative Systems

Qualitative methods of job evaluation are distinguished by the fact that they involve the analysis of jobs as a whole. There is no attempt to isolate the components that comprise the position. Essentially there are two qualitative systems.

Ranking

Straight ranking of jobs is the simplest of all job evaluation methods; however, it is effective only where there are relatively few positions to be evaluated (customarily less than 30) and where it is possible to make logical comparisons between jobs with common characteristics, such as clerical, technical, etc. Ranking jobs can be as simple as placing job titles on 3×5 cards, followed by a sorting process that places the jobs in order of their importance to the organization.

To simplify ranking and to make it possible to rank a maximum number of positions, a technique called *paired comparisons* can be used. As illustrated in Figure 21-1, a matrix is constructed such that jobs are listed on both vertical and horizontal axes. Comparisons now are made between two jobs at a time, an easier and less ambiguous process than attempting to rank a number of jobs at the same time. When each job has been compared with all others, it is then possible to add up the relative rankings for each to determine the final listing.

When rankings have been completed, jobs that are considered to be relatively close to each other are grouped, and these groupings are turned into salary grades.

Classification System

This second qualitative approach can be used where an organization has a larger number of positions and where the nature of these jobs may be dissimilar.

In the classification system, jobs are sorted, much as books are sorted in a library. Different categories are defined that describe the level of complexity and the relative importance. For example, the highest classification level might be defined as one that requires a Ph.D. level of education, extensive background and experience in several professional or technical disciplines, and the ability to solve problems of complex nature and that has a critical impact on the organization. In contrast, the lowest classification level might include jobs that are simple and routine in nature, requiring only an ability to read and write, and that consist of duties and functions that can be learned easily in a short period of time.

When the classifications have been defined, and this can be a difficult and challenging assignment, jobs are then reviewed and placed into the correct classifications, just as books are placed according to categories on a library shelf. After they have been placed in appropriate classifications, the jobs are then ranked. The result is a listing of all jobs in the organization from top to bottom. The grouping of jobs into grades would then follow, guided by the classifications.

2. Quantitative Systems

Health care organizations usually are more complex and contain so many jobs that using a qualitative process is imprac-

	Analyst	A/P Clk	Clk/Secy	Clk/typist	Courier	Distribution Clerk	File Clk	Library Clk	Mail Clk	Office Secy	Receptionist	Statistic Clk	TOTALS
Analysis clerk		2	2	1	1	1	1	2	1	2	1	2	16
A/P Clk	1		2	1	1	1	1	1	1	2	1	2	14
Clk/Secy	1	2		1	1	1	1	2	1	2	1	2	15
Clk/Typist	2	2	2		1	2	1	2	1	2	1	2	18
Courier	2	2	2	2		2	1	2	1	2	1	2	19
Distribution Clk	2	2	2	1	1		1	2	2	2	1	2	18
File Clk	2	2	2	2	2	2		2	2	2	1	2	21
Library Clk	1	2	1	1	1	1	1		1	2	1	1	13
Mail Clk	2	2	2	2	2	1	1	2		2	2	2	20
Office Secy	1	1	1	1	1	1	1	1	1		1	1	11
Receptionist	2	2	2	2	2	2	2	2	1	2		2	21
Statistic Clerk	1	1	1	1	1	1	1	2	1	2	1		13

Figure 21-1 Job Evaluation Using Paired Comparison Method

tical. In such cases, one of two quantitative approaches is usually selected. Both of these approaches break the jobs down into compensable parts so that it becomes possible to evaluate the total worth of a job by adding up the values of its compensable components.

Factor Comparison

This method of job evaluation, which has fallen into disuse, is based on a process that compares the degree a compensable factor is present in a particular job with the degree to which it is present in key benchmark jobs. Called *factor comparison,* this process first involves identifying these key benchmark jobs and dividing them into their compensable factors; each factor is then assigned a dollar value, based on the job's total worth in the competitive marketplace.

Alternatively, if a market survey is not used, it is possible to divide each key job into component factors by identifying the percentage each factor represents as a part of the whole. For example, education, experience, working conditions, etc., would each be considered worth a certain percentage of the total value of the job. When these percentages have been established, comparisons are made to other jobs, also by the compensable factors. The committee or individual responsible for job evaluation determines whether other jobs have more or less of that particular factor and assigns a percentage. (When these percentages are totaled, they might add up to more than 100% or less than 100%.)

When all jobs have been evaluated, a salary survey of the market is conducted for each of the key benchmark jobs. When salaries have been established for them, other jobs are slotted in at rates that maintain the same percentages. For example, if the hourly salary for a key benchmark job has been established at $9 and another job is valued at 90 percent of the key job, that second job will be given a salary of $8.10 per hour.

The difficulty with this approach is that in the volatile employment market that exists in a very rapidly changing business environment, the key jobs do not remain constant. Thus, making comparisons to changing key jobs can throw the entire wage structure into disarray. It is for this reason that the point system described below has become the most frequently used method of job evaluation today.

Point Method

The most widely used and popular approach to job evaluation is a system whereby points are awarded to each job, based on the extent to which the job possesses compensable factors as compared with an objective standard rather than another job. For example, different amounts of points would be given for varying levels of education required. Likewise, for a factor isolating the amount of mental demands (nature and complexity of decision making, application of education, etc.) inherent in the job, varying numbers of points would be awarded that reflect the extent to which these mental demands must be met in order to carry out the job functions.

This method is preferred because objectivity is built in and because the system can remain in place over a long period of time, even though individual jobs, and the key jobs used in the factor comparison method, may have changed. Exhibit 21-1 shows how several degrees are defined and points allocated to them.

Obviously, after points are totaled, there is a complete ranking of all jobs that becomes the basis for determining job grades and eventually salary scales.

Hybrid Approaches

Experienced compensation consultants frequently develop and perfect hybrid plans that can be fine tuned to an organization. This generally is not done by the organization itself because the process usually requires a sophisticated compensation administrator. An error in developing the basic plan can be costly in terms of the program's not achieving its goals. In fact, a poorly designed job evaluation system can be counterproductive and further diminish the organization's employee relations and economic health. It is best to use tried and tested plans or to bring in competent, experienced consultants.

CARRYING OUT THE PROGRAM

An organization can develop its own in-house evaluation system; however, if a quantitative approach is to be used, the task of developing a program can be formidable, unless there is a program that is available for adoption. If improper assumptions are made when evaluation values are determined, the results can prove to be unusable. Certainly, an in-house program can be fine tuned to the organization, but because results have to be validated, developing a custom program can be time consuming and costly.

To avoid these difficulties, many an organization either recruits trained compensation specialists as part of its human relations department or retains a compensation consultant to set up a program and train its staff to maintain the system after installation. In the short as well as long run, retaining an experienced consultant is usually the most cost effective method if the consultant will train the organization's staff and then turn the system over to them. A consultant who controls the evaluation process permanently prevents the organization from developing the strength derived from the training of its personnel. In fact, the greatest return on the investment of money and energy results from the selection of a consultant who is willing to delegate most of the work to the organization's staff after training them.

A DETAIL TO ENSURE SUCCESS—EMPLOYEE PARTICIPATION

Whomever is selected to supervise the process, consideration always should be given to the use of a committee for the

Exhibit 21-1 Factor 4—Interrelationships

For other than those supervised:

This factor credits relationships with others to persuade, negotiate with or to influence them. The purpose is to gain understanding and acceptance of the organization's services, objectives, policies, activities, or actions.

The contacts may be with: co-workers in own or other department; client family; physician; representatives of supplies, community agencies, government, other organizations; or other members of the public.

Consider the frequency, variety—but mainly *the importance*—of the contacts whether in person, written or by phone, especially the extent to which the relationship could affect the good reputation of the organization.

Where relationships with patients/clients are involved, evaluate also with Alternative Factor 4A and use higher of the two scores, but not both.

Benchmark	Degree	JOB REQUIRES	Score
	A	Only incidental contacts with others, requiring normal courtesy. Employee works mainly on own.	5
	B	Regular but routine contacts with others in/out of the unit or department.	10 or 15
	C	Contacts inside or outside the organization to: (1) perform for others routine services or procedures; or (2) give or obtain routine information; or (3) coordinate with others in the department in a teamwork role.	25 or 35
	D	Appreciable contacts on a regular basis in and/or out of the department or organization. Discretion and tact are required to give or get specialized information.	45 or 55
	E	Frequent contacts with many others OR extensive contacts with a few categories of people. High degree of discretion and tact to carry out with others specialized services or to interpret and apply department procedures.	70 or 80

actual scoring. Using a single individual, whether an employee or a consultant, can reduce the probability of success and employee support. Moreover, a single individual's values and decisions are easily subject to question and attack by employees, and that single individual does not ensure lasting validity because if he or she is replaced by someone with a different perspective and value system, the scoring of jobs can take different directions. And if the individual doing the evaluation is neither respected nor seen as knowledgeable, the level of acceptance can drop to an unacceptable point. A committee made up of five to eight well-respected senior managers who represent all viewpoints of the organization can assure that the final scores will have the best balance and will be supported by employees who feel their values and interests are represented. A committee also ensures that scoring is consistent over a long period of time: even if committee members are replaced periodically, the value system that has already been established is maintained by the remaining committee members and is taught to the replacements.

The committee, most commonly chaired by the human resources executive, should represent as close to 80 percent of the population of the organization as possible. This immediately builds in a high probability of success because if the committee members agree on the results, they have, in fact, solved most of the potential problems that may arise later. Deliberations by a committee might take longer than those carried out by a single individual, but the extra time is more than made up for by results that assure that the organization has the most sound internal equity system possible.

MAINTAINING THE PROGRAM

As with any good system or mechanical device, careful maintenance is needed if job evaluation is to continue functioning smoothly over a long period of time. Too frequently, an organization makes a sizable investment in a job evaluation program, and then it fails to appoint a specialist capable of keeping the program current and in good working order.

A number of things happen over time. New jobs are created, current jobs change, and responsibilities decrease and increase. Each of these happenings requires new evaluations, reevaluations, and perhaps placements into new or different grades.

No matter how large an organization is, it should have an individual trained in the administration of the job evaluation program. Large organizations can have compensation specialists with training and education, as well as experience in the process. Smaller organizations should invest in the training of an individual on the essentials of compensation administration, though that individual might have access to expert advice from the outside to ensure that the program is maintained, that salary surveys are conducted properly, and that adjustments in the scales are done within sound compensation parameters.

SUMMARY

Job evaluation is a proven, sound, and extremely cost-effective approach to stretching payroll dollars and guaranteeing good employee relations. Job evaluation strategies can be tailored to every type of organization and to all characteristics of an employee work force. And as business competition increases, job evaluation should be seen as an indispensable tool for obtaining the greatest return on payroll dollars and achieving the highest level of employee productivity.

Jerad D. Browdy

Health Care Executive Compensation Trends: Outlook for the Future

22

COMPENSATION PRACTICES AND ATTITUDES

Until recently, health care executive compensation practices were relatively unsophisticated and egalitarian in nature. Typically, the health care executive and key management group, including exempt department heads, received the same general increase as did the rank-and-file employee group. If merit was a factor at the management level, evaluative criteria were generally those of a personal nature, such as "attitude," "dependability," or "reliability." Rarely were appraisals based on the attainment of specific, predetermined, quantifiable objectives. The annual increase was virtually automatic, regardless of performance, and it came to be expected as a matter of "right" by many hospital managers (and still is to some degree). The situation was exacerbated by trustees who felt "everybody deserves something each year."

Fringe benefits were also basically the same for everyone. The chief executive officer was usually provided with a car and club memberships, but the other managers received basically the same benefits as did the general employee group (although the senior management group may have received more vacation time than department heads and rank-and-file employees). All employees, regardless of level, participated in the same ERISA qualified pension plan. If tax-deferred income programs were established for the management group, funding was usually through voluntary salary deductions. Nonqualified, deferred compensation agreements and incentive compensation were virtually unheard of. Indeed, many health care human resource executives were not even familiar with these concepts.

Health care executives were generally not concerned about compensation, and, even more important, their boards did not expect them to be concerned about compensation. The prevalent attitude among trustees (which is still found to some degree today) was that health care executives voluntarily entered the not-for-profit sector knowing full well that their compensation expectations should be below those in the proprietary sector. Health care executives were expected to be altruistic and dedicated to human service. In the same respect, however, some health care executives entered the field because they viewed it as relatively free from stress, risk, and competitive pressures. These individuals were willing to sacrifice compensation for a career in a "safe" environment (which, in fact, it never was).

Of course, this has all changed. Health care executives and trustees are now very much concerned about compensation (but not necessarily for the same reasons).

It is not the intent of this chapter to dwell on all of the issues and factors that have brought about a change in attitudes toward compensation. Let it suffice to say that decreasing access to capital, alternate delivery systems, cost containment legislation, competition, changing organization structures, and merger and acquisition activities have created a high-risk, high-stress environment. There are high rates of turnover and burnout among senior-level executives.

While boards expect their health care executives to be altruistic in nature and devoted to service, they also expect them to be decisive, entrepreneurial in nature, opportunistic, and not averse to risk or competition.

The current pool of management talent possessing these traits is small. In addition, these entrepreneurial executives are

183

telling their boards that they are perfectly willing to risk the consequences of failure, but that they also expect to be well compensated for their successes. This attitude was almost unheard of a few years ago.

The number of executives entering the health care field from industry is growing, particularly in such areas as marketing, information systems, finance, and human resources. These individuals are generally accustomed to a more sophisticated approach to compensation than are health care executives. In this context, as more not-for-profit health care organizations seek executives to manage proprietary affiliates on a full-time basis, they find that such individuals may not respond positively to traditional health care compensation practices.

Physicians are being hired in executive positions with increasing frequency. At this point, they are generally responsible for clinical departments, but it is anticipated that those with managerial talent will be given expanded responsibilities beyond purely medical administration. The compensation of these individuals can present the board and chief executive officer with some complex issues, and the decisions they make as a result will have an impact on the entire management group. For example, should physician managers be paid as physicians or managers? Whatever the decision, it will affect the entire management compensation structure.

Discussions with hundreds of health care trustees and chief executive officers in all types of institutions in all parts of the country during the course of the author's consulting engagements indicate the same concerns. These concerns are categorized in the sections that follow.

Concerns of Trustees

Trustees are seeking definitive ways to evaluate their chief executive officers (CEOs). In many organizations the CEO has been evaluated informally or on an after-the-fact basis. In this respect, evaluation frequently has been based on the "what a good person am I" approach, in which the CEO prepares a list of accomplishments just prior to his or her review date. This list frequently may come as a surprise to the board, which had no input in determining what was expected.

With respect to base compensation, trustees want to ensure that the available salary dollars are reserved for the achievers. They are asking "How high is up?" as they see salary levels increasing. In this regard, they are also beginning to ask another critical question: "How can we continue to reward achievers without continuing to increase base salaries each year?" In this context, both trustees and CEOs recognize that a point is reached at which the annual increase is no longer feasible, regardless of performance. This is particularly true with high-salaried employees.

A recent significant development is the increase in the number of compensation committees being established as part of the board committee structure. This is a critical committee on the industrial board, and it is also being viewed as such by many hospital boards. Such committees are most typically found in multihospital systems and larger medical centers. It is only a matter of time, however, before the smaller community hospital begins to recognize the value of such a committee. Indeed, we are finding board chairpersons in smaller hospitals who are recognizing that membership on an executive committee does not necessarily mean competence in compensation matters.

Concerns of Chief Executive Officers

Chief executive officers are also concerned about the evaluation process. While some are satisfied with the "what a good person am I" approach, many more are concerned because they are uncomfortable with an informal general discussion. They feel that their performance should be evaluated within the context of predetermined goals, objectives, and accountability standards. This is particularly the case when the CEO realizes that new programs and services may cause conflicts with the medical staff. The CEO wants assurance that the board is fully aware of and concurs with programs to be undertaken.

Almost without exception, CEOs are concerned about job loss for reasons other than poor performance. Their specific concerns center on medical staff pressures, mergers-acquisitions, and changes in the composition of the board. They are seeking income protection in the event they are terminated through no fault of their own.

Chief executive officers want to be compensated within the context of their responsibilities and achievements. An increasing number of these individuals and their key subordinates are telling their boards that they are willing to forgo the annual increase in lieu of a substantial incentive award or performance bonus based on specific, well-defined achievements.

Chief executive officers and human resources executives are also becoming increasingly concerned about their ability to attract and retain the best-qualified managerial talent, who may no longer respond positively to traditional health care compensation practices.

CHANGES IN EXECUTIVE COMPENSATION PRACTICES

As a result of the factors and attitudinal changes discussed above, the following major changes are occurring in compensation practices for health care executive and key management:

• Pay for performance, including incentive compensation, is replacing the annual longevity increase. Salary increases are being related to performance evaluation based on the attainment of specific, predetermined, quantifiable achievements.

- Salary increases are being deferred for the average or marginal performer until performance improves. This was almost unheard of five years ago and is proving to be a traumatic experience for those executives and managers who view the annual increase as a "matter of right."
- Until the Tax Reform Act, senior-level health care executives were being provided with institution-funded, long-term supplemental benefits and deferred compensation programs with increasing frequency. These typically took the form of cash value insurance; matching or institutional, tax-deferred income programs; and non-qualified, deferred compensation agreements. The basic reasons were as follows:
  1. Trustees wanted to retain their most competent executives through some type of "golden handcuffs."
  2. An increasing number of senior-level executives were at a base salary level such that typical hospital pension benefits would incur a financial hardship on the executive at retirement.
  3. An increasing number of CEOs were at a base salary level such that IRS regulations placed limitations on the maximum defined benefit or defined contribution programs.
  4. Trustees were beginning to recognize that at the high-salaried level, capital accumulation and tax-deferred income arrangements may be more attractive than base salary, per se.
  5. Trustees wanted to make early retirement attractive for the senior-level executive who may be showing signs of "burnout" in his or her middle fifties.

It should be noted that the Tax Reform Act has restricted contributions to tax deferral programs. However, such restrictions do not preclude consideration of non-qualified, deferred compensation arrangements, such as "Rabbi Trusts," Key Man, and split dollar insurance. However, many executives are now opting for cash rather than deferred compensation. Many, particularly the younger individuals, feel that retirement programs, per se, are not attractive because of the uncertainties in today's health care climate.

- There are greater differentials in fringe benefits between executives and their subordinates. It is now recognized that a completely egalitarian fringe benefit program may demotivate executives and managers, especially those designated for promotion from within. Again, however, the Tax Reform Act provides for nondiscriminatory welfare benefits (health and life insurance). Distinctions can be made for selected executives, but the value of such benefits will be treated as taxable income.
- Perquisites have become an important element of the executive and key management fringe benefit program. Common "perks" for CEOs include automobiles, club memberships, financial counseling (also for senior-level executives), mandatory annual physical examinations, and spouse travel at hospital expense on business trips. Home computers, personal counseling services, and educational sabbatical leaves are also beginning to be seen. Perquisites are often viewed as an important psychological reward for executives and managers. It remains to be seen how valuable they will be if affected by future changes in tax legislation.
- Trustees are recognizing that some singular achievements may be better compensated through substantial "bonus" awards than a salary increase.
- Formal employment contracts are being provided to CEOs to guarantee them income protection in the event that they are terminated for reasons other than poor performance. These contracts often provide for the possibility of incentive compensation.
- Typically, the midpoints of salary ranges were based on the average or going rate in the external market. Now we are seeing more CEOs and trustees who want the ranges structured on the 75th percentile (or higher) of the market.
- The objective-setting process is becoming more definitive. Expected results by designated dates and specific accountabilities are spelled out in detail. Even more important, individual objectives frequently must be defined within the context of "corporate" objectives. This is a traumatic experience for those health care managers who have never been held accountable for specifics and who have never considered the impact of their actions on the organization as a whole.

An interesting development, and one we have suspected for some time, is that compensation differentials based on institution size are beginning to diminish. This is particularly true at the vice-president and department-head levels. In September 1988, this author's firm conducted a salary survey among 130 specifically selected health care institutions located across the country. The primary comparative factor was expense budget. The diminishing differentials are evident on the graphs in Figures 22-1 through 22-4. The data substantiate trends we have seen in this direction for the past several years.

The reasons for this "gap narrowing" appear to be as follows:

- There is a decreasing pool of management talent in a highly volatile and competitive recruiting environment.
- There is a growing perception, with which the author agrees, that the mere size of an institution is not necessarily an indication of its complexity. For example, a 120-bed specialty hospital with extensive teaching and research programs may have a larger expense budget and more employees than a general, acute care hospital with 400 beds.

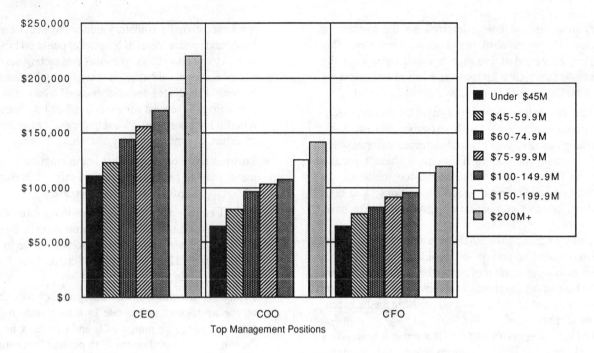

Figure 22-1 1988 Salary Survey Summary for Top-Management Positions—All Participants (Based on Expense Budget)

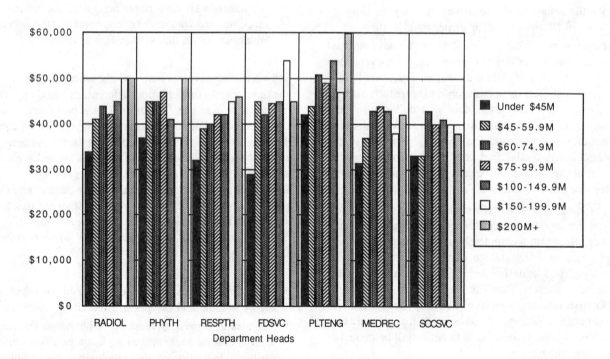

Figure 22-2 1988 Salary Survey Summary for Vice-Presidents—All Participants (Based on Expense Budget)

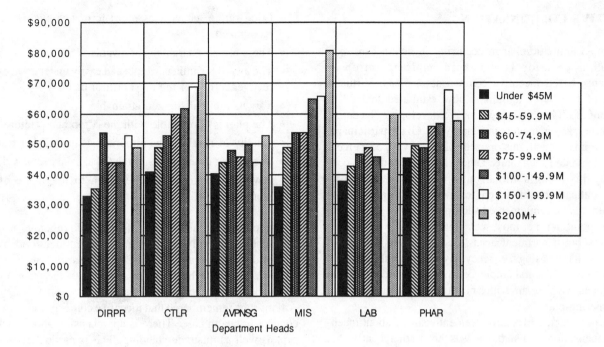

Figure 22-3 1988 Salary Survey Summary for Department Heads: Part I—All Participants (Based on Expense Budget)

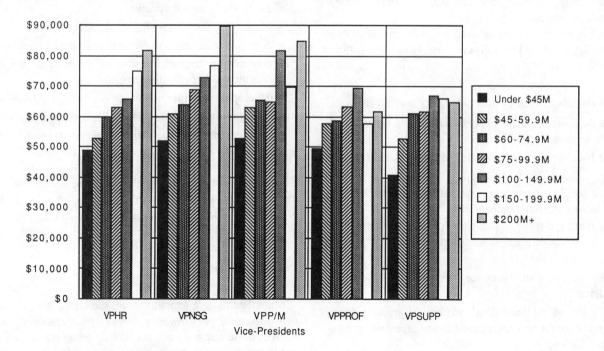

Figure 22-4 1988 Salary Survey Summary for Department Heads: Part II—All Participants Expense Budget

INCENTIVE COMPENSATION

The most dramatic change occurring in health care executive compensation is the rapid implementation of performance-based incentive compensation plans. Virtually unheard of five years ago, it is now estimated that 20 to 25 percent of all hospitals have, or are developing, incentive plans for their key management employees. Of the participants in the aforementioned, customized salary survey, 53 percent have implemented such plans. Other customized surveys conducted by this author's firm among specifically selected participants indicate that anywhere from 40 to 60 percent of the respondents have implemented such plans.

At this point in time, most such plans cover the key executive group, but department heads are being (and should be) included with increasing frequency. By the end of the century, if not sooner, all hospital employees may be included in some type of incentive program which may take the form of a profit- or gainsharing plan.

For many years, CEOs have been enthusiastic about incentive compensation plans, but it was not until recently that trustees have become receptive to the concept. As was indicated, trustees are seeking to reward the achievers without continuing to increase base salaries each year. They are also beginning to recognize that some achievements, whether accomplished by a group or by an individual, deserve some type of special compensation consideration. They are, of course, discovering that the "entrepreneurs" they are seeking for their key executive positions respond more positively to this type of compensation arrangement than to the traditional health care compensation program.

While trustees are becoming receptive to the incentive concept, they are almost universally concerned about the following issues:

- that awards be based on extraordinary performance
- that the financial condition of the institution warrant such compensation
- that fiscal performance not be the total basis for awards

These are legitimate concerns and will be addressed in this discussion of incentive compensation.

While there are many approaches to incentive compensation, the most viable plans share common characteristics.

- They are not a substitute for a competitive base salary structure.
- They are not a "back door" method of granting salary increases or circumventing established salary administration policies.
- They encourage teamwork and cooperation among the eligible group.
- Awards are based on specific, not general, achievements.
- Group and individual effort is recognized.

- Long-range as well as short-term achievements are recognized.
- There are no guarantees of awards.
- The award formula is simple and easily understood by the recipients (one of the most critical factors).
- Targets are realistic and attainable.
- The plan is compatible with the corporate "culture."
- Quality of results is as important as quantity of results.
- The timing of awards is unrelated to salary review dates.
- Awards are significant enough to make the effort worthwhile.

While the actual mechanics of award and funding formulas should be relatively simple and easily understood by all involved, there are a number of critical issues that should be addressed prior to the actual final design of the plan(s) most appropriate for the organization.

It must be remembered that incentive compensation is a new concept in health care. There is apprehension about the concept as well as misunderstanding. This is particularly true in situations in which those in the proposed eligible group have never had their performance measured in specific, predetermined, quantifiable terms.

Basically, the issues that should be addressed by the CEO and the chairman of the board are as follows:

- defining the terms
- determining the purpose and philosophy of the plan
- establishing award criteria
- identifying the group eligible for incentives
- assessing attitudes and receptivity to the concept
- determining the relationship of the plan to the basic executive compensation program
- developing administrative and control procedures
- determining emphasis of the plan (group or individual)
- selecting the plan type(s) most appropriate for the organization (including funding and award formulas)

Once agreement has been reached on these issues, the actual mechanics (design) of the plan can then be undertaken. Each of these issues will be addressed on the following pages.

Defining the Terms

Many health care executives use the terms *incentive compensation* and *performance bonus* synonymously. While related, these terms do not necessarily mean the same thing, and those charged with developing an incentive plan will have to assure that the participants readily understand the differences.

The performance bonus is usually an after-the-fact type of award that may be discretionary in nature or may be based on some significant, unpredicted achievement. A bonus may be awarded, for example, to the key executive group because the hospital has had a good year, although this may not have been previously defined. In other words, the performance may be based on significant achievements that have not been defined in quantitative terms.

Incentive compensation, in the literal sense, is an award based on the attainment of specific, predetermined targets that are usually expressed in quantitative terms. In other words, incentive compensation is based on predictive factors, while the performance bonus is often based on retrospective factors. Health care executives unaccustomed to having their performance evaluated in predetermined, quantifiable terms are more comfortable with the performance bonus concept. In some cases, a performance bonus might be a viable first step toward the development of a more comprehensive incentive plan. In fact, this is not an uncommon approach.

Determining the Purpose and Philosophy

The critical first step will be to determine the basic purpose of the plan. Specifically, the plan is to accomplish the following:

- Reward extraordinary effort and achievement beyond the scope of "normal" or expected job performance.
- Encourage teamwork and cooperative efforts necessary to reach a common corporate goal.
- Supplement a low or uncompetitive base rate structure.

In most cases, the first two comprise the major purposes of incentive plans. In a few rare situations, the third has been a primary factor, but in this consultant's opinion, this is a poor premise for an incentive program and may only exacerbate a bad situation.

Establishing Award Criteria

Every organization is different, and award criteria that are appropriate for one institution may not be appropriate for another. The most effective criteria are those based on the mission of the organization. The board and the CEO should determine the role of the institution in the community and the steps necessary to fulfill that role. The board must determine what steps can be taken within the range of "normal" or expected performance and what steps will require extra effort of the eligible group. The board also must determine whether the mission, with respect to incentive targets, can best be accomplished through group or individual effort.

Award criteria can be based on a variety of factors, which might include the following:

- strategic long-range plans
- state, local, and national hospital association data

- budget reports and financial statements
- Joint Commission on Accreditation of Health Care Organizations (JCAHO) reports
- the objective-setting process

Typically, the primary award criterion is fiscal performance, but this should not negate the importance of establishing quality and nonfiscal targets. It also should be noted that where fiscal performance is the major criterion, it is that performance over which the eligible group has direct and immediate impact. Price increases and extraordinary accounting items should not be a consideration.

In recent plans developed by the author, award criteria have included

- net operating income as a percentage of gross revenues
- decrease in cost per case
- decrease in daily room rate
- reduction in departmental cost
- gain in market share
- new program development and implementation
- affiliation agreements
- increase in positive patient responses
- physician recruiting
- measurable improvements in quality of care

In virtually all cases, these were established as primary corporate incentive targets within which individual targets were identified and agreed on.

Identifying the Eligible Group

Identifying the eligible group can be one of the most perplexing elements of incentive plan design. Initially, eligibility in many plans is restricted to the key officer group (president and vice-presidents). However, the agreed-on award criteria will ultimately determine the eligible group. It may very well be that additional positions may have to be included based on their impact on attaining corporate incentive targets.

Suggested guidelines for determining eligibility are as follows:

- The position is one on which the institution is absolutely dependent to assure fiscal viability and a competitive market position.
- The decisions and judgments of the executive impact across organizational lines.
- The executive is directly responsible for implementing board policies.
- The executive is directly responsible for substantial fiscal, material, and human resources

While initial eligibility may be restricted to a relatively small group, the ultimate goal should be to eventually include as many management positions as possible in some type of plan. A timetable for such implementation should be developed as part of the final plan design.

Eligibility determination also will require consideration of such factors as the differences between line and staff executives with regard to award criteria, minimum service requirements, and overall performance rating (many plans exclude executives whose performance evaluation is less than satisfactory). Ultimately, the most critical question in determining eligibility is "Who has the most direct impact and influence on the attainment of corporate targets?"

It is imperative that the attitudes of those in the eligible group toward the incentive concept be assessed as one of the first steps in the process. These attitudes will indicate if the organization is ready for the further development of an incentive plan.

Recognizing the concept is new in health care, apprehension and concern are often expressed by those to be included in a plan. In general, the achievers (or those who view themselves as such) are receptive to the idea. Executives responsible for the "business" functions are also generally more receptive than are those responsible for direct patient care functions. These concerns are especially evident in institutions in which individual performance has not been evaluated in definitive terms, if at all.

These concerns are frequently expressed in the following manner:

- The predetermined incentive targets may not be valid (depending on who establishes them).
- Quality will suffer, particularly if fiscal performance is the primary award criterion.
- The plan will be divisive and result in an unhealthy competitive climate in the eligible group.

It is not unusual for those in the proposed eligible group to express concern about whether the plan is "equitable." They should understand that the plan may not be equitable in the sense that everyone will receive identical awards. However, they have every right to expect that the plan will be administered in a fair and rational manner.

These concerns may or may not be legitimate, but if raised, they must be addressed. However, as was indicated, these concerns are most likely to be expressed in those situations in which salary increases for the management group have been virtually automatic without regard to individual performance.

Determining Relationships Between Incentive and Base Compensation Programs

Incentive awards should not be timed to coincide with annual salary review dates. It is imperative that those in the eligible group not view the incentive award as an additional salary increase. This can easily occur if the salary review and incentive award dates coincide or are close together. Typically, awards are timed to coincide with the end of the fiscal year or the date of the auditor's report. This is particularly the case where awards are fiscal in nature.

Developing Administrative and Control Procedures

Responsibility for administration of the agreed-on plan must be established early in the process. The issue is basically whether primary responsibility rests with the CEO or with the board (chairperson, executive committee, or compensation committee). Generally, the board approves the concept, including funding formulas and award parameters, and establishes the corporate targets in concert with the CEO. The board also determines incentive award levels for the CEO but allows him or her latitude in establishing individual targets for subordinates.

In some cases, the board will insist on maintaining total control over the program, including determining award levels for all those in the eligible group. In other situations, the board will wish only to be involved in determining the incentive award for the CEO and to be informed of his recommendations as a courtesy. In still other cases, particularly in large organizations, responsibility for administration may be delegated to the vice-president of human resources. In the early stages of plan development, however, it is common for the board to be actively involved in the administration of the incentive plan.

Determining Emphasis and Selecting the Plan(s)

As was mentioned, there are many approaches to incentive compensation. Ultimately the plan will have to be tailormade for the organization because a plan that is appropriate for one organization may not be appropriate for another.

Incentive plans fall into the following broad categories:

- *Discretionary.* Awards are usually not related to specific, predetermined targets. The performance bonus is frequently a discretionary award.
- *Formula.* Award levels are based on the attainment of specific, quantifiable, predetermined targets.

Of course, there are variations within each, but the majority of incentive plans being developed in health care are formula programs in which incentive targets are based on the corporate mission and/or strategic plan.

Within the context of the plan type, the following questions must be addressed:

- Should the plan emphasize group or individual performance?
- Should there be minimum and maximum award levels?

- Should the incentive fund be a percentage of the payroll of the eligible group, a percentage of savings or net income, or a percentage of range midpoints?
- Should there be a discretionary element in a formula plan?
- Should there be a provision for long-range awards?

Various models should be reviewed and tested before agreement is reached on the final funding and award formula.

Most important, a "trigger" point should be established at which it will be determined if the incentive fund will be generated. For example, regardless of individual or group effort, it is suggested that the incentive fund not be distributed unless the following preconditions have been met:

- Institution net income reaches or exceeds predetermined level
- Controllable costs do not exceed a predetermined level

Once the aforementioned issues have been addressed and agreed on, the plan manual can be written and distributed to those in the eligible group. However, there are several other important factors that must be considered.

- The plan must meet the test of IRS regulations with respect to 501(c)(3) organizations. In this context, it is suggested that quality and nonfiscal criteria be considered, as well as fiscal performance.
- There must be a timetable for implementation. The actual plan design, including discussion of all the previously mentioned issues, need not be a time-consuming or lengthy process. However, once incentive targets are established, it may take a year or more to determine if they have been attained. Those in the eligible group will have to understand that awards, if any, may not be made for a year or more after the plan design has been approved. This is a critical factor not often understood by those in the eligible group. It is essential that communications be maintained with these individuals during the design process to ensure that false expectations are not raised.

Decisions also will have to be made with respect to forfeiture in case of termination and payments to deceased or permanently disabled executives. Provisions also should be made for the voluntary deferment of awards in accordance with the institution's salary deferral program.

Finally, it should be recognized that the plan will not remain static. While the basic concept will remain unchanged, award criteria will vary from year to year, depending on the needs of the organization, as will award levels, which are dependent on the financial condition of the organization.

One of the basic characteristics of a viable incentive plan is that it is *not* a substitute for a competitive base salary structure. Such a structure, based on market trends in comparable organizations, should be in place before any work proceeds on the incentive plan.

Most incentive plans are predicated on the assumption that awards will be based on "extraordinary" achievements or results. Therefore, it is first necessary to establish the parameters of "ordinary" or expected performance. A basic performance appraisal program should be in place to ensure that those in the eligible group are accustomed to being held accountable for working within the parameters of specific, quantifiable objectives.

Individual interviews should be conducted with those in the potential incentive-eligible group to determine their understanding of and receptiveness to the incentive concept.

Therefore, it is recommended that no incentive plan be developed until a preliminary study has been conducted to ensure the organization is ready for a plan in terms of the aforementioned factors. The study should include a review of the current base salary structure, an evaluation of the objective-setting and performance appraisal protocols to ensure they are compatible with the incentive concept, and an assessment of individual attitudes toward the concept.

MARKET CONSIDERATIONS

The basis of any sound compensation program is a comparison of common benchmark positions in comparable organizations. While many salary surveys have been conducted in the health care field, a goodly number of them actually do a disservice to the participants because they do not take into consideration the realities of the health care environment.

Bed size has been a common comparative indicator in many salary surveys. In the author's opinion, this is no longer a valid factor as institutions downsize but expand their services. Expense budget, revenue, scope of services, and organization structure are the more reliable indicators.

We have seen many surveys that do not take into consideration the differences in compensation practices between free-standing hospitals and multihospital systems. The differences can be substantial. "Corporate" executives are generally paid more than their counterparts in free-standing hospitals. Executives in system-owned hospitals in which the local CEO reports to such a corporate officer rather than a local board are usually paid less than their counterparts in free-standing hospitals. Product-line management and the establishment of in-house "mini-businesses" can impact on compensation practices.

Even the best surveys only reflect what individuals are actually being paid. Survey averages may not reflect actual market conditions as replacement costs may be higher. Even more important, purely local data may not be sufficient as the market for health care executives is national, not local, in scope. We find that the salary differentials based on geographic area are insignificant.

FUTURE TRENDS

The future is here! While there is much speculation about what hospitals will look like by the twenty-first century, there is little doubt about the future of health care management. It is expected that we will see the following occur:

- "lean and mean" organization structures—fewer layers of middle management
- greater expectations of trustees
- more physician executives
- more nonhealth care MBA executives in significant positions
- product managers responsible for "mini-businesses"

All of these will have, and, indeed, are already having, a profound impact on health care executive compensation programs. Total compensation "packages" will begin to approximate those in the industrial sector. This will cause conflict and adverse reaction in many communities as local hospital compensation practices become a matter of public knowledge, but it will be necessary to attract and retain the types of executives needed to assure the continued viability of private, not-for-profit health care. The primary basis for salary increases at all levels will be performance—measured in specific, quantifiable terms. Incentive compensation and performance bonuses for singular achievements will be common.

Health care executives who view themselves as "doers" and achievers have complained about the field's lack of recognition for their efforts. This recognition is now occurring. The compensation future is bright for those individuals who are, indeed, entrepreneurs and risk takers and who, without sacrificing their devotion to service, can maintain the highest standards of care. However, it is not bright for those individuals who fail to recognize that the "old days" (if, indeed, they existed) of a risk-free, stress-free, and noncompetitive environment are gone. It will be (and already is) a cause of apprehension among those health care managers who have never been held accountable and who have viewed the annual increase as a guaranteed, automatic process that their compensation will be based on performance.

James A. Rodeghero

Managing Physicians' Compensation: Issues, Perspectives, and Approaches

23

As the health care industry continues to deal with a changing economic, social, and operating context, the role of the core provider—the physician—is changing as well. The same factors driving other sectors of the industry to search for new strategies are forcing a re-evaluation of the physicians' roles and the methods for compensating and managing their contributions to the total health care delivery system.

The Hay Group has been taking a lead with clients in all sectors of the health care industry to analyze physicians' compensation trends and to design and install compensation programs for physicians in group practices, hospitals, and insurance plans.

THE CONTEXT: CREATING A NEED FOR NEW APPROACHES TO PHYSICIANS' COMPENSATION

Hospitals have long realized that sound operating practices and quality of care are critical to success. The physician, however, is the control point for filling beds, requesting therapeutic and diagnostic procedures, and creating demand for other services and products. Without good relations with the physician staff, the hospital cannot hope to survive in the overbedded competitive market of the 1990s. Yet pressures to fill beds while controlling costs can lead to frustration in dealing with physicians who are essentially independent contractors; their goals and priorities are often not aligned with the strategies of the hospital.

Insurers also recognize the key linkages between their economic survival and the physician. But insurers must work with physicians to ensure that services are delivered or requested in a cost-effective manner within the reimbursement guidelines of the patient's medical plan. This can create competing priorities between the insurer and the physician. As insurers look to control costs, fees for physicians' services come under scrutiny and are cut wherever possible.

At the same time, physicians themselves are looking for new approaches to managing their practices. As they see their own earnings erode, they are looking for profitable linkages with the other components of the total delivery system. They recognize the very real probability that the historic practice and management freedoms they have enjoyed, as well as their earning levels, may be gone forever.

In this context all parties are rethinking traditional approaches to compensating physicians. These parties must creatively balance the competing economic forces affecting physicians' incomes. They also must create reasonable linkages between the contribution of physicians to the delivery system and equitable and competitive income levels.

HOW PHYSICIANS' COMPENSATION FITS IN THE HEALTH CARE INDUSTRY REVOLUTION

Each segment of the health care delivery system—physicians, insurers, hospitals—has a different perspective for compensating physicians. But all agree that determining competitive and equitable income levels for physicians will be important in the overall success of the health care economic equation. Even though the physician's role is rapidly changing (as technologies, ancillary providers, and alternate delivery systems rise in prominence), the center of the provider system is still the physician.

Whether acting as a "gatekeeper" or direct provider of services, the physician still determines the core aspects of managing patient care in the U.S. health care system. Deciding how to balance this role within a competitive environment with shrinking resources will become a central issue in designing physician compensation plans.

This fundamental economic issue is being questioned by providers, academics, payers, and regulators from distinctly different perspectives. Recent efforts to measure the "relative value" of medical subspecialties have met the mixed response: predictably each constituency sees these efforts from its parochial viewpoint. Although all concerned parties know that the "ultimate" relative value of physicans will be based on a combination of society's values, economics, and technology, the complexity of planning, conducting, and interpreting the necessary research precludes a simply resolution of the fundamental dilemma.

SPECIAL PROBLEMS IN DESIGNING PHYSICIAN COMPENSATION PLANS

Setting Competitive Rates. Traditional approaches to ensuring competitive compensation opportunities have relied on using marketplace data for determining rates for jobs or functions. While some industries have developed sophisticated and wide-ranging data bases for comparisons, few *professions* have developed reliable compensation data bases. Available physicians' compensation data range from association or local surveys to national listings of average specialty rates. However, the quality and validity of these surveys rarely meet the standards set in other sectors of the health care industry, and valid data linking productivity, organizational context, and other causal factors to compensation levels are virtually nonexistent. Coupled with constant changes in reimbursement levels and the relative differentials between specialty income levels, setting competitive rates for physicians using available data sources is often frustrating or impossible. Thus, Hay set out in 1988 to build a national data base that would provide the requisite quality, with findings updated annually.

Developing Viable Systems in a Changing Environment. Perhaps the greatest source of frustration to industry executives or physicians themselves in designing physician compensation plans is the unpredictable change in the environment itself. For example, if a compensation plan takes into account the actual financial value of procedures performed, then it must be able to predict reimbursement levels and collection rates; however, insurers may change reimbursement policies at any time, and the ability of the payers (patients and insurers) to pay is constantly changing. To design a viable plan under these conditions requires extremely sophisticated accounting systems and an inordinate degree of administrative flexibility.

Motivating Professionals Who Have a Long History of High Earnings and Special Social Status. Compared to designing compensation plans for traditional employee groups, physicians present some special problems for which there are no precedents. In the United States, society's long-standing appreciation of physicians' special talents (to heal the sick and save lives) has resulted in high earnings for physicians. The expectations of physicians have been maintained at these levels for many years, and although we all recognize the importance of controlling health care costs, we still place a premium on the availability of the best health care in the world and hesitate to take actions that may demotivate the providers who control the quality of care.

Dealing with Shifting Industry Economics and Control. As the purchasers of health care services (employer coalitions, union health trusts, managed care systems) gain more economic clout, the relative control and influence that individual physicians have within the health care chain has diminished. How to compensate physicians in this unprecedented environment—characterized by lessening control over their own destiny and income—is truly a critical and difficult issue.

Balancing Ethics and Quality of Care with Economic Realities. Overriding concerns for delivering high-quality care present another problem in designing compensation programs for physicians. On the one hand, no one would imply that a physician's compensation level would determine the quality of care provided. Yet payment systems hesitate to allow compensation plans that link pay levels to cost control efforts or any behaviors that may effectively restrict access to care. This is based on the assumption that physicians should not be concerned with medical practice decisions that may affect quality or access if those decisions are linked to their personal income in any way. If a compensation plan allows for linkages between access to care and physician income, all parties will share in the concern that quality may be compromised.

Adapting to Legal and Regulatory Constraints and Unknown Futures. Just as reimbursement plans have sought to balance quality with economic reality, the government has taken an active role in controlling many of the factors that directly affect the resources available for compensating physicians. For example, the Medicare program will not allow physicians' compensation plans to include incentive components that reward doctors for directly controlling costs. This is in a climate of falling reimbursement rates, thereby limiting available resources for physician's incomes. Again, the fear that physicians may—deliberately or inadvertently—restrict access or quality has created a situation in which the very behaviors Medicare should seek to motivate must be outside the compensation plan's scope. Balancing the risks of linking rewards to quality measures presents one of the most important challenges in designing physicians' compensation plans.

To further frustrate the design of viable physicians' compensation plans, the future of this regulatory environment is unknown. Predicting the outcomes of the economic, social, and political contingencies that will guide this environment would take a soothsayer with prescient abilities. In the absence of accurate prediction, compensation plan design may be fraught with pitfalls and require such frequent revisions that continuity—a key factor in successful compensation plans in any environment—may be compromised.

Accounting for the Variety of Employment/Compensation Settings for Physicians. Unlike traditional employment roles, physicians operate in a variety of contexts. In general, the "job" of a physician is to provide medical care, but the roles in an HMO, a hospital, a clinic, a group practice, a medical school, or an industrial setting may be significantly different. In each situation, although providing care is the core "accountability," other components of "job content" may have important implications for a physician's "success" or contribution to the organization. The sum of the relevant job content components should be balanced in determining compensation levels. However, the full content of physicians' roles has been difficult to measure. And the compensation programs that allow for creating motivating linkages between position content and income levels may be difficult to define and measure—or may be precluded from compensation plans as noted above.

Measuring Physician "Performance." Because physicians were long accustomed to a fee-for-service environment in which demand exceeded supply and reimbursement plans allowed costs to be passed through to payers, the concept of their "performance" was moot. In today's environment, however, the traditional rules do not apply, and the concept of assessing physicians' relative levels of performance or contributions to the total delivery system has significant implications. The concept of measurement is at the core of many of the issues outlined above. Simple measures such as billings or numbers of patients seen or numbers of procedures or hours worked all fail to capture the complex nature of the physician's role in the health care delivery system. The increasing importance of care management and utilization review mechanisms adds another layer of complexity to measurement.

THE TRADITIONAL APPROACHES TO COMPENSATING PHYSICIANS

Although physicians in private or group practice have had a need for compensation programs for years, the programs they developed were essentially income distribution plans for their partnerships or professional corporations. Physicians in medical schools worked under traditional faculty plans, and the occasional compensated medical director in a hospital or insurance setting received honoraria or was given a negotiated contract. All these were based on two fundamental approaches.

1. *Fee-for-service/productivity plans.* Most physicians in private or group practice could link their compensation levels to billings; any variable compensation component

(incentives, bonuses, profit shares) could be based on achieving preset targets, or a percentage of billings.

2. *Base salary.* Physicians in HMO settings where the panel sizes, the size and utilization rates of member populations, and the overall plan economics were stable (or at least predictable) could be paid with straight base salaries, and their "jobs" could be structured into predictable schedules and patient loads.

These approaches were suitable in a simpler and more stable environment. But today's environment demands new approaches with built-in controls and distribution schemes.

IS THERE A "BEST" METHOD FOR DESIGNING PHYSICIAN COMPENSATION PLANS?

Hay's experience in working with physicians and with health care industry executives to design physicians' compensation plans has shown that there is no "one best way." We have used a variety of project methodologies to design plans that fit the organization's needs and have found that the "right plan" is typically quite different from one organization to another, depending on the mission, philosophy, strategy, and culture of each.

Still, there are some commonalities in working with a client to design a compensation plan for physicians.

- *Study the culture.* The organization (and often the community) culture plays a critical role in determining the type of compensation plan that will be most effective in a given setting.
- *Deal with the economic realities.* This is often a critical aspect in designing a plan, requiring in-depth analysis of the organization's historic, current, and anticipated financial posture, as well as of the external forces that affect the physicians' practices. For example, if a medical group plans to move into providing prepaid care, it must recognize the differing impact of this decision on various subspecialists and general practitioners.
- *Work closely with the physicians who will be affected.* Physicians typically are intellectually curious. However, compensation plan design is often new to them. It is critical that the plan be designed conjointly to ensure full understanding and commitment.
- *Be sure the measures are valid.* Measuring the outcomes of physician behavior and then linking these outcomes to compensation plan components are the critical technical aspects in plan design. Ensuring that the measures fit the organization's culture and strategy and that the measures do not create anxiety or administrative burdens is necessary for the plan to succeed.
- *Communicate, communicate, communicate.* Without full explanation and disclosure throughout the plan design, at implementation, and through ongoing feed-

back loops, the compensation plan will not get the needed trust and commitment. Physicians want to be kept fully informed.

TRENDS IN PHYSICIAN COMPENSATION PLAN DESIGNS

Three trends are clearly evident as we look at the approaches to physicians' compensation being considered and tested throughout the health care industry.

Formally Structured Plans

Although it may seem obvious, very few physician compensation plans are actually "structured" in the same sense that health care industry executives would expect of their own compensation plans. The trend to formally define physicians' compensation arrangements with their "employer"— whether it be the partnership/corporation in a group practice, insurers, or the hospital—is the first clear signal that this area will become more sophisticated and predictable in the coming years. All the issues discussed earlier speak to the need for structure. Defining and documenting a plan is a necessary first step before the actual plan can be redesigned to ensure that the organization's goals are clearly linked into the manner in which physicians are compensated.

Contingent Compensation Approaches

The use of incentives, productivity bonuses, profit sharing, and other contingent compensation models is the "hot topic" in designing new physician compensation plans. As discussed earlier, measuring the physician's contribution to the organization and the total delivery system, as well as regulatory and reimbursement constraints, presents a major hurdle to designing and implementing effective incentive systems—but also affords the greatest potential to link physician behavior to compensation within the organization's goals and the context of the evolving health care delivery system.

Competitive Data Sources

With the increase in formally structured plans, the pressures from payers to control costs, and all parties' interest in using contingent approaches to physician compensation planning, there is increasing pressure for reliable and valid external reference points. It is no longer acceptable to base negotiations for capitation rates or physicians' salary levels on a quick phone survey of incomes of colleagues in the same specialty. These pressures are leading both to the development of more relevant data bases and to increasing sophistication among users of such data.

FUTURE DIRECTIONS: WHAT'S NEXT?

Hay's experiences in working with all segments of the health care delivery system on the tough issues and design challenges in physicians' compensation suggest that some of the current trends will continue and that the field will quickly increase in sophistication. These changes are creating several near-term issues.

- Interest in the use of incentives and other contingent approaches should force resolution of many of the measurement issues. This also should lead to clarification of the intent of regulatory and reimbursement constraints on using incentive compensation components that are linked to cost control and the management of care by physicians. Checks and balances that integrate professional control and financial monitoring should predominate over regulatory strictures as this area increases in importance and sophistication.
- The wide differentials between specialties will continue to shrink as payers and the general public reappraise the relative values of "care providing" versus "procedure-oriented" specialties. Although it is doubtful that pediatricians and neurosurgeons will ever have equivalent incomes, the differential will continue to shrink to more reasonable levels (some surveys now show as much as a 300-percent difference!).[1]
- Overall compensation levels for physicians involved only in care delivery will probably decline. Everyone expects this outcome, but there may be some important twists which provide the opportunity for many physicians to retain their historic earning levels, including job enlargement (the trend among physicians to move into related aspects of the delivery system, such as care/case management); joint ventures resulting in investment in new products, services, or ventures; and product/service differentiation between generalists and truly distinctive tertiary care providers. There will always be a market for the specialist with significantly different skills and the ability to advance the forefront of medicine—whether it be through new administrative approaches or therapies. These physicians will continue to command premium compensation levels.

CASE STUDY: REDESIGNING COMPENSATION IN GROUP PRACTICES

Hay has recently completed the redesign of a number of base and incentive compensation plans for large multispecialty clinics. Although each organization was unique, a consistent key outcome in each project was the articulation of the issues that had been "bundled" into physicians' perceptions of their compensation plan. For example, dissatisfaction with one incentive plan was really rooted in mistrust of the financial productivity: the physicians did not like to have their incentive based on an accounting system that could not reliably separate bookings from actual collections or consistently deal with changes in reimbursement levels.

The resulting plans all had a number of factors in common:

- substantial emphasis on ongoing communication/education
- provisions for flexible administration (Recognizing the inevitability of exceptions is clearly important in these plans.)
- allowance for the professional control of quality of care issues (Physicians are justifiably hesitant to allow administrators to "measure" quality, and we have found that internal controls established on a professional basis are the best way to ensure compliance with an organization's high standards of quality, ethics, and professionalism.)

- well-documented plan administration materials—with full disclosure of the plan's mechanics, but confidentiality of actual income levels
- uses of multiple sources for comparison with the external market (In the absence of any one reliable data base, we have helped these clients to develop the in-house sophistication to analyze, integrate, and use multiple datapoints to increase reliability in setting target rates for specialties. As an important side benefit, this approach significantly increases the trust of the physicians participating in the new plans.)

NOTE

1. *The Hay Group/Harvard University 1988 Physicians Compensation Survey.* Los Angeles, Calif.: The Hay Group, p. 5.

Charles L. Joiner

Performance Appraisal 24

Perhaps more so than other organizational executives today, health managers are under extreme pressure to contain cost and improve efficiency of operation. To be competitive in the health industry, these managers must develop and adopt new methods and techniques to improve the performance of their organizations. Before prospective reimbursement systems were implemented, many health executives generally ignored industrial models for management practice. However, much has occurred in recent years to push the management of for-profit and not-for-profit health care organizations into a position of strength regarding the transfer of management knowledge and technology to health care institutions.

One area of management not yet developed to its potential in the health field is performance appraisal (PA). Interestingly, this field holds great opportunity for improving management of health organizations and yielding sizable dividends at both the individual and the organizational levels. Through the proper design, implementation, and maintenance of a dynamic performance appraisal system, individual and organizational performance may be monitored and enhanced, resulting in a more efficient and effective organization.

The need to develop a superior and effective performance appraisal system (PAS) in a health care organization can be described in clear and simple terms. Indeed, health care organizations are so employee intensive that salaries and wages comprise as much as 60 to 70 percent of the institution's total operating cost are not unusual. Such data reveal the clear linkage between the successful operation of the organization and the effective and efficient performance of its employees. A

Note: Reprinted from Strategic Management of Human Resources in Health Services Organizations by M.D. Fottler (Ed.), pp. 319–347, with permission of John Wiley & Sons, Inc., © 1988.

good performance appraisal system can help the organization attract and retain highly qualified employees. Health administrators should clearly understand the reasons for implementing a performance appraisal system that is effective in promoting organizational goals as well as in developing human resources.

The development of a performance appraisal system should be a key part of management's responsibility for a variety of reasons.

1. Evaluation of employees is an important management task, since managers must be able to make administrative decisions that cause changes in employee status.
2. Management needs to have current information on the performance of individual units and departments. Through the evaluation of individual performance, management can obtain information about the unit of which the individual is a part.
3. Performance appraisal systems provide managers with information about employees' skills and abilities. These data help to validate or change the organization's selection procedures, and they provide the basis for recommendations on employee training programs.
4. The performance appraisal system provides valuable information on the quality of supervision.
5. The performance appraisal system, if successfully implemented, provides useful information for analyzing the role of management in effecting changes in the performance and development of employees.

Performance appraisal is one of the most important processes in any organization. However, from the employee perspective, all too often organizations implement performance appraisal systems as a punishment rather than to assist the employee. If this attitude pervades an organization, it is difficult to realize the positive outcomes possible for employees and organization alike. How, then, can an organization establish a performance appraisal system that will yield desirable results for all? Admittedly, an answer to this question is easy to prescribe but difficult to implement with consistency. In any system, special emphasis should be given to the human side of appraisal since, in the final analysis, the best system may be only as effective as it is perceived to be by the employees. If the system is to be perceived by employees as effective, all responsible levels of management must implement it fairly and consistently.

A brief overview of history, methods, evaluation, and problems provides background for discussion concerning strategic performance appraisal, application of management by objectives (MBO) for health care organizations, and linking rewards to performance.

HISTORICAL DEVELOPMENT

The first recorded performance appraisal system in industry was developed by Robert Owens in Scotland around 1800 (Harr and Hicks 1976). Owens placed a colored block at each workman's place to designate how well the worker had performed the previous day. Different colors indicated various levels of performance.

Formal appraisal systems were first utilized in the United States by the federal government and by certain city administrators in the middle to late 1800s. Frederick Taylor and his work measurement programs laid the groundwork for performance appraisal in business, which began shortly before World War I. Soon, in 1916, Walter Dell Scott began the development of the man-to-man rating chart that was widely used to identify and evaluate military leaders during World War I. These early appraisal systems were related to various numerical efficiency factors developed from both work simplification studies and time and motion studies popularized by the work of industrial engineers (Harr and Hicks 1976).

The graphic rating scale approach was developed in the 1920s. It required the rater to evaluate an individual on a continuum of "poor" to "excellent" for several characteristics. Human relations was strongly emphasized by management in the 1930s and 1940s, as evidenced by appraisal systems that focused on rating personality and behavior traits of employees.

During the 1950s the concept of management by objectives began to emerge when firms such as the General Electric Company began to focus on detailed planning processes for their organization. General Electric first identified the elements of management by objectives in its extensive planning for reorganization in the period 1952–1954. Peter Drucker emphasized the need for establishing objectives both for the entire organization and for its individual managers, and for

then measuring performance against the objectives. Douglas McGregor added to the impetus for management by objectives when he criticized trait appraisal systems as requiring the rater to "play God" (Harr and Hicks 1976).

In 1971 the Supreme Court mandated that any form of testing procedure for a specific job must relate directly to the job tasks to be performed [*Griggs v. Duke Power Co.*, 401 U.S. 424 (1971)]. This decision contained major implications for the construction of performance appraisal tools and the use of performance appraisal results. For example, using a test of mental ability for purposes of selection or promotion is illegal if no correlation can be established between the test and the performance of a specific job. When used as tools for selection, transfer, or promotion, performance appraisals are considered tests, and the 1971 Supreme Court decision applies (Harr and Hicks 1976).

Reinforcing the Supreme Court decision in *Griggs v. Duke Power* are the guidelines issued by the Equal Employment Opportunity Commission (EEOC) in 1970 outlining employee selection procedures. These guidelines require employers using tests to have available data demonstrating that the tests are predictive of, or significantly correlated with, important elements of work behavior (McCormick 1972).

The topic of performance appraisal is now receiving considerable attention in many organizational settings. This attention has evolved from new demands for performance accountability brought about by cost containment efforts and reduced revenues during times of economic downturn in which expectations of high performance have continued. Additionally, recent EEOC rulings and court decisions have alerted employers to possible discriminatory effects of their performance appraisal systems to determine the degree to which the objectives of the appraisal systems are met and to ascertain whether any discriminatory effects are present.

Sashkin (1981) points out that performance appraisal is, or should be, a major concern of all middle- and upper-level management. One reason for his concern is that federal courts increasingly are hearing cases in which plaintiffs argue on behalf of management that EEOC guidelines and those of other agencies actually have contributed to unfair and illegal employment practices. The alleged unfair practices include promotions, demotions, transfers, and terminations based on performance appraisal data.

These developments and others should be considered in any organization's evaluation of its performance appraisal system. It also is important that management have a comprehensive understanding of the most commonly used methods of appraisal. A summary of such methods follows.

COMMON PERFORMANCE APPRAISAL METHODS

Numerous methods exist for evaluating performance; these generally are classified as comparative methods and absolute standards. An organization should choose a method based on two criteria: the factors the organization desires to measure, and the method that applies best to the nature of the organization.

Comparative Methods

The comparative methods compare one employee to another in order to determine performance ranking. *Straight ranking* merely asks the rater to list employees, beginning with the best employee and ending with the weakest employee. In *alternative ranking*, the most common ranking method, the rater repeatedly chooses the best and weakest employees, each time choosing from the names remaining. The process is continued until all employees have been placed on the ranking list, with the last two employees being ranked in the middle (Glueck 1978).

In *paired comparison* one employee at a time is compared to all other employees. Each time an employee is ranked higher than another employee, a tally is placed by the higher-ranking person's name. The employee with the most tallies is considered to be the most valuable, and the others are placed in order according to the number of tallies by their names. *Forced distribution* asks the rater to assign a certain proportion of the employees to one category on each criterion. For example, 10 percent of employees might be in the "superior" category, 20 percent in "good," 20 percent in "average," continuing to "poor" (Glueck 1978).

Comparison methods are useful in making decisions regarding promotion and selection from within a work unit, and this is their major advantage. However, the use of more than one rater is advisable to obtain more accurate ratings.

Comparison methods are problematic in that they are time consuming and useful only for relatively small groups of employees. Also, an employee's performance rating is based on other employees' work rather than on desired performance. Comparisons can lead to judgment of personality rather than of performance. Finally, ranking assumes equal distance between employees' ranks, an assumption research shows to be unwarranted.

Absolute Standards

Through the use of standards, each individual is evaluated against written standards, and several factors of performance are measured. In one such method, the *weighted checklists method* (see Figure 24-1), the rater identifies, and assigns a weight to, each of the tasks to be evaluated. The employee then is scored on each task to determine overall performance. The checklist calls for a simple "yes-no" judgment (Harr and Hicks 1976).

The major disadvantage to the use of a weighted (or nonweighted) checklist is that it does not reveal the degree with which a specific behavior occurs, requiring only a mere yes-no judgment.

	Delivery of Patient Care	Yes	No	N/A
60%	A. Evaluate and intervene when necessary in nursing care delivered by other non-RN personnel in his or her unit.			
40%	B. Provide skillful and safe care to patients as indicated in patient chart and nursing care plan.			

Figure 24-1 Example of Weighted Checklists

In the *forced-choice method* the rater selects statements that best fit the performance characteristics of the individual employee. The rater does not know the value assigned to each characteristic, and consequently forced choice can reduce bias. However, this advantage can become a disadvantage if the rater is offended by the confidential weights assigned to the statements.

Graphic rating is the most commonly used method for performance appraisal. The scale requires the rater to choose a value or statement along a continuum that best fits the employee for each criterion being reviewed. The advantage of a graphic scale is that it shows the degree to which an employee performs a job or task (Douglas et al. 1985).

As a result of the shortcomings of the critical incidents method, the *behaviorally anchored rating scale* (BARS) was developed. The BARS uses characteristics judged to be critical to job performance and rates the degree to which each characteristic is attained by the employee. The employee's performance is determined by summing the values assigned to each of the critical indicators and/or characteristics (Douglas et al. 1985).

The main disadvantage of the BARS is that its development is time consuming because separate scales are needed for each job. BARS, however, offers objectivity, which is lacking in such clearly subjective appraisal methods as comparative methods and essays. BARS has been used effectively in hospital work units of nurses and ancillary personnel; such successful usage is due to the dimensionality of the BARS scale, which permits identification of separate components of complex job behaviors. BARS demonstrates a necessary movement toward evaluations that are developmental rather than merely evaluative. Such developmental evaluations, being behaviorally based, then provide the basis for changes in behavior.

A system developed from the BARS model, the behavioral observations scale (BOS), attempts to eliminate some of the disadvantages of BARS. The development of the BOS also begins with the identification of critical incidents, which are then categorized according to behavioral dimensions. The behavioral dimensions usually contain five to eight items each, and these are used to rate employee performance. A frequency format is developed in which the highest number corresponds

Table 24-1 Criteria for Choice of Performance Evaluation Techniques

Evaluative base	Graphic rating scale	Forced choice	MBO	Essay	Critical incidents	Weighted checklist	BARS	Ranking	Paired comparison	Forced distribution	Performance test	Field review
Developmental cost	Moderate	High	Moderate	Low	Moderate	Moderate	High	Low	Low	Low	High	Moderate
Usage cost	Low	Low	High	High supervisory costs	High	Low	Low	Low	Low	Low	High	High
Ease of use by evaluators	Easy	Moderately difficult	Moderate	Difficult	Difficult	Easy	Easy	Easy	Easy	Easy	Moderately difficult	Easy
Ease of understanding by those evaluated	Easy	Difficult	Moderate	Easy	Easy	Easy	Moderate	Easy	Easy	Easy	Easy	Easy
Useful in promotion decisions	Yes	Yes	Yes	Not easily	Yes	Moderately	Yes	Yes	Yes	Yes	Yes	Yes
Useful in compensation and reward decisions	Yes	Moderately	Yes	Not easily	Yes	Moderately	Yes	Not easily	Not easily	Yes	Yes	Yes
Useful in counseling and development of employees	Moderately	Moderately	Yes	Yes	Yes	Moderately	Yes	No	No	No	Moderately	Yes

Source: "Performance Evaluation and Development of Personnel," and "Performance Evaluation and Promotion," *Foundations of Personnel,* Business Publications, © 1979.

with "almost always," and the lowest number corresponds with "almost never." A comparison of BOS with BARS reveals that BOS does not require the appraiser to regularly record the occurrence of critical incidents. Instead, BOS asks the rater to evaluate the employee on a variety of behaviors that have been determined to be critical to good or poor performance (Douglas et al. 1985).

Management by objectives (MBO) is a result-based evaluative program in which goals are mutually determined by supervisors and subordinates, and employees are rated on the degree to which these goals are accomplished. MBO stresses the value and importance of employee involvement and encourages discussion of employee strengths and weaknesses. The supervisor acts as a counselor rather than as a judge in aiding the employee in reaching his or her full potential (Levitz 1981).

MBO has become popular for several reasons. First, it promotes better communication and interaction between the superior and subordinate. Additionally, the process of MBO development forces the organization and individual units to recognize and coordinate goals. Also, employees gain understanding of work objectives and come to know what is expected of them. Critical to MBO is the review process in which the supervisor discusses performance with the employee and makes recommendations for future performance (Levitz 1981).

Tables 24-1 and 24-2 may assist managers in reviewing various organizational performance appraisal techniques in terms of cost and applicability (Glueck 1978).

Although an understanding of the most commonly used methods of performance appraisal is helpful, equally important is a review of significant theoretical and philosophical differences in evaluating methods of performance appraisal to date.

EVALUATION OF PERFORMANCE APPRAISAL

"All organizations, whether in the private, public, or non-profit sectors, face the problem of engaging the energies of their members in the task of reaching their goals" (Brinkerhoff and Kanter 1980, 3). To solve this problem, organizations must devise ways to influence and handle the behavior of their members, correcting deviation and rewarding good performance. Performance appraisals constitute one of the major tools used in the organizational control process. At the same time that some form of performance appraisal is a tool in organizational control and decision making, it can be seen as a way of both rationalizing and clarifying the employment relationship, and protecting the individual from arbitrary discipline or the results of non-performance-based favoritism (Brinkerhoff and Kanter 1980).

Therefore, it is important to assess objectively the process of performance appraisal, both theory and practice. This assessment includes a review of the purpose of performance appraisal, a review of the task characteristics important for the PA process, and a summary of performance appraisal system problems.

Purpose of Performance Appraisal

Performance appraisal has served two purposes: evaluation (as the term *appraisal* implies) and development (Kearney 1977). Brinkerhoff and Kanter (1980) point out that the evaluative function of PA refers to assessment of the extent to which progress toward goals (which we can define as desirable end states) has been furthered by the appraisal effort. This purpose of PA is historically oriented; past performance is reviewed in light of results or outcomes. PA for evaluation historically has served as the basis for decision making regard-

Table 24-2 Recommendations on Evaluation Techniques for Model Organizations

Type of organization	Graphic rating scale	Forced choice	MBO	Essay	Critical incidents	Weighted checklist	BARS	Ranking	Paired comparison	Forced distribution	Performance test	Field review	Assessment centers
Large size, low complexity, high stability	X	X	X		X	X	X	X	X	X	X	X	X
Medium size, low complexity, high stability	X		X	X	X	X	X	X	X	X			X
Small size, low complexity, high stability	X		X	X	X			X	X	X			
Medium size, moderate complexity, moderate stability	X		X	X	X	X		X	X	X			X
Large size, high complexity, low stability	X		X	X	X			X	X	X		X	X
Medium size, high complexity, low stability	X		X	X	X			X	X	X			
Small size, high complexity, low stability	X		X	X	X			X	X	X			

Source: "Performance Evaluation and Development of Personnel," "Performance Evaluation and Promotion," *Foundations of Personnel*, Business Publications, © 1979.

ing promotions, transfers, and salary adjustments. It also can be used as a basis for allocating terminations, particularly in an organization that has decided to reduce its work force.

PA's developmental function is forward looking, aimed at enhancing the future capacity of organization members to be more productive, effective, and/or satisfied (Brinkerhoff and Kanter 1980). For developmental purposes PA facilitates improvement in job skills and motivation, as well as career planning and effective coaching between managers and subordinates.

Cummings and Schwab (1973) offer the following useful framework for analysis of the different approaches to performance evaluation: the system is best for the organization and makes its greatest positive contribution in the area of job satisfaction and productivity when the philosophy and operation are that of a developmental program. The time orientation concentrates on future performance rather than on management's assessment of past performance. A developmental system improves performance through personal growth, whereas a judgmental system attempts to improve employee performance through changing personnel and the reward system. A significant aspect of a developmental program is the means by which it achieves its objectives. Specifically, a developmental system includes both a goal-setting process and developmental programs (e.g., management by objectives). Judgmental programs attempt to measure past performance and use a variety of methods such as rating scales and ranking systems.

The methods of operation of these two extremely different systems have strong implications for the way in which the rater is viewed by the employee. In a developmental system, the rater is viewed as a counselor or coach, and the rater views the role as providing encouragement to the employee in the process of personal development. The evaluative system places the rater in the role of judge, one who must assess the value of the employee's performance. Consequently, the individual being rated in an evaluative system frequently is passive or defensive about previous performance. In a developmental system, however, the employee is actively involved in a learning process and in planning for future improvement in job performance.

An assumption of this chapter is that all managers are involved in performance appraisal, regardless of whether it is properly organized and whether it is judgmental or developmental. All managers should be involved actively in organizationwide appraisal systems that are strategically focused and developmental. The role of performance appraisal in health organizations is becoming more and more crucial to institutional effectiveness. Therefore, it seems reasonable that management should spend an appropriate amount of time in analyzing its performance appraisal needs and in developing a system that can be effective in meeting those needs.

Tasks Characteristics

Brinkerhoff and Kanter (1980) stress three characteristics of tasks that have strong impact on the PA process: complexity, clarity, and predictability.

Complexity

As pointed out by Dornbusch and Scott (1975):

the more complex the task, the more complex is the evaluation process required. If the task entails many activities and there are numerous properties of interest in connection with the activities or outcome, then the process of arriving at a valid and reliable performance evaluation is likely to be complicated. (p. 145)

Therefore, the most technically accurate evaluations generally have been limited to jobs that have relatively simple content and unambiguous measures of performance.

Clarity

Clarity concerning tasks and goals is another characteristic that influences the PA process (Brinkerhoff and Kanter 1980). In other words, knowledge of, and/or agreement on, what is to be done must be clear both to management and to the employee. Tasks with specific objectives on which organizational members can agree lend themselves to implementation and subsequent measurement that form a good basis for relatively straightforward performance evaluation.

However, tasks characterized as ambiguous pose problems for performance appraisal. Diffused goals, moreover, provide little help in determining what to measure and/or what standards should be employed in the evaluation process. Conflicts and disagreements commonly occur when goals and tasks are vague and ambiguous.

Predictability

Predictability is another factor particularly relevant for evaluations based on outcomes (Brinkerhoff and Kanter 1980). If the tasks are predictable, the relationships between quality of performance and amount and/or quality of outcome are relatively constant. Typing a letter is a good example of a predictable task in which examination of the outcome provides an accurate picture of performance.

On the other hand, unpredictable tasks do not allow accurate assessments of performance based on outcomes. Such tasks are common in areas where knowledge of cause-and-effect relations is not complete and ambiguous standards for assessing performance are being used (Thompson 1967). Brinkerhoff and Kanter (1980) have stated that as uncertainty in jobs increases (e.g., difficulties of measuring results, time lag between action and results), so does the tendency to use social characteristics in making decisions about who should occupy those jobs (Kanter 1977; Scott 1978). Therefore, it is precisely the difficulty of doing objective appraisals of performance in areas high in uncertainty (such as risky ventures) and higher-level management strategic decisions that results in the appearance of bias through reliance on subjective factors such as trust and loyalty.

Brinkerhoff and Kanter (1980) also point out that the PA process is not an independent one but is structurally linked to a variety of other features and processes of the organization. The structural characteristics that have a direct impact on performance appraisal systems include task interdependence, observability of task performance, the structuring of the authority system, power differentials, and the nature of communicated appraisals.

In summary, what develops from a given PAS depends largely on purpose, task features, and characteristics of the organizational structure. Basically, PA data may tend to be unreliable or misleading from the standpoint of the organizational and social psychological issues. However, most of the appraisal literature, with its technical focus on scientifically developed rating instruments, fails to recognize the realities of practice that contribute to this unreliability. Brinkerhoff and Kanter (1980) conclude that data from formal performance measures tend to be most reliable when the following conditions exist.

1. The purpose of the appraisal is clear.
2. Tasks are simple.
3. Goals for the tasks are clear.
4. Outcomes are predictable.
5. Tasks are relatively independent.
6. Task performance is observable.
7. Criteria of performance are set by those later assessing performance.
8. Appraisers feel secure in their own jobs and have no personal stake in hurting the performers.

This conclusion suggests that single measurement systems based on formal checklists and ratings by the supervisor should be used only for the more routine tasks in organizations, which are likely to meet these criteria. On the other hand, as uncertainty grows—or complexity, interdependence, power concerns, and/or multiple appraisal purposes grow—so should the number of additional features and sources of data used for the appraisal system.

Sashkin (1981) developed a brief questionnaire (Exhibit 24-1) to elicit a rough evaluation of an organization's appraisal system. The questionnaire is based on three basic objectives of performance appraisal.

1. Performance appraisal systems should generate information needed for short- and long-range administrative actions, such as salary decisions, promotions, and transfers (all short-range) or human resources planning and managerial succession (long-range).
2. Appraisal systems should let subordinates know where they stand and how well they are doing, as well as any changes in their behavior the superior wants.
3. Appraisal systems should provide a means for coaching and counseling subordinates, to train and develop them to their full potential.

It is evident that no single system is appropriate or effective for every organization or category of employees. To further assist in the evaluation of an organization's appraisal system, Sashkin (1981) has developed the following 10 questions or rules of thumb:

1. Are managers rewarded for developing their subordinates?

Exhibit 24-1 Organizational Performance Appraisal Questionnaire Evaluation (OPAQUE)

Instructions

Respond to the following six statements by indicating the extent to which you agree (or disagree) that the statements accurately describe performance appraisal in your organization. Some statements refer to your experiences in appraising your subordinates' performance; others refer to your experiences in being appraised yourself. Try to reflect as accurately as you can the current conditions in your organization based on your experiences.

SA = Strongly Agree   A = Agree   ? = Neither Agree nor Disagree   D = Disagree   SD = Strongly Disagree

1. I have found my boss's appraisals to be very helpful in guiding my own career development progress.	SA	A	?	D	SD
2. The appraisal system we have here is of no use to me in my efforts toward developing my subordinates to the fullest extent of their capabilities.	SA	A	?	D	SD
3. Our performance appraisal system generally leaves me even more uncertain about where I stand after my appraisal than beforehand.	SA	A	?	D	SD
4. The appraisal system we use is very useful in helping me to clearly communicate to my subordinates exactly where they stand.	SA	A	?	D	SD
5. When higher levels of management around here are making major decisions about management positions and promotions, they have access to and make use of performance appraisal records.	SA	A	?	D	SD
6. In making pay, promotion, transfer, and other administrative personnel decisions, I am not able to obtain past performance appraisal records that could help me to make good decisions.	SA	A	?	D	SD

Source: © 1981 by Marshall Sashkin. Used by special permission. All rights reserved.

2. Do managers receive skill training and assistance in using the system and, specifically, in being helpers or counselors?

3. Are job descriptions or specific job goal documents based on behavioral characteristics or job-relevant performance?

4. Are employees actively involved in the appraisal process?

5. Does mutual goal setting take place?

6. Do the appraisal sessions have a problem-solving focus?

7. Is the judge role clearly separated from the helper/counselor role?

8. Do the paperwork and technical assistance required by the appraisal system place an unreasonable workload on managers?

9. Are peer comparisons a central feature of the appraisal process?

10. Is information that is needed for administrative action accessible and effectively used?

Managers should be equipped with some understanding of the purpose and complexity of valid performance appraisal. They also should be aware of the variety of problems that may be encountered in the development, implementation, and operation of a performance appraisal system.

Performance Appraisal System Problems

The development, implementation, and operation of a performance appraisal system is a major undertaking. Such a system may fail to bring the organization the desired results for a variety of reasons, ranging from problems in the development stage to the problem of reviewing the system.

Developmental Problems

Several problem areas may be encountered when an organization attempts to implement a PA program. One is designing the best possible system to meet the needs of the organization. The design of the "best" system should comprise an objective program that will evaluate employees on the basis of behavior that can be observed and easily measured. Use of the essay format or a comparative method probably will not result in an objective, accurate evaluation of performance.

Second, a PA system ideally should be equally effective in evaluating employees at all levels in the organization. However, use of the same approach to evaluate everyone may not yield the desired result. In a hospital, for example, use of a critical incidents method for housekeeping staff may be appropriate, but for managers and top-level executives this technique would not measure adequately such qualities as goal attainment and leadership ability.

A third factor crucial to the developmental stage is that of ownership of the PA system; those who will use the system—the employees—should own it. Studies show that a system seen as the personnel department's project is less likely to be accepted and to survive in the organization. Therefore, the employees must be involved in the developmental stage.

Finally, the goals and objectives to be measured must be tied into the organization's strategic plan. This linkage ensures coordination of different units, with each working for the long-term advancement of the organization. Unless the organization considers the strategic long-range plan, its work to obtain short-term performance improvements may at the same time be sabotaging future success in reaching long-range goals.

Implementation Problems

Several problems may arise in the implementation stage. For example, a lack of commitment from the organization will cause employees to lose faith in the system, believing that it will be short-lived. Management should show commitment by implementing the system throughout the entire organization, or from top management down, as evidence of top-level and managerial support.

A second possible problem area is training and education. Those who will be using the system should be thoroughly educated in its purpose and process. Such education includes training raters on evaluating employees. Training reduces evaluator resistance to the system while aiding in getting the most accurate information on performance. All raters should get practical, hands-on experience during the training sessions.

Even the most careful construction of an appraisal tool will not eliminate the need for training raters. Training is necessary to minimize rating errors because a biased, distorted, or inaccurate evaluation diminishes employees' motivation and allows management to make inaccurate personnel decisions, which in turn defeat the purpose of the system. To be successful at reducing rater errors, management should recognize the importance of training sessions in which the future evaluators can practice skills taught and receive immediate feedback.

Operational Problems

One of the most common problems in the operation of a system is rater error. Identifying rater error can be very difficult if an employee is evaluated solely by one supervisor. Common rater errors include the following:

1. *Central tendency and leniency.* The rater evaluates all employees as average, excellent, or poor. A rater who has this tendency should be made aware that such information is not very valuable and should be asked to rate employees from best to worst for each element of the job. This exercise will aid the evaluator in revealing more accurately the performance of those being evaluated (Lowe 1986).

2. *Halo effect.* Some raters judge all performance based on one area in which performance is good or poor (Lowe 1986). That is, the evaluator gives similar ratings for all performance areas even though the performance varies from area to area. This is possibly the most common rater error.

3. *Contrast effects.* The rater evaluates the individual relative to other employees rather than on the requirements of the job. A rater who is tempted to change an individual's rating after rating others is probably making a contrast error. Most people assume that performance in a work unit should follow a normal curve; this is incorrect and can lead to a violation of EEOC regulations.

4. *Similar-to-me.* The tendency to judge more favorably people perceived as similar to the rater should be avoided (Glueck 1978).

Crucial to the operation of a PA system is prompt feedback and guidance for the evaluated employee. Feedback allows the system to move from merely being evaluative to being also developmental (Glueck 1978). For example, if feedback is provided three months after the evaluation, performance may have changed, and the postevaluation may praise or correct behavior that no longer exists. Prompt feedback, when directly associated with the period under evaluation, can help to maintain good performance or to change poor performance. Prompt feedback in the form of a face-to-face meeting between the supervisor and subordinate is crucial to the operation of a performance appraisal system. The rater counsels the employee to help him or her to reach full potential.

Finally, the operation of a system must include periodic review.

A rigid performance appraisal system cannot survive successfully in a dynamic organization. The system will require periodic alterations; a yearly review is advisable. The review should gather input from participants at all levels to accomplish a dual purpose: to assess the participants' level of satisfaction in the system and to determine changes that can be made to improve system effectiveness.

Critical to the building of a strategic human resources management system is the recognition that the functions of performance appraisal comprise a significant part of the overall strategic human resources management process. These ideas are discussed in the sections that follow, along with the application of management by objectives.

STRATEGIC ROLE OF PERFORMANCE APPRAISAL

Latham (1984) defines strategic planning as the process through which the basic need of an organization is identified, its objectives are set, and the allocations of resources to achieve these objectives are specified. Latham further notes that performance appraisals often are viewed as retrospective because they emphasize what occurred in the past. Yet the success or failure of strategic plans rests, in large part, with management's ability to identify the key actions that must be performed to formulate and use the steps that will lead to the attainment of the organization's long-range goals. Therefore, performance appraisal must be the process through which the critical job behaviors of management are identified, the specific objectives of each individual manager are set, and the steps or resources needed to obtain them are agreed on.

A few organizations have formal appraisal systems to evaluate top-level managers on how well they perform against the organization's strategic plan. The prevailing attitude seems to be that good measurement indicators simply do not exist. Frequently, emphasis is placed on managerial style or charisma rather than substance, and/or on whether a given result was achieved, with little or no questioning as to how it was achieved. For example, a chief executive officer may appraise a senior vice-president primarily on whether a set of objectives was pursued in a manner similar to the way in which the CEO would have pursued them. Creativity and divergence of thinking are consequently stifled. Quite common are appraisal measures that reward managers for attending to the "bottom line" of their respective functions, without taking note of how their actions, or those of their people, affected the operation of other departments. No formal assessment is made to determine whether they and their subordinates behaved in a unifying or integrated way with colleagues so that the organization's overall mission could be achieved. Organizational behaviors of these types emphasize why many strategic plans are not carried out successfully (Latham 1984).

Fundamental to the understanding of the strategic role of performance appraisal is the recognition of the dual nature or purpose of the process.

Dual Nature of Strategic Performance Appraisal

The purpose of strategic performance appraisal is twofold (Latham 1984). First, the performance appraisal instrument defines what is meant by implementation and adherence to a strategic plan related to the individual employee. Therefore, when the strategic plan changes, the evaluation instrument should be reviewed for necessary modification and revision. It is through the use of the evaluation instrument that the second objective of performance appraisal is attained: namely, to bring about and sustain effective and/or efficient job performance. This can be done either through self-management or through coaching and counseling other people.

Performance appraisal is the sine qua non of a strategic human resources management system. This is because a performance appraisal system should make explicit what effective and efficient behavior is required of an individual employee for the organization to implement its strategic plan. Just as a nursing services department is concerned with the quality of patient care, the maintenance department is concerned with the operation of equipment, and just as housekeeping is concerned with maintaining a sanitary

environment, the human resources system should be concerned with identification of what the people in nursing services, in maintenance, and in housekeeping must do to be proficient in their respective functions. In a similar way, it should be determined what top management must do to implement the strategic plan once it has been formulated (Latham 1984). The outcomes of these analyses translate into an appraisal instrument that is valid in that people are being evaluated on areas that are important to the attainment of their departmental and/or organizational objectives. To the extent that valid performance appraisals are done, valid decisions can be made regarding which employees should be rewarded. To the extent that valid performance appraisals are not made, it is impossible to make valid selection and reward decisions.

Valid performance appraisals are also critical to health care training programs because they identify people who lack the ability to perform effectively in their jobs. Use of a valid appraisal instrument makes it possible to identify not only those who need training but also the type of training needed.

The strategic purpose of PA cannot be achieved without the implementation of a PAS designed to assist in blending organizational goals with those of individual employees, to assist in the strategic planning process and in the accomplishment of organizational mission. When a properly designed PAS is implemented with consistency, it becomes the cornerstone of an effective human resources management system. As such, the PAS serves a number of strategic functions, some of which are as follows.

Strategic Functions of the Performance Appraisal System

Douglas et al. (1985) list five strategic functions of the PAS

1. to provide a major source of human resources planning information
2. to provide a control mechanism for management
3. to activate and support the motivation system
4. to provide a means of employee development
5. to provide a basis for justifying personnel actions

Human Resources Planning

If done properly, PAS should form the basis for important records including data on each employee's special abilities. This information can be particularly important in identifying managerial talent. The human resources planning aspect of the PAS is significant in terms of strategic plans as well. Each employee's permanent personnel records should include a complete evaluation of her or his background, ability, and potential. The records also should include a summary of work history, education, and training, as well as assessments of factors such as motivation, leadership skills, and potential for assuming greater organizational responsibilities.

Control and Motivation of Personnel

Performance appraisal systems, which contain the justification for distributing the rewards and punishments that organizations have to offer, should be the heart of any motivation system. In concept or theory, any organization should strive to distribute its available resources so that excellent or good performers are rewarded more than average or poor performers. Accomplishing this objective depends largely on the ability of the institution to develop reasonably objective appraisal measures and methods, and then to relate the rewards directly to these objectives and measurements. If success is achieved in these areas, the problems or perceptions of inequity will be reduced, though probably not eliminated.

An extremely important aspect of motivation is goal setting. Much evidence points out that people with explicit performance goals do better than people with vague performance objectives, such as "Do the very best you can." Many studies also indicate that difficult goals produce higher performance than easy goals, although some work suggests that the goals must be limited to what is realistically possible. Unrealistic goals may simply cause people to become discouraged and unproductive.

The idea of control also is related to motivation. Key components of control are goals, measurement, and feedback. Douglas et al. (1985) indicate that good appraisal systems are supported by measurement, progress is noted according to those measures, and feedback occurs to an area in which changes can be made. Control is necessary to enable both management and employees to make associations between behavior and output. The same measures also can be useful in determining rewards.

Personnel Development

One of the primary reasons for PA in any organization should be to assist employees in developing their skills to their maximum potential. The control aspect of PA can help employees make adjustments through better performance. In addition, objective appraisal can help in identifying weaknesses as well as strengths of each employee. Such weakness may be dealt with through planning recommendations communicated to the employee at the time of the appraisal interview.

Justification of Personnel Actions

The performance appraisal process is extremely important in providing information. It requires justification for promotion, transfer, and demotion or termination. This is particularly true in view of civil rights legislation and EEOC regulations. However, any good performance appraisal system must have a carefully thought-out plan of objective measurement and a documentation process. Although judgment is extremely important in many aspects of management, a performance appraisal system that relies almost exclusively on supervisors' judgment will be very difficult to defend. Documentation of objective measurement is essential. If a record of well-designed and properly conducted appraisals is available and indicates consistency, important personnel actions such as promotions or terminations can be justified on the basis of objective, documented information.

To serve the purpose and functions of strategic performance appraisal, the organization must establish and effect a PAS that has application and acceptability throughout the organization. One system with this potential is management by objectives, presented as a strategic appraisal system for health care organizations.

MANAGEMENT BY OBJECTIVES (MBO): A STRATEGIC APPRAISAL SYSTEM

Although no performance appraisal system that exists will meet all the needs of a given organization, the MBO concept is more broadly applicable and fundamentally sound than most other systems. Of particular relevance to this chapter is the possible linkage of the MBO concept to management's strategic planning functions.

The term "management by objectives" was used first by Peter F. Drucker more than 30 years ago. Drucker (1954) pointed out that in this system, each manager should have clear objectives that are identified with and support those of high levels of management. Individuals thus can develop an understanding of their own objectives, as well as those of their managers, and the organization. Many authors have supported the MBO concept developed by Drucker. Douglas McGregor (1960) brought the concept into the performance appraisal arena by advocating that MBO be used to encourage the discussion of employee strengths and potential, making the superior more a counselor than a judge. Whereas Drucker first viewed MBO as a method of integrating the activities of an organization, McGregor developed the idea of applying MBO as a performance appraisal technique. In recent years, the MBO approach has been recommended as an appraisal technique that should be linked to management's strategic planning process.

Definitions

Although a variety of definitions of MBO programs exist, some common elements are present (Cummings and Schwab 1973):

1. goal setting
2. involvement of managers in participation in the formulation of personal goals and methods to accomplish these goals
3. periodic reviews of progress toward the accomplishment of these goals

4. evaluation of performance
5. self-appraisal
6. feedback and evaluation
7. suggestions for development and training

As demonstrated by the common elements listed above, the real process may be viewed as a cycle of events that includes planning, setting objectives and goals, negotiation, performance, review of performance, and evaluation and feedback. Figure 24-2 shows a model objective-setting process, and Figure 24-3 presents an overview of the MBO cycles.

McConkie (1979), who further identified common elements from various authors' descriptions of MBO and their explanations of how performance appraisal should be conducted under MBO, found that almost complete agreement existed on three items specific to goal setting in MBO programs. These items indicated that goals and objectives should be specific, should be defined in terms of measurable results, and should reflect both individual and organizational perspectives.

The ideal objective list tells managers and employees:

1. what should be done
2. when it should be completed
3. when it actually is completed
4. what priority each objective has
5. the percentage of time of the total each objective uses
6. what authority level the employee has to implement plans
7. what is being done to develop each employee
8. how well the employee performs
9. when objectives are to be reviewed
10. the total job expected

It appears that with the linkage of MBO to performance appraisal to establish an effective system that provides a setting for managers and subordinates to set objectives against which performance is measured, management receives better data than are obtained from other traditional methods. Using these concepts, McConkie (1979) concluded that MBO could be defined as follows:

> a managerial process whereby organizational purposes are diagnosed and met by joining superiors and subordinates in the pursuit of mutually agreed upon goals and objectives, which are specific, measurable, time bounded, and joined to an action plan; progress and goal attainment are measured and monitored in appraisal sessions which center on mutually determined objective standards of performance. (p. 37)

It is important to note that the key areas of management involvement that contribute to the success of MBO programs relate to administration's understanding of and commitment to the various features of the system.

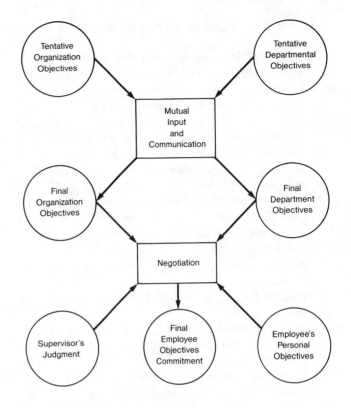

Figure 24-2 The Objective-Setting Process

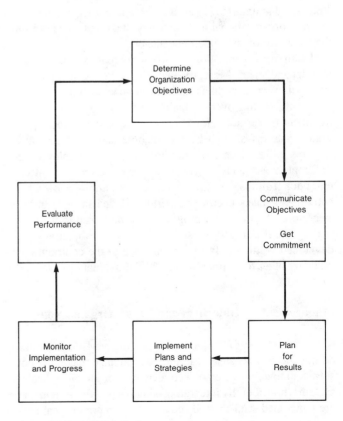

Figure 24-3 The MBO Cycle

Management by Objectives As an Appraisal System

Migliore (1979) describes a frame of reference for the implementation of the MBO program that is based on identifying purposes, objectives, and desired results, and in evaluating performance in the following nine-step process:

1. defining the organization's purpose and reason for being
2. monitoring the environment in which it operates
3. assessing the organization's strengths and weaknesses realistically
4. making assumptions about unpredictable future events
5. prescribing written, specific, and measurable objectives in principal result areas that contribute to the organization's purpose
6. developing strategies on how to use available resources to meet objectives
7. making long-range and short-range plans to meet objectives
8. appraising performance constantly to determine whether it is meeting the desired pace and remaining consistent with the defined purposes
9. Re-evaluating purpose, environment, strengths, weaknesses, and assumptions before setting objectives for the next performance year

This system clearly reflects the intent to match the program to organizational goals, and this is particularly important for strategic planning. However, it is sometimes difficult to bring together organizational units in a way that takes advantage of the existence of such interdependencies.

Health care organizations present numerous examples of the interdependencies. Most, for example, bring together persons from different disciplines to perform specific functions that contribute to the overall quality and efficiency of patient treatment or service. However, a successful treatment program, in terms of both health outcome and cost, generally requires a high degree of coordination among employees in different departments. These personnel represent very different backgrounds, training, and understandings of what activities or tasks need to be performed and in what order. Therefore, the treatment program must be linked to the total management perspective so that individual objectives are developed within the frame of reference of the contributions made by other departments and other individuals.

Management by Objectives and Health Organizations

Gerstenfeld (1977, 52) indicates that many MBO programs do not succeed because of failure to recognize that "it is not sufficient to delineate an objective in one portion of the health system while not fully integrating other parts of the system that are concerned with that objective." It is important that systems of performance appraisal, including MBO, reflect an interest in interdepartmental and, where appropriate, interorganizational management and that health managers understand the many benefits that can accrue from their approach to performance appraisal.

Performance appraisal is not yet widely accepted by individuals in health care settings. Health care employees often feel that evaluation should be performed by peers and not be linked necessarily to the operation or management of an organization. Although such feelings may stem from years of professional training, management of health organizations must have appropriate methods to appraise employees and evaluate the effectiveness of the organization.

In terms of strategic human resources planning and overall management needs, it seems suitable for health care organizations to strive for systems that will contribute to individual growth and development. Some of the traditional methods of evaluation (which are comprised of subjective or trait evaluations, requiring choices on numerical scales or markings on checklists) are not appropriate appraisal tools for many health care employees. Employees simply need an evaluation process in which they participate, one that provides an opportunity to enhance professional skills and will assist workers in making greater contributions to the organization.

An effective evaluation system must be based on observation of skills and performance, not on a laundry list of personal attributes. Job analysis procedures may lead to the development of objective criteria, which then may be used in performance evaluation. These criteria must address both the quality and the quantity of work performed. They also should measure factors over which an employee may have influence, and they should be applied over a realistic period of time (Hand and Hollingsworth 1975).

MBO can be applied effectively in health organizations where there is an integrated management approach and the motivation to have the system work (Gerstenfeld 1977; Hand and Hollingsworth 1975). The primary motivation should be an interest in the development of employees, with rewards to follow for effective and efficient performance. Research also indicates that an MBO program, when combined with other programs such as job enrichment, may enhance both productivity and worker satisfaction (Gerstenfeld, 1977; Hand and Hollingsworth 1975).

Guidelines for Implementing Management by Objectives

When an organization is considering implementation of performance evaluation systems such as MBO, management and employees alike should be aware of the total process from its inception. Through this communication, management and employees can develop an understanding of the commitment needed and the length of time required for a successful program. Listed below are the guidelines Levitz (1981) offers for implementation of an MBO program.

1. Management and employees should be committed to the MBO program and supportive of it. A survey may be necessary to determine how open the organization's climate is.
2. Everyone involved in the process should develop an understanding of the purpose and objectives of the program.
3. Management and other personnel should meet to develop common goals.
4. Departmental objectives should be developed that are consistent with those of the health organization.
5. Job descriptions should be written in result-oriented form, with statements on the measurement of satisfactory performance.
6. Subordinate-superior goal setting should occur at regular meetings.
7. Clear, valid, and measurable objectives for individuals need to be set and agreed upon.
8. Superiors should be trained in evaluation methods, developmental methods, and performance interviewing.
9. Developmental feedback sessions should be scheduled based on individual needs.
10. Employees should view the MBO program as being linked to the reward system.
11. Continual monitoring of the system should occur through a linkage with other management functions.

From the perspective of strategic human resources management, several benefits appear to accrue from the operation of an MBO program, and these make it worthwhile for the management team to invest the resources required for implementation and maintenance of such a system. Levitz (1981) lists several advantages that may result from a successful program:

1. improved direction and planning for activities toward the accomplishment of organizational goals
2. the linking of institutional management functions to control systems through the development of appropriate work standards
3. a reduction in role conflict
4. a better understanding of how performance is linked to rewards
5. increased employee satisfaction through the use of objective criteria
6. the career development of personnel

Through an understanding of the total MBO program and its necessary linkage to performance appraisal, compensation, and other management functions, health care managers can exert better and broader control over performance. The end result will be a more effective and efficient health services organization.

Applications of Management by Objectives

Kessler (1981) indicates that the MBO concept has been used in numerous settings by those who found old ways ineffective, those who tended to be experiment minded, and those who were inclined to research the state of the art or current practices in their organization and felt obliged to pursue the conclusions of that research. Two examples of MBO applications are presented: the GE work planning and review process and the case of a community hospital, St. Charles Hospital in Toledo, Ohio.

The General Electric Work Planning and Review Process

An illustration for application of the MBO program comes from the General Electric Company (GE), noted for its long-standing contributions in human resources management. GE addressed the concept of MBO by focusing on a "work planning and review process" based on certain internal research projects indicating significant opportunities for improved performance and working relationships (Aircraft Engine Division 1986, 4ff). The simplicity of the work planning and review process offers a wide range of applications.

Development of the work planning and review process. To get work done, there must be some form of continuous work planning. Supervisors give tasks and work to their subordinates and have a system to check the work to make sure it is being done properly. However, few supervisors make optimum use of time spent with subordinates because of difficulties inherent in the supervisor/subordinate relationship (e.g., operational problems, pressure of the business, and problems in communication). Concurrently, most subordinates want to do the job and most often feel that they do not understand fully what the boss expects of them. They desire clearer knowledge of how the boss thinks they are doing. Most subordinates want the feelings of accomplishment, interesting work, and additional responsibilities. They want the opportunity to offer suggestions to their superiors and to have those ideas weighed carefully, even though they may not be accepted. In other words, supervisors want to do a better job of managing, and subordinates want to improve their own performance. A question GE faced was, How do we set up conditions whereby people can be helped to do a better job?

We had hoped that its performance appraisal process would help, but research indicated that it did not. The biggest problem was found to be the conflicting roles of the supervisor as both counselor and judge. Because performance appraisal was tied so closely to salary decisions, the supervisor was forced to play the role of judge with regard to salary action, while at the same time the role of a counselor had to be assumed when the supervisor was advising employees on improving their work performance. These two roles simply did not seem compatible, and in the new approach they were separated. The next question was, How is it possible to provide a climate in which managers can act as helpers for their subordinates in improving work performance? The answer found by GE was "work planning and review."

What is work planning and review? Kessler (1981) points out that the work planning and review process consists of periodic informal meetings between subordinates and the supervisor. The meetings are oriented toward the daily work and result in mutual planning of the job and solving of problems that arise in the course of getting it done, and a progress review. The process, which does not involve formal ratings, was designed to take advantage of principles that relate to requisite conditions for subordinate motivation and performance enhancement. The three motivational principles are as follows:

1. An employee needs to know what is expected on the job.
2. An employee needs to know what progress he or she is making.
3. An employee needs to be able to obtain assistance when and as needed.

Figure 24-4 shows how the principles apply to the job.

A Community Hospital Example

Large profit-making corporations can use [a work planning and review process], but can it work in small, nonprofit type organizations such as a community hospital? An application in such a setting is illustrated by the goal-setting process of St. Charles Hospital in Toledo, Ohio. This is a medium-sized Catholic community hospital involved in an organizational development (OD) program over several years. The goal-setting process is viewed as an integral part of the OD activities and congruent with their basic principles and values.

Over the last several years various refinements in the process evolved. Changes were designed to encourage more ownership and commitment to the goals, simplify the paperwork, provide better linkage of individual objectives to key goal areas developed by top management, and focus more attention on results to be achieved rather than having fuzzy work plans or outcomes. More complex goals involving an integrated effort with other functions were developed as the skill and confidence level of managers improved.

The current process begins with an annual planning meeting by top management of the hospital to identify broad major categories of prime interest and high priority for the coming

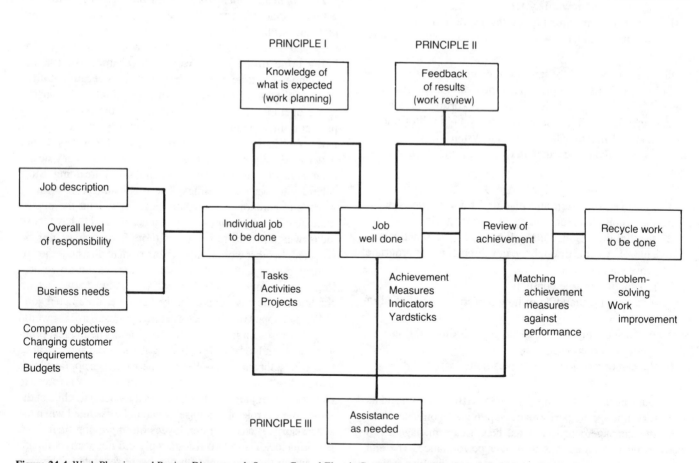

Figure 24-4 Work Planning and Review Diagrammed. *Source:* General Electric Company, Aircraft Engine Division, "Increasing Management Effectiveness through Work Planning," p. 4, General Electric Co, 1968.

year. From this, more detailed identification of related goals in each category is completed with accountability assigned to a specified member of top management. Budgeted resources are renewed to confirm allocation or adjustments. This process recently resulted in 6 broad categories and, subsequently, 46 specific goals for the hospital.

The six key goal areas are patient services, organizational development, education, physical plant, external affairs, and operational issues. Examples of specific goals in the patient services area are the "development of a program for nursing regarding role and duty to monitor quality of care," and "research feasibility of nurse practitioners and physician assistants to define role, assess feasibility, and determine training needed." Under organizational development, a goal specifies "identification of two unproductive norms evident in employee behavior as focus for management skill training." The operational issues cover a wide variety of matters such as a goal to "research and evaluate a new hospitalwide telephone system" and "develop an orientation program for new physicians added to the medical staff."

Department heads in collaboration with their respective division heads select goals applicable to their functional area. Goals requiring integration with functional interfaces are planned jointly, with a series of subgoals and work plans developed accordingly. In addition, intradepartmental goals and plans are developed based on the need and priority as perceived at that level. For example, a goal to revise certain internal scheduling routines for a department to improve efficiency could be of major importance to the department but not impact others directly. In effect, department heads have the responsibility to strike a balance between stated hospital goals where they have a participatory role and their own departmental objectives within the framework of allocated resources.

Goals and work plans are reviewed by division heads (top management team) to assure proper application of criteria for a well-stated goal, logical and complete work plans to achieve the result (including time frames and accountability), and appropriate measurements of progress, completion, and how well done.

Communication with all members of management on the final plans is done through group meetings to share the composite result. Other sharing techniques can be developed so long as adequate information is conveyed to those impacted, where coordinated efforts are required, and when a general overview of the coming year's work stimulates support and commitment from the total organization. Further communication usually takes place throughout all levels of the organization consistent with a participating style of management. Periodic reviews of progress or modification are necessary to maintain momentum, awareness, and commitment.

Developing and consistently implementing a strategic performance appraisal system to meet the needs of a particular organization can be a very rewarding process. For the PAS to be effective, however, it must be linked properly to a strategically designed reward system. A brief discussion of this relationship between extrinsic rewards and job performance follows.

EXTRINSIC REWARDS AND JOB PERFORMANCE

The findings of management studies vary substantially in rating such factors as pay and other extrinsic rewards in their relationship to job performance. However, many advantages are obvious when rewards are tied to performance, and this section advances strong support for this position. A variety of other rewards such as recognition and praise are equally important and should be used to complement the basic extrinsic rewards.

Lawler (1973) emphasized that the relationship between extrinsic reward level and performance has a crucial influence on organizational effectiveness. When extrinsic rewards are related to performance, the results are higher motivation and a tendency for turnover to be concentrated among the poor performers. Despite the obvious advantages of having rewards tied to performance, many organizations do not adopt this practice. Although there are some situations in which tying rewards to performance is dysfunctional, some organizations do not relate rewards to performance even when doing so would be highly functional.

Lawler's (1973) discussion of extrinsic rewards stresses the importance of who receives the extrinsic rewards given out by an organization. Each organization has a limited quantity of rewards to give. How they are distributed determines who will continue to work for an organization, how hard people will work, and the attitudes of employees toward the organization. Extrinsic rewards represent an investment in people, and such enhancements should be a crucial issue in any organization. Indeed, one effective way to understand an organization is to look at the actual distribution of its extrinsic rewards and how the arrangement is perceived by the employees. Determination of the relationship between extrinsic reward satisfaction and performance in an organization also can provide important information about the eventual impact of an organization's reward distribution system. A strong positive relationship between satisfaction and performance usually indicates a reward system that is functioning well and is rewarding good performance.

On the other hand, a negative relationship between satisfaction and performance indicates a poorly functioning reward system and should be taken as a warning. Specifically, such relationships mean that motivation is likely to be low because rewards are not clearly tied to performance. They also mean that turnover in the organization is likely to be centered among the high performers, a costly and extremely negative result for an organization attempting to improve its effectiveness or market share. Therefore, a performance appraisal system not linked to extrinsic rewards will not be as successful in motivating employees as one that is appropriately linked to these rewards. Generally, when performance measures are used, productivity will increase, and when pay-for-performance incentives are added, productivity can be expected to increase more significantly.

In summary, a positive relationship between extrinsic rewards and a good PAS should yield big motivational dividends within the organization, laying a solid foundation for other complementary rewards available within the organization.

SUMMARY

This chapter has advanced the case of performance appraisal as one of the most important processes in any organization. In some manner, all organizations do it, but the results may be either positive or negative.

Performance appraisal is not new; nor is there a single system appropriate for all organizations. This is particularly true in health organizations, which employ a multiplicity of highly trained individuals with widely diverse backgrounds, skills, and developmental needs.

A review of methods and of theories concerning the evaluation of performance appraisal provided background for discussion focused on the strategic role of performance appraisal within the human resources management system. The MBO method was selected as the PAS with the most comprehensive application for health care organizations, and guidelines for the implementation of such a system were given. Two case examples served to provide insight into the actual application process for two different organizations.

The importance of tying rewards to job performance, although not the primary focus of this chapter, was discussed briefly. If the PAS is to be a positive motivational force, it must be administered consistently by all levels of management and linked directly to the organization's reward system.

Any organization should seek to develop the PAS that best meets its needs. Special emphasis should be given to the human side of appraisal since, in the final analysis, the best system may be only an effective as it is *perceived* to be by the employees.

REFERENCES

Aircraft Engine Division. *Increasing Management Effectiveness through Work Planning*. New York: General Electric Company, 1986.

Brinkerhoff, Derick W., and Rosabeth Moss Kanter. "Appraising the Performance of Performance Appraisal." *Sloan Management Review* 21, no. 3 (Spring 1980): 3–16.

Cummings, L.L., and D.P. Schwab. *Performance in Organizations: Determinants and Appraisal*. Glenview, Ill.: Scott, Foresman & Co., 1973.

Deets, Norman R., and D. Timothy Tyler. "How Xerox Improved Its Performance Appraisals." *Personnel Journal* 65, no. 4 (April 1986): 50–52.

Dornbusch, S.M., and R.W. Scott. *Evaluation and the Exercise of Authority*. San Francisco: Jossey-Bass Inc., Pubs., 1975.

Douglas, John, Stuart Klein, and David Hunt. *The Strategic Managing of Human Resources*. New York: John Wiley & Sons, Inc., 1985. 391–405.

Drucker, Peter F. *The Practice of Management*. New York: Harper & Row, 1954.

Gerstenfeld, Arthur. "MBO Revisited: Focus on health systems." *Health Care Management Review* 2, no. 4 (Fall 1977): 51–5.

Glueck, William F. "Performance Evaluation and Development of Personnel" and "Performance evaluation and promotion." *Foundations of Personnel*. Plano, Tex.: Business Publications, 1978. 283–334.

Hand, Herbert H., and H. Thomas Hollingsworth. "Tailoring MBO to Hospitals." *Business Horizons* 18, no. 1 (February 1975): 45–52.

Harr, Linda Pohlman, and Judith Rohan Hicks. "Performance Appraisal: Derivation of Effective Assessment Tools." *Journal of Nursing Administration* 6, no. 7 (September 1976): 20–29, 37.

Holley, William H., and Hubert S. Feild. "Performance Appraisal and the Law." *Labor Law Journal* 26, no. 7 (July 1975): 423–30.

Kanter, R.M. *Men and Women of the Corporation*. New York: Basic Books, 1977.

Kearney, W.J. "Performance appraisal: Which way to go?" *MSU Business Topics* 25, no. 1 (Winter 1977): 58–64.

Kessler, Theodore W. "Management by objectives." In *Handbook of Health Care Human Resources Management*, edited by Norman Metzger, 181–92. Rockville, Md.: Aspen Publishers, Inc., 1981.

Latham, Gary P. "The Appraisal System As a Strategic Control." In *The Strategic Role of the Human Resource Management*, edited by Charles Fombrun, Noel M. Tichy, and Mary Anne Devanna. New York: John Wiley & Sons, Inc. 1984.

Lawler, E.E., III. *Motivation in Work Organizations*. Pacific Grove, Calif.: Brooks/Cole, 1973. 113–47.

Levitz, Gary S. "Performance appraisal in health organizations." In *Handbook of Health Care Human Resources Management*, edited by Norman Metzger, 225–38. Rockville, Md.: Aspen Publishers, Inc., 1981.

Lowe, Terry R. "Eight Ways To Run a Performance Review." *Personnel Journal* 65, no. 1 (January 1986): 60–62.

McConkie, Mark L. "A Clarification of the Goal Setting and Appraisal Process in MBO." *Academy of Management Review* 4, no. 1 (1979): 29–37.

McCormick, R.R. "Can We Use Compensation Data To Measure Job Performance Behavior?" *Personnel Journal* 51, no. 12 (December 1972): 918–22.

McGregor, Douglas. *The Human Side of Enterprise*. New York: McGraw-Hill Book Co., 1960.

Migliore, R. Henry. "The use of long-range planning/MBO for hospital administrators." *Health Care Management Review* 4, no. 3 (Summer 1979): 23–28.

Sashkin, Marshall. "Appraising appraisal: Ten lessons from research for practice." *Assessing Performance Appraisal*, 120–28. San Diego, Calif.: University Associates, 1981.

Scott, W. Richard. "Organizational effectiveness: Studying the quality of surgical care in hospitals." In *Environment and Organization*, edited by M. Meyer. San Francisco: Jossey-Bass Inc., Pubs., 1978.

Thompson, J.D. *Organizations in Action*. New York: McGraw-Hill Book Co., 1967.

Gregory T. Finnegan
Fred W. Graumann

25

Guest Relations: Creating a Supportive Environment for Patients, Visitors, and Employees

INTRODUCTION—THE HEALTH CARE ENVIRONMENT

When a patient becomes an inpatient in an acute care facility, that person loses all identity and status (is not a carpenter, homemaker, salesperson, or executive—but a patient); is placed in a dehumanized environment (gives up clothing and jewelry representing status, style, and individuality—for a dressing gown, most frequently open in the rear); generally knows little about what is going to be done to/for him/her (generally has not enough medical knowledge to make an informed judgment); has to give up desired foods; and so on.

While that phenomenon has moved in one direction, another force, consumerism—a movement that has at its heart the desire to be treated fairly and individually—has grown. Meanwhile, the American economy continues to be in transition from a manufacturing economy, to a service economy, to an information economy.

One result of these many forces has been the desire/demand of the patient to be treated like a customer and to recapture some sense of control. There is no question that there are continuing driving forces for change (Eck et al. 1988).

Some surveys done regionally and across the country show that between 81 and 98 percent of patients surveyed are satisfied with the care they received (Pascoe, Wilson, and Worsfold 1978). But still, the health care industry is under pressure to provide high quality–high tech–high touch care, to contain costs, to reverse the trends in malpractice litigation, and to demystify medicine. All this has taken place while the pay-ment system has changed to require the institution providing such care to compete not only for resources to provide care, but also for patients.

Within the last 10 years, the demand for guest relations has emerged as a response to attract and retain customers—to become "user friendly." Guest relations programs have to do with not only sensitivity to increased self-awareness of what we do, but also sensitivity to an even greater critical view of how we do what we do. They begin with a focus on the other person—the patient, the visitor, the other employees. Especially in the health care industry it is a combination of the golden rule, "Do unto others as you would have them do unto you," and its more modern counterpart, "Do unto others as they would have you do unto them." It is the focus on those who receive our products and services: what they need, in what form, and how we will know that what we do is helpful to them. Knowing the extent of our success in accomplishing these has important implications for the quality of care and for our financial survival (Neuhauser and Murphy 1988).

The message of the guest relations program is to provide excellence in a team manner. Administrators would like to see employees believe and act on this mindset: "The way I handle each situation before me can prove to be the determining factor in the decision of a patient or visitor as to whether their total experience is a positive one." Several studies show that the patient's perception of employee competence directly affects that patient's satisfaction (Cleary and McNeil 1988). Such a framework—worked any number of ways—actualizes the hospital service imperative: namely, to ensure that all who require service, visit the sick, or work in this environment will be treated both in terms of medical care and on a personal level in a courteous, professional, and caring manner. The issue is how to get there.

Five years ago a multidisciplinary task force at Robert Wood Johnson University Hospital was charged with the responsibility of identifying the "right" customer relations program for us. This effort ended in frustration because what was available in the marketplace was very expensive, was recast from another industry (airline, hotel, etc.) and did not quite fit us, or, if health-care-based, had been designed to specifically meet the needs of the originating organization. Additionally, many of the products we reviewed were based on negative feedback and examples of people doing things wrong. They concentrated more on what not to do than on what to do.

TRADITIONAL APPROACHES TO PROGRAM METHODOLOGIES

Traditional approaches suffer from a use of methods that neither support the objectives of a guest relations program nor fulfill the message inherent in such a program. In the traditional approaches, guest relations programs seem to use traditional teaching methods to a large extent. The predominant method is still to *lecture*, sometimes with *videos/films* and simple discussion, in *multiple sessions* to deliver the message. There are problems with each of these three methods.

The basic lecture approach is to *tell* people what to do. This is not necessarily bad. Using the leadership model by Hersey and Blanchard (1982), the "tell and sell" approach provides the correct leadership style in many circumstances. In fact, such a style could be said to be seriously lacking in many companies and health care organizations. The "tell and sell" approach suggests a leader who uses persuasion to convince subordinates of the correctness or appropriateness of a decision or policy. The telling or lecture approach in guest relations, however, can ignore three somewhat overlapping sensitivities.

1. A telling and selling approach, though focused on people *and* getting the job done, works best with people who are new or inexperienced, and generally not with the more mature and accomplished professional.
2. An approach that spells out what things to do/not do—a lecture approach—turns the presenter into a preacher.
3. Those who sit and listen to a lecture may very well perceive themselves as being "talked down to" and can feel insulted that an underlying message is that they do not do the very things being espoused.

So, too, videos and films are routinely used in training to demonstrate how to do something. The expectation of the viewers will be that these are the best examples of doing something specific the right way. These portrayals, however,

can rarely succeed because of too many elements that can go wrong.

- The visuals never include enough examples or situations that encompass enough of the guest relations imperative.
- The scripts have actors saying things that don't ring true, that sound stilted, or that seem unrealistic.
- The scripts concentrate on what not to do and contain many examples of people doing the wrong things.
- The actors overact or offer expressions that exaggerate the point the script and story are trying to make, thus portraying the characters—nurses, housekeepers, clerks, etc.—as very insulting, sarcastic, and unfeeling.

Do these exaggerated scenes occur in a hospital—or in any organization in the world? Yes, absolutely they do. But are they the norm? More likely the scenes that actually take place involve simpler actions, such as forgetting, not listening, not following up, etc.

Here is the dilemma. If such scenes are the norm for an institution, then the above approaches might very well be very effective. If the managers of a particular organization can say, "We have serious problems!" and those examples represent the problems, this overall approach can work. On the other hand, if such is not the case, the negative focus not only misrepresents the issues of a particular institution, but also fails to give people credit for the majority of their existing guest relations sensitivities. The result can be that a work force will not see a gap between their current performance and the desired performance, but rather they may feel insulted and not motivated toward improvement.

These lecture and video/film methods are typically used in a program that requires people to attend multiple sessions. The result all too often is that people start to miss sessions. They create the need to miss: census is up, too busy, have a conflict, forgot. Succeeding groups of employees then fail to attend the sessions. The word is out: the program is a turkey. The organization's managers support the employees, and, ironically, their lack of leadership in support of a guest relations effort may make them look bad to their staff. Administrators find themselves between a rock and a hard place. "It's not playing well out there." Another program—this time the guest relations program—fails like many others and dies from lack of support. The initial message of providing treatment in a personal, courteous, professional, and caring manner is replaced with another: "We're no worse than anyone else," "We provide quality when we can get around to it," or "We do our best to avoid unpleasantness to all."

These methods fail to get commitment. The lecture approach is the method that is least successful at getting commitment. The key to such a successful effort is using methodologies that support the commitment of people to a desired end. Teaching deductive reasoning by the deductive method, for example, will greatly aid the learning of the method.

On reflection, we felt that the best of these commercially available programs could be reduced to a number of principles. Armed with these distilled principles, we decided to "build our own." How to get commitment is the next key issue.

STRATEGY TO ACHIEVE ORGANIZATION COMMITMENT

No matter what form the guest relations program takes, whether home grown or store bought, and no matter how it is designed, whether small or large, the vital link between desire and reality is commitment. The problem for many organizations when they try to get commitment for a program is that they have a poor track record of getting commitment on other programs—especially on programs that try to instill or sell some idealized performance at the worker level.

All too frequently the performance desired by the top for the bottom is just that—for the bottom. Either the same performance doesn't apply to the top, or the top allows for token gestures for a very specific period of time, at which point perquisites and privilege prevail.

Guest relations programs can be deadly to administrations. Failure to see any change at the administrative level will probably ensure failure to see change at any level. Guest relations is first and foremost a test of leadership. As a special program it tests leadership in terms of support and follow-up (Peters and Waterman 1982). "Do we really have to go? Do we really have to do something new?" How our formal and informal leaders answer such questions determines whether leadership is seen as strong or weak: "Do we have to do it?" "Well, if you're too busy, don't worry about it."

What could become a point of true leadership becomes the abdication of the leader's role in deference to the uninspired convenience of the banal and commonplace. The employee who is to rejuvenate a lost sense of "customer satisfaction" draws the conclusion that "it doesn't really matter." Commitment begins somewhere, and commitment begets commitment.

We see four elements to getting the work force—employees, supervisors, and managers—to support a worthy goal: involvement, clear expectations, feedback, and demonstration by management of some changes.

Involvement

The Japanese offer example enough of the power of involvement of employees *before* management decision making and action: improved product, service, market share, and world consumer respect. Too often we still decide and act—and then involve. The purpose of involvement is to make a product or service better, while at the same time providing someone with the opportunity to feel some modicum of control

and ownership over her or his needs to create and be a part of what is happening. Millions of beautiful plants die each year because they are not nurtured. The failure to nurture results when people feel no ownership of or caring for the plant. The initial bonding of parents to a newborn is powerful in bringing forth the nurturing instincts of the parents. Involvement is a process that bonds people not only to the output of a new program, but also to the principles of it (Peters and Austin 1985).

Managers, like subordinates, frequently decry the feeling, and the fact, that they are not consulted; nobody in upper management asks for their opinion. They want to feel involved, but seldom are. If guest relations is a test of leadership, management needs to feel involved. Managers need to have input into critical points, such as how the program is handled in their area, and involvement in identifying what constitutes excellent performance in their area. The simple integration of efforts begins here in a process of employees and managers working toward a common goal of improvement (Kanter 1983).

Clear Expectations

Any human being, given the physical and mental capabilities, can perform in a desired manner if provided with clear expectations—that is to say, desires or worthy performance must be clearly stated in positive terms. Workers should be able to say to themselves, "I will succeed by doing the following. . . ."

If an individual cannot enumerate exactly what constitutes desired behavior, he or she will, in the best case, provide it only on a spot basis or will, in the worst case, not provide it at all. McDonald's Corporation takes the time to first spell out what each person does in general—provide quality, service, value, and cleanliness. Then it spells out the specific tasks that illustrate the accomplishment of the desired general performance goals. If you do not see good performance in your local McDonald's, you are witnessing failure to execute what is already known; the fault is with management (Peters and Waterman 1982).

Feedback

The roles of the manager and the supervisor need clear articulation. Their roles involve the need to look for and recognize the positive and to coach the less-than-expected performance. The critical issue, after being able to articulate what desired performance is, is to look for it to happen. Managers need to work at catching employees doing something right and reinforcing it.

The same holds true for upper-level managers who must show support by including guest relations in regular meetings with their department heads. This models the performance expectation of the department head for her or his employees.

Tom Peters, coauthor of *In Search of Excellence* and *Passion for Excellence* in a *Hospitals* magazine interview said, "Hospital administration should constantly be on the lookout for the good things employees do and ought to acknowledge them with a note, a simple "thanks" or maybe a dinner for two" (1987, 91).

In *The One Minute Manager*, Kenneth Blanchard and Spencer Johnson espouse a motto: "Help people reach their full potential; catch them doing something right" (1981, 39).

Feedback becomes statements and actions that confirm desired performance, identify undesirable or less-than-desired performance, and coach for improvement. Like the nurse who cannot treat an infection if she can't identify it, we cannot congratulate or correct performance if we don't look for it first.

Then, recognition is the next key. The cornerstone of exceptional work group performance is to look for the positive and worthy performance and then recognize and reward it. Spotting aberrant behavior and correcting it is still critical, but secondary to looking for things done right.

The managers and supervisors must see that their roles of being a positive model and giving regular, ongoing feedback are inextricably intertwined. Part of one's right to coach another toward worthy performance is that that same person exhibits that performance. They need to create their own expectation that there will be a lot of positive performance to recognize and reward.

Upper-level managers need to reinforce the actions taken by their middle managers. They should ask them, "What else can we do?" They need to cheerlead middle managers and supervisors and always ask them for testimony of good performance. They need to ask for and coach to get specific answers. Again, this attention to detail and this spirit of the program are then being modeled for the middle managers and supervisors.

Management's Demonstration of Change

Asking people to do anything without adequate reason to do it invites criticism and, worse, benign neglect. Before creating strategies to answer all the criticisms, questions, and complaints, the more important issue is what management will do—and, more succinctly, do differently. There has to be some discernible difference in action and attitude that will be clearly observable and will provide some model for the value and inherent benefit of what the new program requests. Like the new CEO who paints the lobby to leave a sign that there is someone new here and that something else new will probably happen, administrators and managers must clearly demonstrate change that will be perceived as cause and effect by employees.

Managers and supervisors need the support of upper-level management as they prepare and face their employees. Managers and supervisors need to show some changes in their areas that indicate a greater sensitivity to patients, visitors, and other employees. If the demonstration of commitment by management and upper management is to be fulfilled, there has to be

conversation between management levels and agreement on what changes will take place to support the mission and principles of the new program. The conversations are successful when managers and supervisors can identify what is being done through management decision making and action. This will give employees confidence that managers and supervisors will support the cause and rally these employees to its targets.

Upper management should look for ways for the board to be involved. These can include planned or unplanned donations or activities. Donating funds for pictures to hang in a barren waiting room is an example of an unplanned donation. A planned donation takes place when a planned improvement provides an opportunity to make a link between the program and the planned improvement. Though not cause and effect with regard to the program, it shows the integration of activity in a common purpose.

No matter how good people feel about the program, there have to be changes to point to. Everyone—employees through upper management—needs to know that as a result of his or her efforts specific improvements occurred. If the program is to benefit patients, there should be a series or list of accomplishments. The same is true for visitors and employees. People need to see the fruits of their labor. (Making blankets available in clinical areas for patients awaiting testing, adding public telephones for families/visitors in waiting areas, providing information to those waiting—all represent the kinds of thou-ordered sensitivity guests are looking for.) The integrity of the program and its longevity require the evidence and track record of proven success. People identify with success and will be inclined to keep their performance focused over the longer haul and provide in very conscious ways the excellence in performance that is desired.

GOOD PERFORMANCE REQUIREMENTS

Achieving the desired outcome of any guest relations program requires a model that views performance in a systematic way. The principles we have delineated thus far suggest that the positive, face-to-face outcomes of customer orientation and customer satisfaction do not occur merely because people are inherently good; nor do they occur because people are asked to do them. People excel in their performance when their performance is seen as part of a larger system that supports people in their efforts to perform well and do worthwhile work (Gilbert 1978). Six elements need to be in place in order to support desired performance. These elements comprise the basic requirements of a performance model that exemplifies a systems view of ensuring good performance.

Feedback

Feedback needs to be clear. The biggest single cause of performance deterioration over time, or performance failures of any kind, is the lack or inadequacy of feedback. When people get no feedback on their performance, they will often draw erroneous conclusions.

- "I must be doing well; nobody says anything."
- "Nobody says anything, and nothing happens when I don't do *X*, so I guess *X* must not be that important."
- "When I take a short cut and do just *X* instead of *X* and *Y*, it is easier for me, and no one seems to care or notice."

These examples are not meant to suggest that people are bad. In fact, people draw logical conclusions about their performance when working in a vacuum without feedback. The first two examples are very rational conclusions to make. Work groups typically have a strong sense of what is very important. Unfortunately, that primary attention usually goes to solving problems and putting out fires. The "important" things are always talked about and worried about. The "important" things involve overtime and extra work and expense control.

Setting up a simple feedback system on a particular performance will dramatically improve that performance. Feedback tells people first and foremost that a particular activity is important, no matter how simple or commonplace it may seem. Throughout the working day, week, and month, people need ongoing feedback. Providing this feedback as close in time to the performance as possible enhances the desired outcome by reinforcing the good or appropriate performance and identifying and correcting the less desirable.

Clear feedback is feedback that is simple, so that people can understand the message. Telling someone to answer the phone "better" is too vague and subject to misinterpretations and frustration. Clear feedback stems from performance requirements that tell an employee to answer a phone by the third ring and say, "Good morning, Accounts Payable Department." Clear feedback is to say, "I've noticed that in the last three or four calls you have made an obvious effort to answer the phone by the third ring. I appreciate that. It gives the right message to the callers." Another example of clear feedback is to say, "Don't forget to say 'Good morning' when you answer the phone. It's a friendly tone that will be appreciated by the callers." This type of feedback should occur as often as is necessary for the employee to correctly interpret the desired performance level.

Procedures

Procedures need to work for the patient, as well as for the organization. Problems involving the way we get things done—procedures and tasks—constantly occur and result in inconveniences to patients and visitors, extra work for employees, and poor to bad communication between patients/visitors and employees and among employees. Inherent flaws in procedures can be at least twofold.

1. The procedure doesn't work well; because it is not designed well enough to accomplish a specified goal, it needs to be redesigned. For example, one way to make sure that Admitting gets all registration forms from every outpatient service is to require patients to go to Admitting as a final stop. The result can be complaints and noncompliance, especially if there is a penalty for not going to Admitting.
2. The procedure works well when standing by itself; the problem is that it doesn't work well in the context of other procedures that must be completed or that it doesn't fit within certain time periods. The procedure in question or another procedure may have to be altered to accommodate the contextual constraints. For example, having Admitting do an insurance verification at the point of admission can become time consuming and frustrating to patients, visitors, and employees, and, therefore, a new procedure may be needed.

Consequences of Performance

Consequences of performance need to be appropriate—i.e., the desired consequence for the desired behavior should be positive. At the very least, there should not be a negative consequence for the desired behavior. Neither should there be a positive consequence for doing an undesirable or competing behavior. One can predict what will happen when a behavior is positively reinforced: it will be repeated. Sadly though, managers find it difficult to provide meaningful positive reinforcement and recognition. Managers fear that "if I reward them today, I may have to reward them tomorrow." As a result, we tend to celebrate birthdays in the work group and not accomplishments.

A serious problem occurs when people do what is asked of them and something punishing happens to them. Often addressing all of the elements of the performance model will create changes in procedures that will of themselves remove the anger and frustration caused by the way things get done. When people are able to get their work done in the most efficient and effective manner, they will be less frustrated and less inclined to express frustration and anger, thus helping to avoid poor relationships. Improving feedback, changing procedures, improving the environment, improving skill, and increasing knowledge—these are the ways to remove "bad" consequences.

Another serious problem occurs when positive consequences occur for people who are either doing the wrong things or doing secondary things at the expense of more important activities. While people may avoid painful activities, they may still choose to do things that may be counterproductive to the goals of the work group. People cannot be blamed for trying to make their jobs easier or more convenient. Many innovations result from this desire. The problem occurs when a less-than-desirable behavior that is more pleasant is performed at the expense of the group's effectiveness.

Environment

The environment must support good performance. Managers can hope for good performance if resources are not available, but they cannot expect it. Employees need the appropriate support of people, supplies, and equipment. Floor plans need to support the flow of work and should be changed if they sufficiently impede the job's getting done. In addition to functional support, the environment should be sufficiently attractive to create a pleasant atmosphere. Moving things around, recreating supply space, or simply standardizing where things are kept or done can improve people's performance by reducing irritable inconveniences.

Skills

People need the skill to do the job. One simple question to ask about performance that is not up to standard or is not being done at all is "Could an employee do it if his or her life depended on it?" In almost every case you will find that the answer is "yes." This will tell you that the poor performance is caused by a system problem; in other words, the problem has to do with feedback, procedures, consequences, or the environment. If, on the other hand, the answer is "no," then this suggests that people lack the capacity to do the task. The issue of skill is one of capacity to do something. Some people can pass CPR tests that are written, but they fail actual performance tests. They *know* how to do CPR, but they lack the *capacity* to do CPR. Skill, or capacity, is easily addressed by giving an individual opportunity to practice. While this is generally not a guest relations issue, it can be when cultures and language are an issue with a work force.

Knowledge

People need to know what to do. People often have fuzzy expectations about what they really are supposed to be doing in certain situations. Overall, most people in most circumstances perform well. But for everyone there are certain situations that arise that make it difficult to perform as desired. A nurse may know how to treat an infected site, but perhaps he or she is not as certain how to identify all the signs that indicate when an infection is beginning. The result in this case is that without the knowledge necessary to discern when to act, the infection gets very serious before treatment begins.

Once clearly identified, knowledge deficiencies are the easiest to correct. If escorts do not know how to engage people in simple conversation, they need to be trained. If nurses do not know how to identify all signs of infection, then train them. In

both examples, the training should include some practice to help the knowledge facilitate a new skill.

Initial Program Strategy

Based on all the principles stated thus far, we began with a five-point strategy for success. The five elements begin with defining the mission and end with making changes. Everything in between is a controlled attempt to work at successfully influencing people to consciously and actively involve themselves in the guest relations effort. The strategy begins with the broad goal made more tangible in the language of the health care worker. Involvement, evaluation, and change follow. The steps are

- Define the mission.
- Create clear expectations.
- Create feedback within work groups.
- Correct procedural and environmental problems.
- Make easier improvements quickly.

Define the Mission

Failure occurs in most work groups—and in most organizations—because people work with only a fuzzy sense of mission. The focus of the guest relations effort on patient-centered satisfaction behavior, procedures, and environment makes the message of mission real to employees (Cleary and McNeil 1988). The switchboard operator and the radiology file room receptionist who say their mission is to answer phones are not focused well to provide quality care. More than likely the fault is not theirs. The mission of the operator and the file room receptionist is to provide people with access to the information they need. That is a closer statement of their mission. Answering the phone is merely the vehicle provided to achieve the mission.

Create Clear Expectations

We borrow from Tom Peters when we tell employees that creating a memorable responsiveness and distinction comes from doing a thousand things a tiny bit better, not one thing a thousand percent better. That is Excellence. Excellence comes from people, not technology. Excellence is about caring, people, consistency, eye contact and gut reaction. Excellence comes from the belief that anything can be made better, and that Excellence is universally achievable (Peters, 1985).

The service imperative that cries for excellence, as we see it, is that patients bring an expectation when they use a health care service. They expect that in this experience they will be treated clinically and personally in a courteous, professional, and caring manner. Each element is important in providing excellence in guest relations.

Courtesy is increasingly a higher expectation as more and more people in this country work in service companies where customer relations and customer satisfaction are conditions of employment, performance evaluation, and promotion. *Hospitals* magazine reported a survey of 1,000 nationwide health care consumers by Professional Research Consultants, Inc., and *Hospitals*. The question was, "When selecting a hospital, what do you consider 'very important'?" Respondents rated staff courtesy first, ahead of technology, variety of specialties, M.D. recommendation, cost of service, proximity to home, and religious affiliation ("M.D. Influence" 1987). People draw immediate conclusions when someone is not courteous. This casts doubt on the outcome of the rest of their encounters with staff and departments.

Professionalism is the ability to predict and repeat excellence (Cleary and McNeil 1988). It is the ability to control the situation or treatment with clients and move it toward a successful conclusion. And, most importantly, it is the ability to recognize the need for control by the patient over what is happening.

Professionalism is an expectation in any medical facility where so many people receive so much training. The lay public is mostly unable to judge clinical competence. They are, however, very able to judge its delivery and the amenities surrounding it. People treated poorly as a result of staff, department, or hospital procedure will question individual, work group, department, and hospital competence. They can conclude that we don't know what we are doing or that the right hand doesn't even know that the left hand exists. Simple human responses, such as listening, answering questions, and encouraging questions, help support the professional image (Matthews and Feinstein 1988).

Caring is what health care delivery is all about. Hospitals must be caring places. Caring is greatly appreciated by all human beings. They are touched deeply when anyone shows them caring. Caring is greater than courtesy. Courtesy is answering questions; caring is looking for the answers when you don't have them. Courtesy is responding to people; caring is talking to them to help get them comfortable in their surroundings. When courtesy is not extended, people get angry. When caring is not extended, people will probably not notice its absence. When courtesy *is* shown, people appreciate it, but they have an expectation that that is the *least* they will get. When caring is shown, people notice it and feel very good about themselves, the situation they are in, the people showing the caring, the work group, the department, and the hospital. The demonstration of caring is the strength of the health care worker. Caring is exhibited by a smile, one's tone of voice, and attempts to solve problems. These become the basis for much of the patient's evaluation of service (Spicer, Graft, and Rose 1988).

What constitutes excellence in courtesy, professionalism, and caring requires a list of specific desired behaviors. This is

what will be in evidence if we are providing excellence. Patients, visitors, and other employees will see it, but we who provide the service to those three groups will be able to articulate it. We will change specific performance from the vague to the specific. Where we now say, "The doctor will be right with you," we may say, "The doctor will be with you in 15 minutes." In this example, we can create satisfaction by providing a more accurate and realistic patient expectation (Jensen 1988). We will leave nothing to chance. We need to get beyond good intentions.

We want to be able to recreate the motivation of clinical people when they first started saving money to go to school to become a nurse, X-ray technician, lab technician, physician, etc. We also want to get nonclinical people to acknowledge the added value they derive from working in a health care environment. Although it is clear that many health care professionals feel strongly about the contribution they make to humanity and society, the identification is made by environmental services workers, secretaries, accounting clerks, and other nondirect patient care workers as well.

Finally, we want all employees, clinical and nonclinical, to see the value of their individual contributions in the context of the teamwork, cooperation, and mutual respect that is achievable by a group of individuals committed to a common mission.

How do we get the articulation of behavior that is the focus of the commitment? Ask employees for it! In fact, the major activity of the entire effort is to ask employees, as many as possible, to identify what would be observable if their work group were providing excellence better than any other work group providing the same service. That list becomes the focal point of several activities to follow, but primarily it is the articulation of what we will do to provide excellence. This list is not all inclusive. Rather, it becomes a list of what to focus on now. The list will be redone regularly so as to become an ongoing attempt to answer this basic question: "What else should we be doing?"

Create Feedback within Work Groups

Following from the performance model, creating a feedback loop from clients—patients, visitors, and employees—is important. Asking for feedback regularly on specific performance parameters suggests a healthy work group intent on service and integrity. The feedback is on the clear expectations identified by the employees of the work group. The feedback loop is twofold: employee self-assessment and client evaluation.

Once the desired performances of excellence are identified, all employees in the area should complete a self-assessment on how well they feel they are performing them as a group. An employee may feel that he or she is doing specific performances extremely well, but that the same performances are not done well by the group in general. The self-assessment asks each employee to identify for each performance how often he or she feels it is done and how well it is done when it is done.

A summary of the total assessment will be shared with all employees. The list can be summarized by ranking the performances from the most frequently done to the least frequently done. This initial assessment raises four issues.

1. What are the three highest-rated performances?
2. What are the three lowest-rated performances?
3. What can we do to increase the frequency and quality of the lowest performances?
4. How will our self-assessment compare to our client's evaluation?

When employees get the results of this survey of colleagues, they are given the dates for client evaluations and asked to create an action plan to improve the frequency of the performances rated very low. Employees are very interested in the results of these self-assessments.

The second step in the feedback loop is to get patients, visitors, and employees to evaluate a work group. The performances identified by a work group as constituting excellence are used in the self-assessment as well as the client evaluation. The client summaries will also be shared with employees and compared, and the same four questions apply as listed above for their self-assessment. The outcome of the client survey is used in the same manner as that of the self-assessment. An action plan for improvements is made, to be reported to staff within the month. One element of this plan is to determine the frequency of patient/visitor/client evaluations.

Correct Procedural and Environmental Problems

The work done with the work group and its clients will raise issues about problems created by faulty procedures or the environment. Clients may be required to wait or return to an area or be forced to walk over a long distance in a hospital because of procedures that are themselves incomplete or poorly designed. Clients may have to return to a department because no one checked their paperwork there, and they may easily get lost because of inadequate signage. Identifying these problems and working toward resolving them will create simple improvements in administrative areas and clinical areas alike (Kazemek and Mizaur 1987; Tabak 1987).

Many of these problems cause great aggravation to patients, visitors, and employees. Correcting them will reduce frustration, while reinforcing the message of the guest relations effort: excellence that exhibits treatment in a courteous, professional, and caring manner.

Make Easier Improvements Quickly

Like the new CEO who paints the lobby to make a statement, management must make as many changes identified in this process as possible—and as quickly as possible. The action of making improvements is itself a statement of purpose, resolve, and commitment under the umbrella of guest relations. Action says that the effort is very important. Words are wasted; actions do speak louder than words. The actions tell employees that we are listening to patients, we are listening to visitors, and we are listening to you. Who is doing the listening? The employees' administrators, department heads, and supervisors are listening. The message receives testimony by action; this effort is important—thus, simple evaluation surveys become an active management tool (Kerruish, Wickings, and Tarrant 1988).

IMPLEMENTATION STRATEGY—PHASE 1: DEPARTMENTAL

The following is offered as a 10-step process from meeting initially with the manager to drafting a six-month plan for improvement. The entire process can take one year and could be considered the first phase of a two-year, two-phase effort. The steps are as follows:

1. The first step is for the program coordinator to meet with the department manager and discuss the overall department plan. The entire series of steps will be laid out for the manager. The objective is to sell the manager on the process that includes input from employees, supervisors, and managers and that will gain commitment, give credit to employees for what they do well, and focus their efforts in a more articulated way to improve customer satisfaction in a nonthreatening, rather than a negative or condescending, way. Managers need to begin having the expectation that they will have to make some changes and that those changes will be their statement of the value of excellence in guest relations.

2. The second step is to meet with department supervisors and orient them to the program and their role in it. The stress is on the value of their modeling guest relations behavior in a positive way, looking for correct and desired performance (catching people doing something right), offering feedback, and positively reinforcing desired behavior when it happens. These are the key supervisory responsibilities in creating a client-centered culture. Guest relations needs to be defined beyond interpersonal issues. Guest relations is first and foremost an interpersonal focus—but it is also procedural and environmental. Supervisors need to create an expectation that some things may have to be changed—if only a little—if they create situations that are in themselves working against good guest relations. Supervisors will need examples: one example: patients who must return unnecessarily to a department because of incomplete paperwork are victims of a procedural flaw; another example: patients who wander through

the corridors looking for a department because of the absence or inadequacy of signage are victims of environmental flaws. Improvements will be interpersonal, procedural, and environmental.

3. The third step is to meet with department staff to identify excellence in guest relations. If all of the staff cannot be included, then representatives—at least 20 percent of the work group—need to be identified. The criteria for selecting representatives are that they have some proven sensitivity to customer satisfaction and that they are not shy in a group. The question for the group is simple and will be answered in two sessions: "If we are providing guest relations better than anyone else providing this department's service, what would someone see?" The group should then be told that answers need to be observable and specific. These answers will relate to interpersonal communication—that is obvious—but they should also identify procedural and environmental snafus that make us all look bad: the cold waiting room, the absence of a public restroom or telephone, etc.

4. The fourth step is to meet again with the manager and the supervisors to share the results of the employee sessions. The main purpose now is to ask the supervisors and the manager the same question you asked of employees. It is now their turn to identify what excellence looks like. They are encouraged to consider issues that should have been identified by employees because they are problems. For example, answering the phone correctly or quickly (e.g., by the third ring) may have been an issue at one time, but was not mentioned by employees as an issue of excellence. Now, it can be added. The second task is to identify from the procedural and environmental grouping those items that are within the control of the manager and can be improved now and those that will take inquiry and/or money to improve. A simple plan for follow-up on these should be established. The goal is to give status reports on these when it comes time to see employees and discuss guest relations.

5. The fifth step is to meet again with employees in the department. This employee session introduces the goal of excellence and specifies the final list of excellence items identified by the staff in the department. The whole plan is presented for discussion and questions/answers. The final activity is to have the staff do a self-assessment as to how well they feel the work group as a whole accomplishes each item along two parameters: the first is frequency; the second is a subjective view of how well each item is done when it is done. The staff should fill out a self-assessment for the department as well as one for themselves individually. The department self-assessment is handed in; the individual self-assessment is kept by the employee. The individual self-assessment is a self-assessment of each employee's own performance. Retaining a copy allows

her or him to keep a list of the issues of excellence, as well as providing a personal benchmark for future surveys.

6. The sixth step is to meet once again with the manager and the supervisors. This manager/supervisor follow-up meeting includes review of the summary of the surveys before returning them to the employees. The goal of this session is to review the role of the supervisors and the manager in improving performance. The emphasis is on routine checking of performance with an effort to look for the positive to happen. Then the focus shifts to feedback and recognition of good performance. The major objective is persuasion: persuading the supervisors and the manager to see the power in positive reinforcement and to identify the supervisory activities required to provide it.

7. The seventh step is to meet again with employees. This employee follow-up meeting to share the results of the self-assessment is critical. The staff is given credit for the three highest-rated items and asked to review the three lowest-rated items. The question regarding the three lowest-rated items is "What can we do to increase the frequency and quality with which we do the three lowest-rated items?" Suggestions are noted, and a simple plan is made. The objective is to get agreement on doing something to improve the lowest items. Then the dates of the patient/visitor evaluation are scheduled. This period of evaluation should last for one week to one month.

8. The eighth step is to conduct the patient/visitor evaluation. The appropriate client audiences are asked to fill out surveys about the performance of the work group. For clinical areas these audiences are patients and visitors; for some support areas, like Accounts Payable, the audience may be employees. The questions should be designed to elicit a yes/no response. For example, one issue of excellence might be worded as follows: "Did we greet you when you entered our department?" The choices would be "yes," "no," "yes, in an excellent manner," or "was not an issue for me." When summarized, we can tell staff the total percentage who said "yes" we did do something. We can also tell staff what percentage judged the task to be done "in an excellent manner." We can also offer some indication of the relative importance of some items. For instance, suppose 99 percent of the respondents answered this question: "Did we demonstrate an attempt to listen to you through making eye contact, facing you, and acknowledging what you said?" The large response to that question suggests that this issue is very important to all clients—patients, visitors, and employees.

9. The ninth step is to meet again with employees to share the results of the client survey. Employees receive the summary of the client evaluations at this follow-up meeting and are asked to compare it with the results of

their own evaluation. Both the highest- and lowest-rated items are compared. Employees are also asked to identify how their perceptions differ from and match those of the clients. As was done for the self-assessment, it is important to recognize the items that clients rate the highest for the work group. Employees then make a simple plan to improve on the lowest items. The meeting ends with the determination of when the next client evaluation will take place.

10. The tenth step is to have a wrap-up meeting with the manager. The purpose is to draft a simple plan for activities that can occur in the department during the remainder of the year. For each activity the issue will be to determine the frequency and dates of occurrence. A list of activities includes:

a. supervisory monitoring of activities of guest relations performance
b. supervisory reporting of monitored activities
c. employee recognition events
d. goal-setting activities
e. guest relations reporting in regular staff meetings
f. specific dates to repeat client evaluations
g. specific dates to discuss and revise/add to original issues of excellence
h. Additional programs that will maintain or improve excellence in guest relations (e.g., programs on telephone courtesy, dealing with difficult situations, and dealing with others' feelings).

IMPLEMENTATION STRATEGY—PHASE 2: ORGANIZATION

Phase 1 described a department-specific process that involves the individuals and work groups of a department. Phase 2 is a hospitalwide effort that has three components: public relations, supervisory meetings, and employee meetings.

Public Relations

One failure of many guest relations efforts is that they begin with a public relations effort. The thinking is that the awareness factor is being addressed with something substantive to follow. A better approach is to create the substance first and then gernerate the PR. The PR effort is akin to the new CEO's painted lobby. It is a reminder that something new is happening. A PR effort needs to include many elements. They can include, but are certainly not limited to, the following:

- choosing an employee of the month
- publishing letters in the hospital newspaper that have been written by patients, visitors, and employees giving credit for excellence performance

- providing a monthly focus—e.g., eye contact—that is seen on posters, tent cards, and newspapers and covered in department meetings
- holding frequent Guest Relations Days in the cafeteria during which food is given away
- giving free meal passes periodically to employees who exhibit good guest relations (these can be provided ''on the spot'' by supervisors to reinforce positive behaviors)
- implementing a suggestion program
- placing tent cards in the cafeteria and on patient trays that identify an interpersonal issue of excellence as listed on patient/visitor evaluations.

Supervisors should meet at least twice a year. These meetings should be multidisciplinary and should review the themes of providing leadership, looking for the positive, offering feedback and recognition, and coaching. In effect, the sessions should be mini-training sessions around these themes. However, the primary goal is to encourage group discussion as to what is easy and what is difficult to do. Skill building is involved in such things as approaching a frustrated employee to offer coaching or giving positive feedback to a sarcastic employee. The sharing of problems is a support to supervisors who typically work alone. Not only is this support in keeping with the message of the program, but also it models the behavior supervisors are being asked to model for the employees.

Employee meetings should also be scheduled annually. The employee meetings held earlier were department meetings that dealt with what happened in individual departments and with what their patients said about their own performance. For many organizations these may represent one of the few times the work group discusses service excellence. This second set of employee meetings, like the second set of supervisory meetings, should be multidisciplinary. Participants should represent a cross-section of the hospital with an appropriate mix of nurses, clinical technicians, support service workers, finance employees, etc. The objective is to address the teamwork issues. The meeting should have the following agenda as a minimum:

- Provide feedback on what patients, visitors, and employees are saying about hospital services. The source of this information is the hospital's regular patient questionnaire and the new client evaluations. The perspective is first and foremost that which is positive. People need to be given credit for their good performance. It is in that context that they will work toward improvements.
- Identify procedural and environmental changes that have been made. Changes are the result of people working together. The message is successful teamwork in terms of identifying a problem or need and then doing something about it.
- Get suggestions for what else should be done. This open-ended discussion can be the source of hospitalwide client

evaluations to be performed in the following month, creating the questions that are to be asked of patients, visitors, and employees. The results will then be shared with all employees. These employee meetings can be stretched out over six months to allow for six hospital-wide monthly client evaluations and their results.

HOW WILL WE KNOW IF WE SUCCEED?

Success comes from listening to people—patients, visitors, and employees. Management needs to show its commitment by making or allowing some changes, while at the same time recognizing the interpersonal improvements made by the staff.

With reference to procedural and environmental changes, the intention is to attack a list of those problems where we "shoot ourselves in the foot." These are the things that happen daily, and sometimes hourly, that aggravate, frustrate, and anger. The rework, the resteps, the repeat filling out of forms, the hurry up and wait moments, and then the resulting expression of feelings—these comprise this unfortunate list.

The measure of success is the visible changes in these same items. Some procedural shortcomings can be corrected immediately. If people are constantly having to go back to a department, a system of checking paperwork before people leave the department should be instituted. Other procedural improvements require more time (e.g., computer program changes) or a lot of money (e.g., a more convenient stairway or entrance). The absolute bottom line to procedural and environmental issues is that the systems affecting patients must be user friendly and that the systems affecting employees be employee supportive (Spicer, Graft, and Ross 1988).

The evaluations done by patients, visitors, and employees tell members of a work group what they do well and where they need to improve the specific performances they have identified as demonstrating excellence in guest relations. The same evaluations can provide other suggestions for improvements. The evidence that work group members are responsive to the information they receive will be observable and can be tracked through key questions.

First, what steps is the work group taking to improve performance? What improvements are visible? What reports can supervisors and managers make that show improvements in performance? How often do supervisors check guest relations performance? How often is guest relations performance discussed in the work group? How often during the year does the work group review client evaluations? How often does the work group review its initial items of excellence and then make changes—both adding and subtracting to reflect further focus on client satisfaction and response to their prior evaluations?

These questions drive the desire to create an audit trail that shows improvement in guest relations. Action plans need not be a paper exercise if supported by varied activities of review, discussion, response, and follow-up.

If a work group makes a concerted effort to improve what they and their clients initially judge to be poor or infrequent performance, then successive client evaluations should show an improvement. For example, clients in Radiology say that they wait a long time and that no one says anything to them. In fact, this was an item of excellence that Radiology identified. It was worded as follows: "Check every 15 minutes with patients who must wait; apologize for the wait and explain the delay." The staff self-assessment and the first client evaluation showed this to be the lowest-rated item. Staff, while acknowledging it as an issue of excellence, knew that they were poor at doing it. In fact, we have noted that the staff of almost every department knows what to do to create excellence and has an accurate idea of how to accomplish it. In the example above, the staff should be able to get testimony that they are doing this more frequently. In fact, the department could make it *the* objective of the month for everyone to do this. It can become a singular effort with daily feedback by supervisors who can query patients on how well this is being achieved.

The issue is not to argue that excellence won't occur without this focus—or that in the following month things will be as they were. The issue is that we can achieve excellence when we want to. We know what it looks like and how to do it. More clearly, the point is that if we gear ourselves to a service imperative, we can deliver higher-quality care and satisfaction not from the old model reflecting an emphasis on technology, but rather from a new model that says we will provide you with the best clinical care in ways that you will understand and appreciate.

Another source of evidence on improvements leading to excellence is what clients have to say both orally and in writing. Managers and supervisors should log complaints and compliments before the improvement efforts begin. Complaints should go down and compliments up. Letters received should also be logged and shown to staff. The letters of complaint should receive close scrutiny. Over time they should decrease and letters of compliment increase.

CONCLUSION

The approach we took was to maximize the commitment of employees through involvement and clear expectations of what good performance is in guest relations. While we do not advocate training materials as a major focal point of our program, we do not mean to suggest that program materials are not helpful. This approach suggests that guest relations is a feedback issue for most organizations. Improve the feedback, and the performance will increase. We suggest that by and large guest relations is not an issue of knowledge or skill. In most cases people can provide excellence. Excellence, however, needs to be defined, and people need to get recognition and positive reinforcement when they provide it.

We can recommend this approach as a main focus of a guest relations effort. It plugs people into the effort in a substantive way as participators. The feedback loops and issues of excellence create the drive and structure for the use of the traditional approaches.

REFERENCES

Blanchard, K., and S. Johnson. 1981. The one minute manager. New York: The Berkley Book Publishing Group.

Cleary, P., and B. McNeil. 1988. Patient satisfaction as an indicator of quality care. *Inquiry* 25 (Spring 1988): 25–36.

Eck, S., et al. 1988. Consumerism, nursing and the reality of the resources. *Nursing Administration Quarterly* 12, no. 3 (Spring): 1–11.

Gilbert, T. 1978. *Human competence*. New York: McGraw-Hill Book Co.

Guest relations—The competitive edge through concern for customers. 1985. *Profiles in Hospital Marketing* 19, no. 7 (July): 86–87.

Guest relations: A source of competitive advantage. 1988. *Hospital Guest Relations Report* 3, no. 5 (May): 10–11.

Hersey, P., and K. Blanchard. 1982. *Management of organizational behavior: Utilizing human resources*. Englewood Cliffs, N.J.: Prentice-Hall, Inc.

Inguanzo, J., and M. Harju. 1985. Creating a market niche." *Hospitals* 59, no. 1 (January 1): 62–83.

Jensen, J. 1988. Patient surveys help measure satisfaction. *Modern Healthcare* 18, no. 17 (April 22): 40–41.

Johnson, D.E.L. 1986. Patient's healthcare needs dictate who influences choice of providers. *Modern Healthcare* 10, no. 12 (May 9): 42.

Kanter, R. 1983. *The change masters*. New York: Simon & Schuster.

Kazemek, E., and D. Mizaur. 1987. Service strategy improves guest relations. *Healthcare Financial Management* 41, no. 5 (May): 104.

Kerruish, A., I. Wickings, and P. Tarrant. 1988. Information from patients as a management tool—Empowering managers to improve the quality of care. *Hospital and Health Services Review* 84, no. 2 (April): 64–67.

MacStravic, R.S. Customer-oriented medical records can promote patient satisfaction. *Health Progress* 69, no. 3 (April): 66–70.

Matthews, Dale, and A. Feinstein. 1989. A review of systems for the personal aspects of patient care. *American Journal of the Medical Sciences* 295, no. 3 (March): 159–71.

M.D. influence on consumers waning slightly. 1987. *Hospitals* 61, no. 9 (May 5): 44.

Measuring the impact of guest relations. 1986. *Hospital Guest Relations Report* 1, no. 12 (December): 8–11.

Miller-Bader, M. 1988. Nursing care behaviors that predict patient satisfaction. *Journal of Nursing Quality Assurance* 2, no. 3: 11–17.

Neuhauser, P., and E. Murphy. 1988. Guest relations programs: How to measure success. *Journal of Healthcare Education and Training* 3, no. 1: 20–23.

Pascoe D., A. Wilson, and J. Worsfold. 1978. Patients' attitudes to health care: A literature review. *World Hospital* 14 (August): 167–70.

Personal service approach teaches employees job ownership. 1988. *Hospital Guest Relations Report* 3, no. 2 (February): 4–7.

Peters, T. 1987. In search of excellence: A road map for CEOs. *Hospitals* 61, no. 9 (May 5): 91–92.

Peters, T., and N. Austin. 1985. *Passion for Excellence*. New York: Random House, Inc.

Peters, T., and R. Waterman. 1982. *In search of excellence*. New York: Harper & Row.

Powills, S. 1986. Will the customer please stand up? *Hospitals* 60, no. 13 (July 5): 34.

Risser, N.L. 1975. Development of an instrument to measure patient satisfaction with nurses and nursing care in primary care settings. *Nursing Research* 24, no. 1 (January-February): 45–52.

Room service—Turn hospital stays into "Getaways." 1988. *Profiles in Healthcare Marketing* 29, no. 1 (January): 17–19.

Spicer, J., M. Graft, and K. Ross. 1988. A systems approach to customer satisfaction. *Nursing Administration Quarterly* 12, no. 3 (Spring): 79–83.

Subtlety, not hoopla or banners, key to new guest relations effort. 1987. *Hospital Guest Relations Report* 2, no. 11 (November): 5–6.

Tabak, E. 1987. The relationship of information exchange during medical visits to patient satisfaction: A review. *Diabetes Educator* 13, no. 1: 36–40.

Task groups lay guest relations foundation at Danbury Hospital. 1987. *Hospital Guest Relations Report* 2, no. 3 (March): 4–6.

Ware, J.E., A. Davies-Avery, and A. Stewart. 1978. The measurement and meaning of patient satisfaction. *Health & Medical Care Services Review* 1, no. 1 (January-February): 1–15.

Lawrence C. Bassett

Putting Creativity To Work: A Serious Look at Suggestion Plans

26

Although prudent managers acknowledge that employees can generate profitable ideas, it is surprising how little effort they devote to bringing these ideas to the surface. In fact, it almost appears that health care organizations are set up to discourage initiative and the development of creative thinking.

Managers rarely are actively encouraged to innovate, and little priority is given to any formal method of motivating employees to develop their ideas. Health care organizations tend to have more of a caste system than is traditionally found in the private sector of industry because they place so much emphasis on degrees, licenses, certification, and levels of education. The result is almost a natural repression of original thought.

For example, a suggestion by a hospital nurse's aide on improving nursing technique would receive little serious consideration if routed through normal channels. Nurse's aides are not expected to know enough about or have the necessary training in professional nursing practice. Similarly, natural barriers exist in nearly every sector of the organization, resulting in the loss of a potential wealth of "genius."

As the health care industry undergoes profound change because of unprecedented financial pressures, there has been an attempt to break down these barriers. Quality circles (QCs), for example, have been adopted by many health care organizations, though some of the elements that must be present if a QC program is to work negate the energy spent in establishing them. The success of a QC program is frequently tied to the overall corporate culture within the organization and the level of employee relations that exists. Thus, as successful as such an approach can be, there are inherent difficulties that preclude the quality circle approach from being universally successful.

Because health care organizations have to become more competitive and financially stable, a new look at an old tool—the suggestion program—is definitely warranted. Suggestion programs can be installed in any organization, even one with a "cool" employee relations climate. Suggestion plans, which have excellent track records, can be introduced with minimal investment. Of course, we are not talking about placing a suggestion box in a cafeteria or other frequently visited location. Such a move is simplistic and usually ill advised. What is called for is a careful look at how suggestion plans work, how they can be established, and how they can be operated successfully.

An analysis of where and why suggestion plans succeed, based on the author's almost 25 years of experience as a consultant, reveals a number of common elements that form the basis of an effective strategy. While not every program should be a do-it-yourself exercise, the steps outlined below should make it possible for a health care organization to determine how best to proceed, given its unique characteristics.

- *Developing an organizational commitment to succeed.* Shortly after the turn of the century, Congress deliberated a bill that would have closed the Patent Office. The rationale was that there was nothing left to invent. As naive as this appears today, it is not far from the naivete modern-day managers exhibit with regard to finding better ways of doing things.

It is one thing to say that employees have good ideas, but another to believe it. No suggestion program, or for that matter any plan, succeeds unless those directing its course believe in attaining a positive outcome. An emotional and organizational commitment to harvest employee ideas is not easily secured. It is important for those in leadership positions to recognize the potential of the work force and, perhaps, to review the experiences of companies that have nurtured their suggestion programs over a period of years.

According to the National Association of Suggestion Systems, an association comprised of organizations that have suggestion programs, millions of dollars of ideas are developed and put to work each year. Moreover, rather than running out of ideas over a period of years, organizations tend to find there is a steady flow of suggestions from new and long-term employees. In a meeting held on December 14, 1988, Gene Johnson, director of the association, stated that in 1987 over $2 billion in increased revenue or savings was obtained by the approximately 1,250 members of the National Association of Suggestion Systems. There were $150 million paid in awards. The eye-opening part was that the average award for each suggestion accepted was $8,000.

People have ideas, and good ideas frequently come from unexpected sources and unsung employees. The value of these ideas is frequently tremendous, and a system that stimulates and channels these contributions is a management tool with the potential to bring about an excellent return on investment.

- *Building the foundation of a successful suggestion program.* The second foundation element for a successful program is the development of a formal and effective way of channeling ideas into a format that facilitates rapid analysis and implementation. With an effective and well-understood procedure and with carefully designed guidelines and rules, an organization can build and sustain a momentum that leads to an ongoing supply of fresh ideas.

*   *   *   *

> *Merely building a suggestion box is similar to placing a pail in the ocean and hoping that a fish will swim into it. You may get some thoughts, but suggestion boxes unaccompanied by a formal, well-communicated, and well-publicized program will merely become a repository for more candy wrappers, cigarette butts, and miscellaneous gripes.*

*   *   *   *

Clearly, when employees see that management is serious about enlisting their help in supplying ideas, they will respond with the same seriousness. They will see a suggestion box or other simplistic approach as only a half-hearted effort at getting something for nothing.

- *Implementing a generous award system that is as big time as the ideas being sought.* Skimpy rewards bring skimpy results. If management is seeking heavy weight ideas, it must establish an awards system that communicates its commitment by demonstrating its willingness to share the benefits of the suggestion. Employees do not want to be exploited; they see an awards system as a form of communication and respect.

In a pragmatic sense, a liberal reward system pays off royally. The satisfaction of seeing an idea implemented, magnified by a tangible return, is highly motivational. When employees share in the benefits, they will provide, over the long run, a harvest of additional ideas that might otherwise have gone to waste.

As a general rule, the value of awards should be approximately 20 percent of one year's savings or of revenue gain averaged over three years. How this is determined is discussed later.

- *Ensuring rapid evaluation, communication of decisions, and implementation of suggestions.* If there is one common characteristic of successful suggestion programs, it is that ideas are evaluated and implemented soon after they are made. In fact, the success of a plan is directly proportional to how quickly employees get feedback and how quickly their ideas are implemented. This is such an important factor that it may be possible to have a successful program without tangible rewards just as long as ideas are implemented within a few days of being communicated. Prompt attention and action are an enormous award itself. They are evidence of management's concern and interest and provide great psychological and professional satisfaction. Such rapid processing is also both feasible and practical.

- *Providing promotion and publicity.* If a momentum is to be developed and sustained, a carefully prepared communication strategy is critical. While employees must become aware of the rules, it it more important to convince them of the value of investing the time and effort required.

A well-planned and well-executed communication program prevents initial enthusiasm from waning. There is no question that, after a period of time, employees have to dig deeper for innovations. An ongoing, well-planned publicity campaign can eliminate much of the mental laziness that might beset employees. If the communications program is well organized, if winning ideas and the awards they earn are publicized, and if messages of encouragement and motivation are expressed, suggestion programs can produce a high level of activity on a permanent basis.

These five considerations can serve as a checklist to help ensure a good return on investment. Each point is part of a mosaic that, when brought together, can result in an organization that is economically stronger, is competitively more secure, and has employees who have a high level of morale and satisfaction. What follows is a step-by-step plan for implementation, which, when tuned to the characteristics of the organization, will result in a successful program.

APPOINT AN EXECUTIVE IN CHARGE

A good deal of importance should be associated with the responsibility for developing the suggestion program. It is not an assignment to be given out casually to a junior member of the administrative staff to help fill in a work schedule. Rather, it should be given to a manager with a reputation for creativity and for getting things done.

The individual (or individuals) must have the respect of employees and be seen as having substantial organizational clout. If the program is headed by someone who is weak and not respected, the time and energy needed to overcome employee inertia and skepticism could be formidable. In fact, giving the assignment to a key member of management is in itself a fairly good indication that the program will get off the ground successfully.

DEVELOP A THEME AND THE PROCEDURES TO CARRY IT OUT

If employees are expected to be creative, it makes sense to establish a theme that is itself creative. The theme provides a framework for public relations efforts and a focus to prompt employee participation. For example, one program the author helped develop was called the Idea Investment Club, which recognized that dividends (awards) would be given as employees invested their ideas in their hospital. The theme made sense in today's financially oriented world, and it encouraged employees to invest in their own future as they helped their organization succeed.

The development of an appropriate theme is an excellent way of generating employee interest and enthusiasm. Offering the first award to the individual who submits the winning suggestion achieves a number of start-up goals.

Once the theme has been established, the development of procedures is facilitated. For example, following the Investment Club theme, the suggestion form can be put into the form of an ''application for membership.''

* * * *

HELPFUL TIP

The suggestion form should include questions that require the employee to think through the idea in practical terms. Exhibit 26-1 shown below illustrates several questions that are designed to put a greater burden on the employee

to think through the suggestion in practical terms. Frequently, an idea appears practical until the employee makes such an analysis. At that point it becomes clear either that the benefit isn't as great as anticipated or that the negatives that had not been considered outweigh the advantages.

* * * *

An employee who thinks through details that otherwise might have been overlooked may also provide additional information without which the evaluation process might have been delayed. Even more important, rejecting an idea in which the employee believes can be discouraging and counterproductive. When the individual is guided by the process to analyze the suggestion in greater detail, he or she may be led to reject the idea, do additional research, or improve the suggestion. However, should the idea still be rejected, the employee will have a better understanding of management's reasoning. For example, employees are quick to recommend the purchase of equipment and devices before they learn the cost or determine the frequency of use. When they have done some necessary research and have come to understand the complete set of pros and cons, they will tend to be more supportive of the final decision.

The completed application should be expedited into the evaluation process. Whether the suggestion is sent in an envelope, placed in a strategically located container, or given directly to an individual, the employee should know that it will be reviewed and evaluated within a period of two work days.

* * * *

HELPFUL TIPS

The use of brightly colored or distinctive envelopes to convey the idea form provides a sense of urgency and enables a suggestion to stand out from other envelopes and material. It also communicates a sense of importance which further enhances the program.

* * * *

If a container is used (note the word *box* has been avoided), it, too, should be distinctive and carry out the theme in some fashion.

* * * *

DETERMINE AN AWARD SYSTEM

When considering awards, two issues must be addressed: first, a formula for valuing an idea must be developed; second, the form in which the award will be given must be determined.

The first issue is easier to handle. Research has shown that on average an idea survives in its original form for three years.

Exhibit 26-1 Sample Suggestion Form

For Committee Use

Date Received _____

Idea Number _____

Idea Investment Club Application

Name: _____ Position: _____

Date: _____ Department: _____

Who else provided background and/or assistance in designing idea?

_____

Idea: (Describe your idea in detail.) _____

_____

_____

_____

_____

_____

_____

_____

_____

_____

_____

End Results To Be Achieved: (List benefits of idea.)

a. Financial or economic "payoff": (Give dollar estimate and specific area of savings or profit.)

_____

_____

_____

b. Improvement in work efficiency: _____

_____

_____

_____

c. Improvement in patient care: _____

_____

_____

_____

d. Other improvements or results to be attained: _____

_____

_____

_____

Exhibit 26-1 continued

What Costs Or Other Investments Are Needed To Implement Idea?

a. What equipment, construction, etc. might be necessary?

_____

_____

_____

_____

b. Dollar estimate to implement and maintain the idea: _____

_____

_____

c. How much time is required to implement? _____

_____

_____

_____

d. Other possible considerations needed before implementation is possible:

_____

_____

_____

_____

How Soon Will Results Be Obtained? (Over what period of time?)

a. How quickly will there be positive returns? _____

_____

_____

_____

b. For how long will the benefit be realized? _____

_____

Who Should Be Responsible For Implementing The Idea?

a. Employees, departments? _____

_____

_____

_____

b. What role would you want to play in adopting the idea? _____

_____

_____

_____

_____

Exhibit 26-1 continued

(This page is for use by The Review Committee only.)

Committee Member Analysis (Attach additional pages if necessary)

What information is incomplete or invalid? _____

_____

_____

What additional data is needed, and from whom? _____

_____

_____

What are the probable chances of success? _____

_____

Estimated return on investment (benefit less cost of implementation):

First Year   _____

Second Year   _____

Third Year   _____

What other positive impact will be attained? _____

_____

_____

Recommendation for award: _____

_____

_____

Reason for non-acceptance: _____

_____

_____

Would any modification justify re-submission? _____

_____

_____

All ideas, plans, documents, equipment and devices including patents and copyrights for which an award is granted become the property of the Berkshire Medical Center.

_____   _____

Date   Employee Signature

After that time, business conditions generally change to the extent that the suggestion has lost its value or is replaced by a different machine, procedure, or service. Thus, it is helpful to determine the full value of an idea by considering its impact over a three-year period. (This also negates the problems associated with start-up costs and initial investments.)

Normally, an award should be based on an annualized figure averaged on a three-year benefit period. (Dividing the three-year total benefit by 3 gives the annualized benefit for purposes of computing an award.)

Frequently, there is a tendency by managers to worry that they may be "giving away" more than they have to. In actuality, the more that is provided in an award system, the more productive the program becomes.

A safe but effective formula that protects the organization, while making the effort worthwhile to the employee, is to give an award worth 20 percent of the base average value.

Some organizations put a cap at 15 percent, but others go as high as 25 percent. In determining which is the best figure, consideration should be given to whether the evaluation of quality suggestions, which cannot be formulated into a dollar benefit, will be so frequent as to warrant a more conservative award. In actuality, a 20 percent payout—or a 5:1 return—builds in a good deal of latitude and a cushion for absorbing quality suggestions.

Several questions all rasied by the second issue. Who gets the award? Nonmanagement employees? Supervisors? Volunteers? Physicians? Should the quality of awards given to managers be the same as for those given to nonmanagement employees?

Answers are born out of the intent of the program—namely, to get profitable ideas. The argument that managers are expected to come up with sound suggestions and ideas as part of their regular job ignores the basic facts of human nature. Whether a person is a manager or not, the challenge inherent in any form of contest stimulates thinking that probably would not have been attempted otherwise. An organization with strong feelings about not providing awards to managers may derive some philosophical satisfaction but will get few tangible suggestions from this group. As far as the other members of the health care organization are concerned, the better question is this: why not include them with an award that has been modified to suit?

The simplest and easiest award to administer—cash—is also the most frequently used. On the other hand, providing tangible gifts adds an emotional factor that sometimes stimulates a much higher level of motivation than money. Many suggestion programs are built on an award system that offers catalog gifts designed for that purpose. Pictures of luxuries and "dream" vacations can have a powerful impact. From an employer's standpoint, the total value of the gift exceeds its cost. Though an item may call for the same dollars as a cash award, a momentum is developed because every time the employee looks at or uses the award, there is a subtle call for a repeat effort.

* * * *

HELPFUL TIP

When pricing out the value of a tangible award, build in the payment of taxes. This has two desirable effects: the employee does not have to lay out any money to enjoy the gift, and the size of the award might seem even greater than cash when the employee realizes that the taxes have been paid. It is to the organization's benefit to use a system of tangible awards, and announcing that taxes will be paid might tip the balance in the minds of employees in preferring this system over cash awards.

* * * *

In providing awards to managers, there are additional methods of payment, if cash or gifts are not used. Awards can be granted in the form of credits toward salary reviews or possible promotions. Physicians, volunteers, and incidental members of the organization can be given special "recognition" awards: tickets to dinner or a show, special pins, scrolls, or plaques. If a suggestion from a member of one of these groups is of unusual significance or benefit, an award of greater value can be provided. This is not an exception to the rule; it is merely recognition that an exceptional effort should receive exceptional recognition.

* * * *

HELPFUL TIP

Whatever the amount or form of the award, a certificate or a custom-designed pin helps publicize the program and, when presented to and worn by the employee, is a form of continued advertising. In the case of an "investment club," the certificate could be in the form of a "share" of the organization's future, and the pins granted could be club membership pins.

* * * *

EVALUATE THE SUGGESTION

Suggestions can be evaluated quickly, particularly if the suggestion form requires the employee to do much of the basic investigation and pricing out. The most expeditious way of evaluating a suggestion is to use a committee comprised of individuals with insight and know-how in various phases of the organization's operations. When an idea falls into a specific target area, the committee member with expertise in that area should review it, almost upon receipt.

* * * *

There is no need for a committee to gather together to review every suggestion made. This wastes time and is ineffective.

* * * *

As a way of moving a suggestion along rapidly, the chairperson of the committee, normally the individual in charge of the program itself, should have the authority, along with the evaluator, to approve certain awards without further deliberation by other members of the committee.

* * * *

The baseline amount for these awards can be a minimal $200–$300 or as high as $1,000. However, the combination of a relatively low award and a high probability of success minimizes the risk and makes the decision organizationally sound.

* * * *

When a suggestion is more complex or calls for a higher award, discussion by the full committee, based on the analysis and recommendation of the specialist, is appropriate. And, obviously, should a suggestion cut across disciplines, the decision should be a collaborative one.

Respected, decisive, and knowlegeable people must be chosen to serve on the committee. Further, in order to avoid a slowing down of the process during times of heavy workloads, a substitute for each committee member should be available. Providing such a backup enables the process to continue in high gear.

* * * *

The general rule should be that an employee receives a response to his or her suggestion within 72 hours, excluding weekends and holidays. Experience has shown that frequently a response can be given within 24 hours, even with some fairly complex ideas.

* * * *

Should there be an occasion when a decision cannot be given within the time frame, the employee should be told of the delay, the reason, and the new timetable. This maintains the integrity of the process.

* * * *

HELPFUL TIP

The greatest possible impact on the employee is attainable when the acceptance of her or his suggestion is communicated personally by a member of top management, preferably the CEO, in the presence of the employee's supervisor and/or department head. Even for less valuable suggestions, it is desirable to include top management. Small ideas, when there are enough of them, add up to a significant total.

* * * *

A written communication at the time of a suggestion's acceptance also is important. It is a document that can be kept (and sometimes cherished) by the individual, and it helps avoid any misunderstanding as to the nature of the award, degree of acceptance, etc.

EMPLOYEE COMMUNICATION, PUBLICITY, AND OTHER FINE POINTS

A suggestion program that carries a theme should be backed by a communication program that is well designed and well executed. Posters, procedure books, and, if tangible gifts are used, specially designed catalogs have to be prepared in advance. Under no circumstance should a program be announced by a simple memo. It lacks the pizazz, depth, and showmanship that a program promoting creativity deserves.

Distributing special premiums to kick off the program and giving small awards to every submitter of a suggestion within the first three to six months stimulate excitement and enthusiasm.

Posting suggestions at a central location, even rejected ones, shows that the program has achieved a momentum and triggers additional ideas. A central scoreboard showing the number of ideas submitted and the amount of awards given out is also a sound device. Because these figures only go up, the numbers can be dramatic reminders of the program, particularly after a period of several years.

The possibilities for publicity are nearly endless. Newspapers, particularly those in smaller communities, are more than pleased to publish pictures and stories of sizable achievements. Other formal communications media, such as in-house publications, should continually capitalize on accepted suggestions.

Much publicity can be generated when the program includes special awards for suggestions sought to solve specific problems or answer specific questions. Awards for the best suggestion from a shift, from a department, or during a particular week to solve a targeted problem can be offered from time to time to generate enthusiasm.

* * * *

HELPFUL TIP

In return for publicity, hotels, restaurants, and some airlines are willing to barter services. At the least, the organization can make a special arrangement that enables the award to be greater than what might normally have been possible.

* * * *

Suggestion programs work. They increase profitability, improve morale, and build teamwork. They have been proven and time tested. When properly planned and implemented, they can give any health care organization an excellent return on investment.

Martin H. Meisel

27

Making the Most of Your Executive Search Firm: Searching for Godot

Imagine this scenario: You are the human resources manager of a medium-sized hospital in Des Moines, Iowa. Your chief financial officer has walked out, taking half the accounting department with him. A cursory investigation reveals political intrigue, hurt feelings, and low morale among the remaining staff.

For about a month, business goes along more or less as usual, while display ads for the position appear in the *Des Moines Register*, the *New York Times* and the *Chicago Tribune*. The cost of advertising so far has been about $20,000 and the meter is still ticking, but response to the ads has been dismal; only a handful of résumés have come in, despite the significant volume of advertising, and few even look like they are worth interviewing. The situation in your hospital is now steadily deteriorating, and you are beginning to wonder who actually would relocate to take the position if they were aware of the chaotic circumstances.

Things are beginning to look impossible, and it seriously occurs to you for the first time that you may need to consider an executive search and recruitment firm. Until now, you have resisted for most of the usual reasons: neither you nor the hospital has ever used a search firm before; you have a twinge of guilt about "stealing" from someone else—you know how you would feel if one of your key people were recruited; and you lack knowledge about "headhunters" and their methods. The hospital trustees are intent on recruiting from the outside, and because your efforts at finding someone through advertising are languishing, it seems you will have no choice but to consult a search firm.

Now what do you do? How do you select a search firm? How much should they charge, and what should you expect

from them? What do you need to do to make the search productive and ultimately to locate a candidate who will not only fill the position, but also function well in it?

These are some of the questions to be addressed here.

FINDING A SEARCH FIRM

Generally, the right time to call in a search firm is after you have attempted some kind of search on your own, but have failed. Most organizations will want to do an initial search themselves. This in-house search not only will give you an opportunity to think about what you want, but also will convince you and your superiors that a professional executive search firm is necessary. Many companies spend literally tens of thousands of dollars on advertising before reaching this conclusion.

In cases in which there is an existing professional relationship between a hospital or company and a recruiter, the human resources manager who is experienced in the use of professional search firms will probably be in a position to judge whether the search is impossible to handle in-house and, if so, will retain a search consultant at the inception.

Executive search firms come in all shapes and sizes, from international organizations doing millions of dollars in business annually and capable of searching the globe for the right person, to "boutique" operations specializing in certain areas or industries and completing a limited number of national searches each year.

The size of the firm you select is not as important as its quality; specialization is critical, especially in the increasingly complex health care field. Given this, the best way to find a search firm is by getting a referral from someone in the field. Begin by contacting your colleagues at hospitals, wherever they may be located. Inquire about their organization's use of consultants and their experiences with previous searches. Ask if they know anyone else who uses professional search firms. Contact administrators at the medical school affiliated with your institution who may be able to refer someone to you. Utilize your contacts with the American Hospital Association or other industry organizations. You also may want to contact the Association of Executive Search Consultants, which will refer you to recruiters in your field.

The list of search consultants you will be choosing from probably will not include local names unless you are located in or near a major metropolitan area. This is not important because the firm will be looking for candidates throughout the country. If you are located away from a major metropolitan center, a firm's location in a large city will be a tremendous advantage to you.

When you have reduced your choices to the two or three firms that appear to be the most suitable for your particular search, you should contact and interview each one. This is similar to interviewing a candidate for any staff position in your organization.

First, obtain information on the backgrounds of the executives who are the principals in the search organization, ascertain their experience in the hospital field, and ask for the names of their other clients in that field. Discuss their long-standing client relationships, and ask about their completion record. The completion record for a competent executive search firm should be high, somewhere around the 85-percent level. If a search firm is not doing this level of work (exclusive of situations in which the client has withdrawn the search for internal reasons unrelated to the performance of the search consultant), it is unlikely that the search firm will be able to perform productively for you.

Finally, use your instincts and "gut" reactions to determine the attitude of the firm, and ask yourself frankly whether or not you could work comfortably and closely with the firm's personnel for several months. When you have obtained all the basic prerequisite information, focus on this personal relationship aspect. The relationship between a search firm and the human resources manager at the hospital must be one based on openness, mutual trust, and understanding. If this relationship exists, the search is much more likely to produce a "good fit" and an executive who not only can perform the job functions but also can blend into the culture of your organization.

After your interviews with the search firms, the next step is to call the references provided by the firms and obtain information about other institutions' firsthand experiences. If two or more of the references from any firm appear, however subtly, to indicate a bad experience, you will probably want to consider eliminating that firm as a possibility. In the final analysis, you should usually select the firm that has had the most experience successfully placing executives in your field, to which you instinctively have a positive reaction, and for which references seem to be honestly evaluating a good performance.

WHAT YOU PAY FOR AND WHAT YOU SHOULD EXPECT

It is only partially true that executive searches are very expensive. While it may cost $30,000 or more to place an executive, many organizations spend much more than that attempting to find candidates through display advertising that fails. In actual dollars, and in terms of what you get for the money, executive search is the most efficient way to spend your recruitment budget.

Even with extensive advertising, it would be almost impossible for a human resources department to conduct a truly nationwide search. On the other hand, an executive recruiter has the ability to perform exactly this kind of search, using a wide variety of tools and contacts.

The savings in time also are significant; using executive search frees the human resources personnel and other hospital executives to focus on the operation of the hospital, which does not require any less attention because a search is being undertaken. The human resources department does not spend valuable time finding and interviewing mediocre candidates and valuable dollars bringing them to the hospital's location. Also, if one of those mediocre candidates somehow does obtain the position and does not meet expectations, it would be necessary to repeat the entire search at the same high cost as the initial search.

When you work with professional recruiters, their most valuable asset is objective judgment. The value of this cannot be overstated. Equally as important as their judgment is the quality of their objectivity. The recruiters' objectivity enables them to view the nuances of your organization and the position without preconceived opinions. Their experience enables them to screen candidates beyond surface qualifications and personality. A search firm may be working with state-of-the-art technology, huge data bases, and contacts from Oxford, Maine, to Oxnard, California. But without judgment, all the equipment in the world is worthless.

As a hospital administrator very close to the situation, it may be impossible for you to be completely objective. You see things as an "insider." The recuiter has an "outsider's" distance from the situation. This long view has a second major benefit: many top executives in any field are insecure about their own positions and may seek to fill a vacancy with someone who is the least threatening to them. Hiring on that basis is unlikely to produce an executive who can really handle the position. A recruiter considers only a candidate's personal and professional qualifications and presents only strong candidates for consideration.

You are paying for a recruiter's expertise—not only in recruiting, where it probably far exceeds yours, but also in her or his area of specialization. Recruiters are in the business of knowing people, knowing how to find them if they do not know them, and communicating effectively with them. They have extensive knowledge of what is happening in your business because that information is essential to their business.

Another crucial benefit you purchase when you work with an executive recruiter is access. Executive search seeks out the people who do not read the "help wanted" ads. Consider the fact that the most probable candidates for your position are likely to be happily employed elsewhere and are not actively looking for a job. You probably will not know who these people are, and even if you do, you cannot approach them without professional assistance except at the risk of embarrassment. If, for example, you represent a major metropolitan hospital and want to recruit the executive vice-president of a hospital across town, you certainly would not just call him or her on the telephone and ask if he or she wanted a new job. You could, however, retain an executive search consultant to do it anonymously.

For many organizations, being anonymous is crucial to an effective search, and executive search firms have the ability to shield the identity of the searching organization until the last phases of the process. The ability to maintain anonymity is one reason search firms can be so effective. They can help avoid uncomfortable situations, hard feelings, or even charges of direct raiding. You may even want to conduct your search without the knowledge of other executives in your hospital, for whatever reasons. A search firm can accomplish this for you.

Other advantages of the professional search process include the precision that you can obtain only as a result of the depth of research most recruiters will do for a search. A search firm has the ability to match a specific person with a specific need. In addition, search firms adhere to extremely high standards of integrity in searching for candidates, checking their professional and educational credentials, and evaluating their references. A recruiter also will seek and consider the comments of former employees and coworkers to obtain a total picture. This can be tremendously important as increasing emphasis is placed on leadership qualities, honesty, integrity, team playing, and other personal traits. A search firm will recommend only those candidates whom they feel are ideally suited and truly qualified for the position.

There is the instructive story of an executive working in the health care field who began his career as a financial officer, then climbed the ladder to chief financial officer, and finally became the president of a hospital. Then he moved on to become the president of another hospital, and then another one. He never kept any position for more than two years, knowing better than anyone that he was not qualified to do the job. Eventually, as soon as he was installed in a new position, he would begin looking ahead for the next one. Sometimes he got fired, other times he resigned, only to repeat the process. Finally, the man's reputation caught up with him, and he was unable to remain in the hospital field. He is now employed in the import/export business in Florida.

How could this happen? How could he have deceived so many people? This man had a dynamic personality and a talent for saying the right thing at the right time. He was aided and abetted by the people who interviewed and hired him and who were susceptible to his charms. It was the perception that sold—not the reality. This is as true in recruitment as it is in politics or advertising. The fact that this man could insinuate himself into so many organizations at such high levels demonstrates all too well the pitfalls of the nonprofessional search process.

It is very unlikely, however, that this man could have been able to easily impress a professional recruiter. A professional recuiter has the experience and training—and the responsibility—to look beyond the obvious, to be skeptical, to thoroughly examine each potential candidate. The recruiter's entire focus and reputation depend on the ability to produce the right candidate. The human resources manager has many other responsibilities and a multitude of everyday crises, which make it difficult for her or him to match the professional recruiter's complete concentration on the search.

FEE FOR SERVICES

In executive search, the standard fee for services is one-third of the annual salary and benefits package of the executive who is finally placed. The client also is expected to reimburse the search firm for all the costs of the search, including long-distance telephone calls, airfare, hotels, meals, and other expenses involved in the search and interview process.

What happens if a search is withdrawn after work has begun? The client will be expected to pay all or most of the fee and all travel- and interview-related costs that have already been incurred. The later in the process the search is withdrawn, the higher the percentage of costs the client will pay because a search firm is charging for the time consumed in a search. The search process is very costly in terms of time and effort, often involving the work of numerous outside researchers and other sources who must be paid even if the client decides to cancel. You should not embark on a search with an executive recruiter until you are sure that a particular position must be filled and that no one within your organization is promotable to the position.

During a search you should expect results commensurate with the price you are paying. If, for example, the search produces three final candidates that you are not satisfied with, the search firm will produce three more, until you find a satisfactory candidate. And if the person recommended by the executive search firm does not work out within a given period of time, usually six months to a year, then the firm will usually reopen the search at no cost to the client. This should be clarified in your letter of agreement or contract with the search firm, as should other details which will be discussed later.

In some rare instances, the search cannot be successfully completed, and it becomes impossible to find a suitable candidate. The client will be expected to make full payment, even if the position is not filled. This is comparable to working with any other professional; sometimes an attorney will lose the case, sometimes a doctor will lose the patient, but the work has been done, and the client or patient will be required to pay for the services. This should not alarm you because "impossible to complete" searches often result from situations on the client side that you can control or that should be a signal to you not to involve a search firm—for example, when each member of your selection committee has a totally different viewpoint on the kind of person needed to fill a particular position.

You should expect to pay a retainer fee to the recruitment firm at the beginning of the search: approximately one-third of the total fee will be due on signing the contract. A professional search usually takes three to four months, and the client will be expected to pay another third of the fee at the beginning of each of the second and third months. At the end of the search and after salary negotiations have been completed, the client pays any additional amount due to the search firm.

At this point I would like to mention the existence of what are euphemistically known as "contingency search firms." These are really high-priced, glorified employment agencies that have been able to obtain listings in some executive search directories. These operations can be identified in three ways: the volume of work they do will be considerably higher than that of an executive search firm, the cost of their services is likely to be considerably lower, and they usually promise results in much less time than would a professional executive search firm. In actuality, they have neither the time nor the expertise to complete the search. They will send you any résumé that vaguely fits your job description and may be working on a hundred "searches" at one time. I mention their existence only as a caution. It is inappropriate to compare this kind of service to the highly personalized, professional, focused attention you receive from a true executive search firm.

LETTER OF AGREEMENT

Regardless of the relationship between the recruiter and the hospital, it is advisable for both parties to sign a letter of agreement stating the exact terms of their arrangement. It is probably not necessary to have a formal contract; a letter of agreement usually suffices. The letter would be drafted by the search consultant and sent to the executive at the hospital for signature.

Let us use a hypothetical example of a hospital looking for a director of finance and administration with an estimated starting salary of $100,000. The typical letter of agreement should cover the following points:

- The title of the position should be clearly identified.
- The estimated starting salary and, based on that salary, the estimated fee for the search (which in this case would be one-third of the estimated starting salary, or $33,333.33) must be specified. The letter of agreement should state that the initial retainer is one-third of the total amount, payable on signing the agreement, and that two additional monthly retainers will be billed during the

course of the search at the previously agreed-on times, usually in equal monthly installments. The maximum to be billed in advance of completing the search should be one-third of the estimated base salary. The monthly retainers are then applied as credit against the final fee.
- If the search takes longer than three months, then the search firm will continue the search at no additional fee to the client until it is successfully completed.
- Travel, telephone charges, and other expenses will be billed to the client monthly. Out-of-state travel is to be undertaken only with the prior consent of the client; any extraordinary expenses also must receive the client's prior approval.
- The client will receive written progress reports from the search firm.
- The search firm, after interviewing and recommending final candidates, will send detailed information on these individuals' backgrounds to search committee members prior to the final interviews.

These basic points should be incorporated in any agreement letter. Any other services or information that you might require in your particular search must be included in addition to these major points. You also might want to send the final draft of the letter to your legal department for approval, depending on the policy of your organization.

THE PRELIMINARIES

As the hospital human resources manager or the executive charged with the responsibility for a search, you must become the full partner of the executive recruiter. This involves considerably more frankness than in normal day-to-day business; the relationship is comparable to that between an attorney and a client. If an attorney does not have an accurate and complete picture of everything affecting the client, then it becomes difficult or impossible to properly advise the client.

The most important information that you need to provide to the search consultant is an accurate, detailed description of the job's responsibilities and a personality profile of the ideal candidate. Although this definition may be modified in the process of the search, it is essential to express your thoughts, and those of the hospital's board and possibly other key executives, about the kind of person you are seeking. Before meeting with the executive search consultant, you, and anyone else whose opinion will affect the final decision, should spend time discussing the position's requirements and the kind of professional qualifications relevant to that position.

Among the other basic information that you need to provide to the recruiter is the salary range of the position, as well as a comprehensive list of the benefits. This list should include all aspects of compensation, such as relocation costs, insurance, retirement plan, tax-deferred savings plan, a company car or house, organization memberships, tuition reimbursement, country club membership, travel, expense accounts, and any other benefit or possible benefit the hospital is willing to provide for this position.

The executive search consultant must understand every nuance of the job. You must provide the executive search consultant not only with a complete list of responsibilities in your job description, but also with an indication of the experience it will require to execute them. This information should include a detailed organizational chart and two lists, one of all the key people to whom the new executive will be reporting and one of all the key people who will be reporting to the new executive. This is important because there is far more to a search than merely matching qualifications. The recruiter will want to meet the people with whom the new executive will be working on a day-to-day basis to get a better understanding of the position and its interaction with other positions.

Give the search consultant a description of the hospital and its place in the community, including the institution's brochures, annual reports, newsletters, fund-raising literature, and similar material. Also considered basic information is a detailed description of the community and region of the country where the hospital is located, including descriptions of real estate and real estate taxes, life style, the cultural life, the school system, even the weather—any information you would want to have before relocating.

Do not underestimate the value of your location. One school of allied health professions, located in the downtown section of an East Coast metropolitan area, thought its location was not desirable and tried to ignore or understate it in catalogues and student recruitment literature. When students at the institution were surveyed, a surprisingly high percentage of them said that they had chosen the school, in part, because it was located in an urban setting. The school then began promoting itself by highlighting its location as part of an overall increase in recruitment efforts. Today, the institution is showing above average progress in combating its applicant pool shortages.

There is a lesson here for executive search. Give a totally accurate picture to the executive search consultant; it can only help. Every area has its negative and positive aspects. If an executive search consultant has the most complete information, he or she can present the position honestly and accurately, but also positively.

Finally, you should be prepared to speak frankly about the politics and problems in your organizations. Many health care facilities and other human services organizations may think they do not have any politics; unfortunately, every organization everywhere does. If the situation is a relatively pleasant one, so much the better; if it is Machiavellian, or worse, the executive search consultant needs to know this to conduct an effective search for a candidate who can handle such a situation. It may even be necessary for the human resources manager to do some sleuthing to find out, for example, the employees' perspectives on the previous executives who have held this position and on the situation in the department as they see it. You also should provide the executive search consultant

with any information that you gleaned from the exit interview, if there was one. In some cases, it may be necessary for the search firm to find a candidate who can handle morale problems and is experienced in damage control—qualities that might have to take precedence over, or be as important as, all other qualifications. The honest exchange of information between the client and the recruiter can often be the first step toward correcting the situation. Any information you give to your executive search consultant is strictly confidential.

THE SEARCH

After all the preliminary information has been obtained and the necessary discussions have taken place, the next step is to make a list of target companies or health care facilities that will be used, in part, to conduct the search. The executive search consultant will probably already have an extensive list, but the input of the client organization can be very helpful.

Then there should be a review of any possible candidates in those organizations who might be suitable for the position. Regardless of the origin of the names, when they are provided to the recruiter, they become the property of the search. Anyone who applies directly to the institution after a search has begun must be referred to the executive search firm. It is unethical and unprofessional to search yourself once you have retained a search firm. It is also pointless and self-defeating because you are already paying for the search firm's services.

The recruiter will now begin the search. This is a lengthy and carefully organized process of telephone calls, researcher input, résumé reviews, telephone interviews, in-person interviews, and the continual generation of new names of potential candidates. The interviews may take place at the search firm's office, but in most cases the recruiter will need to travel to final interviews.

Toward the end of the process, the search firm may place classified ads in newspapers in several regions to make sure that they have not missed any potential candidates.

The executive search firm and the human resources director usually screen three final candidates to be interviewed by the search committee. Personnel from the executive search firm may be present at the interviews and assist or speak at the request of the client. The executive search consultant's objectivity enables her or him to assess an interview without bias. After the candidates have been interviewed, the recruiter should indicate to you any negative or positive opinions. Obviously, the three final candidates are the ones whom the recruiter has found to be the most qualified, but his or her judgment can be helpful in selecting a final candidate.

When a final candidate has been selected, salary negotiations begin. The search firm can participate as actively in this process as the client wishes. Recruiters have experience in the negotiation process and knowledge of the candidate, the position, and what is being done at other institutions. A compensation specialist also may be used in the salary negotiation, if the institution has a budget for this expense and feels that it is necessary.

Once you have become a client of a search firm, the firm will normally not recruit anyone from your organization for a period of up to two years from the time of their last assignment from your organization. This can be stipulated in the letter of agreement. Some organizations keep executive search firms on retainer so that these firms will never recruit from within their institutions.

PSYCHOLOGICAL TESTING

Many questions are asked about the psychological testing of candidates. Is it necessary? Is it effective? Perhaps this story will serve as an example.

Many years ago a Wall Street firm apparently had been persuaded to use psychological testing for their candidates for executive positions. They sent five candidates for a trial test. After testing the candidates, the psychological evaluators advised the company that it was fortunate to have retained their services because all the candidates were psychologically unfit for the position. This company never used psychological testing again because it had sent its five most promotable managers as test cases, and they were the candidates deemed totally unfit for the hypothetical position in question.

However, if a client requires psychological testing, the search firm certainly should cooperate. There is some question, however, about subjecting executive candidates to psychological tests, lie detector tests, drug tests, and whatever else may come next as a substitute for the most important reason you have retained an executive search firm—objective judgment.

CONCLUSION

It is a tremendous responsibility for one individual to administer the human resources of an entire hospital or hospital department. Even if you are not charged with the final hiring decision, you may be faced with numerous choices that will be critical in determining who the final candidate will be. Working closely and effectively with your executive search consultant can eliminate most of the risk and make the process less stressful and far more productive. The importance of complete honesty between you and your search consultant cannot be repeated too often. You are involved in the complex process of fitting one particular human being into one specific situation. Everything about the situation, the people involved, and any unusual circumstances must be on the table.

To say that trust must be at the heart of the relationship between the executive search consultant and the human resource manager is not to say that you should abandon your own feelings, intuition, and opinions. Although an executive search consultant's judgment, discrimination, and insight are the most valuable commodities that you are buying when you invest in executive search, you always should express any objections or observations that you may have. Tell the recruiter exactly what you are thinking. This kind of open discussion leads to a more effective and successful relationship. Ask questions, even if the answers seem obvious. Never guess, and never assume. You have the right, and the obligation to your organization, to know everything about how your search is being conducted.

Finally, when things look impossible, keep the faith.

James J. Gallagher

How To Hire the Best Outplacement Services

28

If you haven't had much experience with outplacement firms—or if you could use some guidelines on how to pick the best sources for your company, or even for yourself—here is a checklist to help you locate the combination of quality and service that is most likely to satisfy your needs.

This may not be the ultimate word on the subject of selecting outplacement services. But it is the product of my own 18 years in the field and the wisdom accumulated along with my associates in our consultations with literally thousands of terminated executives and professionals.

It helps, I have found, to think of selecting outplacement services like shopping for a new car. First of all, you don't do it that often. Then, just like the first time you entered a new car showroom, you don't know how much to believe of what you hear at an outplacement firm.

It's always hard to separate sales hype from substance. But after buying a few new cars, you learn, for one thing, to get beyond the salesperson. At a car dealer, for instance, I visit the service department late Saturday morning, when I'm most likely to be there looking for help. I listen to how the service people treat customers—and then decide whether to get serious with a salesperson.

Such experience has taught me to look for substance over slick whenever I make a major purchase. I've learned that it takes time to investigate before making a decision, but it is time well spent. The time is particularly worthwhile in a major decision where tangible measurements are hard to pin down and a lot depends on gut feelings. Such is the case when the

new direction of an individual's career is the goal, and outplacement is the vehicle.

Metaphor aside, there are rational principles to guide the buyer of any professional service, whether it be outplacement, heart surgery, legal assistance, or even the college for your oldest child. The checklist starts with three categories: competency, compatibility, and commitment to the customer. Here are specifics so that you can apply those principles to your search for quality outplacement.

A. COMPETENCY

Short of buying the car or going through outplacement, it is difficult to forecast how well the choice is going to satisfy your needs. In the case of new cars, most of us have to rely on trial and error. When that isn't acceptable, or when, in outplacement, there isn't enough time, there are some pieces of data that can provide good clues. Apply the questions in this category first to the outplacement firm. Then, you can apply each of the questions as well to the individual consultants you meet there.

- *What are the track record and reputation of the firm?*
- *How long has the firm been in the outplacement field?*
- *Does it specialize in outplacment and other forms of transition counseling, or divide its energies in other forms of consulting such as compensation and benefits?*
- *How long has it worked with your company?* (No experience need not be bad because it means that the firm is

going to work hard to make sure the first client is successful.)

- *What other companies does it regularly work for?*
- *How often has the firm worked with similar clients?* (Salary level, age, specialty, any unique factor like cultural background or family status, e.g., the recently divorced nuclear power plant manager who is more fluent in his native Chinese dialect than in English.)
- *How successful is the firm with clients from companies like yours?* Outrageous claims like jobs in three weeks will alert you to the hard sell. Ask what criteria the firm uses for predicting length of job search (the old rule of thumb—one month per $10k in salary—is long outdated). Since most firms claim success, be sure to get specific examples of how they measure it.
- *How is the firm different from other outplacement firms?* Simply excuse yourself from further discussion with the consultant who tells you that all outplacement firms are alike and do the same things. Challenge the source of disparaging criticism of other firms. An honest consultant speaks to the strengths of his or her own firms, knows what they are, and the types of clients for whom they are best suited. (It is true that some outplacement firms are better for certain types of clients. Find out whether you are one of those types.)
- *Ask for references who can attest to the firm's work. This is tricky because a conscientious consultant will not violate confidentiality by revealing client names.* You might ask anyhow, just to see how the consultant handles the question. But also, ask around the company, among colleagues at other companies, and among friends for referrals.

B. COMPATIBILITY

Outplacement firms are staffed by people who guide and assist clients in the job search and career-planning process. It is the individual people at the firm who will give you the feel that you fit in well. So remember to ask individual consultants all the questions above that relate to firms. And in addition, there are more questions for them below.

Since it is unlikely—and not desirable—that a client works with a single individual at a firm, you will need to become familiar with the variety of professional staff a firm offers. Meet several of the consultants at least briefly, but be sure to spend at least an hour with the individual who will be your main contact person.

You may need a second visit at the firm that meets your criteria listed above to reassure yourself that the consultants also meet your criteria. Then discuss with the consultant issues like those that follow:

- *Does the consultant speak openly about his or her experience?* How much experience have they had, in outplacement and in business? How long with the firm?

- *Is there good personal chemistry?* Is this a person you can have confidence in?
- *Has this consultant made a successful career change, lost a job, made a successful recovery, i.e., experienced what clients go through?* Job search is truly like riding a roller coaster; you don't really know what it's like unless you've done it.
- *Familiarity of the consultant with your particular field is not so important as most clients first believe.* Outplacement training and coaching are applicable across the board. It's like being taught to give speeches. The basic techniques apply no matter what you talk about or who is in the audience. A competent consultant doing good work will bring out the best in a client from any field.
- *Familiarity with a candidate's specific job is not as important as most candidates believe.* A seasoned consultant has worked with clients from a range of levels, titles, and experience. It may be comforting to a client to know that the consultant has been a corporate officer, for example. But a more important question is how well the consultant can now coach the client in doing interviews and making important career decisions.
- *How good are the consultant's contacts to help a client in search?* Be suspicious of a consultant who even infers that he or she has contacts that will place a client. Outplacement firms simply do not place people in jobs. Search firms do that. Outplacement firms do have job banks, job listings, and sophisticated computerized sources of data on companies, and many have good contacts with search firms. All of these support, but do not replace, the client's own high level of job search activity.
- *Will the consultant tell the client what he or she needs to hear or wants to hear?* If a client can put aside what is desired, an initial meeting with a consultant can yield valuable advice. For example, don't be afraid to ask the consultant, "What problems do you see that I might have in my search?" One of our staff members got that question from an overweight computer engineer. Overcoming his own reluctance to hurt the client's feelings, the consultant advised: "Your external appearance contradicts your intellectual strengths and professional competence. Plainly speaking, you have to lose weight." The client winced and said, "I want to start working with you today. You're the only outplacement consultant honest enough to tell me the truth."
- *Is the nonprofessional staff friendly and cheerful?* A good indicator of the "backstage" workings of a firm can come from clues a visitor picks up front stage. Expression of courtesy from the receptionist and the politeness used among the administrative staff in talking to each other can hint at how comfortable a client would feel spending a lot of time there.
- *Are the values expressed by the consultant consistent with those of the client?* The degree of respect a consultant

shows for your opinions, how the consultant talks about other clients, how well the consultant listens and responds—all these are often indicators you can rely on.

- *Will the consultant talk about other cases, the difficult ones as well as the successes?* How does the consultant justify the occasional "failure"? And how does the consultant distinguish between success and failure?
- *Is the consultant the kind of person a client would feel comfortable talking with about personal goals, achievements, and disappointments, not just in the career, but in life as well?*
- *Conversely, is the consultant comfortable talking about personal history, job changes, and the experiences that qualify the consultant to give advice on critical life decisions?*

C. COMMITMENT

Any professional, to deserve the name, must put the interests of the client in first place. As a potential client, it is legitimate for you to make sure that the success of the job search or career change will be the priority of both the firm and the consultant.

Oddly enough, the structure and financing of the firm are more important in this consideration that most people would realize.

- *Who owns the firm?* It's a legitimate question since it has implications for how the firm is managed, how the professionals are compensated, and how much of the firm's income is committed to servicing of clients versus support of corporate overhead.
- *Do the owners of the firm practice outplacement?* Think of going to a law firm, a dentist, or heart surgeon. You want to be sure that the professional doing the work is backed up by supervisors who also know what needs to be done and who will commit resource like time and support services. Professional firms that maintain high quality have historically been the ones in which the practitioners administer the firm and the administrators are qualified practitioners. Too many outplacement firms are modeled after business organizations rather than professional ones. Since it is often difficult to tell from what is said, clients need to ask whether they are talking to the sales, administration, or production departments. The safest course is to talk to a consultant who, like a doctor or lawyer, both sells the service and performs the work.
- *How are the consultants compensated?* If the professional you are talking with is paid on the basis of new business developed, that person's interests have to be more in selling the service than in delivering it. A potential new client needs to be aware of the difficulty in this conflict.
- *Is the consultant full time, part time, or temporary?* Because of the rapid growth in the outplacement field and

the competitive tactics of the recent entrants to it, a number of firms list on their rosters people whose real commitments are elsewhere. They may not be on call when a candidate has a question. Therefore, ask the right question up front: "Are you available here on a full-time basis?"

- *How heavy a workload does the consultant carry?* The bulk of the head-to-head work in a job search is completed within the first two weeks after starting with the outplacement firm. The rest is follow-up and requires less time. Three to four "starts" a month and a caseload of about 25 clients at a time will keep most consultants reasonably busy, but available.
- *Does the consultant schedule follow-up sessions, or wait for the client to call "when you think you need help?"*
- *How available are the office service facilities? Are the ones you are shown the ones clients in your category really use?* Generally, desk space or private office space at an outplacement firm is not reserved, but available on a first-come basis. That is not always told to clients up front. Be sure to ask specifics on this.
- *How flexible will the consultants be, given a client's particular situation?* Some outplacement firms boast about being "flexible" and accuse others of being "too structured." Any professional service needs to follow some defined procedures. Think of the way a physical examination follows a normal routine. But the doctor stops the procedure to investigate a symptom that shows up and then returns to the scheduled procedure. Claims of "flexibility" are made by consultants who "wing it" through their cases, and who are probably not giving their clients full attention or services. A reasonable degree of discipline with consistency of procedures throughout the firm, I have found, is the only way to guarantee quality service. Seasoned consultants will tailor their meetings to the unique needs of individual clients, and rely on their own past experiences to adapt to the program. But they'll cover all the bases.
- *What if a client wants to change careers instead of just looking for a new job?* You'll find that all outplacement consultants are career changers themselves—nobody grew up to do this work because it only started 20 years ago and became common less than 10. In a thorough outplacement program, detailed career assessment and planning are part of the initial work. Be sure to understand how these are done and what the client's part in them has to be. You'll probably find, as do most people, that the exercise is the most interesting and most selfishly beneficial thing a client has done in years.
- *How much training has the consultant had in the outplacement process?* Listen for the "fudging" in this reply. Training in outplacement firms ranges from "Read through this manual; your first client arrives in the morning," to the 400 plus hours of cognitive learning, observation, and supervised work that a firm invests in new

consultants. Don't be afraid to ask what was involved in the training and who supervised it. You don't want the client's job search to be the consultant's trial and error.

- *To whom is the consultant loyal, the company that's paying the bill or the candidate?* This question should be asked more often, because it puts a focus on the multi-level relationship maintained by an outplacement consultant. The consultant is paid by the employer to serve the needs of the individual client. The employer needs to know that the work is done, so the consultant sends reports. However, the confidentiality of the client cannot be compromised in those reports. If a client is uncomfortable about this issue, discuss it openly with the consultant.

- *What if the client needs services in another city or country?* Most corporate executives these days conduct national-scope searches. A firm needs resources available throughout the United States and even around the world. Most outplacement firms claim such affiliations. But the availability of resources is questionable in the case of franchise holders or casual relationships. So don't hesitate to get specific if you anticipate a need.

- *Can you sort out what are referred to as "bell and whistles" offered by some outplacement firms?* Great lobby decorations, computer printouts, complicated job and data banks, health club memberships, and 24-hour call-in counselors may appeal to some clients. The question to ask is whether they are what you need or just distractions from good old-fashioned head-to-head consulting by competent professionals.

D. CHARACTERISTICS OF OUTSTANDING CAREER COUNSELORS

- The counselor should have a *strong and distinct character*; she or he should not be overbearing or arrogant, but a person of definite principles and values.

- The good practitioner is *self-assured*, confident, and has solved his or her own problems of identity. This feature is needed because a good counselor spends much of every day revealing a good deal of self to the client. We do serve—like it or not—as role models for the people we assist.

- There is an air of *seasoning* and an evident *maturity* about an effective counselor, which does not necessarily correlate with age.

- The *ability to communicate* clearly and effectively goes nearly without saying.

- There is a *commitment to succeeding* in the context of both personal life and business. This is essential in the conselor if it is to be transmitted to the client. The success of the client, more than just the social good it does generate, is also a positive measure of the professional success of the counselor.

- An ironic sense of *pleasure at beating the system* also helps. The effective counselor assists a client in overcoming years of ingrained culture and mythology. There is a whole system of beliefs encrusted with notions of being "out of work and useless," of being a "failure" and losing the identity we all get from our jobs. These powerful shibboleths challenge all but the strongest spirit.

- And, the most important of all we have found for outplacement counselors is the *ability to smile*—more specifically, to be that upbeat kind of person who can see the good in most dismal events, who is confident of the happy endings when all looks pretty sad and dreary at the beginning.

FINAL NOTE

While there is no agency to provide a seal of approval in the 20-year-old outplacement field, a prospective client can look for a firm's membership in the Association of Outplacement Consulting Firms. This is a five-year-old group that sets standards of stability and practice for its members. It provides grievance procedures for complaints against them.

If your conclusion by now is that I have presented the need for a prospective client to be cautious in selecting outplacement services—you are absolutely correct. We would all like it to be different, but the fast growth of outplacement, the ease of entry into consulting businesses generally, and the lack of legal regulation have attracted opportunists masquerading as professionals. That is not surprising in this world.

People who interview outplacement firms, either for their companies or for themselves, are generally experienced managers. They are hard to fool. But the emotions around job loss run high, and often cloud up the selection process. It may be difficult for them, in this situation, to transfer the knowledge learned elsewhere.

You have just read the caveats involved in sensible selection of this important service. To those must be added, unfortunately, another that originated 20 centuries ago. The Romans coined the phrase *caveat emptor*—"let the buyer beware." It still applies in most of our dealings, including when you shop for outplacement services.

Robin Gourlay

29

Negotiations for Managers

WHY NEGOTIATE?

Everyone needs negotiating skills. In any organization, especially one as involved as the National Health Service (NHS), people are going to disagree. Unless there is a good way of resolving these disagreements, the conflict will escalate, and become destructive both of individual relationships and of the objectives which the NHS is trying to achieve.

Negotiations are a way of bringing about agreement. We typically think of neotiations in industrial relations terms, where management and trade unions bargain with each other over a negotiating table. Often these negotiations hit the headlines, and it is sometimes difficult for outsiders to understand why the two parties can't reach agreement. This is not necessarily because of any inherent "badness" in either of the parties, but because of a lack of skill in one party or another in searching for creative answers, which meet the needs of both.

Negotiations take place between individuals, when one person is trying to persuade another to accept his or her point of view. We don't always call these negotiations but in effect that is the process being used.

Negotiations happen at all times and in all places. It is quite wrong to think of them only as set pieces where one party confronts the other with its demands.

The more that you practice negotiations, the more skillful you will become at resolving disagreements. It is when people do not have these skills that they are fearful and embarrassed

Note: Excerpted and reprinted with permission from *Negotiations for Managers* by Robin Gourlay, published by the Health Services Manpower Review, Keele, Staffordshire, England, 1987.

by conflicts and disagreements. Instead of searching for a solution they back away, and either give in grudgingly, or alternatively attempt by different means to dominate the other party.

Neither of these strategies is necessarily in the best interests of the individuals. They store up problems for the future. By having skills in negotiating agreements you will feel a great deal more confident about managing your part of the organization, influencing others, and, above all, achieving objectives which are in the best interests of the patients.

CAN EVERYTHING BE NEGOTIATED?

We have said that negotiations are about achieving agreement, but are there situations where it is quite impossible to achieve agreements? The answer is of course "yes." Not everything can be negotiated. No one can compel you to negotiate. Negotiations are essentially a voluntary relationship between the two parties. If one party believes that they are unlikely to achieve anything of value from the negotiations, they will withdraw and find some other way of resolving the disagreement.

This often happens when terrorists take hostages and demand to negotiate their release. Many countries now refuse to negotiate, believing that by so doing they may encourage the terrorists to take further hostages. In this sense a country is unwilling to take part in the negotiations, because it believes that it can achieve better results by not being involved. Not everything is negotiable!

Issues are only negotiable when both parties believe it is worth their while being involved in negotiations. This does mean that sometimes an early strategy of potential negotiators is to persuade the other party that it is worthwhile attempting to resolve the difference through negotiations.

It is worth considering this a little further. What in essence are the factors that would prevent someone from trying to resolve her or his differences through negotiation?

The first of these is where one party genuinely believes it is unlikely to gain anything from the negotiations. In this case it is obviously up to the other party to demonstrate the potential benefits that can be derived from negotiations. But it may be that the sticking point for the other party is a question of principle or values. They believe that they will not compromise these. In this case the negotiator has first of all to indicate a recognition of these values or principles, and then to persuade the other that any outcomes of the negotiations will be in accord with the principles or values.

This is particularly important for Health Service professionals, who have very strongly held convictions and beliefs about the nature of their work. For example, doctors believe that they must have clinical responsibility for the patient at all times and that they alone can prescribe the treatment to be provided by other professionals to "their" patients.

There have been many conflicts in the NHS about this, most of them remaining unresolved, creating a sense of dissatisfaction and demotivation. To achieve the agreement of medical staff to "allowing" others more responsibility, it must, at the very outset be made clear that this does not jeopardize the principle that the doctors do have overall responsibility for the patient. By safeguarding this value or principle we are more likely to achieve some agreement on the relationship between the doctor and other staff on the way the patient's treatment should be managed.

WHAT DO WE NEGOTIATE ABOUT?

Negotiations are about achieving agreement where there is currently a difference. What are the causes of differences or disagreements in any organization? There are many. Differences, as we said in the previous section, may be about values. Where these are strongly held it is unlikely that negotiations will bring about a change in the values and principles themselves. This is the case of the martyr who preferred to die rather than sacrifice his beliefs.

It is important for organizations to have a firm set of values, which provide the basis for the everyday conduct of individuals. It is right that these values should not be negotiable. On the other hand there are values and principles which for a variety of reasons become inappropriate. Yet individuals cling to the past. Differences then arise between the old order and the new, which are perhaps best settled through some form of negotiation. We recall an example of where a consultant refused, as a matter of principle, to allow curtains around "his" beds because of the possibility of cross-infection.

Negotiations led to screens, then an experiment with curtains until he was negotiated away from his principle!

Differences also arise about objectives, and the priorities that attach to them. For example, in the Health Service there is frequent discussion over whether to invest in new equipment, or additional staff, or new buildings.

Often there are no hard and fast criteria which enable a decision to be reached on the amount which should be devoted to each. Such decisions are arrived at through negotiation. Another example might be a discussion between medical staff on how many beds particular specialties should have. Again there are no hard and fast rules which provide an answer to this. The best result can often be achieved through skillful negotiation.

Individuals' interests and needs can also conflict. It may be that an individual wishes to have a few days on holiday, but his manager requires him to undertake a particularly important assignment which needs to be completed whilst he is away. It would be easy for the manager to prevent the subordinate from going on holiday, but this would give rise to considerable frustration and dissatisfaction on the part of the subordinate.

Negotiations, if they are skillfully conducted, can lead to a decision which meets both the needs of the manager, and those of the subordinate.

ARE THERE OTHER WAYS OF OVERCOMING DIFFERENCES BETWEEN PARTIES?

The negotiating process is not the only way that decisions can be reached. Group discussions are a very effective way of achieving agreement, particularly where there may be many individuals involved, with a variety of views.

For example, many management meetings which discuss strategic issues aim to achieve agreement through consensus. Consensus is a state of mind where all the individuals commit themselves to the decision although the decision itself is not necessarily unanimous.

Another and frequently employed way of resolving disagreements is through voting. Voting has the advantage of speed, but it can leave a sizable minority who remain unconvinced by the majority's view, and therefore uncommitted to the decision which has been reached.

A third approach is sometimes called "bulldozing" or "railroading." Here one or two powerful individuals assert their decision over the views of others, by force of personality, or the exercise of naked power. Obviously such decisions do not necessarily earn the commitment of those who have been "bulldozed." There is a significant danger that the implementation of the decision will be less than effective.

The final way of resolving differences is a bit like "railroading." This is the use of threats. Threats are made to seek compliance of the other, and unless such compliance is forthcoming there is the possibility that the threat will be implemented.

You can see that there are a number of ways in which differences can be overcome. Perhaps the ideal is that of consensus. It requires that the views of all have been taken into account, and as a result everyone feels committed to the outcome even though the decision does not necessarily represent their own preferred position.

However, consensus can be difficult to achieve, particularly where beliefs and values are strongly held, or interests diverge considerably. In this situation the most appropriate process is that of negotiation. Skillfully conducted, negotiation can actually achieve a decision similar to that of consensus. Both parties feel that their needs have been satisfed and are committed to implementing the decision.

All the other processes leave a minority of individuals dissatisfied, and there are dangers where commitment to a decision is minimal.

WHAT IS CONFLICT?

Conflicts and disagreements are inevitable in any organization. Conflicts may be between individuals, groups of staff, or professionals. They can be about the allocation of resources, the way in which patients should be treated, the management of particular individuals, and so on. The common feature is that there is a disagreement that needs resolution if progress is to be made.

It is the manner of this resolution which gives rise to two theoretically distinct processes for conflict resolution. We say ''theoretically'' because it is helpful in analyzing the nature of conflict to distinguish between the two types, although most conflict resolution strategies are an amalgam of both approaches. But more of this later.

Distributive Conflict

Distributive conflict is what the person in the street would associate with the word *conflict*. The essence of distributive conflict is that the conflicting parties perceive there to be only one cake and that their objective is to gain the greater share of this for themselves. What one party wins, the other loses. Distributive conflict is ''win/lose.''

If you do perceive the conflict in which you are involved in distributive terms, then your strategy will be to behave very purposefully in pursuit of your own goals and interests. You will appear absolutely committed to these, and give the impression that there is little chance that you will move away from them. You will tend to use secrecy to disguise your real requirements and may well misrepresent these to the other. You will try to take him by surprise, and catch him off balance. You may use threats and bluffs to bolster your own position. You will view the other party as your opponent and develop a negative stereotype of him, using fairly uncomplimentary language to describe his behavior.

Most individuals would probably not own up to using this strategy for resolving conflict. But in many experiments in which we have been involved, it is nearly always the case that the parties to the negotiation, initially at least, perceive the conflict in distributive terms, and behave in the way we have described. They are going to win, and the other to lose.

In many organizations including the Health Service the consequence of this is considerable organizational politicking. Individuals try to gather supportive groups around them so that they are able to argue their case from a powerful base. People preserve their own territories very strongly, believing that an empire enhances their power and status. Where they are unable to win in the conflict, is it passed up the line for resolution; people cannot be seen to lose.

Similarly risk taking is discouraged. Failure is not acceptable in organizations where power is derived from winning. In these organizations there is little commitment to overall organizational objectives. Individuals, groups, and professions pursue their own objectives, believing that these actually represent the best interests of the organization as a whole. Organizational change is stultified. Change implies risk from which some will win and some lose.

We have tried to describe an atmosphere of an organization where conflict is seen in win/lose terms (i.e., distributively). You may think the descriptions are a little extreme, but look at your own organization, and observe whether you note any of these characteristics.

Integrative Conflict

Conflict is managed on an integrative basis when both parties believe that there is a possibility that their own interests and those of the other party can be satisfied as a result of the negotiations. They perceive the conflict in ''win/win'' terms.

The negotiating processes for integrative conflict are very different from those of distributive conflict. In this case behavior is purposeful in pursuing goals which are held in common. There is in other words a superordinate goal to which both parties commit themselves. Behavior tends to be more open with people sharing their own perceptions of the issues between them, and being willing to explore a wide range of alternatives. There is no attempt to disguise their needs. They are accurately represented to the other. Behavior tends to be predictable, so that the other party is not taken by surprise. The whole essence of the approach is to build trust between the parties, so that creative resolution of the conflict can be found. Hence threats or bluffs are not used; what is used is a logical and rational approach to problem solving.

Where this is the prevailing mode of resolving conflict within the organization, you will find a much greater commitment to overall objectives, to which end groups and individuals are willing to modify their own particular requirements. Creativity is likely to flourish because people are not afraid of taking risks. There is not an atmosphere where failure is punished. Groups and individuals are encouraged to resolve their own differences. They are not passed up the line to superiors for resolution.

In a sense the prevailing process for managing conflict on an integrative basis is much more akin to that of group consensus decision making. Why therefore do not more individuals and organizations try and encourage a resolution of conflict on the basis of integrative problem solving?

This is not the place to search for an answer to this question, but we suspect that the educational and cultural background of individuals must have a large part to play in determining the prevailing mode of conflict resolution within organizations.

Where the organization stresses competition for improving performance, and recruits individuals who are competitive, then one would expect to find a "win/lose" culture. On the other hand where the values of collaboration are emphasized, one would expect more of an integrative approach to conflict resolution.

In the Health Service it could be assumed that the superordinate goal of patient welfare would inevitably lead to negotiations of an integrative nature. Regrettably this is not the case, possibly because of the competitiveness between professional and organizational groups for power. It is this which leads to a predominantly distributive culture. This though does not mean that it must always be like this. Individuals who are skillful in negotiations are able to influence the processes used by others.

For example, it is quite possible to turn what might start off as a "win/lose" negotiation into a "win/win" negotiation. This does however mean that the negotiator has to know how to handle distributive negotiations, so that he can persuade the other of the value of tackling the negotiations in a "win/win" manner.

COMMUNICATING IN THE NEGOTIATION

Negotiations are interpersonal relationships in which communications play a vital role. For there to be an outcome in which both parties win, it is essential that each be able to communicate clearly with the other. Yet the emotions generated by the conflict or difference of opinion can make listening to the other's point of view extremely difficult. It requires a real effort of will to hear the arguments of the other party, and understand the logic behind them. A negotiator who is a skilled listener will have a head start over someone who is less skilled.

To begin, let us explore what might impede or distort the communications between two negotiators. For most communications, there is always some distortion between what someone intends to say and what is actually received by the recipient of the communication. If we can identify the causes of this distortion, then it is probably that we will be able to impove the quality of the communication. We can boil down the main causes of communication distortion to two factors.

The first of these are "filters." Filters are "psychological blocks" which in some way or another distort what another person says to us.

The second cause of distortion is that of "double messages." Here a communicator is sending more than one message at the same time. It is worthwhile examining each of these in a little more depth.

Filters

1. The first filter is that of assumptions. We often assume for example that we know what the objectives and needs of the other party are.

   We may assume that a party wants to sell their house for as much money as possible. This could be quite incorrect. They will want money, but what may be of overriding importance to them is a quick sale as they are emigrating in a few weeks. Never assume that you know what the other side requires. Always take time and trouble to find out for yourself what their objectives and needs are.

2. A second filter is concerned with preconceptions. Because our minds make connections very easily, we make inferences from little bits of information that we glean from our surroundings.

   For example, if the other party dresses well and gives off an air of affluence and status, we may well be somewhat deferential. Our preconception may enable him or her to exert power and influence over us during the negotiations. But it does not cost much to dress well, or even hire an expensive car for a day, to give such an impression. If the deal is an important one, it may be well worthwhile for someone to go to the trouble of trying to influence your preconceptions toward him or her to gain an advantage.

   Similarly when we are negotiating with, say, a senior representative of another authority, we may imbue the other negotiator with power and influence which she or he does not possess. Preconceptions do influence our behavior and attitudes toward others.

   Contrariwise, you need to think about the impression you wish to create on the other party. You need to consider what clothes you should wear, and what "trappings" of power might accompany you to the negotiating table!

3. A third and particularly important filter in negotiations is that of defensiveness. Defensiveness allows us to protect ourselves from criticism. It works by ascribing blame for faults in our own behavior or actions to others.

   In negotiations it may be the case that the other party is critical of your stance and arguments on quite rational grounds. It is important for you to be able to accept these criticisms without becoming defensive. By "hearing" and accepting them you will be in a better position to resolve the problems that lie between you and the other.

If on the other hand you react defensively and reject the criticism, there is considerable danger that the negotiations will escalate into attack and counterattack, the purpose being to score points, rather than to achieve agreement.

There are many other filters, such as prejudice, strong emotions, and fear. These filters can inhibit the communications between parties. Particularly they may prevent you from genuinely "hearing" what the other party is saying to you. In a negotiation it is absolutely essential that your listening skills be at peak perfection. Later on in this chapter we will describe a method which you can use to improve these skills.

Double Messages

Let us now turn to the other cause of distortion in the communication process. This one occurs when the communicator sends more than one message at the same time.

"Double messages" occur particularly frequently with unskilled negotiators. For example, you have probably heard the negotiator who opens by saying: "I am being very generous to you in this" or "Let me be quite honest and frank with you." Somehow you know that these communications actually conceal a covert communication which may be the exact opposite of what is being said.

Researchers[1] into communications in negotiation coined a phrase for these types of communications. They called them "irritators"; they have this effect on the receiving party!

Double messages like defensiveness can lead to defend/ attack spirals. The receiver of the double message may challenge the integrity of the sender, and complain that the offer is not generous; nor is he being honest. These criticisms give rise to defensiveness in the other, and the negotiations escalate away from the substantive issues into personal vilification.

A way of dealing with double messages is to "level" with the other by describing your feelings to the communication. So when somebody says to you: "This is very generous," you may respond by saying: "I accept that you may consider your offer generous but it actually makes me feel a little suspicious. I ask myself why are you being generous to me?" If you respond in this way, you are not being evaluative or passing a judgment on the other. You are merely reflecting your own feelings which the other can hardly deny.

Returning again to the research into communications in negotiation, we find that effective negotiators more frequently "level" with the other party than less effective negotiators. They are more open about how they feel; progress being made; and their attitudes towards the other. The researchers called this "feelings commentary."

So far we have considered some of the distorting factors in the communication process. Earlier we promised to give you an idea for handling these. This is "paraphrasing."

Paraphrasing

Paraphrasing is a communications technique which many of us use quite unconsciously. All paraphrasing does is to "play back" to the other party what you think he said. Although simple to explain, it requires a mental discipline to do.

If you say to yourself that you will paraphrase, then it forces you to listen and concentrate a great deal harder on what the other is saying. By paraphrasing you will give the other party an opportunity to correct any misunderstandings which have occurred during the communication. Sometimes it is useful to get the other party to paraphrase what you have said so that you can ensure that your communication has been properly received.

A way of doing this is to say to the other, "I am not sure that I explained the last point very well. I wonder if you could just play it back to me to make sure that I got it across properly."

You will note that in this choice of language you are not questioning the listening ability of the other, but are taking any blame for a faulty communication on yourself. You are avoiding the possibility of their becoming defensive.

When we ask participants in our negotiating skills course to paraphrase, a number of them do find it quite difficult. They observe how much more effort they have to give to concentrate on what the other party is saying. Many times they find that they are working out their response to the point made by the other, before the other has actually finished speaking! By doing this they have not "heard" the last part of the communication. Another very interesting feature of paraphrasing is that it actually improves the relationship between the parties. Bearing in mind that what we are trying to do is to meet the needs of both parties, this can best be done where the relationship is sound. On the other hand where a great deal of attack and counterattack takes place, then listening will be jeopardized and the chances of understanding the needs of the other severely curtailed.

Communications are not only verbal. There are nonverbal elements to communications, and as a negotiator it is important that you understand these. Occasionally you may want to use them to influence the behavior of the other.

Nonverbal Behavior

There have been many books written about nonverbal behavior. Some would argue that you can divine the most secret of motives from nonverbal behavior. We do not go this far! But we do believe that you can use nonverbal behavior to influence the behavior of others. For example, if you sit forward and maintain eye contact with the other, it demonstrates an interest in what they are saying. If on the other hand you lounge back in your chair with your arms folded, and do not maintain eye contact, it is quite difficult for the other party to communicate with you. You are showing complete disinterest.

We have a colleague who has used this technique in nego-tiating quite often. For example in some negotiations to do with an organizational change, the trade unions wished to negotiate about the gradings of jobs with management. Man-agement were adamant that they were not going to negotiate on this. Whenever the issue was raised by the trade unions, the management negotiator would slump back in his chair, drop eye contact, and fold his arms. This behavior resulted in the trades union negotiators' never pursuing the point beyond a few half-hearted protestations!

What is going on is that certain behaviors of the other party are rewarded, by signs of interest and involvement, whereas other behaviors are not rewarded.

Look also for unconscious nonverbal behaviors. As you get to know the other party they may have particular mannerisms. When, for example, an agreement is about to be reached, one negotiator whose mouth goes dry at this point quite naturally licks his lips. The other party knows that when this happens there is no need to offer any further concessions to clinch the deal.

We have already referred to the research into communica-tions during negotiation. The section "Teamworking in Nego-tiations" looks a little more comprehensively at the results of this research.

Communications Research

There is quite a difference between the way in which effec-tive negotiators communicate and those who are less effective.

Effective negotiators quite frequently label their commu-nication. For example, they might say, "I am going to ask you a question. . ." or "I will put a proposal to you. . . ." The value of doing this is that the intention of the communication is quite clear. There can be no ambiguity about its purpose.

The one communication which they did not label was when they were disagreeing with the other. On these occasions they built up a logical case as to why the view of the other party was not acceptable, and allowed the case to speak for itself.

We have already referred to attack and counterattack, or what some people call *defend/attack spirals*. These can occur when the negotiations become a battle between personalities. It is very important to avoid this happening. You should be tough on the problem, but treat the other party with courtesy and respect. A useful maxim to bear in mind when negotiating is to separate the people from the problems. In this way you will avoid the possibility of slipping into defend/attack spirals.

The researchers also found that effective negotiators do not meet a proposal with a *rapid counterproposal*. If they feel unable to accept the proposal made by the other, they give their reasons for disagreeing with it and then make their own counterproposal. By doing it in this way they indicate that they have given consideration to the arguments of the other and not just dismissed them out of hand.

One of the temptations that less-skilled negotiators fall victim to is to leave some loose ends untied. There is a fear that

by raising issues which have not been absolutely resolved, they may jeopardize the whole agreement. Skilled negotiators do not allow this. They make sure that *all the ends are neatly tied*. They use phrases like: "Are we agreed?" and "Can I get clear that this is what we have ended up with?" and so on.

TEAMWORKING IN NEGOTIATIONS

Teams play an important part in negotiations. You may negotiate as part of a team, or possibly on behalf of another team of people, where you act as their representative.

Because the process of negotiations is quite complex we suggest that in any negotiations of importance, you should have a negotiating team. The team might be as small as two people, or possibly as large as six or seven people. Once it gets beyond this number then it is difficult to manage, and some team members will appear to take no part in the negotiation.

We have been involved in national negotiations on pay and conditions of service in the NHS, where each side was com-posed of about 20 people or so. This meant that the actual negotiations went on between only one or two individuals, whilst the others looked on. We do not think that this is a very efficient use of people's time, and certainly makes the man-agement of the negotiating team very difficult.

There are two types of teams involved in negotiations. The first is the direct team where team members themselves are directly involved in the negotiation over the table. The second is the indirect team; that is the group of people on behalf of whom the direct team is negotiating. They both have important but distinct parts to play in the negotiating process.

The Direct Team

The composition of the direct team is a matter of judgment. One rule that we would suggest is that the "ultimate decision maker" should not be a member of the direct team. By excluding him or her from the negotiations it allows for his or her intervention at a later stage, which could be particularly valuable if the negotiations appear to be becoming dead-locked. Otherwise the team composition should reflect those who have a genuine interest in the outcome, who possess some negotiating skills, and who are able to fulfill the roles described later.

The value of the team is that it can bring more minds to bear on the problem or conflict of the negotiation. A particularly useful feature is to have one team member acting as the "devil's advocate," when you are planning the negotiations. Not only will the devil's advocate find potential weaknesses in your own arguments but by having to rehearse your arguments before the devil's advocate, you will develop a strong commit-ment to your point of view. This will enable you to enter the negotiations feeling confident about the logic of your case.

The devil's advocate prevents you from living in a fool's paradise.

Sometimes teams develop a cozy atmosphere and are unwilling to discuss the potential weaknesses of their own arguments, fearing that this may upset other team colleagues. This has been called "group think." By legitimizing the role of devil's advocate, group think is avoided.

Another valuable feature of having more than one person involved in negotiations is that different styles can be used. At a simple level this could be the lead negotiator taking a hard line, whilst a colleague, perhaps outside the formal negotiating arena, takes a much softer line with the other party.

A more sophisticated version of the hard and soft negotiating ploy was once used by the treasurer and personnel manager of a health authority when negotiating with some ambulancemen. In this case they had agreed that the treasurer would take the hard line, arguing that no concessions could be made because of the procedures and regulations. The personnel manager on the other hand would appear to argue with him apparently on behalf of the staff, suggesting that it was permissible to make a particular concession which would be of value to the staff. During this interchange the staff themselves sat back and watched the two managers appearing to argue the case amongst themselves. When they had arrived at a prearranged point, the personnel manager turned to the ambulancemen and said, "Well I think that is all we can do. Obviously the treasurer has moved as far as he can." The staff nodded their agreement to this observation and accepted the outcome of the negotiations, in which they had actually taken little part.

There are specific roles too, that need to be filled in the direct team.

The Lead Negotiator

The first and most obvious role is that of the lead negotiator. It is this person's job to argue his or her side's case with the other. It is he or she who proposes particular points of view and responds to the others' arguments. The lead negotiator may of course change during the course of the negotiation. Some teams organize themselves so that they have a prearranged signal to bring someone else in as the lead negotiator.

The Process Analyst

A second role is that of the process analyst. The person filling this role has the responsibility for working out what is going on between negotiators. Someone once referred to this rather colorfully as the "interpersonal underworld." The process analyst tries to assess the effect of your team on the other team. He or she looks at the nonverbal behavior of the others to see whether there are any clues which may help his or her team in coming to a settlement. Although we suggest that the process analyst's role is a distinct one, the skills of process analysis should form part of every negotiator's armoury. It is essential for you to be aware of the interaction and feelings of the other team and their relationship with you and your team.

The Recorder

A third very important role is that of the recorder. The recorder's responsibility is to draft the agreement reached between the parties. He or she should keep a record of the concessions offered and accepted so that when the final agreement is reached, he or she already has a draft of this prepared. We have known some particularly skillful recorders who, when asked by their team leader, were able almost instantaneously to produce a draft agreement which proved acceptable to both sides. But as you draft it, you know exactly what is meant by it. This could be helpful in any subsequent debate.

The Space Creator

The final role is one that we call the "space creator." Negotiations are a bit like a game of tennis. If your lead negotiator is served an ace, he or she is not able to respond immediately. He or she will feel embarrassed and lose some degree of confidence. To overcome this, the space creator leaps into the negotiation and talks more or less about anything, until the lead negotiator has recovered his or her composure. At this stage the lead negotiator interrupts whatever the space creator is saying and carries on with the negotiations.

The role of space creator may seem a rather difficult one to fulfill. But we know of colleagues who are frequently called on to do this, especially when their own lead negotiator feels uncomfortable. This is particularly the case when the other side accuses him or her of some incompetence or another and he or she feels so angry that the escalation into "defend/attack" spirals is close at hand. The space creator is able to defuse the situation.

Ideally, negotiating team members should become familiar with each other, and know how to help each other during the course of negotiations. It is obviously important that they should have eye contact with their team colleagues so that they know when they can be of most assistance. Direct teams therefore should organize the seating arrangements so that communication is possible without having necessarily to pass notes to each other.

Indirect Teams

Indirect teams are so important that we suggest that if you do not have one, then you should invent one! Indirect teams are those groups of people on whose behalf the direct team is negotiating. Sometimes the direct team can be a vast number of people such as the membership of a trade union. On other occasions the team may only be the family of the negotiator, when, for example, he or she is negotiating the purchase of a house or car.

The indirect team should agree with the negotiator what negotiating discretion he or she has. They should describe the parameters within which the settlement should be reached. They should work with the negotiator in developing the strategy and objectives for the negotiation. Many times they will be able to provide the negotiating team with backup information which will help in the negotiation. They need to demonstrate their commitment to the team, and to the negotiated agreement. On rare occasions the indirect team may enter the negotiations, but only when the final stages are reached and all that remains is often the symbolic signing.

The indirect team provides power for the direct team. This is why we suggest that if you cannot readily identify the indirect team, then you should invent it. It may be that you feel that you need time to think about a proposal. By having to refer back to an indirect team you are able to have this time. Further, if on consideration you wish to reject the proposal, you can ascribe this rejection to the decision of the indirect team.

You may think that this is a rather cowardly way of progressing, but let us refer you to an editorial which appeared in the *Times* newspaper on March 1, 1982. The occasion was the highjacking of an aircraft and hostages by Tanzanian terrorists. The aircraft landed in Britain and the negotiations began. The *Times* reports these as follows:

> A negotiator of junior rank is preferable, since he can say with truth that he has no power to deal with certain requests, but most consult and so can play for time. Time, though it prolongs the hostages' ordeal, can save their lives. A human bond develops between them and their captors, the captors unwittingly become dependent upon the police with whom they are negotiating, so the police gather more information about the character of the terrorists, their numbers of weapons and exact locations.[2]

Another example of the relationship between a direct and indirect team was graphically described to us by a colleague who negotiates on behalf of management of the New York hospitals.

> At one of our seminars he showed a TV programme which was made about the bi-annual negotiations over pay between management and Trade Unions. The negotiations took place in a large room. Down the centre of this room was a long table, on one side of which sat management, and on the other the staff-side representatives. Behind the staff representatives were a large number of their members. At the time of the TV programme the negotiations had reached a difficult spot, when neither side appeared to be willing to make any further concessions.
>
> After a few opening skirmishes the Trade Union negotiator became increasingly violent, throwing ashtrays and paper darts at management. They were rude and abusive. This built up to a crescendo during which the Trade Union members started shouting and jeering, encouraging their representatives to further heights of violence and aggression. After suffering for some time this invective, management stood up and walked out of the negotiating room to the jeers and catcalls of the Trade Union members.
>
> The next scene on the TV film was the self same Trade Union representatives and management talking quietly and privately alone, obviously genuinely trying to find some form of settlement.[3]

Normally it would be difficult to excuse the behavior of the staff side negotiators, but it was evident that they needed to demonstrate to their own direct team that they were working hard to achieve the best settlement possible. One way of demonstrating this to the indirect team was to vilify management.

The relationship between the direct negotiating team and the indirect team is crucial. Unless managed with care, it can create some stressful dilemmas. In a way, the American illustration highlights these.

DILEMMAS OF THE NEGOTIATOR AS A REPRESENTATIVE

Negotiating representatives obviously want to do well on behalf of the team or organization which they represent. This powerful motivation to succeed causes the first problem: that of the *hero/traitor dilemma*.

The pressure is to succeed and to return home the conquering hero, earning the praise and plaudits of the indirect team. After all, one knows what happens to traitors, or those who let the side down. This pressure causes the other dilemma: that of *logic/loyalty*.

Normally most people use logical and rational thought to resolve difficulties. In negotiations the loyalty to one's own team and the pressure to do well can cause the normal rational processes to fly out of the window, and to be replaced by illogical arguments born of the heat of the moment. This dilemma or pressure makes it difficult to "genuinely hear" what the other side is saying. If the negotiator is losing, he or she becomes more and more desperate to find ways in which his or her position can be bolstered so that he or she can win. It is not unknown for this dilemma to cause negotiators to make palpably untrue statements as they desperately try to support their case. We will discuss how stress caused by these dilemmas can be managed later.

We have proposed that there are two teams involved in the negotiations, the direct team and the indirect team, and we have suggested how the relationships between these should be managed. You, of course, will meet the direct team of the other party and may become frustrated by their delaying tactics, when they constantly have to refer to the indirect team for fresh instructions.

Ideally *you* should aim to deal with the person who can make the decision. Some put this rather crudely, as dealing with the "organ grinder," rather than the "monkey." By *you* having a relationship with the decision maker *you* can be quite certain that he or she hears your arguments as you express them, rather than through an intermediary. *You* can find out directly what his or her objections might be to your proposals. *You* have the opportunity to persuade him or her of the value of what you are saying.

For these reasons your aim should be to negotiate with the decision maker. If on the other hand the other party accuses you of being the monkey and wishes to negotiate with the organ grinder, you should make it plain that you do have the power to make decisions. It is important therefore that in your own discussions with the indirect team you are clear about the boundaries within which you can negotiate. This clarity will give you scope for movement, and also very importantly reduce the pressure of the ''hero/traitor'' and ''logic/loyalty'' dilemmas.

PROCESSES AND PHASES

Here we deal with the heart of negotiating. This is where the real bargaining takes place.

We have divided the latter part of this section up into parts which relate to the various phases of a negotiation. The phases are set out sequentially. It is important to note that they are often iterative. By this we mean that as you start negotiating you may have to revise your negotiating strategy as you find out more about the needs of the other party, and their objections to your arguments.

We will begin by looking at a variety of negotiating behaviors that you may meet. In the previous section on team management we discussed the role of the process analyst. It is his or her job to consider these behaviors and to review their impact on you. Similarly he or she may want to discuss your negotiating behavior and its appropriateness.

Negotiating Behavior

In describing these behaviors we believe it helpful to take the view that they are performed quite deliberately by the other party. There is a significant value in this.

First, if you assume that the other party's behavior is quite deliberate and that his or her intention is to unsettle you in some way, this knowledge will in itself prevent you from becoming unsettled.

Second, by viewing the other's behavior as being rational, it is actually easier to deal with. I don't know about you but I find it difficult to deal with people who are drunk, because their behavior is irrational and unpredictable.

Third, some of the behaviors have quite a dramatic content and you can actually enjoy their performance!

The Aggressive Opener

The aggressive opener begins his act even before you have sat down at the negotiating table. He accuses you of all sorts of wrongdoings and incompetence. He alleges that you have told untruths and that he is having the greatest difficulty in talking to someone as lowly as yourself.

As you can guess the whole intent of this is to disconcert you, and make you feel apprehensive. In the ''good old days'' of industrial relations in the NHS, this was often used by shop stewards in the manual unions. They tried to assert their equality with management by behaving aggressively.

How should you cope with the aggressive opener?

First, do not get sucked into the argument and return kind with kind. You can sit out the performance and ask politely when the other is ready to begin negotiating. Alternatively, you may decide to withdraw from the negotiating room and explain that you will return when the other is ready to begin negotiations.

Putting the ''Mockers On''

This is similar to the aggressive opener, but takes place after you have put a carefully considered proposal to the other side. This is greeted with mocking and shallow laughter. It reminds us of the famous tennis player John McEnroe's phrase, ''You can't be serious.'' There is no doubt that this can be just as disconcerting as the aggressive opener.

We have known one colleague who, exhausted through protracted negotiations, had his latest proposal met with this behavior and responded with the outburst, which was eventually published in the local newspaper: "It is alright for you, we represent professional people, you represent 'bloody scrubbers.'" As you might imagine it took quite some time to recover the position.

There is an important lesson though in this. These aggressive styles are intended to provide a reaction. Typically such reactions are either of ''fight'' or ''flight.'' The above quotation represents the ''fight'' reaction, but just as damaging might be an ill-considered concession to ease the pressure.

The Long Pause Negotiator

For many people long pauses are embarrassing, and they will do almost anything to fill in the silence. The long pause negotiator takes advantage of this human frailty. She may ask a question and receive an answer, but before reacting she allows a silence. It is almost inevitable that the answerer will then go on to amplify his answer, giving further information which may be of value to the negotiator.

We recall a colleague describing how he was negotiating with the vendor of a house. He naturally asked why the vendor was selling. The reply was that he was leaving the district. Then the prospective purchaser allowed a silence. The vendor, embarrassed by the silence, explained that they were actually emigrating, and that they had booked a passage in three weeks time. This information was important to the prospective purchaser, because he knew that the vendor's needs were for a quick completion and not necessarily for a large amount of money.

Silences, even though short, may appear to go on for a long time. Try not to be embarrassed by them. Remember that the longest negotiating silence on record lasted four and a half hours. It occurred between the North Koreans and Americans when they were negotiating a Panmunjom.

The Interrogator

The interrogator is a little like a TV interviewer; he asks a lot of questions but will never reply to yours. This is intended to put you under pressure to make you disclose more information than you may at that time want to reveal.

Perhaps unfortunately, we are brought up always to answer the question. Maybe in this particular case the best policy is not necessarily to answer, but to request the interrogator to reply to your question before you reply to his.

The Cloak of Reasonableness

The cloak of reasonableness is a behavior used by a negotiator who is attempting to win your confidence. She explains how well she does understand what you are saying and all that she wants in the whole wide world is to help you. She might appeal to your finer emotions in that in return for the help she is proffering you, you will help her by making the concessions that she wants.

A favorite phrase of the negotiator who uses the cloak of reasonableness is: "Surely you trust me, don't you?" The answer to this question is that trust has nothing to do with the negotiating relationship. Remember, as we have said before, that you should separate the people from the problem. Certainly be considerate to the individual but be tough and unyielding, if that suits your negotiating stance, on the issue.

Divide and Conquer

As its name implies this aims to create dissension in the other team. It is most often used when one party believes it is making little progress with the lead negotiator of the other side, and turns to another member of the team and asks him or his views.

The aim is to flatter the team member to whom the question is being asked; he is made to feel important and perhaps to hold the key to a successful outcome of the negotiation. Nonverbal behavior is used to encourage him to speak; eye contact, smiles, and nods when he talks all reinforce his behavior. Having now been given the limelight the team member may now say just a little more than his colleagues would wish at this juncture of the negotiation.

It is for this reason that team members should have eye contact with each other to avoid the potential of divide and conquer.

Billy Bunter

Billy Bunter behavior can be particularly exasperating. The essence of Billy Bunter is to appear unintelligent and dense. Billy Bunter demands that everything be explained two or three times over, and even then he pretends not to understand it. The effect of this behavior is that it may make you appear patronising, or if sufficiently annoyed you may lose control of your own emotions.

A way of dealing with Billy Bunter is to address your comments to other members of the team, and if they appear to

PROCESS OF BARGAINING

Interactions and Feelings of the Negotiators

Figure 29-1 Process of Bargaining

understand what you are saying, to invite them to take a short break so that they may discuss your proposal amongst themselves.

There are many other behaviors that you will experience as a negotiator. Be prepared for them and reckon that they are being used for the sole purpose of enabling the other side to achieve their objectives more quickly.

If we now look at Figure 29-1 you will see that we have considered the top loop of the process of bargaining. We have been examining the behavioral interactions and feelings that can be generated during the negotiation. It is for the process analyst to be particularly aware of what is going on and to alert the team if the negotiation is going away; but it is not his or her sole responsibility. All team members should tune into the "process" themselves and assess how the negotiations are proceeding.

TASK OF THE NEGOTIATION

We shall not dwell too long on this second element of the process of bargaining.

The task of the negotiation is what the issue is all about. It is surprising how many people enter a negotiation without being fully briefed about the task. In the early days in the National Health Service when incentive bonus schemes were being negotiated between trade unions and management, it was often the case that management were ill prepared about, for example:

- the nature of the bonus scheme
- the current level of earnings
- the current level of sickness, etc.

The trade unions however had done their homework thoroughly and were conversant with all these aspects. This gave them tremendous advantage when negotiating with an unsophisticated management.

Sometimes the task of the negotiation involves the manipulation of numbers. Many people are worried by numbers and feel embarrassed by their slowness in adding up or in understanding the implication of figures. So that they do not demonstrate this incompetence to the other party, they may well take the figures on trust. *This is dangerous*!

It is essential that every aspect of the task be fully understood. If you do not understand the way in which particular figures have been arrived at, you must demand that the other party go through the calculations with you slowly. If they are unwilling to do this, you must insist on a break so that you can, with your team, take each stage of the calculation, step by step. *Never ever take figures on trust*! You must fully understand how they have been derived and what their implications are.

If part of your negotiations involves reference to legislation, or procedures which have been agreed nationally, it is essential again that you be familiar with these.

It is the height of folly to go into negotiations not being fully briefed. You may believe that your wits will see you through. Many times they will. But there will be times when your knowledge is inadequate, and your reluctance to admit this might eventually lead to some embarrassing results for you and for your organization.

PHASES OF BARGAINING

Each researcher into negotiations suggests different words for the various phases of bargaining. Obviously there are no hard and fast descriptions to these phases. We hope that the way we have broken up the negotiation into phases will be helpful to you when you are planning what needs to be done. Don't forget that as we said at the outset of this chapter, these phases may be iterative as you find out more about the other party.

For example, you may believe that you are close to a settlement, when suddenly the other party brings to the negotiation another matter for which you had not planned. This does not matter. But it does mean that you might need to return to the early phases of the negotiation and not automatically agree there and then. As you will see when we talk about the phase concerned with moving toward settlement it is sometimes a deliberate ploy to bring in, at a late stage, an unanticipated issue.

1. Discovering the Other's Needs

We have deliberately stressed the point once or twice that negotiations are about meeting the needs of the other party, as well as your own needs. Obviously you stand less chance of satisfying the other party's needs if you are unaware of what these are. It is most important that effort be put into trying to discover what the other requires. It is also important to differentiate between a position and a need.

For example, a doctor might argue the case for beds, explaining that he is unable to reduce his waiting lists unless he has additional facilities. This represents his position. His needs are to have increased capacity which could be brought about by, for example:

- reducing the existing length of stay of patients
- rearranging operating schedules
- having more intensive nursing for his existing patients

If the issue is negotiated on the basis of the position that he demands, then deadlock is likely to arise. The skilled negotiator gets behind this position statement and tries to assess what the actual needs are.

The more thorough the preparation in this phase, the more likely you are to identify a range of needs which the other has. By doing this you avoid the danger of *single-issue negotiations*.

It is most important that you do not negotiate about a single issue. Single-issue negotiations create "win/lose" outcomes. They are essentially distributive in nature. Negotiations need to be about a multiplicity of issues. This stage of discovering the others' needs gives you the opportunity to broaden the agenda of the negotiation. A domestic example might illustrate this:

> Imagine two children sitting down to tea. There is one cake, which has to be divided into two between them. On the face of it this is an archetypal distributive type of negotiation. The agenda though can be broadened by introducing the idea that one of them should cut the cake, whilst another should choose. Another way of broadening the agenda would be that one chooses today and the other chooses tomorrow. Another way is that he who has the first choice has to do the washing up!
>
> All these are quite legitimate ways of broadening the agenda, and changing perceptions about the nature of conflict from distributive, to integrative.

A little technique to help you broaden the agenda and identify the other party's needs is something that we call the *accept/reject test*. By undertaking this analysis you will be able to identify on what issues the other party might agree and those on which they will disagree. This enables you to begin formulating your strategy for the movement stage.

The Accept/Reject Test

1. On your "ART" test form, Exhibit 29-1, first of all identify the topic on which you will be negotiating. For our purposes let us say that you wish to install a new machine in the laundry to increase the output.
2. Having done this, list down in the first column all the issues that you as management need a decision on. In our example such issues could be:
   - timing of machine's installation
   - reduction in the labor force
   - increased productivity
   - retraining of the operatives
   - other new staff arrangements

Exhibit 29-1 Accept/Reject Analysis

"ART FORM"
TOPIC: Introduction of new machine into Plant *X*

Issues for Management

Issue	Desired Decision	A/R
1. Timing of installation	In 6 months' time	A
2. Reduction in labor force	By 2 percent	R
3. Increase in productivity	By 10 percent	R
4. Retraining of operatives	Prior to machine's installation	A
5. New staff arrangements	Round the clock including weekends	R

Issues for Shop Stewards

Issue	Desired Decision	A/R
1. Need for new machine	Proof through costing figures	A
2. Increase in pay for operatives	By 5 percent	A
3. Redundancies	None	A
4. Control of new machine's speed	By operatives themselves	R
5. Loss of bonus during installation	None	A

---

3. Once you have made such a list from your point of view, try to put yourself in the shoes of the shop stewards, with whom you are going to negotiate, and make out a similar list, but from their perspective. You might consider that their list would include such things as:
   - whether there is a need for the machine
   - increased pay for operatives using it
   - whether there will be any redundancies
   - who will control the speed of the machine
   - potential loss of bonus payments whilst the machine is being installed

   If you do this analysis thoroughly you will have a pretty comprehensive list of their needs.
4. Having completed these "issue lists" you must then identify the desired decisions (DDs). For you these would be the outcomes on which management would willingly agree. Try to be as specific with your DDs as possible. Then go on to consider the DDs for the other party. What are those outcomes which the shop steward would see as their DDs?

Now we come to the test itself.

For your list ask yourself whether the other party is likely to accept any of your DDs. If "yes" put an A in the final column. If "no" put R.

For the shop steward's list ask yourself whether you as management would be willing to accept his DDs. Do the same A and R analysis.

At the conclusion of the "accept/reject" test you will have identified a series of issues for both yourself and the other party.

If you have done your homework well you will know what they are likely to accept and reject. In other words you will know their needs. You will also know on what issues agreement is likely to be forthcoming.

As you will see in the movement phase, the skill is in linking these issues together so that you obtain something to meet your needs from the other party, in exchange for something of value to the other party which helps them meet their needs, but is of little value to you.

Finally don't forget that not all needs are necessarily directly related to the issue under negotiation. People have psychological needs which are just as important in negotiations. An American psychologist, Abraham Maslow, proposed that everyone has a hierarchy of needs, and once a lower order need has been satisfied the individual is motivated to satisfy the next level of needs.

Maslow began by proposing that we all have needs for

- food
- shelter
- warmth

Then came the needs for

- security
- safety
- companionship—the social need.

For our purposes the next need is particularly important. This is that of esteem or status.

The Need for Esteem or Status

Individuals want to do well and to be recognized as doing well by their colleagues. It is one of the paradoxes in negotiations that unskilled negotiators seem to aim their tactics at deliberately frustrating the satisfaction of this need. People who have had their self-esteem knocked will try and recover their prestige, probably at the expense of the offending party in the future. This is why it is so important to separate the person from the problem. It is unwise to frustrate the need for status and self-esteem. It is much more profitable to find ways of satisfying this at minimal cost to yourself, in return for a concession from them that you really do want.

Have you ever come across the situation where a friend has come back with a bargain? He has been pleased with his prowess at negotiating a significant price reduction. When you ask him whether he really needed the commodity that he has bought, he may, a little shamefacedly, confess that he didn't really need it, but it was after all a bargain!

What has happened is that the negotiator who sold him this commodity has appealed to his wish to do well, and was able to satisfy this wish by selling him "a bargain." The actual commodity was almost an irrelevance.

This need of pride or self-esteem is frequently involved in negotiations. Many negotiators when they talk about the other saving face are actually talking about a way of satisfying this need, because the other party might have made substantial concessions which may get them into difficulty with their indirect team and thereby store up trouble for future negotiations.

Self-Actualization

The final need proposed by Maslow is one which he called self-actualization. This need is satisfied through people's having the opportunity to use their talents as fully as possible. It is not so relevant to the negotiator as the ego or status need, except that a concession can be made which actually enables this need to be satisfied.

We have spent some time discussing the first stage of the negotiation, because it provides the foundation on which your strategy for achieving movement will be built.

We have also concentrated particularly on the other party because we have noted how much attention negotiators often pay to determining their own requirements and what they want from the negotiators, but how little they pay to what the other party might require. If the negotiation is to have a "win/win" outcome, it is essential that as much effort be devoted to considering the other party, as to considering yourself. You may think this unduly altruistic. It is not. By meeting their needs you are much more likely to be able to satisfy your needs.

A lot of the preparatory work during this first phase will take place outside the negotiating room. In the negotiations itself you will still, in the early stages, be concentrating on the needs and requirements of others. To do this you will have to listen well to what they say, paraphrasing back to them your understanding of their arguments. Also try to use a number of open-ended questions beginning with words like

- How?
- Why?
- Where?
- When?
- What?

Don't forget the value of silence. There is a great tendency particularly in the early stages of the negotiations to feel a little apprehensive and to gabble on. Relax, and use your communicating skills to help you to understand the other party better.

2. Structuring Expectations

The purpose of this phase is to influence the other about the boundaries of potential settlements:

- It brings down exaggerated expectations.
- It ensures that there is not too wide a gap between the hopes of both parties.

Like the previous phase, work in this one goes on outside the negotiating room as well as inside. The most obvious use of this phase in recent times has been by the government, when they announce their expectations about pay level settlements. The purpose of doing this is to reduce the expectations that some negotiators might have of high settlements.

Similarly in international negotiations, prior to nations' leaders meeting, many articles appear in the press. The purpose is often to reduce the other party's expectations of an easy settlement, or even of necessarily actually achieving a settlement at all.

This chapter is being written just after Mrs. Thatcher's visit to the Soviet Union. Prior to this visit, articles appear in *Pravda* critical of her and her international stance. This was clearly an effort by the Soviet government to condition Mrs. Thatcher's expectations about potential settlement areas. Many of the articles were critical, and yet the relationship between Mikhail Gorbachev and Margaret Thatcher seemed to be extremely cordial. A very powerful approach to structuring expectations, which is based on the integrative negotiating model, is to try and obtain agreement about the principles which should underpin the results of the negotiation.

For example, in negotiating the price of a house, you might agree in advance that the eventual settlement should be within a certain percentage of what other houses have sold for in the neighborhood.

In Health Service negotiations an obvious principle should be that patients do not suffer as a result of the negotiation, or failure to reach an agreement.

When you are actually in the negotiating room a most effective way of structuring expectations is to make an offer which you know may be some distance away from the settlement point. If, for example, as a supplies manager you are negotiating some discount on a particular set of commodities, you might start with demanding an extremely high discount. The effect on the other party is to immediately make her realize that she is going to have a tough job on her hands to achieve the sort of settlement that she may want. Secondly, she may not pitch her own offer in quite as extreme a form as she intended. If the gap appears to be too wide, there is a fear that it may not be bridgeable.

An illustration of this is where you are hoping for a discount of 15 percent, you might pitch your opening demand at 25 percent. If she was only going to offer you a discount of 2½ percent there is such a huge difference between you that she may well open up at a figure closer to yours.

You are structuring her expectations. Be careful, of course, that your expectations are not similarly structured. Stick to your original view. Gaps can always be bridged if both parties genuinely want a settlement.

Finally, expectations can be structured through the use of power building tactics. When you think of it, any car dealer or shop which puts a price on a particular commodity is in effect structuring expectations. This is a means of using the power of the printed word to structure law expectations.

In our society it is unlikely that many people will negotiate about these prices. They are after all there in black and white. Yet we know of colleagues who have negotiated discounts in many stores such as Debenhams, Dixons and Currys where prices have been clearly displayed. The power of the written word can be challenged! One tip from this is the use of written documents to support your case and structure the other's expectations. On the other hand you should not have your expectations so structured. You should be willing to negotiate about almost anything!

3. Moving toward the Settlement

In this phase most of your time will be spent around the negotiating table. You will of course have done your homework thoroughly, and made sure you are not in a single-issue negotiation. You will have broadened the agenda to include a multiplicity of issues so that you have maximum opportunities for meeting needs. You will have identified concessions that you can make which you think are important to him or her, but cost you little. An early temptation is to make a concession to get negotiations going. Anxiousness may excite you into "making progress" too fast. Do not fall into this trap!

In negotiations there is no such thing as a free concession. Any negotiator who is worth his or her salt will, when offered a free concession, accept it happily and then demand another concession. You will say to yourself that you have given a little way already so what does it matter to give a little more, and anyway the concession is of no value to you. So you concede, and then the other will demand yet another concession, and so on until you say "stop" and stand there naked in front of him or her!

It might remind you of the old aphorism "Give him an inch and he will take a yard!"

In the jargon of psychology what you are doing each time you offer a free concession is rewarding his or her behavior of demanding such a concession, and as everyone likes his or her behavior rewarded, the other will continue to demand.

So how do you get the negotiations going?

There is a sentence which all negotiators should commit to heart. It goes like this: "If you do this for me, then I will do that for you." This approach using "If . . . then" gives no hostages to fortune. What you are offering as a concession is conditional upon you getting something back in return. What you offer will have been derived from your analysis of needs, and ideally should be something which costs you little but is of value to the other party.

This phase of the negotiations should be a really creative phase where both parties are working together to invent options which enable each of them to satisfy their own needs.

Do not be afraid of broadening the agenda still further to take into consideration issues which were not there initially. If this does happen then you may well want to adjourn with your team to consider afresh some of the ideas that are emerging. You may need to brief the indirect team about the progress of the negotiations and to request them to find out more about the needs of the other party.

If the negotiation is going well, you will make progress toward an agreement. The timing of this progress is important. If you move too quickly, you may build up the expectations in the other party that you are anxious to settle. If on the other hand you move too slowly, then you create frustration and resentment.

A fascinating illustration of moving too quickly to agreement was given in a television program which followed the negotiations between the journalists and management of the *Daily Mirror* newspaper. What happened was that management had planned what their opening offer would be, where they hoped to eventually settle, and the point beyond which they would not go.

Unfortunately they moved, in the course of one evening, from their opening position to their ultimate position, and made many concessions on the way. The journalists' representatives were eventually convinced that management had reached their ultimate position and would go no further.

But when they relayed this to their members, the latter quite naturally responded saying that they had only been negotiating for about 12 hours and already had gained a 50 percent increase. Any party that is willing to move that quickly must have more up its sleeve. The industrial action continued for another three or four weeks, and eventually collapsed as management were unable to make any further concessions.

During this phase of moving toward a settlement there will be many proposals made to you. Do be careful not to reject such proposals with a rapid counterproposal. Make sure that you understand what is on offer and if you are unable to accept it, give your reasons in a firm and positive way.

Do make sure that the other party with whom you are negotiating is empowered to make decisions. If they have to return to the indirect team for fresh instructions each time you make an offer, they have obviously been briefed very tightly. You should point out that this is not a true negotiation and you must negotiate with those who can make the decision. Otherwise a lot of time will be wasted. Inevitably there will be occasions when they need fresh instructions, just as you will. But there should be a broad area in which they can negotiate without having to refer back.

4. Achieving Agreement

In the previous phase you will have been recording the agreements reached on the offers and concessions made by both parties. Now we come to the close of the negotiation, when the package gets wrapped up.

Don't be afraid of making progress slowly through small movements. There is often an overeagerness to get it all over and done with as quickly as possible, by offering a number of concessions in a complex package. But making small movements in the negotiation builds trust between the parties, as each one tests the other out in terms of their genuineness in wanting to achieve an agreement that is in the best interests of both.

Small movements are also easier to agree on rather than having to swallow a huge chunk all at once. If you can ensure that the process of small achievements is one where the word "yes" is used, often a positive attitude develops toward the relationship and the eventual outcome.

There is a psychological theory which proposes that if you can persuade the other party to respond to you in a positive way over a number of occasions, it becomes increasingly more difficult for him or her to say "no" to any one particular issue. Always try therefore to make it easy for the other to say "yes." Do this by making your offers clear and unambiguous, be quite explicit as to what you are expecting in return for your concession using the "if . . . then" formula, and make progress in small stages.

A fascinating feature of this phase used by some negotiators is the "nibble."

The nibble is the final demand made by the other party just as you believe the negotiation is completed. We recall the nibble used very successfully in one negotiation between hospital management and their catering staff.

The catering staff had been out on strike for about two weeks over a change in rota arrangements. Negotiations had been going on for some time and eventually it looked as though agreement was in sight. Both parties returned rather wearily to the negotiating room and as had been expected agreement was quickly reached. As everyone was closing their books and heaving a sigh of relief, the trade union negotiator turned to management and asked: "Of course you will be paying my members whilst they have been out on strike, won't you?" Management's immediate response was: "No. We will not." The trade unionist replied that in this case the deal was off. Both parties separated.

Management, who had been doing the catering themselves, preparing salads and wheeling trolleys around the ward, were very tired. After the elation of achieving the agreement, the exhaustion of seeing it scuppered was too much. They returned to the negotiating room and invited the other side to join them. They conceded and agreed to pay the catering staff whilst they were out on strike!

Another and more trivial example of the nibble at work was given to us by a friend who is a photographic buff. He says that whenever he goes to buy a lens for his camera, he invites the salesperson to "throw a filter in" for free as well. Evidently this works nearly every time!

It is very important during this phase that you summarize the agreements that have been made and make sure that both parties understand. Do not be tempted to leave loose ends. These will only store up difficulties for the future.

5. Reviewing the Agreement

In complex negotiations which may give rise to new systems and procedures, it is often a good idea to build in a time when the agreement can be reviewed and perhaps renegotiated. It is not always possible to know how agreements will actually work out in practice. And neither party may want to commit themselves irrevocably to something which turns out to be contrary to their interests.

It is wise therefore to agree on a time at which the agreement will be reviewed and a mechanism to review it. Don't forget to consider what the scope is for renegotiation if it is decided that the agreement is not satisfactory. By creating a review mechanism you do allow both parties to develop a confidence in taking a risk with the agreement. They know that if it does not work out, then it can be changed.

TARGET SETTING

The process of setting targets is important for the negotiator. Targets provide the boundaries within which the negotiations can take place. Targets are the mirror image of concessions. Targets are what you wish to achieve, and concessions are what you are willing to trade to achieve your targets. Targets should be set in conjunction with the indirect team, so that both parties' expectations are realistic.

One of the most interesting findings of research into target setting is that those who set themselves challenging targets to achieve during the negotiation do better than those who do not set themselves such a challenge. Give yourself something to stretch for and you are more likely to achieve it. We also know from the research that those who do not do so well in the negotiations are those who make "free" concessions.

Researchers have also analyzed the power of the deadline for negotiators, and found that the unskilled negotiator is likely to make many more concessions as deadlines become closer. So remember that whenever you make a concession always obtain something in return, and make progress through small agreements.

Target Points

Target points create the framework for your negotiation. You should have three target points in mind:

- The first is the ideal settlement.
- The second is your fallback position.
- The third is realistically where you might expect to settle.

As negotiations contain a number of elements it is quite probable that you may have a number of scenarios which represent the three target points. It is important that these be made explicit and debated with the indirect team. Through this debate you will sharpen the range into one or two descriptions of the target points that represent the boundaries to the negotiation.

1. Determining Target Points

The ideal settlement represents the best possible outcome for yourself. But we often constrain our thinking about what would be best for ourselves, by imagining the difficulties that we will encounter in achieving this. Remember the results of the research; give yourself an ideal settlement which represents some difficulty for you to achieve.

We remember a friend describing how he negotiated for the purchase of a piece of land from his neighbor:

> He had calculated that the land was worth approximately 500 pounds to him, although he would have been willing to have paid up to 600 for it. Ideally he hoped to pay no more than about 150 for the land. So he set himself a challenging target to try and buy the land from his neighbor for 100 pounds.
>
> He opened the negotiations at 50 pounds, and watched his neighbor closely. A little to his surpise the neighbor responded by a counterproposal of 150 pounds. Already he had an offer well below the level at which he might have expected to settle. You might conclude therefore that he shook his neighbor warmly by the hand and gave him the 150 pounds! If he were to have done this though he would have caused frustration in the other. He might have left the negotiation believing that he would have gotten more for his land! So the negotiation progressed toward the movement stage. The agenda was broadened to include the payment of the solicitor's fees.
>
> The eventual outcome was the purchase of the price of land for 100 pounds, plus the payment of the neighbor's legal fees which amounted to about 30 pounds.

This story illustrates the value of setting a challenging target. It could have been very easy for our friend to have opened the negotiations at, say, 300 pounds expecting to settle somewhere around 500 pounds. But by deliberately setting himself a difficult objective to achieve, he was able to save himself a lot of cash.

BATNA. The fallback position has more of a logic to its determination. Some writers on negotiations refer to this as the BATNA. BATNA stands for: Best Alternative To a Negotiated Agreement.

What you have to do in planning the negotiations is to decide what you would do if they broke down. What, in other words, is the best alternative to achieving your objectives that you can identify without having to negotiate.

For example if you are buying a new car and selling your old one, the garage will give you a trade-in price for your old vehicle. You may decide to sell it privately. If you do, it is worth negotiating any price which is even minimally above that which the garage is offering you. The price being offered by the garage is your BATNA.

The BATNA in effect represents a contingency plan for implementation, if you believe that you will gain nothing from the negotiations at all.

The realistic settlement point must be determined by your analysis of what the other party's needs are in conjunction with your own needs. If you suspect initially that a realistic settlement point is unacceptable to you, then you will have to devise strategies aimed at structuring the other's expectations to bring them more in line with where you wish to settle. But just as you have identified a challenging ideal point, also be challenging about the realistic point, too.

2. Revealing Your Target Points

Knowledge of target points is valuable to the other party. If they know what you want, they can then exert the maximum concession from you, in return for enabling you to achieve your target point. It is important not to reveal all your aspirations at once.

We are reminded of an illustration of how this went wrong when a purchaser was negotiating for the purchase of goods from another company. Unfortunately the company selling the commodities was running into serious cash-flow problems. During a round of golf, one of the employees of the company casually mentioned this to an employee of the purchasing company. This news got back to the purchaser's negotiator who then framed his offer to give the vendor a minimal amount of cash for the commodities, but to pay within seven days of delivery. This met the high priority need of the vendor for having cash, but denied him the opportunity of extracting from the purchaser a higher price for the commodity.

This reminds us of the poster displayed around the country during the war, which said, "Careless talk costs lives." In our case, "Loose talk can lose negotiations."

Many negotiators are trained to discover the target positions of the other party. For example, if you trade in your car, the first question the salesman will ask you is how much you want for it. Not what he is willing to offer for it. Because we are so conditioned to answer questions, we immediately reply to the salesman's question letting him know our target point from the outset.

We have heard of a more interesting variation on this, where the salesman guaranteed to offer the best price in town. He said that he would write down on his card the offer he would make, seal it in an envelope and pin it on the notice board behind him. The customer could then go anywhere else in the town and return with the best price that he had obtained. This, of course, the customer did and came back with the best price. The salesman then took the envelope from his notice board, opened it, and read from the card that he was willing to offer 50 pounds more than the best price.

The creative approach found out the target point, and also won the salesman the business.

Other ways of finding out target points are to make offers which you know the other party will refuse, but are likely to respond to by explaining where they hope the settlement might be. Of course you will by now have developed your communications skills, and simply by listening and using silence, you will be surprised how much people will reveal to you of what they are hoping to gain from the negotiation.

On the other hand if you were asked about where you expect and hope to settle, reveal this information with circumspection. You may wish to reply in a deliberately vague way, or even to suggest that this is not quite the right time to talk about these matters, and let us just explore the issues that lie between us.

You may have observed those demonstrators at big exhibitions who are able to hold the rapt attention of their audience, whilst they demonstrate their goods. And any questions about price before they have finished their demonstration are gently dismissed until they have shown all the potential benefits of their products. Although not strictly negotiations, this technique is a useful one to employ if you are not ready to reveal your target points at the particular stage of the negotiations.

POWER

Power is an inevitable ingredient of negotiations. The way that you perceive the other party, and their perceptions of you, are influenced by the power that they attribute to you.

In many of the early negotiations between management and trade unions in the NHS, management often perceived themselves to be in a much weaker position than the trade unions. They argued that whatever happened, hospitals had to be kept open, and patients treated. Any threat therefore to disrupt hospitals by the other side was met by early concessions from management. As soon as management recognized that they could close hospitals, then the power equation became more balanced. Interestingly, in talking to trade unionists about this stage of negotiations they similarly felt less powerful than management, believing that they could not allow their members to stay out on strike for any length of time as they had insufficient funds to pay them.

Power is a perceptual matter.

In integrative negotiations it is easier to obtain a "win/win" outcome when power is perceived to be equal. If one side feels unduly weak it may fear having to make a lot of concessions and thereby "lose" the negotiations. It becomes resistant to the proposals of the other side, being suspicious of them.

The skillful use of power also structures expectations. If your analysis suggests that the other side sees themselves as much more powerful than yourself, or that you perceive yourself to be in a weaker position, it is valuable to be able to enhance your power base and thereby structure expectations that the negotiations are not going to be a walkover.

Six Power-Building Questions

The following questions can be used by negotiating teams as a way of trying to achieve equality in the power balance. These questions provide a focus for your thinking. The answers are not always self-evident. You have to be a little creative in thinking about how you can use the questions to enhance your power base.

1. *Is there some action we can take now which we are not presently taking?* This is perhaps the most obvious question. Trade unionists often answer it by taking industrial action. In this type of situation management sometimes respond by using the media. It is said that Michael Edwardes, whilst he was Chairman of British Leyland, used the newspapers to influence the attitudes and behavior of employees at Cowley. In this way he was able to communicate more directly and powerfully with his work force. He enhanced management's power base in relation to that of the shop stewards. An example of this in the National Health Service was found when some van drivers were persuaded back to work by the following editorial that appeared in a local paper:

> *Patients Hurt by Impatience*
> According to George Bernard Shaw, the worst sin we can commit against our fellow creatures is not to hate them but to be indifferent to them. That, said Shaw, is the essence of inhumanity.[4]
>
> Was it indifference to their fellow creatures that caused six hospital van drivers, all members of the National Union of Public Employees, to refuse to carry out deliveries and collections?
>
> An immediate result of their industrial action was the postponement of 19 operations. If any of the NUPE six had ever been in the situation of the 19 on the brink of operations they would surely not have wished this delay on the luckless patients-to-be.
>
> All the men want, said a NUPE spokesman, is for the hospital authorities to consider introducing an incentive scheme. The authorities reply that this, as NUPE well knew, was to be discussed at a meeting already planned for next Thursday.
>
> If the drivers were sincere in their protestations that they did not wish to cause suffering they would have delayed their action until they knew the result of next Thursday's talks.
>
> The public, not least those directly affected by the action of the six drivers, will see this as an example of wildcat action bearing the hallmarks of Shaw's essence of inhumanity.

2. *Is there anything that we can get the other side to do that they are not presently doing, which could enhance our power base?* Managers often feel under severe pressure when the comfort or lives of patients are at stake. Such pressure can cause them to make concessions which they may regret in the future. When this was the case for one Health Service Manager he asked himself this question. The situation was as follows:

> The staff at a laundry were taking strike action.
> This means that no clean linen was being delivered

to the wards on which there were elderly and incontinent patients. The manager had already exhausted his stock of disposable sheets, and was now faced with a possibility of the old people having to remain in bed in the most distressing of circumstances. As the laundry was not on the site of the hospital, he invited the shop stewards to join him on a ward round and see that conditions in which the elderly patients were having to exist. The shop stewards accepted this invitation and were themselves so distressed at these conditions that they immediately allowed clean linen to be delivered to the ward.

This action took a great pressure off management and enabled them to negotiate a deal acceptable to both parties over the eventual manning of the laundry.

3. *Is it possible to get both sides to take some action that they are not presently taking?* With this question we are searching for potential areas of cooperation which could lead the negotiations to more of a "win/win" outcome. A good example of two sides taking action was during the ambulancemen's dispute:

In one hospital the beds were becoming congested with patients who needed to be moved out, but who could not go to another hospital because the ambulancemen refused to take them.

Management and the representatives of the ambulancemen joined together to try and solve this problem. They agreed on the criteria for emergency and urgent cases, and accepted that such patients must be admitted to hospital. As this meant moving existing patients out of the beds, the ambulancemen's representatives agreed to this. This then allowed for a more acceptable negotiation about other issues to take place.

4. *Are we doing something now which, if we were to stop, would enhance our power base?* Perhaps the best illustration of an answer to this question occurred when a group of staff were taking industrial action, and unknown to management were being paid whilst they were on strike. Management perceived themselves to be at deadlock, because it cost the staff so little to remain on strike. The obvious answer was to stop paying the staff.

Although this example may seem a little trite, it is important not to assume that instructions have been given to stop pay. In this case no such instructions had been given, and this question provoked a response which soon brought the action to an end.

5. *Can we stop the other side from taking some action that they are presently taking!* This is a key question when industrial action is taking place in the Health Service. Again referring to the early days of these problems in the NHS when one strategy sometimes used by management was to send a telegram to the Secretary of State, the following situation arose:

Laboratory technicians were refusing to undertake certain tasks, thereby bringing a large part of the hospital to a grinding halt. To stop them from taking such action, management agreed to support the union's argument in a telegram addressed to the Secretary of State. Although this caused problems for the future, it did enable the hospital to continue working.

6. *Can we prevent both sides from taking some action that we are both presently taking?* An interesting illustration of an answer to this question was during the coal miners' dispute.

Each side had been haranguing the other on the front pages of the newspapers. This clearly was creating problems for reaching an agreement. It created antipathy and hostility. Management suggested that this was not in the best interests of either the union or themselves, and it was agreed that no further releases would be made to the press.

These six power-building questions are particularly useful for complex negotiations, many of which do take place in the NHS. Don't forget though that their intention is to try to equalize power. If the other party perceives you as being extremely powerful, they may feel forced to make concessions during this negotiation, but be determined to get their own back in the future.

We have said that power is a perceptual matter. It is now time to examine what causes these perceptions and how you might influence or change them.

Sources of Power

You are a more influential negotiator when you have a strong commitment to your objectives. Obviously such commitment should not lead to intransigence, but a demonstration that you really are determined to achieve a "win/win" outcome will enhance your negotiating strength. When we discussed teamwork, we talked about the value of the devil's advocate. He is particularly important in testing out your own arguments, and as these are tested and you rehearse them, you will become increasingly committed to your viewpoint.

Another source of power which we have touched on is that of the written document or procedure. There was a fascinating illustration of this in one of the "Candid Camera" episodes on TV.

The "Candid Camera" team had put up a notice on a road leading into Delaware, in the United States. The notice which looked highly official said "Delaware Closed."

People would drive up to the notice, stop, and ask one of the team: "What's going on in Delaware? I live there. Tell me when it will be open again."

Find documents which give a legitimacy to your own arguments. But for your part don't forget that documents are just man-made artifacts, and can be challenged in just the same way as the view of an individual can be challenged.

Power is enhanced when you are seen as being willing to take risks. You may recall the risk that President Sadat of Egypt took when he traveled to Israel to address their parliament. He must have immeasurably enhanced his negotiating position in the eyes of the Israelis and the West in taking such a risk which could and did alienate some Arab states.

Power is also born of confidence. By carefully planning the negotiation, by building up a reputation for yourself as a negotiator, by knowing your way round all your documents you will feel confident about your ability to handle the negotiations. This confidence will come across to the other party and be influential in determining the relationship which they will have with you.

From another angle we are sometimes overawed by other people. They appear very powerful, enjoying a high status and always getting what they want.

It is akin to a respect for authority. We mentioned earlier that trade union negotiators are trained to view themselves as the absolute equals of management when they are negotiating, even though during the normal working day they may be subordinate in the hierarchy. If you perceive someone to be more powerful than yourself and you feel that this may inhibit your negotiating abilities, then one little trick to play on yourself is to imagine them standing naked in front of you! This brings us all down to common human elements which, I am told, are about 90 percent water anyway!

Similarly if you are negotiating with an expert, you may feel anxious about his or her depth of knowledge, and power of reason. The trick here is to flatter the expert's ego and invite him or her to explain to someone who really is not as intelligent as he or she, those matters that he or she is expert upon. Recall the importance of satisfying people's needs!

In this situation do not be afraid of the foolish question. After all, that was what the court jester was employed for in medieval times. It was his job to puncture the "group think" that surrounded the monarch when at court with all his favorites. He had to test the experts with his foolish questions.

Finally let us return to the points made in the opening part of this section, with a story.

> You may think that a prisoner locked up in a cell has little power over the warders. That would accord with our perceptions and that of the warders. But there was one creative prisoner who saw that he did have power, and he used this to get a much-needed cigarette.
>
> As the warder walked past he asked if he could have a cigarette. The warder replied rather curtly in the negative! The prisoner asked himself the question, "Can I do something which I am not presently doing which might enhance my base of power?"
>
> He came up with the answer that he could threaten to bang his head against the bed, and blame the warder for beating him up. So he made the request again, but this time explained what would happen if he were not given a cigarette. As it cost the warder little to provide the cigarette, and could have been a tedious, and possibly dangerous exercise for him to explain how the prisoner gained his injuries, he gave the prisoner his packet of cigarettes.

Power you see is perceptual.

STRESS IN THE NEGOTIATIONS

Negotiations can be stressful. Although we do not make a mountain out of this, we do think it useful to consider the causes of stress, and to consider some ways in which preventive measures can keep stress from becoming so great that it becomes dysfunctional.

Stress in a modicum dosage is very useful. The adrenalin flows, and our wits become that much quicker. Our energy levels are high, and we can carry on for much longer than we would normally expect to undertake managerial chores.

But when stress becomes dysfunctional, it severely affects our abilities to plan and organize work and information. We can feel threatened by it, and it may induce feelings of uncertainty and panic. This, as you might imagine, is a very dangerous state for a negotiator to get into. His or her behavior is likely to be irrational to others, and he or she may go to extremes throwing all the concessions away, or becoming deliberately obstinate, and difficult. This turning point, when stress ceases to be useful, and becomes destructive, varies from individual to individual. An important part of the process analyst's role is to examine what is happening in the team in terms of stress management, and if he or she believes that the negotiations are being badly influenced because of undue stress, to propose an adjournment.

Equally, each individual should tune into his or her own stress management abilities. If your jaws clench, or your neck is sore, or your head aches, then it is time for you to take a break.

First though, let us consider the causes of stress.

Causes of Stress

There are probably as many causes of stress from the negotiation as there are problems to be tackled. We have tried to classify them in terms of their origins so that practical steps can be taken to mitigate their effect.

1. Stress from the Home Environment

It is often very difficult for colleagues not involved in the negotiation to wonder why it is taking so long to get an agreement. We remember one negotiation in which we were involved, when the Chairman of the Health Authority was totally unable to understand the reason why it was taking so long to reach an agreement.

The essential issue was about who should manage domestic staff: the ward sister or the domestic superintendent. But this issue spilled over into interunion rivalry, and what became necessary was an agreement between three parties, which was very difficult to achieve.

Coincidental with this pressure is the feeling that you might be letting your colleagues down. This is the epitome of the "hero/traitor" dilemma. It is particularly acute if you are uncertain about the bargaining discretion that you have. Most readers will not be full-time negotiators, and will have other work to do. Negotiations however do take up a lot of time, and there is always the nagging anxiety as to what is arriving on the desk, and remaining untouched, while you are involved in the drama of the negotiations.

One particular cause of stress from "the home" is the fear about your own career prospects. One personnel manager who is a very skillful negotiator had allegations made against him by trade unionists claiming that he was untruthful and dishonest. Obviously such allegations, whether they are true or not, may stick and severely affect the career prospects of a manager.

What should you do about these causes of stress? First, do keep your colleagues fully in the picture and in particular agree with the indirect team on the parameters for your negotiation. Also keep others informed. We know of one health authority which, when there is the threat of a prolonged industrial relations negotiation, sets up an incident room. The purpose of this is to produce a daily bulletin on the progress of negotiations. In this way all staff are kept informed of what is happening.

It is particularly important that your manager know what progress is being made. Do not let him or her live in a "fool's paradise" giving him or her only the good news. If there are problems and difficulties, explain them, and invite his or her help in resolving them. If you let him or her think that all is going well, and then you are unable to deliver, you will feel considerably stressed.

Finally, and perhaps a counsel of perfection, do organize yourself so that you have time. If you can have somebody look after your desk, then do so. Try and agree with your manager and your colleagues on some way in which they can temporarily deal with the daily issues that are normally your bread and butter.

2. Stress from Yourself

Your self-esteem is bound up in the outcome of the negotiation. If the other party is managing the negotiation extremely distributively, and you feel yourself losing, this creates considerable stress and anxiety. The temptation is therefore to counterattack, after which the negotiation escalates into a bitter "win/lose" battle. This is perhaps the most difficult cause of stress to deal with. What can you do?

How To Get Out of a "Win/Lose" Battle. First of all, do plan for the potential of this outcome. In discussions with the indirect team, hypothesize what would happen if the other side were so adamant that they would not budge and were going to win at whatever cost. Prepare for this contingency. For example, build up stocks of commodities that might be threatened by any industrial action.

Remember also the golden rule that there is no such thing as a free concession even in these extreme circumstances.

Never try to placate the other party with a concession in the expectation that they will suddenly turn nice, and give you something that you want. Always use the "if . . . then" formula.

If the stress is becoming great, and you can sense from your physiological reactions that you are not going to cope with it as well as you would wish, take a break; go for some fresh air; and have a stock-taking session with your team. You may want to change the lead negotiator, or even bring in somebody who is not currently involved in the negotiations. You must use these ideas carefully so that the other side does not perceive it as a sign of weakness.

3. Stress from the Negotiating Process

Negotiations require concentration, and concentration for any length of time is tiring. As you feel tired you may begin to feel that you are losing a grip on the negotiation. To illustrate this, I use what I am sure is an apocryphal story about the Japanese, who took advantage of this.

When a European team of negotiators was about to negotiate in Japan, they would arrive at the Tokyo airport, and be met by their hosts. They would be escorted to the hotel, and then invited out to dinner and a cabaret, complete with sake. At about three in the morning, the Europeans would be feeling decidedly tired and jet lagged, and would clamber wearily into their beds.

The negotiations were due to start at nine o'clock that morning. As they got dressed, breakfasted, and went down to the negotiating room, their hosts of the night before were nowhere to be seen. Instead there was a fresh team of young Japanese negotiators ready to go.

You can imagine the outcome of the negotiations.

We are told that the art of coarse rugby adopts a similar tactic. The visiting team is met by the "home drinking team" and entertained liberally in the pavilion. The "home playing team" is limbering up on an adjacent pitch, but out of sight. At two-fifteen when the whistle blows for the off, the visiting team is feeling decidedly inactive. The home team wins hands down.

Someone in one of our seminars volunteered to lead a dummy negotiating team to go over to Japan and be entertained in the lavish manner, whilst he would allow the real negotiators to have gone there a week or so before, to get acclimatized!

Seriously, what should you do about managing the negotiating process, so that it does not become too stressful?

Managing the Negotiating Process To Avoid Stress. Obviously try and start the negotiations in a fresh state of mind. A not unusual ploy used by trade union negotiators is to cause a significant problem to occur at about four o'clock on Friday, when the managers are hoping to relax after a heavy week. Clearly it needs an exercise of judgment as to whether the problem is so acute that it has to be negotiated there and then, or whether it can wait until Monday.

If you do have to negotiate abroad give yourself at least 36 hours to become acclimatized to the culture, the food, and the time zone.

Negotiating is a very seductive process. Time flies when you are negotiating, and you may find yourself still at it well into the night. On occasions this may be essential in order to conclude the final stages of a deal. Otherwise ask yourself whether it is strictly necessary, and whether or not you would be better off having a break.

If your granny had ever been a negotiator, and perhaps she was, I am sure she would have given you the following tips:

- Don't have heavy meals or drink while negotiating,
- Make sure that you take exercise and fresh air,
- If you feel unwell, then close the negotiations for the time being, explaining that you are feeling ill and need to have a break,
- Finally, sleep long and well in your own bed at night.

4. *Stress from the Other Side*

When we discussed the behaviors of a negotiator, we commented that many of these were used deliberately to create stress on you. The logic is that by being stressed you will respond with either "fight" or "flight." Whatever you do is likely to lead to problems in the negotiation which the other can exploit.

We recall one negotiation where the other side tried to create considerable stress on management. From the trade union's point of view the negotiation had not been going well. They decided to bring in a fresh negotiator. Management learned that this new negotiator had followed his apprenticeship in trade union affairs with Jimmy Hoffa's union in the United States. The teamsters' union was not known for its gentlemanly conduct!

The new negotiator arrived on site, and much to management's horror was dressed in black homburg hat, a black shirt, black trousers and a white tie, and spoke with an exaggerated transatlantic twang.

Management could see that any attempt to handle the negotiations in an integrative manner was out of the question. This was made particularly apparent when the negotiator started talking about dressing up the management team in concrete overcoats!

In fact, the tactic had completely the opposite effect. It became an amusing spectacle to see this negotiator propose the use of strong-arm tactics, which were so entirely alien to the British culture, and which were not even supported by his own members!

The other side's loss of temper, breaking into tears, using abusive language, and hurling epithets at you can cause stress. What should you do about this?

First, and perhaps the best advice, is to admire the performance. If you recognize that what is being done is being done deliberately then, as we have argued earlier, it is easier to manage. But remember, you do not have to take abusive language. You may decide to leave the negotiations.

If you do leave, make sure that you have an avenue for returning. For example, you might decide that one of your team should "accidentally" meet a member of the other team, and raise with him the nature and progress of the negotiations. An individual-to-individual discussion is perhaps best in persuading the others that these sorts of tactics are not going to lead to a resolution, and that you genuinely want to try and achieve an outcome which is in the best interests of both parties.

DEADLOCK

Although we have stressed that negotiations are about meeting your needs and the needs of the other party, i.e., they are integrative negotiations, it is still likely that you will meet negotiators who perceive the conflict very much in "win/lose" terms. They will create deadlock either because they are unwilling to move, or because they feel that this will cause you to move. It is possible that the interests of both parties are so incompatible that there is no chance of a negotiated agreement. In this case you will have to fall back to your BATNA (i.e., your Best Alternative To a Negotiated Agreement).

But on most occasions, there will be a chance of achieving agreement. It is very unlikely, in the Health Service, that there is so much incompatibility between the parties that an accord cannot be achieved on at least some of the issues.

This brief section makes some suggestions on how you can move out of deadlock. In many ways it requires you to replan the negotiations from the outset, really testing your understanding of the other party's needs, and examining the validity of your own needs. A good way to do this is by going back to the ART form described in the "Processes and Phases" section.

What this forces you to do is to "fractionate" the problem. In other words try to break the problem up into as many little bits as you can and see whether movement cannot be achieved on just one element at a time. The smaller you make the issue, then the easier it may be to achieve agreement.

Another approach, apart from the ART form of fractionating the problem, is force field analysis.

Force Field Analysis

In a typical negotiation there may be many issues and individuals involved. To consider these in any systematic way you must be clear about what the key issues are and who the key individuals are. Once you know with whom you are really having to deal, you can then put yourself psychologically into his or her shoes and begin the process or identifying the forces at play upon him or her.

A little technique to help you to do this is force field analysis. This is a way of picturing the pressures that are causing someone to behave in a particular way. It is suggested that the present situation, which might give the appearance of stability, is in fact a dynamic situation wherein the driving forces for change are equally balanced by the restraining forces. Force field analysis is the term used for identification of these forces. The negotiator needs to be able to identify those forces which are working on the other side—which might drive the other party to change and which might restrain him or her from changing. For example, in a negotiation the driving forces for change might be:

- pressure from a small group of constituents
- the shortage of time due to deadlines
- the desire of the negotiator to achieve something

whereas the restraining forces might be:

- a larger group of constituents not wanting change
- the problems of communicating the change to the constituents
- a change in jobs which might emerge from the agreement, etc.

Having identified these forces, the next step is to increase the effect of the driving forces and reduce the effect of the restraining forces. However, at this stage a subtlety creeps in. It is more effective to reduce the effects of the restraining forces than to increase the effects of the driving forces. The reasons for this are that people can resist the continual promotion of "it will be good for you" but are more likely to change if the impediments in the way of change are reduced.

Having gotten so far in the analysis of the forces at work on the other side, the negotiator must decide what it is possible for them to do and how the forces can be altered so that such an action would appear attractive to them.

It is also important to examine the power relationship. Does the other party feel so powerful that they can overwhelm you or, on the other hand, do they feel so weak that they believe that you are trying to overwhelm them?

We recall one chairman of a Health Authority who believed that it was in the best interests of the Authority for there to be a stronger staff side, and so actually encouraged them to develop their own abilities as negotiators. His rationale was that if management are always seeming to overwhelm the staff, then in the longer term this would lead to a much more militant staff side, who could pose more difficult problems for management in the future. And even the existing situation was unhealthy. It is not unknown for the weaker party to be intransigent and disruptive so that they can "prove their point" and not be bullied by the stronger side.

Finally let us consider the use of threats and offers when deadlock occurs.

Threats and Offers

There is often a temptation in negotiations to use threats to force people to agree. But threats actually harden people's attitudes. Even though a party may concede under a threat, they will try to avoid this happening again by counter-attacking.

Threats are not a very effective way of breaking deadlock. They will already have been taken into account by the other party, when they decided to "deadlock." If the deadlock has lasted a while, the threat is more likely to engender an attitude of "we have stuck it so far, a little more won't hurt." It is also quite difficult for a single member of a team to speak up, and say that he or she thinks the threat ought to be taken more seriously, and a concession made. Peer group pressure will tend to make him or her conform to the general approach taken by the team.

If threats don't work, then will offers? Providing offers are formulated appropriately, they may be able to move the negotiation on. The offer has to be clear and easily understood. It will probably not relate to the substantive issue of the negotiations, but more to the process of resolving the deadlock.

For example, an offer might be to set up a joint group to look at the problem, or to call in an arbitrator to help both parties resolve the sticking point, or to hold a meeting on neutral territory.

Another idea for an offer might be to propose that agreement should be reached about what the disagreement is. This will crystalize the area of conflict, as well as generating a greater understanding about each party's need and positions. Furthermore it moves the negotiation from ingrained "no's" to some tentative "yes's." Other offers could have to do with principles on which an eventual agreement should be based.

All these offers require the other party's involvement, but move the focus of the negotiation away from the major issues, to more procedural matters. This is a useful way of breaking deadlocks.

One final point about deadlock. If you are deadlocked, the stress and tension levels will rise. After all, as a negotiator your very reason for existence is to achieve agreement. Here this need is being thwarted. Relax, though, because research demonstrates that even those who deliberately cause deadlock feel just as much tension as the other party.

NOTES

1. N. Rackham and J. Carlise, "The Effective Negotiator," *Journal of European and Industrial Training*, no. 7 (1978):

2. *London Times*, March 1, 1982, p. 1.

3. Movie presented at a seminar sponsored by the Association of Human Relation Administrators of New York City, April 1985.

4. George Bernard Shaw, *Devil's Disciple* New York: Penguin Books, Inc., 1950.

Norman Metzger

Lessons in Management from Baltasar Gracian

30

Much has been made of a book written 24 centuries ago—Sun Tzu's *The Art of War*. It is heralded as a CEO's guide to victory. In an article in *Success*,[1] it is reported that "it's cited regularly by real-life CEOs, generals, politicians and lawyers. . . . And it was on corporate raider Asher Edelman's required readings for his Columbia Business School course in takeovers."

CEOs have also been enamored of Machiavelli. In an article that appeared several years ago, Clemens and Mayer[2] note that "the most effective raider of them all" was Nicole Machiavelli, author of the Renaissance classic *The Prince*. They depict Machiavelli's book as being largely "about the arcane craft of seizing, and then managing, takeover targets." Top management's love affair with Machiavelli was explored extensively in a book by Richard Buskirk.[3] Why the preoccupation of CEOs with strategies of battles and historical comments on power and privilege? Let us balance this preoccupation with a conciliatory historical lesson, given to us by Baltasar Gracian.[4]

Gracian was a member of the Society of Jesus who wrote extensively at the beginning of the seventeenth century. His authoritative *Oraculo Manual y Arte de Prudencia* is a collection of 300 paragraphs excerpted and edited by Don Vincencio Juan de Lastanosa, who published it for him as well in 1650. De Lastanosa introduces his text as follows:

Note: Quotations reprinted from *A Truth Telling Manual: The Art of Worldly Wisdom of Baltasar Gracian*, translated by Martin Fisher. Courtesy of Charles C Thomas, Publisher, Springfield, Illinois.

May this volume serve as the menu card of reason at the feast of the intellectuals, and thus as a register of the choice morsels being served in all the other works, to the end that their general wisdom may be enjoyed more widely.[5]

A sampling of this "menu card of reason" follows.[6] It is well to note that Gracian's gems of profundity and words of wisdom would serve CEOs much better, indeed more productively, than would those of Machiavelli or Sun Tzu.

- *Harness the imagination: sometimes curbing her, sometimes giving her reign, for she is the whole of happiness. . . .*

  Ah yes! What we need are CEOs with imagination and vision. These are the leaders.

- *A just man. He stands on the side of the right with such conviction, that neither the passions of the mob, nor the violence of a despot can make him overstep the balance of reason.*

  Justice in all dealings is the hallmark of great leaders.

- *Take no part in foolish enterprises; much less in schemes more likely to injure than to enhance your reputation.*

  Alas! Some of our politicians or leaders should have read Gracian.

- *Think, and most about that which is most important: all the fools get lost because they do not think; they never see the half of things, and knowing neither their loss nor their profit, they make small effort in either direction.*

  We are warned about emotional decision making, for if CEOs think and engender thinking subordinates, we have the making of greatness. Thinking is not scheming. Gracian goes on to comment further about thinking.

- *Think as the few, speak as the many. To swim against the current is just as useless for setting a matter right, as it is dangerous to the swimmer.*

  What Gracian offers us is a behest to be creative, yet to understand the currents of our time. He warns us against shrewdness to excess and against deceit.

- *Be shrewd, but not too shrewd. . . . Deceit fills the world, wherefor be double suspicious. . . . To have considered well how to proceed is a great advantage for the day's work.*

  Plan, but do not let shrewdness engulf your creativity. Gracian goes on to offer sound advice to CEOs (although his advice was more universal than that), referring to some of the latent failings of leaders.

- *Temper your antipathies. We seem to hate with pleasure, and even before we have looked; and always does this inborn and vulgar aversion arise against the most eminent of men.*

  How often we find CEOs to be preoccupied, blame throwing, and hating. Becker[7] warns us that "We can establish our basic organismic footing with hate as well as by submission. In fact, hate enlivens us more, which is why we see more intense hate in the weaker ego states. The only thing is that hate, too, blows the other person up larger than he deserves."

- *Do nothing to make you lose respect for yourself, or to cheapen yourself in your own eyes; let your own integrity be the standard of rectitude, and let your own dictates be strictive and the precepts of law.*

  Here Gracian warns all CEOs about the need to display integrity and to be a role model in demeanor. As the protestors at the 1968 Democratic convention chanted, "The whole world is watching."

- *Never lose your head, matter of great practical wisdom, never to let it get away from you: it marks the great man, and of noble heart, for all greatness is hard to throw off balance.*

  Controlling one's temper and criticizing subordinates in private may appear old-fashioned, but, nonetheless, these are still the mark of a sensitive leader. Along with this edict for controlling one's temper, a leader must have patience.

- *A man who can wait, for it marks a great heart endowed with patience; never to be in undue haste, or excited. Be first the master of yourself, and you will thereafter be the master of others; one must journey far through time to get to the core of anything.*

  Prudent waiting, Gracian tells us, brings "season to accomplishment, and rightness to what is hidden." These words from the beginning of the seventeenth century seem even more appropriate in the helter-skelter world of competition and the battle for market share.

- Gracian even has words regarding leaving with grace, advice most outplacement experts would subscribe to. *Make a good exit. He who enters the house of fortune through the gate of pleasure leaves it through the gate*

of sorrow; and conversely, keep in mind therefore the curtain, paying greater heed to the happy exit than to the applauded entrance. This advice is equally as valid to those who ride the crest thinking not of tomorrow.*

  A.W. Housman[8] most poignantly addressed quite the same theme (although the leaving he described was an early death).

  The time you won your town the race
  We chaired you through the market-place;
  Man and boy stood cheering by,
  And home we brought you shoulder high.

  . . . .

  Smart lad, to slip betimes away
  From fields where glory does not stay
  And early though the laurel grows
  And withers quicker than the rose.

  Tomorrow always comes for those CEOs bathed in the glory of the moment.

- *Know how to escape grief, a profitable maxim, for it is the way to escape regret. . . . Be not the purveyor of scandal, or yet its recipient, for forbid its entrance much less give it aid.*

  Sound advice not only for CEOs but certainly for presidents and mayors. He warns us of those who "cannot live without daily dirt."

- *Know how to refuse since you cannot accede everything, or to everybody. It becomes important to know how to accede; and especially in those who command; for here enters manner. The no of one man has more esteem, than the yes of another; for a no that is gilded may be more satisfying than a yes unembellished.*

  Gracian continues to refer to the importance of interpersonal relations. *How* we say something is just as important as *what* we say. Rejection is a very difficult pill to swallow. But, on the other hand, rejection with sensitivity can, indeed, mitigate the pain.

- *A man of decision. . . . Some men are so incapable of decisions they need constantly to be prodded from without; and this springs at times less from a confused judgment, since theirs may be unusually clear, than from the unwillingness to act.*

  The troops often are waiting for their leader. Making a decision may at times be more important than the quality of the decision.

- *Not unapproachable. . . . To be unapproachable is a vice of men who do not know themselves, in that they confuse their spleen with their splendor: the road to affection does not lie in surliness.*

  My God! This man of the seventeenth century anticipated critical failings of leaders in the twentieth century. Too often leaders are blame throwers. At other times, they sequester themselves in offices where they are out of touch with the people.

- *Put yourself in the middle of things, to get at once at the heart of the business.*

  Recent books on management keep urging CEOs to get out of their offices, to see life as it really is on the floor. Gracian never misses a beat. He is the best of management consultants.

- *Alert when seeking information we live for the most part by what is told us; it is little that we see; thus we live in the faith of others; the ear is the side door of truth, but the front door of falsehood.*

    There is a need to filter the truth from the words. How often CEOs are faced with what I call the "Emperor's New Clothes Syndrome." Too often, subordinates tell their bosses what they want to hear. As Gracian warns us,

    It requires the whole attention at such times to discover the intent of the newsbearer. . . .

- Gracian even addresses the modern problem of burnout.

    Know how to renew your glitter. It is the birthright of the phoenix: even the best go stale, and so its fame, for familiarity kills admiration, wherefor something fresh even though mediocre comes to outshine the greater virtue, grown old. Bring about, therefore, your rebirth, in courage, in spirit, in fortune, in everything. Clothe yourself in new and shining armour, and rise again like the sun: change the theatre for your appearance, in order that your absence from the one may evoke desire, and your novelty in the other, applause.

    We are warned about the rut. Yesterday's brilliance becomes stale much like yesterday's bread, and the need to renew ourselves is a constant one.

- *Know how to profit through your enemies. . . . To a wise man, his enemies availed him more than to a fool, his friends.*

    Without paranoia Gracian alerts us to the use of our enemies. Enemies may be viewed as challenges, as spurs to creativity.

Too often we become experts and, in our expertise, tend to forget that there is more to life. The ideal CEO is a "Renaissance man." Let us once again go back to Gracian.

- *An all-round man. To be a man of many sides, is to count many men.*

    A long time ago a wise man said to me, "Do something, do it well, and have several sidelines." The CEO who does not read becomes the captive of his or her eroding expertise. We must go beyond the *Harvard Business Review* to Plato, Da Vinci, and Mozart.

- *The shortest road to bring somebody is to know whom to follow.*

    Who are the role models of today's CEOs? Gracian advises us that we must have some contrast in our contacts. He goes on to say,

    Avail yourself of this courteous admonition in the choice of your friends, and your fellows, so that through the meeting of the extremes there may arise a most sensible mien.

- In the dog-eat-dog milieu of the twentieth century, once again we look back to this sage of the early seventeenth century for advice.

    Never the cheap rival. Every effort to outshine an opponent lowers the standing, for competition resorts at once to mud-slinging, in order to besmirch.

This admonition seems to have been resisted in our political campaigns and, equally as ugly, in the advertising trend toward downgrading the competitor's product.

- One of my favorite aphorisms appears in the works of Gracian.

    Never out of stubbornness hold the wrong side, just because your adversary anticipated you, and chose the right, for then you are beaten from the start and will have to retire in disgrace; the right is never saved through the wrong.

    It is difficult, but critical, that we admit our mistakes and that we change our position when facts are clearly presented that alter our understanding. Charles Darwin apprised the same: "I have steadily endeavored to keep my mind free so as to give up any hypothesis however much beloved (and I cannot resist forming one on every subject) as soon as facts are shown to be opposed to it."

- Gracian preceded our interest in participatory management by urging us to listen to others.

    Open to suggestion. None is so perfect that he may not at times need a monitor, for he is incurably the fool who will not.

- We must, at times, listen to foolish suggestions, and Gracian has some wise advice along those lines.

    Know how to suffer fools. . . . At times we suffer most those upon whom we most depend.

    When a CEO can encourage people to speak up—even though they may present inane views—at times he or she may be shocked by their brilliance.

- Too often we say things in anger that can have disastrous effects.

    Mark your words, as a matter of caution when with rivals, and as a matter of decency when with the rest. There is always time to add a word, but none in which to take one back.

- There were times while reading Gracian's *Manual* that I have said aloud, "How does he know these people that I have come across?" Such a time was reflected in reading this aphorism:

    Do not fall into the class of the colossal asses. Such are all the pompous, the presumptuous, the stubborn, the capricious, the too easily led, the freaks, the affected, the facetious, the faddists, the perverse, the sectarians of all kinds, and the whole generation of the intemperate; monsters all of them, of impertinence.

    He asks the question "Who can bring order out of such general confusion?" That is the job of the CEO. In referring to the "faddists," Gracian continues his admonition.

    To keep free from the popular inanities, marks especially good sense.

    Very often CEOs get on the bandwagon of the latest management fad, whether it be MBO, quality circles, etc. Popularity alone is not enough; there must be a fit, a time, and a need.

- Gracian underscores a flexible response in this admonition:

    When unable to wear the lion's skin, clothe yourself in the fox's . . . where force fails, try art; over one road, or another, either the highway of courage, or the byway of cunning: more things have been gained by knack, than by knock, and the wise have won more oftener than the valorous, and not the other way about.

- Gracian knows about inspiration and, indeed, knows that leaders with a vision can present a motivating climate.

  Know how to put fire into your subordinates.

  Leaders need to set the challenge, to design the incentive, to inspire.

Martin Fischer, in translating Gracian, has done us an enormous service. He comments that "It is easy to imagine that Gracian was simply too sharp for his time or for succeeding times, as Aristophanes or Dr. Swift or Voltaire, and in the same fashion."[9] I do not believe that Gracian or even Fischer thought of the *Manual* as a bible for CEOs. But I do!

Clemens and Mayer[10] tell us that there are lessons to be learned from the authors of the classical Renaissance and industrial eras, which could provide a new management perspective. They talk about "The Classic Touch" and recommend to us Homer's Achilles, Shakespeare's Othello, and Miller's Willie Loman. To this I add, Gracian's *Manual*.

Let me conclude with one of the last of Gracian's aphorisms:

Three things make the superman, and they are the greatest gifts of divine generosity: a fertile mind, a deep understanding, and a cultivated taste.

NOTES

1. Sun Tzu, "The Art of War," *Success* (September 1978): 56–57.

2. John K. Clemens and Douglas F. Mayer, "History's First Takeover Expert: Before Pickens, There Was Machiavelli," *The New York Times,* 2 March 1986.

3. Richard A. Buskirk, *Modern Management and Machiavelli* (Boston: Cahners Books, 1974).

4. *A Truth Telling Manual: The Art of Worldly Wisdom of Baltasar Gracian,* trans. Martin Fischer (Springfield, Ill.: Charles C Thomas, 1945).

5. Ibid.

6. Ibid., pp. 34, 38–39, 43, 50, 52–53, 56, 57, 59–60, 62–63, 66, 73, 75–77, 128, 134, 139, 151, 159, 206, 245.

7. Ernest Becker, *The Denial of Death* (New York: Free Press, 1973), 145.

8. A.E. Housman, "To an Athlete Dying Young" in *Immortal Poems of the English Language*, ed. Oscar Williams (New York: Washington Square Press, 1960), 486.

9. *A Truth Telling Manual*, p. 7.

10. John J. Clemens and Douglas F. Mayer, *The Classic Touch: Lessons in Leadership from Homer to Hemingway* (Homewood, Ill.: Dow Jones–Irwin, 1987).

Part II

Employee Benefits

Employee fringe benefits continue to become more expensive, with the cost of providing health care benefits leading the way. The increasing demand for such benefits, in addition to radical changes in demographics and accelerating costs of services, has made benefits administration both complex and time consuming for human resources executives. One of the authors in this section points out:

> Employers and employees have found, much to their dissatisfaction, that an increasing portion of the budget for the total compensation package has to be earmarked for health care instead of salary increases and other benefits, such as educational assistance programs.

Spiraling health care costs now represent 11.5 percent of our gross national product; just two decades ago these costs accounted for less than 6 percent. Recent projections forecast a rise to 15 percent of the gross national product by the year 2000.[1]

In an article in *The New York Times* of February 21, 1989, Glenn Kramon reports that a Wyatt Company survey found that medical claims rose 13 percent between 1987 and 1988, averaging $1,568 per employee, excluding dental costs and health care costs for retirees.[2] Another survey by A. Foster Higgins & Company indicated that total health care costs rose 19 percent in 1988 alone, and 43 percent in just four years, to $2,354 per employee in 1988.[3]

For the human resources director, the need persists to become more knowledgeable about and sophisticated in providing the greater health protection necessary to attract and retain employees. This responsibility has been further complicated by new laws and many new restrictions, such as Section 89 of the Internal Revenue Code dealing with nondiscrimination in health and welfare plans; COBRA, or the Consolidated Omnibus Budget Reconciliation Act of 1985 and 1986; and, of course, the daddy of them all, the Employee Retirement Income Security Act (ERISA), which was passed in 1974.

We have brought together a group of authors with unparalleled knowledge and experience in the field. We are fortunate to have articles by several principals of William M. Mercer Meidinger Hansen, Inc., a firm of consultants; several prominent attorneys who specialize in benefits law; and a group of consultants and practitioners, all of whom afford us an unusual opportunity to look at the varied implications of maintaining benefits for our employees. Even with the national drive to shift the cost of employee benefits to a sharing model, wherein employees pay a fair share, hospitals still are paying the greater portion of the cost of employee benefits.

In this section you will have an opportunity to consider COBRA, the implications of ERISA for human resources directors, retirement plans in not-for-profit institutions, the responsibilities of pension plan trustee, and efforts to manage the medical cost of hospital workers' compensation claims, as well as a recent burden—long-term care insurance—and a recent phenomenon—pension plan terminations and reversions—and a most popular new option—flexible benefit plans. Also included is a discussion of a recent trend—reducing costs

271

through controlling, monitoring, and redirecting health care utilization.

In 1987, Americans spent $500 million on health care. This represented an increase of 9.8 percent over the preceding year and constituted 11 percent of the gross national product.[4] Health benefits costs skyrocketed during 1988; for no other reason, human resources directors must be au courant on the options.

NOTES

1. Jan M. Roser, "Your Money," *New York Times*, 11 March 1989, p. 36.

2. Glenn Kramon, "Employers of 90's Caught in Middle," *New York Times*, 2 February 1989, sec. D2.

3. Ibid.

4. Andrew H. Malcom, "In Health Care Policy, the Latest Word Is Fiscal," *New York Times*, 23 October 1988, sec. E3.

James R. Hudek
Kenneth A. Mason

31

The Technical and Miscellaneous Revenue Act of 1988 (TAMRA)

The Technical and Miscellaneous Revenue Act of 1988 (TAMRA) effects a number of changes in the tax laws governing employee benefit plans. This chapter describes some of the more significant changes in that Act. To wit: Section 89 Nondiscrimination Requirements; COBRA Sanctions; Legal and Educational Assistance Plans; Cafeteria Plans; ESOPs; Defined Benefit Pension Plans; Governmental Plans; and Church Plans.

SECTION 89 NONDISCRIMINATION REQUIREMENTS

Testing Year and Date

As originally enacted, the nondiscrimination rules of Internal Revenue Code Section 89 were required to be satisfied on each day of the plan year. TAMRA simplifies this requirement in at least two respects. First, an employer having multiple plans subject to Section 89 may select a single 12-month "testing year"—even if none of the plan years corresponds to that period. If this option is elected, all plans of the same "type" (i.e., governed by the same Code section) must have the same testing year.

Second, the employer may designate any day within the testing year as the "testing date." The employer must then demonstrate compliance with Section 89 on only that single day. Of course, any changes in plan design or in the benefits elected by highly compensated employees will require that the employer again demonstrate its satisfaction of Section 89's requirements. As was true of the testing year, an employer's

testing date must be the same for all of its plans of the same type. If the employer fails to designate a testing date, compliance with Section 89 must be demonstrated as of the last day of the applicable testing year.

Generally, an employer's designation of the testing year or testing date may be changed only with Internal Revenue Service (IRS) consent. TAMRA does delay this restriction as to testing *date* changes for one year—allowing employers to designate one testing date for years beginning in 1989 and another date for years beginning in 1990.

Comparability

The easiest way to establish compliance with Section 89 is to satisfy the "80-percent coverage test." This may be done by showing that at least 80 percent of an employer's employees are covered by the same plan. The same rule applies if at least 80 percent of the employer's employees are covered by a *group* of plans, so long as those plans are "comparable." Prior to TAMRA, the definition of comparability required that the least valuable of the employer's plans have a value of at least 95 percent of that of the most valuable plan. TAMRA eases this comparability test by substituting 90 percent for 95 percent. Indeed, TAMRA would even permit a plan with a value equal to only *80 percent* of another plan to be considered comparable to that plan, *if* the 80-percent coverage test were made a *90-percent* test. That is, if the 80-percent comparability rule is elected, the employer must demonstrate that at least 90 percent of its employees are covered under "comparable" plans.

TAMRA includes a number of other revisions to Section 89's comparability rules. For instance, a plan may be considered comparable to even a substantially more valuable plan if a sufficient percentage of participants in the more valuable plan are non–highly compensated employees. There is also a "safe harbor" rule, which looks at the cost to *employees* of participating in plans for which a sufficient percentage of employees are eligible. These and other revisions to the comparability rule should be examined before an employer discards the possibility of satisfying the 80 percent coverage test.

Temporary Valuation Rules

Section 89 calls on the IRS to issue regulations informing employers how to value health coverage benefits. Pending the issuance of such valuation tables, TAMRA provides that valuations arrived at for purposes of COBRA's health care continuation requirements may be used under Section 89 as well. Typically, these valuations should be computed by an actuary.

Treatment of Former Employees

Section 89 mandates that its nondiscrimination requirements be met with regard to an employer's *active* employees and, separately, with regard to the employer's *former* employees. TAMRA substantially eases this requirement with regard to former employees by permitting employers to disregard former employees who separated from service prior to January 1, 1989. Even under TAMRA, however, benefit increases received by any such former employees after Section 89's effective date must satisfy the nondiscrimination requirements. Because discrimination could also occur by reducing the benefits provided to non–highly compensated former employees, benefit *reductions* after the effective date must also satisfy Section 89's requirements.

TAMRA does permit employers to ignore certain post-1988 changes in benefits provided to former employees who separated from service prior to 1989. For instance, any federally mandated benefit increase may be ignored. Employers may also ignore benefit increases that are provided to such former employees on the same basis as to employees who separate from service *after* 1988, so long as such benefit increases are nondiscriminatory with respect to the later-separating employees. In any event, these special "former employee" rules do not apply to former employees who are re-employed by their employer after December 31, 1988.

Exceptions to Section 89

Prior to TAMRA, all employers were within the scope of Section 89. TAMRA provides that plans maintained by a church for church employees need not satisfy Section 89's requirements. For this purpose, the definition of "church" is the same as that applicable to the exclusion from FICA taxes, and thus includes certain church-controlled organizations.

TAMRA also makes it clear that any plan having *no* non–highly compensated employees is not subject to Section 89's nondiscrimination rules. Indeed, this exception applies separately with regard to an employer's active employees and former employees. Thus, if all of an employer's former employees are highly compensated, the employer need not satisfy Section 89's nondiscrimination tests with regard to its former employees.

Determination of Part-Time Status

For purposes of Section 89, part-time employees who normally work fewer than 17½ hours per week may be disregarded. Moreover, proportionate adjustments may be made to an employee's employer-provided benefit if the employee normally works fewer than 30 hours per week. TAMRA provides that an employee's "normal" weekly work hours are to be based on the average weekly hours worked in the portion of the testing year prior to the testing date. If that period contains fewer than 60 days, however, the determination of weekly hours should be based on the average weekly hours worked during the *prior* testing year. In the event that an employee failed to work at least 60 days during the prior testing year, the determination of weekly hours should be based on the employee's *scheduled* hours for the longer of (1) the next 60 days or (2) the remainder of the testing year. Under any of these rules, however, periods during which an employee does no work for the employer are to be disregarded.

80-Percent Test for Small Employers

TAMRA provides a transitional rule for employers having fewer than 10 employees. In satisfying the 80-percent coverage test, such small employers may disregard certain part-time employees. For plan years beginning in 1989, employees who normally work 35 hours or less per week may be disregarded. For 1990 plan years, only employees who normally work 25 hours or less may be disregarded. Starting in 1991, the usual rule applies—permitting the employer to disregard only employees who normally work fewer than 17½ hours per week. Many small employers may find this provision helpful in easing their transition to compliance with Section 89.

Interaction With Multiemployer Plans

Employers who both contribute to a multiemployer plan on behalf of certain employees *and* maintain their own plan on behalf of other employees will face additional complications under Section 89. For instance, the two groups of employees must normally be aggregated before the employer conducts the various Section 89 eligibility and coverage tests. In some respects, however, TAMRA will assist such employers. For instance, although an employer must normally adopt the same testing year and testing date with regard to all of its plans of the same type, TAMRA provides that an employer need not adopt the same testing year and date as that adopted by a multiemployer plan to which the employer contributes.

Similarly, Section 89 provides for the exclusion of several categories of employees from the pool as to which the eligibility and coverage tests are to be conducted—and then denies the exclusion as to any employees who would be covered under *any* of the employer's plans. For instance, although employees under age 21 may normally be excluded from the Section 89 calculations, an employer with even a single plan covering 18- to 21-year-olds would be required to test *all* of its 18- to 21-year-olds. TAMRA provides some relief to employers who contribute to multiemployer plans by providing that these exclusions will not be lost simply because certain otherwise excludable employees are covered under the multiemployer plan. Thus, although a multiemployer plan might cover an employer's 18- to 21-year-old bargaining unit employees, the employer may continue to exclude its 18- to 21-year-old non–bargaining unit employees when conducting the Section 89 tests.

Finally, employers who contribute to a multiemployer plan will appreciate a TAMRA provision that eases their task of valuing the benefits provided to their participating employees. Rather than using the yet-to-be-produced IRS valuation tables, such a contributing employer may set the value of each participant's employer-provided benefit equal to the corresponding plan contributions. Then, under regulations issued by the IRS, that contribution amount may be allocated among the plan's various benefits on the basis of the plan's prior year's claims or premiums. The employer may be required to modify this allocation, however, if it varies materially from either the plan's overall allocation of benefits *between* highly compensated and non–highly compensated employees or the plan's allocation of benefits *within* either group of employees. Moreover, an employer that contributes to a multiemployer plan on behalf of any "professional" is ineligible to use this special valuation rule.

Effective Date

The TAMRA changes described above are effective as of Section 89's effective date. Thus, they apply as of the first plan year beginning after December 31, 1988. Although some employers have apparently considered changing their plan year to delay Section 89's effective date, the Conference Committee Report to TAMRA specifically directs the IRS to disregard such changes for effective date purposes.

Moreover, employers having plans with differing plan years will be required to include *all* of those plans in the first year's calculation—even those plans as to which Section 89 is not yet effective. If the total benefits are found to be discriminatory, the discriminatory benefits must be prorated among all of the employer's plans—causing highly compensated employees in an otherwise nondiscriminatory plan that is subject to Section

89 to include a portion of that discriminatory excess in their gross income.

Section 89(k) imposes a number of plan "qualification" requirements. Among these is a requirement that any plan subject to Section 89 be in writing. TAMRA provides that employers have until the *end* of the plan year beginning in 1989 to comply with this written plan requirement.

Other Section 89 Changes

TAMRA makes many other revisions to Section 89. Some of these include

- authorization of certain sampling procedures;
- rules on permissive and mandatory plan aggregation;
- simplification of the "sworn statement" requirements;
- revision of the family coverage rules;
- a simplified definition of highly compensated employees (available only to employers having significant business operations in significantly separate geographic areas);
- revised "safe harbor" rules for separate lines of business or operating units; and
- clarification of possible employer and employee sanctions.

COBRA SANCTIONS

Overview

Prior to passage of TAMRA, the sanctions for an employer's failure to comply with COBRA's coverage continuation requirements were quite severe. The noncomplying employer was denied all tax deductions for contributions to its group health plans, and the employer's highly compensated employees were required to include in their gross income the value of their employer-provided health coverage. Effective with the first plan year beginning in 1989, however, TAMRA repeals both of these sanctions and replaces them with an excise tax. Not surprisingly, this excise tax is nondeductible.

Calculation of Excise Tax

The excise tax will be imposed at the rate of $100.00 per day of noncompliance with respect to each qualified beneficiary, up to a limit of $200.00 per day for each family. The tax will run from the date of the COBRA violation until that violation is corrected or, if never corrected, six months after the end of the 18- or 36-month maximum coverage period. For this purpose, a violation is "corrected" if the COBRA rules are retroactively satisfied to the extent possible and the qualified beneficiary is placed in as good a financial position as he or she would have been in if full COBRA coverage had been offered, elected, and paid for.

Inadvertent or Promptly Corrected Violations

Unlike the existing COBRA sanctions, the excise tax will be excused in certain cases of inadvertent or promptly corrected violations. For instance, if an employer has no actual knowledge of a COBRA violation, the excise tax will not begin to accrue until the employer either learns or should have learned of the violation. Alternatively, where a violation is due to reasonable cause and not to willful neglect, no excise tax will be imposed if the violation is corrected within 30 days after it occurs. Note, however, that both of the rules described in this paragraph are subject to an important exception. If the employer receives a notice of audit from the IRS before the violation is corrected, the employer loses the protection of these rules. Moreover, the employer is then subject to a minimum tax of at least $2,500 (or, if the violation is more than *de minimis*, $15,000).

Entities Liable for Payment of Excise Tax

TAMRA extends liability for COBRA sanctions beyond the employer. Third-party administrators and insurers are also liable for an excise tax if they are responsible for administering or providing plan benefits pursuant to a legally enforceable written agreement, and then cause a violation of COBRA by failing to perform one or more of the responsibilities set forth in that agreement. Moreover, if an insurer provides health benefits to an employer's active employees, that insurer may be subject to an excise tax if it fails to make the same benefits available to COBRA-qualified beneficiaries within 45 days after a written request therefor by the employer, plan administrator, or qualified beneficiary. Note that the insurer will also be responsible for providing coverage during the initial 45-day period, but will avoid imposition of the excise tax if coverage is made available prior to the expiration of that period.

Waiver of Excise Tax

TAMRA also grants the IRS discretion to waive all or any portion of an excise tax in the case of a violation due to reasonable cause and not to willful neglect. The tax may be waived only to the extent that its imposition would be ''unduly burdensome'' relative to the violation involved. The IRS is to make this waiver decision on the basis of the seriousness of the violation, and not on the taxpayer's ability to pay the tax.

Other COBRA Changes

Although both houses of Congress considered a number of other COBRA modifications during the 1988 session, these were not enacted into law. Thus, for example, employers may continue to terminate COBRA coverage on a COBRA beneficiary's becoming covered under another group health plan. It seems likely, however, that this and other COBRA changes will eventually be enacted in future technical corrections bills.

LEGAL AND EDUCATIONAL ASSISTANCE PLANS

Prior to TAMRA, the primary legal authority for excluding from an employee's gross income amounts contributed by his or her employer to an educational assistance program was scheduled to expire in the taxable year beginning after December 31, 1987. The exclusion for amounts contributed to a group legal services plan was scheduled to expire in the taxable year ending after December 31, 1987. TAMRA retroactively restores the authority for both exclusions, but provides for only a one-year extension of each. Thus, the educational assistance exclusion will expire with the last taxable year *beginning* on or before December 31, 1988; and the group legal assistance exclusion expired with the last taxable year *ending* on or before December 31, 1988. Of course, one or both such exclusions may be renewed again in the next tax bill.

CAFETERIA PLANS

Prior to the 1986 Tax Reform Act, Section 125 of the Internal Revenue Code required that cafeteria plan participants be allowed to choose among two or more benefits consisting of cash and ''qualified benefits.'' For this purpose, qualified benefits include certain benefits that are otherwise excludable from an employee's gross income. The 1986 Act modified the definition of ''cafeteria plan'' to include a plan that provides *only* nontaxable benefits. TAMRA retroactively repealed this new definition, thus restoring the law to its pre–1986 Act form.

The result is twofold. First, a plan offering participants a choice among only nontaxable benefits will not be required to comply with Section 125's restrictions. On the other hand, any employer *seeking* to establish or maintain a cafeteria plan must ensure that participants are offered the option of receiving their plan benefits in cash. Recently drafted cafeteria plans may not provide for such a cash option, and would thus need to be amended.

ESOPS

The 1986 Tax Reform Act required that participants in an Employee Stock Ownership Plan (ESOP) be granted the right to diversify the investments in their plan accounts once they attain age 55 and have 10 years of participation in the plan. The actual diversification elections would have been permitted during the first 90 days of each of the five plan years beginning with the second plan year after the plan year in which the participant satisfies the age and participation requirements.

Under TAMRA, the diversification elections must be permitted during the first 90 days of each of the *six* plan years beginning with the *first* plan year after the plan year in which the participant satisfies the age and participation requirements.

Under the effective date contained in the 1986 Act, some employers should have permitted diversification elections during the first 90 days of the 1988 plan year. Recognizing that many employers were awaiting further legislative clarification of these rules, however, TAMRA provides that employers who should otherwise have permitted a diversification election during 1988 may delay that election until 1989. Such employers must nonetheless permit diversification elections to be made over a full six-year period.

DEFINED BENEFIT PENSION PLANS

Employer Reversions

Prior to TAMRA, an employer was subject to a 10-percent excise tax on reversions of assets from qualified plans. The tax was payable by the last day of the second month following the calendar quarter in which the reversion occurred. TAMRA modified these rules in at least two respects. First, the tax rate has been increased from 10 percent to 15 percent. That increase is effective for reversions received after October 20, 1988, unless notice of the intent to terminate the plan was provided before October 21, 1988. Second, the deadline for payment of the tax has been shortened. Effective for reversions received after December 31, 1988, the excise tax must be paid by the end of the *first* month following the *month* in which the reversion occurs.

As passed by the Senate, TAMRA would have imposed a 60-percent excise tax on employer reversions. As part of the compromise by which the 10-percent rate was increased to only 15 percent, the IRS agreed to impose a temporary moratorium on employer reversions from terminated plans. That moratorium remained in effect until May 1, 1989. Congress is now considering further action to discourage or prevent employers from receiving reversions from qualified plans.

Allocation of Excess Assets during Plan Spin-Offs

Currently, qualified plans must provide that, in the case of a plan merger, consolidation, or transfer of assets or liabilities, each participant in the plan involved will have accrued benefits after the merger, consolidation, or transfer that are at least equal to the benefits he or she would have received if the plans had instead been terminated. This rule also applies to plan spin-offs—that is, the splitting of one plan into two or more plans. The effect of this rule is to permit all of an existing plan's excess assets to be allocated to any one of the plans remaining after a spin-off or similar transaction. TAMRA specifically addresses this possibility by requiring that, within a controlled group of corporations, the excess assets be allo-

cated proportionately among the plans remaining after a plan spin-off or similar transaction. This requirement is effective with respect to transactions occurring after July 26, 1988.

Minimum Funding Standard for Multiple-Employer Plans

Currently, the minimum funding requirements of Code Section 412 are applied to multiple-employer defined benefit pension plans on a planwide basis. That is, each contributing employer is *not* required to satisfy those requirements. Under TAMRA, the minimum funding standards are to be applied on an employer-by-employer basis—treating each employer as if it maintained a separate plan. The only exception to this rule occurs if the plan's method for determining required contributions assure that each employer will contribute at least the amount that would be required if each employer were indeed maintaining a separate plan. Moreover, if the plan's funding method satisfies this requirement, the plan will be required to file only a single Form 5500 and a single Schedule B. (*Note:* The changes discussed in this paragraph appear not to apply to *collectively bargained* "multiemployer" plans.)

GOVERNMENTAL PLANS

Required Beginning Date

The 1986 Tax Reform Act required that both private and governmental plans initiate distributions no later than April 1 of the calendar year following the calendar year in which a participant attains age 70½. TAMRA repeals this requirement with regard to governmental plans. Thus, as was the case prior to the 1986 Act, participants in governmental plans may delay their distributions until the *later* of the date described above or April 1 of the calendar year following the calendar year in which the participant *retires*.

Minimum Participation Rule

The 1986 Tax Reform Act also enacted a rule requiring a minimum number of plan participants. Under this rule, both private and governmental plans are required to have the participation of at least 50 of the employer's employees or, if a lesser number, 40 percent of the employer's employees. Although TAMRA does not repeal this requirement, it does provide that the minimum participation rule does not apply with respect to employees who were governmental plan participants as of July 14, 1988. This special rule applies only to plan years beginning before January 1, 1993. The effect of this rule is to grant governmental employers an extended period of time within which to consolidate existing plans into plans large enough to satisfy the 50-employee or 40-percent rule. At the same time, any governmental plan that added participants after

July 14, 1988, must satisfy this minimum participation rule as of the first plan year beginning after December 31, 1988.

CHURCH PLANS

Section 89 Exemption

As noted previously in this chapter, TAMRA exempts church plans (including plans maintained by qualified church-controlled organizations) from Section 89's nondiscrimination requirements.

Required Beginning Date

TAMRA treats church plans just as governmental plans in repealing the 1986 Tax Reform Act's more stringent required beginning date. Distributions from church (and church-controlled organization) plans must now begin by April 1 of the calendar year following the *later* of the calendar year in which the participant attains age 70½ or the calendar year in which the participant retires.

Alexander Sussman
Howard L. Kane

32

Coping with Section 89: A Compliance Strategy

INTRODUCTION

The Tax Reform Act of 1986 (TRA–86) introduced a new section to the Internal Revenue Code. This Section 89 arbitrarily sets up the criterion of nondiscrimination as the test of qualification for favorable tax treatment that all employee benefit programs must satisfy to avoid significant tax penalties to both the sponsoring employer and the plan's participants.

Hospitals will find it almost impossible to meet this test without significantly changing their benefit programs because these programs were designed primarily to deliver specific benefits to specific groups rather than to offer uniform, hospitalwide benefits. Hospitals typically employ a wide range of employees, and it is, therefore, particularly difficult, if not impossible, to design employee benefit programs that uniformly meet the needs of all subclasses of employees. For example, significant retirement programs may be most desirable for physicians but may be less desirable than comprehensive medical plans from the point of view of nurses and other relatively lower paid hospital staff.

Therefore, employee benefit programs in hospitals have historically been developed based on the perceived needs of their various types of employees. Moreover, such benefit programs for unionized employee groups developed through the collective bargaining process and, as such, reflect the relative wages, working conditions, and benefit priorities of the collective bargaining parties, rather than the efforts of hospital administrators to establish uniform programs for all employees, regardless of income level.

The process of developing benefit plans for hospital employees has worked quite well in the past, in that these benefit plans were targeted to the specific needs of the various employee subgroups. However, this ability to target specific benefit programs to the needs of specific hospital employee groups has now been seriously undermined, perhaps unintentionally, as a result of TRA–86.

One example of such affected coverage would be the death benefit protection which is generally greater for higher-paid administrative staff than for union employees under multiemployer group benefit plans. Large multiemployer health benefit plans were developed through the collective bargaining process and were specifically designed to meet the needs of lower-paid employees. As a result, the trustees of such plans considered, as their first priority, applying available funds to comprehensive health care insurance protection rather than to higher death benefits and/or disability income coverages. Section 89 would classify this condition as "discriminatory" and thereby require that the higher-paid administrative staff pay current income tax on the actuarial value of its additional group life insurance coverage. This includes amounts of coverage under $50,000, as well as the amounts over $50,000 that are currently subject to imputed income and, therefore, income tax. This tax liability will arise even if the higher-paid group does not have other benefit programs as valuable as those provided to the lower-paid group.

Because such additional group life insurance coverage would be currently taxable to each of the members of the administrative staff, it is the obligation of the hospital to report this "taxable income" to the employees and to the federal government. This means that the hospital must be able to identify each and every potentially discriminatory situation, quantify the extent of such discrimination, and report these amounts to employees concerned and to the federal government on a timely basis.

To do this, the hospital must compare the relative value and extent of employee participation in each of its life and health insurance benefit plans to determine whether Section 89 discrimination exists. This is particularly difficult and incredibly complicated because Section 89 views any difference within a particular plan as two separate plans. For example, if employee health care coverage is provided at no cost to the employee, but dependent health care coverage requires an employee contribution, Section 89 would view this as two different plans. Therefore, if the rate of participation in the dependent medical program is higher among the highly compensated employees (as specifically defined in TRA–86) than among lower-paid employees, Section 89 views this as discrimination in favor of highly compensated employees. As a result, the value of this extra coverage would be taxable to these employees.

Because lower-paid employees usually decline dependent health care coverage if their working spouses are covered for such benefits through group payments at their places of employment, Section 89 suggests that sworn statements be obtained from employees who decline dependent health coverage, stating that such coverage is provided to their dependents under other programs. If such statements are not obtained, then these employees must be included in the measurement process, thereby increasing the likelihood that the hospital would be deemed to be sponsoring a program that violates the discrimination provisions of Section 89, which would, in turn, trigger the tax ramifications described above.

Because of its complexity, we have decided not to burden the reader with an exhaustive presentation of the provisions and workings of Section 89, particularly the mathematical benefit discrimination tests which, in our opinion, are likely to be modified by regulation and corrective legislation. We believe that it is of greater initial benefit to first examine Section 89's particular impact on hospitals. Section 89's strong impact on hospital employee programs results not only from the wide range of occupational skills and income levels previously described, but also from the diverse and often unique employment relationships that have developed to meet staffing requirements.

Before we examine specific situations, it is important to point out that hospital administrators must be alert not only to the possible need to significantly restructure certain of their group benefit programs to avoid Section 89 discrimination but also to an alternative course of action. This alternative course will be to acknowledge that taxable extra coverage exists in certain instances, add the value of such additional coverage to the employees' cash income, and have the employees so affected pay the additional income tax for such extra coverage. This option is attractive when both the incremental value and the resultant tax are small.

In conclusion to this introduction, it is important to note that significant annual administrative responsibilities and costs quite likely will be added because of the plan analysis, data gathering, and testing necessary to demonstrate that the requirements of Section 89 have been met for any particular year under audit. Let us now examine certain illustrative examples of the unique impact of Section 89 on hospital employee benefit programs.

THE EFFECTS OF SECTION 89

Part-Time Employees

Because hospitals serve their respective communities on a continuous, 24-hour basis and must always have a wide variety of services readily on call, it is often vital for them to employ a significant number of part-time employees.

As an example, hospitals typically employ large cadres of "permanent part-time" nurses who regularly work at least 17½ hours per week. (Under Section 89, employees who work at least 17½ hours per week must be considered for benefit discrimination purposes.) Although such permanent part-time nurses are usually covered for health care insurance benefits, they are often required to contribute toward the cost of the coverage of their spouses and dependent children. As described above, to the extent that these employees decline to participate in such contributory plans, the chance is greater that the hospital will fail to meet the Section 89 discrimination test with respect to such plans.

There are other circumstances in which part-time employees work at least 17½ hours per week, but, instead of having to make contributions for dependent coverage, lesser benefits or, in some cases, no benefits for certain coverages are afforded these part-time employees. This practice also increases the chance that the hospital will fail to meet the Section 89 discrimination test.

Physicians and Independent Contractors

Physicians and other relatively highly paid professionals comprise an important subset of the highly compensated employee group against which Section 89 discrimination is measured. As a result, it is important that hospital administrators review the specific arrangements with each such professional to determine whether an employment relationship exists or whether the relationship is that of independent contractor.

To the extent that a professional is an independent contractor, his or her group benefits need not be considered for testing purposes. This is likely to help the hospital satisfy the Section 89 discrimination criteria by removing some of the "discriminatory" benefits from the testing process.

Leased Employees

Many hospitals enter into employee leasing arrangements in order to meet staffing requirements and to obtain relief from burdensome personnel administration requirements. For purposes of Section 89, leased employees are treated as regular hospital employees—that is, as if their health and welfare benefits are provided by the hospital (even if such benefits are actually provided by the leasing company). As a result, the plans of the leasing company will directly affect the hospital's Section 89 compliance.

Courtesy Programs

Because hospitals are by definition providers of health care services, many hospital employees request and receive medical services directly from staff physicians, laboratory technicians, and radiology specialists. Therefore, the question arises as to whether this is a plan of benefits that must be included for Section 89 testing.

We think that such arrangements are not employee benefit plans for Section 89 testing purposes unless the hospital formally sponsors the program as an internal preferred provider organization (PPO). If this is the case, then the program's benefits and eligibility for participation requirements must be considered for Section 89 benefit discrimination testing purposes.

These examples serve to illustrate how Section 89 uniquely impacts on hospitals. Although hospital administrators will probably find other Section 89 compliance problems as they begin to deal with the new law, we believe that these examples will help in their approaches to Section 89 compliance.

ADOPTING A COMPLIANCE STRATEGY

Under Section 89, almost all health and welfare plans will be subject to two compliance standards.

1. qualification requirements which set minimum standards in plan administration and benefit communications
2. nondiscrimination tests which determine whether a particular plan disproportionately favors highly compensated employees.

Plan Qualification

1. *Requirements.* For qualification purposes, plans must be in compliance by the end of the first testing year beginning on or after January 1, 1989. The qualification requirements are as follows:
   - The plan(s) must be in writing.
   - Employees' rights must be legally enforceable under the plan(s).
   - Employees must be given reasonable notification of the benefits available under the plan(s).
   - The plan(s) must be established and maintained with the intent to be permanent or indefinite.

2. *Includable plans.* Qualification requirements cover the following types of plans:
   - Hospitalization
   - Medical
   - Dental
   - Vision
   - Hearing
   - Prescriptions
   - Accidental Death and Dismemberment
   - Business Travel Accident
   - Physical Exams
   - Smoking Session
   - Weight Control
   - Employee Assistance Programs (EAPs)
   - Executive Benefits
   - Group-Term Penalties
   - Long-Term Disability
   - Salary Continuance
   - Eating Facilities
   - Employee Discounts
   - No-Cost Services
   - Cafeteria Benefits
   - Student Loans
   - Educational Assistance
   - Voluntary Employees Beneficiary Association (VEBAs)
   - Group Legal Assistance
   - Short-Term Disability
   - Dependent Care Assistance
3. *Noncompliance penalties.* Failure of the plan(s) to comply with the qualification requirements will result in *all* participating employees' being taxed on *all* benefits or services received under the plan(s).

Nondiscrimination Tests

As previously indicated, benefit discrimination exists only to the extent that employee benefit programs disproportionately favor highly compensated employees. Therefore, the first step is to identify the individuals who comprise the highly compensated employee group.

In general, a highly compensated employee is one who, during the current or preceding (plan) year, met at least one of the following criteria:

- earned more than $75,000 indexed annually for inflation ($81,720 in 1989)
- earned more than $50,000 indexed annually for inflation ($54,480 in 1989) and whose earnings were within the highest-20-percent group

- owned more than 5 percent of the company
- was an officer of the company earning more than $45,000 indexed annually for inflation ($49,032 in 1989)

It is important to remember that in cases in which a hospital is a member of a controlled group of corporations as defined in the Internal Revenue Code, all Section 89 tests must encompass all the corporations in the controlled group.

In the unlikely event that no hospital employee satisfies the highly compensated definition, the hospital automatically meets Section 89's nondiscrimination requirements.

Next, hospital administrators should identify all employees who may be excluded from testing in accordance with Section 89. The following employee categories may be excluded:

- employees working less than 17½ hours per week
- newly hired employees with less than six months of service (core plan testing) or less than one year of service (non–core plan testing)
- part-time employees normally working fewer than 17½ hours per week
- seasonal employees normally working fewer than six months per year
- employees under age 21
- nonresident aliens
- employees under collective bargaining—but only if they have negotiated no welfare benefits of any kind
- students working for the schools they attend, provided the services they perform are FICA exempt and they are eligible for core medical coverage

The "All or Nothing Rule" states that if just one person from a group of excludable employees (not including nonresident aliens) is provided coverage, then the group must be included in testing.

Finally, after each plan of benefits has been identified for Section 89 testing purposes and the appropriate employee categorizations have been accomplished, Section 89 nondiscrimination testing can commence. The new nondiscrimination tests apply only to group life insurance and to accident and group health care benefits. In order to possibly help the em-ployee pass the tests with respect to group life insurance, other benefit plans may be combined with the group life insurance program for testing purposes.

The following will serve as a checklist of plan tests that must be carried out:

- 80-percent test (based on actual participation in the plan)
- 50-percent test (based on eligibility to participate in the plan)
- 90-percent test (based on net employer contributions)
- 75-percent test (based on the relative values of benefits provided to various employee subclasses)

In addition to the tests described above, a discrimination provision test must also be passed. This test primarily requires that a plan not contain provisions that discriminate in favor of the highly compensated in any quantifiable way.

Noncompliance Penalties

If the plan fails to pass the nondiscrimination tests, highly compensated employees will be taxed on their "discriminatory benefit" excess. If the employer fails to report income on its employees' W-2 forms, that employer will be liable for a nondeductible excise tax on the total value of coverage at the highest individual tax rate.

CONCLUDING COMMENTS

When the Tax Reform Act of 1986 added Section 89 to the Internal Revenue Code, it established stringent compliance rules for employee health and welfare plans. Because of these broad changes, and the difficulty in initially interpreting and applying the new rules, we expect that many clarifications and allowances for good faith compliance attempts will be made.

For these reasons, we urge that hospital plan administrators approach Section 89 with caution and, wherever possible, look to eliminate obvious benefit design flaws, particularly if the incremental cost of correcting them is small. In this way, many of the burdensome testing tasks may be eliminated.

Phyllis C. Borzi

33

COBRA Update:

Summary of Health Insurance Coverage Act of 1985 (Title X of the Consolidated Omnibus Budget Reconciliation Act of 1985, P.L. 99-272), As Amended by Section 1895(d) of the Tax Reform Act of 1986 (P.L. 99-514)

IN GENERAL

Certain qualified beneficiaries—surviving spouses, divorced spouses, spouses of Medicare eligible employees, dependent children, and employees who have either terminated employment or reduced their hours—who would otherwise lose their group health coverage are entitled to elect to continue coverage under their group health plan at their own expense for up to three years (18 months for terminated and reduced-hour employees).

WHY DID CONGRESS ENACT THIS LAW?

- Concern about access to affordable health care
  1. 85 percent of insured individuals have employer-sponsored group coverage
  2. Relatively high cost of individual coverage (for some, unavailable at any cost) and inability of most Americans to pay all medical expenses out of disposable income
- Different from mandated benefits: access to coverage vs. specification of the content of the plan

---

Note: Reprinted with permission from *Employee Benefits Annual 1987: Proceedings of the Annual Employee Benefits Conference*, Vol. 29, published by International Foundation of Employee Benefit Plans. Statements or opinions expressed are those of the author and do not necessarily represent the views or positions of the International Foundation, its officers, directors, or staff.

- Preventive cost shifting; perception that failure to address the problem would result in greater federal and other expenditures in the future
- Understood some adverse selection would result and tried to minimize it

WHAT LAWS ARE AMENDED?

Title X of COBRA makes parallel changes in the Internal Revenue Code of 1954 (IRC), Title I of the Employee Retirement Income Security Act of 1974 (ERISA), and the Public Health Service Act (PHSA). All references in this text are to these laws as amended by COBRA and the Tax Reform Act of 1986.

WHAT REGULATIONS APPLY?

All references in this text to IRS regulations or to questions and answers (Q&A) are references to the proposed regulations on continuation coverage requirements of group health plans issued by the Internal Revenue Service on June 15, 1987, and published in the *Federal Register* of that date beginning on page 22,716.

Those regulations will be effective only when final regulations are published in the *Federal Register*. For the period between the date of enactment of COBRA and the effective date of final regulations, the plan and the employer must operate in good faith compliance with a reasonable interpretation of the statute. In its proposed regulations, the IRS indicated that if, after September 14, 1987, an employer or plan complied with the provisions of the proposed regulations, it would consider the employer or plan to be acting in good faith compliance with a reasonable interpretation of the statute. The IRS also indicated that compliance with the proposed regulations was not the only way to demonstrate good faith compliance, but that compliance with the regulations would be a safe harbor for purposes of the tax sanctions of COBRA, since the determination of whether an employer's or a plan's actions constitute good faith compliance is ultimately a facts and circumstances test. Finally, the IRS regulations point out that there may be nontax consequences if an employer or a plan fails to comply with the parallel requirements found in Title I of ERISA (or, in the case of state and local employers or plans, with the parallel requirements found in the Public Health Service Act).

The Department of Labor issued guidance on some of the notice issues shortly after the law was passed, but before Congress adopted technical corrections to COBRA in the Tax Reform Act of 1986 and the Omnibus Budget Reconciliation Act of 1986 (relating to health benefits in bankruptcy). See ERISA Technical Release No. 86-2 (reprinted in *BNA Pension Reporter*, Vol. 13, No. 26, 1184, June 30, 1986).

WHAT EMPLOYERS ARE REQUIRED TO PROVIDE COVERAGE?

- All private companies and state and local governments employing at least 20 employees on a typical business day during the preceding calendar year [see Q&A-9(b) and (c) for guidance on the 20-employee rule].

- Special rule for *multiemployer plans:* if *all* contributing employers have fewer than 20 employees, the group health plan is exempt from continuation coverage requirements.

- Special rule for *multiple employer welfare arrangements* (MEWAs) as defined in Section 3(40) of ERISA; each employer maintaining the plan is considered a separate employer [Q&A-10(d)].

- Includes taxable and tax-exempt employers.

- *Employer* includes members of controlled group [as described in IRC Section 414(b), (c), (m), or (o)] and successor employers (Q&A-5); special controlled group rules apply for determining whether the plan is a small employer plan (see Q&A-9).

- Excluded: churches, federal government (more limited legislation affecting former spouses' right to continue health coverage was previously enacted in the 98th Congress).

Note: In addition to the general exemption for group health plans of small employers (see Q&A-9), group health plans maintained for employees by the District of Columbia, U.S. territories or possessions, or their agencies or instrumentalities are also exempt.

IRC Sections 162(i)(2) and 106(b); ERISA Section 601; PHSA Section 2201.

WHAT IS A GROUP HEALTH PLAN?

- A plan providing medical care [as defined in IRC Sec. 213(d)]; includes all benefits described in IRC Section 162(i), including medical, vision, dental, prescription drugs, and so forth (Q&A-7).

- The method of providing benefits is irrelevant: The new law affects both insured and self-funded plans, and also HMOs, IPAs, PPOs, cafeteria plans, flexible benefit arrangements, and so forth (Q&A-7 and -14).

- Access to an on-site facility of the employer is not required if the facility provides free first aid care for on-the-job injuries for employees only [Q&A-7(e)].

- Plans providing for medical care are arrangements that include specific treatment for physical conditions or health problems; employer-sponsored arrangements providing for benefits or services that are merely beneficial to general good health are not subject to continuation requirements (e.g., the right to elect continued access to a substance abuse program must be provided but not the right to continued access to a company swimming pool open to all employees and their families) [Q&A-7(b) and (c)].

- A single group health arrangement may be considered to be two or more separate plans; under IRC regulations, each different benefit package or option will be treated as a different plan (Q&A-10).

IRC Section 162(i)(3); ERISA Section 607(1); PHSA Section 2208(1).

WHAT IS A COLLECTIVELY BARGAINED GROUP HEALTH PLAN?

- The plan must cover only employees and former employees (and their families) covered under a collective bargaining agreement; if the plan covers nonbargaining unit employees as well, it will be treated as two separate plans with each plan independently subject to COBRA (Q&A-12).

- Employees of an employee representative and of the plan itself are treated as if they were covered under a collective bargaining agreement for purposes of these rules [Q&A-12(b)].

WHAT TRIGGERS THE CONTINUATION COVERAGE REQUIREMENT?

The right to elect to continue group health coverage must be provided to a ''qualified beneficiary'' upon the occurrence of a ''qualifying event.''

IRC Section 162(k); ERISA Section 602; PHSA Section 2202.

WHAT IS A QUALIFYING EVENT?

- The death of the covered employee.
- The termination of employment (other than by reason of gross misconduct) of the covered employee (regardless of whether the termination was voluntary or involuntary) (Q&A-18 and -19).
- A reduction of hours of the covered employee (includes leaves of absences and strikes) (Q&A-19).
- The divorce or legal separation of the covered employee from the employee's spouse.
- A covered employee becomes entitled to benefits under Medicare.
- A dependent child ceases to meet the plan's definition of a *dependent*.

Note: For a qualifying event to occur, the above event must result in loss of coverage. The loss of coverage, however, need not be immediate (Q&A-18). But *both* the event and the loss of coverage must occur after the plan first becomes subject to COBRA (Q&A-20 and -21). ''Loss of coverage'' includes any change in terms and conditions of coverage. If coverage is reduced or eliminated in anticipation of a qualifying event, that reduction or elimination is disregarded in determining whether a qualifying event has occurred (e.g., if the plan is terminated in anticipation of a plant closing so that when the layoff occurs, arguably no qualifying event could have occurred because no one was covered; if the covered employee removes his or her spouse from the health plan in anticipation of a divorce or legal separation, so that arguably there is no coverage to continue) [Q&A-18(c)].

IRC Section 162(k)(3); ERISA Section 603; PHSA Section 2203.

WHAT IS GROSS MISCONDUCT!

- Generally determined by the facts and circumstances surrounding the termination
- Intended by the conferees to represent circumstances that were rare and involved extremely serious conditions (e.g., dismissal for habitual lateness, excessive absenteeism, or doing nonunion work are not normally examples of gross misconduct)

- Clearly more than a dismissal for cause (that standard appeared in the Senate bill and was rejected by the conferees)

WHO IS A QUALIFIED BENEFICIARY?

- A covered employee who terminates employment for other than gross misconduct (includes voluntary quits and retirees).
- A covered employee who loses coverage because of a reduction in hours worked (either a voluntary or involuntary reduction).
- Any person who, on the day before the qualifying event, is a beneficiary under the plan as the spouse or dependent child of a covered employee.
- Q&A-16 generally describes who is considered a covered employee.
- A qualified beneficiary who has elected continuation coverage may add covered dependents (e.g., newborns, new family members) under the same terms and conditions that active workers could add dependents. Those newly covered persons, however, cannot themselves become qualified beneficiaries [Q&A-17(a)]. Similarly, if a qualified beneficiary does not elect continuation coverage during the election period, but later is added to the continuation coverage of a person who did elect to continue coverage, the former qualified beneficiary does not become a qualified beneficiary (e.g., the spouse of the covered employee declines coverage when the covered employee terminates coverage; one year later, the covered employee on continuation coverage adds his or her spouse to the plan; one month later, the covered employee dies; the spouse does not have COBRA rights) [Q&A-17(b)].

IRC Section 162(k)(7)(B); ERISA Section 607(3); PHSA Section 2208(3).

Note: Nonresident aliens with no source of income in the U.S. are not included in the definition of *qualified beneficiary*.

WHAT TYPE OF COVERAGE IS REQUIRED?

- In general, the same coverage as the qualified beneficiary had the day before a qualifying event occurs.
- In general, qualified beneficiaries are treated the same as active workers, except that qualified beneficiaries cannot be compelled to take ''noncore'' coverage (e.g., vision and dental coverage); if actives are automatically covered under a plan providing medical, vision, and dental benefits, qualified beneficiaries can elect either medical only, or all three types of benefits (medical, vision, dental); qualified beneficiaries *do not* have to be given the right to

elect only vision or only dental unless active employees have that choice (Q&A-22 through -31).

- If coverage is modified for any group of similarly situated beneficiaries, continuation coverage must be modified for qualified beneficiaries in connection with that group (Q&A-23).
- See Q&A-28 for a discussion of how plan deductibles are treated and Q&A-29 for a discussion of how plan limits are treated.

IRC Section 162(k)(2)(A); ERISA Section 602(1); PHSA Section 2202(1).

- Continuation coverage cannot be conditioned on evidence of insurability.

IRC Section 162(k)(2)(D); ERISA Section 602(4); PHSA Section 2202(4).

Note: COBRA does not create new rights to elect coverage for persons not already covered under the plan. For example, if a married employee with individual coverage is laid off, his or her spouse does not have the right to elect continuation coverage.

WHAT IS THE DURATION OF COVERAGE?

- Maximum periods:
  1. 18 months in the case of a termination of employment or reduction in hours.
  2. 36 months for all other qualifying events.

     These maximums are measured from the date of the qualifying event (i.e., the triggering event, even if the loss of coverage occurs at a later date) (Q&A-39).

     Note: Multiple qualifying events are possible during the period of continuation coverage; however, the total period of coverage is capped at 36 months (beginning on the date of the first qualifying event) regardless of how many qualifying events occur. In addition, the subsequent qualifying event must occur during the period of continuation coverage (Q&A-40).

IRC Section 162(k)(2)(B)(i); ERISA Section 602(2)(A); PHSA Section 2202(2)(A).

- Coverage terminated earlier if one of the following occurs:
  1. The employer (on a controlled group basis) ceases to provide any group health plan coverage to any employee.
  2. Coverage ceases under the plan because of failure to make timely payment of required premium (a Tax Reform Act provision clarifies that payments will be considered to be timely if made within 30 days of the due date or whatever longer period that might apply to or under the plan) (Q&A-48 discusses what is timely payment).

3. Qualified beneficiary becomes entitled to Medicare.
4. Qualified beneficiary becomes covered under another group health plan.

Q&A-38; IRC Section 162(k)(2)(B)(ii) through (iv); ERISA Section 602(2)(B) through (D); PHSA Section 2202(2)(B) through (D).

HOW IS THE COST OF COVERAGE CALCULATED?

- A plan can require the qualified beneficiary to pay the total cost of coverage (both the employer and the employee shares), but the premium cannot exceed 102 percent of the cost of coverage for similarly situated beneficiaries with respect to whom a qualifying event has not occurred.
- *Cost of coverage* means cost to the plan; employers that subsidize coverage are not required to continue that subsidy (e.g., the employer charges $50 for family coverage even though it costs $100; the employer can charge a qualified beneficiary electing family coverage $102).
- The premium for self-insured plan must be a reasonable estimate of the cost based on either
  1. An actuarial basis, taking into account factors prescribed by Treasury regulation, or
  2. The comparable cost for similarly situated beneficiaries for the same period occurring during a prior "determination period" (i.e., any 12-month period), adjusted by the GNP deflator (calculated by the Department of Commerce and published in the *Survey of Current Business*) for the 12-month period ending on the last day of the sixth month of the prior 12-month period (e.g., the premium for calendar year 1987 would be calculated by adjusting the cost of the plan for similarly situated beneficiaries for the 12-month period beginning October 1, 1985, and ending September 30, 1986, by the GNP implicit price deflator for the 12 months ending June 30, 1986).
  3. The premium is locked in for 12 months. (*Note:* It is not a 12-month period that is different for each qualified beneficiary; see Q&A-45).
  4. The qualified beneficiary must be allowed to pay the premium monthly (Q&A-48).
  5. The first payment is due no later than 45 days after the election to continue coverage is made and must cover the retroactive period (date of qualifying event to date of payment) (Q&A-47). *Note:* The 30-day grace period for making timely payments does not apply to this 45-day period.
  6. The COBRA Conference Report specifically states that separate risk categories for qualified beneficiaries cannot be set up, nor can the premium be based on categories that would violate Title VII or the Equal Pay Act.

7. Q&A-44 through -48 generally discuss cost and payment issues; the Treasury expects to issue separate proposed regulations dealing with cost issues in the future.

IRC Section 162(k)(2)(C) and (4); ERISA Sections 602(3) and 604; PHSA Sections 2202(3) and 2204.

WHAT ARE THE NOTICE REQUIREMENTS?

- General Notice:
1. At the time the plan first becomes subject to the act, the plan administrator must give written notice to covered employees and their spouses of their new rights to continuation coverage. New employees hired subsequent to that time, and their spouses, must also be given notice.
Note: Although providing a new employee with a summary plan description (SPD) that includes a description of COBRA rights might be sufficient notice with respect to that employee, the statute clearly requires that the spouse of that employee must also be notified of COBRA rights.
Sections 10002(e) and 10003(c) of COBRA.
2. See Labor Department Model Statement, ERISA Technical Release No. 86-2 (see *BNA Pension Reporter*, Vol. 13, No. 26, p. 1184, June 30, 1986).
Note: This model notice was issued prior to the adoption of technical corrections to COBRA in the Tax Reform Act so it does not necessarily represent the current state of the law in every respect.
3. DOL indicates that a first class mailing to the last known address of the employee and his or her spouse is one way of satisfying this notice requirement.
4. The COBRA Conference Report specifically rules out posting at the work place as a method for complying with this notice requirement.
5. In addition to the special notice described above, a description of continuation coverage rights must be included in the plan's summary plan description.
- Specific Notice to Plan Administrator When a Qualifying Event Occurs:
1. The *employer* has 30 days from the qualifying event to notify the plan administrator in the case of a covered employee's death, termination of employment, reduction of hours, or Medicare entitlement.
2. The *covered employee or qualified beneficiary* must notify the plan administrator within 60 days of the qualifying event in the case of a divorce, legal separation, or when a dependent becomes ineligible for coverage under the terms of the plan.
- Notice by Plan Administrator to Qualified Beneficiary:
1. Within 14 days after receiving the specific notice described above, the plan administrator must notify

each qualified beneficiary of the beneficiary's right to elect continuation coverage.
2. Notice to the spouse is considered to be sufficient notice to dependent children if the children reside with the spouse at the time the notice is being given.

IRC Section 162(k)(6); ERISA Section 606; PHSA Section 2206.

Note: Some have advised clients that, if the employer is also the plan administrator, the 30-day and 14-day time frames described above must be shortened to 14 days. The proposed IRS regulations do not address this issue. Therefore, it would be reasonable for the employer to assume that the two time periods are separate, and employers that are also plan administrators are to be treated no differently than employers that do not administer their plans.

WHAT ARE THE ELECTION REQUIREMENTS?

- Each qualified beneficiary is entitled to an election period of no less than 60 days from the later of
1. The date coverage terminates under the plan because of a qualifying event, or
2. The date the beneficiary receives notice from the plan administrator of his or her right to elect continuation coverage.
- Any election to continue coverage by a qualified beneficiary who is a spouse of a covered employee or covered employee (in the case of termination of employment or a reduction in hours) to continue coverage is considered an election by all covered beneficiaries.

Note: Because each qualified beneficiary is entitled to a separate election, if the covered employee does not elect to continue coverage, the employee's spouse and dependents may elect continuation coverage. In addition, if there is a choice of types of coverage under the plan, each qualified beneficiary is entitled to make an individual selection with respect to the type of coverage (Q&A-37).

IRC Section 162(k)(5); ERISA Section 605; PHSA Section 2205.

WHO PAYS FOR COVERAGE DURING THE ELECTION PERIOD?

- If a qualified beneficiary elects coverage, coverage must be provided retroactively from the date that coverage would otherwise have been lost [Q&A-34(a)]. Accordingly, the qualified beneficiary must pay for the period of retroactive coverage in the first premium payment (due no later than 45 days after coverage is elected) (Q&A-47).
- Under indemnity and reimbursement arrangements, an employer could either provide for plan coverage during

the election period or, if the arrangement so provides, drop the qualified beneficiary and retroactively reinstate him or her once the election is made and the premium is paid [Q&A-34(b)]. (*Note:* Many insurance contracts permit retroactive reinstatement, but only with evidence of insurability. Remember that requiring such evidence is not permitted under COBRA.)

- Under other types of arrangements (e.g., HMOs), qualified beneficiaries can be forced to choose between electing and paying for coverage, or paying the reasonable and customary charges for services; the employer can also treat the use of services as constructive election [Q&A-34(c)].

Note: It is critical that the election form indicate who pays for coverage (and the procedure to be followed if either of the two above approaches is adopted) during the election period and until the first premium comes in so there will be no confusion.

WHAT DOES COBRA REQUIRE WITH RESPECT TO A CONVERSION OPTION?

If the plan provides a conversion option at the end of the period of continuation coverage, qualified beneficiaries must be permitted to enroll in any conversion health plan generally available under the plan (Q&A-43).

IRC Section 162(k)(2)(E); ERISA Section 602(5); PHSA Section 2202(5).

HOW IS THE LAW ENFORCED?

Three federal laws are amended by COBRA so three types of sanctions are imposed.

1. Under the *Internal Revenue Code*, Section 162(i) is amended to deny the business expense deduction for contributions to any group health plan maintained by the employer unless all the group health plans of the employer meet continuation coverage requirements of new Section 162(k). In addition, Section 106 is amended to deny the exclusion for employer contributions to group health plans on behalf of any highly compensated employee [as defined in Section 105(h)(5)] unless all group health plans of the employer meet the continuation coverage requirements. How the tax sanctions work is set forth in Q&A-2 through -4 of the proposed IRS regulations.
   Note: The Tax Reform Act of 1986 provides a new definition of *highly compensated employees* [new IRC Section 414(q)] that would apply for purposes of COBRA.
2. Under *ERISA*, a new Part 6 is added to Title I containing the continuation coverage requirements. Thus the nor-

mal ERISA enforcement provisions contained in Part 5 (e.g., civil suits in federal court for injunctive relief and/ or damages and ERISA's $100-a-day penalty for failure to provide notice) are available to aggrieved parties and the Secretary of Labor to enforce the new requirements against plans and employers subject to ERISA.
3. Under the *Public Health Service Act*, a new Title XXII is added requiring that, if a state receives Public Health Service Act funds, each group health plan maintained by that state, any political subdivision of that state, or any agency or instrumentality of that state or political subdivision must provide continuation coverage. This requirement is enforced by granting private rights of action for appropriate equitable relief by aggrieved parties against the state, political subdivision, or agency or instrumentality. PHSA Section 2207.

WHEN ARE THE CONTINUATION COVERAGE REQUIREMENTS EFFECTIVE?

- In general: plan years beginning on or after July 1, 1986.
- Special rule for collectively bargained plans; plan years beginning on or after the later of
  1. Date on which the last collective bargaining agreement relating to the plan expires (disregarding extensions agreed to after the enactment of COBRA), or
  2. January 1, 1987.

Sections 10001(e), 100029(d) and 10003(b) of COBRA.
Note: See Q&A-13 for a discussion of what is considered the plan year and Q&A-12 for a discussion of what is a collectively bargained plan.

ARE STATE HEALTH INSURANCE CONTINUATION LAWS PREEMPTED?

A number of states have enacted laws requiring group health insurance contracts and policies to provide for continuation coverage on the occurrence of certain events. In this regard, questions have been raised concerning the effect of these state laws on plans required to comply with the federal continuation coverage provisions enacted under Title X of COBRA.

Title X did not amend the preemption provisions of ERISA Section 514. Accordingly, the same pre-emption principles established prior to the enactment of Title X applicable to state insurance laws continue to apply. Under ERISA Section 514, state laws that regulate insurance are not pre-empted. Even though employee benefit plans subject to Title I of ERISA may not be considered insurance companies or insurers subject to state insurance regulation, plans that elect to insure their benefits through an insurance carrier subject to state regulation are, nonetheless, required to provide benefits in accordance with state insurance law, according to a U.S. Supreme Court decision (*Metropolitan Life v. Massachusetts*). Accordingly, plans subject to the Title X continuation coverage provisions that insure their benefits will have to satisfy the federal standards established by Title X of COBRA, and insurance contracts that fund those plans will have to satisfy any applicable state insurance laws, including those that require continuation coverage provisions. On the other hand, employee benefit plans subject to Title I of ERISA that are not insured (e.g., unfunded plans and self-funded/self-insured plans) will only be subject to those standards established under federal law.

With respect to how the maximum federal period of continuation coverage should be calculated, it is reasonable for a group health plan to take into account any period of continuation coverage provided under the plan (whether required by state law or voluntarily provided) after the date of the qualifying event if the coverage would otherwise meet the requirements under COBRA with respect to type of coverage, premium, evidence of insurability, notice, and election. In other words, if a plan already provided a period of continuation coverage under terms and conditions no less favorable to qualified beneficiaries than the COBRA requirements, the periods of coverage could run concurrently (Q&A-41).

WHO HAS REGULATORY AUTHORITY?

The Conference Report allocates regulatory authority as follows:

- The Secretary of Labor—reporting and disclosure
- The Secretary of the Treasury—coverage, deductions, and income inclusions
- The Secretary of Health and Human Services—applicability to state and local governmental plans of substance of regulations issued by the Departments of Labor and the Treasury

In addition, the conferees stated that regulations were to be prospective only and that, pending issuance of regulations, employers must act in "good faith compliance with a reasonable interpretation" of the provisions of the act.

Note: Subtitle F of the Omnibus Budget Reconciliation Act of 1986, P.L. 99-509, amends the health insurance continuation rules described above by adding a series of requirements that relate to health benefits for retirees, their spouses, and dependent children, and for persons who were covered under the group health plan as surviving spouses when an employer is in bankruptcy. The amendment establishes a new qualifying event, a new class of qualified beneficiaries, and a new period of continuation coverage for certain qualified beneficiaries.

The new qualifying event is a proceeding under Chapter 11 of the Bankruptcy Act, commencing on or after July 1, 1986, that results in loss of health insurance coverage for qualified beneficiaries. "Loss of coverage" includes substantial elimination of coverage within one year before or after the filing of the bankruptcy petition.

The new class of qualified beneficiaries includes retirees (who retired on or before the date of the qualifying event) and any other individuals (including spouses, dependent children, and surviving spouses) who, on the day before the qualifying event, are beneficiaries under the plan.

The period of continuation coverage for those qualified beneficiaries who are eligible for coverage as a result of the new qualifying event can be much longer than the period under the other qualifying events. Any person who, on the day before the new qualifying event, was covered under the plan as a retiree or as a surviving spouse has the right to elect continuation coverage for life. After the retiree's death, however, a second qualifying event is triggered that entitles the spouse and dependent children to elect 36 months of continuation coverage.

An employer can cease continuation coverage for qualified beneficiaries who are entitled to coverage as a result of this new qualifying event under all but one of the same circumstances under which coverage can be terminated for qualified beneficiaries who are entitled to elect continuation coverage on the basis of any of the other qualifying events. For this group of qualified beneficiaries only, however, entitlement to Medicare does not terminate coverage.

Finally, although the amendments made in P.L. 99-509 related to the new qualifying event are generally effective as if they had been included in the original COBRA legislation, a special effective date provision makes it clear that, with respect to the new qualifying event, the amendments apply retroactively to plan years ending during the 12-month period beginning July 1, 1986. Thus the general effective date and the special effective date for collectively bargained plans contained in the original COBRA legislation are overridden. Because of this retroactive effect, a special notice rule is provided that gives employers 30 days from the date of enactment to notify the plan administrator that a qualifying event has occurred.

Mark E. Brossman

34

ERISA and Multiemployer Employee Benefit Funds

The Employee Retirement Income Security Act (ERISA)[1] was passed in 1974 to comprehensively regulate pension and welfare benefits. Prior to the passage of ERISA many employees failed to receive promised benefits. For example, Studebaker was unable to pay pension benefits, and this tragedy was repeated in numerous smaller situations. ERISA sets forth detailed requirements for pension and welfare benefit plans.

ERISA COVERAGE

ERISA covers "employee pension benefit plans" and "employee welfare benefit plans" broadly defined. Employee pension benefit plans include any plan, fund, or program that provides retirement income to employees or results in the deferral of income by employees for periods extending to the termination of covered employment or beyond.[2]

Employee welfare benefit plans include any plan, fund, or program established or maintained by an employer, labor organization, or both to provide participants and/or their beneficiaries with insurance or other benefits in the event of sickness, accident, disability, death, or unemployment; vacation benefits; apprenticeship or other training programs; day care; scholarship funds; prepaid legal services; etc.[3] Generally severance pay plans are covered; however, certain severance pay plans may be viewed as pension plans if benefits are contingent on retirement, exceed double the employee's final annual compensation, or are not completed within 24 months of termination from service.[4]

Regulations provide that certain benefits are not covered by the definition of employee welfare benefit plan; these include unfunded sick pay, vacation pay, military leave pay, jury duty, training pay, educational leave pay, scholarship plans, on-premises recreation, dining or first aid facilities; inservice bonuses or holiday gifts, remembrances, employee discounts, hiring halls, strike funds, and 100-voluntary, employee-paid, and employee-sponsored group insurance programs.[5] ERISA also does not cover governmental plans, church plans, workers' compensation, unemployment or disability benefit plans, plans maintained outside the United States primarily for nonresident aliens, and unfunded excess benefit plans.[6]

TAFT–HARTLEY REQUIREMENTS

Since the decision of the U.S. Supreme Court in *Inland Steel Co. v. NLRB,*[7] in which the Court held that pension benefits are a mandatory subject of bargaining, there has been a tremendous growth in collectively bargained benefit plans.

The framework for collectively bargained funds was established by the Taft-Hartley Act of 1947.[8] The Taft-Hartley Act outlawed payments by employers to union representatives, except for certain limited purposes. The major exception is payments to a trust fund established for the sole and exclusive benefit of employees. Taft-Hartley, however, placed several restrictions on the operation of these funds.

- The payments are held in trust for the purpose of paying for the benefit of employees, their families, and their dependents.

The author acknowledges, with great appreciation, the assistance of Kenneth C. Morgan and Robin M. Pugh in the preparation of this chapter.

- The detailed basis on which such payments are to be made is specified in a written agreement.
- Employees and employers are equally represented in the administration of the fund.
- In the event of deadlock on the administration of the fund, an impartial umpire shall decide the dispute.
- An audit by an independent accountant must be made at least annually.
- The purposes of the trust are limited to providing certain benefits, such as pensions, annuities, medical or hospital care, disability pay, life insurance, vacation pay, holiday pay, severance pay, etc.[9]

Multiemployer trust funds deliver benefits to approximately 10 million participants and to approximately 20 million spouses and dependents. There are in excess of 2,000 multi-employer-sponsored defined benefit pension funds and over 3,000 health and welfare funds.[10]

INTERNAL REVENUE CODE REQUIREMENTS

Several provisions of the Internal Revenue Code apply to employee benefit plans. If an employee benefit plan is tax qualified, several advantages accrue. First, employer contributions to the qualified trust are deductible as a business expense. Second, the dollar value of the benefits accruing to or purchased by the employee is not taxed to that individual. Finally, the income received by the trust fund is free of all taxation.

ERISA PROVISIONS

Fiduciary Requirements

Prior to the enactment of ERISA, common law fiduciary principles governed the conduct of trustees of employee benefit plans. The common law "prudent man" rule was set forth in *Harvard College v. Amory*.

All that can be required of a trustee . . . is, that he shall conduct himself faithfully and exercise a sound discretion. He is to observe how men of prudence, discretion and intelligence manage their own affairs. . . .[11]

ERISA strengthened the common law standards and established federal law standards for reviewing fiduciary conduct. ERISA sets forth fiduciary duties, in part, as follows:

[a] fiduciary shall discharge his duties with respect to a plan solely in the interest of the participants and beneficiaries and—

(A) for the exclusive purpose of:
(i) providing benefits to participants and their beneficiaries; and

(ii) defraying reasonable expenses of administering the plan;

(B) with the care, skill, prudence, and diligence under the circumstances then prevailing that a prudent man acting in a like capacity and familiar with such matters would use in the conduct of an enterprise of a like character and with like aims;

(C) by diversifying their investments of the plan so as to minimize the risk of large losses, unless under the circumstances it is clearly prudent not to do so; and

(D) in accordance with the documents and instruments governing the plan insofar as such documents and instruments are consistent with the provisions of this title or Title IV.[12]

The Prudence Rule

On the surface the ERISA fiduciary standards appear to set forth the common law "prudent man" rule. A careful reading, however, makes it clear that the ERISA standard is much more comprehensive. Most commentators agree that the ERISA rule constitutes a "prudent expert" rule. A fiduciary's conduct will be evaluated by comparing his or her actions with the actions that a "prudent man acting in a like capacity and familiar with such matters would use in the conduct of an enterprise of a like character and with like aims. . . ."[13] For example, the actions of a trustee of one fund will be judged by determining how trustees of other funds would react in a similar situation. Thus, ERISA sets forth an extremely rigorous standard of fiduciary conduct. Compliance with the prudent expert rule is determined on a case-by-case basis, following an analysis of all the facts and circumstances.

The Exclusive Purpose Rule

ERISA requires a fiduciary to discharge his or her duties for the *exclusive* purposes of providing benefits to participants and their beneficiaries and of defraying reasonable expenses of administering the plan. Similarly, under the Internal Revenue Code in order for a pension plan to constitute a tax-qualified trust, the trust must be for the "exclusive benefit" of an employer's employees or their beneficiaries.[14]

The Solely-in-the-Interest Rule

ERISA also requires a fiduciary to discharge his or her duties with respect to a plan "solely in the interest of the participants and beneficiaries."[15] The Taft-Hartley Act permits the payment of employer contributions to a labor-management trust fund, provided that union and employer representatives share equally in fund administration and that the trust is established "for the sole and exclusive benefit of the employees of such employer and their families and dependents."[16]

Many commentators compare the solely-in-the-interest rule to the common law duty of loyalty. The solely-in-the-interest rule prevents union or management trustees of Taft-Hartley funds from making decisions from a union or management perspective. As a fiduciary, decisions must be apolitical.

The U.S. Supreme Court, in *NLRB v. AMAX Coal Co.,*[17] discussed the issue of whether employer-selected trustees of a Taft-Hartley fund are also collective bargaining representatives. The Court stressed that trustees bear an "unwavering duty of complete loyalty to the beneficiary of the trust, to the exclusion of the interests of all other parties."[18] The Court noted that ERISA's fiduciary duties vest all authority in the trustees alone, and not in the employer or union. The fiduciary provisions of ERISA were designed to prevent a trustee "from being put into a position where he has dual loyalties, and, therefore, he cannot act exclusively for the benefit of a plan's participants and beneficiaries."[19] The Court concluded that an employee benefit fund trustee is a fiduciary whose duty to the trust beneficiaries must overcome any loyalty to the interest of the party that appointed him.

In a corporate fund situation, the same considerations apply. For example, during a hostile takeover attempt, the trustees of a corporate pension plan declined to tender the plan's corporate shares and purchased additional corporate shares at a total cost of approximately $45 million dollars. The U.S. Court of Appeals for the Second Circuit, in *Donovan v. Bierwirth,*[20] reviewed these trustees' actions and found violations of ERISA. The court held that the trustees failed to make a careful and impartial investigation and failed to make their decision "with an eye single to the interests of the participants and beneficiaries."[21] The court noted that some of the trustees were also corporate directors and had already decided to fight the tender offer. Trustees must always act impartially, not as management or union representatives.

The Plan Documents Rule

ERISA also requires fiduciaries to act "in accordance with the documents and instruments governing the plan. . . ."[22] Under ERISA, every employee benefit plan must be established and maintained pursuant to a written instrument.[23] Thus, trustees and all fiduciaries should be very familiar with the trust agreement and the plan of benefits. Frequently, the trust agreement sets forth the powers and duties of the trustees regarding the plan.

The Diversification Rule

ERISA requires fiduciaries to diversify investments of the plan so as to minimize the risk of large losses, unless under the circumstances it is clearly prudent to not do so. Pursuant to the congressional Conference Report, the degree of investment concentration that would violate the diversification requirement cannot be stated as a fixed percentage because the facts and circumstances of each case must be analyzed. However, the following factors should be considered in reviewing the diversification scheme of any plan:

- purpose of the plan
- amount of the plan assets
- prevailing financial and industrial conditions

- type of investment
- distribution as to geographic location
- distribution as to industries
- dates of maturity.[24]

The Conference Report stated that a plan should not invest an unduly large portion of the trust property in one type of security.

Regulations concerning the prudent rule and pension plan investments under ERISA were issued by the U.S. Department of Labor, effective July 23, 1979.[25] The department noted that the relative riskiness of a specific investment or investment course of action is not *per se* prudent or imprudent. Rather, the prudence of an investment decision must be judged by reference to the role of the proposed investment in relation to the overall plan portfolio.

Prohibited Transactions

ERISA sets forth specific restrictions relating to the exclusive purpose and the solely-in-the-interest rules. The prohibited transaction section codifies and spells out in detail long-accepted fiduciary principles. ERISA details a variety of prohibited acts as follows:

(1) A fiduciary with respect to a plan shall not cause the plan to engage in a transaction, if he knows or should know that such transaction constitutes a direct or indirect—

(A) sale or exchange, or leasing, of any property between the plan and a party in interest;

(B) lending of money or other extension of credit between the plan and a party in interest;

(C) furnishing of goods, services, or facilities between the plan and a party in interest;

(D) transfer to, or use by or for the benefit of, a party in interest, of any assets of any plan; or

(E) acquisition, on behalf of the plan, of any employer security or employer real property in violation of section 407(a) [limiting plan holdings to "qualifying" employer securities or real property that does not exceed 10 percent of the fair market value of plan assets].

(2) No fiduciary who has authority or discretion to control or manage the assets of a plan shall permit the plan to hold any employer security or employer real property if he knows or should know that holding such security or real property violates section 407(a).[26]

Thus, ERISA precisely spells out conduct that is banned. ERISA is broader than the common law because it includes parties in interest as well as fiduciaries. The term *party in interest* is broadly defined. A party in interest means a fiduciary (including, but not limited to, any administrator, officer, trustee, or custodian), counsel, or employee of a plan; a person providing services to the plan; an employer, any of whose employees are covered by such plan; an employee organization, any of whose members are covered by such plan; a direct or indirect owner of 50 percent or more of certain stock, capital interest, or profits interest of a partnership or of the beneficial interest of a trust or unincorporated enterprise that is an employer or employee organization; a relative of the above; corporations, trusts, partnerships, or estates 50-percent owned by the above; and an employee, officer, director, or 10-percent shareholder of the above.[27]

ERISA also prohibits transactions involving self-dealing or breach of the duty of loyalty by fiduciaries. ERISA states

> (b) A fiduciary with respect to a plan shall not—
> (1) deal with the assets of the plan in his own interest or for his own account,
> (2) in his individual or in any other capacity act in any transaction involving the plan on behalf of a party (or represent a party) whose interests are adverse to the interests of the plan or the interests of its participants or beneficiaries, or
> (3) receive any consideration for his own personal account from any party dealing with such plan in connection with a transaction involving the assets of the plan.[28]

ERISA excludes a number of specific actions from the long list of prohibited transactions and provides an exemption procedure.[29] A party seeking an exemption must prove that its proposed action is administratively feasible, in the interest of the plan and its participants and beneficiaries, and protective of the rights of these participants and beneficiaries. For example, ERISA specifically permits contracting or making reasonable arrangements with a party in interest for office space or for legal, accounting, or other services necessary for the establishment or operation of the plan, if no more than reasonable compensation is paid therefor.

The Internal Revenue Code (IRC) contains prohibited transaction provisions corresponding to those set forth in ERISA, which are applicable to qualified pension plans.[30]

Fiduciary Liability

ERISA provides that

> (a) Any person who is a fiduciary with respect to a plan who breaches any of the responsibilities, obligations, or duties imposed upon fiduciaries by this title shall be *personally liable* to make good to such plan any losses to the plan resulting from each such breach, and to restore to such plan any profits of such fiduciary which have been made through use of assets of the plan by the fiduciary, and shall be subject to such other equitable or remedial relief as the Court may deem appropriate, including removal of such fiduciary. A fiduciary may also be removed for a violation of Section 411 of this Act [prohibiting individuals convicted of or imprisoned for certain crimes from holding positions].
> (b) No fiduciary shall be liable with respect to a breach of fiduciary duty under this title if such breach was committed before he became a fiduciary or after he ceased to be a fiduciary.[31]

Thus, ERISA established *personal* liability for fiduciary breaches.

Cofiduciary Liability

In addition, ERISA provides that a fiduciary is liable for a co-fiduciary's breach of duty in the following circumstances:

> (1) if he participates knowingly in, or knowingly undertakes to conceal, an act or omission of such other fiduciary, knowing such act or omission is a breach;
> (2) if, by his failure to comply with section 404(a)(1) in the administration of his specific responsibilities which give rise to his status as a fiduciary, he has enabled such other fiduciary to commit a breach; or
> (3) if he has knowledge of a breach by such other fiduciary, unless he makes reasonable efforts under the circumstances to remedy the breach.[32]

In the situation described in paragraph (1) above, a fiduciary must have knowledge of an impropriety of another fiduciary and must also either participate in the impropriety or undertake to conceal the impropriety of such other fiduciary.

Liability under paragraph (2) above is based on the general situation in which a fiduciary, through failure to adhere to the general fiduciary obligations, sets the stage for a breach of duty by his or her cofiduciary. The example given in the Conference Report on ERISA involves two-cotrustees of a plan who jointly manage the plan assets. Trustee A improperly allows Trustee B to have custody of all the assets and makes no inquiry as to his or her conduct. Trustee B is thereby enabled to sell the property and to embezzle the proceeds. As a result, Trustee A is liable for a breach of fiduciary duty.[33]

Liability under paragraph (3) above is premised on the situation in which a fiduciary has knowledge of a breach of duty by one of his or her fellow fiduciaries and fails to make reasonable efforts to remedy that breach. The critical question in this situation, of course, is what constitutes reasonable steps in a particular situation. The Conference Report gives some indication as to the types of steps a trustee might be expected to take if that trustee has knowledge of a cofiduciary's impropriety. The Conference Report states that a trustee may be required to "cure" a cofiduciary's impropriety, assuming that the trustee has the proper authority to do so. Alternatively, the Report notes that a trustee might be required "to notify the plan sponsor of the breach, or to proceed to an appropriate Federal court for instructions, or to bring the matter to the attention of the Secretary of Labor."[34] The Conference Report further states that the proper remedy will turn on the facts and circumstances involved in each case and "may be affected by the relationship of the fiduciary to the plan and to the cofiduciary, the duties and responsibilities of the fiduciary in question, and the nature of the breach."[35]

Named Fiduciary

ERISA provides that the written instrument establishing an employee benefit plan shall provide for one or more "named fiduciaries who jointly or severally shall have authority to control and manage the operation and administration of the plan."[36] The term *named fiduciary* means

> a fiduciary who is named in the plan instrument, or who, pursuant to a procedure specified in the plan, is identified as a fiduciary (A) by a person who is an employer or employee organization with respect to the plan or (B) by such an employer and such an employee organization acting jointly.[37]

The purpose of the named fiduciary requirement is to enable employees and other interested parties to determine who is responsible for operating the plan.

It is preferable to state explicitly the named fiduciary. However, the clear identification of one or more persons, by name or title, combined with a statement of their authority to control and manage the operation and administration of the plan, satisfies the named fiduciary requirement. For example, it is satisfactory to state that the joint board of trustees in a union-negotiated plan is the named fiduciary. In a corporate plan, the document may designate the corporation as the named fiduciary.

Allocation of Fiduciary Duty

ERISA permits the allocation of fiduciary responsibility. A plan shall describe any procedure regarding the allocation of responsibilities for the operation and administration of the plan.[38]

ERISA permits a plan to expressly provide for a procedure to allocate fiduciary responsibilities (other than trustee responsibilities) among named fiduciaries and permits named fiduciaries to designate persons other than named fiduciaries to carry out fiduciary responsibilities (other than trustee responsibilities) under the plan.[39] A trustee responsibility is any responsibility provided in the plan's trust instrument for managing or controlling the assets of the plan, other than a power under the trust instrument of a named fiduciary to appoint an investment manager.

If named fiduciaries of a plan allocate responsibilities in accordance with a written plan procedure, a named fiduciary will not be liable for acts or omissions of the other named fiduciaries in carrying out the allocated responsibilities, except as provided by ERISA's general rules of fiduciary responsibility. If the plan instrument provides for a procedure under which a named fiduciary may designate persons who are not named fiduciaries to carry out fiduciary responsibilities, named fiduciaries of the plan will not be liable for acts and omissions of a person who is not a named fiduciary in carrying out such delegated duties, except as provided by the general rules of cofiduciary liability and the rules relating to the selection of persons to carry out fiduciary duties.

Investment Manager

ERISA states that a named fiduciary with respect to control or management of the assets of the plan may appoint "an investment manager or managers to manage (including the power to acquire and dispose of) any assets of a plan."[40]

ERISA defines investment manager as:

> any fiduciary (other than a trustee or named fiduciary, as defined in section 402(a)(2))—
> (A) who has the power to manage, acquire, or dispose of any asset of a plan;
> (B) who is (i) registered as an investment adviser under the Investment Advisers Act of 1940; (ii) is a bank, as defined in that Act; or (iii) is an insurance company qualified to perform services described in subparagraph (A) under the laws of more than one State; and
> (C) has acknowledged in writing that he is a fiduciary with respect to the plan.[41]

Such delegation must take place pursuant to a written authorization in the trust agreement. When proper delegation of investment responsibility takes place, the investment manager or managers become fiduciaries to the plan, and a concomitant limitation of liability protects the delegating trustees. Specifically, ERISA provides that when a proper delegation takes place to an investment manager, no trustee shall be liable for acts or omissions of such investment manager or managers or shall be under an obligation to invest or otherwise manage any asset of the plan which is subject to the management of such investment manager.[42] Trustees must act responsibly in selecting an investment manager and in continuing to use such investment manager.

Bonding and Fiduciary Liability Insurance

ERISA contemplates the need for plans and trustees to be protected by insurance. Two sections are particularly relevant in this regard. Section 412 requires all plan fiduciaries and all persons who handle funds or other property of a plan to be bonded. In general, the amount of a bond will be approximately 10 percent of the amount of funds handled, although the statute prescribes upper and lower limits. It is permissible for a plan to pay the cost of obtaining the necessary bonding. Bonding protects the plan from actual misappropriation or embezzlement.

ERISA Section 410 addresses exculpatory provisions and the issue of fiduciary liability insurance for plans and for trustees. ERISA bars exculpatory clauses and states that except as provided in Section 405 "any provision in an agreement or instrument which purports to relieve a fiduciary from responsibility or liability for any responsibility, obligation, or duty under this part shall be void as against public policy."[43] Thus, trustees are personally liable for their negligent acts, whether by omission or commission.

Fiduciary insurance protects a plan from losses resulting from fiduciary breaches that may or may not have benefited the breaching fiduciary personally. For example, a fiduciary breach involving an imprudent investment might cause a loss to the plan without a corresponding benefit to the fiduciary who made the investment decision.

ERISA permits a plan to purchase insurance for its fiduciaries or for itself if the insurance permits recourse by the insurer against breaching fiduciaries. ERISA further permits a fiduciary to purchase recourse insurance to cover his or her own liability. It is also permissible for the appointing union to pay the premiums for the fiduciary's recourse insurance.

Taft-Hartley trust funds typically pay the cost of the fund's insurance. The trustees' employers (the contributing companies or the union) pay the cost of the recourse insurance. Insurance companies typically set the recourse premiums quite low (approximately $25–$50 per year), and each trustee arranges to have the fund reimbursed for the appropriate amount.

Reporting and Disclosure

ERISA sets forth detailed reporting and disclosure requirements for benefit plans.[44] Among the reports required are an Annual Report (Form 5500), Summary Annual Report, and Summary of Material Modifications. In addition, a Summary Plan Description (SPD), written "in a manner calculated to be understood by the average plan participant, and . . . sufficiently accurate and comprehensive to reasonably appraise such participants and beneficiaries of their rights and obligations under the plan" must be furnished to all participants and beneficiaries.[45] Any participant or beneficiary who makes a written request to the administrator of an employee benefit pension plan shall have a right to a statement of that individual's benefit rights, including the total benefits accrued and the nonforfeitable pension benefits accrued.[46]

Participation and Vesting

ERISA provides detailed participation and vesting rules for pension plans.[47] Generally, an employee must be permitted to participate in a pension plan at the later of age 21 or after one year of service.[48] The Tax Reform Act of 1986 significantly changed the minimum vesting standards of ERISA, as well as the corresponding provisions in the IRC. ERISA now provides one of three options.

1. An employee who has completed at least 5 years of service has a nonforfeitable right to 100 percent of the employee's accrued benefit derived from employer contributions.
2. An employee has a nonforfeitable right to benefits as follows:

Years of Service	Nonforfeitable Percentage
3	20%
4	40
5	60
6	80
7 or more	100

3. With respect to multiemployer plans, an employee who has completed 10 years of service has a nonforfeitable right to 100 percent of the employee's accrued benefit derived from employer contributions.[49]

ERISA also provides that in the case of a vested participant who retires, the accrued benefit payable shall generally be in the form of a joint and survivor annuity.[50] The above is a brief summary of the participation and vesting provisions of ERISA. The effective dates and the detailed requirements of these provisions should be carefully reviewed.

Funding

ERISA sets forth minimum funding standards for pension plans.[51] These requirements are beyond the scope of this chapter.

Administration and Enforcement

ERISA specifically permits a panoply of lawsuits to be commenced against trustees. Under ERISA Section 502, the following civil actions, among others, are contemplated:

- by a participant or beneficiary for certain information from a plan administrator in order to recover benefits due under the terms of the plan, to enforce rights under the plan, or to clarify rights to future benefits under the plan
- by the Secretary of Labor or by a participant, beneficiary, or fiduciary for appropriate relief for a breach of fiduciary duty
- by a participant, beneficiary, or fiduciary to enjoin any act or practice that violates Title I of ERISA or the terms of the plan and to obtain other appropriate relief to redress such violations or to enforce any provisions of Title I or the terms of the plan
- by the Secretary of Labor or by a participant or beneficiary for appropriate relief for an administrator's failure to provide a report of a participant's benefits rights
- by the Secretary of Labor to enjoin any act or practice that violates Title I of ERISA or to obtain other appropriate equitable relief to redress such violation or to enforce any provision of Title I
- by the Secretary of Labor to collect any civil penalty assessed because of a prohibited transaction
- by a participant or beneficiary for an administrator's noncompliance with either the notice requirements of ERISA Section 606(1)(4) (group health plan coverage continuation requirement) or a request for information which the administrator is required by Title I to furnish to a participant or beneficiary (Administrators may be personally liable up to $100 a day from the date of the noncompliance for a violation under this section.)[52]

ERISA Section 510 also provides a cause of action for interfering with the rights of the participant or beneficiary if the defendant is discharged, suspended, disciplined, or discriminated against the plaintiff because he or she has given certain information or has testified in an inquiry relating to ERISA or the Welfare and Pension Plan Disclosure Act.

Continuation Coverage under Group Health Plans

The Consolidated Omnibus Budget Reconciliation Act of 1985 (COBRA) amended ERISA and the IRC to require employers to offer continuation coverage to their group health plan beneficiaries on the occurrence of certain qualifying events that would cause the beneficiary to lose coverage under the plan.[53]

Plan Termination Insurance

ERISA created a termination insurance program to help protect participants and beneficiaries from losing retirement benefits on plan termination. This program is administered through the Pension Benefit Guaranty Corporation (PBGC), a nonprofit organization in the U.S. Department of Labor.[54] The termination insurance is funded through premiums paid to the PBGC. The PBGC uses these premiums to guaranty certain benefits on plan termination.[55]

Plans may be terminated voluntarily or involuntarily. The PBGC may terminate a plan because of its failure to meet minimum funding requirements and for other specified reasons.[56] A multiemployer plan also may be terminated by an amendment (1) freezing participants' credited service for all purposes under the plan or (2) causing the plan to become an individual account plan, or by the withdrawal of every employer from the plan.[57]

If a multiemployer plan is terminated by amendment, an employer that has not withdrawn must continue to contribute to the plan at a rate no less than the employer's highest rate of contribution in the five preceding plan years. The PBGC, however, may approve a reduced rate if the plan is, or soon will be, fully funded.[58]

If a multiemployer plan is terminated by mass withdrawal and if the value of the plan assets is less than the value of nonforfeitable benefits, benefit payments must be suspended, and the plan must be amended to reduce benefits.[59] The benefit reduction must take effect no later than six months after the plan year in which it is determined that the value of nonforfeitable benefits exceeds the value of the plan assets. Benefits are reduced only to the extent necessary to pay all nonforfeitable benefits when due and to the extent the benefits are not eligible for a guaranty by the PBGC.[60]

The PBGC guaranties multiemployer plan benefits only if the plan is insolvent[61]—that is, if the plan's available resources are insufficient to pay benefits when due for the plan year.[62] The PBGC will not guaranty benefits or benefit increases that have been in effect for less than 60 months. The PBGC also will not guaranty benefits or benefit increases that have been in effect for less than 60 months before the plan year in which a plan amendment reducing benefits is taken into account for determining the minimum contribution for a multiemployer plan in reorganization.[63]

PBGC-guaranteed benefits are less than the benefits a participant would ordinarily receive under the plan. The guarantied monthly benefit equals the participant's years of credited service multiplied by the sum of (1) 100 percent of the benefit accrual rate up to $5.00 and (2) 75 percent of the lesser of either $15.00 or the accrual rate in excess of $5.00. The 75 percent rate is reduced to 65 percent for certain insolvent plans that do not meet minimum funding requirements.[64] For example, assume a participant with 30 years of credited service has accrued a monthly benefit of $450 under a multiemployer plan. The participant's accrual rate is $15 ($450/30), of which $12.50 is guaranteed by the PBGC ($5 at 100 percent and $10 at 75 percent). Thus, the participant's PBGC-guaranteed benefit equals $375 ($12.50 × 30).

PBGC-guaranteed benefits are also subject to an aggregate limit. The aggregate guaranteed benefit paid to a participant from the PBGC under all single employer and multiemployer plans cannot exceed the actuarial value of a monthly benefit of a life annuity commencing at age 65 equal to $750 miltiplied by a fraction. The numerator of the fraction is the contribution and benefit base determined under the Social Security Act in effect at the date of plan termination, and the denominator is $13,200 (the contribution and benefit base in effect in 1974).[65] In 1988, the maximum aggregate benefit equaled $1,909.09.[66]

CONCLUSION

ERISA is a complex and continually changing statute. Any individual who deals with multiemployer benefit funds is wise to follow legal developments, attend educational seminars, and obtain expert assistance.

NOTES

1. 29 U.S.C. § 1001 *et seq* (Supp V-1988).
2. ERISA § 3(2), 29 U.S.C. § 1002(2).
3. ERISA § 3(1), 29 U.S.C. § 1002(1).
4. *See* 29 C.F.R. § 2510.3-2(b) (1988).
5. 29 C.F.R. § 2510.3-1.
6. ERISA § 4(b), 29 U.S.C. § 1003(b).
7. 336 U.S. 960 (1949).
8. 29 U.S.C. §§ 141–188 (1976).
9. 29 U.S.C. § 186(c).
10. *Multiemployer Trust Funds,* in Employee Benefits Basics (1988).
11. 26 Mass. (9 Pick.) 446 (1830).
12. ERISA § 404, 29 U.S.C. § 1104.
13. ERISA § 404(a)(1)(B), 29 U.S.C. § 1104(a)(1)(B).
14. I.R.C. § 401(a) (1986).
15. ERISA § 404(a)(1), 29 U.S.C. § 1104(a)(1).

16. 29 U.S.C. § 186(c)(5).

17. 453 U.S. 322 (1981).

18. *Id*. at 329.

19. *Id*. at 334, *quoting* H.R. Conf. Rep. No. 1280, 93d Cong., 2d Sess. 304 (1974).

20. 680 F.2d 263 (2d Cir.), *cert. denied,* 459 U.S. 873 (1982).

21. *Id*. at 271 (citations omitted).

22. ERISA § 404(a)(1)(D), 29 U.S.C. § 1104(a)(1)(D).

23. ERISA § 402, 29 U.S.C. § 1102.

24. H.R. Conf. Rep. No. 1280, 93d Cong., 2d Sess. 304 (1974).

25. 29 C.F.R. § 2550.

26. ERISA § 406, 29 U.S.C. § 1106.

27. ERISA § 3(14), 29 U.S.C. § 1002(14).

28. ERISA § 406(b), 29 U.S.C. § 1106(b).

29. ERISA § 408, 29 U.S.C. § 1108.

30. I.R.C. § 4975.

31. ERISA § 409, 29 U.S.C. § 1109.

32. ERISA § 405, 29 U.S.C. § 1105.

33. H.R. Conf. Rep. No. 1280, 93d Cong., 2d Sess. at 300.

34. *Id*.

35. *Id*.

36. ERISA § 402(a)(2), 29 U.S.C. § 1102(a)(2).

37. ERISA § 402, 29 U.S.C. § 1102.

38. ERISA § 402(b)(2), 29 U.S.C. § 1102(b)(2).

39. ERISA § 405(c), 29 U.S.C. § 1105(c).

40. ERISA § 402(c)(3), 29 U.S.C. § 1102(c)(3).

41. ERISA § 3(38), 29 U.S.C. § 1002(38).

42. ERISA § 405(d)(1), 29 U.S.C. § 1105(d)(1).

43. ERISA § 410(a), 29 U.S.C. § 1110(a).

44. ERISA §§ 101–111, 29 U.S.C. §§ 1021–1031.

45. ERISA § 102(a)(1), 29 U.S.C. § 1022(a)(1).

46. ERISA § 105(a), 29 U.S.C. § 1025(a).

47. ERISA §§ 201–211, 29 U.S.C. §§ 1051–1061.

48. ERISA § 202(a)(1)(A), 29 U.S.C. § 1052(a)(1)(A).

49. ERISA § 203, 29 U.S.C. § 1053.

50. ERISA § 205, 29 U.S.C. § 1055.

51. ERISA §§ 310–306, 29 U.S.C. §§ 1081–1086.

52. ERISA § 502, 29 U.S.C. § 1132.

53. ERISA §§ 601–608, 29 U.S.C. §§ 1161–1168.

54. ERISA § 4002(a), 29 U.S.C. § 1302(a).

55. ERISA authorizes the establishment of four insurance programs. The first is a program for ''basic'' retirement benefits which are vested under the terms of the plans up to certain limits. The second, which may be established at the discretion of the PBGC, would guarantee ''nonbasic'' benefits. The other two programs are supplementary programs for multiemployer plans: one reimburses multiemployer plans for uncollectible withdrawal liability payments; the other guaranties benefits that would be basic benefits except for limits imposed on multiemployer plans. Separate premiums are charged for each kind of coverage. This chapter, however, is limited to a discussion of the ''basic'' coverage for multiemployer plans. Multiemployer plans must pay a premium of $2.60 per participant for plan years beginning on or after September 27, 1988, for the basic coverage. ERISA § 4006(a)(3)(A)(iii)(IV), 29 U.S.C. § 1306(a)(3)(A)(iii)(IV).

56. ERISA § 4042, 29 U.S.C. § 1342.

57. ERISA imposes liability on an employer that withdraws from a multiemployer pension plan. In general, an employer's withdrawal liability would be its proportionate share of the plan's unfunded vested benefits. ERISA § 4041A, 29 U.S.C. § 1341a. Employer withdrawals and withdrawal liability are beyond the scope of this chapter.

58. ERISA § 4041A(e), 29 U.S.C. § 1341a(e).

59. ERISA § 4041A(d), 29 U.S.C. § 1341a(d).

60. ERISA § 4281(c), (d), 29 U.S.C. § 1441(c), (d).

61. ERISA § 4022A(a), 29 U.S.C. § 1322a(a).

62. ERISA § 4245(b)(1), 29 U.S.C. § 1426(b)(1); ERISA § 4281(d)(2), 29 U.S.C. § 1441(d)(2).

63. ERISA § 4022A(b)(1), 29 U.S.C. § 1322a(b)(1).

64. ERISA § 4022A(c), 29 U.S.C. § 1322a(c).

65. ERISA § 4022B, 29 U.S.C. § 1322b.

66. 29 C.F.R. § 2621 app. A.

Mary S. Case

Back to Basics: Funding and Plan Design for Health Care Employers

35

INTRODUCTION

In many respects, health care employers face the same employee benefit challenges as do other employers: they must attract and retain the highest-caliber employees, and they must be concerned about the costs they incur in providing competitive compensation and benefit packages to those employees. However, in their dual position as employers/purchasers of benefits and as providers of those same benefits, health care institutions face some unique issues and have some unique opportunities. The twofold purpose of this chapter is, first, to review the general subject of the funding of employee welfare benefit plans and, second, to raise some issues and opportunities in funding and plan design that are unique to health care employers.

A PRIMER ON FUNDING CONTRACTS

The business of insurance is like all other businesses: there is no free lunch. Any decision relating to the funding of an employee benefit program involves a trade-off between the degree of risk transferred from employer to insurer and the expenses associated with that risk transfer. The general rule is that the greater the risk retained by the employer, the lower the expense associated with risk transfer. In the less-than-perfect world of insurance underwriting, this is not always the case: mispriced insurance contracts can result in either short-term gains or short-term losses to the employer (and the insurer). However, over the long run, the net price of an insurance contract should bear a direct relationship to the amount of risk assumed by the insurer.

All funding contracts for employee benefit plans fit onto a spectrum of risk-reward trade-offs. In the following diagram, the far left side of the spectrum represents the lowest risk assumption–reward potential to the employer and the far right represents the greatest risk assumption–reward potential to the employer.

```
                          Incurred      Paid
◄—Pooled—Conventional—Minimum—Minimum——Self-Funded—►
                          Premium     Premium
```

The characteristics of these various types of contracts are described below.

Types of Funding Contracts

Pooled Contracts

The most conservative contract—a pooled contract—involves assumption by the employer of a fixed and determined risk, with no potential reward if the actual cost of the contract—to the insurer—is lower than expected. Personal homeowner's insurance coverage, HMOs, insurance policies covering small groups, and volatile or unpredictable insurance risks [such as accidental death and dismemberment (AD&D)] are examples of pooled contracts. The term *pooled* is used because all such contracts of a similar nature are combined to create a large premium pool over which the risk is spread.

Under these contracts, the employer's risk is equal to the premium it pays for coverage: if the claims and expenses are greater than were assumed in setting the premium level, the adverse experience represents a loss to the insurer. If, on the other hand, the actual cost of the contract is less than was assumed, the favorable experience results in a gain to the insurer.

Pooling can manifest itself either as a stand-alone contract or as insurance within a larger, experience-based contract. An example of the former is an AD&D contract; an example of the latter is the provision of a pooling, or specific stop-loss, level for large death or health insurance claims within an experience-based contract. Under such a pooling arrangement, individual or aggregate claims in excess of a predetermined level are disregarded in evaluating the group's experience. No matter where it appears, pooling represents the substitution of a fixed cost—an insurance premium—for the variable cost of claims and expenses.

Conventional Contracts

The next type of contract is the conventional insurance contract. This type of contract is also called experience-rated or participating (because the policyholder may participate in any surplus realized by the insurer). The term *experience-rated* can be confusing: it can refer either to the use of prior experience to establish rates for the future, which is frequently the case under pooled contracts, or to the retrospective evaluation of experience at the end of a policy year to determine the true net cost of the contract. To avoid this confusion, this chapter will use the term *conventional* to mean a contract under which a retrospective evaluation of experience determines the net cost.

Where pooled contracts represent "true" insurance, conventional contracts provide "budget" insurance. The insurer establishes a premium for the policy year—generally based on prior experience—that represents the employer's maximum cost for that period. If the premium turns out to be higher than required, the employer receives credit for the surplus—through a refund or possibly a prospective rate credit. If the premium turns out to be deficient, the insurer will generally carry its deficit forward—with interest—for possible recovery from future surpluses. Because of this deficit recovery provision, the contract provides only budget insurance: as long as the contract remains in force, the employer will eventually pay the actual claims and expenses incurred under it.

A conventional contract becomes true insurance only on policy termination, at which time the insurer is left holding any existing deficit, with no future opportunity for recovery. Because of this possible risk, some insurers do not return surpluses on termination, or they treat off-anniversary terminations differently from on-anniversary terminations; some contracts also provide for open-ended terminal liabilities, effectively eliminating any element of "pure" insurance protection. Finally, in recognition of the incentive to terminate that a large deficit can create, some insurers are willing to limit deficit recovery to minimize the risk of cancellation.

Because the insurer must share gains with the employer and still has at least a terminal risk of a deficit, the premium under a conventional contract generally includes an allowance—or margin—to protect the insurer from unexpectedly high claims. This margin essentially represents an intended refund. In exchange for the assumption of this increased risk—through higher premiums—the employer is given the potential reward of a lower net cost if experience is better than expected. In recognition of employers' cash-flow concerns, insurers are usually willing to waive payment of the margin unless the year-end accounting indicates that it is necessary. This is called a *retrospective premium arrangement*. In some cases, a "retro" merely represents deferred payment of the margin already included in the premium; in other cases, it represents an additional liability to the employer—over and above the normal premium. In these cases, the employer should realize a reduction in the risk charge made by the insurer.

Minimum Premium Contracts

Immediately to the right of the conventional contract on the risk-reward spectrum is the minimum premium (also called excess risk or split-funded) approach to funding benefits. Minimum premium contracts are essentially cash-flow variations on conventional contracts. Under a minimum premium contract, the employer pays a small portion of its total liability as premium—to cover expenses and any other fixed charges, such as charges for pooling—and funds its claims through a bank account. The employer realizes two types of gains from implementing a minimum premium contract: improved cash flow, because it funds claims as they are paid instead of through a level premium, and reduced expenses, because premium taxes are avoided on the amounts funded through the bank account. (This second advantage—which reflects the position that the claims paid out of the bank account are self-funded, and hence not subject to taxes payable on premiums—is under siege by state governments: California won a court battle to charge premium taxes on bank account deposits, and other states are likely to follow suit.)

The primary cash-flow advantage of minimum premium contracts over conventional contracts occurs in the first year of the contract, when the reserves for incurred and unreported claims would normally be funded through the conventional premium payments. Due to the lag between the dates on which claims are incurred and the dates on which they are paid, paid claims in the first year will generally represent 75–80 percent of the full incurred claim level. Under most minimum premium contracts, the employer retains for its own use the cash that the insurer would hold under a conventional contract to fund the lag in claim payments.

There are two primary varieties of minimum premium contracts: those that provide insurance on an incurred claim basis and those that provide insurance on a paid, or cash, claim basis. The incurred variety provides for payment to the insurer on contract termination of a pre-established reserve liability, in exchange for which the insurer will assume responsibility for any claims incurred under the contract prior to termination.

This type of minimum premium is a pure cash-flow variation on the conventional contract: the risk to the employer is close to identical. To the insurer, there is the slight additional risk that the employer will not be able or willing to pay its reserve liability on termination and that the insurer will have an unfunded liability for incurred but unpaid claims. As a result, some insurers establish a slightly higher risk charge for this type of contract than for a conventional contract.

Under a paid claim minimum premium contract, the employer retains both the cash and the liability for incurred but unpaid claims on contract termination; the insurer's risk relates solely to the paid claim budget each year. Under this type of contract, the employer assumes greater risk and should realize a reward through a reduced risk charge.

Self-Funding Contracts

On the far right side of the risk-reward spectrum is the uninsured, or self-funded, contract—also called ASO (for administrative services only) and self-insured. Unless the employer purchases stop-loss insurance to protect itself from higher-than-expected claims—either in the aggregate or for large individual claims—the employer is entirely at risk. The only services it purchases—from an insurer or third-party administrator—are claim adjudication and payment services. In view of the unlimited risk assumed by the employer, the net cost for this type of contract should be the lowest of all.

It merits mention that self-funded health plans are exempt from minimum benefit standards imposed by state insurance laws (due to an ERISA pre-emption). In some states, the added flexibility in plan design is significant—particularly for mental health and substance abuse benefits—and should be considered along with the purely financial issues. This exemption applies only to state insurance laws, not to any other state laws directed at employers.

Factors To Consider in Selecting a Funding Contract

The type of funding contract that is appropriate in a given situation depends on a number of factors: the type of coverage involved, the size of the insured group, the employer's ability to assume financial risk, and sometimes the employee relations impact of various funding alternatives.

Type of Coverage

For certain types of coverage, insurance is the only viable alternative. Low-volume, high-volatility coverages such as AD&D, should generally be pooled (except in the case of huge contracts); life insurance should be insured (i.e., not self-funded) because self-funded death benefits are taxable income to the beneficiary, while insured death benefits are not. (There is one exception to this rule: up to $5,000 in self-funded death benefits may be excluded from the beneficiary's taxable income. Employers that provide small death benefits—for example, to retired employees—may want to consider self-funding those benefits to reduce their expenses.)

Disability is a coverage that may lend itself to self-funding: short-term disability costs are predictable for even small groups, and long-term disability plan costs and cash needs are similar to those of pension plans, which are largely self-funded. There is no potential for a severe cash drain due to a catastrophic disability claim: the liability may be large, but the payments will be made gradually over time.

Size of the Group

Generally, the larger the group insured, the more predictable the risk and the more attractive the right side of the funding spectrum.

Employee Relations

Employee relations may come into play in two different ways. First, it may be desirable from the employer's perspective to have an independent third party involved in adjudicating and assuming risk for certain types of claims. This concern frequently outweighs the financial advantages in self-funding disability claims. (Another disability-related issue is that tax withholding is mandatory for self-funded disability benefits, while it is voluntary for insured benefits. While the ultimate tax treatment is the same, the withholding issue can sometimes be an obstacle, particularly in collective bargaining situations.)

Employee relations may also affect a funding decision if employees have concerns about the employer's ability to pay the promised benefits. An insurer provides a layer of insulation from any real or perceived financial risk from the employer's financial condition.

In evaluating alternatives presented by insurers, employers should consider these issues, their own risk tolerance, and the appropriateness of the risk-reward trade-offs.

FUNDING CHALLENGES AND OPPORTUNITIES FOR HEALTH CARE EMPLOYERS

As both purchasers and providers of health care services, health care employers have a unique financial opportunity for their health care plans, as well as some special challenges.

The opportunity relates to the health care employer's ability to self-fund and administer a large portion of employee health care claims without an appreciable change in the level of risk to which it is exposed—through self-funding and self-administration of claims incurred in its own facilities. The proportion of claims incurred internally will vary for different types of hospitals in different types of communities; however, nearly all hospitals receive substantial claim reimbursements from the insurers of their own employee benefits plans. In most cases, the reimbursement will be less than the amount charged by the insurer—due to the presence of administration and risk charges—resulting in a loss on each dollar of claims incurred in-house. (In some cases, the reimbursement may be even lower relative to the charge. Several years ago we discovered that one hospital client was being charged at Blue Cross's average discount or differential, but that its actual reimbursement agreement with Blue Cross provided for a greater than average discount. As a result, the hospital was being charged 95 cents for every dollar of claims, but was being reimbursed only 90 cents.)

Hospitals that have significant volumes of in-house utilization may want to consider carving those claims out of their insurance contracts and establishing internal administrative and accounting procedures to monitor them.

This opportunity presents some unique challenges to those hospitals that decide to pursue it. Issues that must be considered in evaluating internal self-funding include

- *Effect on the remaining contract*. The premium "credit" given for the claims carved out will not equal the estimated volume of in-house claims, but it should be fairly close. Otherwise, the employer may assume an inappropriate level of risk for the claims incurred at other facilities. In addition, the administrative expense factors and risk charge factors associated with the remaining smaller contract will probably be higher. In evaluating the potential savings from self-funding/administration, these increased expenses should be netted out.

- *Need for appropriate accounting procedures*. To ensure that the human resources department is appropriately charged for employee admissions and that the admitting department is appropriately credited with the patient revenue, internal accounting procedures will need to be developed. Beyond the internal credits/charges, books must be carefully maintained for rate-setting and financial-reporting purposes.

- *Risk*. There are two elements of risk that should be evaluated in looking at internal self-funding. First, on the insurance side, the employer is substituting the variable cost of claims for the potential fixed cost of an insurance premium. If the insurance premium is underpriced and the resulting deficit will not ultimately be paid by the employer, the employer's net costs under the self-funded approach will be higher. Second, on the cash side, insurance contracts may provide a more predictable and reliable influx of cash, which may be important to a hospital's operations.

Obstacles to the successful implementation of an internal self-funding program may be raised by the insurer, particularly if the health care benefits are insured by the local Blue Cross organization. The health care employer that insures its health care program with Blue Cross may encounter less flexibility in financial matters than it would with a commercial insurer; of course, the existence and extent of this problem will vary by Blue Cross organization. Any inflexibility must be considered from the perspective of the health care employer's total relationship with Blue Cross.

PLAN DESIGN OPPORTUNITIES FOR HEALTH CARE EMPLOYERS

In addition to the funding opportunities that exist for health care employers, these organizations' dual positions as both purchasers and providers present opportunities for creative plan design. Hospitals with relatively low occupancy rates may wish to design their health care plans to encourage greater use of their own facilities by employees. Those with higher occupancy rates may want to evaluate the costs of treating employees at others' facilities relative to the patient revenue that might be forgone if an employee occupies a bed that could be sold at "retail."

Such an incentive program can be carefully designed to encourage specific types of employee admissions. For example, a coastal town's hospital may have extremely high occupancy in the summer months, but it may want to encourage employee admissions in the off-season. Certain high-margin admissions—such as maternity admissions—may be attractive at any time.

One issue that health care providers definitely have in common with other employers is the adverse selection that occurs when young, healthy employees elect to participate in health maintenance organizations (HMOs): when the generally low variable cost associated with these employees' claims is replaced by the fixed cost of the HMO, the employer's total health care expenditures inexorably rise. In addition to outright benefit incentives to use their own facilities, health care employers have an opportunity to use existing physician networks and facilities to make their indemnity plans compete more effectively with HMOs. The cost to a hospital of setting up a preventive care program for its employees may be outweighed by the savings that result from attracting the younger, healthier employees back from the HMO alternative. The hospital could also consider becoming part of an HMO network and sharing in any gains resulting from selection.

In addition to these opportunities, health care employers are faced with something of a dilemma as they grow increasingly concerned about the costs of their health care programs. The tactics traditionally used by other employers—increasing employee cost sharing through deductibles and coinsurance and effecting cost management through outside utilization review firms—may raise complicated questions if implemented for a hospital's health care plan. Properly communicated and designed, the cost management approach should be beneficial to health care employers, as it is to other employers.

Additional challenges specifically facing health care employers include the potentially complicated task of meeting the compensation and benefit needs of a generally young, largely female work force. This situation often makes flexible compensation programs attractive to hospital management. Finally, with their usually high complement of part-time employees—who are generally not eligible for benefits—health care employers may have difficulty in passing the new nondiscrimination tests for health and life insurance plans under Section 89 of the Internal Revenue Code. The tax implications of failure to pass the tests may bring about a reassessment of the role and compensation of part-time employees.

CONCLUSIONS

Health care employers, like other employers, are faced with increasingly complex employee benefit decisions. Several years ago, the most difficult evaluations related to the financial arrangements for benefit plans. Today, these issues remain and have been joined by a host of new complexities stemming from changes in the legislative and employee relations environments. As health care and other welfare benefits continue to occupy a major position on Washington's legislative agenda, the area promises to become even more complicated.

While health care employers have some unique opportunities in funding and designing their benefit plans, the process they follow to evaluate the available alternatives should be the same as that of any other organization. Any decision about an employee benefit plan—whether relating to its design, funding, administration, or tax treatment—should be made only in the context of carefully considered business plans and human resources objectives.

Arnold Milstein
Janet R. Douglas
Gail E. Nethercut

Managing the Medical Cost of Hospital Workers' Compensation Claims

36

The emotional and physical stresses of providing patient care in hospitals are significant. This makes hospitals a substantial source of work-related injuries and workers' compensation claims.

Hospital human resources managers are in a pivotal position to reduce the incidence of these injuries and their costs once they occur. This chapter focuses on how the medical costs of workers' compensation claims can be reduced.

A human resources manager's opportunity to apply the information in this chapter will depend on multiple factors. Probably the most important factor is whether the hospital's workers' compensation program is insured through a carrier. If so, the information in this chapter will provide a useful template against which a carrier's medical cost containment efforts can be evaluated. If not, this chapter can help shape a customized strategy for medical cost containment to be implemented by the hospital's internal or third-party workers' compensation claims administration staff.

IS WORKERS' COMPENSATION A FAVORABLE ENVIRONMENT FOR CONTAINMENT OF MEDICAL COSTS?

In an atmosphere of purchaser activism in controlling medical costs, workers' compensation has remained a backwater, largely unaffected by the strong currents of change in adjacent

Note: Portions of this chapter are reprinted from "Controlling Medical Costs in Workers' Compensation" by Arnold Milstein, Gail Nethercut, and Michael Martin with permission of *Business & Health*, © April 1988.

employee health plans. Is this passivity justified by a relatively less favorable environment for medical cost containment?

Six features of the workers' compensation environment have special implications for the development of medical cost containment programs. Three of these are favorable, and three are unfavorable.

Unfavorable Features

Differing State Laws

Workers' compensation laws vary by state. This forces employers and workers' comp carriers to develop *custom* medical cost containment strategies for each state in which they operate. For payers whose work force is highly dispersed, this requirement can be administratively daunting.

Psychological Entitlement

Workers' compensation care occurs in a psychological atmosphere of entitlement on the part of the injured worker. The sense that the employer is at least partly responsible for an injury creates within the injured worker a natural inclination for redress and balance. What an injured worker may consciously and/or unconsciously seek from his or her employer and providers in order to feel a sense of balance will depend on the circumstances of the injury, the worker's relationship with his or her employer, and his or her uniquely personal perspectives on these two realities.

If an injured worker's sense of balance is not satisfied by the simple provision of *medically necessary* services and compensation for lost work time, additional medical services and costs will be incurred. One-hundred-percent employer coverage of medical expenses and the resulting absence of financial barriers to service use increase this potential for unnecessary services.

Litigation Risk

In most states, injured workers may retain attorneys to represent their interests. Because legal services usually are covered in full by the employer (or workers' compensation carrier) and are readily accessible via public advertising, barriers to litigation are very low. In addition, the average total medical and nonmedical costs of litigated cases run two to three times the cost of nonlitigated cases.[1] Accordingly, medical cost containment methods that increase the risk of litigation by creating the appearance of short-changing necessary care are unlikely to be cost effective.

Favorable Features

Employer Right To Select Providers

In employee medical benefits programs, employers have no right to direct employees to specific providers. In contrast, many workers' compensation laws give employers such a right of direction. The strength of these laws varies; therefore, it is necessary to check individual state workers' compensation statutes. In Colorado, for example, it is comparatively absolute. In California, it is absolute for the first 30 days after injury but is often not strictly exercised due to employer fear of litigation. In Oregon, employer right of direction has no legal support. Clearly, states with stronger employer right of direction represent a much more favorable environment for preferred provider programs and, in states with *absolute* employer direction, for prepaid, HMO-like solutions.

Concentration of Diagnoses

The majority or workers' compensation cases and payments originate in musculoskeletal injuries, and the lion's share of these are back and neck problems.[2] This concentration of diagnoses allows a highly focused approach to medical cost containment. Inpatient and outpatient utilization review or case management protocols need only be developed for a relatively narrow range of injuries in order to cover a majority of cases. This enables more rapid refinement of techniques, greater specialization of cost containment personnel, and, on average, better performance from medical cost management mechanisms.

Well-Developed Resources for Prevention and Case Management

While preventive care and case management are relatively new concepts for employee health benefits, they are long established in the world of workers' compensation. All large employers and workers' compensation carriers have loss control or risk management staff to survey and minimize sources of job-site injury. Similarly, workers' compensation claims examiners have traditionally assumed responsibility for case management via personal contact with injured workers and providers, in addition to the more limited role of individual bill adjudication which typifies the world of employee health benefits. Workers' compensation rehabilitation nurses were the forerunners of today's case managers for employee benefit plans and preceded them by at least 10 years.

HOW DOES PROGRAM IMPLEMENTATION DIFFER FROM MEDICAL COST CONTAINMENT PROGRAMS FOR EMPLOYEE HEALTH BENEFIT PROGRAMS?

The design and implementation of medical cost management programs for workers' compensation programs differ from those of employee health benefit programs in three key respects: (1) the role of computerized review of physician bills; (2) the use of utilization review; and (3) channeling to preferred providers.

Computerized review of physician and other nonhospital bills constitutes a much larger opportunity for medical cost savings than on the employee benefit side, where this technique is embryonic, at best. This is a direct outgrowth of the fact that, in most states, providers are legally *prohibited* from collecting reimbursement from injured workers. This enables employers and carriers to cut back reimbursement for unreasonable physician fees without fear of the employee relations problems caused by balance billing of patients by providers whose fees were cut back. Computerized bill review originated in states with legally mandated workers' compensation fee schedules and is now migrating to Texas and other states where statutes limit a payer's obligation to "reasonable" fees. Computerized physician bill review, which has expanded to encompass abusive billing practices and overutilization in addition to unreasonable unit prices, accounts for the majority of workers' compensation medical cost containment program savings in many states.

Utilization review (UR) in workers' compensation differs in two major respects from similar programs in employee medical benefits programs. First, the source through which nonemergency care is brought under the *preservice* scrutiny of UR staff is the provider rather than the patient. This is a direct outgrowth of the injured worker's freedom from economic responsibility for services. This freedom (1) motivates providers to obtain the *payer's* commitment to reimbursement prior to rendering expensive inpatient or outpatient services; and (2) prevents the use of coverage incentives to motivate patients to initiate preservice UR procedures. Secondly, in order to minimize the risk of patients' misinterpreting responsible UR as unjustified scrimping, UR in the world of workers' compensation tends to be transparent to the patient. This contrasts with UR for employee benefit plans in which the patient's economic stake in medical costs is often explicitly communicated to patients.

The long-term success of preferred provider programs ultimately depends on an employer's ability to channel patients to preferred providers. Increased patient volume typically constitutes 90 percent of the rationale by which providers offer price discounts and multiple other benefits to purchasers in preferred arrangements. The ability of a workers' compensation payer to effectively channel patients depends, in turn, on two factors.

The first factor is the degree to which state workers' compensation laws enable an employer to control choice of provider. As previously indicated, this varies dramatically among states. In most states, the ability of an employer to direct injured workers to preferred providers is permitted, rather than mandated or prohibited. The second factor is the skill with which legally permissible channeling is planned and implemented. Key components of skillful channeling programs include methods to maximize (1) immediate reporting by workers to supervisors of job-related injuries; (2) routine referral by work-site supervisors to appropriate and convenient preferred providers; and (3) the satisfaction of work-site supervisors, claims examiners, and injured workers with the performance of preferred providers. The best-planned channeling mechanisms cannot survive preferred providers who build bad reputations with any of these three groups based on unpleasant demeanor, failure to share information, or prolonged patient waiting room time.

WHAT ARE THE BASIC PROGRAM MODULES IN A WORKERS' COMPENSATION MEDICAL COST CONTAINMENT PROGRAM, AND HOW MUCH CAN THEY SAVE?

Programs to contain workers' compensation medical costs are built around five basic modules: prevention, bill audits, utilization review, case management, and preferred provider arrangements.

Prevention

The most effective form of cost containment for workers' compensation, in both human and financial terms, is the prevention, whenever possible, of work-related injury and illness. Provision of a safe work environment is a matter of law. However, despite the fact that hospitals have access to a greater body of knowledge in the area of accident prevention than do most other employers, hospitals continue to be hazardous places in which to work. There are four major ways in which hospitals can reduce the risk of claims for work-related injury and illness among their employees.

Preplacement Physical Examinations

Certain categories of hospital workers fall in high-risk groups for injury and illness. These include nurses and housekeeping personnel. Frequently the injury or illness results from an inappropriate match between the employee's physical capacity and the requirements on the job. For example, a nurse with a history of back pain is injured while lifting a heavy patient in the intensive care unit, or a housekeeping aide with a known history of asthma develops severe allergies to dust and disinfectant. In both cases, the employee files a workers' compensation claim and is found to be incapable of doing the job.

The use of a system providing for preplacement physical examinations based on legally defensible, physically based job descriptions and matching the employee to the requirements of the job will reduce human suffering and numbers of claims filed. The identification through a physical examination of pre-existing medical conditions cannot, because of the Rehabilitation Act and Equal Opportunity laws, allow an employer to discriminate against an employee. It can, however, permit the employee to be placed in a work environment in which the risk of aggravation of the existing condition is minimized. In the case of the two examples given, the nurse could have been placed in an ambulatory setting where lifting was not required, and the housekeeping aide could have worked in food service. The result might well have been avoidance of injury and illness to the employees and considerable cost savings to the employer.

Injury-Specific Prevention Programs

Where there is known risk of injury due to the nature of the job, employees should be educated in techniques to minimize that risk. In a hospital environment there are certain prevalent risks: those related to the handling of patients, from either physical lifting or exposure to infection; and those related to the handling of toxic substances found in various hospital departments, particularly radiology and pathology. In the case of each identified risk, there should be written protocols and staff education. Nurses required to lift patients, for example, should be trained in low-risk lifting techniques. Appropriate, safe methods of dealing with infection control must be taught to all exposed staff. In the case of toxic substance handling, all employees must, by law, be informed of the nature of the substance and risk that they face. They must also be taught, and monitored, for compliance with strict rules for material handling.

Employee Communications

In hospitals, as with other industries, employees are more likely to file a workers' compensation claim and ultimately litigate their claim, when the underlying relationship between employer and employee is poor. The critical time for preventing breakdown in communication is in the immediate post-injury period. The employee who feels that the employer is concerned about him or her and is doing everything possible to ensure the best possible treatment for the injury will respond very differently from the employee who encounters apathy or indifference or who feels that the employer is trying to short-change him or her on his or her "rights."

The employer should ensure that lines of communication are kept open with the employee, that reasonable requests are met with responsiveness, and that an adversarial relationship is not allowed to develop.

An investment in a little tender loving care at the time of injury, coupled with flexibility in planning for return to work, will generally pay dividends to the employer in the form of suits avoided and length of absence from work shortened.

Stress Management

The great majority of hospital employees work in an environment where they have been exposed to reduction of hospital beds, merger with another hospital, or acquisition by a multihospital chain. Mergers, acquisitions, and downsizing lead to increased workers' compensation claims and greater utilization of health benefits in general.

Causal pathways are multiple. The stresses associated with upheavel of this nature are known to produce psychosomatic illnesses. Fear of losing one's job or major changes in administrative policy or corporate identity can also lead to a marked increase in anxiety and a consequent increase in workers' compensation claims. Legitimate accidents occur when employees are not giving their full attention to the task at hand. Substance abuse, already a critical problem with some hospital employee groups, increases in direct proportion to stress and disruption in the work environment. In addition, a blunt fact of life is that workers' compensation "pays better" than unemployment. Whether at a conscious or unconscious level, employees may seize on real and imaginary injuries and illnesses as an escape from a threatening and difficult situation at work or home.

Hospital administrators need to be alert to these relationships between stress and workers' compensation claims and to provide effective support for employees, especially during periods of organizational change.

Bill Audits

Bill audit programs are directed at bills from both hospitals and practitioners. While an audit of your hospital's bill on your own workers' compensation case may, in most cases, be futile, an audit of bills from other hospitals is and can be an important source of savings. In most states, *hospital bill audits* seek to uncover several sources of unwarranted charges including (1) services unrelated to the work injury; (2) services not ordered by a physician; (3) services not actually provided; and (4) excessively marked-up drugs and supplies.

Audits of *bills from physicians*, chiropractors, and other practitioners are directed at (1) fees in excess of a state work-

ers' compensation fee schedule, if any, or in excess of "reasonable," if such review is permitted by a state's workers' compensation law; (2) billing abuses, such as billing a 12-item automated blood test as if 12 individual blood tests were performed; and (3) services unrelated to the work injury.

In some states, hospital bill audits are successful in reducing hospital charges by an average of 18 percent net of audit fees.[3] In states like California with workers' compensation fee schedules for physicians, audit programs are able to reduce physician bills by an average of 14 percent net of audit fees.[4]

Utilization Review

Since most state statutes prohibit billing the patient for treatment of work-related injuries, most hospital billing departments and physician office staff seek treatment authorization before elective treatment and as soon as possible after emergency treatment. This represents an opportunity to link utilization review to most hospitalized cases. In its most successfully executed implementation, utilization review has reduced hospital utilization more than 29 percent below state norms for workers' compensation hospitalization.[5] Utilization review of outpatient services, while now in the pilot test stage in several instances, is too new to allow meaningful assessment of its cost effectiveness or describe its most promising methods of implementation.

Case Management

Case management in workers' compensation relies on a team of three players. First, the workers' compensation *claims examiner* serves as the coordinator of all information and interventions. Second, the *rehabilitation nurse* is responsible for assuring clinically appropriate assessment and intervention plans for cases that the claims examiner has referred because of their apparent opportunity for case management. Third, the *work-site supervisor* usually plays an essential role in providing information about job demands and working with the claims examiner and rehab nurse to structure transitional jobs, when feasible, to allow the earliest reasonable date of return to work.

The latter activity, which is referred to as "return to work programs" or "modified work programs," is often an essential method of preventing solidification of a worker's self-image as a disabled person. Because no data exist on average total medical costs and disability days associated with particular work injuries, estimates of the savings from cases referred for case management cannot be made meaningfully.

Preferred Provider Arrangements

Referring injured workers to preferred providers is supported explicitly by some state workers' compensation statutes, permitted by most, and prevented in very few cases. Critical to the success of these programs are assurance that work-site supervisors, claims examiners, and rehab nurses consistently refer injured workers to preferred providers and careful specification and enforcement of preferred provider obligations.

In workers' compensation care, preferred provider obligations should encompass the following critical elements: (1) favorable unit prices; (2) compliance with the PPO's utilization review and quality assurance mechanisms for inpatient and outpatient care; (3) when referral is necessary, use of other preferred providers; (4) timely submission of routinely required reports and special reports requested by claims examiners; (5) telephone responsiveness to claims examiners and rehab nurses; (6) cooperation in helping rehab nurses plan the earliest reasonable date for return to work.

While the full economic benefit of well-functioning preferred provider relationships in workers' compensation has not been fully calculated, savings from favorable unit prices are, by themselves, proving to be significant where there is an oversupply of providers. In urban areas of California, preferred physician prices have averaged 8–10 percent below the state's medical fee schedule, which is generally considered quite low relative to usual and customary physician fees.[6] In these same geographic areas, preferred inpatient prices have typically been negotiated at 25–35 percent below hospital retail charges.[7]

Special Challenges in a Hospital Functioning as Its Own Preferred Provider for Workers' Compensation Care

The hospital, as an employer, faces unique problems when also serving as the provider of care, particularly in the case of workers' compensation claims.

It is extraordinarily difficult for a physician or therapist to be objective in managing a case when the patient is a coworker. Pre-existing relationships frequently alter the interpersonal dynamics such that the treating physician will grant the patient unwarranted autonomy in setting the course of treatment and projected return-to-work date. The tendency to err on the "safe side" is magnified when physician and patient know each other. Further, when a physician's treating habits are known to patients, there is an impact on selection. Those not wishing to return to work promptly can select physicians who are known to follow slow, conservative treatment regimens.

Fear of reinjury as a result of returning a patient to work too soon is more problematic for physicians when they expect to come face to face with that patient in their place of work every day.

It is very important that the employee health service recognize the impact of interpersonal relationships and ensure that treating physicians, in particular, are selected for their fairness and objectivity. Written criteria for management of all aspects of employee health will also discourage employees from taking advantage of their employer, the hospital.

This same problem of conflicting objectives and loyalties can occur between risk managers and financial officers of large hospitals. Many times it is only the risk manager who is confronted with the vexing medical losses incurred via the hospital's workers' compensation program. Medical/Clinical directors, on the other hand, view the provision of services to the hospital's injured workers as a legitimate source of revenue. These two individuals must be brought together on an ongoing basis to assess and resolve these conflicting objectives.

Execution is Pivotal

Careful planning and implementation of medical cost containment programs for workers' compensation programs are the key to maximum program results. In evaluating the performance of computerized physician bill review, UR, and preferred provider arrangements in the workers' compensation setting, we have found a *three to fourfold variation* in net savings. Execution is the pivotal factor underlying these large variations in results.

Employers and carriers that have pioneered in the thoughtful implementation of comprehensive strategies to control workers' compensation medical costs have already reaped substantial savings. Using very conservative methods of calculation, carriers like Industrial Indemnity[8] and Crum and Foster[9] Commercial Insurance and self-insured employers like Safeway Stores[10] have already reduced workers' medical costs in excess of 15–20 percent, net of implementation expenses. Ratios of savings to implementation costs are roughly 7:1. Early evaluation shows no adverse impact on quality of care. Program enhancements to increase net savings beyond these significant yields are already being planned and implemented. For example, employers like Carter Hawley Hale and Chevron are maximizing the efficiency of preferred provider arrangements by combining employee benefit care and workers' compensation care in unified preferred provider contracts.

Workers' compensation medical care is the last preserve of uncontrolled fee for service medicine in America. For those employers and carriers that take care in understanding its unique characteristics, the opportunity to generate substantial savings without jeopardizing quality of care is great.

NOTES

1. Johnson, G. Personal correspondence, 1986.

2. Johnson, G., and Murphy, W. "Industrial Indemnity," 1987 (internal document). San Francisco, CA: William M. Mercer Meidinger Hansen Medical Audit Services.

3. William M. Mercer Meidinger Hansen Medical Audit Services. "Medical Cost Containment Impact Report Prepared for Safeway Stores." San Francisco, CA: author, 1987.

4. Ibid.

5. William M. Mercer Meidinger Hansen Medical Audit Services. "Medical Cost Containment Impact Report Prepared for Industrial Indemnity." San Francisco, CA: author, 1987.

6. Johnson, G., and Murphy, W. "Industrial Indemnity Network." 1988 (internal document). San Francisco, CA: William M. Mercer Meidinger Hansen Incorporated.

7. Ibid.

8. Johnson, G., and Murphy, W. "Industrial Indemnity Network," 1988.

9. William M. Mercer Meidinger Hansen Medical Audit Services. "Medical Cost Containment Impact Report Prepared for Safeway Stores." San Francisco, CA: author, 1988.

10. William M. Mercer Meidinger Hansen Medical Audit Services. "Medical Cost Containment Impact Report Prepared for Crum & Foster." San Francisco, CA: author, 1989.

Richard E. Johnson

Flexible Benefit Plans

37

Those plan sponsors that have implemented successful flexible benefit plans have been involved in one of the most talked about areas of human resources. The flex plans implemented in the past that have not lived up to expectations have, in part, not gone through a logical process. The most important principles to remember are these:

- Flex is a process.
- Keep the material simplified.
- Organize and plan.

PURPOSES

This chapter has two main purposes: (1) to allow plan sponsors to ascertain if a flex plan is practical, and (2) to assist those who decide to implement a flexible benefit plan. In many cases when a new plan or product comes along, there are those in the benefits field who decide these new concepts will provide a cure-all for a plan sponsor's problems. Some have said flex does that. The fact of the matter is that it does not, and flex is certainly not for everybody. So you need to ask yourself many questions. Your answers to these questions will allow you to ascertain if flex is appropriate.

The following provides an overview of areas for review.

A DEFINITION OF FLEX PLANS

Let's first look at this author's general definition of a flexible benefit plan.

A plan that allows employees to use specific dollars assigned to benefits, in the manner that best meets their personal needs. It involves employees and their families directly in the decisions on how much to select and spend for each benefit. It provides a means for employees to know the real cost/worth of their benefits.

Flex allows employees to use specific dollars to purchase benefits, thereby tailoring the plan to their personal needs. For most people the choices to date are between an indemnity plan and a health maintenance organization (HMO) or preferred provider organization (PPO) option. But they probably have never taken a hard look at benefits within the benefit plan, and that certainly is what a flex plan does. It also shows employees the cost and worth of their benefits, in many cases for the first time.

A PROCESS AND AN ENVIRONMENT FOR CHANGE

There are two general points you need to keep in mind. First, flex plans are simply a process. From the time you start to look at flex, through design and implementation, it is a process. In particular, flex is an ongoing process. It is neither a quick fix nor a short term solution, primarily because there are substantial start-up costs, especially for a full flex program. It is important to keep this in mind. Once you have implemented the flex plan, you have to immediately start planning for your second and subsequent years.

Second, flex plans provide an ideal environment for change. With so many changes in employee benefits, especially at the federal level, it is my opinion that flex plans will become even more prevalent, regardless of what form future legislation takes, because they provide opportunities for employee choice. If there is a tax cap, for example, it will at least give employees a choice of how much they want to be taxed, unlike today's traditional plans.

Flex plans certainly are challenging. They will challenge you, your carriers, and your advisors. They are manageable, assuming you decide to go through a logical process and cover all the bases. As long as you do that, they really work out quite well and can accomplish a lot of different things for you.

THREE KEY CONSIDERATIONS

There are three key considerations.

1. The plan sponsor is involving its employees in the cost of benefits, probably for the first time. If benefits become more taxable, we believe flex plans will become even more popular.
2. It is important to allow employees the opportunity to choose benefits to meet their personal needs. The demographic change in the work force has been substantial.
3. Great value is gained by the plan sponsor in examining all its benefits in total.

What typically happens when benefit plans are reviewed is that the health and welfare benefits are viewed separately from retirement, compensation, or other benefits. You might look at health costs or health plans as one aspect and not relate them to your pension plan(s). That can lead to missed opportunities and can cause problems.

Consideration needs to be given to

- benefits as compensation
- rising health costs—cost management benefits
- work force demographics
- uncertainty of future legislation

One of the most challenging is the uncertainty of future legislation. If you decide to go through a flex process, you are going to need to keep on top of proposed legislation.

REASONS FOR THE POPULARITY OF FLEX PLANS

There are probably six general reasons for the popularity of flex plans.

1. One is the changing work force. It was not too long ago that 45–50 percent of the work force in the United States was comprised of working males with female spouses at home. Now, these males comprise about 20 percent of the work force, and 45–50 percent of the remaining work force is made up of employees whose spouses are working. The traditional plans that have been designed and implemented over the years have not changed, and, as a result, the work force and the plan designs are out of balance. A flex plan offers a good environment in which to balance your work force with your benefits.
2. The same concept applies to cost management benefits. If you are looking at implementing preadmission certification or other review programs, such as outpatient surgery, outpatient testing, individual case management, or other cost management changes, a flex plan is a good environment in which to implement those types of benefits and make them an integral part of your organization's health plan options.
3. Flex plans have a tendency to ease the pressure for additional benefits. Instead of putting in a benefit change under a traditional plan that may impact on, say, 20 percent of the work force, through a flex plan you are designing benefits, so that people can pick and choose benefits and benefit levels based on their own personal needs. Instead of giving an across-the-board benefit increase that may not impact on everybody, you can satisfy employees' needs by offering different types of benefits within a flex plan.
4. Obviously, a flex plan can generate a lot of employee appreciation, assuming it is done well. Employees then have the ability to pick and choose the types of benefits that best fit their personal needs.
5. Financial security is the fifth reason for popularity. The financial issue boils down to 401(k) plans. A 401(k) plan may provide an additional vehicle for the employee's financial security over and above other defined contribution or defined benefit plans that a plan sponsor may offer.
6. Financial budget considerations are an often overlooked reason. The financial aspect plays an important role in budgeting from the standpoint that with flex plans, you set predetermined dollar figures, instead of having the cost of benefits set your budget. Say you have a flex plan, and you decide to contribute $100 per month per employee. That's a lot easier to budget than if you have to determine what the actual cost of the benefits is going to be because predicting benefit costs can be difficult. So it is a nice way to change your budget scenario to one based on dollars, rather than on benefits. You are changing from a retrospective to a prospective approach.

TYPES OF FLEX PLANS

A flexible benefit plan is any plan that lets participants choose some or all of their benefits. The choices can be

- among different levels of one type of benefit (e.g., different health plans)
- among different types of benefits (e.g., life insurance, dental coverage, and cash)

Depending on what the plan sponsor wants to accomplish, a flexible benefit plan can include any or all of the following:

- cash
- health benefits
- group term life insurance
- accidental death and dismemberment
- long-term disability coverage
- short-term disability coverage
- dependent care
- vacation/sick leave
- 401(k) savings plan contributions

A flexible benefit plan that usually offers a choice between cash (or other permissible taxable benefits) and nontaxable benefits is a cafeteria plan. Cafeteria plans are regulated by Section 125 of the Internal Revenue Code (IRC). According to Section 125, a cafeteria plan has the following features:

- It is a written plan.
- All participants are employees.
- It offers a choice among two or more benefits—the choice may be among cash (or other permissible taxable benefits) and benefits the IRC defines (by statute) to be nontaxable in a cafeteria plan.

A *qualified cafeteria plan* is a plan that meets Section 125 requirements. Essential among those requirements (and in addition to those features listed above) are the nondiscrimination standards. These standards require that a plan not give a significantly greater benefit to highly compensated members of the group.

Qualified plans protect participants from constructive receipt. This means that as long as their plan is qualified, participants in Section 125 cafeteria plans will be taxed on the basis of the choices they make, rather than on what benefits are available to them. Section 125 provides that if a cafeteria plan is a qualified plan, all participants in that qualified plan will be taxed only on the taxable benefits they choose. If a cafeteria plan fails to qualify by favoring the highly compensated members of the group in terms of eligibility and contributions or benefits, then the highly compensated members will be taxed on the value of the taxable benefits available to them. All other members of the group will continue to be taxed just on the value of the taxable benefits they choose.

Except for 401(k) plans, a cafeteria plan may not include any benefit that defers compensation in any way. This means that no benefits may be carried over from plan year to plan year. Also, money put into a flexible spending account cannot

be returned to participants as cash at the end of the year; this is often called the "use it or lose it" requirement.

Section 125 cafeteria plans can be either benefit based plans or flexible spending accounts (FSAs). *Benefit-based cafeteria plans* offer choices among benefit coverages (e.g., health benefits, life insurance, etc.) and cash. Modular plans and core-plus-options plans are examples of benefit-based cafeteria plans. FSAs let participants choose between pretax reimbursement of certain eligible expenses and cash.

In order to understand flexible benefit plans, it is important to understand how each of the three general designs works. The following is a discussion of FSAs and benefit-based plans—modular plans and core-plus-options plans—in terms of their features and design considerations.

The Flexible Spending Account

A flexible spending account, or FSA, is a type of cafeteria plan that gives participants a choice between taxable cash and pretax payment of nontaxable expenses. When participants pay for eligible, nontaxable expenses with pretax compensation, they get the benefit of immediate tax relief.

Some of the expenses an FSA can cover are

- health plan premiums
- medical expenses not covered by the plan sponsor's plan (or any other plan the participant might have) or expenses the Internal Revenue Service considers deductible (IRC Section 213 expenses)
- dependent care expenses (within IRC Section 129 guidelines)

From a participant's point of view, the FSA operates like a personal checking account with respect to deposits and disbursements. Deposits enter the account as plan sponsor contributions. In general, plan sponsor contributions are made through a salary deferral agreement. This agreement lets employees decide whether to take salary currently as taxable wages or to put it into an FSA. Because this represents a choice between cash and nontaxable benefits, an FSA funded by salary deferral falls within the Section 125 definition of a cafeteria plan. Such FSAs must meet all Section 125 requirements. Salary deduction contributions are pretax contributions; they enter the account before federal (FIT and FUTA), Social Security (FICA) [except for 401(k) plans], and, in some jurisdictions, state and local taxes are deducted. Even though the money appears to come from employees' wages, salary reduction contributions are defined by the Internal Revenue Service (IRS) as plan sponsor contributions because the employee has technically chosen nontaxable benefits in lieu of cash compensation.

Disbursements are made from the FSA to pay for eligible nontaxable expenses. The final responsibility for the tax status of a filed expense rests with the participant; that is, the person who files for and receives FSA reimbursement of an ineligible expense is responsible for all taxes, penalties, and interest charges attributable to that expense.

Section 125 regulations place restrictions on FSA plan operations. These restrictions have a potential impact on an individual's finances and should cause employees to decide very carefully about participating. These restrictions are as follows:

- Salary deferral elections *for each type of benefit* are to be made before the beginning of the plan year. Once made, *they cannot be changed* unless an employee experiences a change in family status, including a spouse losing employment.

- Because money allocated for each type of benefit must be kept separate from money allocated for every other type of benefit, separate subaccounts must be set up for each type. Benefits in one subaccount cannot be funded by contributions toward another. For example, money earmarked for child care cannot be used to pay for a medical service, even if the child care account carries a surplus and the health care account has a zero balance.

- Money left in the FSA at the end of the year cannot be carried forward into the next year, nor can it be given to the employee as taxable income. Any money left in the account at year-end must be forfeited by the employee. In other words, the employee must expect to "use it or lose it."

From a plan sponsor's point of view, the FSA is a way to provide some benefit flexibility with little additional expense. A plan sponsor implementing an FSA will incur costs for

- adapting the payroll operation to handle salary reductions
- monitoring compliance with Section 125 nondiscrimination requirements
- maintaining a record keeping–administrative system of individual accounts, or contracting with a third party to do so
- communicating with employees to explain the benefits and the risks of participating in an FSA.

Modular Plans

A flexible benefit plan of the modular design presents participants with a choice of predesigned benefit packages. Each package contains a fixed combination of benefit plans put together to meet the needs of a particular segment of the employee group. The price to employees for each package is determined by

- the cost of the benefit module
- the contribution the plan sponsor makes toward it

When the cost of the benefit module exceeds the plan sponsor's contribution, the difference is charged as an employee contribution. When the plan sponsor's contribution is more than the cost of a module, employees choosing that module will receive the difference to purchase additional benefits, to contribute to a 401(k) plan, or in cash. This cash is considered a taxable benefit. A modular plan could look like the plan shown in Table 37-1.

When employees have the chance to choose their benefits, they usually know what they need, and they will select accordingly. For example, employees who opt for a rich health plan are the ones who feel their use of benefits will exceed their contribution. Employees who anticipate being well withdraw support from the rich plan and pick a module with a less rich health plan.

Care has to be taken in designing the benefits because if the rich plan experiences high claim usage relative to other plans, it will lose support: the lower coverage plans will attract the good risks, and a pattern of *adverse selection* starts. As the costs of the health plans grow further apart, the pattern of adverse selection gets worse. The ultimate effect of adverse selection is that plan sponsors may experience an increase in overall costs if they have diverted the plan differential to cash or other unrelated benefits.

Putting benefit plans together in fixed packages or modules can help combat adverse selection. The modules can be designed so that individual coverages within each package appeal to different members of the group and the trade-offs within each package (e.g., a slightly lower health plan in exchange for dental benefits) are acceptable ones.

Consider the example shown in Table 37-2. Module 1 would appeal to any or all of the following:

- a person who anticipated that his/her health care expenses would not exceed the contribution plus deductible

- someone who wants dental benefits and is willing to take some risk in the health care area

- an employee who does not need large life insurance amounts or could find life insurance more economically outside the group but wants dental benefits and vision care coverage

- someone who does not use dependent care services and does not want to make higher contribution for his/her benefits

Table 37-1 Modular Plan

Module 1	Module 2	Module 3	Module 4
Health: Plan A	Health: Plan B	Health: Plan C	Health: Plan A
Dental: No	Dental: No	Dental: Yes	Dental: Yes
Vision: No	Vision: Yes	Vision: Yes	Vision: Yes
Life: 1 × AE	Life: 2 × AE	Life: 3 × AE	Life: 3 × AE
Dep. Care: Yes	Dep. Care: No	Dep. Care: No	Dep. Care: No
Cash Back: Yes	Cash Back: No	Cash Back: No	Cash Back: No
Cost To Employee:			
None	$	$$	$$$

Table 37-2 Module Plan Designs

Module 1	Module 2
Health: $300/600 deductible	Health: $100/200 deductible
Dental: Yes	Dental: No
Vision: Yes	Vision: No
Life: 1 × annual earnings	Life: 3 × annual earnings
Dependent Care: No	Dependent Care: Yes
Cash Back: Yes	Cash Back: No
Employee Contribution: $ -0-	Employee Contribution: $$

Module 2 could be chosen by

- someone who uses dependent care services but does not need dental or vision care benefits
- an employee who wants life insurance at group rates
- a person willing to make a larger contribution for extra health protection

Each of these modules meets different needs. The cost of each benefit within the modules is stabilized somewhat by the support given by other benefits that may not be used to their full extent. For instance, because it includes dependent care benefits and more life insurance, as well as extra health benefits, Module 2 would be chosen by people who will use the extra health benefits *and* by people who will not. The people who pick that module for its life insurance or dependent care benefits rather than for its health benefits help even out the cost of the higher health care plan.

The difference among modules and the plans within them should be meaningful, but not radical. No single module should contain all the richest benefits offered. Additionally, if the health plan in force before flexible benefits was a very rich plan, it will almost never be included in one of the modules, not only because of the potential for adverse selection but also because of plan sponsor's cost management objectives. Plan sponsors often use the attractiveness of benefit flexibility to introduce medical plans with cost management features.

Plan sponsor contributions should probably be the same for each module so that the difference in the cost of each is covered by employee contributions. Employee contributions can be made on a priority basis through a salary reduction agreement.

The modular approach is a conservative approach to flexibility. The spectrum of choice it offers to employees and the added risk it presents to plan sponsors are greater than those contained in conventional plans or FSAs, but less than those of a core-plus-options plan. Initially, the modular approach is also a more costly approach to flexibility than the FSA, but it is probably less costly than a core-plus-options plan.

The plan sponsor wanting to implement a modular plan must be prepared to

- adapt the payroll operation to handle salary reductions
- establish a specific data link between the human resources and payroll departments to manage benefit eligibility information

- maintain a record keeping/administration system of individual accounts or contract with a third party to do so
- coordinate enrollment/eligibility with the entities handling claim administration for various coverages (and levels of coverage)
- develop the ability to monitor compliance with non-discrimination rules on an ongoing basis
- communicate with employees initially and during the plan year
- develop or find pricing expertise and design capabilities

On an ongoing basis, systems linkages, employee communications, and relationships with the pricers and designers must be maintained. Monitoring Section 125 compliance must be done on a regular basis.

Core-Plus-Options Plans

A core-plus-options plan is more flexible than either an FSA or a modular plan. It allows employees to make selections among various options that complement a fixed core of benefits.

The core plan is usually a skeleton plan that provides floor levels of several types of benefits. The core plan sometimes serves as the minimum level of coverage that plan sponsors require for their employees. To assure employees that flexibility should not cause them a loss of benefits, plan sponsors may tie their contribution during the first year to pre–flexible plan contributions. After the first year, plan sponsor contributions generally reflect flexible plan performance. Plan sponsors often fix contributions to cover the cost of the core plan for each employee and may include part or all of core plan dependent costs.

Because of cost management objectives and the likelihood of adverse selection, the pre–flexible benefit health plan is usually modified and offered either as a part of the core plan or as an option. Health benefits that give more protection than the core are offered as options.

Core plans can include new categories of coverage. These new categories should be ones that are interesting and useful to employees and that experience cost increases at a slower rate than traditional health benefits. The following cost management benefits are good examples:

- preadmission certification
- length of stay and concurrent reviews
- second surgical opinion
- outpatient testing
- outpatient surgery
- individual case management
- generic drugs

Just as making benefit-by-benefit choices adds flexibility for employees, it adds a greater likelihood of adverse selection for plan sponsors. A core-plus-options plan's best defense against adverse selection is found in sound plan design and pricing strategy and in an effective communications program. A plan sponsor will be interested in the total cost of the flexible plan. Those involved in pricing should be able to anticipate the total cost of that plan. With enough information about the people in the group and how they will choose benefits, plan pricing may be structured to emphasize the cost-effective benefits that an employer wants to highlight. The core plan can be designed as a module that contains costs, provides a stable base, and appeals to a large segment of the group.

The difference between the core benefit and the richest benefit option in any category should be meaningful, but not radical. Plan sponsor contributions should not extend far enough to pay for the richest benefits in all categories.

The core-plus-options approach gives the plan sponsor the greatest potential for flexibility, risk, and reward. It also generally has the greatest initial cost.

In order to launch a core-plus-options plan, a plan sponsor must be prepared to

- adapt the payroll operation to handle salary reductions
- establish a specific data link between the human resources and payroll departments to manage benefit eligibility information
- maintain a record keeping/administration system of individual accounts or contract with a third party to do so
- coordinate enrollment/eligibility with the entities handling claim administration for various coverages (and levels of coverage)
- develop the ability to monitor compliance with non-discrimination standards on an ongoing basis
- communicate with employees initially and during the plan year
- develop or find pricing expertise and design capabilities

The tasks listed are the same as those required to establish a modular plan, but the content of each task is greater for core-plus-options plans. For example, the concept and mechanics of choosing benefits may present a greater communications challenge with core-plus-options plans than with the other types of flexible benefit approaches.

Once the plan is up and running, the plan sponsor must continuously monitor compliance with Section 125, communicate with new and existing employees, and maintain design and pricing expertise and all systems linkages.

ADMINISTRATIVE CONSIDERATIONS

This may be the area that is most overlooked. A computerized system is needed to administer your flex plan. As an example, whether you have 100 employees, 1,000 employees, 10,000 employees, or 100,000 employees covered under a flex plan, you will have 100, 1,000, 10,000, or 100,000 individual accounts. A system needs to be in place, and the plan sponsor needs to ascertain if this can be done internally. If not, then you need to hire an administrator. It is critical that this process be started when you start the flex process. Don't wait. As you develop the system, make sure you document it. An administrative procedures manual is extremely helpful. It not only details the system but also is a handy reference and good training tool for new employees.

The administrative requirements of a flexible benefit plan with several options, as well as a flexible spending account, would include all of the following:

- *Election forms*: forms with clear instructions on the choices available
- *Record keeping*: a data base of employee choices (These data should be screened to identify election form errors and to be sure all employees have made elections. The plan sponsor must either develop a system to provide the record keeping/administration functions or discharge this responsibility to a third party. *This is a critical aspect of a successful program and must be developed in the early stages of the plan design.*)
- *Benefit determination*: determining that the expenses submitted for reimbursement are eligible for reimbursement and are not duplicate expenses and that the limits for reimbursement have not been exceeded
- *Benefit payment*: reimbursement of eligible expenses either through payroll or by separate check
- *Payroll/W–2 reporting (to employees)*: a means of interfacing the record keeping/administration system data base with payroll if pretax salary deferral, after-tax deferral, or additional employee cash is involved
- *Payroll withholding*: modification of the payroll system if pretax salary deferral is used to handle the FIT, FUTA, FICA, and state and local withholding properly
- *Expense records*: maintaining records on the nature and magnitude of expenses reimbursed under a flexible spending account (Individual record keeping of this type can be useful in determining employee needs for the future.)

In addition to the systems, an administrative procedures manual, systems specifications, and program specifications need to be developed.

The following features of a flexible benefit plan may make its administration different from that of traditional benefit plans:

- The cost for a particular benefit may vary by individual based on individual information, such as age and sex.
- Each individual employee is allocated an amount of ''money'' that he or she may ''spend'' for the benefits selected.
- Employee contributions (if any) for benefits may be deducted as *pretax* payments.

- Traditionally, payroll deductions for benefit contributions are identified by separate deductions in the payroll process. With a flex plan, there may be a single composite deduction for all benefits purchased.
- Employees may be able to increase direct pay above the level that existed prior to the institution of the flex plan.
- A flexible benefit plan usually introduces an annual enrollment process. An individualized enrollment form is required for each employee, identifying the cost of each benefit he or she may select and the amount of "money" (the employer-provided contribution) that he or she has to spend to "buy" benefits. This also entails the validation of the elections made by each individual.
- New benefits may be added to the flexible benefit plan which require initial and ongoing administration.
- Both employer and employee contributions are considered employer funds for benefit and tax purposes.

The administrative requirements for a flexible benefit plan can be categorized into three major areas: enrollment, payroll/accounting, and ongoing administration/record keeping.

There are some aspects of system development that you need to be aware of. Election forms typically will have confidential information, such as salaries, and you need to be sensitive to this. It is important to make sure that the record keeping/administration can be done. The more complex your plan is, of course, the more complex that will be. Since plan administration is such an integral part of a successful flexible benefit plan, the plan sponsor should carefully review the following checklist:

General Issues

- Are flex plan participants located in more than one location? If so, are the payroll and benefits administration functions centralized or decentralized? Is the same payroll system used for all participants, or are different payroll systems involved?
- Are benefits administration functions currently performed by a computerized personnel system? If so, is the personnel system integrated with the payroll system (do they share the same master file, etc.)?
- Will the flex administration system be a stand-alone system, or will it be incorporated as changes to or additional modules in an existing personnel system?
- Can the payroll system accommodate the necessary deductions for both pretax and after-tax deductions?
- What are the *additional* staffing requirements within the benefits department?
- What are the training requirements for *current* benefits staff?
- What are the capabilities and *availability* of internal computer personnel for assisting in both setting up the required systems and performing the ongoing process requirements?

- Will new hires enter the flex plan only during the annual enrollment process, or will they be admitted throughout the year shortly after their date of hire?
- Will the administration system need to perform ongoing processing and reporting tasks for non–flex participants (i.e., new hires and part-time employees)?
- What types of status changes and other data changes must be accommodated by the system during the year? What are the procedures and sources of data for processing changes?
- How will various information and account balances in the flex administration system be reconciled to the payroll system and other accounting requirements, such as the general ledger?
- What are the specific conditions under which changes in the employee's original elections will be permitted during the year? What procedures will be followed to make such changes?

Enrollment Process

- What is the source of data for building the initial master file in the flex administration system (payroll master, personnel master, multiple sources, etc.)?
- Will the enrollment form be individually printed by computer for each participant? Will salaries be on the form?
- Will the computer support system be used to assist in the logistics of the enrollment meetings (helping to schedule employees for specific meeting times, print enrollment forms in meeting assignment order, print labels, etc.)?
- What edit checks on the employee elections (for accuracy and reasonableness) must be performed by the system?
- Will a correction statement and a confirmation statement be generated by the system? What is the procedure to be followed in distributing, collecting, and processing corrections and confirmations?
- What is the exact procedure to be followed when an employee does not complete an enrollment form?
- Will additional enrollment forms for specific benefit coverages need to be completed if certain flex options are elected (dependent care, etc.)?
- Should the system produce enrollment status reports to assist in monitoring the progress of the enrollment process?
- How will the election results be communicated to various administrators and carriers who need to know which options have been selected (medical, life, LTD, etc.)? Should they be in the form of report listings, on magnetic tape, etc.?
- What are the requirements for management reports concerning the results of the entire election process?
- How will the payroll deduction information be communicated to the payroll department? How will this information be incorporated into the payroll system?

- What are the exact timing requirements for all the functions performed during the enrollment process?

Reimbursement Account—FSAs

- Does the reimbursement account involve only one benefit type (e.g., health care) or some combination of different types (health, dependent care, and legal)?
- If there is more than one benefit type, will separate reimbursement checks be generated, or will payments be combined in one check?
- Are the deposits to the reimbursement account from salary deferral only, plan sponsor contributions, or some combination? If plan sponsor contributions are involved, is the deposit made in one lump sum (i.e., at the beginning of the year) or on a pro-rata basis over each payroll period throughout the year?
- How often will employee requests for reimbursement be processed (e.g., once a month)? What documentation is required along with the request form? Specifically, is an EOB (explanation of benefits) form required from the carrier or claims administrator for nonreimbursed health care expenses?
- Who will adjudicate reimbursement payment requests, and what procedures will be followed?
- Where will the reimbursement checks be generated (i.e., the reimbursement processing system, accounts payable, a carrier, etc.)? What auditing controls and procedures are required by accounting?
- What type of statement will be used to communicate account status information to participants? Will it be handled on the stub of the reimbursement check or on a separate employee statement? Will statements be issued only to participants who are receiving payments in the current month or to all participants in the reimbursement account?
- What is the procedure for handling payment requests that are greater than the current balance in the account?
- Will terminated participants be permitted to submit requests for payment for some period of time after termination? How long after the end of the year will requests for payment from the prior year be accepted?
- What management reports are required?
- How are deposits credited and the reimbursement system reconciled with actual payroll deductions in the payroll system? Will the payroll system "drive" the reimbursement system directly?
- Will a minimum amount be required on payment requests (for example, $50)?
- Will interest be credited to account balances? If so, what is the exact procedure for determining the amount and the timing?

Regarding benefit determination and benefit payment, you are going to have people making different types of choices.

You need to make sure the system is set up to track benefits for each individual. The same applies to benefit payments. For example, if you have a dependent care plan, who will process checks, what dollar minimums will be set for reimbursement of expenses, and how often will payments be issued? There needs to be interface with the payroll department because you will have taxable and nontaxable benefits in the plan, and reporting and withholding need to be considered.

AREAS UNIQUE TO PUBLIC SECTOR SPONSORS

There are certain areas unique to public sector plan sponsors. These areas have been changed by the Tax Reform Act of 1986.

401(k) Plans

Until the Tax Reform Act was passed, public-sector plan sponsors could have a 401(k) profit-sharing plan as an integral part of a flexible benefit plan or as a freestanding plan in conjunction with a flexible benefit plan. A qualified 401(k) plan allows employees to defer receipt and taxation of a portion of their income until retirement, termination, or hardship.

The following issues need to be addressed in formulating a 401(k) profit-sharing plan as one of the benefit options available under a flexible benefit plan. The following two issues are key to understanding the ramifications of adopting a 401(k) plan:

1. the individual participant's maximum benefits and contributions under the 401(k) plan and other employer retirement plans
2. distribution rules for 401(k) profit-sharing plans

Although the maximum benefit and contribution rules are somewhat complex, the plan sponsor needs to monitor all rules for each participant.

Maximum Contributions and Benefits

The maximum contribution rules fall into two main categories: those applicable to retirement plans qualified under IRC Section 401(a) and those pertaining to eligible state and local government deferred compensation plans under IRC Section 457.

The qualified retirement plan rules, in turn, include two primary limitations on plan sponsor contributions to defined benefit plans and defined contribution plans [i.e., 401(k) profit sharing]. First, IRC Section 415 limits benefits under a defined benefit plan and contributions to a defined contribution plan with respect to each participant. (All types of plan sponsors are subject to the Section 415 limits.) Second, IRC Section 404 limits the amount of contributions to a qualified retirement plan that a plan sponsor may deduct for income tax purposes. [Since public entities and 5021(c)(9) trusts are not subject to income tax, they are not affected by the Section 404 limitations. The Section 404 limitations apply to the private sector.]

Availability of 401(k) and 457 Plans

Government and tax-exempt organizations may not have 401(k) plans, except for grandfathered plans adopted before

- July 2, 1986, for tax-exempt organizations
- May 6, 1986, for government organizations

Collectively bargained plans are grandfathered if adopted

- before January 1, 1989, or the expiration of the last bargaining agreement made before March 1, 1986, whichever is earlier
- but not earlier than July 2, 1986, for tax-exempt organizations, or May 6, 1989, for government organizations

Grandfathered government plans are subject to the new 401(k) nondiscrimination rules for fiscal years beginning in 1989. Until then, they are subject to the old 401(k) rules. Grandfathered tax-exempt plans were subject to the new rules beginning in 1987.

Implications

Public sector plan sponsors with grandfathered 401(k) plans may find them somewhat less attractive because of new non-discrimination and withdrawal rules. However, plan sponsors will probably want to keep their 401(k) plans for the following reasons:

- 457 plans assets are not kept in a separate trust and are subject to creditors' claims, while 401(k) plans have irrevocable trusts.
- 401(k) plan distributions can be rolled over into IRAs, while 457 plan distributions cannot be.
- 457 plans cannot have employer contributions.

Plan sponsors may want to keep or establish 457 plans as well to accept salary deferrals that cannot be put into 401(k) plans because of stricter nondiscrimination tests.

Social Security Coverage

Certain public-sector plan sponsors do not participate in Social Security. This seems especially common among state governments and police and fire departments.

The public-sector plan sponsor that does not participate in Social Security needs to take care in designing a flexible benefits plan, especially if it has active employees age 65 and over. This is especially true with regard to disability and health coverages.

Filing Requirements

Public entities are exempt from the reporting requirements of ERISA; *however*, public entities with cafeteria plans must file a Form 5500 for the cafeteria plan *only*. The Form 5500 instructions explain which items need to be completed when filing for a cafeteria plan. Also, the Schedule A to Form 5500 is required only for Department of Labor purposes and is not required for entities that are exempt from Title I of ERISA (such as public entities).

TAXATION ISSUES

The issue of taxation for flex plans is very cloudy. So if you are in the process of implementing a flex plan or if you decide you want to implement one, make sure that you stay on top of the existing and proposed legislation.

The following IRC sections and IRS regulations are applicable to flexible benefit plans:

IRC Sections

• Section 79	Group term life insurance
• Section 105	Accident and health plans
• Section 106	Employer contributions to accident and health plans
• Section 120	Group legal plans
• Section 125	Cafeteria plans
• Section 129	Dependent care assistance programs
• Section 401(k)	Cash or deferred profit-sharing plans

IRS Regulations

• 1.79	Group term life insurance
• 1.105	Accident and health plans
• 1.106-1	Employer contributions to accident and health plans
• 1.120	Group legal services
• Proposed cafeteria regulations	Proposed regulations
• 1.125	Cafeteria plans
• 1.401(k)-1	Profit-sharing plans

Although the overall objective of the flexible benefits program is to allow employees to enjoy the greatest possible degree of choice and efficiency of compensation within the confines of the employee benefits program, legal and tax issues must be addressed at the outset. Certain benefits will generate taxable income to the employee. Any direct cash that is received will have to be included in the employee's W–2 earnings in the year in which it is received. In addition, the employee life insurance and long-term disability insurance plans may result in a taxable event, depending on the plan design.

COBRA

Although the changes brought about in benefit plans by the Consolidated Omnibus Budget Reconciliation Act of 1985 (COBRA) is a separate subject, two areas indirectly impact on flexible benefit plans.

1. Since plan sponsors need to have record keeping/administrative systems in place to adequately handle the notification and tracking requirements imposed by COBRA, consideration should be given to developing one system to handle both flex and COBRA record keeping/administration functions.
2. Plan sponsors will need to allow employees and their dependents the ability to choose the various flex health options, whether an employee participates in the flex plan or not.

Tax Reform Act of 1986

Certain changes adopted in the Tax Reform Act of 1986 have a direct impact on cafeteria plans and 401(k) plans.

Cafeteria Plans

The following four general changes to cafeteria plan rules were effective January 1, 1989.

1. A plan that offers a choice only among nontaxable benefits (where there is no cash option) is now subject to the cafeteria plan rules.
2. Each option offered under a cafeteria plan must now satisfy the nondiscrimination rules applicable to welfare plans. These rules take the place of the old tests.
3. If a cafeteria plan discriminates, all benefits received by highly compensated employees (HCEs) will become taxable.
4. A salary reduction feature of a cafeteria plan is not subject to FICA or FUTA taxes.

In essence, health and group term life insurance plans must satisfy complex nondiscrimination tests that include determining the value of coverage. Since the issue of Section 89 testing is being decided in Congress, careful scrutiny to congressional action is necessary.

Qualification Requirements. Each plan must also meet certain qualification requirements.

- The plan must be in writing.
- Employees' rights must be legally enforceable.
- Employees must be notified of available benefits.
- The plan must be for the exclusive benefit of employees.
- The plan must be intended to be permanent.

Highly Compensated Employees. It is important here to understand the definition of highly compensated employees. The determination of highly paid employees is based on an analysis of the entire employee population. The highly compensated group includes

- a 5 percent owner in the current or preceding plan year
- the top one-fifth of all employees ranked by compensation (Employees earning $50,000 or less in the current or preceding plan year will not be considered highly paid, even if they are in the top one-fifth.)
- employees earning more than $75,000 in the current or preceding plan year
- officers of the employee organization who earn more than 150 percent of the Section 415 defined contribution limit [The Section 415 defined contribution limit is presently $30,000 and is to be indexed in the future by the consumer price index (CPI). If no officer earns this much, then the highest-paid officer is considered highly compensated. No more than 50 individuals and no fewer than 10 percent of the organization's employees, up to 3, will be considered highly compensated according to this criteria.]
- certain former employees who were in the highly paid group at any time after age 55

If members of the same family are employed by the same employer, proving nondiscrimination becomes more complicated. If one family member is considered in the highly paid group as a 5 percent owner or one of the 10 highest paid employees, then compensation from the employer and benefits received from the plan by the other family members will be counted as having been received by the highly paid employee.

Disability income coverage will not have to meet nondiscrimination tests because employer-paid disability benefits are taxable. A few disability plans, such as travel accident coverage, will have to meet nondiscrimination tests.

401(k) Plans

Internal Revenue Code Section 401(k) allows employees to save on a tax-deferred basis by entering into salary deferral arrangements with their employer. The Tax Reform Act of 1986 makes significant changes in 401(k) plans and also has provisions that apply to all kinds of savings plans, whether or not they include pretax employee contributions.

Maximum Salary Deferral. Although 401(k) plans have always had to meet special nondiscrimination deferral tests to assure that highly paid employees do not take substantially greater advantage of this tax shelter than do lower-paid employees, the Tax Reform Act modified the old laws. The special 401(k) nondiscrimination tests were made more stringent beginning January 1, 1987.

COMMUNICATION

Communication is obviously one of the most important aspects of a flex plan. For a flex plan to be successful, you need to address the following issues:

- Employees are going to have increased choices. In a majority of cases, employees are going to be asked for the first time to choose benefits based on their personal needs.
- For a full flex plan, employees are going to be asked to make different choices.
- There are going to be some difficult choices to make. Let us look at an example of what can be done in this area. Assume you have a modular plan with a core-option health plan and a high-option health plan. You have situations in which both spouses work. In order to make sure people don't opt for the high option without considering the core option, a sample newsletter could explain coordination of benefits (COB). Because COB is fairly complex to understand, you should try to explain it in the simplest terms. Tell people that if their spouse is working at either your company or somewhere else, the core option may make sense for them because through coordination of benefits, they may get 100 percent of allowable expenses. This is the type of communication you want when you are going through a flex process. (You may even want to name your core or indemnity plan option the COB plan.)
- Harmful choices are always going to be made. People are going to make mistakes. There are two ways to limit that. First, provide very good communication. Second, give employees an annual open enrollment.
- Flex plans and any other employee benefit areas need to have two-way communication. One of the unfortunate things that happens is that plan sponsors have a tendency not to get employees involved in selecting benefit options or making choices. Plan sponsors should ask employees what they would like to see. We always recommend two-way communication, and there are effective ways to do this. You can set up committees, roundtable discussions, focus groups, surveys, anything that gets the employees involved. Employee feedback is critical, and you will be surprised at the good ideas employees have. Such communication is beneficial, and it really helps produce an excellent final product.
- When you talk about salary deferral, people will think you are making a change and taking something away

from them. Of course, that is not the case; you simply need to make sure that, through your communication process, people come to understand what *salary deferral* means. The same applies with pretax versus after-tax. It is simply a new concept for most people. You need to explain to employees what these terms mean and what happens to their benefits.
- Salary deferral has potential effects on pay-related benefits. Life insurance and retirement/pension plans are two examples. If you have a salary deferral feature, you need to make sure employees understand that life insurance and retirement benefits will still be based on their gross salary, not their net salary.

A Four-Phase Approach

This four-phase approach is a planned, tested, and successful communication strategy.

1. First is the announcement phase during which you introduce the flex concepts to the employees. You accomplish this through such vehicles as letters, brochures, posters, and announcement kits.
2. The second phase is the education phase. During this phase you will educate employees regarding benefits and choices. Attention is focused on how benefits will meet their individual needs. The vehicles that you can use are newsletters, special bulletins, and highlight brochures.
3. Third is the enrollment phase. Of importance here is the employees' "comfort zone." Depending on the type of plan you have today, their comfort zone may be fairly small, especially if they have only been asked to choose between an indemnity plan and an HMO option. As they make their choices within the flex plan, make sure through communications that you broaden their comfort zone, so that they feel comfortable in making the choices.
4. The last phase is the follow-up phase. You will review the results and find out what people chose. You should always send employees statements confirming their selections to make sure those statements balance with what the employee actually chose. You can also do post-enrollment surveys to find out why they selected what they did, whether they liked the process, whether they understood everything, etc.

The bottom line is to simplify. The simpler you can make the flex plan communication process, the better off enrollment will be. Give yourself 12 to 18 months from the time you start until the time you actually implement the program.

Develop a theme for the flex plan, and run it through all communications. You will also need to develop enrollment forms, a team leader meeting guide, a summary plan description, and the plan documents.

Don't overlook communication. It is an integral part of a successful flex plan.

STEP–BY–STEP PROCESS FOR SUCCESSFUL IMPLEMENTATION OF A FLEXIBLE BENEFIT PROGRAM

The process described here works whether you are a Taft-Hartley trust fund or a private or public sector plan sponsor. You come up with an organized schedule, a well-thought-out decision-making process, based on your knowledge of why you want to do what you want to do, and a work plan for implementation. Remember that, especially in the flex area, plan sponsors and employees may be reviewing the overall impact of benefits for the first time. Benefits have been on the fringe for a long time. Now they are starting to be looked on more as an integral part of compensation.

Key Objectives

A successful process is centered around key objectives. Examples include the following:

- The flex plan must be perceived by employees as a program of quality and of value to them personally.
- The flex plan must be viewed by employees as an integral part of their compensation.
- The flex plan must involve a partnership between employees and the plan sponsor aimed at cost management.
- The flex plan must be cost effective in that it delivers value within specific cost guidelines, *both short and long term*.
- The flex plan must be responsive to individual employees' needs and choices.
- The flex plan must be competitive.

Statement of Compensation and Benefits

First, develop a statement of compensation and benefits. This is a written document that states the plan sponsor's philosophy and objectives for compensation and benefits. It will serve as an important basis in establishing the plan design for a new flexible benefit program. It should also provide a basis for any other planned changes that may be made to the overall program during the next three to five years.

This process has normally never been done. However, it makes sense to develop such a statement because once you have a general document spelling out your goals, everything else seems to flow well. From this statement you will set three criteria: policy objectives, funding expense objectives, and investment policy objectives.

How do you establish this statement? You do it through these seven basic steps.

1. Interview key personnel.
2. Develop a statement of the plan sponsor's objectives.
3. Summarize current provisions.
4. Identify deviations between desired objectives and current provisions.
5. Make recommendations to bring the plan provisions/funding and expense objectives/investment objectives into line with desired objectives.
6. Quantify the costs/administrative criteria required to implement the recommendations.
7. Finalize plan design/funding and expense criteria/investment policy.

The three major products that come out of this statement are general philosophy objectives, specific plan objectives, and flexible budget objectives.

General Philosophy Objectives

For general philosophy objectives, the following are typically the points we see in a flex plan:

- to attract and retain competent employees
- to enhance employee morale
- to provide incentives to use benefits wisely
- to assist in meeting employees' needs for protection and financial security
- to provide information that is easily understood by employees
- to offer tax-efficient compensation
- to allow employees to plan for their own financial needs

Specific Plan Objectives

For specific plan objectives, you review each benefit. When you focus on a certain benefit, you often overlook others. As an example, if you decide to implement, change, or redesign your life insurance and your disability coverage, most people will typically look at their life insurance plan and their disability plan independently and redesign each, but they will never consider their retirement plan(s), which may have death and disability provisions. By using a benefit-by-benefit approach, you will examine all the areas in your program to make sure that if areas overlap, you will include them and come up with an overall plan of benefits.

Flexible Benefit Objectives

When you get into flex benefit objectives, there is no question that program costs depend on the type of plan. Some plan sponsors spend hundreds of thousands of dollars in implementing a flex plan. You do not need to do that, but the cost does depend on the type of plan you design, the communication effort, and the record keeping/administrative requirement. Good estimates of cost factors can be developed. It will save surprises throughout the process.

Work Plan

Once you have gone through the benefit-by-benefit objectives and have received input from staff and employees, you are now ready to start designing the type of flex plan you want.

Make sure you come up with a work plan. It should consist of two areas: the scope of the project and the timing. The scope of the project is important; you need to list it out, make sure you have covered all your different areas, and then make sure that you keep it updated as you go through the process. The timing is also critical. If you are going to implement a full flex plan, make sure that you give yourself at least 12 to 18 months. You'll need it. If you go with a mini-flex, give yourself 6 to 12 months. Don't sell yourself short on time.

Project Organization and Management

Pick advisors who have done flex before. There's no sense paying for somebody's education. There are consulting firms in the United States that have experience in flex.

A steering committee is an excellent vehicle if it is comprised of a group of employees who represent a cross-section of the organization. This committee puts together the proposed benefit design and oversees all the different areas. These people are in an ideal situation. They can ''break the ice'' when they go back to talk to their peers about the types of things being considered during the design phase.

Make sure you take minutes at all the meetings because a lot of things will be discussed. Provide periodic reports to the CEO, the administrator, etc. You have already gone through your objective-setting process, and you have established a generic statement based on employee input, so you are simply updating them with these reports. This keeps top management involved throughout the entire process—and that really makes a big difference.

Pricing

One of the key aspects of a flexible benefit plan is that pricing/underwriting factors must be successfully applied to the various plans, but primarily to the health coverages. (This is not as significant a consideration under a flexible spending account, though still meaningful.)

During the plan development, underwriting and funding aspects of a flexible benefit plan should emphasize protection against adverse selection within the plan. While it is virtually impossible to totally prevent adverse selection in any type of plan that allows choice among types and levels of benefits, it is possible to minimize this occurrence. It should be emphasized that the benefit elections made by employees and the financial experience of each option must be closely monitored each year, and the appropriate changes in plan design and/or funding necessary to preserve the financial integrity of the plan must be instituted in subsequent years.

The first step is to have the entity performing the actuarial/underwriting services gather appropriate data. Examples of information needed follow:

A. *General Information*

1. organizational chart
2. major employee classifications (such as supervisory staff, hourly employees, part-time employees) and the estimated number of employees in each classification
3. employee handbook (summary plan description)
4. summary information on the plan sponsor
   - strategic plan
   - anticipated new services
   - related useful information
5. demographic information
   - part-time and full-time employees
   - male and female employees
   - employees with dependent families
   - age groupings of employees
   - compensation levels of employee groups
   - families with more than one person employed by the plan sponsor
6. samples of employee communication materials

B. *Benefit Plan Information*

1. summary plan descriptions and contracts/policies for all benefit plans (including separate books for different classifications where appropriate)
   - life insurance and AD&D
   - sick leave and paid time off
   - accident and sickness
   - long-term disability
   - short-term disability
   - vacation policy
   - holidays
   - health plan
   - health maintenance organization (HMO)
   - salary savings program
   - pension plan
   - discounts, recreational
   - other
2. pension plan actuarial valuation for latest two years
3. employee census data
   - identification (name and Social Security number)
   - date of hire
   - date of birth
   - hours worked, if available (scheduled hours)
   - compensation (rate or year to date)—both gross salary and W–2 salary, if different
   - sex

- number of dependents
- marital status
- classification code
- benefit participation (medical, life, AD&D, savings)
4. contribution rates and the last three years' worth of monthly claims experience information for each benefit plan

Once the data have been received, the actuary/underwriter can develop cost factors based on the plan design.

Examples of Plan Pricing

1. Assuming a plan sponsor has four modular health plans to choose from, the scenario shown in Table 37-3 can be drawn.

2. This example discusses a variety of potential medical plan options, construction of the employee budget, and establishment of the price of the option.

Consolidation. All indemnity plans are replaced with a single indemnity plan. Its salary-related deductible and other cost containment features, coupled with the benefit of consolidation, make this an attractive strategy.

The employee can choose between the indemnity plan and HMOs. The deductible of the indemnity plan is

Salary Level	Deductible
Less than $30,000	$100
$30,000–$40,000	$150
More than $40,000	$200

If the indemnity plan is fairly rich, it is not the intent of this strategy to move employees into substantially less valuable coverages.

Shifting. The indemnity plan(s) are retained, and a new indemnity option is added. It has a high salary-related deductible. This feature, coupled with other cost containment features, aims to move employees into less expensive alternatives. Option prices of existing indemnity plan(s) will be expensive.

The employee can choose among existing indemnity plan(s), HMO(s), and the new indemnity plan with its high deductible:

Salary Level	Deductible
Less than $30,000	$ 600
$30,000–$40,000	$ 800
More than $40,000	$1,000

For each of these strategies, you can look at different ways to establish a plan sponsor's budget and to set option prices:

Budget	Option Price
Same for everyone	Composite
Same for everyone	Family subsidy
Family subsidy	Composite
Salary subsidy	Composite
Salary subsidy	Family subsidy

Regardless of how pricing is done, it needs to be carefully thought out to avoid potential problems in future years.

Table 37-3 Flexible Benefit Plan Pricing

Plan	(1) Expected Enrollment (%)	(2) Relative Value (%)	(3) Explicit Antiselection (Census) (%)	(4) Implicit Antiselection (Health) (%)	(5) Self-Supporting Rates (%)
A	10%	86%	−15%	−19%	59.2%
B	25	100	− 5	− 6	89.3
C	25	108	4	2	114.6
D	40	114	4	7	126.9

(5) = (2) × (100% + (3)) × (100% + (4))

Plan	(6) Stand-Alone Plan Rates	(7) Flexible Benefit Plan Rates	(8) Monthly Employee Contribution	(9) Max. Annual Deductible Out-of-Pocket Expenses
A	$31.87	$21.94	−$11.15	$2,000
B	37.06	33.09	-0-	1,000
C	40.02	42.47	9.38	200
D	42.25	47.03	13.94	100

(6) = (2) × $37.06

(7) = (5) × $37.06 ($37.06 is the rate for Plan B as a stand-alone plan.)

Benefit Pricing Computer Models

Benefit Pricing Computer Models

Benefit pricing models that usually run on personal computers are now available for pricing medical and dental plan options.

When rating a flexible benefit program, in addition to the usual trend factors of inflation and utilization, the underwriter/actuary must be able to access the value of the different medical and dental options and determine the impact of changing employee election patterns. Typically, the information available is 12 to 24 months of paid claims data, two years of employee election patterns, and, if applicable, any changes in the design of the options. A pricing model provides (1) a framework in which to evaluate a plan's experience in incorporating election and plan changes, (2) a planning tool with which to estimate the impact of any proposed plan design changes, and a method by which to determine option prices. It does this by utilizing a statistical model to predict the distribution of medical and dental expenses. This distribution is then used to calculate the impact of different plan designs on paid claims and to determine what effect different employee election patterns will have on paid claims.

Pricing models usually consist of integrated worksheets. The worksheets are designed to review historical experience, utilizing data from prior years to the rating year; to determine the plan values for the rating year, relative to the prior year; and to assist the user in setting the flex prices and contribution strategy for the rating year. After specific data are input, the model calculates plan values at several participation points and then interpolates between those values based on the actual elections to determine the value for that year.

It is important to understand that determining what the price structure should be and the possible election outcomes is the role of the plan sponsor and its consultant. A benefit pricing computer model is designed to aid the plan sponsor and the consultant with those issues by providing a format with which to measure the impact of any assumption on the plan. It should be viewed as a tool, not as an absolute.

Benefit Order of Selection

One other area for consolidation is benefit selection, especially in a flexible benefit approach. In order to make sure all employees have funds available for their benefit selections, the plan sponsor may have to prioritize the benefits in order of selection. This selection order will need to be outlined in the communication vehicles and the enrollment form. Sample benefits in order of selection are

1. health (it is important that this be first)
2. disability
3. life/AD&D
4. dependent life
5. dependent care

If the employee has any funds remaining from the plan sponsor contribution and the salary reduction after selecting the five benefits, then the employee can allocate his/her remaining funds to a 401(k) plan and/or cash.

Critical Path

A critical path is an ideal tool for documenting everything you are going to have to do for a flex plan project. Pick a key employee as the overall coordinator, and make sure that employee keeps track of everything as you go through this process.

SUMMARY

To summarize, the most important thing to remember is that flex is a process. This process will continue as long as you have the flex plan in existence. You need to organize. As long as you keep it organized, flex is a logical process, and it will work. Simplify wherever you can, especially in communication. Remember that people are going to be looking at new concepts for the first time.

The three keys to success are these:

- Flex is a process.
- Keep the material simplified.
- Organize and plan.

Patricia Berger-Friedman

38

Current and Future Perspectives on Wellness

THE STATUS OF HEALTH CARE COSTS

Employers and employees have found, much to their dissatisfaction, that an increasing portion of the budget for the total compensation package has to be earmarked for health care instead of salary increases and other benefits, such as educational assistance programs.

Strong evidence links life styles to health risk and to consequent health care utilization and costs. Recent reports state that as much as 50 percent of health care expenditures could be eliminated by more healthy life styles. In addition, 75 percent of deaths annually have been linked to health-damaging behaviors, ranging from smoking and substance abuse to job-related stress and sedentary life styles ("Delaware Insurance Commissioner's Report" 1986, 13).

Life styles have a significant impact on personal health, as well as on the financial health of employers. A recent study by the U.S. Centers for Disease Control examining the 10 leading causes of death among Americans cited individual life style behaviors as contributing to 48.4 percent of all deaths ("Delaware Insurance Commissioner's Report" 1986, 13).

During the last decade, awareness of the relationship between life style and health has increased. To date, the results have been encouraging:

- a 20-percent decline over the last 15 to 18 years in the proportion of people who smoke, representing a 72-percent nonsmoking adult population
- a 12–22-percent reduction in the proportion of the population with high serum cholesterol

- a 10–15-percent reduction in the consumption of foods high in saturated fat and cholesterol
- a 100-percent increase in the proportion of adults who exercise regularly
- an increase of 36 percent, from 1983 to 1986, in the number of Americans who consistently use seat belts (Jensen 1987, 1)

In spite of these encouraging trends, the fact remains that health care costs have continued to escalate in alarming proportions. In 1987, Americans spent $500 billion on health care. This represents an increase of 9.8 percent over the preceding year and a total of 11 percent of the gross national product, up from 6 percent in 1965 (Kramon 1989).

More importantly, the proportion of health care expenses borne by private industry has increased even more dramatically, and there seems to be little hope of a reprieve in the near future. It is not unusual for benefits costs to approximate more than 4.3 percent of total compensation.

Since the early 1980s, employers have taken numerous initiatives aimed at reducing the increase in health care costs. A recent survey conducted by the Health Research Institute (1987, 5) revealed that 93.6 percent of the respondents used traditional short-term cost containment and cost-shifting measures, such as increased deductibles, copayments, and employee contributions to medical plan premiums.

More sophisticated measures have also been developed with the aim of reducing costs by controlling, monitoring, and redirecting health care utilization. These include, but are not limited to, preadmission, concurrent, and retrospective review; preadmission testing; second surgical opinion; outpatient surgery; birthing centers; discharge planning; home care; hospice care; and managed care programs, such as PPOs and HMOs.

Although these programs appeared to have stemmed the tide of increasing costs in the mid-1980s, health care costs have again begun to surge in the late 1980s. Average premium increases in 1987 and 1988 were in excess of 25 percent and are expected to hit 30 percent in 1989 (Kurtzman 1988). In 1989, spending on health care is expected to rise at a minimum of 8.2 percent, more than double the inflation rate (Kurtzman 1988).

The last decade has shown us that controlling the utilization of health care services and redirecting patients to less costly types of care have not had the result on health care costs that was originally projected. Advanced technology has contributed greatly to increasing health care costs. Other major reasons cited include, but are not limited to, the following:

- increased specialization within the medical profession
- increases in consumer demand
- malpractice costs
- aging of the population
- mismanagement of the health care system
- most importantly, providers' increased prices.

The evidence suggests that the insurance industry and employers need to go one step farther by controlling the utilization of health services through the promotion of wellness and healthy life styles among employees and their families. Employers are approaching wellness in two distinct ways. First is the traditional way of promoting wellness through employer-sponsored wellness programs. The second approach involves incentive rating structures in health insurance that reward healthy life styles. The remainder of this chapter will focus on these approaches.

BACKGROUND ON WELLNESS DEFINITIONS

Wellness is defined as a state of optimal physical and mental health and well-being. It encompasses much more than simply the absence of illness. Wellness fosters improved health and better performance and can best be achieved through health promotion, health protection, disease prevention, and social support (Jensen 1987, 2).

Health promotion should introduce and foster positive personal habits through education: weight management and nutrition, stress management, physical fitness, back care, smoking cessation, and medical education or self-care programs (Jensen 1987, 2).

Health protection is the legal and organizational policies and practices of occupational and environmental health and safety (Jensen 1987, 2). Also included are immunizations and screenings for such diseases as high blood pressure, heart disease, and cancer and disease prevention.

Social support is the emotional life and the bolstering that comes from peers, friends, and family (Jensen 1987, 2). Thus, to achieve wellness is to optimize well-being through the way individuals lead their lives.

Wellness can be promoted through formal and informal channels. Wellness programs that identify individuals at risk through health risk appraisals and follow-up programs tailored to the individual's needs represent a comprehensive and formalized approach to wellness promotion. Most current traditional health benefit plans are strictly treatment oriented. Benefit plan changes that reward health rather than sickness—such as reimbursement of well baby care, immunization expenses, and annual physicals on an age-adjusted schedule—are easy ways to informally promote the concept of wellness.

THE HISTORICAL PERSPECTIVE

Wellness is not a new concept in corporate America. The first work-site wellness program was sponsored by the National Cash Register Company in 1894. The company authorized morning and afternoon exercise breaks for employees and built a 325-acre park equipped with a gym (Jensen 1987, 2). Unfortunately, National Cash Register's commitment to wellness did not spread rapidly through corporate America. In fact, it has taken nearly a century for wellness to have a significant impact on the corporate attitude toward benefit planning.

Benefit plans mirror society's attitudes toward health. At the time National Cash Register was offering a wellness program, most life-threatening illnesses were acute, infectious diseases: pneumonia, influenza, and tuberculosis. During the early to mid-1900s, public and private health measures were focused on treating these traditional "killers." Little attention was paid to health promotion.

Since the 1950s, technology has developed to the point that these diseases no longer prove to be the threat they once were. However, we have created a society focused on cure, not prevention. As a result of changes in our Western life styles, smoking, sedentary office jobs, and drinking and driving have replaced these traditional "killers" with chronic long-term illness: cancer, heart disease, and hypertension.

In the past, diseases had a simple cause-and-effect relationship with various viruses and bacteria. Today's killers are not associated with any direct causal agent. They are linked to a number of risk factors—characteristics associated with the development of the top causes of death. These include

- improper diet, especially a high level of cholesterol which clogs the arteries
- obesity
- smoking
- high blood pressure

- lack of exercise
- stress
- alcoholism

The cost of unhealthy life styles includes, but is not limited to,

- *hypertension:* resulting in $2 billion in lost workdays per year and serving as the primary cause of hospitalization
- *stress:* costing employers as much as $17 million each year in productivity losses
- *smoking:* costing employers from $624 to $4,611 a year in illness, accidents, disability, and death (McCoy 1988, 278)

It seems clear that healthier life styles can prevent many of today's killer diseases and help control health care costs.

While it appears obvious that corporate America should focus its attention on this area, it has been a slow process. Not until the 1970s did many large employers draw attention to themselves and the corporate commitment to wellness with their extensive and costly physical fitness centers. Cost containment and health promotion were not the original impetus for these programs. Picking up on the boom created by the fitness craze at that time, corporate sponsors became involved looking to get in on the fun and to reinforce the national attitude and their own corporate image. Fitness and physical conditioning became synonymous with wellness.

Wellness, as we defined it earlier, however, encompasses more than physical fitness. In fact, a wellness program that is targeted only at physical fitness may be failing to meet the full needs of the employee population.

The success of a wellness program is dependent on the extent to which it is incorporated with the corporation's overall benefit planning strategy. The objectives should be reasonable and attainable within the commitment of the employer's financial resources, goals, and philosophies. Some of the more common reasons for initiating a wellness program were identified by a recent Washington Business Group on Health survey.

- to encourage individual responsibility for health
- to focus on high-risk populations
- to enhance corporate image
- to improve employee job satisfaction
- to reduce turnover
- most importantly, to control health care utilization and costs.

From a planning perspective, the most important aspects of a wellness program are

- to develop a program that identifies the health needs of employees and dependents
- to target the program to meet those needs

- to support employees and dependents who participate in the program
- to evaluate the program

An employer can use several mechanisms to develop a program that identifies its employees' health needs: examine medical claims and disability information, analyze employee risk factors, and survey employees' attitudes toward their own health. For example, an employer thinking about starting a weight loss program would need to know how many employees are overweight, how many think they are overweight, and how many are interested in participating.

A number of different tools can be used to assess employee attitudes and life styles. The most common is a variation of the health risk appraisal or health risk assessment. This tool provides employees with personal information about the manner in which their current behavior, habits, and health conditions may affect their future health. These assessments can be sophisticated and computerized surveys or simple checklists with questions about daily habits, such as eating, managing stress, and exercising.

Once employees' needs are identified, a responsive wellness program must be shaped. Surveys and utilization studies will help determine employees' attitudes and their level of knowledge about health care issues. The results should guide program development. The program should achieve one or more of the following goals:

- provide information about health
- foster awareness about health
- identify alternatives so employees can make informed decisions and change personal behaviors that affect their own mental and physical well-being

An easy approach to wellness promotion involves benefit plan design. Surprisingly, the increasing evidence of the value of wellness and the new employer interest in wellness have had little impact on benefit planning. Benefit plans have remained focused on the diagnosis and treatment of disease—not on its prevention. In the wake of rapidly increasing premium costs, employers are changing plans toward catastrophic prevention rather than first dollar coverage for primary care services. A typical benefit plan pays 100 percent for treatment in an emergency room, 80 percent for treatment in a doctor's office, and nothing for a vaccination or other preventive health measure.

RESULTS OF WORK–SITE WELLNESS PROGRAMS

Once a wellness program has been established, how are results measured? As with any business decision, among the major considerations are the cost to initiate a program and the end result in terms of company profits. Will the company recover its investment through reduced medical care costs and decreased absenteeism, or are the results nonquantifiable?

Until recently, the financial benefits of a work-site wellness program were qualitative, not quantitative. However, several recent studies—most notably, a recent survey by the federal Office of Disease Prevention and Health Promotion (ODPHP)—have made a strong argument in favor of the economic advantages of a work-site wellness program. The ODPHP survey reports general benefits, as well as measurable results, from five companies that instituted work-site wellness programs. The survey stated the following:

- 59.6 percent of the respondents claimed improved employee health because of nutrition education in a health promotion program.
- 57.5 percent claimed improved employee health because of high blood pressure control.
- 46.5 percent cited stress management activities as increasing worker productivity (Behrens and Weiss 1988, 3–5).

AT&T's Total Life Concept

The Total Life Concept (TLC) was designed initially to help employees cope with stress after the corporate divestiture. Based on the trends observed, if the program were to continue for the next decade, savings of $72 million from reduced heart attacks and $15 million from reduced cancer occurrences could be achieved. The program also had a sentinel effect on nonparticipants. These nonparticipants had improved perceptions of AT&T, even though they were not directly involved in the program (Behrens and Weiss 1988, 14).

Johnson & Johnson's Live for Life

Johnson & Johnson operated a pilot comprehensive health promotion program, tracking 11,406 employees in 18 states over a five-year period, starting in 1979. Program participants had half the increase in hospital costs of those employees who did not participate. Hospital costs for participants doubled over the study period, while costs for nonparticipants increased four times.

Annual savings were projected at $1 million if the program were offered to all J&J employees (Behrens and Weiss 1988, 16).

Blue Cross/Blue Shield of Indiana's Stay Alive and Well

Blue Cross/Blue Shield of Indiana's (BCBSI) Stay Alive and Well program for its own employees focuses on health risk identification and reduction. It was made available to all BCBSI's 2,400 employees, spouses, and retirees on a voluntary basis.

Results showed an average savings in health care claims per employee of $143.60, a savings to cost ratio of 1.45 to 1. A five-year evaluation of the program showed that although the number of medical claims for program participants was higher, claims were for low-cost routine care that, ultimately, resulted in lower overall health care costs (Behrens and Weiss 1988, 17).

INSURANCE PREMIUMS TIED TO LIFE STYLE

Another emerging approach to wellness promotion will not require a formal employer-sponsored program, but rather employer acceptance of new insurance products. There appears to be growing interest and support for tying health insurance premiums to life styles. Although this concept is not new to the life insurance industry, which has been offering premium reductions for nonsmokers, it has been viewed more cautiously by the health insurance industry.

The National Association of Insurance Commissioners (NAIC) charged its Health Promotion and Chemical Abuse Task Force with studying the legal and cost benefit issues related to health insurance incentives for minimizing health risk factors. In response, the task force's report focused on healthy life styles as a way to control costs (NAIC Proceedings, 660).

In addition, the NAIC developed a model regulation that establishes voluntary certificate programs whereby health insurance companies can offer financial incentives and disincentives to those who practice healthy life style behaviors. To date, only the Insurance Commissioner of Delaware has adopted a regulation similar to that of the NAIC. The regulation requires that

health insurance benefit programs offered in Delaware provide actuarially sound economic incentives and disincentives to enrollees in both employee group and direct pay plans. The incentives provided should be in the form of premium reductions and/or direct financial rebates to those individuals who validate participation in Certified Health Promotion Programs. The disincentives should be in the form of increased deductibles and/or co-payment schedules, set forth in the health care benefit program.

These incentives/disincentives would be applied to those health seeking behaviors having the greatest impact on health status such as (1) no smoking; (2) regular exercise; (3) weight maintenance; (4) blood pressure screening; (5) stress control; (6) non-abuse of drugs and (7) moderate alcohol consumption ("Delaware Insurance Commissioner's Report" 1986, 83).

The most convincing support for this type of legislation was provided by a recent study conducted by Control Data. The five-year study of 15,000 Control Data employees showed a strong correlation between life style and health care costs. The study concluded that health care costs for obese employees were 11 percent higher than those for nonobese employees and that workers who routinely failed to use seatbelts spent 54 percent more days in the hospital than did those who used seatbelts (Behrens and Weiss 1988, 10).

Control Data's study was based on information provided by its employees on seven factors: exercise, weight, smoking, hypertension, alcohol use, cholesterol level, and seatbelt use. Workers were then divided into high-risk, moderate-risk, and low-risk categories, based on standardized health risk profiles. The medical claims of persons in each category were tracked and compared.

The Control Data study is the first of several major research efforts. The Centers for Disease Control and the Carter Center of Emory University are in the early stages of a study comparing death and illness data to various life style factors.

Several insurance companies are offering group health insurance plans that are tied to employee life styles. Prudential is marketing a product called HealthSketch. The employer's cost to operate the program will be based in part on how their employees answer more than 50 questions on such issues as family health history, stress management, and seatbelt use (Kramon 1987). The Travelers has a discount health plan, currently available to groups of 100 or less employees, that deducts a percentage of the standard premium. To qualify, groups must first complete a questionnaire that includes questions on smoking, drinking, weight, and blood pressure. Greater weight is given to smoking in the rating process (Kramon 1987).

While the research and continually rising health care costs seem to argue in favor of these programs, there are legal, administrative, and ethical issues that still need to be addressed. These include, but are not limited to, the following:

- Some employees may view surveys of their health habits as an invasion of privacy.
- The monitoring of employee behavior after working hours may be impossible. For example, how does an employer or insurer verify that an employee is using his or her seatbelt?
- What criteria are used to select the risk factors or types of behavior that justify different rates?
- What about those cases in which the individual practices unhealthy behavior—e.g., smoking—but currently suffers no major ill effects?

- How do you factor in the life styles of children and spouses if not all family members practice the same behaviors?
- How do you ensure that individuals do not misrepresent themselves? ("Questions" 1983)

Hopefully, the ongoing research and further study in this area will answer some of these questions and encourage more insurance companies to develop and offer such products.

REFERENCES

Behrens, R., and J. Weiss. 1988. Worksite wellness media report research update, 1988. Washington, D.C.: Washington Business Group on Health, Office of Disease Prevention and Health Promotion, Public Health Service, U.S. Department of Health and Human Services.

Bly, J.L., R.C. Jones, and J.E. Richardson. 1986. Impact of worksite health promotion on health care costs and utilization. *Journal of the American Medical Association* 256:3235–40.

Delaware Insurance Commissioner's report on health care cost containment and quality enhancement. 1986. *NAIC proceedings*, vol. II. Executive summary. Kansas City, MO: NAIC.

Gettings, L., and N.E. Maddox. 1988. When health means wealth. *Training and Development Journal* 42, no. 4 (April): 81–85.

Health Research Institute. 1987. *Corporate wellness programs, 1987 biennial survey results, participant report.*

James, F.E. 1988. Study lays groundwork for tying health costs to workers' behavior. *Wall Street Journal*, 11 April.

Jensen, D.W. 1987. *Worksite illness, a new and practical approach to reducing health care costs.* Paramus, N.J.: Prentice-Hall Services.

Kramon, G. 1987. The wellness discount plans. *New York Times*, 22 September, sec. D.

———. 1989. Taking a scalpel to health costs. *New York Times*, 8 January, sec. 3.

Kurtzman, J. 1988. Prospects. *New York Times*, 27 November, sec. 3.

Levinson, D.N. 1988. Personal perspective, incentives for healthy lifestyles can pay off for workers, employers. *Business and Health* 5, no. 3 (January): 60.

McCoy, J. 1988. Wellness program can be a cost effective solution to soaring health costs. *Journal of Compensation and Benefits* 3, no. 5 (March-April): 278–84.

National Association of Insurance Commissioners. 1986. *NAIC proceedings*, vol. II. Kansas City, MO: NAIC, Health Promotion and Chemical Abuse (B) Task Force.

Participants' attitudes about health promotion reshape Control Data's Staywell Program. 1987. *Spencer's Research Reports* 5 (February): 33–36.

Questions concerning the feasibility of rating health insurance policies on the basis of individual life style. 1983. (September 7): 1–3.

Sciacca, J.P. 1987. Viewpoint—the worksite is the best place for health promotion. *Personnel Journal* 6, no. 11 (November): 42–49.

Daniel H. Mundt

Self-Funding Health Care Benefits

39

REASONS FOR BEING SELF-FUNDED

A very small publication, yet one that I think is extremely helpful, is *Considerations in Self-Insurance,* May 1987, published by the International Foundation and available from their Information Services. It outlines some of the considerations in self-funding.

When you look at cost savings, be aware that self-funded plans do not pay state taxes. This subject is addressed in "The Relationship Between ERISA Preemption and Federal and State-Mandated Benefits" by Timothy J. Parsons, which is another chapter in this book.

Parsons states that if you are buying stop-loss insurance, individual or aggregate, you may be in the position that what you have done is created a situation where you may be subject to state taxation on all claims that are paid if the excess carrier pays claims directly to the participants. There is a cost savings because you have no retention by the insurance company, and you are not involved in profit as far as the insurance company is concerned.

The second reason for being self-funded is the plan itself and the schedule of benefits can be more suited to the beneficiaries. You can add restrictions or benefits in ways that could not be done under state statutes and in most instances that you cannot negotiate with insurance companies.

Note: Reprinted with permission from *Employee Benefits Annual 1987: Proceedings of Annual Employee Benefits Conference, Vol. 29,* published by the International Foundation of Employee Benefit Plans. Statements or opinions expressed are those of the author and do not necessarily represent the views or positions of the International Foundation, its officers, directors, or staff.

The funds we work with regularly have discussions about what the benefits should be and the way the program should be developed, particularly in the area of cost containment. There is a tremendous amount of flexibility in self-funding not generally available in other programs.

Cost containment for self-funded programs as well as for other programs will be the key subject that we will face within the next several years. The self-funding approach gives the flexibility to achieve better cost containment.

Third, you have better control. You avoid the detailed state statutes with their restrictions. A Minnesota case is one of the leading cases involving the electrical workers' union. *St. Paul Electrical Workers Welfare Fund v. Markman,* found at 490 Fed. Suppl. 931 (D.C. Minn. 1980), holds that self-funded plans were exempt from state regulation and were governed by ERISA only.

Another case, *Farmer v. Montsanto,* 517 S.W. 2d 129, a Missouri Supreme Court decision in 1974, tells us self-funding is not insurance. Those types of decisions made it possible for self-funded plans to operate in a manner that the trustees felt was in the best interest of the fund and the participants.

Fourth, you get better involvement of the trustees and the plan participants. My observation is that it has become more and more apparent that trustees will not have any choice as to whether they are going to be involved or not. In fact, they will have to be involved. Two articles in this book by Marc Gertner tell you the same thing. Self-funding is the best way or the best mechanism for being involved.

Fifth, you increase your investment income because the fund—not the insurance company—holds its reserves. You no longer have a monthly premium payment that is going out. Rather, you are paying out your claims and your expenses on a pay-as-you-go basis.

HOW TO DEVELOP THE PLAN

When you are developing the plan, it is important to review the benefits of self-funding with the consultant, the attorney, and the administrator. Recently, I had an interesting experience with that when a fund in our area went through a conversion, or change, from an insured to a self-funded plan. About seven years ago a large national organization reviewed this plan. At that time, the plan was told it had what the consulting firm called an economic reserve. For six years I have been interested in seeing that fund go to a self-funded status.

One year ago the same consulting firm wrote a report that made no mention at all of the economic reserve, which had been the impediment in the first instance to that fund's being self-funded. After approximately one year's work, that fund is operating on a self-funded basis. Without any question, the experience that fund has had to date—and that it will have—will prove how intelligent they were to move from an insured status to a self-funded status.

Second, as you are developing a plan you should review the provisions that will need reviewing, revising, and drafting to allow for self-funding status.

Third, you should deal with the insurance carrier that you have. Again, this is an education in experience. In this same fund, as we were working toward trying to get the money back that the insurance company had been holding in reserve, the insurance company came back with the report indicating how much money there was.

Our law office looked at this, reviewed it with the consulting firm, and told the consulting firm that we felt there was an error in the insurance company's computations. The consulting firm looked at it again and told us they felt they were still correct. We told the firm that in our opinion it was not correct. About five or six hours later, the firm called back. They said they had checked this matter out and that the insurance company was approximately $70,000 short in the money they were going to remit to the fund.

When you are dealing with your previous carrier, it is critical to have people involved in getting your money back that has been held in reserve or for claim payments. These people must understand what they are doing because often large amounts of money are being held.

Fourth, you must review and complete for the trustees' approval the necessary amendments.

Next, you must notify the emloyers and the employees that the plan has a self-funding status. Our experience consistently has been that when the employees realize what is being done and the reason for it, they find this a better way to go than being insured. They participate, they understand, and they are intelligent. Once employers understand what you are trying to do, they find they are satisfied with this particular approach.

In most of our funds, the employers are permitted to participate in the plan itself. This makes the employers not only more aware of what is happening with the contributions, but also gets them involved in terms of what the plan itself is doing.

Also, you must look at the whole administrative matter with regard to using a third-party administrator or salaried administrators, and those who are working for the fund itself. We have worked with both and believe that either way is satisfactory and effective.

Then it is necessary to prepare a plan document, a summary plan description in plain language rather than in insurance language or legalese. In the State of Minnesota and in quite a number of other states in which we practice, the legislature has mandated that insurance policies cannot be written in legal language or insurance language. Rather, the policies must be written in plain language that the average person can understand.

Self-funded plan descriptions and summary plan descriptions should be written in "plain" language. Plan documents and the summary plan description should be an effort to tell people in a way that they can understand what their benefits are and how the plan operates.

Also, it is necessary to prepare plan rules and regulations. Those are important because once you get into the program, you will discover that changing those benefits, changing the plan rules and regulations to the detriment of the participants, could be a legal disaster for you. So, it is important that when you put your material together in the first instance, you have thought this through clearly with the trustees and understand what you intend to do with respect to various parts of the particular plan with which you are working.

Next, we will look at stop-loss insurance. It may surprise you that plans we operate with that are self-funded do not use stop-loss insurance. We have operated plans for as long as 10 and 12 years without any stop-loss insurance and have had no problem at all. We looked at this particular area several years ago; at that time we were told that we could buy stop-loss insurance without any problem.

But we found out that if we were going to buy stop-loss insurance, we had to agree to give the stop-loss carrier our group life insurance. We discovered by talking with the agent of our previous carrier in one of the plans that he believed the trustees would be making a major mistake if they gave up the life insurance. He pointed out that the number of claims we had in our group life as against the premium that had been collected was so small that we could generate over a period of time a reserve that we could protect ourselves with.

So we have operated a number of plans without any stop-loss insurance. At the beginning, we were a little nervous. But we have developed reserves and have used those as our basis for protecting the fund.

Also, you must decide who will pay the claims. Will you have someone in the fund office, a third-party administrator, or an insurance company under an administrative services only (ASO) contract? Trustees must look at these choices carefully and consider, in terms of their involvement, the time and effort they wish to put in and what the considerations are as to expenses.

EXPERTS NEEDED

When you are looking at self-funding, I believe the attorney, the accountant, and the investment manager are all important, but the most important person is the administrator. Unless you have good administration, you can forget about being successful with respect to self-funding. Trustees cannot possibly police the plan. Remember that the trustees are volunteers who come together usually once a month or every two or three months. They may have committees handling a particular area, but they are basically volunteers who are not there on a daily basis. You cannot afford to have the attorney there on a daily basis, and you certainly do not want to have the accountant there on a daily basis. So it falls to the lot of the person who is doing the administration to have judgment and intelligence enough not only to understand the plan, but also to administer it in a fair and even-handed manner.

A question often raised is whether the attorneys who are representing your fund are knowledgeable or not? Do they really understand what ERISA and COBRA mean, and the effects of the various legislation, and the impact of state-mandated benefits or federally mandated benefits?

A consultant can be helpful in some instances. You may want to consider having a doctor or dentist on retainer to give you advice on medical or dental problems. Acountants are important in terms of filing, auditing your fund, being certain you have been paying out the benefits, and receiving the contributions to which you are entitled.

One of our funds is fortunate to have someone who is a business agent and who has become an expert in electronics, data processing, and computer programming. Not only does the person understand the computer and the fund itself, but also he understands the participants and types of problems that are involved.

INVOLVEMENT OF TRUSTEES

What about the involvement of trustees? Trustees are fiduciaries in every sense of the word. I have listed some areas for involvement. One of the things that a representative from the Department of Labor emphasized in one of the other sessions was that he and the Department of Labor are going to look at the process that we follow.

One reason I like self-funding is that it makes the trustees get involved. They ask questions; they want to know. Is the cost they are paying for their legal representative a fair and reasonable cost?

As trustees, you have a responsibility. Those of you who are working as trustees, with attorneys, administrators, or consultants, should be sure you understand what you are getting for what you are paying. You cannot and do not have the privilege, whether you are insured or self-funded, to allow people to simply collect money from the fund without understanding what they are doing and being sure you are getting value for your services. You must watch each other. If a trustee strongly objects to an action, he or she should request the minutes to show that. Self-funding makes you get involved. I think the best thing that can happen to a health fund is for you to be involved.

You must watch the administration. What is being done? What is happening with claims? Are claims being processed properly? Are the correct amounts being paid? You should be pulling out 100 claims a year and giving them to a neutral third party who is informed and intelligent and who understands what is going on. Have those claims checked as to the validity of their payment against your plan. The review of claim payments is critical. When you are self-funded and you are operating and involved, you will understand what is being done.

Are you going to be an investment manager? No. But are you going to understand what the investment managers are doing? Yes. You must know what your investment managers are paying for brokerage commissions.

When you are self-funded, you *do* pay attention. You do not have the luxury of saying that the insurance company is taking care of all those problems, and you are responsible for understanding what is being done with your investment.

You participate in the meetings and the minutes. There is no such thing as a stupid question, only stupid answers. For years I taught school at the University of Minnesota in Duluth. I always enjoyed the interchange with the students who asked questions because it gave me an opportunity to help them learn and understand. That is what should go on in the trust meetings. When you are self-funded, you will be involved.

We have to act as trustees, not as representatives of union or management. Sometimes that is hard to do. All of us who have sat at the bargaining table and then sat in trust agreement know how difficult that can be.

We are involved in handling appeals and sometimes referring these matters to either medical or dental people who are consultants. Those are important matters.

In 1984, at the International Foundation annual conference in Orlando, Florida, I presented a paper on a model appeals procedure. If you do not have an appeals procedure in your particular fund, you should either get that material or something comparable to it from the International Foundation of Employee Benefit Plans. Then you should study the information. Appeals are mandatory under federal law so you should understand what you are doing.

You must stay abreast of developments and changes and comply with the law. Again, when you are self-funded, you are directly involved, and you tend to stay more up to date or informed than you do when you are letting somebody else take the responsibility for the fund and the payment of the claims.

Liability coverage for fiduciaries is becoming a serious matter. The Department of Labor requires that a summary annual report be sent to all participants to describe the plan.

Consider using the summary annual report as a public relations document to tell the participants how well the program is operating. Too many times, we allow somebody to write that in a very sterile manner, one that does nothing to promote the fund or tell people what their benefits are.

GOVERNMENT INVOLVEMENT

Next is the matter of government involvement. You have reporting requirements, and you must determine whom the trustees are going to charge with the responsibility for making the federal filings and determine that the filings are being made as required.

You have the whole matter of bonding, errors, and omissions. You have the whole subject of state and federal regulations and pre-emption questions. It is a very, very important subject for self-funded plans. For example, in Minnesota and a number of other states that we are in, there are mandated benefits that self-funded, jointly administered plans under ERISA do not comply with. With our self-funded programs, we regard ourselves as being regulated solely under federal law by ERISA. Although we receive inquiries from a state almost every year on one or more funds because we are self-funded, we have taken the position consistently and have maintained that we are not subject to any state-mandated benefits or regulations.

We are all concerned about the effects of COBRA and its administration.

Also, I have noted the summary annual report, the summary plan description update, and the future with respect to legislation and lobbying efforts.

With all the funds we work for, we are currently greatly involved with cost considerations. We are looking at plan design. What kinds of benefits are we providing to our people? What have we done with respect to those particular areas?

One of the tremendous advantages about self-funding is that you do not have to sit and argue with the insurance company about what the plan design will be. Those of you who are trustees and plan administrators or consultants have a feel for the people who are participants in that plan. You understand what their needs are. You have a perception of what kinds of benefits will best serve the needs of the participant in that plan. For example, in some of the plans, we look at things such as X-ray diagnostic lab work. And where before we had been at $50 or $100, we increased it to $300 or $500 to encourage people to get attention not in a hospital setting, but in outpatient facilities.

It is important for us to watch our administrative expenses for the administration itself and for the experts. The Department of Labor has told us they will look at what the trustees have done and what we, who are the experts, are doing. They will evaluate whether or not you, the trustees, have done some type of comparison shopping in obtaining the experts, what kind of services you are getting, and whether you are aware of what your cost is in terms of the benefits the fund receives from the experts.

My experience consistently is that when people are self-funded, they are more involved in each one of these areas. I have become convinced that the people who are there as the business representatives and those who are there as the union representatives and who put on the trustees' hat can all understand the various legal requirements. They might not understand this in a technical sense of being prepared to write a brief or go to court, but they understand in the sense of being willing to spend the time so they know what the requirements are and then can proceed to protect the fund and the participants by their active involvement.

COST CONSIDERATIONS

The area of benefits paid out is of obvious concern. We have found that it is important in this area to be sure we are involved with claims utilization review and monitoring by a line of coverage. Several of our funds have a printout showing the trustees on a quarterly basis exactly what is happening by line of coverage utilization.

Cases that are a problem area and appeal cases that require the full action of the board of trustees are best handled by a self-funded plan. There are many ramifications to some of these cases. We have had difficult cases that had we turned them over to an insurance company, it could have created major problems. Instead, they were resolved by the board of trustees after a thorough discussion and an interested participation by the plan administrator.

Obviously, flexibility with regard to new medical techniques is important. We are all concerned about AIDS, its expense, and its cost.

Recently, someone indicated that the cost was approximately $100,000 per AIDS case. It is important to be consistent and evenhanded in dealing with the matter of claims.

Also, under cost considerations, the collection of employer contributions is important. You should have a formal written delinquency procedure because that type of procedure is noted by the Department of Labor when it audits the fund. We use field auditing of the employers. I believe it is unfair competition for one employer to avoid making payments to the fund. All employers should be treated alike. It is amazing that you need to audit only a few employers to get an effect on all employers. It is not fair to employees for their claims to be either held up or denied.

We have found ourselves in the position of saying that field auditing is important. Again, in our experience, it only takes a few audits a year to send a message to the contributing employers that they must keep up with their particular area of contribution.

Finally, you should look at the long-term cost of retired employee benefits. In this area, self-funded plans have a tremendous advantage over insured plans. I do not know all the answers with respect to the area of retiree benefits and costs.

I believe there is a great difference of opinion between those who are younger and who are participating in making contributions as against those who have retired and who have paid money in for a long period of time to a fund. In many instances, those retirees feel the necessity of having the right to continue to receive benefits even if on some limited basis.

Also, I suggest that you participate in the International Foundation for Employee Benefit Plans. For a long time, I have felt that it is critical and essential for any of us connected with these funds to have an ongoing education. The funds that we have do participate and make an effort to obtain an up-to-date understanding of what it means to be an involved trustee.

CONCLUSION

I have listed some reasons why I feel that if you are not self-funded, you should give serious consideration to it.

1. You have a fiduciary responsibility to look at self-funding. You do not have any choice in the matter. In fact, if the history of most of the funds that have gone to self-funding is favorable and saves money, then fiduciary responsibility says you should look seriously at self-funding your group health benefits.
2. Self-funding is the best vehicle for controlling costs at a time when costs are going to continue to escalate.
3. In the field of benefit schedules, self-funding gives you more flexibility with respect to the schedule of benefits for participants and the retirees.
4. Payments for health care benefits constitute large amounts for employers and employees. This is critical for the employees, their members, and their participants. I believe that the self-funded approach gives the best opportunity to get a good schedule of benefits at a cost the employers can afford.
5. As more responsibility is shifted from the government sector to private plans, self-funding will become more important.
6. Finally, I believe that the self-funded plan operated by a committee of trustees can provide benefits better and more cheaply than can insured plans.

Anthony J. Gajda

Long-Term Care Insurance

40

Long-term care insurance appears to be today's most widely discussed new benefit.

Long-term care has evoked a great deal of interest among employee benefits personnel, human resources personnel, and legislators in Washington for a variety of reasons.

In order to understand long-term care as an employee benefit, it is first necessary to understand why long-term care is an issue today. It is then necessary to understand the factors and elements that must be considered in designing a long-term care employee benefit plan. Finally, it is necessary to understand how a long-term care benefit plan should be implemented.

WHY NOW?

Long-term care is an issue today for a variety of reasons. First, the size and the composition of the work force have been changing during the past several decades, and this has had an important effect on long-term care.

1. As more and more women enter the work force, they are no longer available to care for elderly relatives and parents.

Note: Reprinted with permission from Vol. 14, No. 1, March 1989 *Employee Benefits Journal*, published by the International Foundation of Employee Benefit Plans. Statements or opinions expressed in this article are those of the author and do not necessarily represent the views or positions of the International Foundation, its officers, directors, or staff.

2. As families become smaller, there are fewer and fewer children available to take care of elderly relatives and parents.
3. As families become more mobile, distances of as much as 3,000 miles may separate a child from a parent or aged relative who requires care.

As the health care system becomes more and more successful in treating acute health care conditions, such as heart disease, stroke, cancer, etc., people will live longer and thus have more opportunities to acquire the debilitating chronic conditions that require long-term care.

More and more people are becoming aware of the extraordinary costs of long-term care.[1] For example, in New York City one very fine nursing home charges $65,000 for inpatient care. Even the commonly cited cost of $22,000 a year for nursing home care as the average cost in this country is based on Medicare reimbursement rates for nursing homes, which are typically below the prevailing costs of nursing homes that are charged to self-paying patients. In fact, it's quite reasonable to think of the average cost of a nursing home in the United States as about $35,000 a year. When one considers that the typical nursing home confinement is approximately two years, then the total cost of the nursing home confinement today is about $70,000.

But the real catalyst in the discussion and the attention that long-term care is receiving is Department of Health and Human Services Secretary Otis Bowen.

In October 1986, Secretary Bowen released a report on catastrophic health care costs.[2] That report cited the virtual absence of insurance for long-term care costs—either skilled nursing home care, custodial care or home health care—and the need to educate the public about the need for protection against expenses running as high as $70,000 to $100,000 for one confinement. Foremost among Secretary Bowen's recommendations were that the public be educated about costs and that both the private and the public sector undertake efforts to find ways of protecting the public against these extraordinary costs.

Most long-term care costs are currently paid by personal expenditures or Medicaid. Other government and private programs account for about 9 percent of total payments for nursing home costs today. (See Table 40-1.)

Because of the size and magnitude of nursing home costs, 70 percent of single persons become impoverished within three months of their confinement to a nursing home.[3]

When the patient has a spouse, 50 percent of those patients become impoverished within six months of being confined to a nursing home.[4]

Most elderly persons are simply not aware that they are at risk for expenses that can literally use up a lifetime's savings in a mere 3 or 6 or 9 or 12 months.

Survey after survey has shown that the elderly believe that nursing home costs are covered either by Medicare, which they are not; by their retiree medical plans, which they are not; or by their supplemental Medicare or Medigap policies, which they are not.

The risk of an elderly person's being confined to a nursing home increases at a very, very rapid rate after age 65. As Table 40-2 shows, between age 65 and age 74, the risk of being confined to a nursing home is 1 in 100. Between ages 75 and 84, that risk increases to 7 in 100, and at and after age 85, that risk increases to 23 in 100.

As a nation, we can expect for the demand for long-term care to increase significantly through the end of this century.

Table 40-3 shows that the population age 65 and over will increase by 80 percent between the year 1980 and the year 2000, from 25 million to 45 million. Table 40-3 also shows that the population age 85 and over will increase at an even faster rate, from 2.2 million in 1980 to 5.6 million in 2000.

Table 40-1 Source of Payment for Nursing Home Expenses

Source of Payment	Portion of Nursing Home Expenses
Personal Expenditure	50%
Medicaid	41
Other Government	4
Medicare	2
Private Insurance	2
Miscellaneous	1
TOTAL	100%

Source: "Long-Term Fact Sheet," Health Insurance Association of America; "Task Force on Long-Term Care Policies," U.S. Department of Health and Human Services.

Table 40-2 Probability of Nursing Home Confinement

Age	Probability of Confinement
65–74	1%
75–84	7%
85 and Over	23%

Source: "Long-Term Fact Sheet," Health Insurance Association of America; "Task Force on Long-Term Care Policies," U.S. Department of Health and Human Services.

Table 40-3 Selected Population Data

Age 65 and Over	
1980	25 million
1990	38 million
2000	45 million
Age 85 and Over	
1980	2.2 million
1990	3.5 million
2000	5.6 million

Source: U.S. Census Bureau, "Projections of the Population in the U.S." May 1984; Series P25, No. 952.

This growth in the aged population of the United States probably reflects success in three areas.

1. Medicare
2. Acute health care
3. Social Security

Medicare, which was created in 1965, made health care available to approximately 20 million aged persons at that time. Medicare provides health care to those over age 65, and it can reasonably be concluded that the availability of health care has helped to lengthen the lives of the aged.

Successes in the acute health care area with pacemakers, bypass surgery, cancer chemotherapy, trauma, etc., have been successes against diseases and conditions which, in the past, would have resulted in death.

Social Security has increased the income of the elderly significantly over the past several decades, and the simple availability of enough money to buy food, to pay for housing, etc., has also contributed to the increasing life expectancy of the elderly in this country.

There will be more successes in treating acute health care conditions. Even greater strides will be made against cancer, heart disease, and stroke. And the improvement of life styles generally throughout the U.S. populace will contribute to longer life.

But, even without any further acute health care successes, the growth in the population of the aged in the United States is going to significantly increase the demand for long-term care services.

Applying the utilization rates shown in Table 40-2 to the population data shown in Table 40-3 demonstrates that the demand for nursing home care will increase by about 80 percent between the year 1980 and the year 2000.

With respect to the supply of nursing home beds, the future is not bright.

In a report of the Department of Health and Human Services Task Force on Long-Term Care Insurance, the supply of nursing home beds in this country was estimated to be 1.6 million. That same report revealed that there was a shortage of approximately 250,000 nursing home beds.[5] More recently, the Brookings Institution published a report on long-term care and reported that the occupancy rate of nursing homes in the United States is 92 percent.[6] This seeming inconsistency is explained by the fact that nursing home beds are simply not distributed optimally throughout the United States.

Many nursing home beds are located in areas of little demand while areas of high demand have few beds. While the U.S. average of nursing home beds per 1,000 persons aged 65 and over is 54.8, the supply ranges from 18.7 in New Mexico and 23.7 in Florida to 87.8 in Nebraska and 95.4 in Iowa.

Clearly the expected increases in demand for nursing home care together with the current shortage of nursing home beds suggest that the cost of nursing home care will increase at a rapid rate throughout the balance of this century. As nursing home costs increase, the horror stories that appear in the media about the impoverishment of people who have worked long lifetimes and expected to retire with dignity, security, and independence but who have unfortunately acquired a chronic debilitating disease that requires long-term care and thus consumes that patient's entire life savings will grow. As those stories grow in number and in severity, there will be increasing attention paid to ways by which the aged can protect themselves from these kinds of expenses.

LONG-TERM CARE INSURANCE

In designing a long-term care insurance program, there are more issues to be dealt with than are found in health insurance plans, medical insurance plans, or other typical group insurance plans.

Those issues include

1. coverage
2. funding method
3. plan design
4. pricing strategy
5. utilization management
6. convertibility/renewability

Coverage

A typical employee benefit plan provides benefits to the employee or retiree, the employee's or retiree's spouse, and the employee's or retiree's children. In a long-term care pro-

gram, the possible classes of coverage also include parents of the employee and parents of the employee's spouse, as well as retirees and spouses of retirees.

Funding Method

With respect to funding long-term care insurance programs, there are basically three approaches that can be considered.

First, the plan can be an employee-pay-all program, which is the arrangement in all existing group long-term care insurance programs. In such a program, the employee pays 100 percent of the premiums due, usually via payroll deduction. In some instances when spouses, parents, and parents-in-law are covered, the plan sponsor arranges for premium bills to be sent to the employee's home.

Second, the employer can pay all or part of the long-term care insurance premium. However, because of gray areas in the Internal Revenue Code, it is not clear that an employer could take a deduction for any payments toward long-term care insurance, and consequently employers are not contributing to such programs at this time.

Third, Section 125 of the Internal Revenue Code may be a vehicle for employees to make contributions to a long-term care insurance program. While one sponsor of a group long-term care insurance program has arranged for employees to pay required premiums through the vehicle of a Section 125 salary reduction plan, it is not clear from the Internal Revenue Code that such an arrangement will be treated as an allowable deduction. The principal obstacle to either an employer contribution or employees' contributions via Section 125 is that long-term care and long-term care insurance are not addressed in the Internal Revenue Code. In other words, those sections of the Internal Revenue Code that describe the employee benefits for which an employer will receive a tax deduction do not include long-term care, long-term care benefits, or long-term care insurance.

Because of the interest by some insurance companies and some employers, requests have been made to the Internal Revenue Service for private letter rulings regarding the treatment of long-term care as an employee benefit. In addition, the American Council on Life Insurance and the Health Insurance Association of America have drafted legislation that, among other things, would result in the treatment of long-term care and long-term care insurance as deductible benefits for tax purposes.

Plan Design

One of the most rapidly evolving long-term insurance program issues is that of plan design. The variety of plan design issues can be grouped into six classes. Each of those classes is described below.

1. *State Minimum Standards*. Many states have regulated long-term care insurance for years, if not decades. While

regulation has been aimed at individual long-term care insurance plans, some states have already adopted the model long-term care insurance regulatory language promulgated by the NAIC (National Association of Insurance Commissioners). It is important to ensure that any plan design for a group long-term care insurance program recognizes the minimum standards of insurance in those states in which such insurance is regulated.

2. *Scope.* A long-term care insurance program can include care in a skilled nursing facility and care in a health-related or a custodial care facility. Long-term care insurance can also include home health care, adult day care, social health maintenance organizations, payments to a continuing care retirement community, etc. The preferred plan design will include each of these types and modalities of long-term care services. The broader the scope of service, the less likely it is that a patient will use an inappropriate long-term care service in order to receive benefits.

3. *Single Option/Multi Option.* A decision must be reached by the employer designing the plan with regard to the number of options that will be made available in a long-term care insurance program. The employer could offer a single level of long-term care insurance benefits, or the employer could offer two or more levels of long-term care insurance benefits. For example, the employer might offer a $100-a-day nursing home benefit with a $50-a-day home health care benefit. Or the employer might offer a choice of a $100-a-day nursing home benefit, a $75-a-day nursing home benefit, or a $50-a-day nursing home benefit with home health care benefits equal to one-half of the benefit paid for nursing home care.

4. *Benefit Eligibility.* There are two types of eligibility that must be decided in a long-term care insurance program. First, the eligibility for participation can be made available to all incumbent employees or all retirees under a certain age. Eligibility for participation can be limited by medical underwriting and/or limitations or exclusions of pre-existing conditions.

   Second, the eligibility for benefit payment usually requires a deductible expressed either as days of nursing home confinement or as days of home health care. A typical long-term care insurance program would be made available to incumbent employees without medical underwriting but with a pre-existing conditions limitation and a requirement that the employee pay for the first 100 days of nursing home confinement or the first 100 days of home health care services before the insurance program would begin to pay benefits.

5. *Benefit Maximums.* In all of the plan designs to date, the maximum benefits payable are expressed either as a number of days of benefit payment or as a dollar amount; for example, 1,460 days of benefits, or as a dollar amount—for example, $146,000. In the instance of a maximum expressed as days, that maximum can easily

be converted into a dollar maximum, and in the instance of a maximum expressed in dollars, that can easily be converted into a maximum expressed in days.

6. *Inflation Protection.* The earlier discussion about the risks and costs of long-term care describes conditions in both the demand and the supply of long-term care health services that suggest that the cost of those services will be subject to high inflation at least through the end of this century. Consequently, in the design of a long-term care insurance program some consideration must be given to whether or not an explicit inflation escalator will be contained in the plan. For example, the plan may provide that the benefits will increase by 3 percent per year in response to expected inflation. While this is the preferred design, it is also a very expensive design. An alternative approach would permit those employees who elect to participate in the plan to re-enroll every several years and thereby purchase new benefits in response to the inflation that occurred in the years between re-enrollments. If the re-enrollment approach is used, then employees would enroll initially at a premium rate based on their age at that time and then could buy successive layers of additional protection where the premium would be based on their age at the time they elected each successive layer of additional protection.

Pricing Strategy

The employer who is designing and offering a long-term care insurance program must also make a decision about premium pricing strategy. All long-term care insurance programs to date have contained premium rates that are based on the age of the covered person at the time coverage is elected. (This will be referred to as an entry age pricing strategy.) A second pricing strategy is one which would require a level premium from all participants regardless of their attained age.

The primary concern in the design of a long-term care insurance program is to avoid adverse selection (the condition where those persons who will likely use the benefit elect the coverage in numbers disproportionate to their numbers in the entire eligible population). An entry age pricing strategy is very much preferred because premium rates based on age will minimize selection costs: younger employees who have a lower risk of long-term care services will have a lower premium, while older employees and retirees who have a much higher risk of long-term care services will have a much higher premium.

If a level premium is charged, then that level premium would be based on the mix of older and younger ages in the eligible population. Consequently, older employees would find the premium rate charged for the long-term care insurance plan to be very attractive, while younger employees would find the premium rates very unattractive. The result would be a disproportionate enrollment of older employees who are more likely to require long-term care services. This dynamic would eventually lead to a spiraling of long-term care insurance costs and probably to a point where the plan would have to be terminated because of the rapid increase in premium rates.

Utilization Management

Utilization management has been found to be very successful in eliminating and reducing unnecessary and inappropriate acute health care services. Unfortunately, the evidence to date in long-term care is that utilization management will not necessarily reduce utilization. Because a large amount of long-term care services is now provided informally by relatives and friends, a long-term care insurance program would probably lead to a substitution of paid health care services for informal, unpaid health care services. Utilization review and utilization management, indeed, might even lead to an increase in costs because of the substitution of more professional health care services for the less professional, informal services that may be available today.

Further, the cost difference between inpatient and outpatient care for acute health conditions can be substantial: $700 to $1,000 or more per day of inpatient care versus $40 to $70 for home health care. Yet, the cost difference between inpatient and outpatient care for long-term care services is much smaller: $70 to $120 or more per day for confinement care versus $40 to $70 per day for home health care. The much smaller savings that can be produced by shifting long-term care from an inpatient setting to an outpatient setting sharply reduces the opportunity for savings through utilization management.

Convertibility/Renewability

Finally, a plan sponsor must address the issues of renewability and convertibility. Renewability means that premium rates cannot be raised for individual participants or specific classes of participants; renewability means that premium rates if increased must be increased for all persons in a particular class. Convertibility means that the employee has the right to continue to pay directly for long-term care insurance if the employee leaves employment. To date, the long-term care insurance programs contain guaranteed renewability provisions, and all provide for the direct payment of long-term care insurance premiums by employees who are no longer eligible for the plan through their employer.

THE IMPLEMENTATION OF A LONG-TERM CARE BENEFIT PLAN

The evaluation of the feasibility, the design, and the implementation of a flexible benefit plan involves the same principles as the evaluation of the feasibility, the design, and the implementation of any benefit plan. However, there is a different emphasis in a long-term care plan.

Following are the two major steps in the offering of a long-term care benefit plan to employees:

1. feasibility
   - planning
   - demand analysis
   - preliminary design
2. implementation
   - final design
   - carrier selection
   - communication and enrollment

Planning

The necessary first step at the planning stage is to establish the objectives for the long-term care benefit plan.

Objectives will include such items as the purpose for offering the long-term care plan; the group of employees, retirees, and dependents to whom the plan will be offered; the level of benefits and scope of the plan; the short-term and long-term cost considerations; etc.

Objective setting is the point at which the commitment of the employer must be established. Long-term care, unlike other benefits, requires a great deal of education of employees so that they will understand the risks that they face. If a long-term care benefit plan is going to be successful, it is essential that senior and executive management be solidly behind the program.

It is also essential that benefits managers be behind the plan. Benefits managers will be responsible for the education and communication and will have to be, if not enthusiastic, at least supportive of the concept of long-term care insurance.

During the planning stage it is necessary to evaluate existing programs offered by insurance carriers. This is particularly important at this time because of the rapidly evolving nature of long-term care insurance products that are being offered by insurance carriers.

Finally, there is a need to examine the demographics of the population to whom the benefits will be offered. If a company is relatively young with a relatively young work force and no retirees, the education and communication elements of the long-term care benefit plan will be different from the education and communication elements of a long-term care benefit plan offered in an older company with an older work force and a large number of retirees. Demographic analysis should also include an estimate of the number of spouses, parents, and parents-in-law who will be offered the plan.

Demand Analysis

While estimates should, by this point, have been made about the reception of a long-term care benefits plan by the work force, it is now necessary to start quantifying employee attitudes toward a long-term care benefits plan.

Traditionally, focus groups and questionnaire surveys are used to gain an understanding of employees' attitudes toward benefits and toward benefit needs. In the instance of long-term care, focus groups and questionnaire surveys should be used, but must be augmented by a significant education element.

It does little good to query employees about their demand for long-term care insurance if employees are not aware of the risks that they face from long-term care expenses. Consequently, focus group sessions should begin with a description of long-term care, the risks of long-term care, and the costs of long-term care. This should include an explanation of the fact that long-term care expenses are not covered by the employee benefit plan, Medicare, or supplemental Medicare policies.

The focus groups should be used in the traditional fashion, i.e., as a basis for preparing a questionnaire survey of all employees. Focus group participants should be selected to represent the different demographic groups among the work force and should be used to test understanding of long-term care as well as to design questions about long-term care that will be easily understood by employees.

The questionnaire survey is then used to gather information from all employees.

Finally, a very successful technique for gathering an understanding of how employees will receive a long-term care benefits plan is to conduct mock enrollments.

A mock enrollment is just what it says: employees are gathered together and given a presentation of the long-term care benefits plan; are given an opportunity to ask questions about the long-term care benefits plan; and are then asked to complete an enrollment form on which they either elect long-term coverage or decline long-term coverage. The mock enrollment is a very effective means for gauging the receptivity of employees to the long-term care benefits plan.

Preliminary Design

At this stage in the project a great deal of information will have been gathered.

1. the objectives of management in offering a long-term care benefits plan
2. a survey of available insurance products in the market
3. a quantitative analysis of the demographics of the work force
4. the level of understanding of long-term care by the work force
5. estimates of the enrollment participation level from the mock enrollments

On the basis of this information a preliminary long-term care benefits plan design is constructed. The preliminary design will be the basis for examining the administration requirements, i.e., payroll and personnel systems and pro-

cedures that will have to be modified if a long-term care benefit plan is offered. The preliminary design will also be used to develop a communications strategy.

Final Design

After the administration requirements associated with a long-term care benefits plan have been identified, it may be necessary to modify the design in some fashion to accommodate existing administrative systems. Additionally the pricing of the long-term care benefits plan will have to be established.

Carrier Selection

After the final plan design has been established, specifications for that design are submitted to insurance carriers, and proposals are requested.

It must be kept in mind that long-term care insurance is still in its infancy. Of those carriers that are now offering long-term care insurance products, each is emphasizing a different aspect of long-term insurance. Consequently, it is unlikely that carriers that submit proposals for the long-term care benefits plan will be proposing identical insurance arrangements. With other employee benefits, the fact that there are differences in the insurance products proposed by carriers can be problematical. With long-term care insurance though, those differences may in fact simplify the task of carrier selection. For example: if the plan design requires some type of cash value or paid-up or vested benefit, then those carriers that do not offer such a product can be immediately disregarded.

After the long-term care insurance proposals are received, it is essential that meetings be held with the proposing insurance carriers in order to negotiate very clearly the terms of their proposals. Because long-term care insurance is a relatively new product, insurance carriers very often are stepping very slowly but are willing to discuss variations in coverage terms, in benefit terms, in policy accounting, etc.

This willingness of insurance carriers to discuss the terms and provisions of their proposals can allow an employer to tailor the long-term care benefits plan more closely to the needs of employees.

While it may not seem important in the first year of a long-term care plan, the employer should negotiate the types of management information reports that will be supplied by the insurance carrier. These management information reports can be used to monitor the emerging experience of the plan, to highlight any weaknesses in the plan, and to develop a better sense of the long-term cost of the plan.

Communication and Enrollment

The communication program can govern the success or failure of the long-term care benefits plan. An effective communication program will build anticipation, step by step, toward the announcement of the plan. An effective communication program will educate employees about long-term care expenses.

While the employer who is designing the communication program must educate employees about long-term care, the employer must be equally cautious about overloading employees with information. A long-term care benefit plan is an entirely new benefit for employees, and the education/communication program should be one that delivers materials in a phased basis with incremental additions to the information distributed.

SUMMARY

Long-term care is a relatively new employee benefit issue and virtually unheard of two years ago. Long-term care plans have been implemented in a handful of companies and government retirement systems.

Long-term care has become an employee benefits issue because of the growing awareness of the risks of long-term care to the elderly and the costs of long-term care.

Long-term care benefit plans provide a means for protecting against the expenses of long-term care.

While the design and implementation of a long-term care benefit plan involve the same general principles as the design and implementation of any employee benefit plan, there is a basic difference. That difference lies in the fact that employees must be educated about the risks and expenses of long-term care so that employees can make informed judgments about whether to participate in an employer-sponsored long-term care benefit plan.

NOTES

1. Bowen, Otis. *Catastrophic Medical Care*. Washington, D.C.: Department of Health and Human Services, October 1986.

2. Ibid.

3. William M. Mercer Meidinger Hansen Incorporated. *Long-Term Care: The Newest Employee Benefit*. San Francisco, CA: author, 1988: 3.

4. Gajda, Anthony J. "Long-Term Care: Who'll Pay the Bills," *Personnel* (November 1988): 62.

5. U.S. Department of Health and Human Services. "Report to the Secretary by the Task Force on Long-Term Care Policies." Washington, D.C.: author, September 21, 1987.

6. Rivlin, Alice W., and Wiener, Joshua M. *Caring for the Elderly*. Washington, D.C.: Brookings Institute, 1988.

Thomas J. Welling

After Tax Reform: Retirement Plans in Not-for-Profit Institutions

41

The days of tailor-made retirement and tax-deferred investment plans for the senior staff at not-for profit institutions are gone, probably forever. One of the objectives of the Tax Reform Act of 1986 (TRA–86) was to require even-handed treatment of high-paid, middle-income, and low-paid employees. Although one could argue that the Congress was guilty of overkill, it would be difficult to argue that this objective was not met. Following TRA–86, retirement plans can no longer be used as a device for providing additional tax-deferred compensation for a select group of high-paid employees.

However, TRA–86 went well beyond "leveling out" the retirement benefits of employees at all salary levels. It created a series of new restrictions and excise taxes which were intended, as one pundit noted, to make sure that retirement benefits fall within the guidelines of "not too soon, not too late and not too much." The remainder of this chapter is devoted to providing an understanding of where we were before TRA–86 and what we face in the post–tax reform world of retirement plans in not-for-profit institutions, with special attention to Section 403(b) tax-sheltered annuities.[1]

BACKGROUND

For smaller-size institutions, prior to tax reform, it was not unusual for nonunion employees to be in a defined benefit pension plan, while the employer also contributed to a tax-sheltered annuity (TSA) plan for a few high-paid employees. At some large institutions, the defined benefit plan very often included only lower-paid employees, while employer contributions to the TSA plan provided basic retirement benefits for

higher-paid employees. At other large institutions, defined benefit plans were used only for union employees, while a TSA plan served as the basic retirement plan for all nonunion employees; in this situation it was not unusual for the employer contributions to the TSA plan to increase with the rank of the employee. For example, the employer might contribute 6 percent or 7 percent of pay for rank-and-file employees and 10 percent or 15 percent of pay for more senior staff members. In addition, all employees would generally be permitted to make voluntary contributions to the TSA plan to the extent that the law permitted.

NONDISCRIMINATION REQUIREMENTS

For institutions that have a single defined benefit pension plan in which most or all nonunion employees participate, compliance with the nondiscrimination requirements of TRA–86 is not likely to be too onerous. If the employer contributes to a TSA plan on behalf of a few high-paid employees, then ceasing such contributions may be all that is necessary to comply with the law. On the other hand, if most nonunion employees are in a TSA plan to which the employer contributes varying percentages of pay based on rank, it is likely that these employer contributions will have to be adjusted, so that they are not considered discriminatory in favor of highly compensated employees.[2]

The institution with rank-and-file employees in a defined benefit plan and higher-paid employees in a TSA plan has an even more complicated problem because the law now requires that each retirement plan pass one of the following three coverage tests:

1. *The Percentage Test.* A plan will pass this test if it benefits at least 70 percent of non–highly compensated employees.
2. *The Ratio Test.* A plan will pass this test if it benefits
   - a percentage of non–highly compensated employees which is at least 70 percent of
   - the percentage of highly compensated employees benefiting under the plan.
3. *The Average Benefit Percentage Test.* A plan will pass this test if
   - the plan benefits such employees as qualify under a classification set up by the employer and found by the Secretary [of the Treasury] not to be discriminatory in favor of highly compensated employees, and
   - the average benefit percentage for non–highly compensated employees is at least 70 percent of the average benefit percentage for highly compensated employees.[3]

The definitions of highly compensated and non–highly compensated employees are contained in the Internal Revenue Service's (IRS) Proposed Temporary Regulations which were published in the *Federal Register*.[4]

TAX-SHELTERED ANNUITIES AND DEFINED BENEFIT PLANS

The institution with a defined benefit pension plan for rank-and-file employees and a tax-sheltered annuity plan for senior staff (generally, high-paid employees) may well have to choose between one plan or the other. Maintaining both plans and bringing them into compliance with the law, so that each of them passes at least one of the coverage tests without violating the general prohibition against discriminating in favor of non–highly compensated employees, may prove to be far too costly, administratively too burdensome, or simply impossible. Consequently, many institutions (which find that they can only continue one type of plan due to the non-discrimination requirements of the law) will probably terminate the defined benefit plan. One of the reasons for this result would be that institutions are likely to do what they need to do in order to attract and retain senior staff, and the tax-sheltered annuity has been the plan of choice for these employees for many years. Although it is likely that the percentage of pay contributed by the employer to the tax-sheltered annuity plan on behalf of senior staff will be reduced in order to stay within the institution's budget, while adding the rank-and-file employees to the plan, most institutions will not further distress their senior staff by terminating the tax-sheltered annuity plan. The appeal of the tax-sheltered annuity plan is due to

the following typical characteristics that are attractive to participants:

- a choice of investment alternatives
- portability
- 100 percent immediate vesting
- a loan provision
- access to funds on termination of employment
- a wide variety of payout options at retirement

In addition to the institution's inclination to try to accommodate the senior staff by retaining the tax-sheltered annuity plan, there are a number of other reasons why the termination of the defined benefit plan will be the alternative of choice. In fact, these same reasons have produced an unprecedented number of defined benefit pension plan terminations in the last several years by both for-profit and not-for-profit employers, in and out of the health care field.

THE FUTURE OF DEFINED BENEFIT PLANS

Starting with the Employee Retirement Income Security Act of 1974 (ERISA), the federal government has implemented many changes that diminish the appeal of defined benefit plans to employers. These include, but are not limited to,

- the creation of the Pension Benefit Guaranty Corporation (PBGC)
- the significant increase in annual PBGC premiums from $1 per participant in 1974 to $16 per participant in 1988, plus an additional premium charge of up to $34 per participant for underfunded plans
- the subjecting of the employer to a liability equal to the full amount of underfunding (if any) in the event of a plan termination
- a significant reduction in the flexibility that the employer has with respect to actuarial assumptions (This minimizes the employer's cash-flow flexibility in funding the plan.)
- accelerated vesting requirements
- preretirement death benefits
- a significant diminution in the ability to integrate a defined benefit plan with Social Security
- a reduction in the maximum benefit for higher-paid employees
- a reduction or, in many cases, an elimination of favorable tax treatment for lump sum distributions
- an excise tax on asset reversions (It was originally 10 percent and was just increased to 15 percent, with the likelihood that it will increase significantly in the future. Although this excise tax does not generally apply to not-

for-profit employers, future legislation may require excess assets to be allocated among plan participants, thereby providing benefits to participants in excess of accrued benefits at the time of plan termination. This would diminish the amount that would otherwise be paid to the employer in the event of plan termination.)

- IRS plan comparability requirements (It will be increasingly difficult to establish ''comparability'' between a defined benefit plan and a defined contribution plan, such as a TSA plan, to the satisfaction of the IRS, and yet comparability of the two types of plans is the only basis on which an employer could maintain one type of plan for lower-paid employees and another type of plan for higher-paid employees. Prior to TRA–86, Revenue Procedure 81-202 provided guidance on how to establish the comparability of a defined benefit plan and a defined contribution plan. The successor to Revenue Procedure 81-202 is expected to be significantly more restrictive. Although nothing has yet been officially published at the time of this writing, senior officials at the Department of Treasury and the IRS have stated that the fundamental principle that will guide the IRS on this issue is that two plans will not be considered comparable if any highly compensated employee is expected to receive a benefit greater than any non–highly compensated employee. Averaging of benefits and contributions is not expected to be permitted in order to determine the comparability of two plans; comparability may have to be established by viewing each participant's benefits or contributions in relation to every other participant's benefits or contributions.)

For these reasons and a variety of others, it is not difficult to imagine a future in which the only defined benefit plans are Social Security (a ''pay as you go'' retirement plan which is even more directly subject to the machinations of the political system) and collectively bargained defined benefit plans for union employees. The irony of this situation is that many members of Congress, at least those most actively involved with retirement plan legislation, express enthusiasm for defined benefit plans, while they support legislation that undermines the viability and attractiveness of such plans to employers. ''The path to perdition is paved with good intentions'' could be the epitaph for defined benefit plans because most of the legislation is intended to benefit and better protect the participants in such plans. The problem is that many of the legislative changes cited previously make these plans more expensive to maintain and more difficult to administer.

On the other hand, the legislators are on the right track when they recognize that we have a more portable work force—a work force in which many employees not only do not work for the same employer for an extended period of time but also, in fact, have significant gaps in their working experience. These gaps are attributable to numerous factors, including the return to school for advanced degrees, maternity and paternity leaves, child care, and layoffs, among others. This has prompted the concern over lengthy waiting periods, extended vesting schedules, and lack of portability. It has also contributed to the concept of IRA rollovers.

Oddly, the Congress has not yet embraced the concept of defined contribution plans as the most appropriate mechanism for providing retirement benefits in this environment. Perhaps the reason that Congress favors defined benefit plans instead of defined contribution plans is that the employees, rather than the employer, bear the investment risk in a defined contribution plan. However, employees who are unemployed by choice or by chance for several years or who work at several jobs over their lifetime would realize far more favorable results if they always participate in defined contribution plans instead of defined benefit plans (even if the vesting schedules in both are identical). The reason for this is that on termination of employment under a defined benefit plan, the normal retirement benefit is determined and remains unchanged until the employee reaches normal retirement age; on the other hand, the balance in an employee's account under a defined contribution plan continues to be invested on behalf of the employee and can be expected to increase until retirement.

One of the proposed methods for enhancing defined benefit plans is to allow for portability. Although the exact nature of such portability has not yet been defined, it could mean that employees would be able to withdraw the present value of their accrued benefits on termination of employment. Even with portability of this nature, employees would still be greatly disadvantaged if they have several job changes over their working lifetimes. The reason is that the amount needed to fund a benefit in a defined benefit plan for a younger employee is only a fraction of the amount needed to fund the same level of benefit for an older employee. For example, although the employer's contribution to the defined benefit plan may be 8 percent of the payroll of all eligible employees, it could cost 17 percent of pay to fund a benefit for an older employee and only 2 percent or 3 percent of pay for a younger employee. This differs radically from the defined contribution plan where (typically) the same contribution is allocated to each employee's account, irrespective of age. As a result, employees in the defined contribution plan would have significantly greater sums invested on their behalf in the early years. These funds are invested, and the employees in the defined contribution plan benefit from the investment earnings and growth of these funds over an extended period of time. If the funds are in a defined benefit plan, the employer benefits from the investment earnings and growth of the fund. This is why portability in defined benefit plans is not as beneficial for many employees as participating in a defined contribution plan is.

For the reasons stated previously, tax-sheltered annuity plans will be continued as the basic retirement plan at many not-for-profit health care institutions. In light of this, it is appropriate to consider the other hurdles that have been placed on the path of participants and administrators by the Tax Reform Act of 1986. These include a new limit on elective deferrals by employees; restrictions on withdrawals; an excise tax on early withdrawls; rules on when distributions must commence, how much must be paid out, and when it must be paid; and penalties for failure to comply. There is even a new excise tax on receiving too much from or accumulating too much in retirement plans.

LIMITS ON CONTRIBUTIONS

In addition to the limitations that already existed under Internal Revenue Code (IRC), Sections 403(b) and 415, TRA–86, further limits elective employee deferrals to TSA plans to $9,500 annually. However, a "special catch-up" rule allows employees of certain organizations with 15 or more years of service to contribute an additional $3,000 annually, up to a lifetime maximum of $15,000.[5] Besides limiting the amount of elective deferrals, the law now requires that the employer include the amount of elective deferrals on the W–2 form issued to each employee.

In combination, the maximum annual employee and employer contributions may not exceed $30,000; this $30,000 limit is unchanged by the Tax Reform Act of 1986. Although both the $30,000 and $9500 limits are scheduled to increase with inflation in the future, the terms of the law are such that it will be several years before this indexing takes effect.

PREMATURE WITHDRAWALS

Among the most onerous provisions of the Tax Reform Act of 1986 are the restrictions and excise taxes that apply to premature withdrawals.[6] Specifically, withdrawals or distributions from qualified plans and tax-sheltered annuity plans prior to age 59½ are subject to an excise tax equal to 10 percent of the portion of the distribution that is includible in gross income, unless the distribution meets one of the exceptions under the law. The 10 percent excise tax will not apply to distributions made under the following circumstances:

- death
- disability
- termination of employment after age 55
- the beginning of lifetime annuity benefits on separation from service
- for tax deductible medical expenses
- pursuant to a qualified domestic relations order

The Tax Reform Act of 1986 originally contained a provision, effective January 1, 1989, which limited withdrawals of employee elective deferrals before age 59½ to separation from service, death, disability, and hardship.[7] However, the Technical and Miscellaneous Revenue Act of 1988 (TAMRA) now provides that the withdrawal restrictions will apply only to

- elective deferrals (and earnings on those elective deferrals) made after December 31, 1988
- earnings on the December 31, 1988, elective deferral account balance.[8]

Assuring compliance with these rules is going to present a formidable challenge for employers. First, a procedure will have to be established to determine whether or not a participant who claims to have terminated employment or attained age 59½ has actually terminated employment or attained age 59½. Second, the December 31, 1988, elective deferral account balance will have to be reduced by the amount of each inservice withdrawal. Finally, the reduced December 31, 1988, elective deferral account balance must be maintained on the file in order to determine the maximum permissible amount of subsequent inservice withdrawals by each participant prior to age 59½.

Failure to comply with the restrictions on withdrawals of elective deferrals could result in the IRS's concluding that an employee's total account balance is taxable to the employee as ordinary income because the annuity contract does not meet the requirements of a 403(b) annuity contract.

HARDSHIP WITHDRAWALS

One of the exceptions to the restrictions on inservice elective deferrals prior to age 59½ is hardship. In the Final Regulations on Section 401(k) plans, the IRS provides the following definition of hardship:

> A distribution is on account of hardship only if the distribution is made on account of an immediate and heavy financial need of the employee and is necessary to satisfy such financial need. The determinations of the existence of an immediate and heavy financial need and of the amount necessary to meet the need must be made in accordance with nondiscriminatory and objective standards set forth in the plan.[9]

The IRS also provides the following examples of immediate and heavy financial need:

- medical expenses incurred by the employee, the employee's spouse, or any dependents of the employee
- purchase of a principal residence of the employee
- payment of tuition for the next semester or quarter of postsecondary education for the employee and his or her spouse, children, or dependents
- the need to prevent the eviction of the employee from his or her principal residence or foreclosure on the mortgage of the employee's principal residence[10]

The Regulations then provide guidance on the circumstances under which a distribution is necessary to satisfy the financial need of the individual. The requirements listed by the

IRS are met if the employer reasonably relies on the employee's representation that the need cannot be relieved

- through reimbursement or compensation by insurance or otherwise
- by reasonable liquidation of the employee's assets, to the extent such liquidation would not itself cause an immediate and heavy financial need
- by cessation of elective contributions or employee contributions under the plan
- by other distributions or nontaxable (at the time of the loan) loans from plans maintained by the employer or by any other employer, or by loans from commercial sources on reasonable commercial terms.[11]

In order to provide employers with a safe harbor for making determinations on hardship requests, the Regulations stipulate that a distribution will be deemed to be necessary to satisfy an immediate and heavy financial need of an employee if all the following requirements are satisfied:

- The distribution is not in excess of the amount of the immediate and heavy financial need of the employee.
- The employee has obtained all distributions, other than hardship distributions, and all nontaxable loans currently available under all plans maintained by the employer.
- The plan, and all other plans maintained by the employer, provides that the employee's elective contributions will be suspended for at least 12 months after receipt of the hardship distribution.
- The plan, and all other plans maintained by the employer, provides that the employee may not make elective contributions for the employee's taxable year immediately following the taxable year of the hardship distribution in excess of the applicable limit under Section 402(g) for such next taxable year less the amount of such employee's elective contributions for the taxable year of the hardship distribution.[12]

Although we do not yet know whether these same hardship rules will apply to TSA plans, it is likely that they will. The result for employers that choose to offer a hardship provision in their TSA plans will be another administrative burden and another level of complexity with which they will be forced to cope.

UNIFORM MINIMUM DISTRIBUTION RULES

The Tax Reform Act of 1986 significantly changed the rules for the timing and the amount of distributions from tax-sheltered annuity plans.[13] Exceptions to the new rules can be favorable to participants, but these exceptions complicate the process of determining when distributions must commence and how much must be distributed.

The new rules are referred to as the uniform minimum distribution rules (UMDRs). This name is descriptive because, for the first time, IRAs, TSAs, and qualified retirement plans will be governed by essentially the same rules regarding the minimum amount of each distribution and the timing of these distributions. In brief, each participant in a TSA plan must receive the first distribution by April 1 of the year following the calendar year in which the participant attains age 70½. If the participant does not begin an annuity payout, then the minimum annual distribution must be an amount at least equal to the previous December 31 balance in the participant's account divided by the participant's life expectancy or the joint life expectancy of the participant and the participant's beneficiary.

In order to provide for a transition between the old rules and the new UMDRs, the law contains two provisions favorable to TSA participants.

1. The December 31, 1986, balance in TSA contracts is not subject to the new UMDRs.[14]
2. Participants who attained age 70½ prior to January 1, 1988, may delay commencement of their required distributions until they retire.[15]

The good news about the application of the UMDRs to TSAs is that it is no longer necessary for a participant to roll over TSA assets into an IRA in order to avoid an annuity payout when the participant reaches the age at which distributions must begin. Instead, providing that the insurance company and the plan administrator (if the TSA is a plan covered by ERISA) will allow this alternative, the participant can choose to have a distribution commence from the TSA without beginning an annuity payout. This alternative greatly enhances the flexibility that the participant has in determining how much to have distributed each year from the TSA because the UMDRs only dictate the minimum amount that must be withdrawn each year; the participant can be given the option to have a greater amount distributed in any given year.

The first reaction to this might very well be that this is not too exciting; after all, the participant could roll over the TSA into an IRA and have the same flexibility. The problem with the IRA rollover approach is that it is not always possible to meet the requirements for either a partial or a total IRA rollover; from an investment point of view, it may not even be desirable. In addition, a rollover into an IRA would subject the December 31, 1986, TSA account balance to the UMDRs when they would otherwise be exempt.

Although the UMDRs may provide some additional flexibility for participants in their retirement planning, they also present a number of problems. These include

- making the required distribution at a date earlier than under prior law
- paying a 50-percent excise tax penalty, beginning in 1989, on the amount by which the minimum required distribution exceeds the actual amount distributed in any year

- maintaining a record of, and properly adjusting, the December 31, 1986, account balance (For example, an individual who takes a distribution in excess of the required minimum distribution in a given year must subtract the "excess" from the December 31, 1986, account balance for purposes of determining the minimum distribution amount in subsequent years. In addition, any withdrawal made subsequent to December 31, 1986, and prior to the date of the first required minimum distribution must also be subtracted from the December 31, 1986, account balance for purposes of determining which assets are not subject to UMDRs.

- Calculating the required minimum distribution each year and being sure that the distributions are made on a timely basis

- Complying with the Retirement Equity Act of 1984 (This law requires that benefits for married participants be paid in the form of a qualified joint and survivor annuity, unless the spouse waives this form of payout. This requirement only applies to plans that are subject to ERISA. The waiver must be obtained from the spouse within the 90-day period immediately prior to the date of each distribution, unless an annuity payout has been elected.)

- Amending the TSA plan document to reflect the UMDRs.

EXCESS DISTRIBUTION TAX AND EXCESS ACCUMULATION TAX

One of the lesser known changes in the tax law as a result of the Tax Reform Act of 1986 was the introduction of a 15-percent excise tax on excess distributions and excess accumulations.[16] Excess distributions are those retirement distributions an individual receives in excess of a specified amount in a single calendar year, and excess accumulations are those retirement assets in an individual's retirement plans in excess of a specified amount at the time the individual dies. The retirement plans referred to in the law include tax-sheltered annuities, qualified employer retirement plans, and IRAs; non-qualified deferred compensation plans are not included.

It may be possible for some individuals to minimize the impact of these taxes by electing "grandfather" treatment of the assets in their retirement plans as of August 1, 1986. In order to be eligible for this grandfather treatment, the total of an individual's retirement plan assets had to be at least $562,500 as of August 1, 1986. However, it may not be in the best interests of some individuals to elect grandfather treatment. For someone who expects to take substantial distributions during the next several years, it could be counterproductive. The reason for this is that distributions in 1988 in excess of $150,000 were subject to the 15-percent excess distributions tax if grandfather treatment was not elected. However, the $150,000 was reduced to $117,529 if grand-

father treatment was elected; the $150,000 and the $117,529 are referred to in the law as the "threshold" distribution amounts. Since the $117,529 is indexed to inflation, while the $150,000 is not, it is reasonable to expect that the indexed threshold amount will surpass the $150,000 within the next several years. After the indexed amount reaches or exceeds $150,000, the grandfather election might not result in a reduction in this tax, but it could not result in an increase in the amount of excise tax due.

The deadline for electing grandfather treatment of the August 1, 1986, assets was the date by which individuals had to file their 1988 income tax return, including extensions.

NONQUALIFIED DEFERRED COMPENSATION PLANS

Nonqualified deferred compensation plans have frequently been used by employers in order to provide benefits or defer income in excess of the statutory limits for certain high-paid employees. In some instances, voluntary deferrals by such employees have also been permitted under the terms of non-qualified deferred compensation plans. The advantages to the employee of participation in such an arrangement are that the amount deferred is not currently taxed and that the investment earnings on the deferred amount are not currently taxed. Only at the time that payments are actually received (or made available) to the employee does the employee have to pay tax; the tax liability is based on the amount actually received (or made available) in the particular tax year of the employee. Ever since the maximum annual contribution to tax-sheltered annuity plans was reduced to $30,000, effective January 1, 1983, nonqualified deferred compensation plans have become increasingly popular.

However, TRA–86 effectively eliminated new plans of this type for employees of not-for-profit institutions, unless there is a "substantial risk of forfeiture" provision in the plan. This means that the employee would lose the money that was deferred unless he or she worked for the employer for the period of time specified in the agreement between the employee and the employer. This type of arrangement is described in IRC Section 457(f).

Another type of deferred compensation plan is described in IRC Section 457(b) as an "eligible deferred compensation plan"; this is defined as a plan established and maintained by an eligible employer

- in which only individuals who perform service for the employer may be participants
- which provides that, generally, the maximum amount that may be deferred under the plan for the taxable year shall not exceed the lesser of
  1. $7,500, or
  2. 33⅓ percent of the participant's includible compensation

The problem with utilizing this type of deferred compensation plan in the not-for-profit institution is that contributions to a TSA plan reduce the maximum allowable contributions to an "eligible deferred compensation plan" dollar for dollar. For instance, if the contributions for an employee to a TSA plan exceed $7,500 in a given year, then there can be no contributions for that employee to the eligible deferred compensation plan of that employer in that same year.

RETIREMENT PLANNING "WISH LIST"

At the top of this list is the wish that Congress will take a lengthy sabbatical from pension legislation and devote its attention to other matters for the next several years. The passage of new pension laws each year, and sometimes more than one law in a single year, is counterproductive for both employees and employers. Instead of energy, time, and money being devoted to designing, implementing, and communicating enhancements to their retirement plans, employers have had to focus on compliance with ever-changing, frequently onerous, often useless, and sometimes contradictory legal requirements.

The automatic joint and survivor rules and the pre-retirement death benefit requirements are examples of governmental intrusion where no need was established and no measurable benefit has been attained. Furthermore, employers are saddled with an increased administrative burden, while participants are aggravated by the necessity to obtain spousal waivers from an estranged or recalcitrant spouse or to establish to the satisfaction of the plan administrator that the spouse is among the missing. This is rivaled by the situation in which uniform minimum distribution rules require that employees begin receiving retirement benefits at age 70½, even if they are still employed, while the Age Discrimination in Employment Act requires that these same employees be continued as active participants in the same retirement plan from which they are receiving benefits.

Second on this short wish list is the hope that the new pension laws, when they are inevitably passed, will not apply new restrictions or taxes to benefits that accrued or contributions that were made prior to the change in the law. Examples of these types of after-the-fact changes in TRA–86 are the 10-percent excise tax on premature withdrawals and the 15-percent excise tax on excess distributions and excess accumulations.

The third wish is for nonqualified deferred compensation plans of nongovernmental, not-for-profit institutions to be exempt from IRC Section 457. Employee stock ownership plans (ESOPs), incentive stock options (ISOs), and stock bonus plans are compensation arrangements that are unavailable to not-for-profit institutions by their nature. Nonqualified deferred compensation plans should not have been added to that list, and a legislative remedy would be most welcome in order to give not-for-profit institutions some reasonable chance to compete for the services of the most capable individuals.

The final wish on the list is for employers and their consultants to be successful in their joint efforts both to establish retirement plans that are beneficial to employees and to communicate the characteristics of these plans to employees, so that they are understood, appreciated, and utilized in the most effective way.

NOTES

1. IRC § 403(b).
2. IRC § 401(a)(4).
3. IRC § 410(b).
4. 53 Fed. Reg. 4,965, 4,999 (1988).
5. IRC § 402(g)(8).
6. IRC § 72(t)(2).
7. IRC § 403(b)(11).
8. TAMRA § 1011A(c).
9. IRS § 1.401(k)-1(d)(2)(i).
10. IRS Reg. 1.401(k)-1(d)(2)(ii).
11. IRS Reg. 1.401(k)-1(d)(2)(iii).
12. Ibid.
13. IRC § 403(b)(10).
14. TRA '86 § 1852(c)(3).
15. IRS Reg. 1.403(b)-2, Q-1, A(c).
16. IRC § 4980A.

Jack M. Marco

Pension Plan Trustee Responsibility: Investment Performance Measurement

42

INTRODUCTION

Investment performance measurement services have become widely accepted by employee benefit plans and their investment professionals. However, this industry is still relatively new, with most of its growth occurring in the late 1960s and 1970s. The following chapter will discuss some of the reasons for the expansion of the performance measurement industry, the benefits of establishing a formalized investment program, and the process of performance evaluation.

EXPANSION OF THE PERFORMANCE MEASUREMENT INDUSTRY

Three of the major factors that have contributed to the expansion of investment performance measurement center around legislation, growth of pension fund assets, and disillusionment of trustees with their investment managers.

In the 1950s, the banking industry developed a method to calculate rates of return that would allow for an equitable comparison of two investment managers. However, legislation in the mid-1970s complicated this task for trustees of employee benefit plans. In 1974, the Employee Retirement Income Security Act (ERISA) was enacted, which affected many aspects of the design, cost, and administration of benefit plans. More specifically, it clearly documented the fiduciary liability of trustees of employee benefit plans.

Plan sponsors, particularly trustees of Taft-Hartley pension funds, found themselves in an impossible situation. First, their professional experience and training were generally unrelated to the financial markets, so they had to rely on those who were the "experts" in the field. Second, the trustees' jobs on the funds were part time and unpaid. They had little time or interest in becoming the "prudent expert" dictated by fiduciary standards and later ERISA.

Added to this was a growing competition for the management of these pension fund assets. With no formal process of measuring investment returns, plan sponsors (trustees) became confused and frustrated in attempting to get a handle on how well their investors were doing. This frustration then turned to a healthy skepticism about the data trustees were receiving from their portfolio managers.

From the portfolio managers' perspectives, it didn't make much sense to focus on the shortcomings of the results; rather, these managers found positive things to talk about at trustee meetings. And if the results were good, there was every reason to embellish the success.

Salespeople vying for the opportunity to manage a portion of a plan's assets presented their firms' performance in even more creative ways. Certain portfolios and special time periods were selected to represent the organization's track record. Indices used for comparison were less than objectively chosen. Caveat emptor was never more important.

For many years local banks and insurance companies were successful at obtaining pension plan business and were given full discretion to invest the assets with no limits on risk and no standards for performance. These banks and insurance companies presented themselves and were received by the trustees as "experts." To the trustees this meant that they would always get positive rates of return, well ahead of the interest assumed by their actuary and certainly ahead of inflation. The portfolio managers did little to alter that perception.

In 1973 and 1974, with the tremendous losses in the stock and bond markets, portfolio managers' "expert" status was re-evaluated. Not only had they fallen behind the interest assumption and then raging inflation, but also they had lost money! Certainly it was time to find the real experts and replace these underachievers.

The portfolio managers responded that they hadn't done so badly, given the market's condition. They explained that there was a risk-reward trade-off and that this kind of experience must be expected. Portfolio managers had set themselves up as experts, and experts should have known not to invest in those markets at that time. Earlier they had thrived on their unrealistic expert status, and now they were losing business due to this same misconception.

Who were to be hired as the new experts? Those shrewd investors who now knew that stocks were no place for a pension fund. Unfortunately, these experts lost these same clients a few years later, having missed one of the strongest bull markets of the decade.

In hindsight it all looks pretty silly and unfortunately costly for plan sponsors and beneficiaries. We are all wiser for this experience; however, our human nature will always confound the process and keep it interesting.

Many of these problems still exist today in varying degrees, but trustees and investment professionals have learned from their experiences and have a much better handle on how to deal with the management and evaluation of pension fund investing. The following sections provide guidelines on how to approach the issues of investing pension assets and monitoring the process by (1) establishing an investment program, (2) developing investment guidelines, and (3) measuring performance.

ESTABLISHMENT OF AN INVESTMENT PROGRAM

One of the most useful parts of any labor-management agreement is the part of the contract that describes the job: the expectation of the employer and the task of the employee. If written well and clearly understood by both, harmony should be enhanced at the work place. If, on the other hand, the job description is vague, it increases the possibility that the employee and employer will have different expectations and could result in neither party's being satisfied.

Furthermore, the employer's judgments about superior or inferior performance may be based on expectations not shared by the employee. The result is apt to lead to unnecessary employee turnover and lower productivity, which are costly to both sides. Certainly then, a clear, unambiguous job description precludes a great deal of problems and enhances the objectives of the employer, while allowing the employee the opportunity to be as productive as possible.

Similarly, trustees of pension funds are the employers of investment management organizations. Particularly in jointly trusteed funds, these "employers" (both labor and management representatives) should understand the importance of establishing a clear, unambiguous job description for their "employees" (money managers). I call this job description *Investment Manager Guidelines*. I shall come back to these guidelines later in this section.

Prior to the trustees' deciding what they expect each of their investment managers to do, they must determine what they want out of their entire investment program. Despite the number of different portfolios in the pension fund or the number of money managers that the fund retains, there is *one* pension fund portfolio of assets. The results of that portfolio (the kinds of returns it will produce) will be greatly dependent on the structure designed either purposefully or inadvertently by the trustees.

Statement of Investment Policy

Many plan sponsors spend far too much time dealing with the performance of a single manager to the detriment of their understanding of the entire fund's performance. With this in mind, let us begin with a game plan for the entire fund and later determine what roles the investment managers will play. This game plan is called a *Statement of Investment Policy*.

Following are the elements of a complete Statement of Investment Policy.

Introduction

The introduction should specify the name of the fund and its purpose.

> The purpose of the American Workers Local 100 Pension Fund is to provide retirement benefits for the members of Local 100. The goals and objectives described below are to enhance the value of this fund.

Description of Responsibilities

An important aspect of the Statement is a specific description of those responsibilities that are retained by the trustees and those that are delegated. The fund attorney is likely to be particularly interested in this section. It should be noted that the trustees are accepting the responsibility for determining long-term policy without attempting to direct short-term strategies.

> The Board of Trustees of the American Workers Local 100 Pension Fund assumes the responsibility for establishing the investment policy described below which is to guide the investment of pension trust assets. The investment policy has been arrived at on consideration by the Board of the potential financial implications of a wide range of policies. Furthermore, it describes the degree of

pension fund investment risk that these plan fiduciaries deem appropriate.

Investment managers appointed to execute the policy will invest plan assets in accordance with the policy and with their judgments concerning relative investment values. In particular, the investment manager is accorded full discretion, within policy limits, all federal and state laws, and the terms of their own engagement, to (1) select individual securities; (2) make periodic adjustments to the proportions of equity or fixed-income securities and cash equivalents; and (3) diversify plan assets.

Rate of Return Objective

The language for this section is the easiest to write and the most difficult to determine. It is essential to discuss such objectives with the actuary and the financial consultant to the plan. The question to be considered and deliberated by the trustees is "What do you hope to accomplish by investing these assets?" Typical objectives include

- maintaining a level of assets at least equal to the present value of vested liabilities (fully funded)
- producing earnings, so that benefits may be increased at the rate of 2 percent per year without additional contributions
- assuring that the assets will never be less than 85 percent of vested liabilities.

These goals may or may not be reasonably attainable. The fund actuary will communicate to the trustees what rate of return is necessary to achieve these goals, while the financial consultant can advise the trustees on which asset mixes are most likely to achieve these goals. These goals are simply that—goals. It should be clear to all that they are not benefit changes. This goal setting and analysis result in a rate of return target sometimes described in absolute terms but more frequently described relative to inflation.

> The Board has established a *real* (over inflation) return objective of 3 percent per year over market cycles. The investment policy has been formulated to offer a high likelihood of realizing this particular return.

Investment Policy

The investment policy is the result of the study used to determine the rate of return objective above. The fund's financial consultant usually recommends a few different policies designed to achieve the objective, and the trustees then select the policy with which they feel most comfortable. In order to achieve a certain level of return, a commensurate level of risk must be taken. To prevent asset values from declining below a certain level, a limit must be set on the amount of risk the fund is prepared to take. In general, pension fund investments in equities (common stock) present the greatest risk, followed by real estate, bonds, and finally cash equivalents (short-term investments).

> Up to 40 percent of the market value of pension assets may be invested in equity securities and up to 10 percent in real estate. The remaining assets may be invested in BAA-or-better-rated publicly traded fixed-income securities and cash equivalent securities rated A1 or P1.

Liquidity

The fund actuary typically projects the relationship between the contributions to the fund and the benefits and expenses paid out of the fund in their annual valuation. If contributions are expected to exceed payments for the foreseeable future, no special arrangements need be made. However, if cash needs to be withdrawn from the plan to pay benefits and expenses, it should be noted in the liquidity section.

> There is a need for a degree of liquidity in this fund because contributions may not be sufficient to meet benefit payments. The fund administrator will provide the investment manager with projected liquidity needs on an annual basis.

Structure

There are many approaches to structuring an investment program, ranging from one balanced manager (one firm investing all of the assets) to a large number of specialists. The options should be discussed with the fund's financial consultant. When the decision is made, the structure of the fund should be described in writing, so that it can guide the selection of investment managers and serve as a reference in the future.

> Forty percent of the fund's assets will be allocated equally between two equity managers with complementary styles. Ten percent of the fund's assets will be allocated to a real estate manager. Fifty percent of the plan's assets will be directed to three fixed-income managers: 20 percent to a bond index fund manager, 20 percent to an active bond manager, and 10 percent to a guaranteed investment contract (GIC) manager.

In addition to all of the items described above, the trustees may wish to consider restrictions on particular investments (e.g., companies doing business in South Africa). It is also desirable to add language describing the review process for the policy.

> Periodic review of this statement will be made by the Trustees to evaluate its appropriateness.

Investment Manager Guidelines

It is necessary to provide investment managers with their job description: Investment Manager Guidelines.

Guidelines for the equity managers should be clear and specific as to expectations. Restrictions should not be arbitrary, or they may interfere with the investment firm's ability to perform its task. Investment guidelines have been written specifying parameters for nearly every aspect of the manager's activity: cash reserve levels; price/earnings, market/book, and debt/equity ratios; industry weightings; diversification levels; and turnover. As to the appropriate price/earnings ratio for an equity manager, placing a specific limit or range on this measure does not necessarily reduce risk. More likely than not, it will interfere with the productivity of the manager. Moreover, if such a limit is written so broadly as to make certain it will not interfere with the manager's job, one should question its effectiveness.

The same can be said about asset mix. In general, equity managers purchase domestic common stocks and cash equivalents. Some guidelines have been written setting a minimum exposure to equities. Certainly trustees should expect the vast majority of the assets held by an equity manager over time to be equities. However, if in the managers' judgment the outlook for common stocks is bleak, then trustees should give the managers an unrestricted opportunity to invest in cash equivalent securities until they are secure in moving to the riskier asset. Requiring managers to hold equities against their better judgment is counterproductive.

> Twenty percent of the plan assets will be directed to a value manager and twenty percent to a growth stock manager. The equity managers may invest in domestic common stocks and cash equivalent securities rated A1 or P1. They may invest up to 100 percent of the assets in their portfolio in common stocks or cash equivalent securities. They are responsible for diversifying the portfolio to avoid large losses.

The performance targets for the equity managers should be clear and realistic and should take into account the particular style for which the manager was hired.

> The equity managers are each expected to provide a rate of return 5 percent greater than inflation over a full market cycle. Over this same period of time, the managers are expected to exceed the return of the S&P 500 as well as the median return of a data base of managers with a similar style.

The fixed-income manager guidelines should follow the same principles as the equity manager guidelines.

> The bond index fund manager will receive 20 percent of the fund's assets and manage a portfolio of publicly traded fixed-income securities so as to match the return of the Shearson Lehman Government Corporate Bond Index. It is expected that this portfolio will match the returns of this index within 0.5 percent annually.

In describing the role of active bond managers, it is appropriate to limit the quality of the bonds to be held, as well as their maturity. These are the key elements of risk, and the trustees' tolerance for risk should be described, so that the

investment managers know in advance how to structure their portfolios.

It is assumed here that if the trustees plan to severely limit the risk in bonds—for example, by allowing only short-term U.S. government bonds—the financial consultant took that into consideration in developing a rate of return objective.

> The active bond manager may invest in publicly traded fixed-income securities rated BBB or higher by Moodys or BAA by Standard and Poors and in short-term cash equivalent securities rated A1 or P1. The average maturity of the portfolio may not exceed 12 years.
>
> The active bond manager is expected to achieve a rate of return 2 percent higher than inflation over a market cycle and in excess of the Salomon Brothers Broad Bond Index over the same time period. Furthermore, the bond manager is expected to exceed the median return of a data base of bond managers of pension funds. The bond manager is responsible for diversifying the fixed-income portfolio to avoid large losses.

Real estate guidelines should vary based on the kind of real estate chosen. For example, we assume a pure equity position as opposed to mortgages. Here, again, overdrafting is not helpful.

> The real estate manager may invest in income-producing real estate properties. The manager is responsible for diversifying the portfolio geographically, as well as by type of property (e.g., retail, office, industrial, residential). Properties should be owned or co-owned without leverage.
>
> The real estate portfolio is expected to provide a rate of return 5 percent higher than the rate of inflation over a market cycle. Furthermore, the portfolio should exceed the median return of a data base of similar real estate portfolios over the same period.

Finally, it is recommended that Investment Manager Guidelines close with a caveat that puts responsibility on the money manager to consult with the trustees if, for any reason, this manager believes these guidelines are not in the best interests of the plan. For example, in the early 1980s an equity manager came to a board of trustees and asked that he be allowed, for a short time, to invest a portion of his portfolio in 3- to 5-year U.S. government bonds rather than in equities. He felt interest rates would decline and the capital appreciation potential from those bonds was greater than the opportunities he saw in the stock market. He was given that latitude with the understanding that he was still going to be judged as an equity manager. It turned out as the manager had predicted, and the fund benefited from the manager's recommendations.

> The investment managers should notify the trustees if, in their judgment, it is appropriate to manage the assets outside of these guidelines.

Much more can be said about the Statement of Investment Policy and Investment Manager Guidelines, particularly as they relate to some of the new securities available to pension funds. The issues raised here, however, are the needs to develop a game plan and to communicate clearly with the plan's investment managers. These actions will provide a framework for the ongoing supervision of the program called *Investment Performance Measurement*.

INVESTMENT PERFORMANCE MEASUREMENT

The Statement of Investment Policy and Investment Manager Guidelines establish goals for the performance of a plan. The first purpose of performance measurement is to see if those goals are being met for the total fund and also for the individual portfolios.

The second purpose is to understand the reasons for the performance experience to help determine what, if any, action is required to better achieve the plan's goals.

Answering the First Question: What Is the Bottom Line?

It is not difficult to calculate the earnings of the plan. First, we identify the opening amount (for the period), then the contributions or distributions, and finally the plan's worth at the end of the period. This provides the rate of return. That is the bottom line:

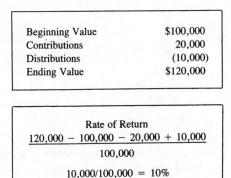

Beginning Value	$100,000
Contributions	20,000
Distributions	(10,000)
Ending Value	$120,000

Rate of Return

$$\frac{120,000 - 100,000 - 20,000 + 10,000}{100,000}$$

$$10,000/100,000 = 10\%$$

There are a number of enhancements available for this formula to more precisely state the rate of return (e.g., providing for the actual date of the cash flows in and out of the fund); however, they do not merit discussing in this context.

If the first rate of return represents the annual experience of the total fund including all the assets and all the money managers, how does one judge that rate? This is the most important fact in any performance review. Comparisons are not simple because several relevant benchmarks can be utilized.

The first benchmark should be the goal set by the Statement of Investment Policy (e.g., "to earn 3 percent per year over the rate of inflation on average"). A relevant benchmark for inflation is the consumer price index (CPI) published by the government. This rate was in the 4.5 percent area in 1989.

A second comparison should be against a data base of similar benefit funds. The key word here is *similar*. Similar goals and similar asset mix are important. Taft-Hartley plans, for example, are best measured against other Taft-Hartley plans. Because they are similarly structured and similarly regulated, they have very similar characteristics. The point of such a comparison is to determine how the plan's total fund return compares to that of other funds like it. Let us assume we know how 10 other similar funds performed in the same year. Their rates were 13.0, 6.9, 9.3, 8.6, 9.5, 7.2, 12.5, 11.6, 10.7, and 7.0, and our plan's rate was 10 percent. A simple average of these numbers results in a mean of 9.7 percent, which could be a benchmark used to determine if our plan performed above average. However, no one fund that was surveyed actually provided a 9.7 percent return.

A preferred method is to stack these rates up, from the lowest to the highest, and see where the plan fits.

13.0
12.5
11.6
10.7
10.0 ←
9.5
9.3
8.6
7.2
7.0
6.9

The middle number (9.5 percent) can be chosen as the median fund performance. Finally, this group can be divided into approximate quarters for further description.

13.0	
12.5	Top quarter
11.6	
10.7	
10.0	Median
9.5	
7.2	
7.0	Bottom quarter
6.9	

A bar chart is most frequently used to enhance the description of relative performance.

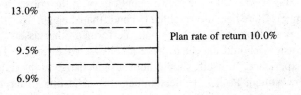

This graph helps to quickly identify the fact that the fund performed better than average and to show the results that were achieved by similar plans.

Dividing the data base into percentiles provides an even more precise description of the location of the fund. This simply means that all of the funds in the data base are divided into 100 equal groups (it helps to have more than 100 funds in the data base). If the plan falls in the 1st (highest) group, it is said to be in the 1st percentile. If the plan is in the 50th group or 50th percentile, it is said to have median results. The 100th percentile is, of course, the lowest group. In the example above, the plan would rank in approximately the 40th percentile.

One final benchmark for the total plan performance is a "passive" portfolio: in other words, a portfolio of similar asset mix with the equity portion earning the return of a market index (S&P 500 Index), the bond portion earning the return of a bond index (Salomon Brothers Broad Bond Index), and the real estate portion earning the return of a real estate index (Evaluation Associates Index). This approach is designed to answer the question "How has the plan performed using investment managers versus owning the entire markets in the same proportions?" Today, more than ever before, this is a relevant comparison because the passive approach is readily available through the use of index funds.

Example:			*Return Policy*
S&P 500 Index	14.6% × 40%	=	5.84%
Salomon Bros.	8.7% × 50%	=	4.35%
E.A. Real Estate	9.0% × 10%	=	0.90%
			11.09%

The conclusions drawn from comparing the total fund's performance to the Statement of Investment Policy, to similarly managed plans, and to a passive approach are as follows:

- The fund made $10,000, which is a 10-percent return.
- The fund exceeded the long-term inflation goals of the CPI plus 3 percent.
- The fund outperformed more than half of the peers.
- The fund underperformed with respect to the passive approach.
- Three out of four isn't bad!

The second goal of performance measurement is to help understand the reasons for the performance results described above. The first question worth asking relates to the asset mix of the fund (set by the Investment Policy). If the chosen asset mix is more heavily weighted to bonds than the plan's peers in a period when bonds have underperformed other assets, the trustees should expect to have a below-median result. That experience, in itself, should not cause a change in the fund's Investment Policy. Understanding this asset mix difference helps trustees understand performance that may, at first blush, cause unwarranted disappointment. Similarly, an asset mix that happens to be advantageous at one point in time should not lead one to expect above-median relative performance.

Further explanations of fund performance can be found by studying the results of individual investment managers to see how each one's role added to or detracted from the total plan results.

Evaluating Equity Managers

One additional certainty in life, besides death and taxes, is the cyclical nature of the stock market, not only in the inevitability of bull and bear markets but also in the rotation in favored areas of the market. We have all heard of the "nifty-fifty" of the bull market of the sixties—when those relatively few very large companies went up and up. This period was followed by a focus on small companies, then growth stocks, then high-dividend stocks, then back to big companies.

The dominant issues that have a major impact on the direction of the market are also quite changeable. It was the price of oil and Middle East politics that moved the markets in the late 1970s, while the value of the dollar and interest rates dominated in the 1980s. The only reasonable conclusion given to us by the past is that the future is unpredictable!

Most investment managers today follow a defined approach to managing stocks. The three major categories are growth, value and yield.

1. *Growth:* An emphasis on companies with *earnings* that have been growing or are expected to grow faster than others. The theory is that the price of the stock will increase as these earnings rise. Assets are not as important.
2. *Value:* A focus on companies with *assets* that are understated and consequently with stock prices that are undervalued by the marketplace. The theory here is that sooner or later the marketplace will understand the true value, and the price of the stock will go up—or that another company will come along and take it over at a higher price. Growth in earnings is not as important.
3. *Yield:* A concentration on stocks that have *dividend* payments higher than the market averages. The yield managers typically argue that these stocks are less volatile because a greater part of the return is based on the dividends than on the less predictable fluctuations in the price.

There are many versions of these styles. One important component is the size of the companies purchased. Regardless of the growth, value, or yield emphasis, there are periods of time when larger "nifty-fifty" stocks are market leaders, rather than over-the-counter stocks, and vice versa.

In evaluating equity managers, it is important to understand their styles of management. If the Investment Policy and structure of the plan call for a variety of equity managers, it is not enough to compare their performances against one another. Each style of management is favored in certain market conditions and not in others. It is, therefore, necessary to compare each equity manager to other managers with similar style. For example, the most appropriate comparison for the performance of a yield manager is against the performance of other yield managers. After all, if they were hired because of this specialization, other indices and data bases of managers that practice other speculations would be meaningless.

However, it is more difficult to find peer group data bases for some styles. The most common problem is market timers, those managers who move between stocks and short-term instruments, trying to be in the right place at the right time. Since data bases of this style are not available (there are not enough market timers to create a significant data base), other measures must be used. The easiest measure is to compare the manager's performance without the use of cash equivalents to its total account performance. This will immediately tell you if the nonequity investments added to or detracted from performance.

Evaluating Fixed-Income Managers

Evaluating fixed-income managers is somewhat different from evaluating equity managers because there are no generally accepted style groupings. The most common benchmarks for fixed-income managers are market indices and data bases of bond managers.

In the fixed-income area, there are a number of viable indices, as opposed to the S&P 500 Index which is the dominant common stock index. The two most frequently used bond indices are the Salomon Brothers Broad and the Shearson Lehman Hutton Government/Corporate. They are both designed to indicate the performance of the entire publicly traded bond market. They both have an average maturity of approximately nine years. However, the Salomon Index includes mortgage-backed bonds, which are widely used in pension portfolios, giving it a slight edge over the Shearson Index, which does not include these issues.

Data bases of fixed-income portfolios of pension funds are also useful benchmarks for measuring bond managers. It is assumed that all the manager portfolios in this data base are designed to "beat" the popular indexes. However, should a plan hire a fixed-income manager to concentrate on shorter maturities, exclusively U.S. government issues, or mortgages, more appropriate data bases or market indices should be chosen for performance benchmarks.

Understanding Performance

Once superior, average, or inferior performance has been determined for each manager, it is important to understand how these results were achieved. For example, while trustees would be inclined to be satisfied with superior results from an equity manager, appropriate efforts should be directed toward determining whether or not the manager took unusual risk to achieve those results.

A group of trustees was cautioned about celebrating a 45-percent return from their equity management firm in 1980 because it had achieved that result with 70 percent of its assets in energy-related stocks. It was hard to be concerned about "risk" after having been rewarded so handsomely for taking it. Unfortunately, the portfolio manager maintained the energy concentration in the following years as that sector fell dramatically out of favor. The portfolio gave back that 45-percent gain and much more.

It is also important to understand the reasons for investment results, in order to continue a healthy dialogue with the plan's investment managers. If trustees know why a manager has underperformed prior to meeting, they can then evaluate the manager's response as an explanation is given for the problem and corrective action is suggested.

Meetings with Portfolio Managers

Trustee meetings with their investment managers do not have to be boring and unproductive. First, the trustees must decide what they want out of the discussion, and, second, they must communicate such requirements to the managers in advance. Too often these meetings are viewed as pro forma and end up wasting much time. Trustees need to hear the managers' analyses of their performance. (The performance results should be presented by someone else more objective.) Among the most disturbing presentations are those from managers who have just produced poor results and do not acknowledge this. Instead, they talk only about the future and avoid, as much as possible, past results. Conversely, managers who admit, up front, the disappointing results and proceed to describe how they misjudged events should give trustees a sense of confidence that improvements can be made.

Trustees also need to know what the managers plan to do in the future, both near term and long term. This is critical, not primarily to approve or reject their strategies, but rather to understand them for future evaluation. This discussion helps reinforce the managers' understanding of their roles and the trustees' understanding of their approach to money management.

Time is important, and a time limit should be established for managers. Depending on the frequency of the meetings, no less than 30 minutes and no more than 60 minutes should be set aside for these reviews. These interviews should take place at least annually and perhaps more frequently, depending on the number of managers retained. Between meetings, quarterly performance reviews are important, not to make judgments about a manager's capabilities but to follow trends of performance as they occur.

When To Fire a Manager

When an investment manager is hired, trustees are convinced that the management firm has a process and that its people are capable of providing superior results. Trustees have this confidence partly because of the past record of the firm.

When a manager's performance declines, trustees naturally begin to re-evaluate their decision to hire the firm. Their confidence is shaken. Likewise, when key people leave the firm or when the management style appears to be shifting, trustees tend to lose the confidence that prompted them to hire the firm initially.

Each one of these events—poor performance, personnel changes, and style alterations—may be reason, if severe enough, to discharge the manager. The important steps for the trustees are, first, to be constantly aware of these issues; second, to discuss concerns openly with the manager; and, third, to evaluate the response of the firm. Finally, trustees must determine whether or not they have confidence that the firm has the performance capability, personnel, and process to produce superior results in the future. Absent that confidence, the manager should be terminated. Academics tell us that a full market cycle is necessary to make a fair evaluation of an investment manager. This assumes, however, that the personnel and process are intact and that the performance in the short term is reasonable. Without these factors there will be (and should be) a loss of confidence, and the manager should be removed before the market cycle is completed.

Who Should Do the Measuring?

The process of performance evaluation was developed to provide trustees with an objective measurement of the success of a plan, and particularly of its investment managers. The investment manager is the wrong person to furnish such evaluation. He or she understands the issues well but is too close to the process, and it is, therefore, unrealistic to anticipate an objective perspective.

In the early years, the introduction of an objective, third-party evaluation accomplished a great deal by reducing the misinformation supplied by portfolio managers and salespeople; however, it put undue emphasis on short-term performance results. This added unnecessarily to manager turnover, and frequently the issues became more confused by a plethora of esoteric and sometimes useless measures. Since then, there have evolved many fine performance evaluation consulting firms that have become much more knowledgeable from these past experiences and are capable of providing an objective review of a manager's performance. For trustees to have confidence in the objectivity of the evaluator, it is important to know whether there is a conflict of interest. On too many occasions, trustees are shocked to discover that their evaluator is reviewing a manager from whom they are accepting fees for other services rendered by the consulting firm. Objectivity in these cases is at best suspect, and at worst nonexistent.

CONCLUSION

The experience of the past several decades has demonstrated the need for pension plan sponsors to have a structured program for their investments. Developing a Statement of Investment Policy aids trustees and plan professionals in understanding the financial needs of the plan and in focusing on the overall investment goals of the program. Furthermore, fine tuning these goals to specific Investment Manager Guidelines leads to a more productive relationship with investment management. Finally, a regular process of performance evaluation, based on the Statement of Investment Policy, will allow plan sponsors to fully supervise and maintain their investment program and achieve "prudent expert" status.

Richard E. Berger

43

Pension Plan Terminations, Asset Reversions, and Possible Medicare Claims on the Reversion

A defined benefit pension plan is a long-term commitment. The plan sponsor that undertakes to provide retirement benefits has made a promise that may not be fulfilled until the death of the youngest employee. But long-lived is not the same as immortal. Moreover, a pension plan can be terminated for a number of reasons, even shortly after becoming effective.[1] Herein we will explore the recent history of terminations, along with the decision whether or not to terminate, and conclude with the implementation of a termination. Special attention will be paid to Medicare's financial interest in certain plan terminations.

INTRODUCTION

A defined benefit pension plan obligates its sponsor over an indefinite period, practically and legally. By the time a plan has been in operation for five years, some benefit commitments have been made that may not be satisfied for the greater part of a century. Consider a participant who leaves the company at age 30, after five years of service. Under a plan that pays annuities starting at age 65, 50 or more years could pass before the last pension payment is made that was credited during that brief period of employment. Plan sponsors earn favorable tax treatment for contributions and benefits by establishing a permanent arrangement.[2] Failure to meet the requirement of permanency can cause a reversal of past years' tax advantages.

Ironically, the extended nature of the defined benefit promise gives rise to effects that motivate sponsors to terminate their plans. First, the process of funding a pension plan can lead to the build-up of "excess" assets, which a plan sponsor may seek to recover after a plan termination. In its most extreme form, "funding" a pension plan may mean making contributions as benefits are disbursed, the "pay-as-you-go" method. This method is not allowed for the funding of tax-qualified plans by the IRS and could lead to the build-up of large, unsecured liabilities, like those found in governmental plans and corporate postretirement medical programs.[3] In practice, contributions are made far in advance of the actual benefit payments that they are designed to fund.

As part of the actuarial valuation of the pension plan, contributions are determined based on expected annual earnings of the pension fund that accumulate before benefit payments are made. In the case of a plan that bases benefits on final average pay, the actuarial valuation also embodies certain assumptions concerning future compensation levels. The basic premise of the actuarial valuation is that of an ongoing plan: the target aimed at is in the future. Three factors may make adequacy over the long haul a surfeit right now. First, the current price of benefits, as reflected in annuity purchase or lump-sum cash-out rates, may be significantly lower than the long-term price that is reflected in the valuation investment return assumption. Second, the assets in the pension fund may have had an unusual run-up in value, common in the mid-1980s. Third, the projected benefit levels that are targeted by the valuation are higher than those that have been earned to date. The operation of any combination of these factors may create a unique opportunity for the plan sponsor. A company may be able to terminate its plan, purchase or otherwise liquidate its benefit obligations, and recoup a large reversion that may be used for other corporate purposes.

Employers have a legal right to terminate defined benefit plans, although the circumstances under which terminations may take place have been narrowed in the last several years in response to congressional concerns and the financial difficulties of the Pension Benefit Guaranty Corporation (PBGC). Unless there are obligations external to the plan itself, such as under collective bargaining agreements, the termination of a defined benefit plan is considered to be a business decision within the discretion of management. This is a reasonable rule because employers would be less eager to enter into unbreakable agreements. Much of the development in pension legislation, starting with the Employee Retirement Income Security Act in 1974 (ERISA), has been designed to restrict the freedom of plan sponsors in determining the form and funding of retirement programs. As the flexibility has been decreased and as the complexity and compliance costs of laws and regulations have been increased, the defined benefit plan has become less attractive to employers. Employers, especially smaller ones, have backed away from a commitment that may be held hostage to future legislative goals. Since ERISA, companies have favored the defined contribution plan, a trend motivated, at least in part, by the desire to avoid an indefinite promise to employees.

Terminations have come into the forefront of pension issues because of a number of highly publicized asset reversions and a controversy over ownership of plan assets and the security of benefit promises. Table 43-1 shows the number of plan terminations, along with the total assets and reversions involved, for the period 1981–87. To put these numbers in perspective, there were 224,474 defined benefit plans with $786 billion in assets in 1985.[4] In other words, terminations affected approximately 1 percent of defined benefit plans, and 2 percent of their total assets were recovered by plan sponsors during 1981–87.

What was more significant was the number of large reversions to well-known corporations and the ensuing controversy over the appropriateness of such actions. Listed in Table 43-2 are the largest reversions in the last six years, by company and amount.

During the same time period, approximately 50 hospital plans were terminated, but the numbers were more modest in terms of both the participants involved and the reversions (see Table 43-3). The typical hospital plan termination (when assets were sufficient) involved a reversion of a few million dollars. Where data were available, the terminated plan was generally replaced with a successor defined benefit plan or a defined contribution plan.

In some cases, retirees and labor unions have contested the employer's right to recoup the excess assets. In the *Blessitt* case, a court ruled that participants were entitled to future benefits in addition to those already earned. That decision was later vacated as being totally inconsistent with law and precedent. The principle that benefit commitments extend only to accrued benefits is now being appealed, and indications are that it will be reaffirmed.[5]

Table 43-1 Pension Plan Terminations

Year of Termination	Number of Plans	Number of Participants	Total Assets (in millions of dollars)	Total Reversion (in millions of dollars)
1981	35	30,512	$ 341.6	$ 158.6
1982	82	123,587	1,136.8	403.9
1983	166	168,549	3,431.7	1,608.3
1984	331	382,188	7,426.8	3,564.8
1985	581	695,248	15,055.3	6,663.7
1986	265	262,795	8,932.7	4,292.4
1987	219	195,656	4,313.0	1,723.2
TOTAL	1,679	1,858,535	$40,637.9	$18,414.9

Source: Pension Benefit Guaranty Corporation, Completed Reversion Cases as of March 31, 1988.

Table 43-2 Plan Reversions

Company	Year of Termination	Number of Participants	Total Reversion (in millions of dollars)
United Air Lines	1985	14,929	$962.0
FMC Corp.	1985	11,156	726.0
Union Carbide	1985	1,920	504.0
Phillips Petroleum	1986	11,160	400.0
Getty	1984	9,293	360.9
Celanese	1984	7,292	325.8

Source: Pension Benefit Guaranty Corporation, Completed Reversion Cases as of March 31, 1988.

There is another side to the picture, however: that of the termination of underfunded plans. The PBGC was entrusted with the insurance of pension benefits that were inadequately funded. In exchange for a per capita premium, plan benefits would be guaranteed up to certain limits. Unfortunately, the premium was set too low, and companies with poorly funded plans were able to dump the liabilities on the PBGC. The results were a large deficit for the PBGC and ever-increasing premiums for plan sponsors. In belated recognition of this problem, Congress restricted the circumstances under which underfunded plans can be terminated to corporate liquidation and to certain bankruptcy reorganizations.[6]

The jury is still out on reversions. In 1984, the Reagan administration promulgated guidelines for reversions that were intended to protect plan participants, while continuing to allow terminations and reversions.[7] Congressional critics were unsatisfied and continued to press for greater restrictions on the activity. Late in 1988, attempts were made to attach a provision requiring a temporary 60 percent excise tax on any reversion to various pieces of legislation in order to allow Congress time to "study" the issue further. Such an excise tax would have effectively stopped any reversion activity by eliminating most of the possible benefits to the sponsor. In the end, the 10 percent excise tax was permanently increased to

Table 43-3 Hospital Plan Reversions

Hospital	Year of Termination	Number of Participants	Total Reversion (in millions of dollars)
Beth Israel Med. Center	1985	1,664	$15.1
Germantown	1987	1,200	13.5
Charleston Area Med. Center	1985	6,920	13.5
St. Luke's Roosevelt	1985	2,965	9.6
L.I. Jewish Med. Center	1985	2,220	8.1
Stanford	1986	1,098	7.8

Source: Pension Benefit Guaranty Corporation, Completed Reversion Cases as of March 31, 1988.

15 percent,[8] and pressure was put on the Treasury Department to look more closely at reversion cases.[9] Congress has also reduced the full-funding threshold above which companies are prohibited to make deductible contributions to their plans, probably reducing the size of future reversions.[10] In summary, the conditions under which plans may be terminated and the freedom with which excess assets may be recovered have been tightened in recent years, with more restrictions possible in the near future.

THE DECISION TO TERMINATE

A plan sponsor may decide to terminate a defined benefit plan for several reasons, the most publicized of which is a desire to recover "excess" assets. The possibility of a substantial reversion increases with the presence of a number of contributory factors. Among these factors are (1) a long-established plan, (2) a plan that is salary related, (3) a history of conservative funding, and (4) superior asset performance. Although there is no firm rule for determining when a plan has been long established, we mean one that has been in existence for 15 years or more and that has not had major benefit improvements recently. Salary-related plans, particularly those that base benefits on pay in the years immediately before retirement, are more likely to have a surplus of current assets over current benefit liabilities and, therefore, excess assets to be recovered. As noted above, funding for these plans is designed to be adequate to provide anticipated benefit levels and may, therefore, be more than sufficient to fund current, lower benefits. This effect is much less pronounced in the case of a career average plan, which accrues benefits based on earnings during each year of an employee's career, and a typical collectively bargained flat-dollar plan. Funding can be considered conservative if the investment return assumption used to develop contributions is low; if the funding method is of the entry age, frozen initial liability, or aggregate type;

and/or if the sponsor has tended to make annual contributions significantly greater than the minimum required. Finally, several years of excellent asset performance (i.e., compared to the rate assumed) may have generated a surplus.

The conditions listed above may have given rise to a surplus. How does an employer determine if a surplus actually exists? In other words, if the employer uses plan assets to satisfy all current benefit obligations, will there be any assets left over? An approximate answer to this question may be found through an examination of the plan's current actuarial valuation report or a brief discussion with the plan's enrolled actuary. The assets available are relatively easy to identify: the market value of assets, including any contributions that are due and unpaid and that are required to meet minimum funding standards.

Identifying the corresponding benefit liabilities requires more guesswork. The quickest estimate for benefits already earned to date will be found in the accounting information for the plan or in the accounting for the company. Under Statement of Accounting Standards Number 35, the plan must provide the present value of accumulated plan benefits as of the valuation date. The actuary has determined this number based on benefits that have been earned to date and a set of actuarial assumptions. In most cases, the assumptions used will be the same as those used to determine contributions, except for the discount rate. The usefulness of this present value as a proxy for termination liabilities hinges on the level of the assumed discount rate. If a plan is terminated, the obligations to plan participants must be satisfied in one of two ways: through the purchase of annuities or through the payment of lump-sum benefits. The purchase price of an annuity depends on interest rates, the size of the total purchase, and the length of time before pension payments are to begin. Generally, the smaller the total purchase or the longer the period before benefits are paid, the higher the purchase price. Annuities must be purchased for benefits that are in pay status. Other participants may be given lump-sum settlements, which must be determined based on the assumptions of the Pension Benefit Guaranty Corporation (PBGC).

Primary among PBGC assumptions is a set of graduated interest rates, with the highest used for benefits currently payable and the lowest used for benefits that are deferred for 15 or more years. As of this writing, the rate for immediately payable annuities is 7.75 percent; depending on the mix of participant ages, the effective rate for PBGC purposes should fall in the 6–7 percent range. In the current economic climate, annuity purchase rates are likely to fall in the 7–9 percent range, except for the largest plans.

If the discount rate for Financial Accounting Standards (FAS) 35 purposes lies in these ranges, the present value of accumulated benefits can be used as an approximation of what it would cost to settle pension liabilities. By comparing this cost to the assets available for benefits, the plan sponsor has some idea of the financial results of a plan termination. This rough measure should indicate whether a significant reversion could be gained, whether the plan is clearly underfunded, or whether assets and liabilities are roughly equal. In any case, the prudent sponsor should consult with the plan's enrolled actuary in developing any approximations. Changing financial conditions that affect asset values, such as the October 1987 market skid or the significant long-term interest rate fluctuations that can influence annuity purchase rates, may swing a plan from a surplus to an underfunded position, or vice versa. This "rule-of-thumb" approach provides a useful check, while avoiding the expense and complication of a full-blown termination calculation, which involves soliciting annuity quotes and valuing plan liabilities on a PBGC assumption basis.

Besides the desire to recover a surplus, an employer may have other reasons for terminating a defined benefit plan. The desire to reduce costs may be a motivation. If the plan has sufficient assets to cover its liabilities on a termination basis, an employer could terminate and reduce its future contributions to zero. Perhaps the sponsor wishes to switch to the defined contribution approach, for one or more reasons. Because of the growing complexity of administering defined benefit plans, a company may prefer the relative simplicity of a defined contribution plan. Many employers have chosen defined contribution plans because the type of employer commitment made is not open ended: there are no liabilities beyond the contributions made. The chances of additional costs being imposed by legislation are diminished. A defined contribution plan may also have greater appeal to a younger, more mobile work force.

DRAWBACKS TO PLAN TERMINATION

Plan termination has hidden and not-so-hidden costs. As outlined below, any termination is a complex, lengthy, and expensive procedure. When a reversion is involved, special costs and problems arise, the most immediate of which is the taxation of the amounts recovered. Even if ordinary taxes are avoided due to favorable circumstances, a nondeductible excise tax of 15 percent is imposed on any reversion. In order to terminate a plan, an employer must vest all participants in their accrued benefits, which means that some employees who might have left the plan with no vested benefits will receive benefits on plan termination.[11]

The scope of benefit liabilities that must be satisfied on plan termination has expanded in recent years and is still unclear in certain respects. The inclusion of such elements as early retirement subsidies for participants who have not met the eligibility requirements is one factor that may increase the cost of terminations. If a successor defined benefit plan is established that is identical to the terminated plan, a sponsor will probably face higher future costs. The excess amounts that are recovered would have served to moderate contribution levels, as they covered some of the liabilities under the plan. Other entities, such as Medicare, may claim a share of the surplus under the principle that cost-based reimbursement took an overstated pension cost into account. To the degree that a reversion represents a retroactive lowering of pension costs, these claims may have some merit.

If a termination is undertaken to reduce costs, employees may feel that something has been taken away, equivalent to a reduction in pay. This can lead to bitterness among employees if the terminated plan is not supplanted by some other benefit, such as a successor plan or a defined contribution plan. Finally, a defined contribution plan has shortcomings of its own: employees bear the risk of poor investment performance, and the benefits may be inadequate at retirement, especially for short-service employees.

ALTERNATIVES TO TERMINATION

In some cases, alternatives to termination may exist. While no mechanism is yet available for the recovery of excess assets short of termination of the pension plan, contributions to the plan may be reduced for a number of years in several ways.

If the plan is of the final average pay type, it could be converted to a career average plan and updated periodically to keep up with inflation. In other words, benefits could be determined on a final pay basis as of a particular date and then continued on a career average form. If the updates are done periodically, costs will approximate those under a final pay plan but will be deferred.

As an alternative to termination, benefit accruals can be frozen. This will eliminate the plan's normal cost; however, the past service cost may continue if the plan is underfunded. If such a step is taken, plan participants will have to be notified, with corresponding negative publicity.

In case of temporary business hardship, an employer may apply for a waiver of minimum funding standards of the plan. If granted by the Internal Revenue Service (IRS), a waiver allows a plan sponsor to defer a contribution to the plan and pay it back over a period of not more than five years.[12] This tactic may be used when a short respite from contributions is needed but will not permanently reduce them.

IS THE TERMINATION LEGAL?

Given the financial feasibility of termination, attention should be turned to the legal aspects. Does the plan document permit unilateral termination of the plan? Would termination violate collective bargaining agreements or any other legal obligations outside the plan? If a reversion is sought, does the plan permit any excess assets to be recovered by the plan sponsor after all obligations to participants have been satisfied? Prior to the enactment of the Omnibus Budget Reconciliation Act of 1987, plans that lacked a provision allowing a reversion could be amended just before the termination to allow a reversion. Now, plan amendments permitting reversions that were adopted after December 17, 1988, do not become effective before the end of the fifth calendar year following the date of adoption.[13]

If the plan is being terminated within a short time after its adoption, questions may be raised by the IRS about the legitimacy of the arrangement. One of the requirements that must be met by any tax-qualified plan is permanency.

According to the Internal Revenue Code (IRC), a plan must be a bona fide arrangement that is maintained for the exclusive benefit of employees.[14] A company needs to demonstrate a dramatic reversal in business fortunes, such as bankruptcy or inability to remain in business without release from plan commitments, to justify the early termination of a pension plan. Failure to meet a facts-and-circumstances test may result in the retroactive disallowance of tax deductions for plan contributions. Further, the termination must not be part of a strategy to favor the prohibited group of employees—i.e., officers, shareholders, or the highly compensated.[15] According to IRS regulations, a pension plan must contain provisions that restrict the benefits to the 25 most highly compensated employees in the case of termination before the plan has been in effect for 10 years.[16]

Finally, plan sponsors must be careful that their plans incorporate all required amendments up to the date of termination. The IRS has taken the position that plans must comply with certain legal requirements, even if the plan is soon to terminate. Failure to review such obligations can result in delays in carrying out the termination.

MEASURING PLAN SUFFICIENCY

If a legal review of the plan documents and related agreements show that a termination is feasible, the next step is to determine whether or not plan assets are sufficient to meet all benefit obligations to participants. If assets are sufficient, then the employer may undertake what is known as a *standard termination*. If assets are exceeded by the amount required to meet all benefit obligations, the plan may only be terminated under a *distress termination* procedure, unless the company makes contributions sufficient to cover the deficit. A distress termination, as its name implies, may be undertaken only when the employer and all members of the employer's controlled group are in extreme financial difficulty. Specifically, this means liquidation proceedings or reorganization (with the approval of the bankruptcy court) where the termination is necessary for the employer to continue in business. Because the circumstances under which a distress termination can occur are limited, we will confine our attention to standard terminations.

The first step in a standard termination is to select a proposed termination date and identify the assets and liabilities as of that date. The market value of assets will be used for this purpose because any smoothed value that is used for funding is inappropriate when accounts are being settled. The determination of the liabilities is more complicated, involving the calculation of the accrued benefits of plan participants and the selection of appropriate assumptions for valuation of the benefits. For retired participants and those who could receive benefits immediately, this means selecting an interest rate that reflects the current prices for annuity purchases from an insurance company. The plan's actuary can estimate this rate based on the size of the potential purchase and information about other recent annuity purchases. For benefits that are not presently payable, the actuary must use assumptions set by the PBGC. Each month, the PBGC publishes a series of interest rates to be used in valuing terminating plans in conjunction with other assumptions as to expected retirement ages and mortality.

Although these calculations should give the plan sponsor a good idea of whether or not a standard termination is possible and, if so, the size of any reversion, circumstances may change by the time the actual termination is effected. The accrued benefits at termination, as calculated on a participant-by-participant basis, may differ from those estimated in the valuation, especially if the accrual of additional benefits has not been frozen. The sponsor should be careful not to overlook the accrued benefits of participants who have separated from employment but have not yet incurred a break in service. Actual annuity purchase rates may also differ from those estimated, and the PBGC assumptions may have changed by the actual termination date. Finally, asset performance before the termination may change the surplus.

Once the decision has been made to terminate the plan, two measures will protect any surplus if they are promptly effected. First, the plan sponsor should freeze benefit accruals as of a specific date, which will prevent the accrued benefits of participants from increasing. Second, asset values should be locked in by switching from more volatile securities to ones less subject to fluctuation.

MEDICARE AND REVERSIONS

In the typical plan termination, after the employer satisfies benefit commitments to participants, what remains in the pension fund reverts back to the sponsor. But a hospital is not a typical plan sponsor in this respect. Medicare may assert a claim to a portion of the excess to the degree that past reimbursements reflect pension costs. To understand the basis for Medicare's potential claims, we must examine reimbursement rules and recent Health Care Financing Administration (HCFA) administrative decisions.

For services covered under reasonable cost methods, Medicare authorizes reimbursement for pension costs if they are actuarially determined under a formal plan meeting a number of standard ERISA-type requirements.[17] Costs under a plan are divided into current service costs and past service costs, which are basically any "adjustments" to a pension plan that increase or decrease liability, amortized over not less than 10 years.[18] A provider is allowed to pay each of these costs in accordance with the sponsor's accounting policy. Excessive payments (in excess of current and past service costs) may be carried forward and considered as payments against a future liability. Based on the guidelines in the *Provider Reimburse-*

ment Manual (Health Care Financing Administration) an employer seems to have considerable freedom in the funding of a plan, as long as the employer sticks to a consistent funding policy. However, several important questions linger unaddressed. How do you carry forward excess payments: Is all the excess applied to the next year's reimbursement, or is it amortized? If no excessive contributions have been made, but an excess that is subject to reversion has arisen, are the contributions retrospectively excessive? Several decisions of the Provider Payment Reimbursement Board (PPRB) hint at a Medicare position on reversions.

The PPRB recently decided a case in which an intermediary reduced the allowable pension costs below those claimed. The board found that the intermediary's reduction of pension costs to the minimum levels was proper, despite the provider's claim that up to a 10-year amortization of past service costs was allowed. The provider claimed that payments that did not exceed the total unfunded liabilities were not excessive. In the course of presenting its findings, the PPRB noted that the actuarial assets of the plan exceeded the actuarial value of the accumulated benefits by $3 million. In the board's opinion, "there was excess funding of $3 million, which should have been treated as a prepayment. . . ."[19] Even though the contributions were not intrinsically excessive (given an established, consistent funding policy), the board thought that the "excess" should have been carried forward to future years. Curiously, the PPRB didn't go beyond the reduction to minimum contributions to the prepayment position. In his review of this decision, the HCFA administrator agreed with the PPRB, noting that provision of pension costs in excess of the minimum was not "necessary" and should be reimbursed in future periods.[20]

In a second decision arising from a review of a PPRB decision, the HCFA administrator provided more insight into the treatment of "excessive" pension costs. In the case under review, a hospital claimed its normal contribution of 10 percent of payroll. All parties agreed that the pension fund had assets that exceeded "the amount required to insure payment of future obligations" by $1.8 million.[21] What was at issue was how quickly the "overfunding" should be reflected, not whether it should affect Medicare reimbursement. The intermediary argued that the excess should be amortized over 10 years, while the provider stated that it should be allowed to make its customary contribution. A third party, the Bureau of Eligibility, Reimbursement, and Coverage (BERC), disagreed with the 10-year amortization, insisting on the application of the entire excess against the current year's contribution. The administrator agreed with the BERC and ruled that the entire excess should be applied to the current year's contribution, which, being less than the excess, was disallowed in its entirety.[22]

Although neither of these decisions explicitly involves a reversion, they both seem to imply that a reversion would have to be taken into account in the reimbursement basis. Not only that, but a reversion would have to be netted against pension contributions immediately. If no successor plan is established and no future contributions are made, would the reversion be netted against all other charges? Would it be reflected in the first year or the first few years? If a successor plan is adopted, would the reversion be reflected each year only to the extent of the year's contribution?

Depending on the answers to these questions, a reversion may hold no advantages to a hospital sponsor that is totally dependent on Medicare reimbursement. Although not explicitly addressing the issue of reversions, the *Provider Reimbursement Manual* indicates that "unvested benefits" that were provided for under Medicare reimbursement rules should be used to reduce the costs in the year that they are realized.[23] The financial impact of Medicare's claims against an asset reversion cannot be ignored; the entire decision to terminate may turn on the size of the potential claim. Before any reversion is sought, therefore, plan sponsors must be very careful to seek the advice of counsel with regard to Medicare claims.

In practice, Medicare's claims against a reversion are likely to be small because of the changes in hospital reimbursement that went into effect in 1983. Effective for cost-reporting periods starting after September 1983, hospitals were reimbursed for inpatient services based on a fixed amount per Medicare discharge.[24] The new prospective payment system reimburses hospitals on the basis of diagnostic-related groups, which makes the question of pension costs moot. In certain exceptional cases, such as psychiatric and rehabilitation hospitals, the cost-based reimbursement system is continued.[25] Services other than those rendered on an inpatient basis are still covered by the old system. Generally, the exclusion of inpatient services from the cost-based system means that most hospital reversions will be affected only slightly by Medicare claims. In short, unless Medicare advances a theory that it is entitled to some share of a reversion because of pre–September 1983 payments, most hospitals should be able to receive reversions free of any such claims.

THE MECHANICS OF THE TERMINATION

Assume that after careful consideration of all aspects of a plan termination, the assets have been found sufficient to cover benefit liabilities, and the decision has been made to proceed. In order to effect the termination, the plan administrator must first secure the legal authority to terminate the plan.

A resolution by the board of directors that specifies a termination date is necessary to start the process. The termination date should be selected so that there is sufficient time to complete the procedure, including notification of various third parties. If the employer has not yet moved to freeze accruals under the plan, then that step should be undertaken, along with notification of plan participants (at least 15 days before accruals cease).[26] With accruals frozen, the plan administrator must assemble participant data that will be used to calculate termination benefits for the purposes of soliciting annuity quotes from insurance companies, calculating lump sums, and notifying participants of their benefit amounts.

At least 60 days prior to the proposed termination date, the plan administrator must provide all affected parties with a written notice of intent to terminate (NOIT), which discloses the intention to terminate and the proposed termination date.[27] Included in the class of affected parties are all plan participants, beneficiaries, alternate payees under qualified domestic orders, and employee organizations (such as unions) that represent plan participants and any parties designated to receive such notice on behalf of an affected party. The NOIT must be mailed or delivered to each affected party.

After notifying the affected parties, the plan administrator must notify the PBGC of the proposed termination.[28] Included in such notice must be an enrolled actuary's certification of the projection of plan assets and liabilities as of the proposed termination date and a statement that assets are projected to be sufficient to provide for all benefit liabilities as of that date. The plan administrator must also certify the completeness and correctness of the information on which the actuary's determination is based.

Concurrently with the filing with the PBGC, the plan administrator must mail or personally deliver to each participant and beneficiary a notice of plan benefits. The date of this mailing must be disclosed in the PBGC filing. Included in the notice of plan benefits are the amount and form of each participant's benefit as of the proposed termination date, along with the data and assumptions used to develop the benefit and its actuarial present value. Except in the case of benefits that have a present value of less than $3,500, the plan administrator must give the participant or beneficiary the option to receive the benefits in annuity form.[29] Because plan participants have several choices in handling their distributions, with different tax consequences, the plan administrator may wish to provide tax information at this time.

After the PBGC has received the submission from the plan administrator, a 60-day review period begins. If the PBGC finds that any of the notification requirements have not been satisfied or that assets are not sufficient, it will issue a notice of noncompliance. Otherwise, after 60 days have elapsed and within 30 days of the elapse of the 60-day period, the plan administrator may begin distribution of the assets in lump-sum or annuity form, as appropriate.[30] Within another 30 days of the final distribution of the assets, the PBGC must be notified that the assets have been distributed and that all benefit liabilities have been satisfied. Given that the plan documents allow it, subject to any claims by Medicare and the 15 percent excise tax under the Internal Revenue Code, amounts remaining in the trust fund may revert to the employer.

CONCLUSION

The termination of a pension plan is a complex procedure and should not be done without careful premeditation, especially in the case of a hospital that may face claims by Medicare against any reversion. Even so, termination might be the best alternative available, and the decision to terminate may be made. Because laws and regulations have changed significantly in the past few years and are likely to change more in the near future, plan administrators should be careful to review any proposed terminations with the plan's enrolled actuary and legal counsel.

NOTES

1. I.R.B. 1969-4, Rev. Rul. 69-24.
2. I.R.C. Reg. § 1.401-1(b)(2) (September 24, 1956).
3. I.R.C. § 412 (1986).
4. Federal Reserve Bulletin, November 1988, at 719.
5. *Blessitt v. Retirement Plan for Employees of Dixie Engine Co.*, 848 F.2d 1164 (1988).
6. ERISA § 4041(c), 29 U.S.C. § 1341(c).
7. P.B.G.C. News Release No. 84-23, May 23, 1984.
8. I.R.C. § 4980 (as amended by the Technical Corrections Act of 1988).
9. Letter from the Treasury Department to Sen. Howard Metzenbaum, October 22, 1988.
10. I.R.C. § 412(c)(7).
11. I.R.C. § 411(d)(3)(A).
12. I.R.C. § 412(d).
13. ERISA § 4044(d), 29 U.S.C. 1344(d).
14. I.R.C. § 401(a)(2).
15. I.R.B. 1969-4, Rev. Rul. 69-24, Rev. Rul. 69-25.
16. I.R.C. Reg. § 1.401-4(c)(2) (September 24, 1956).
17. Provider Reimbursement Manual, Part I, § 2142 (September 1983).
18. *Id.*, at § 2142.5.
19. P.P.R.B. Hearing Dec. No. 88-D10, Dec. 16, 1987.
20. P.P.R.B. Hearing Dec. No. 88-D10, Dec. 16, 1987.
21. P.P.R.B. Hearing Dec. No. 87-D51, Feb. 25, 1987.
22. P.P.R.B. Hearing Dec. No. 87-D51, Feb. 25, 1987.
23. Provider Reimbursement Manual at Part I, § 2140.3.
24. Title VI, Social Security Amendments of 1983, 42 U.S.C. 1305.
25. *Id.*
26. ERISA § 204(h), 29 U.S.C. 1054(h).
27. P.B.G.C. Reg. § 2615.4 (August 20, 1980).
28. *Id.* at § 2616.4.
29. I.R.C. § 417(e)(2).
30. ERISA § 4041, 29 U.S.C. 1341.

Jeffrey P. Petertil

Retiree Welfare Benefits

44

INTRODUCTION

Health needs do not stop at retirement. For that reason, employers that offer health and welfare benefits to active employees are usually reluctant to deprive retired employees of these valuable benefits. Retired employees made strong contributions to the organization during their working years and often find life and health insurance prohibitively expensive in their older years. Thus, many employers extend these benefits to the retirees and their families.

Common employee benefits that are extended to retirees include life insurance and medical insurance. Dental and vision insurance are not as frequently extended to active employees as the other two, and it should not be surprising that they are also not often extended to retirees. The costs for these services are not particularly great and are unlikely to cause financial hardship if insurance is not available. The same cannot be said of life insurance and health insurance.

Life Insurance

Life insurance needs are not as great in the retirement years as in the active years, when families are being raised. Future

Note: This chapter is based on parts of the study note: *Plan Design for Retiree Welfare Benefits,* Society of Actuaries, Schaumburg, Illinois, © 1988. Permission has also been granted by the International Foundation of Employee Benefit Plans, Brookfield, Wisconsin, to include material from *Health Care Cost Management,* © 1986, and *Managing Corporate Health Care Costs,* © 1986.

income needs are not as great and will be provided in large part by personal savings and retirement income plans. Permanent insurance purchased during the working years may exist and provide adequate coverage. Reductions in life insurance amounts needed in retirement years often make the purchase of life insurance, even at the higher term rates for the older ages, more manageable for those in their retirement years.

Active employees are usually offered a life insurance benefit that is a flat amount or a percentage of salary. The flat amount may be periodically adjusted for inflation, while the salary-based amount will automatically adjust. This basic layer of life insurance for the employee will usually be completely subsidized by the employer. Optional layers may be offered to the employee and dependents with little employer subsidy. The first layer will usually be term insurance, while the optional insurance may be term, permanent, or universal life.

For retirees, optional amounts and dependent coverage are usually not available from employers, and the basic insurance amount will not be adjusted for past employment inflation. In fact, many plans for retirees call for *reductions* in face amounts, with typical reduction timing tied to retirement at age 65 or age 70. For instance, a plan that offers active employees two-times-salary coverage might give retirees one-times-final-salary coverage until they reach age 65, 60 percent of final salary with a $10,000 minimum at age 65, and maybe a reduction to $10,000 for all retirees at age 70. This last amount might be seen as a burial and estate settlement amount.

While it is possible for life insurance plan design for retirees to be more complex than the example cited above, it is more often simpler, possibly $10,000 for any retiree. In contrast, retiree health insurance plans are more complicated, with no two plans likely to be exactly the same. For this reason, most of the discussion here will focus on retiree health insurance.

Health Insurance

The need for health care does become more serious after retirement. For that reason, most of the employee plans that have been extended into retirement and the government program for the elderly, Medicare, have found that their expenses are much higher than it was originally thought they would be. These retiree health plans have become quite expensive and face future costs that in some cases are astronomical, and yet many people would say that retiree health plans are inadequate to meet the needs of the elderly.

As evidence of the inadequate nature of private and public plans, it is noteworthy that the Reagan administration, an administration that prided itself on its conservatism and lack of interference in private enterprise, introduced the idea of an additional government plan of catastrophic health coverage for the elderly. (This eventually passed as the Medicare Catastrophic Care Act of 1988 and will be discussed in more detail later.) For this administration to consider such a plan is, in the opinion of many, an admission of current inadequacy by one of the last groups expected to admit it.

How have we reached this point? Part of the answer is seen in the fact that we interchange as though they were synonymous the words *elderly* and *retirees*. These two words have very different connotations. Retiree has essentially a good connotation. Retirees receive pensions. We may look forward to being retirees, but few of us look forward to being elderly. The elderly need health care and health care financial security.

Many of the people involved in designing and implementing employee health benefit plans originally were on the pension side of the benefit situation. This is true not only for private employers, but also within the government, and continues to this day in some areas. Many of those who set up Medicare had been instrumental in setting up Social Security.

There are many differences between setting up a health care security plan and setting up a financial income security plan, such as the Social Security program or a private retirement income plan. These differences have become apparent in the last dozen years for Medicare and the last five or six years for private employer health plans. A great deal of expertise about health care is needed for anyone designing retiree health benefit plans. The emphasis should be on knowledge of health care for the elderly, as well as on knowledge of benefits for retirees.

In this discussion we will deal with the interaction of government plans and private plans. We will also discuss health care needs that will not be covered by either of these programs and that the individual retiree alone will have to finance. At the present, most retiree health plans are essentially active employee plans, modified to recognize Medicare as a primary financing mechanism. They have not been designed with the needs of retirees who might be classified as elderly in mind.

The subject of postemployment health care benefits has received increasing attention in the last few years. The main concern has been with the benefits paid to retirees and their dependents for health care expenses. The passage of the Consolidated Omnibus Budget Reconciliation Act of 1985 (COBRA), however, enlarged the definition of postemployment benefits to include health coverage after employment for just about anyone who had been covered during employment, including voluntary terminations and divorced spouses. COBRA also included retirees who were not entitled to Medicare benefits. Health coverage must be offered at cost, in accordance with COBRA, to retirees for 18 months after their retirement or until they become entitled to Medicare.

The coverage mandated for retirees by COBRA was similar to the coverage that many plan sponsors were already offering to their retirees in some subsidized fashion. Surveys completed in the mid-1980s by the major benefits consulting firms consistently showed that a majority of the organizations surveyed provided medical coverage for retired employees. With larger corporations, the percentage approached 90 percent or more.[1] Surveys asked questions about the extent of the coverage in comparison to that provided to active employees and generally found that only a distinct minority of the companies provided a lower level of benefits to retirees than to actives. This set of statistics indicates the genesis of retiree medical benefits. They were often simply an extension of active medical coverage to retirees, with little thought given to plan design.

HISTORICAL PERSPECTIVE

Retiree coverage was granted by corporations in the 1950s and 1960s when it truly seemed to be a fringe benefit. It was often a negotiated benefit put on the bargaining table in place of an increase in pensions. Although medical costs were rising during this time, the corporations conferring the benefit felt that it was relatively inexpensive in light of their cost analysis and the position of Medicare, which was introduced in 1965, as the primary payer of the medical benefits for retirees. Few employees were expected to retire before age 65, which was the Medicare eligibility age. All plans had provisions for integrating with Medicare, so that a retiree did not get duplicate payments from both Medicare and the employer plan. Plans offered to active employees usually had strong coverage of hospital and physician charges, and this was extended to retirees with the assumption that the cost after Medicare integration was not consequential.

Coverage of long-term care or prescription drugs was minimal and sometimes nonexistent for active employees. These costs are not significant for most people under the age of 60. Prescription drugs are, however, a major cost for those in retirement, and long-term care can be a tremendous cost to the elderly or their families. This difference between the health care needs of actives and those of retirees was ignored, however, in the early plan designs.

Medicare offers substantial coverage to those over 65 who are hospitalized. In a recent year, three-fourths of the hospital costs of those over 65 were covered by Medicare.[2] In the same year, about half of the physician costs were covered by Medicare. Virtually none of the cost of nursing home care or prescription drugs was covered by Medicare. These figures all predate the expansion of Medicare through the Medicare Catastrophic Care Act of 1988 which is to be phased in over five years, beginning in 1989.

Medicare paid a greater percentage of hospital and physician services in the late 1960s than it did in the 1980s, and, given this fact, the employer payments for retirees were relatively low for this benefit at that time in relation to the cost of pensions for retirees or the cost of medical care for the active employees. In the ensuing years, however, retiree medical payments have been rising at an alarming rate. The rising cost focused attention on the long-term cost implications of this benefit. There was a growing awareness that the cost of the benefit would not be measured simply by the payments made in any one particular year. Analogies to the expensing and funding of pension benefits were pointed out.

Cost of Plans

Costs of retiree welfare plans can be measured in a number of ways, including current payments, future payments, and present value of liabilities. The last measure involves an actuarial valuation similar to a pension valuation. Such a valuation would examine all the liabilities and the current and future cost projections and put a time value on the cash flows, using a discount rate in the same manner as a pension valuation.

The resulting present value depends on a number of factors, including the services covered, current claim costs, average age at retirement, male-female makeup of the group, and quite a few other things. But what studies have found time and again is that the amounts are large. The amounts are often larger than pension liabilities. The amounts are often larger than corporate surplus. This tends to make people pay attention.

The liabilities are definitely significant. Many of the retiree plans offer lifetime coverage. This lifetime coverage is not only for the retiree but also for the spouse. This means that the health care coverage extends through all illnesses including terminal illnesses for one, and probably two, people. It is not surprising then that current payments are merely an indication of the coming complications.

It does not help any that many plan sponsors are not even familiar with their current plan costs. This occurs because costs are often hidden through miscoding of retiree claims as active claims, through acceptance of insurance company premium rates as the true costs (when in reality the insurance premium rates may hide the retiree cost by a factor of as much as two or three), and through the misunderstandings of the workings of Medicare.

In attempting to value current costs and future liabilities, it is wise to enroll the services of a trained health care actuary or data analyst. Too often, projections of costs are made by people with a pension benefit background or with experience only in looking at the health care costs for active plans. Skilled health care actuaries reviewing the postemployment welfare projections determined by those less experienced in this field are accustomed to finding results that are off the mark by a substantial factor. Often it is not the projection methods themselves that were in error, but rather the initial determination of what current costs truly were.

Demographic and Economic Factors

Assuming that current costs can be determined correctly, what are the other factors that make those current costs only the tip of a very large financial iceberg? For one, in most cases the retiree population is still growing; the number of retirees at the present time is only a fraction of what it will be 20 or 30 years from now. Other factors are that retirees use more medical care than do active employees and that Medicare does not pay for as much of the retiree costs as is sometimes assumed. Additionally, Medicare has cut back on the proportion of health care that it finances. This means that the plans that integrate with Medicare are usually left holding the bag and paying out the greater proportion of costs.

Health costs for those who retire early are more costly because of the fact that more years of life are involved but, more importantly, because one who retires before age 65 does not have a Medicare program as the primary payer. That means that the employer plan is the primary, and often only, coverage that is available before age 65 for early retirees.

What also must be remembered is that, on average, medical prices increase faster than other economic costs. Finally, medical use per capita has been increasing at a very rapid pace, regardless of what the prices of those medical services are. There has been a plateau in the last few years as the Medicare DRG program and private programs have reduced the use of hospitals, but it is likely that medical utilization will continue to rise in the years to come. All these factors combine to mean that even if current costs are less than $1,000 per retiree on an annual basis, the likely liability that an employer is faced with for an individual retiring in 1989 at age 62 with a younger spouse is upward of $20,000 to $50,000 when measured as the present value of future benefits. This would mean that the retirement of 20 employees could imply a liability of $1 million of retiree health care.

When confronted with these rising costs, many employers took steps to limit their financial obligations. These steps included implementing plan changes that often had the effect of shifting costs onto retirees. Numerous lawsuits were brought to stop these plan changes and were, for the most part, successful in limiting the changes that employers could make for plans where past promises to retirees implied a contract between employers and former employees. Most publicized of these was the *Bethlehem Steel* case, in which the company made reductions in benefits for those already retired and the retirees brought a class action lawsuit against the company. The retirees prevailed in the trial court, and the case was settled before it went to appeal. The trial court essentially said that benefits could not be changed for those already retired, and, although the settlement did result in some slight cutbacks, precedent was set with this case.

Other cases have limited employers' rights to change benefits for retirees, implying that reductions in the postemployment benefits of those still active would also be restricted. The *White Farm* case implied that federal common law applied to vest retiree welfare benefits but was overruled by an appeals court that held vested rights might be found in a plan or contract but not in common law.[3]

For now, it appears that the employer's right to change benefits for those already retired is limited by past actions and that there are also limits on changes that can be made for those active employees who are not far from retirement age. The biggest lesson from the court cases is to be sure that what you are communicating to your members is what you truly intend your commitment to be.

Legislation

Congress did enact legislation in 1986 that guaranteed retiree medical coverage for a certain group for a certain length of time, but the language was so narrow as to apply only to the retirees impacted by the LTV bankruptcy. The quick passage of the legislation, however, is one indication of the seriousness with which Congress is approaching the vesting issue. It will be examined even more closely in the years to come.

There is also concern among some congressional staffers about discrimination in the administration and design of plans for both active employees and retirees. Most observers, on the other hand, do not feel that discrimination in welfare plans is a large problem. The Tax Reform Act of 1986, however, includes nondiscrimination provisions. The initial reaction, inside the Internal Revenue Service (IRS), as well as outside among employers, is that the burden of compliance will far outweigh the reduction in discrimination.

EXPENSING AND FUNDING ISSUES

Most employers or labor-management funds have been funding these benefits on a pay-as-you-go basis. Their accounting has reflected the pay-as-you-go basis also. As was mentioned earlier, the pay-as-you-go basis can lead to a misleading idea of what actual plan costs are likely to be in the future. Thus, the pay-as-you-go expensing and funding are probably a far cry from what will actually be seen in the future.

FASB Action

In 1984 the Financial Accounting Standards Board (FASB) indicated that it required footnote disclosure of postemployment welfare benefits other than pension benefits in annual reports for 1984 and following years. It appears that FASB will move toward implementation of expensing over the working lifetime of the employees over the next four or five years. We can expect a standard similar to that for pension benefits by the early 1990s.

The implication is that the courts and the accounting profession feel that benefits that were promised for life should be considered vested and should be expensed over the working lifetime of the employees. This leaves the question of where the money is to come from. Very little prefunding of benefits has been done in the past, and, if it is to be done in the near future, it will not be done under advantages that are similar to those for pension prefunding.

Relevant Tax Code Sections

Those employers that are interested in pursuing prefunding have looked at the federal Tax Code sections that allow them some tax advantages in prefunding welfare benefits. The first of these is the use of a trust fund under Section 501(c)(9) of the Internal Revenue Code. This was the funding vehicle used by most of those firms that were funding before the 1984 tax act. That act, referred to as DEFRA, appears to have shut the door on funding through a 501(c)(9) trust because the amount that can be contributed is limited in its deductibility and the assets that are funded will not have tax-exempt investment income. This has severely limited interest in use of the 501(c)(9) trusts.

Section 401(h) of the Internal Revenue Code makes provision for the funding of welfare benefits through a pension trust. This section of the Code had been around for a number of years without anyone's taking advantage of it. Interest arose only after the passage of DEFRA in 1984, when Section 501(c)(9) became no longer the favored funding vehicle. Section 401(h), however, is limited in that the benefits are subordinate to pension benefits and the amount contributed is determined as a fraction of the pension contribution. This makes it unlikely that an adequate amount of funding can be obtained through a 401(h) arrangement.

Many plans that have a pension surplus would be interested in using that surplus to pay for welfare benefits, but the IRS has indicated that no transfer of pension assets for the payment of welfare liabilities will be permitted. People in the federal government have been studying the problem and do realize that little funding will occur without federal tax encouragement. Since advance funding is a key to the financial stability of retiree benefits, it is likely that some type of tax advantages will be forthcoming in the next few years.

The legal cases combine with the uncertainty about FASB expense standards and federal government action to create a cautionary environment for plan design changes. Nevertheless, certain points have become quite clear.

1. Retiree health programs insure exactly that segment of society that needs health care the most—the elderly and the disabled.
2. The future trend of health care costs is very uncertain, but there is generally agreement that in the foreseeable future, as a portion of gross national product, health care costs will continue to increase. The uncertainty involves what the rate of increase will be and how long it will last.
3. Most retiree health programs imply a long-term commitment by the plan sponsor.
4. The federal government's Medicare program covers many of the costs of retiree health care, but the government has tended to shift costs to the private sector. The expansion of Medicare through the 1988 Medicare Catastrophic Coverage Act has reinforced the role of the government, but the commitment for the longer term is uncertain.

THE ROLE OF MEDICARE

In considering the plan design of a retiree health program, one must always keep in mind the substantial role played by Medicare in determining the day-to-day administration of these benefits, as well as the overall philosophy of the private sector in conferring these benefits. When Medicare was introduced in 1965, the idea was simple: government would relieve those over 65, and (later) those under 65 who are on disability, of the financial burden of extreme health care costs. In particular, hospital costs were to be primarily financed by the government, with some physician costs and other health care costs also financed through the Medicare program.

In its early years, Medicare did relieve a very large portion of this financial burden. But over the years, as cost implications became apparent, the Medicare program was gradually cut back. More and more of the financial burden was placed on the retiree or the plan that stood secondary to Medicare. This reached a point where Medicare was expected to pay only about 45 percent of the 1988 health care bill for those over age 65.[4]

In reaction to growing complaints that the Medicare program was inadequate in its coverage of health care costs, Congress in 1988 passed a bill expanding coverage, the Medicare Catastrophic Coverage Act (MCCA). The law established a series of additional benefits that were to become effective at different points in time, ranging from the beginning of 1989 into 1993. For 1989 Medicare was to pay all inpatient hospital bills beyond an initial deductible; in 1990 ancillary costs for Medicare recipients will be covered more fully; prescription drug costs will be covered by Medicare in increasing amounts from 1990 to 1993.

The benefits are being changed in phases due largely to administrative reasons, but there are also some financial causes. The federal budget deficit grew alarmingly throughout the 1980s, and the possibility of financing the Medicare improvements from general revenues was never considered practical. Instead, financing via additional premiums and a tax surcharge on Medicare recipients was adopted. At the time of this writing, this financing route was generating considerable controversy among the more vocal Medicare recipients, and, under their influence, certain members of Congress had introduced laws to delay the effective date of MCCA and review certain provisions. With full implementation of MCCA still in question, therefore, the most useful point of reference for those wishing to understand the interactions of Medicare and retiree medical plans is probably Medicare as it existed in 1988 before the passage of MCCA.

Medicare is divided into Hospital Insurance (Part A) and Supplemental Medical Insurance (Part B). Part A covers hospital care, and Part B covers physician care. This is a working definition, although other coverages exist.

Part A was designed so the retiree would pay a deductible that was to be set at a level about equal to one day's hospital care. There is another cost-sharing provision: Part A hospital coverage does not extend to all days in a hospital—after 60 days, reimbursement is cut back somewhat.

The hospital deductible was based on a formula and between 1981 and 1986 rose from $204 to $492, for an average annual increase of 19 percent. The 19-percent average annual increase contrasted dramatically with much lower increases in most other costs over the same period of time. Comparable annual percentage increases for the consumer price index in general and the medical care component in particular were 5 percent and 8½ percent, respectively. Congress stepped in and changed the formula, with the result that the deductible rose ''only'' to $520 in 1987 and $540 in 1988.

The initial deductible is not the only cost-sharing element that has been indexed and increasing. The inpatient hospital coinsurance and the nursing home care copayment are indexed, using the same rate of increase as the hospital deductible.

Part B, the physician coverage, was designed to cover physicians' costs. Coverage is available only on payment of a monthly premium by the enrollee. The monthly premium does not cover the full cost of Part B, which is in large part subsidized by the government.

The Part B premium can also change from year to year depending on the formula, which is different from the Part A formula. While the increases from 1981 to 1987 were not particularly steep, in 1988 the premium increased from the 1987 level of $17.90 to $24.30. To the extent that a plan pays for Part B, the plan is subject to cost increases beyond the employer's control.

Other changes that have been made over the years have had similar cost implications. One of the first was that Medicare's definition of reasonable and customary charges for physicians was considerably different from that of many insurers. The gap between reasonable and customary for Medicare and for a corporate plan may be considerable and is often financed by the private plan.

Diagnostic-Related Groups (DRGs) and the prospective payment system initiated in late 1983 had a tremendous impact on medical care financing in the United States. Whether this will have a positive impact on private retiree health plans remains a subject of debate, but it has been an administrative change applied to Medicare. Medicare is not a static plan. It is always undergoing changes, and the government has reserved the right to be flexible. Legislation in the early 1980s led to Medicare's taking a secondary role and employers' taking a primary role in the coverage of people eligible for Medicare but covered under plans for active employees. Employers are wary of such a reversal of roles in relation to retirees, and those involved in plan design must be aware of this possibility.

When private plan coverage exists but Medicare is primary, the plan provisions must define the relationship with Medicare. It can be done in one of two ways.

1. Coverage is defined as if Medicare were absent, but the benefit provides for an offset of Medicare reimbursement. This is referred to as Medicare integration, and three examples are given later.
2. The plan is designed to fill in coverage that Medicare does not provide. This is the equivalent of Medicare supplement policies sold by insurance companies to individuals. The coverage may specifically refer to Medicare (e.g., Part A hospital deductible), or it may define the coverage without reference to Medicare (e.g., $500 for the first day of hospitalization). The coverage can, when combined with Medicare coverage, be a retreat from the active plan coverage, or it can be an expansion of the active coverage, even moving into the area of chronic care. Such coverage has gone by different names, including Medicare fill-in, Medicare supplement, or Medigap insurance.

INTEGRATION OF THE PRIVATE PLAN WITH MEDICARE

If the usual course of continuing the active plan is chosen, a procedure must be established for integrating with Medicare when the coverages coincide. There are three common ways of integrating: coordination, exclusion, and carve-out.

The Medicare *coordination* provision treats Medicare as any other primary insurer would be regarded under a secondary payment provision. The retiree plan, as secondary payer, pays up to the amount it would pay as primary payer with the exception that it will not pay benefits already paid by Medicare. This practice usually means that the retiree will not have to pay the deductible or copayments of *either* Medicare or the retiree plan.

The Medicare *exclusion* is a plan provision that states that the benefit amount will be calculated by determining what the

Table 44-1 Coverage Example

	Medicare Pays	Calculation	Group Plan Pays	Member Pays
Coordination	$600	$1,100-$600	$500	$ 0
Exclusion	$600	8($500-$100)	$320	$180
Carve-out	$600	$800-$600	$200	$300

plan covers, subtracting Medicare payments, and then determining what the plan pays on the resulting amount. This will usually result in a lower copayment and possibly a lower deductible payment by the retiree than a carve-out provision.

The Medicare *carve-out* is a plan provision that states that the benefit amount will be calculated by determining what the retiree plan will pay in the absence of Medicare and then paying that amount less what Medicare pays. If there is a deductible or copayment required under the plan, the retiree will have to pay it before the plan pays.

As an example, let us look at a covered expense of $1,100. We will assume Medicare pays $600 and the private plan provides for 80 percent copayment after a $100 deductible. In the absence of Medicare, the plan would pay $800. As shown in Table 44-1, the payment will be different with each of the three integration approaches. Although the uses and definitions of the terms in Table 44-1 are becoming common, they are by no means universal. In particular, carve-out is sometimes used to refer to any integration provision. Plan sponsors should ascertain how retiree claims are being integrated with Medicare.

ELEMENTS OF RETIREE PLAN DESIGN

It has been mentioned that for the majority of plans currently in force, the elements of plan design were simply carried over from the active plan. This means that from inception the needs of the retirees were not looked at in a different manner from the needs of the active employees. We have seen that indeed they may be quite different. Plan design in the future is much more likely to take specific retiree needs into account than it has in the past.

The four basic plan design questions are

1. Who will be eligible for coverage?
2. What coverage and benefits will they receive?
3. How much will it cost, and who will pay for it?
4. For how long a period of time will the coverage be promised?

These questions are not unique to retiree health plan design; they should also be asked for active plan design (although the last question is usually assumed to be answered by the length of employment). The questions should be answered in the context of the needs of the plan sponsor and the constraints that derive from financial and other considerations. The following discussion indicates provisions that might be included in a plan design. It will be clear that there is an enormous number of possible combinations for plan design. The challenge is not only to understand the long-term financial implications of any of the combinations selected but also to balance the social benefits with the financial constraints.

Eligibility Criteria

Many of the current retiree health plans offer complete coverage for life to anyone who retires from the organization and receives an immediate pension, no matter how small the pension. Less frequently, plans confer eligibility on terminated vested former employees. For employees with short service or early retirement the financial implication can be that the retiree health benefit is worth as much or more than the pension benefit. An awareness of this has led to several eligibility approaches that offer a rich plan to retirees and yet avoid the high cost. One approach is to extend the benefit for only a limited period following retirement and not for life. Another approach is to extend lifetime coverage to all retirees but full coverage only to those who have given substantial employment service. A third approach would recognize the disparity between the plan costs for those eligible for Medicare and those not eligible and adjust benefits according to some established policy. These three approaches are discussed in detail below.

Although the typical plan offers lifetime coverage, extension of benefits for a limited period following retirement is an approach used by a number of plan sponsors. The period of time varies from plan to plan. Since most plans allow a 30-, 60-, or 90-day extension on termination from the group for *active* employees, an extension equally long is almost always provided to retirees. (COBRA now requires an 18-month extension for retirees not eligible for Medicare, but theoretically this mandated plan is to cost the employer nothing.) Some employers provide retirees one or two or as many as five years of benefits beyond retirement. Other plan sponsors continue coverage until age 65 or age 70. Each extension format will have its own associated costs, and those are likely to differ between covered groups. Multiemployer trusts set up under collective bargaining agreements may continue benefits for a certain period of time for all members.

Lifetime coverage with benefits or contributions varying by length of service has attracted a good deal of attention. Such an approach may reward longer lengths of service with greater benefits or, in some cases, a smaller retiree contribution. For example, where there is a plan deductible, it may be lower for each five years of service. The portion of Medicare Part B premium paid by the plan sponsor could be varied by length of service. A plan's copayment amount, maximum out-of-pocket expense, or lifetime maximum could likewise be varied. Separate benefits, such as home health care, nursing home care, dental care, or prescription drugs, can be offered to only those who have considerable service. Periodic contributions required for maintenance of the retiree's coverage or for

dependent coverage can be lowered or eliminated according to qualifying service.

The variations are probably infinite, but care must be taken that the provisions are understood by both retirees and active employees who will become eligible. The value of the benefits for each service level must also relate to the value placed on the length of service by the plan sponsor.

Benefits based on Medicare eligibility and retirement age are also attracting attention. The reason for this is the disparity between the average annual cost of coverage for a retiree eligible for Medicare and a retiree not eligible. A reason for adjusting benefits by retirement age is a longer life-in-retirement expectancy of the younger retiree. An employer that provides a reduced pension benefit for early retirement should, in theory, offer even a greater reduction (because of Medicare) in the health benefit to assure equity with those who retire at the assumed retirement age of 65. Benefit reductions could use most of the approaches appropriate for length of service adjustments as discussed above. Considerations such as the duration of reductions (lifetime, age 65, etc.) and the handling of dependent coverage also must be taken into account.

Each of the three approaches briefly summarized above has its advantages and disadvantages. The extension approach limits the sponsor's liability in time and, thus, dollars but leaves the retiree vulnerable to high costs beyond coverage termination. (The highest medical costs are incurred, not surprisingly, in the last two years of life.) The service-related benefit provides lifetime security and recognition of work contributions but leaves the plan sponsor with a somewhat open-ended financial liability. The retirement age benefit also leaves an open liability, although providing a lifetime benefit and recognizing future costs and Medicare reimbursement.

Coverage

A number of questions must be answered about the type of coverage that will be provided. Among these are

- Will the emphasis be on acute care, such as hospital and physician treatment, or will coverage extend to chronic care and associated costs, such as prescription drugs and nursing home care?
- Will the basic format be base hospital plus supplementary major medical coverage or comprehensive medical?
- Will HMO or PPO enrollment be allowed or required?
- How will the plan integrate with Medicare?
- Will the Medicare Part B premium be covered?
- Will spouses and other dependents be covered, and, if so, will that coverage extend beyond the retiree's death?

These and other questions about the extent of coverage must be asked as the plan is designed. Different coverages will be appropriate for different plans, often in correlation with coverage under the active plan. The advantages and disadvantages of each must be considered, but here we will simply note a few points specific to coverage of retirees.

Cost containment features incorporated in the active plan should, for the most part, be carried over into the retiree plan if at all possible. The need for efficient, appropriate care does not stop at retirement; rather, that is when it is needed most. Nevertheless, most cost containment provisions are aimed at an appropriate use of hospitals. When retirees become eligible for Medicare, however, Medicare takes on primary responsibility for hospital bills. Effective hospital utilization review may therefore result in little savings to the plan sponsor and, in fact, may shift utilization to outpatient services where Medicare is secondary and the plan sponsor is primary.

A major thrust of plan redesign for active medical plans in the late seventies and early eighties was to switch base hospital plus supplementary major medical plans to comprehensive major medical plans. A prime motivation was to introduce a greater degree of cost sharing by the employee. When payment is secondary to Medicare and coverage extends over a long period of time, however, the effectiveness of a switch to a comprehensive plan should not be overrated.

Coverage for spouses and other dependents may multiply plan costs by a factor of two or three. There have been very few attempts to introduce the concept of actuarial equivalence into retiree health plans in a fashion parallel to the joint and survivor annuity in pension plans. Typically, dependent coverage parallels retiree coverage, often with a higher contribution. Differentiation of coverage will be considered by more and more plans in the future.

To the extent that managed care systems, such as HMOs and PPOs, are used, effective design may differ for retiree plans. Many retirees do move from the geographic area of their former job, but many do not.

Cost can be controlled somewhat by schedules—surgical, dollar per day, etc. This usually results in gradual benefit cutbacks by erosion due to inflation, but that may fit into the long-term plan philosophy.

Finally, the implications 25 or 50 years into the future deserve consideration. Since court cases imply that unfavorable changes cannot be made after an employee retires, the long-run implications of changes are all important. Particularly, the plan designer should be aware of what might happen in case of Medicare cutbacks, either gradual or abrupt.

Length of Eligibility

The retiree needs the coverage for life, and that is the period for which many employers have extended their plans. Eligibility sometimes has gone beyond the retiree's life to cover the surviving spouse or other dependents until their deaths.

In the case of extended eligibility it becomes important to include language in the plan document that reserves the employer's right to make future plan changes. The flexibility to make future changes is key to financial control in the future and can be severely limited by inappropriate communication

or plan provisions. The plan changes that might be considered can often be written into the plan. An example is the indexing of provisions such as deductibles and out-of-pocket maximums. Language that relates these to a formula that will change the amounts over time provides built-in protections against the probable increases in plan costs.

Extension of coverage for a period less than life was mentioned in an earlier section. It should be remembered, however, that the greatest need for health care may be in the later years of life. Lifetime health care coverage extends through all illnesses, including terminal illness, for one and probably two people. It is not surprising, then, that current payments will certainly increase in future years.

Plan Costs

The retiree's health care bill will be shared by the plan sponsor, Medicare, and probably the retiree. A pertinent plan question is "What is the division of cost?" Recent studies have shown that Medicare now pays on average less than half an eligible person's health care bill. Of course, Medicare pays nothing for an ineligible retiree under age 65.

What is the appropriate payment level for the plan sponsors and for the retiree? That depends on the sponsor's philosophy. Points to consider are

1. Average payment levels for health care are likely to increase at a faster rate than are many other financial variables. If, for instance, the employer decides that it is appropriate for the retirees to pay one-third of the cost, the absolute dollar amount is likely to increase year after year at a rate greater than a retiree's income increases.
2. The retiree contribution should not be equated with the retiree's share of the health bill. The latter is larger because of plan exclusions. Some would say that in fairness, over the long term, the larger the plan exclusions are, the smaller the retiree contributions should be. This would equalize the proportion of total costs paid by the retiree for the combination of covered and uncovered expenses.
3. Retiree contributions have to be age rated to, at least, the extent of taking Medicare eligibility into account. In addition, there is statistical evidence to indicate that the cost increases with age. The average 85-year-old will have about twice the cost of the average 65-year-old. Should the contributions reflect this disparity? If age rating is not introduced beyond an over/under age 65 basis, a certain cost shift between retiree generations will occur. This may be a problem, however, if the contribution required from the retiree is more than the cost of an age-rated Medicare supplement insurance policy. The usual problems associated with adverse selection will occur. Better risks may not enroll. An additional complication may be that young retirees who opt out of the plan in favor of individual insurance may wish to return to the plan at a later (and higher cost) age.

Measurement of Liabilities

The measurement of the long-term cost of the benefit obligation is a subject attracting increased attention from experienced health care actuaries and others, notably the Financial Accounting Standards Board. It is obvious that the more complex the eligibility criteria, the plan coverage, and the length of eligibility are, the more complex the valuation is. Nevertheless, the tools do exist for accurate valuations of the comparative differences between different plan design costs.

Most actuaries experienced in the measurement of welfare obligations agree that conceptually the three key elements of measurement are the quantification of current costs, the mathematical model of future costs, and the reconciliation of the first two elements.

The benefit obligation can be measured with enough accuracy to make management decisions about whether to implement or curtail retiree medical and life plans. As to whether the obligation can be measured with enough accuracy to determine optimal plan design, the answer is "yes" or "no," depending on the needs of the plan's sponsor. Another question is "Are two actuaries valuing the same plan, independent of each other but in agreement on the future course of plan design, plan population eligibility, interest rates, and Medicare, likely to agree in their results?" The answer is most likely to be "no."

That is in contrast to pension valuations. Asking a similar question, "Would two actuaries valuing the same pension plan, independent but in agreement on future plan design, population, interest rates, and Social Security, agree in their results?" the answer is likely to be "yes." But the pension people have had 30 or 40 years of discussion and have not had to deal with health care benefits and data.

Thus, while group actuaries might agree on the general magnitude of the answers and the comparative value of different plan designs, there is not yet general agreement about the way claim costs should be measured and how the trend of claim costs in the future will proceed.

Two plan designs that greatly simplify the valuation and may greatly reduce the financial obligation of the plan sponsor have recently attracted considerable attention. These are the defined contribution approach and the defined dollar benefit approach. Under the defined contribution approach, the contribution for the current year is defined, but the ultimate benefit is not. Under the defined dollar benefit approach, the ultimate benefit is defined by a dollar amount with a certain accumulation of that amount being attributed to the current-year contribution. Either way, the plan sponsor avoids much of the uncertainty of what the future financial outlay will be. This is in contrast to a defined service benefit where the coverage is defined as in most active plans but the dollar amount remains uncertain until all claims exposure has passed. Of course, while both of these approaches help the plan sponsor with financial control, they leave most retirees financially insecure.

One final aspect of plan design that must not be ignored is the tax nature of any benefits. The growth of health care as an employee benefit has been fueled in large part because the benefit has not been taxable to the individual employee but has been tax deductible to the plan sponsor. This has been true for retiree benefits, as well as active benefits. On the other hand, if the retiree benefit can be construed as cash to the retiree, rather than claim payments to a provider, the benefit may no longer be tax exempt. The employer should also take care in plan design that the retiree health benefit cannot be construed as deferred compensation. Tax laws concerning retiree health benefits may be subject to a good deal of change in the years to come.

NOTES

1. Jonathan C. Dopkeen, "Postretirement Health Benefits," *Health Services Research* 21, no. 6 (February 1987).

2. "National Health Expenditures, 1986–2000." *Health Care Financing Review* 8, no. 4 (Summar 1987).

3. *Eardman v. Bethlehem Steel Corp.*, No. 84-274E (W.D. N.Y. September 17, 1984); *Hansen v. White Farm Equipment Co.*, No. C82-3209 (N.D. Ohio September 20, 1984; *Hansen v. White Farm* (6th Cir. May 1986).

4. "National Health Expenditures, 1986–2000."

Part III

Labor Relations

The most recent data issued by the Bureau of National Affairs (BNA) indicate that unions organized 85,695 employees in 1,699 elections held in 1987.[1] This was a decrease from the 1984 results, when unions organized 88,874 employees in 1,862 elections. A more significant piece of data reflects unions' successes in elections and, indeed, sheds light on the critical area of labor relations in the health care industry. The national figures on union victories in 1988 stood at 46.3 percent of the elections. A component of that figure is the success rate of unions in health care organizations: such unions prevailed in over 56 percent in 1987.[2] Although merely 20 percent of all health care workers are members of unions, and about the same percentage of hospitals have at least one union contract, the specter of unionization once again looms on the horizon in the health care industry.

Hospital mergers, acquisitions, and closings have led to layoffs; there are shortages of nurses and allied health professionals; and fixed reimbursements from third-party payers and higher expenses have forced hospitals to cut costs. All of these, he states, make hospitals ripe for unionization. Whether Burda is right or not about the effects of the financial pressures on hospitals throughout our country, a recent development will certainly set off a new wave of organizational activities. The National Labor Relations Board plans to establish eight broad categories of hospital employees as appropriate separate bargaining units. Most unions believe that there will be significant gains, based on this move away from recent restrictions on the number of units considered appropriate.

Whether the union movement is dead or alive is considered in one of our chapters in this section. The rulemaking controversy is discussed by representatives of the hospital industry and the chairman of the National Labor Relations Board, and a series of chapters deals with the disciplinary process and the grievance procedure.

John Dunlop tells us, "The basic features of the U.S. industrial relations arrangement have not been altered, although the output of this system may be expected to change in the new environment."[3] Whether the labor-management relationship will be altered in the foreseeable future or not, human resources directors and labor relations executives in the health care industry have a busy time ahead.

This section is dedicated to considering the types of situations that must be addressed in the coming decade.

NOTES

1. *BNA Daily Labor Report* 15 (25 January 1988): B–1.

2. Ibid.

3. John Dunlop, "Have the 1980s Changed U.S. Industrial Relations?" *BNA Daily Labor Report* 130 (7 July 1988): D–1.

Norman Metzger

The Union Movement: Dead or Alive

45

In articles published by the Bureau of National Affairs (BNA) in their *Daily Labor Report* in May 1988, John Dunlop and Audrey Freedman discuss this question: "Have the 1980s changed U.S. industrial relations?" Dunlop concludes

> The basic features of the U.S. industrial relations arrangement have not been altered, although the output of the system may be expected to change in the new environment. The labor movement in the United States is here today. It is adapting its methods to the new environment; already we have seen the reversal of a number of prominent losses and the penetration of some new fields.[1]

On the other hand, Freedman states

> The collective bargaining system, with its heavy flavor of formal legalistic, adversarial maneuvering, is giving way to a more fluid, adaptive business-dominated behavior. Those old-line labor experts who adjust to the new environment are invaluable in responding wisely to the new forces at work. Those old hands who cannot perceive business needs are having to give way before line managers who may not know of the historical background of union relations, but they do know what has to be done to keep the business prospering.
>
> There are a lot of electrical sparks coming from "inexperienced" line managers, and the course of bargaining is not as predictable or smooth and familiar as it once was. But changes are being forced. They are not temporary. We are not looking at a segment of a cycle that will reverse itself and return to the 1950s. This change is for good.[2]

Whether you agree with Dunlop or with Freedman, the specter of the demise of the union movement is an old one. I have, in the course of four decades in labor relations, been asked to attend the wake for the union movement on several occasions. Many management labor relations practitioners, wizened and hoary from decades of adversarial unionism, were always quick to forecast the demise of the union movement. You cannot pick up a newspaper or a national magazine without finding a surprisingly large percentage of articles on the weakening of the union movement; many of them are often directed toward a discussion of what unions can do to "transform" themselves.

Let us get the statistics out of the way.

- Union membership failed to keep up with employment growth in 1987.
- Union membership of the wage and salary work force over the age of 16 fell below 17 percent (at its apex in 1945 union membership was approximately 36 percent of the work force).
- It is interesting to note that this decline in union membership is a worldwide phenomenon. With the exception of the Scandanavian countries, which have upward of 90 percent union density, union membership has fallen off in Italy, the United Kingdom, the Netherlands, and even Japan.
- No industrial democracy has as low a union density as the United States does.
- The work place has been transformed dramatically due to a change in its composition.
    1. Of all first-time mothers, 48 percent return to work after the child is born.

2. Of mothers with children younger than age three, 50 percent are working.

3. The percentage of dual-income households stands at 67 percent.

4. Union membership is more prevalent among men (29.9 percent) than among women (12.6 percent) and more prevalent among blacks (22.6 percent) than among whites (16.3 percent) or Hispanics (17.1 percent).

5. Workers age 35 to 65 have the highest unionizing rate (about 22 percent), followed by the 25- to 30-year-old group (15.7 percent). Workers under 25 and over 64 have the lowest rates (less than 10 percent).

6. Union membership rates in various industries are as follows:
   (a) government: 36 percent
   (b) transportation and public utilities: 33.5 percent
   (c) manufacturing: 23.2 percent
   (d) construction: 21 percent
   (e) mining: 18.3 percent
   (f) finance, insurance, and real estate: 2.3 percent
   (g) agriculture: 2.2 percent

- During the past 15 years the fastest-growing area of the economy is the temporary work force. Now, 22 percent of American workers work part time, and 62 percent of all part time employees are women. Of individuals over age 70, 1.1 million work part time. Two-thirds of the part-time jobs involve clerical responsibilities, while the remaining one-third usually includes health care and manufacturing.

- The percentage of service workers organized today is 10 percent.

- In 1950 unions organized 750,000 new employees. In the 1980s this has dropped below 100,000.

- Every year since 1974 unions have lost more representation elections than they have won, and the numbers of representation elections and employees covered by each election have declined annually. In 1986 there were only approximately 3,000 representation elections that covered a total of 75,000 employees.

- During the 15-year period from 1970 to 1985 the number of decertification elections tripled, and unions lost 75 percent of those elections.

- Unions must organize 465,000 new members each year to stay even with the total percentage of the work force. But during recent years they have organized only a total of 200,000 each year.

- Union membership among health care workers has increased during the 1980s and now stands at 20 percent of the industry. Health care employers lose 55 percent of all representation elections.

- Labor's public approval rating has dropped from 76 percent in 1957 to about 55 percent today, according to a Gallup poll.

- The manufacturing sector will generate almost no new jobs in the next 13 years.

- Nine million new jobs were created in such service industries as health care, finance, real estate, and insurance during the recent decade.

- Today 47 percent of the work force consists of native white males, many of whom are middle aged. By the year 2000 that percentage will drop to 15 percent.

- Five-sixths of new entrants of the U.S. work force between now and the year 2000 are likely to be women, members of minority groups (especially Hispanics and Asian Americans), and immigrants. Of this group, about 66 percent will be women and 29 percent will be non-white—twice the current levels.

- Union membership as a percentage of the total number of wage and salary workers in the United States continued to decline in 1987, but the decline in total membership was comparatively small for the third consecutive year.[3]

The bottom line is that many of the new workers who have joined the work force recently, and who will be joining the work force, have and will have different concerns, biases, and ideas about work place relationships than do traditional union members. The new work force members will change its composition to one that will have less than the median level of education, will not be comfortable speaking English, and will fear that union involvement can cost them their jobs and immigration status. Others will face racism or ethnic prejudice in hiring and promotion. Women will tend to make less money and have lower-status jobs than male coworkers. The great bulk of employment and employment opportunities will be in the mini-economy (all small businesses) for the remainder of this century. The challenge then for unions will be to organize workers in smaller units. And now, with the rulemaking power of the National Labor Relations Board (NLRB), we will "enjoy" more units then we had hoped for.

WHY MANY MANAGEMENTS OPPOSE UNIONIZATION

- In a nonunionized enterprise the employer has great latitude in the running of the operation and directing its employees.

- Freedom to introduce technology that displaces employees without first making provisions for economic security for the affected employees is available in union-free environments.

- The work schedule can be unilaterally altered.

- In unionized institutions the work environment is transformed: there is increased formalization of behavior with rules for many activities previously handled in an informal, personal manner.

- In a unionized environment seniority governs overtime distribution, vacation scheduling, promotional opportunities, etc.
- Generally speaking, employers oppose unionizing because of the necessity to engage in bilateral decision making and the concomitant reductions in flexibility of operations and restrictions on the scope of management decision making, as well as the style of employee relations.
- Many managements believe that the scope of negotiations with unions becomes the battlefield on which the fight for power takes place.
- Nonunion enterprises can introduce such varying programs directed toward improving the motivational milieu and increasing the commitment of employees as

1. gain sharing
2. participatory management
3. merit pay systems
4. employee democracy programs

All of these can be introduced in a nonunion organization without the need to negotiate, and without management's having to deal with the typical union response toward such programs—suspicion and concern over the erosion of union power.

THE GROWTH OF MANAGERIAL OPPOSITION

Freeman and Medoff in their book *What Do Unions Do?* tell us about the "union prevention business." They identify three basic forms of management opposition to unions.

1. The first strategy involves "positive labor relations." Here we are dealing with what I fondly refer to as Metzger's First Rule of Labor Relations: an organization that provides all the benefits and protection afforded by a union contract—such as competitive wages and fringes, a seniority system, and a grievance and arbitration procedure—need not be unionized.
2. The second strategy they discuss is to conduct tough legal campaigns. The key term here is *legal*. This includes communication with workers and immediate supervisors. It also includes predictions about the negative aspects of unionism and references to the union's strike record. Most importantly, it deals with the availability of legal means by which to delay elections and attempts at getting the best possible bargaining unit configuration.
3. The third approach is to break the law. I shall deal with that shortly.[4]

It is well to look at the effects of some of these approaches, as shown in Table 45-1.

Very few management practitioners wish to talk about the illegal approaches to maintaining nonunion status. Since I, myself, have not ever been involved in such practices, I once again went to the literature and offer you the following:

- From the 1960s to the 1980s the number of charges involving employer unfair labor practices rose fourfold. The number of charges involving firing for union activity rose threefold. The number of workers awarded back pay or ordered reinstated to their jobs rose fivefold.
- One in twenty workers who favored the union was fired.
- There is roughly one case of illegal discharge deemed meritorious by the NLRB for every NLRB representational election.
- Managerial opposition to unionism, and to illegal campaign tactics in particular, is a major, if not *the* major determinant of NLRB election results.[5]

The review of the effects of management's opposition on union decline when either legal or illegal practices are used follows:

- The percentage of wins for unions depends on the amount of company communication. If the company is silent, the union win rate goes up. If the company has an extensive communication program during the organization drive, the company's win rate goes up appreciably.
- In general, the percentage of wins for unions depends on the extent of company opposition. Again, if the company remains neutral, the union win rate goes up.
- A time delay between election and petition has a significant effect on union losses.
- Union win rates are lower in elections in which management argues about the bargaining unit before the Regional Board.
- Probably one of the most significant statistics is that the percentage of wins for unions falls if the company hires consultants.[6]

In addition to the typical union-busting activities described before, there has been a radical change in management's approach to employees in many institutions, with an eye toward maintaining nonunion status. Management has adjusted more quickly than have labor unions to the changing needs developing from the changing composition of the work force.

The key components of the unions' base of power—the detailed contract, the narrow job designs, and the emphasis on stability—are now being challenged by management with the introduction of new forms of employee participation, more flexible forms of work organization, and technological changes. Management is better addressing the radical change

Table 45-1 Legal and Illegal Company Opposition and Union Success in NLRB Elections: Twelve Studies

Study	Finding	Study	Finding
1. Conference Board, Study of 140 Drives Attempting to Organize White-Collar Units, 1966–67.	Percentage of wins for union depends on amount of company communication. Written or no communication 85 Meetings with workers 51 Meetings and written communication 39	8. U.S. General Accounting Office, Analysis of 400 8(a)(3) Illegal Firings or Other Cases of Discrimination for Union Involvement, 368 Representation Elections, 1981.	Unions were more successful in campaigns in which no employer discrimination occurred than in those which involved an unfair labor practice charge. Success rate: no violation 45 violation 38
2. AFL–CIO, Study of 495 NLRB Elections, 1966–67.	Percentage of wins for union depends on extent of company opposition. No opposition 97 Some opposition 50 Wages increased 37 Surveillance of union, firing workers 43	9. Aspin, Study of 71 NLRB Elections in which Reinstatements Were Ordered, 1962–64.	Percentage of wins for union depends on firing, with unions doing worse unless reinstatees return to job before election. All elections in region 62 With 8(a)(3) firings 48 Election held before 8(a)(3) case is settled or discriminatee refuses to return to job 41 Election held after discriminatee returns to job 67
3. Prosten, Analysis of Probability of Union Win in 130,701 Elections, 1962–77.	Percentage of wins for union falls with time delay between election and petition; is lower in election in which management argues about district before Regional Board (stipulated elections).		
4. Lawler, Study of 155 NLRB Elections, 1974–78.	Percentage of wins for union falls if company hires consultant. If no consultant 71 If consultant 23	10. Getman, Goldberg, and Herman, Analysis of 1,293 Workers in 31 Elections in 1972–73.	Percentage of workers voting union reduced by sizable, but statistically insignificant, amount by management campaign tactics.
5. Drotning, Study of 41 Elections Ordered Void and Rerun by NLRB, 1956–62.	Nature of employer's campaign influences voting. Average number of employer communications per election Union losses 12.5 Union wins 8.6	11. Dickens, Analysis of 966 Workers in 31 Elections, 1972–73.	Percentage of workers voting union reduced by employer activities. Legal campaign −10% Illegal campaign −4% Employer threatening acts against pro-union workers −15% Percentage of elections unions would win in simulation model. No campaign or light campaign against 53–67% Intense campaign 22–34% Campaign with violations 4–10%
6. Roomkin and Block, Study of 45,115 Union Representation Cases, 1971–77.	Percentage of wins for union decreases with delay between petition and actual election. 0–1 months 50 2 months 45 3 months 41 4–7 months 30 8–12 months 30		
7. Seeber and Cooke, Analysis of Proportion of Workers in States Voting for Union Representation, 1970–78.	One percentage point increase in proportion of elections to which employers "consent" to the election district (rather than objecting to NLRB) increases union success by one-half percentage point.	12. Catler, Study of 817 NLRB Elections Reported on AFL-CIO Organizing Reports, 1966–77.	Company campaigning activities, unfair labor practices, and delay reduce union success, with the percentage of union wins lowered by 10 points by unfair labor practice.

Sources: (1) Edward R. Curtin, *White-Collar Unionization* (New York: National Industrial Conference Board, 1970). (2) Statement of William Kirchner, Director of Organization, AFL–CIO, on *A Bill to Amend the National Labor Relations Act in Order to Increase Effectiveness of the Remedies: Hearings on H.R. 11725 Before the Special Subcommittee on Labor of the House Committee on Education and Labor*, 90th Cong., 1st Sess., 1967 12, 15. (3) Richard Prosten, "The Longest Season: Union Organizing in the Last Decade," Proceedings of the Thirty-first Meeting of the Industrial Relations Research Association (Madison, Wisconsin, 1978): 240–49. (4) John Lawler, "Labor-Management Consultants in Union Organizing Campaigns" (Paper presented at the Thirty-fourth Annual Meeting of the Industrial Relations Research Association, Washington, D.C., 1981). (5) John Drotning, "NLRB Remedies for Election Misconduct: An Analysis of Election Outcomes and their Determinants," *Journal of Business* 40, no. 2 (April 1967): 137–48. (6) Myron Roomkin and Richard Block, "Case Processing Time and the Outcome of Elections: Some Empirical Evidence," *University of Illinois Law Review* 5, no. 1 (1981): 75–97. Calculated from tables 2 and 4. (7) R. Seeber and W. Cooke, "The Decline of Union Success in NLRB Representation Elections," *Industrial Relations* 22, no. 1 (Winter 1983): 33–44. (8) United States General Accounting Office, *Concerns Regarding Impact of Employee Charges Against Employers for Unfair Labor Practices* (Washington, D.C.: GAO–HRD 82–80, June 21, 1982). (9) Leslie Aspin, *A Study of Reinstatement Under the National Labor Relations Act* (Ph.D. diss. MIT, 1966). (10) Jules Getman, Steven Goldberg, and Jeanne Herman, *Union Representation Elections: Law and Reality* (New York: Russell Sage Foundation, 1976). (11) William F. Dickens, *Union Representation Elections: Campaign and Vote* (Ph.D. diss. MIT, 1980). (12) Susan Catler, "Labor Union Representation Elections: What Determines Who Wins?" (Senior thesis, Harvard University, 1978).

Source: What Do Unions Do? by Richard B. Freeman. Freeman and James L. Medoff. Copyright © 1984 by Basic Books. Reprinted by permission of Basic Books, Inc., Publishers.

in the work force than is the union by implementing more flexible and less formal work practices.

THE UNIONS' LAGGING PERCEPTION OF THE CHANGING ENVIRONMENT

Too little has been said about the changing configuration of employer-employee relationships, specifically the changing role of the supervisor.

Although the health care industry lags far behind in radical changes in supervisory-subordinate relationships, this is not so in an overwhelming number of areas outside of health care where unions were once quite successful. The modern company today spends a great deal of time on experimentation and implementation of management programs to increase employee commitment. Sixty years after Hawthorne, we are finally seeing a major change in management structures with more attempts to address commitment, fulfilling and meaningful work, and increased motivational opportunities. Quality of life programs—or whatever name one wishes to apply to such programs—are more prevalent today than in the past. Empowering workers, which means giving them more ability to make independent judgments regarding discipline, promotion, job assignments, etc., blurs the line between supervisors and workers. The Japanese model, which appears to be an anathema to unions, is creeping along and may well be a factor in the decline of the union movement.

Confrontational approaches to solving work problems, which unions were so adept at, have little or no appeal to younger workers and to older workers. More and more workers seem to be expressing a need for individualized due process rather than for the collective due process that results from a union contract. Managements are getting sophisticated enough to understand that maintaining nonunion status does not entitle them to having no due process system. One of the most interesting comments that I have come across was that in recent years "the locus of critical decision making in industrial relations and the power to influence events have shifted to activities above and below the level of negotiating collective agreements."[7]

The name of the game is no longer adversarial labor relations. Many workers are now turned off by the constant threats and rhetoric surrounding employer-union confrontations at negotiating time. The strike as a useful process in settling disputes is now more in question than ever before. Workers' needs are rarely addressed through the strike mechanism. Profit sharing, gain sharing, employee stock ownership plans, bonus incentives, and performance-based pay systems are of much more interest to workers than is obvious from the negative reaction of unions to such plans.

The critical point from this analysis, which questions the union movement's touch with reality, was expressed in a book entitled *The Transformation of American Industrial Relations:*

> Union leaders will be under intense pressure in many situations to recoup the cuts in wages and fringe benefits

that were made during the concessionary era. But the biggest challenge for unions by far will be to find ways to integrate collective bargaining activities with the expanding range of activities emerging at the workplace at strategic levels.[8]

The real question is whether unions can find ways to meet the needs of those "new work groups" for whom the traditional package of union services has little appeal and is often irrelevant.

WHAT'S AHEAD?

Kochan and others[9] suggest some alternate scenarios, as follows.

Scenario 1 sees private sector unionization continuing to decline, with public sector unionization remaining stable. This scenario envisions the organized labor force at only 15 percent in 1990. Unions will be concentrated in the public sector in health care and in those industries that are highly organized at this time, including defense contractors, utilities, and aerospace firms. Union-management relations will become more adversarial and less innovative. Management opposition will intensify. Under this scenario they see the reliving of past history—intensified labor-management conflicts—and if the political pendulum swings back the enactment of new labor laws and the tightening of old laws, management will speed the pace of outsourcing and technological change in order to further reduce vulnerability to unionization.

Under Scenario 2 they envision labor law reform to eliminate delays and provide stiff penalties for illegal conduct. With this reform, unions would increase their organizing success rates with low-wage workers in service industries and in small bargaining units. But this would not make any significant difference in the unionizing rate of large firms or in the quality of the relationship in existing bargaining units.

In Scenario 3 labor law reform would be continued with innovations in bargaining relationships. Improvements in economic performance and the quality of labor-management relations would lead to a stabilization in employment and union membership around the current levels. Again, the inroad for unions would be in the low-wage service sector.

Scenario 4 envisions new organizing strategies. This utopian view encompasses fundamental shifts in the values, strategies, policies, and practices of all parties to industrial relations.

The authors are not convinced which script will emerge, but they are clear about one thing: unions will continue to face intense pressure to modify their traditional strategies in order both to cope with changes in business and human management strategies and to give workers more say over the issues that affect their working lives.

Charles McDonald[10] of the AFL–CIO points out a "sophistication gap" that has developed between management and labor in the handling of organizing campaigns. It is clear that management has experimented with and implemented a much more enlightened view of satisfying worker needs than the traditional union approach: ''self-managed'' work teams, problem-solving groups (which are widely used in Japan), and redesign committees incorporate broader participation of workers—quite a different scene from what was evident in the traditional work place of the past where unions found a high degree of alienation and were able to capitalize on that.

Gus Tyler of the International Ladies Garment Workers Union makes clear the problem for unions.

> Given solutions that were valid fifty years ago are not valid—or equally valid—today because, in no small measure, the problems have changed.
> The differences that have developed over a half century are not quantitative alone, they are qualitative; they are not incremental, they are gross.[11]

The old premises of unionism—people with jobs, governments with power to regulate their domestic economy, individuals with ''definable careers''—will be shaken if not shattered. Tyler offers a most incisive point when he says

> The factors of production are portable; capital, technology, raw materials, and managerial know-how. They can be moved easily and swiftly. Multinational corporations scour the planet to find out where best to allocate their resources to produce more cheaply, to pay the least taxes, to maximize after-taxes returns.
> This internationalization of the economy gives capital an almost unbeatable advantage over labor: the former is mobile, the latter is not.
> Unions and nations are flat-footed losers in a contest with these fleet-footed financial folk.[12]

It is clear to me that unions must reassess their approaches to organizing because they are facing the most serious challenge to their power and influence since the National Labor Relations Act was passed over 50 years ago. Let us review the bidding, which was exquisitely outlined in a BNA Special Report on *Unions Today: New Tactics to Tackle Tough Times*.

- The unionized segment of the work force has been shrinking for three decades.
- Unions have never won more than one-half of NLRB elections since 1974.
- Decertification attempts are succeeding more often.
- Concession bargaining, although on the wane, has changed the structure of collective bargaining.
- Nonunion employees are receiving bigger pay boosts than are unionized workers, although their pay remains below that of unionized workers.
- The public's opinion of unions has declined dramatically in the last two decades.[13]

There should be deep concern for the future of the union movement as it relates to the health and prosperity of our economy. Unions have been a force in the dramatic rise of the middle class and in the decrease in the exploitation of workers over the past 50 years. Even the threat of unionization serves its purpose. If there is truly a ''sophistication gap'' between unions and managements with regard to approaches to worker satisfaction, some of it may be a result of ''unions keeping managements honest.'' The boisterous threatening union leader/organizer has little attraction for the majority of today's American working people. The traditional adversarial relationship, which often is present in unionized enterprises, addresses little of the employees' needs for fulfilling and meaningful work. Internecine battles between union leaders for power within their unions turns off many members. The quality of union stewards has not kept up with the quality of supervisors. The cry for ''taking over the plant'' is comedic and has as much effect long range as does singing ''Solidarity Forever'' or other ''inspiring'' union songs.

Let me now share with you my own vision of what is in store for us during the rest of this century (there is only a decade left). I do not envision a return to the ''old days.'' Labor act reform will be minimal. Even with the obviating of delays between the petition and the election date, unions will be faced with a more difficult mix of employees than in the earlier days—as I had mentioned before. In my own industry—health care—more and more is being done to change the supervisory-subordinate relationship. Less and less exploitation is permitted. Competitive wages flow from the market, as do competitive fringes. Sophisticated approaches, such as gain sharing and incentives, are being widely introduced. A greater sensitivity to what attracts employees to unions is the rule, not the exception. I, therefore, believe that, absent the ''exploitation'' factor, future union organization will be among professionals whose critical needs are not the traditional needs of the organized, but spring from the needs for power, professional independence, and protection of their ''turf.'' Therefore, reluctant administration and medical staff relationships will exacerbate these concerns and make these groups—nurses, doctors, social workers, and other professionals—more vulnerable. I do not see unions going much above the 20 percent level of density in health care. Looking out from the health care industry into the country as a whole, international competition will not abate. The mobility factor will be even more acute as far as where products will be made, and the mass introduction of robots and advanced technology will further reduce the need for highly paid blue-collar workers. We will, therefore, be firmly entrenched as a service economy, and even in those areas foreign competition will be keen.

In a book I read a while back, the author prognosticates about the twenty-first century and sees bidding for work—not only manufacturing work but also services—on an international computerized basis where every home (in Malaysia, Hong Kong, Brunei, etc.) will have a personal computer so that the occupant can bid on the service needed.[14] Given that international economy—and the almost insignificant level of manufacturing that will be handled in the United States—if unions are to thrive, they must address the problems of the newly shaping work arena. I am not sanguine about union leadership's coming to grips with anything other than the traditional problems of wages and fringe benefits. These issues will still need to be addressed, but much more than that is necessary for the union movement to stop its dramatic decline. The seer whom I mentioned earlier talks about a union movement in the United States of less than 10 percent of the work force. I have not come across in the literature any ''experts'' who predict anything more than a level of 15 percent.

DO WE REALLY WANT LABOR ON THE ROPES?

That was the question addressed by Jack Barbash.[15] With the growth and success of the resistance movement to unionization, some observers have come to grips with the very real possibility of the demise of a strong union movement in the United States. Richard Lyles believes that unions are on their way out.

> By the year 2000 the term ''bargaining unit'' will be a phrase from a forgotten era. 21st Century historians will look back on this time right now—let's say about 1982 to the mid-1990s—and they will call it the management revolution. I think it will be every bit as significant as the Industrial Revolution. Part of what they'll talk about in the management revolution is the dying out of trade unions as bargaining units. Unions will still exist as fraternal organizations or social organizations, similar to professional organizations today. But in terms of bargaining units, where they collectively determine the destiny of hundreds of thousands of individuals at one time, I don't think that is ever going to happen again.[16]

Richard Lehr and David Middlebrooks see something different in the trends.

> There will be fewer elections but they will be a result of alternate organizing approaches not because of the decline in the attraction of employees to unions . . . . The most successful union in organizing employees has been the United Food and Commercial Workers. This union is a combination of the former meat cutters and retail clerks unions. From 1983 through 1986 this union organized 65,000 new members per year and has set its goal at 100,000 new members per year through the 1990s. The National Union of Hospital and Health Care Employees, Local 1199, won approximately 70% of representational elections held in 1986, compared to a 50% success rate among all of the unions attempting to organize health care employees.[17]

They go on to quote the American Hospital Association which stated that ''Union membership among health care workers increased 6% in 1980 to 1985, and 20% of the industry is unionized. Health care employers lost 65% of all representation elections held.''[18]

Let us get back to Barbash and the question ''Do we really want labor on the ropes?'' He believes that the general attitude, which is imbued with a strong anti-union animus, leaves us with ''disturbing questions for the future of industrial relations in the United States.''

- Since trade unions have contributed to the stability of democratic societies throughout the West, will labor's decline in the United States unsettle that equilibrium?
- Will the benign aspects of human resources management continue in the absence of organized labor's countervailing power?
- Will public regulation fill the vacuum created by labor's decline? If so, employers' strategic choices will not be between unions and a union-free environment but between collective bargaining and public regulation.
- Will massive layoffs, plant closings, and wage cuts create a backlash if labor market conditions tilt again in favor of employees?[19]

Barbash concludes his answer to the question above with the following:

> A return to open struggle between management and organized labor would be detrimental for American business and for the national interest as well. The new realism of American unions, it seems to me, offers a more promising foundation on which to build the next era of industrial relations.[20]

CONCLUSION

Many academics and practitioners are grappling with the demise of the union movement during the Reagan years. The question of whether we can have a prosperous economy with higher productivity without unions is not easy to answer. Rod Willis answers his own question, ''Could our economy run smoothly without unions?'' with a very quiet ''maybe.''

> Unless the underlying causes that give them birth disappear entirely—causes such as low wages, unsafe working conditions, health hazards, arbitrary firings and layoffs—it's a safe bet that something very similar would soon spring up to take their place. In the meantime, managers need to find better ways to work not against unionized employees for U.S. businesses to remain competitive.[21]

I take that a step further. This new era—an era of human capital—will be with us for the foreseeable future. The challenge is to establish new rules and new approaches. Never has there been a greater opportunity to re-establish sound relationships with employees, notwithstanding the presence of the union, and not only as a deterrent to union organizing. It is one thing to take full advantage of the marketplace—in the possible continued eroding of union power—but another to bring employees into the mainstream of the difficult management of health care institutions during the rest of this century. In this new competitive marketplace additional approaches to labor relations will be strained, if not completely outmoded. It is clear that labor relations, as it has been defined in the past, will not be center stage and, at best, will be a sideshow. The spotlight in the large arena will be on human resources programs. In the midst of enormous financial pressures on institutions, shortages of skilled and professional employees, and reorganizations, hospital administration must pay equal attention to meeting employee needs and to developing programs that maximize employee commitment. If labor relations will, indeed, take a back seat, which is long overdue, we must start to think of our employees not as adversaries, but as partners. We cannot permit unions to get in the way of that partnership. Maybe they won't want to when they see our determination.

NOTES

1. John Dunlop, "Have the 1980s Changed U.S. Industrial Relations?" *BNA Daily Labor Report* no. 130 (7 July 1988): D–1.

2. Audrey Freedman, "How the 1980s Have Changed Industrial Relations," *BNA Daily Labor Report* no. 130 (7 July 1988): D–10.

3. *BNA Daily Labor Report* no. 15 (25 January 1988): B–1.

4. Richard B. Freeman and James L. Medoff, *What Do Unions Do?* (New York: Basic Books, 1984), 230–33.

5. Ibid., 232–233.

6. Ibid., 234–235.

7. Thomas A. Kochan, Harry C. Katz, and Robert B. McKersie, *The Transformation of American Industrial Relations* (New York: Basic Books, 1986), 237.

8. Ibid., 240.

9. Ibid., 250–53.

10. Charles J. McDonald, "Planning for the Future: Implementing the AFL/CIO Report," in *Industrial Relations Research Association Series, Proceedings of the Thirty-ninth Annual Meeting,* Madison, Wisconsin (December 28, 1986): 280.

11. Gus Tyler, "Labor at the Crossroads," in *Unions in Transition,* ed. Semour Martin Lipset (San Francisco: ICS Press, 1986), 376.

12. Ibid., 381.

13. Bureau of National Affairs, *Unions Today: New Tactics to Tackle Tough Times,* Special Report (Washington, D.C.: Bureau of National Affairs, 1985), 1.

14. Norman Macrae, *The 2025 Report* (New York: Macmillan Publishing Co., Inc., 1984), Chapter 8 passim.

15. Jack Barbash, "Do We Really Want Labor on the Ropes?" *Harvard Business Review* 63, no. 4 (July-August 1985): 10–21.

16. Richard I. Lyles, "The Management Revolution and Loss of Union Clout," *Management Review* (February 1988): 25–26.

17. Richard I. Lehr and David J. Middlebrooks, *The New Unionism: A Blueprint for the Future* (New York: Executive Enterprises Co., 1987), 4.

18. Ibid., 12.

19. Barbash, "Do We Really Want Labor on the Ropes?" 8.

20. Ibid.

21. Rod Willis, "Can American Unions Transform Themselves?" *Management Review* 77, no. 2 (February 1988): 21.

Rhonda Rhodes

Rulemaking in the Health Care Industry

46

On July 2, 1987, the National Labor Relations Board (Board or NLRB) announced its intention to engage in rulemaking for the health care industry, proposing that certain types of bargaining units would be appropriate in health care institutions.[1] Over the next three months, the Board held four public hearings at which 144 persons testified and submitted 3,545 pages of testimony. When the period for written comments closed on December 20 of that year, the Board had received additional comments from 315 organizations and individuals.

One year later, on July 1, 1988, at an open meeting required by the Government in the Sunshine Act, the Board met to further discuss this issue. Specifically, the Board addressed the questions of whether it should engage in rulemaking and, if so, what the configuration of the rules would be. Speaking as chairman of the NLRB, James Stephens stated that the record justified engaging in rulemaking for the following reasons:

- the lack of adequate success of the case-by-case approach in determining unit configurations in the health care industry
- the consistent voting patterns of various Board members on this matter since the passage of the Health Care Amendments to the Taft-Hartley Act (Act) in 1974 (1974 Amendments)
- the fact that formal rulemaking was not inconsistent with the Board's past practices
- the lack of merit, in the Board's opinion, of the arguments presented by the health care industry against rulemaking during the hearings in 1987

Consequently, on September 1, 1988, the Board published its Second Notice of Proposed Rulemaking (SNPR) in which it modified its original proposal to provide for up to eight units in all acute care hospitals (except nursing homes and psychiatric hospitals, and except in what the Board defined as "extraordinary circumstances").

1. all registered nurses
2. all physicians
3. all other professionals
4. all technical employees
5. all skilled maintenance employees
6. all business office clerical employees
7. all guards
8. all other nonprofessional employees.[2]

An Editorial Note: On July 25, 1989, Judge James B. Zagel (U.S. District Court in Chicago) issued a permanent injunction against the NLRB's implementation of rulemaking to determine health care bargaining units. Judge Zagel based his decision on Section 9(b) of the NLRA which provides that the Board must decide the appropriate unit "in each case" and on Congress' admonition against proliferation of bargaining units in the health care industry. This decision was appealed immediately by the Board to the Seventh Circuit Court of Appeals (Chicago), but a decision is not expected by the Seventh Circuit until at least the end of 1989. In the meantime, the Board has indicated that representation petitions in the health care industry will be processed under the guidelines in effect prior to the Board's rulemaking attempt.

At the close of the comment period on October 17, 1988, the Board had received 1,550 additional comments. Although the Board had originally planned to issue the final rule within 30 to 45 days after the close of the comment period, up to as late as March 1989 the Board has been unable or unwilling to finalize the modified rule.[3]

The focus of this chapter is on presenting the historic context of the Board's first attempt to engage in rulemaking for this specialized industry, presenting the industry position in light of what occurred at the hearings, and discussing whether the Board has the power to engage in rulemaking and whether its attempt to do so contravenes the legislative intent of the 1974 Amendments.

HISTORIC CONTEXT OF THE BOARD'S ATTEMPT TO ENGAGE IN RULEMAKING

The controversy over what constitutes appropriate bargaining units in the health care industry began when Senator Taft introduced Senate bill S. 2292 on July 31, 1974. The bill included a five-unit statutory presumption (covering professional employees, technical employees, clerical employees, service and maintenance employees, and guards), proposed as a compromise to address the industry fears of unwarranted bargaining unit fragmentation in health care institutions. Hearings were held on the Taft proposal, as well as on legislation submitted by Senators Cranston and Javits, which would have provided a simple elimination of the not-for-profit health care institution exemption in the Act. However, the compromise approach avoided the adoption of a specified number of bargaining units and instead, in both the House and Senate Committee Reports, inserted language requiring the Board to prevent proliferation of bargaining units in the health care industry.[4] Rather than adopting a straight-line approach to the proliferation issue, the remarks of Senators Taft and Williams reveal that Congress was content with continuing to allow the Board to do what it had done for 40 years—decide the appropriate units based on facts and circumstances before it on a case-by-case basis—with a specific admonition not to allow undue unit proliferation in that decision making.[5]

However, the initial Taft proposal was not submitted to a vote in Congress or to the Labor Committee of either House, and, therefore, it should not be accorded any deference in defining the legislative intent with respect to the 1974 Amendments.[6] In fact, the Committee Reports supporting the legislation that was ultimately adopted show that the compromise reached between the statutorily mandated number of bargaining units and the straight exemption approach strongly favored a case-by-case determination of appropriate bargaining units in health care institutions. The Committee Reports reflected the compromise in the following manner:

EFFECT ON EXISTING LAW BARGAINING UNITS

Due consideration should be given by the Board to prevent proliferation of bargaining units in the health care indus-

try. In this connection, the committee notes with approval the recent Board decisions in *Four Seasons Nursing Center*, 208 NLRB No. 50, 85 L.R.R.M. 1093 (1974), and *Woodland Park Hospital*, 205 NLRB No. 144, 84 L.R.R.M. 1075 (1973) as well as a trend toward broader units enunciated in *Extendicare of West Virginia*, 203 NLRB No. 170, 83 L.R.R.M. 1242 (1973).[7]

Accordingly, it is apparent that any arbitrarily proposed number of bargaining units in health care institutions, whether imposed by statute or by rule, was expressly disavowed by Congress in enacting the 1974 Amendments.[8]

Moreover, the plain wording of Section 9(b) of the Act, construed in light of the legislative history of the original Wagner Act and that of subsequent amendments to the Act, reveals that Congress intended the Board to resolve unit determinations by adjudicated case decisions rather than by rulemaking.

The text of Senate bill S. 1958, which was introduced by Senator Wagner and which ultimately became the core of the National Labor Relations Act, originally did not contain the language "in each case" in Section 9(b). In fact, Section 9(b) of S. 1958 initially read as follows:

(b) The Board shall decide whether, in order to effectuate the policies of this Act, the unit appropriate for the purposes of collective bargaining shall be the employer unit, craft unit, plant unit, or other unit.[9]

Although the House bills on the National Labor Relations Act contained the same Section 9(b) language,[10] a subsequent House bill, H.R. 7978, altered Section 9(b) as follows:

(b) The Board shall decide *in each case* whether, in order to effectuate the policies of this Act, the unit appropriate for the purposes of collective bargaining shall be the employer unit, craft unit, plant unit, or other unit.[11]

In the House Labor Committee Report on H.R. 7978, Representative William Connery explained that the "in each case" phrase was intentionally added to the proposed legislation.

Section 9(b) provides that the Board shall determine whether, in order to effectuate the policy of the bill (as expressed in Sec. 1), the unit appropriate for the purposes of collective bargaining shall be the craft unit, plant unit, employer unit, or other unit. This matter is obviously one for determination in each individual case, and the only possible workable arrangement is to authorize the impartial governmental agency, the Board, to make that determination[12]

Subsequently, the House amended S. 1958, crafting Section 9(b) into the form that eventually passed Congress and was signed into law. The House Report accompanying this amendment again stressed the fact that a unit determination "is obviously one for determination in each individual case . . . ."[13] These amendments were accepted by the House-Senate Conference Committee.[14]

This compels the conclusion that the legislative history of Section 9(b) supports the plain language of the Act: unit determinations must be made "in each case." This case-by-case approach to such determinations was a deliberate decision of Congress, and not simply the result of poor drafting of the language of the Act. However, in its attempt to now mandate rules, the Board ignores the command of Section 9(b) that unit determinations be made on an adjudicatory basis.

THE INDUSTRY POSITION

Evolution of the Health Care Industry

Since 1974 the health care industry has become uniquely diversified and dynamic. Technological improvements and changes in methods by which health care providers are reimbursed have caused hospitals to continually revise their methods of operation and governance, as well as the internal structures pursuant to which patient services are provided. Thus, an objective analysis of the testimony and comments the Board received during the rulemaking process manifests the need for the Board to continue its case-by-case approach in determining the appropriate number of bargaining units in this industry.

The Impact of PPS on Labor Relations

After the Medicare prospective payment system (PPS) was implemented in 1983, hospitals were forced to re-examine the way in which services were provided. Medicare's revenues comprise a substantial portion (e.g., 25–40 percent) of most hospitals' patient care revenues. Obviously, the federal budget for Medicare has serious implications for the financial viability of many hospitals. To survive the continual erosion of Medicare dollars, health care providers have had to take all necessary actions including staff, bed, and service reductions or to initiate other creative changes to minimize their losses.

Additional statistics demonstrate that the health care industry faces unparalleled pressures. Kenneth Abramowitz, a senior research analyst at Sanford C. Bernstein & Co., New York, and the author of "The Future of Health Care Delivery in America," has estimated that about 16 percent of the nation's bed capacity, or 172,500 beds, will shut down between 1985 and 1990.[15] Inflationary pressures faced by hospitals have increased, while revenue margins continue the downward spiral begun in 1985. Inpatient admissions have continued to decline, falling 1 percent from the first half of 1986. This is troublesome when coupled with the fact that the growth in outpatient visits has moderated during the first half of 1987, rising 5.9 percent compared with 8.5 percent in the first half of 1986. Admissions on the inpatient side have consistently fallen since the first quarter of 1983; hospitals admitted 1 million fewer patients in the second quarter of 1987

than they did in the first quarter of 1983. Moreover, the length of stay increased slightly in the first half of 1987 due to increasing patient acuity.[16] For most hospitals, then, reducing the length of stay as a cost containment measure is impractical. On the other hand, expense growth is continuing at the same rate as it did in 1986. Total expenses during the first half of 1987 rose at an annual rate of 9.8 percent, but inpatient revenues rose at a 7.9 percent annual rate, while outpatient revenues slowed from an 18.5-percent annual growth rate in 1986 to a 16.7-percent annual rate growth in 1987.

Rural hospitals have been especially hard hit by the changes in Medicare and Medicaid reimbursement, increased competition, diagnostic-related groups, and diversification of health care services outside of inpatient facilities. In response, those rural hospitals have initiated significant diversification programs to provide all forms of health care to the community apart from inpatient acute care. Thus, the number of hospital-based programs in outpatient departments, psychiatric outpatient services, rehabilitation outpatient services, alcohol/chemical dependency outpatient services, home health care services, and health promotional services has dramatically increased in the past four years.[17]

DIVERSIFICATION: THE HALLMARK OF HEALTH CARE DELIVERY TODAY

Because of financial constraints and reduced utilization due to shorter lengths of stay, hospitals of all types and sizes have developed new types of related health care services on an outpatient as well as inpatient basis. The foremost of these alternate services are long-term care and skilled nursing care, which promise to consume a greater percentage of health care dollars as a larger segment of the population ages and as the demand for such care increases. America's aging population has created markets for health care specialties in the treatment of specific conditions, such as heart disease, Alzheimer's disease, and various forms of cancer. The kinds of facilities that currently provide these services include diagnostic imaging centers, pain centers and pain clinics, birth centers, hospices, home health care organizations, rehabilitation centers, ambulatory care centers, free-standing ambulatory surgery centers, mental health centers, alcohol and drug abuse centers, nursing homes and extended care facilities, and independent clinical laboratories.[18]

Between the years 1985 and 2050 the population aged 65 and older will increase from 25 million to almost 70 million; between 1983 and 1985 the number of skilled nursing facilities in hospitals grew 50 percent.[19] Skilled nursing care includes nursing, rehabilitative, and dietary services, as well as lower levels of personal care provided by home aides and orderlies on a 24-hour basis. The services are less expensive, as well as less intensive, and are provided by nurse aides, orderlies, licensed practical nurses, and rehabilitative and physical therapy personnel. Untrained aides and orderlies, together with registered nurses, provide most long-term nursing care.[20]

Hospitals are using part-time workers in increasing numbers to accommodate the rapid fluctuations in inpatient census and the reduction in full-time employee schedules. In addition, shortages of nurses, physical therapists, occupational therapists, pharmacists, and other professionals account for the reduction in many full-time professional staffing positions.

Key to this change are the reduced skill levels of employees. The Care Giver Project, initiated by National Medical Enterprises, Inc., identifies and determines the minimum skill levels necessary to perform patient services based on an analysis of education, training, and licensure. This project is so important because of the demand for a reduction in pay or cost for health services and the health manpower crisis caused by insufficient resources.[21]

Moreover, hospitals are utilizing other specialized services provided by multiple employee classifications working together and marketing these services to their communities. For example, arthritis affects 37 million Americans and, according to the Arthritis Foundation, costs $9 billion annually in lost wages and prescription drugs.[22] Hospitals are now developing specialized arthritis units to teach patients to cope with this condition. Notwithstanding such diversification, specialized services provided by a cross-mix of professional and nonprofessional employees, working as a team, represents the future of health care and supports the contention of the health care industry that the Board's attempt to engage in rulemaking is anachronistic.

MULTISKILLED HEALTHCARE EMPLOYEES

Multiskilled health care workers are an integral part of the profile of the industry today for several significant reasons. First, the need to provide high-quality, cost-effective patient care continues despite the changes in the reimbursement system that have compelled the increase in the number of these multiskilled workers. Moreover, these employees are indispensable in providing continuity of care. They have become essential components of the team approach to health care because of their flexible skills and diverse backgrounds. Another positive aspect of utilizing multiskilled employees is demonstrated by increased worker satisfaction in an industry plagued by severe employee shortages and high attrition rates.

The need and desire for multiskilled health care personnel have been revealed in several studies on this topic. For example, the School of Allied Health Professionals at Hahnemann University conducted a study that focused on interest in multiskilled practitioners in Philadelphia.[23] Fifteen percent of the hospital administrators surveyed, along with 29 percent of the directors of nursing, reported that multicompetent practitioners were currently employed in their respective institutions. Additionally, 68 percent of hospital administrators and 56 percent of the directors of nursing responded that they were willing to hire multiskilled employees.

The industry's response to multiskilled health care workers, as evidenced above, is overwhelmingly positive.[24] However,

the viability of this option, as well as the resultant evolutionary personnel patterns, is jeopardized by the Board's proposed unit configurations.

This profile of the health care industry shows that the Board's attempt to promulgate rules is unrealistic and unworkable. In fact, the Board's proposed rules do not comport with the realities of the industry, either as it exists today or as it will exist in the future. Finally, the definition of employee functions on which the Board has based its proposed unit configuration ignores the interdependence, integration, and coordination of services and, furthermore, represents a threat to the delivery of effective and cost-efficient health care.

THE RULEMAKING CONTROVERSY

The 1987 Hearings

In 1987, the U.S. Court of Appeals for the District of Columbia reversed its decision in *St. Francis Hospital II* and remanded it to the Board.[25] Shortly thereafter, in the matter of *St. Vincent Hospital and Health Center and Montana Nurses Association*,[26] the Board held oral argument regarding what constitutes appropriate bargaining units in the health care industry. Frustrated with the lack of judicial approval of its bargaining unit decisions, the Board announced that it would consider utilizing rulemaking to determine the industry's bargaining units.

Beginning on August 17, 1987, the Board held a series of hearings in Washington, in Chicago, in San Francisco, and again in Washington to receive the testimony of labor, management, and other interested parties on the matters presented in the NPR.[27] The American Hospital Association, several state and metropolitan hospital associations, and a number of individual health care providers submitted both oral and written testimony. All the major labor organizations that have sought to organize health care employees also presented testimony. The AFL–CIO, the Service Employees International Union, the American Nurses Association, and the International Union of Operating Engineers were present during almost all of the proceedings. It is indicative of the importance that labor placed on these hearings that several unions had representatives attend daily and that union representation virtually always outnumbered industry representation by at least two or three to one. Labor generally argued against any distinction between large and small hospitals and in favor of even more bargaining units than the six originally proposed by the Board. Labor also discounted the changes occurring in the industry and suggested that such things as product line management and multidisciplinary terms were meaningless to employee organizing and the manner in which health care is currently delivered.

On the other hand, representatives from the health care industry argued that rulemaking was inappropriate for this specialized industry and that the Board should decide representation issues on a case-by-case basis, applying the disparity of interest test. The industry also urged that the distinction between hospitals with large and small beds be changed and that only three units (all professionals, all nonprofessionals, and guards) be deemed appropriate. Extensive evidence was presented by the industry about the widely varying patterns of organization of different health care institutions (e.g., children's hospitals and psychiatric hospitals) and about the extraordinary and rapid changes occurring in the industry. In December 1987, several months after the conclusion of the hearings, both labor and management filed extensive written comments.

At approximately this time, Board Member Wilford Johansen announced his intention to retire from the Board; simultaneously, Chairman Donald L. Dotson's term expired. Then, in July 1988, Board Member Marshall Babson announced his intention to recuse himself from the Board's deliberations on this issue and stepped down from the Board. However, Member Johansen accepted an interim appointment to the Board and, at the July 1, 1988, open meeting, Chairman Stephens and Board Members Cracraft and Johansen split 2 to 1 in favor of rulemaking. In spite of having barely enough members to even do business, the two members of the majority of the Board decided to proceed with rulemaking!

The two members of the majority announced four major changes in the rule as it was originally proposed. First, the number of units was expanded from six to eight, with the addition of units for business office clerical employees and skilled maintenance workers. Second, the distinction between large and small hospitals was dropped. Third, psychiatric hospitals and nursing homes were excluded from the application of the rule. Fourth, the rule would apply to all pending cases instead of only to cases filed after the adoption of the rules. Both Chairman Stephens and Board Member Cracraft stated that they did not accept the industry's evidence and believed that its presentations were driven more by financial concerns than by concerns for guaranteeing employees the right to organize. They also stated that the record developed in 1987 demonstrated that multiple units do not undermine functional integration of work. Also, multiple units neither result in an increase in proliferation, strikes, jurisdictional disputes, and wage whipsawing nor substantially increase industry costs.

Nonetheless, in order to attempt to ensure that due process had been satisfied, the Board included in the SNPR an exception for "extraordinary circumstances." According to the Board, this exception was provided to allow for the possibility of individual treatment of uniquely situated acute care hospitals, so as to avoid accidental or unjust application of the rule. However, the Board stated its intention to construe the exception narrowly, so that it does not provide an excuse or opportunity for redundant or unnecessary litigation and the resultant delay. The Board said

> To satisfy the requirement of "extraordinary circumstances," a party would have to bear the "heavy burden" to demonstrate that "its arguments are substantially dif-

ferent from those which have been carefully considered at the rulemaking proceeding," as, for instance, by showing the existence of such unusual and unforeseen deviations from the range of circumstances revealed at the hearings and known to the Board for more than 13 years of adjudicating cases in this field, that it would be unjust or an abuse of discretion for the Board to apply the rules to the facility involved.[28]

Accordingly, we may expect the application of the extraordinary circumstances exception to be rare.

The Board's Alleged Power To Engage in Rulemaking

In his dissent in the SNPR, Board Member Johansen stated: "With all due respect, I disagree. Rulemaking in regard to health care units is neither desirable nor appropriate."[29] Because of the many questions surrounding the interpretation of congressional intent, the proper scope of review, and the Board's duty and authority under the Act, Board Member Johansen expressed his view that these questions should be submitted to the Supreme Court. He also stated his opinion that Section 9(b) of the Act mandates that the Board decide in each case what the appropriate units might be.

The reason for this approach, apparent from the debates over the Wagner Act, is that unit determinations depend so greatly on the facts of the particular case that a case-by-case determination is unavoidable. However, the Board has attempted to ignore the plain language of Section 9(b) in both notices of proposed rulemaking. Although the Board asserts in the SNPR that it has the authority to promulgate rules to assist it in representation cases,[30] the "rules" cited by the Board were developed by adjudication, not rulemaking through the Administrative Procedure Act. Although it may be true that the cited rules could have been adopted in the latter fashion, none of these rules involved the formulation of bargaining units, and they related to other types of representation matters not falling within the scope of Section 9(b).

The authority the Board cites to justify its departure from the mandate of Section 9(b) are the remarks of Kenneth Culp Davis, an expert in the field of administrative law.[31] However, Professor Davis's remarks neglect to take into account both the language of Section 9(b) and its legislative history. Hence, any rule proposed by the Board that ignores such a clear legislative directive impermissibly expands the agency's power and runs contrary to the statute itself, rendering the rule a legal nullity.[32]

Since the passage of the 1974 Amendments, every court of appeals, except one, that has addressed the issue has agreed that in determining health care bargaining units, the Board must employ standards different from those applied to other industries. The Board's opinion that "congressional and industry concern with proliferation was directed towards the fifteen to twenty-plus units that had arisen in the health care and other industries prior to the amendments and the possibility of scores of units if each hospital classification were permitted to organize separately" results from its improper construction of what Congress meant by the term "undue proliferation."[33] The Board has attempted to buttress its reasoning by referring to Senator Taft's remarks concerning Congress's desire to avoid in the health care industry the unit patterns of other industries, particularly of the construction trades.

The 1974 legislative history fails to support the Board's contention that so long as it avoids the construction industry pattern of multiple craft units, it is honoring the congressional admonition. Precisely the same argument was made by the Board in *Allegheny General Hospital*, in which the Board reviewed the history of the congressional admonition and concluded that Congress did not intend that the Board depart from the "community of interests" test applied to the formation of bargaining units in general industry.[34] Utilizing this analysis, the Board concluded that a proposed unit of maintenance employees "does not even remotely resemble the pattern of the construction industry" and was not unduly proliferative.[35]

In his dissent in that case, Board Member Penello criticized the Board's interpretation of the 1974 legislative history and its "bold repudiation of Congress' directive. . . to avoid proliferation of bargaining units in the health care industry."[36] He belittled the Board majority's attempts to construe Senator Taft's concerns about proliferation as simply his desire to avoid application on the craft-laden construction industry model to health care institutions. Board member Penello concluded, based on his own review of the legislative history, that Congress intended the unit proliferation admonition to preclude the Board from applying the traditional "community of interests" criteria to health care units without considering the public interest in limiting their number.

The U.S. Court of Appeals for the Third Circuit ultimately rejected the Board's reasoning in *Allegheny General Hospital* as being inconsistent with the Board's earlier decision in *St. Vincent's Hospital*.[37] Even before that ruling, however, the U.S. Court of Appeals for the Second Circuit, in *NLRB v. Mercy Hospital Association,* had the opportunity to consider the Board's and Board Member Penello's conflicting views on the 1974 legislative history and rejected the Board's conclusion that all that Congress wanted to avoid was the approval to separate units for every professional employee or job classification.[38]

None of the remarks of Congress in the 1974 legislative history identifies the specific numbers "fifteen to twenty" as the level of bargaining units that Congress deemed "proliferative." In fact, the legislative history likewise fails to support the Board's contention that the framers of the 1974 Amendments wanted to avoid the 15 to 20 units that the Board asserts were normally found in the health care industry at that time. Rather, the record reflects that the industry was largely unorganized at that time and that great numbers of bargaining units were not developing. However, the Board's current contention that eight units are not unduly proliferative, because Congress was concerned with the specter of twice that number, is not borne out by the legislative history of the 1974 Amendments.

Recent Decisions

The Board's recent decisions demonstrate its traditional position that petitioned-for units for separate groups of health care workers are not warranted.

The decisions in *St. Vincent Hospital*,[39] and *St. Francis III*[40] are in direct opposition to the proposed rules. During the rulemaking process, the Board decided *St. Vincent Hospital* and found that in the face of a petition for a unit of registered nurses (RNs), the smallest appropriate unit is one composed of all professional employees. Significantly, the Board found that nurses are assigned to divisions other than patient care services, have daily contacts with other professional employees, serve on multidisciplinary hospital committees, and work shifts in common with medical technologists, pharmacists, and physical therapists. The Board indicated what it believed to be the normal relationship between nurses and other professions; it found that this relationship did not present "sharper than usual" differences and did not justify a separate RN unit. None of the testimony the Board received in the rulemaking process modifies that result; nor can it now justify the Board finding that a separate RN unit is warranted in every hospital throughout the country.

The courts have continually urged the Board to follow the congressional admonition to avoid the proliferation of health care bargaining units and have supported the Board when it properly adhered to the congressional intent. In *NLRB v. HMO International/California Medical Group Health Plan, Inc.,* the U.S. Court of Appeals for the Ninth Circuit found not only that RN units are not presumptively appropriate but also that RNs are not even presumptively Section 2(12) employees. Thus, the court required that the Board examine the individual circumstances not only of each case but also of each employee or employee group.[41] Previously, the Board rejected an all-RN unit in *Mt. Airy Psychiatric Center*.[42] Most recent, of course, is the Board's decision in *St. Vincent Hospital*.[43]

In *Vicksburg Hospital, Inc. v. NLRB*, both the Board and the U.S. Court of Appeals for the Fifth Circuit found that a separate unit of technical employees was not appropriate.[44] The court found that the Board's certification of a combined service maintenance and technical unit was appropriate, which is particularly interesting in light of the congressional mandate against undue proliferation of bargaining units in the industry.

Even more resoundingly the courts have found that separate units of maintenance employees are not appropriate.[45] There is simply no judicial support for the suggestion that skilled maintenance employees should have a unit separate from other service and maintenance employees.

The courts have been equally and uniformly insistent that the Board not adopt any sort of *per se* rule or otherwise fail to exercise its unit determination judgment in each individual case. In *Memorial Hospital of Texborough v. NLRB*, U.S. Court of Appeals for the Third Circuit held that Section 9(b) of the Act "requires the Board to exercise its discretion as to an appropriate unit in each and every case" and concluded that it could not delegate that authority by giving comity to a state labor relations board decision.[46] The Third Circuit continued to adhere to this view as it chastised the Board for refusing to follow judicial precedent in *Allegheny General Hospital v. NLRB*.[47] The Ninth Circuit also rejected any *per se* policy or irrebuttable presumption of certain appropriate units in *NLRB v. St. Francis Hospital of Lynwood*.[48] Further undercutting the Board's intent to enact rules is the Second Circuit's decision in *Trustees of the Masonic Hall and Asylum Fund v. NLRB*, in which the court affirmed the Board's unit determination, but only after its own factual analysis, indicating in dictum that it would not necessarily have done so in each and every instance.[49] The court stated: "If the Board gives due heed to Congress and looks at the employment circumstances of each health care institution, it is inevitable that in certain cases certified units will not be consistent."[50] Just as the courts did not allow such results in adjudicatory proceedings, it is safe to predict that they will not allow them to stand when challenges to the rulemaking are brought.

CONCLUSION

An objective analysis of the testimony and empirical evidence received at the hearings and in the written comments compels the conclusion that the Board should continue its case-by-case approach in determining the appropriate number of bargaining units in this specialized industry. The current law, set forth in decisions such as *St. Francis II*,[51] provides the Board with appropriate parameters for making unit determinations consistent with the congressional mandate to avoid proliferation of health care bargaining units, while retaining the flexibility of the case-by-case approach. Should the Board decline to return to the case-by-case approach, the American Hospital Association (AHA) has suggested that it would support an alternative that would better follow the legislative intent, provide for fair bargaining representation, safeguard improved care of the ill, and possibly reduce unnecessary litigation. An example of such a guideline, suggested to the Board in the AHA's comments to the SNPR, would be for the Board to adopt the following rebuttable presumption:

> In considering the question of appropriate bargaining units in the health care industry, the Board will presume that multi-disciplinary units (such as all professional or all non-professional employees) can fairly and effectively represent hospital workers in collective bargaining unless a petitioner can show by clear and convincing evidence that: (1) a multidisciplinary unit does not or will not reasonably represent its members; or (2) a different unit determination is consistent with or outweighs the strong public interests protected by non-proliferation of bargaining units.[52]

This concept addresses the concerns Congress expressed in 1974, safeguards the rights of employees to organize, allows the petitioner in a representation case to adduce evidence that may compel the finding of a smaller unit, and satisfies the judicial criticisms of the Board's prior health care unit determinations in which the Board failed to justify its permission of smaller units in particular cases. Such an approach clearly is more adaptable and able to accommodate the concerns of hospitals, their employees, and their unions in the dynamic health care environment than are the inflexible directives embodied in the proposed rules.

Whether the Board returns to the traditional case-by-case adjudication, or whether it chooses to adopt the alternative suggested by the AHA, the Board's foray into rulemaking lacks a sound legislative or judicial basis. The proposed rules as we currently see them are the Board's folly, but despite the litigation that is sure to follow, we must be fearful if they are not.

A FINAL NOTE: N.L.R.B. FINAL DECISION ON BARGAINING UNITS

At a meeting held on Thursday, March 23, 1989, the National Labor Relations Board voted 4-1 to issue a Final Rule regarding bargaining units in the health care industry.

The four-member majority reaffirmed the eight-unit structure proposed in the September 1, 1988 Notice of Proposed Rulemaking, as follows: all registered nurses, all physicians, all other professional employees, all technical employees, all skilled maintenance employees, all business office clerical employees, all other service and maintenance employees, and all guards.

Several changes were made in the September 1, 1988 Notice of Rulemaking. An addition will be made to consider very small units, defined in concept as "fewer than five or six members," as an "extraordinary circumstance" so as to permit a hospital to litigate the issue of whether such a unit should be combined with a larger unit over a union's objection. Thus, for example, a hospital could argue that three skilled maintenance employees must be included in the larger "other service and maintenance" unit rather than having separate bargaining rights.

Second, the four-member majority voted to exclude rehabilitation hospitals from the coverage of the Final Rule. The Rule will be revised to provide that the designated units may be combined only pursuant to a union-filed petition, and that a hospital may not raise the issue of combining units on its own, except as may be provided in the revision to the "extraordinary circumstance" noted above.

In summary, the Board majority reconfirmed substantially all of the positions advocated by organized labor as contained in the September 1, 1988 Second Notice of Proposed Rulemaking. Health care industry arguments and presentations were for the most part ignored.

Procedurally, Board staff must now redraft the Rule and associated Commentary to reflect the changes noted above for final approval by the Board. Thereafter, the Final Rule will be published in the *Federal Register* and, pursuant to the provisions of the Administrative Procedure Act, will become effective thirty days thereafter. Should the Final Rule be published in the form approved March 23, 1989, the American Hospital Association intends to mount a prompt legal challenge to the publication, validity, and content of the Final Rule.

NOTES

1. In fact, on May 15, 1987, during a discussion of *St. Vincent Hospital and Health Center and Montana Nurses Association*, 285 N.L.R.B. 64 (1987), the Board voted 3 to 2 to engage in rulemaking regarding the determination of appropriate health care bargaining units. However, the Board did not give the public notice of this meeting because the discussion occurred in the middle of a session on a case in progress. A written transcript of the meeting was made available, and on July 2, 1987, the Notice of Proposed Rulemaking (NPR) was published (52 Fed. Reg. 25,142). In that notice, the Board proposed six units for hospitals with 100 beds or more (encompassing nurses; physicians; all other professionals; technical workers; service, maintenance, and clerical workers; and guards) and four units for hospitals with fewer than 100 beds and for all nursing homes (covering all professionals; technical employees; service, maintenance, and clerical workers; and guards).

2. 53 Fed. Reg. 33,900 (1988).

3. On March 23, 1989, the Board held another open meeting, in which it addressed several concerns raised in the second round of comments. First, because rural hospitals might have units with as few as two or three people in them (thus presenting a problem in terms of proliferation and costs), under the "extraordinary circumstances" exception, litigation should be allowed over a proper unit where the unit composition is less than five or six employees. Second, rehabilitation hospitals will be excluded from the application of the rule. Third, the definition of acute care hospital will be revised to include a second definition used by the American Hospital Association. In this respect, the Board also decided to establish a reference point for the average length of stay and provide that the hospital should have the burden of showing whether it is an acute care facility. Last, the rule would be clarified to state that a unit may be combined only when petitioned for by a union and that an employer is precluded from arguing that a combination is appropriate.

4. *See* Legislative History, 1974, at 113–14 (remarks of Senator Taft).

5. *See id.* at 113–14, 362–63.

6. U.S. v. Price, 361 U.S. 304 (1960).

7. S. Rep. No. 93-766, 93d Cong., 2d Sess. 5(1974); H.R. Rep. No. 93-1051, 93d Cong., 2d Sess. 7 (1974), reprinted in Legislative History, 1974, 12, 274–75.

8. The cases referred to as the "compromise" on the bargaining unit question are instructive. In *Four Seasons Nursing Center*, maintenance employees were included in a unit of service employees. In *Woodland Park Hospital*, the Board dismissed a petition requesting a separate unit of technical employees. In *Extendicare*, the petitioners sought separate units for licensed practical nurses (LPNs), service and maintenance employees, and all technical employees. The Board, however, stated that a separate unit of technical employees would create "unwarranted fragmentation," and, accordingly, such a unit was rejected. Nevertheless, the Board approved a combined unit of technical, service, and maintenance employees and a separate unit of LPNs. Careful consideration of these decisions in the context of the SNPR discloses that the rules are inconsistent with the Board's decisions, which utilized a case-by-case approach.

9. I Legislative History of the National Labor Relations Act, 1935, at 1300 (1949).

10. *See* H.R. 6187 and H.R. 6288, 74th Cong., 1st Sess. (1949), *Reprinted in* II Legislation History of the National Labor Relations Act, 1935, at 2449, 2464 (1949).

11. H.R. 7978, 74th Cong., 1st Sess. (1935), *reprinted in* II Legislative History, 1935, at 2903 (emphasis added). Identical language to H.R. 7978 was present in an earlier version of the bill, H.R. 7937, 74th Cong., 1st Sess. (1935). *See* II Legislative History, 1935, at 2850.

12. H.R. Rep. No. 969, 74th Cong., 1st Sess. (1935), *reprinted in* II Legislative History, 1935, at 2930.

13. *Id.*

14. *See* II Legislative History 1935, 16 at 3253–54, 3256.

15. Abramowitz, *The Future of Health Care Delivery in America.*

16. Mary Gallwan, *Second Quarter Shows Signs of Downturn* 61 Hospitals, pp. 40-44 (November, 1987).

17. *Id.* at 48.

18. Herman Smith Associates and the Health Industry Manufacturers Association, *HIMA Alternate Site Project Series*, Mod. Healthcare 16 (January 3, 1986): 65.

19. Paul J. Kenkel, *More Hospitals Enter Long-Term Care Business* 17 Mod. Healthcare 16, p. 65 (November 20, 1987).

20. *Id.*

21. Testimony of Lawrence J. Donnelly, Director of Clinical Systems Development, before the National Labor Relations Board, 7 October 1987, W.Tr., 4063–64.

22. K.E. Super, Women slow to respond to bone scanning services while arthritis units show promise. 17 *Mod. Healthcare*, pp. 40, 42 (July 31, 1987).

23. Low & Weisbord, *The Multicompetent Practitioner: A Needs Analysis in an Urban Area*, 16 J. Allied Health 29 (February 1987).

24. The multiskilled work force is not a system unique to the health care industry. Variations of this system, such as the increased knowledge-based system by which pay levels are linked to increased knowledge and skills, are utilized by Firestone, Ford, Johnson & Johnson, and Proctor & Gamble. Jenkins & Gupta, *The Payoffs of Paying for Knowledge*, 42 Nat'l Productivity Rev. (Spring 1985).

25. Electrical Workers (IBEW) Local 474 v. NLRB, 814 F.2d 697 (D.C. Cir. 1987).

26. 285 N.L.R.B. 64 (1987).

27. 52 Fed. Reg. 25, 142 (1987).

28. 53 Fed. Reg. 33,900, 33,932–33 (September 1, 1988).

29. *Id.* at 33,935.

30. *Id.* at 33,901

31. *See* K.C. Davis, Administrative Law Text § 6.04, at 145 (3d ed. 1972).

32. *See* Federal Election Comm'n v. Democratic Senatorial Campaign Comm., 454 U.S. 27, 31–32 (1981); SEC v. Sloan, 436 U.S. 103, 117 (1978).

33. 53 Fed. Reg. 33,933 (September 1, 1988).

34. *Allegheny Gen. Hosp.*, 239 N.L.R.B. 872 (1975), *enforcement denied*, 608 F.2d 965 (3d Cir. 1979).

35. *Id.* at 879.

36. *Id.*

37. *See* Allegheny Gen Hosp. v. NLRB, 608 F.2d 965 (3d Cir. 1979); St. Vincent's Hospital v. N.L.R.B., 567 F.2d 588 (3rd Cir. 1977).

38. 606 F.2d 22 (2d Cir. 1979), *cert. denied*, 445 U.S. 971 (1980).

39. St. Vincent Hospital and Health Center and Montana Nurses Association, 285 N.L.R.B. 64 (1987).

40. Electrical Workers (IBEW) Local 474 v. N.L.R.B., 814 F.2d 697 (D.C. Cir. 1987).

41. N.L.R.B. v. HMO Int'l/Cal. Medical Group Health Plan, 678 F.2d 806 (9th Cir. 1982).

42. 253 N.L.R.B. 1003 (1981).

43. St. Vincent Hospital and Health Center v. Montana Nurses Association, 285 N.L.R.B. 64 (1987).

44. 653 F.2d 1070 (5th Cir. 1981).

45. Notwithstanding the D.C. Circuit's remark regarding the Board's denial of a separate maintenance unit in Electrical Workers (IEBW) Local 474 v. NLRB, 814 F.2d 697 (D.C. Cir. 1987), the Board reaffirmed its decision and rationale that a separate maintenance unit was inappropriate under a disparity of interest test. *St. Francis Hosp. III*, 286 N.L.R.B. 123 (1987).

46. Memorial Hosp. v. NLRB, 545 F.2d 351 (3d Cir. 1976).

47. Allegheny Gen. Hosp. v. NLRB, 608 F.2d 965(3d Cir. 1979).

48. 604 F.2d 404 (9th Cir. 1979).

49. 699 F.2d 626 (2d Cir. 1983).

50. *Id*. at 637–38.

51. *St. Francis II*, 271 N.L.R.B. 948, 116 L.R.R.M. 1465 (1984).

52. "Supplemental Comments of AHA on Proposed Rules and Bargaining Units in the Health Care Industry," October 17, 1988, p. 7.

Susan Warner
Brian G. Costello
Julius M. Steiner

Eight Bargaining Units 47
in the Health
Care Industry:
Invidious Discrimination
in the Work Place?

Since 1974, when Congress extended the protection of the National Labor Relations Act (NLRA) to private nonprofit hospitals, the National Labor Relations Board (NLRB) has taken literally hundreds of thousands of pages of testimony in numerous cases in order to determine appropriate bargaining units in the health care industry.[1]

An enormous amount of attention was given to the Health Care Amendments[2] and to their underlying philosophy,[3] primarily because of the concern over nonproliferation of bargaining units in health care. The basis for this concern is the need to accommodate the public's right to continuity of health care with the right of health care employees to engage in collective bargaining.

Disputes over these competing interests have manifested themselves in incongruities between the NLRB and the courts regarding what legal standard to apply in determining bargaining units in health care (i.e., community of interest test or disparity of interest test).[4] Additionally, various members of the Board, the courts, and others in the legal profession have questioned the nexus between Congress' objective of insuring continuity of health care and its means of accomplishing that objective (nonproliferation of bargaining units).

Now using unprecedented substantive rulemaking powers, the NLRB has proposed new rules for determining appropriate bargaining units in the health care industry.

The Board's proposal sets forth eight bargaining units that will be found appropriate in "acute care" hospitals. These bargaining units are (1) registered nurses, (2) physicians,

(3) all professionals except for registered nurses and physicians, (4) technical employees, (5) skilled maintenance employees, (6) business office clerical employees, (7) all other nonprofessional employees, and (8) the statutorily required security guards.

The Board published a Notice of Proposed Rulemaking (NPR) and then held hearings in Washington, Chicago, and San Francisco, and heard testimony from over 140 witnesses, "representing a broad spectrum of industry, labor, and academia."[5] After receiving written comments from over 300 individuals and organizations, the Board issued a second NPR, stating that the findings in the rulemaking record support finding a total of eight bargaining units.

Thus, attention is again being given to the two sides of the "nonproliferation" coin, this time in the framework of the proposed rules. But no attention has been given to another interest that also must be balanced: one that is so obvious that it has been overlooked completely. This interest did not exist in the 1930s when the NLRA came into being and was still in its infancy when the Health Care Amendments were passed in 1974, for the Civil Rights Act was only passed in 1964, and while Executive Order 11246 (the "Affirmative Action Order") was issued in 1964–1965,[6] Revised Order No. 4 was not published until 1971.[7] So it seems that no one has addressed the potentially devastating effect of so many bargaining units in the health care industry on females and minorities.

It is our position that the Board's proposal will not facilitate employee and labor relations in health care facilities. In fact, it is our position that these units will have the effect of perpetuating race and sex discrimination in the work place.

PROPOSED BARGAINING UNITS V. SEX/RACE DISCRIMINATION

It is submitted that hospitals, which are subject to Affirmative Action and to Title VII of the Civil Rights Act of 1964, will be placed in a position that will defeat their efforts to integrate their work force and to provide opportunities for minorities and females.

The implementation of the proposed rules will place many hospitals in a "double-bind" situation: being held accountable under Affirmative Action requirements for facilitating integration and upward mobility of minorities and females versus acquiescing to negotiating with unions representing bargaining units which, for all practical purpose, are segregated by sex, or race, and, because of the nature of labor contracts, will almost ensure that these units remain segregated.

It must be remembered that hospitals are a labor-intensive industry. They are a unique industry in that their labor force is normally comprised of over 70 percent females. One need only examine and compare the proposed bargaining units against each other with empirical data to begin to understand the discriminatory effects of permitting eight bargaining units in hospitals—effects that our social legislation has attempted to eradicate. The empirical data are telling.

Registered Nurses

The Board proposes a separate unit for registered nurses. The Board asserts that "RNs are unique in that their profession alone requires continuous interaction with patients. Nursing practice acts require that RNs monitor and assess patients around-the-clock, based on a cluster of knowledge which they possess as opposed to a single skill."[8] This analysis is correct. But empirical data also reflect that registered nurses, as a class of employees, are dominated by females (95–98 percent). If the Board's proposed unit of registered nurses becomes reality, then overwhelming female domination will continue, and the breakdown of a traditionally female work force into a more disparate work force will become virtually impossible.

Furthermore, the Board noted that "As a result of their special responsibilities and unusual schedules, nurses have special bargaining interests such as scheduling, shift differentials and premium pay, time off for continuing education, and floating and orientation training."[9]

In contrast, when analyzing a physicians' unit, the Board proposes a separate unit because of their "singular responsibility for directing all other patient care employees, substantially greater compensation, and their interest in bargaining about medical education, malpractice insurance, and input into patient care decisions." The Board, in short shrift, notes, "At the same time, physicians have little interest in issues of special concern to RNs or other professions."[10]

In fact, one would be hard-put to find a professional nurse today who does not have an "interest in bargaining about medical education, malpractice insurance, and input into patient care decisions," and nurses would agree that it is they, not physicians, who, on a daily basis, are "singularly responsible for directing all other patient care employees." On the other hand, physicians (especially house staff) should be—and many are—concerned about scheduling, shift differentials and premium pay, and time off for continuing education.

What is the difference then? The concerns are the same; the sex is different. Nurses are 95–98 percent females[11] (primarily white, usually from 80 to 95 percent), while physicians are dominated by male employees.

Physicians

In this proposed group the demographics are virtually opposite of that of registered nurses—empirical data at one large medical center reflect 83-percent male domination (primarily white) in the physician group. If this proposed unit were adopted, the perpetuation of a male-dominated segment of the work force would continue, and the bargaining strengths of this particular unit, which often result in higher pay and richer benefit plans, will be reflective of this male-dominated statistic.

Technicals

The Board has found that most technicals are classified as working in a medical laboratory, respiratory therapy, radiography, or emergency medicine or as licensed practical nurses. The empirical data consistently reflect that these technical classifications in hospitals are female-dominated groups (72–78 percent), thus again perpetuating work force sex discrimination.

Interestingly, technicals earn approximately $2,000 per year more than service employees. Here the Board notes that "Cross-training of technicals was shown to have occurred almost exclusively with other technicals, thus *maintaining the integrity* of the technical classification."[12] (Emphasis added) Our point exactly. For less than 50 percent of the technicals are minorities, while in the service classification, "Other Nonprofessionals," approximately 90 percent are minorities.

Other Nonprofessionals (Service and Unskilled Maintenance)

The Board proposes that all remaining nonprofessional (primarily service and unskilled maintenance in hospitals) employees constitute an appropriate bargaining unit except for security guards. Empirical data reflect that the "Other Nonprofessional" job classification is dominated by minorities (89–94 percent). This group is, according to the Board's findings, the lowest paid of all classifications.

Business Office Clericals

The Board proposes that business office clericals constitute a separate appropriate unit, a position contrary to the original position articulated by the Board. Business office clericals, clearly, are female dominated (89–93 percent of the business office clerical work force is female). This, too, would have the effect of perpetuating a female-dominated classification. "On average, business office clericals earn $2,000 more than top service employees, ..." [13] Why? One reason may be that this group is almost 50-percent white, compared to only approximately 10-percent white in the service group.

Skilled Maintenance

The Board is now proposing that skilled maintenance employees constitute a separate bargaining unit. According to the Board, the most recent Bureau of Labor Statistics data show that skilled maintenance employees in private hospitals earn wages that average 25 percent more than technicals (technicals are comprised of approximately 72 percent females), almost 60 percent more than business office clericals (89 percent females), and 76 percent more than service employees (89 percent minorities). Empirical data reflect that skilled maintenance job classifications have less than 20-percent female participation and less than 30-percent minority participation. Skilled maintenance is a white male–dominated job classification (85 percent males; 75 percent white). If this job classification were to be perpetuated in a bargaining unit classification, the higher-paying salaries granted to white males would be perpetuated.

Other Professionals

The Board proposes that a unit of all other professionals would be appropriate as "other professionals do not want to be organized with RNs, and the fact that separate units of RNs and physicians have tentatively been deemed appropriated." [14] Empirically, the work force group "Other Professionals" is dominated by females (64–68 percent) with only 27 percent minorities. Again, this type of a unit would have the effect of perpetuating work force segregation.

EFFECT ON UPWARD MOBILITY

Historically, each bargaining unit would negotiate its own collective bargaining agreement. Most items covering terms and conditions of employment would be included in language articulated by the bargaining unit contract including job seniority provisions. It is rare that one bargaining unit contract would "accept" or "recognize" the bargaining unit seniority of another contract. This seriously hinders the progression of minorities and females from lower-paying job group classifications. The overall effect may even totally preclude the upward mobility of minorities and females.

For example, if a female in the business office clerical bargaining unit were to obtain outside schooling and education, thus allowing her to move into a professional job classification covered by another contract, the employee would have to make this move *without* the protection of seniority she had gained in the business office clerical unit. Employees are reluctant to forgo their seniority rights even though it means upward mobility from a professional and economic standpoint. The position taken by the Board articulating these eight units will drastically reduce any upward mobility from job classifications that are traditionally filled by minorities and females—something that Congress has gone to great lengths to address in the bulk of its social legislation passed since the 1930s.

CONCLUSION

The statistics reveal that the Board's proposed eight bargaining units will have a disastrous impact on minorities and females in the work place. First, employees would be segregated into job categories that are dominated either by sex or by minority classification. Second, because of traditional positions regarding seniority within separate bargaining units, the upward mobility and the "breaking out" of females and minorities from traditional job classifications will be strongly curtailed, if not eliminated. Therefore, we strongly recommend to the Board that it eliminate or withdraw its proposal for eight bargaining units and limit bargaining units in health care institutions to two appropriate units—that is, a unit of professionals and a unit of nonprofessionals, plus the statutorily required guards unit. Alternatively, the Board should return to the doctrine established in *St. Francis II,* [15] where the Board began to apply the "disparity of interest" test.

Unless the National Labor Relations Board wishes to be instrumental in fostering segregation and discriminatory disparities in wages and benefits and in substantially hindering the upward mobility of minorities and females, it must abandon the eight-unit concept.

NOTES

1. 170 DLR E-1(9/1/88).

2. See United States Statutes at Large, 93rd Congress, 2d Session 1974, Volume 88, Part 1, pp. 1–1362, Public Laws, for the specific amendments regarding health care, and see 88 Stat. 395–96 (1974) for the statute in its entirety.

3. 120 Cong. Rec. 12,943–45 (1974).

4. *St. Francis Hospital (I)*, 265 N.L.R.B. 1025, 112 L.R.R.M. 1153 (1982) and *St. Francis Hospital (II)*, 271 N.L.R.B. 948, 116 L.R.R.M. 1465 (1984), *remanded sub nom; St. Francis Hospital vs International Brotherhood of Electrical Workers*, Local union No. 474, AFL-CIO, case 26-CA-10060 (*St. Francis II*).

5. 170 DLR E-1 (9/1/88).

6. C.F.R. 339 (1964-1965 Compilation), *reprinted in* 42 U.S.C. § 2000e note, issued on September 24, 1965, as amended.

7. Regulations issued by Office of Federal Contract Compliance Programs (OFCCP) are published at 41 C.F.R. Chapter 60 (1980) and include, inter alia, Part 60-2, known as Revised Order No. 4, affirmative action requirements applicable to nonconstruction workers. Chapter 60 of Title 41 of the Code of Federal Regulations was amended to include Part 60-2 on December 4, 1971, 36 Fed. Reg. 23152, No. 234.

8. 170 DLR E-2 (9/1/88).

9. *Id.*

10. *Id.*

11. The source for the specific minority and female percentages in this paper is the 1987 Affirmative Action Plan for a large, urban hospital and medical center in Philadelphia. Informal discussions with the chief human resource officers at eight additional major urban hospitals confirmed similar statistics. Additionally, according to the 1980 census, EEO Special File, occupations by race and sex for the Philadelphia/New Jersey Standard Metropolitan Statistical Area (SMSA), category 95, "Registered Nurses," the percentage of females among those employed nurses was 94.8 percent and the percentage of minorities among those employed nurses was 16.4 percent. The Scientific Manpower Commission also published data regarding professional women and minorities.

12. 170 DLR E-3 (9/1/88).

13. *Id.*

14. 170 DLR E-2 (9/1/88).

15. *St. Francis Hosp.*, 271 N.L.R.B. 948 (1984).

James H. Stephens

The NLRB's Health Care Rulemaking: Myths versus Reality

48

In reflecting on the Board's fiftieth anniversary, Professor Charles Morris wrote a provocative article recently in the San Diego Law Review entitled *The NLRB in the Dog House—Can an Old Board Learn New Tricks?*[1] Featured prominently was an appeal to the Board to engage in substantive rulemaking—a course of action largely ignored by the Board over the last half century.

The Board, even if it is an "old dog" in some people's eyes, last year decided to accept this challenge of learning this "new trick." The Board embarked on this course, however, not because it is trying to overcome any anxieties it may have had over its institutional expertise, its stamina, or its political courage. Rather, we concluded that there was a fundamental problem which needed attention. That problem has centered around the use of the case-by-case adjudicatory method of unit determinations in the health care field. As anyone who has had any experience in this area can attest, things have been in a state of disarray for a long time. The traditional way of determining appropriate bargaining units simply has not worked. We thus initiated rulemaking with the hope that it will lead us out of the quagmire left by case law.

Professor Morris, of course, has not been a voice crying in the wilderness in his advocacy of rulemaking. In fact, over the years the Board has been criticized by judges, and even Board Members, for not utilizing its rulemaking powers to bring

about more stability in the law. The late Justice Douglas urged this, as have such prominent jurists as Judge Posner of the Seventh Circuit Court of Appeals. Former Members Dennis and Zimmerman while on the Board both urged resort to rulemaking in this specific area of health care unit determinations. At this very conference, in October 1984, former Chairman Miller made these observations:

> The Board has now had enough experience in hospital cases that I would have thought it would now be equipped to adopt some helpful rules to guide us all. Indeed, in the whole field of unit determination, it is my own opinion that rulemaking could be a useful exercise.[2]

Other distinguished members of the labor bar have endorsed rulemaking as well. In a very recent law review article which in part commented on our proposed rulemaking, one of the prominent figures of the New York management bar, Edward Silver, of the firm of Proskauer, Rose, Goetz, and Mendelsohn, said, "After 50 years, the Board should be able to draw upon its experience and codify at least some of its labor law policy into rules of general application."[3]

When we embarked on this undertaking in July of 1987, we posed two questions: (1) Should there be rulemaking in this area? and (2) If so, what should the rule contain?

Our initial proposal would have established six units as appropriate. Following publication of the proposal in the Federal Register, hearings were held in Washington, in Chicago, in San Francisco, and again in Washington.

The evidence received far exceeded, in both detail and exhaustiveness, what we had expected. The transcript of the

Note: Reprinted with permission from Remarks presented at the Southwest Legal Foundation Conference on October 13, 1988, Dallas, Texas, by James H. Stephens, Chairman, National Labor Relations Board, Washington, D.C. (Contains several revisions to the speech originally presented at the 1988 conference.)

hearings totals 3,545 pages; 144 individuals came in person to testify, representing every broad job classification under consideration; written comments, totaling about 1,500 pages, from 315 individuals and organizations, were received. After reviewing all the evidence and comments, we were far better qualified to resolve the issues raised in the first notice.

We reached an important milestone in July of 1988 in deciding to answer the first question in the affirmative—that we should pursue rulemaking to conclusion. We also agreed to consider modifications in the proposed rule based on the evidence gathered. On September 1, the Board published in the Federal Register a second notice containing the proposed modifications, together with over 30 pages of explanation and summaries of the evidence. The comment period will close on October 17.

I thought this conference would provide an appropriate forum to share some observations about this historic rulemaking proceeding. Since a few more days remain in the comment period, I will address the more preliminary issue of whether the Board should have undertaken rulemaking and refrain from discussing the rationale behind the specific aspects of the rule as it appeared in the second notice. I would like to approach this topic from a particular perspective—examining the myths versus the reality of this rulemaking.

It was only after spending a number of years in Washington working in the Congress that I came to appreciate the old saying that, in politics, perception is reality. The merits of a proposal—whether a bill or an administrative regulation—will not necessarily carry it through to enactment or promulgation. Rather, it must in many cases pass through the gauntlet of public opinion. This includes not only the public at large, but also the labor-management bar in particular.

For those who oppose the rulemaking, and who are looking for ways to throw up obstacles to stop it in its tracks, this time period in the rulemaking process provides an opportunity for them to turn public opinion against it. That campaign is already underway, as evidenced by some of the written inquiries being sent to us from Capitol Hill.

In some instances, a misconception will be launched into the public domain by someone, with no apparent ax to grind, who thinks he is just reporting the facts accurately. Yet, such a report can reinforce in the minds of the public that something is amiss with rulemaking.

In the end, though, as the public and the bar become more acquainted with the reality of what we are doing, it is my hope that the objections of the alarmists will be seen for what they are—mythology.

In the interest of injecting a dose of reality into the public debate about the Board's rulemaking, I will attempt today to "demythologize" seven myths which I have come across to date.

Before turning to the first "myth," let me just summarize very briefly the main features of the proposed rule as revised.

It approves eight units for acute care hospitals, absent a showing of extraordinary circumstances: all registered nurses; all physicians; all professionals except for registered nurses

and physicians; all technical employees; all skill maintenance employees; all business office clerical employees; all guards; and all other nonprofessional employees. The separate guards unit is mandated by Section 9(b)(3) of the Act, and physicians' units are rare. As a practical matter, then, this is a six-unit rule.

Nursing homes and psychiatric hospitals are not covered. Unions are permitted to petition for combined units, which the Board may find appropriate. In addition, the Board is proposing that it honor nonconforming stipulations submitted by the parties. Finally, a narrowly tailored "extraordinary circumstances" exception is included which allows the parties to demonstrate that, despite the Board's enunciated rule, the unit being sought is not appropriate in a particular case.

Now let's turn to the myths.

Myth No. 1

The NLRB is for the first time "allowing" employees to organize in hospitals.

Reality: As I intimated, the public's perception of the NLRB's activities is shaped in no small measure by newspaper accounts. To illustrate how false impressions can be generated, listen to this headline of *The New York Times* of September 1 for its story on the rule: "Labor Board To Allow Health Worker Unions." To the layperson, this headline clearly suggests that the Board has run amuck. It reads as if the Board is bestowing some new right or privilege heretofore not enjoyed by health care employees. The fact, however, is that it was a strongly bipartisan Congress that made the decision 14 years ago to extend fully the NLRA's protection to the health care field.

Closely related to this myth is another one derived from a newspaper account of our rulemaking.

Myth No. 2

In reporting on the second notice, *The Wall Street Journal* ran this curious headline, "NLRB Proposes Hospital Staffs Form into Units." This carries the obvious suggestion that the Board is somehow behind an effort to foster organizing in the health care field. This notion is perhaps reinforced by the reported comments of union leaders who see rulemaking as a great boon to organizing.

Reality: The fact is that we are simply trying to afford to health care workers the same opportunity afforded to workers in other industries, namely, the right to vote in a timely manner on whether to be represented by a union. The emphasis, I think, should be on "timely manner." As President Reagan stated on the occasion of the NLRB's fiftieth anniversary: "Our system of peaceful industrial relations, and the national labor policy that has evolved from the Act, rest on this principle of free choice."

If organizing does increase as the result of this rule, it will be because employees have exercised their individual choice to be represented. If people find that objectionable, it is a matter with which Congress must deal. In short, as I see it, we are merely following the original intent of Congress.

Myth No. 3

The case-by-case determination of appropriate units is superior to rulemaking because it represents a careful, searching analysis of the specific facts of each case.

Reality: As careful and efficient as the traditional method usually is, it has become an obstacle to the fair administration of the Act. The history of representation cases in the health care industry has been delay, compounded by more delay. By the time the unit issue is decided, the employees originally interested in union representation may not even be working in the bargaining unit any more. Moreover, for obvious reasons of time and expense the union may have long since given up its efforts to persuade employees of the merits of organizing.

Ever since Congress enacted the Health Care Amendments of 1974, the Board has struggled to develop understandable and meaningful guidelines which can be quickly and easily applied in the field and uniformly approved in the courts of appeals. Under the existing case-by-case approach, as it emerged in health care cases, a petitioning union can be forced to litigate virtually every job classification at a hospital, as the targeted employer tries to include as many employees as possible in the unit. The hearings literally go on for weeks, generating enormous legal expense, producing thousands of pages of record, and leading to enormous delays in processing the case through the Board. During the course of our rulemaking hearings, one management attorney conceded, in an off-the-record conversation, that his firm figured that any health care representation case was good for three thousand pages of transcript at a minimum.

Even after all this delay and expenditure in developing excruciatingly detailed records, there is little evidence that they affected the voting patterns of the Board Members. During the course of our rulemaking, we asked that the Representation Appeals Unit prepare a survey of Board Members' votes in health care cases between 1974 and 1984. To my surprise, the survey showed that the individual Board Members' votes are virtually 100-percent uniform anyway, regardless of the content of different records. As if that were not enough, the Board and the parties then must face the perils and uncertainties, to say nothing of the additional legal expense, of judicial review by courts of appeals, which are badly splintered on interpreting the 1974 Amendments.

Now at this point in our discussion it may be appropriate to consider how the Board got itself into this dilemma.

There are, I think, two main reasons: First, Congress itself must bear initial responsibility for leaving a cloud of ambiguity over the amendments. But, secondly, the Board must bear equal, if not greater, responsibility for not adequately grappling with this ambiguity.

Congress began consideration of proposals to include non-profit hospitals under the National Labor Relations Act in 1972, two years before final passage. In support of the legislation, the unions noted that hospitals originally were included under the Wagner Act in 1935, but were later excluded by the Taft-Hartley Act in 1947. Proponents of the 1947 exclusion had argued successfully that nonprofit hospitals are charitable institutions which generally serve low-income people and which are funded mainly by voluntary donations from the community. Such institutions therefore should not have to operate under the rigors and burdens of commercialized labor-management relations, the proponents argued.

By 1972, however, the unions were able to portray the operation of nonprofit hospitals in a much less sympathetic light. They pointed to the unfavorable working conditions and lower economic lot of many hospital employees, and the propensity of hospital management to resist organizing by engaging in what would otherwise be unfair labor practices. The unions also demonstrated that most of the serious disputes and work stoppages in the industry related to initial recognition and work jurisdiction questions.

In an unusual political development, at least when it comes to labor legislation, both liberal and arch-conservative members of Congress coalesced in support of the amendments. Given the prospect which this consensus meant for passage of the amendments, the hospital industry mustered an array of opposing arguments, which may be summarized as follows:

1. Allowing employees to organize is ill-suited to an industry undergoing dynamic changes in the manner in which it delivers its services to the public.
2. With coverage under the National Labor Relations Act (NLRA), there will occur a proliferation of bargaining units, which will have the following adverse consequences:
   a. The designation of relatively small bargaining units would greatly enhance the wholesale disruption of health care, as other units respect the picket lines thrown up by such units;
   b. Rigid craft lines would evolve similar to those in the construction industry, leading to jurisdictional disputes, picketing, and work stoppages;
   c. Unions would compete for higher wages by "whip-sawing" hospital employers, resulting in higher labor costs;
   d. Hospitals would incur higher costs in administering multiple contracts.

Interestingly, the opponents of the rulemaking have relied essentially on these same "dire prediction" arguments that were raised during the debates over the 1974 Amendments. Congress, of course, determined that these perceived problems were not serious enough to justify rejecting the bill outright. Rather, to the extent there were legitimate concerns,

Congress engrafted certain safeguards into the legislation itself. These are essentially prophylactic measures, under Sections 8(d) and 8(g), that are designed both to promote bargaining and to minimize resort to strikes and picketing.

As to the overall concern about unit proliferation, the congressional committees, in report language, directed the Board to avoid the problem. But significantly Congress itself stopped short of giving the Board specific directives in the statute itself.

Like the Congress, the Board has now concluded that none of the industry's assertions is compelling enough to abandon the proposed rulemaking. Nevertheless, as is apparent from some of the comments being sent to the Congress objecting to what we are doing that the nonproliferation issue has become the subject of Myth No. 4.

Myth No. 4

In adopting the rule, the Board is ignoring the congressional admonition against unit proliferation.

Reality: I will explain why this argument is fallacious in some detail because it is the industry's principal objection to the rule.

During the congressional hearings on the Amendments, hospital witnesses related their experience in several states where nonprofit hospitals were subject to state labor relations laws. New York and Massachusetts were singled out. The New York State Labor Board, for instance, was accused of Balkanizing hospitals into no less than 21 separate units.

Over the next year, the hospitals hammered away at the point that coverage under the Act would produce similar fragmentation. They pointed to the Board's experience in the construction and printing industries as examples of what would likely take place in their own industry. In each of those industries, witnesses identified the number of units as exceeding a dozen. Perhaps the apogee of things to come was predicted by the Colorado Hospital Association. It pegged the potential number of health care units at approximately 200.

Once it became obvious that legislation was going to pass, the industry finally agreed to support its own proposed amendments to the Act. These amendments would have limited the number of bargaining units to four, while leaving intact the separate guards' unit required under existing law. Thus in 1974 the industry was willing to live with five units: an all-professional unit; an all-technical unit; an all-clerical unit; other employees, including service and maintenance; and guards. On the eve of Senate hearings in 1973, Senator Taft introduced a bill incorporating the industry's proposal.

Although some unions found the Taft proposal acceptable, others objected, as did the AFL–CIO. The upshot was that, as enacted, the amendments did not include the four-unit limitation. Section 9 of the Act, which sets forth the Board's unit determination authority, was left untouched. The industry had to take solace in hortatory language in the committee reports,

warning the Board not to allow unit proliferation. But there was nothing in the legislative history to suggest that the Board should not continue to apply the traditional community of interest standard.

If one reads the entire legislative history to the 1974 Amendments, as I have done—and that includes the floor debates, the committee reports, and all the hearing transcripts of the House and Senate hearings—one glaring fact stands out: neither in committee nor on final passage did Congress identify any specific number of bargaining units as crossing the threshold of undue proliferation in the health care field. As between the high, double-digit numbers feared by witnesses during congressional hearings and the five units that the industry was willing to live with, the eight proposed in our second notice comes very close to the latter number.

Voltaire, that prominent philosopher of the French Enlightenment, reportedly said that "History is the trick which the living play on the dead." I would suggest that with respect to our rulemaking, the legislative history being retold by the opponents of rulemaking is just such a trick. But it is being played on the living. And in this instance, it is working men and women whose franchise is being effectively nullified.

Earlier, I said the Board had to accept its share of the blame for getting itself into this quagmire over hospital units. This is shown by considering some of the major hospital cases decided since the 1974 Amendments and their reception in the circuit courts.

In 1975, the year after the Amendments were enacted, the Board attempted to implement them seemingly in one fell swoop by handing down a cluster of decisions broadly approving separate units for registered nurses; business clericals; service and maintenance workers; and technical employees. But the Board soon ran into trouble in the circuits. Moreover, an early attempt to bring the issue to the Supreme Court proved unsuccessful.

There is no need to recount the complete chronology of disappointments in the courts, except to make two personal observations.

First, soon after its initial decisions, the Board seemed to start down the path toward proliferation by approving small, craft-specific maintenance units. For example, in *St. Vincent Hospital*, 223 N.L.R.B. 638 (1976), *enforcement denied*, 567 F.2d 588 (3d Cir. 1977), the Board unanimously approved a four-person boiler operator unit. Significantly, three Members in a plurality and a concurring opinion completely avoided any discussion of proliferation. Similarly, in another instance, the Board seemed to abdicate its own responsibility by adopting a state labor board's determination as to the appropriateness of a maintenance unit. *Memorial Hospital of Roxborough*, 220 N.L.R.B. 402 (1975), *enforcement denied*, 545 F.2d 351 (3d Cir. 1976). The reviewing courts rejected these decisions, but not because the threshold of undue unit proliferation had been crossed in either case. As I read the courts' opinions, their concern was the Board's failure to articulate the limits which the nonproliferation policy might impose if not in the immediate cases, then at least in future cases.

Secondly, I think the Board provided unnecessary opportunities for the various circuit courts to develop varying interpretations of the 1974 Amendments. The Board's position in several nursing unit cases illustrates this point. In one instance, the Board adopted what was, in effect, an *irrebuttable* presumption that a registered nurses unit was appropriate. The Board rejected an employer's proffer that an all-professional unit was more appropriate in that particular case, despite the fact the Board had not had the advantage of any broad, empirical evidence before adopting the presumption. *St. Francis of Lynwood*, 601 F.2d 404 (9th Cir. 1979). In another case, the Board failed to adequately explain why certain nursing employees were excluded from a registered nurses unit. *HMO International*, 678 F.2d 806 (9th Cir. 1982).

These cases enabled the Ninth Circuit to adopt the "disparity of interest" test, which requires the Board to look for "sharper than usual differences" among employees to justify a separate unit. Other circuit courts generally have not been so stringent as the Ninth or Tenth Circuits on this issue. Still, they have insisted that the Board expressly take undue proliferation into account in each case. In any event, what developed were differing tests among the circuits, due in part to the apparent vagaries in the Amendments' history.

Meanwhile, in the last five years, the Board twice attempted—without success—to craft a more acceptable standard. First, it adopted a seven-unit-plus-guards standard in the *St. Francis I* decision in 1982. But before that test could be applied and tested, the Board reconsidered the decision and in 1982 issued *St. Francis II*, which as a practical matter allows for only four units—professionals, technicals, other nonprofessionals, and guards. That decision is the subject of the next myth.

Myth No. 5

The disparity of interest standard adopted in 1984 in *St. Francis II* is a model of clarity and should be preserved.

Reality: The *St. Francis II* opinion was anything but a clear standard. Indeed, within two months after it was issued, former Chairman Miller observed at this annual conference that the plurality opinion "offers very little guidance to either management or unions as to just what units will be approved in the future."[4] But, equally significant, the *St. Francis II* opinion was resoundingly rejected by the D.C. Circuit Court of Appeals in March 1987.[5] In fact, the court's rejection of the Board's new standard was, in my view, the straw that broke the camel's back and prompted us to undertake rulemaking.

The D.C. Circuit flatly dismissed the disparity of interest standard and was the first circuit court to fault the Board for giving too much weight to the legislative history on undue proliferation. The court held that the words of the statute, not the committee reports, are the law. And the only relevant statutory words were those of Section 9(b), which requires

that we "assure to employees the fullest freedom" in organizing, which the disparity test did not provide.

The panel majority (Judge Harry Edwards and Judge Joyce Green) strongly intimated that the Board had to apply the traditional community of interest standard unless it came up with adequate reasons for changing the standard. However, the court said it was the Board's prerogative to decide.

Now some people argue that the D.C. Circuit presented us with a golden opportunity to obtain assured review in the Supreme Court. This leads us to what I identify as the next myth.

Myth No. 6

Appealing *St. Francis II* to the Supreme Court would obviate the problems that rulemaking is attempting to resolve.

Reality: I personally don't think the Supreme Court would have given us a definitive answer. While admittedly there is a divergence of views among the circuit courts, an important aspect of the *St. Francis II* court's decision, in my mind at least, weighed against seeking review: Judge Buckley, a conservative Reagan appointee, filed a concurring opinion in which he agreed with his colleagues that the Board had placed too much emphasis on the committee reports in adopting the disparity of interest standard.

The fact that Judge Edwards and Judge Buckley, who are poles apart philosophically, could agree on this significant point of statutory interpretation created substantial uncertainty whether the Supreme Court, regardless of its philosophical makeup, would resolve the entire controversy by adopting a clear, simple, predictable rule. All that it was likely to do was tell the Board what, if any, weight was to be given to undue proliferation as a general matter. Indeed, it would be unprecedented for the Court to usurp our responsibility in the first instance to develop the specific appropriate units. We need only recall how the Court in its 1976 *South Prairie Construction Co.* decision faulted a court of appeals for taking on itself the initial determination of a unit question.[6] Thus, I foresaw another year or so of further delay if the issue went to the Court, with the likelihood that it would direct us to try once again to fashion a workable standard.

Let me conclude with what I think is the most far-fetched, but perhaps most pernicious myth espoused to date.

Myth No. 7

This rulemaking will open the floodgates to other types of rulemaking. To be more blunt, the thinly veiled fear is that a Democratic Board sometime in the future will cite our health care rules as precedent for promulgating as administrative regulations the provisions of the 1977 Labor Law Reform Bill.[7]

Reality: There is simply no sentiment on the Board to engage in rulemaking in other areas. Whatever its merits, rulemaking was chosen as a means of last resort in the face of repeated failures of the traditional method of determining units.

Moreover, I simply doubt whether rulemaking is appropriate for addressing a whole host of issues under the statute. For instance, if the Board adopted a rule defining "supervisors," it would add nothing to promoting efficiency; we still would have to examine the facts of each case. Likewise, with respect to the 1977 Labor Law Reform bill, its most controversial features—I refer to the provisions calling for double back pay, debarment, "make whole" orders that impose a first contract on parties, union access to private property—could not be implemented short of amendments to the Act.

In closing, I hope my remarks have provided some insight into the Board's decision to proceed with rulemaking, sorting out the myths from the reality. I wish to emphasize once again that our decision to engage in this historic action came down to these two points:

First, after struggling with this issue for 14 years, we became convinced that the traditional case-by-case approach just won't work in this field. The new rule, we hope, will streamline the administrative process by eliminating delays and protracted hearings inherent in the old approach.

Secondly, and more fundamentally, the Board has a duty to implement the decision Congress made in 1974 to extend the Act's coverage to health care facilities. With this rule, we are trying to bring to hospital employees the same rights employees in other industries now enjoy. They deserve no less. Under the old approach, with its self-imposed obstacles, hospital employees effectively are deprived of their right to vote.

Not all employers, of course, have taken unfair advantage of the traditional approach. But enough have. Our intent is not to give an advantage to either unions or management, but rather to enforce the law as it was enacted by Congress. In my view, this all adds up to good policy and makes for good government.

We are conscious that the rule will be challenged in court just as the case-by-case method was challenged. If the courts reject our efforts here, another half century may pass before the Board again ventures down the road of rulemaking.

However, I am confident that we will prevail and that what we are doing is right and salutary. Our case for the rule is absolutely solid and supported by empirical evidence; we have looked at the issue from a variety of perspectives, examined an array of concerns, and presented a reasoned analysis.

I believe that the Board has fulfilled the letter and spirit of the statutory standards of the rulemaking process. And if there ever was an area where Congress envisioned the administrative process to engage in rulemaking—this is it.

NOTES

1. 24 San Diego L. Rev. 9 (1987).

2. Miller, remarks at the 31st Annual Institute on Labor Law sponsored by the Southwest Legal Foundation, Dallas, Texas, October 18, 1984.

3. Silver & McAvoy, *The National Labor Relations Act at the Crossroads*, 56 Fordham L. Rev. 181, 198–99 (November 1987).

4. Miller, remarks.

5. *IBEW, Local Union 474 v. NLRB*, 814 F.2d 697 (D.C. Cir. 1987).

6. *South Prairie Constr. Co. v. Local 627, Operating Engineers*, 425 U.S. 800, 804–05 (1976).

7. H.R. 8410, 95th Cong., 1st Sess. (1977).

Amarjit S. Sethi

49

Information Technology and Collective Bargaining

INTRODUCTION

The latter part of the twentieth century finds the Western world facing major problems of technological change and readjustment that involve organizations in both business and public sectors. Both sectors will play major roles in the search for solutions to these problems both within and outside of a collective bargaining framework to meet a wide range of expectations. Although there has been a tremendous growth in technology in general in the past several decades, the coming period represents fundamental shifts in a whole range of information technologies. One of the key challenges in the field of human resources management is that of a range of effective joint management and union strategic choices which are critical in mitigating the potential adverse impacts of information technology (IT).

According to Jacques Ellul (1964: 25) technology, or technique as he calls it, "is the totality of methods rationally arrived at and having absolute efficiency (for a given stage of development) in every field of human activity." In a broader sense, technology "is the organization and application of knowledge for the achievement of practical purposes. It includes physical manifestations such as tools and machines, but also intellectual techniques and processes used in solving problems and obtaining desired outcomes" (Kast & Rosenzweig 1985: 208).

The term IT refers to the totality of dynamic and complex information technologies covering microelectronics, computers, and telecommunications, including the following components: hardware, software, ergonomic work stations, expert systems, knowledge-based systems, data base systems, advanced telecommunications (telematics), office automation systems, robotics, computer integrated manufacturing systems, and development of the next generation of super computers and fifth-generation technology. Table 49-1 shows some of the functions and applications of IT.

According to Bell (1973) information and not capital is a strategic resource of the new age, characterized as an "information society" (Masuda 1980; Naisbitt 1982; Porat 1977). The actors in an industrial relations system must confront one of the chief distinctive features of an information society, namely, the widening base and power of knowledge made possible by technological advances. "The productivity of knowledge has already become the key to productivity, competitive strength, and economic achievement. Knowledge has already become the primary industry, the industry that supplies the economy the essential and central resources of production" (Drucker 1980).

Porat (1977) measured the information economy in the United States and concluded that it accounted for more than 46 percent of the gross national product and more than 53 percent of income earned. Out of the 19 million new jobs created in the United States during the 1970s, only 5 percent were in manufacturing and only 11 percent in the goods-producing

Note: Adapted from A.S. Sethi, "The Future of Collective Bargaining in an Information Society," in A.S. Sethi (Ed.), *Collective Bargaining in Canada*, © Nelson Canada, A Division of International Thomson, 1120 Birchmount Road, Scarborough, Ontario, MIK 5G4.

411

Table 49-1 Information Technologies: Functions and Applications*

Data Collection	Weather Prediction	Radar, Infra-Red Object Detection Equipment, Radiometers
	Medical Diagnosis	CAT-Scanners, Ultrasonic Cameras
Data Input	Word Processing	Keyboards, Touch-Screens
	Factory Automation	Voice Recognizers (Particularly for Quality Control)
	Mail Sorting	Optical Character Readers
Storage	Archives	Magnetic Bubble Devices, Magnetic Tape
	Accounting Systems	Floppy Disks
	Scientific Computation	Wafer-Scale Semiconductors (Still in Research Phase), Very-High-Speed Magnetic Cores
	Ecological Mapping	Charge-Coupled Semiconductor Devices, Video Disks
	Libraries	Hard Disks
Information Processing	Social Security Payments	General Purpose "Mainframe" Computers, COBOL Programs
	Traffic Control	Minicomputers
	Distributed Inventory Control	Multi-User Super-Micros, Application Software Packages
	Medical Diagnosis	"Expert" Systems
	Engineering Design	Spreadsheet Application Packages, Microcomputers
	Scientific Computation	Supercomputers: Multiple Instruction–Multiple Data (MIMD) Processors, Vector Processors, Data Driven Processors, FORTRAN Programs
	Ecological Mapping	Array Processors, Associative Processors
	Factory Automation	Robotics, Artificial Intelligence
Communications	Office Systems	Local Area Networks, Private Branch Exchanges (PBX), Editor Applications Packages
	Teleconferencing	Communications Satellites, Fiber Optics
	Rescue Vehicle Dispatch	Cellular Mobile Radios
	International Financial Transactions	Transport Protocols, Data Encryption, Integrated Services Digital Networks (ISDN)
Data Output and Presentation	Word Processing	Personal Computers, Printers (Impact, Ink Jet, Xerographic)
	Management Information	Cathode Ray Tubes, Computer Graphics
	Pedestrian Traffic Control	Voice Synthesizers

*This list is not exhaustive; any given technology may also be used for some of the other applications mentioned.

Source: Reprinted from *Information Technology and R&D*, p. 309, Office of Technology Assessment, Washington, D.C., February 1985.

---

sector as a whole (Naisbitt 1982: 17), and almost 90 percent were in information, knowledge, or service jobs. As the public sector is primarily a service industry, the impact of IT on jobs in this sector will be turbulent.

The public sector workers and managers must cope with the difference between the knowledge needed for task execution and the knowledge available to them. This uncertainty emanates from two sources: lack of knowledge about how to perform a task and lack of knowledge about what to do when exception conditions are created (Perrow 1967). Exception conditions primarily arise from variations in inputs (e.g., in the situations of clients or conditions of raw materials) and in variations in the performance of tools. In order to deal with technological uncertainty, an operational collective bargaining system in the health care industry needs to consider some strategic choices that can be applied by employers and unions to improve organizational productivity/effectiveness, as well as accommodate patients' and employees' needs for flexibility, quality of worklife, and self-actualization. In this process, health care unions have the social responsibility to make strategic preventive choices; health care organizations have the social responsibility to examine alternatives that accommodate erupted jobs, technological stress or technostress, patient concerns, and employee well-being.

TECHNOLOGICAL PERSPECTIVES AND COLLECTIVE BARGAINING POLICIES

Management and unions in health care need to understand and develop perspectives to manage IT effects. There are five such perspectives that can serve as a foundation for employer policy and union response to that policy that can be covered as part of the technology agreement in the process of collective bargaining. These include

1. *Rational Efficiency Perspective.* Organizations computerize in order to pursue long-standing goals of efficiency and cost effectiveness. Pursuing the policies of rationalization, computerization is viewed as the most rational technological innovation (Attewell & Rule 1984). Unions need to develop a proactive strategy to cope with this perspective.
2. *Technological Imperative Perspective.* Jacques Ellul (1964) so cogently held the view that technological development is the product of a mind-set that demands a self-sustaining development of technology. In this sense, technology becomes autonomous and a catalyst for change in organizational behavior and thereby impacts on the collective bargaining system.

3. *Political Perspective*. Another explanation, of particular interest to unions, is that changes in information technology may be changes in power relations (Downs 1967; Laudon 1964). As reported by Attewell and Rule (1984) IT developments may actually be the source of satisfying management's political goals.

4. *Ethical Perspective*. Unions may question the ethics of technological growth not only on the grounds of the job insecurity that it may cause, but also on the basis of the philosophical view that computers reduce human dignity, responsibility, and autonomy. The questions that need to be explored are: Is human thought entirely computable? What limits, for example, should be pursued in the ultimate computerization of a professional worker?

5. *Strategic Choice Perspective*. This view holds that IT brings diverse changes in the already complex health care work environment and demands a strategic understanding, by both management and unions, of the ways in which work environments are influenced by technology so that the agenda of collective bargaining can cope with technological uncertainties, with the twin objectives of increasing organizational effectiveness as well as quality of worklife.

One example of interest to bargainers relates to conclusions about the use of Cathode Ray Tubes (CRTs) or Video Display Terminals (VDTs). Studies indicate that it is not the use of a CRT display per se, but rather the psychosomatic stress workers experience when using office automation systems that is the source of consistent reports of worker complaints (Dainoff et al. 1981; Ghiringhelli 1980; Turner 1984). The implication for bargainers is to understand that simply controlling the use of the CRT display will not remedy the stressful situation, but strategies will have to be negotiated to focus on the "network environment" (including job satisfaction, emotional exhaustion, absenteeism, or performance) in controlling the use of computer systems. It is thus imperative for bargainers to understand the ergonomic and stress factors in formulating their positions on technology and working conditions (WHO 1985).

The organizational structure and thereby the collective bargaining system are thus challenged by the new technology. As reported by Turner (1984) the restructuring of work permitted by the new technology has a greater impact on operators than the technology itself. In a study of 620 claims representatives in the Social Security Administration in the United States, it was found that claims representatives using the parallel on-line interface had a poorer work environment than operators using the serial system. Although the task environment, the quality of worklife, and performance are all influenced by IT (e.g., a computerized application system), the resulting interactions are complex, requiring innovative negotiating strategies for a strategic management of the whole job. Productivity and quality of worklife can actually compete (Turner & Karasek 1984).

We cannot provide clear evidence for the support of one technological view as against another cited above. The various studies have reported a mixed picture insofar as the effects of computer innovations are concerned (Dutton & Kraemer 1978; King & Kraemer 1980; Laudon 1964; Weber 1959). Advocates who argue that technology is autonomous (Ellul 1964; Winner 1977) state that we are caught in the inevitable historical struggle when we develop technology for the sake of technology. Management often takes the position that technology increases productivity and efficiency, whereas unions will argue that technology may not automatically increase quality of worklife.

TECHNOSTRESS AND COLLECTIVE BARGAINING

Our view is that IT produces its own social stress, which we have identified as technostress. Technostress is a perceived and dynamic state of uncertainty in the face of technological change that occurs at individual, organizational, and societal levels. "Technostress" refers to uncertainty experienced by the person in different contexts in adapting to the new technological development. In negotiating new technology-related provisions in the health care industry, negotiators on both management and union sides can benefit by an increased awareness of technostress at work.

Technostress is not an isolated category of merely response, but a state of adaptation combining (1) sources (e.g., technology), (2) dimensions (how the source is transmitted and perceived), and (3) responses (reaction to uncertainty). These responses are moderated by characteristics such as locus of control, individual ability, time pressures, relative power, ambiguity of tolerance, field dependence, availability of feedback, and task and group cohesiveness (see Exhibit 49-1).

Exhibit 49-1 Dimensions of Technostress

Factual Factors[a]
• Number of Technological Elements
• Rate of Technological Change
• Heterogeneity of Elements
• Clarity of Elements
• Relationship among Elements
• Predictability of Change

Value Factors[a] (Moderating Variables)	
• Relative Power	• Tolerance of Ambiguity
• Time Pressure	• Field Dependence
• Importance of Issue	• Availability of Feedback
• Individual Ability Interdependence	• Task and Group Cohesiveness
• Locus of Control	

[a]The "factual" and "value" factors are interrelated and separated here for showing their importance in the experience of technostress.

Source: Reprinted from *Strategic Management of Technostress in an Information Society* by A.S. Sethi, D. Caro, and R.S. Schuler (Eds.), p. 488, with permission of C.J. Hogrefe Publishers, Toronto, Lewiston, NY, © 1987.

Technostress is a dynamic adaptive state which has three key ingredients in the environment: the nature of stressor, the reaction or response to this stressor, and results from this reaction, leading again to a cycle of new reactions and formulations by management, workers, and unions. There are two components to technostress:

1. Technoeustress
2. Technodistress

This is based on the assumption that technology can have differential effects on their users.

Technoeustress is the stress that is beneficial or has a positive effect on the functioning of the individual and his/her contribution to the level of organizational productivity. Organizational performance and quality of worklife concerns are given equal emphasis jointly by management and unions. [A striking example is the sponsorship of joint Quality of Work-life (QWL) activities by General Motors (GM) and the United Automobile Workers (UAW), recognizing the positive outcomes for GM and the UAW.] *Technodistress* is that stress that has a negative impact on the individual's functions with consequent negative effects on the overall industrial relations system. In a technodistress context, workers suffer through developing a high level of anxiety and associated psychosomatic illnesses, and management and unions suffer through a higher level of labor relations conflict and reduced organizational commitment.

STRATEGIC CHOICE AND NEGOTIATING SKILLS

We define strategic choice as

1. An awareness of the aim by a dominant coalition (such as management or unions) which is shaped by existing values and transactions within the health care environment;
2. Internalization of that aim in a given environment;
3. Proceeding to identify, negotiate, and exploit (often opportunistically) events and broader circumstances within the environment in ways which one believes will bring oneself nearer the desired aim. The choices are in determining what events to ignore, or exploit to achieve the aim. Essentially what is being created is an "agenda of negotiation" through the use of strategies for achieving desired aims.

This definition of strategic choice has three key elements: vision, values, and decision. The awareness of technological aims by management and unions involved in the health care industry requires some vision about the future. Values are conceptions—explicit or implicit—of the desirable situations or states of consciousness that underlie decisions, and decisions are those negotiated choices that take management,

workers, or unions nearer to the aims. Vision, values, and decisions thus interact in the determination of collective bargaining aims in health care organizations. Strategic choice, in a technological change context, implies internalization of the aim of managing technology effectively for both management and unions; identifying and assessing organizational and technological environments; and selecting those strategies that reduce negative uncertainty (technodistress) and increase opportunity (technoeustress).

The effective coping with technostress by health care management and unions may help them to increase their respective power base (Goh 1985; Hinings et al. 1974; Pfeffer et al. 1976). One of the key negotiating skills needed, therefore, is strategic planning in order to effectively cope with IT impacts. Walton (1985: 560) describes the importance of planning skills required in implementing IT changes as follows:

1. Work systems based on the new technology often require less skill and knowledge, but sometimes these new systems result in more jobs being upgraded than downgraded. System design can influence that outcome.
2. The technical system can increase the flexibility of work schedules to accommodate human preferences, or it can decrease flexibility and require socially disruptive work schedules.
3. New systems often contribute to social isolation, but sometimes they have the opposite effect. Similarly, they often separate an operator from the end result of his or her effort, but occasionally they bring the operator in closer touch with the end result. Seldom are these planned outcomes, but they can be.
4. These systems sometimes render individuals technologically obsolete because of changed skill and knowledge requirements, but they also open up new careers.
5. New technology can change the focus of control—toward either centralization or decentralization.
6. New information systems can change—for better or worse—an employee-typist into a subcontractor operating a terminal out of his or her home.

Technostress can be positive if preventive strategies are adapted. Parties in health care collective bargaining can display their skills and awareness in negotiating meaningful contract provisions by anticipating human effects of new technology. The proposition is that negotiating technology provisions requires the competence and skills to formulate and make strategic decisions. To quote Schönpflug (1983: 355):

Prospective planning, clear priority of decisions, and wise renunciation of goals of low priority may help to prevent multi-demand situations. . . . Lack of prospective planning, inability in setting priorities and blind fixation to various incentives may . . . serve as the *via regia* to the creation of an entangling situation, finally also leading to fatigue. This, at least, is one of the lessons taught by the theory of action and its good companion, the theory of behavior economics.

A STRATEGIC CHOICE MODEL FOR MANAGING IT IN HEALTH CARE

The approach that we have taken is that it is not technology alone that causes productivity increases (or decreases) (as measured in the context of a health care delivery system), or tends to improve (or lower) quality of worklife, but new values emerge from the impact of new technology. These values emanate from the interaction of the work environment and persons in that environment, requiring strategies (that need to be formulated by health care management and unions) directed not only toward changing the person or the work environment but toward developing new assumptions about how the technology is to be integrated into the working environment. We call this conceptual framework a strategic choice model, as presented in Figure 49-1.

The proposition is that technology is the facilitator of a wide range of strategic choices at both micro and macro levels. Preventive and proactive strategies are significant in increasing the competence of management and workers in coping with impacts of new information technology in promoting not only productivity and competitive service but also quality of worklife (Turner & Karasek 1984). When these strategic choices, for example, are considered by health care managements and unions, the agenda and process of a collective bargaining system can be accordingly structured to achieve both organizational effectiveness and quality of worklife. In the technologically renewed collective bargaining process, both management and unions have the social responsibility to examine alternatives that prevent job burnout and protect job security, as well as promote employee education and well-being. The government has also a critical role to play in ensuring through responsive regulation that the parties use the organizational collective bargaining systems in ways that utilize the tremendous power and flexibility of IT in ways that help to keep technological impacts under human control. Figure 49-1 illustrates this process at both micro and macro levels.

In a review of recent research on positive and negative impacts of technology in relation to the issue whether technology controls workers or workers control technology, Alcalay and Pasick (1983: 1980–1) came to the following tentative conclusions:

1. The use of new technologies can increase job strain, job overload and underload and can decrease the level of workers' control over work.
2. Technologically intensive work can have an impact on the individual's social support networks.
3. Workers who benefit the most from the use of new technologies are usually high-level management and/or professionals.
4. Workers who suffer the most from technology-centered tasks are in lower status, blue collar or clerical positions.

Collective bargaining is a continuing process of interactions ranging from free strategic choice to complete environmental determinism. This view allows both proactive as well as reactive behaviors on the part of actors (workers' unions, management, and government) in the collective bargaining process. The issue is not that of strategic choice versus environmental determinism but rather understanding the dimension emcompassing a continuum ranging from determinism to voluntarism. As explained by Hrebiniak and Joyce (1985: 337), "choice and determinism are not at opposite ends of a single continuum of effect but in reality represent two independent variables, and . . . the interaction of independence of the two must be studied to explain . . . behavior." Collective bargaining is viewed as a dynamic process, revealing several options to parties, that may involve a number of possibilities in a given situation.

The practical result of employing a strategic approach is the determination on part of parties to engage in what Kochan and others (1984) have called "strategic bargaining." According to Kochan and others (1984: 17–18), strategic bargaining includes

> negotiations that specifically involve tradeoffs of changes in wages, benefits, or other contractual provisions in exchange for new investment or employment commitments. A recent example is the agreement between several electric companies and the International Union of Electrical Workers (IUEW) in Lynn, Massachusetts whose workers would be IUEW members in return for major changes in the way work is scheduled, jobs are organized, and compensation is determined. . . . The key feature of strategic bargains is that they build on and reinforce the sharing of information and the improved workplace relationships that have grown out of QWL processes.

The interdependence and interactions between strategic choice and environmental determinism define collective bargaining behavior. In order to explain change and conflict within collective bargaining, we need both variables: strategic choice and environmental determinism. Collective bargaining thus needs to focus on interactions and interdependence between the two in varying degrees; thus signifying the dynamic nature of bargaining transactions (Miles & Snow, 1978). Our theoretical premise is to emphasize that models relying on the conceptual construction of competing explanations of cause and effect may not be sufficient to capture the complexity and spirit of collective bargaining. The strategic approach, it is hoped, emphasizes multiple and often competing assumptions, foci, and explanations of cause and effect.

The principle of redefinition of goals (and values) is clearly demonstrated in the case of technological change in the private sector where unions and managements have voluntarily negotiated the emergence of new plants, work design systems, and associated contractual relationships. Kochan and others (1984: 18) illustrate this practice as follows:

> General Motors and the United Automobile Workers Union have a number of . . . new plant agreements in place. Project Saturn (the joint GM–UAW study group

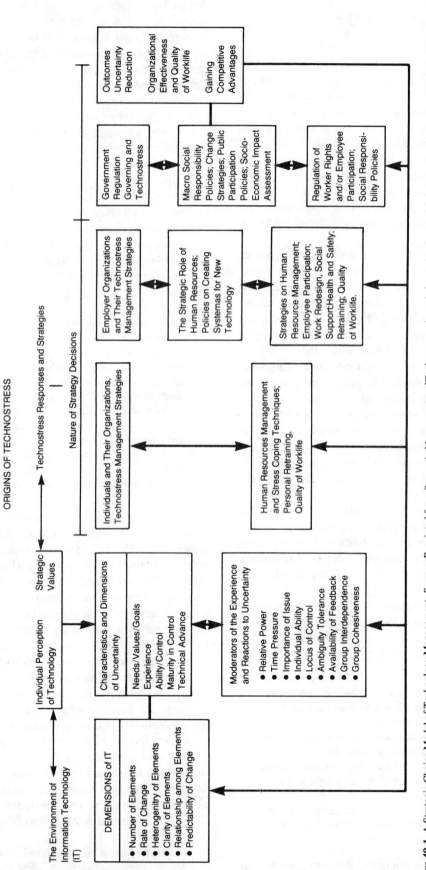

Figure 49-1 A Strategic Choice Model of Technology Management. *Source:* Reprinted from *Strategic Management of Technostress in an Information Society* by A.S. Sethi, D. Caro, and R.S. Schuler (Eds.), p. 21, with permission of C.J. Hogrefe Publishers, Toronto, Lewiston, NY, © 1987.

exploring alternative ways to build small cars) is of enormous scale and already has involved extensive involvement by the UAW in business decisions, thereby making it an extremely important example of such processes. Phillip Morris and the Tobacco Workers have a new plant in Alabama operating with jointly planned innovative work practices. Such agreements will test whether new plants designed with up-to-date technology and with a flexible/ high participation workplace industrial relations system can match or better the performance of new nonunion plants. Evaluation of these experiments must await further time to amass significant experience and comparative data.

The hypothesis is that technological impacts can be positive if preventive strategies are adopted by managements and unions in a cooperative collective bargaining system. Alcalay and Pasick (1983: 1082) state:

> Where innovations are simply adopted by virtue of their proclaimed benefits and intended functions, and where the work environment is structured around such innovations, technology may indeed be in control. However, where planning takes into account benefits, functions and possible unintended consequences, and the work environment, including new technologies, is structured around the health and well-being of workers, then technology is certainly the object of human choice.

Based on a review of several successful companies in the United States that have implemented IT, Benjamin and others (1984: 3:10) support the proposition that IT impacts can be utilized by management (and unions) to gain competitive advantage through generating awareness of the potential benefits of IT, and by creating a cultural environment in which ''information technology is considered an important strategic weapon.''

Recent ILO-initiated research shows that the impact of microcomputers on an organization can lead to perceived stress where there is (1) an uncooperative labor-management system, (2) a lack of supportive management, (3) unclear job definitions, and (4) a high level of physical environmental stressors (Fraser 1983; ILO 1984; Levi 1984; Rada 1980; Wereneke 1983). A recent empirical study supports the proposition that technological innovation produces a lack of fit between demands made by the technology and the needs, skills, procedures, structures, and equipment embodied in the social and technical structure of organizations. The result is that new technology raises both cognitive and motivational problems with which managers, staff specialists, and workers and their unions have great difficulty in coping (Blumberg & Gerwin 1984).

Effects of New Technology

Some of the frequently described effects of information technology include job insecurity, monitoring, machine pac-

ing, monotonous and repetitive work, environmental conditions (e.g. temperature, air quality, and ergonomic problems), and lack of worker participation and control. On the effects of automation, Arndt and Chapman (1984: 32) conclude

> The automation of offices has led to increasing concerns about new or more extreme sources of stress including increased boredom, monotony, job insecurity, job future uncertainties, lack of job control, increased monitoring, job fragmentation, alienation and job dissatisfaction. Broad statements about the effects of automation are difficult to make. It has been suggested that automation offers the opportunity to eliminate tedious, difficult and boring work. It would appear that in some cases this is indeed possible. However, management [and unions have] choices concerning how automation will be used. At one extreme the technology can be introduced under the control of workers to make their jobs easier. At the other extreme, workers are told exactly how to do the work and are closely monitored. . . . It appears that the former option is being primarily reserved for professional and managerial uses of new technologies.

Figure 49-2 summarizes the critical areas of information technology, particularly in relation to fifth-generation technologies. The impacts are multidimensional, affecting all facets of our society. A collective bargaining system cannot escape these technological impacts, and is thus influenced by pressures from the environment to adapt to technological change.

New Technology and Health Effects

Clerical employees in both private and health care sectors have been increasingly using video display terminals (VDTs) to perform their work. It is estimated that by 1990 about 40 million American workers will be using VDTs on the job (Bureau of National Affairs 1984).

Although studies reporting health effects of VDTs are inconclusive, Sauter and others (1982) are correct in concluding that stress does predict health complaints, job dissatisfaction, and emotional states for both VDT and non-VDT work. Technological stress or technostress has both negative and positive impacts. On the positive side the new technology has the enormous potential for increasing productivity, upgrading job tasks, and increasing employee earning power (Pava 1983). On the negative side the new technology may result in job displacement, machine control, resistance to change, information overload, and performance monitoring (Arndt & Chapman 1984).

Further epidemiological research is needed to measure the impact of radiation from VDTs on pregnant women workers (Cox 1980; Labour Canada Task Force 1982). A higher incidence of visual complaints among VDT operators in comparison to traditional office workers has been reported in several studies. The VDT constitutes a hazard if the cause of the complaint can be related to image quality or screen

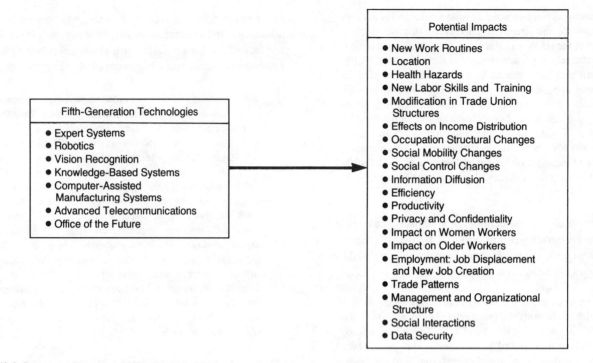

Figure 49-2 Summary of Impacts of Fifth-Generation Technology. *Source:* Reprinted from *Strategic Management in an Information Society* by A.S. Sethi, D. Caro, and R.S. Schuler (Eds.), p. 358, with permission of C.J. Hogrefe Publishers, Toronto, Lewiston, NY, © 1987.

flicker. The VDT represents a risk factor if the vision complaint arises because of the more intensive and sustained nature of the VDT task.

A large number of reputable scientific surveys on radiation emissions from VDT have been carried out in various parts of the world, investigating emission measurements for X-ray, microwave, radiofrequency, extremely low frequency, infrared, and visible radiations. VDTs have no components that can generate microwave radiation. Some low-frequency (up to 150 kilohertz) radiofrequency radiation has been detected very close to the surface of some VDTs. However, the levels fall off so rapidly with distance that at the position of the operator they are either nondetectable or significantly lower than the most restrictive standard in the world (Health & Welfare Canada 1983).

The health hazards of IT relate to various environmental factors such as air quality, temperature, musculoskeletal stress, visual stress, psychological stress, noise, and accidents. Table 49-2 summarizes the analysis of potential hazards and control strategies.

A 1977 NIOSH study in the United States (Colligan et al. 1977) reported that out of 130 occupations studied, secretaries, office managers, and manager-administrators were among the top 12 occupations in terms of stress-related disease. This finding was corroborated by the Framingham Heart Study in which coronary heart disease rates were found to be almost twice as great among women holding clerical jobs as among housewives (Haynes & Feinleib 1980).

The sources of technodistress for clerical workers include monitoring, machine pacing, lack of promotional opportunities, low pay, monotonous and repetitive work, environmental conditions (e.g., temperature, air quality, and ergonomic problems), lack of feedback, and underutilization of skills (Arndt & Chapman 1984).

Technoeustress can occur as a result of work simplification realized through the use of microelectronics. However, technoeustress can be converted into technodistress and decreased job satisfaction if the introduction of IT leads to fragmentation of jobs and increased repetitiveness. Research indicates that machine pacing does lead to high job tension, underutilization of abilities, frequent health complaints, and a variety of psychosomatic disorders (Murphy & Hurrell 1979). We should, however, be cautious in assigning all negative impacts of IT on office workers. Arndt and Chapman (1984: 34-35) have assessed it as follows:

> The results of studies comparing VDT and non-VDT work tend to confirm the theory that broad generalizations about the effects of new office technologies should not be made. For example, Sauter et al. (1982) reported that "VDT work did not contribute to psychological distress or job dissatisfaction to any greater extent than non-VDT clerical work," among the group of workers studied. Other studies have reported similar findings (Coe et al. 1980; Dainoff et al. 1981). Thus, the conclusion that VDTs and related technologies do not have to increase psychological stress and job dissatisfaction seems warranted. In fact, a number of studies report some positive aspects and feelings about VDTs (Cakir et al. 1978; Dainoff et al. 1981; Gunnarsson & Ostberg 1977; Gunnarsson & Soderberg 1980; Hunting et al. 1981; Johansson & Aronsson 1980)

Table 49-2 Strategies for Controlling Potential Hazards in Offices

	Potential Health Effects*	Potential Hazards	Hazard Control
Air Quality	Irritation, Discomfort, Outbreaks of Disease Sensitization	Formaldehyde, Ozone, Organics, Allergens, Micro-Organisms	Ventilation, Substitution Enclosure, Filtering
Temperature	Discomfort	Heat, Cold, Humidity, Air Circulation	Radiant Control, Air Circulation, Different Location, Individual Control, Humidity Control
Musculoskeletal Stress	Neck, Shoulders, Back, Arms Fatigue and Chronic Disorders	Workstation Design, Chair Design, Task Repetitiveness, Constrained Posture	Furniture Ergonomics, Task Redesign, Job Enlargement, Rotation, Rest Breaks, Exercise
Visual Stress	Eyestrain, Burning or Itching	Lighting, Close Work, Quality of VDT and Other Viewed Material, Dry Air, Stress	Vision Exams, Illumination Controls, Equipment Design, Rest, Exercise, Work Layout
Psychological Stress	Anxiety, Tension Stress, Boredom, Headaches, Job Dissatisfaction, Alienation, Absenteeism, Turnover, Behavioral Problems (smoking, drinking), Ulcers, Coronary Heart Disease, Diabetes and Other Diseases	Repetitiveness, Monotony, Monitoring, Lack of Promotional Opportunity, Lack of Job Security, Lack of Control, Pacing, Piecework, Work Environment	Stress Management, Wellness, Exercise, Job Redesign, Worker Control, Job Enlargement, Job Enrichment, Rotation, Environmental Control
Noise	Irritation, Interference, Distraction	Conversations, Equipment, Ventilation Systems	Barriers, Equipment Design, Enclosures, Absorption
Accidents	Traumatic Injuries	Work Surfaces, Furniture, Equipment, Lifting	Guarding, Hazard Removal, Training
Radiation	None Yet Established	Low-Level Radiation	Shielding, Low Voltage, Alternative Designs, Work Removal, Time Limits

*Almost all potential hazards may affect health indirectly by causing emotional stress, especially air quality, temperature, and noise.

Source: Reprinted from *Potential Office Hazards and Controls* by R. Arndt and L. Chapman, pp. 123–124, Office of Technology Assessment, Washington, D.C., 1984.

especially relating to making certain tasks easier. At the same time, a number of studies have clearly indicated that VDT tasks with certain characteristics are more stressful than both non-VDT and other types of VDT work (Cakir et al. 1978; Elias et al. 1980; Gunnarsson & Ostberg 1977). The most frequently mentioned variables were monotony and boredom, monitoring, piecework, loss of control over work pace, technical problems of interruptions, and production quotas.

The overall conclusion of research studies on VDT (Smith, 1982) is that job design factors, primarily highly paced work, lack of control, and deadlines, are more prevalent in some types of VDT work than in others. These factors have been shown to be related to many of the health complaints that are reported by VDT operators and could be linked to serious health disorders.

The Issue of Privacy

Privacy is centered on the rights of individuals to safeguard the access to and availability of information pertaining to their private lives. Regulation should provide adequate safeguards for the protection of privacy and individual liberties.

Westin (1979: 3) explains the issue of privacy as follows:

Privacy is the claim of individuals, groups, or institutions to determine for themselves when, how, and to what extent information about them is communicated to others. Viewed in terms of the relation of the individual to social participation, privacy is the voluntary and temporary withdrawal of a person from the general society through physical or psychological means, either in a state of solitude or small-group intimacy or, when among larger groups, in a condition of anonymity or reserve. The individual's desire for privacy is never absolute, since participation in society is an equally powerful desire. Thus each individual is continually engaged in a personal adjustment process in which he balances the desire for privacy with the desire for disclosure and communication of himself to others, in light of the environmental conditions and social norms set by the society in which he lives. The individual does so in the face of pressures from the curiosity of others and from the processes of surveillance that every society sets in order to enhance its social norms.

Collective bargaining, although not an all-purpose institution, may be used as a mechanism, in addition to responsive regulation, where provisions concerning privacy may be developed.

LABOR MARKET IMPACTS

Impact on Employment

IT may lead to job displacement as well as result in job creation. Rada (1980: 105–106) explains the consequences of IT as follows:

> It would seem that a transition is taking place from a society with unemployment to one that no longer needs its full potential labour force to produce the necessary goods and services under current conditions of work. It is doubtful whether measures such as early retirement, shorter working hours, and the creation and development of small business and new products and services will have much effect on job creation. Nevertheless, the need to meet the educational, cultural and social ends inherent in such a transition, plus cultural resistance, could lead to job creation in some fields. A transition of this nature will not be free from turmoil while the population tries to adjust to new life styles.

Servan-Schreiber, head of France's World Centre for Computer Science and Human Resources, estimates that by 1990 50 million people in the industrialized Western world will be jobless because of high technology (Servan-Schreiber 1981).

Professor Tom Stonier predicts (in Forrester 1981) that by early in the next century we will require only 10 percent of today's labour force to satisfy our production needs. Choate (1982) estimates that as the American economy robotizes and domestic jobs are lost to foreign production, 10–15 million manufacturing jobs may be lost along with a similar number of service jobs.

Impacts of Robotics

The three key impacts of new technology are on job displacement, new job creation, and new training requirements. One such example is the impact of robotics on industry.

Hunt and Hunt (1983) predict a strong growth in the utilization of industrial robots in the decade of the 1990s. They forecast that the total robot population in the United States, for example, by 1990 will range from a minimum of 50,000 to a maximum of 100,000 units representing an annual growth of 30–40 percent. Although job displacement will not be a major problem according to these authors, some occupational areas such as painting and welding will need to adapt to new changed circumstances. Insofar as job creation is concerned, Hunt and Hunt (1983) estimate about 32,000 to 64,000 new jobs will be created by robots in the United States by 1990 within four broad areas: robot manufacturing, direct suppliers to robot manufacturers, robot systems engineering, and corporate robot users.

The new technical skills required by robotics technology will need a well-planned training policy by corporations in order to cope with new technical and scientific demands that will be required in the newly created jobs.

In summary we agree with Hunt and Hunt (1983) that the impacts will be evolutionary. Hunt and Hunt (1983: 181) explain it as follows:

> Industrial robots are simply one more piece of automated industrial equipment, part of the long history of automation of production. Robots will displace workers in the same way that technological change has displaced workers. There is a possibility that this job displacement will be a significant problem, particularly in a given occupation or industry or geographical area. There is also the certainty that robots will create new jobs. Most of these will be quite different from the kinds of jobs eliminated. It is not time to panic, it is time to begin rational planning for the human resource implications of robotics.

Impact of New Technology on Women Workers

The majority of women are employed in the tertiary sector of the economy and in nonmanual occupations which are affected by the new technology. In the United States, about half of the labour force works in the information-related occupations (Porat 1971; Bird 1980), and about one-third of all women workers are concentrated in white-collar or clerical occupations, which will be affected by the advent of information technology. Parties engaged in formulating collective bargaining strategies in health care need to take into account the needs of women workers who will increasingly face the impacts of IT (Wereneke 1983).

Impact on Unions

Information technology gives managers enormous new powers to process information and use it for achieving their goals. In so doing, this integrated control paradoxically permits production to be fragmented, affecting the international division of labour. The powerful ideology of technology makes it imperative for unions to develop coherent preventive strategies for dealing with technostress and encouraging workers to participate in the decision-making process.

Some of the union techniques in coping with IT practiced in Sweden and shared by the United States are pertinent (LO 1982). These include policies on advance notice, consultation, and full information on what the technological effects will be on employment, work environment, job organization, and training. According to the Swedish trade union report (LO 1981), workers are becoming more isolated, and conversations are being replaced by anonymous messages on visual display units. Employees are subjected to more supervision with computerized evaluation of individual performance contributive to new stresses. The Swedish trade union movement offers the following union strategies to cope with technostress:

- Legislated right to codetermination and the acceptance of a free collective bargaining system
- Better trade union control over the work environment regulations
- Right to work on computerization issues during working hours without deductions from pay
- Right of unions to consult experts.

Labour-Management Relations and IT

Improved labour relations is the key in coping with technostress effectively in the health care sector as well as in the U.S. economy as a whole. In the case of Japan, for example, strategies include an improved structural base for labour-management relations emphasizing consultation and training at all levels. Training has the dual objective of meeting human resources needs and safeguarding jobs, whereas dialogue through consultation in labour relations has the possibility of converting technodistress into technoeustress. If labour and management fail to accommodate technostress and IT changes, the stability of labour-management relations will be threatened (ILO 1984).

In order to cope with technostress, the system of cooperation between management and unions, as demonstrated by GM and the UAW, must work effectively. Some means must be found for labour and management to get together and resolve the questions covering employment, wages, hours of work, work organization, safety and health, job satisfaction, and the distribution of resources.

There will be greater demand in the health care industry for general skills such as strategic planning, team working, and conceptual skills, in addition to technical and scientific skills. The training system will need to make structural and attitudinal adjustments to meet new IT-related training needs. These strategies include modernization and rationalization through the promotion of the application of information technology throughout the health care industry and the economy as a whole. Early training in data processing and IT in secondary school curricula will need to be matched by continuous life-long training and education.

Training and the Older Worker

Studies in the United States and Canada that have explored the impact on workers of plant closings and layoffs find that age significantly influences the success of finding another job. Unemployment resulting from IT will probably have a more serious impact on older workers between the ages of 45 and 65.

Some employers fear that hiring older workers will add extra costs to their pension plans, thus producing a bias in favour of hiring younger workers.

INFORMATION TECHNOLOGY: UNION'S PERSPECTIVE

One striking example of how computers can impact on the union's power to strike was demonstrated in the case of air traffic controllers. The Professional Air Traffic Controllers Organization (PATCO) walked off the job on August 3, 1981. The Reagan administration gave the strikers 48 hours to return to work or face permanent dismissal. The result was that 12,000 air traffic controllers were fired and the union decertified. As Shaiken (1984: 248) reported, the government skillfully used computer technology to keep air traffic moving, thus "gutting the strikers' leverage." "The government's expanded bargaining power means it can now implement . . . options to increase automation more readily and is moving aggressively to do so" (Toong & Gupta 1982: 1:54). According to a Rand Commission report, the critical questions are: "Should we strive for a system in which the machine has the primary responsibility of control and human expertise is used in a secondary, backup fashion? Or should men, in spite of their intrinsic limitations, retain primary contact responsibility and utilize machine aids to control their activities?" (Wesson et al. 1981: 23). Shaiken (1984: 254–55) states

> The story of the confrontation between PATCO and the FAA underscores the potential importance of computers in labor-management relations in general and strike situations in particular. On the one hand, computer technology and telecommunications make possible central direction of far-reaching activities, concentrating enormous power into relatively few hands. The few dozen controllers in Gander, Newfoundland, for example, demonstrated their ability to halt virtually all trans-Atlantic flights for a number of tense hours near the beginning of the strike. Had a few more PATCO members joined the strike, the air traffic system of the entire country would have been tied in knots. On the other hand, complex computer systems often lend themselves to operation by a reduced and less skilled work force in an emergency situation. The leverage for the air controllers evaporated because less-experienced workers could successfully take over the job.

Another example in which computers caused a shift in the balance of power was provided by an office workers' strike during a 1980–81 dispute between Blue Shield of California and 1,100 members of the Office and Professional Employees Union (OPEU) Local 3 in San Francisco. Shaiken (1984, 258–259) states

> As the 133-day strike began, the company adopted a carefully prepared contingency plan. This plan included assigning all available supervisors to computer banks in the claims-processing area, hiring and quickly training 350 new workers, and routing some claims processing to non-union offices as far away as Los Angeles. The various offices were linked together through computers and telephone lines irrespective of picket lines. In addition, train-

ing the new workforce was made far easier because computers had been used to simplify tasks. As a result, Blue Shield asserted that it was able to maintain near-normal operations with far fewer workers. After the strike, the company refused to return 448 jobs to the main office.

Unions need to develop and make strategic choices in coping with technological change. Shaiken (1984: 263) sums up the scope of such strategies based on recent historical events as follows:

> If new strategies are not developed by labor, its power could become increasingly eroded—first at the bargaining table, and ultimately in the society itself. The strike of the Communications Workers of America (CWA) against AT&T and the Bell System in the fall of 1983 is one more example of union leverage being sharply curtailed. While the strike disrupted certain services, such as telephone installations, the telephone company nonetheless was able to continue its core operations uninterrupted for over three weeks. Ironically, the strike occurred against a backdrop of near record profits for the telephone company and at a time when its relations with its union were among the most cordial of major U.S. industries. The company was obviously using power to protect its interest not simply in 1983 but for years to come in a deregulated market. If unions are weakened at the bargaining table in this way, then the erosion of the power of the labor movement in the society is not far behind. To the extent that power shifts in management's direction in negotiations, new industries, particularly high-tech industries, could become even more difficult to organize. None of this grim scenario for labor is inevitable. But in an age of high technology, "business as usual" is no longer a tenable strategy for unions.

As a proactive strategy for influencing the course of technology, unions and managements can use a "Technology Bill of Rights," rooted in the concept that "the introduction of new technology is not an automatic right of management but a process subject to bargained development" (Shaiken 1984: 270). There are four key assumptions of this concept, and three key hypotheses, as explained below (Shaiken, 1984).

Assumptions

The design of new technology can be strategically based on the following assumptions:

1. The quality of worklife is as important as productivity.
2. The social aspects of technological change are as important as economic benefits.
3. Workers (and their organizations) have a right to participate in the decisions that affect their work.
4. The benefits of technology should be shared by employers and workers.

Hypotheses

The three key hypotheses include (Shaiken 1984: 272–273)

1. New technology must be used in a way that creates or maintains jobs.
2. New technology must be used to improve the conditions of work.
3. New technology must be used to develop the industrial base and improve the environment.

The implication of a Technology Bill of Rights are explained by Shaiken (1984: 273–278) as follows:

> The implementation of a Technology Bill of Rights would obviously require profound changes at the collective bargaining table and in the political area. Unfortunately, the swift introduction of new technology won't wait until the proper mechanisms are available to deal with it. . . . Ultimately the issues transcend collective bargaining and their political character becomes apparent. . . . The design of machines reflects social values as well as technical needs. The ideas and experiences of those who are affected by new designs can help ensure that computerization will be a force that aids in liberating people rather than a vehicle for increased authority and control.

COLLECTIVE BARGAINING PRACTICES, 1980–1984

Ornati (1985) analyzed the contractual clauses dealing with technological change by using the data from a *Comparative Survey of Major Collective Bargaining Agreements*, issued by the Industrial Union Department, AFL–CIO (Prosten 1980, 1982, 1984). Each of these surveys summarizes, by type of contract clause and benefit, the contents of 100 collective agreements. As summarized in Table 49-3, there appears to be a clear change in contractual clauses by 1980 to provide for protection from technological impacts.

Ornati (1985: 6–7) analyses the data (contained in Table 49-3) as follows:

> At least some union employees have gained job security in the language of contracts as negotiated over the last four years. The requirement of advanced notification to the union appears more frequently ($+7$); there is an increase in the number of contracts with an outright prohibition of layoffs ($+3$). Along with expanded employment protection there is a diminution in preferential rehiring by seniority (-5) and an increase in the number of companies with no specific job security clause. The major development is in the expansion of workers' rights to have training for new jobs (an increase over 1980 of 10 covered companies) coupled with a major use in severance pay ($+8$). The changes . . . seem to indicate a trend in which unions and managements have expanded the job security

Table 49-3 Contractual Arrangements Dealing with Job Security

	1980	1984	
1. No Special Provisions, Seniority Rules Apply	4	0	−4
2. Special Provisions in Local Agreement	2	1	−1
3. Contract Provides Advance Notice to Union	24	31	+7
4. Contract Sets Up Special Company/ Union Committee	7	9	+2
5. Contract Provides for Negotiation of Rights	7	8	+1
6. Attention Clause for Greater Job Security	2	3	+1
7. Contract Prohibits Layoff	6	9	+3
Workers Have Right To:			
a. Training for New Job	11	21	+10
b. Bump into Another Job/Same Plant	8	8	0
c. Transfer to Replacement Facility	5	5	0
d. Preferential Hiring, Same Plant	9	8	−1
e. Preferential Hiring, Other Plant	8	6	−2
f. Retain Prior Seniority When Hired at Other Plant	5	3	−2
8. Layoff with Recall Rights	10	11	+1
9. Severance Pay	14	22	+8
10. Moving Expenses	7	5	−2

Source: Reprinted from *Comparative Survey of Major Collective Bargaining Agreements* by R. Prosten, AFL–CIO, Washington, D.C., 1980, 1982, 1984.

of workers presumably capable of acquiring new skills and knowledge, while older workers presumed not as able to adapt to the new technologies are being "phased out" with various types of severance pay.

RIGHTS ARBITRATION AND TECHNOLOGICAL CHANGE

Ornati (1985) conducted an inquiry into the impact of contractual restraints, precedent, and arbitrators' values as moderators of the impact of technological change. Twenty-nine cases (drawn from BNA and CCH arbitration reports) from 1976 to 1984 were analyzed, dealing with grievances arising from manpower impacts, pursuant to the introduction of new technology. In a detailed survey of 16 cases, the researcher found that management was sustained in 14 of the 16 cases; the union's grievance was upheld entirely only in 2 and in part in 2 others. On the whole, 88 of the awards went in favour of management. The major issues as a result of technological change included (a) job elimination, (b) assignment of work in an out-of-bargaining unit, (c) changes in wages; and (d) job classification changes.

An analysis of the arbitration awards for the period 1980–84 revealed that arbitrators followed well-established criteria, such as "the centrality of the contract viewed in its totality, the importance of the wording of the management rights clause,

the parties' duty to negotiate and binding nature of precedent" (Ornati 1985: 8). The two key considerations arbitrators have constantly considered are the parties' willingness to negotiate and the economic necessity for introducing technological change. Precedent is given "explicit weight" in decisions that "permit management to eliminate jobs or transfer duties of a position or a classification when technological developments require it" (Ornati 1985: 9).

The researcher found that the most challenging cases were those dealing with new technologies that led to work assignment out of the bargaining unit. Ornati (1985: 10) reports

> The Arbitrator is brought face-to-face with the central characteristics of the newer technologies; still a substitution of capital for labor, the machine now is a substitute for brain rather than brawn. What we see here is the compressing of control functions (as in Drano Co. Case . . .) where all timekeepers were displaced or in the Eaton Corporation Case . . . where the quality control function was removed from the jurisdiction of layout craftsmen, or the enlargement of the information requirements for the control of subsidiary activities (as in the case of the Ben Secours Hospital, Inc. . . .) where the coding process of what was earlier an essentially clerical process, was enlarged requiring the operator to have knowledge of biology, physiology and medical terminology.

The rationale of the arbitrators in out-of-bargaining-unit work cases was based on multiple factors that included (a) management's right, (b) the time needed to phase out an employee's work before a new computer system is involved, (c) joint determination by union and company to establish exactly how much of a job is still left after automation, (d) union jurisdiction, (e) costs involved in retaining employees, and (f) union's legitimate claims.

Based on the preceding survey analysis of rights arbitration of cases involving technological issues, Ornati (1985: 16) arrived at the following conclusions:

1. While the cases surveyed clearly point to more basic and, so to speak, discontinual, changes in operating processes in the 1980's, the principles that guide arbitrators have *not* changed.
2. While arbitrators are clearly aware of the environmental changes that have been impacting our industries, these have not visibly influenced their decisions. The data deny my hunch that arbitrators in their case-by-case examination of the interaction of facts and contractual texts would have softened the employment impact of the new technologies. "It all depends on the circumstances" and "the contract is what we are guided by" are still at the core of what we do and precedent is what we follow—with care.
3. While surveys of available contracts show that new clauses increasing job security are being introduced, these do not appear to have limited management's freedom to implement new techniques.

4. The cases reviewed suggest that in the 1980's we will see an expansion of arbitral jurisprudence as to employee training rights.
5. When confronted with managerial clauses that are imprecise, and when the totality of the contract does not explicitly deny it, management is viewed as fundamentally free to assign work and pay as business need seems to require it. Indeed, recent arbitrators' obiter dicta, like in those of the past, show a broad internalization of the importance of technological change and of its related constructive/destructive influence.

Unionization Trends

Clerical workers affected most by new technology have expressed dissatisfaction with the manner in which management has introduced technology. In a 1984 survey, only 21 percent of nonunionized clerical employees felt they were treated fairly by employers, thus making them a ripe area for further unionization (Schieman et al. 1984).

Collective bargaining agreements have begun to include provisions that address technological issues affecting clerical workers. Mills (1986: 513) reports

> Collective bargaining agreements . . . have begun to include provisions for clerical work. The Newspaper Guild, the Service Employees, and the Communication Workers, among others, are unions which have contracts with provisions specifically designed for clerical work. The agreement between District 925 and the Equitable, for example, provides medical vision care for users of VDTs and requires installation of screens to reduce glare, detachable keyboards for greater operator flexibility and adjustable chairs. Further, no employee can be required to work at a terminal without a break for more than two consecutive hours.

Although the effort to organize clerical workers has been strong, success for unions has been limited relative to the size of the unorganized clerical work force. The public sector employees (government) and private universities and colleges have been the major targets in unionization drive (Mills 1986). Unions that have succeeded in organizing clerical workers include the United Auto Workers, Teamsters, Hotel Employees and Restaurant Employees International Union, and the Service Employees International Union. Women's organizations, such as Nine-to-Five, have supported the cause of unions as clerical workers are primarily women. Mills (1986: 513–514) states

> Clerical workers are the great frontier of unionism in the United States today. In terms of potential number of new employees, they far outdistance other groups. . . . Reports of high job dissatisfaction among clerical workers suggest that unionism may be attractive, but the enrollment of large numbers of clerical workers into the unions remains only a future possibility.

Another area for union growth is the high-technology industry. It is estimated that by 1990 there will be about 3 million employees in high-tech manufacturing, representing 15 to 20 percent of all manufacturing. Mills (1986: 514–515) summarizes these trends as follows:

> Unionization efforts in high-tech differ in an important way from the structure of unionism as it has developed in most of our other manufacturing industries. Collective bargaining in steel, autos, apparel, textiles, etc., is largely confined to production and maintenance employees. Professional and technical staff (scientists and engineers, in particular) are largely unrepresented by unions. There are, however, some exceptions to this, and employee organizers in high-tech industry hope to capitalize on the exceptions to organize not only production and maintenance employees in high-tech but also professional and technical staff. . . . It would be an interesting twist in history if the first major breakthroughs for collective bargaining in high-tech were to occur not among production workers (as they did in the 1930s and 1940s in other manufacturing industries), but rather among engineers, scientists, and technicians.

NEW TECHNOLOGY AGREEMENTS ABROAD

Britain

A new technology agreement, entered between union(s) and management in a given organization, covers a wide variety of subjects including job security, consultation and disclosure of information, health and safety, and sharing benefits. The specific nature of an agreement will be determined by (1) the relative strength of parties, (2) the environment and skills of negotiators, (3) the level and elements of new technology, and (4) the general climate of industrial relations (Benson & Lloyd 1983). A survey of 70 agreements, in the United Kingdom, conducted by Benson and Lloyd (1983: 176) suggests that health and safety is the most strikingly precise of the issues agreed; the others—such as job security, consultation and disclosure, and sharing benefits—are usually either tentative or vague, and all depend heavily on the maintenance of considerable strength and vigilance on the part of the unions.

New technology agreements potentially open the way for union involvement in corporate planning. Unions in the United Kingdom have generally cooperated with large-scale nationalizations resulting from new technology. The Trade Union Congress (TUC) issued a position paper, "Employment and Technology" in 1979 and accepted that "technological change and the microelectronic revolution are a challenge but also an opportunity" (Benson & Lloyd 1983: 168) and endorsed the establishment of new technology agreements, where possible. The TUC's framework, for these agreements, provides a "checklist for negotiators." This checklist includes 10 guidelines, which can assist negotiators anywhere in the formulation of new technology agreements (Benson & Lloyd 1983: 172):

1. Objective of "change by agreement": no new technology to be introduced unilaterally; status quo provisions recommended.
2. Challenge to union organization: inter-union collaboration in negotiations; build up of technical expertise by unions; technology stewards.
3. Access to information: all relevant information to be provided to union representatives before decisions taken; linked to regular consultation on company plans.
4. Employment and output plans: preferably no redundancy agreements or improved redundancy payments if impossible; planned approach to redeployment and relocation of workers; pursue commitment to expanding output.
5. Retraining: provision of training, priority for those directly affected by new technology; principle of maintained or improved earnings during retraining.
6. Working hours: scope for reducing working hours and systematic overtime.
7. Pay structures: avoid disruption to pay structures and polarization of workforce; ensure income levels maintained and improved; move towards single status and equal conditions.
8. Control over work: union influence over systems design and programming; no computer-gathered information to be used in work performance measurement.
9. Health and safety: stringent standards for new machinery and processes including visual display units.
10. Review procedure: joint union/management study teams to monitor developments and review progress.

Technological uncertainty can be channeled into productive outcomes, provided preventive strategic choices are made jointly by management and unions. The union movement, as Manwaring (1981: 7) has argued, has recognized the new IT impacts on job security, but it believes

> that extension of traditional collective bargaining relationships will ensure that the era of the chip will not be characterized by the "collapse of work" but by widespread benefits to union members. The "silicon dream" is of increased leisure and higher material standards of living brought about by shopfloor bargaining over the introduction of new technology and sympathetic government action.

West European Countries

Information technology has produced tremendous impacts on work organization and collective bargaining systems in European countries. Benson and Lloyd (1983: 179–180) summarize these trends:

> With the exception of the Scandinavian unions, who are in many aspects the trail-blazers, few have approached the

issue in ways similar to those taken by the British unions. The reasons for this lie in the different traditions and practices of the various national labour movements and their perceived need of formal agreements and other structures to regulate technological change.

Many other European labour movements—such as the West German, the Italian, the Austrian, the Finnish, and the Scandinavian—have greater regulation of their activities by statute. . . . In spite of wide variations two common major elements emerge across the Western European industrial relations scene. First, the scope of collective bargaining is continuously expanding to cover issues beyond pay, encompassing the content and structure of work, and second, local bargaining is becoming more important. Both of these developments have assisted the spread of new technology bargaining, especially as it is often seen as a direct threat to jobs. Thus, a number of demands occur in agreements in various countries: joint control over new technology, the provision of information on a routine basis, no compulsory redundancies due to new technology, no work measurement by computerized equipment, and monitoring of health and safety.

IMPLICATIONS FOR COLLECTIVE BARGAINING IN HEALTH CARE

The introduction of new technology raises issues and thereby new choices for health care leaders, not only in job redundancies, but in work organization, union organization, and traditional demarcation lines. Management representatives emphasize their right to adopt and apply new technology, whereas unions have succeeded, to a very limited extent, in negotiating new technological provisions. In the process of change two outcomes are clear. First, technological negotiations are shaped by the balances of power among the various social forces and institutions which govern those forces. Second, there is an indication that IT has created a new value structure in society, in which technological change is perceived as inevitable and progressive, not only by management, but also by arbitrators, and to a significant degree unions themselves. Given the explosive future growth of IT, our proposition is that technological innovation in health care can be guided by strategic choices, developed by management, unions, and government. Walton (1985) argues that IT is less deterministic than other basic technologies that have shaped our industrial system for two main reasons.

> First, the rapidly declining cost of computing power makes it possible to consider more technical options, including those that are relatively inefficient in the use of that power. Second, the new technology is less hardware dependent, more software intensive. It is, therefore, increasingly flexible, permitting the same basic information-processing task to be accomplished by an even greater variety of technical configurations, each of which may have a different set of human implications. (Walton 1985: 561)

A RESEARCH AGENDA ON IT IMPACTS ON HEALTH CARE HUMAN RESOURCES MANAGEMENT

A research strategy exploring labor market IT impacts would cover the issues listed below. This research can be conducted by management, unions, and government to facilitate parties in negotiation in the collective bargaining process.

- Extent of job loss in these health sectors that have rapidly adopted IT
- Nature of specific IT technologies that are most likely to have major health industry labor market effects in the future
- Emerging new skills and the need for restructuring education and training for maximum productivity
- Union and management strategies for adapting to IT impacts in relation to organization of work, pay systems, and industrial relations for organizational effectiveness in health industry
- Union and management strategies in health care human resources management for coping with qualitative effects of IT such as:
  1. part-time/full-time distribution of employment
  2. new employment arrangements such as job sharing, work sharing, and flexible hours
- Emerging new skills and the need for restructuring education and training for maximum productivity
- Union and management strategies for adapting to IT impacts in relation to organization of work, pay systems, and industrial relations for organizational effectiveness
- Quality of worklife programs such as job enrichment, autonomous work groups, worker participation and involvement, and programs based on theory Z concepts (Ouchi 1980)
- Innovative health care human resources management concepts and ergonomic tools including new ways of appraising, remunerating, and motivating staff, including physicians

CONCLUSIONS

One of the key propositions examined is that the perception of technological uncertainty can be the driving force of a productive opportunity and can aid in gaining a competitive edge if this uncertainty is managed strategically at both micro and macro levels of analysis and thus becomes part of an effective industrial relations system (Abernathy et al. 1983; Abernathy & Townsend 1975; Hill & Atterback 1979).

The notion of technostress, understood as technological uncertainty, is both good (eustress) and bad (distress), depending on how technostress is coped with by individuals, organizations, and society as a whole. This coping process raises the issue of competence needed by collective bargaining players to understand and manage technological complexity. At what stage technostress is harmful or dysfunctional is a determination that depends on complex relations between product costs, markets, technology, competition, extent of maturity of the industry involved, managerial competence to manage technological impacts, and union-management cooperation.

There is evidence to show that technological uncertainty associated with information technology is disruptive and makes obsolete existing capital equipment, labor skills, materials, components, management expertise, and organizational capabilities (Abernathy 1978; Clark 1982; Sabel 1981). It destroys the value of present competence in various aspects of production and may alter the relative position of competitors (Abernathy et al. 1983; Tilton 1971). How technological uncertainty is integrated into the production process is rooted in the basic competence of producers, including workers and managers, and their cultural attitudes toward change and uncertainty. Bargaining skills become the critical capacity in responding creatively to environmental change in health care as well as in other private and public sectors.

An analysis of existing collective bargaining practices suggests that information technology continues to be accepted as a prime stimulant to innovation and technological change (Abernathy et al. 1983). The increasing speed and integration of information technology is pervasive in all key industries and services including health care. The overall lesson for health care human resources management is that excellence lies in understanding the complex relations among technology, production management markets, competition, the level of an industry's maturity over time, and the motivations and skills of people involved. The key ingredient in adapting to technology lies in the quality of *adaptation*, i.e., the capacity to influence technologically changed services systems and their linkage with the markets and clients in both private and public sectors. The development and maintenance of a technology strategy as a part of an industrial relations system thus becomes a key process in coping with technological change in health care industry.

The main feature of technological adaptation is the demonstrated capacity of management and unions to go through the painstaking sequence of managing strains that stem from exploring, introducing, maintaining, and changing new technological systems. The underlying assumption is that technological adaptation does not happen of itself—it needs to be strategically managed; this is the essence of human resources strategy: technological excellence requires the skills needed to map out an entirely proactive strategic approach (Rosenbloom 1983; Radford et al. 1983). Put differently, new technologies can have considerable positive results when they are based on strategic human resources management with a skilled and responsive work force in a given industrial relations system in the health care industry. The health care executive and the union leader of the 1990s must not only contribute to the design and delivery of health services, but also research, negotiate, develop, and utilize IT-related human resources management strategies for achieving effectiveness and excellence.

REFERENCES

Abernathy, W.J. (1978) *The Productivity Dilemma*. Baltimore: Johns Hopkins University Press.

Abernathy, W.J.; Clark, K.B.; and Kantrow, A.M. (1983) *Industrial Renaissance*. New York: Basic Books.

Abernathy, W.J., and Townsend, P.L. (1975) Technology, Productivity and Process Change. In *Technological Forecasting and International Trade*, 379–396.

Alcalay, R., and Pasick, R.J. (1983) Psycho-Social Factors and the Technologies at Work. *Social Science Medicine* 17, no. 16: 1075–1084.

Arndt, R., and Chapman, L. (1984) *Potential Office Hazards and Controls*. Washington, D.C.: Office of Technology Assessment.

Attewell, P., and Rule, J. (1984) Computing and Organizations: What We Know and What We Don't Know. *Communications of the ACM* 27, no. 12: 1184–1192.

Bell, D. (1973) *The Coming of Post-Industrial Society*. New York: Basic Books.

Benjamin, R.; Rockart, J.F.; Morton, M.S.; and Wyman, J. (1984) Information Technology: A Strategic Opportunity. *Sloan Management Review*, 3: 10.

Benson, I., and Lloyd, J. (1983) *New Technology and Industrial Change*. London: Kogan Page.

Bird, E. (1980) *Information Technology in the Office: The Impact on Women's Jobs*. Manchester, England: Manchester Equal Opportunities Commission.

Blumberg, M., and Gerwin, D. (1984) Coping with Advanced Manufacturing Technology. *Journal of Occupational Behavior* 5: 113–130.

Bureau of National Affairs. (1984) *Special Report on VDTs and the Workplace*. Washington, D.C.: Bureau of National Affairs.

Cakir, A.; Reuter, H.; von Schmudt, L.; et al. (1978) *Research into Effects of Video Display Workplaces on the Physical and Psychological Function of Persons*. Bonn, West Germany: Federal Ministry for Work and Social Order.

Canada Tomorrow Conference (1983, Nov. 6–9). (1984) *Summary*. Ottawa: Supply and Services.

Choate, P. (1982, July) *Retooling the American Workforce*. Washington, D.C.: Northeast-Midwest Institute.

Clark, K.B. (1982) *The Competitive Status of the Influence of Technology in Determining International Competitive Advantage*. Washington, D.C.: National Academy of Sciences.

Coe, J.B.; Cuttle, K.; McClellan, W.C.; et al. (1980) *Visual Display Units*. Report W/1/80. Wellington, New Zealand: Department of Health.

Colligan, M.J.; Smith, M.J.; and Hurrell, J.J. (1977) Occupational Incidence Rates of Mental Health Disorders. *Journal of Human Stress* 3, no. 3: 34–39.

Cox, E.A. (1980) Radiation Emissions from Visual Display Units. In *Health Hazards of VDTs, 1. Papers Presented at HUSAT Conference*. Loughborough, U.K.: Loughborough University of Technology.

Dainoff, M.; Happ, A.; and Crane P. (1981) Visual Fatigue and Occupational Stress in VDT Operators. *Human Factors* 23, no. 4: 421–437.

Downs, A.A. (1967) A Realistic Look at the Final Payoffs from Urban Data Systems. *Public Administration Review* 27, no. 3: 204–209.

Drucker, P. (1980) Quoted from a speech by N.B. Hannay, Vice-President, Research and Patents, Bell Laboratories, Northwestern University, March 5, in Naisbitt, J. (1982) *Megatrends*. New York: Warner Communications Co.

Dutton, W., and Kraemer, K. (1978) Determinants of Support for Computerized Information Systems: The Attitudes of Local Government Chief Executives. *Midwest Review Public Administration* 12, no. 1: 19–40.

Elias, R.; Cail, F.; Tisserland, M.; et al. (1980) Investigations in Operators Working with CRT Display Terminals: Relationships between Task Content and Psychophysiological Alterations. In E. Grandjean & E. Vigliani (eds.), *Ergonomic Aspects of Video Display Terminals*, 211–218. London: Taylor & Francis.

Ellul, J. (1964) *The Technological Society*. Translated by John Wilkinson. New York: Alfred A. Knopf.

Forrester, T., ed. (1981) *The Microelectronic Revolution*. Cambridge, Mass.: MIT Press.

Fraser, T.M. (1983) *Human Stress, Work and Job Satisfaction*. Geneva, Switzerland: International Labour Organization.

Ghiringhelli, I. (1980) Collection of Subjective Opinions on the Use of VDTs. In E. Grandjean, E. Vigilian: (eds.), *Ergonomic Aspects of Visual Display Terminals*, 227–232. London: Taylor & Francis.

Goh, S.C. (1985) Uncertainty, Power and Organizational Decision Making: A Constructive Replication and Some Extensions. *Canadian Journal of Administrative Sciences* 2, no. 1: 177–191.

Gunnarsson, E., and Ostberg, O. (1977) *Physical and Mental Working Environment in a Terminal-Based Data System*. Research Report. Stockholm: Industrial Welfare Council.

Gunnarsson, E., and Soderberg, I. (1980) *I. Eyestrain Resulting from VDT Work at the Swedish Telecommunications Administration*. Stockholm: National Board of Occupational Safety and Health, Staff Conference.

Haynes, S.G., and Feinleib, M. (1980, February) Women, Work and Coronary Heart Disease: Prospective Findings from the Framingham Heart Study. *American Journal of Public Health* 70, no. 2: 133–141.

Health and Welfare Canada. (1983) *Investigation of Radiation Emissions from Video Display Terminals*. 83-EHD-91. Ottawa: Environmental Health Directorate.

Hill, C.T., and Atterback, J.M., eds. (1979) *Technological Innovation for a Dynamic Economy*. Elmsford, N.Y.: Pergamon Press.

Hinings, C.R.; Hickson, D.J.; Pennings, J.M.; and Schneck, R.E. (1974) Structural Conditions of Intraorganizational Power. *Administrative Science Quarterly* 19: 22–44.

Hrebiniak, L.G., and Joyce, W.F. (1985) Organizational Adaptation: Strategic Choice and Environmental Determinism. *Administrative Science Quarterly* 30: 336–349.

Hunt, H.A., and Hunt, T.L. (1983) *Human Resource Implications of Robotics*. Kalamazoo, Mich.: W.E. Upjohn Institute for Employment Research.

Hunting, W.T.; Laubli, T.; and Grandjean, E. (1981) Postural and Visual Loads at VDT Workplaces, I. Constrained Postures. *Ergonomics* 24, no. 12: 917–931.

International Labour Organization (ILO). (1984) *Automation, Work Organization and Occupational Stress*. Geneva, Switzerland: ILO.

Johansson, G., and Aronsson, G. (1980, July) Stress Reactions in Computerized Administrative Work. *Journal of Occupational Behavior* 5, no. 3: 159–181.

Kast, F.E., and Rosenzweig, J.E. (1985) *Organization and Management*. New York: McGraw-Hill.

King, J.L., and Kraemer, K. (1980) *Cost As a Social Impact of Telecommunications and Other Information Technologies*. Irvine, Calif.: Public Policy Research Organization.

Kochan, T.A.; McKersie, R.B.; and Katz, H.C. (1984) *U.S. Industrial Relations in Transition: A Summary Report*. Paper presented at the Annual Meeting of the Industrial Relations Association, Dallas, Texas.

Labour Canada Task Force. (1982) *In the Chips: Opportunities, People, Partnerships*. Ottawa: Labour Canada.

Laudon, K. (1964) *Computers and Bureaucratic Reform*. New York: Wiley.

Levi, L. (1984) *Stress in Industry. Causes, Effects and Prevention*. Geneva, Switzerland: International Labour Organization.

LO. (1981, September) Facklig data Poletik (Jönköping). Quoted in *Social and Labour Bulletin* 3: 261–262.

Manwaring, T. (1981) Trade Union Response to New Technology. *Industrial Relations Journal* 1:10.

Masuda, Y. (1980) *The Information Society as Post-Industrial Society.* Tokyo: Institute for the Information Society.

Miles, R.E., and Snow, C.E. (1978) *Organizational Strategy: Structure and Process.* New York: McGraw-Hill.

Mills, D.Q. (1986) *Labor-Management Relations.* New York: McGraw-Hill.

Murphy, L.R., and Hurrell, J.J. (1979) Machine Pacing and Occupational Stress. In *New Developments in Occupational Stress*, 17–35. Los Angeles: University of California Press.

Naisbitt, J. (1982) *Megatrends.* New York: Warner Books.

Office of Technology Assessment. (1985, February) *Information Technology and R&D.* CIT-268. Washington, D.C.: U.S. Congress, Office of Technology Assessment.

Ornati, O. (1985) *Rights Arbitration and Technological Change.* Working Paper No. 85-38. New York: New York University.

Ouchi, W.G. (1981) *Theory Z.* New York: Avon books.

Pava, C. (1983) *Managing New Office Technology: An Organizational Strategy.* New York: Free Press.

Perrow, C. (1967) A Framework for Comparative Analysis of Organizations. *American Sociological Review* 32, no. 2: 194–208.

Pfeffer, J.; Salancik, G.R.; and Leblebeci, H. (1976) The Effect of Uncertainty on the Use of Social Influence in Organizational Decision Making. *Administrative Science Quarterly* 21: 227–45.

Porat, M. (1971) *The Information Economy: Definition and Measurement.* OT Special Pub. 77-12(1). Washington, D.C.: U.S. Department of Commerce, Office of Telecommunications.

Porat, M. (1977) *The Information Economy: Definition and Measurement.* OT Special Pub. 77-12(1). Washington, D.C.: U.S. Department of Commerce, Office of Telecommunications.

Prosten, R. (1980, 1982, 1984) *Comparative Survey of Major Collective Bargaining Agreements.* Washington, D.C.: AFL–CIO.

Rada, J. (1980) *The Impact of Micro-electronics.* Geneva, Switzerland: International Labour Organization.

Radford, R., et al. (1983) The View from the Top: Executive Perspectives on the New Industrial Competition. Boston, Mass.: Harvard Business School Working Paper.

Rosenbloom, R.S. (1983) *Research on Technological Innovation Management and Policy.* Greenwich, Conn.: JAI Press.

Sabel, R. (1981) *IBM: Colossus in Transition.* New York: Truman Talley Books—Times Books.

Sauter, S.L.; Gottlieb M.; and Jones, K.C. (1982) A General Systems Analysis of Stress/Strain in VDT Operations. Paper presented at the Conference on Human Factors and Computer Systems, Gaithersburg, Md.

Schieman, W., et al. (1984) *Supervision in the 80s: Trends in Corporate America.* Washington, D.C.: Opinion Research Corporation.

Schönpflug, W. (1983) Coping Efficiency and Situational Demands. In R. Hockey (ed.), *Stress and Fatigue in Human Performance*, 299–326. New York: John Wiley & Sons.

Servan-Schreiber, J.J. (1981, October) *Un Centre Mondial pour le développement des ressources humaines.* Rapport à M. le Président de la République. Paris, France.

Sethi, A.S.; Schuler, R.S.; and Caro, D.H.J. (1987) A Strategic Choice Model of Technostress Management. In A.S. Sethi, D. Caro, and R.S. Schuler (eds.), *Strategic Management of Technostress in an Information Society*, 16–32. Toronto: Hogrefe International Inc.

Shaiken, H. (1984) *Work Transformed: Automation and Labor in the Computer Age.* New York: Holt, Rinehart & Winston.

Smith, M.J. (1982) *Health Issues in VDT Work.* Cincinnati, Ohio: NIOSH.

Tilton, John E. (1971) *International Diffusion of Technology: The Case of Semiconductors.* Washington, D.C.: Brookings Institution.

Toong, H.D., and Gupta, A. (1982, April) Automating Air Traffic Control. *Technology Review* 1:54.

Turner, J.A. (1984) *Computer Mediated Work: A Comparative Study of Mortgage Loan Servicing Clerks and Financial Investment Officers in Savings Banks.* Research Report GBA#84-70. New York: New York University, Center for Research in Information Systems.

Turner, J.A., and Karasek, R.A., Jr. (1984) Software Ergonomics: Effects of Computer Application Design Parameters on Operator Task Performance and Health. *Ergonomics* 27: 6.

Walton, R.E. (1985) Social Choice in the Development of Advanced Information Technology. In M. Beer & B. Spector (eds.), *Human Resource Management*, 557–566. New York: Free Press.

Wereneke, D. (1983) *Personnel Administration Microelectronics and Office Jobs. The Impact of the Chip on Women's Employment.* Geneva, Switzerland: International Labour Organization.

Wesson, R., et al. (1981, November) *Scenarios for Evaluation of Air Traffic Control.* Monograph R-2698-FAA. Santa Monica, Calif.

Westin, A.F. (1979) *Privacy and Freedom.* New York: Atheneum.

WHO. (1985, November 11) *Consultation on Linkage of Occupational Exposure. Information with Morbidity Data: Summary Report.* Geneva, Switzerland: Regional Office for Europe, World Health Organization.

Winner, L. (1977) *Autonomous Technology.* Cambridge, Mass. MIT Press.

E.J. Holland, Jr.

Dealing with Physicians As Employees

50

INTRODUCTION

As physicians grow more and more disenchanted with their role in the health care delivery system and as older physicians are replaced by baby boomers who sometimes have a different work ethic than that of their parents, physicians more and more will look to alternative structures within which to practice their chosen profession. As hospitals seek ways to implement outreach activities and encourage favorable referral patterns in a lawful manner, they more and more will find themselves employing physicians. Whether the employer is a community hospital with employed radiology, anesthesiology, and pathology physicians, or an academic health center with employed faculty, or a preferred provider organization with employed participating physicians, the phenomenon of physicians as employees rather than as independent contractors will continue to grow in the foreseeable future. In fact, by 1985, the overall percentage of employed physicians increased to 25.7 percent, and physicians meeting at an American Medical Association forum cited as the prime reasons the growth of alternative delivery systems, the increase in competitive pressures caused, in part, by a larger physician supply, and the financial security sought by younger physicians.[1]

As the traditional staff physician model for hospital-physician relationships breaks down, health care organizations are being faced with a dizzying array of issues with which they did not have to deal with in the past. Beyond the employee and labor relations expertise required in order to deal with physician employees, one also needs expertise in areas such as taxation, antitrust law, corporate law, professional liability law, insurance law, and third-party (including Medicare and Medicaid)

reimbursement. At each fork in the road the health care organization faces many options and more implications. Because of the many issues involved, health care organization counsel must bring a variety of expertise to the table to deal with them. Few, if any, lawyers I know have enough expertise to deal in depth with all of these issues. Certainly, this author does not have such expertise, and, as a result, this chapter will not attempt to deal with all these issues either. Instead, it will focus strictly on employment-related and contract issues, while acknowledging and covering only in passing a variety of related substantive problems.

EMPLOYEE OR INDEPENDENT CONTRACTOR?

Traditionally, physicians have had and jealously guarded an independent contractor relationship with health care organizations. One is inclined to suspect that the various "corporate practice of medicine" statutes were at least in part a product of medical associations' desires to preserve this relationship. The first thing a health care organization must decide in dealing with its physicians is whether it wishes to maintain the traditional independent contractor relationship or whether it wishes to enter into an employment relationship. The alternative implications are far-reaching.

The Legal Test

Before looking at those implications we should analyze what determines the nature of the relationship. How does one know whether a physician is an employee or an independent contractor? One thing is certain: you frequently cannot tell from what the documents call the physician. Many contracts designate physicians as independent contractors, but, on closer examination, the facts are to the contrary.

The Federal Insurance Contributions Act sets out the appropriate definition of *employee* for our purposes.

> (d) Employee.—For purposes of this chapter, the term "employee" means . . .
>
> (2) any individual who, under the usual common law rules applicable in determining the employer-employee relationship, has the status of an employee; . . .

26 U.S.C. § 3121(d)(2)(1989).

The Code of Federal Regulations provides somewhat more assistance in applying the statute. It first emphasizes that the title alone is not significant.

> (3) If the relationship of employer and employee exists, the designation or description of the relationship by the parties as anything other than that of employer and employee is immaterial. Thus, if such relationship exists, it is of no consequence that the employee is designated as a partner, coadventurer, agent, independent contractor, or the like.

26 C.F.R. § 31.3121(d)-1(a)(3)(1988).

The Regulations go on to add some detail about the definition of common law employees.

> (2) Generally such relationship exists when the person for whom services are performed has the right to control and direct the individual who performs the services, not only as to the result to be accomplished by the work but also as to the details and means by which that result is accomplished. That is, an employee is subject to the will and control of the employer not only as to what shall be done but how it shall be done. In this connection, it is not necessary that the employer actually direct or control the manner in which the services are performed; it is sufficient if he has the right to do so. The right to discharge is also an important factor indicating that the person possessing that right is an employer. Other factors characteristic of an employer, but not necessarily present in every case, are the furnishing of tools and the furnishing of a place to work, to the individual who performs the services. In general, if an individual is subject to the control or direction of another merely as to the result to be accomplished by the work and not as to the means and methods for accomplishing the result, he is an independent contractor.

26 C.F.R. § 31.3121(d)-1(c)(2)(1988).

It is interesting to note that, one sentence later, the regulations go on to observe that

> individuals such as physicians, lawyers, dentists, veterinarians, construction contractors, public stenographers, and auctioneers, engaged in the pursuit of an independent trade, business, or profession, in which they offer their services to the public, are independent contractors and not employees.

26 C.F.R. § 31.3121(d)-1(c)(2)(1988).

The key concepts in this sentence are those of independence and of offering services to the public. One simply cannot jump to the conclusion that the regulation sanctions the designation of all physicians as independent contractors.

In analyzing the employer-employee relationship, the Internal Revenue Service will look primarily at four factors.

> 1. The degree to which the physician is integrated into the healthcare organization;
> 2. The nature, regularity and continuity of the physician's work for the healthcare organization as opposed to himself or for his own patients;
> 3. The authority reserved by the healthcare organization to require the physician's compliance with its policies, procedures and rules; and
> 4. The extent to which the physician is treated in the same fashion as that established for the healthcare organization's other employees.

Rev. Rul. 72-203, 1972-1 C.B. 324. Although the labor law services have reported thousands of cases applying the independent contractor–employee rules, a search of the computer data bases produces remarkably few cases in which the analysis has been done with respect to physicians. The cases that do exist make the point reasonably well, even though some of them are fairly old.

In *Flemming v. Huycke,* 284 F.2d 546 (9th Cir. 1960), the U.S. Court of Appeals for the Ninth Circuit found that an older physician who had sold his practice to his younger colleague and remained for a transitional period was an employee rather than an independent contractor. The court quoted at length from the Code of Federal Regulations materials set forth above and found the employment relationship, even though the agreement between the two physicians made the price of the practice dependent on the older physician's ability to participate, did not specifically give the younger physician the right to discharge the older physician, and provided the older physician the right to retain title to certain equipment; further, the younger physician in no way limited the older physician's methods of treatments and medicine used. The Court of Appeals mentioned but distinguished these factors and found that the key was that the younger physician retained the right to control the activities of the older physician. It is that "right of control" that is determinative.

In a subsequent similar case, *Cody v. Ribicoff,* 289 F.2d 394 (8th Cir. 1961), the Eighth Circuit agreed with the analysis of the Ninth Circuit and refused to give any weight to the fact that the physician employee was referred to as an "associate physician" or even that his remuneration was based on the partnership's income and that he paid certain of his own expenses. Again, the Eighth Circuit emphasized the right that the partnership reserved to control the actions of the employed physician. See also *St. Luke's Hospital Association v. United States,* 333 F.2d 157 (6th Cir. 1964), in which the court found that payments made to residents were not exempt under the Federal Insurance Contributions Act and, therefore, were subject to taxes. Much more recently, a Michigan appellate court found that salaried physicians at city-operated clinics were employees for purposes of the Michigan Employee Relations Act. *City of Detroit v. Salaried Physicians Professional Association,* 418 N.W.2d 679 (Mich. Ct. App. 1987). Therefore, the court found that the proper test was

> (1) Whether the employer maintains control over the manner and means of performing the work as well as the end to be achieved and (2) whether the work done by the individual can be characterized as a part of a common task.

418 N.W.2d at 682. The court went on to observe that the contracts between the physicians and the city were an integral part of the task of providing health care to city residents. The physicians were found to be employees.

The precedents are not talismanic. They require analysis of the precise relationship between the physician and the health care organization. It is clear that many existing relationships are employment relationships, notwithstanding their designation of the physicians as independent contractors. It is equally clear that many future relationships will be the same. The key is to apply the appropriate common law tests, analyze the facts and how the relationship will operate, and then make a conscious decision rather than slip into a situation by accident.

Substantive Considerations

As a health care organization attempts to make the strategic decision whether to employ or to have independent contracts with physicians, it needs to consider a variety of pros and cons. These will vary from institution to institution and from situation to situation. Any laundry list is destined to be too long, too short, or otherwise inadequate. Furthermore, what might be an opportunity in one situation will be a problem in another, and what one person will view as a pro, another will view as a con.

Therefore, rather than attempt a full laundry list or even decide which are the pros and which are the cons, we now will turn briefly to some of the implications of the decision, including a few implications that have the potential for far-ranging impact but that are beyond the scope of this chapter.

The Right of Control

The first implication to be considered of necessity must be the one that determines the status of the physician—that is, the right of control. Clearly, if the health care organization wishes to demand certain standards of practice and to control the method of meeting those standards, including such things as practice schedule, referral patterns, drug and equipment usage, etc., it must retain sufficient control that the organization will become an employer and the physician will become an employee. As stated above in the Code of Federal Regulations, it simply is not possible both to retain control and to maintain an independent contractor relationship.

Certainly, the organization must consider operational efficiency and simplicity issues. These are not legal issues, but instead are management issues. The only point in raising them here is to remind counsel, who seem too often to forget, that the business and operational issues should drive the decision and that the legal analysis simply should be calculated to find a way to implement the desired practical result. Neither approach necessarily is more or less complex or efficient than the other. The patient care objectives, the need for extensive coverage, and the requirement of administrative functions all must be taken into consideration. Counsel first should raise the control issue and then ask the client to outline the desired business objectives. Thereafter, the appropriate vehicle should become clear.

Fraud and Abuse

The Medicare and Medicaid fraud and abuse and anti-kickback laws and regulations also must be considered carefully. This is one of those areas for which a full analysis is beyond the scope of this chapter, but it is so important that a few highlights must be mentioned. Section 1128B(b)(2) of the Social Security Act prohibits the knowing and willful offer or payment of remuneration of any kind, whether direct or indirect, overt or covert, in cash or in kind, to any person to induce that person to refer an individual to another person for purposes of arranging or furnishing services under Medicare or recommending certain purchases or other business arrangements to be paid for by Medicare. Violation is a felony, and conviction is punishable by a fine of not more than $25,000 and imprisonment for not more than five years, or both.

The statute provides a specific exemption for payments by an employer to an employee who has a bona fide employment relationship with the employer. The Office of Inspector General of the U.S. Department of Health and Human Services prepared, recommended, and has circulated a draft of implementing regulations that provide certain safe harbors for practices under the statute. The regulations are proposed to be published as 42 C.F.R. § 1001, and in paragraph (I)(2) the Inspector General specifically adopts the definition of an employee from the Internal Revenue Service set forth in 26 U.S.C. § 3121(d)(2). The Inspector General goes on to suggest that in spite of suggestions to broaden the exemption to apply to independent contractors paid on a commission basis, he has decided to the contrary.

> We have declined to adopt this approach because we are aware of many examples of abusive practices by sales personnel who are paid as independent contractors and who are not under appropriate supervision. We believe that, if individuals and entities desire to pay sales persons on the amount of business they generate, then to be exempt from civil or criminal prosecution, they should

make these sales persons employees where they can and should exert appropriate supervision for the individual's acts.

Proposed as 42 C.F.R. § 1001(I)(2). Assuming these regulations eventually are promulgated and enacted, the safe harbor provides no comfort in any way broader than the statute itself. Thus, the only way to avoid completely the fraud and abuse problem is to make the physician an employee.

Once the health care organization decides not to have physician employees, it must analyze both the proposed regulations and a series of cases, the most important of which is *United States v. Greber*, 760 F.2d 68 (3d Cir.), *cert. denied*, 474 U.S. 988 (1985). There a company that provided Holter-monitor services paid physicians an interpretation fee when the physicians made referrals to the company. The Third Circuit found that the payments violated the fraud and abuse statutes, even though they were in part for professional services, because they also were in part intended to induce the physicians to use the company's services. *Greber* is simply a sign of the ambiguity practitioners must face in this area.

Antitrust Considerations

Antitrust considerations also must play a major part in the decision as to what relationship to create with a physician. As in the fraud and abuse area, simplicity would seem to compel creation of an employment relationship. An exclusive contract with one's own employee certainly will not generate antitrust liability. On the other hand, even though exclusive contracts have been upheld in cases such as *Jefferson Parish Hospital District No. 2 v. Hyde*, 466 U.S. 2 (1984), the very existence of an exclusive contract with independent contractors at least raises the issue and makes planning a defense imperative. Likewise, the case of *Patrick v. Burgett*, 486 U.S. 94 108 S. Ct. 1658 (1988), demonstrates the need for care in granting or denying staff privileges. Avoidance of antitrust risk may not be sufficient justification to enter into an employment relationship, but it may well be a substantial incentive.

Peer Review and Related Issues

The conduct of credentialing, peer review, quality assurance activities, and general utilization review may be significantly different in the employee relationship and in the independent contractor relationship. Again, the employee relationship should make this area simpler and less dangerous. One assumes that if the defendant physicians in *Patrick* all had been employees of the hospital and had decided not to employ an additional physician, they would not have had antitrust liability. The scope of immunity and the requirements of the Healthcare Quality Improvement Act of 1987, 42 U.S.C. § 11101 *et seq.*, are well beyond the objectives of this chapter, but, again, they clearly must be considered, and their impact may differ, depending on how the health care institution resolves the employee–independent contractor issue.

Corporate Practice of Medicine Restrictions

Many, perhaps most, states have some prohibition or restriction on the so-called "corporate practice of medicine." These vary widely from state to state in their terms and application. The reason for these proscriptions are well set out in the case of *Dr. Allison, Dentist, Inc. v. Allison*, 360 Ill. 638, 196 N.E. 799 (1935), which suggested that a corporation simply can't meet the various requirements of education, moral fitness, etc., of the various state licensure laws.

Similar analysis has been applied by other states. On the other hand, the continuing viability of some of these state statutes is in question. For example, federal health maintenance organization law specifically pre-empts state laws on some of these issues [42 U.S.C. § 300e-10(1989)]. Other states, including my own home state of Missouri, have no restrictions on the corporate practice of medicine. See, e.g., *State ex rel. McKittrick v. Gate City Optical Company*, 339 Mo. 427, 97 S.W.2d 89 (1936). In other states there are specific exceptions for hospitals and other nonprofit charitable entities. In a state that has a strict, aggressively enforced statute in this regard, the corporate practice of medicine analysis may be the beginning and the end of the question of whether to have employees or independent contractors. A practitioner is well advised to check first the laws of his or her own state in this regard.

Reimbursement Issues

Methods of Medicare reimbursement also are impacted by the relationship between a physician and a health care organization. Hospitals normally are reimbursed under Part A of Title XVIII of the Social Security Act, 42 U.S.C. § 1395c (1983 and Supp. 1989), *et seq.*, and doctors normally are reimbursed under Part B of the Act, 42 U.S.C. § 1395j (1983), *et seq.* The former generally are compensated on a reasonable cost basis and the latter on a reasonable charge basis. Services rendered by provider-based physicians must be categorized as to whether coverage is provided under Part A or Part B. The Tax Equity and Fiscal Responsibility Act of 1982 (TEFRA) (Public Law 97-248, 96 Stat. 324) made major changes in how provider-based physicians could charge for services under Medicare. "Generally, physicians are considered based in a hospital or other provider if they receive compensation from the provider or another entity for services in the provider." 48 Fed. Reg. 8904 (1983). Both TEFRA amendments to the Social Security Act and the implementing regulations set forth criteria to differentiate between physician services provided by the physician himself or herself and those provided on behalf of the hospital. The distinction is between services.

(A) which constitute professional medical services, which are personally rendered for an individual patient by a physician and which contribute to the diagnosis or treatment of an individual patient, and which may be reimbursed as physicians' services under part B, and

(B) which constitute professional services which are rendered for the general benefit to patients in a hospital or skilled nursing facility and which may be reimbursed only on a reasonable cost basis or on the bases described in Section 1886.

Social Security Act, § 1887(a)(1)(A) and (B), 42 U.S.C. 1395xx (1988), 42 C.F.R. § 405.550 (1988).

To comply with these requirements it is necessary to distinguish in an agreement among physician services rendered to the provider, physician services rendered to the patient, and physician activities, such as research, that are not reimbursable under either part of Medicare. Next, it is necessary to create a system whereby time records or other documentation can be maintained in order to support the allocation. There are limitations on reasonable charge reimbursement under Part B, and those must be observed. Additionally, there are specific requirements for the various types of provider-based physician reimbursement, such as anesthesiology (42 C.F.R. § 405.552), radiology (42 C.F.R. §§ 405.554–405.555), and pathology (42 C.F.R. §§ 405.556–405.557). In deciding on and then drafting a contract with a provider-based physician, whether an employee or an independent contractor, the practitioner must study and apply these and the related regulations.

Malpractice Liability

The questions of professional liability also must be taken into account when deciding on the nature of a proposed relationship between a physician and a health care organization. Traditionally, business entities, including hospitals, have been liable for the negligence of their employees under the theory of *respondeat superior,* but they have not necessarily been liable for the negligence of their independent contractors. Since physicians frequently bear more of the risk of professional liability and are more likely to make actionable mistakes, the traditional law argued strongly in favor of keeping physicians off of hospitals' payrolls.

While, again, a state-by-state analysis is required, that reflex principle may be changing. The watershed case was, of course, *Darling v. Charleston Memorial Hospital,* 33 Ill.2d 326, 211 N.E.2d 253 (1965), *cert. denied,* 383 U.S. 946 (1966), in which the court found that the hospital was liable for having failed to supervise adequately the medical treatment provided by physicians, irrespective of whether they were employees or independent contractors. *Darling* found a duty to investigate, review, and oversee the practices of physicians providing services within the hospital.

In a similar vein, *Johnson v. Misericordia Hospital,* 99 Wis.2d 708, 301 N.W.2d 156 (1981), assigned liability to the hospital for failing to verify properly a surgeon's credentials. Additionally, courts have begun to find hospitals liable under a theory of ostensible or apparent agency. See, e.g., *Northern Trust Company v. St. Francis Hospital,* 522 N.E.2d 699 168 Ill. App. 3d 270 (Ill. App. Ct. 1988), in which the hospital was found liable because, along with the physician, it was found to have led the patient to believe that an agency relationship existed between the physician and the hospital. Similarly, a California appellate court recently found that a hospital might be held vicariously liable for actions of the psychiatrist who clearly was an independent contractor. *Richard F.H. v. Larry H.D.,* 243 Cal. Rptr. 807 198 Cal. App. 3d 591 (Cal. Ct. App. 1988). But, to the contrary, see *Sledziewski v. Cioffi,* 137 A.D.2d 186, 528 N.Y.S.2d 913 (N.Y. App. Div. 1988).

There simply is no way to generalize on what law will be applied in the various states and the hospital that is concerned about liability issues must determine the current and likely state of the law in its state before deciding what type of relationship to establish with its physicians. Generally speaking, hospitals will be liable for the professional negligence of their employees and may or may not be liable under one of the various corporate negligence theories for the negligence of their independent contractors.

Antidiscrimination Laws

The application of various antidiscrimination laws also may have an ambiguous effect on the decision as to what type of relationship to create with a physician. Instinctively, labor lawyers will tell you that the various antidiscrimination statutes (both state and federal), which prohibit discrimination on the basis of race, creed, color, sex, religion, national origin, ancestry, age, and physical handicap (and perhaps a few other attributes), apply only to the employment relationship. Thus, these statutes clearly will come into play if the hospital decides to create an employment relationship with a physician.

The reciprocal principle should be that these rules would not apply to an independent contractor. However, in a recent case the U.S. Court of Appeals for the Eleventh Circuit found that a physician had a cause of action under Title VII of the Civil Rights Act (42 U.S.C. 2000e) and Section 1981 of the Civil Rights Act of 1866 (42 U.S.C. § 1981), even though the physician was not an employee of the hospital. The plaintiff was a resident at one hospital that included in its residency program a rotation to the defendant hospital. The defendant hospital refused to permit the plaintiff to participate in the rotation at its facility, and, as a result, the plaintiff was dismissed from the first hospital's residency program. The Court of Appeals found that the defendant hospital should be liable because it was in a position to interfere discriminatorily with the plaintiff's employment opportunities, even though the defendant hospital was not actually the employer. *Zaklama v. Mt. Sinai Medical Center,* 842 F.2d 291 (11th Cir. 1988).

Similarly, a New York court applied Section 296 of New York's Human Rights Law to a sexually discriminatory evaluation of one physician by another. *Samper v. University of Rochester Strong Memorial Hospital,* 528 N.Y.S.2d 958 139 Misc. 2d 580 (N.Y. Sup. Ct. 1987). The court concluded that the immunity accorded a physician who engaged in an evaluation of another physician did not extend to discriminatory treatment of a participant in a residency program. Again, in

Pardazi v. Cullman Medical Center, 838 F.2d 1155 (11th Cir. 1988), the Eleventh Circuit found a medical center liable for national origin discrimination because its discriminatory denial of staff privileges interfered with the physician's employment contract with his professional corporation.

Fortunately for those states within the Fifth Circuit, that Court of Appeals does not appear to be inclined to take up this analysis. In *Diggs v. Harris Hospital-Methodist, Inc.,* 847 F.2d 270 (5th Cir. 1988), the court declined to find Title VII applicable to a situation in which there was no employer-employee relationship between the physician and the hospital. The court found that there was no evidence in this case that denial of privileges at defendant hospital would interfere with plaintiff's ability to obtain privileges at other hospitals in the same metropolitan area. In distinguishing *Pardazi* and other cases, the court found that whatever opportunities are interfered with must be in the nature of employment relationships that are to be determined by application of the economic realities/common law control test adopted by the court. The court went on to find that the physician's relationships with her patients, even though interfered with by the defendant's discriminatory activity, were not in the nature of employment relationships and, therefore, were not entitled to protection under Title VII or Section 1981. Even the Fifth Circuit's decision indicates some willingness to extend the reach of Title VII beyond the direct employer-employee relationship. Should that continue to occur, the result probably would dissipate any benefit to be obtained by a health care organization from keeping an arms-length relationship with a physician's corporation instead of entering into an employment relationship with the professional employees of the corporation.

Miscellaneous Issues

Finally, there is a variety of miscellaneous matters to be considered when deciding whether to establish an employee or an independent contractor relationship. Among these are withholding and unemployment compensation tax issues, as well as something as esoteric as application of the Railroad Retirement Act in appropriate circumstances. Additionally, hospitals must examine their fringe benefits, and particularly their deferred compensation programs. Section 89 of the Internal Revenue Code (26 U.S.C. § 89) may have traps for the unwary hospital that makes a physician an employee, and those traps may still exist under certain alternative methods of establishing the hospital-physician relationship. Additionally, such matters as the hospital's employee handbook and the medical staff bylaws must be examined to determine their interplay with the alternative possible relationships between the hospital and its physicians. In other words, the basic hospital-physician relationship affects many ancillary matters, all of which must be considered before making the decision as to how to structure the relationship. Once a hospital decides that physicians are to become employees of the institution, it,

like all other employers, has two alternative methods for dealing with the physicians–individual and collective. We now will turn to the implications of those two different methods of dealing with professional employees.

UNIONIZED PHYSICIANS

History

According to a recent article in *Hospitals,* "physicians' unions, in one form or another, have been around for nearly 30 years. Although they have a solid membership core, they have not enjoyed steady growth."[2] *Hospitals* goes on to quote Sanford A. Marcus, M.D., founder and president of the Union of American Physicians and Dentists (UAPD), as saying, "The number of members has risen in spurts and in response to big issues, such as mandatory acceptance of assignment for Medicare. After all, who needs a union when things are rosy?"[3] Nationwide, membership statistics do not seem impressive. UAPD reports some 43,000 members in 17 states. Doctors Council, representing physicians, dentists, podiatrists, and optometrists in New York City, has approximately 2,500 physician members, and other splinter groups have a total of 3,000 members.[4] Nonetheless, as the number of employed physicians increases, it seems that unionization of those physicians also inevitably will increase. Given the increasing pressures on physicians in the health care system, including the report recently issued by Harvard University to the Healthcare Financing Administration on physician fees,[5] any other conclusion seems counterintuitive.

In addition, a significant number of hospitals have been faced with unionization of their house staff officers, medical interns, residents, and fellows. These efforts have occurred primarily in major metropolitan areas and university centers, such as New York, Chicago, and Los Angeles. Many of the existing bargaining units predate the 1974 Healthcare Amendments to the National Labor Relations Act (NLRA).

In a series of cases decided two years after the Healthcare Amendments were passed, the National Labor Relations Board (NLRB) concluded that house staff members primarily are students and, as such, are not entitled to the protections afforded employees by the NLRA. *Cedars-Sinai Medical Center,* 223 N.L.R.B. 251 (1976); *University of Chicago Hospitals and Clinics,* 223 N.L.R.B. 1002 (1976); *Kansas City General Hospital,* 225 N.L.R.B. 106 (1976). As a result of these rulings it is virtually impossible for house staff to force recognition by hospitals. However, some consensual units do survive. The impact of these units can be significant.

In 1975 the Committee of Interns and Residents, which represents the house staff in various New York City hospitals, called a strike which lasted four days and gained the participation of some 3,000 house staff officers. While the phenomenon has not been repeated frequently, its threat must be a concern.

Faculty Practice Plans and Yeshiva

An unresolved issue related in some respects to the educational nature of the house officer's role is the role of members of faculty practice plans. Originally designed primarily to take advantage of increased reimbursement opportunities available to non-hospital-based physicians, these plans are becoming increasingly prevalent at academic medical centers. The model simply is that the faculty members of a medical school incorporate into a separate physicians' group and then contract through that group with the university to provide teaching services and perhaps with the university's hospital to provide patient care services.

The question, from a unionization point of view, is whether the faculty employees of these faculty practice plans could organize and be in a position to negotiate with the plan over wages, hours, and working conditions. At issue will be the application to the Supreme Court's decision in *NLRB v. Yeshiva University,* 444 U.S. 672, 103 L.R.R.M. 2526 (1980). In that case and its progeny, the Supreme Court and the NLRB have found a substantial number of university professors to be managerial employees because of their responsibilities as faculty members in governing the academic institution. The Supreme Court in *Yeshiva* forced the Board to this analysis when it analyzed the role of the Yeshiva faculty as follows:

> The controlling consideration in this case is that the faculty of Yeshiva University exercise authority which in any other context unquestionably would be managerial. Their authority in academic matters is absolute. They decide what courses will be offered, when they will be scheduled, and to whom they will be taught. They debate and determine teaching methods, grading policies, and matriculation standards. They effectively decide which students will be admitted, retained, and graduated. On occasion their views have determined the size of the student body, the tuition to be charged, and the location of a school. When one considers the function of a university, it is difficult to imagine decisions more managerial than these. To the extent the industrial analogy applies, the faculty determines within each school the product to be produced, the terms upon which it will be offered, and the customers who will be served.

NLRB v. Yeshiva University, 444 U.S. 672, 686 (1980).

If these faculty members were employed by a faculty practice plan instead of by the university, would the result have been different? Probably not in the case of Yeshiva University, but subsequent cases make it clear that the Board will examine these matters on a case-by-case basis and look at faculty members virtually on a position-by-position basis. Interestingly, since *Yeshiva,* the Board decided the case of *Montefiore Hospital & Medical Center,* 261 N.L.R.B. 569, 110 L.R.R.M. 1048 (1982). In that case, the Board applied the *Yeshiva* principles in analyzing managerial status but found that the views of physicians primarily were involved in patient care and that their function of overseeing and teaching interns and residents was not managerial because it was not related to the primarily patient care–oriented nature of the hospital's business.

Applying *Yeshiva* and *Montefiore* to the physician employees of a faculty practice plan could be very tricky. Traditionally, faculty practice plans were set up primarily to maximize patient care revenue in order to support the teaching and research functions of otherwise academic physicians. Would the Board faced with unionization by faculty practice plan employees apply the same sort of analysis as it did in *Montefiore*? We simply don't know.

Appropriate Units

The one final question to be addressed before looking at actual negotiations with physicians is that of the appropriate collective bargaining unit. In its proposed hospital bargaining unit rules, 53 Fed. Reg. 33,900 (1988) (to be codified at 29 CFR § 103) the NLRB has found that a separate unit of physicians is appropriate in hospitals. Frankly, this is among the Board's less surprising conclusions in the rulemaking process, but it does not necessarily close the book on these issues. The rule is likely to be the beginning of the analysis of an appropriate bargaining unit, but it certainly will not be the end.

Montefiore and *Yeshiva,* discussed above, raise academic and managerial issues. Additionally, there will be true supervisory issues, and, in the evermore common multihospital systems, there will be community of interest issues among physicians who stay at one facility or who move from facility to facility. In *Manor Health Care Corp.,* 285 N.L.R.B. 31 (1987), the Board once again found single facility units to be presumptively appropriate in health care organizations. Under this presumption one must ask how physicians who rotate among various facilities will be treated in relation to physicians who stay permanently at one or the other of the facilities. Clearly, significant community of interest issues will be raised in these contexts.

Negotiating a Contract

Once one has disposed of the various bargaining unit and coverage issues and actually is faced with a union of doctors across the table, what can be expected? This author has not had the distinct pleasure of sitting across the table from a physicians' union. Such unions simply are not common in the Midwest and, as far as I know, are nonexistent in my four-state region. Nonetheless, conversations with professional practitioners who do negotiate with physicians would lead one to the conclusion (which probably should have been anticipated) that, in their role as organized employees, physicians are not materially different from teamsters or teachers.[6] This author's experience with teachers would indicate that base contract terms for professionals are not materially different from those for unions representing the broadest possible variety of blue-collar workers—at least they need not be.

The preferred approach is to refer professional issues (as opposed to administrative and economic issues, such as wages and hours) to committees or task forces which will function after and outside of collective bargaining.[7] To be sure, the professional sorts of issues should be discussed during the collective bargaining sessions. After all, the cathartic effect of bargaining is one of the true side benefits of having one's employees organize. However, once having dealt with these sorts of issues at the bargaining table, one should attempt to keep them out of the collective bargaining agreement and, if they are not yet resolved, should create professional task forces or committees to pursue them further.

What, then, should the practitioner expect to find in a collective bargaining agreement? Let us look briefly at the types of clauses, their intent, and what management's objective should be for each. (See Table 50-1).

Typically, the negotiator should have with him or her, at the bargaining table, supervising professionals from various key departments. This will allow for reasoned discussion of professional issues and will avoid having the negotiator make a concession that seems innocuous but results in practical difficulties later.

As the number of employed physicians grows, we will have more bargaining units and, of necessity, will obtain much greater experience in collective bargaining with physicians.

NONUNION PHYSICIAN EMPLOYEES

Background

The standard among nonunion employees is that, subject to a variety of state judicial interpretations, they are employees at will and not covered by employment agreements. Physicians, just as many other highly compensated employees, have come to expect different treatment, and, hence, it is likely that the health care organizations employing physicians will be faced with a request for a written contract. These organizations may even wish to initiate such a relationship. That brings us to the last subject of this chapter, negotiation of individual contracts with employed physicians. Again, we will assume that the employee–independent contractor issue has been addressed and resolved in favor of employment status and will address only the creation of the contractual relationship between the organization and the individual physician.

Historically, the most common hospital-based physicians, and, therefore, those most likely to be subject to employment contracts, were the so-called RAP physicians—radiologists, anesthesiologists, and pathologists. Today, however, the changing nature of the health care delivery system has led to physician contracting in virtually every subspecialty.

Negotiating a Contract

Before embarking on physician contract negotiations, the practitioner should be aware of the interplay between and

---

Table 50-1 Clauses in a Collective Bargaining Agreement

Type of Clause and Purpose	Management's Objectives
Purpose and intent: is normally used to express the desire of the parties to engage in mutually beneficial labor relations	Generally not very important to management. Actually it can have some detriment when otherwise meaningless boilerplate is referred to by the union in some arbitration in order to give an arbitrator a rationale for deciding a matter contrary to other language in a contract.
Recognition: generally describes the bargaining unit and confirms that the employer recognizes the union's right to represent the people in that unit	Not required in order to complete a collective bargaining agreement. If this boilerplate type of language is agreed to, it should be modified with language making it clear that nothing in the clause is intended as a grant of exclusive jurisdiction over any particular type of work. Some employers have been surprised that a recognition clause has been interpreted to provide exclusive work jurisdiction.
Management rights: is intended to make clear that management retains certain rights and all rights not specifically ceded to the union or employees in the contract	This clause should be as broad as possible. Frequently, less is more in the sense that drawing a long list of rights may run afoul of the old Latin principle *inclusio unius est exclusio alii* (i.e., if one creates a list, those things left off the list are deemed to have been omitted deliberately). The very right management leaves out of the list may be the one it wants to exercise at a later date. Thus, a very broad but simple statement of the reserved rights theory may be best.
No strike: intended to prohibit any and all strikes or work stoppages during the term of the agreement; the reciprocal usually is that the union requests a parallel no-lockout clause	This clause should be as broad as possible. It specifically should prohibit sympathy strikes and unfair labor practice strikes. Some would say that the no-strike clause really is the only thing management gets from a union contract. If that is true, management should get a good one.

Table 50-1 continued

Type of Clause and Purpose	Management's Objectives
Grievance and arbitration: provides a method of resolving disputes	There are many different kinds of grievance and arbitration procedures. No one is best. However, the clause should be as simple as possible with reasonably short time periods that can result in loss of a grievance if not followed accurately. The scope of the arbitrator's authority should be limited to application or interpretation of the specific terms of the contract.
Wages: establishes the rates of pay for unit members	Clauses should be clear and unambiguous. Management may wish to provide that the rates established are minimums in order to preserve the right to pay in excess of scale.
Fringe benefits: is used to establish a variety of fringe benefit programs	Clauses should be limited to the amount of various payments. Management should resist adopting or incorporating by reference various extraneous trust agreements. Management also should avoid granting unions the right to strike over fringe benefit contribution disputes.
Union security and checkoff: usually establishes a union shop and provides for automatic payment of union dues	These really are the union's clauses. If anything, management should attempt to provide relatively easy and frequent opportunities for bargaining unit members to withdraw both from the union and from the checkoff authorization.
Paid time off: establishes vacation, holiday, sick leave, and other leave times	These clauses are as varied as the bargainers who draw them. They range from the very simple to the very complex. Be sure that management considers various hypothetical applications of the clauses before finally agreeing to them.
Complete agreement: also known as a "zipper" clause; is similar to the complete agreement clauses found in normal commercial contracts	Management wishes to see to it that it will not be required to negotiate during the term of the agreement and that the agreement itself contains all agreements between the parties.
Savings clause: preserves the effectiveness of the bulk of the contract if one portion of the contract is found legally ineffective	Need to ensure continued application of no-strike commitment, even in face of various external changes. This is much like a savings clause in a normal commercial agreement.
Part-time employees: covers whether and how part-time employees can be used	Retain as much flexibility as possible including the right to compensate part-time employees in ways different from those it uses to compensate full-time employees.
Hours of work and overtime: establishes when employees will work and in what situations they will be paid	Avoid excessively complex scheduling provisions, to try to have "normal" hours, rather than "required" hours, and to retain as much flexibility as feasible.
Job promotion and transfer: establishes bidding or similar requirements	Typically management would prefer not to have such a clause, and if it is to be accepted, its practical impact must be studied carefully. Certainly application should be restricted to promotions and transfers within the bargaining unit, and it should have no application to promotions to supervisory positions.
Seniority: establishes what is meant by seniority and how it will be utilized	Again, management may prefer not to have this. If it is to be accepted, the application of seniority should be limited to those specific items or contract clauses to which it will be applicable.
Bargaining unit work: is used to restrict performance of bargaining unit work to members of the unit	Avoid this clause if possible. If accepted, its application should be restricted, and broad exceptions for teaching, oversight, and emergencies should be included.
Discharge and discipline: is frequently used to provide a standard for discharge	Since most arbitrators will imply a "just cause" standard, agreement to such standard by management is not a major concession. Probably management should avoid a laundry list of dischargeable offenses because of the risk of omitting something that will occur. Try to avoid expunging offenses from an employee's record after a certain period of time, particularly after short periods of time. Avoid excessively complex discharge procedures.
Term of agreement: establishes the length of the contract	Management normally likes multiyear contracts, although that is a policy question in each instance. Avoid clauses that have certain parts of a contract surviving even while other parts are up for renegotiation. Avoid having to specify subjects of bargaining in a notice of reopening. It is best simply to provide for termination of the agreement on the predetermined date, subject only to a notice from either party of a desire to renegotiate any term of the agreement.

Table 50-2 Clauses in an Individual Physician Contract

Type of Clause and Purpose	Management's Objectives
Contracting parties: sets forth clearly the precise identity and nature of each party to the contract	The goals are simplicity, clarity, and accuracy.
Legal status of physician: identifies whether the physician is an independent contractor or an employee	Wants a recitation of the factors establishing whichever status has been selected.
Antimoonlighting: restricts the activity of the physician during the term of the agreement	To clearly delineate what is and is not permitted in terms of outside activities or employment during the term of the agreement.
Noncompete agreement: establishes a limitation on the right of the physician to compete with the employer after the termination of the agreement	To establish reasonable restrictions as to time, type of interest protected, and geographic scope of the protection.*
Licensure: establishes the type of licensure required of the physician	The licensure required should be as broad as conceivably necessary for the organization to carry out its objectives. If multistate admission is required, it should be designated here. Similarly, subspecialty board certification, if required, should be established here.
Hours of work and coverage: establishes a specific schedule during which the physician will be available to work	To obtain as much coverage as possible. Be certain that the language is broad enough to cover all needs or that it is alterable at the discretion of the employer.
Compensation: establishes the methods and terms of payments	Some commentators suggest there really should be two different contracts or documents covering this issue, one to establish compensation for patient care and one to establish compensation for services rendered to the hospital. In any event, management must see to it that this clause complies with the various Medicare and Medicaid and other third-party reimbursement mechanisms.
Fringe benefits: establishes various forms of insurance and deferred compensation	Aside from the obvious financial objectives, management must see to it that these provisions comply with ERISA and any other applicable statutes or regulations.
Paid time off: establishes amounts of vacation, holidays, sick leave, etc.	To establish some sort of maximums rather than leave decisions to professional discretion.
Utilization review—quality control—peer review: sets out and defines the terms of the physician's participation in these activities	To obtain understanding that physician is both subject to and must participate in these activities.
Duties and time allocation: sets forth the duties to be performed and, to the extent relevant, the method of allocating time among them	To obtain a clear understanding that the physician is required to engage in patient care, administration, research, teaching, and any other activities to be assigned by the organization. Establish methods of allocating time in order to maximize reimbursement and comply with the various reimbursement regulations.
Hospital staff membership: establishes those hospitals, if any, at which the physician will be required to obtain and retain staff privileges	This should be written to apply to those hospitals to which the physician normally will be expected to admit patients. Preferably it also will provide the opportunity for the organization to require a physician to obtain privileges at other hospitals, at its discretion.
Dispute resolution: establishes procedure for resolving disputes	On this issue a hospital may have different objectives than other health care organizations. A hospital may wish to restrict the physician to use of the procedures set out in the medical staff bylaws. Other organizations may not wish to have any sort of dispute resolution, instead leaving the matter to the civil courts. In any event, whatever is decided on as a policy matter should be set out clearly in this clause.
Professional liability insurance: establishes the mutual agreements with respect to malpractice coverage and premium payments	To be sure to comply with applicable state laws as to coverage requirements. Try to obtain some participation by the physician in the provision of his or her professional liability insurance. Such participation gives the physician a greater ownership of and interest in the insurance policy and compliance with its various requirements.
Indemnification: sets forth the extent to which the physician and the organization will share or allocate possible mutual liabilities	Management must try to obtain the maximum possible indemnification by the physician of the organization for the physician's actions.
Books and records: sets forth the right of access to the respective books and records	Obtain either certain access to the physician's own records or agree to keep those records for the physician in order that they always are under the control of the organization.

Table 50-2 continued

Type of Clause and Purpose	Management's Objectives
Complete agreement: provides that this contract constitutes the full agreement between the parties and is subject to change only by written amendment	To attempt to merge all outstanding discussions as well as any other applicable documents in order to establish which document, if any, supersedes others.
Savings clause: provides continuation of the overall contract, even in the face of a finding that one portion of it is unenforceable	This is virtually the same as the normal commercial agreement. It should be clear that the physician remains responsible for continuing to perform his or her duties, even though some portion of the contract must be changed because of operation of law.
Disability: establishes the responsibility of the parties in the case of disability of the physician	To make the responsibilities of the respective parties clear. Management may wish to insure against this potentiality.
Liquidated damages: sets out damages for breach	This clause should provide a reasonable measure of damages that can be expected to be enforced in the event of a breach by the physician. Damages that are clearly excessive may not be enforceable and so will not have the desired effect.
Ownership of books and records: sets forth the ownership rights of the organization and the physician in records kept and maintained by both	To obtain acknowledgment from the physician that the patient care records are the property of the organization and prohibit their copying or removal from the premises without specific permission.
Due payments: sets forth the various professional societies, if any, for which the organization will pay the physician's membership dues	To provide for a limit in terms of either specific organizations or total funds committed to this item.
Continuing medical education: sets forth the requirements and responsibilities of the parties for maintaining the physician's continuing medical education	To ensure at least minimal compliance by the physician with the required continuing medical education within the jurisdiction. Perhaps require something more than the minimum and establish procedures under which CME programs will be selected and the amount of time to be spent in such activities determined.
Confidentiality: sets forth the confidentiality of books, records, and other information concerning patient care	To obtain assurance from the physician regarding the maintenance of confidentiality, as well as to establish the notion that a breach of confidentiality would be a breach of the underlying agreement.
Notices: Identifies the names and addresses of parties to receive notice as required in the agreement	To place the burden on the physician to provide notification of any change in the place to which he or she desires notices to be sent.
State law: sets out the state law that will govern the agreement	In most instances there really will be no choice here, but where there is some choice and the performance of the agreement will span multiple states, management should seek to create a record that would permit the law of the most favorable or the most convenient state to apply.
Billing assignment: sets out the right of the organization to bill various third-party payers, as appropriate	To ensure compliance with Medicare and Medicaid in particular but also with any other assignment requirements.
Alternative delivery system participation: establishes the terms, if any, under which the physician can participate in various alternative delivery systems	To ensure that other systems in which physician participates are not contrary to the interests of the organization. It should retain the right to approve such participation in advance and the right to withdraw any such permission at its discretion.
Private practice: sets forth the terms, if any, under which the physician can have outside practice income	Management may wish to permit this in order to allow the physician to maximize income without additional cost to the organization. However, it should retain control and the right to require cessation of such activities at its discretion.
Facilities and services: establishes those facilities, services, and materials to be made available to the physician	To establish at least some general guidelines so that the physician is not in a position to demand a broad range of services, equipment, and facilities that the organization is not prepared to provide. This is an area that a physician seeking to sever a relationship might use as an excuse, perhaps claiming that the organization's failure to provide adequate facilities is justification for or is, in itself, a breach.
Provisions of medical services to others: establishes those to whom the physician is required to provide services	If the physician will be required to provide services to fellow employees, students, staff, or various indigent persons, it should be set out clearly in order to avoid disputes later. This clause also should establish how the physician will be compensated, if at all, for such services.

*Enforceability of these restrictive covenants depends entirely on the application of state law. The three principles enumerated above are those under which most states decide the reasonableness of a restrictive covenant. The practitioner must be aware of the law in his or her own state before drafting such a contract term.

among a potential employment contract on the one hand and hospital staff bylaws, employee handbooks, and state statutes on the other. Where multiple documents bear on the employment relationship, it is necessary to establish some order of precedence in case of future disputes.

Perhaps not surprisingly, the types of clauses one finds in individual contracts are not terribly dissimilar from those discussed earlier in relation to union contracts. Let us now turn to the types of clauses one might find in an individual physician's contract and a brief discussion of management's objectives in each instance. (See Table 50-2.)

Any list such as that set out in Table 50-2 is bound to be incomplete. Other terms and conditions may be included in physician contracts, but the ones listed, or variations on them, should cover most situations. Special problems will arise, depending on the precise nature of the health care organization contracting with physicians. No effort has been made to distinguish these types of differences.

Negotiating a contract with a physician can be both a fascinating and a frustrating experience. Perhaps the only people who think they know more about everything than lawyers are doctors (although one must concede it is a close race). As in most negotiations, it is preferable to prepare the first document and begin the negotiations from the institution's perspective. Beyond that, there appear to be no particular secrets or tricks unique to physician negotiations, with one possible exception.

That exception is the way individual physicians may be inclined to use their own attorneys. To paraphrase an old saying regarding union business agents, the only lawyers doctors dislike more than the hospital's lawyers are their own lawyers because they have to pay their own lawyers. You may find you are faced with a physician across the bargaining table who is there without benefit of counsel. After weeks of frustrating negotiations you may finally reach agreement, only to have the physician say that now he or she is going to take the document to a lawyer "just to see if there are any legal problems with it." As we all know, the lawyer will do something to earn his or her fee, and you inevitably will have the contract back with changes. Unfortunately, you already will have made the concessions you are prepared to make, and this postagreement bargaining will become difficult.

Perhaps the best solution is actually to have the physician's lawyer in negotiations from the outset. The only other way to deal with it is to advise the physician at the beginning that he or she should talk to a lawyer throughout the negotiations because you have no intention of making changes after a final understanding is reached. Then you must be prepared to follow through on how you say you will respond.

CONCLUSION

Physicians are fascinating and capable people, and negotiating contractual arrangements with them need not be unpleas-

ant. The health care organization must first decide whether it wishes to employ physicians or deal with them on an independent contractor basis. A number of issues bear on this decision. Once that decision is made and the organization has decided to employ physicians, the contract negotiator (whether dealing with a union or with an individual physician) must consider a checklist of contractual terms and must be certain to coordinate it with various other documents and statutory requirements. If all this is done with care, the result can be a fair and reasonable document that will be the basis for a good relationship between the physician and the health care organization.

NOTES

1. Joyce Ripper, "Physicians Trade Private Practice for Security," *Hospitals* 60–66.
2. "Will Rise in Salaried M.D.'s Prompt Union Growth?" *Hospitals* 62, no. 6 (20 March 1988): 93.
3. Ibid.
4. Ibid.
5. William C. Hsiao et al., "A National Study of Resource-Based Relative Value Scales for Physician Services" (Cambridge, Mass.: Department of Health Policy and Management, Harvard School of Public Health, and Department of Psychology, Harvard University, September 27, 1988).
6. Credit is due here to Norman Metzger, Edmund A. Guggenheim Professor of Health Care Management at the Mt. Sinai School of Medicine in New York City. He has been most helpful in the preparation of this chapter by providing background information and sharing the results of his considerable experience.
7. Professor Metzger reports success with this approach as well.

* * * *

ACKNOWLEDGMENT

A high school English teacher of mine once said, "If you copy from one person it is plagiarism. If you copy from many people it is research." In doing the research for this project I have read the work of many people and have looked at textbooks and casebooks, some of which are cited and some of which are not. Where I have consciously copied, I have given appropriate citations. However, each of us does work that inevitably is the sum of one's own experience and the particularly useful writings of others that one has read. In the latter category I want to acknowledge having read and reread with great interest the work of three skilled health care practitioners—Alex M. Clarke of the Omaha law firm of Baird, Holm, McEachen, Pedersen, Hamann & Strasheim; Joseph L. Hiersteiner of the Kansas City law firm of Smith Gill Fisher & Butts; and Thomas C. Shields of the Chicago law firm of Hopkins & Sutter—all of whom have written and spoken on the subject of contracting with physicians. I particularly have had the pleasure of hearing Messrs. Shields and Clarke speak at several meetings of the American Academy of Hospital Attorneys and must acknowledge use of their materials prepared for the Academy for both annual meetings and other purposes. While I have not consciously copied any of their work, a careful reader may well find some of their ideas in my work, and while they are not responsible for any of my errors, they do deserve some credit for the development of my thinking. My thanks to them.

Norman Metzger

Negotiating and Administering the Contract

51

Negotiators of collective bargaining agreements are skilled practitioners of an art that is little understood. Indeed, collective bargaining is an art, where personalities play a far more important role than any theoretical or academic format that may be suggested by numerous writers. The art of negotiating has been called a neglected one and is far more complex than the mere resolution of the terms of an agreement.[1]

Collective bargaining has been described as a poker game that combines deception, bluff, and luck; as an exercise in power politics; as a debating society marked by both rhetoric and name calling; and as a "rational process" with both sides remaining completely flexible.[2] Probably all of these characteristics at one time or another, in various combinations, are typical of collective bargaining and of negotiating any contract. The hallmarks of a successful bargaining are more complex than trite descriptions of the process. In the final analysis, the charade described above is not as critical as are the personalities involved in the bargaining, the realistic planning of strategy, and the commitment of top administration and trustees of an organization. These, then, are the hallmarks of successful bargaining.

Successful bargaining is built around and on the following cornerstones:

- advance planning of strategies with pragmatism and minimal subjectivity
- selection of a principal spokesperson who is an experienced labor relations individual and who is delegated full responsibility for presenting management's position in the bargaining
- delegation to the principal spokesperson for management of full power to bind management and to make "a deal"

LEGAL DEFINITION OF BARGAINING

Moving from the unilateral determination of policy into the arena of collective bargaining, administrations are faced with the need for a new life style. The National Labor Relations Act (NLRA) requires an employer to recognize and bargain in good faith with a certified union, but it does not force the employer to agree with the union. You may, indeed, yield to the union's persuasions, but on the other hand you may resist such yielding, provided that you have given the union an opportunity to persuade you. The Taft-Hartley Act definition of collective bargaining is pertinent to further discussion of the mutual obligations involved.

> To bargain collectively is the performance of the mutual obligation of the employer and the representative of the employees to *meet at reasonable* times and confer in good faith with respect to wages, hours and terms and conditions of employment or the negotiation of an agreement, or any question arising thereunder, and the execution of a written contract incorporating any agreement reached requested by either party, but such obligation does not compel either party to agree to a proposal or require the making of a concession.[3]

In order to participate in "good faith" bargaining, the employer must be prepared to receive the proposals of the union and meet with the union from time to time to discuss such proposals. After an election has been held and the union has been certified as the bargaining agent for a specific bargaining unit, a request to meet is most often presented in a formal letter to the institution. Management of the health care institution is then legally obligated under federal law to bargain with the union, and to bargain in good faith.

This duty, under the NLRA, to meet and negotiate with the representatives of a majority of one's employees has been interpreted over the years by National Labor Relations Board (NLRB) decisions and court decisions. You may not require, as a condition that the union must meet before you will bargain, that the union give up some rights that it possesses.[4] An express intention not to agree at the onset of negotiations violates the Act. This does not preclude hard bargaining. Such "hard bargaining" is considered bargaining in good faith. Except for an outright refusal to negotiate, bad faith is the strongest evidence of a refusal to bargain; indeed, factors indicative of bad faith of themselves frequently constitute refusals to bargain.[5] It is unlawful to insist that the collective bargaining contract be subordinated to individual contracts or to demand the right to make unilateral changes.[6] You do not fulfill your obligation to bargain by bargaining individually with employees or by offering them individual contracts when bargaining has been requested by the majority representative.[7] It is also unlawful to fail to have your representative available for conferences with the union at reasonable times and places and to fail to appoint representatives with the power to reach agreements. In rejecting union proposals you must submit counterproposals and attempt to reconcile the differences; otherwise, it is considered bad faith.[8] If an understanding is reached, it is an unfair labor practice to refuse to reduce its terms to a written agreement.[9]

The keys then to satisfying the duty to bargain in good faith are approaching the bargaining table with an open mind and negotiating in good faith with the intention of reaching final agreement. The NLRB determines the good faith nature of bargaining by the employer's *entire* conduct during the negotiations. A "take it or leave it" approach, a refusal to furnish information requested by the union during the negotiations, and an intensive communications campaign with employees during the negotiations that is designed to discredit the union are all considered unfair labor practices.[10] When a response to a union demand is made, the institution must be prepared to back up a rejection by providing relevant information to the union or agreeing to be audited.[11] The Supreme Court has held that unilateral changes during talks with the union are, in themselves, unlawful without proof of bad faith by the employer.[12]

MANDATORY BARGAINING SUBJECTS

The NLRA states that where a request for negotiation is made by a union representing a majority of employees in an appropriate unit, the employer must bargain collectively with respect to rates of pay, wages, hours, or other conditions of employment and with respect to questions arising under existing agreements.[13] The National Labor Relations Board has interpreted the term *wages* to include items of value that may accrue to employees out of their employment relationship.

These include wage rates, hours of employment, overtime, and work requirements. In addition, such mandatory items include procedures and practices relating to discharge, suspension, layoff, recall, seniority, discipline, promotion, demotion, transfer, and assignment within the bargaining unit. They also include conditions, procedures, and practices governing safety, sanitation, and protection of health in the place of employment. Indeed, vacations, holidays, leaves of absences, and sick leaves are mandatory subjects of bargaining.

The category of mandatory subjects of bargaining has developed from a long line of NLRB and court decisions. Included below are some of these subjects and references to decisions establishing their mandatory nature:

- discharge of employees (6 L.R.R.M. 674)
- seniority of grievances and working schedules (22 L.R.R.M. 2506, 28 L.R.R.M. 1015, 30 L.R.R.M. 2602)
- union security and checkoff (24 L.R.R.M. 2561, 32 L.R.R.M. 2225)
- vacations and individual merit raises (22 L.R.R.M. 2238, 31 L.R.R.M. 1072)
- retirement and pension and group insurance plans (22 L.R.R.M. 2506, 24 L.R.R.M. 2068)
- Christmas bonuses and profit-sharing retirement plans (21 L.R.R.M. 2057, 33 L.R.R.M. 2567)
- a nondiscriminatory union hiring hall (53 L.R.R.M. 1299)
- plant rules on rest or lunch period (21 L.R.R.M. 1095)
- safety rules, even though the employer may be under legal obligation to provide safe and healthful conditions of employment (66 L.R.R.M. 2501)
- institution-owned houses occupied by employees, as well as the rent paid for the houses (28 L.R.R.M. 2434, 70 L.R.R.M. 2409)
- no-strike clauses binding on all employees in the bargaining unit (22 L.R.R.M. 1158, 43 L.R.R.M. 1507)
- physical examinations employees are required to take (56 L.R.R.M. 1369)
- insurance plans, even though the employer proposed to improve the insurance programs and the expiring agreement contained no provisions concerning the plans (80 L.R.R.M. 1240)
- "most favored nation" clauses (74 L.R.R.M 1230)
- a "zipper clause" closing out bargaining during the term of the contract and making the contract the exclusive statement of the parties' rights and obligations (97 L.R.R.M. 2660)
- inplant food services and prices, even where inplant food services are managed by an independent caterer (101 L.R.R.M. 2222)
- subcontracting unit bargaining work (47 L.R.R.M. 2609, 58 L.R.R.M. 1257)

VOLUNTARY (PERMISSIVE) BARGAINING SUBJECTS

The NLRB has delineated between mandatory bargaining subjects and voluntary bargaining subjects—those that may be proposed but not insisted on as a condition to an agreement.

- a clause making the local union the exclusive bargaining agent, even though the international union was the certifying agent (42 L.R.R.M. 2034)
- a clause requiring a secret ballot vote among the employees on the employer's last offer before a strike could be called (42 L.R.R.M. 2034)
- a clause fixing the size and membership of the employer or union bargaining team (31 L.R.R.M. 2422)
- a requirement that a contract must be ratified by a secret employee ballot (38 L.R.R.M. 2574), though the method of ratification is an internal union concern (73 L.R.R.M. 2097)
- a clause providing that a contract will become void whenever more than 50 percent of the employees fail to authorize the dues checkoff (38 L.R.R.M. 2574)
- a requirement that the union post a performance bond or an indemnity bond to compensate the employer for losses caused by picketing by other unions (32 L.R.R.M. 3684, 49 L.R.R.M. 1831)
- a clause fixing terms and conditions of employment for workers hired to replace strikers (19 L.R.R.M. 1199)
- benefits for retirees (78 L.R.R.M. 2974)
- interest-arbitration clauses calling for arbitration of disputes over the terms of a new contract (93 L.R.R.M. 3055)

IMPORTANT CONSIDERATIONS THAT AFFECT THE BARGAINING MILIEU

There are many forces, external and internal, that affect the bargaining environment and, in the final analysis, affect outcomes. A seasoned negotiator will be familiar with all of these forces.

It is essential to understand not only your own personality, but also the personality of "the other." Warschaw[14] helps us identify certain styles.

- *Jungle fighters* are the most dangerous negotiators of all. They are consummate "con artists." They are win-lose negotiators. They hate to be kept waiting for an appointment; they're the drivers honking in a traffic jam, the patients pacing in the doctor's waiting room.

  Psychologist Harry Levinson told the American Psychological Association at its 1977 conference that "such abrasive personalities are probably the most single frequent cause for the failure of bright men and women in executive ranks."[15]

- The next style is that of *Dictators*. They are win-lose negotiators: they win, you lose. Warschaw says that they are gatekeepers of information: they are assertive, organized, poised, decisive, shrewd, analytical, and efficient. But they are, as well, rigid, isolated, obsessive, opinionated, demanding, self-righteous, judgmental, and intimidating. You learn only what they want you to know. They have little tolerance for mistakes. Many of them are perfectionists, making impossible demands not only of others but also of themselves. I thought it interesting that Warschaw said that they gravitate to those fields in which most people have little experience and knowledge. The field of gynecology is loaded with dictators, she says.

- The next style is that of the *Silhouettes*. Silhouettes fear intimacy of any kind. They are lose-lose negotiators. They do anything and everything to ignore conflict and to avoid exposing their feelings. They have an effective response to pressure, more effective than anger: silence.

- Then we have the *Big-Daddies* and *Big-Mamas*, who are extremely manipulative. They will help you grow, but they must be in charge of that growth. They are successful because they offer the one human commodity that is essential for growth—tender loving care. But Warschaw identifies the fact that they will do so only up to a point— the point at which their control over you is threatened. The big threat in dealing with Big-Daddies and Big-Mamas is that the strokes they offer are so comforting and the rewards so good, you'll never gain the independence you require to reach maturity.

- The next style she identifies are *Soothers*. This style loses more often than any other type of negotiator because
  1. They start off every negotiation expecting to lose.
  2. They won't tell you what they want.
  3. They seldom tell you the truth, if the truth is likely to upset you. Instead, they'll tell you what they think you want to hear.
  4. They'll pretend problems do not exist or gloss over them. They seldom return phone calls.
  5. They are overcome by anxiety during high stress negotiations.
  6. They won't say no out of fear of losing your approval.
  7. They blame themselves too quickly and make concessions too early.

The really successful negotiators are win-win negotiators. They know that negotiating is not solely a question of how much they will win, but also of how much the loss will affect the other person. They are master observers of the human condition. They know their purpose, needs, and goals as well as those of their opponents or partners. They won't humiliate you in public. They don't luxuriate in emotionalism; their regard for others is their greatest strength. They stay focused on the objective. They are risk takers, but such risks are calculated. They don't try to out-muscle a combative force; more often they try to buffer and divert it. They don't feel they need to be loved by everyone. They are objective, nonjudgmental, curious, clear, motivated, specific, sensitive, and open. These people usually wind up with more self-esteem.

The personalities involved have a critical impact on the outcome. Acknowledging this, the selection of the principal negotiator for the institution—the spokesperson— is a threshold decision. Managements often talk about union irresponsibility and about union leaders who, in exercising their "responsibilities," have a punishing effect on their members. Still another pervasive management criticism of the other side of the table is the disconnection of the union representatives from the rank-and-file employees (who are often referred to as "our" employees). It is essential that the management negotiators be fully aware of their counterparts on the union negotiating team. There should be an attempt at an "intellectual" meeting of the minds between the two principal negotiators. It is not uncommon for the tenor of the negotiations and the outcome to be positively or negatively affected by the personalities involved. Friendship is not necessary, but appreciation of the integrity of the negotiators is, indeed, critical.

The past history of management-labor relations in the institution will have a decisive effect on the bargain. It is during the term of the prior contract through the grievance and arbitration mechanism—the shop steward system, the numerous interfacings between labor relations executives and labor union leaders—that a climate is developed. This climate can affect the "trust" element so necessary in the bargaining room.

The general economic conditions and the competitive nature of the industry will be a backdrop for the bargaining of a contract. The free exchange of information on the economic pressures impacting on the institution and the new market situation in health care must be shared in advance of the bargain with the union representatives. The winds of change are blowing in the health care industry. The marketplace is changing; union membership is declining in general in the country, if not in the health care industry. One publication paints the following picture:

> It is no secret that labor unions are losing power, but that doesn't mean companies will ride roughshod over workers. In fact, a remarkable surge of new laws and court rulings are expanding employees' rights. In all, a revolution is in the making.[16]

Another factor impacting on the bargain is the experience of both parties during the life of the contract. A union that is losing members, is faced with massive layoffs, and is unable to fulfill the pressing needs of employees will be ineffective in collective bargaining. A management that is uncommunicative, unresponsive to employee grievances, and authoritarian in its management style will be faced with an uncompromising union negotiating committee.

SELECTING A NEGOTIATING TEAM

Management must make certain decisions *before* selecting the members of its negotiating team. One of the first and most important decisions relates to the character of the approach to the union at the bargaining table. Will the hospital take a hard-nosed approach? Will it attempt to contain the union at each turn? Will it attempt to discredit the union during the bargaining sessions? Will it attempt to change major provisions in the collective bargaining agreement?

The decisive factor in determining the eventual settlement is the makeup of the negotiating team. Much depends on the individual skills and judgments brought into the bargaining arena by the negotiators. Logically the major responsibility for negotiating a contract should be with the management executive who has day-to-day responsibility for labor relations. In most institutions this is the director of personnel or labor relations. Such an individual should be familiar with the composition of the bargaining unit—its longevity, wage structure, grievances, and arbitrations over prior years—and should have an understanding and appreciation of the needs of employees and the needs of the institution. Very often institutions do not employ experienced labor relations executives and, therefore, use labor attorneys to represent the institution in collective bargaining. Such attorneys are well versed in labor law and the realities of collective bargaining. The presence of an experienced labor attorney to direct, guide, and, perhaps, plan the strategy for the administrator's position at the bargaining table is truly an asset. Many institutions use both a labor relations executive or a personnel executive and a labor attorney; the latter takes the role of advisor to the principal spokesperson. In any case, it is essential for a labor attorney to review the proposed language of the contract before it is signed, whether or not he or she is the institution's chief negotiator.

Line administrators normally offer advice and ideas before the negotiations begin. Some are included as members of the negotiating team. The chief executive officer or chief operating officer of the institution does not usually serve on the negotiating committee. It is important to note that the introduction of critical demands and arguments by the union may require the management negotiating team to confer with its principals—i.e., the chief executive officer, the chief operating officer, or the chief financial officer.

It is not unusual to have a key department head on the negotiating team. However, the smaller the number of members on the negotiating team, the more effective the negotiating.

Most union negotiators are skilled practitioners of their art. They are well versed in negotiating techniques. The union negotiating team may include the president and vice-presidents of the local and employees of the institution who have been elected by their co-workers to represent them in the negotiations. This committee is often comprised of the delegates who have been elected to handle the day-to-day problems within the institution, and, therefore, the members are well versed in the grievances and arbitrations which have taken place in prior years. More often than not they are usually the institution's most outspoken and militant proponents of the union, and more often than not they were instrumental in bringing the union into the institution. Many union negotiating teams include a labor attorney, who represents the union. In most instances, the principal spokesperson for the union is the local president.

STRATEGIES FOR BARGAINING

At the outset the institution must decide on the issues that can be compromised and those that cannot be compromised. Strategy must be planned in advance, and experienced labor relations practitioners must supervise the strategic planning and actual conduct of the negotiations.

The preparation for bargaining begins long in advance of the actual face-to-face sessions. Management must gather and organize material obtained both from within the institution and from outside (from other similar institutions and other firms within the community). Such information should include

- the present wage rates operative in the institution, classification by classification
- job descriptions, when available
- the complete review of the fringe benefits program including the costs and areas amenable to savings
- the total number of employees, by classification, in the bargaining unit
- hourly schedules for each classification
- average amount of overtime by classification
- average straight time hourly wage rates
- rates of employee turnover by department
- seniority lists—number of employees with length of service in the 5-, 10-, 15- and 25-year classes
- analysis of experience as to grievances and arbitrations

It is also essential to assemble collective bargaining agreements in effect in other institutions in and out of the area, which may be used by either party to the negotiations. Most important are contracts recently negotiated by the same union. Bade and Stone provide an excellent list of "Do's" and "Don'ts":

- Strategy must be planned in advance. Do not play it entirely by ear. Clear-cut decisions must be made as to those issues that (1) cannot be compromised, (2) can be compromised and to what extent and in exchange for what, and (3) merely represent an antidote to anticipated overreaching in union demands that one recognizes will be dropped when the union does the same thing with its extreme demands. As part of the preparations, a pragmatic anticipation of union demands should be completed.
- Do not start with the hard issues and leave the easy ones for the end. It is best to set a mood for compromise. Do not emphasize technicalities and legalisms at the onset. Develop a mood that is conducive to give-and-take. (The

hallmark of successful negotiators is their understanding that for every take, there may need to be a give.)

- Do not be subtle, pedantic, threatening, or hesitant. Use the right language. Be direct, clear, *calm*, patient, and tolerant. Of course, it may be necessary to play to the bleachers; if so, do not get lost in the feigned emotion.
- Do not exaggerate or misrepresent the facts. A fact is a fact, and there is no substitute for honesty. It has been said many times that although a union might be able to get away with deception, management cannot. Management's position must always be factually defensible. It may be the one the union wants management to have, but if it is supported by facts and is rational, it is the only one that should be taken.
- When responding to the other side's positions, give reasons. A reasoned ''no'' includes the sharing of how the decision was reached.
- Do not make commitments at the table that you do not intend to keep. Do not hide behind tricky, vague, or inconclusive language. If making a commitment is not possible, do not gloss over it with murky language.
- Keep control of the negotiations. It is always best to make proposals or counterproposals the basis of future negotiations. If an issue gets too difficult, too hot to handle, put it aside for the time being.
- When there is agreement on a clause or issue, translate the agreement into actual words that both parties can agree on.
- Do not agree on anything until *everything* has been agreed on. Until the entire contract is negotiated and signed, make sure the union understands that agreement on anything should be considered tentative.
- Thinking of quid quo pro as the order of the day may well be the backbone of successful bargaining. A granting of a concession by management should be related to the granting of an equal concession by the union. Withdrawals of proposals should be mutual. If one party will not listen to the needs of the other, it should be made clear that that party's needs will not be listened to.
- The myth of ''final offers'' must be debunked. Never describe a position as the final offer *unless it is*. Never take the position that ''this is as far as management will go,'' and then go forward while the pronouncement is still clear in the minds of the union.[17]

Raiffa offers a checklist for negotiators.

- First, know yourself.
- Know your adversary.
- Give thought to the negotiating conventions in each context.
- Consider the logistics of the situation.
- Remember that simulated role playing can be of value in preparing your strategy.
- Iterate and set your aspiration levels.[18]

It is important to know whether the person across the table from you is a Jungle Fighter, a Big-Daddy, or a Big-Mama; it is well to know how they have negotiated in the past. As far as knowing yourself, the critical element here is searching for competing and substitute alternatives. The really successful negotiator is not the one who goes in with an all-or-nothing attitude. The really successful negotiator consistently thinks about alternatives and fallback positions.

Be careful of a common failure in negotiations. Max Bazerman states that when both sides start with extreme demands, expecting to compromise somewhere in the middle, they get caught up in the struggle and feel that they have too much invested to back off; thinking that this is so, they each take a hard line instead of adopting conciliatory or problem-solving approaches. Why does this happen? Bazerman says there are at least four complementary reasons.

1. Once negotiators make an initial commitment to a position, they are more likely to know the information that supports their initial evaluation of the situation.
2. Their judgment is biased to interpret what they see and hear in a way that justifies their initial position.
3. Negotiators often increase their demands or hold out too long to save face with their constituency.
4. Finally, the competitive context of the negotiations adds to the likelihood of escalation.[19]

It is important to note that negotiations rarely are strictly competitive, but the players may behave as if they were competitive; the players might consider themselves as strictly opposed disputants rather than jointly cooperative problem solvers. Raiffa points out that we really are not a zero sum society—it is not true that what one gains another must necessarily lose. The trouble is that often we act as if this were the case.[20]

Fisher and Ury, in their excellent book *Getting to Yes*, tell us that principled negotiation or negotiation on the merits can be boiled down to four basic points.

1. *People*: Separate the people from the problem.
2. *Interests*: Focus on interests, not positions.
3. *Options*: Generate a variety of possibilities before deciding what to do.
4. *Criteria*: Insist that the results be based on some objective standards.[21]

Successful negotiations spring from a working relationship of trust. William Ouchi defines trust as consisting "of the understanding that you and I share fundamentally compatible goals in the long run, that you and I desire a more effective relationship together, and that neither desires to harm the other."[22] Successful negotiations occur when the parties believe that neither desires to harm the other.

In order to be a successful negotiator, it is important that you generate a variety of possibilities before deciding what to do. In addition, you must be willing to see the situation as your opponent does. Carl Rogers tells us that when you get into the castle of another person's skin, you are liable to see things the way he or she does; and then you are liable to change. The key to successful negotiations is understanding the other party's positions, stresses, and needs. You've got to be willing to listen and alter your position. Charles Darwin said, "I have steadily endeavored to keep my mind free so as to give up any hypotheses, however much beloved, (and I cannot resist forming one on every subject), as soon as facts are shown to be opposed to it." But, on the other hand, José Ortega y Gasset told us that " it does not worry him that his 'ideas' are not true, he uses them as trenches for the defense of his existence, as scarecrows to frighten away reality."

In order to be a win-win negotiator, you cannot frighten away reality. You cannot stand with positions that are fallible in the face of facts.

It is essential that you understand—not always agree with—the other party's position. Therefore, understanding that interests motivate people, you must direct your attention to interests, not positions. You must attempt to see what motivates the other party. In *Getting to Yes*, it is suggested that if you want someone to listen and understand your reasoning, give your interests and reasoning first and your conclusions or proposals later.[23]

I have identified two typical styles that fail in negotiations. One I call the *Macho* or *Cowboy/Cowgirl* style; that is, the style practiced by negotiators who pit their strength against the other party's strength. It is the dramatic high noon confrontation. Here someone may have to give way, and it usually is a win-lose result, with a great deal of bitterness as far as the loser is concerned. A variation on this, yet still very much a part of the *Macho* approach, is the bottom line approach. A bottom line has been defined by its very nature, a rigid one, as almost certain to be too rigid. It usually is set too high and more often than not does not take into consideration possible options. The second failing style, that of the *Sycophant*, results because very often in our institutions we are forced to redefine reality. We rationalize positions and bury our creativity by submitting. Michael Maccoby describes the dilemma in the following words: "He needs to be liked and accepted by strangers in order to gain a livelihood. The danger for him is not so much that it will harden his heart but that he will lose his integrity, sense of self-esteem and values in an attempt to adapt and ingratiate, to be what others want, to become more marketable."[24] Sycophants are similar to Warschaw's *Soothers*; they expect to lose, they drown their integrity in submission, they are frightened to really state what they want.

One seventeenth-century writer defined the art of negotiations as follows:

The compleat negotiator should have a quick mind but unlimited patience, know how to dissemble without being a liar, inspire trust without trusting others, be modest but assertive, charm others without succumbing to their charms, and possess plenty of money and a beautiful wife while remaining indifferent to all temptation of riches and women.[25]

A rather sexist view. I would not subscribe to this jocular definition entirely, but I offer it as part of the legacy of the win-lose approach to negotiations. Further evidence is presented by Gerard I. Nierenberg, president of the Negotiating Institute of New York City, who describes the successful negotiator as follows:

> The successful negotiator must combine the alertness and speed of the expert swordsman with an artist's sensitivity. He must watch his adversary across the bargaining table with the keen eye of a fencer, ever ready to spot any loophole in the defense, any shift in strategy. He is prepared to thrust at the slightest opportunity. On the other hand he must also be the sensitive artist, perceptive of the slightest variation in the color of the opponent's mood or motivation. At the correct moment he must be able to select from the pallet of many colors exactly the right combination of shades, tints, that will lead to mastery. Success in negotiation, aside from adequate training, is essentially a matter of sensitivity and correct timing.[26]

A former director of the Federal Mediation and Conciliation Services, William E. Simkin, suggests 10 qualifications of the "ideal" negotiator.

> The patience of Job, the sincerity and bulldog characteristics of the English, the wit of the Irish, the physical endurance of the marathon runner, the broken field and dodging abilities of a halfback, the guile of a Machiavelli, the personality probing skills of the psychiatrist, the confidence-retaining characteristics of a mute, the hide of a rhinoceros, and the widsom of Solomon.[27]

Herb Cohen several years ago wrote the book, *You Can Negotiate Anything*, and his basic message was

> You can get what you want if you recognize that each person is unique and that needs can be reconciled. At the same time never forget that most needs can be fulfilled by the way you act and behave.[28]

Some of the best advice I have ever come across was presented by A. Samuel Cook, an attorney whom I knew from his experience with labor unions. He wrote an article called "The Neglected Act of Negotiations" for *The Daily Record* in Baltimore. His advice:

- Understand the satisfaction of needs. He refers to Maslow's hierarchy of human needs. In effect, he is directing your attention to the interests and needs of the other party.
- Preparedness is crucial. You cannot "wing it" and expect to win. Preparation requires, first of all, an intimate knowledge of oneself. Patience is essential. Theodore Voorhees tells us of an occasion when Walter Reuther, the famous union leader of U.A.W., was asked the same question 15 times. He never gave a sign of irritation and answered the question as carefully and as patiently on the fifteenth time as on the first.[29]

- Technical and economic research is essential. If you are bargaining over staffing levels, over your salary, over the salaries of the people who work for you, you should know as much as possible about the marketplace, the economic conditions at your institution, and what the parameters of the economic settlement should encompass.
- The versatile negotiator must learn the art of listening. I believe this is the real key to a win-win negotiator.
- The successful negotiator has the power of persuasion. This includes honest debate, exchange of facts, and arguments seriously considered by both sides with subsequent movement and compromise.[30]

Let me go back to Theodore Voorhees, a distinguished member of the Philadelphia bar, who gave some suggestions for successful negotiations.

- Never go into a negotiating session without advance preparation.
- A skilled and well-prepared opponent comes to the meeting with his or her arguments all lined up, and his or her thrusts may unseat you. You may feel like an ignoramus if you do not respond in some fashion. You may find yourself in a win-lose situation at the losing end of the deal.
- Candor and sincerity are the most powerful weapons of the good negotiator. As soon as the individual you are negotiating with understands that she or he is dealing with a person of integrity, the discussions can proceed with directness, and the time wasted in beating around the bush may be eliminated.
- You should stake out the ground to be covered in the area in which agreement is to be reached. Be practical. Don't set up rigid bottom lines for results.
- In some instances it may be well to delineate at the earliest stage certain basic areas for which no agreement is possible. But remember that an exchange of views can lead to a change in your position.
- The good negotiator takes the initiative, states his or her position, and presents the justification for that position and the arguments that may persuade the other side to accept it. The presentation of your position must be handled delicately. Success will be impeded by your unnecessarily antagonizing the opponent. Win-win is the objective, not win-lose.
- Patience should be preserved at all times. Control of one's temper and constant courtesy are to be recommended.[31]

Let me share with you a most profound code of conduct for negotiators who believe in win-win. This code of conduct, enunciated by Milton Wessel in his book *The Rule of Reason*, has the following salient points:

- Data will not be withheld because they may be "negative" or "unhelpful."
- Concealment will not be practiced for concealment's sake.
- Delay will not be employed as a tactic to avoid an undesired result.
- Unfair "tricks" designed to mislead will not be employed to win a struggle.
- Borderline ethical disingenuity will not be practiced.
- Motivation of adversaries will not unnecessarily or lightly be impugned.
- An opponent's personal habits and characteristics will not be questioned unless relevant.
- Wherever possible, opportunity will be left for an opponent's orderly retreat and "exit with honor."
- Extremism may be countered forcefully and with emotionalism where justified, but will not be fought or matched with extremism.
- Dogmatism will be avoided.
- Complex concepts will be simplified as much as possible so as to achieve maximum communication and lay understanding.
- Effort will be made to identify and isolate subjective considerations involved in reaching a technical conclusion.
- Relevant data will be disclosed when ready for analysis and peer review—even to an extremist opposition and without legal obligation.
- Socially desirable professional disclosure will not be postponed for tactical advantage.
- Hypothesis, uncertainty, and inadequate knowledge will be stated affirmatively—not conceded only reluctantly or under pressure.
- Unjustified assumption and off-the-cuff comment will be avoided.
- Interest in an outcome, relationship to a proponent, and bias, prejudice, and proclivity of any kind will be disclosed voluntarily and as a matter of course.
- Research and investigation will be conducted appropriate to the problem involved. Although the precise extent of that effort will vary with the nature of the issues, it will be consistent with stated overall responsibility to the solution of the problem.
- Integrity will always be given first priority.[32]

It is clear to me that the concept of win-lose, that so preoccupies most individuals who are involved in negotiations of any sort, is counterproductive. We are preoccupied with winning; in almost every aspect of life people want to be winners. The real measure of successful negotiations is when both parties come out thinking they have won. Indeed, negotiations are really a cooperative endeavor. Your focus must be on the converging of interests, the satisfaction of needs of both parties, and an approach that maintains the dignity of both parties. The goal, therefore, is to come up with an arrangement—nothing less than that; an arrangement that satisfies the needs of the parties. I do not want to take a simplistic view that all negotiations concern themselves with a give-and-take, trading, and, in the final analysis, splitting the difference.

Fred E. Jandt, in his book *Win-Win Negotiating*, states it eloquently:

> Positional bargainers articulate certain demands (their "positions") and they measure their success in terms of those demands to which their opposites accede. In positional bargaining, either I win or you win; either the majority of your "positions" prevail, or the majority of mine do.[33]

This is a destructive view. It clearly defines success in bargaining by making the position itself more important than the ultimate objective. Never get mired down into positions. Keep your eye on a point where you and the other party arrive at a mutually beneficial deal. There is an opportunity in sound negotiations to explore mutual problems. Therefore, what some practitioners call *interest bargaining* is the form that I recommend to you. It takes into account the full range of the parties' interests, and, therefore, one negotiates problems rather than demands. Jandt once again comes up with a sound observation.

> Practitioners of interest bargaining investigate the *real*— as opposed to the stated—desires of the opponents. [They] then seek ways to satisfy their opponents' desires—by among other approaches, offering desiderata that they themselves control in exchange for desiderata that their opponents control. ["Desiderata" is defined as "Things lacking but needed or desired."][34]

The key here is to make certain that you and the other party understand any hidden agenda.

There is a phenomenon that I have noted, which I call the *end-game ploy*—in which a "hail fellow well met" aura lulls you into a sense of receptivity directed toward closing the negotiations. Negotiations often are distasteful and tiring. An individual across the table from you may chip away at you near the end. It has also been described by John Illiche in his book *Power Negotiating*. He calls it the "It's-a-Shame-to" technique as in, "Look. We resolved three or four most important issues. *It's a shame to* make that much pressure without resolving the remaining issues. . . . *It's a shame to* give up without giving it a sincere try."[35] What Illiche and I are discussing is the need to keep your eye on closing the deal. You should clearly know when "enough is enough." Or when the negotiations need a "time out."

Two particular salient characteristics of the successful negotiator are the ability to identify alternatives and patience. There is no question that patience is a hallmark of the experienced negotiator. In his book *Give and Take*, Chester Karrass, director of the Center for Effective Negotiating in Los Angeles, writes

> Patience gives an opponent and his organization time to get used to the idea that what they wish for must be reconciled with what they can get. . . . [It gives (opposers) time] to find out how best to benefit each other. Before a negotiation begins it is not possible for either to know the best way to resolve problems, issues, and risks. New alternatives are discovered as information is brought to light.[36]

Beware being in a hurry to close the deal. And beware your opponent's rush to closure. The erosion of patience plays an important role in the end-game ploy. Arbitrary deadlines are usually counterproductive. "Final offers" are usually followed by other offers. Both the arbitrary deadline and the final offer are often a sign of impatience.

The exploration of alternative positions *before* the bargaining begins is a critical and worthwhile investment. A key element in preparing your negotiating positions is an exploration of the possibility of the "nonagreement." You must come to grips with a realistic evaluation of whether *the* agreement is better than *no* agreement; you must understand what the ramifications of "no agreement" are. By exploring alternatives—no matter how unpleasant that exercise might be—one must come to understand that the agreement must satisfy not only your self-interests but the self-interests of the other as well. One-sided solutions can have a worse effect than no solution. What I urge you to do in negotiations is to broaden your options. Look for mutual solutions, and remember that the party is not over when you have made the deal. Remember that stressing shared interests will facilitate agreement. I do not suggest that you lower your expectations. In fact, one of the cornerstones for successful bargaining is a need for pragmatism and minimal subjectivity. You need to set high targets. But there is an inherent risk in aspiring to more in order to get more—"non-agreement!" Effective bargaining requires a flexibility of approach.

Let me add some caveats—or better call them Do's and Do Not's—which may be helpful and which come from my exposure to top-flight negotiators as well as my own negotiation experiences:

- Do not think of negotiations as a Roman gladiator's battle, as a test of strength.
- Preconceived notions of the other party's responses, which bring you into the bargaining with a chip on your shoulder, are to be discouraged.
- Prepare! Prepare! Prepare! Make the hard choices of positions and a realistic analysis of interests before you start.
- Success in negotiating involves an informed awareness and understanding of the compulsions that are operating on the other party. Keep your eye on the "why" of the other party's position.
- Assumptions as to your opponent's understanding of what he or she can gain in a settlement are not to be made lightly.
- Do not make the fatal error of underestimating your opponent.
- Personal integrity and courage are the pervasive traits of successful bargainers.
- Talk less. Listen more.

Once again, let me return to the personalities involved in the negotiating process. Cornelius J. Peck has written on the psychodynamics of the negotiating process. It is strongly suggested that an intuitive understanding of the process of negotiations is probably one of the most valuable traits of the successful negotiator. The significance of understanding personality types involved in a particular negotiation cannot be overestimated. As important is the appreciation of the importance of "being one's real self" in negotiating situations. If you attempt to be someone other than whom you really are, then you will be unlikely to succeed. The reason is clear. You have to rehearse the new role and are likely to make mistakes, and, indeed, the falseness of your adopted position will be clear to the other in the negotiations.

But let us return to the *other* in the negotiations, to the typical personalities that you must recognize and appreciate if you are to succeed in negotiations. An exploration of personality traits, which Peck brought to our attention, is an important element in successful negotiations.

- *Transference*. This is when you attribute to the other in the negotiations value judgments and motivations based not on what you have observed or heard, but on what you are reminded of from other experiences with other people—whose characteristics you attributed to the other. This can be either a positive view of the other or a negative view. If it is a positive view, you tend to be sympathetic to the other's position and are often susceptible to unnecessary concessions or compromises. If it is a negative view, you tend to be defensive or overly aggressive. Transference can result in a feeling that the other is incomplete, unreal, or mechanical. It is, therefore, essential to guard against transference by engaging in introspective evaluation and careful analysis of the real person across the table.
- *Nonverbal communications*. The nonverbal communications of the *other* may be the most important indicator of the ability to gain agreement. An observant negotiator will attempt to understand the signals coming from the person across the table. What was the cause of the obvious indicators of attention? Should you discontinue the negotiations or hasten a conclusion? Such signals include the level of the voice, nervous laughter, giggles, hand gestures, clenched fists, and jabbing motions of the

fingers. Peck reminds us that the person who is confident of her or his position in the negotiations will be willing to sit at the table or desk, whereas the person who is dissatisfied with the current posture of negotiations will be inclined to manifest his or her desire for a change by moving in his or her chair, or even by moving around the room. Eye contact is most important in understanding the body language of negotiations. Looking sidewise and not making eye contact may indicate a lack of confidence in either the accuracy of one's statement or the power of one's position. Lack of confidence may also be displayed by partially covering one's mouth with one's hand while speaking. The positioning of arms and legs often indicates tension, concern, frustration, or openness. I have learned over the years that facing an individual in a chair that is unencumbered by a desk is a sign of openness. I keep my roll-top desk against the wall and put nothing between me and the individual to whom I am talking. If someone I am negotiating with insists on standing up, I will stand up. The successful negotiator watches the physical movements of the other for indications that, more often, are more accurate than the spoken word— physical movements that reflect the other's position and willingness to reach agreement. They are not infallible but cannot be ignored. You must, if you are to become an experienced negotiator, learn which of the nonverbal communications you can trust.

- *Uncertainty, ambiguity, silence, and delay.* The art of negotiating is not for those who have a low threshold for frustration and limited patience. A successful negotiator lives with uncertainty and often sets up conditions of uncertainty so that the other, in the hopes of eliminating such uncertainty, will come to agreement. The use of silence is a profound mechanism in negotiations. Most people cannot tolerate long periods of silence while in the company of others. If you can remain silent, you force the other to speak, to give information, and, more often than not, to look for ways to bring you back into the discussion—possibly by altering a position. Often ambiguity is used by skilled negotiators. I do not recommend it.

- *Sex in negotiations.* It may be that persons prefer to negotiate with members of their own sex, but this is certainly neither possible nor defensible. Peck, from observations, reports that women believe men are more likely to lie in negotiations than women are—he attributes this to the traditional romantic male pursuit of a woman. Best leave this subject by presenting one bit of advice, and that is to carefully evaluate the role of sex in the negotiating process. If the other is a man, does the fact that you are a woman lessen your position? Are sexual stereotypes present in the exchange? Do you bring sexual stereotypes into the room?[37]

The successful negotiator understands the personality across the table from him or her. It is desirable to know in advance the expectations, priorities, and limits established by the other.

DEALING WITH THE POSSIBILITY OF A STRIKE

An important part of planning the strategy for negotiations is making a clear, objective estimate of strike issues. Are there issues that are likely to be critical for the union, thus becoming instigators for a strike? By identifying such issues, the institution need not change its position. Reality-based negotiations are productive ones.

It is essential to forecast the impact of a possible strike. In any industry strikes put economic pressure on both parties: the workers lose wages while the employers lose revenue. The key to a successful strike from a union's viewpoint is to inflict inordinate discomfort, expense, and pressure on the employer so as to effect a compromise or a move toward the union's position. An institution must carefully evaluate the discomfort, the expense, and the pressure it will have to withstand if it is to take a strike. The real losers in strikes of health care institutions are the patients, their families, and prospective patients. The patients may well be deprived of services; they may need to be moved from a struck hospital or nursing home; they may be discharged earlier than they should be. Prospective patients will be troubled by the limited beds available, operations will be delayed, and outpatient care will be discontinued. It is well to state at the onset of discussions of the impact of a strike that such action at a health care facility is the most severe form of labor-management dispute.

Then there are, in any discussion of the impact of a strike, critical factors: the ability of the health care institution to withstand the strike and its willingness to take a strike. There are critical indicators that must be evaluated when estimating the impact of a strike in a health care institution.

- What effect will it have on revenue? Will lost revenue be recoverable in the poststrike period?
- How long will a strike be acceptable? Is there a critical point at which pressure on the institution will be unbearable?
- What support will be available to the institution to make up for the employees who are withholding their services—supervisors, nonbargaining unit employees, temporaries, bargaining unit employees who will cross the picket line?
- Can you replace strikers? A decision must be made as to the policy of replacing the economic strikers with permanent new hires.
- Will striking employees be able to augment or replace their lost income by finding temporary employment elsewhere?
- What is the union's policy on strike benefits?

- What is the hospital's policy on discontinuing benefits coverage for strikers? Health benefits may be covered under a union plan or under the institution's own plan.
- What outside forces may be brought to bear on the institution to avoid or settle a strike?

One of the other considerations is the use of employees from nonstruck hospitals. The ally doctrine is a legal doctrine developed from National Labor Relations Board case law. It defines the rights of third parties who provide assistance to the employer involved in a labor dispute. This doctrine affects a secondary employer who, during the course of a labor dispute, performs work that would have been performed by striking employees of the primary employer. In doing such work the secondary employer loses neutral status and, therefore, is subject to the labor organization involved in the dispute, thus extending its economic activity to the secondary employer. As the reports of both houses of Congress in the deliberation regarding the Taft-Hartley health care amendments stated,

> It is the sense of the Committee that where such secondary institutions *accept the patients of the primary employer*, or otherwise provide life sustaining services to the primary employer, by *providing the primary employer with an employee or employees who possess critical skills such as EKG technicians*, such conflict shall not be sufficient to cause the secondary employer to lose its neutral status [38]

In effect, Congress intended to permit a neutral hospital to accept patients of a primary employer and not lose its status as a neutral as a result. Such a neutral hospital would, however, lose its status if it supplied *noncritical* personnel to a hospital that was experiencing a strike, or if it not only accepted patients from such a hospital but also greatly expanded its noncritical staff in the process. Gradually, the NLRB's exception to the ally doctrine for the health care industry has become dependent on the *urgency* of the medical needs of the patients who were transferred from the primary hospital to the neutral hospital.[39]

THE 1974 AMENDMENTS TO THE NLRA

The 1947 Taft-Hartley Act excluded from the definition of *employer* private, not-for-profit hospitals and health care institutions. The NLRB asserted jurisdiction over proprietary hospitals and nursing homes, but it was not until the 1974 Amendments that Congress, through Public Law 93-360, brought the private, not-for-profit health industry within the jurisdiction of federal labor law. The 1974 Amendments enacted the following changes:

- The exemption contained in Section 2(2) that excluded not-for-profit hospitals from the definition of *employer* was removed.

- A new Section 2(14) was added to define the term *health care institution*. It included any "hospital, convalescent hospital, health maintenance organization, health clinic, nursing home, extended care facility or other institutions devoted to the care of sick, infirm or aged persons." This definition is essential in the determination of which employees would thereafter fall under the special health care provisions and within the scope of the act.
- A new series of special notices applicable to the health care industry and unions representing employees in that industry were enacted. The Section 8(d) notice period for notices of disputes, which by law must be given by one party to the other, was extended from the normal 60 days prior to contract expiration to 90 days, and the period for notices filed with the Federal Mediation and Conciliation Service (FMCS) was extended from the normal 30 days to 60 days.
- A new Subsection 8(g) was added. It requires that a union representing employees in a health care institution give 10 days' written notice to the employer and to the Federal Mediation and Conciliation Service (FMCS) of its intent to engage in a strike, picketing, or other concerted refusal to work.
- Broader sanctions under Section 8(d) of the act provide that employees represented by labor organizations that do not comply with the requirements of the 90- and 60-day dispute notices or with Section 8(g), Strike Notices, would lose their protected status under the act.
- Mandatory mediation of disputes in the health care industry was provided under Section 8(d). The FMCS must mediate health care disputes, and the parties involved in such disputes are compelled to participate in that mediation process. It is an unfair labor practice for a party to refuse to participate in such mediation.
- Section 213, the second special dispute resolution provision, provides that when disputes threaten substantial interruptions of delivery of health care in a community, the director of FMCS may appoint a special board of inquiry to investigate the issues in the dispute and to issue publicly a written report on the dispute.
- A new Section 19 provides for an alternative to the payment of union dues by persons with religious convictions against making such payments. It allows contribution to designated 501(c)(3) charities in lieu of dues.[40]

In an interpretation by the Office of the General Counsel of the NLRB, the following guidelines have been established regarding Section 8(g) notices:

- The notice should be served on someone designated to receive such notice, or through whom the institution will actually be notified.
- The notice should be personally delivered or sent by mail or telegram.

- The 10-day period begins on receipt by the employer and the FMCS of the notice.
- The notice should specify the dates and times of the strike and picketing, if both are being considered.
- The notice should indicate which units will be involved in the planned action.[41]

As with Section 8(d) notices, workers engaged in a work stoppage in violation of the 10-day strike notice lose their status as employees. The NLRB will probably interpret violations of the Section 8(g) notice requirement as a separate and distinct unfair labor practice.

In considering the 1974 Amendments to the NLRA, the congressional committee included the Section 8(g) 10-day strike and picket notice to provide health care institutions with sufficient advance notice of a strike. The committee realized, however, that it would be unreasonable to expect a labor organization to commence a job action at the precise time specified in a notice provided to the employer. On the other hand, if a labor organization failed to act within a reasonable period after the time specified in the notice, such action would not be in accordance with the intent of the provision. Therefore, the committee report of the Amendments provided that

> it would be unreasonable, in the committee's judgment, if a strike or picketing commenced more than 72 hours after the time specified in the notice. In addition, since the purpose of the notice was to give a health care institution advance notice of the actual commencement of a strike or picketing, if a labor organization does not strike at the time specified in the notice, at least 12 hours' notice should be given of the actual time for commencing of the action.[42]

Thus, absent unusual circumstances, a union would violate Section 8(g) if it struck a facility more than 72 hours after the designated notice time, unless the parties agreed to a new time or the union gave a new 10-day notice. Additionally, if the union did not start the job action at the designated time as provided in the initial 10-day notice, it would be required to provide the health care facility at least 12 hours' notice prior to actual commencement of the action. The 12-hour warning must fall totally within the 72-hour notice period.

The committee report notes that "repeatedly serving ten-day notices upon the employer is to be construed as constituting evidence of a refusal to bargain in good faith by a labor organization"[43]—i.e., a violation of Section 8(b)(3). What constitutes "repeatedly serving notice" will have to be defined and interpreted by the NLRB in individual cases. In a memorandum, the Board's General Counsel provided the following guidelines to regional offices regarding the handling of intermittent strikes or picketing situations:

- Where the facts and circumstances of the labor organization strike or picketing hiatus support the reasonable conclusion that the activity has not indefinitely ceased and that it is reasonable to assume that it will commence again, no new notice will be required if the activity recommences within 72 hours of the start of the hiatus; but 12 hours' notice to the institution will be required if the activity is to recommence more than 72 hours from the start of the hiatus.
- Where the facts and circumstances of the hiatus support the reasonable conclusion that the activity has ceased indefinitely and that it will not be resumed in the near future, 12 hours' notice to the institution will be required if the activity is to resume within 72 hours of the start of the hiatus, but a new 10-day notice meeting all the requirements of Section 8(g) will be required if the activity is to resume more than 72 hours from the start of this hiatus.[44]

Exceptions to the requirement that labor organizations provide Section 8(g) notices are indicated in two situations. First, if the employer has committed serious or flagrant unfair labor practices, notice would not be required before the initiation of the job action. Second, the employer is not allowed to use the 10-day notice period to "undermine the bargaining relationship that would otherwise exist." The facility would be free to receive supplies, but it would not be "free to stock up on the ordinary supplies for an unduly extended period" or to "bring in large numbers of supervisory help, nurses, staff and other personnel from other facilities for replacement purposes." The committee reports held that employer violation of the above principles would release the union from its obligation not to engage in a job action during the Section 8(g) notice period.[45]

KEY CONTRACT CLAUSES

Among the many clauses that will be included in a collective bargaining agreement with the union, four have specific interest to any practitioner (for a full list of clauses, see Appendix 51-A). These clauses are

1. union security
2. management rights
3. seniority
4. no-strike

Union Security

Once a union has been certified as the collective bargaining agent for the employees in a hospital, one of that union's primary aims is to get a contractual provision that gives it maximum protection as to its continued existence in that hospital. It, therefore, attempts to bargain some form of compulsory union membership. There are six forms of union security that we will define: an open shop, a maintenance of membership shop, a union shop, a modified union shop, a closed shop, and an agency shop.

The *open shop* offers maximum choice to employees in the bargaining unit. Such employees can join or not join the union and can remain in the union or drop out of the union without losing their jobs.

In the *maintenance of membership shop*, members of the bargaining unit are not required to become members of the union to keep their jobs, but those employees who do decide to join the union must maintain their membership in the union for a specific length of time: either for one year or for the duration of the contract. An escape clause is often included in such a union security arrangement. It clarifies the times at which union members may drop out of the union without losing their jobs. The following is a typical maintenance of membership clause:

> Any employee who is a member in good standing of the union at the end of thirty (30) days from the date the provision becomes effective or who thereafter joins the union during the term of this agreement shall remain a member of the union in good standing as a condition of employment with the hospital.

Another form of union security is the *union shop*. It is found in the majority of collective bargaining agreements and provides that all employees in the bargaining unit must join the union within a specified period of time after hire, usually at the end of a probationary period. In addition, these employees must remain members in good standing during their employment in the hospital. A sample union shop provision follows:

> All employees on the active payroll at the time of the signing of the contract who are members of the union shall maintain their membership in the union in good standing as a condition of continued employment. All employees on the active payroll as of the time of the signing of the contract who are not members of the union shall become members of the union within thirty (30) days after the effective date of the contract. All employees hired after the effective date of the contract shall become members of the union no later than the thirtieth day following the beginning of such employment and shall thereafter maintain their membership in the union in good standing as a condition of continued employment.

A *modified union shop* provides an option to employees presently on the payroll. Those who are members of the union must maintain their membership, but those who have not joined the union need not join. As to new employees, they must join the union within a specified period of time after hire, again usually after the probationary period. This form of union security is a compromise which protects present employees who do not wish to join the union. The movement from a modified union shop is sometimes affected by a clause that states that after a certain percentage of employees have joined the union, all those remaining out must join the union.

The *closed shop* (which was largely outlawed by the Labor-Management Relations Act of 1947, but is permissible under certain state laws for hospitals that are so covered) requires applicants for employment to be members of the union before they can be hired. This form of union security is usually accompanied by union hiring hall provision. The union is notified of employment needs, and it sends applicants to fill the jobs. A sample closed shop clause follows:

> The hospital shall hire only applicants for employment who are members of the union. The union shall furnish such applicants for employment provided that, however, if the union is unable to fill such request, the hospital may hire applicants who are not members of the union, but such applicants must become members of the union immediately upon being hired.

The *agency shop* was a comparatively rare form of union security which had a rebirth as a counterposition of unions to right-to-work laws (operative in several states). These laws outlawed mandatory or compulsory union membership. Here, the employee can join or not join the union and remain a member or drop out, but all employees in the bargaining unit serviced and represented by the union as a condition of employment must pay a service fee to support the union.

In all forms of union security, whether they only partially or totally compel employees of the bargaining unit to join the union, such employees are covered by all conditions of the contract if they are indeed part of the bargaining unit. If the employees are given the option to remain out of the union, they are nonetheless covered by all provisions of the collective bargaining agreement, including the grievance procedure; however, they may not attend meetings, and they may not vote on union issues.

Labor leaders argue in favor of compulsory union membership, and their principle argument revolves around the so-called "free rider" inequity. The "free rider" is a worker who refuses to join the union and is permitted to maintain this position based on a union security clause. This worker, the labor leaders argue, reaps all the advantages hard won by the union in its negotiations with the hospital. The union leaders maintain that the philosophy of compulsory union membership is rooted in a basic democratic principle: the rule of the majority. It is their position that given free choice, the employees will join the union, but they usually remain out due to fear of reprisal or promise of reward on the part of the employer. Management defends its position for optional membership on the basis of the inherent right of the individual to make choices and withhold his/her membership from any organization. Actually there are some advantages to management to agree to a compulsory union security provision. Too often when the employees are given an option to join or not join the union, only the most militant and outspoken critics of management join the union, and their views are not modified by those of more conservative employees. In addition, in a modified union security arrangement, the union continues its drive to enroll employees, often undertaking this activity during the normal workday and throughout the year.

Management Rights

Management and labor have usually agreed that any rights not restricted by the collective bargaining agreement reside in management. The question whether management rights clauses should be expressly included in a contract has been hotly debated over the years. Most managements feel that the right to manage the business or administer the hospital is solely theirs. *But it should be clear that when the administration enters into a collective bargaining agreement with a union, it no longer has the sole authority to administer the hospital.* There are limitations clearly outlined in each of the the contract clauses.

The Supreme Court has ruled that management prerogatives could be exercised only in the cases "over which the contract gives management complete control and unfettered discretion." The Court's decision points out that management retains only those rights specifically outlined in the labor agreement.[46] Almost three-quarters of all collective bargaining agreements contain a managment rights clause. For years, many practitioners presumed that the employer could exercise the right to manage the enterprise and that such a clause was unnecessary. They further warned that in an effort to construct a management rights clause that would outline those rights reserved for management, it was impossible to anticipate all the contingencies that should be included. In supporting their position against the inclusion of the management rights clause, some practitioners felt that in negotiating such a clause, which was indeed the prerogative of management in any case, they would have to grant certain concessions to the union in exchange for what they had obtained. Yet the majority of labor negotiators were convinced by the arguments for inclusion. They felt that the institution needs as much protection as it can get and that the clause outlining management prerogatives is most helpful in adjudicating day-to-day grievances. The battle over the pros and cons for inclusion or exclusion of a managment rights clause in a collective bargaining agreement has become an academic one in light of the decisions of the Supreme Court.

The collective bargaining agreement does indeed limit management's action in those cases outlined in each of its clauses. Management does well to define those areas in which the union waives its rights because most arbitration awards and court decisions have indicated that any management decision or action that affects the employment relationship should be discussed with the union representing the employees unless clearly reserved to management. If management wishes to retain its freedom to act in specific areas without recourse to the grievance and arbitration procedure, then the management rights clause is the proper place to define those areas.

There are two major categories of management rights clauses. One is a brief general clause dealing not with specific rights, but with the principle of management rights in general. The other is a detailed clause that clearly lists areas of authority that are reserved to the management. The key areas of authority that would be included in such a clause are the rights to

- manage and administer the hospital and direct the work force
- hire, discipline, and transfer
- introduce new or improved methods or facilities
- promulgate rules of conduct
- set quality standards
- discontinue jobs
- decide employee qualifications
- subcontract work

An example of a brief encompassing clause follows:

The management of the hospital and the direction of the work forces are vested exclusively with the administration, subject only to the restrictions and regulations governing the exercise of such rights as are expressly provided for in this contract.

Seniority

One of the most important clauses in the collective bargaining agreement, and one which often cuts deepest into management prerogatives, is the seniority provision. The principle of seniority should no longer be at issue between management and the union. Unilateral interpretation and application of seniority, on the part of management, are no longer possible. Seniority simply is that principle under which the employee with the longest service is given preference in such areas as promotions, transfers, layoffs, rehirings, choice of shifts, and choice of vacation periods. Unions tend to seek straight seniority, recognizing no factor other than period of service in gaining preference. To them, strict seniority means job security and is the basic protection against possible biases or acts of favoritism on the part of the administration. They maintain that with the application of strict seniority measures, a more stable, experienced, efficient, and loyal work force will develop. Of course, the administration argues that operating efficiency requires compromise on the position of straight seniority. They would place more emphasis on merit and ability. In its earliest application, the National Railroad Adjustment Board held that seniority is a personal right and "the keystone upon which many rights of individuals under collective bargaining agreements are based."[47]

The right to preference on the basis of seniority exists only by virtue of contractual clauses contained in the collective bargaining agreement. There are two main areas for hospital negotiators to focus on when bargaining a seniority provision. They are the role of ability as it modifies the strict application of seniority and the definition of the seniority unit. The first area has dramatic implications in instances of promotions, layoffs, and rehires. Many agreements provide for a qualifying clause, either the seniority plus ability test or the relative ability test. The *seniority plus ability test* provides preference in promotions or other job rights on the basis of seniority, but the most senior employee must be able to do the work involved: just being able to do the job—not necessarily better than other employees—will suffice under this provision. The *relative ability test* provides for a comparison of the abilities and skills of those employees claiming rights to a job on the basis of seniority. Here, in instances of layoffs, recalls, promotions, or demotions, ability and seniority will be considered, and where ability is relatively equal, seniority will be the governing factor. If ability is not relatively equal, then the more able employee will be granted preference.

The definition of the seniority unit is key to the application of the provisions of the seniority system. The broader the unit is, the more difficult it is for the administration to maintain its control over the efficient operation of the hospital. The narrower the unit is, the more strict the limitation is on the exercise of an employee's seniority rights. Where there is a wide variation in skill requirement for jobs (such as is evident in a hospital), it is more practical to negotiate a departmental or occupational unit. Under departmental seniority, seniority is applied within the employee's specific department. Because that unit is smaller and contains many interchangeable jobs, the advantages are obvious. Departmental seniority sets up separate seniority units for each department.

The most efficient seniority unit for a hospital is the occupational seniority unit. Occupational seniority sets up separate units for employees performing the same type of job. This is far more practical where departments contain a broad spectrum of occupations that are not interchangeable. Hospital unions will usually agree to a compromise between the limited occupational seniority unit and the broader departmental system. This approach is sometimes called *noninterchangeable occupation groups*. After defining the occupational groups in which seniority may be applied, the groups are broadened to include occupations that are clearly interchangeable and, therefore, should form one occupational family.

No-Strike and No-Lockout Clauses

A no-strike clause is probably one of the most important provisions of the agreement for the hospital. It is the administration's assurance of peaceful and uninterrupted operations during the life of the contract. No-strike clauses fall into two categories: unconditional clauses and conditional or contingent clauses. An *unconditional no-strike clause* elicits a firm pledge from the union and its rank-and-file members that they will under no circumstances be involved in a work stoppage or slowdown during the life of the agreement. A *conditional or contingent no-strike clause* prohibits stoppages or slowdowns until certain clearly defined conditions have been met such as (1) the exhausting of the grievance procedure, including arbitration, and (2) the refusal of either party to abide by the decision of an arbitrator. These clauses often provide that strikes or slowdowns are prohibited in matters subject to arbitration and that the union must take certain positive action against any unauthorized (wildcat) strikes if it

is to avoid any liability. Such actions may include informing its members in writing that they must return to work, posting notices on union bulletin boards, or taking ads in local newspapers stating that the strike is unauthorized and that workers should return to work. A union that calls workers out in violation of a no-strike pledge in a contract may be sued for damages that the employer suffers as a result. Nearly all no-strike clauses in collective bargaining agreements contain a quid pro quo for the union, a comparable ban against lockouts by the company.

ADMINISTERING THE CONTRACT

Once a collective bargaining agreement is completed and negotiations are concluded, breathing life into the agreement is a key responsibility of the parties. This includes the disciplinary, grievance, and arbitration procedures.

Discipline

The collective bargaining agreement imposes on the administration limitations in the disciplinary powers that it may exercise. Any limitations of a management right may be counterproductive to the primary goal of establishing an efficient work force. To minimize such limitations, an effective and constructive approach to discipline must be designed and implemented. The limitations imposed on management's right to discipline do not, in themselves, remove from management the right to impose discipline on its employees. The key point about such limitations is that management *may* discipline up through discharge only for sufficient and appropriate reasons. This requires the development of a sound procedure based on due process for disciplining unionized employees. The right to discharge, suspend, or discipline is clearly enunciated in contractual clauses and in the adoption of rules and procedures that may or may not be incorporated in the collective bargaining agreement.

The union's role in the disciplinary process is to vigorously defend the employee in the face of what could be considered unfair management actions. Employees expect the union to come to their assistance. It is the heart of the disciplinary process to ascertain the propriety of the management action. The best way to judge the propriety of a management action in a disciplinary case is to "program" the case to its ultimate conclusion in arbitration. Arbitrators will normally support a management action if they find progressive discipline, which includes verbal reprimands and a full explanation of what is necessary to remedy the situation, followed by a written reprimand for a second infraction with a clear warning of the future penalties that may be imposed. Suspensions may precede the final disciplinary action of termination. In essence, the review of the disciplinary action, which terminates in arbitration, should be directed to ascertaining whether the employee was fully aware of the standards against which his or her behavior was to be measured. These standards include basic rules and regulations that outline offenses that will subject employees to disciplinary action and the extent of such disciplinary action. The question that is critical in all disciplinary actions is this: Is there sufficient reason for such action? Frequently supervisors find themselves on the defensive after having administered discipline, and often have such action overturned due to insufficient evidence and improper remedies, which do not fit into the concept of progressive disciplining. To the arbitrator, discharge is economic death; therefore, the burden of proof lies with management that such action was the only proper avenue of recourse.

Discipline to be effective—to be fair—must be corrective in nature. Justin lists some basic rules of proper disciplinary procedures:

- Discipline to be meaningful must be corrective, not punitive. Corrective discipline encourages the wrongdoer to correct himself or herself and leads to self-discipline.

- When you discipline one, you discipline all.

- Corrective discipline satisfies the rule of equality of treatment by enforcing equally among all employees established plant rules, safety practices, and the responsibility of the job.

- It is the supervisor's job to make the workers toe the line, or to increase efficiency—not the shop steward.

- Just cause or any other comparable standard for justifying disciplinary action under the labor contract consists of three parts:
  1. Did the employee breach the rule or commit the offense charged against him or her?
  2. Did the employee's act of misconduct warrant corrective action or punishment?
  3. Is the penalty just and appropriate to the act or offense as corrective punishment?

- The burden of proof rests on the supervisor to justify each of the three parts that make up the standard of just cause under the labor contract.

- The misconduct or offense charge should be proved by sensory facts. Opinions, feelings, and conclusions should be avoided.

- In drafting rules or writing disciplinary letters, opinions, inferences, and conclusions must also be avoided. Rules should be based on neglect of job, and disciplinary action must be supported by the facts of how, when, and where the employee neglected his or her job.

- To prove a cause for disciplinary action, the circumstantial evidence must permit two reasonable inferences or inescapable conclusions to be drawn:
  1. The circumstantial evidence points to or compels one reasonable finding or conclusion.
  2. The circumstantial evidence excludes all other reasonable findings or conclusions.[48]

It is imperative that management keep a record of each reprimand, warning, layoff, or discharge. Annotations of ver-

bal warnings should be maintained by the supervisors in the department. The procedure for written warnings should include the writing of warnings as soon as possible after the incident. It is important to note on the warning notice the rule violated or the specific provisions of the union contract in question. Explanations should be specific and comprehensive. One helpful device on a warning notice is a special notation, where indicated, that immediate satisfactory improvement must be shown and maintained or further disciplinary action will be taken. The specific action taken by management based on the violation should be clearly noted on the form.

The right to discipline or discharge for proper cause and the right to make rules and regulations governing the conduct of employees are primary management prerogatives. Notwithstanding these rights, the union will attempt to protect the disciplined employee. In the main, collective bargaining agreements permit the employer to discipline or discharge for cause, but they also permit the union to protest such actions through the grievance and arbitration procedure. It, therefore, is essential that just cause be established, that the reasonableness of the action be clear, and that the documentation be complete.

The Grievance Procedure

The grievance procedure is the real heart of the collective bargaining agreement. It is a useful and productive management tool when it makes use of the finding of facts, objective evaluations, and equity. Consistent and fair adjudication of grievances is the hallmark of sound employee-employer relations.

Most grievance procedures contain four steps. The first step in all cases involves the presentation of the grievance by the employee and/or his or her representative to the immediate first-line supervisor. This is an essential cornerstone of a grievance procedure. Since most grievances refer to actions taken by first-line supervisors, a second step taken outside the department or at a higher level in the department is necessary. This second step involves the employee and, once again, his or her representative, where indicated, and a department head or an administrative person outside of the department. The underlying rationale for the third step of a grievance procedure is to provide a final in-house review of the management decision by an individual outside the involved department with a twofold responsibility of ensuring objectivity and evaluating the need for consistency. This third step involves the employee and/or his or her representative and a union official and, in most instances, a labor relations representative of the organization's personnel department. To ensure such objectivity and the evaluation of the need for consistency, it is important to understand the following caveats:

- This cannot be done effectively if the last step remains at the same operating department from which the grievance arose.

- This cannot be done effectively if the management representative at the third step has neither the power nor the inclination to overrule an improper decision.
- This cannot be done effectively if an individual is perceived as anything other than neutral.

The manager has six basic responsibilities during the grievance procedure.

1. hearing the complaint
2. getting the facts
3. making the decision
4. communicating the decision
5. preparing a written record
6. minimizing grievances

The management hearing officer should be guided by the following general principles for effective grievance handling:

- a strong desire to resolve dissatisfaction and conflicts
- an empathy toward employees, an understanding of their problems, and an ability and a willingness to listen and probe for hidden agenda
- a complete knowledge and understanding of personnel policies, procedures, and practices and of the union contract
- a personal commitment to the interest of the institution side by side with a sense of fair play on behalf of the employees

Very few grievances can be adjudicated as soon as they arise. Indeed, haste is not a desirable attribute because the critical aspect of sound administration of the grievance procedure is a thorough investigation, not a quick evaluation. It is essential that in dealing with employees' grievances, the management gain employee commitment and reduce employee dissatisfaction. Therefore, the facts are the key. By uncovering the facts it is possible to discover the underlying causes of grievances, rather than their surface appearances.

Rules for Grievance Administration

The following checklist is provided as a guide for managers involved in administering the grievance procedure:

- *Listen*. Permit the presentation of the full story by the employee and/or the delegate.
- *Try to understand*. Uncover the how, who, what, when, where, and why of the grievance.
- *Separate fact from emotion*. This requires painstaking investigation.
- *Refer to policy and contract provisions*. These are the rules of the road. Do not attempt to rewrite policy and the bargaining agreement at this stage of the game. The role of the supervisor is to interpret such policy and contract provisions as they pertain to the grievance at hand.

- *Remember that your decision may set a precedent*. A decision in one case has a direct bearing on subsequent cases.
- *Consult with others*. It is not a sign of weakness to check with other supervisors who may have had similar grievances and to check with the personnel department.
- *Explain your decision fully*. It is essential to get employee commitment and understanding. Therefore, be explicit and honest in communicating your decision.[49]

In addition to the points covered in the checklist above, the following are essential to the effective handling of grievances:

- Employees deserve a complete and an empathetic hearing of grievances they present.
- The most important job in the handling of grievances is getting at the facts.
- Look for the hidden agenda.
- Hasty decisions often backfire.
- While you are investigating a grievance, try to separate fact from opinion or impression.
- After you have come to your decision, promptly communicate that decision to the employee.
- Remember that you have to sell your decision.
- There is no substitute for common sense in arriving at a decision.
- Written records are most important.
- Follow-up is essential.[50]

Arbitration

Provisions for the use of arbitration to resolve contract interpretation disputes during the life of the contract appear in well over 90 percent of all collective bargaining agreements. Arbitration is the final step in the grievance procedure.

A voluntary arbitration is judicial in nature. When two parties are unable to resolve a dispute by mutual agreement, they submit the particular issue to an impartial person for solution.

There are several types of voluntary arbitration clauses dealing with contract administration disputes. The most common provides for both parties to select an arbitrator each time a dispute arises. Many contracts state that the arbitrator shall be selected through the American Arbitration Association (AAA). When an issue is in dispute, the aggrieved party petitions the AAA, which, in turn, submits a list of arbitrators to both parties. If the two parties cannot agree on which arbitrator to select, the AAA designates the arbitrator. The selection of a separate arbitrator for each issue has the marked advantage of securing a qualified individual to rule on a particular type of dispute.[51]

A less widely used voluntary arbitration clause provides for a permanent arbitrator system. Here both parties mutually select an impartial arbitrator to handle *all* arbitrations during the life of a specific agreement. This has the distinct advantage of providing the parties with a carefully selected individual who has earned the respect of both labor and management and who, because of repeated experiences with the parties, can develop a thorough understanding of the problems and unique difficulties of a particular institution.

An arbitrator's award is mandatory on both parties. The arbitrator's decision is final and binding. The first principle of effective arbitration in contract administration is to obtain an agreement between management and the union as to the type of arbitration desired—i.e., will it be the ad hoc arrangement (selecting a different arbitrator for each case) or the permanent arrangement (selecting an arbitrator for the life of the contract)? Even more critical is the question of the limits or nonlimits on what matters shall be submitted to the arbitrator. In deciding which matters should be submitted to the arbitrator and the arbitrator's authority, contractual definitions must be considered. The arbitrator's authority is limited by the agreement. Typically, he or she is responsible for interpreting or applying a specific clause in the contract. The arbitrator is precluded from adding to or deleting any clause contained in that agreement. Some contracts limit the arbitration process to specific issues and not to all clauses contained in the collective bargaining agreement.

In submitting contract interpretation disputes to an arbitrator, both parties risk losing the decision on matters which they deem to be important, but this is a small price to pay for uninterrupted service. The obvious advantages of continuing operations while deciding disrupted claims arising from interpretation of the contract can easily be recognized. Arbitration neither diminishes nor detracts from the collective bargaining process. Rather, it is an extension of the bargain arrived at during the negotiations. It is an administrative tool for living with the contract. Having adopted the arbitration process voluntarily, both parties are more likely to accept the decision that emanates from the arbitrator.

The AAA provides us with a good arbitration clause of 50 words.

> Any dispute, claim or grievance arising out of or relating to the interpretation or the application of this agreement shall be submitted to arbitration under the Voluntary Labor Arbitration Rules of the American Arbitration Association. The parties further agree to accept the arbitrator's award as final and binding upon them.[52]

A grievance procedure without voluntary arbitration at its terminal step is ineffective. All grievances should be heard, regardless of whether or not they are covered by the definition in the contract. When grievances cannot be settled internally, the disputed matter should be submitted to a disinterested party. In this way, both the union and the aggrieved employee understand that management's decision can be questioned or reviewed by a disinterested and unbiased tribunal.

NOTES

1. A. Samuel Cook, *The Neglected Art of Negotiation* (Baltimore: The Daily Record), (Date unknown.)

2. J.T. Dunlop and J.J. Healy, *Collective Bargaining*, rev. ed. (Homewood, Ill.: Richard D. Irwin, 1955), 53.

3. National Labor Relations Act, 8(d).

4. *Labor Law Reporter* (Chicago: Commerce Clearing House), ¶3130.

5. Ibid., ¶3085.

6. Ibid., ¶3130.16.

7. Ibid.

8. Ibid., ¶¶3105 and 3110.

9. Ibid., ¶3115.

10. Ibid., ¶3095.

11. *1985 Guidebook to Labor Relations* (Chicago: Commerce Clearing House, 1985), 315.

12. *Labor Law Reporter*, ¶3135.70.

13. Ibid., ¶3143.386.

14. Tessa Albert Warschaw, *Winning by Negotiation* (New York: McGraw-Hill Book Co., 1980), 18–61.

15. Ibid., 23.

16. *Business Week*, July 1985.

17. William J. Bade, Jr., and Morris Stone, *Management Strategy in Collective Bargaining Negotiations* (New London, Conn.: National Foremen's Institute, 1951).

18. Howard Raiffa, *The Art and Science of Negotiation* (Cambridge, Mass.: Beltnap Press of Harvard University Press, 1982), 126–27.

19. Max H. Bazerman, "Why Negotiations Go Wrong," *Psychology Today* (June 1986): 56.

20. Raiffa, *Art and Science*, 14.

21. Roger Fisher and William Ury, "Getting to Yes—Negotiating an Agreement without Giving In," *Harvard Negotiation Project* (Boston, Mass.: Houghton Mifflin, 1981), 21.

22. William Ouchi, "Going from A to Z: 13 Steps to a Theory Z Organization," *Management Review* (May 1981): 9.

23. Fisher and Ury, "Getting to Yes," 53.

24. Michael Maccoby, *The Leader, A New Face for American Management* (New York: Ballantine Books, 1981), 48.

25. Cook, *The Neglected Art of Negotiation*, 1.

26. Gerard I. Nierenberg, *The Art of Negotiating* (New York: Simon & Schuster, 1981), 185–86.

27. William E. Simkin, *Mediation and the Dynamics of Collective Bargaining* (Washington, D.C.: Bureau of National Affairs, Inc. 1986), 53.

28. Cook, *The Neglected Art of Negotiation*, 2.

29. Theodore Voorhees, "The Art of Negotiations," *The Practical Lawyer* 13, No. 7 (April 1967): 62.

30. Cook, "The Neglected Art of Negotiation," 2.

31. Voorhees, "The Art of Negotiations," 61–66.

32. Milton Wessel, *The Rule of Reason: A New Approach to Corporate Litigation* (Reading, Mass.: Addison-Wesley Publishing Co., Inc., 1976), 64–65.

33. Fred E. Jandt, *Win-Win Negotiating* (Toronto: John Wiley & Sons, Inc. 1985).

34. Ibid., 70.

35. John Illiche, *Power Negotiating* (Reading, Mass.: Addison-Wesley Publishing Co., Inc., 1980), 103.

36. Chester Karrass, *Give and Take* (New York: Thomas Y. Crowell, 1974), 143.

37. Cornelius J. Peck, *Cases and Materials on Negotiations*, 2d ed. (Washington, D.C.: Bureau of National Affairs, Inc., 1980), 226–36.

38. Senate Committee on 93d Cong., 2d sess., 1974, S. Rept. 766, 5; House Committee on 93d Cong., 2d sess., 1974, H. Rept. 1051, 7 (emphasis added).

39. Norman Metzger, Joseph Ferentino, and Kenneth Kruger, *When Health Care Employees Strike* (Rockville, Md.: Aspen Publishers, Inc., 1984), 17–18.

40. Ibid., 18–21.

41. Ibid., 19.

42. Ibid., 20.

43. Ibid., 20.

44. Ibid., 20.

45. Ibid., 21.

46. Norman Metzger and Dennis D. Pointer, *Labor-Management Relations in the Health Services Industry* (Washington, D.C.: The Science Health Publications, Inc., 1972), 166.

47. *Ibid.*, 168.

48. Jules J. Justin, *How to Manage with a Union* (New York: Industrial Relations Workshop Seminars, Inc., 1969), 294–330.

49. Norman Metzger, *Personnel Administration in the Health Services Industry*, 2d ed. (New York: PMA Publishing Corp., 1979), 265.

50. Norman Metzger, *The Health Care Supervisor's Handbook*, 3rd ed. (Rockville, Md.: Aspen Publishers, Inc., 1988), 91–92.

51. This section has been developed from an article written by the author for *Hospital Progress* in September 1970.

52. *Labor Arbitration, Procedures and Techniques* (New York: American Arbitration Association, 1981), 7.

Appendix 51-A

A Checklist To Be Included in the First Contract

I. RECOGNITION: This clause defines the employees who will be covered by the collective bargaining agreement. It usually contains those jobs to be represented by the union and those to be excluded from the bargaining unit.
Sample:

Bargaining Unit Recognition

Section A. The Hospital recognizes the Union as the sole and exclusive representative of the Employees of the Hospital as hereinafter defined for the purposes of collective bargaining with respect to rates of pay, hours of employment, and other conditions of employment within said bargaining unit.

Section B. Except as hereinafter limited, the term "Employee" as used herein shall apply to and include the following classifications:

Diet Aides
Food Preparer C, D
Mechanic A, B, C, D, E
Maintenance Worker A, B, C
Laundry Worker A, B, C
Nursing Auxiliary A, B, C
Surgical Technician A, B
Orderly
Pharmacy Technician
X-Ray Technician A, B, C
Telephone Operator C, D

Section C. Except as hereinafter limited, the term "Employee" when used in this Agreement shall exclude all other classifications not so included in Section B and shall without limitation, however, exclude the following:

All Professional Personnel
Administrative Personnel
Supervisors
Physicians
Psychologists
Physicists and Similar Professionals
Registered and Graduate Nurses
Practical Nurses
Student Nurses
Social Service Workers
Dieticians

II. UNION SECURITY: This clause states the extent to which employees are required to join a union, maintain their membership, and pay union dues.
Sample:

Union Security

1. All Employees on the active payroll as of July 1, 1988, who are members of the Union shall maintain their membership in the Union in good standing as a condition of continued employment.

2. All Employees on the active payroll as of July 1, 1988, who are not members of the Union shall become members of the Union within thirty (30) days after the effective date of this Agreement, except those who were required to become members sooner under the expired Agreement who shall become members on the earlier applicable date, and shall thereafter maintain their membership in the Union in good standing as a condition of continued employment.

3. All Employees hired after July 1, 1988, shall become members of the Union no later than the thirtieth (30th) day following the beginning of such employment and shall thereafter maintain their membership in the Union in good standing as a condition of continued employment.

4. For the purposes of this Article, an Employee shall be considered a member of the Union in good standing if he or she tenders his or her initiation fee and periodic dues uniformly required as a condition of membership.

5. Subject to Article XXVII, an Employee who has failed to maintain membership in good standing as required by this Article shall, within twenty (20) calendar days following receipt of a written demand from the Union requesting his or her discharge, be discharged if, during such period, the required dues and initiation fee have not been tendered.

III. Checkoff: This clause will outline management's obligation to deduct dues and initiation fees from union members' wages and remit them to the union.
Sample:

Check off

1. Upon receipt of a written authorization from an Employee in the form annexed hereto as Exhibit A, the Hospital shall, pursuant to such authorization, deduct

from the wages due said Employee each month, starting not earlier than the first pay period following the completion of the Employee's first thirty (30) days of employment, and remit to the Union the initiation fee and regular monthly dues, as fixed by the Union. The initiation fee shall be paid in two (2) consecutive monthly installments beginning the month following the completion of the probationary period.

2. Employees who do not sign written authorization for deductions must adhere to the same payment procedure by making payments directly to the Union.

3. Upon receipt of a written authorization from an Employee in the form annexed hereto as Exhibit B, the Hospital shall, pursuant to such authorization, deduct from the wages due said Employee each pay period, starting not earlier than the first period following the completion of the Employee's first thirty (30) days of employment, the sum specified in said authorization and remit same to the Union's Credit Union to the credit or account of said Employee. It is understood that such checkoff and remittance shall be made by the Hospital wherever feasible.

4. Upon receipt of a written authorization in the form annexed hereto as Exhibit C, the Hospital shall, pursuant to such authorization, deduct from the wages due said Employee once a year the sum specified in said authorization and remit same to the Union Fund as the Employee's voluntary contribution to said Fund. It is understood that such checkoff and remittance shall be made by the Hospital wherever feasible.

5. The Hospital shall be relieved from making such checkoff deductions upon (a) termination of employment, or (b) transfer to a job other than one covered by the bargaining unit, or (c) layoff from work, or (d) an agreed leave of absence, or (e) revocation of the checkoff authorization in accordance with its terms or with applicable law. Notwithstanding the foregoing, upon the return of an Employee to work from any of the foregoing enumerated absences, the Hospital will immediately resume the obligation of making said deductions, except that deductions for terminated Employees shall be governed by paragraph 1 hereof. This provision, however, shall not relieve any Employee of the obligation to make the required dues and initiation payment pursuant to the Union constitution in order to remain in good standing.

6. The Hospital shall not be obliged to make dues deductions of any kind from any Employee who, during the dues month involved, shall have failed to receive sufficient wages to equal the dues deduction.

7. Each month, the Hospital shall remit to the Union all deductions for initiation fees and dues made from the wages of Employees for the preceding month, together with a list of all employees from whom initiation fees and/or dues have been deducted.

8. The Hospital agrees to furnish the Union each month with the names of newly hired Employees, their addresses, their social security numbers, their classifications of work, and their dates of hire, and with the names of terminated Employees, together with their dates of termination, and with the names of Employees on leaves of absence.

9. It is specifically agreed that the Hospital assumes no obligation, financial or otherwise, arising out of the provisions of this Article, and the Union hereby agrees that it will indemnify and hold the Hospital harmless from any claims, actions, or proceedings by any Employee arising from deductions made by the Hospital hereunder. Once the funds are remitted to the Union, their disposition thereafter shall be the sole and exclusive obligation and responsibility of the Union.

IV. PROBATIONARY PERIOD: This clause defines the period of time a newly hired employee shall be considered to be on probation.
Sample:

Probationary Employees

1. Newly hired Employees shall be considered probationary for a period of two (2) months from the date of employment, excluding time lost for sickness and other leaves of absence.

2. Where a new Employee being trained for a job spends less than twenty-five percent (25%) of his or her time on the job, only such time on the job shall be counted as employment for purposes of computing the probationary period.

3. The probationary period for part-time Employees whose regularly scheduled hours are fifteen (15) or less shall be twice the length of the probationary period of full-time Employees.

4. Notwithstanding the foregoing, the probationary period for social workers including part-time social workers, according to custom, shall be six (6) months.

5. During or at the end of the probationary period, the Hospital may discharge any such Employee at will, and such discharge shall not be subject to the grievance and arbitration provisions of this Agreement.

V. SENIORITY: This clause outlines the application of seniority to eligibility for holidays, vacations, promotions, transfers, overtime, layoffs, shifts, and shift preferences.
Sample:

Seniority

Section A. Bargaining Unit Seniority is defined as the length of time an Employee has been continuously employed at the Hospital. An Employee shall have no seniority for the first three months of employment, or for the probationary period whichever is longer; but upon successful completion of this probationary period, seniority shall be retroactive to the date of hire. Bargaining Unit Seniority shall apply in the computation of vacation eligibility, holiday eligibility, free day eligibility, sick leave eligibility, and pension eligibility.

Section B. An Employee shall have seniority to be known as Classification Seniority, in each classification in which he or she has completed a probationary period of three months retroactive to the date of his or her employment in that classification.

1. An Employee's Classification Seniority shall be used for the purposes of transfers, promotions, demo-

tions, shift preferences, vacation scheduling, layoffs, recalls, and rehires.

Section C. In case of an indefinite layoff, Employees shall be laid off and recalled by classification within their Department.

1. In the event of a layoff, recall, or promotion within the Bargaining Unit, the following factors shall govern:
    (a) Ability to do the work
    (b) Classification Seniority

2. Where factor (a) above is relatively equal, factor (b) shall be the governing factor.

3. The Hospital shall be the sole judge of the ability of an Employee to do the work.

Section D. The Hospital may make any transfer deemed by it to be expedient, whether within the Department, to another department, or to another shift. When an Employee is transferred to another classification or to another shift, he or she shall maintain seniority in his or her original classification until that Employee has completed the three-month probationary period in his or her new job. Thereafter, his or her Classification Seniority shall be retroactive to his or her date of transfer.

Section E. Seniority shall be broken when an Employee:

1. Terminates voluntarily.

2. Is discharged for cause.

3. Exceeds an official leave of absence.

4. Is absent for three consecutive working days without properly notifying the Hospital, unless proper excuse is shown.

5. Fails to report for work within three working days after being notified by telegram or mail to do so, unless proper excuse is shown.

6. Is laid off for six consecutive months.

Section F. Bargaining Unit and Classification Seniority shall not accumulate during the period of an official leave of absence exceeding one month.

Section G. Employees whose pay is charged to a special or nonbudgetary Fund, and who are informed at the time of their hire or at the time of transfer that their employment is for a special nonbudgetary or research project, shall be excluded from the provisions of this Article. Such employees may be laid off or transferred without regard to seniority.

Section H. Proper notification of absence for purposes of this Article shall be by telephone call to the Employee's supervisor immediately at the start of the work shift.

Section I. Notification of recall from layoff for purposes of this Section shall be by a telegram or a registered letter to the Employee's last known address, as shown by the Hospital's records.

VI. HOURS: This clause states the hours of work, time for lunch, rest periods, and number of days in a regular work week.
Sample:

Hours
1. The regular work week for all full-time Employees shall consist of the number of hours per week regularly worked by such Employees as of June 30, 1988. The regular work week for part-time Employees shall not exceed five (5) days. Such hours, not to exceed forty (40) per week, shall be specified in a Stipulation (Stipulation H) between the Union and the Hospital, to be annexed hereto. Employees shall receive two (2) days off in each full calendar week, except in the event of overtime.

2. The regular work day for all full-time Employees covered by this Agreement shall consist of the number of hours in the regular work week as above defined, divided by five (5), exclusive of an unpaid lunch period, except for those Employees who receive a paid lunch period as of June 30, 1988.

3. The scheduling of weekends off shall be negotiated on a Hospital-by-Hospital basis.

VII. OVERTIME: This clause states when overtime premium pay shall be paid and in what amount. It also covers how overtime hours are to be distributed and the requirements for working such overtime.
Sample:

Overtime
1. Employees shall be paid one-and-one-half times their regular pay for authorized time worked in excess of the regular full-time work week for their classification as set forth in Article XX, Section 1.

2. The following paid absences shall be considered as time worked for the purposes of computing overtime: holidays, vacations, jury duty days, condolence days, paternity day, marriage days, and sick leave days. Unpaid absences shall not be considered as time worked.

3. The Hospital will assign, on an equitable basis, "on call" duty and required prescheduled overtime among qualified Employees. Employees shall be required to work overtime when necessary for the proper administration of the Hospital.

4. There shall be no pyramiding of overtime.

VIII. SHIFTS AND SHIFT DIFFERENTIALS: This clause includes any provisions for special premium pay for work performed outside of the regular day shift.
Sample:

Shifts and Shift Differentials
1. Employees working on shifts whose straight time hours end after seven (7:00) P.M. or begin prior to six (6:00) A.M. shall receive the following differentials:
    (a) Licensed Practical Nurses—An amount equal to three-fourths (¾) of the dollar amount of shift differential paid to Registered Nurses working at the same institution on the same shifts.
    (b) All Other Employees — A shift differential of ten percent (10%) of salary, including specialty differential.

2. Employees shall work on the shift, shifts, or shift arrangements for which they were hired. The Hospital may change an Employee's shift only for good and sufficient reason, and any such change shall apply to the Employee with the least Classification Seniority qualified to do the work.

Whenever the Employee requests a change of shift, approval of such request shall not be unreasonably withheld if a vacancy exists in the classification in which he or she is then working, and if more than one Employee applies, such change shall apply to the Employee with most Classification Seniority qualified to do the work. Notwithstanding the foregoing, an Employee shall have preference in filling a vacancy on another shift in the classification in which he or she is then working over new Employees.

IX. DISCIPLINE: This clause may include work rules and the mechanism for discharging or suspending Employees. *Sample*:

Discharge and Penalties

1. The Hospital shall have the right to discharge, suspend, or discipline any Employee for cause.

2. The Hospital will notify the Union in writing of any discharge or suspension within twenty-four (24) hours of the time of discharge or suspension. If the Union desires to contest the discharge or suspension, it shall give written notice thereof to the Hospital within five (5) working days, but no later than ten (10) working days from the date of receipt of the notice of discharge or suspension. In such event, the dispute shall be submitted and determined under the grievance and arbitration procedure hereinunder set forth in the full Agreement; however, such procedure shall commence at Step 3 of the grievance machinery.

3. If the discharge of an Employee results from conduct relating to a patient and the patient does not appear at the arbitration, the arbitrator shall not consider the failure of the patient to appear as prejudicial.

4. The term "patient" for the purposes of this Agreement shall include those seeking admission and those seeking care or treatment in clinics or emergency rooms, as well as those already admitted.

5. All time limits herein specified shall be deemed exclusive of Saturdays, Sundays, and Holidays.

X. MANAGEMENT RIGHTS: This clause outlines those activities in which management is free to act, subject only to the limitations of the contract. *Sample*:

Management Rights

Section A. The management of the Hospital and the direction of the working forces are vested exclusively with the Hospital. The Hospital retains the sole right to hire, discipline, discharge, lay off, assign, and promote, and to determine or change the starting and quitting time and the number of hours to be worked; to promulgate rules and regulations; to assign duties to the work forces; to reorganize, discontinue, or enlarge any department or division; to transfer Employees within departments, to other departments, to other classifications, and to other shifts; to introduce new or improved methods or facilities; to reclassify positions and carry out the ordinary and customary functions of management, whether or not possessed or exercised by the Hospital prior to the execution

of this Agreement, subject only to the restrictions and regulations governing the exercise of these rights as are expressly provided in this Agreement.

Section B. The Union recognizes that the Hospital has introduced a revision in the methods of feeding patients, which has and will produce a revision in job duties and a reduction in personnel in the Food Service Department. The union agrees that nothing contained in this Agreement shall prevent the implementation of this program and of the specific reductions or of any other similar program to be hereafter undertaken by the Hospital.

Section C. The Union, on behalf of the Employees, agrees to cooperate with the Hospital to attain and maintain full efficiency and maximum patient care, and the Hospital agrees to receive and consider constructive suggestions submitted by the Union toward these objectives.

XI. SEPARABILITY CLAUSE: This clause, sometimes referred to as a savings clause, protects the Agreement from the possibility that any part of it is found to be contrary to the law. *Sample*:

Effect of Legislation—Separability

It is understood and agreed that all agreements herein are subject to all applicable laws now or hereafter in effect and to the lawful regulations, rulings, and orders of regulatory commissions or agencies having jurisdiction. If any provision of this Agreement is in contravention of the laws or regulations of the United States or of this state, such provision shall be superseded by the appropriate provision of such law or regulation, so long as the same is in force and effect; but all other provisions of the Agreement shall continue in full force and effect.

XII. ENTIRE AGREEMENT CLAUSE: This clause, sometimes referred to as a zipper, provides that once negotiations have been completed, no further negotiations are necessary. Both parties mutually waive the right to negotiate on any further subject during the term of the Agreement. *Sample*:

Duration

Section E. The Union, in consideration of the benefits, privileges, and advantages provided in this Agreement and as a condition of the execution of this Agreement, suspends meetings in collective bargaining negotiations with the Hospital during the term of this Agreement with respect to any further demands, except as may be dealt with as a grievance under Article XXII, or except as may be dealt with under Section B of Article XXXI.

XIII. SICK LEAVE: This clause states the eligibility requirements and amount of sick leave negotiated by the parties. *Sample*:

Sick Leave

1. Employees, after thirty (30) days employment, shall be entitled to paid sick leave earned at the rate of one (1)

day for each month of employment, retroactive to date of hire, up to a maximum of twelve (12) days per year. Employees, after one (1) or more years of employment with the Hospital, shall be entitled to a total of twelve (12) additional days of sick leave as of the beginning of his or her second and each subsequent year of employment, provided that at no time will an Employee be entitled to accumulate more than thirty-six (36) working days of sick leave during any one year, including the days earned or to be earned in the current sick leave year.

2. Pay for any day of sick leave shall be at the Employee's regular pay.

3. To be eligible for benefits under this Article, an Employee who is absent due to illness or injury must notify his or her supervisor at least one (1) hour before the start of his or her regularly scheduled work day, unless proper excuse is presented for the Employee's inability to call. The Hospital may require proof of illness hereunder.

4. Employees who have been on sick leave may be required to be examined by the Hospital's Health Service physician before being permitted to return to duty.

5. If an Employee resigns or is dismissed or laid off and has exceeded his or her allowable sick leave, the excess sick leave paid shall be deducted from any moneys due him or her from the Employer at the time of resignation, layoff, or dismissal.

XIV. HOLIDAYS: This clause will include the requirements for eligibility for holiday pay, the number of holidays granted, and the method of payment for such holidays.

Section A. Employees shall be entitled to eight (8) paid Holidays each year as follows:

1. New Year's Day
2. Martin Luther King's Birthday
3. Washington's Birthday
4. Memorial Day
5. Independence Day
6. Labor Day
7. Thanksgiving Day
8. Christmas Day

Section B. To be paid for a Holiday, an Employee must have worked that last complete scheduled shift prior to and the next complete shift after such Holiday unless the absence is authorized or excused.

Section C. Recognizing that the Hospital works every day of the year, and that it is not possible for all Employees to be off duty on the same day, the Hospital shall have the right, at its sole discretion, to require any Employee to work on any of the Holidays, provided however that such Employee shall be given a day off in lieu of such Holiday at the convenience of the Department. Employees who work on a Holiday and cannot be scheduled for a compensatory day off, at the discretion and option of the Hospital, shall in lieu thereof be paid an additional day's pay at straight time, in addition to one-and-one-half times their regular straight time rate of pay for all hours worked on the Holiday.

Section D. Employees shall be entitled to four "free days" with pay in the course of a calendar year in addition to eight (8) paid Holidays listed above. Free days shall be scheduled at the convenience of the Hospital and shall not be taken immediately preceding or immediately following vacation time or a Holiday. Request for scheduling a free day must be made by the Employee at least two weeks prior to the date requested.

Section E. For the purposes of computation of pay for Holidays and free days under this Article, an Employee will be paid for his or her regularly scheduled work day at his or her regular straight time hourly rate.

Section F. Employees will be entitled to time off with pay to vote at regularly scheduled City, State, or Federal elections, in accordance with New York State laws. Such time off will be granted only if the Employee does not have at least four hours' time between the time the polling places open and the start of his or her work schedule or between the close of his or her work schedule and the time the polling places close. Such time off shall not exceed two hours and shall be granted only if the Employee notifies his or her supervisor not more than ten (10) nor less than two (2) days before the day of the election.

A new series of clauses will be included in the new contract covering wages and minimums, vacation provisions, paid leave provisions, no-discrimination requirements, severance pay, uniform allowance, and any agreement on past practices.

Eugene D. Ulterino
Susan S. Robfogel

52

Discipline and Discharge: Avoiding Legal Pitfalls

A hospital's decisions with respect to the discipline and discharge of employees may have a variety of legal consequences. A wide array of state and federal laws have established legal constraints on employers' actions in this area. Law relating to employment discrimination, wrongful discharge, and collective bargaining agreements is particularly important.

FEDERAL AND STATE DISCRIMINATION LAWS

Title VII

At the federal level, Title VII of the Civil Rights Act of 1964 prohibits discrimination in employment on the basis of race, color, religion, sex, or national origin.[1] It is a violation of Title VII to discharge or otherwise discriminate against an individual with respect to compensation, terms, conditions, or privileges of employment based on the protected characteristics. Claims under Title VII are often based on the discipline or discharge of an employee.

Sexual harassment is considered sex discrimination under Title VII. Under Equal Employment Opportunity Commission guidelines

> unwelcome sexual advances, requests for sexual favors, and other verbal or physical conduct of a sexual nature

constitute sexual harassment when (1) submission to such conduct is made either explicitly or implicitly a term or condition of an individual's employment, (2) submission to or rejection of such conduct by an individual is used as the basis for employment decisions affecting such individual, or (3) such conduct has the purpose or effect of unreasonably interfering with an individual's work performance or creating an intimidating, hostile, or offensive working environment.[2]

With respect to discipline and discharge, this means that an employer can be found in violation of Title VII if a supervisor demands sexual favors as a condition of employment or in exchange for favoritism.[3] Thus, an employer can be held liable if a supervisor discharges or disciplines an employee for failing to submit to sexual advances. In addition, if an employer allows a hostile work environment to exist and if an employee resigns as a result of it, the resignation may be considered a constructive discharge in violation of Title VII.[4]

Title VII applies to virtually all private employers, as well as to state and local governments. Remedies may include reinstatement and back pay.

The Age Discrimination in Employment Act

The Age Discrimination in Employment Act (ADEA) prohibits discrimination in employment against employees age 40 or older.[5] The ADEA forbids employers from treating employees differently because they are in the protected age group. An employer may not, for instance, discipline or discharge such an employee based on a belief that the employee is

Note: The authors wish to acknowledge the assistance of Todd Shinaman, our associate, for his valuable contribution in the preparation of this chapter.

465

too old for the job. Mandatory retirement, except in limited circumstances, is prohibited. The ADEA operates in much the same way as Title VII. A successful plaintiff in an ADEA action, however, is entitled to double damages if the employer committed a "willful" violation.[6]

The Rehabilitation Act

The Rehabilitation Act of 1973 requires employers that have federal contracts or subcontracts exceeding $2,500 not to discriminate against "otherwise qualified" handicapped individuals.[7] The act also bars discrimination by recipients of federal financial assistance.[8] A "handicapped individual" is any person who has a physical or mental impairment that substantially limits one or more of the person's major life activities, has a record of such impairment, or is regarded as having such an impairment.[9] "Otherwise qualified" individuals are those who can perform, with or without reasonable accommodation, the duties of the job without endangering the health and safety of the individual and others.[10] The employer may not discipline or discharge an otherwise qualified employee on the basis of handicap and must take reasonable steps to accommodate the handicap.

State Laws

In addition to the federal statutes noted above, many states have enacted legislation prohibiting discrimination in employment on the basis of race, sex, national origin, etc. Some states have also enacted laws requiring hospitals to provide legitimate reasons for terminating a doctor's staff privileges. Other states review hospitals' decisions concerning medical staff not by statute but as a matter of public policy, while still others hold that such decisions are not subject to judicial review.

Discrimination Theories

Many of the cases arising under the statutes noted above are analyzed on the basis of either "adverse impact"[11] or "disparate treatment."[12] Adverse impact occurs when an employment policy, which may be neutral on its face, has a disproportionate impact on a protected group. Disparate treatment occurs when a particular individual is treated differently because he or she is a member of a protected group. This category of discrimination is most often at issue in discipline and discharge cases.

In order to prevail in a disparate treatment case, the employee must first establish a prima facie case. To do this the employee must show

- that he or she was a member of the protected class;
- that he or she was qualified for the job at issue;

- that he or she was adversely affected by an employment action; and
- that the job at issue continued to be available to others.[13]

The burden is then on the employer to articulate a legitimate nondiscriminatory reason for its actions.[14] The ultimate burden of proof, however, remains at all times on the plaintiff, who must then prove that the reason presented by the employer was a mere pretext for actual discrimination.[15]

For example, if a minority employee is discharged, no matter what the reason, he or she may be able to establish a prima facie case. Thus, the employer will have to come forward with a legitimate reason for discharging the employee, such as excessive absenteeism. In order to prevail on the claim, the employee will have to prove, by a preponderance of the evidence, that absenteeism was not the real reason for his or her discharge and that the actual reason was race.

WRONGFUL DISCHARGE

Historically, employers and employees operated under the doctrine of employment at will. Under this doctrine an employment contract without a specified term could be terminated by either party with or without cause. Recently, however, this doctrine has been eroded. In addition to statutes, such as those discussed above, courts have recognized certain causes of action for wrongful discharge.

In recent years wrongful discharge claims have become increasingly prevalent against health care providers, as they have against employers in general. These claims are extremely difficult to defend, and employers lose about 75 percent of them.[16] They are generally based on one of three different causes of action: (1) tort; (2) implied contract; (3) implied covenant of good faith and fair dealing. Under these theories many courts have recognized exceptions to the common law rule of employment at will.

Tort Claims

Some states have recognized an exception to the doctrine of employment at will when an employee's discharge clearly violates established principles of public policy. A variety of grounds for termination have been found in violation of public policy and thus actionable under the tort of wrongful discharge: discharge of an employee solely on the basis of age[17]; discharge for refusing to handle a radioactive cobalt unit[18]; discharge for refusing to commit perjury[19]; discharge for refusing to participate in a price fixing scheme[20]; discharge for serving on a jury[21]; discharge for refusing to date a supervisor[22]; discharge for filing a worker's compensation claim[23]; discharge for filing a lawsuit against the employer[24]; discharge for threatening to report abuse of hospital patients to state authorities.[25]

Some courts have also recognized other torts in relation to employee discharge. These include intentional infliction of emotional distress,[26] intentional interference with economic relations,[27] fraud,[28] and defamation.[29] Although in most of these cases the former employee will have to prove something beyond what is required for the wrongful discharge tort, an employer should consider the possibility of such claims when making discharge decisions.

It should also be noted that many states, including those that do not recognize the wrongful discharge tort, have enacted laws prohibiting discharge for certain retaliatory reasons. Employees may be protected from discharge for actions such as filing worker's compensation claims, reporting illegal activity, and serving as a juror.

Implied Contract Claims

Courts in many states have recognized claims based on statements made in employee manuals and handbooks or oral statements by management. Employees have been successful in establishing an implied just cause requirement based on statements to the effect that an employee would be employed for a certain length of time or for so long as the employee performed satisfactorily and based on certain personnel policies and standards.

These issues arise often in the hospital setting. The Supreme Court of Idaho has held that a hospital was contractually bound by written statements in its employee handbook and providers' manual, as well as by oral statements to the effect that employment would continue unless and until the employee violated the hospital's rules and procedures or did not perform the job.[30] The court held that these statements established a set of standards to be complied with by both employer and employees. A factor contributing to the importance of the documents was that the employees were required to acknowledge receipt of the handbook in writing.

In *Renny v. Port Huron Hospital*, the Michigan Supreme Court held that the existence of a grievance procedure was evidence that a just cause contract existed.[31] The court then held that the grievance procedure did not satisfy the requisite elements of fairness and that the final decision by a management committee was therefore subject to full judicial review. The court refused to grant the deference given to an independent arbitrator's decision regarding just cause.

Implied Covenant of Good Faith and Fair Dealing Claims

Courts in some states have recognized an implied covenant of good faith and fair dealing in the employment context. This implied covenant has been used to protect employees who were discharged for reasons other than just cause.[32] The covenant is most often recognized on the basis of long service, personnel policies, and oral representations.[33] In *Cleary v.*

American Airlines,[34] the court relied on an employee's length of service and the existence of a grievance procedure to imply that the employer had an obligation to engage in good faith and fair dealing rather than in arbitrary conduct. Relatively few states, however, recognize such an implied covenant in the employment context.[35]

COLLECTIVE BARGAINING AGREEMENTS AND THE NLRA

The National Labor Relations Act

Section 7 of the National Labor Relations Act, as amended,[36] ("NLRA"), provides that employees have the right to organize and engage in concerted activity for the purpose of collective bargaining or other mutual aid or protection. Section 8(a)(1) of the NLRA prohibits employers from interfering with employees' Section 7 rights. These provisions are most often applied with respect to union activity, but they also protect concerted activity that is not specifically union oriented. Work stoppages by nonunion employees[37] and safety-related protests,[38] for instance, have been protected.

Section 8(a)(3) prohibits employers from discriminating against employees in order to encourage or discourage membership in a labor organization. In Section 8(a)(3) cases, the burden is on the NLRB's General Counsel to establish by a preponderance of the evidence that protected conduct was a motivating factor in the employer's decision. The burden of proof then shifts to the employer to show that the decision would have been the same despite the protected conduct.[39]

As of 1974, these provisions have applied to virtually all hospitals, for-profit and nonprofit, and they can have considerable impact on discipline and discharge decisions.

Collective Bargaining Agreements

If a union is established as the collective bargaining representative, the employer will almost certainly be required to abide by a just cause standard. Virtually all collective bargaining agreements contain a just cause provision. Few such agreements contain a definition of "just cause," but arbitrators over the years have fleshed out the term's meaning.[40] The important elements include progressive discipline, fairness, and proper investigation.

AVOIDING LEGAL PROBLEMS IN DISCIPLINE AND DISCHARGE

The legal constraints discussed above are quite broad. As a result, an employer should never discipline or discharge an employee without a legitimate, fair, nondiscriminatory reason. In addition, to avoid legal as well as human relations problems, health care employers should take a number of steps to ensure that they do not make promises they do not intend to keep and that their discipline and discharge decisions are fair.

Avoiding Contractual Liability

If an employer wishes to avoid contractual liability for its employment decisions, personnel policy manuals, as well as letters offering employment, should be reviewed to ensure that they do not contain representations by which the employer is unwilling to be bound. Avoid language, for instance, that indicates that an employee may be terminated only for failure to meet performance standards. Even a provision allowing termination when an employee's work "does not measure up to company standards" may be interpreted as a "good cause" requirement.[41] Obviously, such phrases as "permanent employment," "discharge for just cause," "probationary period," and "job security" should be avoided.

Disclaimers

Employers may also insert explicit disclaimers in employment applications, offer letters, and policy manuals in order to ensure at-will employment. Such disclaimers, which assert the right of the employer to discharge employees with or without cause, have been effective against breach of contract claims.[42]

A disclaimer that may insulate an employer from liability, however, may also discourage desirable employment prospects and alienate current employees. Because disclaimer statements eliminate contractual, enforceable job security, employees may be especially susceptible to a union that emphasizes job security as a reason for unionizing. Thus, the potential benefits of a disclaimer must be balanced against the need for a successful recruiting campaign, the importance of maintaining a satisfactory level of employee morale, and the risk of encouraging a union-organizing campaign.

Not surprisingly, the more often disclaimer statements appear in employment materials, the greater the protection they are likely to provide. To maximize effectiveness, therefore, disclaimer statements should appear in your employment applications, letters offering employment, and policy manuals. Should employers choose, however, to strike more of a balance between the benefits and the potential detriments of disclaimer statements, they might merely place a disclaimer in their policy manuals.

Set forth below are some prototype disclaimers which can be used in an employment application, letter offering employment, and policy manual. As always, professional legal advice should be sought in order to ascertain whether these disclaimers would be effective in a given jurisdiction. Employers may want to place the disclaimer in the employment applications and policy manuals in bold-face type in order to establish constructive notice to the employees. Moreover, all job applicants should be required to sign their applications.

Employment Application Disclaimer

I understand that this employment application is not a contract and that if hired, my employment with the hospital can be terminated, with or without cause, and with or without notice, at any time, at the option of either the hospital or myself. I also understand that no hospital official has the authority to make any agreement, oral or written, contrary to the foregoing without written approval of the President.

Letter Offering Employment Disclaimer

This offer of employment is not to be construed as a guarantee of employment for any specific period of time or specific type of work. Your acceptance of this employment offer constitutes an acknowledgment that your employment can be terminated, with or without cause, and with or without notice, at any time, either at your option, or the option of the hospital. Your acceptance also acknowledges that no representative of the hospital, other than the President, has any authority to enter into any agreement for employment for any specified period of time, or to make any agreement contrary to the foregoing.

Policy Manual Disclaimer

This manual is informational only, and is not intended to create any contractual rights in favor of any employee of the hospital. The hospital reserves the right to change the terms of this handbook at any time.

or

The contents of this manual are presented as a matter of information only. The hospital reserves the right to modify, revoke, suspend, terminate, or change any or all plans, policies, or procedures in the manual, in whole or in part, at any time, with or without notice. The language which appears in this manual is not intended to create nor is it to be construed to constitute a contract between the hospital and any one or all of its employees.

Recruiters, persons making job offers, and other personnel should be advised that oral statements may be enforceable contracts and that they should not oversell the hospital, make any representations that contradict written policy, or imply job permanence or that discharge can be for "just cause" only.

Supervisors and others who conduct interviews should be given clear lines of authority and instructions as to what they may say during interviews. Supervisors should limit their discussions to a description of the job and its requirements. It is best if only trained personnel staff are allowed to discuss benefits, salary, and other terms and conditions of employment. Obviously, no representation should be made to the effect that employees will have job security or will not be discharged except for good cause, unless, of course, you are willing to be bound by such representations.

Discipline and Discharge Procedures

Employers should be sure that all rules and standards are articulated in a written policy or otherwise communicated to employees. Employees must be made aware of what is expected of them. One way to ensure this is to develop accurate job descriptions detailing the duties and responsibilities of each job. Prospective employees should be given these descriptions, and interviewers should make certain that they are understood. Such procedures prevent future problems by giving employees accurate expectations and by giving the employer something to point to if the employee does not measure up.

Employees should receive periodic performance evaluations by supervisors trained to give an honest assessment. These evaluations should be developed by job category and should be based on objective indicia of good performance. If an employee has performance problems, the evaluator should tell the employee and document the evaluation or discussion. If this procedure is followed, the employee will not be surprised by any eventual disciplinary action or discharge and will be less likely to feel that he or she is being treated unfairly.

The employer's written personnel policies should include a list of infractions for which disciplinary action will be taken. The policy should list separately those infractions for which discipline and warnings will be given and those for which discharge will be immediate. The employer should clearly state that these lists are not exhaustive and that discipline and discharge will not be limited to listed infractions.

Violations of rules and standards that do not justify immediate discharge should be dealt with through a system of progressive disciplines. If an employee is not performing satisfactorily or has violated a rule, the employee must be notified, first by verbal warning and then, if the situation has not improved, by written warning. The warnings should indicate that disciplinary action or termination may result if the behavior does not improve. Keep thorough records of such warnings and all other disciplinary actions taken with respect to each employee.

Even if a situation involves gross misconduct justifying immediate dismissal, the employee should be suspended pending a complete investigation. The employee should be told precisely what is being charged and should be allowed to explain his or her behavior. The employer should interview witnesses and obtain statements.

The employer should make certain that all its rules and policies are applied fairly. They should be applied evenhandedly and without discrimination to all employees. The employer must find out whether employees guilty of similar conduct in the past have been given the same discipline as is contemplated in the present situation. The seriousness of the discipline should be related to the seriousness of the offense. The past record of the employee should also be taken into consideration.

Some higher, detached management official should assume the "judicial" role when serious infractions are charged. This person should actively search out and question all persons involved. He or she should make certain that the charge did not arise out of purely personal animus on the part of another employee or supervisor. He or she should also check on the consistency of the punishment with respect to seriousness and prior instances of similar conduct.

In order to avoid claims under state and federal antidiscrimination laws, the employer is advised to make certain that the reason for the discharge is not discriminatory. The employer should ascertain whether the rule or policy, although not discriminatory on its face, impacts disproportionately on a certain group because of age, sex, race, national origin, etc. If it does, the employer should satisfy itself that it has a good business reason for the existence of the rule or policy.

In order to avoid sexual harassment claims under Title VII, the employer should have a written policy that defines sexual harassment as set forth above and that prohibits it. The policy should provide that anyone found to have engaged in sexual harassment will be subject to discipline and/or discharge. The policy should also provide an effective means by which an employee claiming to be sexually harassed may bring the allegations to management's attention and have the charges investigated—and have the situation addressed if the charges are found to be true. Claims of sexual harassment should be thoroughly investigated before any action is taken.

Once the decision to discharge is made, the employer should conduct an exit interview with the employee. The employer should provide a candid explanation of the reason for the decision. The employee should be told that the decision is final and should be told what information will be given to prospective employers. The exit interview should be documented, and if litigation is anticipated, a witness should be present.

To avoid potential defamation claims, the employer should take care in disclosing information concerning an employee's discharge. Defamation is the making of a false statement that tends to adversely affect a person's reputation, thereby exposing the person to public hatred, contempt, or ridicule.[43] Defamation claims may arise when an employer disseminates negative information concerning an employee's discharge to other employees or outsiders who do not have a legitimate interest in the information. Such claims may also arise when an employer gives negative references to other employers.

Truth is a complete defense to a defamation claim. Courts have held that an employer also enjoys a qualified privilege protecting it from liability when the employer makes a statement in good faith, with a belief in its truth, on a subject in which it has a legitimate interest, and to a party also having a legitimate interest in the subject matter of the statements.[44] This qualified privilege is lost if the employer makes statements with malice or with reckless disregard for the truth and effect of the defamatory statements on the former employee. With respect to employee references, the privilege can also be lost by volunteering information not requested by the inquiring employer.

Employers can protect themselves from liability by disseminating information only to employees who have a legitimate need to know and by limiting the amount of information given in references. An employer can enjoy maximum protection concerning references by restricting them to an employee's dates of employment and positions held. Such a policy, however, may result in an inability to get references from other employers.

The employer may therefore choose to implement a policy that provides more information but that contains safeguards to minimize the risk of a defamation claim. Such a policy should require employers seeking references to send a written inquiry to the attention of the personnel department. A personnel officer should prepare a written response and/or have the former employee's supervisor prepare the response and return it to the personnel officer. The personnel officer should then review the reference for signs of malice, reckless disregard for truth, or answers that go beyond the questions asked, any of which might destroy the qualified privilege. Individual supervisors should not be permitted to release unreviewed responses.

In addition, employers should request written authorization for making references from departing employees at their exit interviews. This may further protect the employer against potential liability. If an employee refuses to consent, no references should be given for that individual.

Some states, including New York and Virginia, require hospitals to report terminations of certain personnel to a state agency. Such requirements, however, are normally limited to professionals involved in patient care, such as physicians and nurses.

CONCLUSION

Health care providers are subject to a myriad of laws and regulations in almost every area, and employee relations is no exception. Discrimination laws, wrongful discharge claims, and labor laws all place constraints on hospital managers in terms of how they deal with employees. Administrators would do well, however, to remember one basic principle that underlies all this regulation: discipline and discharge decisions should be based on nonarbitrary, nondiscriminatory, and fair criteria. When legitimate reasons exist for disciplining or discharging an employee, the employer can avoid legal problems by taking the steps discussed above. In doing so, the employer will also avoid many of the situations that cause dissension between management and employees.

NOTES

1. 42 U.S.C.A. § 2000e-2 (1981, Supp. 1989).

2. EEOC Guidelines for Sexual Harassment, 29 C.F.R. § 1604.11 (1987); *see also* Meritor Sav. Bank v. Vinson, 477 U.S. 57 (1986).

3. *See, e.g.*, Schroeder v. Schrock, 42 F.E.P. 1112 (D. Kan. 1986).

4. *See* Lamb v. Smith Internatl, 32 E.P.D. ¶ 33,772 (DC Tex. 1983).

5. 29 U.S.C.A. § 621 (1985, Supp. 1989) *et seq.*

6. 29 U.S.C.A. § 625 (1985); *see* Wilhelm v. Blue Bell Inc., 773 F.2d 1429 (4th Cir. 1985) (plaintiff must show that employer knew or showed reckless disregard as to whether its conduct was in violation of ADEA).

7. 29 U.S.C.A. § 793 (1985, Supp. 1989); 41 C.F.R. § 60-741.4 (1988).

8. 29 U.S.C.A. § 794 (1985, Supp. 1989). The law is applicable to hospitals because of their participation in programs such as Medicare and Medicaid.

9. 29 U.S.C.A. § 706(8)(B) (1985, Supp. 1989).

10. 41 C.F.R. § 60-741.2 (1988); *see*, 29 C.F.R. 1613.702(F) (1988).

11. Griggs v. Duke Power Co., 401 U.S. 424, 3 F.E.P. 175 (1971). There is a split among the federal circuit courts of appeal as to whether this theory applies in age discrimination cases.

12. McDonnell Douglas Corp. v. Green, 411 U.S. 792, 5 F.E.P. 965 (1973); Sutton v. Atlantic Richfield Co., 646 F.2d 407, 411 (9th Cir. 1981); Loeb v. Textron Inc., 600 F.2d 1003, 1013 (1st Cir. 1979).

13. *McDonnell Douglas* 411 U.S. 802; *Sutton*, 646 F.2d 411; *Loeb*, 600 F.2d 1013.

14. Texas Dep't of Community Affairs v. Burdine, 450 U.S. 248, 25 F.E.P. 113 (1981); Sutton, 646 F.2d at 412.

15. Burdine, 450 U.S. 254; Sutton, 646 F.2d 412.

16. The Wrongful Discharge of Employees in the Health Care Industry, Legal Memorandum Number Ten, Office of General Counsel, American Hospital Association (1987).

17. Payne v. Rosendaal, 147 Vt. 488, 520 A.2d 586 (Vt. 1986). Note that such a discharge may also give rise to a claim under the Age Discrimination in Employment Act.

18. Wheeler v. Caterpillar Tractor Co., 108 Ill. 2d 502, 92 Ill. Dec. 561, 485 N.E.2d 372 (Ill. 1985), *cert. denied*, 106 S. Ct. 1641 (1986).

19. Sides v. Duke Hosp., 74 N.C. App. 331, 328 S.E.2d 818, *review denied*, 335 S.E.2d 13 (1985).

20. Tameny v. Atlantic Richfield Co., 610 F.2d 1330 (9th Cir. 1970).

21. Nees v. Hocks, 272 Or. 210, 536 P.2d 512 (1975).

22. Monge v. Beebe Rubber Co., 114 N.H. 130, 316 A.2d 549 (1974). Note that such a discharge may also give rise to a claim under Title VII.

23. Frampton v. Central Ind. Gas Co., 260 Ind. 249, 297 N.E.2d 425, 215 Cal. Rptr. 860 (1973).

24. Khanna v. MicroData Corp., 170 Cal. App. 3d 250, 215 Cal. Rptr. 860 (1985).

25. McQuary v. Bel Air Convalescent Home, Inc., 69 Or. App. 107, 684 P.2d 21, *review denied*, 298 Or. 38, 688 P.2d 845 (1984).

26. *See, e.g.*, Meieser v. Du Pont, 792 F.2d 1117, 122 L.R.R.M. 2920 (4th Cir. 1986); Rice v. United Ins. Co., 465 So. 2d 1100 118 L.R.R.M. 2516 (Ala. 1984).

27. *See, e.g.*, Crank v. Intermountain Rural Elec. Ass'n, 765 P.2d 619 (Colo. App. 1988) 3 I.E.R. (BNA) 1049 (1988).

28. *See, e.g.*, Brown v. Lockwood, 76 A.D.2d 721, 432 N.Y.S.2d 186 (1980).

29. *See, e.g.*, Lewis v. Equitable Life Assurance Soc'y of the United States, 389 N.W.2d 876 (Minn. 1986).

30. Watson v. Idaho Falls Consol. Hosps., 111 Idaho 44, 720 P.2d 632 (1986).

31. 427 Mich. 415, 398 N.W.2d 327 (1986).

32. 111 Cal. App. 3d 443, 168 Cal. Rptr. 272 (1980).

33. *See, e.g.*, Cancellrin v. Federated Dep't Stores, 672 F.2d 1312 (9th Cir. 1982), *cert. denied*, 459 U.S. 859 (1982).

34. *Cleary*, 111 Cal. App. 3d at 443, 168 Cal. Rptr. at 272. In *Cleary* the court allowed tort damages for breach of the implied covenant. The California Supreme Court, recently held, however, that damages for such a breach would be limited to contract damages, such as lost wages. *See* Foley v. Interactive Data Corp., 1989 Daily Labor Report No. 2 (BNA) at D-1.

35. 42 U.S.C. § 2000e-2 (1981, Supp. 1989).

36. 29 U.S.C.A. §§ 151–169 (1973, Supp. 1989).

37. NLRB v. Washington Aluminum Co., 370 U.S. 9, 50 L.R.R.M. 2235 (1962).

38. Wheeling-Pittsburgh Steel Corp. v. NLRB, 618 F.2d 1009, 104 L.R.R.M. 2054 (3d Cir. 1980).

39. NLRB v. Transportation Management Corp., 462 U.S. 393, 1113 L.R.R.M. 2857 (1983).

40. *See, e.g.*, Enterprise Wire Co., 46 L.A. 359 (Daugherty, 1966); Texas Internat'l Airlines, 78 L.A. 893 (Dunn, 1982).

41. Tirrano v. Sears Roebuck & Co., 99 A.D.2d 653, 472 N.Y.S.2d 49 (1984).

42. Reid v. Sears Roebuck & Co., 790 F.2d 453 (6th Cir. 1986).

43. Bennet v. Commercial Advertiser Co., 230 N.Y. 125, 127, 129 N.E. 343 (1920).

44. *See, e.g.*, Stillman v. Ford, 22 N.Y.2d 48, 238 N.E. 304 (1968).

Fred W. Graumann
Donald Crow

Documentation

53

For better or for worse, we live in a highly regulated society. Most would agree that while regulation is bothersome, it is a small price to pay for living in a communal society. Philosophers tell us that laws are the price we pay for the safety and convenience of living in this ordered world—that the ability and willingness to inhibit certain behaviors is one of the major differences between modern and primitive humans.

With the proliferation of federal, state, and local laws and regulations, together with the fact that ours is an ever-increasingly litigious society, documentation is more important than ever for the employer. At stake is the ability to successfully defend against an action brought by an employee or governmental agency arising out of circumstances related to employment. The inability to document the employer's side, which frequently involves proving that something did not happen, could cost tens of thousands of dollars, and in not so rare cases, millions of dollars. Most frequently, however, this is an unnecessary expenditure of resources which more appropriately could and should be put to better use.

Webster's *Ninth New Collegiate Dictionary* (1985) defines *documentation* as

> 1): the act or instance of furnishing or authenticating with documents; 2) a: the provision of documents in substantiation also: documentary evidence b(1): the use of historical documents (2): conformity to historical or objective facts (3): the provision of footnotes, appendices or addenda referring to or containing documentary evidence; 3): Information science

This process of documenting, then, is one of the many charges of the employer in the late twentieth century—prove it. This phenomenon has occurred as part of a larger shift in our industrial society—the erosion of the employment-at-will concept, the growth of union strength, and the broad drift toward the notion of an employee's proprietary right to a job.

An internal system designed to continually monitor and evaluate the documentation process is an absolute necessity. Health care institutions have developed systems that successfully document the patient's treatment and recovery, hour by hour, and day by day; yet the same organizations have difficulty defending a wage and hour claim brought by a disgruntled employee.

Why would this circumstance exist? It is our view that there are several primary reasons; among them are (1) the lack of proper (perhaps any) supervisory training as it relates to the documentation process "in the interest of the employer",[1] and (2) the place the human resources function has made for itself in the organization.

Because of the limitations of space, this material will cover only the more critical areas of documentation, together with suggested guidelines to assist the beleaguered supervisor. These guidelines are meant to be representative and instructive and, by no means, all inclusive. In areas relating to the legal processes, counsel should be consulted. Our goal in writing this chapter is to aid in preventing litigation by employee(s) in the first instance and in legally enhancing the employer's case if litigation does occur. In addition, a guide for record retention requirements can be found at the end of this chapter. (See Appendix 53-A.)

Discharge for cause; suspension without pay; claims of illegal discrimination based on age, race, sex, religion, ethnicity, etc.; unemployment insurance claims, wage and hour litigation, workers' compensation requirements, the National Labor Relations Act, and other legislation present the broad framework that gives rise to the need of documentation. This need is generally seen as "defensive administration" but should more accurately be seen in proactive terms.

While legal and business requirements vary by state and/or organizational philosophy, a review of how to approach the issues surrounding the question of discharge presents a sufficiently broad array to use as a diagram for all similar documentation situations.

DISCHARGES OR TERMINATION FOR CAUSE

The discharge of an employee is at best an unpleasant circumstance, and there is some likelihood that an employer-controlled error in judgment has been made—a poor selection of a candidate, an improper offer of employment, limited training, an inadequate employee relations program, or a host of other employer-controlled possibilities may have preceded this act. Sound business practice dictates that labor costs be effectively controlled. Since replacement and retraining are becoming ever more expensive, in terms of both direct and indirect costs, your organization's policies, culture, and values regarding termination should be reviewed with a view to limiting avoidable turnover.

A progressive disciplinary policy is a key to avoiding discharges that may result in successful litigation against the employer. Such a program must be in writing and published—and understood completely by both supervisors and employees. Underlying such a policy are the premises that behavior modification is possible, that the employee wishes to perform successfully, and that education and clarification will result in changed performance. A process of progressive discipline includes several stages.

THE VERBAL CONFERENCE

This conversation between the supervisor and the employee relates to some aspect of work that is not meeting the standards in the eyes of the supervisor or the organization. At its best, this conference is a coaching session; but at the very least, it initiates the progressive disciplinary process. These conversations can occur over a few days or weeks and can be related to the same or different areas of concern. Some supervisors jot down a note in a diary, calendar, or the employee's file each time a counseling takes place. This is not designed to be and will not suffice as a written warning. The *primary purpose* of a verbal conference is to make the employee aware of a problem and to discuss potential solutions. Such conferences should be conducted as close in time as possible to the events and behaviors being discussed (research has shown that reinforcement has the best chance of success if it takes place close to the time of the infraction) and, if the conference is to succeed, in private. Privacy tends to assure two things: first, that the employee is not unintentionally and publicly embarrassed;

and, second, that the employee recognizes the counseling as a significant event in the employment relationship. There is a tendency on the part of the supervisor to put off talking to an employee because of the "discomfort" factor. This is similar to not putting out a fire in a trash can and then having to call the fire department because you can no longer control the fire.

Verbal conferences, particularly when unacceptable performance is being discussed with the employee, can be very difficult. On the other hand, in a great many cases a well-thought-out and properly conducted conference can assist the employee in meeting the supervisor's expectations. Waiting until tomorrow decreases the likelihood of a satisfactory resolution and increases the probability of failure with the employee. Do it now!

WRITTEN OR DOCUMENTED CONFERENCES

When the supervisor arrives at this stage, it is a signal that the verbal conferences, for one reason or another, have not accomplished their goal. The written procedure involves a further discussion with the employee, in private, concerning the areas of performance or the working relationship that are not meeting expectations.

A document reflecting the conversation should be a result and an outcome of the supervisor's investigation and the discussion with the employee. It should be prepared with a sufficient number of copies to assure one copy for the employee, one copy for the department in which the employee works, and one copy for the human resources department. Some supervisors seem reluctant to provide the employee with a copy; but it is counterproductive to prepare a document that may affect the employee-employer relationship and not share it with the party most affected, especially in a system designed to generate behavioral change.

This document can logically be structured to begin with a recitation, where appropriate, of the dates on which verbal conferences on the same, or similar, subjects were held. Thereafter, the specific problems and/or policy infraction must be defined, along with a specific explanation of what is expected from the employee in the future. Additionally, where possible, some comment should be made as to the educational and other efforts made to assist the employee. The closing paragraph should fully indicate the consequences to the employee of continued nonimprovement or noncompliance. Spaces for the supervisor and the employee or witness to sign should be provided. The employee's signature denotes receipt of the document—rather than acceptance of the veracity of the statement. Should an employee refuse to sign the notice, another supervisor should be called in at this point to witness receipt. A simple statement is sufficient: for example, "I have warned John about his job performance and indicated that many of his responsibilities are not being completed properly or on time. This has been detailed in this warning notice which he refuses to sign." Then have the supervisor sign the form in the appropriate area. Offer the employee his/her copy. If (s)he refuses, so indicate on the form, have the supervisor again sign, and then have this placed in the employee's file. The conference should be concluded at this point.

The primary purpose of the signature portion of this notice is to document the fact that the employee was, in fact, warned or counseled about a specific concern. This "signal" puts the employee on notice that the issue or issues being discussed are of sufficient importance to be reduced to writing and to be placed in his or her personnel file. This document should be written in a style designed to underscore the behavioral or performance change desired and not as recrimination or "wrist slapping." Subjective/emotionally charged language should be avoided. If the employee requests to write on the notice, suggest that this be done on a separate sheet of paper, signed, and attached to the counseling notice or on the companion "grievance" form.

Should there be a wide variance between what the supervisor reports and the facts according to the employee, a third party, such as the department manager or employee relations supervisor, should be sought for assistance or the grievance procedure begun.

Many times the counseling process is viewed by the supervisory staff as a laborious, unnecessary, unpleasant requirement of the human resources department to "get an employee fired." If this is the attitude generally shared by the management, the organization has a serious problem.

A progressive discipline program must be viewed as a positive educational process that is aimed at detailing areas of concern to the employer and listing specific corrective action. It should be the objective of each supervisor who uses the process to assist the employee to achieve at least standard performance with the employee's full understanding and cooperation. Unfortunately, supervisors frequently try to "zip" through the process as quickly as possible, creating an adversarial atmosphere, to build a case and get rid of the employee. Instead, every effort should be made to evaluate, discuss, and identify the causes of the problem(s) and the steps to be taken to determine how to satisfactorily correct the performance. These failures, or potential failures, most frequently represent organization failures and not employee failures. The lack of understanding on the part of a supervisor or manager as to the appropriate role to be played, and how that role impacts on patient care as well as on the "bottom line," results from a training or communication slippage of top management.

Supervisors' attitudes determine the success or failure of the process. When problems such as those described above are encountered, a thorough review or audit should be conducted immediately. Potential problem areas such as lack of support from top management, the fact that only one or two divisions in the organization are required to follow the disciplinary counseling procedure, and either improper or no supervisory understanding of the procedures indicate that such a review is required.

In organizations that have a formal human resources department, the director or assigned representative should be available to assist both the supervisor and the employee with the disciplinary counseling/grievance process. When an organization does not have a formal human resources department, someone within the organization must be formally designated, in writing, to provide this assistance. The assignment should be made sufficiently high in the organization to assure "clout," but not so high as to preclude the person's availability.

SECOND WRITTEN COUNSELING REPORT

Organizations vary as to how many written warnings they give in an attempt to change performance prior to discharge. Some use two, three, or more, with the final occurrence resulting in discharge. The thing to remember is that we are describing a system of progressive discipline. In this context, we use the word *progressive* in two ways: first, to describe the objective (i.e., to correct the problem by assisting the employee in resolving the difficulty rather than by punishing); and second, to make it clear to the employee that each succeeding occurrence of documentation has even greater implications of gravity and that this fact is evidenced by the growing amount of documentation.

This procedure should be handled in exactly the same manner as the first written counseling report was handled. A statement should be included indicating that further repetitions of the infraction on the part of the employee will result in further disciplinary action up to and including suspension without pay or discharge. In many organizations, suspension without pay occurs with the second written counseling report.

It is recommended that most discharges be preceded by a suspension without pay.[2] This says to the employee that money is being taken out of his or her pocket; that this is the last chance before severing the employment relationship. Obviously, there are some infractions or violations that do not lend themselves to educational correction, and it is in those instances that discharge takes place with the first occurrence. A list of such offenses can frequently be found in the employee handbook and/or a policy statement covering this subject. The suggested length of time for suspension without pay is generally from two to five working days.

The reasons that two to five days have been recommended are threefold.

1. The suspension of one day may be treated lightly and act as an "additional vacation day."
2. A suspension of greater than five days interrupts the management process (scheduling, continuity, etc.) as much as, or more than, it injures the worker.
3. Most importantly, the purpose of the suspension without pay is to demonstrate to the employee the seriousness of the infraction and the precariousness of the employment relationship—this has been done by taking otherwise paid days away following a verbal conference and one or more written warning notice(s).

This suspension is the "last mile" the employer will generally walk with the employee.

In a unionized setting, many arbitrators have reinstated an employee who has been discharged without a suspension first. In fact, it is probably fair to say that even with a properly documented history including a suspension, many arbitrators will reinstate an employee to his or her former job.

It is strongly recommended that decisions regarding suspension be reviewed with the organization's designated authority in advance of the counseling interview giving rise to the suspension. This review with the director of personnel or other designated person is to assure that all cases follow prior or proper practice. If, for example, a three-day suspension for insubordination represents the organization's precedent, this check will ensure equal treatment for like infractions; then five days might be exceptional and inappropriate.

It should be noted that suspension without pay can be used after the first, second, or third warning. The seriousness of the situation is what determines the sequence. Equally important is that the description of the offense and the sequence of correction efforts be in writing and pursuant to a written policy which is followed in each case. This may be a good place to note again that the purpose of this process is to make every effort to correct the employee performance that is keeping him or her from being productive, while protecting the organization against adverse repercussions. This is a difficult balance to achieve and maintain.

DISCHARGE

As noted, discharge or termination for cause is the most serious negative outcome of the employment relationship. Many perceive it as the "capital punishment" of the employment relationship. The failure is one for both the employer and the employee. Even though it may impact most heavily on the employee, the employer will suffer cost and downtime consequences while seeking a competent replacement. Neither is the capital punishment analogy accurate because not only won't a death take place, but also no incarceration will occur. At its extreme, this is a civil matter, and, while loss of a job is painful, it should be kept in perspective. As with a suspension, discharge must be reviewed by a third party *in advance* of discussion with the employee. This is to assure the organization that all possible steps to forewarn and educate the employee have been taken and that the action being contemplated meets organizational criteria for such action. Please note that we have used the term *third-party review* and not *approval*. Should the department manager or supervisor not agree with the person reviewing the recommendation for discharge, there should be a procedure to allow for a review by the chief executive officer or other assigned senior representative. Again, this should be accomplished *before* discussion with the employee.

Once the recommendation for discharge has been reviewed and agreed on, the employee should be contacted and discharged as soon as possible. A delay in such circumstance serves no useful purpose.

The discharge conference should be private; no other individual should be present except the discharging supervisor and the employee. Very few, if any, employees agree with such a decision, and, therefore, the meeting could go on for hours without a useful result. An argument serves only to escalate the tempers of the parties, and for this reason, we recommend that the meeting last approximately 20 to 30 minutes, at most.

The supervisor should call the employee's attention to past warning notices, the suspension if used, and the circumstances of each. The details leading to discharge should be reviewed and the fact that the employee's services have been terminated effective immediately emphasized.

All pay due to the employee, including accrued vacation or other pay due based on organization policy, should be paid to the employee at that time. There is no benefit to having a discharged employee come back into the work environment at a later date or have him or her wait for the final check(s) to be mailed. This serves only to further anger the employee, who may then think of initiating litigation or going to a state or federal agency for assistance.

Many payroll departments balk at issuing interim paychecks, but all discharged employees should be paid immediately, regardless of the fact that state law frequently allows the employer to delay payment to the next regular pay day.

PURGING EMPLOYEE RECORDS OF WRITTEN WARNING

There should be a formal personnel policy purging written warning(s) from an employee's file after a certain time, frequently 12 to 18 months from the date of the last such warning if there has been no further intervening discipline.

In reviewing written warning notices or records of conferences and the span of time the notices or conferences cover, judgment must be used. Should an employee receive three written notices over 12 months, a discharge for the fourth similar offense after an additional 14 months could probably not be substantiated or defended.

As stated earlier, the primary purposes of the written warning or conference notice are to notify the employee of performance that is not standard and to assist the employee in improving or changing performance in a positive manner. Some supervisors balk at this policy, feeling that written warnings should be retained indefinitely. The prime objective of the progressive discipline process is to detail, in writing to the employee, areas of employer dissatisfaction so that correction and improvement can take place. Most employees understand this and make every effort to do what the supervisor has asked, and little, or no, difficulty is experienced again. The employee should not be forced to "pay" for the remainder of his or her employment for problems or difficulties that are no longer present or relevant.

The table that follows brings into sharp focus the manner in which an employer's discharge process can be documented and validated to any outside representative (investigator). This same charting procedure graphically allows the employer to monitor and collect practices violative of organizational policy. This, in turn, may be used in training and orienting toward performance improvement. Some common practices that will undermine this process are

- absence of a written progressive disciplinary policy
- absence of a third-party review before suspension or discharge
- lack of appropriate and consistent records
- inconsistent enforcement of the written policy
- absence of written and current personnel policies and procedures
- absence of, or limited, training of managers and supervisors with reference to the disciplinary process and its purpose(s)
- failure of the human resources department to establish a system that logs written warnings by infraction to assure consistency of treatment and to facilitate identification of problem areas, policies, or managers

PAST PRACTICES

In almost any litigation, or administrative proceeding, an outside investigator will ask, "What has been done in similar cases in the past?" For the employer to have any chance of being successful, it must be able to show what has actually been done in previous similar circumstances and that this practice is consistent with its published policies, as well as with the action taken in the matter under review. Table 53-1 lists a few selected examples of discharge, displaying common employee claims and examples of how best to refute the charge by proper and adequate documentation.

It is worthy of note that these claims might have been brought before a number of agencies or persons and that a

Table 53-1 Employee Discharges

Reason for Discharge	Employee's Charge	Documentation*
Insubordination	Fired because of union sympathies	Six cases in the past 24 months, each showing similar progressive disciplinary records and each with the same length suspension before discharge
Attendance	Sex discrimination	Eight employees of both sexes discharged with similar warnings and attendance patterns
Poor quality of work	Race discrimination	Five employees of another race discharged in the past 12 months with similar warnings and suspension before discharge
Tardiness	Age discrimination	Seven other employees under and over age 40 discharged under similar circumstances

*See Appendix 53-A.

determination before one body is not necessarily determinative of an outcome before all bodies—for example, a ruling in the employer's favor by the EEOC, NLRB, or Unemployment Insurance Commission may be helpful but does not preclude an employee's success in pursuing his or her claims before others. Further, the claimant frequently has no legal cost because certain of these forums become the petitioner on claimant's behalf. (See Table 53-2.)

Should you answer "no" to more than one or two of the questions in Table 53-2, we would recommend a full and

Table 53-2 Disciplinary Documentation Checklist

	Yes	No
Are there written personnel policies and procedures?	——	——
Have they been reviewed within the last 12 months?	——	——
Are they updated on a regular basis as a matter of policy?	——	——
Do supervisors and managers have easy access to personnel policies and procedures?	——	——
Do employees have easy access to personnel policies and procedures?	——	——
Is there a formal written policy outlining in-hospital third-party review before suspensions and terminations?	——	——
Do supervisors and managers feel that the progressive discipline policy is fairly and equally applied? How do you know?	——	——
Is there regular training of supervisors and managers regarding the organization's obligations toward employees which includes updates on labor law, discrimination law, etc.?	——	——
Do the employees feel the progressive discipline policy is fairly and equally applied? How do you know?	——	——
Does the human resources department have a system of logging disciplinary warnings, conferences, suspensions, and discharges? Is the log available for management review? Does the log reveal consistency?	——	——
Is there a formal written policy requiring the purging and destruction of warning notices after a stated period of time?	——	——
Are monthly (or quarterly) summaries of personnel policies and procedures sent to supervisors and employees or published in the employee publication?	——	——
Is a monthly turnover report listing terminations by department, by reason, by length of service, and for the same period last year distributed to all department managers?	——	——
Are unemployment compensation charges at the lowest maximum level with no chargebacks?	——	——
Has the hospital not lost a case in the last three years involving a discharge that was challenged?	——	——
Can the hospital defend actions brought by an employee or third party successfully based on documentation?	——	——

immediate review of the disciplinary procedure. In any event, these questions and others like them will allow you to begin to gauge the effectiveness of your existing systems.

Executives and practitioners are frequently asked questions regarding statutory record retention requirements. For your convenience, we have included a table displaying these requirements for major pieces of federal legislation. Since regulations change and are periodically amended, this material should be reviewed for accuracy regularly.

NOTES

1. See 29 U.S.C. § 152(11), 1947.

2. F.L. Elkouri and E.A. Elkouri. *How Arbitration Works*, 2d ed. (Washington, D.C.: Bureau of National Affairs, Inc., 1960), 411, 419–20, 423. N. Metzger and D. Pointer, *Labor Management Relations in the Health Services Industry—Theory and Practice* (Washington, D.C.: Science & Health Publications, Inc., 1972), 213–16. M. Hill, Jr., and A. Sinicropi. *Evidence in Arbitration* (Washington, D.C.: Bureau of National Affairs, Inc., 1980), 34–35.

Record Retention Requirements

	90 days	6 mos.	1 yr.	2 yrs.	3 yrs.	5 yrs.	6 yrs.
Payroll Records* (See I Below)							
Fair Labor Standards Act (hereafter referred to as FLSA)					x		
Child Labor Law					x		
Equal Pay Act					x		
Age in Discrimination Act					x		
Certificates, Agreements, Plans, Notices, etc. (See II Below)*							
FLSA					x		
Sales and Purchase Records (See III Below)*							
FLSA					x		
Basic Employment and Earnings Records (See IV Below)*							
FLSA				x			
Equal Pay Act							
Wage Rate Tables for Piece Rates or Other Rates Used in Computing Earnings*							
FLSA				x			
Worktime Schedules Establishing Hours and Days of Employment*							
FLSA				x			
Records of Addition to or Deductions from Wages Paid* (See V Below)							
FLSA				x			
Certificates of Age** FLSA/Child Labor Law	Until Termination of Employment						
Written Training Agreements** FLSA/Child Labor Law	Duration of Training Program						
Job Orders Submitted to Employment Agencies or Labor Unions for Recruitment of Personnel Age in Discrimination Act 29 C.F.R. § 1627.3			x				
Personnel or Employment Records related to job applications, promotions, demotions, transfers, layoff or termination, rates of pay, and selection for training or apprenticeship Age in Discrimination Act 29 C.F.R. § 1602.14		x from date of making record or personnel action, whichever is later; if charge is brought, retain until final disposition					

	90 days	6 mos.	1 yr.	2 yrs.	3 yrs.	5 yrs.	6 yrs.
Executive Order 11246, et al. (See Written Affirmative Action Plan)			x				

Test Papers of Employer-Administered Aptitude or Other Employment Tests
  Age in Discrimination Act
  29 C.F.R. § 1627.3
			x				

Results of Physician Examinations Considered in Connection with Personnel Actions
  Age in Discrimination Act
  29 C.F.R. § 1627.3
			x				

Advertisements for Hiring Personnel
  Age in Discrimination Act
  29 C.F.R. § 1627.3
			x				

Employment Applications for Temporary Positions
  Age in Discrimination Act
  29 C.F.R. § 1627.3
	x						

Employee Benefit Plans, such as pension and insurance plans as well as copies of any seniority and merit systems
  Age in Discrimination Act
  29 C.F.R. § 1627.3
			x
			after termination of Plan				

Written Affirmative Action Plan, including EEO-required records on testing, validation of tests, and results
  Executive Order 11246
  Vietnam Era Veterans
  Readjustment Act
  41 C.F.R. § 60-250.4
  41 C.F.R. § 60-250.52
	Not Specified		x				

Books, documents, papers, and records concerning employment and advancement in employment of handicapped Rehabilitation Act of 1973	Not Specified						

Disabled Veterans and Veterans of the Vietnam Era Readjustment Act (reports to state employment services regarding employment openings and hirings):
Vietnam Era Veterans Readjustment Act
  41 C.F.R. § 60-250.4
  41 C.F.R. § 60-250.52
		x
		after final payment under federal contract					

Record of each occupational injury and illness, including an annual summary, and also a supplemental record in detail according to OSHA Form 101 or Workers' Compensation Form
  OSHA
  29 C.F.R. § 1952.4
						x	

	90 days	6 mos.	1 yr.	2 yrs.	3 yrs.	5 yrs.	6 yrs.
Records on matters for which disclosure is required of any plan descriptions, annual reports, and summary annual reports under ERISA 29 C.F.R. § 486 ERISA 29 U.S.C. § 1027						x	x Not less than 6 years after filing date of report or description required
Records regarding complaints and action taken. Executive Order 11246 Rehabilitation Act of 1973 Vietnam Era Readjustment Act	Not Specified		x x				

I. a. Name in full of employee (as used for Social Security record purposes) and identifying number or symbol, if such is used on payroll records.

   b. Home address, including zip code.

   c. Date of birth, if under 19 years of age.

   d. Sex and occupation (sex may be indicated by Miss, Mrs., Ms., or Mr.)

   e. Time of day and day of week on which employee's work week begins, if this varies among employees; otherwise, a single notation for the entire establishment will suffice.

   f. Regular hourly rate of pay for any week when compensation is due, and any overtime data, as well as any additional payroll data which is pertinent.

   g. Daily hours worked and total hours worked each work week (workday may be any consecutive 24-hour period).

   h. Total daily or weekly straight time and overtime earnings or wages due for hours worked during the workday or work week, including all earnings or wages due during any overtime hours worked, but excluding overtime excess compensation.

   i. Total overtime excess compensation for the work week over and above all straight time earnings or wages also earned during overtime worked.

   j. Total additions or deductions from wages paid each pay period. The employer shall also maintain in individual employee accounts a record of dates, amounts, and nature of the items which make up the total additions and deductions.

   k. Total wages paid each pay period.

   l. Dates of payment and pay period covered.

   Employers shall maintain and preserve records containing all the information and data required by the above section for bona fide executive, administrative, and professional employees (including academic, administrative, personnel, and teachers in elementary or secondary schools). In addition thereto, the basis on which wages are paid must be given in sufficient detail to permit calculation for each pay period of the exempt employee's total remuneration for employment including fringe benefits and perquisites.

   Although there is no specific form furnished by the Wage and Hour Division for calculation of the benefit costs, the data necessary to calculate these costs should be readily available to Wage and Hour audit personnel.

   Walsh-Healey requires the same basic records but also requires records of the worker's sex and identifying number of the contract on which the employee is working.

II. Includes collective bargaining agreements, plans, trusts, employment contracts (where such contracts or agreements are not in writing, a written memorandum summarizing the terms), and certificates and notices listed or named in any applicable section of 516.5 of Regulation 29.

III. A record of (1) total dollar volume of sales or business and (2) total volume of goods purchased or received during such periods (weekly, monthly, quarterly, etc.) and in such forms as the employer maintains in the ordinary course of business.

IV. a. Including all basic time and earning cards or sheets and work production sheets of individuals where all or part of the employee's earnings are determined therefrom.

   b. Wage rate tables which provide piece rates or other rates used in computing earnings.

   c. Work time schedules from last effective date which establish hours and days of employment of individual employees or of separate work forces.

V. a. Records of additions or deductions as provided in Section 516.2 (those items listed under 3-year retention section). See I(j).

b. All employee purchase orders or assignments made by employees, and all copies of additions or deductions statements furnished employees.

c. All records used by employers in determining the original cost, operating and maintenance cost, and depreciation and interest charges, if such costs and charges are involved in the additions or deductions from wages paid.

d. Records explaining the basis for payment of any wage differentials to employees of the opposite sex in the same establishment which may be pertinent to a determination whether such differential is based on a factor other than sex.

*29 C.F.R. § 516.2, 516.3, 516.6, 516.11–516.29.
**29 C.F.R. §§ 516.5, 516.33, 570.6, 570.35A, 570.72.

Source: Federal Register—Guide to Record Retention, National Archives of the United States, 1981.

Michael I. Bernstein

54

What's in a Name: The Discovery in Grievance Handling

Senator Chic Hecht (R-Nevada) reportedly once said he opposed a nuclear waste *"suppository"* in his home state.[1] It is unclear whether Senate administrative aides relied to any extent on this remark when they designated Senator Hecht the Senate's least effective member. It is clear, however, that the senator's malapropism couldn't hurt him when the aides sought out their most likely candidate.

Malapropisms, by definition, are humorous and, witness Mr. Berra, generally harmless. That, unfortunately, isn't necessarily the case with faulty packaging. How a thought, idea, or program is presented, labeled, or classified may well be determinative. The implications can be profound.

Query, for example, whether the term *grievance procedure* is an apt one. Some years ago, I asked a group of managers what the term *grievance procedure* brought to mind. As they responded, I wrote their comments on a chalkboard: "due process," "discipline," "complaints," "day in court," "safety valve," "fair hearing." They cited, as well, the procedure as an indicator of problems, the need for management to be concerned with both real and imaginary issues, and the importance of expeditious processing, predictability, and uniformity in the resolution of problems.

All of these comments, of course, were accurate, and each captured vital and essential aspects of any grievance procedure, whether in a union or union-free setting. Yet none of the managers even thought of the grievance procedure as a vehicle for discovery—a critical vehicle, I might add, given the likelihood that a grievance eventually may resurface in any number of different fora. Indeed, if I were to cite one of management's most common errors, it would be this failure to recognize the best discovery vehicle management has at its command.

How many times have we witnessed a grievance in or en route to arbitration, administrative processing, or litigation where management has learned surprisingly little during the grievance stages about the grievant's case? What *precisely* is the grievant's position? If there are witnesses, who are they, what is it they are prepared to say, and has such been fully investigated? If the grievant was elsewhere, what do we know about his/her alibi and the extent to which it can be substantiated? If there is documentation, will there be any surprises, and have we been apprised of all the documentation on which the grievant relies? If the grievant's position is predicated on a pattern or practice, or a supervisor's representation, do we know the individuals, specific situations, or facts he/she has in mind? To what extent has the grievant been *pinned down* to a fixed position, or details, so that subsequent attempts to alter that position, or its details, can be highlighted?

Why is it too often we first hear the answers to these questions only when in arbitration, administrative hearing, or litigation? Why, when preparing for such, must we merely *speculate* on precisely what the grievant's position will be? Not in every case, but in most, there is no reason whatsoever for management to find itself in such a position. But it does happen—and too frequently.

After much thought I have come to believe the answer in large part lies with the packaging. Here is where the labeling leads us down the wrong path. Call it a *grievance procedure*, and immediately a certain mindset develops. A *grievance* generally entails an *accusation* that management/supervision

483

in some way has acted improperly. That, in turn, often produces a defensive reaction on the part of those involved in the grievance process, even if well intentioned. The initial focus, as a result, is more on justifying management's position, consciously or otherwise. The grievant is allowed to speak, and even conduct a superficial investigation if necessary, but if the grievant can't convince you that management has acted improperly, the grievance is denied.

On its face, that appears reasonable enough, especially if you consider the time limits of a grievance procedure, the busy schedules of those charged with resolving grievances, and their understandable preference to deal instead with their many other concerns and responsibilities.

But is it acceptable or desirable?

Suppose that you were taught that after a grievance is filed, the next step in the procedure is *discovery*—to borrow a term from our litigation process. Assume that nothing is changed in your existing grievance procedure other than the label "discovery," but now each manager/supervisor involved in the process is instructed that his/her express mandate, in resolving the grievance, includes learning as much as possible about the grievant's position and, where appropriate, investigating it before making a decision. More specifically, assume that each such manager/supervisor is advised to ask as many questions as necessary to flush out—*and pin down*—the grievant's position, so that if the grievance reaches arbitration, administrative hearing, or litigation, you are not surprised by the theory of the case, the contract provision(s) (if applicable) on which the grievant relies, the chronology of events, the documentation, and the witnesses.[2]

Not only is a grievance more likely to be resolved—one way or the other—if such an approach is pursued, but also if a case does proceed to arbitration, administrative hearing, or litigation and the theory or material details have changed, management will be in a better position to point such out. At the very least, management will be far more able to anticipate and prepare for the arguments and evidence advanced.

What must be emphasized is that the grievance procedure is, essentially, *management's* own internal procedure. It is not a

procedure supervised or controlled by a court or administrative agency, or even (where one exists) by the union. At no other time will management have such utter control over the process and, for that matter, such relatively unfettered access to potential witnesses. Even where the grievant and/or union refuses to name or produce witnesses, that may well bear either on the credibility of the grievant's and/or witnesses' position thereafter or on the reasonableness and good faith of management's position in acting on the information then available to it. Moreover, in its pursuit of a meaningful investigation of the grievance, management's "license"—indeed, obligation—to question these individuals should go unchallenged; it is to be expected that management will seek to learn as much as possible about the grievance before rendering its decision at each step, and, accordingly, the grievant and/or union is in less of a position to resist.

Contrast this with the discovery procedure of the litigation process. There the parties already are locked into an adversarial proceeding. While discovery in litigation is designed to discourage and minimize surprises, this adversarial relationship and the formality of the proceedings breed a tension and degree of resistance less likely to be present, or justified, in the internal and informal grievance stages controlled by the employer.

In short, there probably never will be an opportunity such as that afforded during the grievance procedure. It offers, as Senator Hecht might have said, a potential "suppository" of vital information.

NOTES

1. "The Election," *Time* (21 November 1988): 83.

2. You might even consider revising the grievance form, to the extent you control it, to include specific reference to the contract provisions, the chronology, the pertinent documentation, and the names and positions of any witnesses. Failing that, a checklist of such areas of inquiry might be distributed to those managers/supervisors involved in the process.

Paul Yager

The Mediation of Grievance Disputes

55

Grievance procedures frequently include a final step which provides for a binding decision by a neutral arbitrator to resolve such disputes when the parties cannot reach agreement short of that step. Advocates and representatives of employer and employee organizations have found that some grievance disputes can be settled short of arbitration with the assistance of a mediator who helps the parties overcome some of the obstacles to settlement by further negotiation. The mediator does not make a binding decision. The mediator provides a forum in which the parties are encouraged to explore settlement prospects that they might not have considered in bilateral negotiations, but that are more accessible when they surface under the auspices of a mediator. Usually the mediation of grievance disputes is not a feature of the standard grievance procedure because not all grievances are perceived as amenable to the mediation process. However, the parties can provide for such a function in the grievance procedure or by a separate agreement.

Note should also be taken that mediation of grievance disputes can be provided in procedures that may be available to deal with disputes that arise between employers and nonrepresented employees, as well as employees represented by unions and other employee organizations.

The mediation process is the continuation of negotiations with the help of a neutral who is knowledgeable about dispute settlement procedures. The mediator can provide the parties with opportunities to consider alternative bases for settlement, to review their options, to explore proposals that they might not explore in bilateral negotiations, and to clarify the meaning of the contract language which each of them interprets differently. The mediator works jointly and separately with the parties. The mediator listens to the positions of the parties and any facts and data about the dispute which they consider relevant. The mediator does not evaluate evidence or credibility because the mediator does not write a decision. The mediator may offer suggestions for terms of settlement and may even make a recommendation for the parties to consider, but the choice of settling the dispute or proceeding to arbitration is the parties'.

Every mediator has a personal approach and method of operating, but all have the same goal: to help the parties achieve a mutually satisfactory settlement.

The parties to a grievance dispute that are prepared to take the matter to arbitration may want to consider whether or not mediation is appropriate. Certain grievance disputes may not be appropriate for mediation, so that moving to mediation is not automatic. However, each party might consider the appropriateness and benefits of mediation before deciding to take a grievance to arbitration.

As arbitration becomes more and more expensive, settlement through mediation—which is usually speedier, less formal, and less complex, and therefore cheaper—may be useful when the amount in dispute is small and no great principle or significant interpretation of the agreement is at stake. When calculating the cost of arbitration, the parties should consider the costs for attorneys and other representatives, the lost-time costs for witnesses and other participants, and the cost of preparation time. Consideration should also be given to the win-lose nature of litigation, such as arbitration. The climate of litigation tends to exacerbate existing tensions. The results are not predictable and may create more problems, and the losing party may be so distressed by the outcome as to seek significant modifications of the contract at the next negotiation, which will create an obstacle to settlement. Arbitration is subject to delays in selecting the arbitrator, scheduling the arbitration hearings, and receiving the decision from the arbitrator. All this can be minimized by attempting to achieve settlement with a mediator.

There are situations wherein work place realities require intensive support by higher levels of management and/or union leadership for the individual supervisors, employees, and members who become involved in grievance disputes. Yet such support may not be warranted by the facts of the dispute. Such disputes wind up in arbitration and become expensive demonstrations of loyalty and support, frequently for a lost cause. The mediation forum is an opportunity to involve the front-line supervisors, the grievant, and the union representative in dialogue which can illuminate the win-lose environment of an arbitration proceeding. The informality of the mediation forum also provides opportunity for fuller participation by the people most deeply involved in the dispute than is allowed in an arbitration procedure in which the professional advocates are usually the chief participants.

The mediation forum provides opportunity for expression of remorse and reconsideration of hasty actions, for encouraging behavior modification, and for illuminating the problems that have created disputes but that are lost to sight when the parties are involved in grievance and arbitration procedures.

Another byproduct of the mediation of grievance disputes is the opportunity to clear up ambiguities in agreement language. The climate is not always favorable to do so, but when it is, all parties benefit by having achieved a better understanding of their commitment to each other. Also, issues that fester during the term of an agreement and then erupt during contract renewal negotiations may be reduced if explored in a less heated forum. Yet another byproduct is the opportunity that the higher echelons of employer and employee organizations have to learn about the realities of the business operation and the relationships in the work place. The responses to the mediator's inquiries about the circumstances of the dispute often reveal conditions to the upper echelons that tend to be overlooked if these questions are not asked.

Although arbitrators' decisions and awards are seldom considered absolutely binding interpretations of the agreement, they do tend to be seen as precedents for the future. When a grievance is settled by negotiation, either with or without a mediator, that settlement can be implemented in such a way as to avoid any precedent-setting implication.

As indicated earlier, there are some disputes that cannot be settled short of arbitration, and it is wise not to try mediation in such situations. If either party is determined to exercise the right to arbitration, further negotiation with a mediator would be a waste of time and money. When one party has to prove a particular version of the facts or the correctness of a certain interpretation of the agreement, further negotiation is not warranted. If the continuation of the negotiation process with a mediator is perceived by any participant as disadvantageous or if the mediator is perceived as unfair or ineffective, the process should go no further. If either or both of the parties are reluctant to discuss a possible settlement because they do not want to weaken their position if they have to go to arbitration, the process should stop because the matter is not appropriate for the mediation forum.

One of the weaknesses of a hierarchical system of dispute resolution is that participants may tend to abdicate their responsibilities to negotiate to settlement at an early stage if they believe they might do better at a later stage. Thus, we might find advocates in bilateral grievance negotiations reluctant to settle because they are anticipating the mediation step. This fault can be eliminated by appropriate training and leadership. Furthermore, it will exist even if there is no mediation step.

When the parties agree to include a mediation step in their grievance procedure, they should formalize that agreement with some form of written statement that also describes the procedure for determining which grievances are subject to or barred from mediation, how the process is initiated, how the mediator is selected, the payment of fees, and the limitations, if any, on the mediator. Fortunately, there are programs in place that can serve as models. The National Academy of Conciliators has such a program. Its rules are presented in Appendix 55-A to this chapter as an example. The American Arbitration Association and many of the statutory mediation services provide mediators and can be helpful in setting up the rules.

It is worth noting that the expansion of dispute resolution procedures does not diminish the effectiveness of keen advocacy. In fact, advocates of the rights and interests of the constituents and clients can undertake more vigorous advocacy when they know that means for resolving disputes are readily available. Negotiation, mediation, and arbitration are devices that provide us with a safety net when the potential cost of vigorous advocacy threatens to exceed our resources and our ability to pursue our goals in a more confrontational arena. We should be prepared to use the safety net when we find ourselves at the brink of disaster.

National Academy of Conciliators
Grievance Mediation Rules and Procedures

PREAMBLE

The National Academy of Conciliators (NAC) is a private, independent, impartial organization which administers dispute resolution procedures.

Grievance Mediation Procedures, administered by NAC, can be provided pursuant to an applicable provision of a collective bargaining agreement, under a personnel policy or, in the alternative, by a standard NAC submission agreement on an ad-hoc basis.

The following rules ("The Rules") govern the initiation, conduct and administration of the NAC Grievance Mediation Procedure.

1. *Initiation of the Grievance Mediation Procedure*

   a. The parties shall submit a request for grievance mediation on a *Request for Grievance Mediation* or NAC *Submission Agreement* Form.

   b. The proper Administrative Fee (as determined under Section Seven (7) of these Rules) shall accompany the request.

2. *Mediator Assignment*

   a. NAC shall assign a mediator within five (5) work days of receiving the request for mediation.

   b. NAC shall provide the mediator with the names, addresses and telephone numbers of the parties and the parties with the name and telephone number of the mediator assigned.

   c. Within five (5) work days of the receipt of the notification of the assignment, the mediator shall communicate with the parties to establish a mediation conference date and location.

   d. The mediation conference shall be held within fifteen (15) work days of the first communication between the mediator and the parties.

   e. Should the mediator assigned be unable to execute his or her responsibilities within the time specified by these

Rules, another mediator shall be assigned unless all the parties mutually agree to retain the mediator and hold the mediation conference on a later date.

3. *The Mediation Conference: Time and Site*

   a. The mediation conference shall be held at a site and at such time as are mutually agreed to by the parties.

   b. Should the parties fail to agree on a site and/or time, the mediator shall select the site and/or establish the time of the mediation conference.

   c. The parties shall notify the mediator of any postponement or cancellation of the conference within forty-eight (48) hours of the scheduled conference. The parties shall also notify NAC, as soon as practicable, of any delay, postponement or cancellation of a mediation conference by a mediator.

   d. Should a party delay, postpone or cancel a mediation conference less than forty-eight (48) hours prior to its scheduled date, that party shall be solely liable for any expenses and fees occasioned by such action, including those incurred by the mediator, and for the NAC administration fees. NAC shall have the sole and exclusive right to make such an assessment.

4. *Conduct of the Mediation Conference*

   a. *Authority of the Mediator*
   The mediator shall have the authority to conduct the mediation conference in such manner as the mediator shall judge will best facilitate the most expeditious disposition of the grievance, consistent with commonly accepted mediation procedures and these Rules. The mediator shall decide questions of interpretation and application of these Rules, and give due consideration to rule changes mutually agreeable to the parties.

Source: Grievance Mediation Rules and Procedures for the Health Care Industry: A Pilot Program, National Academy of Conciliators. Reprinted with permission.

b. *The Mediation Conference*

The mediation conference shall be conducted as an informal procedure in such manner as the mediator determines to be consistent with informal practices, with securing the most expeditious disposition of the grievance, and with the following rules of conduct:

(i) Attendance shall be required of each party to the grievance. There shall be no *ex parte* proceedings.

(ii) Only those other persons who may have a bearing on the resolution of the grievance shall attend the conference; such attendance shall be in such manner and at such time as the mediator may determine.

(iii) Each party shall designate a representative who shall act as spokesperson; provided however, that nothing shall preclude a grievant from making a presentation in order to have the fullest opportunity to be heard; and provided further, that should extraordinary circumstances require more than one spokesperson for any party, the mediator shall designate the number of such spokespersons.

(iv) Either party may present such proof, written or oral, as each shall deem necessary to the presentation of their respective positions without the challenge of materiality or conformance with any rules of evidence.

(v) The mediator shall utilize commonly accepted mediation practices including, but not limited to, joint and separate meetings with any person or persons participating and the proferring of grievance resolution proposals.

(vi) The mediator shall have no authority to compel resolution of the dispute.

(vii) There shall be no permanent record kept of the substance of the mediation conference by the parties.

(viii) Either party shall have the right to withdraw the grievance from mediation, in which event the mediation shall terminate upon the mediator's delivery to the parties of an advisory opinion.

(ix) Should the parties not be able to resolve the grievance to their mutual satisfactions after a reasonable period of conference time, the mediator shall, upon the request of both parties or whenever the mediator shall deem it appropriate, provide an oral advisory opinion, which shall be grounded on findings of fact and conclusions as if the mediator were serving as an arbitrator. The parties may accept or reject the advisory award. Nothing in these Rules shall preclude the parties from accepting the award as final and binding and the parties may agree, at any time, to give the mediator authority to make such a binding resolution.

(x) Contractual time limits for notice to move to arbitration (or the next step of the grievance process) shall be tolled from the date of the joint request for grievance mediation.

5. *Actions on the Conclusion of the Grievance Mediation Conference*

a. Should the grievance be resolved as a result of the mediation process:

(i) The parties shall sign a statement, on a NAC *Grievance Mediation Settlement* Form, that the matter has been resolved and that no party or individual represented by a party shall appeal to or attempt to move in any other forum for the purpose of further proceeding on the issue(s) derived therefrom. The Form shall contain a brief statement of the settlement.

(ii) The final resolution of the grievance shall not constitute a precedent unless the parties agree otherwise.

b. If the grievance is not resolved as a result of the mediation process:

(i) The contractual time for notice to move to arbitration (or the next step in the grievance process) shall commence running on the date on which the mediation process is terminated.

(ii) The mediator may not be the arbitrator in any subsequent arbitration proceeding of the grievance which was the subject of the mediation conference.

(iii) No utterance, action or inaction by any person involved in the mediation process shall be referred to by expression or implication at any arbitration or other proceeding and such subsequent proceedings shall be, in all respects, *de novo*.

6. *Other*

a. All discussions between and among the grievant, disputing parties and/or the mediator shall be privileged and treated as confidential. All notes relating to the events of the conference, except those relating directly to the disposition of the grievance, shall be destroyed by the respective parties.

b. Expenses for attendance of participants (including lost time for employees), other than those of the mediator, shall be borne by the party incurring such expenses unless otherwise agreed.

c. When the parties choose NAC and this Grievance Mediation Procedure, they have agreed to abide by these Rules as established by NAC, that The Rules are binding on the parties, and that they hold NAC, and the mediator appointed by NAC to conduct the mediation conference, harmless from any claim for damages arising from the grievance mediation process.

7. *Fees and Expenses*

    a. The fees and related expenses of the grievance mediation process, including those of the mediator, shall be shared equally by the parties.

    b. The parties shall make payment for the grievance mediation directly to NAC on the basis of the following fee schedule:

(i) Mediator's fees:

first case/day $400

same day $200/case

(up to two (2) additional cases—maximum of three (3) cases in one day)

(ii) Administrative fees:

each case . . . . $ 75/party

Steven G. Allen

Unions and Productivity Growth

56

INTRODUCTION

Until recently, the issue of how unions affect productivity had been explored only with an institutional approach. Slichter, Healy, and Livernash (1960) and Bok and Dunlop (1970) examined the static aspects of this question (such as how unions affect the skill level of the work force or the extent of featherbedding), as well as the dynamics (such as how unions affect technical change or the future of apprenticeship). This approach produced a very comprehensive and balanced view of the factors that enter the unionism-productivity relationship, but yielded very little insight into the magnitude of unionism's impact.

Roughly 10 years ago a group of researchers armed with the thoretical and applied econometric tools of the price theoretic approach to labor issues started to produce quantitative estimates of the impact of unionism across cross-sections of firms or industries. The results of this research, summarized in Freeman and Medoff (1984), show that in most instances productivity is much higher *at a given point in time* under unionism. The main reasons for this seem to be lower turnover, better training, improved communication, and "shock effects" on management. While each of these studies has

some methodological shortcomings, it is rather remarkable that they reach similar conclusions despite differences in level of aggregation in the data, availability of control variables, and econometric specification (and perhaps even more remarkable once one considers the payoffs within the economics profession to anyone who could find higher productivity in the nonunion sector).

These studies have not considered the question of how unions affect productivity *over time*. The use of cross-section data sets has largely precluded the examination of this set of issues, with one notable exception. Connerton, Freeman, and Medoff (1983) use repeated cross-sections to examine how the union-nonunion productivity difference has changed over time in the bituminous coal mining industry. They find that productivity in union mines was 33 to 38 percent higher than in nonunion mines in 1965, but 14 to 20 percent lower than in nonunion mines in 1975 and 1980. They attribute the decline of the union coefficient to the deterioration of labor-management relations during that time period, a perfectly legitimate inference given the theoretical framework within which all these studies (including, of course, my own) have been embedded. The exit-voice model emphasizes turnover, training, and labor-management interaction, but pays scant attention to such dynamic factors as investment in R&D lags in adopting new techniques, and organizational change.

This chapter examines union-nonunion differences in productivity levels at different points in time and in the rate of productivity change over time. The ways in which unions affect the rate of productivity change are examined below. Considering both price theoretic and institutional factors, the impact of unionism on productivity change cannot be predicted *ex ante*. For instance, under certain circumstances

Note: This chapter is an expanded version of the article "Productivity Levels & Productivity Change under Unionism," *Industrial Relations*, Vol. 27, No. 1, pp. 94–113, Institute of Industrial Relations, University of California, Berkeley, © Winter 1988.

Financial support was provided by the National Science Foundation and North Carolina State University. John Abowd, Richard Freeman, Casey Ichniowski, Tom Kniesner, and Sol Polachek provided helpful comments on earlier versions of the paper. Myra Ragland and Katherine Foote were excellent research assistants.

managers may invest more in potentially labor-saving R&D under unionism to reduce inefficiency resulting from higher union wages, whereas in other cases management may be reluctant to invest in R&D because the returns may be appropriated by the union. The interests of union members are equally important. Some unions have used work rules to block the introduction of new technology, while others have accepted wage cuts in return for promises by management to upgrade plant and equipment and thereby increase long-term job security. Just as in the case of cross-section union-non-union differences in productivity levels, the question of whether unions promote or retard productivity change is an empirical issue.

Previous studies of how unions affect productivity change in manufacturing are surveyed. Many studies have found that productivity growth is slower in unionized industries, especially when they use data on two-digit industries. The problem with using such data is that it is impossible to distinguish the hypothesis that unions reduce productivity growth from the hypothesis that the most heavily unionized industries have limited opportunities for productivity growth. The only way to overcome this problem is to use a data set that allows one to make union-nonunion comparisons within a particular sector. Studies using data on individual firms or less aggregated industrial categories tend to find that unionism has no effect on productivity growth, a conclusion which is replicated below over a new data set.

It is widely believed that the negative effects of unions on productivity growth are most likely to arise under craft unionism. To test this possibility, this chapter reports new evidence on the impact of unions on productivity change in construction. Repeated cross-sections of state by industry (two-digit SIC) data from the 1972, 1977, and 1982 Censuses of Construction Industries (CCI) are examined in two different ways. First, following Connerton, Freeman, and Medoff (1983), different union coefficients are estimated for each year. The results for a variety of specifications show that the union coefficient dropped considerably between 1972 and 1982. The next step involves estimating productivity change equations. If a static Cobb-Douglas production function is an accurate picture of reality, productivity change should be a function of the change in unionization (and other variables), not the initial level of unionization (or other variables). If unions affect productivity growth, however, both the change and the initial level of unionization belong in the equation. The evidence strongly supports the latter view. Both the initial level and the change in unionization are inversely correlated with the productivity change.

PRODUCTIVITY CHANGE UNDER UNIONISM

In cross-section analyses union-nonunion productivity differences can arise through a number of mechanisms. Turnover should be lower under unionism because of the greater voice given to workers with regard to personnel policies and outcomes. In addition to freeing resources which would have otherwise been allocated to hiring and training replacements for departed employees, this should also encourage more investment in specific human capital. Collective bargaining also opens up communication channels between workers and management, another aspect of worker voice that sometimes generates suggestions for productivity changes from workers that had been overlooked by managers.

Foremen and supervisors have much less control over promotions and compensation in a union setting. This has ambiguous implications for productivity. While seniority rules interfere with the optimal matching of workers and jobs and the weaker linkage between pay and performance under unionism removes an important incentive for work effort, these changes also eliminate an important source of rivalry among workers and result in greater cooperation. Morale may also be enhanced to the extent that favoritism is no longer a factor in promotions or pay increases.

The "shock effect" of unions on management behavior is another important factor in making cross-section productivity comparisons by union status. In unionized settings, the pressure of higher wage rates induces management to tighten up on any sources of organizational slack. Clark (1980) shows that after a plant is unionized, many management practices change, with a greater emphasis on standards and accountability. In addition to these shock effects, unions also perform certain functions for management, such as explaining changes that are about to be introduced in the plant or, in some cases, administering employee benefits.

Craft union institutions also can have an important impact on productivity. Hiring halls in the construction industry cut employer search costs and reduce the risk of having an inadequate number of workers on a large job. Union apprenticeship programs are the only source of well-rounded craftsmen in that industry. However, craft unions are also responsible for many anachronistic work rules and an occupational jurisdiction system that not only results in overstaffing but also creates conflicts at the job site which frequently result in work stoppages.

Using a Cobb-Douglas production function $Q_t = (A_n + cU_t)L_t^a K_t^b$, the net impact of all these sources of productivity differences between union and nonunion observations in a cross-section can be determined by estimating the parameter c. Suppose now that two cross-section data sets are available. Then, after taking log differences, the parameter c can also be estimated with the equation

$$d\log(Q/L)_t = c*d^U_t + b*d\log(K/L)_t + (a + b - 1)*d\log L_t \qquad (1)$$

In this specification, productivity changes are entirely a function of changes in the percentage of workers unionized, the capital/labor ratio, and the establishment size. If the model has been specified correctly and if there is no measurement error in the data set, one should get the same estimate of c from either the conventional cross-section equation or the log difference equation (1). In cases in which output is measured in terms of value added, the union coefficient will also reflect price differences unless value added has been properly deflated.

The parameter c in (1) is assumed to be constant in each period. This assumption is inappropriate whenever productivity shocks occur within either the union or the nonunion sector. For instance, if relations between labor and management deteriorate, as was the case in the bituminous coal industry in the period examined by Connerton, Freeman, and Medoff (1983), one would expect c to decline. Also, c could change as a result of changes in the sources of union-nonunion productivity differences. For instance, if changes are made in union work rules to allow management greater flexibility in assigning workers to jobs, this would cause c to rise. If c is allowed to vary over time, the product of the change in c and the initial level of percentage unionized must be added to (1).

$$d\log(Q/L)_t = c_t{*}dU_t + b{*}d\log(K/L)_t + (a - b - 1){*}d\log L_t + dc{*}U_{t-1} \quad (2)$$

The assumption of a constant value of c in (1) is also inappropriate when there is a difference in the rate of technical change between the union and the nonunion sectors. Let $d_0 = $ annual rate of technical change under unionism and $d_1 = $ annual rate of technical change in the nonunion sector. Then the production function becomes

$$Q_t = (A_n + cU_t)L_t{}^a K_t{}^b \exp\{(d_0 U_t + d_1(1 - U_t))t\}$$

and the estimating equation is now

$$\begin{aligned} d\log(Q/L)_t = c{*}dU_t &+ b{*}d\log(K/L)_t + (a + b - 1){*}d\log L_t \\ &+ (d_0 - d_1){*}U_{t-1} + d_1 t \\ &+ (d_0 - d_1)t{*}dU_t \end{aligned} \quad (3)$$

As one can see from comparing (2) and (3), changes in labor-management relations (or other factors that may cause c to vary over time) and unequal rates of technical change between the union and the nonunion sectors are econometrically equivalent in terms of their effects on productivity change. In each case both the initial level of unionization and the change in unionization appear on the righthand side of the equation. This means that some care must be taken to examine the institutional setting in any particular analysis before attributing the results to either labor relations factors or union-nonunion differences in technical change.

Unions are likely to influence productivity change through both price theoretic and institutional mechanisms. Changes in the union-nonunion wage gap lead to factor substitution decisions that will change labor productivity but have no effect on total factor productivity. The change in the capital/labor ratio controls for this spurious source of productivity change in (3).

Union wage behavior becomes a more critical factor when the technology itself is endogenous. Tauman and Weiss (1987) show that under certain assumptions, unionized firms are more likely to choose the most productive technology. They consider the case of a duoploy in which one firm is unionized and the other is nonunion. These firms participate in a two-stage noncooperative game with the union. In the first stage the firms choose their technology while the union simultaneously chooses the wage. Output and employment are determined in the second stage. Both firms initially have the same technology, but each can purchase and install a more productive technology at the same cost. Labor is assumed to be the only factor of production, so the more productive technology must be labor saving.

The decision to adopt this technology hinges on product demand. At very low demand levels, neither adopts, and at very high demand levels, both adopt. The key difference between the union and the nonunion firm is that the union charges its firm higher wages at high levels of output, while the nonunion firm pays the same competitive wage at all output levels. Thus, the union firm stands to gain more than the nonunion firm from adopting the more productive technology at some output levels, and it is possible to have a solution in which only the union firm uses that technology.

This result is very sensitive to the assumption that the union selects its wage at the same time that the firms select their technologies. If the union can alter its wage after the technologies have been chosen, it has the ability to appropriate the returns from the increase in productivity. Realizing this, the union firm is less likely than the nonunion firm to adopt the best technology, and it is impossible to have an equilibrium in which only the union firm uses the most productive technology.

Union firms may also want to keep some low productivity capacity in operation as part of a strategy to keep union wage demands in line. Baldwin (1983) shows that when the capital replacement cycle is long relative to the time horizon of the union, in the absence of enforceable long-term wage contracts, it is optimal to invest in both efficient and inefficient capacity rather than to invest only in the former. If firms invest only in the most efficient capacity, they are subject to the risk of higher union wage demands in the future, as pointed out by Tauman and Weiss (1987). However, by investing in both types of capacity, unions will be less likely to make such demands because some of the less efficient capacity would no longer be profitable to operate and employment would fall, lowering the union's utility. Although this strategy results in lower productivity growth in unionized industries, it is optimal from the standpoint of investors because it guarantees them some return on new capital investments.

Both the Tauman and Weiss and the Baldwin models are couched in terms of certain returns to investment in more productive capacity. Nelson (1981) has emphasized that two key aspects in the process of technical change—investment in R&D and the screening and spread of new technology—involve considerable uncertainty. A reasonable argument can be made that unionized firms engaged in innovative activities must deal with an additional source of uncertainty—namely, the reaction of the union. In addtion to the question of how much of the returns to any sort of innovative activity (product or process) will have to be shared with the union, there is also the issue of the willingness of unions to agree to changes in the production process. Not only may the expected returns to innovation be lower under unionism, but also they may be more unpredictable. If so, this would result in an even slower rate of technical change under unionism.

Now consider the institutional effects of unions on productivity growth. In most cases unions do not attempt to prevent management from introducing new techniques, mainly because the consequences of doing so are almost always self-destructive. Two specific cases cited by Bok and Dunlop (1970) are the attempts of the window-glass workers to stop the glass-making machine in 1908 and the efforts of the cigar makers to halt specialization and new machinery. The window-glass union had to be officially disbanded in 1928, while the percentage of workers unionized in the cigar industry dropped from 45 to 20 percent. Instead of obstructing new technology, Bok and Dunlop conclude that "labor leaders have normally chosen to accept new methods and share in the gains which these innovations make possible" (p. 262). A key exception to this general rule, they note, seems to be the case of "older members with a short, remaining work life and with little interest in moving or learning new skills, [who] may even find rational grounds for sacrificing their union in order to prolong their jobs until retirement" (p. 262).

Even if unions rarely attempt to block the introduction of new technology, they can still make the introduction of new technology more costly. In almost every case, management must consult with the union before making any changes in work assignments, skill requirements, number of positions, or plant and equipment. Slichter, Healy, and Livernash (1960) note that this will generally raise questions regarding craft jurisdiction, seniority, wage adjustments, and treatment of any displaced workers. Problems are most likely to arise when management must deal with a number of craft unions simultaneously. Even though management may at times receive highly valuable input from the union, on balance one would expect that the greater cost of introducing new technology under unionism should make the introduction of such technology less likely than in a nonunion setting.

However, there are also many cases in which the unions themselves have actively encouraged firms to make changes that workers believe will lead to more job security and higher wages. Slichter, Healy, and Livernash (1960) note that such a policy "usually is followed when the union is worried about the ability of an industry or a plant to hold its own in competition" (p. 355). For instance, they point out that the engineering departments of the needle trades have at times suggested technological changes to employers and assisted these employers in implementing them, performing a role similar to that of the extension service in agriculture. Unions also have generated technical improvements in plants with profit-sharing or employee participation programs. Currently, the growing emphasis on work organization and efficiency in quality-of-work-life (QWL) programs is another example of unions acting to promote productivity growth. To the extent that workers feel that they are more likely to share in the benefits of QWL programs under unionism, those programs may turn out to be more successful in a union setting than in a nonunion setting. Thus, the "voice" aspects of union behavior are far from irrelevant in the analysis of productivity change.

On balance the above discussion indicates that considering both price theoretic and institutional aspects of union behavior and managerial response, the impact of unions on productivity growth is an empirical question. I turn now to a survey of existing evidence, all of which comes from the manufacturing sector.

PREVIOUS EVIDENCE FROM MANUFACTURING

Only two studies have focused on the effects of unionization on productivity growth. Hirsch and Link (1984) found slower productivity growth in industries in which the percentage of workers unionized is high and in those in which that percentage is rising. Freeman and Medoff (1984) found no correlation between unionization and productivity growth in three different samples. There is, however, additional evidence on this question in a number of other studies in which, although the emphasis has been on estimating the impact of R&D on productivity growth, the percentage of workers unionized has been included as a control variable. The samples in some of these studies are almost identical to that used by Hirsch and Link and to one of the samples used by Freeman and Medoff. Thus, examination of their findings not only provides a wider base of evidence but also serves as an independent check on the robustness of the Hirsch and Link and the Freeman and Medoff results.

The results of all studies of productivity growth that include unionization as a righthand variable are summarized in Table 56-1. All these studies are limited to manufacturing and are grouped in Table 56-1 according to whether they use data on industries (at various levels of aggregation) or firms. For each study the table describes the sample, reports the measures of productivity and unionization, lists the control variables, and summarizes the results for the union variable(s).

The first four studies summarized all use data sets consisting of two-digit industries over various intervals. The first three of these consistently find much slower average annual productivity growth in unionized industries, with the estimates of the union-nonunion difference ranging between 4 and 6 percentage points. Even at the lower bound, this implies that over an 18-year period there will be twice as much productivity growth in a nonunion industry as compared to a unionized industry, implying that unions anathematize economic progress.

There are, however, a number of good reasons to question these findings. The results obtained by Kendrick and Grossman (1980) for the change in the unionization variable imply that a 10-percentage-point increase in unionization results in 1.8-percent faster productivity growth. Although they attribute this finding to the multicollinearity of the change in unionization with other variables, it could just as easily be explained in terms of "shock effects" in cases in which unionization is growing and in terms of increased turnover and lower labor quality in cases in which unionization is falling. Also, Terleckyj's (1980) findings indicate that the estimated effect of the initial level of unionization is very sensitive to which total factor productivity measure is used as the dependent variable. He finds a significant negative union impact on productivity growth for only two out of four measures.

The biggest problem with these results lies in the nature of the data. At the two-digit SIC level of aggregation it is impossible to determine whether unions directly reduce productivity growth or whether unions are most likely to be found in industries with limited opportunities for technical advancement. The percentage of workers unionized is highest in "smokestack" industries, such as primary metals, transporta-

Table 56-1 Studies of Unionization and Productivity Change in Manufacturing

Study	Sample	Measure of Productivity Change and Source[a]	Measure of Unionization and Source[a]	Control Variables[b]	Impact of Unionization on Annual Productivity Growth
Studies using industry data					
1. Kendrick and Grossman (1980)	20 2-digit, 1948–76	Own	Level: K (1973) Change: Own	R&D, CR, FEM, CAPUTIL	3.6 percent slower under unionism; 1.8 percent faster when union share rises by 1 percentage point
2. Mansfield (1980)	20 2-digit, 1948–66	K (1973)	Level: K (1973)	R&D CAT	5.4 to 6.1 percent slower under unionism
3. Hirsch & Link (1984)	19 2-digit, 1957–73	KG (1980) & GJ (1980)	Level: FM (1979) Change: GM (1979)	R&D, CR, PVT, CYC	3.6 to 4.4 percent slower under unionism and 0.5 to 0.0 percent slower when union share rises by 10 percentage points
4. Terleckyj (1980)	20 2-digit, 1948–66	a. K (1973)	Level: Own	R&D CAT, PVT, CYC	a. 4 percent slower under unionism
		b. GJ			b. Insignificant 3 percent slower under unionism
		c. Revised GJ			c. 3 percent slower under unionism
		d. KG (1980)			d. Insignificant 2 percent slower under unionism
5. Terleckyj (1984)	27 2- and 3-digit, 1969–76	GL (1984)	Level: FM (1979)	a. R&D	a. Insignificant 0.5 percent slower under unionism
				b. EMB R&D	b. 1.0 percent slower under unionism
				c. R&D, EMB R&D	c. Insignificant 0.5 percent slower under unionism
6. Sveikauskas and Sveikauskas (1982)	138 3-digit, 1959–69	Own	Level: FM (1979)	DY, SIZE, R&D, CR	Insignificant 0.44 percent slower to 0.01 percent faster under unionism
7. Freeman and Medoff (1984)	a. 176 3-digit, 1958–76	Own	Level: FM (1979)	None	a. Insignificant 0.4 percent slower under unionism
	b. 450 4-digit, 1958–78	G (1984)	Level: FM (1979)		b. Insignificant 0.3 percent slower under unionism
	c. 341 2-digit by state or region, 1972–77	Own	Level: Own		c. Insignificant 0.3 percent slower under unionism
8. Link (1981)	51 firms in 7 industries, 1973–78	Own	Level: FM (1979)	R&D CAT	2.5 percent slower under unionism
9. Link (1982)	97 firms in 3 industries, 1975–79	Own	Level: FM (1979)	a. R&D	a. 10.3 percent slower under unionism
				b. R&D CAT	b. 9.2 percent slower under unionism
10. Clark and Griliches (1984)	924 "businesses" in FIMS data, 1970–80	Own	Level: Own	R&D, R&D CAT, CAPUTIL, REC	Insignificant 1 percent higher under unionism

Notes: The dependent variable is growth in total factor productivity except for the Freeman and Medoff study, which uses growth to labor productivity. All results for impact of unionization are statistically significant at conventionally accepted confidence levels unless noted otherwise.

[a]Key to sources of productivity and unionization measures:

FM = Freemand and Medoff	GJ = Gollop and Jorgenson	K = Kendrick
G = Gray	GL = Griliches and Lichtenberg	KG = Kendrick and Grossman

[b]Key to control variables:

CAPUTIL = Capacity utilization ratio	EMB R&D = R&D embodied in capital goods purchased from other industries	R&D CAT = R&D intensity coefficient allowed to vary for different categories for R&D
CR = Concentration ratio		
	FEM = Percentage female employees	REC = Newness of capital stock
CYC = Index of cyclical instability of industry output	PVT = Share of sales to nongovernmental buyers	SIZE = Shares of workers in firms with 500 or less workers and 2,500 or more workers
DY = Output growth	R&D = Ratio of total R&D to output	

tion equipment, and paper, in which the products and the production processes changed very little over the sample periods examined in these studies. The only way to control for differences across industries in opportunities for productivity growth is to construct a data set with some predominantly union and some predominantly nonunion observations within each industrial category. This can be done by either using a finer level of aggregation than the very crude two-digit level or breaking down the two-digit industries by some other variable, such as location.

The remaining industry studies cited in Table 56-1 follow one of these two strategies. Terleckyj (1984) breaks a few two-digit industries down into their major three-digit components and finds significantly lower productivity growth under unionism in only one out of three specifications—one in which he includes R&D embodied in purchased capital goods but excludes R&D spending. When the latter R&D variable is included (with or without the embodied R&D measure), he finds no link between unionism and productivity growth. In a sample of 138 three-digit industries, Sveikauskas and Sveikauskas (1982) find no correlation between unionization and productivity growth in any of the seven equations they report. Freeman and Medoff examine one sample of three-digit industries, another sample of four-digit industries, and another consisting of two-digit industries broken down by state or region. As noted earlier, in all three cases they find slower productivity growth under unionism, but the relationship is not statistically significant.

The main conclusion that can be drawn from the industry studies surveyed here is that there is little reason to believe that unions have acted as a major obstacle to productivity growth in manufacturing. Although the sign of the union coefficient is almost always negative, in the most careful studies the estimated effect of unions is rather small and estimated with relatively little precision.

The results of three studies using data sets consisting of individual firms or lines of business within a firm are reported on the last three lines of Table 56-1. This type of data provides another way to obtain observations by union status within a particular industry, thus allowing independent variation in unionism and technological opportunities. This flexibility is obtained at the cost of limiting the sample to large, publicly traded firms and, in some cases, measuring unionization inaccurately. Two studies by Link (1981, 1982) find dramatically slower productivity growth in firms that seem to be predominantly unionized. Link's measure of unionization in both of these studies is the percentage of workers unionized in the three-digit industry in which the firm mainly operates. Because his samples are limited to three or seven industries, the meaning of his results is not altogether clear. Clark and Griliches (1984) find productivity grows at a 1-percent faster rate under unionism, but the union coefficient is the same size as its standard error. Thus, the studies using data on firms also fail to provide any conclusive evidence that unions have any direct effect on productivity growth.

Even if there is no direct correlation between unionism and productivity growth, unions could still influence productivity

growth indirectly by reducing R&D, investment, or profits. Research into these issues has just begun, so many of the conclusions reported below should be viewed as preliminary, especially those from unpublished papers. Nonetheless, the weight of this evidence suggests that unions significantly reduce R&D, investment, and profits.

Connolly, Hirsch, and Hirschey (1986) report evidence from a sample of 367 firms from the Fortune 500 that investment in R&D adds less to the market value of firms in unionized industries and that firms in those industries respond to this by investing in less R&D. This means that holding R&D intensity constant in an ordinary least squares (OLS) regression equation may not be the appropriate method for estimating the total impact of unionization on productivity growth. By failing to consider this indirect effect, the studies surveyed above may very well be underestimating the total impact of unionization. Further work with more broadly representative data sets is clearly needed to establish the robustness of Connolly, Hirsch, and Hirschey's findings with respect to union effects on R&D and how this influences estimates of the union impact on productivity growth.

Two recent studies report that unionized firms invest significantly less in plant and equipment than do nonunion firms. Bronars and Deere (1986) obtain this result for 756 publicly traded firms between 1972 and 1976, whereas Hirsch (forthcoming) reaches this conclusion using a sample of 315 Fortune 1000 firms between 1970 and 1980. With less investment one would expect to see reduced growth in the capital/labor ratio, thereby resulting in lower productivity growth. This result could not show up in the studies in Table 56-1 because the productivity measures control for differences in capital intensity.

Finally, there have been 13 recent studies of the linkage between unions and profits. These studies are summarized and critiqued in an excellent survey article by Addison and Hirsch (1989), which the interested reader should consult for references and details. The evidence across all but one of these studies indicates that profitability is sharply lower under unionism. To the extent that this reflects a simple transfer of rents from shareholders to workers, this need not imply lower productivity growth. However, to the extent that reduced profitability diminishes the incentives for innovative activity, the consequence will be inevitably slower growth in productivity.

NEW EVIDENCE FOR MANUFACTURING

Because of the absence of any firm conclusions on the links between unionism and productivity growth in the studies surveyed above, this issue was re-examined over a sample of 74 three- and four-digit industries for which the U.S. Department of Labor (1986) reports indexes of output per employee hour between 1972 and 1983. In addition to the fact that it has not been used in any previous study focusing on unionization and productivity growth, this data set merits examination because the output measures are based mainly on physical quantities,

Table 56-2 Labor Productivity Growth Equations for 74 3- and 4-Digit Manufacturing Industries, 1972–83

	Mean (S.D.)[a]	(1)	(2)	(3)	(4)	(5)	(6)
Constant		1.045	.956	.936	.868	.937	1.016
		(.059)	(.124)	(.098)	(.141)	(.135)	(.125)
Unionization, 1973–75	.505		.186		.155	.096	−.009
	(.139)		(.229)		(.229)	(.230)	(.221)
Change in unionization, 1973–75 to 1983	−.116			−.705	−.668	−.457	−.381
	(.060)			(.510)	(.515)	(.508)	(.509)
Concentration ratio in 1972	.388	.386	.360	.437	.412	.373	.416
	(.217)	(.131)	(.135)	(.135)	(.141)	(.146)	(.144)
Change in concentration, 1972 to 1982	−.003	1.194	1.236	1.170	1.206	1.273	1.340
	(.060)	(.484)	(.488)	(.481)	(.486)	(.492)	(.494)
R&D intensity by use	.028	.831	1.003	1.067	1.197		
	(.056)	(.508)	(.551)	(.533)	(.568)		
R&D intensity by origin	.036					.954	
	(.048)					(.652)	
σ		.240	.240	.238	.239	.243	.245
R^2		.195	.203	.217	.222	.196	.171

[a]The mean (S.D.) of the dependent variable is 1.214 (.262).

which should make them extremely accurate, and because it covers a more recent time period, one during which union density has been declining rapidly.

The percentage of growth in the labor productivity index in each industry is assumed to be a function of R&D intensity, four-firm concentration ratio, and unionization. Scherer (1984) constructed two measures of 1974 R&D activity: one indicating R&D originating in each industry and a second indicating R&D used by each industry. The second measure was obtained by using an input-output table to estimate how much of the R&D originating in a particular industry was used in other sectors. Each measure of R&D spending was converted into a measure of R&D intensity by dividing it by value added in 1974, as reported in the Annual Survey of Manufactures. Both the initial levels and the changes in the concentration and unionization variables were included as righthand side variables. The concentration ratios come from the Censuses of Manufacturing for 1972 and 1982. The initial level of unionization is the value reported by Freeman and Medoff (1984) for production workers from the pooled May 1973–75 CPS tapes; the final level was estimated by the author from the May 1983 CPS pension supplement public use tape. The results are reported in Table 56-2.

Productivity growth is strongly related to concentration and R&D in this sample, but it is unrelated to unionization. Productivity tends to grow slightly faster in industries with high initial levels of unionization and markedly faster in industries in which the percentage of workers unionized is declining most rapidly, but neither coefficient is statistically significant in any specification. In results not reported in Table 56-2, the equations were re-estimated with union variables calculated across all occupations; the union coefficients were even smaller. This new evidence reinforces the main conclusion from the studies surveyed in the previous section—there is no direct connection between unionization and productivity growth in manufacturing.

Table 56-3 R&D Intensity Equations for 74 3- and 4-Digit Manufacturing Industries, 1974

	Dependent Variable	
	Ratio of R&D Originating to Output	Ratio of R&D Used to Output
Constant	.079	.104
	(.020)	(.024)
Unionization, 1973–75	−.122	−.167
	(.039)	(.045)
Concentration ratio in 1972	.050	.020
	(.025)	(.030)
σ	.045	.052
R^2	.141	.161
Mean (S.D.) of dependent variable	.036	.028
	(.048)	(.056)

One limitation of this analysis is that it holds R&D intensity constant, whereas the models discussed in "Productivity Change under Unionism" imply that unions could reduce R&D. Even when R&D intensity is dropped from the model in column 6 of Table 56-2, there is no relationship between unionization and productivity growth. To test the linkage between R&D and unionization directly, each R&D intensity measure was regressed on unionization and the concentration ratio. The results, reported in Table 56-3, show that unionized industries spend much less money on R&D. The ratio of R&D originating to output is 12 percentage points less in an industry in which all production workers belong to unions than in an industry in which none does. The same relationship holds when R&D embodied in purchased materials is factored into the analysis. The ratio of R&D used to output is 17 percentage points lower in unionized industries than it is in nonunion industries. Increased concentration is associated with higher R&D spending in this sample.

Both union coefficients are dramatically larger than the mean of the dependent variable and, if taken literally, imply the mean ratio of R&D to output in unionized industries is negative. This suggests that the model is overly simple. There are many important variables that remain to be considered, along with different possible routes of causation. Nonetheless, the results are very consistent with those of Connolly, Hirsch, and Herschey (1986) and point to the need for more careful analysis of the union-R&D-productivity link in the future. Future analysis should include output growth, and endogenous variable that is likely to be correlated with unionization.

EVIDENCE FROM THE CONSTRUCTION INDUSTRY

Construction is widely thought of as an industry in which very little technological progress has been made and in which there are very limited opportunities for future productivity growth. Government statistics systematically overstate the growth of prices in the industry because they assume prices grow at the same rate as a weighted average of wages and material costs, disregarding the relationship between wages and productivity. This understatement of productivity growth is partly responsible for the view of no technical progress, along with the popular wisdom that the jobs of painters, plumbers, electricians, and carpenters have not changed in at least 30 years. Interestingly, productivity growth in construction was above the nonmanufacturing average between 1948 and 1968. Allen (1985) shows that much of the alleged decline in construction productivity since then is attributable to biases in the data.

Tatum (1984) cites two major sources of innovation in construction. One is changes in the design of projects so that they can be built with less labor or materials. The other is changes in the construction process itself. This can include "(1) development of new construction methods or sequences; (2) application or extension of methods or techniques originally developed to meet other requirements; (3) development and application of new equipment and tools; and (4) scale-up or refinement of existing methods" (Tatum 1984, 311–12). For instance, a case study of the highway construction industry by Koch and Moavenzadeh (1979) shows that the main source of productivity growth in that sector between the 1950s and the 1970s was improvements in equipment. They attribute this to competition among equipment manufacturers, changes in highway design (including some standardization of certain features), relatively stable demand (because of the use of user fees to fund highway construction and repair), and the increased price of labor relative to capital. Rosefielde and Mills (1979) cite other sources of productivity growth including the widespread adoption of power tools and machinery, introduction of larger lifting and moving machinery, changes in the use of building materials that economize in terms of labor time (such as drywall for plaster and movable partitions for walls), and increased use of prefabricated components.

Where do these innovations come from? It is quite clear that they do not come from R&D done by firms in the construction industry itself. Scherer (1984) estimates that these firms spend only $28 million a year for R&D, a small amount compared to the size of the industry. A study recently completed for the Building Research Board of the National Research Council (1986) also found very little government spending on R&D related to construction. One potentially important factor is R&D embodied in capital goods and materials purchased by the construction industry. Scherer estimates that R&D spending by companies in all industries which is used by companies in construction amounts to $432.9 million. It is also clear that some innovations must simply emerge from challenges produced by unique situations or informal worker-management interaction at the job site.

The predominance of craft as opposed to industrial unionism in construction makes this industry an especially interesting case to consider when examining how unions affect productivity growth. Unions are most likely to influence productivity growth in construction through relative factor prices and work rules. The small amount of R&D done by firms in the construction industry makes it unlikely that this route of union influence is very important.

Pooled data from the 1972, 1977, and 1982 Censuses of Construction Industries are used here to estimate the effect of unions on productivity growth in construction. There are separate observations in each year for 3 two-digit industries and 27 states or regions identified in the May 1973–75 Current Population Survey (CPS). The 1972 data set is the same as that in Allen (1984), and the 1977 and 1982 data sets are constructed in exactly the same way. The May 1977–78 CPS is used to estimate the percentage of workers unionized and labor quality for 1977; the May 1979–81 CPS, for 1982.

The productivity variable used in Tables 56-4 and 56-5 is the ratio of output to employment. To convert monetary to real values, variables were deflated to 1972 dollars. The output measure used below is value added, and it was deflated in two different ways. In addition to the deflator for construction industry GNP in the national income accounts, output was also deflated by the Dodge Cost Index (where New York City = 100 in 1972) in some equations. This adjustment roughly controls for differences across states or regions in price levels in 1972 and the rates of price increase since 1972. The capital variable equals the sum of the service flow from owned capital and expenditures on rented machinery and structures. It was deflated with an index of durable equipment prices, weighted by the share of each type of equipment in construction, as reported by Boddy and Gort (1971). The weights for education, age, occupation, and region in the labor quality index are all based on wage equation coefficients for nonunion workers (with separate coefficients for men and women) from the 1977–78 CPS. This removed year-to-year variation in wage equation coefficients as a source of labor quality variation.

Two questions relating to how unions affect productivity over time are examined. Following Connerton, Freeman, and Medoff, I first determine whether the union coefficient is

Table 56-4 Union Coefficients in the Pooled Time-Series Cross-Section Model

	Value Added per Employee in 1972 $		Value Added per Employee in 1972 New York City $	
	(1)	(2)	(3)	(4)
Union	.172	.224	.080	.187
	(.056)	(.072)	(.048)	(.061)
Union * 1977 dummy		−.032		−.109
		(.084)		(.072)
Union * 1982 dummy		−.148		−.250
		(.089)		(.076)

Note: Each equation also contains the following variables: intercept, log (K/L), log (employees per establishment), labor quality index, and binary indicators of Census division (8 categories), two-digit industry (2), and year (2).

Table 56-5 Union Coefficients in the Repeated Cross-Sections Model, by Year

	Value Added per Employee in 1972 $		Value Added per Employee in 1972 New York City $	
	All Occupations	Construction Workers	All Occupations	Construction Workers
Pooled	.172	.344	.080	.166
	(.056)	(.075)	(.048)	(.066)
1972	.354	.622	.182	.344
	(.070)	(.086)	(.059)	(.077)
1977	.148	.312	.051	.021
	(.080)	(.123)	(.076)	(.119)
1982	.050	.331	−.011	.170
	(.134)	(1.75)	(.119)	(.158)

Note: Each equation also contains the following variables: intercept, log (K/L), log (employees per establishment), labor quality index, and binary indicators of Census division (8 categories) and two-digit industry (2).

constant in each of the three cross-sections. I then estimate the effect of both the initial level of unionization and the change in proportion unionized on total factor productivity growth.

Stability of the Union Coefficient

One way to test for changes in the union coefficient over time is to estimate interaction coefficients between the percentage of workers unionized and the year dummies in a pooled time-series cross-sectional model. When the interaction terms are omitted from the model (see Table 56-4), productivity is 19 percent higher in each year for union contractors when the dependent variable is unadjusted for cross-section differences in construction cost and 8 percent higher when the dependent variable has been adjusted for such differences (these are referred to as the NOCS and CS equations below). When the interaction terms are included, the union coefficient indicates the union-nonunion productivity difference in 1972, and the interaction terms indicate the change in that difference over the following 5 and 10 years,

respectively. In 1972 the estimates of the union-nonunion productivity difference range between 20 and 25 percent. This difference narrows substantially over the following 10 years to 8 percent in the NOCS equation and to −6 percent in the CS equation. The hypothesis of equal union coefficients in 1972 and 1982 is rejected at the 10-percent level in the NOCS equation and the 1-percent level in the CS equation.

Another way to examine this issue is to estimate a separate set of cross-section coefficients for each sample year, eliminating the restriction that the coefficients of all variables other than the percentage of workers unionized and the intercept are constant. The results (see Table 56-5) are quite similar. In this case the union-nonunion productivity difference drops from 42 to 5 percent in the NOCS equation and from 20 to −1 percent in the CS equation. To illustrate the robustness of these findings, results are also reported in Table 56-5 for a different union variable—the proportion of production workers who are union members in a given state or region. Even though the estimates of the union-nonunion productivity difference obtained with this variable are much larger in each year, the trend is still the same. The coefficient drops by .291 in the NOCS equation and by .174 in the CS equation.

Finally, the models in Table 56-4 and 56-5 were re-estimated over a data set that was less aggregated in 1977 and 1982 (separate observations for each state). These results, reported in Allen (1988), point to the same conclusion—a dramatic narrowing of the productivity gap between union and nonunion contractors. Thus, all the evidence shows that while productivity in the union sector was much higher than in the nonunion sector in 1972, there was very little difference in productivity 10 years later.

Productivity Growth Models

Estimates of equations (1) and (3) are reported in Table 56-6, along with an extension of (3) in which productivity growth is also allowed to be a function of the initial levels of average establishment size and labor quality [denoted (3′) in the table]. The dependent variable is the change in the log of total factor productivity between 1972 and 1982. Factor shares are allowed to vary by year. The model was also estimated under the assumption of constant factor shares and with labor productivity as the dependent variable. These results were the same as those in Table 56-6 and are not reported.

The estimates of (1) show that productivity growth is slower in state by industry cells where unionization is growing, but the coefficient is smaller than its standard error. These results bear little resemblance to the cross-section results in Table 56-4 and 56-5, indicating either that (1) is not the most appropriate specification for a productivity growth equation or that the cross-section estimates of c are upwardly biased because of correlation between unionization and unobservable or omitted variables.

Two stronger conclusions emerge from the estimates of (3). First, productivity growth is much slower in areas with high

Table 56-6 Change in Total Factor Productivity Equations for Two-Digit Construction Industries Broken Down by State or Region

	Sample Period and Equation								
	1972–82			1972–77			1977–82		
	(1)	(3)	(3′)	(1)	(3)	(3′)	(1)	(3)	(3′)
Intercept	−.289	−.160	−1.187	−.142	−.098	−1.210	−.160	−.060	−.352
	(.028)	(.055)	(.611)	(.021)	(.044)	(.487)	(.025)	(.060)	(.596)
Change in union	−.173	−.456	−.451	.082	.003	.005	−.160	−.303	−.320
	(.200)	(.220)	(.217)	(.144)	(.159)	(.156)	(.168)	(.182)	(.194)
Change in labor quality	−.475	−.739	−.515	−.503	−.484	−.128	.206	−.007	.097
	(.489)	(.480)	(.527)	(.352)	(.352)	(.378)	(.380)	(.391)	(.440)
Change in establishment size	.844	.808	.845	.794	.799	.809	.795	.722	.717
	(.127)	(.123)	(.122)	(.122)	(.121)	(.117)	(.133)	(.137)	(.142)
Initial level of union		−.375	−.516		−.126	−.304		−.277	−.321
		(.140)	(.158)		(.110)	(.134)		(.150)	(.175)
Initial level of labor quality			.584			.636			.196
			(.386)			(.313)			(.379)
Initial level of establishment size			.057			.067			−.004
			(.034)			(.028)			(.034)
σ	.198	.190	.187	.159	.159	.152	.186	.184	.186
R^2	.371	.426	.459	.370	.381	.445	.329	.358	.361
Mean (S.D.) of dependent variable	−.304	−.304	−.304	−.196	−.196	−.196	−.108	−.108	−.108
	(.245)	(.245)	(.245)	(.196)	(.196)	(.196)	(.223)	(.223)	(.223)

Note: There are 81 observations in each equation.

levels of unionization. The union-nonunion difference in productivity growth, in terms of annual rates of change and assuming no productivity growth under unionism, is between 3.8 and 5.3 percent. Second, productivity growth is also much slower in areas in which the proportion of union workers is rising. The change in unionization coefficient falls from −.173 in the estimate of (1) to −.456 in (3). The level of unionization and the change in unionization coefficients are both economically and statistically significant, implying that the specification in (3) is to be preferred to that in (1). To test whether the initial level of unionization is acting as a proxy for initial levels of other variables that might contribute to productivity growth, (3) was extended to include the initial values of the labor quality index and average establishment size. Inclusion of these two variables caused the coefficient of the initial level of unionization to drop even farther from −.375 to −.516.

Are these results sensitive to the time period chosen? The market share of union contractors was falling between 1972 and 1982, but Allen (1988) shows that the rate of decline was steepest after 1977. Also, 1982 was the last year of an extended period of depressed output in construction. To test the robustness of the results in terms of stability over different periods, separate models were estimated for 1972–77 and 1977–82. The results, in the last six columns of Table 56-6, show only one important difference between the two periods. Whereas the initial level of unionization is inversely related to productivity growth in both periods, the relationship between changes in unionization and productivity growth holds up for 1977–82 but not for 1972–77. This probably results from either the relatively modest drop in unionization in the earlier period or the greater variation in the change in unionization in the later period.

If the means of the dependent variables are taken seriously, these results imply that productivity was falling in both the union and the nonunion sectors over this period. Most of this alleged productivity decline results from overestimation of the rate of price increase in construction and the absence of any controls for changes in the mix of construction, as discussed in Allen (1985). Once adjustments are made for these factors, the change in productivity over this period is negligible. If the rate of productivity growth for the industry is assumed to be zero, the estimates of the union-nonunion difference in productivity growth in Table 56-6 still imply that productivity was falling in union construction while rising in nonunion construction.

There are no obvious sources of declining productivity in union construction over this period. Strike activity has fallen since 1975, indicating no deterioration in labor-management relations akin to that in the coal industry. There was no change in this period in the share of workers covered by agreements limiting or prohibiting subcontracting, limiting or regulating crew size, and restricting work by those outside the bargaining unit. Thus, the possibility that productivity in union construction stayed constant, rather than declining, should not be ruled out. The results in Table 56-6 would then imply very rapid productivity growth in nonunion construction.

Regardless of whether productivity in union construction was constant or falling during this period, there is still the question of why the productivity gap between union and nonunion construction narrowed. Most construction-related R&D is done in industries that supply materials and equipment to construction firms. The growth in capital input or the change in the capital/labor ratio is the best available signal of this form of innovative activity in the CCI data. Although included as a control variable in Tables 56-4 through 56-6, one could reasonably argue that to estimate the true impact of unionism, capital must be viewed as an endogenous variable in a system of equations.

To test this, both the change in capital input and the change in the capital/labor ratio were regressed on the exogenous variables in equation (3') over the same sample used in Table 56-6. The strongest correlate of the change in capital and the change in the capital/labor ratio across region-industry cells was the change in labor quality, which had a negative coefficient. The change in unionization and the initial level of unionization coefficients were smaller than their standard errors in both equations. Thus, the change in capital in the CCI data does not seem to be directly linked with the unionization patterns in the CPS data.

A question that cannot be addressed with these data is how to interpret the results in light of the growing share of union workers who seem to be working for nonunion contractors and the growing share of union contractors that have opened nonunion subsidiaries. For instance, the data on capital input indicate that union contractors have invested just as much as nonunion contractors. This finding can be misleading if the union contractors put most of their new capital into their nonunion "double-breasted" subsidiaries.

A number of labor-market related causes of the decline in the union-nonunion productivity difference are discussed in some detail in Allen (1988). The rising share of union members working in the open shop seems to have eroded the training advantage that union contractors once possessed over their nonunion competition. When the share of union members working in the open shop was added to pooled 1972–82 CCI cross-sections (both linearly and interacted with the percentage of union members), the results indicated that this explained as much as half the decline in the union coefficient. It is also likely that the high unemployment rates observed during much of this period significantly eroded the search economies offered by union hiring halls.

CONCLUSION

This chapter has examined the ways in which unions can affect productivity growth and presented evidence from manufacturing and construction. While cross-section studies that estimate union-nonunion differences in productivity levels frequently find productivity to be higher under unionism, the results reported here show that unionism has little effect on productivity growth in manufacturing, whereas it is associated with much slower productivity growth in construction. One possible explanation for this pattern of results is that labor-management relations have deteriorated in construction in the seventies. This would be consistent with the growth of the nonunion sector in construction. Another factor could be the dominance of the craft form of unionization in construction. As noted by Slichter, Healy, and Livernash (1960), the introduction of changes in the work place is much more costly under this form of unionism, and this makes innovation less likely to occur.

There is evidence that the building trades unions are aware of this problem and have begun to do something about it. In a number of areas contractors and unions have formed cooperative associations to generate productivity improvements. In St. Louis PRIDE (Productivity and Responsibility Increase Development and Employment) was launched in 1972. This group, which also includes owners, engineers, architects, and equipment and materials suppliers, has been so successful that employment of union craftsmen has actually increased by 35 percent and the open shop has made little headway in that area. In 1982 the AFL–CIO Building Trades Department and the National Construction Employers Council launched a "Market Recovery Program for Union Construction" which aims to emulate this approach nationwide. The results of these efforts will determine whether the effect of unions on productivity change can vary over time in a particular industry, an issue beyond the scope of this chapter but one that should be examined in future work.

REFERENCES

Addison, John, and Barry Hirsch. 1989. Union effects on productivity, profits, and growth: Has the long run arrived? *Journal of Labor Economics* 7: Forthcoming.

Allen, Steven. 1984. Unionized construction workers are more productive. *Quarterly Journal of Economics* 99 (May): 251–74.

———. 1985. Why construction industry productivity is declining. *Review of Economics and Statistics* 67 (February): 661–69.

———. 1988. Declining unionization in construction: The facts and the reasons. *Industrial and Labor Relations Review* 41 (April): 343–59.

Baldwin, Carliss. 1983. Productivity and labor unions: An application of the theory of self-enforcing contracts. *Journal of Business* 56 (April): 155–85.

Boddy, Raford, and Michael Gort. 1971. The substitution of capital for capital. *Review of Economics and Statistics* 53 (May): 179–88.

Bok, Derek, and John Dunlop. 1970. *Labor and the American community*. New York: Simon & Schuster.

Bronars, Stephen, and Donald Deere. 1986. The real and financial decisions of unionized firms in a dynamic setting. Santa Barbara: University of California. Mimeo.

Clark, Kim. 1980. The impact of unionization on productivity: A case study. *Industrial and Labor Relations Review* 33: 451–69.

Clark, Kim, and Zvi Griliches. 1984. Productivity growth and R&D at the business level: Results from the PIMS data base. In *R&D, patents, and productivity*, ed. Zvi Griliches. Chicago: University of Chicago Press.

Connerton, Marguerite, Richard Freeman, and James Medoff. 1983. Industrial relations and productivity: A study of the U.S. bituminous coal industry. Cambridge, Mass.: Harvard University. Mimeo.

Connolly, Robert, Barry Hirsch, and Mark Hirschey. 1986. Union rent seeking, intangible capital, and market value of the firm. *Review of Economics and Statistics* 68 (November): 567–77.

Freeman, Richard, and James Medoff. 1984. *What do unions do?* New York: Basic Books.

Gollop, Frank, and Dale Jorgenson. 1980. U.S. productivity growth by industry, 1947–73. In *New developments in productivity measurement and analysis*, ed. John Kendrick and Beatrice Vaccara. National Bureau of Economic Research Studies in Income and Welfare, vol. 44. Chicago: University of Chicago Press.

Gray, Wayne. 1984. The impact of OSHA and EPA regulation on productivity. National Bureau of Economic Research Working Paper no. 1405. Cambridge, Mass: National Bureau of Economic Research.

Griliches, Zvi, and Frank Lichtenberg. 1984. R&D and productivity growth at the industry level: Is there still a relationship? In *R&D, patents, and productivity,* ed. Zvi Griliches. Chicago: University of Chicago Press.

Hirsch, Barry. Forthcoming. Innovative activity, productivity growth, and firm performance: Are labor unions a spur or deterrent? In *Advances in applied microeconomics,* vol 5, ed. Albert Link and Kerry Smith. Greenwich, Conn.: JAI Press.

Hirsch, Barry, and Albert Link. 1984. Unions, productivity, and productivity growth. *Journal of Labor Research* 5 (Winter): 29–37.

Kendrick, John. 1973. *Postwar productivity trends in the United States, 1948–1969.* New York: Columbia University Press.

Kendrick, John, and Elliot Grossman. 1980. *Productivity in the United States.* Baltimore: Johns Hopkins University Press.

Koch, Janet, and Fred Moavenzadeh. 1979. Productivity and technology in construction. *Journal of the Construction Division, ASCE* 105 (December): 351–66.

Link, Albert. 1981. Basic research and productivity increase in manufacturing: Additional evidence. *American Economic Review* 71 (December): 1111–12.

———. 1982. Productivity growth, environmental regulations, and the composition of R&D. *Bell Journal of Economics* 13 (Autumn): 548–54.

Mansfield, Edwin. 1980. Basic research and productivity increase in manufacturing. *American Economic Review* 70 (December): 863–73.

National Research Council, Building Research Board Committee on Construction Productivity. 1986. *Construction productivity: Proposed actions by the federal government to promote increased efficiency in construction.* Washington, D.C.: National Academy Press.

Nelson, Richard. 1981. Research on productivity growth and differences. *Journal of Economic Literature* 19 (September): 1029–64.

Rosefielde, Steven, and D. Quinn Mills. 1979. Is construction technologically stagnant? In *The construction industry,* ed. Julian Lange and D. Quinn Mills. Lexington, Mass.: Heath.

Scherer, Frederic. 1984. Using linked patent and R&D data to measure interindustry technology flows. In *R&D patents, and productivity,* ed. Zvi Griliches. Chicago: University of Chicago Press.

Slichter, Summer, James Healy, and Robert Livernash. *The impact of collective bargaining on management.* Washington, D.C.: Brookings Institution.

Sveikauskas, Catherine, and Leo Sveikauskas. 1982. Industry characteristics and productivity growth. *Southern Economic Journal* 48 (January): 769–74.

Tatum, Clyde. 1984. What prompts construction innovation? *Journal of Construction Engineering and Management* 110 (September): 311–23.

Tauman, Yair, and Yoram Weiss. 1987. Labor unions and the adoption of new technology. *Journal of Labor Economics* 5 (October): 477–501.

Terleckyj, Nestor. 1980. What do R&D numbers tell us about technological change? *American Economic Review* 70 (May): 55–61.

———. 1984. Comment. In *R&D, patents, and productivity,* ed. Zvi Griliches. Chicago: University of Chicago Press.

U.S. Department of Labor, Bureau of Labor Statistics. 1986. *Productivity measures for selected industries, 1958–84.* BLS Bulletin 2256. Washington, D.C.: GPO.

William A. Rothman

Strikes in Hospitals, 1981–1987

57

INTRODUCTION

This chapter provides a brief review of strikes that occurred between the years 1981 and 1987. Those health care worker walkouts which had the greatest impact on their communities are delineated. Important legal decisions and the effects of these strikes are also outlined.[1]

GENERAL STRIKES

The years 1981 through 1986 showed fewer strikes in hospitals than in previous periods. However, the length of time employees stayed on the picket lines was longer than in the past. A brief review of some of the longer or more significant work stoppages follows.

In 1982, 85 optometrists struck the Kaiser-Permanente hospitals in San Francisco for two months. The employees, represented by the Engineers and Scientists of California, walked out in a dispute over patient scheduling and the length of the work day. The union leader and seven others were arrested for trespassing. During the strike, Kaiser's 1400 clerical employees (OPEIU) walked off the job, too. The optometrists settled for a compounded 40 percent pay increase and resolution of their schedule problems. The clerical employees' strike lasted one month and ended in increased wages for the workers.

District 1199 workers struck Long Island Jewish Hospital in 1982 for 27 days. The 2300 employees walked out to protest

the hospital's refusal to recognize the union as the bargaining agent for nurses at the hospital's Manhasset division. The strike ended with the hospital and the union agreeing to seek a court resolution of the issues.

Employees at Trumbull Memorial Hospital in Warren, Ohio (AFSCME), struck for 4½ months in a dispute over wages and working conditions in the fall and winter of 1982. The basic issues were settled rather swiftly, and the main stumbling block became return to work procedures. Settlement terms agreed on a return to work over a 29½-month period.

Strikes during 1983 were relatively few and of short duration. The longest reported walkout was in Oakland, California, where service employees (SEIU) were out for nine weeks for economic reasons.

In 1984 employees of Yale University struck in a dispute that brought it national notoriety. Yale–New Haven Hospital, which is one not owned by the university but acts as its medical school hospital, was struck by District 1199 during the overall university dispute (but before the university walkout). The 200 workers, all food service employees, stayed off the job for 10 days. According to the union, a dispute arose during the strike when hospital security guards physically attacked the strikers as they tried to hand out leaflets to coworkers in the hospital's parking garage. Four strikers were arrested. The union reported that an agreement was reached between Yale–New Haven Hospital and the Connecticut Civil Liberties Union "which upholds the union's position that workers and others cannot be prevented from communicating with the hospital's employees or others who use the parking garage." ("Yale-New Haven" 1985)

Note: Reprinted with permission from *Journal of Health and Human Resources Administration*, Vol. 10, No. 1, © Summer 1987.

Employees of a Zelionople, Pennsylvania, nursing home represented by the Teamsters struck for 14 months from November 1983 until February 1985. "The initial reason for the strike centered on what the union claimed were excessive benefit cuts. . . . The permanent replacement of 100 of the strikers . . . however, . . . changed the primary reasons . . . to the issue of agency versus maintenance shop." (*White Collar Report* 1984:56) The strike ended with an agreement that most employees would be under an agency shop.

The summer of 1984 saw 46,000 hospital workers belonging to District 1199 striking 28 hospitals and 24 nursing homes in New York City. During the strike, nurse members of 1199 walked out at some hospitals in violation of their contract. The union was fined $350,000 for civil contempt in not having the nurses return to work. The strike lasted 47 days and ended with the employees accepting an offer of five percent wage increases in each of the next two years.

However, the agreement indicated that it would not take effect until the union and hospitals had established a procedure for a binding determination of the amount that the settlement exceeded income available through a "labor trend factor" and assurances from the state that the hospitals would receive the necessary reimbursement. The union agreed to come up with suggestions for contract savings from a list of options. The strike was "believed to be the nation's largest loss of labor hours ever from a health care strike, with an estimated 13 million hours lost." ("New York City Strike" 1984)

The strike cost a union member an average of $2,500 in wages while each achieved about $1,836 over the two years of the agreement. Interestingly, most of the agreement was never implemented because the parties could never agree on the suggestions for savings. Finally, in October 1986, the hospitals and the union reached an agreement to pay lump-sum equivalents in lieu of the five percent agreed on in 1984. The union members also voted out their old leadership because of the unpopular strike, the leaders' inability to resolve the contract disputes, and accusations of voting irregularites.

In an unusual move in 1985, striking workers at a Minneapolis HMO urged patients to cross picket lines and seek medical services. An SEIU leader said that the HMO gets paid whether or not patients use the services and that "if patients do not use the clinics . . . the clinics will make even more money from the strike since the fees are prepaid." ("SEIU Local" 1985) The strike ended after 10 days.

The longest strike in 1986 occurred when the United Steelworkers of America struck nine hospitals operated by the Appalachian Regional Hospitals in Kentucky, Virgina, and West Virginia. The strike continued for three months. SEIU members struck the Kaiser hospitals in northern California for seven weeks in the fall of 1986 to protest a two-tier wage system and subcontracting as well as such patient care issues as the establishment of a labor-management patient care standards committee to hear complaints about patient care. The union decided to utilize tactics similar to those used by the 1985 Minneapolis HMO workers. "Rather than picket facilities and discourage utilization, the union . . . circulated 250,000 leaflets at businesses whose employees are Kaiser members, encouraging them to seek care. The leaflets [told] members that Kaiser [was] obligated to provide care during the strike or to pay for referral to another facility." (McCormick 1987) The workers settled for a modified two-tier wage plan.

NURSING

Probably the most frequent strikers in the health care field are nurses. The history of nursing shows reluctance by nurses to engage in any but sporadic militant action until the latter part of the 1970s. Elaine E. Beletz (1983:111), a past president of the New York State Nurses' Association, has pointed out why nurses changed their stance:

> Nurses' reluctance to maximize their bargaining power has paralleled other professional groups. However, increasing collective bargaining sophistication, changing norms within professional groups and society at large, the impact of the women's liberation movement and increased professional consciousness have resulted in nurses' increased commitment to the visible demonstration of bargaining power in the labour-management relationship.

The years 1981–87 saw many nurses walking the picket lines, many time for weeks on end. Space limitations allow for discussion of only a few of these strikes.

Nurses at the Berkshire Medical Center in Pittsfield, Massachusetts, struck for 69 days in 1981. The strike, according to those who participated, was caused by a number of issues: lack of respect as professionals by administrators and physicians; anger over understaffing in critical care; poor wages and pensions; and feelings of powerlessness to change their situation. Even five years after the strike, the nurses had bitter feelings about what happened (Forfa, 1987)

The longest nurses' strike (570) days was at Ashtabula General Hospital in Ashtabula, Ohio. The nurses struck from July 21, 1980, until February 8, 1982. The hospital was closed for the first six weeks of the strike, and the emergency room closed for close to a year. Poor communication with administration, wages, reinstatement issues, and establishing a code of ethics were all major issues.

In 1982, 1350 nurses struck four San Jose, California, hospitals. The major issue was comparable pay with pharmacists. Three of the hospitals settled for minimum wage increases after three weeks. In order to force a settlement on the remaining hospital, nurses ceased picketing and attempted to organize a public boycott against the hospital. The strike lasted almost a year.

Burbank Hospital in Fitchburg, Massachusetts, experienced a 176-day walkout over wages of its registered nurses in 1982. The hospital was forced to operate at 40 percent capacity during the strike.

The year 1983 saw a 3-month economic strike by nurses in Akron, Ohio; a 6-week walkout by RNs in Lynn, Massachusetts; a 12-week strike in Buffalo, New York for 800 nurses; and a 54-day strike by RNs and other employees in Hudson, New York.

In 1984 nurses at two Kaiser Foundation hospitals in Los Angeles struck for 31 days over a new contract and RNs at St. Mary Hospital in Hoboken, New Jersey, walked out for 84 days. The latter strike ended when a state senator agreed to act as a factfinder and arbitrator over economic issues of pay, recall, and retroactivity. Norwalk Hospital in Norwalk, Connecticut, was struck for 65 days by its registered nurses over economic issues.

The major strike of the year, however, was in Minneapolis–St. Paul and suburbs where 6300 RNs struck 16 hospitals over job security issues. This was the largest nursing strike ever to occur in the United States. None of the hospitals closed, but all were operating at 30–40 percent of their normal occupancy. According to one report, the nurses wanted "to remove a clause in their contract . . . that gives the hospitals great flexibility in making layoffs. The growth of cost-conscious health maintenance organizations has helped reduce the hospital occupancy rate in the Twin Cities to about 15% . . . . Over the past two years, the hospitals . . . slashed staff and increased the percentage of nurses working part-time to 70 percent from 50 percent." ("A Nurses' Strike" 1984)

The strike ended after 39 days when the hospital agreed to future layoffs by seniority. Two years after the strike, it was reported that "there's still animosity between strikers and nonstrikers. . . . We see it mostly in our critical care area. Traditionally our critical care nurses stayed put, but now they're asking to be transferred to other units. This is a major change and I think it's strictly part of the aftermath of the strike." (Van Meter 1986:84)

In 1986 nursing strikes occurred in Santa Rosa, California (48 days); Oakland, California (5 weeks); Yakima, Washington (2 weeks); and a number of other places around the country for very short times (1–10 days). Waterbury Hospital in Waterbury, Connecticut, was struck for four months by its nurses. The 550-bed hospital was forced to close most of its beds throughout the entire period. (The hospital's service and maintenance employees also struck during part of the four months.)

A 37-day strike at Carney Hospital in Dorchester, Massachusetts, in 1986 resulted from inability to settle wage issues and language over non-nursing duties in an expired contract. The settlement reached included the establishment of a committee to find ways of improving nurse efficiency. The hospital agreed to contribute each year one-half of all savings (up to $200,000) to a fund to be used to hire ancillary staff. ("Boston RNs Win" 1986)

PHYSICIANS

Strikes by physicians, in contrast to the 1970s, were very infrequent since 1980. In 1981 the house staff in Bergen Place, New Jersey, went on strike. According to one news report, this was initiated when the hospital's administrator "peeled a union sticker off a hospital wall and slammed it into the chest of a member of the union's negotiating team. The doctors, already angry over management's alleged failure to bargain in good faith . . . saw the incident as another example of bad treatment." (*White Collar Report* 1981:1258) The strike ended after four days when the hospital presented an apology to the physicians.

The year 1983 saw 15 house physicians strike Interfaith Medical Center in Brooklyn, New York, to protest the hospital's reluctance to recognize the Committee of Interns and Residents as their bargaining agent. The hospital threatened not to certify the striking physicians for completion of a year's residency if they continued their walkout. The strike ended after two weeks when both sides agreed to take the issues to binding arbitration. This was reported to be the longest strike ever staged by the Committee of Interns and Residents. (*White Collar Report* 1985:57) The arbitrator ordered a new election which was won overwhelmingly by the union.

Practicing physicians' protests took place infrequently also. "Strikes" occurred mostly to demonstrate opposition to third-party regulators, payment schemes, and malpractice rates. A massive strike of Ontario's 15,000 practicing physicians in 1982 was held to demand higher fees under the Province's health care system. Doctors stayed away from their offices and refused to perform some services such as prescribing drugs over the telephone. Also in 1982, surgeons in Florida protested rising malpractice rates by refusing to perform elective surgery for one week. The "strike" ended when the state legislators enacted new legislation to cap the costs.

A hiatus in such demonstrations occurred during 1983 and 1984. However, in the summer of 1985, orthopedists in Flint, Michigan, refused all services to emergency room patients due to increased malpractice insurance rates and insurance company threats to discontinue insurance coverage. One orthopedist explained that 90 percent of all suits were a result of services to emergency room patients. They reasoned that, by stopping such services, they were preserving the possibility of continuing care to the rest of the community because they could not practice without insurance. "My entire practice was at risk. The other orthopedists . . . also felt they were in a bad position, because . . . there was little control over the patients we see in the emergency room. . . . It is easy . . . to come to the conclusion to curtail services to those who jeopardize the well being of the patients you are caring for as well as your family and yourself." (Pack 1985)

In February 1986, about 250 Massachusetts physicians participated in a "slowdown" to protest malpractice premium rates. Orthopedists and obstetricians spearheaded the strike by refusing to accept new patients or perform surgery. It was reported that "midwives in the northern Boston area [were] . . . setting up makeshift storefront clinics for newly pregnant women turned away by obstetricians." (*Hospital Week* 1986:3) Orthopedists ended their protest after three weeks and the obstetricians shortly thereafter.

In early 1986, 160 physicians employed by the Group Health Association, a Washington, D.C., HMO, staged a

25-day strike when administrators announced a plan to initiate productivity bonuses. (*Newsweek* 1987:64) The doctors were upset because they thought such a plan would reduce the quality of care and bring about "assembly line medicine" by limiting the time each could spend with a patient. The strike ended with an agreement to set up a union-management committee to review the proposal. During the strike, "the doctors voluntarily agreed to continue to service patients in the emergency rooms, to see their hospitalized patients, and to deliver babies." (*White Collar Report* 1986:59)

Ontario's physicians went on strike again from June 12 to July 2, 1986, to protest provincial legislation banning extra billing. The protest ended because it became apparent to the doctors that "the strike was not positively perceived by the public, the very group the doctors were trying to convince of the harm the legislation will cause." (*White Collar Report* 1986:60)

An interesting viewpoint on physician unions and strikes was raised concerning HMOs:

> The establishment of independent practice associations (IPAs), health maintenance organizations and preferred provider organizations by state and county medical societies represents the de facto unionization of physicians. . . . There's no question that IPAs act like labor unions. . . . After bargaining, some IPA negotiators refused to renew the contract with Intergroup [a Chicago HMO] because it wouldn't meet their demands. In effect they went on strike. . . . (Richman 1986)

The Internal Revenue Service has also "characterized IPAs as providing billing and collection services as collective bargaining representatives devoted to maximizing fees for member physicians." ("Health Care Notes" 1986)

LEGAL

The 1974 Congressional Amendments to the National Labor Relations Act contained a special Section 8(g) requiring unions to give adequate advance notice of a strike. This notice states in part:

> A labor organization before engaging in any strike, picketing or other concerted refusal to work at any health-care institution shall, not less than ten days prior to such action, notify the institution in writing and the Federal Mediation and Conciliation Service of that intention . . . .

A number of decisions concerning Section 8(g) have been made in recent years. In 1981 the National Labor Relations Board (NLRB) ruled that sympathy picketers were required to give 10 days' notice even if the picketers never represented any of the employer's workers. (*White Collar Report* 1982:1319) In a related case in 1983 the NLRB again ruled that a union, which joined nonunion members who were already picketing a hospital, must give 10 days' notice. It was the

majority opinion that Congress, by its putting in the word "any" in Section 8(g), had intended that *any* union must comply: i.e., "any strike, picketing or other concerted refusal to work at any health care institution." *Any* was thus the controlling wording. (*White Collar Report* 1983: 54; Hickey 1983) The NLRB has also ruled that the notice cannot be oral, must be written, and should be served on a high-level manager, and also that a union seeking to represent employees, but neither recognized nor certified, must also give 10 days' notice and that all forms of physical patrolling of an area adjacent to a hospital are picketing rather than handbilling. (Kruchko & Fries 1984)

The U.S. Court of Appeals for the Seventh District ruled that a two-hour wildcat strike by nursing home employees, protesting a management rule, was lawful and did not need the 10-day notice required by 8(g). (*White Collar Report* 1984:56) The NLRB also determined that it was legal for a hospital to demote a supervisor for participating with the rank and file in a strike. (*Health Labor Relations Reports* 1982)

A little-known section of the Medicare reimbursement regulations [405.463(g)(2)] provides exceptions to a hospital's target ceiling in the event of extraordinary circumstances such as a strike. An adjustment can be requested for factors which result in a significant distortion in operating costs. A review of such requests to the Health Care Financing Administration (HCFA), obtained through the Freedom of Information Act, shows that only two have been made (through February 1987): one by Hospital de Diego in San Juan, Puerto Rico, and the other by Akron General Medical Center, Akron, Ohio. Both hospitals incurred a strike in 1982. Neither request was granted. HCFA explained in its letter denying Hospital de Diego's request that

> "The exception for extraordinary circumstances . . . may be granted if the provider can show that it incurred higher costs due to extraordinary circumstances beyond its control. These circumstances include but are not limited to strikes, fire, earthquake, flood or similar unusual occurrence with substantial cost effects. The occurrence of a strike in and of itself does not justify an exception to the rate-of-increase ceiling. We wish to point out that Medicare regulations 42CFR405.463(g) provide that an adjustment will be made only to the extent that the hospital's costs are reasonable, attributable to the circumstances specified, separately identified by the hospital and verified by the intermediary":
>
>> When a strike occurs, the purpose of the exception for extraordinary circumstances is to give the provider relief from the necessity of spreading fixed costs over a reduced number of patient days. Therefore, the provider must submit documentation showing what actions it has taken to reduce the hospital's costs when faced with such circumstances. For example, what actions were taken to reduce variable costs, when were they initiated, by how much were costs reduced, and how long did the extraordinary circumstances last? What data, such as

monthly staffing levels during the period, is available to demonstrate that low staffing existed due to the reasons alleged, and how many months did the low staffing actually continue? Additionally, the prior year cost report as well as the cost report for the fiscal year in which the strike occurred is needed in order to evaluate the impact of the occurrence on the hospital's costs.[2]

CAUSE AND EFFECTS OF STRIKES

A review of the strikes mentioned here shows that the basic cause of most of the walkouts was poor or nonexistent communication between administrators and employees. It is a well-known fact that most strikes are not called over money, benefits, or safety issues but the inability or unwillingness of labor and management to understand each other's views on those issues. Hopefully, the major effect of a strike would be to impress on both sides that communication is necessary to avoid future work stoppages. In most instances, that message seems to have been heard as subsequent contracts appear to have been negotiated without a strike.

Luckily, strikes are a rare occurrence in health care facilities. A 1984 report of testimony by the President of SEIU before the House Subcommittee on Labor-Management Relations reflects the rarity: The Federal Mediation and Conciliation Service, he said, reported that ''strikes occur in less than 5 percent of all health care contract situations and less than 3.3 percent when nursing homes are excluded.'' (*White Collar Report* 1984:56)

The effects of a strike can be devastating. For example, Waterbury Hospital, in Waterbury, Connecticut, reported an $8.5 million loss in its 18-week nurses strike in 1986.

> When it finally ended, there were no winners and every participant and the community at large were losers. The Waterbury Hospital was shaken to its core and the recovery process will take far longer than the strike itself. We have lost a great number of skilled and valued nursing colleagues who have taken permanent positions in other hospitals. They left for a variety of reasons but virtually all were strike related. . . . As a result, the hospital will have to operate at a reduced level of size and activity for many months ahead. This will result in a continued and perhaps permanent loss of both union and non-union jobs. (1986 Annual Report of the Waterbury Hospital)

Waterbury's experience, except for its huge financial loss, exemplifies that of many other institutions. Almost all report severe staff cuts after the strike. Administrators found, because they and their supervisor actually did the work of the general staff during the strike, that many jobs could be streamlined and many tasks consolidated.

Some unexpected effects of the strikes have recently been reported. For example, Standard and Poor's has indicated that strikes might result in negative credit ratings for nonprofit hospitals.

> Citing both the New York City (1984 Local 1199) and Minneapolis–St. Paul (1984 Nurses) strikes as examples, the rating agency said depressed admissions and increased costs per case caused by strikes, as well as contract settlements, are the most obvious credit concerns. Such strikes can result in increased costs and shifts in competitive balance among hospitals in a given service area. (''Strikes Could Hurt'' 1984)

A strike seriously affects the nonstriking workers left in the hospital who must do their own work plus the tasks of those walking the picket lines. Union tactics generally include notifying the local health departments of ''unsafe'' conditions in the hospital. The 1984 Local 1199 New York City strike was no exception. The State Department of Health was asked to inspect the hospitals and subsequently cited 10 hospitals for deficiencies in care and for unsanitary conditions. The ''violations included not fulfilling physician orders, and failing to give some patients complete physical exams before surgery.'' (''New York City Strike'' 1984) (These violations, however, were not considered particularly serious.)

Interestingly, the staff of Mt. Sinai Hospital in New York City studied patient reactions to that strike and found ''that satisfaction levels during the strike were equal to or higher than those obtained pre-strike for most items. Exceptions were in the area of housekeeping and dietary/food delivery. Medical and nursing care scores were higher during than prior to the strike.'' (Rosenberg, Speedling, Rehr, & Morrison, 1983)

The effect on physicians can, of course, be severe, too. In those cases where the hospital has closed or cut the number of available beds, admissions have been eliminated or greatly reduced. Generally, elective surgery has been curtailed. All of these steps have either reduced physician income or forced open alternative delivery sites on them. A report of the Minneapolis–St. Paul 1984 nursing strike reveals some of these effects:

> Some doctors stayed in the hospital overnight and some started making house calls. . . . The strike may have permanently changed the way some doctors practice . . . the shorter stays new mothers had in the hospital during the strike [may] now become mandatory. . . More physicians are taking a harder look at what can be done on an ambulatory basis. People who were reluctant to perform outpatient surgery for simple hernias, rectal lesions, breast biopsies, and D&Cs were forced by the strike to become more aggressive about it. (Crane 1984)

Another report, also citing the effects of the same Minneapolis–St. Paul strike, states,

> The strike effects were immediate. The struck hospitals restricted admissions and arranged earlier discharges. Home care companies were swamped with pre-strike requests for durable medical equipment. . . . The strike

was a catalyst for the change that was to occur in the next two years, that is, a slow reduction in staffing in response to census declines . . . . Other . . . effects . . . have been a two-day reduction in hospital length of stay, more procedures completed in the physicians' offices, and admission of sicker patients. (Adams & Green 1985)

The serious effects of these changes on the hospital, the striking employees, the physicians, and the community should certainly not be overlooked at the bargaining table. The results of a strike, it can be seen, may very well unintentionally affect the entire health care delivery system in the hospital's market area.

NOTES

1. For details of strikes prior to 1982, see William A. Rothman, *Strikes in Health Care Organizations.* (Owings Mills, Md: National Health Publishing, 1983).

2. Letter from HCFA to Hospital de Diego, San Juan, Puerto Rico, obtained through Freedom of Information Act.

REFERENCES

Adams, Alex, and Beth Green. 1985. Nurses on strike. *AAR Times* 9 (September): 34–35.

Beletz, Elaine E. 1987. Nurses' commitment to militance in collective bargaining. *International Nursing Review* 30 (July-August): 111.

Boston RNs win concession on nonnursing work. 1986. *American Journal of Nursing* 85 (September): 1051.

Crane, Mark. 1984. How doctors outmaneuvered a nurses' strike. *Medical Economics* 61 (October 15): 109–115.

Forfa, Lorraine Wells. 1987. Strike: More than two sides. *American Journal of Nursing* 87 (January): 17–19.

Health care notes. 1986. Ernst & Whinney, November. *Health Labor Relations Reports.* 1982. 6 (June 14): 2.

Hickey, Kevin F. 1983. Union must file notice before involvement in picketing. *Health Law Vigil* 6 (April): 9–10.

Hospital Week. (1986) 22 (March 14): 3.

Kruchko, John G, and Jay R. Fries. 1984. Hospital work stoppages—The legal basis and legal response. *Health Care Management Review* 9 (Fall): 35–42.

McCormick, Brian. 1987. Labor union plays hard ball with HMOs. *Hospitals* 61 (January 5): 35.

Newsweek. 1987. (January 26): 64.

New York City strike brings charges of health violations at 10 hospitals. 1984. *Hospital Week* 20 (August 24): 2.

New York City strike called largest, craziest in history. 1984. *Hospitals* 58 (September 16): 19.

1986 Annual Report of the Waterbury Hospital.

A nurses' strike that could be catching. 1984. *Business Week* (June 25): 31–32.

Pack, Larry. 1985. Flint doctor tells why. *Michigan Hospitals* 21 (November): 17–20.

Richman, Dan. 1986. Medical societies' prepaid plans resemble unions, observers say. *Modern Healthcare* 16 (April 25): 29.

Rosenberg, Gary, Edward J. Speedling, Helen Rehr, and Barbara J. Morrison. 1985. Some effects of a hospital employee strike on patient satisfaction. *The Mount Sinai Journal of Medicine* 52 (April): 259–64.

SEIU local encourages patients to cross its picket lines at six twin cities HMOs. 1985. *White Collar Report* 57 (January 30): 83.

Strikes could hurt hospitals' credit ratings, S&P warns. 1984. *Modern Healthcare* 14 (October): 170.

Van Meter, Margaret. 1986. A second look at the Minnesota strike. *RN* 49 (January): 84.

White Collar Report. 1984. 56 (July 4): 13–14.

———. 1981. 1258 (June 26): A10–11.

———. 1982. 1319 (September 3): A4.

———. 1983. 54 (July 22): 81–82.

———. 1985. 57 (June 26): 613.

———. 1986. 59 (April 2): 309.

———. 1986. 60 (July 9): 28.

Yale–New Haven agrees to respect first amendment. 1985. *1199 News* 20 (March): 23.

Charles L. Joiner

Preventive Labor-Management Relations

58

Strategic labor-management relations is concerned with maintaining a positive labor relations climate regardless of whether the organization is unionized. This chapter focuses on the issues necessary for an understanding of how to develop a preventive management program, based on the premise of a management policy to maintain nonunion status. The fundamental principles are applicable, however, even if simply focused on maintaining good relations between management and organized labor.

With well over 3 million workers, the health care industry represents one of the largest work force population groups in the United States. The health care industry also represents one of the largest pools of nonunion employees, and, therefore, a prime target for union organizers. This is particularly true in times of economic stress when management decisions must be made concerning the employment status of many employees, both professional and nonprofessional.

DEVELOPING AN EMPLOYEE RELATIONS PHILOSOPHY AND STRATEGY

Management strategy regarding its desired relationship to labor organizations should be formulated as a part of overall policy development. This strategy formulation must, of course, take into consideration the geographic, demographic,

and historical factors pertinent to its setting. For example, an organization that is located in an area where unionization is prevalent may find it extremely difficult to prevent unionization of groups of its employees even with the best preventive plan. Nonetheless, it is management's responsibility to develop and communicate to its employees the organization's employee relations philosophy.

The organization's employee relations philosophy should be developed on the basis of its objectives regarding such factors as communication with employees, management rights, and unions. If an organization is not presently unionized, management should consider the array of environmental and organizational issues in the process of determining its policy relating to unions. Specifically, management should consider the available strategic options for developing and maintaining a positive employee relations climate.

One option is to adopt a nonunion policy and begin to implement a preventive management program. This option is explored in detail in this chapter. A second option is for management to implement essentially the same program without communicating a formal nonunion policy, depending on its analysis of circumstances and objectives. Regardless of the strategic option chosen, it is essential for management to do the necessary analysis and adopt an appropriate employee relations program focused on maintaining good communication and positive relations.

MAINTAINING NONUNION STATUS

Maintaining nonunion status depends largely on what managers do to prevent the need for a union. This view is based on

Note: Excerpted from "Management's Response to the Union Phenomenon" by Charles L. Joiner and James O. Morris in *Hospital Progress*, pp. 59–63, with permission of The Catholic Health Association of the United States, © May 1978.

509

the philosophy that unionization is preventable if management is doing enough of the "right things." When management actions do not support a positive employee relations climate, workers may find it necessary to seek external help, and, in some situations, they deserve help from a union.

This argument may be supported further by noting that union organizers typically do not attempt to organize an employee group until workers themselves have sought union assistance. Union certification elections seem to suggest that employees really are voting for or against management instead of for or against a particular union. Based on these premises, this chapter seeks to help health care managers by identifying issues important to good personnel relations and the maintenance of nonunion status.

To provide a sound basis for prevention of unnecessary problems, it is essential to understand the historical perspective of the underlying issues including employee perceptions of the need for unionization. The purpose of the chapter, therefore, is accomplished through a review of labor law history and trends, an overview of the fundamental causes of friction between management and labor, a summary of the reasons health care employees give for joining unions, an analysis of the criteria used by union organizers to evaluate health care institutions, and, finally, specific recommendations for establishing a preventive management program and maintaining nonunion status. Since knowledge of the legal framework is essential to any manager who desires to avoid foolish mistakes in the implementation of a well-conceived program, it is appropriate to review labor law history and trends first.

LABOR LAW HISTORY AND TRENDS

The National Labor Relations Act (NLRA) is the foundation for the labor law of the United States. The NLRA, the so-called Wagner Act, was adopted in 1935 and has been amended by the Taft-Hartley Act of 1947, the Landrum-Griffin Act of 1959, and Public Law 93-360 (the Health Care Amendments) in 1974.

The Wagner Act authorized the formation of the National Labor Relations Board (NLRB) to administer the provisions of the act. The Wagner Act encompassed all institutions that had an impact on interstate commerce. The status of nonprofit health care institutions was left to the interpretation of the courts. Proprietary institutions and nursing homes were considered within the jurisdiction of the act. Since by definition governments are not employers, federal, state, and municipal hospitals were specifically exempted from the jurisdiction of the act (Rakich 1973).

Under the protection of the Wagner Act, unions flourished in industries of virtually all types, creating a host of problems regarding the regulation of union-management relations. Industries had to contend with many jurisdictional strikes caused by disputes between competing unions. Some labor leaders, because of their new and unbridled power, refused to bargain in good faith (Rakich 1973). The Wagner Act proved to be inadequate to curb these and other abuses of the bargaining process. Therefore, Congress in 1947 passed the Labor Management Relations (Taft-Hartley) Act. It is this legislation that has become the backbone of the nation's labor laws (Rakich 1973).

The Taft-Hartley Act amended the Wagner Act by listing specific unfair labor practices. In addition, it specifically exempted nonprofit health care institutions from coverage under the act. The status of other types of health care institutions did not change.

In 1959 Taft-Hartley was amended by the Labor-Management Reporting and Disclosure (Landrum-Griffin) Act. Among its many provisions, this act requires employers, including voluntary nonprofit health care facilities, to submit a report to the U.S. Secretary of Labor detailing the nature of any financial transactions and/or arrangements that are intended to improve or retard the unionization process (Rakich 1973).

Until 1967 the courts on a case-by-case basis determined which proprietary health care institutions and nursing homes had an impact on interstate commerce and thus came under the NLRA. As a result of several court cases, the NLRB in 1967 determined that proprietary health care institutions with an annual gross revenue of at least $250,000 and nursing homes, regardless of ownership, with an annual gross revenue of at least $100,000 were covered by the act (Rakich 1973).

With voluntary hospitals comprising the largest sector of the health care industry, it was only a matter of time until they too fell under federal legislation. Their shift in status occurred in 1974, when Congress passed P.L. 93-360 to amend the NLRA. These Amendments, which extended the coverage of the labor laws to include all health care institutions under nonpublic ownership and control, defined a health care institution as any "hospital, convalescent hospital, health maintenance organization, health clinic, nursing home, extended care facility, or other institution devoted to the care of sick, infirm, or aged persons" (Pointer and Metzger 1975, 56).

A decade ago, only about 20 percent of the total nonpublic health care labor force was unionized (Pointer & Cannedy 1974). However, because of their declining rate of growth among blue-collar workers, labor unions are renewing their interest in the organizable group of white-collar employees in the health care industry (Pointer & Metzger 1975; Reed 1970). Attempts have been made in recent years to modify the Taft-Hartley legislation to favor union organizational campaign strategies.

The legislative background and prospects certainly point to difficult times for health care managers seeking to stay nonunion. For a realistic perspective on maintaining nonunion status, management shall have a good understanding of the fundamental causes of labor problems. Reasons for labor-management friction are summarized next.

CAUSES OF LABOR-MANAGEMENT PROBLEMS

Fundamental differences between the goals and objectives of management and labor create friction that cannot be totally explained in terms of desires for higher wages, shorter working hours, or better working conditions. Two fundamental causes of such friction are the issue of management rights and the issue of efficiency versus human value. Management always will assert its right to prescribe certain modes of action or levels of desired productivity to justify its existence or that of the organization. Yet labor unions question whether management should have complete power over the work force. This is a point of conflict. Organized labor attempts to shift the locus of control by seeking to obtain a voice for employees about working conditions and terms of employment.

The question of management's right to govern is paralleled by the question of human value versus efficiency. If management is to achieve its stated goals and objectives, it must maintain efficiency through increased productivity and cost containment. On the other hand, the union seeks to improve its members' standard of living. Neither side may be totally right or totally wrong in its demands, and unfortunate circumstances often trigger open conflict. For example, a management that wishes to improve the existing fringe benefits package for employees may be prevented from doing so by pressures to contain costs. Evidence of this type of conflict in health services organizations is mounting almost daily, especially as new crises (e.g., malpractice insurance rate hikes) arise and cause even greater cost increases.

With an understanding of the fundamental causes of labor problems, administration can begin developing its philosophy for a preventive management program by reviewing research on employee reasons for joining unions. The analysis that follows summarizes findings from a selected number of such studies.

Why Employees Join Unions

The desire to unionize is thought to be centered on three issues: wages, employee dissatisfaction with work benefits, and employee perceptions about the organization as a place to work that could reflect perceptions about management or the employer. However, other factors have contributed to increased union activity in the health care industry. Over the past three decades social turmoil has precipitated civil rights legislation and stimulated changes in the attitudes and social conscience of many individuals. The idea of being represented by a union is not considered as unprofessional as it once was (Phillips 1974; Stanton 1971). The health care industry is just beginning to feel the effects of this turmoil, and the passage of P.L. 93-360 served only to release the pent-up emotions of the industry's workers and union leaders. Recent labor reform efforts are further evidence of labor's continuing struggle to swing the pendulum in its favor.

In a study pertaining to why employees want unions, Brett (1980) found two main factors.

1. An employee's initial interest in unionization is based on dissatisfaction with working conditions and a perceived lack of influence to change those conditions.
2. The likelihood that a coalition of dissatisfied employees will try to organize a union depends on whether they accept the concept of collective action and whether they believe that unionization will yield positive rather than negative outcomes for them.

According to this study, a significant proportion of employees who were dissatisfied with working conditions—particularly job security and wages—voted for union representation. Initial employee satisfaction with working conditions was measured by interview data collected from employees who were asked the eight questions listed in Table 58-1.

As Table 58-1 shows, the level of satisfaction with wages, job security, fringe benefits, treatment by supervisors, and chances for promotion was significantly correlated with a vote for union representation.

Although study findings vary with respect to the factors being measured and the degrees of importance of the factors, a sampling of studies in 11 publications reveals some interesting commonalities in the attitudes of health care workers who seek union representation. Table 58-2 outlines the findings of the search. Although not all inclusive, the data do show that money and fringe benefits are not always the only issues to employees. Other, less tangible factors such as poor communication, poor supervision, bad working conditions, and inconsistently enforced personnel policies carry considerable weight.

The less tangible issues may be just as important to employees. One reason workers frequently mention for joining unions is failure by management to "treat them fairly, decently, or honestly." Employees view management as fair, decent, and honest if it recognizes the need of individuals and treats people with dignity. Issues such as wage disputes, respect, and recognition for loyalty and service to the institution are related to the individual need to be recognized and to be treated fairly. A specific example is employees' feeling that management offers no educational opportunities for upgrading their skills as a means to career mobility (Pointer 1974). Unless these opportunities are available, employees often believe that they are locked into dead-end jobs.

Generally, the reasons health care personnel give for joining unions may be grouped into two broad categories: poor communication and perception of poor treatment. Almost all the reasons are related in some way to communication problems (e.g., little upward communication) or to the employees' belief that they are not receiving fair treatment on specific

Table 58-1 The Correlation between Job Satisfaction and Voting for Union Representation

	Correlation with Vote*
1. Are you satisfied or not satisfied with your wages?	−.40
2. Do supervisors in this company play favorites, or do they treat all employees alike?	−.34
3. Are you satisfied or not satisfied with the type of work you are doing?	−.14
4. Do your supervisors show appreciation when you do a good job, or do they just take it for granted?	−.30
5. Are you satisfied or not satisfied with your fringe benefits, such as pensions, vacations, holiday pay, insurance, and sick leave?	−.31
6. Do you think there is a good chance or not much chance for you to get promoted in this company?	−.30
7. Are you satisfied or not satisfied with the job security at this company?	−.42
8. Taking everything into consideration, would you say you were satisfied or not satisfied with this company as a place to work?	−.36

*$p < .01$; $r = .08$; $N = 1004$

*The negative correlations indicate that employees who were satisfied tended to vote against union representation.

Source: "Why Employees Want Unions," *Organizational Dynamics*, American Management Association. Spring 1980, p. 51. Reprinted, by permission of the publisher, from *Organizational Dynamics*, Spring 1980, copyright © 1980 American Management Association, New York. All rights reserved.

Table 58-2 Reasons Health Care Employees Join Unions: Derived from a Sampling of Studies in 11 Publications

Issue	Publications*										
	1	2	3	4	5	6	7	8	9	10	11
Poor communication	x	x	x	x	x	x	x	x	x	x	x
Personnel policies	x		x			x	x	x	x	x	x
Supervision	x	x	x	x		x	x		x		x
Fringe benefits		x	x			x	x	x	x	x	x
Work conditions		x	x	x	x			x	x		x
Grievances	x	x	x					x			x
Job security	x	x	x		x	x	x				x
Human dignity	x			x	x		x				x
Shift differentials		x	x								x
Wages	x	x	x	x	x	x	x	x	x	x	x

*Numbers correspond to the following chapter references:
1. Stanton (1971)
2. Goodfellow (1969)
3. "Keeping Your Employees' Morale Up" (1974)
4. Imberman (1973)
5. Lewis (1974)
6. Phillips (1974)
7. Rakich (1973)
8. Milliken and Milliken (1973)
9. Sibson (1965)
10. Stanton (1974)
11. Metzger and Pointer (1972)

work-related issues. As a generalization, employees may consider the union alternative when they perceive a prevailing attitude that management does not consider meeting employee needs as a primary goal of the institution. Administrators should find an interesting relationship between why employees join unions and what the union organizer looks for. Although this study does not include a correlation analysis, some relationships are evident between the findings of the two.

What the Union Organizer Looks for

Employees typically try to resolve their problems internally before seeking outside help. Typically, union organizers appear on the scene only if they have been invited. In other words, if a union organizer is involved, it is likely that pro-labor activity has progressed to a serious level.

There is no blueprint the health care manager can use to determine how a union organizer will evaluate a given institution. The method of evaluation depends on the organizing team sent into the area and its previous experience or success. Tactics may vary considerably, depending on the contacts from employees and on management's response to the situation. However, the organizer may concentrate in certain areas, including the following.

Employee Loyalty by Work Shift

Normally, the first shift is the most loyal to the organization, the second shift less loyal than the first, and the third the least loyal. This probably is because new employees usually start on the second or third shift. They see top management seldom or never, and the supervisory force usually is smaller. Thus, there often is no one who can provide consistent supervision (e.g., answering employee questions about personnel policies or benefits). These employees tend to feel overlooked and forgotten. They are more susceptible to the pleas of the union organizer, who usually is available on the later shifts (Goodfellow 1969, 1972; "Keeping Your Employees' Morale Up" 1974).

Female-Male Employee Ratio

Women historically have been less interested in unions than have men. In the past, many women worked to supplement the family income, but this has changed rapidly. Today, women are prevalent in the work force and frequently earn a primary or major part of the family income.

Nursing personnel, a majority of whom are women, are increasingly recognizing the need to organize to improve their status. The American Nurses' Association is attempting to upgrade and negotiate conditions of employment for its membership. Other professional organizations, such as the American Society of Hospital Pharmacists, the American Society of Medical Technologists, the National Association of Social Workers, and the American Dietetic Association, are also actively seeking more voice in the representation of their members ("Goals and Trends" 1972; Matlack 1972; Metzger 1970; Pointer & Metzger 1975; Stanton 1971).

Work Environment

Employees want clean working and eating environments and expect management to provide them. If the health care institution allows the work environment to deteriorate, employees may think that the institution does not care much about them ("Keeping Your Employees' Morale Up" 1974).

Wage Rates

Traditionally, the health care employee has subsidized health care institutions with low wages. This is an injustice to the employee, who must compete daily in the retail market for goods and services. In addition, the institution must have fair and regular wage differentials. Failure to update these differentials will cause a compression effect between the new employees' base pay and the tenured employees' level (Goodfellow 1972; "Keeping Your Employees' Morale Up" 1974; Reed 1970).

Incentive Pay

In areas in which an incentive pay program has been implemented, employees may complain that some of the rates, or daily quotes, are too high. High quotas obviously breed dissatisfaction if management does not respond by re-examining the quotas periodically (Goodfellow 1972).

Overtime Practices

Problems arise when overtime is scheduled for employees without their consent. Management assumes that the worker will not object to the extra hours because of the overtime pay, but this often is not a valid assumption. Overtime can be very disruptive to the employee's family life and leisure time. The union organizer will exploit this point of dissatisfaction and force management to hire additional workers. Inequities in the distribution of overtime represent another aspect of the problem (Goodfellow 1972; Stanton 1971).

Seniority

Although management may prefer to recognize the skill and health of a worker in assigning a new job, it must not overlook the employees' view of seniority. Seniority to them is job security. If management takes the time-honored seniority concept away completely, it is asking for employee dissatisfaction and unionization, particularly in geographical areas where unionization already is well entrenched (Goodfellow 1972).

Promotion Policy

When a new job opens up or an employee leaves, present personnel should be given an opportunity to apply for the position. A good job-posting policy can be extremely helpful. Health care institutions also should have education and training programs available to assist employees' vertical or lateral movement (Joiner & Blayney 1974).

Job Transfers

Most often it is the ambitious employee who would like to be promoted to a more convenient shift or a different job. Research has shown that many times supervisors, who do not want to lose good workers or have to train new ones, sabotage the promotion of ambitious employees. Such practices should be avoided. Frequently, the best employees are those who have worked up the organizational ladder (Goodfellow 1972).

Fringe Benefits

Research has revealed that most managements underrate the value of fringe benefits to the employee. And as employers continue to increase the benefits portion of total compensation, the benefits package is likely to increase in relative importance to employees. With the news media and the next-door neighbor discussing the benefits of union representation, it is foolish for health care management to neglect either to establish a good benefits program or to adequately explain to employees the benefits offered by the institution.

Discipline and Grievance Procedures

If the institution does not provide employees with written rules covering what is not allowed and what is and to what degree, some supervisors may abuse their authority to reprimand. The grievance procedure serves as a safety valve for employees to release their frustration about supervisors or other major problems. Management should develop and implement an internal procedure that employees will use instead of resorting to an outside agency to settle disputes. Management also should review the procedures periodically to make sure they are serving workers' needs. Many grievances, for example, are either about or under the direct control of the employees' immediate supervisors. In these cases, the employees probably will not use the procedure unless there is some provision to circumvent that superior (Clelland 1967; Goodfellow 1972; Sibson 1965).

With an understanding of why health care personnel join unions and some of the criteria by which labor organizers evaluate an institution, management should begin to assess its employee relations climate and to plan its strategy for maintaining nonunion status (Goodfellow 1972; "Keeping Your Employees' Morale Up" 1974).

A PREVENTIVE MANAGEMENT PROGRAM

Assessing an institution's employee relations climate and implementing a program to prevent unionization comprise a process for which a myriad of management responses are possible. Each institution must carefully design a strategy that is both practical and suited to its own particular situation. Recognizing the significant relationship between the reasons given by employees for joining unions and what an organizer looks for, there is substantial reason to believe that the primary causes of unionization include "communication problems" and the perception by employees of "unfair treatment."

Therefore, a preventive management program should be designed with a primary emphasis on improving communication and dealing with employees and related problems in an honest and fair manner. This emphasis is detailed in several ways in the following recommendations for establishing a preventive management program. These recommendations are an outgrowth of previously described employee-related issues and could serve as the general framework within which each management team builds its own strategy.

Nonunion Policy

If a health care institution intends to be nonunion, it should give careful consideration to the development and publication of such a policy. Good labor counsel should be consulted to assist in the development of an up-front nonunion policy and to advise regarding the best alternatives for communicating the policy to all who wish to work at the institution. All prospective employees should be informed in the screening process and given written evidence of the institutional position regarding unions, along with other significant policies. The prospective employee then has the choice of whether or not to work for a nonunion institution. This, in itself, should be an indication of fair treatment. Management should also consider publishing the nonunion policy in the employee handbook for reference during orientation and other group meetings. This policy should include the following key points:

- a resolution committing the administration to provide equitable treatment to all employees in their wages, benefits, hours, and conditions of employment

- a resolution committing adequate funds and time to provide all managers with the information that they need to be effective in employee relations and knowledgeable in ways of avoiding unionization

- a resolution committing administrators to the philosophy that each employee is important as an individual vital to the optimal functioning of the entire hospital team

- a resolution expressing a commitment to oppose efforts of outside organizations to unionize employees (Rutkowski & Rutkowski 1984).

Personnel Selection

Management must have effective policies and procedures regarding selection of new employees. Prevention of labor-management problems begins with the proper matching of personnel to specific jobs. A good wage and salary program including job analyses, job descriptions (with performance objectives), and job evaluation is essential. If good procedures are used for selecting on the basis of both the individual's

qualifications and the requirements of a specific job, the result is likely to be a better fit for the institution and the employee. Concurrently, the institution is likely to avoid many communication and morale problems. A fair wage and salary system provides at least a basis for establishing an objective employee evaluation system.

Employee Attitude Assessment

Employee attitude surveys, when conducted properly, can provide much valuable data to management at nominal costs. The method chosen should be simple to implement and should elicit concise employee responses. The result should be an accurate assessment of the topics surveyed, clearly differentiating between positive and negative attitudes.

Attitute surveying should be done on a planned, periodic basis, so that employees perceive continual concern for their needs and management keeps abreast of fluctuations in worker attitudes. If this procedure is combined with efforts to obtain upward communication through formal or informal channels at all levels of the institution, the results should be a positive change in the attitudes of employees and the development of a management system for dealing with personnel problems before they become sore spots. Once attitudes have been assessed and problems identified, management should be ready to take corrective action, including an appropriate training program.

Probably the single most important part of the attitude measurement analysis process is communication with the employees about

- purpose
- how the data will be analyzed and used
- confidentiality of the individual responses
- feedback concerning the findings
- what changes, if any, they can expect as a result of their participation in the survey

Management should be careful not to make promises that cannot be fulfilled, but should make a strong effort to do whatever is possible to improve employee relations.

In summary, when management asks employees to take valuable time to participate in a survey, it is extremely important for them to feel that the administration values their input and is doing what it can to meet their needs.

Employee Training

Administration should examine its role and responsibilities in training employees as a function of management rather than as a staff function. If this self-examination indicates that management is assuming little, if any, responsibility for employee training, such abdication is very likely to be related directly to workers' perceptions of poor treatment. For employees to perceive fair, honest, or decent treatment, top management must make the commitment to assume responsibility for training and must transmit it down through all levels to first-line supervisors. This is necessary, for example, before management can develop an adequate performance appraisal and reward system that employees will consider equitable.

Once management has made the commitment to assume its training responsibility, it must determine what type of training program to implement. The following questions may provide evaluative insight into employee needs:

- Are employee functions and responsibilities agreed on and clear?
- Do employees have the ability (technical training and experience) to do what is expected?
- Do job descriptions contain specific performance objectives?
- Do employees know what performance standards are being used to evaluate their work?
- Is there a positive relationship between employee performance and reward?

Management implementation of an appropriate training program should have positive effects on employee attitudes and productivity and should be a major asset in eradicating the dead-end job syndrome.

Employee Value Systems

Management should recognize the different types of value systems that exist among various employee groups in both professional and nonprofessional categories. Research has identified as many as seven different employee value systems, varying from tribalistic to existentialist (Hughes 1976). Some examples of responses to the myriad of value systems and needs include flexible work scheduling, earned time programs, methods of job enrichment, and a cafeteria approach to fringe benefits. Management must develop a variety of imaginative ways to respond to the needs of multiple employee "families."

First-Line Supervisors

Management should recognize the importance of first-line supervisors in preventing serious labor problems. The logic is simple. First-line supervisors represent all of management in the operational contact with nonsupervisory personnel. If these supervisors do not have good management skills, the institution is inviting unionization. Frequently, a problem with first-line supervisors is manifested by the number of grievances filed involving situations that are either about or under the direct control of such persons. Management should evaluate the effectiveness of first-line supervisors' employee rela-

tions skills carefully and regularly. When deficiencies are found, management should either assist the supervisor through training or terminate the person, depending on his or her past record and potential.

Performance Appraisal

The institution should establish a performance appraisal policy that reflects management's desire to develop employees to their potential. If management behavior indicates anything else, workers are likely to perceive treatment by supervisors as poor or unfair. Performance appraisal must be done honestly and on a regular basis to be effective in improving the morale and productivity of all employees.

Management's avoidance of an honest appraisal of the nonproductive employee simply demonstrates to all workers that the reward system is inequitable or that the laggards receive the same rewards as those who are productive. This can be interpreted logically by productive employees as evidence that the nonproductive actually are rewarded more than the productive in relation to their effort. If this attitude prevails, management very likely is "teaching" its employees to move toward union thinking. The implementation of a good performance appraisal system depends largely on the management skills of the first-line supervisors. In other words, the appraisal system used is not nearly as important as the people (managers) who implement it. The best system is as weak as the people who operate it.

Disciplinary Policies and Procedures

Management must take great care to apply disciplinary policies and procedures consistently. Consistent and fair application normally can prevent unnecessary employee relations problems and grievances. One basic principle is that management should have "just cause" for imposing discipline. The definition may vary from case to case, but several basic tests can be applied to determine whether "just cause" exists for disciplining employees.

- Was the disciplinary rule reasonably related to efficient and safe operations?
- Were the employees properly warned of potential consequences of violating the rule?
- Did management conduct a fair investigation before applying the discipline?
- Did the investigation produce substantial evidence of guilt?
- Were the policies and procedures implemented consistently and without discrimination?
- If a penalty resulted, was it related to the seriousness of the event as well as the past record of the employee? (Did the punishment fit the crime?)

Some form of grievance procedure should be viewed as a part of any prevention program because employees should be able to complain formally about perceived problems without fear of subjective reprisal. Although any grievance procedure is open to problems of interpretation and application, some basic factors can be applied equally in evaluating the system from the employees' perspective.

- All employees should be able to understand the mechanics of filing a grievance and should know where they can go to ask questions about any step of the system. Thus, the procedure should be written.
- When employees file grievances, they expect prompt action. Promptness is one of the most important aspects of a grievance settlement, and failure to resolve the problem with reasonable speed is likely to lead to adverse employee feelings.
- The first-line supervisor typically is the first step in a grievance procedure. When that individual is perceived to be the problem, however, employees need to know that they can access the grievance machinery without going through the first-line supervisor. However, employees should take every reasonable step to solve the problem with the immediate supervisor before going to someone else with the grievance.

When employees realize that a fair grievance procedure is available and when management is doing what it can to prevent unnecessary problems, the result should be a decreased number of complaints, fair and objective processing of those that are filed, and an employee feeling that management is concerned about employee needs.

Wages

The health care institution should be very careful to stay competitive with regard to wages and should compare its rates at least annually to similar institutions in the same geographical area. Frequently, wage survey data can be found that apply to the local area, but if this is not the case, management should conduct its own survey. Even a sample survey of representative jobs will help keep the institution abreast of trend information. Of course, certain shortage points will have to be dealt with on a case-by-case basis and possibly more frequently than every year. Competitive wages are a necessary condition in any preventive management program, but it should not be concluded that being competitive in wages is sufficient for maintaining nonunion status.

As has been indicated, wages is only one of many factors that may enter into employee decisions to seek union help. Health care no longer is as far behind other industries in wages as it was 15 or 20 years ago, and, indeed, wages may not be the major motivating factor for a significant portion of employees in a given institution. Although there may not be a great

deal that management can definitively conclude from research regarding wages as a motivating factor, the folly of relying totally on competitive wages to prevent unionization can be illustrated best by a review of wage structures in institutions that have had union elections recently.

In summary, the absence of competitive wage levels (particularly in times of double-digit inflation) is a potentially severe problem, but the presence of good wage levels is not sufficient, in itself, to prevent unionization. This is particularly true in multidimensional institutions that employ a diverse group of employees with a variety of value systems.

MANAGEMENT STRATEGY FOR REACTIONS DURING UNION-ORGANIZING CAMPAIGNS

Although many "prevention" steps may have been implemented, managers should not be so naive as to believe that a union organization attempt cannot happen. An extremely important part of a preventive management program is to have a well-planned strategy for reacting if such an attempt does occur.

Brett's (1980) two-point conceptualization of employee reactions during a union-organizing campaign holds important implications for both employers and unions.

1. An employer's antiunion campaign that attempts to persuade employees by emphasizing economic control over them and using fear tactics is unlikely to be successful.
2. The employer's most effective antiunion campaign stresses the desire to remain nonunion; provides factual information pertaining to working conditions, benefits, and so on; and indicates that a labor organization cannot guarantee what conditions will exist under union representation.

SUMMARY

Maintaining nonunion status is an attainable goal. Whether it will be achieved is related directly to the behavioral dedication of management in demonstrating its concern for meeting employee needs fairly and equitably. Although the material in this chapter is not all inclusive and does not offer a formula to guarantee nonunion status, it is suggestive of management practices necessary to prevent communication problems and to avoid employee perceptions of unfair treatment.

The unionization process is highly situational and in some locations may be essentially inevitable. Nevertheless, a positive nonunion philosophy and a preventive management program usually should obviate the need for a labor organization. When employees do not perceive a need for union assistance, the probability is slim that they will elect to begin paying union dues.

REFERENCES

Brett, Jeanne M. 1980. Why employees want unions. *Organizational Dynamics* 8 (Spring 1980) (American Management Association): 48, 49, 51.

Clelland, R. 1987. Grievance procedures: Outlet of employee, insight for management. *Hospitals* 41, no. 18 (August 1): 60.

Goals and trends in the unionization of health care professionals. 1972. *Hospital Progress* 53, no. 2 (February): 40–43.

Goodfellow, M. 1969. If you aren't listening to your employees, you may be asking for a union. *Modern Hospital* 113, no. 4 (October): 4.

———. 1972. Checklist: How the union organizer rates your institution. *Risk Management* 19 (December): 1–6.

Hughes, Charles L. *Making unions unnecessary*. New York: Executive Enterprises Publications, 1976.

Imberman, A.A. 1973. Communications: An effective weapon against unionization. *Hospital Progress* 54, no. 12 (December): 54–57.

Joiner, C.L., and K.D. Blayney. 1974. Career mobility and allied health manpower utilization. *Journal of Allied Health* (Fall).

Keeping your employees' morale up takes more than money, *Hospital Financial Management* 28, no. 11 (November): 24–29.

Lewis, H.L. 1974. Wave of union organizing will follow break in the Taft-Hartley dam. *Modern Healthcare* 1, no. 2 (May): 25–32.

Matlack, D.R. 1972. Goals and trends in the unionization of health professionals. *Hospital Progress* 53, no. 2 (February): 40–43.

Metzger, Norman. 1970. Labor relations. *Hospitals* 44, no. 6 (March 16): 80–84.

Metzger, Norman, and D.D. Pointer. 1972. *Labor-management relations in health services industry: Theory and practice*. Washington, D.C.: Science and Health Publications, Inc.

Milliken, R.A., and G. Milliken. 1973. Unionization—Vulnerable and outbid. *Hospitals* 47, no. 20 (October 16): 56–59.

Phillips, D.E. 1974. Taft-Hartley: What to expect. *Hospitals* 48, no. 13 (July 1): 18a–18d.

Pointer, D.D. 1974. How the 1974 Taft-Hartley amendments will affect health care facilities. *Hospital Progress* 55, no. 10 (October): 68–70.

Pointer, D.D., and L.L. Cannedy. 1974. Organizing of professionals. *Hospitals* 48, no. 6 (March 16): 70–73.

Pointer, D.D., and Norman Metzger. 1975. *The National Labor Relations Act—A guidebook for health care facility administrators*. New York: Spectrum.

Rakich, J.S. 1973. Hospital unionization: Causes and effects. *Hospital Administration* 18 (Winter): 10.

Reed, K.A. 1970. Preparing for union organization. *Hospital Topics* 48, no. 4 (April): 30–32.

Rutkowski, Arthur D., and Barbara Lang Rutkowski. 1984. *Labor relations in hospitals*. Rockville, Md.: Aspen Publishers, Inc.

Sibson, R.E. 1965. Why union in the hospital? *Hospital Topics* 43, no. 8 (August): 46, 48, 54.

Stanton, E.S. 1971. The Charleston hospital strikes. *Southern Hospitals* 39 (March): 39.

———. 1974. Unions and the professional employee. *Hospital Progress* 55, no. 1 (January): 58.

Marco L. Colosi

Substance Abuse: Management Responses

59

INTRODUCTION

The use of illegal substances, commonly referred to as *drug abuse*, *substance abuse*, or *chemical abuse* (which also includes alcoholism), imposes enormous social, political, and economic burdens on society, while at the same time imposing equally significant socioeconomic costs on the American economy.

The seriousness of the extent of substance abuse is finally being realized. Statistics compiled by the National Council of Alcoholism and by the Research Triangle Institute indicate that the total cost of substance abuse in the American economy may be in the range of $60 to $144.8 billion per year.[1] These losses are manifested in the form of lost productivity, turnover, absenteeism, sick leave, drug-related injuries/accidents, increased costs of health benefits, and workers' compensation and disability claims, as well as additional costs for overtime, training, retraining, and security measures. It is estimated that 3 to 7 percent of the employee population use illicit drugs daily and that another 5 to 10 percent of the employee population are likely to have an alcohol problem.[2] The net effect on employers is devastating, and the effects on the business world can be divided into four simple categories, as follows:

1. Workers suffering from alcoholism are at least 25 percent less productive than their coworkers, according to Dr. William Meyer of the U.S. Public Health Service.[3]
2. There are four times more accidents and five times more workers' compensation claims due to substance abuse as compared to all other reasons for claims.[4]

3. Affected employers may have three to nine times more utilization of health benefits related to stress from dependents living with those workers.[5]
4. Substance-abusing employees have an absentee ratio two-and-one-half times higher than that of their coworkers.[6]

The business world is reacting by developing and implementing a variety of antidrug and/or antialcoholism programs. Therefore, it is no wonder that employee substance abuse screening is an increasingly common business response to this societal-employment dilemma. This response is predicated on the belief that the demand for illegal substances will be reduced by raising their noncriminal costs and impact of their use. To an employee who is a substance abuser, this noncriminal cost may manifest itself as work place social ostracism, reprimands, suspension, and even discharge. Needless to say, the noncriminal employment-related consequences could have enormous personal, familial, and sociopsycho-economic effects. From the employer's point of view, this noncriminal employment-related action could also have serious consequences, especially if the substance-abusing employee is in a critical, confidential, managerial, or difficult-to-fill position.

The federal government, various state and local governments and their agencies, and approximately 168 Fortune 500 companies have implemented some form of a substance abuse screening policy and program. The federal government basically has taken the lead in this antidrug arena, as noted in President Reagan's Executive Order 12564 of September 19, 1986, and considerable attention is being given to the many constitutional and legal issues raised by drug testing, especially if it is carried out on a random or mandatory basis. A related dispute in the unionized sector revolves around the negotiability of effecting testing proposals. The entire concept of substance abuse screening is fraught with many legal, social-civil rights, common law, labor relations, and employee morale questions, concerns, and liabilities.

It is obvious why hospitals, as well as other types of companies in the private and public sectors of the business world, are facing higher security, safety, and financial risks from substance-abusing employees. Many employees are using and selling drugs on the job and are often using pilfered hospital or company property as the "currency" with which to buy drugs. These employees who work while under the influence of alcohol or drugs present a serious safety hazard to themselves, their coworkers, and society at large. Moreover, apart from theft and safety issues, drug- and alcohol-impaired individuals are unreliable, error prone, and unproductive. This likelihood is more complicated in hospitals, especially if these individuals have direct access to controlled substances (i.e., drugs, etc.) or obtain indirect access to these substances. Further, employers may incur liability for negligent hiring or negligent supervision when intoxicated or impaired employees injure themselves, coworkers, visitors, or patients while at work. Thus, the questions of risk management and malpractice raise major areas of concern, especially in a period of spiraling jury awards and insurance rates. Coupled with this are declining morale, shifting employee attitudes, and the risk of a negative image for the hospitals, at a time when hospitals are trying to improve their image and become more competitive. Therefore, it is quite evident that for the health care industry and the rest of the not-for-profit and for-profit employers, anti–substance abuse efforts serve many of the same public policy ends as the well-publicized efforts of law enforcement, school, and health officials.

The 1986 report to the President's Commission on Organized Crime, "America's Habit: Drug Abuse, Drug Trafficking and Organized Crime," urged applicant drug screening and employee drug testing with "zero tolerance" for all federal employees. The report also recommended that private employers institute similar programs in their work places.[7] Further, according to the Commission's report, in a recent survey of Fortune 500 companies, 66 percent of the respondents stated that they do not employ applicants who fail substance abuse tests, 41 percent required treatment for current employees who fail, and 25 percent said they discharge drug-using employees.[8] This should be compared to 1982 when less than 10 percent of these employers used screening devices, according to the U.S. Drug Enforcement Administration report of 1986.[9]

Advocates of work place screening argue that strong measures must be taken to reduce the economic loss caused by substance abuse and to protect the public and the workers in an employment setting. Critics of work place screening oppose testing, especially mandatory testing and blanket and random screening, because of the potential erroneous results and the inability of tests to indicate impairment. They also oppose the screening because of the considered violations of constitutional and legal rights posed by drug testing. Further, employers and employees alike lack the understanding of drug and alcohol detection technology and methods necessary to assure their proper and effective use. Therefore, it becomes quite evident that there is good reason why employers that have attempted to develop procedures to control substance abuse have been plagued by legal uncertainty.

The basic premise of this chapter is that informed employers may lawfully and decisively rid their institutions of substance abuse. In addition to the complex legal issues raised by screening, employers must also weigh the impact on employee relations and morale and on their business as a whole. Additionally, the cost of a substance abuse policy must be considered in light of the anticipated benefits before electing to implement a testing program.

Employers may rightfully presume that efforts to reduce or eliminate substance abuse in the work place are generally job related, no matter what the job or the level of the individual in the organization's hierarchy. Nevertheless, the screening or investigatory methods an employer selects will have varying degrees of job relatedness and intrusiveness that may affect employee acceptance and minimize legal risks. The foundations of the screening and investigatory methods rest in the various testing methodologies, their purposes, and the confidentiality of the process, as well as in the confidence that can be instilled in employees regarding the integrity of the program's need and purpose.

TESTING METHODOLOGIES

As employee or applicant screening increases, so does the need to have an informed and knowledgeable management that understands the uses and limitations of chemometric technology. Generally, screening methods that are appropriate for work place testing should be sufficiently precise to support the organization's rehabilitative and/or disciplinary decisions based on positive and confirmed positive results from testing. An employer's ability to minimize the risk associated with testing is directly linked to the design of its substance abuse program. The greater an employer's emphasis on the preservation of the employee's dignity, cooperation, and program acceptance, the less the legal risk. Blood tests and urinalyses are highly accurate in determining whether an employee has alcohol or drugs in his/her system. There are few instances of "false positive" or "false negative" reactions to the test, and these can be controlled through the use of "confirmatory tests" before making any employment decisions.

These tests are less effective, however, with respect to determining when the individual ingested the alcohol or the drug. There are distinct differences between the blood and the urinalysis tests. The blood test is more accurate for measuring the actual quantity of alcohol or drugs in the employee's body, while the amount of alcohol indicated in a urinalysis will be affected by the quantities of nonalcoholic beverages the employee has in his/her system up to the time the test is taken. Thus, in the urinalysis test there is a potential for reduced accuracy in determining the level of intoxication or abuse that does not exist in the blood test. In short, a urinalysis is just as effective as a blood test for substance abuse detection, but it is less effective in measuring the level of that abuse, while the breathalyzer test is preferable to urinalysis for detecting the quantity of alcohol in the employee's system and could be used as an initial or support test. On the other hand, a blood test requires a professional to draw the blood, whereas a urinalysis does not usually require such professional involvement and is therefore more economical. However, a risk exists for the employer because there is a potential for fraud in the urinalysis testing that is conducted without any supervision or observed sample taking. This potential does not exist in blood testing because the "taking" is observed.

Initially, companies usually utilize a relatively low cost test procedure, supported where applicable by a more sophisticated, selective, and accurate technique to confirm any initial positive test results. These "confirmatory screens" are more expensive. The two most widely accepted initial screening methods are

1. immunochemical tests, all referred to as *immunoassays*
2. thin layer chromatography (TLC).

A popular initial screening technique of the immunoassay variety is the enzyme multiplied immunoassay technique (EMIT) marketed by the SYVA company of Palo Alto, California. This technique is a very common, low-cost substance abuse test. Drug specific immunoassays can discriminate but only between the presence or absence of the expected drug or drugs. These assays are designed as a primary screening test to detect positive samples in a given (employee) population, and a negative result is evidence that the drug in question is not present in excess of the detection limit of the assay. In short, it is a good detector test.

The EMIT cannabinoid assay is the most complicated drug test to confirm because, unlike many other techniques, it detects a large number of THC metabolites ($\Delta 9$—Tetrahydrocannabinol). This ability to cross-react with so many THC metabolites was built into the assay to maximize its ability to detect marijuana use. It should be recognized that the test cannot directly measure the level or degree of employee impairment, and little is known about the time length of impairment after marijuana use. But one preliminary Stanford University study of pilots indicates that the seriously impairing effects of a single marijuana cigarette persist for up to 24 hours after inhalation.[10] These findings appear to show a need for further research regarding the effects of marijuana in the work place. However, they also indicate that employee screening that detects recent non-work-hours marijuana use cannot be considered presumptively *non-job-related* because the effects of the use may persist into work hours. Most of the other controlled substances have much shorter detection periods in urine than does marijuana. These laboratory detection periods are sufficiently brief to be considered strongly job-related. Since objective drug tests supplement or supplant less accurate subjective impressions of possible employee drug use, employers should not be faulted so long as the detection limits of objective tests bear a rational relationship to the persistence of impairment.

Another commonly used, and relatively inexpensive, urine drug screening test is the thin layer chromatography (TLC) test. TLC takes advantage of the fact that various drugs interact differently with solvents that are pulled upward by capillary action through a concentrated sample on a prepared plate.[11] It is most frequently used in drug detoxification clinics, methadone maintenance programs, and other large-scale screening programs.[12] It should be noted that if these tests are used alone, they could produce false positives. False positives are really nothing more than unconfirmed positive results from an initial test.

Although the principle behind gas chromatograph—mass spectrometers (GC/MS) is similar to that of TLC, the GC/MS equipment is capable of performing varying chemical analyses or vaporized samples. It is for this reason that GC/MS is acknowledged to be the most sensitive, specific, accurate, and reliable method for confirming the presence of drug abuse in biological samples.[13] Because of this, GC/MS tests are currently becoming the most accepted means of verifying initial positive findings of drug use.

Employers hope that the existence of the substance abuse screening program will deter most abusers from applying and help to detect those who do apply. Somewhat ironically, the deterrence of substance-abusing applicants is probably more valuable than the detection of the abuse after an application has been made. Many potential applicants who use drugs may assume that the screening will detect any past or current substance abuse or use and will not apply for employment.

The concepts inherent in a substance abuse policy and program with a genesis in the testing methodologies have given rise to many issues concerning the potential infringement of these programs on the constitutional rights of the individuals who are required by a corporate policy to participate in a substance abuse program. The American Civil Liberties Union (ACLU) has been quite vocal and active in this area as an advocate of constitutional rights over any involuntary policy or program.

CONSTITUTIONAL CONCERNS

Private sector employers are not bound by the same constitutional restraints that apply to the public sector. In non-union organizations, employers do not have to justify their right to test other than for communications and employee relations purposes. The legal issues in the private sector are not as concretely defined as in the public sector. Thus far, suggestions have been made that state constitutions, some statutory law, and certain common law concepts may impinge on the private sector employers' rights to test. Some experts have suggested that state constitutions with an expressed right to privacy may establish a Fourth Amendment type of privacy requirement for the private sector in that specific state only. Currently there are seven states that have constitutionally expressed a right to privacy: Arizona, Arkansas, California, Florida, Massachusetts, Montana, and Rhode Island. However, no case law has been reported that tests this position, and even if the privacy right were recognized, "reasonable suspicion" or "compelling need" would probably justify that required testing.

Other constitutional issues have also been raised but only in the public sector. These public sector arguments to block drug testing include the Ninth Amendment's right to privacy, as well as the Fourteenth Amendment's equal protection clause and the Fifth Amendment's protection from self-incrimination. At this point in judicial decision making, the Fourth Amendment right to privacy stands as the pre-eminent constitutional barrier to drug testing, at least in the public sector. The Fifth and Fourteenth Amendments' due process rights provide courts with principles that ensure fairness where testing meets the Fourth Amendment standards. While these public-sector-applied constitutional barriers appear formidable, it should be stated that generally courts are allowing testing. The constitutional barriers do not blanketly prohibit drug testing; rather, these principles require that government have a reasonable, legitimate interest in testing and that government test using guidelines that assure fairness and protect employee rights. To be prudent, private sector employers should set up guidelines and policies that provide this protection for their employees, while also enhancing integrity, minimizing liabilities, and ensuring a safe work place.

An employer may wish to test "for cause" when an employee exhibits possible symptoms or behavioral signs of drug or alcohol use or abuse. Currently many employers require a "reasonable suspicion" or some degree of "cause" prior to their requiring a substance abuse test of the employee. Naturally, absent an employee's admission of use or abuse of drugs or alcohol, an employer has no real or direct factual knowledge of that use or abuse. Therefore, "for cause" testing policies rely to some degree on "reasonable suspicion" before testing is triggered. Employers may best support their policies on substance abuse screening by supplementing reasonable suspicion with behavioral, observational, and physiological symptoms-observation techniques on the job. Through this tripartite approach the employer is more likely to find those employees who exhibit present impairment from substance abuse. This tripartite "for cause" selection methodology places the policy and testing selection method in a better legal and practical light.

An alternative "for cause" method for substance abuse screening is the policy that requires testing following certain types of on-the-job accidents or incidents. Irrespective of the method utilized, supervisors who may administer detection programs need to be trained to document their observations at the time of the incidents.

Contrasted to "for cause" screening for which employees are selected based on behavioral or physiological observation, random or periodic testing policies do not have their basis in any evidence of potential employee impairment. Random testing is considered to be more onerous to employees due to the arbitrariness of the testing selection methodology. Further, the random sampling approach has to date been considered totally unacceptable to the courts for the public sector employees, and it faces much uncertainty in the courts for private sector employees, especially because job relatedness is difficult to demonstrate, absent from significant safety, health, or economic impact. If random, periodic, or "fitness for duty" testing is needed, using an approach to minimize the negative employee relations and to detect employee abstinence of drug and alcohol use in order to circumvent testing results, the employer may provide notice of intent to test. This notice is referred to as the *window for testing*.

In the window for testing, employees are given a calendar period during which testing may occur. This approach may make it more difficult for employees to abstain from substance use. In the window for testing concept there could be notice that testing may occur at any time within, for example, a 15-day period (i.e., March 10 through March 25). Thus, to test negative (or below detectable limits) the employee would need to abstain possibly throughout the entire period and for some time prior to that period.

The majority of cases in the public sector hold random testing is unconstitutional. Further, substance abuse testing is considered a *search and seizure*, which causes additional complications and risks in implementing a substance abuse policy and program. To minimize the risks associated with search and seizure, let us also review the employers' and employees' rights and concerns. If an employee is suspected of possession, use, or sale of illegal drugs or alcohol, an employer may determine that the search of the employee's locker, desk, work area, and possessions or the individual him/herself is appropriate. Such searches may be lawful, depending on the state laws and may be effective, depending on the employer-employee labor relationships. On the other hand, the employer risks serious liability if the search is inconsistent with state and federal legal principles and the reasonable business practices doctrine. The key to a successful search policy is communicating the nature of the policy to employees prior to commencing the search program. In those cases in which the employer explained that the search would be done randomly and that the search would cover employee vehicles on company property or employee packages carried on or off the company property, those employees who refused such searches could be and were terminated. Their claim of violation of constitutional and common law rights have thus far been denied. Thus, as supported by *Checkin v. Bellevue Hospital Center* [479 F. Supp. 207 (S.D. N.Y. 1979)], and *Gretencord v. Ford Motor Company* [538 F. Supp. 331 (D. Ky. 1982)], the employer's defense in an employee's suit alleging invasion of privacy is greatly strengthened when the employer has given employees notice of the possibility of and the rationale behind the searches. This notification will have the effect of diminishing an employee's "expectation of privacy" and multiplying the employer's need to know. Naturally, the search philosophy ("reasonable cause" or "random search") and the circumstances surrounding the individual case are important in terms of minimizing liability and enhancing program acceptability.

In other words, absent the existence of a preannounced search policy to which employees may be deemed to have consented voluntarily and without coercion, an employer may *not* conduct a general search. This is true even if the employer has probable cause to believe that the employee possesses or is under the influence of illegal drugs or impermissible alcohol on the company premises. Under these conditions an organization is well-advised to confine the search to items in "plain view," which will be held to contain no reasonable expectation of privacy [*People v. Zelinski*, 24 Cal. 3d 357, 155 Cal. Rptr. 575 (1979)]. The thrust of *Zelinski*, *People v. Patel* [121 Cal. App. 3d 20, 175 Cal. Rptr. 416 (1981)], and *People v. Carter* [117 Cal. App. 3d 735, 172 Cal. Rptr. 863 (1981)] indicates that, absent a communicated search policy, if an item is *not* visible, then the search will be held reasonable only if the affected employee can be said to have had no reasonable expectation of privacy. (See, e.g., *Simmons v. Southwestern Bell Telephone Company* [452 F. Supp. 392 (W.D. Okla. 1978), *aff'd*, 611 F.2d 342 (10th Cir. 1979)] and *Kemp v. Block* [607 F. Supp. 1262 (D. Nev. 1985)].

A different situation arises when the object of the search is not the employee's person or personal property as discussed above, but property supplied by the employer for work-related use. Several cases have held that there is no reasonable expectation of privacy in an employer-owned locker when an established policy of unconsented locker inspection exists. In *United States v. Bunkers* [521 F.2d 1217 (9th Cir.), *cert. denied*, 423 U.S. 989 (1975)], the court held that

> A warrantless search of a . . . locker . . . is upheld because there was no reasonable expectation of privacy for possession in the locker since:
>
> 1. A regulation allowed for such searches when there was reasonable cause to suspect criminal activity.
> 2. The defendant had been fully advised of the regulation and the conditions placed upon her use of the locker and the [employer's] right to search it.

In *Tucker v. Superior Court of California* [84 Cal. App. 3d 43, 148 Cal. Rptr. 167 (1978)], the court held that the employee had a "reasonable expectation" of privacy in his closed but unlocked locker because there was no notice, regulation, or practice within the organization pertaining to locker searches. On the other hand, in the case of *Williams v. Collins* [728 F.2d 721, 728 (5th Cir. 1984)], an employer's search of an employee's desk and office, including a locked desk drawer, without a warrant, when the supervisor also seized personal property in the drawer for safekeeping, was within the outer perimeter of the supervisor's line of duty. In *Williams* the primary issue was whether a federal government employee's supervisor had absolute immunity from common law tort liability for actions taken in dismissing the employee.

A more complicated issue involves the search of employer-owned vehicles that employees use off company property. In this case, the employer's policy should include the fact that the employer retains the right to search the vehicle, wherever the vehicle is located. Even if the vehicle is on the private property of the employee, refusal to permit a search of a hospital vehicle at any time could lead to disciplinary action.

At this point, it becomes obvious that it is difficult to draw conclusions from the two lines of reasoning set forth in *Williams* and *Tucker*, respectively. It is likely, however, that searches will be upheld if the employer has an established policy of inspecting lockers or other property without consent. It appears that once employees are notified that searches of lockers, desks, or other property may occur, they cannot have an expectation of privacy, particularly when the property is the target of potential searches at any time. The employer must take affirmative steps to ensure that the employees are informed of the policy and that the policy is observed throughout the organization.

The employer can justify a search policy by showing that it is intended for the purpose of the protection and safety of the employer's property, employees, visitors, and patients. This justification is supported by state laws and OSHA regulations requiring employers to maintain a safe work environment [*Davis v. Monsanto Company*, 627 F. Supp. 418 (S.D. W. Va. 1986)]. The practical effect of all the above is that search procedures should be announced well in advance and should be described in detail in a written communication to all employees. Employees who are subject to these policies will ordinarily be deemed to have consented to them, but employers should seek express written consent whenever practical before proceeding with an intrusive search. All searches should be conducted so that an employee's dignity is preserved. Searches of areas that are not *explicitly* permitted in the policy manual should be governed by a strict policy requiring a rational basis for believing that there is a violation of the substance abuse policy. Evidence of employee violations of hospital drug or alcohol rules need satisfy only normal company standards for discipline to be imposed. Generally, for employee relations purposes, the hospital standard for disciplinary action should require a good faith belief that a violation has occurred, or is occurring. Such belief requires some credible evidence obtained in a reasonable investigation that conforms with hospital policies regarding investigations. Such evidence need not be convincing "beyond a reasonable doubt" because this standard applies solely to criminal prosecutions. An acceptable investigative standard for employers could be "convincing evidence on the record as a whole." The investigation should follow the hospital's normal due process and the fair and uniform hearing and appeals procedure within the organization's grievance arbitration (union) or complaint (nonunion) procedures.

Further, the following guidelines should be observed when considering employee searches for possession of either stolen goods or prohibited materials, such as drugs or alcohol. These guidelines apply not only to searches of an employee's person but also to searches of personal effects (i.e., automobiles, lunch boxes, etc.) and equipment provided by the hospital for the employee's use (i.e., lockers, hospital vehicles, etc.). For a well-communicated search policy, we suggest the following, which should be referred to as a guide in developing a practical policy that would specifically relate to the needs of the individual employer.

SAMPLE SEARCH POLICY

In order to prevent (1) theft of hospital property and (2) theft of employee property and (3) use or possession of drugs or alcohol, the hospital reserves the right to inspect all bags, lunch boxes, and other parcels on hospital property or whenever an employee enters or leaves the hospital.

Further, the hospital reserves the right to search private offices, file cabinets, credenzas, and desks for the purpose of ensuring that the hospital policies are followed and that hospital property (i.e., company vehicles, tool boxes, lockers, etc.) is used as intended.

SAMPLE LOCKER POLICY

The hospital provides lockers for the use of its employees during work. Each locker has a "master" combination lock which may be opened by the hospital. No other lock may be used on the locker. Unauthorized nonmaster combination locks will be removed by the hospital at the employee's expense, with or without notice, and a hospital master combination lock substituted.

The hospital reserves the right to open and inspect the interior of each locker at any time with or without notice of said inspection. Prohibited materials including nonprescribed illicit drugs, alcohol, and weapons may not be stored in the locker. Lockers will be maintained in a neat and sanitary condition.

The hospital is not responsible for any articles in the lockers that are lost or stolen.

In conclusion, when implementing a substance abuse policy and conducting investigations of an individual's drug or alcohol involvement, an employer must be thoroughly aware of the applicable legal principles and concomitant potential liability.

In short, the employer must take stock of the legal landscape which includes (1) civil rights statutes, (2) handicapped discrimination laws, (3) common law tort theories, (4) labor law [e.g., the National Labor Relations Act (NLRA)], and (5) specific state statutes that may apply to an employer's substance abuse testing policies.

LABOR RELATIONS

Whether or not an employer's work force is unionized clearly affects the legal issue of whether the hospital may unilaterally introduce a substance abuse policy. Unionized hospitals are required by the National Labor Relations Act (NLRA) to bargain collectively over "wages, hours, and other terms and conditions of employment" [29 U.S.C. § 158(d)]; but the National Labor Relations Board (NLRB) has not addressed the issue of whether a substance abuse testing program is a "term" or "condition" of employment. However, the Board, in analogous situations, has held that requiring employees to submit to polygraph testing as a condition of continued employment is a mandatory subject of bargaining [*Medicenter, Mid-South Hospital*, 221 N.L.R.B. 1431 (1978) and *LeRoy Machine Co. Inc.*, 147 N.L.R.B. 670 (1964)]. In these cases the NLRB also held that an employer's policy that requires employees with records of heavy absenteeism to submit to a physical examination is a mandatory subject of collective bargaining. For the probable position the NLRB may assume, refer to *NLRB v. Lovey & Duke Storage Warehouse Co.* [369 F.2d 859 (5th Cir. 1966)].

Although to date the National Labor Relations Board has taken no definitive posture regarding substance abuse, Rosemary Collyer, the NLRB General Counsel, has issued a memorandum stating her legal position (GC 87-5, September 8, 1987). This memorandum states that a drug-testing program for either applicants or current employees is a mandatory subject of collective bargaining under Section 8(d) of the NLRA because this program constitutes a substantial change in the working conditions. The General Counsel also indicates that a union's waiver of its bargaining rights may not be implied; it must be "clear and unmistakable."

The scope of bargaining should include the content, purpose, and disciplinary effect of the testing. However, the NLRB General Counsel has reiterated her position that employers need only bargain in good faith until agreement or impasse. At that point, the employer simply implements its substance abuse policy and programs, unless there is restrictive contract language limiting such action. For example, if the employer had a "for cause" drug testing program in the contract, but wants to implement random testing, it would be required to negotiate over the issue with the union(s). However, if the hospital had a substance abuse testing program on the table during contract negotiations (which it withdrew due to union objections or in exchange for another union concession), the hospital undoubtedly would be considered to have "waived" its right to bargain to impasse mid-term in the contract. By the same token a union may waive its rights to negotiate by failing to respond to an employer's proposal to bargain on the implementation of a substance abuse testing program by a specified date. Such a union waiver, by acquiescence, is also possible through contract language or past practice. However, the waiver of statutory rights must be "clear and unmistakable." It must be pointed out for emphasis that while an employer may rely on its management rights clause or other "zipper" clauses, the NLRB has read these clauses extremely narrowly and has required an unmistakable waiver of the union's right to bargain [see *Teamsters v. Southwest Airlines Company*, 842 F.2d 794 (5th Cir. 1988)].

The NLRB General Counsel considers that the areas of a substance abuse program that are subject to mandatory collective bargaining include

- privacy
- confidentiality
- the chain of custody
- the validity of the laboratory methods involved
- the impact of testing positive
- the impact of false positives or false negatives
- the need for confirmatory tests
- the existence of a rehabilitative philosophy and programs
- employee assistance programs
- the issue of when a violator of the substance abuse program and policy can be discharged.[14]

Notwithstanding the collective bargaining requirement covering a substance abuse policy, thereafter the employer must promulgate rules that must be communicated to all employees. An example of a safety rule would be as follows:

> The use of alcoholic beverages, intoxicants, narcotics, marijuana, or other controlled substances by employees subject to call-in, or their possession or use while on duty and on hospital property, is expressly prohibited. Employees must not report to duty under the influence of any alcoholic beverage or illicit drug(s) including, but not limited to, marijuana, other controlled substances, or medications, including those prescribed by a doctor, that may in any way adversely affect their alertness, productivity, coordination, reaction response, or safety.

Hospitals should also reserve the right to amend, change, or modify policies and rules as circumstances change or as the need dictates. The policy and its amendments naturally need to be communicated to all employees and supervisors. Above all, once a policy or rule is in place, employers must follow it. Any deviation, particularly a significant one, may result in liability and, especially from the viewpoint of nonunionized employees, possibly a breach of contractual obligations (i.e., implied contracts, good faith, and fair dealing, constructive discharge alternatives to test theories, etc.).

Most hospitals that have reason to suspect or that confirm job-related abuse of alcohol or drugs usually desire to take remedial action. The action they may take should be dependent on

- the labor contract in unionized hospitals
- the hospital's communicated policy and rules
- the hospital's past practices

The employee–labor relations success and legal liability of the employer for adverse action will depend on whether the policy and the rules of conduct are considered "reasonable" under the circumstances and whether they are uniformly applied, providing due process and equal protection under the employer's policy. Since a hospital's philosophy, style, work environment, employee relations, corporate culture, and needs vary, the concepts of disciplinary measures and degree

vary accordingly. Basically, there are three approaches to employee discipline.

1. pure discipline
2. the flexible-moderate approach
3. the therapeutic approach

At one end of the spectrum, an employer may decide that violators of the hospital policy must be terminated regardless of potential for rehabilitation. At the other end of the spectrum from pure discipline, an employer may decide to implement a program involving therapeutic or medical treatment, with no disciplinary action (at least initially). However, most hospitals prefer a flexible approach that permits rehabilitation within a disciplinary framework.

Since substance abuse is commonly linked to increased work place hazards, employers will have more latitude to discipline employees if they pose a safety threat to themselves, coworkers, visitors, or patients. As a general rule, restrictive laws affect health care employers the least when the discipline relates to absenteeism, unacceptable performance, or safety violations. Sometimes an employer may need to discharge an employee for violations of the hospital's substance abuse policy, rules, or program. This discipline or discharge should be handled in the same reasonable, investigative, and "due process" manner as any other discipline or discharge situation.[15] Also, if legal counsel is involved in the investigative process, it is possible to protect the confidentiality of the process with documentation based on the legal concepts of attorney-client privilege or work product [*Upjohn v. United States*, 449 U.S. 383 (1981)]. However, caution should be exercised because the attorney could become a material witness [*D.J. Chadbourne Inc. v. Superior Court*, 60 Cal. 2d 723, 388 P.2d 700 (1964)].

When an employer deems that a disciplinary action is necessary, due to a violation of the hospital's substance abuse policy or rules, as based on test results, then the hospital must consider the following criteria often used by arbitrators in deciding a case:

- Was there an impairment of the individual's ability to do the job? This applies regardless of whether the test results indicate use on or off hospital property.
- Was there possession or consumption on the hospital premises and/or during the workday? An arbitrator is more likely to uphold an employer's decision based on the possession of an illicit substance at the work place, as opposed to off the premises. Furthermore, the consumption during the working day of drugs or alcohol is usually the strongest case for an employer.
- If the decision arises because of an employee's off-premises conduct, what is the relationship among the employee's conduct and the employer's business purpose and the employee's work function?
- Is the test part of an overall employer policy to promote alcohol and drug abuse awareness and to provide a condi-

tion for potential rehabilitation prior to discipline, or is the test simply for punitive purposes?

- Has there been some impairment of the individual's ability to do the job, such as (1) absenteeism, (2) decreased productivity, (3) poor performance, or (4) safety violations?

- What are the business justifications for the policy, and how has the policy been communicated?

- Is the rule clear and unambiguous?

- Was the test properly, fairly, and nondiscriminatorily administered?

- Was there reasonable suspicion to justify administering the test?

- Was there a documented chain of custody?

- Was there a confirmatory test?

- Was there due process?

Decisions regarding drug issues in arbitration vary. Generally, the rule is that management has the right to unilaterally establish reasonable rules that are not inconsistent with the union contract.[16] Some issues to consider are

- *Should a test or search require probable cause?* Although the hospital rule should contain probable cause, it should also include specific articulated facts that form the basis for the hospital's belief that the employee is violating a hospital rule (even if most arbitrators do not believe that a rule must have a probable cause requirement to be valid). The key is careful selection of an arbitrator.

- *What should the employer do if the employee refuses to take the test?* In general, a refusal to take a test in the face of a direct order to do so will undoubtedly result in severe discipline. Although an employee has the right of union representation (Weingarten doctrine) during an investigative interview, there is no requirement to inform the employee of that right. If the employer has cause to require the test and the employee refuses, this could be considered insubordination. It should also be noted that there are many arbitrators who have held that refusal to take a test does not constitute insubordination.

- *What is the propriety of the drug test or the search (of lockers, lunch boxes, and purses) and subsequent discipline?* An employer has a right to inspect or search lockers if the hospital provides locks, permits the union representative to be present during the searches, and gives advance notice of those inspections.

- *What are the consequences of extracurricular and off-duty involvement with drugs?* If the behavior harms the hospital's reputation or impairs the employee's ability to perform a job in the work place, then discharge for serious off-duty misconduct is permissible. (An employer's reputation may be at issue if the employer holds a public contract, handles or manufactures drugs, is a hospital, or is a common carrier, etc.).

- *Is there an employer obligation to rehabilitate the employee?* Generally arbitrators are reluctant to order rehabilitation absent some contractual requirements, but arbitrators could reduce discipline contingent on the employee's enrollment in an employee assistance program.

- *What are the standards of proof and sufficiency of evidence?* The degree of proof the employer must produce to establish possession or impairment sufficient to sustain a discharge or discipline, according to a majority of the arbitrators, is "clear and convincing evidence."

- *Should an arbitrator use an adverse inference rule?* Major considerations arise when the employee is a member of management. Can management be treated more stringently if its members themselves abuse the institution's substance abuse policy? The answer to this question is "yes." Management employees who violate the policy can and should be treated more harshly because management employees are in a position of great trust and responsibility. If it appears that management employees "get off easy," then employee morale will suffer, and there is the probability that management will run into many other legal risks and problems due to (1) disparate treatment or (2) inconsistency of the application of policy and due process. The substance abuse policy is for all or not at all.

Finally, it is important to bear in mind that unions may seek to enjoin unilateral implementation of a substance abuse policy. The validity of enforcing a unilateral substance abuse policy implemented after a negotiations impasse, but pending an arbitrator's ruling on its validity, turns on the court's assessment of the danger to employees or public safety in delaying enforcement. The enforcement is measured relative to the injury employees would suffer if subjected to the policy prior to an arbitrated decision. This was exhibited when a federal judge in Washington, D.C., refused to issue a preliminary injunction against the Potomac Electric Power Company, following the issuance of a temporary restraining order (TRO) directing the employer to delay implementation of the substance abuse testing program pending arbitration. This is tantamount to a reverse of *Boys Market* [74 L.R.R.M. 2257 (1970)]. The court in *International Brotherhood of Electrical Workers, Local 1900 v. Potomac Electric Power Company* [634 F. Supp. 642 (D. D.C. 1986)] reasoned that the testing program would not expose employees to any "new" injuries that they were not already experiencing under the employer's prior substance abuse rules and that injunctive relief was therefore inappropriate. However, in *I.B.E.W. Local U-9 v. Metropolitan Edison* [No. 86-4426, slip. op. (E.D. Pa. 1986)], a Section 301 TRO was issued, blocking random drug and alcohol testing pending arbitration, and this was also suggested in the case of *Utility Workers Union of America Local 246 v. Southern California Edison Company* 852 F. 2d 1083 (9th Cir. 1988). However, the Ninth Circuit also held that Section 301 of the NLRA pre-empts the union's claim under a state constitution because the state constitution claims cannot be resolved without reference to the collective bargaining agreement. The court emphasizes the following:

> Resolution of the issue of whether Local 246 has bargained away its members' claimed constitutional rights must rest upon the clauses in the collective bargaining agreement, which recognizes SCE's right to manage the plant, to direct the work force, and to implement reasonable safety rules and require their observance.

The Ninth Circuit declined to hold on the NLRB pre-emption issue but held that the district court lacked jurisdiction of the union's breach of contract claim because the union had not exhausted all its contractual proceedings over the issue. As a result, the court vacated the injunction against the substance abuse testing program.

In summary, sensitive or important business functions should not be in the hands of substance abusers. Thus, strong disciplinary action, including termination, may be required and can be executed with minimal legal risk if the action is based on fair and reasonable policies that have been communicated and followed in good faith. This is accomplished through supervisors who are sensitive to the employees' needs, while balancing the integrity of the employer's policy.

SUGGESTIONS

This section will suggest management approaches in designing a pragmatic substance abuse strategic and operational model that will result in behavioral and attitudinal modifications. This model should be linked to a program of communicated policy leading to positive and stable employee relations. In general, a substance abuse testing policy and program should be only as extensive as is reasonably justified by the specific employer's legitimate need for safety, security, and employee productivity. If "for cause" screening is selected, the hospital must be prepared to justify its suspicion that a particular employee is under the influence of some substance prohibited by company policy or law; and the greater the documentation, the less the legal risk. If an employer can justify a random selection method, an employer should apply it in a wholly objective and nondiscriminatory manner. Employers also should choose test methods and cutoff values having short detection periods in order to minimize intrusion into off-hours and non-employment-related activities. Employers should not require involuntary administration of these tests, although in the employment context the concept of voluntary administration presupposes that employees who refuse to take the test may be permitted to resign or be subjected to some predetermined discipline in lieu of taking the test. The policy may also call for the discharge of employees who refuse to undergo substance abuse screening.

An employer seeking to design a substance abuse testing program should use a quality control procedure checklist[17] for policy development and programmatic implementation. Prior to developing the checklist the employer should identify the specific aspects of its organization that are adversely affected by employee substance abuse. The employer should consider the following:

- The employer must be concerned with patient, visitor, and public safety.
- The safety of employees should also be a concern.
- The potential effects on the hospital's image, due to the community's perception of drug-using employees' effects on patient care, etc., must be considered.
- The potential threat of negligent hiring lawsuits exists.
- Management must consider the effects on the hospital regarding the theft of drugs.
- There should be a review of risk management issues, which will hopefully minimize employer prospective liabilities.
- The employer must identify the problems that exist in the organization and ascertain what the employee needs and attitudes are concerning a substance abuse policy, screening, and an employee assistance program.
- The employer must review the laws and various court decisions in its immediate jurisdiction and review, where applicable, all union contracts and grievance and arbitration clauses.
- The employer should establish a corporatewide policy "top to bottom" with a reasonable accommodation provision. The policy must indicate the type of screening desired—that is, random, companywide, periodic, or reasonable suspicion screening.
- The employer must communicate the policy to all employees and applicants.
- The employer must emphasize the program's confidentiality.

Thereafter, the employer should consider the negative implications of adopting a substance abuse policy, which may include:

- the effect on employee morale
- the cost of testing (The cost could be between $30 and $45 per test, plus confirmatory test costs.)
- the possible duty-to-bargain requirement with unions in a unionized setting
- the possibility of encouraging union-organizing efforts in nonunion hospitals
- potential adverse public or community reactions
- the fact that the hospital may need to make a substantial commitment of people, money, and resources to implement a successful substance abuse program

Prior to reviewing the nine categories in the guidelines checklist for a substance abuse program, the employer has generally identified the above concerns and is now prepared to consider alternatives to a pure substance abuse testing program. For example, the employer has considered and rejected

- providing a voluntary, confidential employee assistance program (EAP) that includes counseling and treatment as well as nonsubstance-abuse-related programs (i.e., marital, legal, financial, psychological, stress, etc.).
- tying the anti–substance abuse policies to a simple rehabilitation program (not disciplinary) only after reviewing the alternatives to a substance abuse policy and the possible negative implications of that policy. At this point an employer has gone a long way toward developing the foundations that will justify the policy. The key here is to document the impracticability of a pure substance abuse test alternative.

At this point the employer is ready to analyze the organization and to document the reasons for the direction that the hospital plans to follow. This checklist is offered to expedite and facilitate your needs analysis; it should be considered illustrative rather than conclusive.

CHECKLIST FOR A SUBSTANCE ABUSE SCREENING PROGRAM

I. *Does the company need a program?*
  A. What experiences, data, risks support the need?
  B. Factors to consider: nature of business; level of absenteeism, tardiness, productivity, health care claims, accidents, workers' compensation claims; perceived magnitude of drug and alcohol abuse in the work place.
  C. Is a policy needed for applicants only or for all employees? An employer generally may require substance abuse screening of an applicant to determine whether the individual is *presently* using substances. It is advisable to test only those applicants who successfully progress to the final stages of the selection process. The applicant may be employed contingent on successfully passing a physical examination that includes a drug/alcohol screening; should the applicant fail to pass the physical because of the positive test result, the applicant should be disqualified (like any other applicant who fails to pass the physical examination for any other reason).
    Further, the employer may desire to maintain an open publication in all advertisements for employment—that is, that the employer is *not only* an "Equal Opportunity Employer" or an "Equal Employment At-Will Employer" but also an "Equal Opportunity At-Will Substance Abuse Screening Employer." This communicates to all potential applicants that you are not only an "Equal Oppor-

tunity Employer," but also an employer that is committed to "employment at will" where applicable, and that is reserving the right to test applicants for substance abuse. This open publication of pre-employment drug and alcohol screening procedures may discourage substance users and abusers from applying for a job opening. This obviously helps reduce your cost per hire.

The employer should also revise employment applications to include the statement that a condition of employment is the successful passing of the physical examination, which includes a substance abuse test. Further, employers should design a "waiver" permitting substance abuse testing only for finalists in the employment process (for a sample waiver form see Exhibit 59-1). It is prudent to have an applicant-employee sign a second waiver permitting future testing (see Exhibit 59-2 for sample).

II. *What will the program philosophy be?*
  A. Will it be disciplinary, rehabilitative, or both?
  B. Will an EAP be used? Will the program be an internal program or a referral program?

III. *Research the law in your jurisdiction* regarding privacy, polygraph statutes, standards for wrongful discharge, statutory restrictions on testing, etc.

IV. *Draft a comprehensive policy.* (A sample is shown in Exhibit 59-3.) Elements of a policy must include the following:
  A. conduct prohibited
  B. substances covered
  C. definition of *use* (e.g., "under the influence," "job performance affected," certain levels of drug or alcohol in body)
  D. exceptions (e.g., prescription drugs, alcohol consumed at business lunches or company parties)
  E. scope of the premises affected (e.g., company vehicles, personal property brought onto the premises, personal vehicles in company parking lots?)
  F. work-related restrictions on off-premises use
  G. procedures and methods to be used (e.g., tests, searches, surveillance)
  H. circumstances leading to screening, searches, etc.
  I. consequences of violation

V. *Become familiar with the accuracy and availability of test procedures.*
  A. Generally less invasive tests are preferable (i.e., urinalysis is preferred over blood sample).
  B. The laboratory should be selected carefully. Employers need to contact and reference-check laboratories to determine which are best qualified and suited for performing substance abuse testing. Particular attention must be given to

Exhibit 59-1 Pre-employment Drug Information and Consent Form and Release

I understand that as part of the employment process, I agree to undergo substance screening for drugs, controlled substances, and alcohol through testing of my blood and/or urine. I also understand that the use, possession, sale, or transfer of alcohol, narcotics, hallucinogens, depressants, stimulants, marijuana, or other controlled substances may affect my eligibility for employment because my potential employment is contingent on, among other things, successful completion of the testing for such substances. I agree to abide by any decision made by the Company in this regard. I hereby authorize any physician or medical facility retained by the Company to collect samples as required and to provide test results and evaluations to Company management, and I release any such person or institution from liability therefor.

I further understand and agree that once employed, if I appear impaired or if reason exists to believe that I have violated the Company policy on drugs, controlled substances, and alcohol, I will be subject to further screening or face disciplinary consequences, up to and including loss of employment. If employed, I recognize and agree that on suspicion of substance possession, in order to determine compliance with the Company's substance policy, the Company may exercise its right to conduct searches of my personal effects and outer clothing as well as my work station, files, locker, personal and company vehicles, and suspected areas of concealment at any time for any reason, with or without notice. I further understand that if the results of substance screening or search indicate that I have violated the Company's policy on drugs, controlled substances, and alcohol, I will be subject to discipline up to and including discharge.

Have you, within the last 60 days, used any narcotics, hallucinogens, depressants, stimulants, marijuana, or other controlled substances?

   Yes _____   No _____

If yes, describe/explain: _____
_____
_____

Please list over-the-counter medication/drugs used within the past two weeks:

Specific Brand Name Medication/Drug	Dosage/Strength per Day	Date/Time Last Dose and Number of Days Used	Reason for Medication
_____	_____	_____	_____
_____	_____	_____	_____
_____	_____	_____	_____

---

1. whether the laboratory performs confirmatory tests (GC/MS) of specimens when initial screens indicate a positive result
2. the laboratory's chain of custody procedures and the documentation methods
3. whether the laboratory provides collection and specimen handling assistance (i.e., chain of custody forms, urine collection bottles, etc.)
4. how long it takes to analyze a specimen and report results

Exhibit 59-2 Employee Authorization Permitting and Recognizing the Employer's Substance Abuse Policy

I understand, agree, and accept that as part of the requirements of my continued employment, I recognize and agree to undergo substance screening for drugs, controlled substances, and alcohol through testing of my blood and/or urine. I also understand that the use, possession, sale, or transfer of alcohol, narcotics, hallucinogens, depressants, stimulants, marijuana, or other controlled substances may affect my eligibility for continued employment because my employment is contingent on, among other things, successful completion of the testing for such substances on an annual basis during the yearly required physical examination, or during a substance screening directed by the employer as part of its (for cause, reasonable suspicion, periodic, or random) substance abuse screening.

I hereby agree to abide by any decision made by the employer in this regard and hold my employer harmless from any decisions arising out of the substance abuse policy.

Having read this policy waiver form, I understand, agree to abide by, and accept this policy as a condition of employment and voluntarily execute this waiver.

_____   _____
Employee   Date

_____   _____
Witness   Date

C. At this point the employer must establish procedures for the taking of the specimens. The employer should consider the following:
   1. Should the specimen be "taken" by the employer's medical personnel in employee health services, or should it be taken by a third party?
   2. Should the taking be observed by a second party who would attest as a witness to the integrity of the taking?
   3. Should the container be sealed in the employee's presence and the employee be required to initial the seal?
   4. Should the chain of custody be documented thereafter?

VI. *Consider carefully under what circumstances tests or screening will be conducted.*
   A. Random tests are inadvisable, except when employees perform work dangerous to themselves or others and when there is reason to believe that widespread or regular abuse is occurring in the work force.
   B. Assuming tests will not be conducted randomly, define the circumstances for conducting them— i.e., after industrial accidents or when there is an objective reason to believe that the employee is under the influence. Further, indicate what symptoms will be used to indicate when an employee is considered "under the influence."

VII. *Develop consent forms for tests.* (A sample test release form is illustrated in Exhibit 59-4.)

Exhibit 59-3 Sample Policy on Substance Abuse

From a humanitarian and business standpoint, the Company is committed to two goals:

1. Maintaining a drug-free work place.
2. Aiding employees who seek help with a drug problem.

Thus we have established the following:

I. *Policy*

The use, possession, sale, or transfer of illegal drugs or alcohol while on Company property, in Company vehicles, or engaged in Company activities is strictly forbidden. Also, being under the influence of drugs or alcohol while on Company property, in Company vehicles, or engaged in company activities is strictly forbidden. A violation of this policy will result in disciplinary action up to and including immediate termination.

The Company reserves the right to take any or all actions deemed to be in its best interests in a given case.

At the same time, the Company has developed and strongly urges use of a rehabilitation program for employees who request assistance. Each case will be evaluated individually to determine the appropriate course of action. However, because the Company is interested in helping troubled employees, requests for assistance with a drug problem will generally be given positive consideration. If a request for assistance is made *after* disciplinary action (short of discharge) has been determined or taken, the manager should help the employee enroll in an appropriate rehabilitation program. If a request is made *after* a decision to discharge the employee has been finalized and/or communicated to the worker, the manager retains the right to determine what, if any, affect the subsequent admission will have on the decision based on the facts of the case. However, the decision to discharge the employee can be modified only after approval from an executive with oversight responsibility at the site.

The Company reserves the right to take any and all actions deemed in its best interests in a given case. We urge all employees to come forward voluntarily and seek assistance.

RELATED PROGRAMS

II. *Drug Screening during Pre-Employment Physical*

As a part of the Company's substance abuse assistance program, once proper medical support is identified for each operating company all applicants that have been selected by a manager or supervisor for employment must submit, without exception, to a urinalysis test for drug and alcohol use before being hired. A positive result will indicate the presence of an illegal drug or an inappropriate level of alcohol or prescription drugs in the body. If an inappropriate amount of prescription drugs is indicated, the results will be reviewed with the applicant before a decision is made in regard to employment. All other positive results (including a refusal to take the test or sign the requisite consent form) will mean the applicant will not be eligible for employment at that time. Test results will remain strictly confidential.

III. *Inspection of Company Property When Appropriate*

In order to determine compliance with the Company's substance abuse policy, the Company reserves the right to inspect its property (including but not limited to lockers, desks, and vehicles) and suspected areas of concealment at any time for any reasons, with or without notice.

IV. *Any Other Means Consistent with the Program and Sound Business Principles*

The Company reserves the right to utilize any other means consistent with sound business principles to determine violations of the substance abuse policy.

Note: All applicable state and federal laws should be reviewed before this policy is instituted.

Exhibit 59-4 Model Substance Abuse Test Release Form

(To be signed in the presence of the Examining Physician)

I certify that the specimen is my urine, that it was voluntarily given for the purpose of alcohol and drug urinalysis, and that the information given in the Pre-employment Drug Information and Consent Form and Release is correct. I authorize the examining physician to convey the results of my physical examination, including the urinalysis, to the Company and agree to release and hold harmless the Company, its officers, agents, and employees from any liability based on the request for, administration of, and use of the results of my physical examination, including the urinalysis.

(Signature) _____

(Date) _____

VIII. *Before implementing a search policy, consider what circumstances will invoke a search.*
   A. Random searches should be avoided unless there is an objective basis for believing that there is a significant amount of contraband being brought onto the premises.
   B. Searches of an individual employee's person or of property within his/her control should be based on objective reasons to believe there is a need for the search.

IX. *When and where do employees have a reasonable expectation of privacy?*
   A. Locked offices?
   B. Locked desks?
   C. Lockers with personal locks?
   D. Personal vehicles?
   E. Company vehicles on private property?
   F. File cabinets?
   G. Credenzas?
   H. Closets?

PROCEDURAL SAFEGUARDS

- Conduct searches with at least two management representatives present.
- Never use force in searches.
- Conduct a search with the employee present whenever possible.
- Develop procedures for preserving contraband that is seized.
- Develop interview procedures to let an employee explain the presence and to identify the contraband.
- Develop a consent form for the search.

Supervisors should not act like diagnosticians; rather, they should concentrate on employee work performance. Supervisory sensitivity to the employee's personal needs should be sufficient for counseling or training employees for better performance. Where substance abuse problems are identified, the supervisor should merely refer the matter to the personnel department or to employee assistance program officials.

Supervisory employees should be coached and trained to identify problematic work behavior and attitude changes in general, as well as signs of substance abuse/use. Such training is important not only to maintain good employee relations, morale, and safety, but also to minimize the possibility that substance use may increase in the work place and to support rehabilitation. A supervisor must be trained to understand his/her responsibilities, as well as how they relate to a substance abuse policy and how they may affect his/her employees in the work setting. These responsibilities include

- knowing the role of a supervisor
- knowing the EAP policy and procedures
- informing employees about the hospital's substance abuse policy and about the employee assistance program
- referring employees, as needed, to an employee assistance program

These responsibilities become the basis for the supervisor's role in assuring a successful substance abuse/employee assistance program and policy.

The keys to an employer's substance abuse program are the role of the supervisor and the training that the supervisor receives in identifying and handling problematic employees. The supervisor's role includes

- monitoring employee job performance and attendance
- documenting any employee deterioration (job related and psycho-socio-peer related)
- when applicable, discussing the need for improvement with the employee (This keeps the relationship on a work-related basis rather than on a substance abuse or clinical-medical basis.)

- setting time horizons for expected job performance improvement
- discussing the case with management and, if applicable, with a union representative
- *always* preserving the confidentiality of the information
- maintaining detailed notes regarding detection symptoms and adverse employee relationships and productivity effects

Supervisors must be oriented to and trained in the means for detecting both drug abuse and alcoholism, as well as in the methods for confronting an employee suspected of alcohol problems or substance abuse.

Supervisors must be trained to recognize and to be vigilant, as well as discrete, when observing alcoholism symptoms. Supervisors detecting the following symptoms must be prepared to document immediately the suspected employee's observed behavior:

- There are usually an uneven work pattern and pace.
- The quality of the work is lower and/or constantly deteriorating.
- The employee has hangovers on the job.
- The employee uses breath purifiers.
- The employee exhibits financial problems.
- The employee is in a depressed condition.
- The employee may even drink on the job or during lunch time.
- The employee begins to exhibit antisocial behavior. He/she avoids peers and his/her supervisor.
- The employee exhibits a flushed face.
- The employee experiences an increased number of minor accidents on or off the job, as well as an increased occurrence of minor illnesses.
- The employee has increased family problems.
- The employee becomes resentful and angry and exhibits the major symptoms of denial.
- The employee becomes forgetful, and there is an increased incidence of equipment and material loss.
- The employee neglects details. There is an increase in the number of errors that he/she commits, and there is also a slowdown in productivity.

Supervisors must also be trained to recognize and to be vigilant, as well as discreet, when observing drug abuse symptoms. Supervisors noting the following symptoms must be prepared to document immediately the suspected employee's observed behavior:

- The symptoms of alcoholism noted above are detected.
- There is an increase in employee theft and/or embezzlement.

- The employee is involved in accidents with increased frequency.
- There is a decrease in the quality of the work performed.
- The employee takes extended coffee breaks.
- The employee's lateness and absentee rates increase above the average, followed by implausible excuses.
- There is an increased number of complaints by others regarding the employee.
- There is an increased number of complaints or grievances by the employee suspected of the substance abuse.
- There is an increase in disciplinary problems.
- The employee exhibits mood swings and personality changes with aggressive behavior.
- The employee also exhibits anger, resentment, and the major symptoms of denial.

If the employee is a cocaine user, additional symptoms include the following:

- The employee exhibits problems with his/her nose. He/she constantly snivels and sneezes.
- The employee has an increased incidence of respiratory problems.
- There is a sudden weight loss, and the employee tends to shy away from foods.
- The employee is irritable.
- The employee exhibits extreme fatigue.
- The employee also exhibits mood swings.
- The employee may even fall asleep on the job.
- The employee may become forgetful.
- The employee exhibits paranoia. He/she may become secretive and suspicious.
- The employee will also exhibit a lessened attention span.

Having reviewed the symptoms of substance abuse that a supervisor must be aware of to maintain a productive and safe work force with high morale, we must now turn to the methodology for dealing with substance abusers in the work place. At this point, let us review the *Do's* and *Don'ts* of how to confront an employee suspected of substance abuse.

Do's

- Preserve employee confidentiality and privacy.
- Confront the suspected employee in private.
- During the meeting maintain a formal and firm atmosphere, but be considerate.
- During the meeting concentrate on the suspected employee's job performance, and offer help.
- At this meeting present documentation to the suspected employee concerning his/her deteriorating job performance.

- At this meeting explain the employee assistance program and how it works, and offer referral.
- Reassure the suspected employee of the employee assistance program's confidentiality.

Do Not's

- Do not attempt to find out what is wrong with the suspected employee. Do not play priest, social worker, advisor, or doctor.
- Do not get personally involved with the suspected employee's family life or personal problems.
- Avoid drawing conclusions or putting tags or titles on the performance-related etiology.
- Do not generalize about the suspected employee's deteriorating job performance.
- Do not moralize.
- Do not be misled by "sympathy getting" stories.
- Never threaten discipline.

After the supervisor has confronted the suspected substance-abusing employee, he/she must continue to follow normal performance appraisal procedures and

- Document further incidents.
- Report the substance of the meeting to management.
- Follow up with the EAP to determine the progress of the employee.

In the discussion that follows, the comprehensive approach of the employee assistance program is more fully reviewed.

EMPLOYEE ASSISTANCE PROGRAMS

Employers should contact drug and alcohol rehabilitation centers to review the possibility of establishing an employee assistance program (EAP). It must be emphasized that EAPs are laudable both from an employee/labor relations point of view *and* from the employer point of view because they support an employer's adverse disciplinary decision if an employee refuses employee assistance or falls off the wagon while in the program. These employee wellness programs are becoming increasingly popular with employers who are adopting some form of employee assistance plan. Too many wellness programs are offered without consideration of other issues related to substance abuse rehabilitation. A recent survey by the Human Resources Group, Inc., a New York–based firm that develops and administers EAPs, found that substance abuse treatment constituted only 14 percent of the EAP usage in 1983 and 15 percent in 1984. In both of these years, substance abuse treatment and counseling was the third most common activity after intervention for psychological and legal problems.[18]

Employee assistance programs vary considerably; some offer confidential counseling and/or referral to independent, free-standing EAPs; others provide in-house services (through the employee health department, the personnel department, or the social service department); and others simply offer employer-sponsored health insurance that covers rehabilitation programs. It needs to be pointed out that hospitals referring employees to outside firms should execute a formal contract that clearly spells out the desired services and provides for indemnification for the hospital against any lawsuits arising out of the employee's use of the independent EAP provider. On referral, the hospital should also have the referred employee execute a "hold harmless" waiver *prior* to referral. Absent either or both of the above, the employer should refer employees to their private physicians.

Further, the employer needs to consider other issues that may arise. For example:

- Will an employee's participation in a wellness program stay a disciplinary or discharge decision, pending the results of the program? As a matter of policy, in most cases it does not. Frequently, employers state to employees that while participation in a wellness program is encouraged, an employee is still held responsible for meeting job expectations and for complying with company policies. However, in those situations in which the employer does *not* specify the implications of participation in a program, the employer may become embroiled in a discharge dispute. Further, if an EAP of some type is offered, participation by the affected employee should not be mandatory.

- If the employee is terminated while enrolled in the EAP, does he/she have the right to coverage at the employer's expense? Usually this is *not* the case.

- Employers who offer wellness programs often want to receive reports concerning the employee's progress. The employer should obtain an executed authorization for disclosure of such information from the employee. In this way, the issues of confidentiality and privilege are resolved. The recent cases of *Davis v. Monsanto Co.* [627 F. Supp. 418 (S.D. W. Va. 1986)] and *Bratt v. IBM* [785 F.2d 352 (1st Cir. 1986)] review the dangers associated with unauthorized disclosures. In essence, even if the employer pays for the treatment, it is the employee's decision whether or not to permit disclosure, unless the employee is dangerous to others.

- The employer needs to establish the parameters of the dialogue with employees with an EAP counselor who visits the facility. The most effective way to limit discussion, but still be able to receive information, is to establish with the resource person the scope of the dialogue, the scope of disclosure to the employer of the subjects that arise, and their policy implications.

Since 66 percent of an EAP's referrals are successfully rehabilitated,[19] employers may wish to seriously consider making an employee assistance program an integral part of their substance abuse policy and program. An employer that considers an EAP must review the legal, employee relations, and cost implications. The employer may seek information from

- National Institute on Drug Abuse
  5600 Fishers Lane
  Rockville, MD 20857
  (301) 443-6245
- Washington Business Group on Health
  229½ Pennsylvania Avenue, S.E.
  Washington, D.C. 20003
  (202) 547-6644
- New York Business Group in Health
  1633 Broadway, 6th Floor
  New York, New York 10017
  (212) 808-0550

How does an employer develop an EAP? Prior to responding, the employer needs to make a business decision. Does the employer want to establish a referral-service employee assistance program or its own employee assistance program? Once this philosophical question is resolved, the employer should follow these easy steps:

- Designate an EAP coordinator.
- Form an EAP Advisory Committee.
- Formulate policy.
- Develop an extensive training program for management, supervisors, and the personnel or human resources department.
- Develop specific procedures to facilitate program implementation.
- Conduct a needs analysis.
- Conduct a survey of community resources.
- Assess existing health insurance coverage and how, when, and to what extent EAP participants are covered.
- Design employee orientation and training for employees and union representatives, where applicable.
- Develop promotional strategies.
- Design an evaluative component.

All the issues and approaches we have reviewed, culminating in EAPs, represent a broad range of choices for employers.

CONCLUSION

The case of *Glenwood P. Roane, Jr. v. Conair Inc.* (KY Cer Ct. No. 88C1670, 9/22/88) provides the perfect negative example of the importance of a well-designed substance abuse policy that has its genesis in a corporate philosophical needs analysis, which becomes the foundation for the development of the thorough review that may justify an employer substance abuse policy, thus minimizing liabilities and legal risk.

EMPLOYEES SUE OVER EMPLOYER'S DRUG TESTING CONDUCT—AIRLINE WORKERS FILE SUIT OVER CONDUCT OF DRUG TESTING

A pilot and four flight attendants are suing Conair Inc. (which is one of the nation's largest regional airlines, employing 350 pilots who fly routes throughout the Midwest and the South) alleging they were "shanghaied" to a local hotel, interrogated about drug use among airline employees, and coerced into giving urine samples in front of two witnesses (*Glenwood P. Roane, Jr. v. Conair Inc.*, KY Cir Ct. No. 88C1670, 9/22/88). According to the lawsuit filed September 22, 1988 in Kentucky's Boone County Circuit Court, the employees were taken to a Greater Cincinnati International Airport hotel under false pretenses by officials of the commuter airline, kept there for up to six hours, had their personal belongings searched, were denied use of telephones, were questioned repeatedly about their own and others' illegal drug consumption, and were threatened with dismissal if they refused to give urine samples.

Plaintiff's attorney is "charging Conair with false imprisonment, assault, defamation, invasion of privacy, intentional interference with employment, and infliction of severe emotional distress. . . ."

After the questioning, four of the five were suspended for a week, even though none of their tests showed evidence of drug use, and one flight attendant was fired for refusing to cooperate with the investigation. In their suit the employees are seeking both compensatory and punitive damages. . . .

Officials for Conair contend the suit's allegations are groundless, stating that any drug testing "was conducted properly, in good faith, and in the best interest of the welfare and safety of the traveling public," and refused further comment on the suit thereafter. Two days before the suit was filed, Conair fired three pilots and two other employees for drug use. These dismissals sprang from the same week-long investigation that promoted the lawsuit. A Company spokesperson said the inquiry began after Conair received information that eight employees were using drugs off duty. While Conair does run a drug test on new hires, it does not have a random testing policy. "However," according to a spokesperson "we do feel compelled to investigate serious allegations that employees might be using drugs."

Grievances have been filed on behalf of the three pilots, according to Air Line Pilots Association who stated that the union has as much of a commitment to "drug-free cockpits" as Conair does, but believes these pilots "should be given the benefit of rehabilitation, as the Company has done in cases of alcohol abuse, rather than firing them." The union said this is the first time Conair has taken this type of disciplinary action in a drug use

case. . . . Responding, Conair notes that it does offer rehabilitation to employees with substance abuse problems who come forward seeking treatment; however, if testing reveals drug use "that is cause for dismissal or at least severe disciplinary action," according to the spokesperson.[20]

This case reveals the important need for a substance abuse policy development model that is well communicated to all employees and that will inure to the employer's benefit in terms of avoiding the types of legal costs and potential damages that resulted from the six causes of action brought in the *Roane* case.

NOTES

1. Bureau of National Affairs, *Alcohol and Drugs in the Workplace* (Washington, D.C.: Bureau of National Affairs, Inc., 1986), 7–9.

2. Eric A. Sisco, *Alcohol and Drug Abuse in the Workplace* (New York: Employment Law Institute, 1987): 2.

3. David J. Middlebrooks, *Current Developments in Employer Strategies for Alcohol and Substance Abuse Issues* (New York: Employment Law Institute, 1986): 1.

4. Ibid., 2.

5. Ibid., 1.

6. "America's Habit: Drug Abuse, Drug Trafficking and Organized Crime," Report to the President's Commission on Organized Crime (Washington, D.C.: 1986) 454.

7. "National Institute of Justice, Research in Brief, *Daily Labor Report*, 5 March 1986, A–12.

8. Michael Allen, "Drug Screening Methodologies," *12 PharmChem Newsletter*, no. 5 (September-October 1983): 4.

9. U.S. Drug Enforcement Administration, *U.S. Drug Enforcement Administration Report* (Washington, D.C.: U.S. Drug Enforcement Administration, 1986): 93.

10. Yesavage, Lerner, Denari, and Hollister, "Carry-Over Effects of Marijuana Intoxication on Aircraft Pilot Performance; A Preliminary Report," *American Journal of Psychiatry* (November 1985): 1325.

11. Allen, "Drug Screening Methodologies," 1.

12. Ibid., 3.

13. "GC/MS Assays for Abused Drugs in Body Fluids," National Institute on Drug Abuse Research Monograph Series 12 (Washington, D.C.: National Institute on Drug Abuse) 1980.

14. N.L.R.B. General Counsel Memorandum GC 87-5, September 8, 1987.

15. R. Baxter and G. Siniscalco, *Managers Guide to Lawful Terminations* (New York: Executive Enterprises Institute, 1983), 105–107.

16. F. Elkouri and E. Elkouri, *How Arbitration Works*, 4th ed (Washington, D.C.: Bureau of National Affairs, Inc., 1985), 533.

17. Richard G. Moon, *Potential Legal Restrictions on Employer Drug and Alcohol Abuse Policies* (Portland, ME: Thompson, Hinckley & Keddy, 1980).

18. Human Resource Group, Inc., *Employee Assistance Programs Survey* (New York: Human Resource Group, Inc., 1984): 19.

19. Benjamin Fiaukoff, Ph.D., clinical psychologist, Ridgewood, New Jersey.

20. Bureau of National Affairs, Inc., "Employees Sue Over Employer's Drug Testing Conduct," *Daily Labor Law Reporter* 22 (February 20, 1989): A-1.

L. Robert Batterman
Bettina B. Plevan

Sex in the Work Place **60**

ANTINEPOTISM RULES

Several business reasons for adopting antinepotism rules were articulated in *Yuhas v. Libbey-Owens-Ford Company*.[1]

> The no-spouse rule is predicated on the assumption that it is generally a bad idea to have both partners in a marriage working together . . . . First, the marital relationship often generates intense emotions which would interfere with a worker's job performance . . . . Second, if an employee who works with his or her spouse became involved in a grievance with the employer or another worker, the two spouses might be expected to take the same side in the dispute, [thus preventing] the expeditious resolution of grievances. Third, if . . . one spouse was promoted to a supervisory position, numerous problems could arise . . . . Finally, a no-spouse rule eliminates the possibility of the already-employed marriage partner intervening in the hiring process on behalf of his or her spouse, to the detriment of the employer and any more qualified persons who did not obtain the job because of this intervention.

Similar arguments have been made to justify policies prohibiting the hiring of close relatives.

There has recently been a trend toward re-evaluation of antinepotism policies, particularly in light of the shrinking labor force in some industries, the advent of dual career couples, and the increased liklihood of employees' marrying someone they meet on the job. In addition, the difficulties associated with deciding which of two married employees should resign or be discharged and administering a no-spouse rule consistently and equitably have led some companies to abandon them.[2]

Challenges to the Legality of Antinepotism Rules Based on Title VII

Antinepotism rules have been challenged by female employees on the ground that the rules discriminate against them on the basis of sex. Courts have applied traditional Title VII analyses in adjudicating these claims.

Disparate Impact Claims

1. *Burdens of proof:* As in other Title VII cases, a plaintiff challenging an antinepotism policy must establish a prima facie case by demonstrating that, although the policy is sexually neutral on its face, its implementation has a "significantly discriminatory pattern."[3] "In making a prima facie case in a disparate impact suit, however, the plaintiff must not merely prove circumstances raising an inference of discriminatory impact at issue."[4]

In its recent decision in *Wards Cove Packing Co. v. Atonio*,[5] the Supreme Court determined the nature of the employer's evidentiary burdens in disparate impact cases once a prima facie case has been established. According to the Court, the burden shifts to the employer to produce "evidence of a business justification for his employment practice." Such justification is found where "a challenged practice serves, in a significant way, the legitimate goals of the employer." *Id.* at 2125-26. While a "mere insubstantial justification" is not sufficient, the challenged practice need not be "essential" or "indispensable" to the business of the employer.[6]

The burden of proof does not shift to the employer, however. Contrary to previous rulings by other courts, the Supreme Court held in *Wards Cove* that the "ultimate burden of proving that discrimination against a protected group has been caused by a specific employment practice remains with the Plaintiff *at all times*."[7]

Although *Wards Cove* involved a race discrimination challenge to a variety of employment policies, including an alleged nepotism policy favoring the employment of relatives of existing employees (as opposed to an anti-nepotism policy), the Court's pronouncements concerning evidentiary burdens and standards would likely be controling in suits challenging anti-nepotism policies as well. Therefore, earlier decisions involving anti-nepotism policies that suggested that the burden of proof or persuasion shifts to the employer after the plaintiff establishes a prima facie case, or that an employer satisfies the requisite showing of business justification by demonstrating that an employment practice was "business-related," are called into question by *Wards Cove*.[8]

2. *Statistical proof demonstrating disparate impact:* Plaintiffs have frequently failed to establish a disparate impact because the sample size was deemed statistically insignificant.

a. In *Harper v. Trans World Airlines*,[9] the plaintiff unsuccessfully challenged a rule prohibiting married couples from working in the same department. Under the rule, TWA would discharge the spouse with less seniority unless the couple decided within 30 days that one spouse would resign. The plaintiff alleged that the rule had a disparate impact on women because women generally had less seniority than men. In support she cited evidence that the wife resigned in four of five instances in which a couple was forced to choose who would resign as a result of the rule. The court found this statistical sample to be too small to have predictive value and thus dismissed the claim.

b. In *Thomas v. Metroflight, Inc.*,[10] the plaintiff was discharged pursuant to the employer's no-spouse rule after marrying a fellow employee. She cited eight instances of intrafirm marriage. In one instance, the rule was enforced by firing the female spouse; in the other seven instances, each couple was permitted to remain at work, either because the rule was overlooked or because the spouses worked in different departments. The court held that "a sample size of two is too small to make even a 100% impact rate significant."[11]

c. By contrast, in *Yuhas v. Libbey-Owens-Ford Company*,[12] the court found that plaintiff sustained her prima facie case of discriminatory impact in challenging a company's antinepotism rule by demonstrating that "seventy-one of the last seventy-four people disqualified under it were women."

3. *Rebutting the disparate impact presumption:* In deciding what evidence is necessary to rebut a prima facie case of disparate impact, the courts appear to be influenced by circumstances suggesting the presence of other discriminatory practices toward women. When the Eighth Circuit found evidence of such circumstances, it insisted on demonstrable proof of business necessity.[13] On the other hand, the Seventh Circuit[14] relaxed the standard to a "business related" test in *Yuhas* in the absence of any extrinsic evidence of intentional discrimination. As noted above, the Supreme Court's recent decision in *Wards Cove* calls both of these decisions into question.[15]

• In *EEOC v. Rath Packing Co.*,[16] the court invalidated a no-spouse rule on finding that the employer failed to demonstrate "business necessity" for the rule. The court held that the problem to be addressed by the no-spouse rule must be concrete and demonstrable, not just perceived, and that the rule must be essential to eliminating the problem, not simply reasonable or designed to improve conditions.

Because it had offered no evidence of the existence of the problems the rule was purportedly designed to remedy—namely, dual absenteeism, problems scheduling vacations, and decreased production or safety—the court found that this test was not satisfied.

The court also stated that it would be inappropriate to lower the employer's burden of proof to "business-related" where, as here, there was a history of intentional discrimination against women at the plant.

• In *Yuhas v. Libbey-Owens-Ford Company*,[17] the court upheld a rule against hiring an hourly employee at its plants when the applicant's spouse was already employed there in the same capacity. The plaintiff's statistical showing of discriminatory impact was rebutted, according to the court, by the employer's demonstration of "business related" reasons for the policy. These reasons included keeping personal problems out of the work place, avoiding the formation of alliances against the employer, and preventing the appearance of bias or favoritism. Although the employer cited no statistics demonstrating that the rule's goals were actually being achieved, the court was satisfied that the rule "plausibly improves" the workplace.

The court was also persuaded by the absence of evidence of actual intent to discriminate. The court found that there was no history of discriminatory intent in the plants and that the disparate impact indicated by plaintiffs' statistics resulted merely from the fact that fewer women had been in the work force. Women have not been "penalize[d] . . . on the basis of their environmental or genetic background," according to the court.[18]

Disparate Treatment Claims

1. *Burdens of proof:* To establish a prima facie case of disparate treatment, a plaintiff must present evidence giving rise to "an inference of unlawful discrimination."[19]

When the plaintiff has done that, the employer need only present a plausible nondiscriminatory explanation for its action to dispel the inference. The plaintiff then has an opportunity to show that the employer's proffered explanation is pretextual; the burden of proof never shifts from the plaintiff.[20]

2. *Application of policy as a basis for discriminatory discharges:* In *George v. Farmers Electric Cooperative, Inc.,*[21] the court upheld a challenge to the application of an antinepotism policy that precluded the employment of "close relatives" on finding that the policy was not properly implemented. The policy permitted the affected employees to decide who would resign but also contained procedures for selecting the employee to be terminated when neither she nor her husband agreed to resign. Even though the policy would have required the plaintiff to be terminated pursuant to a "tiebreaker" system under which the lower-salaried employee was selected, the district court found that plaintiff was in fact chosen for termination because her husband was "head of the household." The Court of Appeals upheld this finding as not clearly erroneous but limited the back pay award to the period between the actual termination and the date the plaintiff would otherwise have been terminated pursuant to the criteria set forth in the policy.

3. *Evidence of incnsistent application of policy as proof of disparate treatment:* In *McDowell v. Mississippi Power and Light,*[22] the company's antinepotism policy provided that close relatives should not "work under the same supervisor or in jobs where the performance of their duties brings them in close contact" and that "discretion must be used in considering the employment of relatives of existing members of the organization." The plaintiff, a female applicant for a position at a nuclear generating facility for which her husband acted as subcontractor successfully challenged the application of the policy to her on grounds of sexual discrimination.

The court found that the company's "application of its antinepotism policy was absolutely without standards,"[23] and that the policy was applied with greater latitude toward male applicants than female applicants. For example, only male applicants had been offered the opportunity to accept jobs on the condition that they would never request transfers to departments in which their relatives were employed.

The court also found that there was a "pervasive sexist attitude," which caused it to discredit the employer's claim that the plaintiff was denied a position because of the policy.

4. *Demonstrating equal application of policy:* The fact that a policy is not in writing will not necessarily result in a finding of uneven application or discriminatory treatment. For example, in *Fitzpatrick v. Duquesne Light Co.,*[24] the court rejected a challenge to the implementation of an unwritten no-spouse policy on finding that the policy had been implemented in a similar fashion on four previous occasions.

State Law Challenges to Antinepotism Policies

Some states have adopted laws prohibiting discrimination on the basis of marital status, giving rise to claims challenging antinepotism or no-spouse policies on the ground that they discriminate on the basis of marital status. The states are divided in their rulings. New York, New Jersey, Michigan, and Hawaii have interpreted their statutes narrowly and have refused to strike down no-spouse rules. On the other hand, Minnesota, Montana, and Washington have interpreted "marital status" to include the identity and occupation of the spouse and on this basis have upheld challenges to no-spouse rules. California and Oregon have enacted statutes that specifically ban no-spouse rules, as opposed to merely prohibiting discrimination based on marital status. These state statutes provide exceptions for business necessity, however.

1. *Narrow interpretation of marital status discrimination laws in New York and elsewhere:* New York Executive Law § 296 prohibits discrimination, *inter alia,* on the basis of marital status. New York courts have rejected the contention that the law prohibits the implementation of no-spouse rules.

In *Manhattan Pizza Hut v. New York State Human Rights Appeal Board,*[25] the New York Court of Appeals refused to find that a no-spouse rule discriminated on the basis of marital status against an employee who was terminated for being married to her supervisor. The court ruled that Executive Law § 296 was intended to protect against discrimination on the basis of one's marital status, not the status of the person to whom one was married. Since the plaintiff's disqualification "was not for being married, but for being married to her supervisor," the court found the law inapplicable.[26]

State laws in Michigan, New Jersey, and Hawaii prohibiting discrimination on the basis of marital status have similarly been found to afford no protection to employees challenging implementation of antinepotism policies.[27]

But see *Kraft, Inc. v. State of Minnesota,*[28] in which the court found that "marital status" did not include the identity and occupation of the spouse and remanded the case for consideration of the question whether the employer's antinepotism policy satisfied the statutory exception for a "bona fide occupational qualification." In *Thompson v. Board of Trustees,*[29] the court found that the plaintiff's rejection because of his wife's employment was discrimination based on marital status and that the employer's showing of business necessity was irrelevant because no "reasonable grounds exception" was written into the statute. In *Washington Water Power Co. v. Washington State Human Rights Commission,*[30] the court upheld regulations, adopted pursuant to a statute prohibiting marital status discrimination, that included the identity and occupation of the spouse within the definition of marital status.

Some of these decisions have implied, however, that marital status discrimination would be found if there were evidence of uneven application of the policy. For example, in *Campbell v. New York State Human Rights Appeal Board,*[31] the court found that refusal to hire the complainant because her husband was already employed did not discriminate when there is no irregular application of the policy. See also *Miller v. Muer Corp.*,[32] in which the court found no discrimination based on marital status but indicated that impermissible discrimination may occur in the antinepotism policy's application; and *Thompson v. Sanborn's Motor Express, Inc.*,[33] in which the court found no conspicuous uneven application of the antinepotism rule, no disparate impact on married people, and no violation of state law against discrimination on the basis of marital status.

2. *Statutory prohibitions on antinepotism policies:* The antidiscrimination laws of California, Oregon, and Washington contain specific limitations on the use of antinepotism policies. For example, California provides

> Sec. 7292.5. Employee Selection
> (a) Employment of Spouse. An employment decision shall not be based on whether an individual has a spouse presently employed by the employer except in accordance with the following criteria:
> (1) For business reasons of supervision, safety, security or morale, an employer may refuse to place one spouse under the direct supervision of the other spouse.
> (2) For business reasons of supervision, security or morale, an employer may refuse to place both spouses in the same department, division or facility if the work involves potential conflicts of interest or other hazards greater for married couples than for other persons.
> (b) Accommodations for Co-Employees Who Marry. If co-employees marry, an employer shall make reasonable efforts to assign job duties so as to minimize problems of supervision, safety, security, or morale.[34]

Similarly, the Oregon antidiscrimination statute requires the employer to demonstrate the existence of a bona fide occupational requirement for refusing to hire a family member.[35]

Decisions interpreting these statutes have generally placed a substantial burden of proof on employees seeking to justify the implementation of antinepotism policies and have invalidated such policies on this basis.

In *City of Simi Valley v. FEHC*,[36] the court found that the employer violated the California statute in applying a no-spouse policy to an applicant without making any "individualized assessment of the work situation." The employer's evidence of potential conflicts of interest was found inadequate because the employer failed to demonstrate that these concerns were actually considered when rejecting the application for employment.

Federal Constitutional Challenges to Antinepotism Rules

Challenges by public employees to antinepotism rules based on constitutional rights to marriage, due process, or equal protection have generally been rejected. The courts have required employers to demonstrate only a rational basis for such rules and have found that test satisfied where the rules are designed to prevent conflicts in the work place.

Right to Marriage Claims

On an employer's demonstration of a rational basis for the policy, courts have upheld no-spouse rules because they do not directly implicate the fundamental constitutional right to marry.[37]

Equal Protection Claims

The failure to include all relationships in an antinepotism policy does not constitute a violation of a spouse's equal protection rights.

1. According to the court in *Sebetic v. Schoenfeld*,[38] "[t]hat the [Law Enforcement Joint Services] Board chose not to go further than it did does not mean that its legitimate objective of preventing avoidable mishaps in the delivery of law enforcement services is not 'rationally furthered' by the choice made."

2. In *Parsons v. County of Del Norte*,[39] the court found that "[i]nquiry into non-familial relationships might easily invite a host of interpersonal conflicts disruptive of morale. Instead, the County has reasonably drawn the line at the immediate family."

3. In *Espinoza v. Thomas*,[40] the court upheld against "equal protection" challenges a policy that prohibited the employment of family members or people in "an espoused relationship," which was defined to mean "two people living together, sharing bed and board, siring children, sharing financial, recreational, social activities together, along with the normal cares and woes of raising a family, without the benefit of a marriage license or marriage certificate."

SEXUAL HARASSMENT

Elements of Sexual Harassment Claims

The EEOC Guidelines define sexual harassment as

> Unwelcome sexual advances, requests for sexual favors, and other verbal or physical conduct of a sexual nature . . . when (1) submission to such conduct is made either explicitly or implicitly a term or condition of an individual's employment, (2) submission to or rejection of such conduct by an individual is used as the basis for employment decisions affecting such individual, or (3) such conduct has the purpose or effect of unreasonably interfering with an individual's work performance or creating an intimidating, hostile or offensive working environment.[41]

These guidelines were generally endorsed by the Supreme Court in *Meritor Savings Bank, FSB v. Vinson.*[42]

1. *Quid Pro Quo Harassment Claims:*

- Conditioning job benefits or continued employment on submission to sexual demands by a supervisor is uniformly considered to be discrimination on the basis of sex and protected under Title VII.[43]
- Liability is not limited to demands of "no promotion without sex." For example, demands that an employee dress a certain way or tolerate, without objection, a sexually hostile environment in order to obtain or retain tangible job benefits constitute *quid pro quo* harassment.[44]

2. *Hostile Work Environment Claims:*

- A claim for environmental harassment is based on the presence of sexually hostile conditions in the work place and is not dependent on any loss of tangible job benefits. In *Meritor,* the Supreme Court recognized that if the plaintiff was subjected to constant demands for sexual favors, she stated a claim for "environmental" harassment even if her submission to unwelcome advances did not affect her job advancement. Moreover, the sexual harassment need not even be directed at the plaintiff.[45]
- Hostile working environments have been found in a variety of circumstances, including situations characterized by
  (1) constant sexual advances, discussion of sexual fantasies (including possibly raping of the plaintiff), physical abuse, and accusations of lesbianism.[46]
  (2) repeated sexual advances, interception of mail, embarrassing remarks in public, and harassment in work assignments.[47]
  (3) "repeated crude sexual advances and suggestive comments" combined with other harassing conduct.[48]

Employer Liability for Sexual Harassment by Supervisors and Other Employees

1. *Quid pro quo harassment claims:*

- In *Meritor,* the Court noted that employer liability should be based on traditional agency principles.[49]
- Federal courts have generally imposed liability for *quid pro quo* harassment by supervisors, even where the employer had no notice of harassment.[50]

2. *Environmental harassment claims:*

- In *Meritor,* the Supreme Court indicated that, in the absence of notice, an employer might not be found liable for environmental harassment if it had implemented a complaint procedure and a policy against discrimination and if the plaintiff had failed to use the procedure to complain of the alleged harassment.[51]
- Consistent with these principles, most cases both before and after *Meritor* have applied a "knew or should have known" standard to all environmental cases, whether or not the acts were committed by supervisors.[52]

Employer Liability Based on Romantic Relationships of Supervisors

1. Title VII claims have been filed by employees who, though not subjected to harassment, were allegedly denied employment opportunities because of the romantic relationship of the supervisor with a coemployee. In an October 25, 1988 memorandum entitled "Policy Guidance on Current Issues of Sexual Harassment," the EEOC noted that Title VII law is unsettled in this area.

- The EEOC Guidelines provide that where employment opportunities or benefits are granted because of an individual's submission to the employer's sexual advances or requests for sexual favors, the employer may be held liable for unlawful sex discrimination against other persons who were qualified for but were denied that employment opportunity or benefit.[53]
- The Second Circuit has ruled that a supervisor's preferred treatment of an employee with whom he was having a romantic affair does not give rise to a claim for sexual harassment by coemployees if the relationship is consensual.[54]

  In *DeCintio v. Westchester County Medical Center,*[55] the supervisor created a new position and established as a job requirement that the person hired be registered by the National Board of Respiratory Therapists—a requirement not necessary for any other position in the unit. The only registered therapist was the supervisor's romantic partner. The promotion of that employee was challenged as discriminatory by a number of male coemployees.

  Reversing the district court, the Second Circuit found no violation of Title VII. "Sex" within the meaning of the statute does not include "sexual liaisons" or "sexual attractions," according to the court. The court distinguished the EEOC Guidelines on third-party claims on the ground that "submission" to sexual advances results only from *involuntary* sexual relationships (i.e., harassment). It reasoned that a contrary "interpretation of Title VII prohibitions against sex discrimination would involve the EEOC and federal courts in the policing of intimate relationships [,] . . . a course [that] is both impracticable and unwarranted.[56]

- The ruling and reasoning in *DeCintio* were adopted in *Miller v. Aluminum Co. of America.*[57] Even though, unlike in *DeCintio,* the plaintiff was female, the court ruled that she failed to state a claim under Title VII because she could not show "that her employer would have or did treat males differently."[58]

- *DeCintio* conflicts with an earlier decision of the New York Supreme Court, Queens County, holding that a cause of action for sex discrimination was stated under both state and federal discrimination laws where a female employee alleged that she was denied employment benefits and ultimately dismissed because her supervisor favored another employee with whom he was having a consensual sexual relationship.[59]

- In *Toscano v. Nimmo,*[60] relying on the EEOC Guidelines, the court held that an employer had violated Title VII on finding that "in order for a woman to be selected [for promotion to a particular position] it was necessary to grant sexual favors, a condition not imposed on men." Although the plaintiff did not allege that she refused specific requests for sexual favors, the court found that she sustained her claim by presenting evidence of both the supervisor's conduct in promoting a coemployee who granted sexual favors and the supervisor's general practice of engaging in provocative sexual conduct toward the plaintiff and other female employees.

  The *DeCintio* court distinguished *Toscano* because "the claim itself was premised on the coercive nature of the employer's acts, rather than the fact of the relationship itself."[61] See also *Priest v. Rotary,*[62] in which the court found that Title VII is violated when an employer conditions preferential treatment of female employees on their submission to sexual advances or other conduct of a sexual nature.

- In *King v. Palmer,*[63] the court ruled that the plaintiff had adequately demonstrated that a sexual relationship between a supervisor and another employee had been "a substantial factor" in the promotion of the other employee and thus was entitled to recovery under Title VII. As noted by both the D.C. Circuit panel and the *DeCintio* court, however, neither party addressed the legal issue of whether Title VII could be extended to remedy claims of unequal treatment resulting from consensual sexual relationships. For that reason, the D.C. Circuit Court declined an opportunity to address the issue *en banc.*

2. More recently courts have found that an employee can state a claim for environmental (as opposed to *quid pro quo*) harassment based on the consensual sexual conduct of other employees if that conduct is so widespread and offensive that it detrimentally affects the employment conditions of other employees.

In *Broderick v. Ruder,*[64] the district court held that "consensual sexual relations, in exchange for tangible employment benefits, while possibly not creating a cause of action for the recipient of such sexual advances who does not find them unwelcome, do, and in this case did, create and contribute to a sexually hostile working environment." On that basis, the court found that sexual promiscuity at a regional office of the Securities Exchange Commission had impaired an attorney's ability to perform her work and receive promotions, in violation of her Title VII rights.

According to the court's findings, the supervisors in the office routinely and openly fondled and kissed coworkers at the work place, made sexually provocative comments, told crude jokes, carried on affairs with secretaries, and advanced employees who were receptive to such sexual advances. The court found that this sexually permissive environment undermined the plaintiff's motivation, contributed to her inability to communicate well with her supervisors, and deprived her of promotional opportunities to which she otherwise would have been entitled.

3. Office romances have also given rise to harassment claims by disgruntled employees after their romance with a supervisory source. No relief under Title VII is available, however, if the court concludes that the original relationship was consensual. As the Supreme Court held in *Meritor,* the plaintiff must establish that she was the victim of unwelcome sexual advances in order to recover under a claim of either *quid pro quo* or environmental harassment.[65]

- In *Koster v. Chase Manhattan Bank,*[66] the plaintiff alleged, *inter alia,* that a bank vice-president caused her to be denied salary increases and a transfer to another department, and later caused her to be terminated, because of her cessation of their sexual relationship. After trial, the court dismissed her claim for sexual harassment on finding no evidence to suggest that the relationship was not consensual. Futhermore, the court found that the plaintiff could not sustain a claim for *quid pro quo* harassment because her former paramour did not participate in any of the employment decisions that she alleged were discriminatory. See also *Anderson v. University Health Center,*[67] in which the court dismissed sex discrimination claims on finding no evidence that the alleged sexual relationship between the coemployee and the supervisor resulted in any favoritism or promotion.

- In *Jensen v. Kellings Fine Foods,*[68] the plaintiff was discharged by her supervisor and his wife, both of whom held stock in the company, after the wife discovered that the plaintiff and her husband were having an affair. The court held that there could be no recovery on grounds of sexual harassment because the supervisor's sexual advances were not unwelcome.

"MARITAL STATUS" DISCRIMINATION CLAIMS

Claims Based on State Laws

The implementation of company no-fraternizing rules has been unsuccessfully challenged on the ground that the rules violate state law prohibitions against discrimination on the basis of marital status.

In *Federated Rural Electric Insurance Company v. Kessler*,[69] the Wisconsin Supreme Court held that a company rule prohibiting the romantic association of any employee of one sex with a married employee of the opposite sex did not impermissibly discriminate on the basis of marital status. The court reasoned that the rule prohibited "a course of conduct rather than a status," that it applied equally to all emloyees regardless of their marital status, and that it was justified by the important public policy of preventing extramarital affairs.[70]

Similarly, in *Sears v. Ryder Truck Rental, Inc.*,[71] the court upheld the discharge of a female employee for dating a male coemployee in violation of a company no-dating rule, rejecting claims that the rule violated Michigan's statute prohibiting discrimination on the basis of marital status. The court found that while "there are strong policy provisions for protecting the marital relationship and marital status, "[s]uch policy considerations do not apply to a mere dating situation, and should not be written into law by a court."[72]

In *Thorrez v. Civil Rights Commission*,[73] the plaintiff unsuccessfully challenged her discharge following the discovery by a coemployee's wife that the two employees were having an affair and the wife's demand that the affair end. The court found under these circumstances that the employer had not discriminated on the basis of sex, but rather merely had implemented a reasonable business decision.

Claims against Public Employers Based on Constitutional Rights of Privacy and Free Association

Employees of governmental institutions or entities otherwise engaged in "state action" may challenge employer restrictions on their romantic relationships on the basis of their rights to privacy and free association under the First, Fourth, and Ninth Amendments to the Constitution. Courts have generally applied a strict scrutiny analysis to such claims, requiring the employer to demonstrate a substantial and demonstrable reason for the policy.

Relationships between Governmental Employees and Nonemployees

Restrictions on the relationships between governmental employees and nonemployees have generally been struck down on constitutional grounds on finding that the rules bear no relationship to any valid governmental interest.

1. In *Thorne v. City of El Segundo*,[74] the Ninth Circuit Court of Appeals held that a police department violated an applicant's constitutional rights to privacy and free association by inquiring during the application process into her former relationship with a departmental employee and then rejecting the application on the basis of that inquiry. The inquiry was found to have no job-related purpose. The court further held that the inquiry violated Title VII because similar inquiries were not made of male applicants.

2. Similarly, in *Briggs v. North Muskegon Police Department*,[75] the court held that the discharge of a police officer for cohabiting with a married woman violated his constitutional rights because neither the officer's personal life nor the public disapproval of his conduct bore any relationship to his job performance.

Relationships between Governmental Employees

Restrictions on relationships between two governmental employees have been upheld where the employer can demonstrate that the restrictions serve a governmental interest.

1. In *Hollenbaugh v. Carnegie Free Library*,[76] the court dismissed constitutional claims for infringement of privacy and equal protection rights brought by two library employees who were discharged for engaging in "open adultery." The court held that the fundamental right to privacy did not protect the right of two people, one of whom was married, to live together in an espoused relationship. Moreover, whatever privacy interest the plaintiff could claim was deemed outweighed by the library's interest in functioning effectively in a small community that strongly disapproved of the plaintiff's conduct.

2. Similarly, in *Kukla v. Village of Antioch*,[77] the court held that the discharges of a police sergeant and a police dispatcher for cohabitation did not infringe on their constitutional rights to privacy and freedom of association. The court found that the right to cohabitation was not entitled to the same level of constitutional protection as the right to marry and thus that the discharges need only be rationally based. Finding that the plaintiffs' relationship could have adversely affected their performance and the department's operations, the court concluded that the employer had made the requisite showing to defeat the constitutional claim.

Challenges to No-Dating Rules by Private Employees Based on Public Policy Grounds

Although claims based on federal constitutional rights to privacy and free association are not available to private employees seeking to challenge the implementation of company rules against dating or cohabitation, similar claims have been alleged on the basis of state constitutional rights or public policy. Since a violation of public policy generally constitutes an exception to the employment-at-will doctrine, an employee might successfully challenge his or her discharge if the state has a defined policy protecting privacy and association rights which a court will be willing to extend to the romantic activity that prompted the discharge.

1. In *United Parcel Service v. Slohoda*,[78] a New Jersey appellate court found that the application of an antifraternization policy to married employees alone would constitute discrimination on the basis of marital status in violation of the state's antidiscrimination law. The plaintiff alleged that he was discharged for having a sexual liaison with a coemployee

while still married to another woman and that unmarried employees of the company were not discharged for having affairs with coemployees. The company maintained that the plaintiff was discharged for misconduct.

In its first ruling in this case, the New Jersey court reversed a grant for summary judgment for the company, finding that "if an employer's discharge policy is based in significant part on an employee's marital status, a discharge resulting from such policy violates N.J.S.A. 10:5-12a."[79] In addition, the court remanded the case for further proceedings on the issue of whether the company's policy breached the plaintiff's right to privacy.

Subsequently, the trial court dismissed the case following the presentation of the plaintiff's evidence at trial because the plaintiff had failed to demonstrate that unmarried employees were treated differently. The appellate court then reversed and remanded the case for further proceedings, finding in part that discriminatory treatment could be proved on grounds other than the unequal application of the no-dating policy to unmarried employees.[80]

2. In *Staats v. Ohio National Life Insurance Co.*,[81] a married employee who was discharged for attending a business convention with another woman alleged that his discharge violated public policy. In dismissing this claim, the court held that "the right to 'associate with' a non-spouse at an employer's convention without fear of termination is hardly the kind of threat to 'some recognized facet of public policy' that the Pennsylvania Supreme Court envisioned. . . . "[82] See also *Ward v. Frito-Lay, Inc.*,[83] in which the court found that an unmarried employee was properly discharged for living with another unmarried employee in the absence of any guaranteed statutory or constitutional right or clearly defined public policy.

3. Courts of other states have similarly found that state privacy rights or public policies did not protect employees against implementation of antifraternization policies. See *Patton v. J.C.Penney Co.*,[84] where the court found an at-will employee was properly discharged for violating a no-dating rule, after having been warned to end the relationship, because his right to privacy gave him rights against governmental infringement and not against a private employer; and *Rodgers v. IBM*,[85] in which no right to privacy was found to be infringed when an at-will employee was discharged for having a personal relationship with a subordinate worker that disrupted normal operating procedures. See also *Trumbauer v. Group Health Corp.*,[86] in which the court found that an employee's challenge to an office romance policy based on speech or association rights was waived by virtue of a collective bargaining agreement between the company and the employee's union.

4. In *Rulon-Miller v. IBM*,[87] the court held that an employer breached an employee's contractual right to privacy when it discharged her for dating an employee in a competing firm. The company had a written policy of protecting the private affairs of its employees. The court found that the employer breached an implied covenant of good faith and fair dealing derived from this policy because it discharged the plaintiff even though her relationship presented no conflicts of interest.

NOTES

1. 562 F.2d 496, 499 (7th Cir. 1977), *cert. denied*, 435 U.S. 934 (1978).
2. Bureau of National Affairs, Corporate Affairs: Nepotism, Office Romance, Sexual Harassment (1988).
3. Dothard v. Rawlinson, 433 U.S. 321, 329 (1977).
4. Johnson v. Uncle Ben's Inc., 657 F.2d 750, 753 (5th Cir. 1981), *cert. denied*, 459 U.S. 967 (1982).
5. Wards Cove Packing Co. v. Atonio, 109 S. Ct. 2115 (1989).
6. *Id.* at 2116.
7. *Id.* (quoting *Watson v. Fort Worth Bank & Trust Co.*, 108 S. Ct. 2777, 2790 (1988) (O'Connor, J.)).
8. *Wards Cove*, infra, at 1721.
9. 525 F.2d 409 (8th Cir. 1975).
10. 814 F.2d 1506 (10th Cir. 1987).
11. 814 F.2d at 1509.
12. 562 F.2d at 498.
13. EEOC v. Rath Packing Co., 787 F.2d 318 (8th Cir.), *cert. denied*, 479 U.S. 910 (1986).
14. 562 F.2d at 498-500.
15. *Wards Cove*, supra, at 1719.
16. 787 F.2d at 318.
17. 562 F.2d at 500.
18. *Id.* at 500.
19. Texas Department of Community Affairs v. Burdine, 450 U.S. 248, 253–54 (1981).
20. *Thomas*, 814 F.2d at 1508 (citing *Texas Department of Community Affairs*, 450 U.S. at 254–56).
21. 715 F.2d 175 (5th Cir. 1983).
22. 641 F. Supp. 424, 427 (S.D. Miss. 1986).
23. *McDowell*, 641 F. Supp. at 428.
24. 601 F. Supp. 160 (W.D. Pa.), *aff'd without opinion*, 779 F.2d 42 (3d Cir. 1985).
25. 51 N.Y.2d 506, 434 N.Y.S.2d 961 (1980).
26. *Id.* at 514, 434 N.Y.S.2d at 965. See also Campbell v. New York State Human Rights Appeal Board, 81 A.D.2d 991, 440 N.Y.S.2d 73 (3d Dep't 1981).
27. Miller v. Muer Corp., 362 N.W.2d 650, 420 Mich. 355 (1984). *See also* Thompson v. Sanborn Motor Express, Inc., 154 N.J. Super. 555, 382 A.2d 53 (N.J. Super. Ct. App. Div. 1977); Moore v. Honeywell Information Systems, Inc. 558 F. Supp. 1229 (D. Haw. 1983) (citing *Manhattan Pizza Hut* and holding that the marital status provision of the state law only prohibits discrimination based on marital status, not discrimination based on the identity of the employee's spouse).
28. 30 F.E.P. Cases (BNA) 31 (S. Ct. Minn. 1979).
29. 627 P.2d 1229 (Mont. 1981).
30. 91 Wash. 2d 62, 586 P.2d 1149 (1978).
31. 81 A.D. 2d 991, 440 N.Y.S. 2d. 73 (3d Dep't 1981).
32. *Miller*, 362 N.W. 2d 650, 420 Mich. 355.
33. *Thompson*, 154 N.J. Super. at 555, 382 A.2d at 53.
34. Cal. Admin. Code tit. 2, div. 4, § 7292.5, 8A *BNA Fair Employment Practices Manual* § 453:875 (1980).
35. Or. Rev. Stat. § 659.340 (1987).

36. 39 F.E.P. Cases (BNA) 863, 868 (Ct. App. Calif. 1985).

37. *See, e.g.,* Keckeisen v. Independent School District, 509 F.2d 1062 (8th Cir.), *cert. denied,* 423 U.S. 833 (1975) (upholding school board no-spouse policy, finding that it was rationally designed to "prevent conflicts of interest and favoritism"); Parsons v. County of Del Norte, 728 F.2d 1234 (9th Cir.), *cert. denied,* 469 U.S. 846 (1984) (rejecting application of strict scrutiny analysis to a constitutional challenge to a no-spouse rule filed by a matron-dispatcher in the sheriff's department who was forced to resign because her husband was a duputy sheriff); Cutts v. Fowler, 692 F.2d 138 (D.C. Cir. 1982) (finding an antinepotism policy was not unconstitutionally applied to a civil servant who was reassigned to a new division at the same grade and salary when her husband became head of her former division).

38. 640 F. Supp. 1274, 1277 (E.D. Wis. 1986), *aff'd without opinion,* 819 F.2d 1144 (7th Cir.), *cert. denied,* 108 S.Ct. 235 (1987).

39. 728 F.2d at 1238.

40. 580 F.2d 346, 347 (8th Cir. 1978).

41. EEOC Guidelines, 29 C.F.R. § 1604.11(a) (19).

42. Meritor Savings Bank, FSB v. Vinson, 477 U.S. 57 (1986).

43. *See Meritor,* 477 U.S. at 63; Rabidue v. Osceola Refining Co., 805 F.2d 611, 618 (6th Cir. 1986), *cert. denied,* 107 S. Ct. 1983 (1987); Henson v. City of Dundee, 682 F.2d 897, 901 (11th Cir. 1982).

44. Priest v. Rotary, 634 F. Supp. 571 (N.D. Cal. 1986).

45. *Meritor,* 477 U.S. at 64-67.

46. Bohen v. City of East Chicago, Ind., 799 F.2d 1180, 1185 (7th Cir. 1986).

47. Woerner v. Brzeczek, 519 F.Supp. 517 (N.D. Ill. 1981).

48. Skadegaard v. Farrell, 578 F. Supp. 1209, 1212 (D. N.J. 1984).

49. *Meritor,* 477 U.S. at 72.

50. Highlander v. K.F.C. National Management Co., 805 F.2d 644, 648–49 (6th Cir. 1986); Katz v. Dole, 709 F.2d 251, 255 n.6 (4th Cir. 1983); Schroeder v. Schock, 42 F.E.P. Cases (BNA) 1112 (D. Kan. 1986).

51. *Meritor,* 477 U.S. at 72.

52. Paris v. Vogt Machine Co., 813 F.2d 786 (6th Cir. 1987); Hensen v. City of Dundee, 682 F.2d 897 (11th Cir. 1982); Katz, 709 F.2d at 251.

53. EEOC Guidelines, 29 C.F.R. § 1604.11(g) (1986).

54. DeCintio v. Westchester County Medical Center, 807 F.2d 304 (2d Cir. 1986), *cert. denied,* 108 S. Ct. 89 (1987).

55. *Id.* at 305.

56. *Id.* at 308.

57. 679 F. Supp. 495 (W.D. Pa. 1988), *aff'd without opinion,* (LEXIS, Genfed library, USAPP file) (3d Cir. 1988).

58. *Id.* at 501.

59. Kersul v. Skulls Angels, Inc., 130 Misc. 2d 345, 495 N.Y.S.2d 866 (Sup. Ct. Queens Cty. 1985).

60. 570 F. Supp. 1197 (D. Del. 1983).

61. *DeCintio,* 807 F.2d at 307.

62. 634 F. Supp. at 571.

63. 778 F.2d 878 (D.C. Cir. 1986).

64. 685 F. Supp. 1269, 1280 (D. D.C. 1988).

65. *Meritor,* 477 U.S. at 68.

66. 687 F. Supp. 848 (S.D. N.Y. 1988).

67. 623 F. Supp. 795 (W.D. Pa. 1985).

68. No., slip op. No. 85-2643 (D. Kan. Feb. 11, 1988).

69. 388 N.W.2d 553 (Wis. 1986).

70. *Id.,* at 560.

71. 596 F. Supp. 1001 (E.D. Mich. 1984).

72. *Id.* at 1005.

73. 278 N.W.2d 725, 88 Mich. App. 704 (Mich. Ct. App. 1979).

74. 726 F.2d 459 (9th Cir. 1983), *cert. denied,* 469 U.S. 979 (1984).

75. 563 F. Supp. 585 (W.D. Mich. 1983), *aff'd without opinion,* 746 F.2d 1475 (6th Cir. 1984).

76. 436 F. Supp. 1328 (W.D. Pa. 1977), *aff'd,* 578 F.2d 1374 (3d Cir.), *cert. denied,* 439 U.S. 1052 (1978).

77. 647 F. Supp. 799 (N.D. Ill. 1986).

78. 193 N.J. Super. 586, 475 A.2d 618 (N.J. Super. Ct. App. Div. 1984).

79. *Id.* at 589, 475 A.2d at 620.

80. *United Parcel Service v. Slohoda,* 207 N.J. Super. 145, 504 A.2d 53 (N.J. Super. Ct. App. Div.), *certification denied,* 104 N.J. 400, 517 A.2d 403 (N.J. 1986).

81. 620 F. Supp. 118 (W.D. Pa. 1985).

82. *Id.* at 120.

83. 95 Wis. 2d 372, 290 N.W.2d 536. (Wis. 1980).

84. 301 Ore. 117, 719 P.2d 854 (Or. 1986).

85. 500 F. Supp. 867 (W.D. Pa. 1980).

86. 635 F. Supp. 543 (W.D. Wash. 1986).

87. 162 Cal. App. 3d 241, 208 Cal. Rptr. 524 (Cal. Ct. App. 1984).

About the Editor

Norman Metzger is the Edmond A. Guggenheim Professor of Health Care Management in the Department of Health Care Management of the Mount Sinai School of Medicine. He is vice-president for labor relations of the Mount Sinai Medical Center in New York City.

He is also an adjunct professor at the Bernard M. Baruch College of the City University of New York in the Department of Management's Graduate Program in Health Care Administration.

Professor Metzger was president of the League of Voluntary Hospitals and Homes of New York from 1968 to 1972 and from 1980 to 1982. He is currently chairman of the League's Labor Relations/Negotiating Committee.

He also served as president of the American Society for Healthcare Human Resource Administration (ASHHRA) for the term 1985–86. In 1987 he was honored with the Society's Exceptional Contribution Award.

Professor Metzger has written over 100 articles on labor relations, personnel administration, and social behavior. He is the author, coauthor, or editor of 15 books. In 1987 he received for the sixth time the Annual Award for Literature given by ASHHRA, in recognition of his outstanding contribution to hospital personnel administration literature.

About the Contributors

Steven G. Allen, Ph.D., is professor of economics and business at North Carolina State University. In addition, Dr. Allen is a research associate of the National Bureau of Economic Research. He earned a B.A. in mathematics with high honors and an M.A. in economics from Michigan State University. He earned his Ph.D. from Harvard. Dr. Allen's research specialties are wage rigidity in the United States, the economics of labor productivity and productivity change, unions and efficiency, trends in unionization, and the economics of pensions. His articles are widely published in many scholarly journals, and he has contributed chapters to a number of books. Dr. Allen is also active as a presenter of papers at professional meetings and conferences.

Laura Avakian is vice-president for human resources at Beth Israel Hospital in Boston, Massachusetts. She earned her M.A. at Northwestern University and her B.A. at the University of Missouri, Columbia. Ms. Avakian is a past president and member of the Executive Committee (1988–89) of the Massachusetts Healthcare Human Resources Association, chairman of the Legislative and Labor Committee (1988–89) of the American Society for Healthcare Human Resources Administration, and associate editor (1989) of the *Health Management Yearbook*.

Lawrence C. Bassett, CMC, is president of The Bassett Consulting Group, Inc., of Thornwood, New York, a member of the ALT Consulting Network. Previously, for 10 years he was president, professional services of Applied Leadership Technologies, Inc., which he founded with several associates in 1976. Mr. Bassett's experience as a Certified Management Consultant includes work in industry, retailing, government organizations, hospitality, and health care. He held important line and staff positions before becoming a consultant in 1966 and has extensive experience in employee/labor relations, organization development, compensation, and sales. He is a frequent speaker and writer and has authored *Achieving Excellence,* published by Aspen Publishers, Inc. In addition, he is on the graduate school faculties of New York University and Fairleigh Dickinson University and is a guest lecturer. For many years he also has been an arbitrator with the American Arbitration Association. Mr. Bassett holds B.A. and M.B.A. degrees from New York University.

L. Robert Batterman, Esquire has been a practicing lawyer for 22 years. He is a partner in the law firm of Proskauer Rose Goetz & Mendelsohn in New York City and represents management in labor relations and employment law. He is a member of various bar associations and professional organizations and writes and speaks frequently at various functions.

Richard E. Berger is an associate with William M. Mercer-Meidinger-Hansen in New York. He is a fellow of the Society of Actuaries and an enrolled actuary.

Patricia Berger-Friedman, M.A., is an associate in Mercer-Meidinger-Hansen's New York office. She has consulted on a range of welfare plan issues including plan design, cost containment, HMOs, flexible benefits, wellness, plan administration, and audits. Prior to joining Mercer in 1983, Ms. Friedman was a consultant with Frank B. Hall's National Benefit Consulting Group, where she specialized in HMO administration and cost containment. She holds a B.A. *cum laude* and an M.A. in health planning from the University of Pennsylvania.

Michael I. Bernstein, Esquire is a partner in the New York City law firm of Benetar Isaacs Bernstein & Schair, which specializes exclusively in the representation of management in the areas of labor and employment discrimination law. He is a former chairman of the New York City Bar Association Committee on Labor Law and of the American Bar Association Committee on Federal Labor Standards Legislation. Currently he is a member of the Executive Committee of the Labor Law Section of the New York State Bar Association.

David A. Bjork, Ph.D., is director of the Hay Group's HMO consulting practice. Located in Hay's Minneapolis office, he specializes in the areas of compensation and organization effectiveness. He has consulted to a wide variety of health care (particularly managed care), financial, and service organizations. He is a major contributor to Hay's annual Health Care Management Company Total Compensation Survey with particular responsibility for executive compensation and the HMO industry. Dr. Bjork earned an A.B. at Harvard, an M.B.A. in finance at the University of Chicago, and a Ph.D. at the University of California at Berkeley. Before joining Hay he taught at the University of California and the University of Chicago. He spent one year as a French Government Fellow and another as a Charles E. Merrill Fellow at the Center for the Study of Public and Non-Profit Institutions, Graduate School of Business, University of Chicago. During the bicentennial year, he worked as a program director for the Smithsonian Institution.

John D. Blair, Ph.D., is a professor of management (College of Business Administration) and associate chairman of the Health Organization Department (School of Medicine) at Texas Tech University in Lubbock. He is also director of the Program in Health Organization Management, Institute for Management and Leadership Research, Texas Tech. Dr. Blair specializes in strategic and stakeholder management for health care organizations.

Phyllis C. Borzi, Esquire has been affiliated with the Sub-Committee on Labor Management Relations, Committee on Education and Labor in Washington, D.C., since 1979. She originally worked for the Task Force on Pension and Welfare Benefit Plans and since 1981 has been counsel for pensions and employee benefits. Ms. Borzi is a graduate of the Catholic University Law School, where she was editor-in-chief of the Catholic University *Law Review*. Her major areas of interest are health and pension issues, and which she has had articles published.

Mark E. Brossman, J.D., earned his B.S. at Cornell University and his J.D. and LL.M. in labor law at the New York University School of Law. He is the author of *Social Investing*

of Pension Funds (IFEBP 1982), as well as numerous articles concerning labor law and ERISA. He is a speaker in the Cornell University Labor Relations Studies on arbitration, ERISA, COBRA, and labor law and is an adjunct assistant professor at the New York University School for Continuing Education.

Jerad D. Browdy formed his own health care consulting firm in 1984, after spending 11 years with Witt Associates where his positions in recruiting and compensation included vice-president for executive compensation services. Mr. Browdy earned his B.S. degree from Northwestern University and his M.S. degree from George Williams College. He is the author of the book *Healthcare Executive Compensation—Principles and Strategies* published by Aspen Publishers. His articles on executive compensation have appeared in numerous health care journals, and he is on the editorial board of *The Healthcare Supervisor* (Aspen Publishers).

Mary S. Case is a principal in Mercer-Meidinger-Hansen's New York office. She joined the firm in 1981 as a consultant specializing in group welfare benefit programs. In her eight years of consulting experience with this organization, Ms. Case has assisted clients of all sizes in the profit, not-for-profit, and public sectors with the design, financial arrangement, administration, and compensation of their group benefit plans. She is a frequent speaker at internal and external seminars, specifically addressing Section 89 and other compliance issues. Prior to joining Mercer-Meidinger-Hansen, Ms. Case was responsible for benefits planning and administration at AmeriTrust Company, headquartered in Cleveland, Ohio. Ms. Case received her B.A. degree *magna cum laude* from Harvard University.

Marco L. Colosi is a vice-president of human resources and labor relations at Bronx-Lebanon Hospital Center in New York. Mr. Colosi holds professorships at the New York Institute of Technology and Pace University, where he teaches on the graduate level. He is past president of the Academy of Employee-Industrial Relations, a member of the Legal Committee of the Greater New York Hospital Association, and a member of the National Academy of Conciliators. Mr. Colosi is the recipient of the NYIT President's Award for Academic Excellence, the Faculty Award, and the Queens County Citation of Honor. He has a master's degree in labor relations from the New York Institute of Technology and is a Ph.D. candidate in labor law. He is also certified as "Employee Relations Society Qualified" (ERSQ) by the Academy of Industrial-Employee Relations.

Michael R. Cooper, Ph.D., is worldwide managing director, Hay Research for Management, The Hay Group, in Philadelphia, Pennsylvania, where he provides firmwide leadership, business development, and client consulting that focuses on diagnosing the client organizations' readiness for transition and assessing employee commitment, attitudes, and values for implementation of business strategy. Dr. Cooper has written many articles and has been invited to speak at executive management meetings for major corporations, associations, and universities. His extensive work on managing organization culture during transition has received widespread coverage by the three major television networks, newspapers such as the *Wall Street Journal* and the *London Times*, and management journals such as the *Harvard Business Review, Business, Leaders, Management Review, Inc. Magazine,* and *Strategic Directions*. His article "Early Warning Signals" was selected from more than 500 periodicals as a most significant business contribution and published in *Best of Business*.

Brian G. Costello, SPHR, is a vice-president of Garofolo, Curtiss & Company, conducting executive searches and related consulting services. He was the senior human resources professional at Hahnemann University, Philadelphia. Mr. Costello has lectured extensively on subjects of interest to hospitals, academic medical centers, professional organizations, and physician groups. In addition, he has written articles for health care publications and has received a national award for literature. Mr. Costello has a B.S. in economics from the Wharton School of the University of Pennsylvania and an M.S. in human resource management from Widener University.

Donald Crow is vice-president for operations at The Methodist Health Care Network (TMHCN) in Houston, Texas, where he is responsible for supervising and coordinating various consulting services for hospitals under contract to TMHCN, the hospital management subsidiary of The Methodist Hospital. Formerly he served as senior management consultant for John Short and Associates in Austin, Texas. Mr. Crow received his B.B.A. in management from Texas A & M University. He is a guest instructor in management at the Southwest Texas University and Hill Junior College and has conducted programs for the American Hospital Association and for Arizona, Arkansas, Florida, Louisiana, South Carolina, and Texas Hospital Associations.

Janet R. Douglas, M.P.H., O.T.R., specializes in the design and evaluation of programs to manage workers' compensation costs for Mercer-Meidinger-Hansen in San Francisco. She has developed and implemented corporate disability management and cost containment projects for large multisite employers, including work capacity evaluations, rehabilitation interventions, and work hardening programs. Previously, she was a manager in the health care practice group at Coopers and Lybrand and lead specialist in occupational medicine. Ms. Douglas received her M.P.H. from the University of Illinois and her dual diploma in occupational therapy in the United Kingdom.

Edward J. Dowling, M.B.A., is vice-president for human resources at the Yale–New Haven Hospital, Connecticut, and is responsible for a broad number of human resource functions, including the recruitment of all staffing at the hospital, employee and labor relations, training and organization development, compensation and benefits, and the hospital's personnel health services. He graduated from Rutgers University and received his master of business administration specializing in personnel administration from the University of Detroit. In addition to his extensive personnel administration experience in the health care field, Mr. Dowling also has a broad background in human resource management in private industry.

Catherine A. Duran, M.B.A., is a research associate for Area of Management and the Institute of Management and Leadership Research, Texas Tech University.

Norbert F. Elbert, D.B.A., is currently the Brown and Williamson Professor of Management and chairman of the Department of Business Administration and Economics at Bellarmine College. He has taught human resources management at the University of the Denver and Northern Arizona University. He received his B.S. and M.B.A. from the University of Louisville and his D.B.A. from the University of Kentucky. He has contributed over 30 articles to scholarly journals, including *Decision Sciences, Health Care Management Review, Academy of Management Journal, Journal of Experimental Education,* and *Journal of Marketing Research*. Dr. Elbert is also an active consultant and trainer to Ford Motor Company and Louisville Gas and Electric Company. He has designed performance appraisal and reward systems for firms in Kentucky, Arizona, Colorado, and New Mexico. He has also coauthored three books, the newest of which is *Personnel* (3d ed.).

Gregory T. Finnegan, M.B.A., is a director of management systems at the Robert Wood Johnson University Hospital, New Brunswick, New Jersey. He holds an M.B.A. from DePaul University. He was formerly director of training and development at Little Company of Mary Hospital and a member of the adjunct faculty for the National College of Education in the M.S. degree program in management and human resource development. He is the author of numerous articles on productivity improvement, job aid development, value analysis, and analysis and improvement of human performance in the work setting, as well as other areas. In 1984 he received the Health Systems Agency Award for Health Promotion.

Thomas P. Flannery, Jr., Ph.D., is a vice-president of the Hay Group and serves as a regional director of Health Care Consulting as well as the general manager of Hay's St. Louis office. His consulting experience is in the areas of organizational effectiveness, including human resources planning and productivity and compensation at the executive, professional, and technical levels. He provides services to a range of private and public clients, with particular emphasis on health care organizations.

Myron D. Fottler, Ph.D., is professor of the Ph.D. program in administration–health services at the University of Alabama at Birmingham. He has a Ph.D. from Columbia University and has published extensively on a wide variety of health care management topics.

Anthony J. Gajda, Ph.D., is an economist with the firm of William M. Mercer-Meidinger-Hansen, Inc., which specializes in employee benefits and pensions. Before joining Mercer in 1983, Mr. Gajda was executive vice-president of Program Planners, Inc., a New York consulting firm. In that position, he directed and managed the firm's activities in employee benefits, pensions, applied economic research, systems development, labor management relations, and health planning; designed health and retirement plans; supervised competitive bidding; negotiated renewal and other conditions; organized cost containment programs; recommended pension valuations and funding methods; and assisted in the selection of actuarial assumptions. Mr. Gajda directed research in the area of public policy, including studies of casino gambling, fire safety laws, and hospital systems, and managed the development of major computer system installations in benefit and pension funds. He received B.A. and M.A. degrees and will be receiving his Ph.D. in economics from the City University of New York.

James J. Gallagher, Ph.D., is a founding partner of King Chapman Broussard & Gallagher, Inc. After 15 years in industry, working with International Nickel Company and several major corporate communications firms in New York City, he headed a think tank and later an innovative community service college in northern New Jersey. In 1970 he founded J.J. Gallagher Associates, Inc., which recently merged with King Chapman & Broussard, Inc., and he has since been active in the development of professional standards in outplacement. Mr. Gallagher was a founder and later served as president of the Association of Outplacement Consulting Firms.

Robin Gourlay is professor of health care management at The International Management Centre in Buckingham, England. He joined I.M.C.B. in May 1986, having previously been regional personnel manager to the Wessex Regional Health Authority. Mr. Gourlay is a director of Marcia Publications Ltd. and Buckingham House Ltd., a parent company for I.M.C.B. He jointly publishes the *Health Services Manpower Review* and publishes and edits the *Journal of Health Care Management*. He is a frequent speaker at seminars on major personnel issues and contributes many articles on general management matters.

Fred W. Graumann, Esquire is senior vice-president for human resources at the Robert Wood Johnson Health Care Corp. in New Brunswick, New Jersey. He was formerly vice-president for human resources at the Children's Memorial Hospital in Chicago. Mr. Graumann has a B.A. from Hunter College and a J.D. from the New York Law School. His related faculty experience was conducted at Columbia University and the State University of New York, and was a part-time assistant professor teaching courses in personnel administration and labor relations in master's program(s) in health care. Mr. Graumann was chairman of the Legislative Committee (1985–87) of the American Society for Healthcare Human Resources Administration. He has lectured to various professional audiences on pay for performance, defined contribution plans, the recruitment dilemma, the new immigration law, and flexible compensation. He is the author of the article "After Bakke Many Questions are Left Unanswered," which appeared in *Hospitals*.

E.J. Holland, Jr., Esquire is a managing partner of the Kansas City law firm of Spencer Fane Britt & Browne. Educated at Rockhurst College and Boston College Law School, he has spent a substantial part of the last 20 years representing employers in labor and employee relations matters and has appeared before the National Labor Relations Board and various courts and administrative agencies. Mr. Holland is a member of the Labor Law Sections of the American and Missouri Bar Associations and a member of the bars of Missouri and the United States Supreme Court. He serves on the Labor Relations Advisory Committee of the American Hospital Association and the Labor Committee of the Missouri Hospital Association. He has written and spoken extensively on a wide variety of labor and employment law issues and has been deeply involved for the last 18 months in the NLRB hospital industry rulemaking.

James R. Hudek, L.L.B., is a managing partner and head of the employee benefits group of the Kansas City law firm of Spencer Fane Britt & Browne. In the past 20 years that he has been with the firm, he has advised clients on their health and welfare plans, pension and profit-sharing plans, and employee benefits trusts. He has spoken extensively on a wide variety of employee benefits law issues, especially Section 89. Mr. Hudek is a graduate of Michigan State University, where he received his bachelor's degree with highest honors. He attended Yale Law School, from which he also received his LL.B. He is a member of the Kansas City Metropolitan Bar, the Missouri Bar, and the American Bar Associations.

Sanford M. Jacoby, Ph.D., is associate professor of human resource management at the Anderson Graduate School of Management at UCLA. He received his A.B. from the University of Pennsylvania and his Ph.D. in economics from the University of California at Berkeley. He has published numerous articles in scholarly journals on such topics as labor economics, business history, comparative industrial relations, and labor law. He is the author of *Employing Bureaucracy: Managers, Unions, and the Transformation of Work in American Industry, 1900—1945*, which won the Terry Award from the Academy of Management. Presently he is writing a book on personnel management in large nonunion companies.

Richard E. Johnson is a principal of William M. Mercer-Meidinger-Hansen, Inc., in Chicago. He is a managing consultant to a wide range of public, private, and labor management trusts. Mr. Johnson's primary consulting emphases are in the areas of flexible benefit plans, cost management/containment for health plans, group consulting, and defined contribution plans [401(d) and 454]. Mr. Johnson is the author of *Flexible Benefits—A How-To Guide* and *Utilization Review—A How-To Guide* published by the International Foundation. He gives speeches and workshops, has written numerous articles, and has participated in numerous education programs. He is the former chairman of Mercer-Meidinger-Hansen's health care consulting practice group. Mr. Johnson holds a B.A. degree from Pacific Lutheran University. He has been named to "Who's Who" over the past eight years.

Charles L. Joiner, Ph.D., is a professor of hospital and health administration and associate dean, School of Community and Allied Health, University of Alabama in Birmingham. He is a graduate of the University of Alabama, where he received his master's in economics and his Ph.D. in business administration. His present responsibilities include graduate courses in human resources management and primary administrative assignments in the areas of finance, personnel, and overall administration. In addition to being the author of numerous management presentations and publications, Dr. Joiner has served as a consultant and training specialist with numerous health care organizations, particularly in the labor relations and personnel areas.

Arnold D. Kaluzny, M.H.A., Ph.D., is professor of health policy and administration, School of Public Health, and director, Program on Health Care Organization, Health Services Research Center, University of North Carolina at Chapel Hill. He received his undergraduate education in economics and chemistry at the University of Wisconsin. He earned both his master's degree in hospital administration and his Ph.D. in medical care organization/social psychology from the University of Michigan. Dr. Kaluzny is also a research associate at the Institute for Research in the Social Sciences and the UNC Lineberger Cancer Research Center. Dr. Kaluzny's long and active research interests involve technology assessment, implementation, program evaluation, and organizational innovation and diffusion. He has been the principal and/or coinvestigator of several large studies, and he currently serves as the principal investigator for a large contract funded by the National Cancer Institute to evaluate the implementation and impact of community clinical oncology programs (CCOPs). Dr. Kaluzny is on the editorial board of *Health Care Management Review* and *Medical Care Review* and has served as an associate editor of the *Journal of Health and Social Behavior*. He is the author of numerous articles and has coauthored several books including *Health Care Management: A Text in*

Organizational Theory and Behavior, 2d ed., with Steve Shortell (Wiley, 1988).

Howard L. Kane, F.S.A., is New York vice-president and chief actuary of Noble Lowndes, a worldwide employee benefits consulting firm. He serves as consultant to major national corporations, jointly trusteed union management employee benefits funds, not-for-profit organizations including hospitals, and professional associations. Mr. Kane graduated from the University of Florida. His professional achievements include fellowship in the Society of Actuaries and membership in the American Academy of Actuaries, as well as being an Enrolled Actuary under ERISA. He is past president of the Pension Council of Long Island, and he has served the Society of Actuaries as a general officer of their Examination and Education Committee and as vice-chairman of the Examination Committee for Enrolled Actuaries under ERISA. Mr. Kane has direct responsibility for all phases of his company's consulting and actuarial services, including actuarial cost valuations, determination of health and welfare contributions, health care cost containment, investment performance monitoring, and numerous other detailed studies necessary in the operation of self-insured retirement, pension, and health benefit programs.

Elliott A. Kellman, M.P.A., is currently senior vice president for human resources at the Baystate Health Systems, a multi-institutional health services organization serving Western Massachusetts. In this capacity he is responsible for all human resource functions within the eight corporations comprising the system including Baystate Medical Center, an 878 bed teaching hospital with more than 4500 employees; and Franklin Medical Center. Previously he was administrative director of human resources at Yale New Haven Hospital and a member of the hospital's senior management group. Prior to his appointment at Yale New Haven Hospital, Mr. Kellman served as vice president of human resources at Bristol Hospital, Bristol, Connecticut, and vice president of professional services and director of employee and human relations at Newport Hospital, Newport, Rhode Island. He was also assistant vice president of human resources for the Hospital Association of Rhode Island. Mr. Kellman is a frequent lecturer on management and human resources strategic planning. He holds both BS and MBA degrees from West Virginia University.

David Lance is the chairman and founder of The American Healthcare Consulting Corporation (TAHCC), a Boston-based management consulting firm, and president of its business sector subsidiary, American Horizon Consulting. These organizations specialize in compensation systems, human resources, analytic tools, organizational development, and representation for unionized and nonunionized employers. His work experience spans over 20 years across three major teaching hospitals and health care systems where he served as vice-president or corporate vice-president for human resources.

Mr. Lance has led institutes in labor relations, preventative labor relations, and administrative management for Cornell's New York State School of Industrial Relations, the Hospital Association of New York State, the New York Joint Educational Program, the Middle Atlantic Healthcare Congress, and the Hospital Financial Management Association. He was the founder and president of the Rochester Regional Personnel Association.

Jack M. Marco is president of the Marco Consulting Group (MCG), an investment consulting firm specializing in multiemployer benefit funds. He currently serves as the consultant to 33 multiemployer plans. MCG is the largest provider of investment consulting services to multiemployer plans. Mr. Marco began his career as an investment consultant in 1977 when he joined A.G. Becker, Inc. In late 1983 SEI Corporation purchased the consulting division of A.G. Becker and named Mr. Marco the national manager of their Taft-Hartley Funds Evaluation Services. Prior to joining A.G. Becker, he was administrative assistant to U.S. Congressman Abner J. Mikva of Illinois. At age 26 he was named by the Governor of Illinois as the director of the Environmental Protection Agency. Mr. Marco received his undergraduate degree in mathematics from Lewis University. His graduate studies were in mathematics at Purdue, Northwestern, and Northern Illinois Universities. He is a frequent speaker on many aspects of benefit funds.

Kenneth A. Mason, J.D., is an associate with the employee benefits group of the Kansas City law firm of Spencer Fane Britt & Browne. Since joining the firm in 1986, Mr. Mason has concentrated his practice in the areas of Taft-Hartley multiemployer funds and the regulation of welfare benefit plans. Mr. Mason addresses groups and businesses on employee benefit topics such as COBRA, Section 89, and qualified plans. He received his bachelor's degree *magna cum laude* in government from Harvard University. He is also a graduate of Yale Law School. Mr. Mason served as a law clerk to the Honorable Earl E. O'Connor, Chief Judge of the U.S. District Court, District of Kansas, from 1984 to 1986. He is a member of the Kansas City Metropolitan Bar, the Missouri Bar, and the American Bar Associations.

Martin H. Meisel is president of Martin H. Meisel Associates, Inc., a management consulting firm which specializes in executive search for the hospital and health care fields. He received an A.B. degree from New York University, where he was elected to Phi Beta Kappa, and did graduate work as a Maxwell Fellow at the Maxwell Graduate School of Syracuse University. He completed his master's course requirements at the New York University Graduate School of Public Administration. Prior to entering the management consulting field, Mr. Meisel headed a successful executive placement service, Executive Talent, Inc. He presently serves on the National Panel of Arbitrators for the American Arbitration Association.

V. Brandon Melton, M.A., serves as corporate vice-president, human resources, for the Catholic Health Corporation, one of the nation's 10 largest health care systems, which is a partnership of eight religious institutes and is comprised of 74 health care facilities in the midwestern and western United States. Mr. Melton is the former executive director of the American Society for Healthcare Human Resources Administration of the American Hospital Association.

Bart Metzger, M.A., has been in the health care human resources field since 1976 and has held administrative-level positions since 1979. He was the associate executive director at Bellevue Hospital Center in New York City from 1979 to 1986 and is currently the director of human resources at Georgetown University Hospital in Washington, D.C. Within the human resources function, his areas of particular interest are organizational development and work place democracy. He has authored and coauthored several articles in these areas for personnel and management journals.

Arnold Milstein, M.D., M.P.E., directs National Medical Audit (NMA), the medical audit services unit of William M. Mercer-Meidinger-Hansen, Inc. NMA specializes in auditing and designing health care controls for large employers, carriers, providers, and government. Dr. Milstein heads a national audit team of 120 NMA physicians. His publications have centered on measuring and maximizing the effectiveness of utilization review. He is the editor of the "Case of the Month" section of *Medical Utilization Review*. The California Chamber of Commerce has published his *Employers' Guides to PPOs and Utilization Review*. Dr. Milstein earned his B.A. in economics at Harvard, his M.D. at Tufts, and his M.P.H. in health services planning at the University of California at Berkeley. He is a board certified physician and an associate clinical professor at the University of California, San Francisco Medical Center. He is a managing director of Mercer-Meidinger-Hansen, Inc.

Daniel H. Mundt, J.D., is the proprietor of the law firm of Mundt & Associates, Duluth, Minnesota, and lectures on business law and government regulations at the University of Minnesota at Duluth. He received his bachelor's degree in business administration, his J.D. degree and his master's degree in psychology from the University of Minnesota.

Gail E. Nethercut, Ph.D., is director of National Medical Audit's workers' compensation medical cost containment practice of Mercer-Meidinger-Hansen in San Francisco. Her areas of focus include program design, program installation and supervision, and financial analysis of program impact. Prior to joining NMA, Dr. Nethercut was director of utilization and health care analysis at Blue Cross/Blue Shield of Florida. She was responsible for the design and evaluation of comprehensive medical cost containment programs which covered over 2 million insureds. Dr. Nethercut received her undergraduate degree at the University of California, Los

Angeles, and her doctorate in health evaluation from the University of California, San Francisco Medical Center. Her publications have encompassed workers' compensation cost containment and a variety of health research subjects.

Mark F. Peterson, Ph.D., is professor of management at the College of Business Administration and director for the Program in International Leadership and Management for the Institute for Management and Leadership Research at Texas Tech University.

Jeffrey P. Petertil, M.B.A., is a consulting principal and group actuary in the Chicago office of Mercer-Meidinger-Hansen, Inc. He has over 15 years of experience dealing with health and life insurance plans. Mr. Petertil is an associate of the Society of Actuaries (SOA), a member of the American Academy of Actuaries (AAA), and a member of the Chicago Actuarial Association. He is currently chairman of the Committee on Health and Welfare Plans of the AAA. He was an original member of the Actuarial Standards Board's Committee on Retiree Health Care Benefits and an organizer and faculty member of the SOA seminars on retiree medical benefits. His papers "Plan Designs for Retiree Welfare Benefits" and "An Actuarial Model of the Cost Projection of Retiree Health Benefits" are part of the examination syllabus of the SOA. Mr. Petertil currently is a member of the Mercer Health Care Practice Group, which provides leadership and coordination nationally for Mercer's health care consulting. He graduated from DePaul University with a B.A. in mathematics. In 1975, he received an M.B.A. from the University of Chicago with a specialty in finance and economics.

Robert L. Phillips, Ph.D., is director of the Institute for Management and Leadership Research and associate professor of management and associate dean for research, College of Business Administration, at Texas Tech University. Dr. Phillips holds a joint appointment with the School of Medicine.

Bettina B. Plevan, J.D., is a member of the law firm of Proskauer Rose Goetz & Mendelsohn in New York City. Her areas of expertise are labor and employment litigation, including Title VII discrimination and sexual harassment suits and employee benefits (ERISA) matters. She earned her J.D. *magna cum laude* at the Boston University School of Law, where she was editor of the *Boston University Law Review*. Ms. Plevan is a member of the ABA House of Delegates, Association of the Bar of the City of New York, Committee on Second Century, Special Committee on the Bicentennial of the Constitution, and Second Circuit Committee on the Bicentennial, and she is vice-president of the Federal Bar Council.

Kevin Renner is an associate with the Walnut Creek, California, office of Hay Management Consultants. He specializes in the analysis, design, and implementation of programs in organization effectiveness, job analysis, base salary, and incentive programs. Mr. Renner has participated in consulting

projects with emerging growth companies and health care organizations. He graduated with honors from the University of California, Santa Cruz, with a B.A. degree in economics/sociology, with an emphasis in applied social psychology. He earned his M.B.A. degree from the University of California at Berkeley, with an emphasis in strategic management and organizational behavior.

Rhonda Rhodes, J.D., is senior counsel in the Office of Legal and Regulatory Affairs at the American Hospital Association. Her practice is limited to labor law and general corporate matters, in which she represents both the health care industry and the management of the Association. Ms. Rhodes testified before the National Labor Relations Board on behalf of the health care industry in August 1987 and directed the industry response to the Board's rulemaking. She has written a number of articles and has spoken at various programs on this subject. Before joining AHA in 1984, Ms. Rhodes was senior attorney at Sun Electric Corp., Crystal Lake, Illinois. Prior to that, she practiced regulatory law for two years at Abbott Laboratories, North Chicago, Illinois, and was associated with the firm of Green & Barnard, also in Chicago. Ms. Rhodes received her B.A. from Northwestern University and her J.D. from De Paul University College of Law, where she was a member of the *De Paul Law Review*.

Susan S. Robfogel, Esquire is a partner in the law firm of Nixon, Hargrave, Devans and Doyle, Rochester, New York, and chairman of the firm's health services practice group. She concentrates in health law and labor and employment relations law representing management. In 1983 she was appointed by President Reagan to the Federal Service Impasses Panel. She was reappointed in 1988. Since 1984, Ms. Robfogel has served by appointment of the Commissioner of Health as a member of the New York State Data Protection Review Board, and she currently is chairman of the Board. She presently is a member of the American Bar Association's Labor Relations Law Section and serves on the Committee on Development of Law Under the National Labor Relations Act and the management subcommittee responsible for preparing the annual supplement to the text entitled *Developments of the Law Under the National Labor Relations Act;* she is also a member of the Municipal Law Section and serves on the Committee on Public Health Care and the Forum Committee on Health Law. She lectures extensively on health and employment law topics.

James A. Rodeghero, Ph.D., is director of physicians consulting of the Hay Group's Los Angeles office. He directs Hay's consulting practice in the area of physicians' compensation effectiveness. Dr. Rodeghero's consulting activities emphasize Hay's strategic management and organizational effectiveness practice as well as reward management. He is experienced in the design and implementation of base salary programs, executive incentive plans, and nontraditional compensation and reward systems. Dr. Rodeghero has led the design, development, and management of Hay's annual Physician's Compensation Survey, the pre-eminent survey in the field. His consulting activities have included the design of compensation and income distribution plans for physicians in clinic, hospital, and managed care settings. His activities have resulted in a variety of innovative approaches to the complex issues surrounding the compensation and effectiveness of physicians for professional services and administrative duties. He holds an undergraduate degree in psychology and natural sciences from St. Louis University and M.S. and Ph.D. degrees in industrial and organizational psychology from Bowling Green State University.

Kent E. Romanoff, M.A., is practice leader, healthcare gainsharing, for the Hay Management Group. He directs Hay's health care consulting practice in northern California. Mr. Romanoff has been instrumental in adapting gainsharing technology to the service sector. His gainsharing design experience encompasses a wide range of health care delivery settings. He also assists clients with a variety of other human resource issues including performance management, total compensation planning, organization effectiveness, and productivity. He speaks and writes primarily on a wide variety of human-resources-oriented topics. Mr. Romanoff is a Phi Beta Kappa graduate of Stanford University where he earned his B.A. and M.A. degrees.

William A. Rothman, M.S., H.A., is former executive vice-president of Gaylord Hospital in Wallingford, Connecticut. He has written six books on labor relations in hospitals, including *Strikes in Health Care Facilities* and *Interviewing for a Career in Health Care.* He is a fellow of the American College of Health Care Executives and the American Public Health Association.

Grant T. Savage, Ph.D., is an assistant professor of management, College of Business Administration, and assistant professor of health organization management, School of Medicine, Texas Tech University. He is an organizational communication researcher specializing in negotiation within and among health care organizations.

Amarjit S. Sethi, Ph.D., is associate professor at the Faculty of Administration, University of Ottowa, Canada. He specializes in health administration, industrial relations, human resources management, and international management. Dr. Sethi is the author of many articles and the editor of several books including *Collective Bargaining in the Public Sector in the United States: A Time of Change* (JAI Press Inc.) and *Human Resource Management in the Health Care Sector: Guide for Administrators and Professionals* (Greenwood Press, 1989). Dr. Sethi has worked as a consultant in health care and international development projects in India, Afghanistan, the United Kingdom, and Canada. He earned his B. Com. in commerce at the University of Agra in India, his M.S. in industrial relations at the University of Wisconsin, and his Ph.D. at the University of Manchester, United Kingdom.

Howard L. Smith, Ph.D., is a professor at the Anderson School of Management, University of New Mexico. He is also a research scientist with the Division of Health Services Research and Education, Lovelace Medical Foundation. He has published and consulted extensively on health services issues in the United States and abroad. His primary interests include strategic management and organization theory topics relative to health care organizations. He has authored several texts including *Essentials of Finance in Nursing, Competitive Hospitals, Prospective Payment: An Operational Approach,* and the *Health Care Supervisor's Guide to Staff Development* with Aspen Publishers, Inc. He earned his Ph.D. at the University of Washington.

Edward J. Speedling, Ph.D., received his Ph.D. in sociology from the City University of New York. Since 1977 he has held a variety of academic and administrative positions at the Mount Sinai Hospital, School of Medicine, and the Graduate Center of the City University of New York. He currently is director of organizational development and associate professor of community medicine at Mount Sinai. Dr. Speedling works to promote effective intraorganizational relationships and a team approach to patient care. He has published in journals across the spectrum of health care. His book *Heart Attack: The Family Response at Home and in the Hospital* (Tavistock, 1982) has reached a wide readership in this country and abroad.

Paula L. Stamps, Ph.D., is a professor at the University of Massachusetts, where she teaches program evaluation, research methods, and ethics. The major thrust of her research has been in the area of occupational satisfaction, which resulted in the publication of the book *Nurses and Work Satisfaction: An Index for Measurement* (Health Administration Press, 1986). Dr. Stamps has also published in the areas of program evaluation and family practice. She has been a visiting professor at Dartmouth College in their Family and Community Medicine Department.

Julius M. Steiner, J.D., received his prelegal education at Temple University, where he received a B.S. in communications. He is an honor graduate of the University of Louisville School of Law, where he received his J.D. degree. Mr. Steiner was admitted to the University of Louisville honor fraternities of Phi Kappa Phi and Omicron Delta Kappa and was a member of the *University of Louisville Law Review.* He is a partner in the firm of Myerson & Kuhn, where his practice is exclusively devoted to the representation of management in every phase of labor relations. Mr. Steiner is the author of numerous articles and texts, including his most recently published book *The Arbitration Handbook: A Guide to Practical and Legal Issues in Labor Arbitration,* and he is a frequent lecturer.

James H. Stephens, J.D., was named the thirteenth Chairman of the National Labor Relations Board by President Reagan on January 7, 1988. He has been a Member of the

Board since November 1, 1983, with a term that expires on August 27, 1990. From 1981 until his appointment as a Board Member, Mr. Stephens had served as labor counsel to the Senate Committee on Labor and Human Resources. He was associate minority labor counsel to the House Committee on Education and Labor from 1977 to 1981; practiced law in an Akron, Ohio, firm from 1973 to 1977; and was a law clerk for Judge Leo A. Jackson, Ohio Court of Appeals, Eighth Appellate District in Cleveland, Ohio, 1971–73. Chairman Stephens received his A.B. from Wittenberg University and his J.D. from Case Western Reserve University.

Alexander Sussman, F.S.A., is New York president and consulting actuary of Noble Lowndes, a worldwide employee benefits consulting firm. He serves as consultant to major national corporations, jointly trusteed union management employee benefit funds, and not-for-profit organizations including hospitals, universities, and charitable foundations. Mr. Sussman graduated from Boston University. His professional achievements include fellowship in the Society of Actuaries and membership in the American Academy of Actuaries. In addition, Mr. Sussman is a Fellow of the Canadian Institute of Actuaries and a member of the International Actuarial Association. He has direct responsibility for all phases of his company's consulting and actuarial services, including actuarial cost valuations, health care cost containment, administration of profit-sharing plans, investment performance monitoring, and numerous other detailed studies necessary in the operation of self-insured retirement, pension, and health benefit programs.

Eugene D. Ulterino, L.L.B., is a partner and chairman of the labor and Employment Law Department of the firm of Nixon, Hargrave, Devans & Doyle. He concentrates on labor and employment law, advising employers on matters involving personnel. Mr. Ulterino received his B.A. degree from the University of Rochester and his L.L.B. degree from the Georgetown University Law Center, where he was a member of *The Georgetown Law Journal*. He is a member of the American Bar Association, Labor Law Section, and a management representative on the Committee on Equal Employment Law. He has lectured at numerous symposia on employment law matters and has authored *The New Technology's Impact on Employer/Employee Relations*, published by the Research Institute of America, Inc.

Susan Warner, J.D., received her prelegal education at Marywood College where she graduated *summa cum laude* with a B.S. degree in business administration. She was awarded a J.D. degree from Temple University School of Law, where she received a Barrister's Award for Trial Advocacy. She has held positions as director of human resources and management of employment/EEO-AA in major health care institutions. Ms. Warner was also the regional manager for a national management consulting firm. Currently, she is director, human resources and administrative

services, United Way of Southeastern Pennsylvania in Philadelphia. Prior to this, she was a member of the law firm of Myerson & Kuhn, and before that she was a partner in a general practice firm concentrating in employment law, criminal law, and family law. Her practice is restricted exclusively to the representation of management in every phase of labor relations and employment law. She is a member of the Philadelphia, Pennsylvania, and American Bar Associations, the Pennsylvania and American Trial Lawyers Associations, and the American Academy of Hospital Attorneys of the American Hospital Association.

Thomas J. Welling, C.L.U., C.H., F.C., established Welling Associates in March 1978 as a firm specializing in retirement plans for not-for-profit institutions. Welling Associates, Inc., is a broker-dealer with the National Association of Securities Dealers, Inc. Prior to the establishment of Welling Associates, Mr. Welling was president of RBH Equities, Inc., and vice-president in charge of the Employee Benefits, Pension, and Estate Planning Department of Rollins Burdick Hunter of New York. He is a registered principal with the National Association of Security Dealers, as well as a chartered life underwriter and a chartered financial consultant.

Carlton J. Whitehead, Ph.D., is professor and area coordinator of management, College of Business Administration, and professor of health organization management, School of Medicine, Texas Tech University. Dr. Whitehead is director of the Program in Organizational Design and Strategic Management, Institute for Management and Leadership Research, at Texas Tech.

James B. Williams is the vice-president and worldwide director of Health Industry Consulting for the Hay Group. Located in Hay's San Francisco/Walnut Creek office, he has expertise in organizational effectiveness, executive/incentive compensation, strategic management, human resources planning, and productivity improvement. Mr. Williams provides overall direction and management to the following major ongoing projects for the U.S. health care industry: Organization Effectiveness/Human Resource Productivity Study (over 35 leading diversified health care systems participate), and Total Executive Compensation (cash and noncash) Survey (over 100 diversified health care systems participate). He graduated *magna cum laude* with a B.S. degree in accounting/business administration from the University of Southern California, where he was a member of Beta Gamma Sigma and received the university's Scholar-Athlete Award. He earned his M.B.A. from the Graduate School of Business, University of Southern California, where he graduated with honors after majoring in organizational behavior and financial management. Mr. Williams is a contributor to the book *Managing Organizational Performance*, a coauthor of the recently published book *Human Resource Planning in the Health Care Organization*, and a coauthor of the soon-to-be published books *Managing and Motivating Health Care Executive Per-*

formance and *Designing and Implementing Gainsharing Programs in the Health Care Industry*.

Sharon Winn, M.S., specializes in simultaneously developing plans, teams, and individuals. She has worked internationally for over 20 years with hundreds of highly trained professionals, governing bodies, and executives. She is certified by the Institute of Management Consultants. She teaches a graduate seminar at the University of Washington entitled "Managing with Professionals," which received the highest possible evaluation. She is also a clinical associate professor, Department of Health Services, School of Public Health and Community Medicine, University of Washington, Seattle.

John A. Witt is national advisor to Witt Associates Inc. Until September 1986, he was president of the firm he founded in 1969. This consulting organization pioneered executive search, board of directors training programs, and executive compensation consulting for hospitals, health care corporations, and health associations. Before organizing his own firm, Mr. Witt was with an international consulting firm in their health care management division. Mr. Witt's special interests include development of boards of directors, and he is a recog-nized authority on boards and board development. He has spoken before almost every state, regional, and national health association in America. He is currently involved in an advanced degree program at DePaul University, where he is continuing his research on the development of boards of directors. He is the author of *Building a Better Hospital Board*, published in 1987 by Health Administration Press.

Paul Yager, M.S., I.L.R., is an arbitrator and mediator. He retired in 1986 as director of the Eastern Region (11 states) of the Federal Mediation and Conciliation Service after having served in Washington, Philadelphia, and New York since 1952. He has earned an M.S. in industrial and labor relations from Cornell University and served as a labor economist with the U.S. Department of Labor. Mr. Yager was actively involved in collective bargaining in the health care industry after the amendment of the National Labor Relations Act (NLRA) in 1974. He has taught labor-management relations and collective bargaining as an adjunct at various universities, has written extensively on the subject, and has lectured both in the United States and abroad. Mr. Yager has been an officer and director of several major professional organizations and has trained mediators and arbitrators in various techniques of dispute resolution.

Index